Morality and the Market

Ethics and Virtue in the Conduct of Business

Eugene Heath
State University of New York, New Paltz

Mc
Graw
Hill

Boston   Burr Ridge, IL   Dubuque, IA   Madison, WI   New York   San Francisco   St. Louis
Bangkok   Bogotá   Caracas   Kuala Lumpur   Lisbon   London   Madrid   Mexico City
Milan   Montreal   New Delhi   Santiago   Seoul   Singapore   Sydney   Taipei   Toronto

ɟ-Hill Higher Education ⚡

A Division of The **McGraw-Hill** *Companies*

ᴋALITY AND THE MARKET: ETHICS AND VIRTUE IN THE CONDUCT
ᴆ BUSINESS

Published by McGraw-Hill, a business unit of The McGraw-Hill Companies, Inc., 1221
Avenue of the Americas, New York, NY 10020. Copyright © 2002 by The McGraw-Hill
Companies, Inc. All rights reserved. No part of this publication may be reproduced or
distributed in any form or by any means, or stored in a database or retrieval system, without
the prior written consent of The McGraw-Hill Companies, Inc., including, but not limited to,
in any network or other electronic storage or transmission, or broadcast for distance learning.

Some ancillaries, including electronic and print components, may not be available to
customers outside the United States.

This book is printed on acid-free paper.

1 2 3 4 5 6 7 8 9 0 QPF/QPF 0 9 8 7 6 5 4 3 2 1

ISBN 0-07-234508-X

Vice president and editor-in-chief: *Thalia Dorwick*
Editorial director: *Jane E. Karpacz*
Sponsoring editor: *Monica Eckman*
Developmental editor: *Shannon Morrow*
Marketing manager: *Daniel M. Loch*
Senior project manager: *Gloria G. Schiesl*
Senior production supervisor: *Sandy Ludovissy*
Design manager: *Stuart D. Paterson*
Cover design: *Emily Feyen*
Cover image: *Erich Lessing/Art Resource, NY*
Compositor: *Carlisle Communications, Ltd.*
Typeface: *9.5/11 Times Roman*
Printer: *Quebecor World Fairfield, PA*

The credits section for this book begins on page 691 and is considered an extension
of the copyright page.

Library of Congress Cataloging-in-Publication Data

Morality and the market: ethics and virtue in the conduct of business / [edited by]
Eugene Heath. — 1st ed.
    p. cm.
  Includes index.
  ISBN 0-07-234508-X
  1. Business ethics. I. Heath, Eugene A.
HF5387 .M654   2002
174.4-dc21
                            2001044972
                            CIP

www.mhhe.com

To my mother and father

Contents

AIII   Regulation 105

AIV   The Moral Conditions of Commerce 146

AV   Ethical Theory 194

Section B
VICE AND VIRTUE IN THE CONDUCT OF BUSINESS

Preface

This anthology is intended for use in classes in business ethics, at both the undergraduate and graduate level, though I would hope that the book might also prove suitable for either topical courses in social and political philosophy or for the general reader interested in the foundations, operations, and effects of business and markets. The book is unlike many other business ethics texts even as it covers many of the traditional concerns of the subject area. It is my aim to provide the reader with a selection of writings that communicate not only the philosophical but also something of the economic, political, sociological, and historical contexts of business ethics. In fulfillment of this aim, I also place particular emphasis on the philosophical relevance of virtue to the practice of business.

Most of the books and anthologies devoted to business ethics cover a fairly standard set of issues, including, for example, the nature and responsibility of the corporation (corporate agency, social responsibility); relations between employers and employees (privacy, whistleblowing, affirmative action, occupational safety); and relations between business and society (pollution and the environment, consumer protection, advertising). Interesting and worthy of examination, many of these topics can be found in this collection. However, this book attempts to address these questions with greater attention to both the economic and moral foundations of public policy as well as to the effects of market institutions in general.

The standard set of business ethics issues and topics, as typically presented within the field, is developed largely in terms of public policy and geared, frequently, toward the ethics of large corporations. However, the ethics of business is not exhausted by discussion of public policy, nor is it a matter of corporate ethics alone. Indeed, to the extent that business ethics focuses only on public policy or on corporations, it runs the risk of becoming increasingly irrelevant to the day-to-day conduct of persons who, as managers, owners, employees, or buyers and sellers, confront a variety of circumstances that call for the exercise of judgment or demand a particular quality of character. In this collection I seek to supplement the traditional slate of business ethics topics by offering a selection of writings on some of the virtues related to commercial life. It must be granted that there is not an abundance of writing on the virtues of commerce or business, nor can I claim to have exhausted the literature, even if it is small.

The structure of the text, distinct from that of many other collections, is organized into three broad topic sections (A, B, and C). Section A focuses on the foundational framework of business and commerce and includes readings on justice, regulatory policy, and, along with selections on philosophical ethics (Aristotle, Kant, Mill), readings on the (neglected issue of the) normative behavioral conditions for effective or successful markets. Section B focuses on the actual operation of business by taking up the way in which virtues may come into play in business life and by considering some of the preeminent ethical issues that arise in the operation of business. Just as Section A focuses on foundations, so does Section C focus on effects, whether these be moral, cultural, artistic, or technological and environmental. With the exception of the topic of the environment, the subjects and readings of Section C are found in no other collection devoted to the ethics of markets and business.

Sections A and C have exactly the same structure, with each subdivision commencing with a substantive introduction that provides background and context for the readings, as well as a brief summary of each selection. Section B has a slightly different structure: Its three subdivisions are divided into further subsections, each of which is preceded by a brief introduction and summaries of the readings. Whether in Section A, B, or C, any introduction can be read independently of the others. It is my hope that the readings will serve the interests of the inquisitive reader and that my introductions will provide helpful background to those new to these issues.

The idea for this text grew out of a desire to provide students in business ethics with a collection of readings of breadth, variety, and historical context. Many of the authors are philosophers or economists, others are sociologists, intellectuals, or writers. The reading selections are not narrowly philosophical, though the aim throughout is one of helping students to think more deeply and widely on the relevant matters—surely a philosophical aim. Many of the articles are from contemporaries but others are not. This is as it should be, for even if the questions of markets and commerce seem preeminently modern, they are not singularly contemporary and, so, we should not go galloping after the most recent article or the most current. Many of the relevant questions are *not* current and some of the most current writing provokes and resonates less well than that of earlier works. Throughout I have sought to include writers of diverse intellectual perspectives and opinions, and I have also readily sought to include thinkers whose work has been ignored or neglected. I lament the fact that the inclusion of so many topics and writers has meant that excisions have had to be made in so many of these selections. I have tried to err on the side of inclusion rather than exclusion, but I sympathize with the reader (or the author) who wishes to have available all of the essay, article, or book. Despite the breadth of the text, I am well aware of the omission of relevant topics, including that of globalization, sexual harassment, and drug testing, to mention but a few. I should have liked to include these, just as I would have preferred to have included readings on other topics too often ignored in the traditional business ethics texts: religious perspectives on markets and business; the relation between the U.S. Constitution and commercial laws and policies; and the possibility and problems of alternatives to markets (for example, market socialism). It has been impossible to include all of these, but what is included should prove both interesting and challenging.

ACKNOWLEDGMENTS

This anthology has suffered long periods of fermentation since it was first conceived and begun in the early 1990s. Several persons reviewed my early lists of reading selections for this text and made helpful comments or suggestions: Scott Arnold (University of Alabama, Birmingham); J. David Blankenship (State University of New York at New Paltz); Kenneth F. T. Cust (Central Missouri State University); Michael DeBow (Samford University); Robert Holyer (Randolph-Macon College); Zbigniew Rau (University of Lodz); Andrew Melnyk (University of Missouri, Columbia); Fred Miller (Bowling Green State University); David Schmidtz (University of Arizona); and Kory Tilgner. In particular, Andrew Melnyk directed me to the work of Samuel Smiles; Robert Holyer to that of Dorothy Sayers. In addition, the following reviewers provided valuable input and feedback on the manuscript: John Rowan (Purdue University, Calumet); Charles T. Hughes (Chapman University); Sally Hardwick (University of Nevada, Reno); Richard Lippke (James Madison University); Kelley C. Smith

(Clemson University); Lawrence P. Ulrich (University of Dayton); Stephen W. White (Auburn University); and W. B. Griffith (George Washington University). I owe special thanks to the Social Philosophy and Policy Center of Bowling Green State University for granting me a Summer Visiting Research Fellowship at which some of the early work was begun on this anthology.

All of the individuals with whom I have worked at McGraw-Hill have performed superbly and congenially. The original sponsoring editor was Sarah Moyers, but it was Monica Eckman who, having assumed the reins, rode herd on an author whose ambitions were often woefully out of sync with his estimates of the time needed for completion. Her eager interest and deft oversight were crucial. Shannon Morrow, the editorial coordinator, proved to be extraordinarily patient and effective even in the most desperate moments, and Gloria Schiesl oversaw, most efficiently, thoughtfully, and helpfully, the final production of the book.

Reva Wolf had the nerve to say that this book would get finished even when I did not think that it would, and for this and for so much more, I owe a debt of gratitude. The book itself is dedicated to my parents, Foster E. and Doris P. Heath, two exemplars of unpretentious honesty, quiet industry, and devotion and dedication beyond self. The debt I owe them cannot be repaid, but I should like to think that one small recompense to them would be that this book would, in some small way, help to improve our thinking and conduct on matters of consequence and, thereby, do some good for some persons somewhere.

Eugene Heath

The Moral and Political Framework of Business

Introduction

Markets and Business

This division of labour, from which so many advantages are derived, is not originally the effect of any human wisdom, which foresees and intends that general opulence to which it gives occasion. It is the necessary, though very slow and gradual consequence of a certain propensity in human nature which has in view no such extensive utility; the propensity to truck, barter, and exchange one thing for another.

Adam Smith[1]

The bourgeoisie, during its rule of scarce one hundred years, has created more massive and colossal productive forces than have all preceding generations together. Subjection of Nature's forces to man, machinery, application of chemistry to industry and agriculture, steam-navigation, railways, electric telegraphs, clearing of whole continents for cultivation, canalization of rivers, whole populations conjured out of the ground—what earlier century had even a presentiment that such productive forces slumbered in the lap of social labour?

Karl Marx[2]

Over the past four hundred years—during what has come to be called the "modern era"—the manner in which persons in the West have come to work and live has undergone dramatic change. Although it has always been the case that some form of trade was necessary if human beings were to meet their needs effectively and satisfy some desires, it has only been in the modern era that commercial exchange has become the primary manner in which we cooperate with one another in order to grow our food, make our products, and exchange our goods. Whether as a consumer who seeks to buy a manufactured article of clothing, a shop owner who searches for a well-trained and productive salesperson,

a contractor who advertises quality buildings at inexpensive prices, or an investor considering whether to buy some shares of a multinational corporation, our lives are inextricably intertwined with commerce.

Because our lives are so enmeshed in commerce, it is of particular interest to consider the value of commercial relations and to examine, from a normative point of view, the foundations, operations, and effects of markets and commerce. One takes up the normative point of view when one considers, in general and without regard to attaining some particular purpose or result for oneself, whether something *ought* to be the case; for example, whether some action should be performed, a

---

1. *An Inquiry into the Nature and Causes of the Wealth of Nations* [1776], edited by R.H. Campbell, A.S. Skinner, and W.B. Todd (Indianapolis, Ind.: Liberty Classics, 1981) I. ii. 2 (p. 25).

2. *Manifesto of the Communist Party* [1848], in *The Marx-Engels Reader,* 2d ed., edited by Robert C. Tucker (New York: W. W. Norton, 1978), 477.

policy implemented, or some character trait cultivated. Such evaluations often take either a moral, political, or cultural form, or some combination thereof. As we explore the foundations, operations, and effects of markets, we will appeal to these types of normative evaluations and to others as well.

The first section of this text (Section A, foundations) emphasizes both the moral or ethical evaluation of the institutional framework that establishes and regulates markets and the ethical and psychological qualities necessary for conducting business in market societies. Section B (operations) focuses on the relation between virtue and commerce, exploring some virtues (and vices) relevant to commercial practice and considering these particular character traits in light of some of the main questions of business ethics. In the final part of the text, Section C (effects), we employ normative evaluations to consider the consequences of markets, inquiring into the effects of commerce on morals, culture and the arts, as well as into certain effects—environmental and technological—of economic growth more generally.

Because any normative evaluation requires some context and background, it is worthwhile to begin with some general observations on markets and business. After that we will examine more closely the nature of normative evaluations.

ECONOMIC SYSTEMS AND THE MARKET

Economic Systems

On any given day we undertake a variety of business exchanges or renew commitments born of commercial transactions—between customer and clerk, employer and employee, stockholder and manager, client and professional. When we meet as buyers and sellers who, generally speaking, wish to buy at the lowest price and sell at the highest, we interact within a particular kind of *economic system* that we call the market. An economic system involves a framework of rules and structures which either specifies or provides the basis for determining four constituents of social cooperation:

- *which* goods are produced (and their quantities and relative importance),
- *how* they are to be produced,
- *who* will produce them, and,
- *how* they can be acquired by, or allocated to, individuals.

These four matters acquire their significance because of scarcity. Our needs and desires seem limitless, but the re-

sources required to make and distribute goods (to satisfy these needs and desires) are finite. Thus, any economic system—market or no—must provide some answer to each of the four preceding questions. The manner in which these questions are dealt with determines, to one degree or another, the kind of economic system in question.

Theoretically, if not historically, there have been at least three economic frameworks that respond to these four questions. In stratified economic systems, such as caste systems or feudal economies, the extent of private property is limited by law or custom, and other significant controls exist over prices as well as the individual's opportunity to alter or change vocation or status. In such systems, there is little room for economic competition among and between buyers and sellers, and many economic decisions are influenced by class or caste. In the fourteenth century prices were more often set by custom than by market forces, and individuals (whether serfs or nobles) were bound to a certain status and vocation. In centralized (or command) economies, the decision as to what is to be produced, how, and for whom, is determined by either an autocratic individual or a centralized decision-making body which may or may not attempt to reach its decisions on the basis of the needs and desires of the citizenry. Centralized economies, the characteristics of which may overlap with stratified systems, may exhibit distinct aims as well as different degrees of centralized decision making and can exist in either dictatorships or democracies. In either case, however, the decisions about production and distribution are determined not by the interaction of independent buyers and sellers but by some governmental body acting for the entire society.

The Market

The third economic system is that of a market. Though markets, or market systems, go by several other names (the free market, free enterprise economy, the competitive system, or capitalism), what unites these terms is that each specifies an economic system of privately owned property[3] in which the interaction of individuals

---

3. It is possible that a market could operate within a system in which property were not privately owned. Historically such markets have been rare, and, thus, as a historical phenomenon the term "market" has, at least informally, been taken to imply a private property market. However, it is at least possible that a market could operate within a system in which property in productive resources was not held privately but was "owned" by the nation as a whole and, accordingly, managed by the central government.

as buyers and sellers coordinates what is produced, how it is produced, who produces it, and how the goods are allocated. Under a market system, the individuals of a society manufacture or exchange goods or services—including inputs to production, such as land, labor and capital, as well as the final products—according to prices which result from their own interactive bargaining, including their decisions to buy or to sell. Neither the government nor the framework of laws specifies exactly which goods will be produced or by what method of production; rather, individuals and firms make decisions as to what to produce, and how, in anticipation of what others want and are willing to purchase. Individuals come together to trade because each places a greater value on the item (or service) to be gained than is placed on the item (or service) to be surrendered. Indeed, it is just because each party places a different, rather than an equal, value on the same item that the exchange occurs!

Business Firms and Profit

Although the exchange of goods often takes place among and between individuals, markets are distinguished by the presence of *firms,* hierarchically arranged (or vertically integrated) organizations devoted to business. Business firms may include single proprietorships or partnerships in which the owners assume responsibility for decision making and have legal responsibility for the actions undertaken in the firm's name. On the other hand, a third type of firm, the corporation (which began to emerge in the sixteenth century), is regarded, legally, as an entity unto itself. The owners (shareholders or stockholders) have a responsibility limited to the amount of money invested. Within the corporation a board of directors, elected by the stockholders, makes decisions about who is to run the firm.

In each of these businesses, the monetary criteria of success and failure are profit and loss. Each firm seeks to manage its resources so that the costs of its factors of production are less than the revenue it receives from the sale of goods or services. Spurred by profit, producers seek the lowest cost of production and are thereby led to commit their labor and resources to those activities that are most highly valued by others. In this way, resources are generally allocated to their most valued uses, and, ultimately, profit and loss are determined by whether or not what is produced is valued sufficiently highly by the consumers. Thus, it is the consumers who, relative to available resources and technology, determine what is produced. (Of course, one may question *how* consumers

come to acquire their desires and preferences, the degree to which these desires and preferences are dependent on self or society, or the extent to which these desires are rational or express a consumer's best and long-term interest.)

In a sense, of course, the profit motive—or a motive analogous to it—also holds for any individual who participates in exchange: Each person seeks to trade an item of lesser value for an item perceived to be of greater value. Similarly, the "division of labor"—or who is to produce what (and who is to provide which service)—is determined by individuals who, bearing divergent talents, skills, and interests, seek to specialize in that area in which they can enjoy the highest return on their labor and effort. The total allocation of goods and services is then determined by the supply and demand for one's labor in conjunction with land rents, interest rates, and the prices of goods and services. What is common to all of the agents—whether as consumers, producers, or workers—is the issue of profit and loss. Will this trade or exchange (of land, labor, or capital) secure for me a higher value, under what conditions, and in what length of time?

The Market Framework

The market framework can be understood to include two related sets of conditions: legal rules and moral, cultural, and psychological conditions. The basic legal framework for a market includes laws that sanction individual private ownership of property, permit the free movement of capital and labor, define and enforce rules of contract, and provide for the administration of justice. In addition, of course, the government may provide goods or services that the market may not provide (for example, dams or parks)[4], regulate the production and sale of goods and services, institute a monetary system, utilize fiscal policies of taxation and spending in the attempt to lessen perceived fluctuations in the market, and redistribute income through taxation, cash payments, or subsidies. Obviously, the legal framework has significant effects on the range and success of markets as well as on the forms and sizes of business firms. However, along with the legal and political framework of a market are the moral, social, and psychological conditions and qualities that serve to en-

---

4. Interestingly, economists long assumed that a lighthouse was a clear and outstanding example of a service that could not be financed or operated by private agents, but in the nineteenth century there were private lighthouses! See, Ronald H. Coase, "The Lighthouse in Economics," *Journal of Law and Economics* 17 (October 1974): 357–376.

courage certain acts, habits, and attitudes that may also affect the long-term success of markets and render more likely certain forms and sizes of business firms. These moral, social, and psychological conditions and qualities would include moral norms and expectations regarding how well individuals can cooperate with one another (norms of trust, responsibility, reliability, honesty, and civility) as well as the extent to which individuals exhibit such traits as industriousness, self-denial, or initiative. Differing laws and morals may have significant effects on the sizes and types of businesses that emerge in a society, on the overall productivity of business firms, and on whether individuals can or will achieve business success, either as owners, managers, or employees.

Obviously, then, markets may vary in their particular manifestations. Historically, an absolutely pure, *laissez-faire,* market has not existed. However, there is evidence that markets have arisen and flourished in just those places in which property, free exchange, and competition were allowed to exist securely over time. Of course, as historical phenomena, each of the economic systems—stratified, command, and market—may have elements of the other. The U.S. economy is an example of a mixed economy with a market orientation.[5] Certain production decisions may be the result of the edicts of governmental bodies, just as economic opportunities and success may be at least partly determined by status, class, customary expectations, or government policy. For example, hiring decisions are affected by laws on affirmative action and discrimination; the price of labor is constrained by minimum-wage laws; environmental laws and regulations influence production methods (and have disproportionate effects on smaller businesses); the rules of the Food and Drug Administration delimit what can be produced; the tax system affects the allocation of resources and incomes (and may also affect, as do regulations, the demand for certain services and professions, including law, accounting, and business advisory services); and familial, social, and moral traditions, social class, and customary habits and expectations may all affect the opportunities of individuals and how those individuals will view, and act on, their available options.

---

5. It might be best to speak of the *orientation* of an economy as either market, command, or stratified, rather than to employ—sometimes unthinkingly—the more general label. Moreover, when evaluating the performance of a mixed economy, it is especially important that one take into account whether the state of affairs (or event) under evaluation is the result of purely market forces or of the forces of command.

EVALUATING THE MARKET

The Market: Foundations, Operations, and Effects

The activities that occur in markets and businesses arise because there is a *legal framework* that defines a set of permissions, requirements, and prohibitions. These include laws regarding property and its proper use, regulations concerning what can be produced and advertised (and under what circumstances), and laws regarding contracts and working conditions. In addition to this legal foundation there are moral, social, and psychological conditions and qualities required for the effective *operation* of (or participation in) markets, and there are moral, cultural, technological, and environmental *effects* of markets. The operation of markets depends not only on whether individuals are rational and capable of discerning and taking advantage of opportunities but whether individuals have moral habits and virtues that serve them well in a legal framework that permits trade and exchange and the formation of businesses and corporations. That our participation in markets occurs against a moral and cultural background should remind us that commerce may also affect that background, altering our moral and cultural heritage for better or worse. Thus we must also evaluate the possibility that markets have consequences that are morally and culturally significant.

Two Types of Evaluation

The foundations, operations, and effects of markets, like that of any economic system, can be evaluated by invoking either criteria of efficiency or normative criteria. An evaluation according to productive performance seeks to determine how well the market (or some aspect of the market) produces goods and services, utilizes resources, or allocates goods and services. The second kind of evaluation considers the foundations, operations, or effects of the market (or some aspect of the market) and subjects these to some standard of morals, politics, or cultural value. For example, the market framework, as a whole system, can be subject to evaluation in terms of either its tendency to generate efficient outcomes or its compatibility with certain moral, political, or cultural criteria. In fact, for much of this century there was a debate as to whether the market system was preferable to a command system such as that exhibited in the communist nations. On the other hand, particular laws, rules, or practices can also be subject to these evaluations: Does this rule or practice contribute to productivity? For example, does a law mandating a minimum wage serve to increase productivity (and lift the wages of those who are the least well off)? Or does the law inhibit productivity and guarantee that those whose labor is not valued as high as the mandated minimum will be left without any work at all? Of course, one may shift one's examination from considerations of efficiency to those of morals or justice. Does a business have a right to request that any potential employee submit to a drug test? Or does such a test violate a right to privacy? Are policies of affirmative-action hiring compatible with justice, or do such policies violate rights? Although any law or regulation may be evaluated as much for its efficiency as for its moral desirability, it should not be assumed that productivity and moral desirability will always coincide. To underscore how these considerations are distinct, let us consider each in turn.

The Market as a Productive System

If we consider the issue of *productivity* (and if we recall that the framework of the market does not specify or determine particular production decisions, prices, or economic patterns), it may seem surprising that a market, as a system, achieves any level of productivity or exhibits any order or regularity at all! One of the chief reasons that we may consider it surprising is that we are disposed, incorrectly perhaps, to believe that any order or design must be the product of a designer.[6] Defenders of the market, however, want to argue that a market framework allows for an order to arise spontaneously, as if guided by an "invisible hand," a phrase originally invoked by Adam Smith:

> [E]very individual necessarily labours to render the annual revenue of the society as great as he can. He generally, indeed, neither intends to promote the public interest, nor knows how much he is promoting it. By preferring the support of domestick to that of foreign industry, he intends only his own security; and by directing that industry in such a manner as its produce may be of the greatest value, he intends only his own gain, and he is in this, as in many other cases, led by an invisible-hand to promote an end which was no part of his intention.[7]

6. Consider William Paley's remark in his *Natural Theology* (1802), chapter two, paragraph 4: "There cannot be a design without a designer; contrivance without a contriver; order without choice; arrangement without anything capable of arranging; subserviency and relation to a purpose without that which could intend a purpose; means suitable to an end, and executing their office in accomplishing that end, without the end ever having been contemplated or the means accommodated to it."

7. *An Inquiry into the Nature and Causes of the Wealth of Nations*, IV.ii.9 (p. 456).

This passage indicates one important aspect of the invisible hand: From impulses that are not directed to a public end there can arise a state of affairs that satisfies the public good. In other words, beneficial results can emerge from the actions of individuals, none of whom intended any such benefit. Just as important, the individual motivated by a private impulse may have greater knowledge of his local surroundings—including knowledge of what others want, what to produce, and how best to produce and deliver it—than does a public official who is motivated, ostensibly, toward the public good. Individuals with differing goals and interests act in accordance with the signals provided by the prices offered on the market. Via these prices, and the profit and loss system, the actions of individuals are coordinated so that resources, labor, and capital are moved toward those areas with the greatest potential for profit and away from those areas with the greatest potential for loss. In this way, prices help individuals, acting on their interests and local knowledge, to produce orderly outcomes that promote the ends of other individuals. Of course, one can inquire into whether the invisible-hand process always functions in a beneficial way or whether individuals always seek or prefer what is most rational. For example, the market may be incapable of producing some goods, and some market interactions may impose costs (externalities) on third parties who want nothing to do with the exchange. These are but a few of the objections and concerns that have been raised with regard to the productivity of markets, and we shall consider these and others in subsequent readings.

Normative Inquiry: Levels and Types

Apart from the evaluation of the market in terms of its productive performance, one can evaluate the market by appeal to *normative standards of value*. A normative evaluation seeks a general answer, recommendation, or guideline as to what *should* be done, either by an individual, a group, or a political body. Thus, a normative response to some conflict, circumstance, or state of affairs offers counsel as to what *ought* to occur, or what ought to be done, and this normativity entails some obligation, recommendation, or guideline that applies to all relevant persons. Most normative appeals invoke concepts and principles concerning morality, goodness, and responsibility, but the realm of the normative may include appeals to aesthetic principles or values concerning art or beauty. In other instances, the normative may make reference to values and concepts concerning knowledge, friendship, or human relations more generally. A normative evaluation may operate at either of two levels, one being that of the application of principles, standards, values, or rules to a particular case (so as to render a judgment about what ought to be done in a certain situation). The other is at a theoretical level at which these principles, standards, values, or rules are explained and justified in terms of a unified normative *theory,* such as an ethical theory.

The most prominent type of normative evaluation is a *moral* evaluation by which one seeks to determine the moral rightness or value of the market framework or of some aspect of that framework, whether these be laws or market institutions, business actions, or qualities of character necessary for business success. (Is it morally right to permit a person or business to advertise a product in such a way that its good qualities are exaggerated and its bad qualities omitted? Does the government have a right to tell the owner of property whom he or she must hire and under what conditions?) However, it must be pointed out that a nonmoral type of normative evaluation may take place at the level of society and culture. With respect to markets and business, this type of assessment seeks to consider the extent to which markets either presuppose or bring about certain features deemed valuable, even if these features are not understood to be moral. Thus, one might evaluate a market by its cultural or aesthetic effects. However, to do so one must pose certain descriptive questions; for example, what are the general civilizational (moral, cultural, or attitudinal) effects (or conditions) of markets? Do commercial societies bring about a greater diffusion of the arts, or do they inhibit artistic creativity? Do markets bring about a form of consumerism that is shallow and alienating?

Normative Versus Descriptive

Although a normative inquiry must rely on adequate and clear accounts of facts, including causes and effects, it is nonetheless very important to recognize that a normative inquiry is distinct from reporting that some practice or act is, as a matter of fact, done in a certain situation. For example, to ask what sort of person I should be is not the same as detailing what sort of person I am. Similarly, knowing how a society operates is not sufficient for knowing how a society *should* operate. (Thus, business law is not the same as business ethics.) Not only are descriptive inquiries distinct from normative, but a description is not by itself an answer to a normative question: That an individual does X does not entail that the person should do X. If one wishes to claim that

what one does is what one should do, then one must first argue that what one does is what one should do! Moreover, knowing what one *should* do does not entail that one will do it.[8] In order to answer the question of what one should do, one must apply a standard, rule, or value to the case under consideration. That still leaves open the matter of justifying that standard, rule, or value. Here again one cannot justify a standard by merely stating that the standard is employed. The standard—whether invoked to support a character trait, a specific act, or an institution—must be justified by giving reasons or some more general value, principle, or theory.

There are several senses in which normative inquiry is related to empirical. In the case of ethical theories one's theoretical perspective on foundational ethical principles may be related to certain broad empirical claims about human nature and the circumstances of society. Nonetheless, there are those, such as Immanual Kant, who claim that a supreme principle of ethics is discernable by pure reason and is, therefore, utterly divorced from empirical considerations. Even so, in the case of the application of a normative theory or principle to some particular state of affairs, it is clear that the determination of what one should do in a certain situation may require that one know, factually, certain features of the situation, including the feasible options, previous actions and decisions, or probable effects. Thus, a normative inquiry into the market requires, at the very least, some knowledge of the foundations, operations, and effects of the market.

Framework or Specific Practice

Just as we saw in the case of evaluations of efficiency, a normative evaluation might judge either the overall framework or some specific aspect, rule, or policy. In the case of the *framework,* one might consider whether the rules and practices presupposed by markets are just. Are they compatible with freedom, equality, virtue, or the good life? For example, Karl Marx, like Adam Smith before him, saw that social patterns were the unintended results of human action. However, unlike Smith, Marx did not see these results as beneficial! For Marx, the patterns of the market seem to acquire an autonomy of their own that overwhelms and immiserates individuals. What is needed, according to Marx, is a political framework in which these seemingly autonomous

---

8. However, the ancient Greek philosopher Socrates thought differently. For Socrates, knowledge of the right course of conduct insured that one would conduct oneself rightly. See Plato's dialogue *Meno* (87c-88d).

market forces are placed under rational direction to insure that the economy actually satisfies human needs and serves the ends of human beings.

A normative inquiry into a market might, in addition, evaluate some *specific practice,* permission, or rule of the market: Does this rule (or this permission) unfairly disadvantage some persons? For example, if the law allows banks or lending agencies to charge high interest rates to persons who have no (or little) collateral or poor borrowing records, does this practice exploit the borrowers or does it merely allow individuals an option which, if rendered illegal, would disappear? Similarly, does the legal requirement of affirmative-action hiring give advantage to minorities and female applicants at the expense of white men? Or would the lack of affirmative action allow white (or male) applicants unfair advantages?

Apart from questions that relate to some specific practice or policy, there remain matters of individual *character* and *judgment.* All actions that are justifiably permitted to an individual need not be morally desirable. Such questions, of course, affect all areas of life, not just business. At a public gathering, one may have a right to freedom of speech, but the freedom provided by that right does not entail that it is morally right or desirable for one to say to a bystander that he or she is the ugliest person on the face of the earth! Thus, that some action is wrong does not entail that the action should be prohibited. (That certain wrongful actions, in particular those that pose physical harm or infringe the rights of others, should be prohibited seems relatively uncontroversial; however, there may be other wrongful actions that should not be prohibited, either because these acts do not put others at risk of harm or because the costs of prohibition might outweigh the benefits.) Within the area of permissions, one must inquire into questions of both action (doing) and character (being): What sort of actions are appropriate? And what sort of person should one be? How should one's business life reflect one's larger life and aspirations? For example, does a business have a responsibility to the community that extends beyond the pursuit of profit? Should a funeral home owner engage in aggressive advertising? Should an employee work no harder than any other employee or actively seek to do the least amount of work possible? Ought an owner or manager be generous as well as prudent in the evaluation of employees? Although the legal framework of the market may leave open to the individual the kind of person he or she wants to be, it may still be the case that certain kinds of qualities of character (virtues) are either required by the market or rewarded by the market. What virtues are necessary in a competitive market? Must one be selfish

in order to get ahead in the market? Is the person of integrity the better manager of a company? Is the conscientious employee preferable to the creative one?

Finally, there are those questions that focus on certain consequences of a market system. Some of these consequences have to do with technological progress as well as the effects of economic growth on the environment. However, there are also normative questions that focus on whether or not there are certain significant moral, cultural, or aesthetic effects of commercial societies. Do markets serve to improve or corrupt morals? Does commerce encourage certain ideas about progress? or certain attitudes about consumption? Does a society devoted to business inhibit or encourage artistic creativity? Although these questions intertwine with the earlier questions, they have a resonance of their own that is worthy of investigation.

Thus, a complete inquiry into the moral foundations, operations, and effects of business and markets will take place in three areas, and we will attempt to address these in the various sections of this text:

A. **The Moral and Political Framework of Business:** What sorts of institutions, practices, or behavior ought to be required, prohibited, or allowed? Are there significant moral, social, or cultural preconditions of markets?

B. **Virtue and Vice in the Conduct of Business:** What qualities are particularly important to business success? What virtues or vices are relevant to understanding one's role as entrepreneur, manager, or employee?

C. **The Consequences of Commerce:** Are there significant moral or cultural effects of markets? How does commerce affect the production and consumption of the arts? What sort of issues arise as economic growth not only generates new technology but fuels concern about the natural environment?

The first area of inquiry provides the background upon which the second and third sets of questions become more understandable. Even if most of us engage in business relations every day of our lives, that itself does not provide any theoretical point of view on the market as an institution. A more complete understanding of the market framework, therefore, makes possible a greater understanding of the second and third sets of inquiries. However, these inquiries may also influence one's evaluation of the market framework. If the market framework generates a society that corrupts moral action and virtue (or requires one to be vicious), then that discovery may require one to revise one's view of the framework.

On the other hand, if the market framework does not corrupt but improves moral possibilities, then that realization may also affect one's evaluation of the framework.

From the long perspective of history, the generation of wealth that has occurred within commercial societies seems extraordinary (even to Karl Marx). It is important to examine (as the authors Rosenberg and Birdzell do) whether the astounding generation of wealth owes something to the institutions, rules, and expectations that, forged over several centuries, define, delimit, and establish the very conditions of the markets in which we do business, exchange goods, and acquire wealth. We should also, therefore, consider the nature of the market as an economic system (Mises) and pose the question of whether there are goods which should not be regarded as *commercial* or *economic* goods (Anderson). Finally, since the participants in markets include not only individuals but organizations called *firms* or *businesses,* we should pause to consider the nature of business and whether we can define what is peculiar to this type of organization (Sternberg).

THE READINGS

Nathan Rosenberg and L. E. Birdzell, Jr.   In the selection *How the West Grew Rich,* Nathan Rosenberg and L. E. Birdzell, Jr., delineate how the wealth that has been achieved in Western societies owes much to market institutions. This wealth has accrued in spite of what they consider to be the "almost unrelieved wretchedness" of most of human history, and it has occurred through an unintended and slow evolution. Thus, the West's economic growth depends not on a benevolent designer or a malevolent conspiracy but on certain institutional features of the societies in which the wealth has accrued. What the authors seek in their explanation is a set of features that together are sufficient to account for the development of wealth in the Western world.[9] After canvassing nine possible explanations—each of which tries to account for wealth by reducing it to one factor—Rosenberg and Birdzell contend that the *proximate* sources of wealth are innovations in trade, technology, and organization and the accumulation of capital, labor, and natural resources. What is *primary,* they argue, is the aspect of innovation, but what accounts for innovation? Here they appeal to systemic or institutional features that are mutually reinforcing: firms, markets, and competition. The first two, developing out of the freedom that emerged with the decline of political and religious controls over society, insure the emergence of competition and with it the concomitant stimulus to innovation. With these institutional features in place the authors delineate eight noteworthy aspects of the growth in wealth. They conclude that "The key elements of the system were the wide diffusion of the authority and resources necessary to experiment; an absence of more than rudimentary political and religious restrictions on experiment; and incentives which combined ample rewards for success, defined as the widespread economic use of the results of experiment, with a risk of severe penalties for failing to experiment."

Ludwig von Mises   Mises characterizes the market as "the social system of the division of labor under private ownership." Distinct from government ownership of the means of production, a market system, contends Mises, allows individuals to serve others as a means to providing for their own ends. The freedom of the market is characterized in terms of a "sphere" within which individuals may "choose between alternative modes of action." In this way, the subjective valuations of consumers determine not only what is produced but the value of one's labor and the income one receives. Indeed, the very survival of a business firm depends on how well it responds to consumers whom Mises describes as "merciless bosses, full of whims and fancies, changeable and unpredictable."

As a result of market activities one may realize a profit or loss, though it is the former that is the aim of one's purposeful action. Mises focuses on the profit-seeking *entrepreneur* who, as distinguished from the technical expert, makes the decision to employ certain factors in the production of certain goods or services; it is the entrepreneur who endeavors to buy the factors of production (land, labor, and capital goods) at lower prices than that at which the final product can be sold. Since no one can foresee the future prices of market goods, there is an opportunity for profit and for loss, the very phenomena that select the more efficient and farsighted entrepreneurs from the less efficient and myopic. Of course, each individual in the market is always striving to sell high and to buy low, and what results from a myriad instances of exchange is an orderly structure of prices, not only for consumer goods but for labor

---

9. To say that "X is sufficient for Y" is to say that the presence of X guarantees the presence of Y. Alternatively, to say that "X is necessary for Y" is to say that the presence of X is required for, but does not guarantee, Y. Thus, oxygen is necessary for combustion, but oxygen does not suffice for combustion. On the other hand, the presence of combustion does guarantee that there is oxygen present.

and other factors of production. The order of prices is subject to revision in accordance with the subjective valuations of consumers.

Elizabeth Anderson   Although Anderson would agree with Mises that market evaluations are subjective, she argues that the economic goods of the market are distinct from other goods, implying thereby that there are certain ethical limits on the goods that should be subject to market exchange. She first outlines how the market embodies an ideal of freedom in the use of commodities. These commodities, she points out, are valued in terms of their "use," and she contrasts how the "use" of commodities—indeed, the very valuation of commodities—is distinct from modes of valuation that involve "respect," personality, or the sharing of goods. Economic goods are those whose production, distribution, and enjoyment are governed by what she describes as five norms of market relations. In contrast, however, to market relations, which are impersonal and involve goods whose use is exclusive to the purchaser, there are noneconomic goods and noneconomic relations. Within "personal relationships," the goods to be realized are shared goods that require one to consider oneself as sharing one's life with another. Unlike market relations, personal ties are governed "by the spirit of the gift rather than the spirit of commercial exchange." After chronicling several ways in which the gift relation differs from commercial exchange, Anderson turns to consider the problems that arise when market norms infiltrate spheres in which personal values and norms should predominate. In the penultimate section of her essay, she describes how the marketplace does not distinguish between ideal goods (such as fraternity and democracy) and ordinary economic goods *or* between desires and needs. The ideal goods of fraternity and democracy are shared values whose realization conflicts with the norms of the market; to be realized at all, these shared goods require provision through political institutions.

Elaine Sternberg   If one is to study the ethics of business, then it should be of interest to distinguish businesses from other types of organizations or associations under which individuals cooperate together. Such is the operating assumption of Elaine Sternberg, who contends that any fair and clear study of business ethics requires that one begin with a definition of "business" that captures its essential purpose, a purpose that differentiates it from other activities or organizations, such as families, clubs, or government institutions. (A definition of business is necessary because otherwise one will not understand the nature of the organization that is under ethical examination and one's inquiry will be likely to mislead rather than inform.) The purpose of business, she says, is the maximization of "owner value over the long term" through the sale of either goods or services. By defining business in this way, she hopes that her definition extends properly only to those enterprises engaged in business and excludes those organizations that are not so engaged.

How the West Grew Rich
The Economic Transformation of the Industrial World

Nathan Rosenberg and L. E. Birdzell, Jr.

Nathan Rosenberg is Fairleigh S. Dickinson, Jr., Professor of Public Policy in the Department of Economics, Stanford University. His most recent book is The Emergence of Economic Ideas *(1994). L. E. Birdzell, Jr., is an attorney and legal scholar. This section is the introductory chapter to* How the West Grew Rich *(1986).*

POVERTY AS A NORM

If we take the long view of human history and judge the economic lives of our ancestors by modern standards, it is a story of almost unrelieved wretchedness. The typical human society has given only a small number of people a humane existence, while the great majority have lived in abysmal squalor. We are led to forget the dominating misery of other times in part by the grace of literature, poetry, romance, and legend, which celebrate those who lived well and forget those who lived in the silence of poverty. The eras of misery have been mythologized and may even be remembered as golden ages of pastoral simplicity. They were not.

Only during the last two hundred years has there come to Western Europe, the United States, Canada, Australia, Japan, and a few other places one of history's infrequent periods when progress and prosperity have touched the lives of somewhat more than the upper tenth of the population. For brevity, albeit at the sacrifice of geographical accuracy, we will call these places, collectively, the West. In England, the United States, and parts of Western Europe, it became evident early in the nineteenth century (and later in other countries of the West) that an unusually high proportion of people were becoming better fed, healthier, and more secure than in the ancient Middle Eastern, Indian, Chinese, Greek, Roman, and Islamic civilizations—that is, than at any other time in human history.

The move from poverty to wealth is, in a social sense, an advance in material well-being. It is not adequately captured in statistics of gross national product, national income, or real wages. Death has always been the ultimate threat, and the move from poverty to wealth is first of all a move away from death. Its first indicators are statistics on life expectancy, death rates, and infant mortality. Famine and hunger are next on the list; again, the move from poverty to wealth is a move from famine and hunger, as indicated statistically by a declining incidence of malnutrition and its related diseases. Plague is the next of the ancient afflictions, and it may be taken as symbolic of all fatal or disabling diseases; the move away from them is another move from poverty to wealth. Poverty tends to be associated with illiteracy, superstition, ignorance, and life lived within an extremely narrow setting. The move from poverty to wealth is a move toward literacy, education, and variety of experience. A life of poverty is a life in which survival is the first and almost the only order of business, in which housing is so crowded as to make privacy unknown, and in which choices are narrowly restricted. The move to wealth is a move toward greater possibilities of privacy and individual choice. . . .

It is, of course, possible for a society to move from poverty to wealth without producing a people serenely satisfied with itself; in fact, it may be doubted that self-satisfied people could move from poverty to wealth in the first place. It is even possible that the psychological restlessness of a people in good physical health will, as a rule, be more intractable than that of a people numbed by hunger. But even though a nation that achieves wealth must expect to support a busy mental-health industry and put up with the social dissonance which goes with an extension of individual choice, there continues to be widespread interest in how such a move is accomplished. It is, after all, in the nature of social change to supply societies with a new set of problems in exchange for an old set, and people are hardly to be blamed for preferring the problems of wealth to those of poverty.

The story of the move from poverty to wealth offers enough mysteries, surprises, exposés, triumphs, and tragedies to make it worth the retelling for its own sake. Moreover, a better understanding of how economic growth came about in the West should be helpful to those Westerners who are concerned with public policy, the comparative significance of the West's many economic institutions, the future of the Western economies themselves, and most of all to those who feel some responsibility for passing along to the next generation an opportunity to better their own conditions at least as much as has the current generation.

GRADUALNESS OF THE GROWTH OF WESTERN WEALTH

As we turn to the problem of explaining Western economic growth, we must begin with its most puzzling aspect: its gradualism.

The advanced Western countries completed their escape from poverty to relative wealth during the nineteenth and twentieth centuries. There was no sudden change in their economic output, but only a continuation of year-to-year growth at a rate that somewhat exceeded the rate of growth of population. . . .

Over a year, or even over a decade, the economic gains, after allowing for the rise in population, were so little noticeable that it was widely believed that the gains were experienced only by the rich, and not by the poor. Only as the West's compounded growth continued through the twentieth century did its breadth become clear. It became obvious that Western working classes were increasingly well off and that the Western middle classes were prospering and growing as a proportion of the whole population. Not that poverty disappeared. The West's achievement was not the abolition of poverty but the reduction of its incidence from 90 percent of the population to 30 percent, 20 percent, or less, depending on the country and one's definition of poverty—a concept that seems to keep growing in content with economic growth itself. The continued expansion of Western economies through the twentieth century created an enormous gap between their wealth and the poverty from which they had escaped, but in which most of the world's people still live. . . .

The explanation of gradual growth, so long continued, has to reside in an institutional mechanism, built deep into the structure of Western economies and continuously seeking out and adopting growth-inducing changes. *Deep* is the key word, for the mechanism is so far buried that it has seemed impossible to many observers that the future could hold anything but stagnation or decline after so long an expansion of production and growth in numbers of people. The rate of growth of output in the last century or so is commonly stated at around 3 percent a year, and in most branches of human experience, this kind of geometric progression, in which each term is 1.03 times the preceding term, tends to run into insurmountable barriers and taper off in considerably fewer than two hundred successive terms. . . .

A[fter] World War I, Oswald Spengler made his widely read prediction of *The Decline of the West*.[1] No reasonable prophet, writing in Spengler's day, could have foreseen that in the next half-century the population of the United States would nearly double and gross national product (GNP) per capita (in constant dollars) would increase more than two-and-a-half times. It is not just that Spengler mistimed his forecast of an inevitable exhaustion of a geometric progression. The more serious point is that Spengler, a thinker of talent and insight, both misconceived and underestimated the forces behind Western progress and just as clearly misconceived and overestimated the forces corrupting and eroding it. He was far from alone.

We will find that the West has created a powerful system for economic growth, of a sort which could keep generating growth and even substantive advances in material welfare for decades after the spirit had burned out of it. The very inertia of such systems makes them deceptive. The people who work within them and who make them work may continue doing what they have always done long after all the incentives for creative work have vanished, leaving the system driven only by habit and the lack of anything better for its people to do. Such a system could run down so slowly, in response to causes separated by so many years from their effect, that by the time its degeneration became apparent, it might be irreversible. Indeed, social systems can continue to expand long after the events that made their collapse inevitable. The stock lesson from history is still supplied by the political empire of Rome rather than by the economic empire of the West: it continued to expand for more than a century after events which all but guaranteed its eventual disintegration.

It is important to keep this long and uncertain time gap between cause and effect in mind when we attempt to evaluate possible explanations of Western growth. Many Western institutions that might help explain the dynamics of Western economies have been substantially changed by the political and social currents of the latter part of the twentieth century. Despite the changes, Western economic growth has continued, and it is even arguable that there has been no long-term deterioration in the rate of growth. This is ground for caution in relying on these changed institutions as explanations of Western growth, but it is not a sufficient reason for ruling them out altogether. The effects of comparatively recent institutional changes may not yet be obvious, or growth might have occurred at a higher rate without the changes. Unhappily for certainty in economic history, there are no conclusive experiments to guide inquiry through the puzzles created by multiple causation, the capacity of human beings and their institutions to adapt to change in ways that obscure its effects, the possibility—even likelihood—that Western growth had different causes at different periods, and the propensity of effects to surface decades after their causes have been forgotten.

SOME PREVIOUS EXPLANATIONS

The causes of the West's rise from poverty to wealth have been extensively explored for a century-and-a-half. The more widely credited explanations are worth a brief preliminary review, both of their truths and their weaknesses.

Science and Invention

The most popular explanations of Western prosperity are focused on science and invention. But why, if science and invention are a sufficient cause of national wealth, were not China and the Islamic nations, which were the leaders in science and invention when the West turned from feudalism and entered into the modern era, the countries that escaped from poverty to riches? Another difficulty with these explanations is that science and invention are forms of knowledge which, one would think, are easily transferable from one society to another by lectures and the printed page. But the difficulty of transferring the keys to economic growth from the West to the Third World has proved far greater than the difficulty of teaching science. We are far from denying that technology was important, but it is evidently not the sole explanation of Western growth.

Natural Resources

Another common explanation of the wealth of nations is that it is a consequence of their natural resources or of their access to natural resources on favorable terms. Karl Marx, for example, attributed some of the new wealth of the West to its imperialist conquests and its commercial acquisitions of raw materials from overseas, beginning in the sixteenth century. The late nineteenth-century imperialists of England, France, Germany, Italy, Belgium, and Holland similarly argued the importance of owning natural resources. And much of the writing on the limits of growth in our own day combines a more sophisticated concept of natural resources with a belief in a simple link between ownership of natural resources and economic growth.

But the prosperity of the Low Countries and Switzerland has long plagued these explanations. More recently, the phenomenal growth and prosperity of Japan have hopelessly undermined them. After World War II, other Western countries with limited natural resources, and now without colonies, have persisted in growing richer while some Third World countries with extensive natural resources have lingered in poverty. In short, natural resource explanations do not fit the facts.

Finally, explanations based on natural resources are subject to the difficulty that a society's economic resources are not its natural resources as such, but a relation, internal to the society, between its natural resources and its organizational and technological skills in extracting or otherwise acquiring and utilizing those natural resources for advancing its people's material welfare. Resources that contribute to economic wealth are not simply material; they are a subtle combination of materials present in nature with the human knowledge and social organization required to use those materials (and, by extension, the efforts of human beings) to satisfy human needs. To the American Plains Indian, for example, the oil, coal, iron ore, forests, and farmlands of North America were not economic resources, but the buffalo herds were resources of the utmost importance. The West's *economic* resources *are* its wealth; the problem is how the West generated the organizational and technological skills required to produce and exploit that wealth.

Psychological Explanations

Marx also, and more emphatically, attributed Western economic growth to the driving force of a competitive economy that pressed capitalists to a frenzied pursuit of ever larger sales and ever larger profits, creating what was, even in his day, a formidable "capitalist engine." He regarded Western technology not as a separate source of growth, but as derived from this driven pursuit of personal riches. But to Marx, the behavior of capitalists was not so much an independent psychological phenomenon as it was a response to the peculiar pressures of capitalist institutions. Capitalist economic growth was not for Marx merely a concession that he was prepared to make for purposes of argument, but a central point of his theory of inevitable revolution. To him, capitalist growth in economic output, by creating the possibility of a better life for workers, made it inevitable that workers would take advantage of the possibility by revolutionary seizure of the means of production. If the theory seems implausible today, it is because seizure of the means of production has not proved to

be a necessary precondition to widespread worker participation in the benefits of economic growth. The essential point for Marx was his belief that capitalism was incapable of translating its great growth potential into higher standards of material well-being for the workers.

Economic growth is unlikely to occur unless the economy is so organized that those who can bring about growth have incentives for doing so, and Marx was no doubt right in stressing the importance of the profit-and-loss incentives supplied by contemporary capitalism. But a century after his death, when we can observe the Third World's efforts to achieve growth, it has become evident that more than incentives are needed. Incentives cannot enable a community to do what it does not know how to do. Knowledge, and an institutional structure which gives knowledge room to grow and incentives room to operate, are at least as important.

The great difficulty of identifying the sources of Western economic growth has led to some psychological explanations which are little short of desperate. One that has gained fairly wide acceptance is that the decline of feudalism was somehow linked to a psychological mutation, creating market institutions out of some new capitalist spirit or out of the intensification of acquisitive impulses above and beyond those that existed in China, India, or Islam. . . . Max Weber questioned the central importance of what he called "the economic impulse":

> The notion that our rationalistic and capitalistic age is characterized by a stronger economic interest than other periods is childish; the moving spirits of modern capitalism are not possessed of a stronger economic impulse than, for example, an oriental trader. The unchaining of the economic interest merely as such has produced only irrational results; such men as Cortez and Pizarro, who were perhaps its strongest embodiment, were far from having an idea of a rationalistic economic life. If the economic impulse in itself is universal, it is an interesting question as to the relations under which it becomes rationalized and rationally tempered in such fashion as to produce rational institutions of the character of capitalistic enterprise.[2]

Luck

We will find that the history of Western economies includes at least three, and perhaps four, groups of events that might fairly be called revolutions. Beginning in the fifteenth century, there was an expansion of trade and commerce that can be viewed as a mercantile revolution. Three centuries later, in the eighteenth century, there occurred the Industrial Revolution. At the end of the nineteenth century and the beginning of the twentieth, the introduction of electric power and the internal combustion engine amounted to a second industrial revolution. In our own day, developments in electronic storage and switching networks, embodied in communications systems and computers, seem likely to lead to an information revolution, if they have not already done so.

One could explain the West's rise to wealth as the consequence of the extraordinary luck of having experienced these four beneficent revolutions in five centuries, just as one might explain the collapse of the antecedent feudal society by the bad luck of having experienced too many plagues, wars, and famines in the fourteenth century. But when lightning has struck four times in one place, it seems appropriate to inquire what it is about the topography of the place that attracts it so persistently.

In another sense, luck is the true explanation, for the origins of Western economic institutions cannot be traced to the wisdom of any identifiable human beings. They are a product of history, unintended consequences of action taken for entirely different reasons. They were well advanced by the time Adam Smith began the modern work of understanding their structure. To this day, that work is nowhere near completion. What produced the wealth of the West was luck in the sense that the results of biological evolution are luck, but still those processes, their results, and their interrelations are abundantly worthy of study.

Misconduct

A different group of explanations of Western wealth has been widely advanced in political discourse. Western wealth has been attributed to various forms of misconduct, some of it highly reprehensible by modern standards, if not by the standards prevailing at the time of its occurrence. The forms of misconduct most commonly charged to Western economies are increased inequalities of income and wealth, exploitation of workers, colonialism and imperialism, and slavery. As devices for encouraging charitable giving, national and international, supporting social legislation, and for checking Western hubris, these explanations have been very useful. There is less to be said for their adequacy as explanations of Western economic growth.

Inequalities of Income and Wealth

Of the explanations of Western wealth which center on misconduct, the most fundamental maintains that inequalities of income and wealth are unjust, but necessary to Western economic systems. Some critics of inequality contend that income and wealth are social products which a society ought to divide equally among its members, so that the inequalities resulting from the operation of capitalist markets are ipso facto unjust. Others allow inequalities to be justified by differences in the economic or social contribution of different individuals or families, but hold that the actual inequalities prevailing in Western countries are not so justified. Either way, it is safe to say that inequalities are not a sufficient explanation of economic growth. Income and wealth inequalities have occurred in earlier Western societies and in a great many non-Western societies without setting off advances in economic welfare comparable to those experienced by the West in the last five centuries. Indeed, many Third World countries today have far greater inequalities than the United States.

Although it is clear that inequality of income and wealth is not a sufficient condition for economic growth, there is some reason to think that it may be a necessary condition. The reason is simple. Wealth may be a social product which originates in a social inheritance, but individuals and nations make very uneven marginal contributions to its production, over and above the original social inheritance. It is those marginal contributions which can be stimulated or repressed by rewards or penalties. A society which wishes to use rewards and penalties to encourage the production of wealth must somehow treat those individuals who make marginal contributions more favorably than it treats those who contribute only their share of the social inheritance. The only reason for stopping short of the conclusion that the resulting inequalities, in some uncertain degree, are an absolutely necessary condition of economic growth is the possibility that there may be ways of inducing people to engage in wealth-producing activity without such large rewards and penalties. To date, the possibility is conjectural, for no advanced society has managed without rewards and penalties, though many have stressed penalties more and rewards less than the West.

Whether inequalities arising from the operation of capitalist markets are unjust, and, if so, to what extent they can be remedied without creating further injustices, are questions with many ramifications, some highly controversial. The difficulties are due only in part to the inherent complexities traceable to the fact that extremely high income and wealth, like extreme poverty, have numerous causes, and their suppression would require a variety of political measures, some less acceptable than others.

A more objective difficulty is that the occupations essential to the orderly functioning of a modern society require widely different talents and skills and vary greatly in working conditions, social and cultural status, risk of unemployment and other forms of loss, and the sense of doing something interesting, valuable, or uplifting. Capitalist markets use variations in money income to match the number of people attracted to each occupation (the labor supply) to the number of jobs available in that occupation (the labor demand). A wage rate that matches supply and demand does not tell anyone what he or she is worth, but only how much can be earned by entering a given job or occupation. It supplies one datum relevant to the individual's choice to enter or leave. In the absence of variation in wage rates, it would be necessary to use some form of compulsory labor to avoid an oversupply of workers in the more attractive occupations and a shortage in the less attractive. Inequalities are thus a socially workable alternative to a system of compulsory labor. . . .

Exploitation

In its dictionary use, *exploitation* is part of all economic activity, if only in the sense of exploiting the actor's economic capabilities. In Marxist terms, the word is used invidiously, to describe the process by which the capitalist class is said to appropriate part of the product of labor, its "surplus value," particularly in industrial modes of production. The question is whether exploitation, even in this special sense, adequately explains Western growth. Its explanatory power seems limited to the growth of Western capital and capitalists' income. It is not helpful in explaining the growth of labor's income, which comprises most of the growth in question.

Even as to capital, exploitation explains accumulation better than it explains the opening up of opportunities for capital investment. Economic growth requires both capital and opportunities to use it profitably, and after the experience of the 1930s, few Western economists believe that the opportunities follow automatically from capital accumulation. Marx argued that capital accumulations supplied capitalists with an incentive to form new industries and develop overseas markets in order to employ the accumulated capital, but the existence of an incentive does not guarantee accomplishment. More recent appreciation of the importance of technological and social change and the expansion of trade in the creation of investment opportunities suggests that causation may have run in the other direction—that is, that the existence of investment opportunities may have been the incentive for the accumulation of capital. This

was especially so in the first stages of the Industrial Revolution, when the builders of the early factories responded to perceived needs for improvements in textile production, with no indication that a desire to utilize whatever surplus capital accumulations may have existed in prefactory England played a part in their efforts. If capital accumulation had been their purpose, the early factories would have been failures, for they required relatively small amounts of capital by comparison to the agriculture, shipping, or mercantile trade of their times.

A type of investment opportunity particularly relevant to exploitation consists in the opportunity to establish a factory where labor can be hired at lower costs than those prevailing among existing competitors. Opportunities of this type have been important in the economic development of Third World countries, but there are many older examples. Employment of factory workers at wages below those of guild artisans was a basic source of complaint in the England of the Industrial Revolution, and wages below those of New England were an important cause of the development of the textile and shoe industries in the American South. Marx would presumably have regarded these opportunities as exploitive, and workers who were being paid the former prevailing wages tended to agree. On the other hand, to countries or regions whose principal economic resource is an abundance of unemployed labor, employment of that labor on the best terms available is likely to seem not only a reasonable path of economic development, but morally imperative.

Whether driving down wages is a systemic or a merely opportunistic characteristic of capitalism is another question. Low wages encourage labor-intensive, rather than capital-intensive, methods of production and so tend to lessen the need for capital accumulation. For this reason, the corporation which replaces an old plant in Chicago with a new one in Korea may actually reduce its need for capital. In practice, however, the main thrust of capitalist development has been toward capital-intensive production. Had low wages been inherent in capitalist systems, one might have expected capitalists to stay with labor-intensive production and apply the money so saved to personal or other uses. Moreover, an international perspective is essential here. Opening a new plant in Korea will tend to *raise* wages in Korea.

As it is, real wage rates in the West have been rising for more than a century. Exploitation can hardly explain that rise. One might even observe that a long-continued rise in wages can make the question of exploitation irrelevant, for not even Marx contended that the expansion of output (which made the rise possible) was solely attributable to the proletariat.

Colonialism and Imperialism

Several explanations turn on the relations between Western countries and other, economically less developed, countries. Marxists describe these relations as imperialism, though the meaning of the term is clouded by differences in its treatment by Marx, Lenin, post–World War II theoreticians, and upward of a hundred years of variation in the economic history and development of both capitalist and precapitalist countries. There is considerable disagreement as to whether capitalism is a progressive force for development in precapitalist societies or an obstacle to it.

Colonialism is a slightly more neutral term for the relations between capitalist and precapitalist countries. In the sense of permanent colonization by residents of a mother country, colonialism is a very ancient practice, more often benign in its effects than colonialism in the later sense of imposing foreign rule on a large native population, after the manner of the British in India or the gradual extension of the Great Russians' domination over their many subject peoples. A mix of the two, in which colonists from a mother country become a significant minority, dominating a culturally different majority descended from earlier inhabitants and not readily admitted to the colonists' economy, is politically explosive, generating the violent modern histories of Algeria, Kenya, and Rhodesia and the contemporary political passions in South Africa. One might even add Ireland to the list.

Westerners began to colonize the American continents, in the first sense of colonialism, in the sixteenth century. Colonization was not entirely a matter of occupying nearly empty real estate, for the casualties included the highly developed Aztec and Inca cultures of Mexico and Peru. In the second sense of colonialism, the West asserted political hegemony over many densely populated and politically organized regions of India, Africa, Southeast Asia, and the East Indies—a process so far advanced by the closing decades of the nineteenth century that the newly formed German Empire complained of the lack of remaining opportunities for colonial enterprise.

If only because colonialism has become synonymous with infamy, it is worth recalling that from the Greek colonization of the Mediterranean to the colonial ventures of the West, some colonies were immensely successful from the viewpoints of both the colony and of its country of origin. Colonialism planted the seeds for the early development of today's North and South American economies—an awesome accomplishment. But the Spanish, Portuguese, English, French, and Dutch colonial experiences and their consequences were various, even in the Americas. Spain and Portugal became major colonial powers without ever becoming advanced capitalist economies, either at home or in their colonies. Their most valuable colonies were in Latin America, and the home countries lost these to independence movements while they themselves were in a precapitalist stage of development.

By far the most striking accomplishment of British colonialism was that it seeded several advanced Western economies, to the substantial benefit of the colonies: the United States, Canada, Australia, New Zealand, Hong Kong, and Singapore. These colonies' economic accomplishments also benefited Britain, for controlled and exploitive trade with an economically backward colony is much less beneficial to an advanced country than its trade with other advanced countries. France built and lost a large colonial empire, remembered for the violent collapse of its Indo-Chinese rule and the almost equally violent end of its rule over what was probably its most economically successful colony, Algeria. In retrospect, there is little reason to think that its colonial ventures contributed positively to France's economic growth.

Sometimes, the claim that Western economic advances arose from imperialism is based on the fact that colonies provided part of the market for the goods produced in the more advanced countries. This line of thought cannot be pressed much beyond the benefits to the individual firms engaged in colonial trade. First, poor and undeveloped countries do not as a rule provide markets large in relation to the output of advanced economies, so that the possibilities of exploitation are relatively small for the advanced economy as a whole. Markets large enough to encourage a major expansion of production in advanced countries are, almost by definition, markets in countries that are themselves economically advanced, though not necessarily industrialized. Second, the more solid benefits of trade with nonindustrialized countries came from trade that was not subject to effective imperialist political control. This trade arose from the development of overseas sources of food in both colonial and politically independent areas of North and South America, Australia, and Africa. It has been of immense economic benefit to the growing populations of Western Europe in the last century and a half, not because of exploitation, but because increased production kept world food prices from becoming a severe burden on European economies.

But the primary reason for doubting that an adequate explanation for Western growth is to be found in imperialism is the absence of any general correlation between the magnitude and timing of Western countries' economic growth and the magnitude and timing of their participation in imperialism. Imperialist Spain and Portugal did not achieve long-term growth; Switzerland and the Scandinavian countries, which did grow, were not imperialist countries; Germany and the United States, which achieved long-term growth, were latecomers to imperialism. Imperialist Britain and Holland grew, but they were already strong before they became imperial powers and they continued to grow after they gave up their empires. The eighteenth- and nineteenth-century history of most imperialist countries makes their economic growth seem more a cause of imperialism, stimulating overseas political adventures in the irresponsible exercise of new-found economic power, than its result. Of course, it is no comfort to non-Western countries injured by Western imperialism to suggest that the injury was gratuitous.

Slavery

Another explanation of Western economic growth stresses slavery. Slavery was rarely, if ever, used in Western industry. The reason was probably not moral, since slavery was an ancient and widespread institution—accepted, at the time of the Industrial Revolution, in English colonies though not in England itself. In the United States, if we wish to believe pre–Civil War Southern slaveholders and modern economic historians, slavery was not found in industry because free labor was available at less cost.

Since slavery was not used in industry, whatever contribution slavery made to Western development depended on the profits realized from the slave trade or on the use of slave labor in producing raw materials for Western factories. Profits from the slave trade were small by comparison to other sources of capital in the Western countries that engaged in it. The principal example of the use of slaves in the production of raw materials for factories is that of the British textile industry and its Southern suppliers. In the decades before the Civil War, England met much of its rapidly growing need for raw cotton by imports from the Southern states, where slave labor was widely used in cotton production. The growth in cotton imports was clearly a consequence, rather than a cause, of Britain's industrial revolution. How much slavery, as an institution, contributed economically to the growth of the cotton textile industry depends on how much the British saved by importing slave-grown cotton rather than cotton grown by free labor in the South, or in Egypt or India. Assuming cot-

ton produced by free labor would have been more expensive, the higher cost would tend to increase the price, and reduce the volume of sales, of cotton and cotton textiles; encourage production of cotton in Egypt, India, and Brazil; reduce the value of Southern cotton plantations; and modestly alter the economic incentives for technological developments in British textile production. The sum of these tendencies is that if the British had not imported slave-grown cotton, there is a reasonable possibility that the rate of growth of the British textile industry might have been a little slower in the years up to 1861.

An earlier use of slavery, notoriously in the West Indies, was in the production of sugar. But sugar was produced for consumption, not as a raw material for European factories.

To Western Europeans, slavery was an institution that arose almost entirely from colonization. The European countries which developed growth economies without colonialism also eschewed slavery. In contrast, Spain and Portugal were early leading colonizers, and both used slavery widely in their colonies. Yet both lagged in the development of modern growth economies. As in the case of imperialism, slavery, as an explanation for Western economic growth, suffers from a mismatch between the practice of slavery and the occurrence of economic growth.

It is worth stressing again that we are concerned with the question of whether colonialism and slavery explain Western economic growth. Whether some of the West's former colonies would have grown more rapidly had they not been colonized is a different question, again with answers that vary from one former colony to another.

What passes for an acceptable explanation often depends in part on the reason one wants an explanation. For some purposes, if one asks how James J. Hill built the Great Northern Railroad, the answer, "By stealing," suffices. But such an explanation would be of no assistance to someone who is contemplating the financing and construction of a railroad. Similarly, for some purposes, a sufficient explanation of how the West grew rich would be, "By the sweat of the poor and the plunder and enslavement of the weak." But if a non-Westerner wants to understand Western economic growth with a view to furthering the economic growth of his or her own country, or if a Westerner wants to understand it in order to safeguard existing growth, further explanation is needed. After all, exploitation has been pervasive outside the West, as well as in the ancient and medieval West itself, without duplicating the modern Western achievement.

AN EXPLANATION FROM HISTORY: A WESTERN GROWTH SYSTEM

Where, Then, Can We Find an Explanation?

The immediate sources of Western growth were innovations in trade, technology, and organization, in combination with accumulation of more and more capital, labor, and applied natural resources. Innovation emerged as a significant factor in Western growth as early as the mid-fifteenth century, and from the mid-eighteenth century on it has been pervasive and dominant. Innovation occurred in trading, production, products, services, institutions, and organization. The main characteristics of innovation—uncertainty, search, exploration, financial risk, experiment, and discovery—have so permeated the West's expansion of trade and the West's development of natural resources as to make it virtually an additional factor of production.

Ours is not the first period of Western European economic advance, though it much exceeds the earlier periods in magnitude. The era of the Roman empire, when England, France, and Spain were Roman colonies, came first. After the fifth century, when the Roman empire collapsed into the Dark Ages, the West suffered economic retrogression, rather than progress, for approximately five centuries. The West then experienced a second period of economic progress, beginning no later than the tenth century: a period of advance from the Dark Ages characterized by an increase in population, a steady extension of agricultural settlement into what had been wilderness, a growth in the number of towns, and appreciable advances in the technologies of war, architecture, transportation, and agriculture. The growth of Northern Europe from the tenth to the fourteenth century was primarily accumulative, as a growing population brought more land under cultivation. Expansion without innovation, however, eventually encounters serious limits to the continued growth of output per capita.

Growth resulting from innovation and growth resulting from the accumulation of capital and labor are not always easy to distinguish. Innovation frequently requires a concomitant growth of capital and labor, and, over a long enough time, some innovation can almost always be detected in even the most conservative expanding economy. The distinction rests partly on which type of growth predominates. It is also partly a question of whether the line of causation runs from innovation, providing opportunities for profitable investment, to the accumulation of capital and other resources, or from the accumulation of capital to the development of opportunities for investment.

Either way, the West has increasingly placed its primary reliance on innovation. As the Western economies expanded, so did their stocks of capital, their expenditures on education, the accumulation of skills by their work forces, and their populations. But the growth of these conventional factors of production was often a response to innovation, the deliberate fulfillment of a precondition to carrying through innovation. The line of causation was not all one way, but investment opportunities traceable to innovation became, predominantly, more the cause than the consequence of the accumulation of capital. Even the rise in population, which was not as rapid as the rate of economic growth, was made possible by innovations in agricultural techniques and the numerous types of innovation, including those in public health, required for urbanization.

. . . [B]oth firms and markets played important parts in innovation, and so did competition. Let us begin with firms.

By the mid-nineteenth century, Western societies had given their enterprises certain rights which can be viewed either as a grant of authority to make a number of decisions which had been made by political or religious authorities in most other societies, or as a grant of freedom from many common types of political or religious control. Four of these rights set the stage for economic growth based on innovation. First, individuals were authorized to form enterprises, with less and less political restriction. The formation of enterprises was extensively restricted by lack of money, lack of talent, or both, but not by lack of license from the political authorities nor by lack of ecclesiastical blessing. Second, enterprises were authorized to acquire goods and hold them for resale at a profit or loss, again with little or no restriction. Third, enterprises were authorized to add activities and to switch from one line of activity to another that seemed more promising, again with little restriction. Political or religious restriction arose only at the outer bounds of the numerous economic choices open to the enterprise: that is, the products or services it would make, how it would make them, the extent to which it would make them or buy them from other enterprises, how it would sell them, and the prices it would charge. Finally, while the assets of the enterprise and such profits as it accumulated from its activities might be taxed at predetermined rates, its property came to be regarded as immune from arbitrary seizure or expropriation by the political authorities.

In sum, the economic enterprise had become a unit for making a wide range of economic decisions, and its gains and losses from the decisions were expected to accrue to the enterprise or, less abstractly, to its owners. Virtually without thought or discussion, the West delegated to enterprises the making of a decision basic in the innovation process: which ideas should be tested and which should be allowed to die. For economic innovation requires not only an idea, but an experimental test of the idea in laboratory, factory, and market. Such tests are costly; they require resources and competence in engineering, manufacturing, and marketing, especially if the innovator is to capture the financial rewards of the innovation. These resources existed in the ordinary firm described in economics textbooks, and they made the firm a readily available unit for organizing innovation.

An essential aspect of the diffusion of authority over economic decisions generally, and innovational decisions in particular, was the emergence of markets. Likewise comparatively free of political and religious controls, markets became institutions for the resolution of the conflicts of interest among enterprises, consumers, and employees. As firms assumed a role in innovation in addition to their more familiar role as producers, markets assumed a role in innovation in addition to their role in determining prices and allocating resources. Markets determined who won the rewards of innovation and the quantum of the reward. The response of the market was *the* test of success or failure of an innovation. Governments could be asked to fund innovations that failed or seemed unlikely to succeed in markets, but the appeals were seldom successful except for military hardware, other products primarily of interest to governments, and research into the public health or food supply.

Competition also became involved in innovation. The market rewards of innovation depended largely on the innovator's ability to charge a high price for a unique product or service until such time as it could be imitated or superseded by others. The rewards depended, in other words, on the innovator's margin of priority in time over imitators and successors. This was true even of patents, which go to the first inventor, and whose economic life is measured by the time it takes to find a better alternative. Given the multiplicity of Western enterprises, the possibility of forming new ones, and the possibility that old ones could shift to new activities, the process of gaining the rewards of innovative ideas takes on the characteristics of a race, informal but still competitive. The competitive nature of the process was intensified by the Western practice of leaving the losers to bear their own losses, which were often substantial. This use of a competitive spur to stimulate change was a marked departure from tradition, for societies and their rulers have almost always strongly resisted change unless it enhanced the ruler's own power and well-being.

In the first centuries of Western growth, Western artisan inventors and their enterprises originated most of their own technology. Western science developed almost independently of Western industry until after 1800. Its contributions to industrial technology, still rare at the beginning of the nineteenth century, became more numerous as the century wore on. The introduction of the industrial research laboratory, toward the end of the nineteenth century and the beginning of the twentieth, systematized the links between science and industry and made it much easier for the West to nourish economic growth by drawing on a growing body of scientific knowledge.

The West's system of growth required a social class with the capacity to effect innovations, with incentives or motives for innovation, with a source of ideas for innovation, and with immunity from interference by the formidable social forces opposed to change, growth, and innovation. Since innovation works against the status quo, the innovating class had to act collectively as though it had more interest in change than in the status quo. Whatever diversity of interest existed among its individual members had to be regularly resolved in favor of the members interested in change.

We have emphasized the part played by innovation in Western growth. The decentralization of authority to make decision about innovations, together with the resources to effectuate such decisions and to absorb the gains or losses resulting from them, merits similar emphasis as an explanation of Western innovation. This diffusion of authority was interwoven with the development of an essentially autonomous economic sector; with the widespread use of experiment to answer questions of technology, marketing, and organization for which answers could be found in no other way; and with the emergence of great diversity in the West's modes of organizing economic activity.

It is not difficult to trace the outlines of the development, in the West, of these aspects of what amounted to a growth system.

The Emergence of an Autonomous Economic Sphere and a Merchant Class

The West's sustained economic growth began with the emergence of an economic sphere with a high degree of autonomy from political and religious control. The change from the coherent, fully integrated feudal society of the late Middle Ages to the plural society of eighteenth-century Europe implied a relaxation of political and ecclesiastical control of all spheres of life, including not only the economy, but also science, art, literature, music, and education.

This relaxation of political control over the economic sphere took several forms. There was an increase in the volume of trade at unregulated prices, as distinguished from trade at prices determined by political authority. This trade, and its profits, helped produce a merchant class who lived by buying and selling, as distinguished from one selling products they had made with their own hands. There was likewise a weakening of guild and government control over starting new businesses. In England, particularly, where the guilds' charters gave them authority over entry into particular lines of trade or manufacture within a town or borough, aggressive individuals could and did evade guild authority by establishing enterprises in the countryside or in other towns or boroughs. There was no sudden repeal of price controls or general deregulation movement; rather, in a development traceable from small beginnings in twelfth-century Northern Italy, enterprising merchants and artisans searched out more and more opportunities for relatively unregulated trade and manufacture until, by the end of the eighteenth century, the older forms of trade by "regulated companies" of merchants or artisans had become moribund. As Adam Smith sardonically observed in 1776, "To be merely useless, indeed, is perhaps the highest eulogy which can ever justly be bestowed on a regulated company."[3]

Innovation by Extension of Trade and Discovery of New Resources

As merchants succeeded more and more in escaping political control, they ventured into trade in more commodities and between more places. The early long-distance trading voyages, which brought exotic products back to European ports from the mysterious East, were enormously profitable when they were successful—scandalously so, to some observers. But for purposes of understanding the elements of Western growth, nothing could be more revealing than the early merchants' discovery of the enormous rewards to be reaped from introducing a new product that was popular with buyers and had no immediate competitors. They may have scandalized their late-medieval colleagues by skimming off consumers' money for exotic foreign goods instead of for the sober products of the local guilds, and they may have outraged their fellow burghers by drawing promising youngsters from honest trades into the hazards of voyages to unknown and often pagan places. But in modern terms, what they did is called innovation and competition by innovation. It would not be easy to overstate their importance to Western economic growth.

One characteristic of an economic system that is closely related to growth is the degree to which the economy employs trade and exchange, both domestic and foreign. This is partly a statistical artifact, since most statistics on economic growth measure the volume of some aspect of trade, but it has a deeper significance also. Exchange does not normally occur unless each party sees some advantage in it: usually, giving something it can produce (or otherwise acquire) more easily than it can produce (or otherwise acquire) what it accepts from the other party in exchange. Many communities have tried to supply most of their own needs by local production, like the manors of medieval Europe or the village economies of the Third World. When such communities begin to meet their needs through trade and exchange with other communities and with foreigners—as happened in England during the decline of the manorial system—the change implies specialized production and a new pattern of trade-based cooperation among the communities. It thus leads to increased wealth.

The Western search for trade was, at least in the beginning, not just for novel or exotic products from the East, but also for more familiar natural resources that could be netted, trapped, mined, felled, or plowed to yield something that could be sold in European markets. Fishermen preceded trappers to North America, and trappers preceded farmers, lumberjacks, and miners. The development of overseas exploration, overseas and domestic trade, and the finding and use of new natural resources were closely linked in an innovational process.

Innovation by Lowering the Cost of Production

The merchants gained wealth by being first with a novel import. When, a little later, enterprising artisans began to circumvent guild restrictions by setting up relatively large shops, or manufactories, outside guild jurisdiction, they extended the merchants' formula of being first, this time to being first with a lower-cost method of production. Late in the eighteenth century, during the Industrial Revolution, this same formula of competing with the status quo by new, lower-cost methods of production was used, this time by introducing more power and powered machinery to production processes.

Innovation by Introducing New Products

Innovation by devising and manufacturing new products was not a high road to great wealth so long as the individual inventor produced on a small scale. There were new products before the factory system—many of them, from improved wagons and carriages to improved clocks and watches. But what the inventive watchmaker or other artisan could collect in premium prices, however superior the product might be, did not add up to a great fortune, simply because the total quantity each sold was small. That changed with the introduction of the factory system of production, and in the nineteenth century, the introduction of new products became highly rewarded (sometimes).

In most societies, new products have tended to be of more interest to the rich than to the poor. It is an oddity of Western economic growth that, while it made some individuals extremely rich, it benefited the lifestyle of the very rich much less than it benefited the lifestyle of the less well-off. The reason is to be found in the nature of the innovations that the West most conspicuously rewarded. Innovations that reduced the cost of producing goods did not appreciably change the lifestyle of people who were abundantly able to pay pre-innovation prices, and the most lucrative new products were those with a market among the many, rather than among the few. Thus the first textile factories produced fabrics of inferior quality, which the rich did not want, and, a century later, the great automobile fortune was Henry Ford's, not Henry Royce's. The very rich were as well-housed, clothed, and adorned in 1885 as in 1985. Improvements in the transportation and preservation of food have benefited both rich and poor, but the main difference in the eating habits of the rich stems from the modern idea that obesity is medically inadvisable. A measured condescension toward innovations in mass entertainment, such as professional sports, movies, television, and rock music, is today almost an indicium of upper-class status, along with education outside the new system of public schools and colleges. It is much easier to think of innovations which benefited only the less well-off than it is to think of innovations which have benefited only the rich, and, in fact, the innovations of positive value to the rich are relatively few: advances in medical care, air conditioning, and improvements in transportation and preservation of food. It is a nice question to what extent modern electric gadgetry compensated the rich for the loss of their servants. The real point, not often recognized but essential to understanding why the benefits of Western growth were so widely diffused, is that the West's system of economic growth offered its largest financial rewards to innovators who improved the life-style not of the wealthy few, but of the less-wealthy many.

. . . The existence of a bias in Western systems toward the development of products and services for mass markets suggests that the differences in products have probably tended to favor the many rather than the few. Near the top of the wealth pyramid, it hardly matters, but a little further down—where one may expect to find people whose self-image of superior cultural and social status is not supported by a correspondingly superior life-style—the resulting exasperation may find expression in the characterization of advanced Western societies as lowbrow, tawdry, vulgar, cheap—or even consumerist.

The Development of Sources of Innovative Ideas

The development of an economic sphere within which individuals were allowed to engage in new ventures, to launch new business enterprises, to change the activities of existing enterprises, and to charge whatever prices seemed likely to yield the highest profits, all without asking official permission, offered immense possibilities of wealth to those who could furnish goods that were too new to the market to have any competitors, and that were highly valued by buyers. But it is one thing to know that both individual and social wealth flow generously from introducing lower-cost methods of producing old products, or from introducing new products, and it is quite another thing to know how to go about generating the required advances in method and product. For this, the Western growth system needed a source of invention. The development of this source followed two roughly parallel paths.

In the seventeenth century, the West developed a mode of scientific procedure conventionally associated with the names of Galileo and Bacon. It was based upon observation, reason, and experiment. By insisting upon the experimental verification of scientific explanations, Galileo and his successors established a general test of scientific truth which enabled scientists specialized in widely different disciplines to accept and use each other's results. The shared method created an organized scientific community, with a division of labor among scientists in numerous specialized fields, all contributing to the accumulation of a coherent body of knowledge. By the close of the seventeenth century, the scale of the West's scientific effort was already overwhelmingly greater than in any contemporary or earlier culture, and so was the West's progress in understanding natural phenomena. Even so, it was little more than the seed of what it was to become.

The advances of the seventeenth century established the method, organization, secular viewpoint, and the early beginnings of the basic knowledge upon which modern Western science has been built. Yet in industrial technology, parallel advances of more direct economic importance originated mostly in hands-on invention and experiment by artisan inventors until late in the nineteenth century. The influence of scientific discovery was indirect, although some chemists formed early links between scientific explanation and industrial practice. The progress of Western industrial technology during the eighteenth and nineteenth centuries was, nevertheless, no less striking than that of Western science.

Today, we recognize a rough division between pure science, which develops explanations for natural phenomena, and industrial science, which develops commercial products and production processes. Late in the nineteenth century, the paths of pure science and industrial technology converged in the fields of chemistry, electricity, and biology. The earlier artisan inventors of industry gave way to professional scientists, simply because industry was now working with phenomena which could be understood only in terms of the explanations devised by pure science, and these explanations were accessible only to specially trained professionals. It was not so much that the possibilities of artisan invention were exhausted as that the expansion of science had opened a new world of professional invention. It thus took approximately two hundred fifty years for Galilean science to reach the point of dominating the West's industrial invention.

Uncertainty and Experiment

Uncertainty runs throughout the process of innovation. The outcome of invention is, by definition of invention, unpredictable. The cost of development is initially unknown, and so are the benefits, dependent as they are on the advantages and cost of the final product and the opportunities for exploiting it commercially before imitators compete down the margin of profit. Human experience, judgment, and planning can reduce the uncertainty, but they can never come close to eliminating it.

The only known device for resolving the uncertainties surrounding any given innovation proposal is experiment, up to and including the manufacture and marketing of a product. Such experiments are costly; on the other hand, the failure to undertake them precludes the possibility of innovation. And the consequences of successful experiments are economic growth. The West has threaded its way between the horns of this dilemma by what amounts to a form of insurance. Authority to undertake an innovation is diffused among a comparatively large number of firms and individuals who can bring together the required money and talent, thus reducing the risk that a desirable proposal may be rejected because of a viewpoint peculiar to a single decision maker. Along with the

authority goes the responsibility: the innovator bears the losses of failed experiments and gains such of the benefits of the successful ones as the innovator can capture.

This system of diffusion of authority, experiment, and responsibility presupposes an ownership relation between the holders of authority to innovate and the required funds, laboratories, factories, and distribution systems. For a socialist system to replicate the Western system for innovation, it would be necessary to give the managers of socialist enterprises roughly the same authority—to determine the uses to be made of the enterprise's assets, what products the enterprise might produce and by what methods, and what prices it should charge—that the owner of a capitalist enterprise possesses. It might not be necessary to give the managers the owners' right to all the profits and all the responsibility for the losses; after all, many Western innovations originated under the direction of managers compensated by salaries and bonuses. On the other hand, the relationship between private owners and a salaried public employee, and some Western innovations have originated in owner-managed enterprises. It is doubtful that a socialist society could be as innovative as the West without using the main substantive features of private ownership of the means of production and without curtailing central authority over the uses of the means of production so greatly as to make the feasibility of planning dubious. Put the other way around, the West's system of innovation is interwoven, probably beyond separation, with its system of private property rights.

Overcoming Resistance to Innovation

The diffusion of authority to initiate innovations served also as the West's way of guarding against a chronic menace to innovative change—the interest of the status quo in suppressing innovation. An innovation will seldom be authorized or financed by government or corporate officials whose careers would be adversely affected by the success of the proposal. Sometimes the success of an innovation means the end of an entire industry, entailing large capital losses as well as the loss to its employees of their human capital of training and experience. The opposition to innovation can be, and has been, very powerful.

The West's methods of overcoming the obstructionism of the status quo included a system of decentralized decision making in capital investment. Not all capital investments fund innovations; a decision is sometimes made, though not often, to spend funds to replace old equipment or rebuild old facilities without modernizing them at all. But a diffusion of the authority to make investment decisions generally is so closely related to the diffusion of authority to select innovations as to make the two practically inseparable.

The comparative impotence of the forces opposed to innovation may have rested ultimately on the general Western belief that innovation is a good thing, but there is little record of its having been debated in those terms. Like the rest of the Western growth system, it originated in a much more devious and far less rational way. During the Middle Ages, guilds and corporations that wished to obtain power to exclude others from their trade got it by purchase of a charter from the Crown. The issuance of such charters was a substantial source of royal revenues. When English judges were presented with the question whether an individual who wished to enter a lawful occupation was liable for the consequent injury to those already there, an eye to the royal revenues made the answer predictable: no charter, no liability. By the seventeenth century, English merchants were strongly resisting the continued issuance of such charters. In this backhanded way, the right of individuals to use their personal efforts and property in trade and manufacturing without having to answer to their competitors became embedded in English law. By the late eighteenth century, when the introduction of the factory system seriously disrupted some types of earlier handicraft production, there was rarely any way to prevent innovation except by force. Force was sometimes employed, but it was illegitimate force, indignantly suppressed by political authorities acting against riots, arson, and sabotage.

Innovation in Organization: Diversity

We have stressed innovation in technology as a major element in the West's growth system. But innovation in organization also played a part worth emphasizing; indeed, it can be reasonably argued that the West's success in technological innovation is attributable to its success in organizational innovation.

From the fifteenth century on, changes in the internal economic organization of Western societies proliferated. The relationship between the political and economic spheres began to change. European governments and merchants joined in the invention of new forms of enterprise, sometimes successfully and sometimes with scandalous or disastrous results. Later, the Industrial Revolution of the late eighteenth century made it necessary to devise new modes of organization for new kinds of economic enterprise. The problem was not simply one of legal forms—corporate, partnership, or proprietorship. There were also the more novel problems of devising ways to organize

groups of workers much larger in number than those employed in artisan shops and specialized to many more skills, of finding ways to minimize the risks of investing great blocks of capital in one enterprise, of deciding what different lines of business should be combined in one enterprise, and of protecting the interests of owners in enterprises increasingly managed by hired professionals. By continuing experiment, the West found solutions to these problems. The solutions were often transient, but the experimental process by which they were found proved basic to Western economic advance.

As the economies of Western countries have grown, and as they have changed both their methods of production and their products, they have constantly modified the size and structure of their enterprise organizations. The size of enterprises and their form of organization (partnership, proprietorship, or corporation) had to be adapted to the new environment of factory, railroads, and the apparatus of urbanization: transport, gas, and electricity. In addition, the competitive element within Western economies, particularly rivalry for the rewards of being first with innovations, led enterprises to try to differentiate themselves from other enterprises in ways that carried a competitive advantage. An attempt to be first with a new product or a lower-cost way of producing an old product is an attempt at differentiation. This combination of necessary adaptation to a changing environment and competitive attempts at self-differentiation has produced a striking diversity in the size, economic functions, and organization of enterprises. . . .

CONCLUSION

Our general conclusion is that the underlying source of the West's ability to attract the lightning of economic revolutions was a unique use of experiment in technology and organization to harness resources to the satisfaction of human wants. The key elements of the system were the wide diffusion of the authority and resources necessary to experiment; an absence of more than rudimentary political and religious restrictions on experiment; and incentives which combined ample rewards for success, defined as the widespread economic use of the results of experiment, with a risk of severe penalties for failing to experiment.

The experiments embraced not simply the abstract creation of a new product or service or a new organizational device, but also the testing of the product or service by actually offering it for public use, and of the organizational device by using it in active enterprises. This type of experiment required an economic sector with autonomy from political intervention, in which experiment could be tried and results used with little outside interference. Experimental adaptation to the inherent diversity of both human wants and the resources available for satisfying them involved self-reinforcing, two-way causation, for experiment created both additional human wants and additional resources, thereby inviting additional diversity in the system for satisfying them. This causal loop generated great diversity of sizes and types of both enterprises and markets. This diversity in the forms of economic life, like the diversity in biosystems, is important not for its own sake but because it is an earmark of successful adaptation and full utilization of the resources available. The thematic terms are thus *autonomy, experiment,* and *diversity.*

This system of commercial experiment owed its accomplishments in part to the immense achievements in another department of Western life—the scientific sphere. But it was not entirely a matter of dependency on science. In the three-cornered relations of technology, the experimental economy, and growth of material welfare, the experimental economy served as a more efficient link between science and growth than any other society had achieved, and the economy was itself the source of much of its own technology.

The system involved, and indeed required, a division of labor among the political, religious, scientific, and economic spheres of social life, which allowed each the degree of autonomy needed to enable it to concentrate on its own affairs with much less interference from the others than has been common in other societies. The result was not just an improvement in the conduct of economic affairs, but also in the conduct of political, religious, and scientific affairs.

It is worth dwelling on the special importance of experiment to organization. The organizational innovator is typically dealing with well-informed and highly intelligent people who react vigorously, ingeniously, adversely, and even vengefully to organizational changes not in their interests—and to a good many changes which are in their interests, at least as perceived by the innovator. It is thus inherent in organizational innovation that the outcome can never be predicted more than tentatively, nor known without experiment. By comparison, physicists, geologists, and biologists work with materials that are sometimes almost perversely resistant to understanding, but such materials only appear to have minds of their own. It is the organizational innovator who is open to counter-invention by those in the organization who are op-

posed to the change, and the uncertainty of the outcome is implied by the definition of *invention.* Of all the fields of human endeavor, none is more unsuited to ideology than organizational innovation, and nowhere else does ideology rise so far above experiment in pressing its claims.

Initially, the West's achievement of autonomy stemmed from a relaxation, or a weakening, of political and religious controls, giving other departments of social life the opportunity to experiment with change. Growth is, of course, a form of change, and growth is impossible when change is not permitted. And *successful* change requires a large measure of freedom to experiment. A grant of that kind of freedom costs a society's rulers their feeling of control, as if they were conceding to others the power to determine the society's future. The great majority of societies, past and present, have not allowed it. Nor have they escaped from poverty.

ENDNOTES

1. Oswald Spengler, *The Decline of the West,* 2 vols (New York: Knopf, 1926–28).
2. Max Weber, *General Economic History* (New York: First Collier Books Ed., 1961), p. 261.
3. Adam Smith, *An Inquiry into the Nature and Causes of the Wealth of Nations,* vol. 2 (New York: Oxford University Press, 1976), bk. 5, p. 735.

QUESTIONS ON ROSENBERG AND BIRDZELL

1. Rosenberg and Birdzell canvas some of the competing explanations for the growth of wealth in the Western world. What are some of these, and why do the authors reject them?

2. Rosenberg and Birdzell argue for a set of features that are sufficient to account for the growth of wealth. What are these features? Are each of these features (or all of them together) *necessary* for the growth of wealth? Are there other features which might also be sufficient or necessary?

3. In what sense can it be said that economic innovation requires not only ideas but a method or field of experimentation? How do firms and markets provide a means for experimentation?

4. The authors state that "the 1985 life-style is clearly preferable" to that of 1885. Do you agree? Why or

why not? Are there any negative side effects to the gains in wealth and productivity noted by Rosenberg and Birdzell?

The Market

Ludwig von Mises

One of the twentieth century's greatest economists and a leader of the "Austrian School" of economics, Ludwig von Mises (1881–1973) is the author of The Theory of Money and Credit *(1912),* Socialism *(1922),* Epistemological Problems of Economics *(1933), and, among other works,* Human Action *(1949), from which this selection is taken. An émigré from Austria in the 1930s, Mises settled first in Switzerland, moving to the U.S. in 1940. Never offered an academic position in the United States, he nonetheless taught for over twenty years at the Graduate School of Business at New York University, though his salary was paid by foundations and businesspersons independent of the university.*

THE CHARACTERISTICS OF THE MARKET ECONOMY

The market economy is the social system of the division of labor under private ownership of the means of production. Everybody acts on his own behalf; but everybody's actions aim at the satisfaction of other people's needs as well as at the satisfaction of his own. Everybody in acting serves his fellow citizens. Everybody, on the other hand, is served by his fellow citizens. Everybody is both a means and an end in himself, an ultimate end for himself and a means to other people in their endeavors to attain their own ends.

This system is steered by the market. The market directs the individual's activities into those channels in which he best serves the wants of his fellow men. There is in the operation of the market no compulsion and coercion. The state, the social apparatus of coercion and compulsion, does not interfere with the market and with the citizens' activities directed by the market. It employs its power to beat people into submission solely for the prevention of actions destructive to the preservation and the smooth operation of the market economy. It protects the individual's life, health, and property against violent or fraudulent aggression on the part of domestic gangsters and external foes. Thus the state creates and preserves the environment in which the market economy can safely operate. The Marxian slogan "anarchic production" pertinently characterizes this social structure as an economic system which is not directed by a dictator, a production tsar who assigns to each a task and compels him to obey this command. Each man is free; nobody is subject to a despot. Of his own accord the individual integrates himself into the cooperative system. The market directs him and reveals to him in what way he can best promote his own welfare as well as that of other people. The market is supreme. The market alone puts the whole social system in order and provides it with sense and meaning.

The market is not a place, a thing, or a collective entity. The market is a process, actuated by the interplay of the actions of the various individuals cooperating under the division of labor. The forces determining the—continually changing—state of the market are the value judgments of these individuals and their actions as directed by these value judgments. The state of the market at any instant is the price structure, i.e., the totality of the exchange ratios as established by the interaction of those eager to buy and those eager to sell. There is nothing inhuman or mystical with regard to the market. The market process is entirely a resultant of human actions. Every market phenomenon can be traced back to definite choices of the members of the market society.

The market process is the adjustment of the individual actions of the various members of the market society to the requirements of mutual cooperation. The market prices tell the producers what to produce, how to produce, and in what quantity. The market is the focal point to which the activities of the individuals converge. It is the center from which the activities of the individuals radiate.

The market economy must be strictly differentiated from the second thinkable—although not realizable—system of social cooperation under the division of labor: the system of social or governmental ownership of the means of production. This second system is commonly called socialism, communism, planned economy, or state capitalism. . . .

If within a society based on private ownership by the means of production some of these means are publicly owned and operated—that is, owned and operated by the government or one of its agencies—this does not make for a mixed system which would combine socialism and capitalism. The fact that the state or municipalities own and operate some plants does not alter the characteristic features of the market economy. These publicly owned and operated enterprises are subject to the sovereignty of the market. They must fit themselves, as buyers of raw materials, equipment, and labor, and as sellers of goods and services, into the scheme of the market economy. They are subject to the laws of the market and thereby depend on the consumers who may or may not patronize them. They must strive for profits or, at least, to avoid losses. The government may cover losses of its plants or shops by drawing on public funds. But this neither eliminates nor mitigates the supremacy of the market; it merely shifts it to another sector. For the means for covering the losses must be raised by the imposition of taxes. But this taxation has its effects on the market and influences the economic structure according to the laws of the market. It is the operation of the market, and not the government collecting the taxes, that decides upon whom the incidence of the taxes falls and how they affect production and consumption. Thus the market, not a government bureau, determines the working of these publicly operated enterprises. . . .

Nothing that is in any way connected with the operation of a market is in the praxeological or economic sense to be called socialism. The notion of socialism as conceived and defined by all socialists implies the absence of a market for factors of production and of prices of such factors. The "socialization" of individual plants, shops, and farms—that is, their transfer from private into public ownership—is a method of bringing about socialism by successive measures. It is a step on the way toward socialism, but not in itself socialism. . . .

For monetary economic calculation is the intellectual basis of the market economy. The tasks set to acting within any system of the division of labor cannot be achieved without economic calculation. The market economy calculates in terms of money prices. That it is capable of such calculation was instrumental in its evolution and conditions its present-day operation. The market economy is real because it can calculate.

CAPITALISM

All civilizations have up to now been based on private ownership of the means of production. In the past civilization and private property have been linked together. Those who maintain that economics is an experimental science and nevertheless recommend public control of the means of production, lamentably contradict themselves. If historical experience could teach us anything, it would be that private property is inextricably linked with civilization. There is no experience to the effect that socialism could provide a standard of living as high as that provided by capitalism.[1]

The system of market economy has never been fully and purely tried. But there prevailed in the orbit of Western civilization since the Middle Ages by and large a general tendency toward the abolition of institutions hindering the operation of the market economy. With the successive progress of this tendency, population figures multiplied and the masses' standard of living was raised to an unprecedented and hitherto undreamed of level. The average American worker enjoys amenities for which Croesus, Crassus, the Medici, and Louis XIV would have envied him. . . .

THE SOVEREIGNTY OF THE CONSUMERS

The direction of all economic affairs is in the market society a task of the entrepreneurs. Theirs is the control of production. They are at the helm and steer the ship. A superficial observer would believe that they are supreme. But they are not. They are bound to obey unconditionally the captain's orders. The captain is the consumer. Neither the entrepreneurs nor the farmers nor the capitalists determine what has to be produced. The consumers do that. If a businessman does not strictly obey the orders of the public as they are conveyed to him by the structure of market prices, he suffers losses, he goes bankrupt, and is thus removed from his eminent position at the helm. Other men who did better in satisfying the demand of the consumers replace him.

The consumers patronize those shops in which they can buy what they want at the cheapest price. Their buying and their abstention from buying decides who should own and run the plants and the farms. They make poor people rich and rich people poor. They determine precisely what should be produced, in what quality, and in what quantities. They are merciless bosses, full of whims and fancies, changeable and unpredictable. For them nothing counts other than their own satisfaction. They do not care a whit for past merit and vested interests. If something is offered to them that they like better or that is cheaper, they desert their old purveyors. In their capacity as buyers and consumers they are hard-hearted and callous, without consideration for other people.

Only the sellers of goods and services of the first order are in direct contact with the consumers and directly depend on their orders. But they transmit the orders received from the public to all those producing goods and services of the higher orders. For the manufacturers of consumers' goods, the retailers, the service trades, and the professions are forced to acquire what they need for the conduct of their own business from those purveyors who offer them at the cheapest price. If they were not intent upon buying in the cheapest market and arranging their processing of the factors of production so as to fill the demands of the consumers in the best and cheapest way, they would be forced to go out of business. More efficient men who succeeded better in buying and processing the factors of production would supplant them. The consumer is in a position to give free rein to his caprices and fancies. The entrepreneurs, capitalists, and farmers have their hands tied; they are bound to comply in their operations with the orders of the buying public. Every deviation from the lines prescribed by the demand of the consumers debits their account. The slightest deviation, whether willfully brought about or caused by error, bad judgment, or inefficiency, restricts their profits or makes them disappear. A more serious deviation results in losses and thus impairs or entirely absorbs their wealth. Capitalists, entrepreneurs, and landowners can only preserve and increase their wealth by filling best the orders of the consumers. They are not free to spend money which the consumers are not prepared to refund to them in paying more for the products. In the conduct of their business affairs they must be unfeeling and stony-hearted because the consumers, their bosses, are themselves unfeeling and stony-hearted.

The consumers determine ultimately not only the prices of the consumers' goods, but no less the prices of all factors of production. They determine the income of every member of the market economy. The consumers, not the entrepreneurs, pay ultimately the wages earned by every worker, the glamorous movie star as well as the charwoman. With every penny spent the consumers determine the direction of all production processes and the details of the organization of all business activities. This state of affairs has been described by calling the market a democracy in which every penny gives a right to cast a ballot.[2] It would be more correct to say that a democratic constitution is a scheme to assign to the citizens in the conduct of government the same supremacy the market economy gives them in their capacity as consumers. However, the comparison is imperfect. In the political democracy only the votes cast for the majority candidate or the majority plan are effective in shaping the course of affairs. The votes polled by the minority do not directly influence policies. But on the market no vote is cast in vain. Every penny spent has the power to work upon the production processes. The publishers cater not only to the majority by publishing detective stories, but also to the minority reading lyrical poetry and philosophical tracts. The bakeries bake bread not only for healthy people, but also for the sick on special diets. The decision of a consumer is carried into effect with the full momentum he gives it through his readiness to spend a definite amount of money.

It is true, in the market the various consumers have not the same voting right. The rich cast more votes than the poorer citizens. But this inequality is itself the outcome of a previous voting process. To be rich, in a pure market economy, is the outcome of success in filling best the demands of the consumers. A wealthy man can preserve his wealth only by continuing to serve the consumers in the most efficient way.

Thus the owners of the material factors of production and the entrepreneurs are virtually mandataries or trustees of the consumers, revocably appointed by an election daily repeated.

There is in the operation of a market economy only one instance in which the proprietary class is not completely subject to the supremacy of the consumers. Monopoly prices are an infringement of the sway of the consumers. . . .

THE PRICING PROCESS

The recurrence of individual acts of exchange generates the market step by step with the evolution of the division of labor within a society based on private property. As it becomes a rule to produce for other people's consumption, the members of society must sell and buy. The multiplication of the acts of exchange and the increase in the number of people offering or asking for the same commodities narrow the margins between the valuations of the parties. Indirect exchange and its perfection through the use of money divide the transactions into two different parts: sale and purchase. What in the eyes of one party is a sale, is for the other party a purchase. The divisibility of money, unlimited for all practical purposes, makes it possible to determine the exchange ratios with nicety. The exchange ratios are now as a rule money prices. They are determined between extremely narrow margins: the valuations on the one hand of the marginal buyer and those of the marginal offerer who abstains from selling, and the valuations on the other hand of the marginal seller and those of the marginal potential buyer who abstains from buying. . . .

The driving force of the market process is provided neither by the consumers nor by the owners of the means of production—land, capital goods, and labor—but by the promoting and speculating entrepreneurs. These are people intent upon profiting by taking advantage of differences in prices. Quicker of apprehension and farther-sighted than other men, they look around for sources of profit. They buy where and when they deem prices too low, and they sell where and when they deem prices too high. They approach the owners of the factors of production, and their competition sends the prices of these factors up to the limit corresponding to their anticipation of the future prices of the products. They approach the consumers, and their competition forces prices of consumers' goods down to the point at which the whole supply can be sold. Profit-seeking speculation is the driving force of the market as it is the driving force of production. . . .

VALUATION AND APPRAISEMENT

The ultimate source of the determination of prices is the value judgments of the consumers. Prices are the outcome of the valuation preferring *a* to *b*. They are social phenomena as they are brought about by the interplay of the valuations of all individuals participating in the operation of the market. Each individual, in buying or not buying and in selling or not selling, contributes his share to the formation of the market prices. But the larger the market is, the smaller is the weight of each individual's contribution. Thus the structure of market prices appears to the individual as a datum to which he must adjust his own conduct.

The valuations which result in determination of definite prices are different. Each party attaches a higher value to the good he receives than to that he gives away. The exchange ratio, the price, is not the product of an equality of valuation, but, on the contrary, the product of a discrepancy in valuation.

Appraisement must be clearly distinguished from valuation. Appraisement in no way depends upon the subjective valuation of the man who appraises. He is not intent upon establishing the subjective use-value of the good concerned, but upon anticipating the prices which the market will determine. Valuation is a value judgment expressive of a difference in value. Appraisement is the anticipation of an expected fact. It aims at establishing what prices will be paid on the market for a particular commodity or what amount of money will be required for the purchase of a definite commodity.

Valuation and appraisement are, however, closely connected. The valuations of an autarkic husbandman directly compare the weight he attaches to different means for the removal of uneasiness. The valuations of a man buying and selling on the market must not disregard the structure of market prices; they depend upon appraisement. In order to know the meaning of a price one must know the purchasing power of the amount of money concerned. It is necessary by and large to be familiar with the prices of those goods which one would like to acquire and to form on the ground of such knowledge an opinion about their future prices. If an individual speaks of the costs incurred by the purchase of some goods already acquired or to be incurred by the purchase of goods he plans to acquire, he expresses these costs in terms of money. But this amount of money represents in his eyes the degree of satisfaction he could obtain by employing it for the acquisition of other goods. The valuation makes a detour, it goes via the appraisement of the structure of market prices; but it always aims finally at the comparison of alternative modes for the removal of felt uneasiness.

It is ultimately always the subjective value judgments of individuals that determine the formation of prices. Catallactics in conceiving the pricing process necessarily reverts to the fundamental category of action, the preference given to *a* over *b*. In view of popular errors it is expedient to emphasize that catallactics deals with the real prices as they are paid in definite transactions and not with imaginary prices. The concept of final prices is merely a mental tool for the grasp of a particular problem, the emergence of entrepreneurial profit and loss. The concept of a "just" or "fair" price is devoid of any scientific meaning; it is a disguise for wishes, a striving for a state of affairs different from reality. Market prices are entirely determined by the value judgments of men as they really act.

If one says that prices tend toward a point at which total demand is equal to total supply, one resorts to another mode of expressing the same concatenation of phenomena. Demand and supply are the outcome of the conduct of those buying and selling. If, other things being equal, supply increases, prices must drop. At the previous price all those ready to pay this price could buy the quantity they wanted to buy. If the supply increases, they must buy larger quantities or other people who did not buy before must become interested in buying. This can only be attained at a lower price.

It is possible to visualize this interaction by drawing two curves, the demand curve and the supply curve, whose intersection shows the price. It is no less possible to express it in mathematical symbols. But it is necessary to comprehend that such pictorial or mathematical modes of representation do not affect the essence of our interpretation and that they do not add a whit to our insight. Furthermore it is important to realize that we do not have any knowledge or experience concerning the shape of such curves. Always, what we know is only market prices—that is, not the curves but only a point which we interpret as the intersection of two hypothetical curves. The drawing of such curves may prove expedient in visualizing the problems for undergraduates. For the real tasks of catallactics they are mere byplay. . . .

The market determines prices of factors of production in the same way in which it determines prices of consumers' goods. The market process is an interaction of men deliberately striving after the best possible removal of dissatisfaction. It is impossible to think away or to eliminate from the market process the men actuating its operation. One cannot deal with the market of consumers' goods and disregard the actions of the consumers. One cannot deal with the market of the goods of higher orders while disregarding the actions of the entrepreneurs and the fact that the use of money is essential in their transactions. There is nothing automatic or mechanical in the operation of the market. The entrepreneurs, eager to earn profits, appear as bidders at an auction, as it were, in which the owners of the factors of production put up for sale land, capital goods, and labor. The entrepreneurs are eager to outdo one another by bidding higher prices than their rivals. Their offers are limited on the one hand by their anticipation of future prices of the products and on the other hand by the necessity to snatch the factors of production away from the hands of other entrepreneurs competing with them.

The entrepreneur is the agency that prevents the persistence of a state of production unsuitable to fill the most urgent wants of the consumers in the cheapest way. All people are anxious for the best possible satisfaction of their wants and are in this sense striving after the highest profit they can reap. The mentality of the promoters, speculators, and entrepreneurs is not different from that of their fellow men. They are merely superior to the masses in mental power and energy. They are the leaders on the way toward material progress. They are the first to understand that there is a discrepancy between what is done and what could be done. They guess what the consumers would like to have and are intent upon providing them with these things. In the pursuit of such plans they bid higher prices for some factors of production and lower the prices of other factors of production by restricting their demand for them. In supplying the market with those consumers' goods in the sale of which the highest profits can be earned, they create a tendency toward a fall in their prices. In restricting the output of those consumers' goods the production of which does not offer chances for reaping profit, they bring about a tendency toward a rise in their prices. All these transfor-

mations go on ceaselessly and could stop only if the unrealizable conditions of the evenly rotating economy and of static equilibrium were to be attained. . . .

The pricing process is a social process. It is consummated by an interaction of all members of the society. All collaborate and cooperate, each in the particular role he has chosen for himself in the framework of the division of labor. Competing in cooperation and cooperating in competition all people are instrumental in bringing about the result, viz., the price structure of the market, the allocation of the factors of production to the various lines of want-satisfaction, and the determination of the share of each individual. These three events are not three different matters. They are only different aspects of one indivisible phenomenon which our analytical scrutiny separates into three parts. In the market process they are accomplished *uno actu.* Only people prepossessed by socialist leanings who cannot free themselves from longing glances at socialist methods speak of three different processes in dealing with the market phenomena: the determination of prices, the direction of productive efforts, and distribution. . . .

COMPETITION

In nature there prevail irreconcilable conflicts of interests. The means of subsistence are scarce. Proliferation tends to outrun subsistence. Only the fittest plants and animals survive. The antagonism between an animal starving to death and another that snatches the food away from it is implacable.

Social cooperation under the division of labor removes such antagonisms. It substitutes partnership and mutuality for hostility. The members of society are united in a common venture.

The term competition as applied to the conditions of animal life signifies the rivalry between animals which manifests itself in their search for food. We may call this phenomenon *biological competition.* Biological competition must not be confused with *social competition,* i.e., the striving of individuals to attain the most favorable position in the system of social cooperation. As there will always be positions which men value more highly than others, people will strive for them and try to outdo rivals. Social competition is consequently present in every conceivable mode of social organization. If we want to think of a state of affairs in which there is no social competition, we must construct the image of a socialist system in which the chief in his endeavors to assign to everybody his place and task in society is not aided by any ambition on the part of his subjects. The individuals are entirely indifferent and do not apply for special appointments. They behave like the stud horses which do not try to put themselves in a favorable light when the owner picks out the stallion to impregnate his best brood mare. But such people would no longer be acting men.

Catallactic competition is emulation between people who want to surpass one another. It is not a fight, although it is usual to apply to it in a metaphorical sense the terminology of war and internecine conflict, of attack and defense, of strategy and tactics. Those who fail are not annihilated; they are removed to a place in the social system that is more modest, but more adequate to their achievements than that which they had planned to attain.

In a totalitarian system, social competition manifests itself in the endeavors of people to court the favor of those in power. In the market economy, competition manifests itself in the fact that the sellers must outdo one another by offering better or cheaper goods and services, and that the buyers must outdo one another by offering higher prices. In dealing with this variety of social competition which may be called *catallactic competition,* we must guard ourselves against various popular fallacies.

The classical economists favored the abolition of all trade barriers preventing people from competing on the market. Such restrictive laws, they explained, result in shifting production from those places in which natural conditions of production are more favorable to places in which they are less favorable. They protect the less efficient man against his more efficient rival. They tend to perpetuate backward technological methods of production. In short they curtail production and thus lower the standard of living. In order to make all people more prosperous, the economists argued, competition should be free to everybody. In this sense they used the term *free competition.* There was nothing metaphysical in their employment of the term *free.* They advocated the nullification of privileges barring people from access to certain trades and markets. All the sophisticated lucubrations caviling at the metaphysical connotations of the adjective *free* as applied to competition are spurious; they have no reference whatever to the catallactic problem of competition.

As far as natural conditions come into play, competition can only be "free" with regard to those factors of production which are not scarce and therefore not objects of human action. In the catallactic field competition is always restricted by the inexorable scarcity of the economic goods and services. Even in the absence of institutional barriers erected to restrict the number of those competing, the state of affairs is never such as to enable everyone to compete in all sectors of the market. In each sector only comparatively small groups can engage in competition.

Catallactic competition, one of the characteristic features of the market economy, is a social phenomenon. It is not a right, guaranteed by the state and the laws, that would make it possible for every individual to choose ad libitum the place in the structure of the division of labor he likes best. To assign to everybody his proper place in society is the task of the consumers. Their buying and abstention from buying is instrumental in determining each individual's social position. Their supremacy is not impaired by any privileges granted to the individuals qua producers. Entrance into a definite branch of industry is virtually free to newcomers only as far as the consumers approve of this branch's expansion or as far as the newcomers succeed in supplanting those already occupied in it by filling better or more cheaply the demands of the consumers. Additional investment is reasonable only to the extent that it fills the most urgent among the not yet satisfied needs of the consumers. If the existing plants are sufficient, it would be wasteful to invest more capital in the same industry. The structure of market prices pushes the new investors into other branches.

It is necessary to emphasize this point because the failure to grasp it is at the root of many popular complaints about the impossibility of competition. Some sixty years ago people used to declare: You cannot compete with the railroad companies; it is impossible to challenge their position by starting competing lines; in the field of land transportation there is no longer competition. The truth was that at that time the already operating lines were by and large sufficient. For additional capital investment the prospects were more favorable in improving the serviceableness of the already operating lines and in other branches of business than in the construction of new railroads. However, this did not interfere with further technological progress in transportation technique. The bigness and the economic "power" of the railroad companies did not impede the emergence of the motor car and the airplane.

Today people assert the same with regard to various branches of big business: You cannot challenge their position, they are too big and too powerful. But competition does not mean that anybody can prosper by simply imitating what other people do. It means the opportunity to serve the consumers in a better or cheaper way without being restrained by privileges granted to those whose vested interests the innovation hurts. What a newcomer who wants to defy the vested interests of the old established firms needs most is brains and ideas. If his project is fit to fill the most urgent of the unsatisfied needs of the consumers or to purvey them at a cheaper price than their old purveyors, he will succeed in spite of the much talked of bigness and power of the old firms.

Catallactic competition must not be confused with prize fights and beauty contests. The purpose of such fights and contests is to discover who is the best boxer or the prettiest girl. The social function of catallactic competition is, to be sure, not to establish who is the smartest boy and to reward the winner by a title and medals. Its function is to safeguard the best satisfaction of the consumers attainable under the given state of the economic data.

Equality of opportunity is a factor neither in prize fights and beauty contests nor in any other field of competition, whether biological or social. The immense majority of people are by the physiological structure of their bodies deprived of a chance to attain the honors of a boxing champion or a beauty queen. Only very few people can compete on the labor market as opera singers and movie stars. The most favorable opportunity to compete in the field of scientific achievement is provided to the university professors. Yet, thousands and thousands of professors pass away without leaving any trace in the history of ideas and scientific progress, while many of the handicapped outsiders win glory through marvelous contributions.

It is usual to find fault with the fact that catallactic competition is not open to everybody in the same way. The start is much more difficult for a poor boy than for the son of a wealthy man. But the consumers are not concerned about the problem of whether or not the men who shall serve them start their careers under equal conditions. Their only interest is to secure the best possible satisfaction of their needs. As the system of hereditary property is more efficient in this regard, they prefer it to other less efficient systems. They look at the matter from the point of view of social expediency and social welfare, not from the point of view of an alleged, imaginary, and unrealizable "natural" right of every individual to compete with equal opportunity. The realization of such a right would require placing at a disadvantage those born with better intelligence and greater will power than the average man. It is obvious that this would be absurd.

The term competition is mainly employed as the antithesis of monopoly. In this mode of speech the term monopoly is applied in different meanings which must be clearly separated.

The first connotation of monopoly, very frequently implied in the popular use of the term, signifies a state of affairs in which the monopolist, whether an individual or a group of individuals, exclusively controls one of the vital conditions of human survival. Such a monopolist has the power to starve to death all those who do not obey his orders. He dictates and the others have no alternative but either to surrender or to die. With regard to such a monopoly there is no market or any kind of catallactic competition. The monopolist is the master and the rest are slaves entirely dependent on his good graces. There is no need to dwell upon this kind of monopoly. It has no reference whatever to a market economy. It is enough to cite one instance. A world-embracing socialist state would exercise such an absolute and total monopoly; it would have the power to crush its opponents by starving them to death.[3]

The second connotation of monopoly differs from the first in that it describes a state of affairs compatible with the conditions of a market economy. A monopolist in this sense is an individual or a group of individuals, fully combining for joint action, who has the exclusive control of the supply of a definite commodity. If we define the term monopoly in this way, the domain of monopoly appears very vast. The products of the processing industries are more or less different from one another. Each factory turns out products different from those of the other plants. Each hotel has a monopoly on the sale of its services on the site of its premises. The professional services rendered by a physician or a lawyer are never perfectly equal to those rendered by any other physician or lawyer. Except for certain raw materials, foodstuffs, and other staple goods, monopoly is everywhere on the market.

However, the mere phenomenon of monopoly is without any significance and relevance for the operation of the market and the determination of prices. It does not give the monopolist any advantage in selling his products. Under copyright law every rhymester enjoys a monopoly in the sale of his poetry. But this does not influence the market. It may happen that no price whatever can be realized for his stuff and that his books can only be sold at their waste paper value.

Monopoly in this second connotation of the term becomes a factor in the determination of prices only if the demand curve for the monopoly good concerned is shaped in a particular way. If conditions are such that the monopolist can secure higher net proceeds by selling a smaller quantity of his product at a higher price than by selling a greater quantity of his supply at a lower price, there emerges a *monopoly price* higher than the potential market price would have been in the absence of monopoly. Monopoly prices are an important market phenomenon, while monopoly as such is only important if it can result in the formation of monopoly prices.

It is customary to call prices which are not monopoly prices *competitive prices*. While it is questionable whether or not this terminology is expedient, it is generally accepted and it would be difficult to change it. But one must guard oneself against its misinterpretation. It would be a serious blunder to deduce from the antithesis between monopoly price and competitive price that the monopoly price is the outgrowth of the absence of competition. There is always catallactic competition on the market. Catallactic competition is no less a factor in the determination of monopoly prices than it is in the determination of competitive prices. The shape of the demand curve that makes the appearance of monopoly prices possible and directs the monopolists' conduct is determined by the competition of all other commodities competing for the buyers' dollars. The higher the monopolist fixes the price at which he is ready to sell, the more potential buyers turn their dollars toward other vendible goods. On the market every commodity competes with all other commodities. . . .

FREEDOM

. . . In the market economy, the laissez-faire type of social organization, there is a sphere within which the individual is free to choose between various modes of acting without being restrained by the threat of being punished. If, however, the government does more than protect people against violent or fraudulent aggression on the part of antisocial individuals, it reduces the sphere of the individual's freedom to act beyond the degree to which it is restricted by praxeological law. Thus we may define freedom as that state of affairs in which the individual's discretion to choose is not constrained by governmental violence beyond the margin within which the praxeological law restricts it anyway.

This is what is meant if one defines freedom as the condition of an individual within the frame of the market economy. He is free in the sense that the laws and the government do not force him to renounce his autonomy and self-determination to a greater extent than the inevitable praxeological law does. What he foregoes is only the animal freedom of living without any regard to the existence of other specimens of his species. What the social apparatus of compulsion and coercion achieves is that individuals whom malice, shortsightedness or mental inferiority prevent from realizing that by indulging in acts that are destroying society they are hurting themselves and all other human beings are compelled to avoid such acts. . . .

Liberty and freedom are the conditions of man within a contractual society. Social cooperation under a system of private ownership of the factors of production means that within the range of the market the individual is not bound to obey and to serve an overlord. As far as he gives and serves other people, he does so of his own accord in order to be rewarded and served by the receivers. He exchanges goods and services, he does not do compulsory labor and does not pay tribute. He is certainly not independent. He depends on the other members of society. But this dependence is mutual. The buyer depends on the seller and the seller on the buyer.

The main concern of many writers of the nineteenth and twentieth centuries was to misrepresent and to distort this obvious state of affairs. The workers, they said, are at the mercy of their employers. Now, it is true that the employer has the right to fire the employee. But if he makes use of this right in order to indulge in his whims, he hurts his own interests. It is to his own disadvantage if he discharges a better man in order to hire a less efficient one. The market does not directly prevent anybody from arbitrarily inflicting harm on his fellow citizens; it only puts a penalty upon such conduct. The shopkeeper is free to be rude to his customers provided he is ready to bear the consequences. The consumers are free to boycott a purveyor provided they are ready to pay the costs. What impels every man to the utmost exertion in the service of his fellow men and curbs innate tendencies toward arbitrariness and malice is, in the market, not compulsion and coercion on the part of gendarmes, hangmen, and penal courts; it is self-interest. The member of a contractual society is free because he serves others only in serving himself. What restrains him is only the inevitable natural phenomenon of scarcity. For the rest he is free in the range of the market. . . .

ENTREPRENEURIAL PROFIT AND LOSS

Profit, in a broader sense, is the gain derived from action; it is the increase in satisfaction (decrease in uneasiness) brought about; it is the difference between the higher value attached to the result attained and the lower value attached to the sacrifices made for its attainment; it is, in other words, yield minus costs. To make profit is invariably the aim sought by any action. If an action fails to attain the ends sought, yield either does not exceed costs or lags behind costs. In the latter case the outcome means a loss, a decrease in satisfaction.

Profit and loss in this original sense are psychic phenomena and as such not open to measurement and a mode of expression which could convey to other people precise information concerning their intensity. A man can tell a fellow man that *a* suits him better than *b;* but he cannot communicate to another man, except in vague and indistinct terms, how much the satisfaction derived from *a* exceeds that derived from *b.*

In the market economy all those things that are bought and sold against money are marked with money prices. In the monetary calculus profit appears as a surplus of money received over money expended and loss as a surplus of money expended over money received. Profit and loss can be expressed in definite amounts of money. It is possible to ascertain in terms of money how much an individual has profited or lost. However, this is not a statement about this individual's psychic profit or loss. It is a statement about a social phenomenon, about the individual's contribution to the societal effort as it is appraised by the other members of society. It does not tell us anything about the individual's increase or decrease in satisfaction or happiness. It merely reflects his fellow men's evaluation of his contribution to social cooperation. This evaluation is ultimately determined by the efforts of every member of society to attain the highest possible psychic profit. It is the resultant of the composite effect of all these people's subjective and personal value judgments as manifested in their conduct on the market. But it must not be confused with these value judgments as such. . . .

In the changing world of reality differences between the sum of the prices of the complementary factors of production and the prices of the products emerge again and again. It is these differences that bring about money profits and money losses. As far as such changes affect the sellers of labor and those of the original nature-given factors of production and of the capitalists as moneylenders, we will deal with them later. At this point we are dealing with the promoters' entrepreneurial profit and loss. It is this problem that people have in mind when employing the terms profit and loss in mundane speech.

Like every acting man, the entrepreneur is always a speculator. He deals with the uncertain conditions of the future. His success or failure depends on the correctness of his anticipation of uncertain events. If he fails in his understanding of things to come, he is doomed. The only source from which an entrepreneur's profits stem is his ability to anticipate better than other people the future demand of the consumers. If everybody is correct in anticipating the future state of the market of a certain commodity, its price and the prices of the complementary factors of production concerned would already today be adjusted to this future state. Neither profit nor loss can emerge for those embarking upon this line of business.

The specific entrepreneurial function consists in determining the employment of the factors of production.

The entrepreneur is the man who dedicates them to special purposes. In doing so he is driven solely by the selfish interest in making profits and in acquiring wealth. But he cannot evade the law of the market. He can succeed only by best serving the consumers. His profit depends on the approval of his conduct by the consumers. . . .

The ultimate source from which entrepreneurial profit and loss are derived is the uncertainty of the future constellation of demand and supply.

If all entrepreneurs were to anticipate correctly the future state of the market, there would be neither profits nor losses. The prices of all the factors of production would already today be fully adjusted to tomorrow's prices of the products. In buying the factors of production the entrepreneur would have to expend (with due allowance for the difference between the prices of present goods and future goods) no less an amount than the buyers will pay him later for the product. An entrepreneur can make a profit only if he anticipates future conditions more correctly than other entrepreneurs. Then he buys the complementary factors of production at prices the sum of which, including allowance for the time difference, is smaller than the price at which he sells the product.

If we want to construct the image of changing economic conditions in which there are neither profits nor losses, we must resort to an unrealizable assumption: perfect foresight of all future events on the part of all individuals. If those primitive hunters and fishermen to whom it is customary to ascribe the first accumulation of produced factors of production had known in advance all the future vicissitudes of human affairs, and if they and all their descendants until the last day of judgment, equipped with the same omniscience, had appraised all factors of production accordingly, entrepreneurial profits and losses would never have emerged. Entrepreneurial profits and losses are created through the discrepancy between the expected prices and the prices later really fixed on the markets. It is possible to confiscate profits and to transfer them from the individuals to whom they have accrued to other people. But neither profits nor losses can ever disappear from a changing world not populated solely with omniscient people. . . .

The vehicle of economic progress is the accumulation of additional capital goods by means of saving and improvement in technological methods of production the execution of which is almost always conditioned by the availability of such new capital. The agents of progress are the promoting entrepreneurs intent upon profiting by means of adjusting the conduct of affairs to the best possible satisfaction of the consumers. In the performance of their projects for the realization of progress they are bound to share the benefits derived from progress with the workers and also with a part of the capitalists and landowners and to increase the portion allotted to these people step by step until their own share melts away entirely. . . .

The entrepreneurial function, the striving of entrepreneurs after profits, is the driving power in the market economy. Profit and loss are the devices by means of which the consumers exercise their supremacy on the market. The behavior of the consumers makes profits and losses appear and thereby shifts ownership of the means of production from the hands of the less efficient into those of the more efficient. It makes a man the more influential in the direction of business activities the better he succeeds in serving the consumers. In the absence of profit and loss the entrepreneurs would not know what the most urgent needs of the consumers are. If some entrepreneurs were to guess it, they would lack the means to adjust production accordingly.

Profit-seeking business is subject to the sovereignty of the consumers, while nonprofit institutions are sovereign unto themselves and not responsible to the public. Production for profit is necessarily production for use, as profits can only be earned by providing the consumers with those things they most urgently want to use.

The moralists' and sermonizers' critique of profits misses the point. It is not the fault of the entrepreneurs that the consumers—the people, the common man—prefer liquor to Bibles and detective stories to serious books, and that governments prefer guns to butter. The entrepreneur does not make greater profits in selling "bad" things than in selling "good" things. His profits are the greater the better he succeeds in providing the consumers with those things they ask for most intensely. People do not drink intoxicating beverages in order to make the "alcohol capital" happy, and they do not go to war in order to increase the profits of the "merchants of death." The existence of the armaments industries is a consequence of the warlike spirit, not its cause.

It is not the business of the entrepreneurs to make people substitute sound ideologies for unsound. It rests with the philosophers to change people's ideas and ideals. The entrepreneur serves the consumers as they are today, however wicked and ignorant.

We may admire those who abstain from making gains they could reap in producing deadly weapons or hard liquor. However, their laudable conduct is a mere gesture without any practical effects. Even if all entrepreneurs and capitalists were to follow their example, wars and dipsomania would not disappear. As was the case in the precapitalistic ages, governments would pro-

duce the weapons in their own arsenals and drinkers would distill their own liquor. . . .

ENDNOTES

1. For an examination of the Russian "experiment" see Mises, *Planned Chaos* (Irvington-on-Hudson, 1947), pp. 80–87 (reprinted in the new edition of Mises, *Socialism* [New Haven, 1951] pp. 527–592).
2. Cf. Frank A. Fetter, *The Principles of Economics* (3rd ed. New York, 1913), pp. 394, 410.
3. Cf. Trotsky (1937) as quoted by Hayek, *The Road to Serfdom* (London, 1944), p. 89.

QUESTIONS ON MISES

1. Mises contends that one is free within a market and that one's actions and decisions are not subject to compulsion and coercion. How does Mises understand freedom? Is there such a thing as "economic coercion" or a "coercive offer"?

2. In what ways are markets analogous to democracies? How do the votes of consumers mirror or diverge from the votes of citizens?

3. Mises writes that "Social competition is consequently present in every conceivable mode of social organization." Do you think he is correct? Does his view depend on a certain view of human nature or assume an inevitable hierarchy in every form of social organization?

4. How do you understand the function of the entrepreneur? How does the entrepreneurial function differ from the managerial? How does profit management differ from bureaucratic management? What does Mises mean when he says, "The only source from which an entrepreneur's profits stem is his ability to anticipate better than other people the future demand of the consumers"?

The Ethical Limitations of the Market

Elizabeth Anderson

Elizabeth Anderson is Professor of Philosophy and Women's Studies at the University of Michigan and the author of many essays in ethics and social and political philosophy. A version of this selection can be found in her book Value in Ethics and Economics *(1993).*

A distinctive feature of modern capitalist societies is the tendency of the market to take over the production, maintenance, and distribution of goods that were previously produced, maintained, and distributed by nonmarket means. Yet, there is a wide range of disagreement regarding the proper extent of the market in providing many goods. Labor has been treated as a commodity since the advent of capitalism, but not without significant and continuing challenges to this arrangement. Other goods whose production for and distribution on the market are currently the subject of dispute include sexual intercourse, human blood, and human body parts such as kidneys. How can we determine which goods are properly subjects of market transactions and which are not? The purpose of this article is to propose a theory of what makes economic goods differ from other kinds of goods, which can help to answer this question.

I propose that we think of economic goods as those goods whose dimensions of value are best realized within market relations. The market, like any other social institution, embodies norms regulating the production, exchange, and enjoyment of goods that are sensitive to some qualitative distinctions among values and insensitive to others. These norms also foster and sustain certain shared understandings of the interactions and relations of the participants and thereby promote particular ideals of self and society. The ethical limitations of the market (or any other system of social relations) can thus be explored in part by seeking the answers to three questions.

First, what dimensions of value in things, relationships, and persons are acknowledged and successfully realized, or ignored and undermined, by the norms of the market? Second, what are the ideals of self and society that the market attempts to embody? Do market institutions embody an adequate interpretation of these ideals, or do they fail to realize the ideals to which they aim to give expression? Third, does the extension of the market to a certain realm undermine the realization of other ideals?

This chapter has four parts. In the first part, I explore the ideals and social relations of the market. In the next two parts, I contrast economic values with the values of personal relationships and of social democracy. For each of these other two spheres of life, several cases will be examined in which values are undermined when the norms of the market come to govern them. In the final section, I draw some general conclusions about the limitations of the market and of welfare economics as a theory of value.

THE IDEALS AND SOCIAL RELATIONS OF THE MODERN MARKET

We can understand the nature of economic goods by investigating the ways we value commodities; the social relations within which we produce, distribute, and enjoy them; and the ideals which these relations are supposed to embody.[1] The most important ideal that the modern market attempts to embody is a particular conception of freedom. On this view, freedom is primarily exercised in the choice and consumption of commodities in private life. It consists in having a large menu of choices in the marketplace and in exclusive power to use and dispose of things and services in the private sphere without having to ask permission from anyone else.[2]

The economic ideal of freedom is closely linked with the way we value commodities. I call this mode of valuation "use" and contrast it in three ways with other modes of valuation that demand constraints on use. First, I follow Kant in contrasting "use" with higher forms of regard, such as respect. To merely use something is to subordinate it to one's own ends, without regard for whatever intrinsic value it might have. For example, several years ago certain owners of David Smith sculptures stripped the paint off of these works because Smith's unpainted works were selling for more money than his painted works were. These owners treated Smith's art as a mere commodity, since they disregarded its intrinsic aesthetic worth in favor of its mere usefulness for their independently defined ends. Second, use is an impersonal mode of valuation. It is contrasted with valuing something for its personal or sentimental attachments to oneself, as when one cherishes an heirloom. A mere commodity is something one regards as interchangeable with any other item of the same kind and quality and something that one is prepared to trade with equanimity for any other commodity at some price. But a cherished item is viewed as unique and irreplaceable. Since it is valued for its special connections to the self, it is sold only under duress, and its loss is felt as a personal one (Simmel, 1978, pp. 123, 404, 407). Finally, use values may be contrasted with shared values, whose value for oneself is dependent on other people also enjoying them. Such values cannot be realized in private acts of use, but rather reside in a shared public understanding of the meanings of the goods. For example, certain sites of historical events may be valued as parts of a national heritage or the layout of a neighborhood valued as the locus of a particular community. Again, the preservation of these values requires constraints on use. For instance, zoning laws may be required to preserve the architectural integrity of a city or rent control required to enable a community's residents to remain living together as members of a community.

The market ideal of freedom has a special connection with the mode of valuation of commodities known as use. For the freedom that the market gives us is the freedom to use commodities without the constraints implied by other modes of valuation. The realization of the noneconomic values that inhere in things often requires constraints on use and, hence, constraints on the degree to which these things are treated as commodities. But to explore these points, we must achieve a fuller understanding of the distinctive character of economic goods. This requires an investigation into the social relations of the market.

Five features of the social norms and relations of the market are particularly important for understanding the distinctive character of economic values. First, market relations are impersonal ones. Second, the market is understood to be a sphere in which one is free, within the limits of the law, to pursue one's personal advantage unrestrained by any consideration for the advantage of others. Third, the goods traded on the market are exclusive and rivals in consumption. Fourth, the market is purely want-regarding: from its standpoint all matters of value are simply matters of personal taste. Finally, dissatisfaction with a commodity or market relation is expressed primarily by "exit," not "voice." That is, one simply drops out of the market relationship rather than sticking with it and trying to reform it from within. Actual market practices often deviate in significant ways from the patterns described here. But these patterns are still characteristic of the market. They express a shared understanding of the purpose and meaning of market relations that I believe every experienced participant in the modern market will recognize. Let us examine each of these features in more detail.

Perhaps the most characteristic feature of market relations is their impersonality. The producers and consumers of economic goods are typically strangers. Each party to a market transaction views one's relation to the other as merely a means to the satisfaction of ends defined independently of the relationship and of the other party's ends. The parties have no precontractual obligations to provide one another with the goods they exchange. They deal with one another on an explicit basis of exchange, in which each good that changes hands has its equivalent in return. The explicit basis of exchange serves to guarantee mobility. If each transaction between buyer and seller can be completed to the reciprocal advantage of each, leaving no unpaid debts on either side,

then nothing ties the parties together over time. They are free to change their trading partners at any time.

The impersonality of market relations thus defines a sphere of freedom from personal ties and obligations. There is another side to this impersonal freedom: one need not exhibit any specific personal characteristics or invoke any special relationships to gain access to the goods traded on the market. The market is open to all indifferently, as long as they have the money to pay for the goods. Money income—not one's personal status, characteristics, or relationships—is what determines one's access to the realm of commodity values.[3]

The impersonality of the market leaves its participants free to pursue their individual interests unrestrained by any consideration of other people's advantage. Each party to a market transaction is expected to take care of himself and not to depend on the other to look after his own interests. Every extension of the market thus represents an extension of the sphere of egoism. Indeed, the market would not be economically efficient if each party to a transaction tried to satisfy the other's preferences at his own expense. The success of a commercial transaction, its bringing benefit to both parties, depends on the possibility of drawing sharp lines between the interests of the negotiators. One must be able to define and satisfy one's interests independently of the other. This is why the market is a domain for the expression of individualism—one cannot function successfully in it without drawing a clear distinction between self and other.

Individuals' interests are independently definable and satisfiable only with respect to a certain class of goods. Such goods have the properties of exclusivity and rivalry in consumption. A good is exclusive if access to its benefits can be limited to the purchaser. If there is no means of excluding people from enjoying a good, it is impossible to charge a price for it. A good is a rival in consumption if the amount that one person consumes reduces the total amount of it available to others (Fisher, 1981, p. 175). The value that can be obtained from commodities is rival, since it is typically realized through personal appropriation and use. Insofar as another person with distinct ends gains control over it, I lose such control and consequently lose the use value of the good. The value of a rival good cannot be given to another without losing it oneself. But many goods are not rival—I do not lose, but rather enhance my knowledge, or my pleasure in a joke, by conveying these goods to others.

A further feature of the market is that it is a want-regarding institution. What it responds to is "effective demand," that is, desires backed up by money or the willingness to pay for things. Commodities are exchanged without regard for the reasons people have in wanting them. This fact has two implications. First, it means that the market does not respond to needs as such and does not draw any distinction between urgent needs and intense desires. Second, the market does not draw any distinction between reflective desires, which can be backed up by reasons or principles, and mere matters of taste. Since it provides no means for discriminating among the reasons people have for wanting or providing things, it cannot function as a forum for the expression of principles about the things traded on it. The market conception of personal autonomy reflects this fact. The market provides individual freedom from the value judgments of others. It does not regard any one individual's preferences as less worthy of satisfaction than anyone else's, as long as one can pay for one's own satisfaction. But it provides this freedom at the cost of reducing preferences, from the market's point of view, to mere matters of taste, about which it is pointless to dispute (Sheffrin, 1978).

A final feature of economic relations is that an individual's influence on the provision and exchange of commodities is primarily exercised through "exit," not "voice" (Hirschman, 1970). The counterpart to the customer's freedom to stop purchasing a particular product or to stop patronizing a particular retail outlet is the producer's freedom to say "take it or leave it." The customer has no voice—that is, no right to directly participate in the design of the product or to determine how it is marketed.

In the light of this account of the norms of the market, we can offer a more precise account of an economic good. A thing is an economic good if its production, distribution, and enjoyment is properly governed by these five norms, and its value can be fully realized through use. These criteria allow us to anticipate the shape of arguments that certain goods should not be treated as commodities. There may be certain values that are realized only if the exchange of particular goods is responsive to personal characteristics or takes place on a nonexplicit basis of exchange. Our ability to realize other goods may be impaired if we view them as exclusive and rival, rather than as shared. In the next section, I show how many of the goods of personal relationships have these characteristics. Some ideals may be realized only if the provision of certain goods is responsive to the needs of others or reflects shared principles and not just individual matters of taste. And the realization of a good as shared, or as reflecting principles, may require that its

distribution be regulated through institutions of voice rather than exit. In the third section of this chapter, I show how many of the goods of social democracy are of this kind.

Since these arguments are based on comparisons of ideal types, some observations about the limitations of ideal typical analysis is in order. Any particular social institution or practice is apt to diverge from its ideal type in multifarious and complex ways and to include mixtures of norms more prominently associated with institutions and practices in other spheres of life. And the norms that presently govern our actual practices often inadequately express the ideals these practices are supposed to embody. The arguments I present are intended to highlight evaluative considerations that find little place in the standard models for criticizing market and other institutions—that is, in welfare economics and in most liberal theories of justice. The standard models highlight other evaluative considerations, such as efficiency, that are also important. Hence, any move from a relative evaluation of ideal types to a relative evaluation of actual practices must be informed by a detailed empirical investigation of the actual norms they embody, an evaluation of how well they combine norms from different spheres, how well these norms express the ideals in terms of which they are justified, and how well the practices fare by other criteria such as justice and efficiency. Since I obviously cannot provide such details here, the cases I discuss should be taken as illustrations of the kinds of arguments I wish to endorse and not as comprehensive evaluations of the practices in question.

THE VALUES OF PERSONAL RELATIONSHIPS AND THE MARKET

The sphere of personal relationships is in many ways the polar opposite to that of market relationships. For, as we shall see, the ideals of personal relationships are embodied in norms of exchange that directly conflict with market norms. Two of many ideals central to the personal sphere of life are intimacy and commitment. Living on intimate terms with another person involves a mutual revelation of private concerns and sharing of cherished emotions that are responsive to the other's personal characteristics. This is the romantic side of personal relations, which involves passion, affection, and trust but not necessarily devotion or long-term commitment to the other person, for the romantic relationship may end as soon as the passions that animate it cool.

The deepest ideal of commitment involves dedicating oneself to living a shared life with another person on a permanent basis. A shared life is not simply a life of long-term cooperation on mutually advantageous terms, as might be true of a business partnership. It is founded on values that the persons committed to each other hold together. The central goods realized in such a life are shared in at least two senses. First, their goodness for each partner partially consists in the facts that the other partner also enjoys them, and that each partner knows this fact and knows that the other knows. One committed and loving partner could not rejoice in living with the other if he knew that the other found the relationship to be oppressive. The goods of intimacy are also shared in this first sense. Second, the realization of the good requires an expansive understanding of the self as including another person. The persons to whom the good is good are not selves regarded as isolated individuals, but selves regarded as members of the committed relationship. Commitment to a shared life, such as a marriage, requires redefining one's interests as interests of the *couple* in the marriage. Insofar as one has this commitment, one's interest in the aims of the marriage can neither be defined nor satisfied independently of one's being joined with one's spouse in marriage.[4] This is why marrying just for money is base: it takes advantage of an institutional form of commitment merely for the sake of lower goods definable independently of it.

These ideals inform the ways we value the people with whom we have personal relationships and the ways we value the goods we exchange with them. In this sphere love, affection, trust, and devotion supercede the formal respect of useful persons (acknowledgment of their autonomy) characteristic of the marketplace. The goods exchanged and jointly realized in friendship are valued less through use than through appreciation and cherishing, for they are tokens of shared understandings, affections, and commitments.

If the ways we value the goods proper to friendship differ from the ways we value commodities, then we should expect that the norms that govern the exchange of these goods should also differ; for different modes of valuation are embodied in different norms of exchange, production, and enjoyment. This is what we do find. A fundamental contrast between the sphere of personal relations and that of the market is that the former is properly governed by the spirit of the gift rather than the spirit of commercial exchange. The goods proper to the personal sphere can only be fully realized if they are given as gifts or established through the exchange of gifts. They are goods that cannot be genuinely procured for oneself by paying others to produce them or by appealing to another's merely personal advantage to provide them. The authenticity and worth of these goods depend on the motives that people have in providing them. Among these goods are trust, loyalty, conviviality, sympathy, affection, admiration, companionship, and devotion. None of these goods can be bought (or extracted by threats), although people often deceive themselves in the attempt, mistaking flattery for admiration and subservience for devotion.

The significance of gift exchange differs from that of market exchange in several respects (Hochschild, 1983; Hyde, 1983; Mauss, 1967; Sahlins, 1972; Titmuss, 1971). In the first place, the exchange of gifts affirms and continues the ties that hold the donor and recipient together. This is why refusing a gift is often an insult to a friend, but refusing a trade is merely an unrealized financial gain to a retailer. To reject an appropriate gift is to refuse to acknowledge or sustain a friendship. One point of gift exchange is to realize a shared value in the relationship itself, whereas the point of a market relationship is purely instrumental and realizes distinct goods for each party. Moreover, while both forms of exchange involve reciprocity, the shape and timing of the return of goods differ in the two cases. In market exchange, a delay in reciprocation (unless explicitly arranged in a contract) is cause for legal action. But the exchange of gifts among friends usually incorporates an informal understanding of reciprocity only in the long term. To be anxious to "settle accounts," as when one person insists upon splitting a restaurant tab exactly in half, calculating sums to the penny, or paying a friend for returning a library book, is to reject the logic of friendship. The delay in reciprocation symbolizes the fact that goods are given for the friend's sake, not for the sake of obtaining some good for oneself in return. Moreover, the accounting mentality reflects an unwillingness to be in the debt of another and hence an unwillingness to enter into the longer term commitments that such debts entail. For the debts of friendship—that is, the goods friends owe to one another—are not of a kind that they can be repaid in such a way as to leave nothing between the friends.

Friendly gift exchange is responsive to the personal characteristics of the friends involved and to the particular qualities of their relationship. We seek to give to our friends gifts that have more than merely generic meaning, gifts whose full meaning is conditioned by who gave the gift, to whom it was given, and the character of their friendship. For the gift is a vehicle for the expression of the friends' mutual understanding of how their relationship stands (or how the giver wishes it to be), and not merely a good of impersonal use value to the receiver.

This fact is evident not only in cases of such material gifts as engagement rings and Valentine's Day chocolates, but also in the exchange of compliments, affections, and jokes. Max knows that Adam is just the person to appreciate *this* practical joke coming from *him,* but takes care to offer a more serious expression of affection to his girlfriend Marsha, who finds practical jokes rather vulgar. This is why cash is usually such an inappropriate gift between friends. Since it can be used by anyone to acquire any commodity, it expresses nothing of the giver's personality, of any particular thought the giver had for the receiver, or of the receiver's interests.

In the light of this brief account of some fundamental differences between the norms of the market and of personal relations, we can explore some of the ways values are undermined when the norms of the market come to govern the exchange of goods proper to personal relations. Consider the following cases of the importation of market norms in the exchange of personal values: prostitution, the exploitative manipulation of gift relations in commercial transactions, the detailed marriage contract advocated by *Ms.* magazine, and the practice of making loans between friends.

Prostitution is the classic example of the debasement of a gift value through its commodification. But what is base about buying and selling sexual "services" on the market? One cannot understand what makes this practice base without understanding the specifically human good achieved when sexual acts are exchanged as gifts. This good is founded on a mutual recognition of the partners as sexually attracted to each other and as affirming an intimate relationship in their mutual offering of themselves to each other. This is a shared good: one and the same good is realized for both partners in their action, and part of its goodness lies in the mutual understanding that it is shared. The couple rejoices in their *union,* and not simply each in his or her own distinct physical gratification. As a shared good, it cannot be realized except through each partner reciprocating the other's gift *in kind,* offering his or her own sexuality in the same spirit in which the other's sexuality is received—as a genuine offering of the self.

When sexual "services" are sold on the market, the kind of reciprocity required to realize human sexuality as a shared good is broken. The prostitute does not respond to the customer as a sexually attractive person, but merely as someone willing to put down the cash. So it is not the customer as a person that attracts the prostitute, but only his or her wealth. This is simply the counterpart to the impersonality of the market: one need not display any personal characteristics to obtain the goods sold there. And the customer seeks only sexual gratification from the prostitute, not a physical union. Sexuality as a specifically human, shared good cannot be achieved except through gift exchange; market motives cannot provide it.

The failure of reciprocity implied in the sale of sexual services signifies not simply a failure to realize a good, but a degradation of the prostitute, whose sexuality is reduced to the status of a mere service to the customer: sexuality is equated with the lesser good of money.[5] The prostitute's subordination is expressed in the fact that (except in the most blatantly alienated and sterile encounters), he or she must confer on the customer all manner of personal attentions, while the customer need pay attention only to him- or herself, recognizing the prostitute only as an object for satisfaction.

The problems entailed by explicitly exchanging sexual acts for money arise in part because sexual acts, insofar as they are more than means for sheer physical gratification, are valuable as expressions of underlying noncommercial motives and understandings. Since the expressive content of actions cannot be traded on the market, only those goods that are valuable to the receiver apart from their being expressions of the giver's motivations are genuine commodity values. The attempt to sell gift values on the market makes a mockery of those values and subordinates the provider of them.[6]

Other values are undermined when goods offered in the spirit of the gift have been solicited in the spirit of commercial exchange. These arise because the forms of reciprocity appropriate to gift (personal) relationships differ from those appropriate to market relationships. One basic kind of exploitation occurs when one party to an exchange gives goods to the other in accordance with the norms of gift exchange, while the other party returns goods in accordance with the norms of market exchange. Since gift exchange does not involve the demand for an immediate quid pro quo, the party taking a market orientation to the transaction can extract a greater share of goods from the gift giver than one returns.

This kind of exploitation occurs when firms attempt to establish a paternalistic relationship with their employees. By putting them in a dependent position and providing, however meagerly, for their needs, the firm can engender feelings of gratitude and loyalty on the part of its employees. These feelings can then be exploited to extract more labor and obedience from the employees. This has been a common practice of employers of migrant farm workers and sharecroppers. The latter are placed in the position of children to their parents because they have nowhere else to turn for the provision of basic needs. This dependency is reinforced by the fact that wages are paid largely in kind rather than cash. Cash payment would free the worker to purchase his needs from another source and thereby enable him to affirm at least some minimal autonomy from the employer.[7] Paternalistic practices are not confined to backward commercial enterprises. Young women training to be flight attendants are housed by airlines in airport dormitories and encouraged to regard their supervisors as substitute parents to whom they can come to confide any personal problems. They are thus encouraged to develop ties of loyalty and trust with their employers and to work for them in this spirit. But at the same time they are constantly reminded that these ties are not reciprocal: poor performance or disobedience can lead to immediate dismissal, since the tight job market ensures no shortage of job applicants (Hochschild, 1983, pp. 89–101).[8]

Even the impersonal exchanges of civility follow the norms of gift exchange and consequently can be exploited in commercial transactions. One common sales technique is to take advantage of people's desire to be polite, by manipulating them into a position in which it seems that they can back out of a deal only by risking offense or awkwardness. So car salesmen ask reluctant customers questions such as, "Do you doubt the integrity of our dealership?" knowing that most people will go to great lengths to avoid giving offense, and that each "no" they receive to questions like this undermines their ability to explain their reasons against signing the dotted line. The salesman's advantage consists in the fact that he participates in the negotiation strictly in accordance with market norms of pursuing maximum personal advantage, while the customer is manipulated into conceding his bargaining edge because he views some of their verbal exchanges as merely polite ones. Since civility often requires that we hide our frank opinions, we feel uncomfortable in explaining exactly why we don't want to buy. The remark delivered in the spirit of civility ("No, I don't mistrust your dealership") is then seized in the spirit of negotiation and used to the salesman's advantage by being interpreted as a literal expression of the customer's belief.

In these cases of exploitation, one party uses the norms of the market to manipulate the exchange of sentiments and civilities that are properly governed by the norms of gift exchange. When both sides adopt the norms of the market to govern the exchange of gift values, we no longer have a case of exploitation, but other losses still occur. Such is the case with the kind of detailed marriage contract advocated several years ago by *Ms.* magazine.[9] In the interests of avoiding the exploita-

tive tendencies of traditional marriages, in which most of the drudgery involved in maintaining a household and raising children is left for the wife to perform, *Ms.* proposed to place the marriage relationship on an explicit basis of exchange. Henceforth, the duties of husband and wife with respect to the household, children, and sexual interactions were to be laid out in detail in the marriage contract.

While the intentions of *Ms.* in promoting equality in marriage are noble, the attempt to enforce this equality by remaking the marriage on the same terms as a business partnership threatens to undermine the goods of commitment and intimacy proper to marriage. For the realization of these goods depends on each partner carrying out the projects and tasks constitutive of their shared life in a spirit of trust and love rather than of contractual obligation and the piece-meal calculation of individual advantage. Giving and receiving in a spirit of trust is itself one of the goods of marriage. The point of marriage in realizing shared goods is obscured by tending to the terms of the explicit marriage contract, which evaluates the marriage in terms of the distinct advantages accruing to each party. And fixing the terms of exchange in advance undermines the responsiveness of the marriage to the changed needs of the partners, as well as the promise it holds out for deepening their commitment in the light of a more articulate understanding of their shared project, which may require a new division of activities between them. Being open to the possibility of renegotiating the contract in the light of changed wants is not the same thing as committing oneself to love and care for one's spouse "for better, for worse" (Hirsch, 1976, pp. 87–88, 99–101).[10]

These examples show how the norms of the market and of personal relationships are not easily mixed, because adherence to these norms secures quite different kinds of goods. Consider, as a final example of this problem, the basis for discouraging friends from making substantial long-term loans to one another.[11] Loaning money to a friend threatens the friendship in at least two ways. By undermining the equality of friends, it fosters resentment on the part of the debtor. And by tying down his financial resources without prospect for gaining from his friend, it undermines the capacity of the creditor to pursue successfully his advantage on the market and thus fosters resentment on his part. It might be thought that charging interest between friends would restore equality and prevent the creditor from thinking he is losing out by loaning to a friend. But this expedient threatens the friendship even more deeply than a loan without interest. To charge the prevailing interest rate is to permit the norms of strangers interacting merely from self-interest to govern the interactions of friends. Such an act encourages the friends to view their interests as sharply divided and to view themselves as having to be on their guard in protection of their interests when dealing with friends. But friendship is supposed to preserve a sphere of relationships in which one does not have to be on one's guard. Successful participation in both spheres of life thus requires an isolation of their respective concerns.

POLITICAL VALUES AND THE MARKET

The preceding section emphasized two qualitative distinctions among goods to which the market is insensitive: between gift values and ordinary exchange values, and between shared goods and divisible goods. I argued that the goods of the personal sphere, which are shared gift values, cannot be adequately realized within the norms of the market. This section will emphasize two further qualitative distinctions among goods that the market does not acknowledge: between ideals and ordinary goods, and between the objects of need and of desire. I shall argue that these distinctions support the application of several norms of democratic political life to the production, distribution, and enjoyment of a variety of goods that could also be provided by the market. As in the case of the economic and personal spheres, the significance of these norms must be understood in the light of the ideals they are supposed to embody. In this section, I focus on two ideals of social democracy: fraternity and democratic freedom.

The ideal of fraternity, while rather vague, seems to involve the following notions. Citizens have fraternal relations with one another when they agree to refrain from making claims to certain goods that come at the expense of those less well off than themselves and when they view the achievement of such relations with their fellow citizens as a part of their own good.[12] People express relations of fraternity with one another in part through providing certain goods in common. Whereas distributing goods through a system of bilateral transactions tends to emphasize either the separateness of persons (in the market) or some special relationship between the two traders (in personal gift relationships), providing goods out of pooled resources obliterates any connection of specific donors with specific recipients. It thereby expresses the idea that the goods are provided by the community as a whole to its members, rather than by some specific individuals to others. Furthermore, where the goods in question are not public but distrib-

uted, distribution takes place in accordance with some conception of members' needs. Fraternal relations are need-regarding, not only want-regarding.[13]

Another aspect to the intuitive idea of fraternity connects it to the democratic tradition. This is the idea that citizens are equals engaged in a common cooperative project. In the democratic tradition, this project is collective self-rule. The political freedom of a citizen is the freedom to participate on terms of equality with fellow citizens in deciding the laws and policies that will govern them all. This freedom is meaningless unless citizens have the goods they need (e.g., education) to participate effectively in the project of self-government. Citizens express their fraternity in part by ensuring that these needs are met through community guarantees or outright provision of the goods in question. But the proper interpretation of citizens' needs and, hence, of the ideal of fraternity is itself a subject for democratic deliberation. Citizens cannot interact with one another in the spirit of fraternity without a shared understanding of this ideal forged through participation in democratic institutions. Democratic freedom and fraternity are thus complementary goods.

These ideals of fraternity and democratic freedom are embodied in three norms that conflict with the norms of the market. First, citizens exercise their freedom in a democracy primarily through voice, not exit. Their freedom is the power to take the initiative in shaping the background conditions of their interactions and the content of the goods they provide in common. It is a freedom to participate in democratic activities, not just to leave the country if their government does not satisfy their desires. Second, an uncorrupted democracy distributes goods in accordance with shared principles (including a shared understanding of citizens' needs), not in accordance with unexamined wants. Decisions must be justified in terms acceptable to the public. Third, the goods provided by the public body are provided on a nonexclusive basis—everyone, not just those who pay, has access to them. The different norms of decision-making in the market and in democracy are reflected in the different interpretations of respect we apply to these two spheres. To respect a customer is to respect her privacy by not probing more deeply into her reasons for wanting a commodity than is required to effectively satisfy her want. There is little scope here for challenging her own estimation of what is valuable. But to respect a fellow citizen is to take her reasons for advocating a particular position seriously. It is to consult her judgment about political matters, to respond to it in a public forum, and to accept it if one finds her judgment superior to others'.

Many goods can be secured only through a form of democratic provision that is nonexclusive, principle- and need-regarding, and regulated primarily through voice. To attempt to provide these goods through market mechanisms is to change the kind of good they are for the worse. They contribute to human flourishing in lesser ways when they are provided through the market than when they are provided on a democratic basis. Goods of this kind I shall define as "political goods." This conception of political goods can shed light on two kinds of proposals for subjecting goods to market control. The first is the proposal for "dividing the commons." Many goods, such as streets, parks, and schools, are presently provided on a public, nonexclusive basis and/or subject to public control. Some people argue that freedom (and sometimes also efficiency) would be enhanced if such goods were completely divided into privately owned or controlled parcels that would then be provided on an exclusive basis. The second is the proposal for converting the public provision of goods in kind to the provision of their cash equivalents. I argue that both kinds of proposals fail to recognize the goods realized through democratic provision and also embody a flawed conception of freedom when they are applied to the goods discussed. Let us turn first to the various proposals to "divide the commons."

Since Locke wrote his *Two Treatises of Government,* the argument that both individual freedom and efficiency would be enhanced if publicly provided goods were completely divided into privately controlled parcels has been an enduring one in Western political thought, particularly in libertarian circles. The basic idea behind all of these proposals is that freedom is enhanced when people are granted the power of exit from common control of a good. I argue, however, that in these cases the freedom of exit is no substitute for the loss of voice and of nonexclusive access to the goods in question. Some forms of freedom can be secured only through institutions of voice established over goods to which public access is guaranteed.

Let us begin our investigation of this problem with a relatively uncontroversial case: the value of public streets and parks. Some libertarians have suggested that a system of private, toll-charging roads would be superior to a public system, since these would be paid for through voluntary user fees rather than a coercive tax system, which charges people whether or not they want to use the roads (Rothbard, 1978, Ch. 11). The idea that such a system would enhance individual freedom is

rather curious, however. Under a system of public roads, no one need ask anyone else's permission to travel anywhere these roads go. If all roads are privately owned, one must ask the permission of each owner to visit people in areas accessible only by such roads and subject oneself to whatever terms the owner demands for using these roads. Nearly everyone would be subject to arbitrary restraints on their freedom of association by others.[14] Next to this loss, the restriction on my freedom entailed by taxation to maintain public roads is trivial. I would even be reluctant to characterize it as a loss of *freedom* at all—merely a loss of money.

The mistake in the libertarian picture seems to lie in the view that individual freedom is always increased when the common is divided into parcels over which individuals have exclusive control. While this regime would enable each person to be a despot in the territory she owns, she would be a mere subject to others everywhere else. This conception of freedom fails to grasp the point that some freedoms can only be exercised in spaces over which no individual has more control than others. These are the public spaces of free association among equals. I want to make two claims about such goods. First, freedom with respect to these goods requires the right of participation in their enjoyment and control, and not just the right of exit. If the primary spaces of free public association are appropriated by private persons, this amounts to a private appropriation of political power, similar to that found in a comprehensive system of private roads. Second, the goods provided by spaces of free public association are qualitatively different from those provided by exclusive spaces that ostensibly provide the same goods. For these goods extend beyond the privately conceived purposes of each individual using them.[15] Association in public spaces is needed to cultivate relations of civility among citizens of all walks of life. And relations of civility are indispensable for democratic politics.

Consider the goods that are provided by a successful city park. One good lies in its being open without charge to any member of the public. The fact that all members gain access to the park freely and in the same way prevents invidious distinctions from arising among them, enabling all to meet each other on terms of equality—in contrast, say, with an exclusive country club. By providing the park as a common good, citizens thus express fraternal relations with one another. A second good lies in its being a locus for spontaneous interaction and political activity. The users of the park, who may each have separate reasons for being there, together create a lively scene of diverse people and purposes, with many occasions for spontaneous interactions that can build a spirit of trust and civility among the users. Joggers meet on the same trail, one dog takes an interest in another, leading their owners to stop and chat, an old man catches a stray Frisbee and tosses it back to the players, business people eat lunch on the benches to watch the passing show. In virtue of its diverse and open uses, this kind of public space then provides the occasion for political action. Outside of the media, it is only in lively public spaces that people can rapidly and effectively generate concern and support on matters of the public interest among fellow citizens who are strangers to themselves. Here rallies can attract curious bystanders and petitioners gather signatures from those who would feel intruded upon by a door-to-door canvasser.[16]

Sometimes the spaces of public interaction are enclosed under a roof and subjected to private control. This happens whenever a commercial mall leads to the decline of a downtown business district. May the owners of a mall suppress any speech or political activity in it that they find offensive or opposed to their interests? Insofar as they are granted the right to do so, the value of this space deteriorates from one in which people can meet as equal citizens with common interests to one in which they can meet only as private consumers. And there may be no alternative space that can serve the same public functions as the downtown once did. . . .

So far I have emphasized the ways in which the principle of public access can change the kind of good something is for us by changing the ways in which we can value it. Similar transformations of value occur when we distribute certain goods according to the norms of fraternity rather than those of the market. In both cases, we not only change the ways we value the goods we enjoy, but we also change the ways we appreciate each other when we adopt the nonmarket norms. This insight lies at the foundation of Richard Titmuss' famous argument that human blood should be given only as a gift, not sold as a commodity (Titmuss, 1971). By understanding how his argument exemplifies the approach to value defended here, we can see how it illuminates another dispute about welfare policies, namely, whether welfare should be provided in cash or in kind.

Titmuss' fundamental objection to obtaining the blood supply by paying people to provide it is that this policy undermines fraternal relations among people in the community, whereas a purely volunteer system enhances such relations.[17] In a volunteer system, people agree not to extract payment from those needing blood as compensation for donating it. Their actions follow the norms of the gift rather than the market. But these are the norms of the anonymous gift; they create no personal bonds, since no one knows whose blood is transfused into a patient. Blood is regarded as a common resource available to any member of the public. In other words, the provision of blood under the volunteer system follows the norms of fraternity, as I have previously defined this ideal.

As in the case of personal values, the value of blood to both the recipient and the donor is partially dependent on the motives for which it is given, and enhanced when these motives are not commercial. Attempting to increase the blood supply through financial incentives rather than appealing to a sense of civic duty or fraternity promotes the social expectation that people may feel entitled to some merely personal advantage for donating their blood. This attitude makes it seem as if small acts contributing to the health of one's neighbors should be seen merely as inconveniences requiring compensation instead of as enhancing the spirit of the entire community. And this atmosphere of expectations really does make blood donation an onerous task. Patients, forced to pay extravagant amounts for blood, must put pressure on their relatives to donate to keep down costs. The typical circumstances under which people do in fact donate are ones of stress, duress, and punishment. The poor who desperately need money, prisoners who hope to gain parole, and relatives who face the choice of severe financial burden or donation provide most of the supply. But when blood donation is a habit born of a sense of civic duty or benevolence, no such punitive or burdensome circumstances accompany its donation, and the act of giving without pay enhances the donor rather than diminishing her. Virtue *can* be its own reward, but it ceases to be so once people are paid for it, even if some still volunteer. As Peter Singer pointed out, the significance of my volunteer donation is trivialized when other blood is paid for. If blood is also a commodity, then all I have given to the recipient is the cash equivalent of the blood, not the gift of life itself (Singer, 1973, pp. 315–16).

This suggests that there is some good inherent in providing goods in kind rather than in cash. Welfare economics takes the opposed view. According to its analysis, the welfare of the recipient is always increased when she receives her welfare payment in cash rather than in kind. For the cash-equivalent payment offers her more freedom of choice, she could use it to purchase the good for which it was a substitute, but she may wish to purchase preferred bundles of goods that would contribute to her welfare even more. While there is some appeal to this position, it seems that most of us have the intuition that some goods, such as medical care, are still better provided in kind. Is this simply a patronizing position? Why not let the poor decide whether they will spend a cash donation to purchase medical insurance or some other good that they might prefer? Do we not arbitrarily reduce the recipients' welfare by preventing them from exercising this choice?

There is a value, however, in collectively taking a stand on what goods the community regards as so important that it would be a disgrace to let any of its members fall short in them (Kelman, 1986; Thurow, 1977). The ability to take such a stand depends on being sensitive to the distinction between urgent needs and merely intense desires. The scale of urgency is an objective one that the whole community can recognize. It plays a public role in expressing shared principles and fraternal bonds among community members that the policy to simply indulge in individuals' subjective tastes cannot do. Given that we do recognize the distinction between urgent needs and intense desires, we can see that for a community to treat these two as on a par is to trivialize and debase the concerns of those who have the needs and to hold itself hostage to those with extravagant tastes (Scanlon, 1975). To distribute welfare payments on a want-regarding rather than a need-regarding basis would be, for instance, to treat the gourmet's anxiety at her lack of ostrich tongues on a par with the handicapped person's need for a wheelchair.[18]

But what lies at the basis of this distinction between needs and wants? It is our capacity to draw distinctions of worth among goods. In the case of the gourmet and the handicapped person, we understand that gastronomic pleasures are less important to leading a worthwhile life than the power to move about freely without depending on others. For the latter power is needed to lead a life of autonomy and to pursue worthwhile activities such as the development of one's talents. To lack the power to pursue such ends leaves one's life not merely frustrated, as when we lack certain pleasures, but degraded. Moreover, to lack the power to govern one's life in accordance with distinctions of worth between goods is itself debasing.[19] But such distinctions are not the product of private fancy. I cannot draw them in my own life except against a background of shared social understandings that recognizes them.

The social practice of distributing goods in accordance with need-regarding rather than want-regarding principles is one means of fixing these social understandings, thereby enabling us to lead not merely pleasurable but worthwhile lives. . . .

CONCLUSION: SOME ETHICAL LIMITATIONS OF THE MARKET

. . . We have seen that the realization of some values demands that they be open to the public (nonexclusive), or confined to people who have personal ties to one another, or done for reasons other than merely personal advantage, or held to be valuable as a matter of ideals rather than as a mere matter of taste, and so forth. This is to say that the realization of some values demands that certain goods be produced, exchanged, and enjoyed outside of market relations, or in accordance with nonmarket norms.

I have emphasized in particular two classes of goods whose realization must take place within nonmarket norms of exchange: gift values and shared values. Gift values differ from commodity values in that their worth is at least partially constituted by the nonmarket motives for which they are given. They are valued as tokens of love, admiration, respect, honor, and so forth, and consequently lose their value when they are provided for merely self-interested reasons. What is important about these goods as gift values is the fact that they express the giver's acknowledgment and affirmation of a certain relationship to the beneficiary, or of some characteristic she has, which is valued for its own sake.

Shared values differ from commodity values in that their being good for a group of people cannot be fully analyzed in terms of their being independently good for each member of the group, considered in isolation. Part of their being good consists in the fact that they are understood to be held in common—that everyone in the group both acknowledges the thing to be good and participates in its benefits. The value of any noninstrumental relationship is shared in this sense. The realization of shared values needs to take place within social relations that differ from market relations in at least three respects. First, since these values are sustained in part through a common activity of working out how they are valuable for the group, their realization requires a forum for working out these understandings together. Most of these values must be provided by the same people who enjoy them. The people who enjoy the good need to have the opportunity to participate in shaping its character. These characteristics require institutions of voice rather than of exit alone. Second, since part of its value lies in the fact that all members of the relevant group have access to it, some provision must be made for opening access to those members of the group who lack the ability to pay for their share of the costs of providing it. Shared goods are undermined by the market norm of restricting access to those who can afford to pay for it. Finally, since the value of shared goods is realized not in individual, exclusive appropriation and use but in common activities, rights over the physical vehicles of these values cannot be fully distributed in exclusive bundles. This was the basis for my arguments against "dividing the commons."

Gift values and shared values are not the only kinds of goods that are improperly treated as commodities, but our investigation of the problems that arise in attempting to regard them as commodities suggests the general form of arguments that certain goods should not be treated as economic values. By recognizing what this general strategy is, we can both make sense of the heretofore vague objections that some goods should not be treated as commodities and apply it to new cases. When the good in question is something or service to be marketed, the argument is as follows: for a certain dimension of value to be realized in a good, or for the good to serve as the vehicle for the realization of our ideals, the production, distribution, and enjoyment of this good must take place within the context of certain social relations. To trade the good on the market, or otherwise to subject its conditions of valuation to market forces and market norms, is to remove it from these social relations or to undermine their integrity. When the good in question is an ideal, the argument is that the social relations that most adequately embody the ideal are undermined when people adopt market norms to regulate their interactions in these relationships. Then we can say that the ideal is not an economic good, where to regard an ideal as an economic good is to regard it as best embodied in market relations.

Arguments of this form do not conclusively show that the goods in question may never be traded on the market. It may be that the distinctive dimensions of value in the goods can be preserved short of prohibiting their sale. Zoning laws represent an attempt to preserve certain public goods while allowing a private market in land. More importantly, the good in question may have more than one dimension of value. Prohibiting or regulating the sale of goods prevents certain economic goods from being realized. If the Grand Canyon is perma-

nently preserved from strip-mining in appreciation of its aesthetic value, its commercial value is unrealized. An argument against marketing a good is stronger if it shows not just that a noneconomic value is lost in marketing it, but that the value is degraded or perverted in marketing the good.[20]

The market has traditionally been defended on two grounds: for its efficiency and for its embodiment of a particular conception of freedom. This argument exposes a serious limitation on the market's claim to efficiency. The market cannot make claims to superior efficiency when it changes the qualities of the goods it provides, since claims to efficiency are valid only when ends are unchanged by alternate means of provision. My account also raises questions about the adequacy of the economic ideal of freedom. The market promises us freedom from the value judgment of others. How much I choose to value a commodity is independent of how much others choose to value it. We have seen, however, that giving a good a place on one's preference ranking is not all there is to valuing a good, unless that good is the object merely of a direct primitive liking. The freedom to value a good as much as one wishes is not the freedom to value it in any *way* one wishes. For the ability of an individual to value a good in some ways requires her participation in a social practice in which others understand its value in the same way. Outside of shared understandings, one can value things only as objects of primitive appeal. And some ways of valuing goods require a shared understanding that the goods are not commodities. The ideal of freedom as consent has also emerged somewhat tarnished. When the outcome of bargaining is influenced by a manipulation of one party's commitment to norms of civility or gratitude, the normative significance of his consent is diminished.

Finally, we may note that the market ideal of freedom is just one among others. Sometimes the realization of one ideal of freedom conflicts with the realization of another. The market ideal interprets freedom as freedom from ties of obligation to others. Committed or involuntary relationships with other people are viewed as entanglements, as constraints on personal autonomy. But we are not free to pursue the goods of deepest significance to human life under these conditions. The personal sphere offers us a different ideal of freedom. Within committed and intimate relationships, we are free to reveal ourselves to others, without having our self-disclosure become the object of another's manipulations. In the market, on the other hand, the successful bargainer must hold his concerns and desires in reserve, lest they be used by the other party to gain a negotiating edge. The sphere of democratic politics offers a different challenge to the market ideal of freedom. The market ideal identifies freedom with the power to exclude others from participation in decisions affecting one's property. But when some realms are completely divided into pieces of private property, nearly everyone is excluded from decision-making power over central areas of their lives. Democratic freedom, on the other hand, is freedom to participate in collective decisions. It is a freedom to be included, rather than to exclude others. When exit is impossible, when decisions concern shared goods, or when freedom can be effectively exercised by all only in public spaces of free and equal association, the freedom of democratic participation supercedes the exclusive freedom of the market.

To argue that the market has limits is to acknowledge that it also has its proper place in human life. There is a wide range of goods that *are* properly regarded as commodities. Among these are the conveniences, luxuries, delights, gadgets, and services found in ordinary stores. The modern market produces and distributes these goods with unsurpassed efficiency and in unsurpassed abundance. It is a good not only to have these goods, but to be able to procure them freely through the anonymous, unencumbered channels the market provides. For harm is done both to personal autonomy and to the integrity of friendship when one's access to consumer goods is dependent on personal connections with political cadres, foreigners, or other well-placed individuals, as is often the case in socialist countries. The difficult task for modern societies is to reap the advantages of the market while keeping its activities confined to the goods proper to it.

ENDNOTES

1. Economic goods are not confined to things or commodities; they can include economic relations, activities, and ideals as well. Things or services are "economic" insofar as their values are best realized through being traded on the market or otherwise treated in accordance with market norms—that is, as commodities. Ideals are "economic" insofar as they are best embodied in practices and relations governed by market norms. Norms are here understood as rules by which the participants in a practice govern and evaluate their behavior, or standards by which they understand the meanings of what they do or value. Often norms are justified as attempts to realize ideals to which we are committed.

The investigation needed to determine the nature of economic goods is a historical and empirical study of the norms and social understandings that govern market practices. What we discover from such investigations of different practices is similar to what Michael Walzer (1983) called the social meanings of goods. I generally endorse Walzer's view that goods can be usefully viewed as occupying different, although often overlapping, spheres of life. However, since social meanings are endlessly nuanced, constantly changing and being reinterpreted, the generalizations I make here about social meanings and norms should not be taken to be unqualified, much less a priori claims. Since modern social practices are deeply pluralistic, I also do not wish to suggest that I have offered an exhaustive account of the values of any particular sphere of life. In every case, the claims I make here should be taken as invitations to further detailed empirical investigation. In taking social meanings as the starting points for ethical argument, I also do not mean to suggest that they are beyond criticism. After all, I criticize later the economic ideal of freedom that informs many of our social practices. A general account of how to criticize social meanings is the task of another paper, however.

2. Friedman (1962) had a particularly clear exposition of the implications of this view.

3. Both aspects of the impersonal freedom of the market are the result of a long process of historical and legal development. My account of the market ethic and its development is indebted to the discussions by Atiyah (1979), Hirschman (1977), Horwitz (1977), Nelson (1969), Polanyi (1944), Simmel (1978), and Weber (1968). In particular, I have been influenced by Polanyi's thesis that societies need to constrain the extent of the market in order to protect themselves.

4. I owe this account of shared goods to Rawls (1971, pp. 523–26) and Taylor (1987).

5. This implied hierarchy of values, according to which one's sexuality is a higher and deeper (more intimate) value than any commodity, is founded on the public meanings embodied in our social practices and not on the possibly idiosyncratic intentions or feelings of individuals who may engage in them. The understanding that a person's sexuality reaches deeper into the self than money, that it is therefore a good that is different in kind from and higher than money, also lies behind our judgment that rape is a deeper violation of the person than robbery. One who would deny that prostitution is degrading would thus be hard pressed for an explanation of why rape is a more serious crime than robbery. To claim simply that rape results in more "disutility" than robbery is not enough—the question is why this is true, and how the claim can be substantiated. Since no one has provided an adequate account of how interpersonal comparisons of subjective utility can be made, it would seem that the basis for the judgment about utilities lies not

in such a comparison, but rather in the publicly accessible meanings of the acts themselves: the shared understanding that rape is more degrading than robbery.

6. One could imagine forms of "prostitution" that, while offered on the market, diverge from market norms in ways that could rescue the practice form the criticisms made here. For example, Schwarzenbach (1990) defended a conception of prostitution as a form of sex therapy practiced by professionals who help people liberate themselves from sick, patriarchal forms of sexuality. Such a practice would diverge from the ideal type of market relations presented here in many ways, especially insofar as it is informed by the norms and ideals of a profession. Professional services, such as legal, medical, and educational services, provide a classic case of "mixed" goods whose production and distribution is determined partly by market norms and partly by nonmarket, professional norms. Notoriously, market norms pose a constant threat to the integrity of professional norms. Yet, market norms may still be needed to ensure the efficient production and allocation of professional services, or to realize certain freedoms for their practitioners or customers.

7. Of course, the mere substitution of cash for in-kind payment does not obviate the exploitative character of such relationships. The firms still take advantage of their employees' duress and lack of decent alternatives; but they would be less likely to be able to evoke the ties of children to parents from which an extra margin of effort or obedience can be extracted from workers, if their dealings with employees were blatantly self-interested instead of ingratiatingly paternalistic.

8. While gift norms can be used by employers for exploitative purposes, there may be cases where employers themselves come to be guided by them. See Akerlof (1982).

9. "To Love, Honor, and . . . Share: A Marriage Contract for the Seventies," *Ms.* vol. 1, no. 12 (June 1973), pp. 62–64, 102–3.

10. My claim here is not that bargaining can never take place in a worthwhile marriage, but that where the norms of bargaining predominantly govern the relations of the partners, the integrity of their marriage is threatened.

11. It seems obvious to us that friends are not liable for each other's debts. Yet, it was not until the sixteenth century that in England it came to be seen as a foolish act rather than an act of true friendship to guarantee a friend's debts. This change is due to the fact that the present radical separation of the spheres of personal relationships and economic relationships is the product of a long historical development. For some of the details of this history, see Nelson (1969, esp. pp. 142–43). Of course, it is possible that we could rework our practices and understandings of friendship and credit, so

that the threats posed to success in each of these practices by combining them would not come about. Ideal-typical analysis does not preclude the reformation or combining of practices in new ways. It simply points out the conflicts and tensions among our present practices, and the conceptions of value they reflect, which would have to be adequately dealt with by any proposal to combine them.

12. Here I am generalizing John Rawls' account of fraternity and of the good of a social union (1971, pp. 105ff, 520–29).

13. On the significance of communal provision, see Sahlins (1972, pp. 188–91).

14. This might violate the norm of impersonality that I previously attributed to the market. However, libertarians do reject the view that impersonality is an appropriate norm to impose on people's use of their private property. Robert Nozick argues that a libertarian would have to accept a proviso on property acquisition that prevents people from trapping others in a small territory. But his proviso doesn't prevent private interference with others' freedom of movement that is less drastic than complete entrapment. For the libertarian account of freedom doesn't acknowledge that the restrictions mentioned count as interferences in others' freedom at all, since the freedom of movement we are concerned with here is not embodied in some property right. See Nozick (1974, pp. 55, 178–82).

15. Welfare economists differ from libertarians on the issue of dividing common goods that are nonrivals in consumption. It is a theorem of welfare economics that nonrival goods may be more efficiently provided on a nonexclusive (public) basis than on an exclusive one. However, even this view does not recognize the fact that providing a good on an exclusive basis may not merely provide it less efficiently, but change the kind of good it is for the worse. I thank Howard Wial for this point.

16. This account is indebted to Jane Jacobs' (1961) rich description of the goods of public parks and streets.

17. Titmuss has a second argument against selling blood, which relies on the facts that we depend on donors' honesty about their health to keep the blood supply safe and that the prospect of cash reward tempts unhealthy people to donate. In fact, there are many goods for which we are not in a position to verify whether the things offered to us really have the characteristics that make them good, or that are so complex that the costs of supervising the process by which they are provided are prohibitively high. In these cases, we have no choice but to grant a large degree of discretionary power to the providers, on condition that they exercise this power as a trust and not as a private right to exploit

for merely personal advantage. This is one powerful basis for opposing the commercialization of hospitals, elementary and secondary schools, and prisons. The profit motive offers a constant incentive for violating this trust, while the complexity of the goods guarantees a wide variety of opportunities for doing so undetected by the public.

18. This is not to claim that providing certain needs on a means-tested basis is better than other alternatives. Arguably, fraternity would be better expressed by making health care a right of all citizens, provided equally on a public basis. Furthermore, the actual meaning of any given form of cash or in-kind provision—whether it expresses respect or contempt for its recipients—depends on the details of its enactment and administration. For example, the petty regulations attending the food stamp program seem more designed to exercise public control over consumption habits of the poor than to express fraternity with its recipients.

19. Thomas Scanlon expressed this idea in the notion (following Rawls) that we are responsible for our ends (Rawls, 1982, pp. 168–71; Scanlon, 1975, pp. 663–66). One account of distinctions of worth between goods, and its connection with responsibility for one's ends, is provided by Charles Taylor (1985, esp. vol. 1, essays 1, 2, and 4, and vol. 2, essay 9).

20. The view developed here does not depend on postulating the existence of completely isolable spheres of social practices. Talks of "spheres" is useful, however, because the norms within which we produce and distribute goods typically come in bundles, with distinct bundles defining different spheres. Still, the different norms in the bundles can be separated and combined in different ways, and new norms invented, resulting in hybrid practices, or even in the creation of very new kinds of practices. I would hope that the kind of analysis developed here would be used as an opportunity to think of new kinds of practices that could help us move beyond the sterile dichotomy between market and state that informs so much contemporary political disagreement. The key question to be asked is, "What sets of norms are best for realizing these values?" and the answers need not be confined to the bundles of norms presently in operation.

REFERENCES

Akerlof, George. 1982. "Labor Contracts as Partial Gift Exchanges." *Quarterly Journal of Economics* 97:543–69.

Atiyah, P. S. 1979. *The Rise and Fall of Freedom of Contract.* Oxford: Clarendon Press.

Fisher, Anthony C. 1981. *Resource and Environmental Economics.* Cambridge: Cambridge University Press.

Friedman, Milton. 1962. *Capitalism and Freedom.* Chicago: University of Chicago Press.

Hirsch, Fred. 1976. *Social Limits to Growth.* Cambridge, MA: Harvard University Press.

Hirschman, Albert O. 1970. *Exit, Voice and Loyalty: Responses to Decline in Firms, Organizations, and States.* Cambridge, MA: Harvard University Press.

———. 1977. *The Passions and the Interests: Political Arguments for Capitalism before Its Triumph.* Princeton: Princeton University Press.

Hochschild, Arlie. 1983. *The Managed Heart: Commercialization of Human Feeling.* Berkeley and Los Angeles: University of California Press.

Horwitz, Morton J. 1977. *The Transformation of American Law: 1780–1860.* Cambridge, MA: Harvard University Press.

Hyde, Lewis. 1983. *The Gift: Imagination and the Erotic Life of Property.* New York: Random House.

Jacobs, Jane. 1961. *The Death and Life of Great American Cities.* New York: Random House.

Kelman, Steven. 1986. "A Case for In-Kind Transfers." *Economics and Philosophy* 2:55–73.

Mauss, Marcel. 1967. *The Gift.* Translated by Ian Cunnison. New York: W. W. Norton.

Nelson, Benjamin. 1969. *The Idea of Usury: From Tribal Brotherhood to Universal Otherhood.* 2nd ed., enlarged. Chicago: University of Chicago Press.

Nozick, Robert. 1974. *Anarchy, State, and Utopia.* New York: Basic Books.

Polanyi, Karl. 1944. *The Great Transformation.* Boston: Beacon Press.

Rawls, John. 1971. *A Theory of Justice.* Cambridge, MA: Harvard University Press.

———. 1982. "Social Unity and Primary Goods." In *Utilitarianism and Beyond,* edited by Amartya Sen and Bernard Williams, pp. 159–85. Cambridge: Cambridge University Press.

Rothbard, Murray. 1978. *For a New Liberty.* New York: Collier (Macmillan). Revised edition of first Collier edition.

Sahlins, Marshall. 1972. *Stone Age Economics.* New York: Aldine.

Scanlon, Thomas. 1975. "Preference and Urgency." *Journal of Philosophy* 72:655–69.

Schwarzenbach, Sibyl, 1990. "Contractarians and Feminists Debate Prostitution." *NYU Review of Law and Social Change* 18 (1991).

Sheffrin, Steven. 1978. "Habermas, Depoliticization, and Consumer Theory." *Journal of Economic Issues* 7:785–97.

Simmel, Georg. 1978. *The Philosophy of Money.* Translated by Tom Bottomore and David Frisby. Boston: Routledge and Kegan Paul.

Singer, Peter. 1973. "Altruism and Commerce: A Defense of Titmuss against Arrow." *Philosophy and Public Affairss* 2:312–20.

Taylor, Charles. 1985. *Philosophical Papers.* 2 vols. Cambridge: Cambridge University Press.

———. 1987. "The Political Consequences of Communitarianism." Lecture delivered at Harvard University, February 12, 1987.

Thurow, Lester. 1977. "Government Expenditures: Cash or In-Kind Aid?" In *Markets and Morals,* edited by Gerald Dworkin, Gordon Bermant, and Peter Brown, pp. 85–106. New York: Wiley.

Titmuss, Richard M. 1971. *The Gift Relationship: From Human Blood to Social Policy.* New York: Pantheon Books.

Walzer, Michael. 1983. *Spheres of Justice.* New York: Basic Books.

Weber, Max. 1968. *Economy and Society.* 2 vols. Edited by Guenther Roth and Claus Wittich. Berkeley and Los Angeles: University of California Press.

QUESTIONS ON ANDERSON

1. How does Anderson describe the five aspects of market relations? Are these features essential or necessary to *any* economic system? Are there other relations of markets that she has not mentioned?

2. How does Anderson describe how gift exchange differs from market exchange? What are some of the shared values that Anderson believes can be realized only through nonmarket institutions?

3. Of the public provision of city parks, Anderson states: "By providing the park as a common good, citizens thus express fraternal relations with one another." What are "fraternal relations"? (Is "fraternity" distinct from "civility"?) How might these be expressed through the provision of a public park? Do you think that "fraternal relations" are important in a society? Why or why not? Do markets impede fraternal relations? Does the centralization of government impede or encourage fraternal relations among citizens?

4. How does Anderson describe the sort of values that are realized by providing certain goods "in kind" rather than in cash? Do you agree? Why or why not?

The Nature of Business

Elaine Sternberg

Elaine Sternberg is Research Fellow in Philosophy at the Centre for Business and Professional Ethics, University of Leeds. Reflecting her experience as both a philosopher and an investment banker, her works include Just Business: Business Ethics in Action *(1994/2000) from which this extract is taken,* The Stakeholder Concept: A Mistaken Doctrine *(1999), and* Corporate Governance: Accountability in the Marketplace *(1998).*

THE DEFINITIVE APPROACH

A fundamental prerequisite for understanding business ethics is understanding exactly what business is. Unless business's distinctive purpose is clearly understood, business is likely to be confounded with other activities and associations, and evaluated by inappropriate standards. Defining business precisely is far from an academic trick; precise definition is a technique often required in business. Technical specifications rely on exact definitions and descriptions; so do most kinds of contracts. Financial statements depend on strict definition: to draw them up or to use them, it is necessary to understand what differentiates 'current assets' from 'non-current assets' and 'net operating profit' from 'net profit.' In tackling business ethics, it is business itself that needs to be defined.

Isn't it obvious what business is? Surely businesses are easy to pick out and identify? Some certainly are: it is generally accepted that Marks and Spencer and IBM are businesses, while St. Paul's and Cambridge are not. But is the village fête? What about the German industrial/financial complexes, and the Japanese *keiretsu?* And is the (UK) Post Office a business? Is the National Health Service? Merely dealing with vast sums of money does not automatically make an organisation a business. And at the other end of the scale, a business must be distinguished from a profitable hobby. In order to identify the very subject matter of business ethics, it is necessary to understand precisely what business is. Unless business is clearly differentiated from organisations and activities which it may closely resemble, it will be impossible to determine what is good in or for *business.*

The first step in understanding business, is to recognise that business is something very specific and limited. Despite widespread belief to the contrary, business is not even the whole of economic life, far less the whole of life. Business is neither the same as, nor a substitute for, other associations or activities; it is but one small part of human existence, albeit an extremely important one. In highlighting the fact that business has boundaries, and that it specifies something particular and distinctive, the classic business pronouncement that 'Business is business' expresses a fundamental truth. But though 'Business is business' is both true and significant, and basic to any proper understanding of business and business ethics, it does not specify what makes business different from all other undertakings and organisations. What does that is business's characteristic objective.

THE DEFINITIVE GOAL OF BUSINESS

The defining purpose of business is maximising owner value over the long term by selling[1] goods or services.[2] This simple statement is the key to understanding business, and consequently one of the foundations of understanding business ethics. Elucidating its meaning, and setting out its implications, will take up the rest of this chapter and, *inter alia,* much of the book.

To some, defining business in this way may seem obvious, even trivial. Until quite recently, after all, an even narrower definition of business—in terms of owner profits—was taken for granted by most business people and commentators. Even now such key business studies as corporate finance still take financial gains for owners to be the evident and undisputed end of business.

Increasingly, however, such a narrow definition of business has come to seem controversial. The trend has been to see business not as something that exists solely for the financial benefit of its owners, but as something with a myriad of other objectives, social and psychological, political and economic. As the objectives have multiplied, so have the groups to which business is assumed to be accountable. It has become almost commonplace for owners to be reduced to just one of the many 'stakeholders' whose interests must be served. Since these proliferating objectives and interested parties are of growing importance, they cannot be ignored. But nor can they serve to define business.

It is important to explain just why and in what ways they cannot. . . .Those who treat business as more inclusive than it is make. . . [a fundamental] mistake. By substituting a comprehensive, pretentious notion of business for the narrow, prosaic one, they sharply reduce their chances of achieving either objective. The broad objectives they are seeking are beyond the range of business, while the goal that should be their focus is ignored.

Maximising long-term owner value[3] may well be a less noble objective than curing the ills of the world[4]— but if it is, then so is business. To reject maximising long-term owner value as the defining purpose of business because it is too paltry and too insignificant, or because business is too important to be restricted to a narrow commercial end, is to mistake the function of definition: the purpose of defining a term is not glorification, but

clarification. Accepting a definition is not the same as approving of what is defined; precise definition is equally a precondition for criticising and rejecting a subject. To incorporate extraneous elements into the definition of business simply because they are perceived to be good, or important, is to distort the truth. It is to confuse the desirable with the essential, rather as one might do by including electric windows and a sunroof in defining 'motorcar': a car without those accessories might possibly not be worth having, but it is nonetheless a car.

The need to define business narrowly is not an ideological requirement, but a logical one: business that is everything to everyone is not anything at all in itself. A concept that excludes nothing is useless; since it refers equally to everything it cannot distinguish one thing from another.[5] A category that is too broad is correspondingly uninformative. To investigate business ethics, it is therefore not enough to focus on 'human activity' or even 'socially beneficial commercial activity'; a concept of business that cannot distinguish it from a charity or a hobby will not do. A definition that incorporates all social goals into the purpose of business, risks making business meaningless.

It may be protested that defining business narrowly is unrealistic. Actual business organisations pursue all sorts of objectives, and do so as a matter of course. Actual businesses sponsor the arts and give to charity and constitute social communities. Indeed, businesses are obliged by law to do things other than maximise long-term owner value: in many jurisdictions they are required to act as tax collectors in respect of VAT and income taxes. That actual organisations undeniably do pursue such varied ends, however, does not count against the strict definition of business: it simply means that such organisations are not exclusively businesses.[6]

It is precisely because most large commercial organisations pursue a variety of objectives that defining business strictly is so important. For unless the specifically *business* activity can be clearly identified, and distinguished from all the other things that such organisations do, the role that business should play within the multi-purpose organisation cannot even be discussed. In order to rank or reconcile or evaluate an organisation's possibly incompatible aims, one must first know what they are, and how they differ.

Although business is inseparably intertwined with other activities and objectives in practice, it can nevertheless be distinguished from them conceptually. Differentiating for analytical purposes that which is inseparable in fact is a technique often used in business. 'Lines of business' and geographical contributions are routinely separated out to give a better understanding of what is going on, even when they are not actually free-standing. And financial modelling depends heavily on the technique: in estimating business's future performance, variables are often isolated in order to sensitise projections. Strict definition of business is an attempt to isolate business itself.

In effect, strict definition is an attempt to provide a 'pure play' on business. Businesses sometimes restructure or create separate classes of equity to allow investors a purer play on some sub-set of their complex activities.[7] In like fashion, a clear definition of business permits examination of business itself, free of extraneous considerations. When the specifically business aspects of a multipurpose organisation are clearly identified, their ethical status can more realistically be assessed. And when business is not just one obscure end hidden amongst the many—often unconsidered and ill-assorted—objectives that characterise most actual firms, the core business goal is more likely to be achieved. . . .

WHAT BUSINESS IS NOT

In order to be useful for specifying or evaluating business, the definition of business must identify that which characterises business alone. What differentiates business from everything else is its purpose: maximising long-term owner value by selling goods or services. Only this definitive goal is essential to business. All other goals are at best incidental to business, and are justified for business only insofar as they contribute to achievement of the definitive goal. Many of the commonest characterisations of business are therefore radically incorrect.

The purpose of business is not to promote the public good.[8] Business is a prime contributor to the public good, but that role does not distinguish it from the other activities—medicine and education, for example—that also are; promoting the public good therefore cannot be the definitive purpose of business. Similarly, business does not exist to foster employees' physical or psychological well being; still less is its goal their ultimate fulfilment. Nor is it the aim of business to provide full employment for the nation's labour force or even jobs for local workers. Business's purpose is not to serve the interests of customers or of managers or of the community. Such positive benefits routinely result from business, but they do not constitute its defining aim.

Equally, business's definitive purpose is not to produce goods or services, or to add value. Producing goods or supplying services and adding value are, of course, indispensable elements of doing business: unless it produces goods or supplies services, business will have nothing to sell, and no way of maximising long-term owner value. But producing goods and services and adding value are not exclusive to business, and therefore cannot serve as business's defining goal. The army, the courts and housewives supply services, and children's carpentry classes produce goods, but they are not businesses. Similarly, though cooking a meal, tidying a garden and telling a joke all add value, they do not normally constitute businesses.

To focus on business's function as a producer, supplier or adder of value is to misconstrue business's purpose. If the nature of the goods or services, or the way they are produced, takes priority over maximising long-term owner value, then the activity involved is not business. An organisation whose guiding principle is producing the absolutely best widgets (e.g., engines, books, healthcare) or the very cheapest ones—*independent of the consequences for long-term owner value*—is not operating as a business . . . even if, incidentally, it sells the widgets profitably.

Business is also not a charity or a church, a school or a club; it is not, except incidentally, an agency of government or of social policy. Since, however, business is so often confused with such organisations and activities, it is worth examining in some detail how they differ from business. Failure to differentiate them clearly is responsible for some of the seemingly most fundamental and intractable problems of business ethics.

Family

All too frequently, managers boast that they treat their employees like 'one big happy family.' The ethical difficulty is not (just) that they may be hypocritical in making that claim, but even worse, that they might not be. The more literally managers consider their staff to be an extended family, the more likely it is that basic moral issues will be confused, and that the ends of both business and of family will be subverted.

Different things count as correct conduct for families and businesses, because families and businesses have different functions. Families exist for the mutual care and support of family members, particularly those, like children and the very old, who are less capable of looking after themselves. A family takes care of its members simply because they are family, without any particular regard for reciprocity or merit; family members are kept and cared for, come what may. Business, in contrast, only exists to maximise long-term owner value. As a result, those who undermine achievement of that end are rightly penalised or dismissed. It is as 'dysfunctional' for a business always to excuse errant action as it is for a family never to.

What is appropriate conduct also differs with respect to financial support. Given the family's caring function, family resources are typically allocated on the basis of current need: those who cannot contribute are supported by those who can. Within a business, in contrast, all must contribute, and resources are allocated in proportion to contributions made to the business goal. A firm that stresses its 'family' character, and tolerates or indulges non-performance, is unlikely to achieve its business ends. But in going out of business, it does not thereby become a family. Far from it, it makes achievement of real family goals—the goals of actual families—less rather than more feasible.

Club

Just as a business is not a family, nor is it a club. A club is typically defined by its members' shared interests, amusements or values. The defining objective need be nothing more than the members' wish to associate with people who are in some way like themselves, and to exclude all others: consider small boys who club together precisely to exclude even smaller boys. What differentiates a club from other associations is that, subject only to the law and its articles (if any), the criteria determining a club's membership and activities are simply whatever the club's members please.

As a result, clubs and businesses have very different approaches to recruitment. For a club, the sole criterion of a suitable new member is acceptability to the existing members. Business, in contrast, has a definitive purpose to accomplish, and selects candidates for their ability to contribute to it: recruits qualify because of their ability to maximise long-term owner value, not their congeniality.

Hobby, Game

Just as business as an association differs from a social club, business as an activity differs from a hobby. A hobby is something done in one's spare time to pass the time agreeably. As pleasurable pastimes, hobbies by their nature are subordinate to most other activities: when duties or even other pastimes call, hobbies are typically forsaken. Business, in contrast, has a serious purpose; its commitment to maximising long-term owner value means it cannot be abandoned just because it ceases to be fun or convenient. Business commitments affect people's lives and livelihoods, and should not be undertaken lightly; when business creates expectations, it has a responsibility to correct or to fulfil them.

Like hobbies, games are conducted primarily for amusement, and even more than clubs, games are defined by their rules. The notion that business might be a game is therefore implausible. It has, however, arisen frequently in connection with the (mistaken) view that separate and less stringent moral standards apply to business. It will therefore be considered and refuted in *Just Business's* Chapter 3 discussion of the principles of ethical business.

Government

Businesses are also definitively different from governments. Actual institutions, of course, are often complex mixtures. Governments are deeply involved in business, in regulating and in owning vast commercial organisations; conversely, businesses are often required by law to act as agents of the state. Businesses also require effective corporate governance.[9] Nevertheless the definitive functions of business and government are radically different, and can and must be distinguished if they are properly to be understood. When they are, it will be seen that businesses are not unethical for lacking stakeholder representation and employee 'rights.'

The purpose of business is to maximise long-term owner value by selling goods or services. The essential function of government, in contrast, is to provide the framework within which business and all other purposes can peaceably be pursued.[10] To achieve this equally limited but fundamental end, government and its officially designated agents—mainly the armed services and the police—normally have a monopoly on the legitimate use of physical violence.[11]

This definitive power of government has several important consequences. Crucially, it makes consent an essential condition of legitimate government. Since government has the power forcibly to deprive the governed of their lives,[12] liberty and property, it is vital that those subject to its power have a say in how that power is used. Because those from whom consent is required, and to whom the government is legitimately accountable, are too numerous to do the job in person, representatives are frequently employed.

Comparable representation is inappropriate in business for anyone except shareholders. First, it is not justified. Unlike government, business cannot legally use force to compel anyone to do anything; it cannot even enforce its own contracts without recourse to the courts. Since business has no coercive power, participants in a business have no need for a vote in the business in order to ensure their freedom from that power.

Those who do not wish to comply with a decision or a policy can simply leave;[13] in business, unlike in government,[14] participants can vote with their feet. The choice to become, or to stay, a participant in a particular business is a matter of voluntary contractual agreement.

Moreover, unlike citizens who are all[15] equal under the law, participants in a business are not all equal, or equally entitled to a vote. Within the business, the owners and their interests are paramount, and are so by the very nature of business. This does not mean that employees and other stakeholders do not count, or that they cannot influence the outcomes of businesses. But their concerns are important to the business only insofar as they influence the maximising of long-term owner value. Far from business's being accountable to its employees, it is the employees who are properly accountable to the business: employees and managers are agents of the business, not vice versa. Those who seek 'industrial democracy' are as much mistaken as those who endorse 'corporate government.'[16]

The notions of freedom of speech and other political rights also do not apply within business. Such rights exist[17] as a means of limiting coercive powers. Since business has no coercive power, specific rights to protect against abuse of it do not make sense. Business must, of course, respect the civil and natural rights of all members of society; business should never be above the law. But in their capacity as participants in a business, stakeholders have no rights other than those explicitly conferred on them by law and contract.

. . .Using business resources for non-business purposes is tantamount to *theft:* an unjustified appropriation of the owners' property. Managers who employ business funds for anything other than the legitimate business objective are simply embezzling: in using other people's money for their own purposes, they are depriving owners of their property as surely as if they had dipped their hands into the till.

That the diverted resources are applied to ends that are commonly regarded as laudable, or as 'social responsibilities.' does not make the act of diverting them any less larcenous. However worthy the charity being helped, if the employee uses company time and telephones to solicit contributions rather than business, he is cheating the business's owners. Despite what might be called the 'Robin Hood Syndrome,' stealing from the rich to give to the poor is still stealing; so is all embezzling from business owners to give to others. Wrongdoing is not annulled by worthy motives[18] or by applying the ill-gotten gains to popular ends. Had the proceeds of the Great Train Robbery been donated to charity, the monies used would still have been stolen, and the robbers would still have been thieves. . . .

'MAXIMISING LONG-TERM OWNER VALUE' EXPLAINED

It should now be clear that much depends on properly identifying the purpose of business. It is therefore important to dispel any misunderstandings that might arise concerning the business definition and its components.

The first point that needs clarification is the relationship that the elements of the business definition bear to one other. 'By selling goods or services' indicates how long-term owner value is to be maximised. Business is not about maximising long-term owner value through theft, or alchemy, or increasing or preserving personal assets. Adding a loft extension to one's house, polishing the family silver, and getting interest on one's savings can all enhance the value of what one owns, but they are not the same as doing business. Business is only conducted when long-term owner value is maximised by selling goods or services.

Conversely, 'selling goods or services' only constitutes business when it is conducted so as to 'maximise long-term owner value.' Business activities and decisions—about what sort of widgets to sell, and how to price them, and whether widget components should be produced or bought in—are characterised by their reference to expected effects on maximising long-term owner value. If selling striped widgets contributes more to long-term owner value than selling spotted ones, then a business will concentrate on stripes.

'Maximising long-term owner value' qualifies not only 'selling goods or services,' but everything that the business does. To maximise long-term owner value by selling goods or services a business has to perform ancillary activities: it must produce or acquire those goods or services; it must also distribute them. Consequently, a business normally must, among other things, own assets and arrange finance and employ staff; simply by existing, it automatically plays a part in a community, and may even constitute a community of its own. The extent to which ancillary purposes and incidental activities should be pursued by business, and the way in which they should be pursued, are governed by the definitive need to maximise long-term owner value.

'Maximising long-term owner value' normally operates as a criterion within a business, rather than in the choice of which business to pursue initially. When starting a business, the choice of what goods or services to sell will reflect the founders' interests, opportunities and available capital as well as the comparative gains to be made from different lines of activity. If maximisation were necessary for choosing which business to start, most coeval businesses would pursue the same market niche. Once a business is underway, however, and capital has been committed on the understanding that a particular line of business is being pursued, all deviations from that line must be justified on the grounds of maximising long-term owner value. . . .

The Meaning of 'Owner Value'

Financial vs. Moral Value   . . . In the definition of business, 'value' is simply financial value. Contributions to financial value may not always be immediately obvious: they may well be indirect, qualitative and only evident over the long term. But in the end, activities must contribute to financial value to be appropriate for business.

That business is devoted exclusively to financial value does not, of course, deny the validity or importance of other values, be they ethical or spiritual or artistic. Indeed, financial value, though an end in itself for business, is both a product of, and a precondition for, the myriad other values held by individuals. In stressing the primacy of financial value within business, nothing is being asserted about the relative rankings of values; the definition does not imply that financial value is more important than other values, for owners or anyone.

It is also important to recognise that in defining business by reference to maximising financial value, nothing at all is being suggested about motivation.[19] No view is being taken about the reasons why people either do go or should go into business, or about the value of financial versus other incentives for affecting their performance within business. People are in fact motivated by all sorts of different things. That they are, however, is not an argument against business's essence being maximising long-term owner value; business's connection to financial value is logical, not psychological.

What if owners want something other than maximum financial value from their enterprises? Examples are not hard to find. 'Ethical investment' is becoming more prominent, and firms have increasingly been stressing their explicitly non-financial aims. Moreover, the Anglo-Saxon emphasis on owner value is not equalled in other major commercial centres. Japanese *keiretsu* have traditionally been more concerned with achieving market share to save jobs, while the German industrial complexes have focused on consolidating power. Owners are perfectly entitled to devote their organisations to all sorts of ends. To the extent that they

pursue something other than maximum long-term owner value, however, they are simply not engaging in business.

Owner Value vs. Wealth, Assets, Revenues   But why specify the defining purpose of business in terms of maximising owner *value?* Why not wealth, or assets or revenues? The defining purpose of business could well be specified in terms of maximising wealth. The main reason for preferring the term 'value' is that it carries no suggestion of opulence. A very small business, which generates only meagre sums for its owners, can nevertheless be as much of a business as one that produces great riches: in this, as in so much else, size is not important.

'Value' is preferable to 'assets' and 'revenues' for a more significant reason: not all assets are worth having. An unused building may incur property taxes while generating no income, and constitute a financial liability. The purpose of business is not simply to amass things, but to maximise the financial worth of the owners over the long-term. For the same reason, it is not the purpose of business to maximise revenues or turnover or unit sales, all of which may generate losses. What is important about business activity is not its level, but its outcome: volume without value is seldom worth pursuing.

Owner Value vs. Profits   Should business therefore be identified with maximising profits, as it so very often is? There are two important reasons why not. The first is that profits, like earnings per share, return on investment and all other accounting measures, are notoriously slippery. By determining the timing of a firm's actions, management can shape the reality that financial statements report. And given the opportunities for (completely legal) creative accounting and 'window dressing,' those reports can also be 'massaged' to suit management purposes.[20] Even when managers are scrupulously pursuing the owners' objectives, the ambiguity and flexibility of accounting standards allow external analysts to disagree significantly about what actual profit levels are.

The second reason why profits are an inadequate measure of owner value is that they import an intrinsically but inappropriately short-term bias: 'profits' usually means 'current period accounting profits.' By referring only to a single, short, historical span, current period profits do not make allowance for the investments—in research and development, in capital equipment, in training, in restructuring—that may be necessary to improve the business over the long term. Current period profits are not designed to take into account the future consequences of present action.

A thing's value, in contrast, is normally influenced by its future potential as well as by its past and by its present. The value of a piece of land is typically determined not just by its historical cost and its location, but by the likely availability of planning permission. As a result, calculations of value automatically recognise the importance of investment now for generating improved results later. Equally, calculations of value require paying heed to the consequences of business actions. Improper action that yields immediate profits may lead to actual and opportunity costs in future, and produce a net reduction of financial value. Value is therefore more satisfactory than profit for specifying the definitive end of business. . . .

Owner Value vs. Share Price A much more plausible candidate for owner value, at least of public quoted companies, is the share price. Notionally, the share price reflects the present value of the future cash flows expected from dividend payments[21] over the indefinite future. And according to efficient market theory, the share price incorporates all the information available at a given time about a corporation's performance and prospects. Market capitalisation should therefore represent what a corporate business is worth to its owners, the shareholders.

Share price has two major advantages as a measure of owner value. Unlike accounting measures, it is not directly manipulable by management. On the contrary, it exhibits the market's assessment of managements, and of managements' likely achievements. In addition, since the share price reflects future cash flows, it automatically takes into account the future effects of current actions, and consequently does not suffer from the short-term bias of historical, single-period measures.

But though the share price may be the best surrogate available at any time, it is nevertheless not a fully adequate measure of owner value. First, the best information available at any given time may still be incomplete, or simply inaccurate. When, for example, the stock market Crash of 1987 expressed a major shift in investor sentiment, whole sectors were marked down indiscriminately; in the crisis atmosphere, the likely effects on particular companies of, for instance, changing exchange rates, were inadequately differentiated. Until corrections were made some time later, the share prices of individual companies did not accurately reflect owner value.

Such errors do not only arise in crises. Some firms coast on their reputations long after they have ceased to deserve them, and thereby command a price that exceeds their real value. Equally, a low share price may reflect an inadequately understood business product,

process or policy. While poor communications to shareholders may be paralleled by equally poor sales descriptions to customers, they need not be. There may actually be 'fundamental' value that the market has failed to appreciate. 'Unlocking' such value is often the objective of acquisitions, 'de-mergers' and buyouts.

A second and more basic problem is that share price is only a plausible measure of owner value for quoted companies. Share prices are not readily available for private companies, and may be manipulable when a liquid market does not exist. Even more fundamentally, neither shares nor share prices exist for the very many businesses that are not corporate in form. So although share price may be a good surrogate for owner value in quoted companies, it cannot be the definitive measure of business.

Owner Value Defined The best way to measure owner value is to use that component of share price that is transferable: discounted future cash flows. Owner value consists of the present value of the future cash flows that the owners will obtain from the business. Those cash flows are normally of two kinds: distributions from the business, in the form of dividends or other payouts, and the capital gains or losses that are realised when (the owner's financial interest in) the business is sold.

Though estimating such future cash flows is one standard way of valuing businesses, most business decisions do not require estimating the value of a business as a whole. All they require is estimating the marginal effects on owner value of alternative courses of action. Even calculating the relative contributions of specific programmes is not easy; such calculations still require reliable information, and careful judgement in the choice of assumptions and discount rates. They are, nevertheless, calculations that businesses are accustomed to making, especially in connection with evaluating major capital projects. They are less familiar in considering personnel or policy proposals largely because explicit calculation is not necessary when the answers are obvious or immaterial. Whether or not evaluating it requires a mathematical computation, however, 'owner value' serves as a valuable criterion: it indicates what considerations are relevant when business decisions have to be made.

Owners vs. Others
Shareholders Why is the relevant value that of the owners? The purpose of business cannot be maximising shareholder value, because not all businesses are

corporations: shareholders are only one kind of business owner. Sole proprietorships and partnerships abound, especially in respect of smaller businesses, and are as legitimate a form of business organisation as the limited liability company and its international equivalents. Maximising shareholder value is the purpose of corporate business, not of business as such.

Stakeholders   An equally popular but more pernicious mischaracterisation of business is that which defines business in terms of 'stakeholders' rather than owners. The term 'stakeholder' was originally used to designate those groups without whose support the business could not survive,[22] those in which the business had a stake: not just its owners, who provided the initial capital, but its employees and its customers, its suppliers and its lenders, the community and even the legal system. Increasingly, however, the meaning of 'stakeholder' has been reversed, and the term has been used ever more widely, to include everything and everyone who might have a stake in the business or be affected by it.[23] In this extended sense it has been taken to include the media, competitors and terrorists,[24] and even encompasses future generations and nameless sea creatures.[25]

The stakeholder theory of business typically holds that business is accountable to all its stakeholders, and that the role of management is to balance their competing interests.[26] Though increasingly popular, and indeed sanctioned by law in some jurisdictions,[27] this characterisation of business is nonetheless wrong: stakeholder theory incorporates at least four fundamental errors.

First, in maintaining that all stakeholders are of equal importance to a business, and that the business ought to be answerable equally to them all, stakeholder theory confounds business with government. Because of the nature of government, citizens are equal under the law, and are entitled to representation and a vote in the way things are run. As argued above, however, participants in a business are not. Stakeholder theory asserts that they are, by mistakenly regarding stakeholders in a business as citizens of that business.[28]

Second, and even more fundamentally, stakeholder theory rests on a confusion about the nature of accountability. Starting from the fact that business is affected by and affects certain groups, the theory concludes that the business should be accountable to them. But this is nonsense. Business is affected by all sorts of things—by gravity and the weather and interest rates—and it affects the Gross National Product and traffic conditions, but it is not accountable to them. Equally, the business is not, and could not rationally be, accountable to terrorists or competitors. That the business must take them into account, does not give them any right to hold it to account. Nor does the fact that they are affected by the business, give them any right to control it.

The same is true for suppliers and lenders, employees and customers. To recognise that a business affects them, and must to some degree be functionally responsive to them, is quite different from saying that it is accountable to them. The business must indeed take them into account. But it is answerable to them only insofar as its specific contractual arrangements or laws have made it so.

There are, of course, a variety of ways in which a business might have rendered itself accountable to those counterparties. It might, for example, have entered into written contracts: loan agreements, or contracts of employment, or long-term purchasing arrangements. The business might also have bound itself by creating expectations that it now should honour; some contracts are implicit and unwritten. In all such cases, however, the accountability stems from the nature of the specific contracts entered into, not from the stakeholder relationship as such. The only stakeholders to which the business is automatically accountable are its owners.[29] And the reason why the business is accountable to them, is simply because it belongs to them: it is their property.

The third reason why the stakeholder theory cannot be a proper account of business, is that it effectively destroys business accountability. In substituting a notional accountability to all stakeholders for direct accountability to owners, the stakeholder approach to business makes it impossible to hold business properly to account. And that is because a business that is accountable to all, is actually accountable to none: accountability that is diffuse, is effectively non-existent. This sad truth is known to all executives who have struggled with 'matrix management.' When several groups or individuals are theoretically in charge, each has an excuse for not taking responsibility; getting things right is always someone else's job. Multiple accountability can only function if everyone involved accepts a common purpose that can be used for ordering priorities.

But therein lies the fourth problem with the stakeholder account of business: it provides no such criterion. In rejecting the maximisation of long-term owner value as the purpose of business, and requiring business instead simply to 'balance' the interests of all stakeholders, stakeholder theory discards the objective basis for evaluating business action. How are those conflicting interests to be balanced? Are they all strictly equal? Are some more important than others? If so, which are they?

And when, and by how much, and why? Since stakeholder theory offers no substantive business purpose, it provides no guidance at all as to how competing interests are to be ranked or reconciled. It consequently provides no effective standard against which business can be judged.

It is interesting to note that some of the most prominent advocates of stakeholder theory have been just those with most to gain from avoiding accountability: business managers.[30] By substituting a vague notion of 'balancing interests' for a measurable standard of financial performance, stakeholder theory frees business managers to pursue their personal ends. Stakeholder theory allows them to take lavish salaries and extravagant perks, and enables them to protect their powers by rejecting takeovers that would maximise owner value. . . .

Customers, Employees, Managers If the purpose of business cannot be to serve the interests of stakeholders collectively, might it not be to benefit specific stakeholder groups?

The customer is traditionally king: perhaps, as many commentators have claimed, serving the interests of customers is also the purpose of business. Customers are indeed vital for a business's very existence: there is no business without selling, and no selling without customers. And treating customers well is essential for achieving business success: the customer is not always right, but in most circumstances the business benefits from acting as though he were.

Nevertheless, serving customers' interests cannot constitute the definitive purpose of business. First, serving customers does not distinguish business from all the other sorts of organisations that also provide services: fee-paying schools, for instance. If it were claimed that business differs because its purpose is to serve customers' financial interests, that still would not do. For if that really were business's objective, it would give its goods away—and would not long survive. Even if it covered its costs, such an organisation would be conceptually indistinguishable from a consumer charity.

Similarly, an association whose purpose is promoting the interests or expressing the wishes of its employees, is not a business but an employee club. Consider the all too common phenomenon of shop customers' wanting assistance while oblivious staff chatter amongst themselves. If the purpose of business were furthering employee interests, the staff would be justified in serving their own convenience rather than the customers. But they are not, because promoting employees' interests is not the purpose of business.

Nor can the purpose of business be serving that subset of employees consisting of its managers. Given the disjunction between ownership and control that is characteristic of large corporations, and the remoteness of most shareholders, the managers and directors are frequently left free to treat the business as though it were their property. But this simply reflects a defect of corporate governance. Far from owning the business, or constituting its reason for being, managers are merely agents of the owners, charged with maximising long-term owner value.

The Meaning of 'Long-Term'

Though the phrase 'long-term owner value' has been used throughout in characterising the defining purpose of business, inclusion of the words 'long-term' is, strictly speaking, superfluous:[31] a thing's value normally reflects its potential. A car that has been driven 100,000 miles normally sells for less than one with low mileage. And a business with a backlog of new products, or a well-developed and popular brand image, will normally represent greater owner value than one with overhanging litigation or exposure to declining markets.

Though strictly unnecessary, 'long-term' is included in the formula to highlight the simple but too frequently overlooked fact that actions have long-term consequences, in business as elsewhere. It is therefore vital for businesses to take into account the future effects of their current actions. 'Long-term' serves as a reminder that though consequences may be temporally distant, and correspondingly uncertain, they are nonetheless real.

'Long-term' is also included as a reminder that business is normally assumed to be a sustained activity, not a temporary one. An isolated transaction does not usually constitute a business; a fly-by-night operation is a business deviation. Owner value is normally to be maximised on the assumption that the business will be around to reap the consequences of its current actions. Accordingly, in determining whether to undertake a complex restructuring programme, the high initial costs must be netted against the benefits likely to accrue over future years. Equally, the increased current profits that may result from sharp practice must be weighed against the long-term costs of covering up and of alienating stakeholders. When courses of action are assessed, their future consequences must not be ignored.

In most circumstances a business will be able to generate greater owner value if it operates over an extended period: the sum of future values will normally be greater if there are more of them to aggregate. But though there is often a presumption that businesses are perpetual, the object of business is not survival at any cost. If a business is generating losses, and is likely to continue to do so, its disposal value may well exceed its value as a going concern. When that is so, then owner value is maximised by selling the business, or winding it up. Reference to the long-term provides no excuse for incompetence or lack-lustre performance in the meanwhile: owner value is unlikely to be maximised if the business's short-term decisions are wrong.

The Importance of Maximising   It is essential that the objective be to maximise owner value, not just to increase or promote, secure or sustain it. Less stringent objectives than maximising fail to differentiate business from other activities. If there were no requirement for owner value to be maximised, any activity or association that increased owner value through occasional sales would thereby qualify as a business. Hobbyists making casual sales would constitute businesses, as would families selling their houses.[32] But, of course, they are not.

Only maximising[33] provides a sufficiently clear-cut, hard-edged criterion of business action. All sorts of things can create or conserve or even augment owner value; if business's goal were simply to further or to enhance owner value, there would be no business reason to choose one alternative rather than another. When, in contrast, the purpose is to maximise value, the choice is clear: the policy, project or course of action to be pursued is that which is likely to produce the greatest return over time.[34]

Maximisation reinforces business's long-term view: future periods must be included in the calculation. The very need to be forward-looking can, however, make maximising long-term owner value seem an awkward criterion to apply. The owner value of a course of action can only be definitively determined in retrospect; even then, the values that might have resulted from alternative programmes remain unknown. In the absence of a reliable time machine, it is therefore difficult to know which of several courses of action will actually produce the greatest value.

The difficulty of foreseeing the future does not, however, disqualify maximising long-term owner value as a useful business criterion. To the extent that forecasting outcomes is a practical problem, it is one that besets all forward-looking criteria: the effects of current action on future share prices, or profits, or sales would be equally hard to predict. In each case, the criteria operate by specifying the terms of reference for business decisions, the standard against which proposals must be measured. Since the ultimate outcomes cannot be known at the time decisions are taken, decisions are based on the extent to which proposed actions are expected to achieve the desired goal. And that is a matter for judgement based on reasoned argument and objective evidence. The outcomes may not be available, but the reasons why particular actions are expected to lead to them can be subjected to critical scrutiny.

By indicating the grounds on which business action must be justified, 'maximising long-term owner value' specifies the sorts of arguments and the kinds of evidence that must be adduced to justify business decisions. All assumptions, factual data and judgements must be evaluated against the objective of maximising long-term owner value. It is not enough to show that a project is expected to increase current profits, or that it exceeds a hurdle rate for return on investments, or that all the directors like it. To justify a course of action one must instead show why and how the action can be expected to maximise long-term owner value, taking into account all the factors, positive and negative, that are likely to affect owner value over the foreseeable future. A proposal whose connection with maximising long-term owner value is remote, or that seems likely to produce less long-term owner value than an alternative, is one that the business should not adopt. Satisfying the criterion does not, of course, guarantee that long-term owner value actually will be maximised, but it does ensure that action will be directed at the right objective.[35]

The Role of Rational Self-Interest   Long-term owner value is likely to be maximised when business owners pursue their enlightened self-interest.[36] The notion of self-interest is normally presumed to incorporate an element of optimisation. Moreover, the considerations that are essential for maximising long-term owner value are closely akin to those that qualify the pursuit of self-interest to be called 'enlightened' or 'rational': the future consequences of actions must always be taken into account, and immediate effects must be balanced against wider and more distant ones.

Rational self-interest and maximising long-term owner value require taking into account behaviour by, and to, all those who regularly interact with the business. One of the most valuable uses of 'stakeholder' is as a reminder of, and a convenient shorthand label for, all those groups whose actions and attitudes must be considered in assessing whether a course of action is likely to maximise long-term owner value.

Although its responsibilities to stakeholders are limited, the business cannot afford to ignore any stakeholder concern that might affect long-term owner value. It is not just the actions of owners that affect the operations of the business, but also those of employees and customers, suppliers and lenders and regulators. Their tastes and preferences, including their moral preferences, will influence their willingness to deal with the business, and thus must be considered in assessments of long-term owner value. It is as important to be straight with suppliers as with shareholders, as necessary to be fair to employees as to customers.

Rational self-interest and maximising long-term owner value also require reciprocity: behaviour both by, and to, all stakeholders must be taken into account. In business it is as vital that owners behave responsibly as that employees do, as important for borrowers to be honest as it is for lenders. When the nature of business is properly understood, and the components of maximising long-term owner value are fully appreciated, it should be clear why it is normally true both that 'bad ethics is bad business' and 'good ethics is good business'. . . .

ENDNOTES

1. Selling here includes leasing, renting, etc.
2. Or both. . . .
3. 'By selling goods or services' should be assumed . . . the defining purpose of business is always the same, though the shorter form of words will often be employed for convenience.
4. Though it might equally be a necessary condition for doing so. . . .
5. For a fuller discussion of these and related points, see Aristotle, *Metaphysics,* especially Books IV and XI.
6. See also Preface of Sternberg, Elaine, *Just Business: Business Ethics in Action,* second edition, Oxford University Press, 2000; first edition: Little, Brown & Co., 1994; Warner Paperback, 1995.
7. Consider the General Motors Class E shares issued to reflect the performance of the once-independent Electronic Data Services, and the split of the Racal Group into Vodaphone, Racal Electronics and Chubb Security.
8. The famous slogan 'The public good be damned' can be seen as a pithy reminder of this crucial fact.
9. For a comprehensive discussion of corporate governance, and a defence of the Anglo-Saxon model of corporate governance, see Sternberg, Elaine, *Corporate Governance: Accountability in the Marketplace* (henceforth *CGAIM*), Institute of Economic Affairs, 1998.
10. Like actual commercial organisations, actual governments do much more in practice, and arrogate to themselves many diverse functions and objectives. That they do so, however,

in no way undermines the correctness of the definition. For a fuller exposition of this notion of the role of government, see, for example, Hayek, Frederich A., *The Road To Serfdom,* University of Chicago Press, 1944, especially Chapter VI, and Friedman, Milton, *Capitalism and Freedom, op. cit.,* especially Chapter II. For its philosophical underpinnings, see Hobbes, Thomas, *Leviathan,* and the works of Michael J. Oakeshott, especially *On Human Conduct,* Oxford University Press, 1975, Section II.

11. Except for self-defence.
12. By conscription into the armed forces, and in some jurisdictions through capital punishment.
13. Subject, of course, to fulfilling any contractual or other commitments they might have undertaken.
14. The choice to live outside the jurisdiction of government is no longer available.
15. Except for those who are underage, convicted felons or mentally defective.
16. Not to be confused with corporate governance.
17. When they do . . . it is arguable that unlike American citizens, whose Bill of Rights is set out as a series of amendments to the (written) Constitution, British subjects had only the right of *habeas corpus* prior to the incorporation of the European Convention on Human Rights into UK law. Even if such rights are considered to be 'natural rights' (see Chapter 6 of Sternberg, Elaine, *Just Business: Business Ethics in Action, op. cit.*), however, they operate chiefly as a limit on coercive force.
18. Though such motives may sometimes make criminals less blameworthy; for a fuller discussion of motives and actions see the Preface and Chapter 4 (Acts vs Motives section) of Sternberg, Elaine, *Just Business: Business Ethics in Action, op. cit.*
19. See also the Preface and Chapter 4 (Acts vs. Motives section) of Sternberg, Elaine, *Just Business: Business Ethics in Action, op. cit.*
20. In some sense, of course, all measures are influenced by management: if management had no effect, it would not be worth having. But as discussed in Chapter 7 of Sternberg, Elaine, *Just Business: Business Ethics in Action, op. cit.,* accounting measures are exceptionally susceptible to management control; even auditing presents few limits on their being used to promote the ends of managers rather than owners.
21. When a share is sold, the price received reflects the further dividends forgone; that price will crystallise a capital gain if it is greater than the price paid for the shares.
22. Reportedly in a 1963 internal memo at the Stanford Research Institute; Freeman, R. Edward, *Strategic Management: A Stakeholder Approach,* Pitman Publishing Inc., 1984, p. 31.
23. Freeman, *op. cit.,* p.vi.
24. *Ibid,* p. 52.
25. The UK Co-operative Bank explicitly includes both 'past and future generations' in its list of stakeholders; Kellaway,

Lucy, 'Stakeholders step up for the generation shuffle,' *Financial Times,* 17 March 1997, p. 16. Consider as well the future generations, of whatever species, in whose name ecologists protest against various perceived depredations, and the nameless sea creatures allegedly threatened by, e.g., the disposal of the Brent Spar oil rig at the bottom of the ocean.

26. For a comprehensive analysis of the defects of the stakeholder doctrine, see Sternberg, Elaine, *The Stakeholder Concept: A Mistaken Doctrine,* Foundation for Business Responsibilities, Issue Paper No. 4, November 1999, and *CGAIM, op. cit.,* Chapter 6.

27. By, for example, Pennsylvania's notorious anti-takeover Act 36 of 1990.

28. It is noteworthy that stakeholders are commonly described as representing 'constituencies,' which in turn are identified with interest groups. The notion that an elected representative's function is to represent the special interests of his particular electors rather than the nation as a whole is itself a debatable, though increasingly common, view of political representation.

29. The fact that business can be held to account by government is a function of the coercive power of government, not its notional role as stakeholder. The extent to which government has any *right* to control business in this way is a quite separate matter, and is a key issue of political philosophy.

30. See, for example, The Business Roundtable, *Corporate Governance and American Competitiveness,* March 1990, p. 13. The Roundtable did, however, repudiate the stakeholder doctrine in 1997.

31. I am grateful to Daniel Moylan for this observation.

32. That is not to say that families are, or should be, content to receive less than the best price available. The point is simply that selling a house in order to obtain a different location or space is different from selling the house simply to maximise financial gain, as a property dealer might do.

33. Or 'optimising' to the extent that it means the same thing.

34. Being obliged to maximise owner value is also what makes the business sensitive to stakeholder preferences; it is thus an important element in the operation of social responsibility. See Social Responsibility Revisited in Chapter 10 of Sternberg, Elaine, *Just Business: Business Ethics in Action, op. cit.*

35. For a further discussion of the way in which decision criteria rather than actual outcomes determine the correctness of actions, see the discussion of Fiduciary Responsibility in Chapter 4 of Sternberg, Elaine, *Just Business: Business Ethics in Action, op. cit.*

36. In their capacity as owners; the same effect should be achieved when there are adequate mechanisms for ensuring that managers (and directors) identify with the business purpose.

QUESTIONS ON STERNBERG

1. How does Sternberg define the purpose of business? How does she distinguish "business" from some other types of organizations?

2. Consider each aspect of Sternberg's definition. Do you agree with her definition? Why or why not? Can you think of any counterexamples to her definition?

3. Do you think that there is a single general purpose which all businesses exemplify? Or can there be a variety of business purposes some of which are exemplified by some businesses, others of which are exemplified by other businesses? (If you adopt this approach, then what is it that unifies these business firms as businesses?)

4. Is it important to have a definition of "business" prior to engaging in the ethical examination of commerce? Why or why not?

FOR FURTHER READING

The History of Business and Markets

Ashton, T. S. *The Industrial Revolution: 1760–1830.* Oxford University Press, 1948.

Bethell, Tom. *The Noblest Triumph: Property and Prosperity Through the Ages.* New York: St. Martin's, 1998.

Bordo, Michael D., Claudia Goldin, and Eugene N. White, eds. *The Defining Moment: The Great Depression and the American Economy in the Twentieth Century.* Chicago: University of Chicago Press, 1998.

Braudel, Fernand. *The Structures of Everyday Life: Civilization and Commerce, 15th–18th Century.* Vol. I. New York: Harper and Row, 1982.

———. *The Wheels of Commerce: Civilization and Commerce, 15th–18th Century.* Vol II. New York: Harper and Row, 1983.

———. *The Perspective of the World: Civilization and Commerce, 15th–18th Century.* Vol. III. New York: Harper and Row, 1984.

Diamond, Jared. *Guns, Germs, and Steel: The Fates of Human Societies.* New York: W. W. Norton, 1997.

Easterly, William. *The Elusive Quest for Growth.* Cambridge: MIT Press, 2001.

Gordon, John Steele. *The Business of America.* New York: Walker & Company, 2001.

Hartwell, R. M., ed. *Causes of the Industrial Revolution in England.* London: Methuen, 1967.

Hayek, F. A. *Capitalism and the Historians.* Chicago: University of Chicago Press, 1954.

Hirschman, Albert O. *The Passions and the Interests: Political Arguments for Capitalism Before Its Triumph.* Princeton, N.J.: Princeton University Press, 1977.

Jones, Eric L. *The European Miracle.* Cambridge: Cambridge University Press, 1987.

Landes, David. *The Wealth and Poverty of Nations.* New York: Norton, 1998.

Macfarlane, Alan. *The Origins of English Individualism.* New York: Cambridge University Press, 1978.

McCloskey, Deirdre, ed. *Second Thoughts: Myths and Morals of U.S. Economic History.* New York: Oxford University Press, 1993.

Mokyr, Joel. *Levers of Riches: Technological Creativity and Economic Progress.* New York: Oxford University Press, 1990.

North, Douglass C., and Robert Paul Thomas. *The Rise of the Western World.* Cambridge: Cambridge University Press, 1973.

Polanyi, Karl. *The Great Transformation: The Political and Economic Origins of Our Time.* Boston: Beacon Press, 1957.

Powelson, John P. *Centuries of Economic Endeavor.* Ann Arbor: University of Michigan, 1994.

Rothbard, Murray N. *America's Great Depression.* Los Angeles: Nash Publishing, 1972.

Weber, Max. *The Protestant Ethic and the Spirit of Capitalism* [1904–1905]. New York: Charles Scribner's, 1958.

Markets and Economics

Bowles, Samuel, and Herbert Gintis. *Democracy and Capitalism: Property, Community, and the Contradictions of Modern Social Thought.* New York: Basic Books, 1986.

Friedman, David. *Hidden Order: The Economics of Everyday Life.* New York: Harper Collins, 1995.

Friedman, Milton. *Capitalism and Freedom.* Chicago: University of Chicago Press, 1963.

Heilbroner, Robert. *The Nature and Logic of Capitalism.* New York: Norton, 1986.

Hazlitt, Henry. *Economics in One Lesson.* New Rochelle, New York: Arlington House, 1979.

Heyne, Paul. *A Student's Guide to Economics.* Wilmington, Del.: ISI Books, 2000.

Kirzner, Israel M. *The Economic Point of View.* Princeton, N.J.: Van Nostrand, 1960.

Lane, Robert E. *The Market Experience.* Cambridge: Cambridge University Press, 1991.

Mill, John Stuart. *Principles of Political Economy.* Edited by Jonathan Riley. Oxford: Oxford University Press, 1994.

Miller, David. *Market, State, and Community: Theoretical Foundations of Market Socialism.* Oxford: Clarendon Press, 1989.

von Mises, Ludwig. *Socialism.* Indianapolis: Liberty Classics, 1979.

Reisman, George C. *Capitalism.* Ottawa, Ill.: Jameson Books, 1996.

Rhoads, Steven E. *The Economist's View of the World: Government, Markets, and Public Policy.* Cambridge: Cambridge University Press, 1985.

Rothbard, Murray. *Man, Economy, and State: A Treatise on Economic Principles.* 2 volumes. Princeton, N.J.: D. Van Nostrand Co., 1962.

———. *Power and Market.* Kansas City: Sheed Andrews and McMeel, 1977.

Schumpeter, Joseph A. *Capitalism, Socialism, and Democracy.* New York: Harper and Row, 1942.

Schweickart, David. *Against Capitalism.* Boulder, Colo: Westview Press, 1996.

Smith, Adam. *An Inquiry into the Nature and Causes of the Wealth of Nations.* Edited by R.H. Campbell, A.S. Skinner, and W.B. Todd. Indianapolis: Liberty Classics, 1981.

Wiles, P.J.D. *Economic Institutions Compared.* New York: Wiley, 1977.

Williamson, Oliver E. *The Economic Institutions of Capitalism.* New York: The Free Press, 1987.

Justice

I affirm that the just is nothing else than the advantage of the stronger.

Thrasymachus[1]

Without justice, what are kingdoms but great robber bands?

St. Augustine[2]

Political power, then, I take to be a right of making laws and penalties of death, and consequently all less penalties, for the regulating and preserving of property, and of employing the force of the community, in the execution of such laws, and in the defence of the commonwealth from foreign injury; and all this only for the public good.

John Locke[3]

We may often fulfill all the rules of justice by sitting still and doing nothing.

Adam Smith[4]

As an economic system a market is established by a framework of legal rules that set up standards of permissible, prohibited, and required behavior. These rules either *pro*scribe certain types of actions (e.g., a law that prohibits the infringement of property rights), *pre*scribe other actions (e.g., a regulation that requires that a business be accessible to disabled persons), or place conditions on the legal performance of other actions (e.g., a law demands that an enforceable contract take a certain form). In these ways, legal rules define rights to property (in land, labor, and capital), allow for the creation of business firms, determine the limits for the exchange

1. As spoken in Plato's *Republic.* See *Plato: The Collected Dialogues,* edited by Edith Hamilton and Huntington Cairns (Princeton N.J.: Princeton University Press, 1980), 338c.

2. *The City of God* [413–426], IV. 4, in Augustine, *Political Writings,* translated by Michael W. Tkacz and Douglas Kries (Indianapolis, Ind.: Hackett Publishing, 1994), 30.

3. *Second Treatise of Government* [1689–1690], edited by C. B. MacPherson (Indianapolis, Ind.: Hackett Publishing, 1980), book II, chapter 1, section 3 (p. 8).

4. *The Theory of Moral Sentiments* [1759], edited by D. D. Raphael and A. L. Macfie (Indianapolis, Ind.: Liberty Classics, 1982) II.ii.I.10 (p. 82).

of goods and services, and describe the parameters under which contracts are binding and competition may occur. In addition, the government may establish a monetary system, prescribe for the taxation of profits, earnings, and income, and issue a variety of laws and regulations which, for better or worse, will affect the conduct of individuals, organizations, and firms. In any market system, some combination of laws, institutions, and regulatory rules will hold sway, establishing and influencing markets, businesses, and commerce. In addition, there will coexist another powerful set of rules, norms, traditions, and habits which guide the behavior of individuals; these will include moral obligations and nonmoral customs (not all of which may even be articulated by the individuals who abide by them).

It should be clear, therefore, that the foundational laws and regulations of a society, enforced by the authority of government, provide the very basis and foundation of a market system, defining the types and limits of exchange, contracts, and business organizations, as well as other more general rights and duties. It is important that these foundational laws and regulations be morally legitimate if our conduct is to be legitimate, and *justice* is the essential quality of legitimate law. In order, therefore, to begin a moral and political examination of the foundations of markets, we must explore this most important moral and political concept. In particular, we will consider some of the leading theories of justice, examining divergent *principles* or *standards* of justice and relating these to the legal framework of markets. Do certain principles support or conflict with the laws and regulations that underlie market systems? Are the foundations of markets compatible with justice? These are *moral* questions that can be answered only if we consider certain theories of justice. What is justice? What does it demand? Are the demands of justice compatible with markets? With state intervention? Or with equality?

The focus of our concern is, then, *normative* and *moral*. We will be considering the principles that *ought* to guide our judgments and actions, regardless of whether those principles do, in fact, support or justify the legal framework of our actual society. Moreover, we shall see how some philosophers offer conceptions of justice critical of market institutions (Nielsen), how others see the market as essentially entailed by justice (Hayek, Nozick), and how some understand justice to be neutral with respect to certain aspects of the market (Rawls). Before we turn to the readings, it will be helpful to consider more generally the idea of justice and its relation to law and markets.

JUSTICE: INTRODUCTORY CONSIDERATIONS

The Preeminence of Justice

Since the age of classical Greece, the idea of justice has taken a preeminent role in any consideration of the human condition. For both Plato and Aristotle justice was the defining virtue of the human being and the essential characteristic of a good society. Although the conception of justice adumbrated by the Greeks is different from that of modern thinkers, many would still agree that "Justice is the first virtue of social institutions."[5] In what ways is justice a preeminent standard of conduct and policy? In the first place, justice serves as the standard that determines the appropriate status of values (such as liberty and equality), for it is justice that establishes the parameters of human freedom and equality and defines our enforceable duties to one another. The obligations of justice are, therefore, some of the most important and primordial of ethical demands and thus, the complaint of *injustice* is one of the most serious moral complaints that one could lodge against an action, practice, policy, or law. The importance of justice is registered further in the fact that the obligation to be just is the sort of obligation whose nonfulfillment is punishable. In other words, the duty to be just is a duty which may be coercively enforced. It is in this sense that justice is sometimes called a "perfect" duty; unlike an imperfect duty, such as the obligation to help those less fortunate, a perfect duty is one to which compliance is enforceable; an imperfect obligation is one whose compliance is not enforceable.

Kinds of Justice

Although justice has a direct relation with the law, it is important to recognize that justice should not be identified solely with conformity to the law. Even if we sometimes speak about justice as if it entailed nothing more than conformity to the law, any assertion that justice amounts only to conformity to law must implicitly presuppose that the law is just. However, our concern is precisely that of considering the principles according to which laws can be adjudged to be just.

In this regard, it is worth pointing out that theories of justice are sometimes classified as either *distributive* or *retributive*. As opposed to retributive justice, which deals with conditions of legitimate punishment and is

---

5. John Rawls, *A Theory of Justice* (Cambridge: Harvard University Press, 1971), 3.

therefore not of our concern, "distributive justice" is typically described as concerned with the distribution or allocation of responsibilities, rewards, and benefits. As one of our authors (Nozick) suggests, this often-used phrase seems to imply that there is some set of things, ready made and waiting for distribution, that are to be allocated in some just manner. However, things such as wealth, resources, rewards, and power are not just lying around waiting to be distributed; rather, these "things" are products of human activity, effort, and creativity. Surely justice must take into account not only the allocation of goods but how these goods come into being and whether effort, application, or creativity have any relevant connection to principles of justice. To imply that these items need only be allocated, without reference to their creators, might favor one theory of justice over others. Therefore, it seems wise to dispense with the phrase "distributive justice" and to employ the more simple term "justice." In so doing, we should think of justice not as a method of allocation or distribution but as a concept concerned, more generally, with establishing the legitimate limits and possibilities of human interaction. It is in this sense that justice has to do with claims to liberty, rights, resources, respect, and equality. To better understand the nature of justice, we should first consider why there is any need for justice at all.

The Circumstances of Justice

Those who live under a just system of law live under legitimate and reasonable constraints. These constraints allow individuals to live peacefully and cooperatively. Why are such constraints necessary? This sort of question reminds us that justice is a legitimate response to certain circumstances of the human condition. The eighteenth-century philosopher David Hume recognized and articulated the circumstances of justice, stating two conspicuous conditions that establish a need for justice: scarcity of resources and limited benevolence. Hume first notes how finite goods require that we have some measure by which to determine the legitimacy of our claims to things:

> For what purpose make a partition of goods, where every one has already more than enough? Why give rise to property, where there cannot possibly be any injury? Why call this object *mine,* when upon the seizing of it by another, I need but stretch out my hand to possess myself to what is equally valuable?[6]

6. David Hume, *An Enquiry Concerning the Principles of Morals,* edited by L. A. Selby-Bigge, revised by P. H. Nidditch (Oxford: Clarendon Press, 1975), Section III, Part I (p. 184).

Hume also notes a second circumstance of justice, namely, that our goodwill and benevolence are so often limited to family and friends. If all human beings were "so replete with friendship and generosity, that every man has the utmost tenderness for every man, and feels no more concern for his own interest than for that of his fellows,"[7] then there would be no use for justice. Whether or not human benevolence is so limited, Hume's suggestion may be broadened to include the idea of divergent ends. It is not simply that our benevolence is limited as that one person's good may differ or conflict with another person's ends. Unless individuals have the same hierarchy of goals and agree to work together for these goals, then we need a legitimate standard by which to determine which of our divergent ends may be pursued, under what circumstances, and with what effects. These circumstances—scarcity, limited benevolence, and divergent ends, perhaps supplemented and enriched with additional assumptions about human rationality or our limited information about other persons, places, and circumstances—provide conditions that would make social cooperation difficult if not impossible. Without some sort of enforceable rules or standards by which to adjudicate and evaluate competing claims to goods, resources, or respect, there would be the sort of conflict that would diminish the very possibility of stable, ongoing human interaction.

THE IDEA OF JUSTICE

There may be a variety of principles or rules that would adjudicate conflict, but which of these would be legitimate? Which principles would be just? Throughout the course of history there have been differing formulations or theories of justice. Although many of these share a certain basic outlook on the principles of justice, their theoretical justifications often differ, and the implications of their principles may differ as well. Some theories give greater emphasis to liberty than to equality; some allow for a stronger role for state action; others contend that much of what governments do is itself unjust. These differences can be seen in the theories elucidated in the readings that follow.

The Formal Concept

For now it is important to recognize something of the general conceptual structure of any theory of justice. To begin, we can note that any formulation of a theory of

7. *An Enquiry Concerning the Principles of Morals,* 184–185.

justice expresses both a *formal* and a *material* (or substantive) component. The same formal element is found in any theory of justice; however, the material content of the divergent principles of justice will sometimes differ, and it is here that controversy arises. In simple terms, the formal idea of justice is that of treating "like cases alike." Whatever the principle or rule of justice, that principle is to be applied to each and every instance for which it is relevant. For example, in the case of education, if a professor has a view as to what constitutes an excellent (or "A") paper, then if the professor reads a paper whose characteristics would call for the application of an excellent grade ("A"), it would be formally unjust *not* to give that paper the excellent grade. Thus, a professor who has some principle about what qualities merit the grade of A should apply that grade to each paper that displays the similarly relevant characteristics of excellence. None of this tells us, however, what these characteristics of excellence are or whether the award of a grade is the best or appropriate means of recognition.

Consider another example. Suppose that a law places a tax of ten percent on all aluminum manufacturers except those whose owners contribute to the majority political party. Such a law would seem to violate the idea of formal justice. That some aluminum manufacturers contribute to the majority party and others do not, does not seem to be relevant to whether or not a tax should be applied to the business. In this instance the rule to be applied is that of a policy of taxation, but the characteristic according to which that policy is to be applied would seem to be irrelevant to the policy. If *formal* justice means treating equals equally or like cases alike, then it must follow that there must be not only some quality or attribute by which cases are deemed to be relevantly similar. There must also be some material rule or principle to apply just in those cases in which individuals have the relevantly similar attributes. In other words, if formal justice demands that relevantly similar individuals are to be treated in relevantly similar ways, then a theory of justice must make some reference to both the relevant attributes of individuals *and* to the rule or principle by which these individuals are to be treated.

It is at this juncture that controversy arises. Although in the case of aluminum manufacture there may be agreement that, barring some unusual set of circumstances, a contribution to the majority party is not relevant to a tax policy (and thus not a relevant difference between one business and another), in many other cases there will be controversy either about the principle itself or about the sort of material differences or similarities deemed relevant to the application of the principle.

The Material Concept: Principles and Attributes

In moving from considerations of formal justice to an examination of material justice, we need to address two issues: What is the rule or principle to be applied? And what are the relevant attributes of those to whom the principle is applied? Individuals can be said to bear certain qualities which entitle them to a certain kind of treatment; because of these qualities one can say that an individual *deserves* certain things, is *entitled* to, or has a *claim* on certain things (a claim that cannot be ignored). Among other things, these qualities may include particular individual traits, or they may include some fact about the individual, such as having done or performed a certain action or having been subjected to a certain set of circumstances (e.g., poverty). These qualities will bear a close logical link with the principle that is to be applied. For example, if individuals possess rationality, then it might be argued that all rational individuals are to be considered as bearers of rights. Alternatively, if under another conception of justice it is demanded that individuals be given some spheres of liberty, then under what conditions can individuals make a claim to liberty? What attributes must individuals have if the principle of liberty is to be applied to them? Or if justice demands that individuals have a minimum income, then under what conditions is this rule to be applied to individuals? Similarly, it might be argued that justice requires that insofar as human beings have similar types of needs, then so should they either have *equal* resources or resources *sufficient* for meeting these needs (regardless of whether these resources are allocated equally).[8] Another theory might point out that needs alone ignore individual initiative and effort and that insofar as individuals make similar efforts, then so should they receive similar rewards.

Figuring prominently in theories of justice is the particularly human characteristic of rationality or reason. However, the appeal to rationality has been invoked to justify principles of rights (and liberty) as well as egalitarian principles. For example, John Locke (1632–1704) considered human beings to be bearers of

---

8. The latter has been suggested by Harry Frankfurt, who writes, "Mere differences in the amounts of money people have are not in themselves distressing. We tend to be quite unmoved, after all, by inequalities between the well-to-do and the rich; our awareness that the former are substantially worse off than the latter does not disturb us morally at all. . . . The fact that some people have much less than others is morally undisturbing when it is clear that they have plenty." "Equality as a Moral Ideal," in *The Importance of What We Care About* (Cambridge: Cambridge University Press, 1988), 146–147.

inalienable rights, and it was by respecting these rights—to life, to liberty, and to the acquisition of property—that one complied with the demands of justice. Robert Nozick extends Locke's account to argue that autonomous individuals have rights and that insofar as their interactions are voluntary and violate no rights, then individuals are *entitled* to their wealth and resources and may use these as each sees fit (compatible with a like use for other rightsholders). On the other hand, others might argue that justice is founded on the fact that each of us has made a rational agreement to abide by certain rules and that it is in light of that agreement that we adhere to rules of justice. This is the idea of a social contract, an idea delineated in the seventeenth century by Thomas Hobbes (1588–1679). In the twentieth century John Rawls has reinvigorated the basic idea of a social contract, contending that rational individuals would agree, from a hypothetical situation, that justice would include a principle of liberty and a principle of equality, the latter of which would insure that no inequality should be tolerated unless it worked to benefit the least well-off. On the other hand, F. A. Hayek contends that the law should not seek to advance any particular interest but should be abstract and universal; only in this way does the law serve the general interests of everyone. This sort of theory resembles *utilitarian* theories which ally justice with the advancement of the good of all. (The utilitarian holds that there is but one supreme moral principle, the maximization of some intrinsic good, whether that be pleasure, happiness, or the satisfaction of preferences. Rules of justice should be constructed to advance the realization of utility.) Another theory is articulated by Kai Nielsen, who contends that there are several distinct, or plural, grounds for the claims of justice and that these include goods whose realization requires a commitment to democratic socialism.

We can summarize some of the attributes or characteristics which serve as conditions for the application of some principle(s) of justice.

Relevant Attributes
General human needs
Rationality
Rational agreement
Effort
Productivity
Contribution to common good
Contribution to maximization of utility

Such are but some of the characteristics in virtue of which a principle is applied to individuals. But what are some of the principles that are applied? Some of these are summarized in the following table.

Principle to Be Applied
That all have equal resources, incomes, or wealth
That all have equal opportunity
That all have equal liberties
That all have equal rights
That inequalities of wealth be permitted only if they advantage the least well-off
That utility be maximized
That all persons be subject to the same general, abstract, and purpose-independent rules

Clearly, then, to consider the question of justice is to enter into a central and profound question of political philosophy. The philosophical grounding of a conception of justice may require, or allude to, considerations of human nature (what are the range and limits of human behavior and cognition?); conceptual meaning (what is a "right"? what is "liberty"?); and epistemology (by what method or form of argument can we establish these claims?). That there are divergent theories does not entail that there is no right or wrong answer as to the nature of justice, only that the inquiry is difficult and complex.

Justice and Markets

Conceptions of justice may be considered in both abstract and concrete ways. An abstract consideration offers an account of the basic principles but does not apply these to practical cases. It is, however, in the application of the principles of justice that one can see how these principles may either justify or condemn economic systems (whether these be market systems or socialist systems), as well as specific laws or regulations. In any commercial society, for example, the rewards one achieves in the marketplace will be a function of effort, ability, and luck. One salesperson may work very hard but have little ability to connect with customers. Another salesperson, blessed with the "gift of gab," may produce huge sales with little effort. The rewards of each of these persons may be further affected by economic circumstances, technological developments, and political events that are unforeseen. Are the rewards that these persons acquire just? One might argue, as Nozick or Hayek would, that insofar as these rewards have been acquired voluntarily, then so are they justly acquired. One might seek to alter these through private acts of benevolence or charity, but it would be impermissible to alter these through some coercive mechanism. On the other hand, Rawls might argue that the differential rewards arise because of natural and social contingencies that are arbitrary and undeserved; because of this, inequalities in income or wealth should be tolerated only insofar as these serve to help those persons who are least well-off.

If, as Rawls suggests, justice has to do with meeting human needs, then one might ask whether these needs are met best through an unfettered market or by a government providing certain social services, limiting the maximum hours that can be worked, and so on. The market rewards those who best satisfy the most ardent and widespread consumer desires, but this may result in the enrichment of film stars or sports figures while rewarding others at a much, much lower magnitude. This may be quite compatible with justice, especially if justice is conceived less in terms of meeting needs than in terms of rights to life, liberty, and property; on the other hand, if the principles of justice have a strongly egalitarian element, then differential rewards may be seen as irrelevant to the moral qualities of human beings, thus providing the groundwork for policies of income redistribution.

RECENT CHALLENGES

The Communitarian Challenge

In recent years, two challenges have arisen to the reigning ideas of justice. The first of these suggests that most theories of justice have a mistaken understanding of the individual and that such theories attempt to define principles of right action without any reference to any concept of good. However, the communication argues that individuals, as moral agents, must be understood, not as mere rational agents who exist prior to any society or community, but as individuals who are constituted in terms of their relation to some historical community which itself manifests some shared conception of good. In this sense, who we are cannot be defined apart from the community or apart from some notion of the good. What is right (just) depends on what is good; justice (or right) is not defined prior to some notion of goodness. The communitarian stance seems to allow for various perspectives on economy and society, some emphasizing a redistributive role for the state (or one which serves to limit market exchanges in favor of some overarching conception of good), others placing stress on religious, historical, or traditional concerns. The unifying elements of these perspectives are that individuals are constituted within a community and that any account of justice must take into account the nature of the goods within that community. For the communitarian, we are not bare individuals whose choices, desires, and wants have no reference to some shared ideas of the society. That is why one of the prominent defenders of the communitarian ethic writes:

> [W]e cannot regard ourselves as independent in this way without great cost to those loyalties and convictions whose moral force consists partly in the fact that living by them is inseparable from understanding ourselves as the particular persons we are—as members of this family or community or nation or people, as bearers of this history, as sons and daughters of that revolution, as citizens of this republic. Allegiances such as these are more than values I happen to have or aims I 'espouse at any given time.' They go beyond the obligations I voluntarily incur and the 'natural duties' I owe to human beings as such.[9]

The Feminist Challenge

Another challenge—one that also contends that the aims and desires of individuals are shaped by the community (and that this must be taken into account by those who theorize about justice)—is put forth by a dominant strand of feminist political thought. Contending that traditional political theory, and traditional accounts of justice, overlook the way in which society is structured along lines of gender, these feminists argue that the distinction between a public realm and a private domestic realm must be reevaluated and that the rights and duties of the public sphere—long the single focus of theories of justice—cannot be understood or justified independent of the manner in which both the private and public sphere are governed so as to favor one sex over another.[10] By this account, a theory of justice should take into account the manner in which gender has affected, in both the public realm and the familial, the opportunities and possibilities for both men and women. For some, justice demands a gender-free society, the attainment of which entails that steps must be taken to diminish the power of traditional sex roles. How is this to occur? It is argued that because of the differentiation and inequalities of traditional sex roles, a market in which men and women were free to contract with one another in business and to trade as they wish would merely perpetuate inequality. The government, therefore, should strive to insure that females as well as males are treated equally

9. Michael Sandel, *Liberalism and the Limits of Justice* (Cambridge: Cambridge University Press, 1982), 179.

10. One feminist critique is that of Susan Moller Okin, *Justice, Gender, and the Family* (New York: Basic Books, 1989).

and that gender distinctions are eliminated. The government should establish laws of affirmative action hiring, enact programs of comparable pay for comparable work (the idea of "comparable worth"), mandate equal opportunities for employment and childrearing (involving flexible work time, child care, mandatory maternity or paternity leave), and enact laws against sexual harassment. In future sections of this text we shall examine the issue of affirmative action (section BIII), but for now it is worth pointing out the seriousness of this feminist challenge, in particular, the difficulty and complexity of its assumptions, be they factual assumptions about gender roles and human nature, assumptions regarding the nature and value of equality, or the assumption (common to certain strands of feminism) that contract and market exchange, unless suitably constrained, are incompatible with gender equality.

In any discussion of theories about humanity and society, one must strive to be clear not only about principles of right and wrong but also about the factual circumstances of the world in which these principles are to be applied. Thus, it should seem clear that any examination of the foundations of markets must take into account both abstract considerations and concrete applications. To begin our examination of these issues, let us turn to four twentieth-century conceptions of justice and markets.

THE READINGS

F. A. Hayek   Hayek offers a view of justice that is grounded in a conception of equality before the law, a law that itself is based on a conception of society as a "self-generating or spontaneous order . . . an order which made it possible to utilize the knowledge and skill of all members of society to a much greater extent than would be possible in any order created by central direction. . . ." The government should insure a legal and constitutional framework that, by establishing abstract rules of justice, will provide the best conditions for a "spontaneous order." This order, which coordinates the dispersed and fragmented knowledge of a variety of individuals—thereby producing a more complex society than could be achieved by deliberate arrangement—has no overall purpose, hierarchy of ends, or specific results. Government should limit itself to providing, in a nonmonopolistic manner, the services that the market cannot provide and to enforcing rules of justice. These rules are characterized by four criteria: They apply to conduct (and not to states of affairs), function as prohibitions, restrain infringements of property, and exemplify universalizability. Because

Hayek holds that a liberal order would not have a specific goal, that order, or "catallaxy," is optimal in the sense that it "may aim, and ought to aim, at increasing the chances of any member of society taken at random of having a high income, or, what amounts to the same thing, the chance, that, whatever his share in total income may be, the real equivalent of this share will be as large as we know how to make it."

John Rawls   One of the most celebrated of the current theories of justice, Rawls' work is for many the starting point of contemporary political philosophy. For Rawls, the principles of social justice emerge out of a hypothetical social contract whose conditions of agreement are "fair." Rawls characterizes this contractual situation as one in which rational persons would come together behind a "veil of ignorance," under which each person is to deliberate as if ignorant of his or her social status, class, income, education, race, intelligence, or particular skills or tendencies. Given the veil of ignorance— and assumptions concerning human rationality and mutual disinterest—any agreement reached will be fair in the sense that it abstracts from socioeconomic conditions and natural qualities that, Rawls asserts, are morally arbitrary.

In this initial hypothetical situation individuals would agree upon two principles.

> [E]ach person is to have an equal right to the most extensive basic liberty compatible with a similar liberty for others.
>
> Social and economic inequalities are to be arranged so that they are both (a) to the greatest benefit of the least advantaged and (b) attached to offices and positions open to all under conditions of fair equality of opportunity.

The first principle, which includes the right to hold *personal* property, governs the rights of citizens; the second concerns social and economic inequalities. The first principle is *prior* to the second and cannot, therefore, be sacrificed for some social or economic advantage; each principle has implications for determining the moral status of commerce and markets.

In the last section of the reading, Rawls considers some of the practical economic implications of his theory of justice, pointing out that if public goods are to everyone's advantage, then it would be rational to employ coercion to fund these goods. Although Rawls asserts that "there is no essential tie between the use of free markets and private ownership of the instruments of production," Rawls seems to endorse market prices even as he draws a distinction between the "allocative" and the "distributive" function of prices. Nonetheless, Rawls remains indifferent as to whether the individual firms are privately owned or state owned, or directed by managers or by some democratic process.

Robert Nozick   Intended in part as a response to Rawls' work, Nozick's *Anarchy, State, and Utopia* begins with this bold assertion: "Individuals have rights, and there are things no person or group may do to them without violating their rights."[11] Drawing from the Lockean natural rights tradition, which holds that individuals have rights to life, liberty, and to the just acquisition of property, Nozick contends that the only sort of state that is compatible with these rights is a minimal (or "night watchman") state whose activities would be limited to the protection of rights and the adjudication of conflict. What sort of theory of justice accords with this view?

Nozick refers to his theory of justice as the "entitlement" theory, one which would require the explication of two sub-theories concerning (1) how one could justly acquire property (or a holding) in a resource that was previously unowned, and (2) how one could justly transfer one's (justly acquired) holdings to another person. (A third aspect of Nozick's theory considers the explication of a principle of the rectification of injustice.) Describing his theory as both a historical and unpatterned theory, Nozick elaborates an example intended to show that patterned theories of justice may require "continuous interference with people's lives," for these theories require a redistribution of holdings that will violate rights. Nozick also suggests that "taxation of earnings from labor is on a par with forced labor." The selection concludes with Nozick's considerations on equality of opportunity and the voluntariness of exchange (even when one's options are limited).

Kai Nielsen   Nielsen defends one version of a democratic socialist account of society, arguing that, in comparison with a pure model of capitalism, the pure model of socialism better serves three widely held values: autonomy, democracy, and equality. Any society that operates in accordance with these values will be a just society. Defining capitalism in terms of the private ownership of productive property, and socialism as the public ownership of that property, Nielsen contends that capitalism will rend society into classes but that socialism will be classless. If autonomy is the ability to set ends for oneself and to pursue those ends without unjustified interference, then, as Nielsen characterizes matters, socialism is compatible with

greater autonomy for more persons and with diminished interference in the exercise of autonomy. In addition, although capitalist society is compatible with political democracy, and although it does permit individual firms to have workplace democracy, it does not allow for workplace democracy across the entire society. Finally, the very idea of moral equality ("that everyone's life matters equally") is rendered possible only under democratic socialism.

The Principles of a Liberal Social Order

F. A. Hayek

F. A. Hayek (1899–1993) taught at the University of Chicago and at the University of Freiburg. A recipient of the Nobel Prize in Economics (1974), he is the author of numerous works in economics and in social and political philosophy, including The Road to Serfdom *(1944),* The Constitution of Liberty *(1960), and* Law, Legislation, and Liberty *(1979).*

By 'liberalism' I shall understand here the conception of a desirable political order which in the first instance was developed in England from the time of the Old Whigs in the later part of the seventeenth century to that of Gladstone at the end of the nineteenth. David Hume, Adam Smith, Edmund Burke, T. B. Macaulay and Lord Acton may be regarded as its typical representatives in England. It was this conception of individual liberty under the law which in the first instance inspired the liberal movements on the Continent and which became the basis of the American political tradition. A few of the leading political thinkers in those countries like B. Constant and A. de Tocqueville in France, Immanuel Kant, Friedrich von Schiller and Wilhelm von Humboldt in Germany, and James Madison, John Marshall and Daniel Webster in the United States belong wholly to it.

This liberalism must be clearly distinguished from another, originally Continental European tradition, also called 'liberalism' of which what now claims this name in the United States is a direct descendant. This latter view, though beginning with an attempt to imitate the first tradition, interpreted it in the spirit of a constructivist rationalism prevalent in France and thereby made of it something very different, and in the end, instead of advocating limitations on the powers of government,

11. *Anarchy, State, and Utopia* (New York: Basic Books, 1974), ix.

ended up with the ideal of the unlimited powers of the majority. This is the tradition of Voltaire, Rousseau, Condorcet and the French Revolution which became the ancestor of modern socialism. English utilitarianism has taken over much of this Continental tradition and the late-nineteenth-century British liberal party, resulting from a fusion of the liberal Whigs and the utilitarian Radicals, was also a product of this mixture.

Liberalism and democracy, although compatible, are not the same. The first is concerned with the extent of governmental power, the second with who holds this power. The difference is best seen if we consider their opposites: the opposite of liberalism is totalitarianism, while the opposite of democracy is authoritarianism. In consequence, it is at least possible in principle that a democratic government may be totalitarian and that an authoritarian government may act on liberal principles. The second kind of 'liberalism' mentioned before has in effect become democratism rather than liberalism and, demanding *unlimited* power of the majority, has become essentially anti-liberal.

It should be specially emphasized that the two political philosophies which both describe themselves as 'liberalism' and lead in a few respects to similar conclusions, rest on altogether different philosophical foundations. The first is based on an evolutionary interpretation of all phenomena of culture and mind and on an insight into the limits of the powers of the human reason. The second rests on what I have called 'constructivist' rationalism, a conception which leads to the treatment of all cultural phenomena as the product of deliberate design, and on the belief that it is both possible and desirable to reconstruct all grown institutions in accordance with a preconceived plan. The first kind is consequently reverent of tradition and recognizes that all knowledge and all civilization rests on tradition, while the second type is contemptuous of tradition because it regards an independently existing reason as capable of designing civilization. (Cf. the statement by Voltaire: 'If you want good laws, burn those you have and make new ones.') The first is also an essentially modest creed, relying on abstraction as the only available means to extend the limited powers of reason, while the second refuses to recognize any such limits and believes that reason alone can prove the desirability of particular concrete arrangements. . . .

The first kind of liberalism, which we shall henceforth alone consider, is itself not the result of a theoretical construction but arose from the desire to extend and generalize the beneficial effects which unexpectedly had followed on the limitations placed on the powers of government out of sheer distrust of the rulers. Only af-

ter it was found that the unquestioned greater personal liberty which the Englishman enjoyed in the eighteenth century had produced an unprecedented material prosperity were attempts made to develop a systematic theory of liberalism, attempts which in England never were carried very far while the Continental interpretations largely changed the meaning of the English tradition.

Liberalism thus derives from the discovery of a self-generating or spontaneous order in social affairs (the same discovery which led to the recognition that there existed an object for theoretical social sciences), an order which made it possible to utilize the knowledge and skill of all members of society to a much greater extent than would be possible in any order created by central direction, and the consequent desire to make as full use of these powerful spontaneous ordering forces as possible. . . .

The central concept of liberalism is that under the enforcement of universal rules of just conduct, protecting a recognizable private domain of individuals, a spontaneous order of human activities of much greater complexity will form itself than could ever be produced by deliberate arrangement, and that in consequence the coercive activities of government should be limited to the enforcement of such rules, whatever other services government may at the same time render by administering those particular resources which have been placed at its disposal for those purposes.

The distinction between a *spontaneous order* based on abstract rules which leave individuals free to use their own knowledge for their own purposes, and an *organization or arrangement* based on commands, is of central importance for the understanding of the principles of a free society and must in the following paragraphs be explained in some detail, especially as the spontaneous order of a free society will contain many organizations (including the biggest organization, government), but the two principles of order cannot be mixed in any manner we may wish.

The first peculiarity of a spontaneous order is that by using its ordering forces (the regularity of the conduct of its members) we can achieve an order of a much more complex set of facts than we could ever achieve by deliberate arrangement, but that, while availing ourselves of this possibility of inducing an order of much greater extent than we otherwise could, we at the same time limit our power over the details of that order. We shall say that when using the former principle we shall have power only over the abstract character but not over the concrete detail of that order.

No less important is the fact that, in contrast to an organization, neither has a spontaneous order a purpose nor need there be agreement on the concrete results it will produce in order to agree on the desirability of such an order, because, being independent of any particular purpose, it can be used for, and will assist in the pursuit of, a great many different, divergent and even conflicting individual purposes. Thus the order of the market, in particular, rests not on common purposes but on reciprocity, that is on the reconciliation of different purposes for the mutual benefit of the participants.

The conception of the common welfare or of the public good of a free society can therefore never be defined as a sum of known particular results to be achieved, but only as an abstract order which as a whole is not oriented on any particular concrete ends but provides merely the best chance for any member selected at random successfully to use his knowledge for his purposes. Adopting a term of Professor Michael Oakeshott (London), we may call such a free society a *nomocratic* (law-governed) as distinguished from an unfree *telocratic* (purpose-governed) social order.

The great importance of the spontaneous order or nomocracy rests on the fact that it extends the possibility of peaceful co-existence of men for their mutual benefit beyond the small group whose members have concrete common purposes, or were subject to a common superior, and that it thus made the appearance of the *Great* or *Open Society* possible. This order which has progressively grown beyond the organizations of the family, the horde, the clan and the tribe, the principalities and even the empire or national state, and has produced at least the beginning of a world society, is based on the adoption—without and often against the desire of political authority—of rules which came to prevail because the groups who observed them were more successful; and it has existed and grown in extent long before men were aware of its existence or understood its operation.

The spontaneous order of the market, based on reciprocity or mutual benefits, is commonly described as an economic order; and in the vulgar sense of the term 'economic' the Great Society is indeed held together entirely by what are commonly called economic forces. But it is exceedingly misleading, and has become one of the chief sources of confusion and misunderstanding, to call this order an economy as we do when we speak of a national, social, or world economy. This is at least one of the chief sources of most socialist endeavour to turn the spontaneous order of the market into a deliberately run organization serving an agreed system of common ends.

An economy in the strict sense of the word in which we can call a household, a farm, an enterprise or even the financial administration of government an economy, is indeed an organization or a deliberate arrangement of a given stock of resources in the service of a unitary order of purposes. It rests on a system of coherent decisions in which a single view of the relative importance of the different competing purposes determines the uses to be made of the different resources.

The spontaneous order of the market resulting from the interaction of many such economies is something so fundamentally different from an economy proper that it must be regarded as a great misfortune that it has ever been called by the same name. I have become convinced that this practice so constantly misleads people that it is necessary to invent a new technical term for it. I propose that we call this spontaneous order of the market a *catallaxy* in analogy to the term 'catallactics,' which has often been proposed as a substitute for the term 'economics.' (Both 'catallaxy' and 'catallactics' derive from the ancient Greek verb *katallattein* which, significantly, means not only 'to barter' and 'to exchange' but also 'to admit into the community' and 'to turn from enemy into friend.')

The chief point about the catallaxy is that, as a spontaneous order, its orderliness does *not* rest on its orientation on a single hierarchy of ends, and that, therefore, it will *not* secure that for it as a whole the more important comes before the less important. This is the chief cause of its condemnation by its opponents, and it could be said that most of the socialist demands amount to nothing less than that the catallaxy should be turned into an economy proper (i.e., the purposeless spontaneous order into a purpose-oriented organization) in order to assure that the more important be never sacrificed to the less important. The defence of the free society must therefore show that it is due to the fact that we do not enforce a unitary scale of concrete ends, nor attempt to secure that some particular view about what is more and what is less important governs the whole of society, that the members of such a free society have as good a chance successfully to use their individual knowledge for the achievement of their individual purposes as they in fact have.

The extension of an order of peace beyond the small purpose-oriented organization became thus possible by the extension of purpose-independent ('formal') rules of just conduct to the relations with other men who did not pursue the same concrete ends or hold the same values except those abstract rules—rules which did not impose obligations for particular actions (which always presuppose a concrete end) but consisted solely in prohibitions from infringing the protected domain of each which these rules enable us to determine. Liberalism is therefore inseparable from the institution of private property which is the name we usually give to the material part of this protected individual domain.

But if liberalism presupposes the enforcement of rules of just conduct and expects a desirable spontaneous order to form itself only if appropriate rules of just conduct are in fact observed, it also wants to restrict the *coercive* powers of government to the enforcement of such rules of just conduct, including at least one prescribing a positive duty, namely, the rule requiring citizens to contribute according to uniform principles not only to the cost of enforcing those rules but also to the costs of the non-coercive service functions of government which we shall presently consider. Liberalism is therefore the same as the demand for the rule of law in the classical sense of the term according to which the coercive functions of government are strictly limited to the enforcement of uniform rules of law, meaning uniform rules of just conduct towards one's fellows. . . .

Liberalism recognizes that there are certain other services which for various reasons the spontaneous forces of the market may not produce or may not produce adequately, and that for this reason it is desirable to put at the disposal of government a clearly circumscribed body of resources with which it can render such services to the citizens in general. This requires a sharp distinction between the coercive powers of government, in which its actions are strictly limited to the enforcement of rules of just conduct and in the exercise of which all discretion is excluded, and the provision of services by government, for which it can use only the resources put at its disposal for this purpose, has no coercive power or monopoly, but in the use of which resources it enjoys wide discretion. . . .

Liberalism has indeed inherited from the theories of the common law and from the older (pre-rationalist) theories of the law of nature, and also presupposes, a conception of justice which allows us to distinguish between such rules of just individual conduct as are implied in the conception of the 'rule of law' and are required for the formation of a spontaneous order on the one hand, and all the particular commands issued by authority for the purpose of organization on the other. This essential distinction has been made explicit in the legal theories of two of the greatest philosophers of modern times, David Hume and Immanuel Kant, but has not been adequately restated since and is wholly uncongenial to the governing legal theories of our day.

The essential points of this conception of justice are (a) that justice can be meaningfully attributed only to human action and not to any state of affairs as such without reference to the question whether it has been, or could have been, deliberately brought about by somebody; (b) that the rules of justice have essentially the nature of prohibitions, or, in other words, that injustice is really the primary concept and the aim of rules of just conduct is to prevent unjust action; (c) that the injustice to be prevented is the infringement of the protected domain of one's fellow men, a domain which is to be ascertained by means of these rules of justice; and (d) that these rules of just conduct which are in themselves negative can be developed by consistently applying to whatever such rules a society has inherited the equally negative test of universal applicability—a test which, in the last resort, is nothing else than the self-consistency of the actions which these rules allow if applied to the circumstances of the real world. These four crucial points must be developed further in the following paragraphs.

Ad(a): Rules of just conduct can require the individual to take into account in his decisions only such consequences of his actions as he himself can foresee. The concrete results of the catallaxy for particular people are, however, essentially unpredictable; and since they are not the effect of anyone's design or intentions, it is meaningless to describe the manner in which the market distributed the good things of this world among particular people as just or unjust. This, however, is what the so-called 'social' or 'distributive' justice aims at in the name of which the liberal order of law is progressively destroyed. We shall later see that no test or criteria have been found or can be found by which such rules of 'social justice' can be assessed, and that, in consequence, and in contrast to the rules of just conduct, they would have to be determined by the arbitrary will of the holders of power.

Ad(b): No particular human action is fully determined without a concrete purpose it is meant to achieve. Free men who are to be allowed to use their own means and their own knowledge for their own purposes must therefore not be subject to rules which tell them what they must positively do, but only to rules which tell them what they must not do; except for the discharge of obligations an individual has voluntarily incurred, the rules of just conduct thus merely delimit the range of permissible actions but do not determine the particular actions a man must take at a particular moment. (There are certain rare exceptions to this, like actions to save or protect life, prevent catastrophes, and the like, where either rules of justice actually do require, or would at least generally be accepted as just rules if they required, some positive action. It would lead far to discuss here the position of such rules in the system.) The generally negative character of the rules of just conduct, and the corresponding primacy of the injustice which is prohibited, has often been noticed but scarcely ever been thought through to its logical consequences.

Ad(c): The injustice which is prohibited by rules of just conduct is any encroachment on the protected domain of other individuals, and they must therefore enable us to ascertain what is the protected sphere of others. Since the time of John Locke it is customary to describe this protected domain as property (which Locke himself had defined as 'the life, liberty, and possessions of a man'). This term suggests, however, a much too narrow and purely material conception of the protected domain which includes not only material goods but also various claims on others and certain expectations. If the concept of property is, however, (with Locke) interpreted in this wide sense, it is true that law, in the sense of rules of justice, and the institution of property are inseparable.

Ad(d): It is impossible to decide about the justice of any one particular rule of just conduct except within the framework of a whole system of such rules, most of which must for this purpose be regarded as unquestioned: values can always be tested only in terms of other values. The test of the justice of a rule is usually (since Kant) described as that of its 'universalizability,' i.e., of the possibility of willing that the rules should be applied to all instances that correspond to the conditions stated in it (the 'categorical imperative'). What this amounts to is that in applying it to any concrete circumstances it will not conflict with any other accepted rules. The test is thus in the last resort one of the compatibility or non-contradictoriness of the whole system of rules, not merely in a logical sense but in the sense that the system of actions which the rules permit will not lead to conflict.

It will be noticed that only purpose-independent ('formal') rules pass this test because, as rules which have originally been developed in small, purpose-connected groups ('organizations') are progressively extended to larger and larger groups and finally universalized to apply to the relations between any members of an Open Society who have no concrete purposes in common and merely submit to the same abstract rules, they will in this process have to shed all references to particular purposes. . . .

The character of those universal rules of just individual conduct, which liberalism presupposes and wishes to improve as much as possible, has been obscured by confusion with that other part of law which determines the organization of government and guides it in the administration of the resources placed at its disposal. It is a characteristic of liberal society that the private individual can be coerced to obey only the rules of private and criminal law; and the progressive permeation of private law by public law in the course of the last eighty or hundred years, which means a progressive replacement of rules of conduct by rules of organization, is one of the main ways in which the destruction of the liberal order has been effected. . . .

The difference between the order at which the rules of conduct of private and criminal law aim, and the order at which the rules of organization of public law aim, comes out most clearly if we consider that rules of conduct will determine an order of action only in combination with the particular knowledge and aims of the acting individuals, while the rules of organization of public law determine directly such concrete action in the light of particular purposes, or, rather, give some authority power to do so. . . .

A state of affairs as such, as we have seen, cannot be just or unjust as a mere fact. Only in so far as it has been brought about designedly or could be so brought about does it make sense to call just or unjust the actions of those who have created it or permitted it to arise. In the catallaxy, the spontaneous order of the market, nobody can foresee, however, what each participant will get, and the results for particular people are not determined by anyone's intentions; nor is anyone responsible for particular people getting particular things. We might therefore question whether a deliberate choice of the market order as the method for guiding economic activities, with the unpredictable and in a great measure chance incidence of its benefits, is a just decision, but certainly not whether, once we have decided to avail ourselves of the catallaxy for that purpose, the particular results it produces for particular people are just or unjust.

That the concept of justice is nevertheless so commonly and readily applied to the distribution of incomes is entirely the effect of an erroneous anthropomorphic interpretation of society as an organization rather than as a spontaneous order. The term 'distribution' is in this sense quite as misleading as the term 'economy,' since it also suggests that something is the result of deliberate action which in fact is the result of spontaneous ordering forces. Nobody distributes income in a market order (as would have to be done in an organization) and to speak, with respect to the former, of a just or unjust distribution is therefore simple nonsense. It would be less misleading to speak in this respect of a 'dispersion' rather than a 'distribution' of incomes.

All endeavours to secure a 'just' distribution must thus be directed towards turning the spontaneous order of the market into an organization or, in other words, into a totalitarian order. It was this striving after a new conception of justice which produced the various steps by which rules of organization ('public law'), which were designed to make people aim at particular results, came to supersede the purpose-independent rules of just individual conduct, and which thereby gradually destroyed the foundations on which a spontaneous order must rest.

The ideal of using the coercive powers of government to achieve 'positive' (i.e., social or distributive) justice leads, however, not only necessarily to the destruction of individual freedom, which some might not think too high a price, but it also proves on examination a mirage or an illusion which cannot be achieved in any circumstances, because it presupposes an agreement on the relative importance of the different concrete ends which cannot exist in a great society whose members do not know each other or the same particular facts. It is sometimes believed that the fact that most people today desire social justice demonstrates that this ideal has a determinable content. But it is unfortunately only too possible to chase a mirage, and the consequence of this is always that the result of one's striving will be utterly different from what one had intended.

There can be no rules which determine how much everybody 'ought' to have unless we make some unitary conception of relative 'merits' or 'needs' of the different individuals, for which there exists no objective measure, the basis of a central allocation of all goods and services—which would make it necessary that each individual, instead of using *his* knowledge for *his* purposes, were made to fulfil a duty imposed upon him by somebody else, and were remunerated according to how well he has, in the opinion of others, performed this duty. This is the method of remuneration appropriate to a closed organization, such as an army, but irreconcilable with the forces which maintain a spontaneous order.

It ought to be freely admitted that the market order does not bring about any close correspondence between subjective merit or individual needs and rewards. It operates on the principle of a combined game of skill and chance in which the results for each individual may be as much determined by circumstances wholly beyond his control as by his skill or effort. Each is remunerated according to the value his particular services have to the particular people to whom he renders them, and this value of his services stands in no necessary relation to anything which we could appropriately call his merits and still less to his needs.

It deserves special emphasis that, strictly speaking, it is meaningless to speak of a value 'to society' when what is in question is the value of some services to certain people, services which may be of no interest to anybody else. A violin virtuoso presumably renders services to entirely different people from those whom a football star entertains, and the maker of pipes altogether different people from the maker of perfumes. The whole conception of a 'value to society' is in a free order as illegitimate an anthropomorphic term as its description as 'one economy' in the strict sense, as an entity which 'treats' people justly or unjustly, or 'distributes' among them. The results of the market process for particular individuals are neither the result of anybody's will that they should have so much, nor even foreseeable by those who have decided upon or support the maintenance of this kind of order.

Of all the complaints about the injustice of the results of the market order the one which appears to have had the greatest effect on actual policy, and to have produced a progressive destruction of the equal rules of just conduct and their replacement by a 'social' law aiming at 'social justice,' however, was not the extent of the inequality of the rewards, nor their disproportion with recognizable merits, needs, efforts, pains incurred, or whatever else has been chiefly stressed by social philosophers, but the demands for protection against an undeserved descent from an already achieved position. More than by anything else the market order has been distorted by efforts to protect groups from a decline from their former position; and when government interference is demanded in the name of 'social justice' this now means, more often than not, the demand for the protection of the existing relative position of some group. 'Social justice' has thus become little more than a demand for the protection of vested interests and the creation of new privilege, such as when in the name of social justice the farmer is assured 'parity' with the industrial worker.

The important facts to be stressed here are that the positions thus protected were the result of the same sort of forces as those which now reduce the relative position of the same people, that their position for which they now demand protection was no more deserved or earned than the diminished position now in prospect for them, and that their former position could in the changed position be secured to them only by denying to others the same chances of ascent to which they owed their former position. In a market order the fact that a group of persons has achieved a certain relative position cannot give them a claim in justice to maintain it, because this cannot be defended by a rule which could be equally applied to all.

The aim of economic policy of a free society can therefore never be to assure particular results to particular people, and its success cannot be measured by any attempt at adding up the value of such particular results. In this respect the aim of what is called 'welfare economics' is fundamentally mistaken, not only because no meaningful sum can be formed of the satisfactions provided for different people, but because its basic idea of a maximum of need-fulfilment (or a maximum social product) is appropriate only to an economy proper which serves a single hierarchy of ends, but not to the spontaneous order of a catallaxy which has no common concrete ends.

Though it is widely believed that the conception of an optimal economic policy (or any judgment whether one economic policy is better than another) presupposes such a conception of maximizing aggregate real social income (which is possible only in value terms and therefore implies an illegitimate comparison of the utility to different persons), this is in fact not so. An optimal policy in a catallaxy may aim, and ought to aim, at increasing the chances of any member of society taken at random of having a high income, or, what amounts to the same thing, the chance that, whatever his share in total income may be, the real equivalent of this share will be as large as we know how to make it.

This condition will be approached as closely as we can manage, irrespective of the dispersion of incomes, if everything which is produced is being produced by persons or organizations who can produce it more cheaply than (or at least as cheaply as) anybody who does not produce it, and is sold at a price lower than that at which it would be possible to offer it for anybody who does not in fact so offer it. (This allows for persons or organizations to whom the costs of producing one commodity or service are lower than they are for those who actually produce it and who still produce something else instead, because their comparative advantage in that other production is still greater; in this case the total costs of their producing the first commodity would have to include the loss of the one which is not produced.)

It will be noticed that this optimum does not presuppose what economic theory calls 'perfect competition' but only that there are no obstacles to the entry into each trade and that the market functions adequately in spreading information about opportunities. It should also be specially observed that this modest and achievable goal has never yet been fully achieved because at all times and everywhere governments have both restricted access to some occupations and tolerated persons and organizations deterring others from entering occupations when this would have been to the advantage of the latter.

This optimum position means that as much will be produced of whatever combination of products and services is in fact produced as can be produced by any method that we know, because we can through such a use of the market mechanism bring more of the dispersed knowledge of the members of society into play than by any other. But it will be achieved only if we leave the share in the total, which each member will get, to be determined by the market mechanism and all its accidents, because it is only through the market determination of incomes that each is led to do what this result requires.

We owe, in other words, our chances that our unpredictable share in the total product of society represents as large an aggregate of goods and services as it does to the fact that thousands of others constantly submit to the adjustments which the market forces on them; and it is consequently also our duty to accept the same kind of changes in our income and position, even if it means a decline in our accustomed position and is due to circumstances we could not have foreseen and for which we are not responsible. The conception that we have 'earned' (in the sense of morally deserved) the income we had when we were more fortunate, and that we are therefore entitled to it so long as we strive as honestly as before and had no warning to turn elsewhere, is wholly mistaken. Everybody, rich or poor, owes his income to the outcome of a mixed game of skill and chance, the aggregate result of which and the shares in which are as high as they are only because we have agreed to play that game. And once we have agreed to play the game and profited from its results, it is a moral obligation on us to abide by the results even if they turn against us.

There can be little doubt that in modern society all but the most unfortunate and those who in a different kind of society might have enjoyed a legal privilege, owe to the adoption of that method an income much larger than they could otherwise enjoy. There is of course no reason why a society which, thanks to the market, is as rich as modern society should not provide *outside the market* a minimum security for all who in the market fall below a certain standard. Our point was merely that considerations of justice provide no justification for 'correcting' the results of the market and that justice, in the sense of treatment under the same rules, requires that each takes what a market provides in which every participant behaves fairly. There is only a justice of individual conduct but not a separate 'social justice.'

We cannot consider here the legitimate tasks of government in the administration of the resources placed at its disposal for the rendering of services to the citizens. With regard to these functions, for the discharge of which the government is given money, we will here only say that in exercising them government should be under the same rules as every private citizen, that it should possess no monopoly for a particular service of the kind, that it should discharge these functions in such a manner as not to disturb the much more comprehensive spontaneously ordered efforts of society, and that the means should be raised according to a rule which applies uniformly to all. . . . In the remaining paragraphs we shall be concerned only with some of the functions of government for the discharge of which it is given not merely money but power to enforce rules of private conduct.

The only part of these coercive functions of government which we can further consider in this outline are those which are concerned with the preservation of a functioning market order. They concern primarily the conditions which must be provided by law to secure the degree of competition required to steer the market efficiently. We shall briefly consider this question first with regard to enterprise and then with regard to labour.

With regard to enterprise the first point which needs underlining is that it is more important that government refrain from assisting monopolies than that it combat monopoly. If today the market order is confined only to a part of the economic activities of men, this is largely the result of deliberate government restrictions of competition. It is indeed doubtful whether, if government consistently refrained from creating monopolies and from assisting them through protective tariffs and the character of the law of patents for inventions and of the law of corporations, there would remain an element of monopoly significant enough to require special measures. What must be chiefly remembered in this connection is, firstly, that monopolistic positions are always undesirable but often unavoidable for objective reasons which we cannot or do not wish to alter; and, secondly, that all government-supervised monopolies tend to become government-protected monopolies which will persist when their justification has disappeared. . . .

The application of this same principle that all agreements in restraint of trade should be invalid and unenforceable and that every individual should be protected against all attempts to enforce them by violence or aimed discrimination, is even more important with regard to labour. The monopolistic practices which threaten the functioning of the market are today much more serious on the side of labour than on the side of enterprise, and the preservation of the market order will depend, more than on anything else, on whether we succeed in curbing the latter. . . .

In conclusion, the basic principles of a liberal society may be summed up by saying that in such a society all coercive functions of government must be guided by the overruling importance of what I like to call The Three Great Negatives: Peace, Justice and Liberty. Their achievement requires that in its coercive functions government shall be confined to the enforcement of such prohibitions (stated as abstract rules) as can be equally applied to all, and to exacting under the same uniform rules

from all a share of the costs of the other, noncoercive services it may decide to render to the citizens with the material and personal means thereby placed at its disposal.

QUESTIONS ON HAYEK

1. What is an "order"? How do you understand the phrase "spontaneous order"? In what sense is this an *order?* In what sense is this order *spontaneous?*

2. Hayek's defense of a spontaneous order seems to rest, in part, on an assumption about the limits of individual knowledge. How does Hayek think that our knowledge is limited, and why might a spontaneous order take advantage of our knowledge in a way that a centralized agency could not?

3. Does Hayek provide a good account of the rules of just conduct? Why does he claim that "a state of affairs . . . cannot be just or unjust as a mere fact"? Do you agree with this contention? Why or why not?

4. Summarize Hayek's account of justice. What does this model of justice entail about the size and extent of the market? The proper role of the state? Does Hayek's account set up firm boundaries between appropriate and inappropriate actions of government?

A Theory of Justice

John Rawls

John Rawls is Professor Emeritus of Philosophy at Harvard University and the author of Political Liberalism *(1993) and* The Law of Peoples *(1999). This selection is from his noted work,* A Theory of Justice *(1971).*

JUSTICE AS FAIRNESS

The Role of Justice

Justice is the first virtue of social institutions, as truth is of systems of thought. A theory however elegant and economical must be rejected or revised if it is untrue; likewise laws and institutions no matter how efficient and well-arranged must be reformed or abolished if they are unjust. Each person possesses an inviolability founded on justice that even the welfare of society as a whole cannot override. For this reason justice denies that the loss of freedom for some is made right by a greater good shared by others. It does not allow that the sacrifices imposed on a few are outweighed by the larger sum of advantages enjoyed by many. Therefore in a just society the liberties of equal citizenship are taken as settled; the rights secured by justice are not subject to political bargaining or to the calculus of social interests. The only thing that permits us to acquiesce in an erroneous theory is the lack of a better one; analogously, an injustice is tolerable only when it is necessary to avoid an even greater injustice. Being first virtues of human activities, truth and justice are uncompromising.

These propositions seem to express our intuitive conviction of the primacy of justice. No doubt they are expressed too strongly. In any event I wish to inquire whether these contentions or others similar to them are sound, and if so how they can be accounted for. To this end it is necessary to work out a theory of justice in the light of which these assertions can be interpreted and assessed. I shall begin by considering the role of the principles of justice. Let us assume, to fix ideas, that a society is a more or less self-sufficient association of persons who in their relations to one another recognize certain rules of conduct as binding and who for the most part act in accordance with them. Suppose further that these rules specify a system of cooperation designed to advance the good of those taking part in it. Then, although a society is a cooperative venture for mutual advantage, it is typically marked by a conflict as well as by an identity of interests. There is an identity of interests since social cooperation makes possible a better life for all than any would have if each were to live solely by his own efforts. There is a conflict of interests since persons are not indifferent as to how the greater benefits produced by their collaboration are distributed, for in order to pursue their ends they each prefer a larger to a lesser share. A set of principles is required for choosing among the various social arrangements which determine this division of advantages and for underwriting an agreement on the proper distributive shares. These principles are the principles of social justice: they provide a way of assigning rights and duties in the basic institutions of society and they define the appropriate distribution of the benefits and burdens of social cooperation. . . .

The Main Idea of the Theory of Justice

My aim is to present a conception of justice which generalizes and carries to a higher level of abstraction the familiar theory of the social contract as found, say, in Locke,

Rousseau, and Kant.[1] In order to do this we are not to think of the original contract as one to enter a particular society or to set up a particular form of government. Rather, the guiding idea is that the principles of justice for the basic structure of society are the object of the original agreement. They are the principles that free and rational persons concerned to further their own interests would accept in an initial position of equality as defining the fundamental terms of their association. These principles are to regulate all further agreements; they specify the kinds of social cooperation that can be entered into and the forms of government that can be established. This way of regarding the principles of justice I shall call justice as fairness.

Thus we are to imagine that those who engage in social cooperation choose together, in one joint act, the principles which are to assign basic rights and duties and to determine the division of social benefits. Men are to decide in advance how they are to regulate their claims against one another and what is to be the foundation charter of their society. Just as each person must decide by rational reflection what constitutes his good, that is, the system of ends which it is rational for him to pursue, so a group of persons must decide once and for all what is to count among them as just and unjust. The choice which rational men would make in this hypothetical situation of equal liberty, assuming for the present that this choice problem has a solution, determines the principles of justice.

In justice as fairness the original position of equality corresponds to the state of nature in the traditional theory of the social contract. This original position is not, of course, thought of as an actual historical state of affairs, much less as a primitive condition of culture. It is understood as a purely hypothetical situation characterized so as to lead to a certain conception of justice.[2] Among the essential features of this situation is that no one knows his place in society, his class position or social status, nor does any one know his fortune in the distribution of natural assets and abilities, his intelligence, strength, and the like. I shall even assume that the parties do not know their conceptions of the good or their special psychological propensities. The principles of justice are chosen behind a veil of ignorance. This ensures that no one is advantaged or disadvantaged in the choice of principles by the outcome of natural chance or the contingency of social circumstances. Since all are similarly situated and no one is able to design principles to favor his particular condition, the principles of justice are the result of a fair agreement or bargain. For given the circumstances of the original position, the symmetry of everyone's relations to each other, this initial situation is fair between individuals as moral persons, that is, as rational beings with their own ends and capable, I shall assume, of a sense of justice. The original position is, one might say, the appropriate initial status quo, and thus the fundamental agreements reached in it are fair. This explains the propriety of the name "justice as fairness": it conveys the idea that the principles of justice are agreed to in an initial situation that is fair. The name does not mean that the concepts of justice and fairness are the same, any more than the phrase "poetry as metaphor" means that the concepts of poetry and metaphor are the same.

Justice as fairness begins, as I have said, with one of the most general of all choices which persons might make together, namely, with the choice of the first principles of a conception of justice which is to regulate all subsequent criticism and reform of institutions. Then, having chosen a conception of justice, we can suppose that they are to choose a constitution and a legislature to enact laws, and so on, all in accordance with the principles of justice initially agreed upon. Our social situation is just if it is such that by this sequence of hypothetical agreements we would have contracted into the general system of rules which defines it. Moreover, assuming that the original position does determine a set of principles (that is, that a particular conception of justice would be chosen), it will then be true that whenever social institutions satisfy these principles those engaged in them can say to one another that they are cooperating on terms to which they would agree if they were free and equal persons whose relations with respect to one another were fair. They could all view their arrangements as meeting the stipulations which they would acknowledge in an initial situation that embodies widely accepted and reasonable constraints on the choice of principles. The general recognition of this fact would provide the basis for a public acceptance of the corresponding principles of justice. No society can, of course, be a scheme of cooperation which men enter voluntarily in a literal sense; each person finds himself placed at birth in some particular position in some particular society, and the nature of this position materially affects his life prospects. Yet a society satisfying the principles of justice as fairness comes as close as a society can to being a voluntary scheme, for it meets the principles which free and equal persons would assent to under circumstances that are fair. In this sense its members are autonomous and the obligations they recognize self-imposed.

One feature of justice as fairness is to think of the parties in the initial situation as rational and mutually disinterested. This does not mean that the parties are egoists, that is, individuals with only certain kinds of interests, say in wealth, prestige, and domination. But they are conceived as not taking an interest in one another's interests. They are to presume that even their spiritual aims may be opposed, in the way that the aims of those of different religions may be opposed. Moreover, the concept of rationality must be interpreted as far as possible in the narrow sense, standard in economic theory, of taking the most effective means to given ends. I shall modify this concept to some extent, as explained later, but one must try to avoid introducing into it any controversial ethical elements. The initial situation must be characterized by stipulations that are widely accepted. . . .

One should not be misled, then, by the somewhat unusual conditions which characterize the original position. The idea here is simply to make vivid to ourselves the restrictions that it seems reasonable to impose on arguments for principles of justice, and therefore on these principles themselves. Thus it seems reasonable and generally acceptable that no one should be advantaged or disadvantaged by natural fortune or social circumstances in the choice of principles. It also seems widely agreed that it should be impossible to tailor principles to the circumstances of one's own case. We should insure further that particular inclinations and aspirations, and persons' conceptions of their good do not affect the principles adopted. The aim is to rule out those principles that it would be rational to propose for acceptance, however little the chance of success, only if one knew certain things that are irrelevant from the standpoint of justice. For example, if a man knew that he was wealthy, he might find it rational to advance the principle that various taxes for welfare measures be counted unjust; if he knew that he was poor, he would most likely propose the contrary principle. To represent the desired restrictions one imagines a situation in which everyone is deprived of this sort of information. One excludes the knowledge of those contingencies which sets men at odds and allows them to be guided by their prejudices. In this manner the veil of ignorance is arrived at in a natural way. This concept should cause no difficulty if we keep in mind the constraints on arguments that it is meant to express. At any time we can enter the original position, so to speak, simply by following a certain procedure, namely, by arguing for principles of justice in accordance with these restrictions. . . .

Two Principles of Justice

I shall now state in a provisional form the two principles of justice that I believe would be chosen in the original position. In this section I wish to make only the most general comments, and therefore the first formulation of these principles is tentative. As we go on I shall run through several formulations and approximate step by step the final statement to be given much later. I believe that doing this allows the exposition to proceed in a natural way.

The first statement of the two principles reads as follows.

> *First:* each person is to have an equal right to the most extensive basic liberty compatible with a similar liberty for others.
>
> *Second:* social and economic inequalities are to be arranged so that they are both (a) reasonably expected to be to everyone's advantage, and (b) attached to positions and offices open to all.

There are two ambiguous phrases in the second principle, namely "everyone's advantage" and "open to all." Determining their sense more exactly will lead to a second formulation of the principle [on p. 83]. . . .

By way of general comment, these principles primarily apply, as I have said, to the basic structure of society. They are to govern the assignment of rights and duties and to regulate the distribution of social and economic advantages. As their formulation suggests, these principles presuppose that the social structure can be divided into two more or less distinct parts, the first principle applying to the one, the second to the other. They distinguish between those aspects of the social system that define and secure the equal liberties of citizenship and those that specify and establish social and economic inequalities. The basic liberties of citizens are, roughly speaking, political liberty (the right to vote and to be eligible for public office) together with freedom of speech and assembly; liberty of conscience and freedom of thought; freedom of the person along with the right to hold (personal) property; and freedom from arbitrary arrest and seizure as defined by the concept of the rule of law. These liberties are all required to be equal by the first principle, since citizens of a just society are to have the same basic rights.

The second principle applies, in the first approximation, to the distribution of income and wealth and to the design of organizations that make use of differences in authority and responsibility, or chains of command. While the distribution of wealth and income need not be equal, it must be to everyone's advantage, and at the same time, positions of authority and offices of command must be accessible to all. One applies the second principle by holding positions open, and then, subject to this constraint, arranges social and economic inequalities so that everyone benefits.

These principles are to be arranged in a serial order with the first principle prior to the second. This ordering means that a departure from the institutions of equal liberty required by the first principle cannot be justified by, or compensated for, by greater social and economic advantages. The distribution of wealth and income, and the hierarchies of authority, must be consistent with both the liberties of equal citizenship and equality of opportunity.

It is clear that these principles are rather specific in their content, and their acceptance rests on certain assumptions that I must eventually try to explain and justify. A theory of justice depends upon a theory of society in ways that will become evident as we proceed. For the present, it should be observed that the two principles (and this holds for all formulations) are a special case of a more general conception of justice that can be expressed as follows.

> All social values—liberty and opportunity, income and wealth, and the bases of self-respect—are to be distributed equally unless an unequal distribution of any, or all, of these values is to everyone's advantage.

Injustice, then, is simply inequalities that are not to the benefit of all. Of course, this conception is extremely vague and requires interpretation.

As a first step, suppose that the basic structure of society distributes certain primary goods, that is, things that every rational man is presumed to want. These goods normally have a use whatever a person's rational plan of life. For simplicity, assume that the chief primary goods at the disposition of society are rights and liberties, powers and opportunities, income and wealth. (Later on in Part Three [of *A Theory of Justice*], the primary good of self-respect has a central place.) These are the social primary goods. Other primary goods such as health and vigor, intelligence and imagination, are natural goods; although their possession is influenced by the basic structure, they are not so directly under its control. Imagine, then, a hypothetical initial arrangement in which all the social primary goods are equally distributed: everyone has similar rights and duties, and income and wealth are evenly shared. This state of affairs provides a benchmark for judging improvements. If certain inequalities of wealth and organizational powers would make everyone better off than in this hypothetical starting situation, then they accord with the general conception.

Now it is possible, at least theoretically, that by giving up some of their fundamental liberties men are sufficiently compensated by the resulting social and economic gains. The general conception of justice imposes no restrictions on what sort of inequalities are permissible; it only requires that everyone's position be improved. We need not suppose anything so drastic as consenting to a condition of slavery. Imagine instead that men forego certain political rights when the economic returns are significant and their capacity to influence the course of policy by the exercise of these rights would be marginal in any case. It is this kind of exchange which the two principles as stated rule out; being arranged in serial order they do not permit exchanges between basic liberties and economic and social gains. The serial ordering of principles expresses an underlying preference among primary social goods. When this preference is rational so likewise is the choice of these principles in this order. . . .

Now the second principle insists that each person benefit from permissible inequalities in the basic structure. This means that it must be reasonable for each relevant representative man defined by this structure, when he views it as a going concern, to prefer his prospects with the inequality to his prospects without it. One is not allowed to justify differences in income or organizational powers on the ground that the disadvantages of those in one position are outweighed by the greater advantages of those in another. Much less can infringements of liberty be counterbalanced in this way. Applied to the basic structure, the principle of utility would have us maximize the sum of expectations of representative men (weighted by the number of persons they represent, on the classical view); and this would permit us to compensate for the losses of some by the gains of others. Instead, the two principles require that everyone benefit from economic and social inequalities. It is obvious, however, that there are indefinitely many ways in which all may be advantaged when the initial arrangement of equality is taken as a benchmark. How then are we to choose among these possibilities? The principles must be specified so that they yield a determinate conclusion. I now turn to this problem.

Interpretations of the Second Principle

I have already mentioned that since the phrases "everyone's advantage" and "equally open to all" are ambiguous, both parts of the second principle have two natural senses. Because these senses are independent of one another, the principle has four possible meanings. Assuming that the first principle of equal liberty has the same sense throughout, we then have four interpretations of the two principles. These are indicated in the table.

| | "Everyone's advantage" | |
"Equally open"	Principle of efficiency	Difference principle
Equality as careers open to talents	System of Natural Liberty	Natural Aristrocracy
Equality as equality of fair opportunity	Liberal Equality	Democratic Equality

I shall sketch in turn these three interpretations: the system of natural liberty, liberal equality, and democratic equality. In some respects this sequence is the more intuitive one, but the sequence via the interpretation of natural aristocracy is not without interest and I shall comment on it briefly. In working out justice as fairness, we must decide which interpretation is to be preferred. I shall adopt that of democratic equality, explaining in this chapter what this notion means. The argument for its acceptance in the original position does not begin until the next chapter.

The first interpretation (in either sequence) I shall refer to as the system of natural liberty. In this rendering the first part of the second principle is understood as the principle of efficiency adjusted so as to apply to institutions or, in this case, to the basic structure of society; and the second part is understood as an open social system in which, to use the traditional phrase, careers are open to talents. I assume in all interpretations that the first principle of equal liberty is satisfied and that the economy is roughly a free market system, although the means of production may or may not be privately owned. The system of natural liberty asserts, then, that a basic structure satisfying the principle of efficiency and in which positions are open to those able and willing to strive for them will lead to a just distribution. Assigning rights and duties in this way is thought to give a scheme which allocates wealth and income, authority and responsibility, in a fair way whatever this allocation turns out to be. The doctrine includes an important element of pure procedural justice which is carried over to the other interpretations.

At this point it is necessary to make a brief digression to explain the principle of efficiency. This principle is simply that of Pareto optimality (as economists refer to it) formulated so as to apply to the basic structure.[3] I shall always use the term "efficiency" instead because this is literally correct and the term "optimality" suggests that the concept is much broader than it is in fact.[4] To be sure, this principle was not originally intended to apply to institutions but to particular configurations of the economic system, for example, to distributions of goods among consumers or to modes of production. The principle holds that a configuration is efficient whenever it is impossible to change it so as to make some persons (at least one) better off without at the same time making other persons (at least one) worse off. Thus a distribution of a stock of commodities among certain individuals is efficient if there exists no redistribution of these goods that improves the circumstances of at least one of these individuals without another being disadvantaged. The organization of production is efficient if there is no way to alter inputs so as to produce more of some commodity without producing less of another. For if we could produce more of one good without having to give up some of another, the larger stock of goods could be used to better the circumstances of some persons without making that of others any worse. These applications of the principle show that it is, indeed, a principle of efficiency. A distribution of goods or a scheme of production is inefficient when there are ways of doing still better for some individuals without doing any worse for others. I shall assume that the parties in the original position accept this principle to judge the efficiency of economic and social arrangements. . . .

There are, however, many configurations which are efficient. For example, the distributions in which one person receives the entire stock of commodities is efficient, since there is no rearrangement that will make some better off and none worse off. The person who holds the whole stock must lose out. But of course not every distribution is efficient, as might be suggested by the efficiency of such disparities. As long as a distribution leaves some persons willing to swap goods with others, it cannot be efficient; for the willingness to trade shows that there is a rearrangement which improves the situation of some without hurting that of anyone else. Indeed, an efficient distribution is one in which it is not possible to find further profitable exchanges. In that sense, the allocation of goods in which one man has everything is efficient because the others have nothing to give him in return. The principle of efficiency allows then that there are many efficient configurations. Each efficient arrangement is better than some other arrangements, but none of the efficient arrangements is better than another. . . .

There are, I shall assume, many efficient arrangements of the basic structure. Each of these specifies a particular division of advantages from social cooperation. The problem is to choose between them, to find a conception of justice that singles out one of these efficient distributions as also just. If we succeed in this, we shall have gone beyond mere efficiency yet in a way compatible with it. Now it is natural to try out the idea that as long as the social system is efficient there is no reason to be concerned with distribution. All efficient arrangements are in this case declared equally just. Of course, this suggestion would be outlandish for the allocation of particular goods to known individuals. No one would suppose that it is a matter of indifference from the standpoint of justice whether any one of a number of men happens to have everything. But the suggestion seems equally unreasonable for the basic structure. Thus it may be that under certain conditions serfdom cannot be significantly reformed without lowering the expectations of some representative man, say that of landowners, in which case serfdom is efficient. Yet it may also happen under the same conditions that a system of free labor cannot be changed without lowering the expectations of some representative man, say that of free laborers, so this arrangement is likewise efficient. . . .

Now these reflections show only what we knew all along, that is, that the principle of efficiency cannot serve alone as a conception of justice.[5] Therefore it must be supplemented in some way. Now in the system of natural liberty the principle of efficiency is constrained by certain background institutions; when these constraints are satisfied, any resulting efficient distribution is accepted as just. The system of natural liberty selects an efficient distribution roughly as follows. Let us suppose that we know from economic theory that under the standard assumptions defining a competitive market economy, income and wealth will be distributed in an efficient way, and that the particular efficient distribution which results in any period of time is determined by the initial distribution of assets, that is, by the initial distribution of income and wealth, and of natural talents and abilities. With each initial distribution, a definite efficient outcome is arrived at. Thus it turns out that if we are to accept the outcome as just, and not merely as efficient, we must accept the basis upon which over time the initial distribution of assets is determined.

In the system of natural liberty the initial distribution is regulated by the arrangements implicit in the conception of careers open to talents (as earlier defined). These arrangements presuppose a background of equal liberty (as specified by the first principle) and a free market economy. They require a formal equality of opportunity in that all have at least the same legal rights of access to all advantaged social positions. But since there is no effort to preserve an equality, or similarity, of social conditions, except insofar as this is necessary to preserve the requisite background institutions, the initial distribution of assets for any period of time is strongly influenced by natural and social contingencies. The existing distribution of income and wealth, say, is the cumulative effect of prior distributions of natural assets—that is, natural talents and abilities—as these have been developed or left unrealized, and their use favored or disfavored over time by social circumstances and such chance contingencies as accident and good fortune. Intuitively, the most obvious injustice of the system of natural liberty is that it permits distributive shares to be improperly influenced by these factors so arbitrary from a moral point of view.

The liberal interpretation, as I shall refer to it, tries to correct for this by adding to the requirement of careers open to talents the further condition of the principle of fair equality of opportunity. The thought here is that positions are to be not only open in a formal sense, but that all should have a fair chance to attain them. Offhand it is not clear what is meant, but we might say that those with similar abilities and skills should have similar life chances. More specifically, assuming that there is a distribution of natural assets, those who are at the same level of talent and ability, and have the same willingness to use them, should have the same prospects of success regardless of their initial place in the social system, that is, irrespective of the income class into which they are born. In all sectors of society there should be roughly equal prospects of culture and achievement for everyone similarly motivated and endowed. The expectations of those with the same abilities and aspirations should not be affected by their social class.[6]

The liberal interpretation of the two principles seeks, then, to mitigate the influence of social contingencies and natural fortune on distributive shares. To accomplish this end it is necessary to impose further basic structural conditions on the social system. Free market arrangements must be set within a framework of political and legal institutions which regulates the overall trends of economic events and preserves the social conditions necessary for fair equality of opportunity. The elements of this framework are familiar enough, though it may be worthwhile to recall the importance of preventing excessive accumulations of property and wealth and of maintaining equal opportunities of education for all. Chances to acquire cultural knowledge and skills should not depend upon one's class position, and so the school system, whether public or private, should be designed to even out class barriers.

While the liberal conception seems clearly preferable to the system of natural liberty, intuitively it still appears defective. For one thing, even if it works to perfection in eliminating the influence of social contingencies,

it still permits the distribution of wealth and income to be determined by the natural distribution of abilities and talents. Within the limits allowed by the background arrangements, distributive shares are decided by the outcome of the natural lottery; and this outcome is arbitrary from a moral perspective. There is no more reason to permit the distribution of income and wealth to be settled by the distribution of natural assets than by historical and social fortune. Furthermore, the principle of fair opportunity can be only imperfectly carried out, at least as long as the institution of the family exists. The extent to which natural capacities develop and reach fruition is affected by all kinds of social conditions and class attitudes. Even the willingness to make an effort, to try, and so to be deserving in the ordinary sense is itself dependent upon happy family and social circumstances. It is impossible in practice to secure equal chances of achievement and culture for those similarly endowed, and therefore we may want to adopt a principle which recognizes this fact and also mitigates the arbitrary effects of the natural lottery itself. That the liberal conception fails to do this encourages one to look for another interpretation of the two principles of justice.

Before turning to the conception of democratic equality, we should note that of natural aristocracy. On this view no attempt is made to regulate social contingencies beyond what is required by formal equality of opportunity, but the advantages of persons with greater natural endowments are to be limited to those that further the good of the poorer sectors of society. The aristocratic ideal is applied to a system that is open, at least from a legal point of view, and the better situation of those favored by it is regarded as just only when less would be had by those below, if less were given to those above.[7] In this way the idea of *noblesse oblige* is carried over to the conception of natural aristocracy.

Now both the liberal conception and that of natural aristocracy are unstable. For once we are troubled by the influence of either social contingencies or natural chance on the determination of distributive shares, we are bound, on reflection, to be bothered by the influence of the other. From a moral standpoint the two seem equally arbitrary. So however we move away from the system of natural liberty, we cannot be satisfied short of the democratic conception. This conception I have yet to explain. And, moreover, none of the preceding remarks are an argument for this conception, since in a contract theory all arguments, strictly speaking, are to be made in terms of what it would be rational to choose in the original position. But I am concerned here to prepare the way for the favored interpretation of the two principles so that these criteria, especially the second one, will not strike the reader as too eccentric or bizarre. I have tried to show that once we try to find a rendering of them which treats everyone equally as a moral person, and which does not weight men's share in the benefits and burdens of social cooperation according to their social fortune or their luck in the natural lottery, it is clear that the democratic interpretation is the best choice among the four alternatives. With these comments as a preface, I now turn to this conception.

Democratic Equality and the Difference Principle

The democratic interpretation, as the table [on p. 80] suggests, is arrived at by combining the principle of fair equality of opportunity with the difference principle. This principle removes the indeterminateness of the principle of efficiency by singling out a particular position from which the social and economic inequalities of the basic structure are to be judged. Assuming the framework of institutions required by equal liberty and fair equality of opportunity, the higher expectations of those better situated are just if and only if they work as part of a scheme which improves the expectations of the least advantaged members of society. The intuitive idea is that the social order is not to establish and secure the more attractive prospects of those better off unless doing so is to the advantage of those less fortunate. . . .

To illustrate the difference principle, consider the distribution of income among social classes. Let us suppose that the various income groups correlate with representative individuals by reference to whose expectations we can judge the distribution. Now those starting out as members of the entrepreneurial class in property-owning democracy, say, have a better prospect than those who begin in the class of unskilled laborers. It seems likely that this will be true even when the social injustices which now exist are removed. What, then, can possibly justify this kind of initial inequality in life prospects? According to the difference principle, it is justifiable only if the difference in expectation is to the advantage of the representative man who is worse off, in this case the representative unskilled worker. The inequality in expectation is permissible only if lowering it would make the working class even more worse off. Supposedly, given the rider in the second principle concerning open positions, and the principle of liberty generally, the greater expectations allowed to entrepreneurs encourages them to do things which raise the long-term prospects of laboring class. Their better prospects act as incentives so that the economic process is more efficient, innovation proceeds at a faster pace, and so on. Eventu-ally the resulting material benefits spread throughout the system and to the least advantaged. I shall not consider how far these things are true. The point is that something of this kind must be argued if these inequalities are to be just by the difference principle. . . .

The Tendency to Equality

I wish to conclude this discussion of the two principles by explaining the sense in which they express an egalitarian conception of justice. Also I should like to forestall the objection to the principle of fair opportunity that it leads to a callous meritocratic society. In order to prepare the way for doing this, I note several aspects of the conception of justice that I have set out.

First we may observe that the difference principle gives some weight to the considerations singled out by the principle of redress. This is the principle that undeserved inequalities call for redress; and since inequalities of birth and natural endowment are undeserved, these inequalities are to be somehow compensated for.[8] Thus the principle holds that in order to treat all persons equally, to provide genuine equality of opportunity, society must give more attention to those with fewer native assets and to those born into the less favorable social positions. The idea is to redress the bias of contingencies in the direction of equality. In pursuit of this principle greater resources might be spent on the education of the less rather than the more intelligent, at least over a certain time of life, say the earlier years of school.

Now the principle of redress has not to my knowledge been proposed as the sole criterion of justice, as the single aim of the social order. It is plausible as most such principles are only as a prima facie principle, one that is to be weighed in the balance with others. For example, we are to weigh it against the principle to improve the average standard of life, or to advance the common good.[9] But whatever other principles we hold, the claims of redress are to be taken into account. It is thought to represent one of the elements in our conception of justice. Now the difference principle is not of course the principle of redress. It does not require society to try to even out handicaps as if all were expected to compete on a fair basis in the same race. But the difference principle would allocate resources in education, say, so as to improve the long-term expectation of the least favored. If this end is attained by giving more attention to the better endowed, it is permissible; otherwise not. And in making this decision, the value of education should not be assessed solely in terms of economic efficiency and social welfare. Equally if not more important is the role of education in enabling a person to enjoy the culture of his society and to take part in its affairs, and in this way to provide for each individual a secure sense of his own worth.

Thus although the difference principle is not the same as that of redress, it does achieve some of the intent of the latter principle. It transforms the aims of the basic structure so that the total scheme of institutions no longer emphasizes social efficiency and technocratic values. We see then that the difference principle represents, in effect, an agreement to regard the distribution of natural talents as a common asset and to share in the benefits of this distribution whatever it turns out to be. Those who have been favored by nature, whoever they are, may gain from their good fortune only on terms that improve the situation of those who have lost out. The naturally advantaged are not to gain merely because they are more gifted, but only to cover the costs of training and education and for using their endowments in ways that help the less fortunate as well. No one deserves his greater natural capacity nor merits a more favorable starting place in society. But it does not follow that one should eliminate these distinctions. There is another way to deal with them. The basic structure can be arranged so that these contingencies work for the good of the least fortunate. Thus we are led to the difference principle if we wish to set up the social system so that no one gains or loses from his arbitrary place in the distribution of natural assets or his initial position in society without giving or receiving compensating advantages in return.

In view of these remarks we may reject the contention that the ordering of institutions is always defective because the distribution of natural talents and the contingencies of social circumstance are unjust, and this injustice must inevitably carry over to human arrangements. Occasionally this reflection is offered as an excuse for ignoring injustice, as if the refusal to acquiesce in injustice is on a par with being unable to accept death. The natural distribution is neither just nor unjust; nor is it unjust that persons are born into society at some particular position. These are simply natural facts. What is just and unjust is the way that institutions deal with these facts. Aristocratic and caste societies are unjust because they make these contingencies the ascriptive basis for belonging to more or less enclosed and privileged social classes. The basic structure of these societies incorporates the arbitrariness found in nature. But there is no necessity for men to resign themselves to these contingencies. The social system is not an unchangeable order beyond human control but a pattern of human action. In justice as fairness men agree to share one another's fate. In designing institutions they undertake to avail themselves of the accidents of nature and social circumstance only when doing so is for the common benefit. The two principles are a fair way of meeting the arbitrariness of fortune; and while no doubt imperfect in other ways, the institutions which satisfy these principles are just.

A further point is that the difference principle expresses a conception of reciprocity. It is a principle of mutual benefit. We have seen that, at least when chain connection holds, each representative man can accept the basic structure as designed to advance his interests. The social order can be justified to everyone, and in particular to those who are least favored; and in this sense it is egalitarian. But it seems necessary to consider in an intuitive way how the condition of mutual benefit is satisfied. Consider any two representative men A and B, and let B be the one who is less favored. Actually, since we are most interested in the comparison with the least favored man, let us assume that B is this individual. Now B can accept A's being better off since A's advantages have been gained in ways that improve B's prospects. If A were not allowed his better position, B would be even worse off than he is. The difficulty is to show that A has no grounds for complaint. Perhaps he is required to have less than he might since his having more would result in some loss to B. Now what can be said to the more favored man? To begin with, it is clear that the well-being of each depends on a scheme of social cooperation without which no one could have a satisfactory life. Secondly, we can ask for the willing cooperation of everyone only if the terms of the scheme are reasonable. The difference principle, then, seems to be a fair basis on which those better endowed, or more fortunate in their social circumstances, could expect others to collaborate with them when some workable arrangement is a necessary condition of the good of all.

There is a natural inclination to object that those better situated deserve their greater advantages whether or not they are to the benefit of others. At this point it is necessary to be clear about the notion of desert. It is perfectly true that given a just system of cooperation as a scheme of public rules and the expectations set up by it, those who, with the prospect of improving their condition, have done what the system announces that it will reward are entitled to their advantages. In this sense the more fortunate have a claim to their better situation; their claims are legitimate expectations established by social institutions, and the community is obligated to meet them. But this sense of desert presupposes the existence of the cooperative scheme; it is irrelevant to the question whether in the first place the scheme is to be designed in accordance with the difference principle or some other criterion.

Perhaps some will think that the person with greater natural endowments deserves those assets and the superior character that made their development possible. Because he is more worthy in this sense, he deserves the greater advantages that he could achieve with them. This view, however, is surely incorrect. It seems to be one of the fixed points of our considered judgments that no one deserves his place in the distribution of native endowments, any more than one deserves one's initial starting place in society. The assertion that a man deserves the superior character that enables him to make the effort to cultivate his abilities is equally problematic; for his character depends in large part upon fortunate family and social circumstances for which he can claim no credit. The notion of desert seems not to apply to these cases. Thus the more advantaged representative man cannot say that he deserves and therefore has a right to a scheme of cooperation in which he is permitted to acquire benefits in ways that do not contribute to the welfare of others. There is no basis for his making this claim. From the standpoint of common sense, then, the difference principle appears to be acceptable both to the more advantaged and to the less advantaged individual. Of course, none of this is strictly speaking an argument for the principle, since in a contract theory arguments are made from the point of view of the original position. But these intuitive considerations help to clarify the nature of the principle and the sense in which it is egalitarian. . . .

These remarks must suffice to sketch the conception of social justice expressed by the two principles for institutions. Before taking up the principles for individuals I should mention one further question. I have assumed so far that the distribution of natural assets is a fact of nature and that no attempt is made to change it, or even to take it into account. But to some extent this distribution is bound to be affected by the social system. A caste system, for example, tends to divide society into separate biological populations, while an open society encourages the widest genetic diversity.[10] In addition, it is possible to adopt eugenic policies, more or less explicit. I shall not consider questions of eugenics, confining myself throughout to the traditional concerns of social justice. We should note, though, that it is not in general to the advantage of the less fortunate to propose policies which reduce the talents of others. Instead, by accepting the difference principle, they view the greater abilities as a social asset to be used for the common advantage. But it is also in the interest of each to have greater natural assets. This enables him to pursue a preferred plan of life. In the original position, then, the parties want to insure for their descendants the best genetic endowment (assuming their own to be fixed). The pursuit of reasonable policies in this regard is something that earlier generations owe to later ones, this being a question that arises between generations. Thus over time a society is to take steps at least to preserve the general level of natural abilities and to prevent the diffusion of serious defects. These measures are to be guided by principles that the parties would be willing to consent to for the sake of their successors. I mention this speculative and difficult matter to indicate once again the manner in which the difference principle is likely to transform problems of social justice. We might conjecture that in the long run, if there is an upper bound on ability, we would eventually reach a society with the greatest equal liberty the members of which enjoy the greatest equal talent. But I shall not pursue this thought further.

Economic Systems

. . . Political economy is importantly concerned with the public sector and the proper form of the background institutions that regulate economic activity, with taxation and the rights of property, the structure of markets, and so on. An economic system regulates what things are produced and by what means, who receives them and in return for which contributions, and how large a fraction of social resources is devoted to saving and to the provision of public goods. Ideally all of these matters should be arranged in ways that satisfy the two principles of justice. . . .

I should like to conclude with a few comments about the extent to which economic arrangements may rely upon a system of markets in which prices are freely determined by supply and demand. Several cases need to be distinguished. All regimes will normally use the market to ration out the consumption goods actually produced. Any other procedure is administratively cumbersome, and rationing and other devices will be resorted to only in special cases. But in a free market system the output of commodities is also guided as to kind and quantity by the preferences of households as shown by their purchases on the market. Goods fetching a greater than normal profit will be produced in larger amounts until the excess is reduced. In a socialist regime planners' preferences or collective decisions often have a larger part in determining the direction of production. Both private-property and socialist systems normally allow for the free choice of occupation and of one's place of work. It is only under command systems of either kind that this freedom is overtly interfered with. . . .

It is evident, then, that there is no essential tie between the use of free markets and private ownership of the instruments of production. The idea that competitive prices under normal conditions are just or fair goes back at least to medieval times.[11] While the notion that a market economy is in some sense the best scheme has been most carefully investigated by so-called bourgeois economists, this connection is a historical contingency in that, theoretically at least, a socialist regime can avail itself of the advantages of this system.[12] One of these advantages is efficiency. Under certain conditions competitive prices select the goods to be produced and allocate resources to their production in such a manner that there is no way to improve upon either the choice of productive methods by firms, or the distribution of goods that arises from the purchases of households. There exists no rearrangement of the resulting economic configuration that makes one household better off (in view of its preferences) without making another worse off. No further mutually advantageous trades are possible; nor are there any feasible productive processes that will yield more of some desired commodity without requiring a cutback in another. For if this were not so, the situation of some individuals could be made more advantageous without a loss for anyone else. . . .

A further and more significant advantage of a market system is that, given the requisite background institutions, it is consistent with equal liberties and fair equality of opportunity. Citizens have a free choice of careers and occupations. There is no reason at all for the forced and central direction of labor. Indeed, in the absence of some differences in earnings as these arise in a competitive scheme, it is hard to see how, under ordinary circumstances anyway, certain aspects of a command society inconsistent with liberty can be avoided. Moreover, a system of markets decentralizes the exercise of economic power. Whatever the internal nature of firms, whether they are privately or state owned, or whether they are run by entrepreneurs or by managers elected by workers, they take the prices of outputs and inputs as given and draw up their plans accordingly. When markets are truly competitive, firms do not engage in price wars or other contests for market power. In conformity with political decisions reached democratically, the government regulates the economic climate by adjusting certain elements under its control, such as the overall amount of investment, the rate of interest, and the quantity of money, and so on. There is no necessity for comprehensive direct planning. Individ-

ual households and firms are free to make their decisions independently, subject to the general conditions of the economy.

In noting the consistency of market arrangements with socialist institutions, it is essential to distinguish between the allocative and the distributive functions of prices. The former is connected with their use to achieve economic efficiency, the latter with their determining the income to be received by individuals in return for what they contribute. It is perfectly consistent for a socialist regime to establish an interest rate to allocate resources among investment projects and to compute rental charges for the use of capital and scarce natural assets such as land and forests. Indeed, this must be done if these means of production are to be employed in the best way. For even if these assets should fall out of the sky without human effort, they are nevertheless productive in the sense that when combined with other factors a greater output results. It does not follow, however, that there need be private persons who as owners of these assets receive the monetary equivalents of these evaluations. Rather these accounting prices are indicators for drawing up an efficient schedule of economic activities. Except in the case of work of all kinds, prices under socialism do not correspond to income paid over to private individuals. Instead, the income imputed to natural and collective assets accrues to the state, and therefore their prices have no distributive function.[13]

It is necessary, then, to recognize that market institutions are common to both private-property and socialist regimes, and to distinguish between the allocative and the distributive function of prices. Since under socialism the means of production and natural resources are publicly owned, the distributive function is greatly restricted, whereas a private-property system uses prices in varying degrees for both purposes. Which of these systems and the many intermediate forms most fully answers to the requirements of justice cannot, I think, be determined in advance. There is presumably no general answer to this question, since it depends in large part upon the traditions, institutions, and social forces of each country, and its particular historical circumstances. The theory of justice does not include these matters. But what it can do is to set out in a schematic way the outlines of a just economic system that admits of several variations. The political judgment in any given case will then turn on which variation is most likely to work out best in practice. A conception of justice is a necessary part of any such political assessment, but it is not sufficient. . . .

ENDNOTES

1. As the text suggests, I shall regard Locke's *Second Treatise of Government,* Rousseau's *The Social Contract,* and Kant's ethical works beginning with *The Foundations of the Metaphysics of Morals* as definitive of the contract tradition. For all of its greatness, Hobbes's *Leviathan* raises special problems. A general historical survey is provided by J. W. Gough, *The Social Contract,* 2nd ed. (Oxford, The Clarendon Press, 1957), and Otto Gierke, *Natural Law and the Theory of Society,* trans. with an introduction by Ernest Barker (Cambridge, The University Press, 1934). A presentation of the contract view as primarily an ethical theory is to be found in G. R. Grice, *The Grounds of Moral Judgment* (Cambridge, The University Press, 1967). See also §19, note 30.

2. Kant is clear that the original agreement is hypothetical. See *The Metaphysics of Morals,* pt. I (*Rechtslehre*), especially §§47, 52; and pt. II of the essay "Concerning the Common Saying: This May Be True in Theory but It Does Not Apply in Practice," in *Kant's Political Writings,* ed. Hans Reiss and trans. by H. B. Nisbet (Cambridge, The University Press, 1970), pp. 73–87. See Georges Vlachos, *La Pensée politique de Kant* (Paris, Presses Universitaires de France, 1962), pp. 326–335; and J. G. Murphy, *Kant: The Philosophy of Right* (London, Macmillan, 1970), pp. 109–112, 133–136, for a further discussion.

3. There are expositions of this principle in most any work on price theory or social choice. A perspicuous account is found in T. C. Koopmans, *Three Essays on the State of Economic Science* (New York, McGraw-Hill, 1957), pp. 41–66. See also A. K. Sen, *Collective Choice and Social Welfare* (San Francisco, Holden-Day Inc., 1970), pp. 21f. These works contain everything (and more) that is required for our purposes in this book; and the latter takes up the relevant philosophical questions. The principle of efficiency was introduced by Vilfredo Pareto in his *Manuel d'économie politique* (Paris, 1909), ch. VI, § 53, and the appendix, § 89. A translation of the relevant passages can be found in A. N. Page, *Utility Theory: A Book of Readings* (New York, John Wiley, 1968), pp. 38f. The related concept of indifference curves goes back to F. Y. Edgeworth, *Mathematical Psychics* (London, 1888), pp. 20–29; also in Page, pp. 160–167.

4. On this point see Koopmans, *Three Essays on the State of Economic Science,* p. 49. Koopmans' remarks that a term like "allocative efficiency" would have been a more accurate name.

5. This fact is generally recognized in welfare economics, as when it is said that efficiency is to be balanced against equity. See for example Tibor Scitovsky, *Welfare and Competition* (London, George Allen and Unwin, 1952), pp. 60–69 and I. M. D. Little, *A Critique of Welfare Economics,* 2nd ed. (Oxford, The Clarendon Press, 1957), ch. VI, esp. pp. 112–116. See Sen's remarks on the limitations of the principle of efficiency, *Collective Choice and Social Welfare,* pp. 22, 24–26, 83–86.

6. This definition follows Sidgwick's suggestion in *The Methods of Ethics,* 7th ed. (London, 1907), p. 285n. See also R. H. Tawney, *Equality* (London, George Allen and Unwin, 1931), ch. II, sec. Ii; and B. A. O. Williams, "The Idea of Equality," in *Philosophy, Politics, and Society,* ed. Peter Laslett and W. G. Runciman (Oxford, Basil Blackwell, 1962), pp. 125f.

7. This formulation of the aristocratic ideal is derived from Santayana's account of aristocracy in ch. IV of *Reason and Society* (New York, Charles Scribner, 1905), pp. 109f. He says, for example, "an aristocratic regimen can only be justified by radiating benefit and by proving that were less given to those above, less would be attained by those beneath them." I am indebted to Robert Rodes for pointing out to me that natural aristocracy is a possible interpretation of the two principles of justice and that an ideal feudal system might also try to fulfill the difference principle.

8. See Herbert Spiegelberg, "A Defense of Human Equality," *Philosophical Review,* vol. 53 (1944), pp. 101, 113–123; and D. D. Raphael, "Justice and Liberty," *Proceedings of the Aristotelian Society,* vol. 51 (1950–1951), pp. 187f.

9. See, for example, Spiegelberg, pp. 120f.

10. See Theodosius Dobzhansky, *Mankind Evolving* (New Haven, Yale University Press, 1962), pp. 242–252, for a discussion of this question.

11. See Mark Blaug, *Economic Theory in Retrospect,* revised edition (Homewood, Ill., Richard D. Irwin, 1968), pp. 31f. See the bibliography, pp. 36f, esp. the articles by R. A. deRoover.

12. For a discussion of this matter, with references to the literature, see Abram Bergson, "Market Socialism Revisited," *Journal of Political Economy,* vol. 75 (1967). See also Jaroslav Vanek, *The General Theory of a Labor Managed Economy* (Ithaca, Cornell University Press, 1970).

13. For the distinction between the allocative and the distributive functions of prices, see J. E. Meade, *Efficiency, Equality and the Ownership of Property* (London, George Allen and Unwin, 1964), pp. 11–26.

QUESTIONS ON RAWLS

1. "It seems to be one of the fixed points of our considered judgments that no one deserves his place in the distribution of native endowments, any more than one deserves one's initial starting place in society." Do you agree with this claim? If it is true, what moral relevance does it have? Explain.

2. How does Rawls characterize the initial situation? Do you agree that this is a fair situation? Would you

choose the two principles of justice? Would you order these principles as Rawls has done? Why or why not?

3. Why does Rawls choose the "difference principle" as his favored interpretation for the second principle of justice? What considerations lead him to his conclusion? Do you agree with these considerations?

4. Do you believe that Rawls' two principles of justice provide any justification for market institutions and, if so, which ones? Do his principles provide a justification for governmental action within the economic system? Explain.

The Entitlement Theory

Robert Nozick

Robert Nozick is Pellegrino University Professor of Philosophy at Harvard University and is the author of Philosophical Explanations *(1981),* The Examined Life *(1990),* The Nature of Rationality *(1993),* Socratic Puzzles *(1997) and* Invariances *(2001). This reading is an excerpt from* Anarchy, State, and Utopia *(1974).*

DISTRIBUTIVE JUSTICE

The minimal state is the most extensive state that can be justified. Any state more extensive violates people's rights. Yet many persons have put forth reasons purporting to justify a more extensive state. It is impossible within the compass of this book to examine all the reasons that have been put forth. Therefore, I shall focus upon those generally acknowledged to be most weighty and influential, to see precisely wherein they fail. In this chapter we consider the claim that a more extensive state is justified, because necessary (or the best instrument) to achieve distributive justice; in the next chapter we shall take up diverse other claims.

The term "distributive justice" is not a neutral one. Hearing the term "distribution," most people presume that some thing or mechanism uses some principle or criterion to give out a supply of things. Into this process of distributing shares some error may have crept. So it is an open question, at least, whether *redistribution* should take place; whether we should do again what has already been done once, though poorly. However, we are not in the position of children who have been given portions of pie by someone who now

makes last minute adjustments to rectify careless cutting. There is no *central* distribution, no person or group entitled to control all the resources, jointly deciding how they are to be doled out. What each person gets, he gets from others who give to him in exchange for something, or as a gift. In a free society, diverse persons control different resources, and new holdings arise out of the voluntary exchanges and actions of persons. There is no more a distributing or distribution of shares than there is a distributing of mates in a society in which persons choose whom they shall marry. The total result is the product of many individual decisions which the different individuals involved are entitled to make. Some uses of the term "distribution," it is true, do not imply a previous distributing appropriately judged by some criterion (for example, "probability distribution"); nevertheless, despite the title of this [section], it would be best to use a terminology that clearly is neutral. We shall speak of people's holdings; a principle of justice in holdings describes (part of) what justice tells us (requires) about holdings. I shall state first what I take to be the correct view about justice in holdings, and then turn to the discussion of alternate views.[1]

THE ENTITLEMENT THEORY

The subject of justice in holdings consists of three major topics. The first is the *original acquisition of holdings,* the appropriation of unheld things. This includes the issues of how unheld things may come to be held, the process, or processes, by which unheld things may come to be held, the things that may come to be held by these processes, the extent of what comes to be held by a particular process, and so on. We shall refer to the complicated truth about this topic, which we shall not formulate here, as the principle of justice in acquisition. The second topic concerns the *transfer of holdings* from one person to another. By what processes may a person transfer holdings to another? How may a person acquire a holding from another who holds it? Under this topic come general descriptions of voluntary exchange, and gift and (on the other hand) fraud, as well as reference to particular conventional details fixed upon in a given society. The complicated truth about this subject (with placeholders for conventional details) we shall call the principle of justice in transfer. (And we shall suppose it also includes principles governing how a person may divest himself of a holding, passing it into an unheld state.)

If the world were wholly just, the following inductive definition would exhaustively cover the subject of justice in holdings.

1. A person who acquires a holding in accordance with the principle of justice in acquisition is entitled to that holding.
2. A person who acquires a holding in accordance with the principle of justice in transfer, from someone else entitled to the holding, is entitled to the holding.
3. No one is entitled to a holding except by (repeated) applications of 1 and 2.

The complete principle of distributive justice would say simply that a distribution is just if everyone is entitled to the holdings they possess under the distribution.

A distribution is just if it arises from another just distribution by legitimate means. The legitimate means of moving from one distribution to another are specified by the principle of justice in transfer. The legitimate first "moves" are specified by the principle of justice in acquisition. Whatever arises from a just situation by just steps is itself just. The means of change specified by the principle of justice in transfer preserve justice. As correct rules of inference are truth-preserving, and any conclusion deduced via repeated application of such rules from only true premises is itself true, so the means of transition from one situation to another specified by the principle of justice in transfer are justice-preserving, and any situation actually arising from repeated transitions in accordance with the principle from a just situation is itself just. The parallel between justice-preserving transformations and truth-preserving transformations illuminates where it fails as well as where it holds. That a conclusion could have been deduced by truth-preserving means from premises that are true suffices to show its truth. That from a just situation a situation *could* have arisen via justice-preserving means does *not* suffice to show its justice. The fact that a thief's victims voluntarily *could* have presented him with gifts does not entitle the thief to his ill-gotten gains. Justice in holdings is historical; it depends upon what actually has happened. We shall return to this point later.

Not all actual situations are generated in accordance with the two principles of justice in holdings: the principle of justice in acquisition and the principle of justice in transfer. Some people steal from others, or defraud them, or enslave them, seizing their product and preventing them from living as they choose, or forcibly exclude others from competing in exchanges. None of these are permissible modes of transition from one situation to another. And some persons acquire holdings by means not sanctioned by the principle of justice in acquisition. The existence of past injustice (previous violations of the first two principles of justice in holdings) raises the third major topic under justice in holdings: the rectification of injustice in holdings. If past injustice has shaped present holdings in various ways, some identifiable and some not, what now, if anything, ought to be done to rectify these injustices? What obligations do the performers of injustice have toward those whose position is worse than it would have been had the injustice not been done? Or, than it would have been had compensation been paid promptly? How, if at all, do things change if the beneficiaries and those made worse off are not the direct parties in the act of injustice, but, for example, their descendants? Is an injustice done to someone whose holding was itself based upon an unrectified injustice? How far back must one go in wiping clean the historical slate of injustices? What may victims of injustice permissibly do in order to rectify the injustices being done to them, including the many injustices done by persons acting through their government? I do not know of a thorough or theoretically sophisticated treatment of such issues.[2] Idealizing greatly, let us suppose theoretical investigation will produce a principle of rectification. This principle uses historical information about previous situations and injustices done in them (as defined by the first two principles of justice and rights against interference), and information about the actual course of events that flowed from these injustices, until the present, and it yields a description (or descriptions) of holdings in the society. The principle of rectification presumably will make use of its best estimate of subjunctive information about what would have occurred (or a probability distribution over what might have occurred, using the expected value) if the injustice had not taken place. If the actual description of holdings turns out not to be one of the descriptions yielded by the principle, then one of the descriptions yielded must be realized.

The general outlines of the theory of justice in holdings are that the holdings of a person are just if he is entitled to them by the principles of justice in acquisition and transfer, or by the principle of rectification of injustice (as specified by the first two principles). If each person's holdings are just, then the total set (distribution) of holdings is just. To turn these general outlines into a specific theory we would have to specify the details of each of the three principles of justice in holdings: the principle of acquisition of holdings, the principle of transfer of holdings, and the principle of rectification of violations of the first two principles. I shall not attempt that task here.

HISTORICAL PRINCIPLES AND END-RESULT PRINCIPLES

The general outlines of the entitlement theory illuminate the nature and defects of other conceptions of distributive justice. The entitlement theory of justice in distribution is *historical;* whether a distribution is just depends upon how it came about. In contrast, *current time-slice principles* of justice hold that the justice of a distribution is determined by how things are distributed (who has what) as judged by some *structural* principle(s) of just distribution. A utilitarian who judges between any two distributions by seeing which has the greater sum of utility and, if the sums tie, applies some fixed equality criterion to choose the more equal distribution, would hold a current time-slice principle of justice. As would someone who had a fixed schedule of trade-offs between the sum of happiness and equality. According to a current time-slice principle, all that needs to be looked at, in judging the justice of a distribution, is who ends up with what; in comparing any two distributions one need look only at the matrix presenting the distributions. No further information need be fed into a principle of justice. It is a consequence of such principles of justice that any two structurally identical distributions are equally just. . . . Welfare economics is the theory of current time-slice principles of justice. . . .

Most persons do not accept current time-slice principles as constituting the whole story about distributive shares. They think it relevant in assessing the justice of a situation to consider not only the distribution it embodies, but also how that distribution came about. If some persons are in prison for murder or war crimes, we do not say that to assess the justice of the distribution in the society we must look only at what this person has, and that person has, and that person has, . . . at the current time. We think it relevant to ask whether someone did something so that he *deserved* to be punished, deserved to have a lower share. Most will agree to the relevance of further information with regard to punishments and penalties. Consider also desired things. One traditional socialist view is that workers are entitled to the product and full fruits of their labor; they have earned it; a distribution is unjust if it does not give the workers what they are entitled to. Such entitlements are based upon some past history. No socialist holding this view would find it comforting to be told that because the actual distribution *A* happens to coincide structurally with the one he desires *D, A* therefore is no less just than *D;* it differs only in that the "parasitic" owners of capital receive under *A* what the workers are entitled to un-

der *D,* and the workers receive under *A* what the owners are entitled to under *D,* namely very little. This socialist rightly, in my view, holds onto the notions of earning, producing, entitlement, desert, and so forth, and he rejects current time-slice principles that look only to the structure of the resulting set of holdings. (The set of holdings resulting from what? Isn't it implausible that how holdings are produced and come to exist has no effect at all on who should hold what?) His mistake lies in his view of what entitlements arise out of what sorts of productive processes.

We construe the position we discuss too narrowly by speaking of *current* time-slice principles. Nothing is changed if structural principles operate upon a time sequence of current time-slice profiles and, for example, give someone more now to counterbalance the less he has had earlier. A utilitarian or an egalitarian or any mixture of the two over time will inherit the difficulties of his more myopic comrades. He is not helped by the fact that *some* of the information others consider relevant in assessing a distribution is reflected, unrecoverably, in past matrices. Henceforth, we shall refer to such unhistorical principles of distributive justice, including the current time-slice principles, as *end-result principles* or *end-state principles.*

In contrast to end-result principles of justice, *historical principles* of justice hold that past circumstances or actions of people can create differential entitlements or differential deserts to things. An injustice can be worked by moving from one distribution to another structurally identical one, for the second, in profile the same, may violate people's entitlements or deserts; it may not fit the actual history.

PATTERNING

The entitlement principles of justice in holdings that we have sketched are historical principles of justice. To better understand their precise character, we shall distinguish them from another subclass of the historical principles. Consider, as an example, the principle of distribution according to moral merit. This principle requires that total distributive shares vary directly with moral merit; no person should have a greater share than anyone whose moral merit is greater. (If moral merit could be not merely ordered but measured on an interval or ratio scale, stronger principles could be formulated.) Or consider the principle that results by substituting "usefulness to society" for "moral merit" in the previous principle. Or instead of "distribute according to moral merit," or "distribute according to usefulness to society," we might consider "distribute according to the weighted sum of moral merit, usefulness to society, and need," with the weights of the different dimensions equal. Let us call a principle of distribution *patterned* if it specifies that a distribution is to vary along with some natural dimension, weighted sum of natural dimensions, or lexicographic ordering of natural dimensions. And let us say a distribution is patterned if it accords with some patterned principle. (I speak of natural dimensions, admittedly without a general criterion for them, because for any set of holdings some artificial dimensions can be gimmicked up to vary along with the distribution of the set.) The principle of distribution in accordance with moral merit is a patterned historical principle, which specifies a patterned distribution. "Distribute according to I.Q." is a patterned principle that looks to information not contained in distributional matrices. It is not historical, however, in that it does not look to any past actions creating differential entitlements to evaluate a distribution; it requires only distributional matrices whose columns are labeled by I.Q. scores. The distribution in a society, however, may be composed of such simple patterned distributions, without itself being simply patterned. Different sectors may operate different patterns, or some combination of patterns may operate in different proportions across a society. A distribution composed in this manner, from a small number of patterned distributions, we also shall term "patterned." And we extend the use of "pattern" to include the overall designs put forth by combinations of end-state principles.

Almost every suggested principle of distributive justice is patterned: to each according to his moral merit, or needs, or marginal product, or how hard he tries, or the weighted sum of the foregoing, and so on. The principle of entitlement we have sketched is *not* patterned. There is no one natural dimension or weighted sum or combination of a small number of natural dimensions that yields the distributions generated in accordance with the principle of entitlement. The set of holdings that results when some persons receive their marginal products, others win at gambling, others receive a share of their mate's income, others receive gifts from foundations, others receive interest on loans, others receive gifts from admirers, others receive returns on investment, others make for themselves much of what they have, others find things, and so on, will not be patterned. Heavy strands of patterns will run through it; significant portions of the variance in holdings will be accounted for by pattern-variables. If most people most of the time choose to transfer some of their entitlements to others only in exchange for something from them, then a large part of what many people hold will vary with what they held that others wanted. . . .

To think that the task of a theory of distributive justice is to fill in the blank in "to each according to his _____" is to be predisposed to search for a pattern; and the separate treatment of "from each according to his _____" treats production and distribution as two separate and independent issues. On an entitlement view these are *not* two separate questions. Whoever makes something, having bought or contracted for all other held resources used in the process (transferring some of his holdings for these cooperating factors), is entitled to it. The situation is *not* one of something's getting made, and there being an open question of who is to get it. Things come into the world already attached to people having entitlements over them. From the point of view of the historical entitlement conception of justice in holdings, those who start afresh to complete "to each according to his _____" treat objects as if they appeared from nowhere, out of nothing. A complete theory of justice might cover this limit case as well; perhaps here is a use for the usual conceptions of distributive justice.[3]

So entrenched are maxims of the usual form that perhaps we should present the entitlement conception as a competitor. Ignoring acquisition and rectification, we might say:

> From each according to what he chooses to do, to each according to what he makes for himself (perhaps with the contracted aid of others) and what others choose to do for him and choose to give him of what they've been given previously (under this maxim) and haven't yet expended or transferred.

This, the discerning reader will have noticed, has its defects as a slogan. So as a summary and great simplification (and not as a maxim with any independent meaning) we have:

> *From each as they choose, to each as they are chosen.*

HOW LIBERTY UPSETS PATTERNS

It is not clear how those holding alternative conceptions of distributive justice can reject the entitlement conception of justice in holdings. For suppose a distribution favored by one of these nonentitlement conceptions is realized. Let us suppose it is your favorite one and let us call this distribution D_1; perhaps everyone has an equal share, perhaps shares vary in accordance with some dimension you treasure. Now suppose that Wilt Chamberlain is greatly in demand by basketball teams, being a great gate attraction. (Also suppose contracts run only for a year, with players being free agents.) He signs the following sort of contract with a team: In each home game, twenty-five cents from the price of each ticket of admission goes to him. (We ignore the question of whether he is "gouging" the owners, letting them look out for themselves.) The season starts, and people cheerfully attend his team's games; they buy their tickets, each time dropping a separate twenty-five cents of their admission price into a special box with Chamberlain's name on it. They are excited about seeing him play; it is worth the total admission price to them. Let us suppose that in one season one million persons attend his home games, and Wilt Chamberlain winds up with $250,000, a much larger sum than the average income and larger even than anyone else has. Is he entitled to this income? Is this new distribution D_2, unjust? If so, why? There is *no* question about whether each of the people was entitled to the control over the resources they held in D_1; because that was the distribution (your favorite) that (for the purposes of argument) we assumed was acceptable. Each of these persons *chose* to give twenty-five cents of their money to Chamberlain. They could have spent it on going to the movies, or on candy bars, or on copies of *Dissent* magazine, or of *Monthly Review.* But they all, at least one million of them, converged on giving it to Wilt Chamberlain in exchange for watching him play basketball. If D_1 was a just distribution, and people voluntarily moved from it to D_2, transferring parts of their shares they were given under D_1 (what was it for if not to do something with?), isn't D_2 also just? If the people were entitled to dispose of the resources to which they were entitled (under D_1), didn't this include their being entitled to give it to, or exchange it with, Wilt Chamberlain? Can anyone else complain on grounds of justice? Each other person already has his legitimate share under D_1. Under D_1, there is nothing that anyone has that anyone else has a claim of justice against. After someone transfers something to Wilt Chamberlain, third parties *still* have their legitimate shares; *their* shares are not changed. By what process could such a transfer among two persons give rise to a legitimate claim of distributive justice on a portion of what was transferred, by a third party who had no claim of justice on any holding of the others *before* the transfer? To cut off objections irrelevant here, we might imagine the exchanges occurring in a socialist society, after hours. After playing whatever basketball he does in his daily work, or doing whatever other daily work he does, Wilt Chamberlain decides to put in *overtime* to earn additional money. (First his work quota is set; he works time over that.) Or

imagine it is a skilled juggler people like to see, who puts on shows after hours.

Why might someone work overtime in a society in which it is assumed their needs are satisfied? Perhaps because they care about things other than needs. I like to write in books that I read, and to have easy access to books for browsing at odd hours. It would be very pleasant and convenient to have the resources of Widener Library in my back yard. No society, I assume, will provide such resources close to each person who would like them as part of his regular allotment (under D_1). Thus, persons either must do without some extra things that they want, or be allowed to do something extra to get some of these things. On what basis could the inequalities that would eventuate be forbidden? Notice also that small factories would spring up in a socialist society, unless forbidden. I melt down some of my personal possessions (under D_1) and build a machine out of the material. I offer you, and others, a philosophy lecture once a week in exchange for your cranking the handle on my machine, whose products I exchange for yet other things, and so on. (The raw materials used by the machine are given to me by others who possess them under D_1, in exchange for hearing lectures.) Each person might participate to gain things over and above their allotment under D_1. Some persons even might want to leave their job in socialist industry and work full time in this private sector. I shall say something more about these issues in the next chapter. Here I wish merely to note how private property even in means of production would occur in a socialist society that did not forbid people to use as they wished some of the resources they are given under the socialist distribution D_1.[4] The socialist society would have to forbid capitalist acts between consenting adults.

The general point illustrated by the Wilt Chamberlain example and the example of the entrepreneur in a socialist society is that no end-state principle or distributional patterned principle of justice can be continuously realized without continuous interference with people's lives. Any favored pattern would be transformed into one unfavored by the principle, by people choosing to act in various ways; for example, by people exchanging goods and services with other people, or giving things to other people, things the transferrers are entitled to under the favored distributional pattern. To maintain a pattern one must either continually interfere to stop people from transferring resources as they wish to, or continually (or periodically) interfere to take from some persons resources that others for some reason chose to transfer to them. (But if some time limit is to be set on how long people may keep resources others voluntarily transfer to them, why let them keep these resources for *any* period of time? Why not have immediate confiscation?) It might be objected that all persons voluntarily will choose to refrain from actions which would upset the pattern. This presupposes unrealistically (1) that all will most want to maintain the pattern (are those who don't, to be "reeducated" or forced to undergo "self-criticism"?), (2) that each can gather enough information about his own actions and the ongoing activities of others to discover which of his actions will upset the pattern, and (3) that diverse and far-flung persons can coordinate their actions to dovetail into the pattern. Compare the manner in which the market is neutral among persons' desires, as it reflects and transmits widely scattered information via prices, and coordinates persons' activities. . . .

REDISTRIBUTION AND PROPERTY RIGHTS

Apparently, patterned principles allow people to choose to expend upon themselves, but not upon others, those resources they are entitled to (or rather, receive) under some favored distributional pattern D_1. For if each of several persons chooses to expend some of his D_1 resources upon one other person, then that other person will receive more than his D_1 share, disturbing the favored distributional pattern. Maintaining a distributional pattern is individualism with a vengeance! Patterned distributional principles do not give people what entitlement principles do, only better distributed. For they do not give the right to choose what to do with what one has; they do not give the right to choose to pursue an end involving (intrinsically, or as a means) the enhancement of another's position. To such views, families are disturbing; for within a family occur transfers that upset the favored distributional pattern. Either families themselves become units to which distribution takes place, the column occupiers (on what rationale?), or loving behavior is forbidden. We should note in passing the ambivalent position of radicals toward the family. Its loving relationships are seen as a model to be emulated and extended across the whole society, at the same time that it is denounced as a suffocating institution to be broken and condemned as a focus of parochial concerns that interfere with achieving radical goals. Need we say that it is not appropriate to enforce across the wider society the relationships of love and care appropriate within a family, relationships which are voluntarily undertaken?* . . .

Proponents of patterned principles of distributive justice focus upon criteria for determining who is to receive holdings; they consider the reasons for which someone should have something, and also the total picture of holdings. Whether or not it is better to give than to receive, proponents of patterned principles ignore giving altogether. In considering the distribution of goods, income, and so forth, their theories are theories of recipient justice; they completely ignore any right a person might have to give something to someone. Even in exchanges where each party is simultaneously giver and recipient, patterned principles of justice focus only upon the recipient role and its supposed rights. Thus discussions tend to focus on whether people (should) have a right to inherit, rather than on whether people (should) have a right to bequeath or on whether persons who have a right to hold also have a right to choose that others hold in their place. I lack a good explanation of why the usual theories of distributive justice are so recipient oriented; ignoring givers and transferrers and their rights is of a piece with ignoring producers and their entitlements. But why is it *all* ignored?

Patterned principles of distributive justice necessitate *re*distributive activities. The likelihood is small that any actual freely-arrived-at set of holdings fits a given pattern; and the likelihood is nil that it will continue to fit the pattern as people exchange and give. From the point of view of an entitlement theory, redistribution is a serious matter indeed, involving, as it does, the violation of people's rights. (An exception is those takings that fall under the principle of the rectification of injustices.) From other points of view, also, it is serious.

Taxation of earnings from labor is on a par with forced labor.† Some persons find this claim obviously

---

*One indication of the stringency of Rawls' difference principle is its inappropriateness as a governing principle even within a family of individuals who love one another. Should a family devote its resources to maximizing the position of its least well off and least talented child, holding back the other children or using resources for their education and development only if they will follow a policy through their lifetimes of maximizing the position of their least fortunate sibling? Surely not. How then can this even be considered as the appropriate policy for enforcement in the wider society?

†I am unsure as to whether the arguments I present below show that such taxation merely *is* forced labor; so that "is on a par with" means "is one kind of." Or alternatively, whether the arguments emphasize the great similarities between such taxation and forced labor, to show it is plausible and illuminating to view such taxation in the light of forced labor. This latter approach would remind one of how John Wisdom conceives of the claims of metaphysicians.

true: taking the earnings of *n* hours labor is like taking *n* hours from the person; it is like forcing the person to work *n* hours for another's purpose. Others find the claim absurd. But even these, *if* they object to forced labor, would oppose forcing unemployed hippies to work for the benefit of the needy. And they would also object to forcing each person to work five extra hours each week for the benefit of the needy. But a system that takes five hours' wages in taxes does not seem to them like one that forces someone to work five hours, since it offers the person forced a wider range of choice in activities than does taxation in kind with the particular labor specified. (But we can imagine a gradation of systems of forced labor, from one that specifies a particular activity, to one that gives a choice among two activities, to . . . ; and so on up.) Furthermore, people envisage a system with something like a proportional tax on everything above the amount necessary for basic needs. Some think this does not force someone to work extra hours, since there is no fixed number of extra hours he is forced to work, and since he can avoid the tax entirely by earning only enough to cover his basic needs. This is a very uncharacteristic view of forcing for those who *also* think people are forced to do something *whenever* the alternatives they face are considerably worse. However, *neither* view is correct. The fact that others intentionally intervene, in violation of a side constraint against aggression, to threaten force to limit the alternatives, in this case to paying taxes or (presumably the worse alternative) bare subsistence, makes the taxation system one of forced labor and distinguishes it from other cases of limited choices which are not forcings.[5]

The man who chooses to work longer to gain an income more than sufficient for his basic needs prefers some extra goods or services to the leisure and activities he could perform during the possible nonworking hours; whereas the man who chooses not to work the extra time prefers the leisure activities to the extra goods or services he could acquire by working more. Given this, if it would be illegitimate for a tax system to seize some of a man's leisure (forced labor) for the purpose of serving the needy, how can it be legitimate for a tax system to seize some of a man's goods for that purpose? Why should we treat the man whose happiness requires certain material goods or services differently from the man whose preferences and desires make such goods unnecessary for his happiness? Why should the man who prefers seeing a movie (and who has to earn money for a ticket) be open to the required call to aid the needy, while the person who prefers looking at a sunset (and hence need earn no extra money) is not? Indeed, isn't it surprising that redis-

tributionists choose to ignore the man whose pleasures are so easily attainable without extra labor, while adding yet another burden to the poor unfortunate who must work for his pleasures? If anything, one would have expected the reverse. Why is the person with the nonmaterial or nonconsumption desire allowed to proceed unimpeded to his most favored feasible alternative, whereas the man whose pleasures or desires involve material things and who must work for extra money (thereby serving whomever considers his activities valuable enough to pay him) is constrained in what he can realize? Perhaps there is no difference in principle. And perhaps some think the answer concerns merely administrative convenience. (These questions and issues will not disturb those who think that forced labor to serve the needy or to realize some favored end-state pattern is acceptable.) In a fuller discussion we would have (and want) to extend our argument to include interest, entrepreneurial profits, and so on. Those who doubt that this extension can be carried through, and who draw the line here at taxation of income from labor, will have to state rather complicated patterned *historical* principles of distributive justice, since end-state principles would not distinguish *sources* of income in any way. It is enough for now to get away from end-state principles and to make clear how various patterned principles are dependent upon particular views about the sources or the illegitimacy or the lesser legitimacy of profits, interest, and so on; which particular views may well be mistaken.

What sort of right over others does a legally institutionalized end-state pattern give one? The central core of the notion of a property right in *X,* relative to which other parts of the notion are to be explained, is the right to determine what shall be done with *X;* the right to choose which of the constrained set of options concerning *X* shall be realized or attempted.[6] The constraints are set by other principles or laws operating in the society; in our theory, by the Lockean rights people possess (under the minimal state). My property rights in my knife allow me to leave it where I will, but not in your chest. I may choose which of the acceptable options involving the knife is to be realized. This notion of property helps us to understand why earlier theorists spoke of people as having property in themselves and their labor. They viewed each person as having a right to decide what would become of himself and what he would do, and as having a right to reap the benefits of what he did. . . .

When end-result principles of distributive justice are built into the legal structure of a society, they (as do most patterned principles) give each citizen an enforceable claim to some portion of the total social product;

that is, to some portion of the sum total of the individually and jointly made products. This total product is produced by individuals laboring, using means of production others have saved to bring into existence, by people organizing production or creating means to produce new things or things in a new way. It is on this batch of individual activities that patterned distributional principles give each individual an enforceable claim. Each person has a claim to the activities and the products of other persons, independently of whether the other persons enter into particular relationships that give rise to these claims, and independently of whether they voluntarily take these claims upon themselves, in charity or in exchange for something.

Whether it is done through taxation on wages or on wages over a certain amount, or through seizure of profits, or through there being a big *social pot* so that it's not clear what's coming from where and what's going where, patterned principles of distributive justice involve appropriating the actions of other persons. Seizing the results of someone's labor is equivalent to seizing hours from him and directing him to carry on various activities. If people force you to do certain work, or unrewarded work, for a certain period of time, they decide what you are to do and what purposes your work is to serve apart from your decisions. This process whereby they take this decision from you makes them a *part-owner* of you; it gives them a property right in you. Just as having such partial control and power of decision, by right, over an animal or inanimate object would be to have a property right in it.

End-state and most patterned principles of distributive justice institute (partial) ownership by others of people and their actions and labor. These principles involve a shift from the classical liberals' notion of self-ownership to a notion of (partial) property rights in *other* people. . . .

May a person emigrate from a nation that has institutionalized some end-state or patterned distributional principle? For some principles (for example, Hayek's) emigration presents no theoretical problem. But for others it is a tricky matter. Consider a nation having a compulsory scheme of minimal social provision to aid the neediest (or one organized so as to maximize the position of the worst-off group); no one may opt out of participating in it. (None may say, "Don't compel me to contribute to others and don't provide for me via this compulsory mechanism if I am in need.") Everyone above a certain level is forced to contribute to aid the needy. But if emigration from the country were allowed, anyone could choose to move to another country that did not have compulsory social provision but otherwise was (as much as possible) identical. In such a case, the person's *only* motive for leaving would be to avoid participating in the compulsory scheme of social provision. And if he does leave, the needy in his initial country will receive no (compelled) help from him. What rationale yields the result that the person be permitted to emigrate, yet forbidden to stay and opt out of the compulsory scheme of social provision? If providing for the needy is of overriding importance, this does militate against allowing internal opting out; but it also speaks against allowing external emigration. (Would it also support, to some extent, the kidnapping of persons living in a place without compulsory social provision, who could be forced to make a contribution to the needy in your community?) Perhaps the crucial component of the position that allows emigration solely to avoid certain arrangements, while not allowing anyone internally to opt out of them, is a concern for fraternal feelings within the country. "We don't want anyone here who doesn't contribute, who doesn't care enough about the others to contribute." That concern, in this case, would have to be tied to the view that forced aiding tends to produce fraternal feelings between the aided and the aider (or perhaps merely to the view that the knowledge that someone or other voluntarily is not aiding produces unfraternal feelings). . . .

EQUALITY OF OPPORTUNITY

Equality of opportunity has seemed to many writers to be the minimal egalitarian goal, questionable (if at all) only for being too weak. (Many writers also have seen how the existence of the family prevents fully achieving this goal.) There are two ways to attempt to provide such equality: by directly worsening the situations of those more favored with opportunity, or by improving the situation of those less well-favored. The latter requires the use of resources, and so it too involves worsening the situation of some: those from whom holdings are taken in order to improve the situation of others. But holdings to which these people are entitled may not be seized, even to provide equality of opportunity for others. In the absence of magic wands, the remaining means toward equality of opportunity is convincing persons each to choose to devote some of their holdings to achieving it.

The model of a race for a prize is often used in discussions of equality of opportunity. A race where some started closer to the finish line than others would be unfair, as would a race where some were forced to carry heavy weights, or run with pebbles in their sneakers. But life is not a race in which we all compete for a prize which someone has established; there is no unified race, with some person judging swiftness. Instead, there are different persons separately giving other persons different things. Those who do the giving (each of us, at times) usually do not care about desert or about the handicaps labored under; they care simply about what they actually get. No centralized process judges people's use of the opportunities they had; that is not what the processes of social cooperation and exchange are *for*.

There is a reason why some inequality of opportunity might seem *unfair*, rather than merely unfortunate in that some do not have every opportunity (which would be true even if no one else had greater advantage). Often the person entitled to transfer a holding has no special desire to transfer it to a particular person; this contrasts with a bequest to a child or a gift to a particular person. He chooses to transfer to someone who satisfies a certain condition (for example, who can provide him with a certain good or service in exchange, who can do a certain job, who can pay a certain salary), and he would be equally willing to transfer to anyone else who satisfied that condition. Isn't it unfair for one party to receive the transfer, rather than another who had less opportunity to satisfy the condition the transferrer used? Since the giver doesn't care to whom he transfers, provided the recipient satisfies a certain general condition, equality of opportunity to be a recipient in such circumstances would violate no entitlement of the giver. Nor would it violate any entitlement of the person with the greater opportunity; while entitled to what he has, he has no entitlement that it be more than another has. Wouldn't it be *better* if the person with less opportunity had an equal opportunity? If one so could equip him without violating anyone else's entitlements (the magic wand?) shouldn't one do so? Wouldn't it be fairer? If it *would* be fairer, can such fairness also justify overriding some people's entitlements in order to acquire the resources to boost those having poorer opportunities into a more equal competitive position?

The process is competitive in the following way. If the person with greater opportunity didn't exist, the transferrer might deal with some person having lesser opportunity who then would be, under those circumstances, the best person available to deal with. This differs from a situation in which unconnected but similar beings living on different planets confront different difficulties and have different opportunities to realize various of their goals. There, the situation of one does *not* affect that of another; though it would be better if the worse planet were better endowed than it is (it also would be better if the better planet were better endowed

than *it* is), it wouldn't be *fairer*. It also differs from a situation in which a person does not, though he could, choose to *improve* the situation of another. In the particular circumstances under discussion, a person having lesser opportunities would be better off if some particular person having better opportunities didn't exist. The person having better opportunities can be viewed not merely as someone better off, or as someone not choosing to aid, but as someone *blocking* or *impeding* the person having lesser opportunities from becoming better off.[7] Impeding another by being a more alluring alternative partner in exchange is not to be compared to directly *worsening* the situation of another, as by stealing from him. But still, cannot the person with lesser opportunity justifiably complain at being so impeded by another who does not *deserve* his better opportunity to satisfy certain conditions? (Let us ignore any similar complaints another might make about *him*.)

While feeling the power of the questions of the previous two paragraphs (it is *I* who ask them), I do not believe they overturn a thoroughgoing entitlement conception. If the woman who later became my wife rejected another suitor (whom she otherwise would have married) for me, partially because (I leave aside my lovable nature) of my keen intelligence and good looks, neither of which did I earn, would the rejected less intelligent and less handsome suitor have a legitimate complaint about unfairness? Would my thus impeding the other suitor's winning the hand of fair lady justify taking some resources from others to pay for cosmetic surgery for him and special intellectual training, or to pay to develop in him some sterling trait that I lack in order to equalize our chances of being chosen? (I here take for granted the impermissibility of worsening the situation of the person having better opportunities so as to equalize opportunity; in this sort of case by disfiguring him or injecting drugs or playing noises which prevent him from fully using his intelligence.[8]) *No such consequences follow.* (Against whom would the rejected suitor have a legitimate complaint? Against what?) Nor are things different if the differential opportunities arise from the accumulated effects of people's acting or transferring their entitlement as they choose. The case is even easier for consumption goods which cannot plausibly be claimed to have any such triadic impeding effect. *Is* it unfair that a child be raised in a home with a swimming pool, using it daily even though he is no more *deserving* than another child whose home is without one? Should such a situation be prohibited? Why then should there be objection to the transfer of the swimming pool to an adult by bequest?

The major objection to speaking of everyone's having a right *to* various things such as equality of opportunity, life, and so on, and enforcing this right, is that these "rights" require a substructure of things and materials and actions; and *other* people may have rights and entitlements over these. No one has a right to something whose realization requires certain uses of things and activities that other people have rights and entitlements over.[9] Other people's rights and entitlements to *particular things (that* pencil, *their* body, and so on) and how they choose to exercise these rights and entitlements fix the external environment of any given individual and the means that will be available to him. If his goal requires the use of means which others have rights over, he must enlist their voluntary cooperation. Even to *exercise* his right to determine how something he owns is to be used may require other means he must acquire a right to, for example, food to keep him alive; he must put together, with the cooperation of others, a feasible package.

There are particular rights over particular things held by particular persons, and particular rights to reach agreements with others, *if* you and they together can acquire the means to reach an agreement. (No one has to supply you with a telephone so that you may reach an agreement with another.) No rights exist in conflict with this substructure of particular rights. Since no neatly contoured right to achieve a goal will avoid incompatibility with this substructure, no such rights exist. The particular rights over things fill the space of rights, leaving no room for general rights to be in a certain material condition. The reverse theory would place only such universally held general "rights to" achieve goals or to be in a certain material condition into its substructure so as to determine all else; to my knowledge no serious attempt has been made to state this "reverse" theory. . . .

VOLUNTARY EXCHANGE

Some readers will object to my speaking frequently of voluntary exchanges on the grounds that some actions (for example, workers accepting a wage position) are not really voluntary because one party faces severely limited options, with all the others being much worse than the one he chooses. Whether a person's actions are voluntary depends on what it is that limits his alternatives. If facts of nature do so, the actions are voluntary. (I may voluntarily walk to someplace I would prefer to fly to unaided.) Other people's actions place limits on one's available opportunities. Whether this makes one's resulting action nonvoluntary depends upon whether these others had the right to act as they did.

Consider the following example. Suppose there are twenty-six women and twenty-six men each wanting to be married. For each sex, all of that sex agree on the same ranking of the twenty-six members of the opposite sex in terms of desirability as marriage partners: call them A to Z and A' to Z' respectively in decreasing preferential order. A and A' voluntarily choose to get married, each preferring the other to any other partner. B would most prefer to marry A', and B' would most prefer to marry $A,$ but by their choices A and A' have removed these options. When B and B' marry, their choices are not made nonvoluntary merely by the fact that there is something else they each would rather do. This other most preferred option requires the cooperation of others who have chosen, as is their right, not to cooperate. B and B' chose among fewer options than did A and A'. This contraction of the range of options continues down the line until we come to Z and Z', who each face a choice between marrying the other or remaining unmarried. Each prefers any one of the twenty-five other partners who by their choices have removed themselves from consideration by Z and Z'. Z and Z' voluntarily choose to marry each other. The fact that their only other alternative is (in their view) much worse, and the fact that others chose to exercise their rights in certain ways, thereby shaping the external environment of options in which Z and Z' choose, does not mean they did not marry voluntarily.

Similar considerations apply to market exchanges between workers and owners of capital. Z is faced with working or starving; the choices and actions of all other persons do not add up to providing Z with some other option. (He may have various options about what job to take.) Does Z choose to work voluntarily? (Does someone on a desert island who must work to survive?) Z does choose voluntarily if the other individuals A through Y each acted voluntarily and within their rights. We then have to ask the question about the others. We ask it up the line until we reach A, or A and B, who chose to act in certain ways thereby shaping the external choice environment in which C chooses. We move back down the line with A through C's voluntary choice affecting D's choice environment, and A through D's choices affecting E's choice environment, and so on back down to Z. A person's choice among differing degrees of unpalatable alternatives is not rendered nonvoluntary by the fact that others voluntarily chose and acted within their rights in a way that did not provide him with a more palatable alternative.

We should note an interesting feature of the structure of rights to engage in relationships with others, including voluntary exchanges.* The right to engage in a certain relationship is not a right to engage in it with anyone, or even with anyone who wants to or would choose to, but rather it is a right to do it with anyone who has the right to engage in it (with someone who has the right to engage in it . . .). Rights to engage in relationships or transactions have hooks on them, which must attach to the corresponding hook of another's right that comes out to meet theirs. My right of free speech is not violated by a prisoner's being kept in solitary confinement so that he cannot hear me, and my right to hear information is not violated if this prisoner is prevented from communicating with me. The rights of members of the press are not violated if Edward Everett Hale's "man without a country" is not permitted to read some of their writings, nor are the rights of readers violated if Josef Goebbels is executed and thereby prevented from providing them with additional reading material. In each case, the right is a right to a relationship with someone else who *also* has the right to be the other party in such a relationship. Adults normally will have the right to such a relationship with any other consenting adult who has this right, but the right *may* be forfeited in punishment for wrongful acts. This complication of hooks on rights will *not* be relevant to any cases we discuss. But it does have implications; for example it complicates an immediate condemnation of the disruption of speakers in a *public* place, solely on the grounds that this disruption violates the rights of other people to *hear* whatever opinions they choose to listen to. If rights to engage in relationships go out only half-way, these others do have a right to hear whatever opinions they please, but only from persons who have a right to communicate them. Hearers' rights are not violated *if* the speaker has no hook to reach out to join up with theirs. (The speaker can lack a hooked right only because of something he has done, not because of the *content* of what he is about to say.) My reflections here are not intended to justify disruption, merely to warn against the too simple grounds for condemnation which I myself have been prone to use. . . .

ENDNOTES

1. The reader who has looked ahead and seen that the second part of this chapter discusses Rawls' theory mistakenly may think that every remark or argument in the first part against alternative theories of justice is meant to apply to, or antic-

ipate, a criticism of Rawls' theory. This is not so; there are other theories also worth criticizing.

2. See, however, the useful book by Boris Bittker, *The Case for Black Reparations* (New York: Random House, 1973).

3. Varying situations continuously from that limit situation to our own would force us to make explicit the underlying rationale of entitlements and to consider whether entitlement considerations lexicographically precede the considerations of the usual theories of distributive justice, so that the *slightest* strand of entitlement outweighs the considerations of the usual theories of distributive justice.

4. See the selection from John Henry MacKay's novel, *The Anarchists,* reprinted in Leonard Krimmerman and Lewis Perry, eds., *Patterns of Anarchy* (New York: Doubleday Anchor Books, 1966), in which an individualist anarchist presses upon a communist anarchist the following question: "Would you, in the system of society which you call 'free Communism' prevent individuals from exchanging their labor among themselves by means of their own medium of exchange? And further: Would you prevent them from occupying land for the purpose of personal use?" The novel continues: "[the] question was not to be escaped. If he answered 'Yes!' he admitted that society had the right of control over the individual and threw overboard the autonomy of the individual which he had always zealously defended; if on the other hand, he answered 'No!' he admitted the right of private property which he had just denied so emphatically. . . . Then he answered 'In Anarchy any number of men must have the right of forming a voluntary association, and so realizing their ideas in practice. Nor can I understand how any one could justly be driven from the land and house which he uses and occupies . . . every serious man must declare himself: for Socialism, and thereby for force and against liberty, or for Anarchism, and thereby for liberty and against force.' " In contrast, we find Noam Chomsky writing, "Any consistent anarchist must oppose private ownership of the means of production," "the consistent anarchist then . . . will be a socialist . . . of a particular sort." Introduction to Daniel Guerin, *Anarchism: From Theory to Practice* (New York: Monthly Review Press, 1970), pages xiii, xv.

5. Further details which this statement should include are contained in my essay "Coercion," in *Philosophy, Science, and Method,* ed. S. Morgenbesser, P. Suppes, and M. White (New York: St. Martin, 1969).

6. On the themes in this and the next paragraph, see the writings of Armen Alchian.

7. Perhaps we should understand Rawls' focus on social cooperation as based upon this triadic notion of one person, by dealing with a second, blocking a third person from dealing with the second.

8. See Kurt Vonnegut's story "Harrison Bergeron" in his collection *Welcome to the Monkey House* (New York: Dell, 1970).

*Since I am unsure of this point, I put this paragraph forward very tentatively, as an interesting conjecture.

9. See on this point, Judith Jarvis Thomson, "A Defense of Abortion," *Philosophy & Public Affairs,* I, no. I (Fall 1971), 55–56.

QUESTIONS ON NOZICK

1. How is Nozick's theory *unpatterned* and *historical?* Using Nozick's schema, how would you characterize Rawls' theory?

2. What is the point of the Wilt Chamberlain example? What does Nozick intend his example to show? What do *you* think that it shows?

3. Why does Nozick claim that "taxation is on a par with forced labor"? If the government taxes those who work, should it force those to work who are not working? What if their work were essential to helping the least well-off?

4. In what way(s) is Nozick's entitlement theory dependent on a theory of rights? How do you understand the nature of these rights? How would society differ if we were to recognize such rights?

A Moral Case for Socialism

Kai Nielsen

Kai Nielsen is Professor Emeritus of Philosophy at the University of Calgary, Canada. He is the author of Equality and Liberty: A Defense of Radical Egalitarianism *(1985),* God, Scepticism and Modernity *(1989), and* Ethics without God *(1990).*

I

In North America socialism gets a bad press. It is under criticism for its alleged economic inefficiency and for its moral and human inadequacy. I want here to address the latter issue. Looking at capitalism and socialism, I want to consider, against the grain of our culture, what kind of moral case can be made for socialism.

The first thing to do, given the extensive, and, I would add, inexcusably extensive, confusions about this, is to say what socialism and capitalism are. That done I will then, appealing to a cluster of values which are basic in our culture, concerning which there is a considerable and indeed a reflective consensus, examine how capitalism and socialism fare with respect to these values. Given that people generally, at least in Western societies, would want it to be the case that these values have a stably exemplification in our social lives, it is appropriate to ask the question: which of these social systems is more likely stably to exemplify them? I shall argue, facing the gamut of a careful comparison in the light of these values, that, everything considered, socialism comes out better than capitalism. And this, if right, would give us good reason for believing that socialism is preferable—indeed morally preferable—to capitalism if it also turns out to be a feasible socio-economic system.

What, then, are socialism and capitalism? Put most succinctly, capitalism requires the existence of private *productive* property (private ownership of the means of production) while socialism works toward its abolition. What is essential for socialism is public ownership and control of the means of production and public ownership means just what it says: *ownership by the public.* Under capitalism there is a domain of private property rights in the means of production which are not subject to political determination. That is, even where the political domain is a democratic one, they are not subject to determination by the public; only an individual or a set of individuals who own that property can make the final determination of what is to be done with that property. These individuals make the determination and not citizens at large, as under socialism. In fully developed socialism, by contrast, there is, with respect to productive property, no domain which is not subject to political determination by the public, namely by the citizenry at large. Thus, where this public ownership and control is genuine, and not a mask for control by an elite of state bureaucrats, it will mean genuine popular and democratic control over productive property. What socialism is *not* is *state* ownership in the absence of, at the very least, popular sovereignty, i.e., genuine popular control over the state apparatus including any economic functions it might have.

The property that is owned in common under socialism is the means of existence—the productive property in the society. Socialism does not proscribe the ownership of private personal property, such as houses, cars, television sets and the like. It only proscribes the private ownership of the means of production.

The above characterizations catch the minimal core of socialism and capitalism, what used to be called the essence of those concepts. But beyond these core features, it is well, in helping us to make our comparison, to see some other important features which characteristically go with capitalism and socialism. Minimally, capitalism is private ownership of the means of production but it is also, at least characteristically, a social system in which a class of capitalists owns and controls the means of production and hires workers who, owning little or no means of production, sell their labor-power to some capitalist or other for a wage. This means that a capitalist society will be a class society in which there will be two principal classes: capitalists and workers. Socialism by contrast is a social system in which every able-bodied person is, was or will be a worker. These workers commonly own and control the means of production (this is the characteristic form of public ownership). Thus in socialism we have, in a perfectly literal sense, a classless society for there is no division between human beings along class lines.

There are both pure and impure forms of capitalism and socialism. The pure form of capitalism is competitive capitalism, the capitalism that Milton Friedman would tell us is the real capitalism while, he would add, the impure form is monopoly or corporate capitalism. Similarly the pure form of socialism is democratic socialism, with firm workers' control of the means of production and an industrial as well as a political democracy, while the impure form is state bureaucratic socialism.

Now it is a noteworthy fact that, to understate it, actually existing capitalisms and actually existing socialisms tend to be the impure forms. Many partisans of capitalism lament the fact that the actually existing capitalisms overwhelmingly tend to be forms of corporate capitalism where the state massively intervenes in the running of the economy. It is unclear whether anything like a fully competitive capitalism actually exists—perhaps Hong Kong approximates it—and it is also unclear whether many of the actual players in the major capitalist societies (the existing capitalists and their managers) want or even expect that it is possible to have laissez-faire capitalism again (if indeed we ever had it). Some capitalist societies are further down the corporate road than other societies, but they are all forms of corporate, perhaps in some instances even monopoly, capitalism. Competitive capitalism seems to be more of a libertarian dream than a sociological reality or even something desired by many informed and tough-minded members of the capitalist class. Socialism has had a similar fate. Its historical exemplifications tend to be of the impure forms, namely the bureaucratic state socialisms. Yugoslavia is perhaps to socialism what Hong Kong is to capitalism. It is a candidate for what might count as an exemplification, or at least a near approximation, of the pure form.

This paucity of exemplifications of pure forms of either capitalism or socialism raises the question of whether the pure forms are at best unstable social systems and at worse merely utopian ideals. I shall not try directly to settle that issue here. What I shall do instead is to compare *models* with *models*. In asking about the moral case for socialism, I shall compare forms that a not inconsiderable number of the theoretical protagonists of each take to be pure forms but which are still, they believe, historically feasible. But I will also be concerned to ask whether these models—these pure forms—can reasonably be expected to come to have a home. If they are not historically feasible models, then, even if we can make a good theoretical moral case for them, we will have hardly provided a good moral case for socialism or capitalism. To avoid bad utopianism we must be talking about forms which could be on the historical agenda. (I plainly here do not take "bad utopianism" to be pleonastic.)

II

Setting aside for the time being the feasibility question, let us compare the pure forms of capitalism and socialism—that is to say, competitive capitalism and democratic socialism—as to how they stand with respect to sustaining and furthering the values of freedom and autonomy, equality, justice, rights and democracy. My argument shall be that socialism comes out better with respect to those values.

Let us first look at freedom and autonomy. An autonomous person is a person who is able to set her ends for herself and in optimal circumstances is able to pursue those ends. But freedom does not only mean being autonomous; it also means the absence of unjustified political and social interference in the pursuit of one's ends. Some might even say that it is just the absence of interference with one's ends. Still it is self-direction—autonomy—not noninterference which is *intrinsically* desirable. Non-interference is only valuable where it is an aid to our being able to do what we want and where we are sufficiently autonomous to have some control over our wants.

How do capitalism and socialism fare in providing the social conditions which will help or impede the flourishing of autonomy? Which model society would make for the greater flourishing of autonomy? My argument is (a) that democratic socialism makes it possible for more people to be more fully autonomous than would be autonomous under capitalism; and (b) that democratic socialism also interferes less in people's exercise of their autonomy than any form of capitalism. All societies limit liberty by interfering with people doing what they want to do in some ways, but the restrictions are more extensive, deeper and more undermining of autonomy in capitalism than in democratic socialism. Where there is private ownership of productive property, which, remember, is private ownership of the means of life, it cannot help but be the case that a few (the owning and controlling capitalist class) will have, along with the managers beholden to them, except in periods of revolutionary turmoil, a firm control, indeed a domination, over the vast majority of people in the society. The capitalist class with the help of their managers determines whether workers (taken now as individuals) can work, how they work, on what they work, the conditions under which they work and what is done with what they produce (where they are producers) and what use is made of their skills and the like. As we move to welfare state capitalism—a compromise still favoring capital which emerged out of long and bitter class struggles—the state places some restrictions on some of these powers of capital. Hours, working conditions and the like are controlled in certain ways. Yet whether workers work and continue to work, how they work and on what, what is done with what they produce, and the rationale for their work are not determined by the workers themselves but by the owners of capital and their managers; this means a very considerable limitation on the autonomy and freedom of workers. Since workers are the great majority, such socio-economic relations place a very considerable limitation on human freedom and indeed on the very most important freedom that people have, namely their being able to live in a self-directed manner, when compared with the industrial democracy of democratic socialism. Under capitalist arrangements it simply cannot fail to be the case that a very large number of people will lose control over a very central set of facets of their lives, namely central aspects of their work and indeed in many instances, over their very chance to be able to work.

Socialism would indeed prohibit capitalist acts between consenting adults; the capitalist class would lose its freedom to buy and sell and to control the labor market. There should be no blinking at the fact that socialist social relations would impose some limitations on freedom, for there is, and indeed can be, no society without norms and some sanctions. In any society you like there will be some things you are at liberty to do and some things that you may not do. However, democratic socialism must bring with it an industrial democracy where workers by various democratic pro-

cedures would determine how they are to work, on what they are to work, the hours of their work, under what conditions they are to work (insofar as this is alterable by human effort at all), what they will produce and how much, and what is to be done with what they produce. Since, instead of there being "private ownership of the means of production," there is in a genuinely socialist society "public ownership of the means of production," the means of life are owned by everyone and thus each person has a *right* to work: she has, that is, a right to the means of life. It is no longer the private preserve of an individual owner of capital but it is owned in common by us all. This means that each of us has an equal right to the means of life. Members of the capitalist class would have a few of their liberties restricted, but these are linked with owning and controlling capital and are not the important civil and political liberties that we all rightly cherish. Moreover, the limitation of the capitalist liberties to buy and sell and the like would make for a more extensive liberty for many, many more people.

One cannot respond to the above by saying that workers are free to leave the working class and become capitalists or at least petty bourgeoisie. They may indeed all in theory, taken *individually,* be free to leave the working class, but if many in fact try to leave the exits will very quickly become blocked. Individuals are only free on the condition that the great mass of people, taken collectively, are not. We could not have capitalism without a working class and the working class is not free within the capitalist system to cease being wage laborers. We cannot all be capitalists. A people's capitalism is nonsense. Though a petty commodity production system (the family farm writ large) is a logical possibility, it is hardly a stable empirical possibility and, what is most important for the present discussion, such a system would not be a capitalist system. Under capitalism, most of us, if we are to find any work at all, will just have to sell (or *perhaps* "rent" is the better word) our labor-power as a commodity. Whether you sell or rent your labor power or, where it is provided, you go on welfare, you will not have much control over areas very crucial to your life. If these are the only feasible alternatives facing the working class, working class autonomy is very limited indeed. But these are the only alternatives under capitalism.

Capitalist acts between consenting adults, if they become sufficiently widespread, lead to severe imbalances in power. These imbalances in power tend to undermine autonomy by creating differentials in wealth and control between workers and capitalists. Such imbalances are the name of the game for capitalism. Even if we (perversely I believe) call a system of petty commodity production capitalism, we still must say that such a socio-economic system is inherently unstable. Certain individuals would win out in this exchanging of commodities and in fairly quick order it would lead to a class system and the imbalances of power—the domination of the many by the few—that I take to be definitive of capitalism. By abolishing capitalist acts between consenting adults, then (but leaving personal property and civil and political liberties untouched), socialism protects more extensive freedoms for more people and in far more important areas of their lives.

III

So democratic socialism does better regarding the value that epitomizes capitalist pride (*hubris,* would, I think, be a better term), namely autonomy. It also does better, I shall now argue, than capitalism with respect to another of our basic values, namely democracy. Since this is almost a corollary of what I have said about autonomy I can afford to be briefer. In capitalist societies, democracy must simply be *political* democracy. There can in the nature of the case be no genuine or thorough workplace democracy. When we enter the sphere of production, capitalists and not workers own, and therefore at least ultimately control, the means of production. While capitalism, as in some workplaces in West Germany and Sweden, sometimes can be pressured into allowing an ameliorative measure of worker control, once ownership rights are given up, we no longer have private productive property but public productive property (and in that way social ownership): capitalism is given up and we have socialism. However, where worker control is restricted to a few firms, we do not yet have socialism. What makes a system socialist or capitalist depends on what happens across the whole society, not just in isolated firms. Moreover, managers can become very important within capitalist firms, but as long as ownership, including the ability to close the place down and liquidate the business, rests in the hands of capitalists we can have no genuine workplace democracy. Socialism, in its pure form, carries with it, in a way capitalism in any form cannot, workplace democracy. (That some of the existing socialisms are anything but pure does not belie this.)

Similarly, whatever may be said of existing socialisms or at least of some existing socialisms, it is not the case that there is anything in the very idea of socialism that militates against political as well as industrial democracy. Socialists are indeed justly suspicious of

some of the tricks played by parliamentary democracy in bourgeois countries, aware of its not infrequent hypocrisy and the limitations of its stress on purely legal and formal political rights and liberties. Socialists are also, without at all wishing to throw the baby out with the bath water, rightly suspicious of any simple reliance on majority rule, unsupplemented by other democratic procedures and safeguards. But there is nothing in socialist theory that would set it against political democracy and the protection of political and civil rights; indeed there is much in socialism that favors them, namely its stress on both autonomy and equality.

The fact that political democracy came into being and achieved stability within capitalist societies may prove something about conditions necessary for its coming into being, but it says nothing about capitalism being necessary for sustaining it. In Chile, South Africa, and Nazi Germany, indeed, capitalism has flourished without the protection of civil and political rights or anything like a respect for the democratic tradition. There is nothing structural in socialism that would prevent it from continuing those democratic traditions or cherishing those political and civil rights. That something came about under certain conditions does not establish that these conditions are necessary for its continued existence. That men initially took an interest in chess does not establish that women cannot quite naturally take an interest in it as well. When capitalist societies with long-flourishing democratic traditions move to socialism there is no reason at all to believe that they will not continue to be democratic. (Where societies previously had no democratic tradition or only a very weak one, matters are more problematic.)

IV

I now want to turn to a third basic value, equality. In societies across the political spectrum, *moral* equality (the belief that everyone's life matters equally) is an accepted value. Or, to be somewhat cynical about the matter, at least lip service is paid to it. But even this lip service is the compliment that vice pays to virtue. That is to say, such a belief is a deeply held considered conviction in modernized societies, though it has not been at all times and is not today a value held in all societies. This is most evident concerning moral equality.

While this value is genuinely held by the vast majority of people in capitalist societies, it can hardly be an effective or functional working norm where there is such a diminishment of autonomy as we have seen obtains unavoidably in such societies. Self-respect is deeply threatened where so many people lack effective control over their own lives, where there are structures of domination, where there is alienated labor, where great power differentials and differences in wealth make for very different (and often very bleak) life chances. For not inconsiderable numbers, in fact, it is difficult to maintain self-respect under such conditions unless they are actively struggling against the system. And, given present conditions, fighting the system, particularly in societies such as the United States, may well be felt to be a hopeless task. Under such conditions any real equality of opportunity is out of the question. And the circumstances are such, in spite of what is often said about these states, that equality of condition is an even more remote possibility. But without at least some of these things moral equality cannot even be approximated. Indeed, even to speak of it sounds like an obscene joke given the social realities of our lives.

Although under welfare-state capitalism some of the worst inequalities of capitalism are ameliorated, workers still lack effective control over their work, with repercussions in political and public life as well. Differentials of wealth cannot but give rise to differentials in power and control in politics, in the media, in education, in the direction of social life and in what options get seriously debated. The life chances of workers and those not even lucky enough to be workers (whose ranks are growing and will continue to grow under capitalism) are impoverished compared to the life chances of members of the capitalist class and its docile professional support stratum.

None of these equality-undermining features would obtain under democratic socialism. Such societies would, for starters, be classless, eliminating the power and control differentials that go with the class system of capitalism. In addition to political democracy, industrial democracy and all the egalitarian and participatory control that goes with that would, in turn, reinforce moral equality. Indeed it would make it possible where before it was impossible. There would be a commitment under democratic socialism to attaining or at least approximating, as far as it is feasible, equality of condition; and this, where approximated, would help make for real equality of opportunity, making equal life chances something less utopian than it must be under capitalism.

In fine, the very things, as we have seen, that make for greater autonomy under socialism than under capitalism, would, in being more equally distributed, make for greater equality of condition, greater equality of opportunity and greater moral equality in a democratic socialist society than in a capitalist one. These values are values commonly shared by both capitalistically inclined people and those who are socialistically inclined. What the former do not see is that in modern industrial societies, democratic socialism can better deliver these goods than even progressive capitalism.

There is, without doubt, legitimate worry about bureaucratic control under socialism. But that is a worry under any historically feasible capitalism as well, and it is anything but clear that state bureaucracies are worse than great corporate bureaucracies. Indeed, if socialist bureaucrats were, as the socialist system requires, really committed to production for needs and to achieving equality of condition, they might, bad as they are, be the lesser of two evils. But in any event democratic socialism is not bureaucratic state socialism, and there is no structural reason to believe that it must—if it arises in a society with skilled workers committed to democracy—give rise to bureaucratic state socialism. There will, inescapably, be some bureaucracy, but in a democratic socialist society it must and indeed will be controlled. This is not merely a matter of optimism about the will of socialists, for there are more mechanisms for democratic control of bureaucracy within a democratic socialism that is both a political and an industrial democracy, than there can be under even the most benign capitalist democracies—democracies which for structural reasons can never be industrial democracies. If, all that notwithstanding, bureaucratic creepage is inescapable in modern societies, then that is just as much a problem for capitalism as for socialism.

The underlying rationale for production under capitalism is profit and capital accumulation. Capitalism is indeed a marvelous engine for building up the productive forces (though clearly at the expense of considerations of equality and autonomy). We might look on it, going back to earlier historical times, as something like a forced march to develop the productive forces. But now that the productive forces in advanced capitalist societies are wondrously developed, we are in a position to direct them to far more humane and more equitable uses under a socio-economic system whose rationale for production is to meet human needs (the needs of everyone as far as this is possible). This egalitarian thrust, together with the socialists' commitment to attaining, as far as that is possible, equality of condition, makes it clear that socialism will produce more equality than capitalism.

QUESTIONS ON NIELSEN

1. How do you understand the values that Nielsen defends? Why does he hold that these values would be best served by a socialist economy?

2. How does Nielsen characterize the ideal of "autonomy"? How does the market interfere with autonomy? Do you agree? Is there any sense in which a market might support autonomy?

3. Nielsen says that under democratic socialism, the workers would determine, by democratic procedures, "how they are to work, on what they are to work, the hours of their work, under what conditions they are to work . . . what they will produce and how much, and what is to be done with what they produce." How will the workers know what to produce, what quantity, and by what methods? Should the rest of society have a say in what is produced?

4. How is "class" manifested in market societies? Do you think that Nielsen's version of socialism would eliminate classes? Is there a risk that a "new class" of politicians, public administrators, and intellectuals might emerge under such a system? Why or why not?

FOR FURTHER READING

Barry, Brian. *Theories of Justice.* Berkeley: University of California Press, 1989.

Braybrooke, David. *Meeting Needs.* Princeton, N.J.: Princeton University Press, 1987.

Buchanan, Allen. *Marx and Justice.* Totowa, N.J.: Rowman and Littlefield, 1982.

———. *Ethics, Efficiency, and the Market.* Totowa, N.J.: Rowman and Littlefield, 1988.

Buchanan, James, and Gordon Tullock. *The Calculus of Consent.* Ann Arbor: University of Michigan, 1962.

Buchanan, James. *The Limits of Liberty.* Chicago: University of Chicago, 1975.

Cohen, G. A. *If You're an Egalitarian, How Come You're So Rich?* Cambridge: Harvard University Press, 2000.

Dworkin, Ronald. *Taking Rights Seriously.* Cambridge: Harvard University Press, 1977.

Etzioni, Amitai. *The Spirit of Community: Rights, Responsibilities, and the Communitarian Agenda.* New York: Crown, 1993.

Finnis, John. *Natural Law and Natural Rights.* Oxford: Clarendon Press, 1980.

Galston, William. *Justice and the Human Good.* Chicago: University of Chicago Press, 1980.

George, Robert P., ed. *Natural Law, Liberalism, and Morality.* New York: Oxford University Press, 1996.

Havelock, Eric. *The Greek Conception of Justice: From Its Shadow in Home to Its Substance in Plato.* Cambridge: Cambridge University Press, 1978.

Hayek, F. A. *Law, Legislation, and Liberty,* vol. 2, *The Mirage of Social Justice.* Chicago: University of Chicago Press, 1976.

de Jouvenel, Bertrand. *The Ethics of Redistribution* [1952]. Indianapolis, Ind.: Liberty Press, 1990.

Locke, John. *Second Treatise of Government* [1689–1690], edited by C. B. MacPherson. Indianapolis, Ind.: Hackett Publishing, 1980.

Lucas, J. R. *On Justice.* Oxford: Clarendon Press, 1980.

Mansfield, Harvey C. *A Student's Guide to Political Theory.* Wilmington, Del.: ISI Books, 2000.

MacIntyre, Alasdair. *After Virtue: A Study in Moral Theory.* Notre Dame: University of Notre Dame Press, 1981.

Mill, John Stuart. *On Liberty* [1859], edited by George Sher. Indianapolis: Hackett Publishing, 1980.

Miller, David. *Social Justice.* Oxford: Clarendon Press, 1976.

Nagel, Thomas. *Equality and Partiality.* New York: Oxford University Press, 1991.

Nozick, Robert. *Anarchy, State, and Utopia.* New York: Basic Books, 1974.

Okin, Susan Miller. *Justice, Gender, and the Family.* New York: Basic Books, 1989.

Plato. *The Republic.*

Posner, R. A. *The Economics of Justice.* Cambridge: Harvard University Press, 1981.

Rawls, John. *A Theory of Justice.* Cambridge: Belknap Press of Harvard University, 1971.

———. *Political Liberalism.* New York: Columbia University Press, 1993.

Sandel, Michael. *Liberalism and the Limits of Justice.* Cambridge: Cambridge University Press, 1982.

Sen, Amartya. *Inequality Reexamined.* Cambridge: Harvard University Press, 1992.

Sunstein, Cass. *Free Markets and Social Justice.* New York: Oxford University Press, 1997.

Van Creveld, Martin. *The Rise and Fall of the State.* Cambridge: Cambridge University Press, 1999.

Walzer, Michael. *Spheres of Justice: A Defense of Pluralism and Equality.* New York: Basic Books, 1983.

A III

Regulation

In every case of the exploitation of the ignorance of consumers or workers or investors by a businessman, the leading protector of the exploited class is the businessman's competitors. I need not be well informed, because if anyone seeks to profit by my ignorance, his efforts will merely arouse his rivals to provide the commodity at a competitive price. Competition is the consumer's patron saint.

George Stigler[1]

The freely voting rational citizen, conscious of his (long-run) interests, and the representative who acts in obedience to them, the government that expresses these volitions—is this not the perfect example of a nursery tale?

Joseph Schumpeter[2]

'Sweat equity,' though the phrase itself has been recently coined, is as distinctively an American concept as 'equality before the law' and 'liberty.' You could get ahead by plain hard work. No one would stand in your way. Today that is no longer true. American society has erected barriers to individual sweat equity, by saying, in effect, 'Only people who are good at navigating complex rules need apply.' Anyone who has tried to open or run a small business in recent years can supply evidence of how formidable those barriers have become.

Richard Herrnstein and Charles Murray[3]

Obviously modern law has become a series of instructions to administrators rather than a series of commands to citizens.

Theodore Lowi[4]

The legal framework that establishes the rules and institutions of a market may be evaluated according to moral criteria that may include standards of justice. In addition to that legal framework is another set of rules, having the force of law, which are invoked to constrain and guide the actions and decisions of participants in the market. Referred to as "regulations," these rules have been the source of much controversy. They are seen by some as

1. *The Citizen and the State: Essays on Regulation* (Chicago: University of Chicago Press, 1975), 12.

2. *History of Economic Analysis* (New York: Oxford University Press, 1954), 429.

3. *The Bell Curve: Intelligence and Class Structure in American Life* (New York: The Free Press, 1994), 542.

4. *The End of Liberalism* (New York: W. W. Norton, 1969), 144 (emphasis omitted).

the saving grace of the market, there to ameliorate or rectify economic problems, human error, or lack of will, but others view regulations as ineffective impositions that do not improve market imperfections so much as they introduce new problems while raising the costs of doing business or insuring legislative protection for powerful economic interests. What are these regulations that engender such controversy? And how might they be evaluated?

REGULATION: THE BACKGROUND

Definition and Categorization

Regulations may be defined as "general rules or specific actions imposed by administrative agencies that interfere directly with the market allocation mechanism or indirectly by altering consumer and firm demand and supply decisions."[5] What this definition implies is that rules are regarded as regulations in relation to a prior framework that establishes the essential conditions for the operations of markets and business. What is crucial to the idea of a regulation is that it is a rule that can be said to "interfere" with the operation of the market as that market is defined in terms of certain essential conditions. (Of course, it does not seem essential that a regulation be imposed by an administrative agency, even though most of them are; a regulation could be imposed as a result of a specific legislative act of congress. Moreover, it could also be argued that "taxation" is a form of regulation in that most taxes alter economic decision making. For example, taxes affect the decision making of business firms by defining a "taxable income," rates of depreciation, and so on; taxes also affect the division of labor by increasing the demand for lawyers, accountants, and investment advisors.)

It is typically argued that regulatory rules are required if a market is to function in a salutary and beneficial manner. We will address some of these justifications below, but first we should look at how one might categorize the variety of regulations that exist. Some regulations are *economic,* and are justified in terms of some alleged economic need or market imperfection (for example, antitrust regulations, minimum-wage legislation, and many environmental regulations). Other regulations are *social* and are justified in terms of ameliorating some social inequality or improving health, welfare, or behavior (for example, regulations governing working conditions, limiting the smoking of cigarettes

5. Daniel F. Spulber, *Regulation and Markets* (Cambridge, Massachusetts: M.I.T. Press, 1989), 37.

in public and private areas, or establishing procedures for the labeling of food items). Regulations can also be categorized in terms of the type of rule; for instance, some regulatory rules are specific commands that require that one perform some specific action, use resources in some specific manner, or achieve some level of output. Other regulations are more general and allow the individual to utilize discretion in attempting to conform to the rule.

A Brief Historical Perspective

One of the first instances of major regulatory action by the United States government occurred in 1887 with the authorization of the Interstate Commerce Commission to oversee the rates and routes of the railroads. During what historians refer to as the "Progressive Era," between the depression of the 1890s and the entry of America into the first World War, a new outlook arose regarding the relation of private and public authority. In a departure from the attitudes of much of the nineteenth century, it was now suggested that there be increasing governmental guidance over the economy and private enterprise. In 1890 the Sherman Antitrust Act became law. In the subsequent decades of the Progressive Era, the Pure Food and Drug Act (1906), the Clayton Antitrust Act (1914), and the Federal Trade Commission (1914) were established. However, an even greater expansion of regulation occurred during the New Deal of President Franklin Roosevelt. Along with numerous regulatory acts, many of which were passed during the first session of the seventy-third Congress (the "Hundred Days"), regulatory agencies such as the Securities and Exchange Commission (1934), the Federal Communications Commission (1934), and the Civil Aeronautics Board (1938, but eliminated in 1978), were added during his administration. A new round of regulatory legislation occurred during the 1960s and 1970s, but in these two decades the focus was less on economic regulation than on regulation aimed to improve the quality of life or to reform behavior. During this period, the Environmental Protection Agency, the Occupational Safety and Health Administration, the Consumer Product Safety Commission, and the Equal Employment Opportunity Commission were created.

Regulation and the Public Interest

Since the Progressive Era, government regulatory efforts have generally been defended in terms of the public good, a characterization that still survives. After all, in a democratic society, voters elect representatives who are to act as agents of the public good, deliberating and legislating with an eye to the interests of their constituents and to the long-term good of the nation. That is certainly the democratic hope. However, both economists and historians have recently challenged the view that regulation serves the public rather than private interests.[6]

One might evaluate the history of regulation according to three simplified perspectives. There is first the ideal view, which assumes that the good intentions of voters, legislators, and administrators are sufficient for the construction and implementation of regulations that achieve good outcomes. Nonetheless, historical and economic evidence cast great doubt as to whether any such ideal view is a justified account of actual practice. The evidence raises doubts as to whether the good intentions of legislators will ensure that the situation (or problem) that has drawn their attention has been correctly described, that the regulation will be effectively drawn up, or that it will be administered properly. One explanation for the failure of the ideal view is the enormous complexity of society and the difficulty of crafting a regulation adequate to this complexity. Another explanation challenges the assumption that the relevant intentions or motivations are actually oriented to the public good. Perhaps those who are most interested in crafting or administering a regulatory rule have private, rather than public, interests uppermost. Because of the enormous power of the government to shape commerce and to affect our livelihoods, legislators face enormous pressure to craft legislation with an eye toward those businesses or industries that are most powerful politically.

In contradistinction to the ideal view is, then, the theory that regulation is rarely initiated in the public interest and just as rarely achieves any public interest. This view feeds off of the recognition of the complexity of society, but it adds to that assumption the idea that the real motivations of politicians and regulators have less to do with some broad public interest than with something more narrow (though not, for that reason, necessarily selfish)—a private interest.

In addition to these two perspectives is the outlook that accepts much of the warnings of this latter group but still holds that, in spite of the failure of much regulation, regulation can, if adopted carefully, serve properly public ends. The question then arises as to what are the required conditions for *careful* regulation.

6. See, for example, Gabriel Kolko, *The Triumph of Conservatism* (New York: The Free Press, 1963), and *Railroads and Regulation* (Princeton: Princeton University Press, 1965); and George Stigler, "The Theory of Economic Regulation," in *The Citizen and the State: Essays on Regulation.*

ECONOMIC REGULATION

Perfect Competition

The standard justification for economic regulation has been that of "market failure." Market failure is typically defined in terms of a model of "perfect competition." A model of perfect competition is a purely theoretical model employed to explain and predict economic events and processes. Models of perfect competition employ several assumptions, but the most important of these are that (1) for any given item, buyers and sellers are so numerous that the action of no single buyer or seller can affect the price of the good, and that (2) there are no legal barriers to any firm either entering or exiting a market for any particular good. Additional assumptions concern the homogeneity of the goods that are sold, that each firm and each consumer has perfect information concerning the price and quality of the goods that are available, that all firms and consumers are rational, and that property rights are so defined and so certain that all of the costs or benefits of any exchange redound only to parties to the exchange.[7]

In this model of perfect competition, there will be no surpluses or shortages of any goods, and the market will be in equilibrium. At this equilibrium point the market is efficient; in other words, the market is efficiently acquiring the inputs to production, efficiently producing goods, and efficiently allocating these goods to consumers. What is meant by efficiency? In its ordinary meaning, efficiency has to do with using the minimal effort, time, or cost to attain some given end. Similarly, in economic terms an efficient market is one in which for any given output (or value of an output) the means for attaining that output is the least valued of all possible means.[8] However, even if the market is operating efficiently, that alone does

7. The model of perfect competition has come under attack on several occasions. F. A. Hayek, for example, contends that "nothing is solved when we assume everybody to know everything and that the real problem is rather how it can be brought about that as much of the available knowledge as possible is used. This raises for a competitive society the question, not how we can 'find' the people who know best, but rather what institutional arrangements are necessary in order that the unknown persons who have knowledge suited to a particular task are most likely to be attracted to that task." "The Meaning of Competition," in *Individualism and Economic Order* (Chicago: University of Chicago Press, 1948), 95.

8. Economists try to capture this concept of efficiency by using the concept of Pareto optimality (named after the Italian economist and sociologist, Vilfredo Pareto, 1848–1923): A perfectly competitive economy is efficient or Pareto optimal in the sense that it is impossible to make any single person better off without simultaneously making someone else worse off.

not tell us that this market is operating beneficially or to one's moral satisfaction. Theoretically, there are a variety of equilibrium efficient points, and efficiency alone cannot determine which should be preferred. Moreover, since efficiency itself merely tells us that the market is efficiently satisfying preferences, one might still consider whether the preferences are morally suitable, wise, or beneficial. Finally, efficiency is a function of the background conditions out of which the efficient outcome is to emerge, and those background conditions can also be subject to moral evaluation, including an evaluation by some standard of justice. None of this means that efficiency is not important, only that it is not sufficient.

Is it always the case that actual markets are efficient? Or are there certain conditions in which markets simply cannot achieve efficiency? There are generally considered to be at least three major candidates for market failure: monopoly, public goods, and externalities. These market failures provide the strongest reasons for government regulation in the market.

Market Failure: Monopoly

A market dominated by a single seller is a monopoly. Although it may sound simple enough to define the idea of monopoly, it is not so easy to apply the definition to a particular market. A monopolist is a single seller, so it is a single seller of a *product*. But what is the product? Every seller of a particular brand is, in a sense, a single seller of that particular brand, but such sellers are obviously not monopolists. Presumably, the crucial issue in monopoly is the extent to which there is a real option of substituting one product for another, for if there are substitutes for some product, then the consumer has the option of buying from alternative sellers.

The typical response to monopoly is for the government to regulate the monopoly so that its prices are not excessive. Of course, the crucial unknown is what these prices should be. How are the prices to be determined in the absence of competition? Another vital question is whether monopolies are that frequent. Here one must distinguish between so-called "natural" monopolies that would arise in an unregulated market and monopolies—such as the postal service (which holds a monopoly on the delivery of first-class mail)—established by the government. That a monopoly exists by some order of legislation or as a result of legislative barriers to entry (such as regulations that raise the costs of doing business) is not evidence of *market* failure.

Market Failure: Public Goods

A second type of market failure concerns "public goods." The market is able to produce and sell "private goods," which are those goods for which a nonpayer can be excluded and for which consumption is "rivalrous." (Rivalrous consumption occurs when one person's consumption of the good diminishes the availability of the good for others.) Although it is not obvious that the market can produce public goods, it is also not clear which goods are truly public goods. On this question, it is important to distinguish the concept of a public good and those goods that have, historically, been *assumed* to be public goods. Thus, although the post office may be regarded as a public good, it is not obvious that its services fit into the conceptual criteria of public goods. A problem arises for the market provision of goods that are truly public rather than private. The most crucial assumption here is that of excludability: For if nonpayers cannot be excluded (as in, for example, the defense of a nation), then the good can be enjoyed by those who are not paying for the good, thus creating an incentive for each person not to pay anything at all. And if each individual believes that he or she can enjoy the good without paying anything, then no individual will pay for the good and the good will not be produced. In other words, each individual will hope to "free ride" on the payments of other individuals. If all (or most) individuals reason similarly, the good will not be produced at all (even though it is in everyone's interest to have the good produced).

How can this problem of public goods be overcome? One solution is for the government to finance the good via taxation. This, certainly, is part of what Adam Smith meant when he wrote that government would have to build "those public works, which, though they may be in the highest degree advantageous to a great society, are, however, of such a nature, that the profit could never repay the expense to any individual or small number of individuals."[9] However, it is worth noting that the problem of free riding would not exist if there were some ethical norm against it (or, conversely, if there were a norm obligating or urging individuals to contribute toward the production of the public good), a norm that could be maintained without the enforcement of the government. Such a norm would most likely emerge and survive only if the number of individuals required to fund the production of the good is small. A

9. *An Inquiry into the Nature and Causes of the Wealth of Nation* [1776], edited by R. H. Campbell, A. S. Skinner, and W. B. Todd (Indianapolis: Liberty Classics, 1981), V. i.c. (p. 723).

third alternative has been suggested. If the production of a good is either impossible (or prohibitively expensive) because nonpayers cannot be excluded, then the producer of the good could offer a contract to the potential users of the collective good stipulating that the good will be produced only if a certain number of potential users commit to produce the good. In the event that the community does not commit sufficient funds, then any person who has committed funds to the production of the good will receive a refund.[10]

Market Failure: Externalities

Finally, a third kind of market failure is that of externalities or spillovers. For any two-person exchange, an externality occurs when the exchange between the two parties generates a consequence or effect that extends to a third person, who is not party to the exchange. The externality occurs insofar as the effects of the exchange are not contained between or internalized to the transacting parties. If there are effects that are external to the transaction, then the transacting parties do not bear all of the costs or benefits of the exchange, and thus neither party is taking into account all of the costs or benefits which actually occur. Although it is the *negative* externality (or cost) which is the concern, externalities can also be *positive,* as is the case with vaccinations against communicable diseases (which generate positive externalities on those who come into contact with the immunized individual), education, or something as simple as a beautiful flower bed. However, for every neighbor who cultivates a beautiful garden, there is another neighbor who operates an angry lawn mower, thus generating a noise that is a negative externality. More noticeable yet is the negative externality of pollution (discussed further in Section CIV). An industry whose pollutants affect third parties is an industry whose goods are priced to cover only the internal cost and not the external cost.

How might the problems of negative externalities be resolved? One option is simply to ban any activity that produces any negative externality. Obviously, however, this option comes at a high cost, for many instances of pollution arise as effects of processes utilized to produce necessary goods. Another alternative is to levy a tax on the producer of the externality sufficient to cover the cost imposed on others. This option would not mean the end of the externality, but, if successful, this would reduce

pollution to the point at which it costs the polluter more in pollution taxes than is gained by selling the products that generate the side-effect of pollution. A third, and popular, option is some form of regulation that limits externalities either by directly limiting their output or by indirectly prescribing a certain process of production, the effect of which will be a limit on the externalities.

A final option involves property rights. Consider that externalities result because property rights are not clearly defined (or consistently enforced). There are two alternative approaches to the matter of establishing or articulating property rights. R. H. Coase has argued[11] that in the case of externalities it simply does not matter to whom the property rights are assigned. This may sound surprising (and holds true only if one is employing the standard of Pareto optimality), but Coase argues that whoever receives the right—whether it is a right to impose costs or whether it is the right to be free of some externality—is irrelevant as long as the individuals could then bargain over the cost (or price) of allowing an externality, thereby achieving an efficient outcome. An alternative property-rights approach would also allow bargaining, but this approach holds that the original assignation of property rights should not be arbitrary but should be decided on the basis of justice.[12]

Some Costs of Regulation

It is important to remember that the mere claim of a market failure does not provide a sufficient reason for regulation. There is, first of all, the problem of establishing that there is a genuine market failure. If there is such, then the case for government intervention would seem to require (1) that a government regulation can solve the failure or ameliorate it, and (2) that the costs of government action are less than the benefits. Among those costs, one must consider that each new regulation raises the cost of doing business. If that is the case, then insofar as the regulation will affect all businesses, large and small, actual and potential, a regulation will have a much greater cost to the small business than to the large. A large corporation will not only have a larger staff, including full-time attorneys to deal with the vagaries of the legislation, but the cost of the regulation will have a more noticeable economic impact on the smaller firm. Indeed, for businesspersons seeking to enter a market or

---

10. This idea (that of "pre-contract exclusion") is discussed in Earl R. Brubaker, "Free Ride, Free Revelation, or Golden Rule?" in *The Theory of Market Failure: A Critical Examination,* edited by Tyler Cowen (Fairfax, Va.: George Mason University Press, 1988), 93–109.

11. "The Problem of Social Cost," *Journal of Law and Economics* 3 (October 1960): 1–45.

12. See, for example, Murray Rothbard, "Law, Property, Rights, and Air Pollution," *The Cato Journal* 2 (Spring 1982): 55–99.

for those persons running small businesses, regulations sometimes create additional costs that place the new entrant or the small business at a competitive disadvantage. Finally, as regulations become more numerous and complex, they make compliance ever more difficult for the person lacking either education or experience, thus creating another hurdle for success in a competitive market and for upward mobility within society. These are some of the often uncounted costs of the imposition of regulations.

However, there is another cost of regulation that is often unnoticed and is also less economic than political or constitutional. The United States Constitution, Article 1, Section 8, states that Congress has the power "To regulate Commerce with foreign Nations, and among the several states, and with the Indian Tribes." This clause leaves unclear the extent to which Congress may delegate its power to regulate commerce to an administrative agency. Such agencies are, of course, created by Congress and it is Congress which determines their aims, powers, and procedures. Much of this is done because the crafting of regulation requires a level of expertise that most members of Congress do not have. (Of course, there are other incentives for Congress to delegate regulatory power to an agency: Congress can receive credit for acting on some problem but blame a "bureaucrat" if the regulation is onerous; in addition, a member of Congress could subsequently receive adulation for rescuing constituents from entanglements in regulatory "red tape.") However, it is not entirely clear whether these regulatory agencies are legislative or executive. The Constitution creates three branches of government: the judiciary, the legislative, and the executive; however, the creation of large numbers of administrative agencies, which may not only formulate rules, but determine violations and punishments, may threaten the very division of powers set up by the Constitution.[13]

That there might be costs to regulation must not go unrecognized, nor should one ignore any of the potential benefits of a reasonable regulation. What are the criteria of a good regulation? What are some of the problems that have bedeviled the regulations of the past? Is there a tendency, in contemporary democracies, to overregulate? Can businesses be expected to regulate themselves? These are just some of the questions that are addressed by the readings that follow.

13. An excellent account of these constitutional issues can be found in Gary S. Lawson, "The Rise of the Administrative State," *Harvard Law Review* 107 (1994): 1231.

THE READINGS

Nicholas Rescher   Rescher delineates the criteria—individually necessary and jointly sufficient—by which an instance of government regulation would be justifiable. The issue of whether a regulation is desirable hinges on whether the regulation would be in the public interest, and this entails showing that the actual implementation of the regulation would serve the larger public. That a regulation might be in the public interest need not entail that it is feasible. Rescher mentions four reasons as to why a governmental regulation might be less feasible than alternatives. Even if a regulation is desirable and feasible, one must still weigh the costs of the regulation against its benefits, including costs and benefits that are not narrowly economic but moral and social. (For example, one cost might involve the "diminution of the liberty of the individual.") In the last two sections of his essay, Rescher considers how state regulation has, within the past century, taken a new orientation toward regulation for social and economic well-being, with much of this effort motivated by egalitarian concerns. However, as Rescher indicates, regulations motivated by considerations of equality sometimes have unintended consequences, including the diminishment of the very quantity of the service that is to be more equally distributed.

Cass Sunstein   Sunstein considers six paradoxes of the regulatory state, revealing those sorts of regulations that are "self-defeating" in that they bring about results diametrically opposite to the result intended. The elimination of such self-defeating regulations would "eliminate a significant source of regulatory failure." Prior to delineating these paradoxes, Sunstein discusses what he takes to be some of the success stories of regulation, and he notes as well some additional regulatory failures. The heart of the essay is devoted to six paradoxes: that stringent regulation leads to lax regulation; that the regulation of new risks may increase the overall level of risk; that requiring the best technology diminishes incentives to innovation and experimentation; that regulation designed to help those who are not well-off may harm the poor; that disclosure requirements may leave consumers less informed; and that independent agencies are not, in fact, independent. These self-defeating policies often arise because lawmakers and regulators impose "Soviet-style command-and-control regulation," ignoring the dynamic of private choice exercised by consumers, producers, and those who enforce the regulations.

Leland B. Yeager Yeager's essay focuses on how regulation often arises as a particular response to some discrete problem of some specific time or place: "Preoccupation with the immediate and specific is part of the problem with government action." Yeager argues that we should consider principles and systems of rules, rather than specific instances of regulation, for the appeal to instances conceals a "bias" in favor of government regulation and intervention. The origin of this bias is a fragmentation of the knowledge required to determine what sort of rules or regulations would, over time, function best. No one person has either the incentive or the knowledge to consider the long-run consequences of government action, and those who make a political or regulatory decision are typically not those who bear the cost. Even if a single decision seems worthwhile, the accumulation of hundreds of such (worthwhile) decisions may prove less than desirable. Yeager then offers a political analysis of the growth of regulation, noting first that those who would be affected positively by regulation are not only well-informed about the legislation but most eager in pressing their claims on their legislators. Other individuals who might be harmed by the legislation have neither the incentive to inform themselves nor the motivation to advance their concerns to the legislators. These persons are "rationally ignorant and apathetic about the details of public policy." To develop his case Yeager discusses the knowledge, motivations, circumstances, and opportunities that affect individual voters, special interest groups, "hobbyists," politicians, bureaucrats, and judicial courts.

Ian Maitland Maitland describes how the conditions of markets may militate against self-regulation, leaving us to rely on the "legal compulsion" initiated by the state. Maitland contends that the interest of any single firm will often diverge from interests that it has as a member of a larger society. In particular, a society's interest in responsible business conduct is, says Maitland, a public good that may be enjoyed regardless of whether a single firm has contributed toward the production or maintenance of such conduct. However, since no firm is assured that other firms will act responsibly, each firm decides not to contribute to the maintenance of this good because doing so would only place it at a competitive disadvantage. Noting three levels of self-regulation (that of the firm, the industry, and the economy), Maitland contends that the solution may lie in "peak organizations," composed of a variety of industries and firms, that serve as "quasi-public" organizations that go beyond mere private interest. These organizations might enforce a common code of responsible conduct, help secure the relations between corporate managers and stockholders, and constrain the conduct of firms that might otherwise wish to defect from the common code. Maitland considers the possibility that such organizations might take hold in the United States, but he concludes that this possibility seems remote given the "fragmentation of power" in the American political system and the "individualist" culture of the society as a whole.

On the Rationale of Governmental Regulation

Nicholas Rescher

Nicholas Rescher, University Professor of Philosophy at the University of Pittsburgh, is the author of numerous articles and books, including Rationality *(1988),* Luck *(1995), and* Complexity *(1998).*

THREE BASIC PARAMETERS

The theoretical justification of state intervention in the sphere of individual action and initiative depends on three basic issues: Is it *right?* Is it *desirable?* Is it *expedient?* A negative response to any of these questions would suggest that the state's abridgement of individuals' liberty to conduct their affairs in their own preferred ways is inappropriate. Rightness, desirability, and expediency are severally necessary and jointly sufficient to legitimate state regulation of individual affairs. Let us examine these three parameters of the problem more closely.

The Issue of Right?

The state has always impinged heavily on the lives of its individual subjects. It has taxed them, impressed them into its service, dictated where they can and cannot live, and, not infrequently, appointed the time and means of their death. Obscure existence outside the range of the state's sight has usually been the best way to remain outside its reach. "Fortunate," said one of the caliphs, "is the man whom I do not know and who does not know me." But what is, is not necessarily right, and so the big question remains: To what extent is it right and proper for the state to interfere by way of regulation and control in the actions and dealings of its members.

Is it right for the state to take onto itself this or that mode of regulation or control of the activities of its citizens—to fix the rules of the road, say, or to stipulate retirement ages, or to limit the opening hours of bars? Such questions pose the difficult normative issue of the basis on which one is to proceed in determining whether a state acts rightly or legitimately in adopting a certain regulative measure.

Two alternatives arise at this point. On the one hand, one can take the view that it is somehow written large in the scheme of things that the state should exercise certain regulative functions and these only; that this is somehow determined by the general principles of the matter. Such a position in effect has it that it is somehow engraved on bronze tablets delivered from on high—to put it in caricature—what the proper regulative business of the state actually is. The virtually insuperable difficulty here is that of getting hold of the bronze tablets, or, rather, of establishing the general principles that are to effect the determination at issue.

On the other hand, a more relaxed view of the matter is also possible. That is, one can take the view that the proper business of the state is to discharge whatever regulative functions it is assigned by its citizens through the due processes of the political decision-making apparatus at their disposal. If the public wants to charge public authorities with the licensing of TV sets, the monopoly of postal services, or the monitoring of banking transactions, then so be it; the activities and regulations at issue have thereby automatically become part of the "proper business" of the state. The question "Is it right and proper that the state should restrict or regulate the activities at issue?" is on this view effectively settled when the public uses the valid political processes at its disposal to mandate those responsibilities to the state.

But this rather laissez faire approach to the question of the right of the state to take on certain restrictive and regulating functions does not resolve the issue of justification. What it does is simply to displace the entire weight of concern to the issues of desirability and expediency. Beyond question, much can be said for the view that, if and when a viable consensus of the public (acting through the channels of the duly established political process) charges the state with a certain regulative mission, then the question of inherent rightness is closed—for this position bypasses any problematic aspects beyond "the general will" in regard to the normative appraisal of the legitimation of state action.[1] But of course, even with such a view the issues of "Is it desirable?" and "Is it expedient?" still remain wide open. These considerations now come to the center of the stage.

The Issue of Desirability

The question "Is it *desirable* for the state to exercise a certain controlling or regulative function?" comes down to this: Is it manifestly in the best (real) interests of the substantial preponderance of its members that the state should assume this function—in short, is it in "the public interest"? In concrete cases the answer to this question may sometimes be *yes* (e.g., fluoridating water supplies, licensing the construction of nuclear power stations, controlling the distribution of drugs). But sometimes it may be *no* (mandating a certain retirement age) and sometimes *maybe* (prohibiting the use of studded tires on private vehicles, prohibiting the acquisition of gold or of foreign exchange by private individuals). The status of these particular examples is unimportant: they are meant to be no more than suggestive. What matters is the general principle at issue, namely that the question of desirability turns on the devising of a cogent case to show that a *successful* carrying-through of the measure at issue will indeed serve the best interests of a preponderant majority.

It is important, however, to recognize that even after this question of desirability has been settled in the affirmative, the issue of feasibility yet remains wholly untouched, for the question of desirability takes the hypothetical form. Even if the measures at issue were implemented in an efficient, effective, and (relatively) inexpensive manner, would worthwhile results thereby be anticipated? And the important question yet remains very much open, whether this hypothesis—or anything like it—is realized or indeed realizable. It is to this concern that the issue of feasibility is addressed.

The Issue of Feasibility

Even if it is "desirable—in the sense of contributing to "the public interest"—it is still reasonable to raise the question of whether it is actually possible for the state to realize this desideratum. Can the mice bell the cat? Is the state actually in a position to discharge this mission efficiently and effectively? Prohibition was an arrangement that arguably satisfied the criteria of desirability. But it soon came to grief, shattered on the rock of feasibility.

This matter of efficiency and effectiveness poses large and ramified problems. For one thing, it is important to realize that the question of efficiency and effectiveness is generally not so much absolute as relative, a matter of a comparison between alternatives; that is, the question is not just whether the state can achieve the desired results with some degree of adequacy, but whether other, less awesome mechanisms for their realization might actually be superior in this regard. In particular, we must recognize that potent forces are generally at work to militate against the state's assumption of a function when other, less dramatic alternatives may be substituted; this is true regardless of how desirable it is to accomplish the function. These constraints are indicated by the following sorts of considerations:

1. The state—an inherently sluggish and cumbersome agency—is hard to coax into an area of concern, and, once settled there, is even harder to oust when circumstances so develop that this becomes desirable.

2. The state is, in general, a comparatively problematic mechanism of purpose realization, because its pursuit of any given goal is inevitably fraught with political complications.

3. The actual agents through which the state effects its actions—officialdom and its bureaucracy—are generally too insulated against consumer feedback to emerge in fact (rather than theory) as effective servants of the public.

4. The state operates at a disadvantage in that by proceeding within an all-embracing monolithic framework, it loses the benefits of efficiency gained through rivalry and competition among smaller units of operation.

A large variety of considerations of this sort militate toward the conclusion that whenever an agreed-upon goal can be pursued without the state assuming the responsibility of implemention, then this should be done on grounds of feasibility.

In general and *in abstracto* the issue of feasibility turns on matters of cost-effectiveness. Its governing concern is with the question, "Are the specific measures of regulation and control so operable that the benefits at issue with *desirability* are achieved at a practicable cost?" And the costs at issue must be estimated not just in economic terms but in social terms as well, including such matters as a diminution of the liberty of the individual.

THE RATIONALE OF STATE INTERVENTION

Let us pause to consolidate the implications of the preceding deliberations. They indicate that it only makes sense to assign a regulative function to the state—even an inherently meritorious one—when certain conditions are met:

1. Exercise of the regulative function at issue would actually be desirable in terms of the public interest.

2. There is reason to think that the state will prove (in absolute terms) reasonably efficient and effective in achieving the regulative functions at issue, and moreover that it will prove (in relative terms) more efficient and effective than alternative mechanisms would.

3. The overall costs and negative effects incurred through the state's assumption of control are significantly outweighed by the benefits resulting from such control.

From this analysis, then, it emerges that a complex series of conditions must be met if state control or regulation of the personal or economic dealings of its citizenry is to be properly legitimated. Specifically, a convincing case must be established for believing that (1) in the absence of the particular control or regulations there is a real risk of significant harm to individuals or of serious impairment of the public interest; (2) there is reasonable assurance that this danger will be avoided or significantly diminished by the controls at issue; (3) no alternative device less awesome and less cumbersome than actual state intervention is available for attaining the desiderata; and (4) the overall costs and disabilities of implementing the particular controls and regulations in an acceptably efficient and effective way do not exceed the benefits being realized.

Such a process of assessment involves a number of distinct but important factors: (1) the gravity of the potential risk; (2) the probability of the potential risk's realization; (3) the cost of the proposed measures (including the realization that we may be paying an assured price for averting a merely possible danger); and (4) the likelihood that the proposed measures will actually *avert* the potential risk (and not simply deflect it into other channels).

These considerations illuminate the difficulties inherent in establishing a legitimating rationale for measures of state control and regulation. Indeed, they establish a powerful presumption against all such measures. But this presumption is certainly not indefeasible. Although the difficulties in question are real, they are not insuperable. Consider an example of the current standard security measures of weapons control imposed on airline passengers. They do exact from all concerned a price in terms of increased expense, added delays, and some degree of invasion of privacy. But they do provide a substantial benefit in terms of diminishing the inconvenience and safety risks involved in aircraft hijackings. Accordingly, one can reasonably argue in this case that the benefits outweigh the costs and that such controls and regulations are legitimate.

On the other hand, there can be little doubt that this is not true of much current governmental regulation in the economic and social areas. Instances of major expenditures in time, energy, and resources for the realization of minor or nonexistent benefits are legion. To take just one example, the annual cost to society of the paperwork generated by the federal government's insatiable demand for information was estimated at some $100 billion in 1977. Certainly the vast bulk of this cannot be justified on cost-benefit considerations of the sort operative in validating measures of governmental regulation and control.

With respect to feasibility, it must surely be conceded that in some instances we cannot be assured of knowing beforehand if the state can actually administer particular regulations or controls efficiently and effectively—whether, for example, governmental funding of scientific research facilities in colleges and universities will help or hinder the research process it is designed to facilitate. The dangers are certainly there. A program of statutory regulation often makes a leap in the dark—creating a monster that dwarfs the evils it is designed to remedy. (Prohibition affords a good example of this.) Whenever possible it is wisest to proceed by a slow and tentatively experimental process, lest relatively minor evils be traded for even greater ones. (And one of the real problems is that in this sphere of governmental action a "slow and experimental process" is well-nigh impossible to realize.)

QUESTIONS OF PRESUMPTION

It is important to recognize that regulation and control are matters of degree that admit of infinitely varied shadings and gradations. At the top of the scale we have the state's determination as to whether a certain type of good or service should be banned altogether (the sale of fireworks, the screening of pornographic films, the purchase of armaments by private individuals). At the next level come controls over who can provide or receive certain goods or services (child-labor laws, licensing of professionals or airlines or radio stations, licensing of purchases of certain "dangerous" products, etc.). Then come regulations about conditions of operation (closing times for bars). Near the bottom come the mere requirements to provide information (regarding certain banking transactions, for example).

Now in a democratic society there must always be a strong presumption against the control and regulation of individual action by the state. The need for a maximum range of individual liberty is axiomatic within the democratic ethos.

Recognition of the fact that regulation and control *can* be justified is simply the first step toward recognizing that they *must* be justified—that they are not proper and legitimate unless we make sure cost-benefit conditions are satisfied, conditions such as those illustrated in our preceding discussion. The presumption is always against government intervention and in favor of things being allowed to run their own course.

Accordingly, even in cases where state regulation and control is desirable and feasible, it is also desirable that it be accomplished at the minimum level of intervention. Every move toward control or regulation, and every step up the ladder of increased intervention levels must prove itself in terms of benefits to be actually realized.

But while there is a presumption in favor of unfettered liberty, this is certainly a defeasible presumption. We do not operate an unfettered free market in the provision of medical services, or of land utilization because the school of bitter experience has taught us that the consequences are unacceptable. And this is the important factor, for it takes a clear and present danger—a very real risk of some substantial sort—to reverse this standing presumption in favor of "the liberty of the subject."

THE RECENT AGGRANDIZEMENT OF STATE FUNCTIONS

Historically the state has sought to intervene in the affairs of its citizens when necessary for: (1) the survival or aggrandizement of the state itself; (2) the physical safety and well-being of its citizens; (3) the peaceable and orderly settlement of interpersonal dealings; and (4) the creation of major public works and facilities. Considerations of the first kind would yield such measures as the impressment of seamen, conscription in time of war, and the launching of colonies. Those of the second kind would underwrite the quarantine of the victim of a dangerous communicable disease or the maintenance of police forces or the construction of aqueducts. Considerations of the third kind lead the state into the regulation of inheritance, the mechanisms of commercial transaction (including, for example, the management of the coinage, the regulation of property transfers, and other aspects of the economic interaction of one person with another). Finally, those of the fourth kind bring the state into the business of building roads, constructing harbors, or exploring distant shores.

self-evident

However, the past hundred years have seen a major change, with the state assuming substantial functions beyond the four traditional areas of national security, public safety, the settlement of interpersonal disputes, and public works. Specifically, the state has come to assume responsibility for the *economic well-being* of its citizenry and for the "quality of life" in a broader, noneconomic sense that embraces various *social desiderata,* particularly those of promoting equality of opportunity and access.

In respect to these latter items, the question of expediency that has preoccupied us throughout these pages now becomes especially significant; for this question looms extra large with respect to these "new" state functions, seeing that, historically speaking, the state has not evolved with a view to handling these new functions, and that it has had to develop new and sometimes problematic devices to meet them—especially by developing a vastly enlarged and diffused regulative bureaucracy. To clarify this issue, it is useful to look somewhat closely at a particularly important special case: the pursuit of egalitarianism.

EGALITARIANISM AS A SPECIAL CASE

The realization of egalitarian arrangements is something that by its very nature invites state intervention. For only action and coordination at the grandest and most inclusive level can assume uniformity of procedure and process. Thus, a great part of the modern state's best efforts at control and regulation is motivated by the pursuit of justice, fairness, equality of access and distribution, and other such egalitarian goals.

It is at this point that the potential discord between desirability and expediency comes into prominence, for the pursuit of egalitarianism, doubtless laudable as an end, can run into trouble when the correlative measures of regulation and control come to exert—as they inevitably must—a powerful feedback impetus upon the process being controlled. Thus rent-control measures can lose their effectiveness if they engender economic distortions that eliminate the availability of rental property. Or again, there is no point in promoting equality of access to medical services by means that seriously diminish the quality or quantity of the services being delivered.

There is, in sum, no sense in striving for equality of access and distribution by means that degrade significantly the resources available for distribution. A society can only distribute the goods and services it manages to produce. But the egalitarian ethos of our time all too easily fails to deal realistically with this factor of productivity. Consider the following two distributions of shares to individuals:

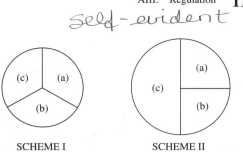

SCHEME I   SCHEME II

Patently Scheme I effects the fairer (indeed a perfectly fair) distribution. From the standpoint of "justice in the narrower sense" it has the clear-cut advantage. But that Scheme II is superior from the standpoint of the interests of all concerned is equally clear: everyone would be the gainer by its adoption. Despite its less *fair* distribution, the advantage from the standpoint of "justice in the wider sense" lies with this scheme. An adequate theory for the evaluation of distributions cannot confine its attention to fairness alone, but must also take into account the crucial factor of production.

Examples of the sort previously indicated underline the critical importance of a principle of production for determining the expediency of regulatory and control measures. Due heed of these factors soon forces the recognition that we must be prepared to acknowledge the superiority of "unfair" distributions whose unfairness "pays for itself" by conducing to the general advantage. We may well be prepared to tolerate discrepancies in the fairness of a distribution in contexts where these *could only be removed by exacting an unreasonable price* from all or most or the least well-off of the individuals involved.

In this connection it is necessary to reemphasize the deliberation already mentioned that the pursuit of inherently desirable ends can run into problems of expediency when it exacts too great a price in the attainment of other desiderata. It can—and often does—happen that measures that, inherently and in themselves, are incontestably desirable create a systematic feedback so that their operation exacts a price not commensurate with the expected benefits. And this sort of phenomenon can totally undermine, on grounds of *expediency,* the legitimacy of measures of control and regulation that aim at inherently proper and desirable objectives.

ENDNOTE

1. In actuality this position is overly simplistic since its conception of rightness is too legalistic and overlooks the underlying issue of justness. Certainly the measures of control or regulation at issue could be unjust—in being discriminatory, for example. For the methodological purposes of this essay we may, however, adopt a suspension of disbelief in this regard.

QUESTIONS ON RESCHER

1. How do you think Rescher understands the concept of "regulation"? Is his concept too broad or not broad enough?

2. Restate in your own words the three criteria for regulation. Do you think these criteria are justified? Do these criteria create a high threshold for the legitimacy of any regulation? Explain.

3. Is egalitarianism "doubtless laudable as an end"? On the other hand, is Scheme II preferable to Scheme I?

Paradoxes of the Regulatory State

Cass R. Sunstein

Cass Sunstein is a Professor of Law and Political Science at the University of Chicago and the author of Democracy and the Problem of Free Speech *(1993),* Legal Reasoning and Political Conflict *(1996), among other books and essays. This essay is excerpted from* Free Markets and Social Justice *(1997).*

By "paradoxes of the regulatory state," I mean self-defeating regulatory strategies—strategies that achieve an end precisely opposite to the one intended, or to the only public-regarding justification that can be brought forward in their support. An example of a regulatory paradox would be a Clean Air Act that actually made the air dirtier, or a civil rights law that increased the incidence of racial discrimination. This definition excludes a number of pathologies of the regulatory state that are clearly related to the phenomenon of regulatory paradoxes, such as strategies whose costs exceed their benefits, or that have unintended adverse consequences. I am interested only in self-defeating regulatory strategies here.

A large literature, inspired by public choice theory and welfare economics, has grown up around the theory that purportedly public-interested regulation is almost always an effort to create a cartel or to serve some private interest at the public expense. Although I shall be drawing on much of that literature here, I do not conclude, as some of that literature appears to, that the appropriate response to regulatory paradoxes is to abandon modern regulation altogether and rest content with the operation of private markets. In many cases, the market itself produces harmful or even disastrous results, measured in terms of efficiency or justice. The appropriate response to the paradoxes of regulation is not to return to a system of "laissez faire," but to learn from past failures. To this end, I outline the lessons, for legislators, judges, and administrators, that are to be drawn from the omnipresence of regulatory paradoxes. My general goal is to describe some reforms by which to restructure regulatory institutions so as to achieve their often salutary purposes, while at the same time incorporating the flexibility, respect for individual autonomy and initiative, and productive potential of economic markets.

I. THE PERFORMANCE OF THE REGULATORY STATE: A PREFATORY NOTE

Empirical assessments of the consequences of regulation remain in a primitive state; but it is possible to draw several general conclusions. I outline some of them here.

In many ways things are getting better, not worse. The average American's life expectancy at birth was 47 years in 1900; it rose to 78 in 1990, partly because the death rate from infectious diseases is less than 5 percent, down from 20 percent in 1900. . . .

Undoubtedly many of these improvements come from social changes having nothing to do with regulation. But the view that regulation has generally proved unsuccessful is far too crude. Some of the progress comes from more and better immunizations, better nutrition, and improved water and sanitation systems, some of which is a result of governmental activity and regulatory controls. In fact, environmental protection has produced enormous gains.[1] Regulatory controls have helped to produce substantial decreases in both the levels and emissions of major pollutants, including sulfur dioxide, carbon monoxide, lead, and nitrogen dioxide. Lead is an especially dangerous substance, and ambient concentrations of lead have decreased especially dramatically, declining 96 percent since 1975; transportation emissions of lead decreased from 122.6 million metric tons in 1975 to 3.5 in 1986. The EPA's phase-down of lead in gasoline was firmly supported by cost-benefit analysis. So, too, carbon monoxide levels fell 57 percent from 1975 to 1991; nixtrous oxide levels fell about 24 percent; and particulate levels fell 26 percent. Most important, the vast majority of counties in the United States are now in compliance with air quality goals. In 1982, about 100 million people lived in nonattainment areas; in 1994, the number was about 54 million.

Water pollution control has shown significant successes as well. Perhaps most important, all sewage in the nation is treated before it is discharged, and the treatment ordinarily brings water to a level safe for swimming. There are many successes with respect to particular water bodies. The Great Lakes are much cleaner than they were in 1965. Phosphorus loading is, for example, substantially down, somewhere between 40 and 70 percent less than in peak years. Levels of PCBs in the Great Lakes are almost 90 percent lower than they were in 1973.

In addition, a number of harmful nutrients have been reduced by nearly 50 percent in national rivers. In 1970, about 25 percent of U.S. river miles were safe for fishing and swimming; the number is now about 56 percent. Industrial pollutants in Chesapeake Bay fell by 53 percent in the brief period from 1988 to 1992. Governmentally required lead and nitrate reductions have produced huge improvements in water quality. Ocean dumping of sludge is now substantially eliminated in the United States. All in all, both air and water are substantially cleaner than they would have been without regulatory controls, and despite a wide range of errors, the American experience serves in some respects as a model for the rest of the world. People continue to be very much concerned about toxic waste sites. But it is notable that since the enactment of the Solid Waste Disposal Act, nearly all toxic byproducts are disposed of in safe ways, and new toxic waste "dumps" are almost entirely a thing of the past.

The risk of a fatal accident in the workplace was reduced by 50 percent between 1970 and 1990, partly because of workers' compensation, occupational safety and health, and other programs. Similarly, automobile safety regulation has significantly reduced deaths and serious injuries.[2] Automobiles are much safer for occupants, and many of the safety-improving features of automobiles are a product of regulatory controls supported by cost-benefit balancing. For example, the requirement that all cars have center-high mounted stop lamps was shown to be highly effective in reducing rear-end collisions. More generally, highway fatalities would have been about 40 percent higher in 1981 if not for governmental controls.[3] Between 1966 and 1974, the lives of about 34,000 passenger car occupants were saved as a result of occupant safety standards. The annual benefits from regulation exceed ten billion dollars. For automobile regulation, in general, the ratio of benefits to costs is extremely high. Indeed, some of the regulations pay for themselves in terms of health and related savings, and the large number of deaths actually prevented is of course a bonus.

More broadly, studies of the costs and benefits of regulatory initiatives show that a number of other measures have produced health and other benefits at especially low costs. Of course, it would be foolish to suggest that government regulation in its current form passes a global cost-benefit test. There is much indeterminacy in the data, and certainly many regulatory efforts have been futile, self-defeating, counterproductive, or much worse. But every detailed study shows a number of regulations that have saved lives at comparatively low cost. . . .

Finally, regulatory successes are not limited to the areas of safety and health. The most important civil rights initiative—the Voting Rights Act of 1965—appears to have broken up the white monopoly on electoral processes in a number of states. Only two years after passage of the Act, the number of registered blacks in the eleven southern states increased from 1.5 million to 2.8 million—an increase of nearly 90 percent. This is an impressive illustration of regulatory success.

Now turn away from voting rights and toward discrimination in general. Though the evidence is more disputed, the better view is that the Civil Rights Act of 1964 has also had important beneficial consequences. The most careful and impressive study shows that this Act had major effects on the manufacturing sector in South Carolina. "Suddenly in 1965 the black share in employment begins to improve when Title VII legislation becomes effective and the Equal Employment Opportunity Commission begins to press textile firms to employ blacks and when Executive Order 11246 forbids discrimination by government contractors at the risk of forfeit of government business."[4] Many other studies reach a broadly similar conclusion: The federal effort to redress race discrimination has had many favorable consequences. There have been gains in the area of sex discrimination as well.

Finally, the Endangered Species Act has saved a number of species from extinction and endangerment.[5] Thus the American bald eagle was, in 1963, thought to be on the verge of extinction; it is now doing much better, and in 1995 its status was shifted from "endangered" to merely "threatened." The number of gray wolves in Minnesota has grown from 500 to 1750 in a relatively short time; there are now about 10,000 adult peregrine falcons in the United States, compared with very few in the early 1970s; sea lions had declined to a population of 30,000 in 1972 and are now up to 180,000; California gray whales recovered to a population of 21,000 in 1994, when they were removed from the list under the Endangered Species Act. In fact, of the 71 species initially listed under the Act in 1973, only seven are gone, and 44 are stable or improving.

On the other hand, regulation has frequently failed. Sometimes it has imposed enormously high costs for speculative benefits; sometimes it has accomplished little or nothing; sometimes it has aggravated the very problem it was designed to solve. For example, the United States spent no less than $632 billion for pollution control between 1972 and 1985, and some studies suggest that alternative strategies could have achieved the same gains at less than one-fifth the cost. There is no doubt that environmental and safety regulation have taken an unnecessarily high toll on the productivity of the American economy. Studies show reduced output in the economy as a whole as 2.5 percent, with a cumulative impact through 1986 of 11.4 percent from the level that would have been achieved without OSHA and EPA regulation.[6]

The fuel economy standards for new cars appear to have produced no substantial independent gains in fuel economy; consumer demands for fuel efficient cars, in response to gas shortages and high gas prices, were leading in the same direction. Worse, the fuel economy standards have led manufacturers to produce smaller, more dangerous cars; an estimated 2200–3900 mortalities were expected over a ten-year period as a result of regulatory changes in 1989 alone.[7] There is little question that the administration of the Natural Gas Act helped produce the energy crisis of the late 1970s—with huge attendant costs to investment and employment—by artificially restraining the price of gas.[8] Some of OSHA's carcinogen regulations impose enormous costs for uncertain gains. Indeed, the pattern of OSHA regulation of carcinogens is a crazy quilt; regulations costing up to $40 million per life saved exist in some areas, with no regulations at all in others. By delaying the entry of beneficial drugs into the market, the Food and Drug Administration has, in many settings, dramatically increased risks to life and health.[9]

Ironically, a large source of regulatory failure in the United States is the use of Soviet-style command-and-control regulation, which dictates, at the national level, technologies and control strategies for hundreds, thousands, or millions of companies and individuals in a nation that is exceptionally diverse in terms of geography, costs and benefits of regulatory controls, attitudes, and mores. A valuable perspective on this problem can be obtained by examining the paradoxes of regulation, which pose a particular dilemma for the administrative state. A government that eliminated self-defeating regulatory strategies would eliminate a significant source of regulatory failure. And although the paradoxes are numerous, six of them have been of major importance in the last generation.

II. THE PARADOXES

I have defined a regulatory paradox as a self-defeating regulatory strategy; but whether a strategy is self-defeating depends on how its purposes are described. Any statute that fails to produce a net benefit to society can be described as self-defeating if its purpose is described as the net improvement of the world. But if the statute's purpose is to benefit a particular group or segment of society, and that purpose is achieved, then the statute is not self-defeating at all. For example, a statute benefiting the agricultural industry at the expense of the public will not be self-defeating if its purpose is described as helping farmers. Throughout this discussion I describe the relevant statutory purposes as public-regarding rather than as benefiting special interest groups.

Moreover, I mean to assess whether a statute is self-defeating by comparing the result it has produced with the likely state of affairs had Congress either enacted a different and better statute or enacted no statute at all. Measured against either of these benchmarks, regulation has produced a wide range of paradoxes.

Importantly, nearly all of the paradoxes are a product of the government's failure to understand how the relevant actors—administrators and regulated entities—will adapt to regulatory programs. The world cannot be held constant after regulations have been issued. Strategic responses, the creation of perverse incentives for administrators and regulated entities, unanticipated changes in product mix and private choice—these are the hallmarks of the paradoxes of the regulatory state. The adoption of strategies that take account of these phenomena would produce enormous savings in both compliance costs and safety and health gains.

Paradox 1: Overregulation Produces Underregulation

The first paradox is that especially aggressive statutory controls frequently produce too little regulation of the private market. This surprising outcome arises when Congress mandates overly stringent controls, so that administrators will not issue regulations at all or will refuse to enforce whatever regulations they or Congress have issued.

The imposition of extremely stringent controls on regulated industries is a common strategy in Congress. Such controls typically ban cost-benefit balancing or indeed trade-offs of any sort. The expectation is that these controls will bring about safety in the workplace, or clean air and water, even if both the agency and industry are reluctant to act, and even if the costs of regulation are high. This strategy was especially popular during the dramatic growth of regulation in the 1960s and 1970s. It both fueled and was fueled by the notion that a safe workplace, or clean air and water, should be treated as involving a right to be vindicated rather than a risk to be managed. Consider President Nixon's proclamation: "Clean air, clean water, open spaces— these should again be the birthright for every American."[10] This form of rights-based thinking was also inspired by evidence that recalcitrant agencies, suffering from inertia or immobilized by the power of well-organized private groups, frequently refused to enforce regulatory controls.

The strategy of imposing stringent regulatory controls or banning cost-benefit balancing is not impossible to understand. It might seem natural to think that if air pollution is a severe problem, the correct response is to reduce it as much as possible; and this idea quickly translates into a command to the EPA to reduce dangerous substances in the atmosphere to a level that will not adversely affect human health. Certainly this seems like a natural thought if health or safety is conceived as a right. Similarly, an obvious method for controlling toxic substances in the workplace is to tell OSHA to eliminate these substances "to the extent feasible." Such strategies might produce too much regulation, but this might be thought a small price to pay for (finally) reducing pollution in the air or deaths in the workplace. In addition, a prohibition on "balancing" might be thought desirable by those fearful that any effort to balance would be distorted by the enforcement agency's undervaluation of life and health, especially in the context of seemingly permanent political divisions between the executive and the legislative branches of government.

But consider the record of both the EPA and OSHA in these settings. Of the several hundred toxic substances plausibly posing significant risks to human health, the EPA had for a long period regulated only seven—five as a result of court orders. The Clean Air Act's severe provisions for listed pollutants, operating in rule-like fashion, led the Environmental Protection Agency to stop listing pollutants at all. Thus, the Act's strict duties of response to danger prompted officials not to recognize the dangers in the first instance. Of the many toxic substances in the workplace, OSHA had for a long time controlled only ten. Stunningly, this is so even though the private organization that once performed some of OSHA's functions had recommended lower exposure limits for hundreds of chemicals.[11] To be sure, those substances that EPA and OSHA regulate

are stringently controlled. The regulatory pattern, however, includes not only substantial overregulation of the substances that are subject to federal standards, but also, and possibly more serious, substantial underregulation of dangerous substances, such as chromium, perchloroethylene, and trichloroethylene.

Despite the stringency of statutory standards, many activities in the United States are entirely free from regulatory controls. There is no evidence that the United States generally does a better job than England in protecting workers and citizens from occupational and environmental hazards, even though the English system consciously allows balancing in most contexts and the American system consciously rejects it.[12] Compare in this regard the pattern under rigid criminal statutes, including the "three strikes and you're out policy" for felons and mandatory minimum sentences. These have often produced underregulation by encouraging prosecutors to indict for lesser charges or by leading prosecutors not to enforce at all.

Statutes containing stringent regulatory requirements have thus yielded no protection at all in many settings. What is responsible for this astonishing outcome? It might be tempting to find answers in the power of regulated industries or in the intransigence and deregulatory zeal of government officials. But the pattern of underregulation can be found in the Carter Administration as well as the Reagan Administration, even though President Carter's appointees, drawn in large number from the consumer and environmental movements, were hardly eager to prevent the government from curbing the proliferation of toxic substances. Elaborate and costly procedural requirements for the promulgation of federal regulations undoubtedly provide some explanation, since the process, including judicial review, has built into it enormous delays and perverse incentives. These requirements surely slow down and deter rule making. Industry has every opportunity and every incentive to fend off regulation by making plausible claims that additional information is necessary before regulation can be undertaken. Here we have a subparadox that might explain the overregulation–underregulation paradox: Procedural protections designed to improve agency rule making may lead to little or no agency rule making. This explanation is not in itself adequate, however, because organized interests have not prevented agencies from being far more aggressive in other settings.

A large part of the explanation lies in the stringency of the regulatory standard itself. A stringent standard—one that forbids balancing or calls for regulation to or beyond the point of "feasibility"—makes regulators reluctant to act. If, as is customary, regulators have discretion not to promulgate regulations at all, a stringent standard will provide them with a powerful incentive for inaction. Their inaction is not caused by venality or confusion. Instead, it reflects their quite plausible belief that the statute often requires them to regulate to an absurd point. If regulators were to issue controls under the statute, government and private resources would be less available to control other toxic substances; domestic industry costs would increase; ultimately, industries competing in world markets would face a serious risk of shutdown. Under these circumstances, a stringent standard will mobilize political opposition to regulation from within and without government. It will also increase the likelihood of judicial invalidation. Finally, it will require agencies to obtain greater supporting information to survive political and judicial scrutiny, while at the same time making it less likely that such information will be forthcoming from regulated class members. All the incentives are therefore in the direction of issuing fewer regulations.

It is thus unsurprising that a draconian standard produces underregulation as well as overregulation. A crazy quilt pattern of severe controls in some areas and none in others is the predictable consequence of a statute that forbids balancing and trade-offs.

The problem goes deeper still. Even if the resistance of the agency has been overcome, and some or many regulations have been issued under a statute calling for stringent regulatory controls, the risk of underregulation does not disappear. Levels of enforcement—inspections and fines—will reflect the agency's reluctance. This has in fact been the pattern with OSHA's safety and health regulations, some of which have been effectively unenforced by Democratic as well as Republican administrations. This, then, is the first paradox of the regulatory state: Stringent regulatory standards produce underregulation.

Paradox 2: Stringent Regulation of New Risks Can Increase Aggregate Risk Levels

Congress is often presented with a risk or problem that can be found in both existing entities and in potential new entrants. For example, automobiles produce carbon monoxide; modern electricity plants emit sulfur dioxide; many existing buildings are inaccessible to the handicapped; and drugs currently on the market pose health hazards to consumers. In such situations, a common strategy has been to impose especially severe limitations on new sources but to exempt old ones. Indeed, such exemptions might be a political prerequisite for enactment of the regulation, since existing companies might otherwise fight very hard against enactment. Congress might require that new automobiles be equipped with pollution control devices, that new plants emitting pollution meet stringent regulatory controls, that new buildings be accessible to the handicapped, and that new drugs survive special safety requirements.

This strategy is a pervasive one in current regulatory law, and it has obvious advantages.[13] Retroactive application of regulatory requirements can be extremely costly; the expense of altering existing practices is often high. Requiring the specified approach only prospectively can achieve significant savings. In addition, it may seem unfair to impose costs on people who would have ordered their affairs quite differently had they been informed beforehand of the regulatory regime.

As a control technique, however, the strategy of imposing costs exclusively on new sources or entrants can be self-defeating. Most important, it will discourage the addition of new sources and encourage the perpetuation of old ones. The problem is not merely that old risks will continue, but that precisely because of regulatory programs, those risks will become more common and last longer—perhaps much longer—than they otherwise would.

Two different phenomena underlie the old risk–new risk paradox. First, those who plan regulatory programs often assume that the programs will not influence private choices. Private choices are, however, a function of current supply and demand. If the program raises the price of new products, it will shift choices in the direction of old risks. Second, a focus on new risks reduces the likely entry of potentially superior sources or technologies and thus perpetuates old ones. Regulatory controls eliminate possibilities that might have turned out to be substantially safer than currently available options. The result is to increase the life of those options.

Examples are not difficult to find. The EPA's program requiring the installation of antipollution technology in new automobiles belongs in the first category. This program has prolonged the use of old, dirty vehicles, retarding the ordinary, salutary retirement of major sources of environmental degradation. Command-and-control regulation of new pollution sources creates incentives to use existing facilities longer, with harmful consequences for the environment. Imposition of high, safety-related costs on new airplanes may well encourage airlines to retain (and repair) old, risky planes.

We might put the EPA's requirement of costly "scrubbing" strategies for new sources of sulfur dioxide in the second category. This rule has perpetuated the existence of old sources of sulfur dioxide, thus aggravating in many parts of the country the very problem it was designed to solve.[14] So too, the imposition of stringent barriers to nuclear power plants has perpetuated the risks produced by coal, a significantly more dangerous power source. And perhaps worst of all, the FDA's stringent regulatory standards for approving new drugs have forced consumers to resort to old drugs, which are frequently more dangerous, more costly, or less beneficial than the new drugs being kept off the market.

A final example of the old risk–new risk paradox is the Delaney Clause, which prohibits manufacturers from using food additives containing carcinogens. Ironically, this provision has probably increased safety and health risks. The Clause forces manufacturers to use noncarcinogenic, but sometimes more dangerous, substances. In addition, it makes consumers resort to substances already on the market that often pose greater risks than new entrants would. Since the newest and best detection equipment is used on proposed new additives, the statutorily prohibited additive may well pose fewer risks to consumers than substances already on the market that were tested with cruder technology. The Delaney Clause defeats its own purpose.[15]

The phenomenon of careful regulation of new risks and lenient or no regulation of old ones may not simply reflect legislative myopia or confusion. Public choice theory provides a plausible explanation for the phenomenon. A system of regulation that imposes controls solely on new products or facilities should have considerable appeal for those in possession of old ones. If new sources will face regulatory costs, the system of government controls will immunize existing producers from fresh competition. Indeed, the regulatory statute will create a partial cartel, establishing a common interest among current producers and giving them a significant competitive advantage over potential new entrants. The victims of the old-new division, however, often do not yet exist. They are usually hard to identify, do not perceive themselves as victims, and are not politically organized.

It may be for this reason that the careful regulation of new risks is such a popular strategy. It is apt to be favored both by existing industry and by many of those who seek to impose controls in the first instance. The potential victims—consumers and new entrants—often have insufficient political strength to counter the proposals. When this phenomenon is combined with the ap-

parently sensible but sometimes self-defeating idea that a phase-in strategy is better than one that requires conversions of existing producers, it is no surprise that the old risk–new risk division remains so popular. It is a perverse strategy, but it is likely to continue, at least so long as there is no shift from command-and-control regulation to economic incentives.

Paradox 3: To Require the Best Available Technology Is to Retard Technological Development

Industry frequently fails to adopt the best technology for controlling environmental or other harms. The technology exists or can be developed relatively cheaply, but polluters simply refuse to use it. Congress and the EPA have often responded by requiring that all industries use the best available technology (BAT). The BAT strategy is pervasive in federal environmental law and may indeed be its most distinctive characteristic.

The BAT strategy is motivated by a desire to produce technological innovation, and here it has a surface plausibility. As discussed previously, recent years have witnessed large decreases in air and water pollution, and these decreases are partly attributable to the use of emission control technologies. Requiring the adoption of the best available control technology seems a sensible way to ensure that all industries are doing their utmost to prevent pollution. This strategy also appears inexpensive to enforce. The government simply decides on the best technology and then requires all industries to comply.

The BAT approach, however, can defeat its own purposes and thus produce a regulatory paradox. It is an extremely clumsy strategy for protecting the environment. To be sure, the approach is a plausible one if the goal is to ensure that all firms use currently established technology. But a large goal of regulation should be to promote technological innovation in pollution control. Regulation should increase rather than decrease incentives to innovate. Government is rarely in a good position to know what sorts of innovations are likely to be forthcoming; industry will have a huge comparative advantage here. Perversely, requiring adoption of the BAT eliminates the incentive to innovate at all, and indeed creates disincentives for innovation by imposing an economic punishment on innovators. Under the BAT approach, polluting industries have no financial interest in the development of better pollution control technology that imposes higher production costs. Indeed, the opposite is true. The BAT approach encourages industry to seek any means to delay and deter new regulation.

Industry will have the information as well as the incentive to persuade administrators, courts, and other authorities that a suggested technology is not "feasible" and should not be required.

If government requires whatever technology is available, then, industry has no economic incentive to develop new mechanisms for decreasing safety and health risks. Moreover, the BAT approach, applicable as it is only to new sources, raises the cost of retiring old facilities, which delays capital turnover and in that way aggravates environmental degradation. The paradox, in a nutshell, is this: Designed to promote good control technology, the BAT strategy actually discourages innovation. It is therefore self-defeating.

Paradox 4: Redistributive Regulation Harms Those at the Bottom of the Socioeconomic Ladder

A common justification for regulation is redistribution. The legislature imposes controls on the market to prevent what it sees as exploitation or unfair dealing by those with a competitive advantage. In principle, the claim for redistribution is often a powerful one. People often enter into harsh deals, simply because their options are so few. In fact, market wages and prices depend on a wide range of factors that are morally irrelevant: supply and demand curves at any particular point; variations in family structure and opportunities for education and employment; existing tastes; and perhaps even differences in initial endowments, including talents, intelligence, or physical strength. So long as the regulation can be made effective and does not produce high ancillary costs (an important qualification), government should not always take these factors as "natural," or let them be turned into social disadvantages.

The inspiration for minimum wage legislation, for example, is easy to identify. Such legislation prevents workers from having to settle for market wages that do not even approach the poverty level and thus offer minimal incentives to work. So, too, occupational safety statutes protect workers against extremely hazardous workplaces; rent control legislation prevents tenants from being subject to unanticipated price increases and perhaps thrown into significantly inferior housing; and implied warranties of habitability protect tenants from living in disgraceful and indeed dangerous apartments.

In all these cases, however, regulation is a poor mechanism for redistributing resources, precisely because it is often self-defeating. The problem is that if everything else is held constant, the market will fre-

quently adjust to the imposition of regulation in a way that will harm the least well off. It is a mistake to assume that regulation will directly transfer resources or create only ex-post winners and losers—an idea exemplified by the assumption that the only effect of the minimum wage is to raise wages for those currently working. An important consequence of the minimum wage is to increase unemployment by raising the price of marginal labor; and those at the bottom of the ladder—the most vulnerable members of society—are the victims.[16] In the same vein, rent control legislation and implied warranties of habitability create incentives for producers (landlords) to leave and disincentives to enter the housing market, with perverse redistributive consequences and especially harsh results for the poor, who may be left without housing at all.[17] It should not be surprising to find that Cambridge, Massachusetts has experienced a dramatic growth in new housing since rent control has been eliminated by state referendum.

Laws forbidding discrimination or requiring affirmative action will to some extent have the same perverse effect, since they will make it more expensive to hire blacks, women, and older people by increasing the likelihood that employers will be subject to a lawsuit in the event of a discharge.[18] Similarly, occupational safety and health regulation does not unambiguously promote the interests of workers. By raising costs, it may depress wages and increase unemployment, thus harming the least well off. In each of these cases, the group that is harmed is likely to be poorly organized and incapable of expressing itself through the political process.

In sum, redistributive regulation will have complex distributive consequences, and the group particularly disadvantaged by the regulation will typically consist of those who are already most disadvantaged. Efforts to redistribute resources through regulation can therefore have serious perverse results.

Three qualifications are necessary here. First, the redistributive regulation, though in some ways perverse, might be part of a system of redistribution that is effective overall. A minimum wage law might be justified as a means of protecting the working poor, if it is accompanied by a welfare system to take care of those who cannot work at all. For this reason, plausible arguments can be made for the minimum wage. It has been argued, for example, that an increase in the minimum wage is necessary to guarantee that work will be sufficiently remunerative to keep people out of poverty and to send a signal about the importance and value of work, thereby increasing the supply of and demand for labor. These effects might outweigh any unemployment effect.

A second qualification of the redistribution paradox relates to the fact that preferences are not static. Preferences are usually taken as exogenous to and independent of the legal rule, but sometimes this is a mistake. If the statute in question transforms preferences and beliefs, the self-defeating effect just described will not occur. For example, laws forbidding sexual harassment aim to alter the desires and beliefs of would-be harassers; and if the laws succeed in this goal, any perverse side effects may be minimal or nonexistent. The same argument may apply to antidiscrimination laws generally. If such laws change attitudes, they may not on balance harm the least well off. There is, however, little empirical evidence on the effects of law in changing preferences and beliefs, and, in any case, this is not likely to result from such redistributive regulation as minimum wage legislation.

The third qualification is that laws that seem to be justified on redistributive grounds are best understood as a response to inadequate information. Occupational safety and health legislation does not transfer resources from employers to employees; but it may be justified as a response to the fact that workers lack information about workplace risks. In the face of inadequate information, a regulatory response may well make sense. In fact, a well-tailored response will make workers better off. But this point leads directly to our fifth paradox.

Paradox 5: Disclosure Requirements May Make People Less Informed

Sometimes markets fail because people are deceived or lack information. Regulatory agencies commonly respond by requiring correction or full disclosure. Congress and agencies have imposed disclosure regulations in many areas, ranging from occupational and environmental risks to potentially deceptive advertising. Here the rationale is straightforward. Whether or not ignorance is bliss, it is an obstacle to informed choice. Surely, it might be asked, regulation cannot be condemned for increasing information?

Disclosure strategies are indeed valuable in many circumstances. But for two reasons, they can be self-defeating. The first is that people sometimes process information poorly. After being given certain data, they actually "know" less than they did beforehand. In particular, when people receive information about probabilities, especially low ones, they frequently rely on heuristics that lead to systematic errors. Thus, for example, people assess probabilities by asking if the event was a recent one, by seeing if an example comes

readily to mind, and by misunderstanding the phenomenon of regression to the mean. In addition, disclosure or corrective language can help straighten out one form of false belief but at the same time increase the level of other kinds of false beliefs.[19] Finally, there is a risk of information overload, causing consumers to treat a large amount of information as equivalent to no information at all.[20] All this suggests that with respect to information, less may be more. Additional information can breed confusion and a weaker understanding of the situation at hand.

The second problem is that a requirement of perfect accuracy will sometimes lead producers or other regulated entities to furnish no information whatsoever. For example, if producers are prohibited from advertising, unless they eliminate all potential deception or offer strong substantiation for their claims, they might not advertise at all. The result will be the removal from the market of information that is useful overall.[21] If advertisers must conduct extensive tests before they are permitted to make claims, they will be given a strong incentive to avoid making claims at all. More generally, almost all substantive advertisements will deceive at least some people in light of the exceptional heterogeneity of listeners and viewers. If this is so, efforts to eliminate deception will significantly reduce advertising with substantive content. . . .

Paradox 6: Independent Agencies Are Not Independent

The distinctive institutional legacy of the New Deal period is the "independent" regulatory agency. An agency is independent if Congress has provided that its members can be discharged by the president only for specified causes. If Congress has so provided, it is ordinarily understood that the president cannot discharge independent commissioners simply because he disagrees with their views, and that his supervisory authority is sharply limited. Independent agencies, some of them antedating the New Deal, include the Federal Trade Commission, the Federal Communications Commission, the Interstate Commerce Commission, and the National Labor Relations Board. The paradox at issue here is one of institutional design rather than substantive regulatory policy.

The argument for the independent agency stems largely from a belief in the need for expert, apolitical, and technically sophisticated administration of the laws. Even if independent agencies achieved this end, we should question the goal itself. Independent agencies often must make important judgments of value and principle, and on those judgments expertise is never decisive. Consider, for example, the decisions of the National Labor Relations Board defining what constitutes an unfair labor practice; the judgment of the FCC about whether licensees are obliged to present programming on public issues, or whether diversity on the basis of race or sex counts in favor of an applicant for a license; and the safety requirements of the Nuclear Regulatory Commission. None of these policies is based solely on technocratic judgments, and so may properly belong—at least in part—in the political rather than the regulatory sphere.

But even if we accept the premise that political independence is necessary, the fact is that independent agencies are not independent at all. Indeed, such agencies are responsive to shifts in political opinion and even to the views of the president.[22] But the problem is even worse than that. The independent agencies have generally been highly susceptible to the political pressure of well-organized private groups—perhaps even more susceptible, on balance, than executive agencies.[23] . . .

Why would agencies independent of the president be so susceptible to factional power? The phenomenon might be explained at least in part by the fact that executive agencies, precisely because they are subject to presidential control, are able to withstand the parochial pressures imposed on "independent" agencies that lack the buffer of presidential oversight. The absence of this presidential buffer leaves agencies vulnerable both to individual members and committees of Congress, which sometimes represent narrow factions and well-organized private groups with significant stakes in the outcome of regulatory decisions. Executive agencies are at least sometimes immunized from those pressures precisely because of the protective, insulating wing of the president. Ironically, independence from the president often appears to be a mechanism for increasing susceptibility to factionalism. . . .

III. TWO QUESTIONS: WHAT WE DON'T KNOW

Causation

It is tempting to react to the regulatory paradoxes by suggesting that the relevant strategies are not self-defeating at all. On the contrary, they might represent a conscious governmental choice and even, on one view, regulatory success. Public choice theory suggests that legislative outcomes are frequently a product of pressure applied by well-organized private groups. It is not

difficult to find "cartels in the closet" to account for many or all of the paradoxes and to make them seem far less mysterious.

For example, the apparently perverse effects of redistributive regulation may be actively sought by the benefited groups. On this account, the purpose of minimum wage legislation might not be to help the poor, but rather to immunize union members from competition by people who are willing to work for low wages by limiting entry into the labor market. Far from being unintended consequences, the harmful effects on those at the bottom of the economic ladder may be actively sought. Looked at from this perspective, minimum wage legislation creates a cartel among those not threatened by unemployment, benefiting them at the expense of new entrants into the labor market.

So, too, independent agencies might be created at the behest of groups that know they will have particularly strong influence over public officials not subject to presidential oversight; or Congress might create an independent agency not to ensure technocracy or neutrality, but to increase the power of its members and committees over agency decisions. Similarly, existing industry, in a bid to reduce competition, might acquiesce in or actively seek regulations distinguishing between old and new risks. It is hardly unusual for companies to enlist regulatory law in the service of cartelization.

The overregulation—underregulation phenomenon has a similar explanation. By adopting a draconian standard, legislators can claim to support the total elimination of workplace hazards or dirty air; but legislators and regulated industries know that administrators will shrink from enforcing the law. A "deal" in the form of a stringent, unenforceable standard benefits the politically powerful actors. Hence, the political economy of overregulation is similar to that of open-ended delegations of administrative authority: In both cases, legislative incentives incline Congress toward broad and appealing statutes that will not in practice harm politically powerful groups. The public is the only real loser.

Explained in this manner, the paradoxes of the regulatory state are not mysterious at all. On the contrary, they are perfectly predictable responses to electoral self-interest and to disparities in political influence.

While explanations of this sort have power in some settings, clear evidence on their behalf is often unavailable. It is of course possible that the seemingly paradoxical effects of regulatory programs actually account for their enactment. But this is only a possibility. To explain a phenomenon by reference to its consequences is bad social science, even though it is pervasive in such widely diverse disciplines as neoclassical economics, Marxism, and sociobiology.[24] In the context of the regulatory state, whether public choice explanations are good ones, rather than merely plausible stories, depends not just on the consequences of regulation, but also on a careful investigation into the actual forces that lead to regulation. In the regulatory sphere, such investigations are infrequent.

The most we can say is that the regulatory paradoxes might reflect the influence of well-organized private groups, and that in some settings there is direct or indirect evidence to support that conclusion. At least thus far, any more global conclusion is not supported by what we know about the facts.

Magnitude

Whether the regulatory paradoxes should cause major concern depends on their magnitude. Here too, much of the relevant information remains to be developed. For example, a decision to focus on new sources of pollution would be understandable if that decision would have only a minor effect in perpetuating old sources. But if the effect is substantial, the regulatory policy would almost certainly be ill-considered. Everything depends on the question: How large is the relevant effect? Similarly, the minimum wage might well be justified if its effect is the unemployment of only a few additional people. The relevant question is the elasticity of the demand for labor. Even if some people are misled by compulsory disclosure of risks, perhaps there will be sufficient gains through reducing others' ignorance to justify the regulation. And even if some producers refuse to advertise at all in the face of a substantiation requirement, perhaps the overall level of information will increase.

Critics of regulation sometimes treat the existence of unintended side effects or partly self-defeating strategies as a reason to abandon regulatory controls altogether. But in order to justify that conclusion, it is necessary to gather detailed evidence on the magnitude of the relevant effects in particular regulated markets and overall. In some contexts, regulation having some self-defeating results will on the whole make things better rather than worse. The American regulatory state, though pervaded by paradoxes, has had a number of substantial successes.

From both theory and experience, it is possible to conclude that the regulatory paradoxes will arise frequently and thus to prescribe efforts to avoid them. Certainly we have far too little information to say, as a general matter, that regulatory programs embodying the paradoxes are by virtue of that fact a bad idea on balance, at least when compared with the preregulatory status quo. Total elimination of such regulatory programs is hardly warranted. Nevertheless, a system that avoided the paradoxes would bring about major improvements. . . .

ENDNOTES

1. See John Graham and Jonathan Wiener, eds., *Risk versus Risk,* pp. 8–11 (Cambridge: Harvard University Press, 1995); Gregg Easterbrook, *A Moment on the Earth* (New York: Viking, 1995). Air and water pollution data can be found in *id.;* CEQ, 24th Annual Report, Environmental Quality (1993).
2. See Robert W. Crandall, et al., *Regulating the Automobile* (Washington, D.C.: Brookings Institution, 1986), pp. 44–74.
3. *Id.* at 75.
4. See James Heckman and John Paynor, "The Impact of Federal Antidiscrimination Policy on the Economic Status of Blacks: A study of South Carolina," 79 *Amer. Econ. Rev.* 138 (1989).
5. See Easterbrook, *supra* note 1; Steven Lewis Yaffee., *Prohibitive Policy: Implementing the Federal Endangered Species Act.* (Cambridge, Mass.: MIT Press, 1982).
6. On productivity losses, see James Robinson, "The Impact of Environmental and Occupational Health Regulation on Producivity Growth in U.S. Manufacturing," 12 *Yale J. on Reg.* 387, 416–17 (1995); on cheaper control strategies, see Thomas H. Tietenberg, *Emissions Trading: An Exercise in Reforming Pollution Policy* (Washington, D.C.: Resources for the Future, 1985), pp. 41–45.
7. See Crandall et al., *supra* note 2, at 157–58 Robert W. Crandall and John D. Graham, "The Effect of Fuel Economy Standards on Automobile Safety," 32 *J. L. & Econ.* 97, 115 (1989).
8. See Stephen G. Breyer, *Regulation and Its Reform* (Cambridge: Harvard University Press, 1982), p. 244.
9. See Henry G. Grabowski and John M. Vernon, *The Regulation of Pharmaceuticals: Balancing the Benefits and Risks* (Washington D.C.: American Enterprise Institute for Public Policy Research, 1983), pp. 10–13, 46–47.
10. Richard M. Nixon, "State of the Union Address," in *Public Papers of the Presidents of the United States:* GPO, 1970, p. 13.
11. See John M. Mendeloff, *The Dilemma of Toxic Substance Regulation: How Overregulation Causes Underregulation at OSHA* (Cambridge, Mass.: MIT Press, 1988), pp. 2, 82.
12. See David Vogel, *National Styles of Regulation: Environmental Policy in Great Britain and the United States* (Ithaca: Cornell University Press, 1986), p. 163.
13. See Peter Huber, "The Old-New Division in Risk Regulation," 69 *Va. L. Rev.* 1025 (1983). See also Michael T. Maloney and Gordon L. Brady, "Capital Turnover and Marketable Pollution Rights," 31 *J. L.*

14. See Bruce A. Ackerman and William T. Hassler, *Clean Coal/Dirty Air: Or How the Clean Air Act Became a Multibillion Dollar Bail-Out for High Sulfur Coal Producers and What Can be Done About It* (New Haven: Yale University Press, 1981), pp. 2, 11–12.

15. See Richard A. Merrill, "FDA's Implementation of the Delaney Clause: Repudiation of Congressional Choice or Reasoned Adaptation to Scientific Progress?," 5 *Yale J. Reg.* 1 (1988). See also Peter W. Huber, *Liability: The Legal Revolution and Its Consequences* (New York: Basic Books, 1988).

16. See Finis Welsh, *Minimum Wages: Issues and Evidence* (Washington, D.C.: American Enterprise Institute for Public Policy Research, 1978). But see David Card and Alan B. Krueger, *Myth and Measurement: The New Economics of the Minimum Wage* (Princeton: Princeton University Press, 1995).

17. See Werner Z. Hirsch, Joel G. Hirsch, and Stephen Margolis, "Regression Analysis of the Effects of Habitability Laws upon Rent: An Empirical Observation on the Ackerman-Komesar Debate," 63 *Cal. L. Rev.* 1098, 1139 (1975).

18. See Richard Posner, "An Economic Anology of Spy Discrimination Laws," 56 *U. Chi. L. Rev.* 1311, 1326, 1331, 1333.

19. See Jacob Jacoby, Margaret C. Nelson, and Wayne D. Hoyer, "Corrective Advertising and Affirmative Disclosure Statements: Their Potential for Confusing and Misleading the Consumer," 46 *J. Mktg.* 61, 70 (Winter 1982); Philip G. Kuehl and Robert F. Dyer, "Applications of the 'Normative Belief' Technique for Measuring the Effectiveness of Deceptive and Corrective Advertisements," 4 *Advances in Cons. Res.* 204, 209 (1976); and Michael B. Mazis and Janice E. Atkinson, "An Experimental Evaluation of a Proposed Corrective Advertising Remedy," 13 *J. Mktg. Res.* 178, 181–83 (1976).

20. See Richard Craswell, "Interpreting Deceptive Advertising" 65 *B. U. L. Rev.* 657, 690–91. (1985).

21. See Howard Beales, Richard Craswell, and Steven C. Salop, "The Efficient Regulation of Consumer Information," 24 *J. L. & Econ.* 491, 520 (1981); and Robert Pitofsky, "Beyond Nader: Consumer Protection and the Regulation of Advertising," 90 *Harv. L. Rev.* 661, 682–83 (1977).

22. See Terry Moe, "Regulatory Performance and Presidential Administration," 26 *Am. J. Pol. Sci.* 197 (1982).

23. See Marvin H. Bernstein, *Regulating Business by Independent Commission* (Princeton: Princeton University Press, 1955), p. 170; and Richard A. Harris and Sidney M. Milkis, *The Politics of Regulatory Change: A Tale of Two Agencies* (New York: Oxford University Press, 1989).

24. The best discussions here are by Jon Elster. See his various criticisms of functional explanations in *Explaining Technical Change: A Case Study in the Philosophy of Science* (Cambridge: Cambridge University Press, 1983); *The Cement of Society: A Study of Social Order* (Cambridge: Cambridge University Press, 1989); and *Nuts and Bolts for the Social Sciences* (Cambridge: Cambridge University Press, 1989).

QUESTIONS ON SUNSTEIN

1. How do you understand the idea of a "regulatory paradox"? Restate the basic idea behind each of the six paradoxes. Can you think of any other paradoxes?

2. What does Sunstein suggest is the cause of these regulatory paradoxes? Is there a solution to these paradoxes or are they inevitable?

3. How important is regulation to the operation of business and markets? To the life of the whole society?

Is There a Bias Toward Overregulation?

Leland B. Yeager

Leland B. Yeager, Professor Emeritus of Economics at Auburn University, is the author of International Monetary Relations: Theory, History, and Policy *(1976),* The Fluttering Veil: Essays on Monetary Disequilibrium *(1997),* Ethics as Social Science: The Moral Philosophy of Social Cooperation *(2001), and numerous scholarly articles in political economy and monetary theory.*

WHAT IS "TOO MUCH" GOVERNMENT?

Often it is appropriate to consider the question of government regulation industry by industry or problem by problem, focusing on specific facts. Heaven knows there has been enough of the opposite: adopting regulations lightheartedly, as if good intentions were justification enough. On the other hand, sometimes it is appropriate to step back from a narrowly factual focus and consider a broader question. Preoccupation with the immediate and specific is part of the problem with government action.[1]

A broader view suggests that our political system harbors a bias toward overactivity. Regulation is just one of several things that government does probably too much of. Such a bias, if it does exist, argues for seeking—or restoring—constitutional restraints on regulatory activity and for not letting each particular issue be decided on its own narrow apparent merits. Despite the scorn of hard-nosed positivists, human rights belong in the discussion.

Strictly speaking, perhaps, what argues for restraint is not an incontestable bias toward too much regulation but a structure of government decision-making in which prospective costs and benefits escape accurate confrontation. The result may be too much regulation in some directions and, in some sense, too little in others. Errors of omission do not cancel out errors of hyperactivity, though, and a case for restraint remains.

What might the ideal amount of government mean? Even without being able to say (and without facing the anarchists' challenge to any government at all), one can still recognize aspects of decision-making processes that tilt the outcome toward too much government. Some utterly familiar facts suggest this conclusion. Admittedly, I may have overlooked some powerful and even overriding biases working in the opposite direction. As a contribution to discussion, though, I report the biases I see and challenge the reader to explain any opposite ones that might override them.

FRAGMENTED DECISIONS AND AGGLOMERATED ACTIVITIES

Almost everyone who plays a part in governmental decisionmaking, from the average citizen on up, has a fragmentary view. No one has, or has reason to seek, a full view of the prospective costs and benefits of a contemplated activity. (Just one kind of relatively specific and obvious example concerns federal sharing in the costs of many state and local projects, with the result that the local authorities are deciding on expenditure of what, from their points of view, are "ten-cent dollars" or "fifty-cent dollars.") Nothing in government corresponds to the market process of spontaneous coordination of decentralized decisions; nothing corresponds to its way of bringing even remote considerations to the attention of each decentralized decisionmaker in the form of prices.[2] Knowledge, authority, incentives, and responsibility are largely fragmented and uncoordinated

in the political and governmental process. Far-reaching and long-run consequences of decisions receive skimpy attention.

One aspect of this fragmentation, noted by Samuel Brittan, is that "the cost of a political decision is borne by people other than the voter. A customer buying a suit or a washing machine has to bear the cost himself." Someone voting for a candidate who makes some attractive promise, however, usually—and realistically—assumes "that others will bear the cost."[3]

Any number of government activities might each seem desirable by itself in the absence of most of the others, but it does not necessarily follow that the whole agglomeration of them is also desirable. To suppose so would be to commit the fallacy of composition, of supposing that anything true of the part or individual must also be true of the whole or group. Adding any particular government function to all the others complicates the tasks of choosing, operating, and supervising those others.[4] The more functions the government takes on and the more complicated they are, the more they must be left to the "experts"; and the people's elected representatives, let alone the people themselves, are less able to exercise close and informed control. The elected representatives, who supposedly should monitor the experts, must largely depend on them for information; and the experts have their own special views about their work. . . .

THE "FLAW" AND THE CASE FOR LIMITS

Overregulation stems from a "basic flaw" in our political system closely related to the flaw noted in current arguments for a constitutional limit to government taxing or spending.[5] Because of its close relation to the present topic, the central argument is worth reviewing. The alternative to such a limit—letting total spending emerge as the sum of individually enacted appropriations—is biased upward. Some people are especially interested in government spending on rivers and harbors and military installations, others in spending for schools and teachers, others in housing subsidies, and still others in energy research contracts. Because of its special interest, each group is well informed about the government action it wants and has arguments for it readily at hand. Furthermore, since the benefits of its favorite program will be relatively concentrated on itself rather than diluted over the entire population, its members have incentives to incur the trouble and expense of pressing the group's views on the legislators. A candidate or legislator, for his part, knows that each special interest cares intensely about what concerns it and fears that losing the support of only a few such interests could cost him election or reelection; so he tends to be responsive.[6]

The links between particular government expenditures and particular tax collections are loose. No one really knows who will ultimately pay for a government program. The voter can drift into thinking that someone else, perhaps "the rich" or the big corporations, will pay or ought to pay. (Not even economists know who ultimately pays the corporate income tax.) It is easy to drift into thinking that the government gets resources out of some sort of fourth dimension. Politicians will not hasten to disabuse voters of this "fiscal illusion." Nowadays, with taxes and inflation being what they are, this illusion is evaporating; but the very fact that the present state of affairs could develop suggests that some such illusion has been at work until recently.

An art-loving journalist has unwittingly illustrated the sort of attitude that expands government activity—and thereby also illustrated the logic of the sort of limit he was complaining against.[7] State and local government actions taken after passage of Proposition 13 in California reveal, he complained, that many officials see the arts as an expendable elitist pursuit. The recent tremendous growth in public funding for the arts had suddenly been thrown into reverse. A 60 percent slash in the budget of a state agency making grants to art programs and individual artists had lowered California to 44th place among all states in per capita funding for the arts. Yet, he continued, the arts pay the wages of hundreds of thousands of people, directly and indirectly. How many restaurants near the Music Center in downtown Los Angeles would remain open without the audiences that the Center draws? The arts offer pleasure and entertainment and stimulation. State and local governments have made too much of a commitment to them to back out now without seriously retarding their progress. "A society that considers it a frill to nourish its soul is in deep trouble." In reply, a reader asked: "What kind of trouble can be expected by a society that depends on government to nourish its soul?"[8] The journalist tacitly accepts the notion that not to finance particular activities by taxes—by compulsion—is to be neglectful of them. . . .

Much the same points that apply to spending apply also to regulation. Some economic interest groups benefit from regulation (perhaps it protects them against competition) and automatically have the information and incentives to press candidates and legislators for what they want. The latter, for their part, are rationally more responsive to special-interest pressures than to the general interest of the average voters, who are rationally ignorant and apathetic about the details of public policy. Furthermore, citizens who identify themselves with some cause—protecting the environment, cracking down on health and safety hazards, developing exotic energy sources, fostering the arts, remedying supposedly unjust inequalities, suppressing (or facilitating) abortion, improving the eating habits of school children, or whatever—take on the political characters of special interests and, like them, tend to have disproportionate influence with politicians or the relevant bureaucrats. The much discussed "new class" of activist intellectuals and publicists belongs in the story. Legislators, bureaucrats, and other members of the government themselves have personal stakes in government activism, though many of them are no doubt sincerely motivated to do good as they conceive of doing good in their own special niches in life.

METHODOLOGICAL INDIVIDUALISM IN ANALYZING GOVERNMENT

None of this amounts to casting aspersions on the moral characters of the people who take part in deciding on government activities. I am simply drawing implications from the fact that these people decide and act within particular frameworks of information, incentives, tests of performance, and rewards.[9] Economists, long successful with methodological individualism in their own field, are now applying that approach to understanding how people behave in the governmental framework. We, the analysts, project ourselves into the role of businessman, consumer, bureaucrat, legislator, political candidate, or whoever it is whose decisions and actions we are trying to understand. We consider his motivations and incentives, perhaps even including the circumstances affecting his self-esteem, as well as the opportunities and constraints he faces. We can draw relevant information from our own personal thoughts, actions, and experiences. Such an approach does not depend on the profundities of psychology. It draws inferences from familiar facts about human nature and about decision-making situations.

Circumstances and Ideas of the Average Voter

The "average voter" is the voter considered at random, otherwise than as a member of any special-interest group. (To take account of *non*voting, perhaps the term should be "average citizen.") He does not automatically possess the information needed to weigh the pros and cons of more or less spending on each special group's favorite project. Furthermore, obtaining such information would cost him money, time, and trouble better devoted to other purposes. He profits more from a day spent learning the strong and weak points of different makes of car or refrigerator, when he wants to buy a new one, than from a day spent trying to learn the advantages and disadvantages of increased government spending on aircraft carriers or urban renewal.

Acquiring and acting on information about public issues has a low payoff because it is a "public good." The standard rationale for having any government at all is that it is necessary to provide public goods, such as national defense, police protection, and the legal system. Their benefits cannot be confined to people who voluntarily contribute money or effort for them. Each person might as well sit back and enjoy a free ride on the expenditures or efforts of others. So government sells public goods compulsorily, for taxes. But no such solution, imperfect as it may be, has been found for the public good of monitoring the government itself.[10] If an average voter should go to the trouble of keeping informed and politically active, most of the benefits, in the form of sounder policy, would accrue to others. While reaping only a very minor share of these benefits, he would have to bear all of his own costs. He has about as little reason to incur them as he would have to stop driving his car to hold down air pollution. He has little incentive to work for what is in the general interest.[11]

Exhorting citizens to study the issues and take an active role in politics largely ignores these facts. It tacitly regards concern with governmental affairs as a noble activity holding a special claim on each citizen's attention. Actually, badgering him to divert his money, time, and energy from work or recreation to political studies that perplex or bore him will contribute little to wise policy-making. It is an imposition, too, if holding down the range of government decisions in the first place could have held down these demands on his attention.

Even if, implausibly, the voter should become well informed and vote accordingly, he cannot express himself on each program separately. If he is voting on issues at all when choosing between candidates, he is voting on policy positions all jumbled together in vaguely specified packages, along with the candidates' actual or advertised personalities. Furthermore, his own monitoring of the government through informed voting (and lobbying) would do little good unless other voters joined him. He is only one out of many, and his own informed vote

would hardly be decisive for the outcome of an election or for the decision on some program. It is rational for him to content himself with superficial notions about election issues, voting for a party label out of habit or for a well-packaged personality out of whim.[12] His position is different from that of people who would reap concentrated benefits from particular programs and have good prospects of promoting government *activism* in their favor. Average and special-interest voters alike, though, enjoy an apparent freedom from personal responsibility in the voting booth; each is acting anonymously along with many others.

It is doubtful that businessmen, as such, have any strong interest in working to limit government intervention. Just because they are the key actors in a free-market economy, it does not follow that the individual businessman finds it in his self-interest to work to preserve such an economy. Businessmen can cope with regulation. Its burdens may not be much worse than those of competition, which, anyway, some kinds of regulation restrain. The prospects for businessmen of ordinary ability relative to the prospects of the most dynamic entrepreneurs may even be better in a highly regulated economy than under substantial laissez faire; enjoying the quiet life may be easier. Hence the pointlessness of businessmen exhorting each other to do a better job of communicating their case to the public. Businessmen as such, rather than simply as human beings, are not the main beneficiaries of a free economy.

With little personal incentive really to understand public affairs, the average voter tends to work with ideas that are in the air. The attitude does seem to prevail widely these days that if anything is bad—pornography, or small children's eating medicine that they shouldn't have, or junk food in the schools—then it is the government's job to suppress it. Similarly, if anything is good—housing, arts, effective drugs, good nutrition—then government ought to promote or subsidize it. . . .

The psychological roots[13] of interventionism include people's tendency to believe what they want to believe and the readiness of politicians to exploit this tendency. In political argumentation, plausibility counts. Mere slogans and name-calling sometimes work. The acceptance of merely plausible arguments is aided by a trait of contemporary thought roughly equivalent to what F. A. Hayek has called "scientism."[14] Just as Chanticleer thought his crowing made the sun rise, so voters and politicians seem to think that their laws are what make good things happen. People are unaccustomed to conceiving of how good results will occur unless they are explicitly sought; the invisible hand is not universally appreciated. When a problem has become politically fashionable, to suggest leaving its solution to private initiative seems callous.[15] Action is considered "positive" and therefore good, while opposition is "negative" and therefore bad.

Support for activism intertwines with the idea that democracy is a good thing. That idea slides into the belief that doing things democratically, that is, through democratic government, that is, through government, is a good thing.

Another reason for the widespread appeal of government intervention is disregard of the incompleteness of knowledge and the costs of information, transactions, and decisionmaking in the public sector while emphasizing such "imperfections" of the private sector. Tacitly, the government is regarded as a philosopher-king, totally benevolent, omniscient, efficient, and effective.[16] Handing over a problem to such an entity seems like solving it.

Special Interests and Synthetic Majorities

So far we have been considering the average voter, his circumstances and attitudes, and the appeals directed toward him. Next we turn to special interests and then to "hobbyists." Politicians are tempted to appease each clamoring interest by helping it get what it wants and to compensate the others by doing the same for them. Under these circumstances, logrolling (explicit in legislatures and implicit in political platforms) assembles majorities out of essentially unrelated minorities. "Minorities rule"[17]—not *the* minority, but an implicit coalition of several minorities. Suppose that for each of three programs, 25 percent of the voters favor it so intensely that they would vote for whichever candidate supports it, regardless of his position on other issues. Seventy-five percent of the voters oppose each program, but only mildly. Suppose, further, that the minority favoring each of the three programs is a distinct group. (To recognize that two or three of the groups have some members in common would complicate the example without affecting its point.) A candidate supporting all three programs would be elected overwhelmingly and be put in a position to work for their enactment, even though 75 percent of the electorate opposed each program. The same sort of implicit log-rolling operates, though less clearly than in this example, in the growth of government budgets. As the example suggests, by the way, the political process affords scope for political entrepreneurship and not just for passive response to existing demands.

Particularly as the vote-trading process spreads out over time and over numerous separate ballots, spurious consensus becomes possible. Policy combinations get adopted that could not have commanded a majority if considered as a whole. The procedure of making decisions year by year leads to commitments to the future growth of spending that are not seen or not appreciated when made, yet are hard to reverse later. Furthermore, the automatic growth of revenue as the economy grows and as inflation proceeds, pushing taxpayers into higher brackets, allows the government to avoid an *explicit* decision to raise taxes to cover increased spending.[18]. . .

Hobbyists

Activists on all sides of the abortion issue are examples of what I call "hobbyists," who engage in political study and activity not so much for obvious material gain as because they have identified themselves with some mission or are seeking an outlet for their energies or a sense of participation in admirable causes. Hobbyists include people who want a federal crash program to cure a disease that killed a relative, or who have lost a child in a boating accident and therefore seek federal regulation, or want subsidies for art or music, or want preservation of the unspoiled wilderness. People acting out of disinterested public spirit count among the hobbyists; the term is not meant disparagingly. Stretched a bit, the term also covers "consumer advocates," who, for the publicity they thrive on, require "a constant supply of new charges against new villains . . . suitably printed in the hot ink of outrage."[19]

By the very nature of their "hobbies," just as by the very nature of special economic interests, most hobbyists are pressing for more government activity. A belief in laissez faire or limited government is itself a hobby for some people, to be sure; but it is just one among a great many hobbies, most of which do tend toward interventionism. It is no real embarrassment for this argument that some intellectuals do take an *anti*interventionist stand. Of course some are libertarians, but psychological factors and aspects of the democratic process make it difficult for their view to prevail in practice.

Hobbyists are charmed at having one central focus, Washington, for their persuasive efforts and charmed by the prospect of using the force of government to *impose* what they want. Success seems easier along that route than along the route of persuading myriads of individuals voluntarily to observe, for example, stricter standards of boating safety. Hobbyists seeking entertainment or a sense of participation are inclined to want to be in fashion. If altruist and interventionist doctrines prevail, they will go along.

The Politician

The politician, to thrive in his career, must recognize the voters as they are—the average voters with their susceptibilities, the special interests and hobbyists with their particular concerns. Like most people, he wants to think well of himself; he wants to think he is accomplishing something. His particular mission in life is to perceive problems and get government programs enacted to solve them.[20] Even when out of office, the politician does not typically strive to limit the scope for doing good in the office he hopes to win at the next election.[21] In office, he wants to carry forth his uncompleted programs and continue serving the public better than his opponents could do.

Publicity is helpful in the quest for votes. (So is having patronage with which to reward supporters, and to which government expansion contributes.) One way to gain favorable publicity is to become identified with one or more problems and with proposals for their solution—pollution, unemployment, the urban crisis, the energy crisis, the expenses of medical care, poverty, inequality, or whatever. It may even count as a solution that the proposed legislation merely creates a new agency assigned to deal with the problem.[22] One reason for delegating work to regulatory agencies is that the legislature has too much to do to consider problems and solutions in detail: legislating, along with the bargaining necessary for it, is a high-cost activity with steeply rising marginal costs.[23] Furthermore, the vagueness inherent in handling a problem by turning it over to a new agency can itself be helpful in lulling possible opposition, just as vagueness in the wording of a proposed international agreement may be helpful in getting all parties to accept it.

The individual advocate of one particular bit of government expansion has little personal incentive to consider the external diseconomies that may result in the form of the enhanced role of inadequately supervised experts and the worsened difficulties of monitoring government. Neither he nor the voters will recognize any responsibility of his for such long-run consequences. Later on, after such pseudosolutions have enhanced the power of administrators, reduced the relative power of the people and their elected representatives, increased the difficulties of monitoring the government, and expanded the scope for court cases, these unin-

tended results will hardly be traced to and blamed on the original sponsors of the legislation. Meanwhile, they get credit for being *concerned* with problems.

Politicians and government officials tend to have short time horizons. Unlike corporation executives, who may hold stock or stock options of their companies and whose performance tends to be assessed and reported on the stock market anyway, government officials hold no shares of stock whose current prices might reflect assessments of the *long-run* consequences of their actions; hence, short-run electoral concerns tend to prevail. How much incentive, for example, do mayors have to mount strong resistance to the demands of unionized city employees? Mayor John Lindsay of New York "took the attitude that he would not be around in ten years. He thought he would be either in the White House or doing something else, so he decided to pay people off with promises of pensions that would come due when he was no longer mayor."[24]

The personal qualities useful in gaining favorable publicity and in political wheeling and dealing are not likely to coincide with the personal qualities of a competent, far-sighted, and courageous statesman. Neither are the qualities of a successful campaigner, which include adroitness in projecting an appealing personality and in cleverly stating or obscuring issues.[25] Similarly, a competent and devoted public servant would have rather different qualities than a personally successful bureaucrat, whose abilities might run more toward cultivating superiors by promoting their personal ambitions.

Exceptions do occur. Why can't a politician see it as his mission in life to do good by resisting and reversing the trend toward ever more government? If that resistance really is in the interest of the average citizen, why can't the politician both serve his self-esteem and win votes by campaigning on such a platform?

Conceivably he might. But these questions, instead of refuting the argument about activist biases, merely note a possible offset. For several reasons, this offset is unlikely to be strong. (The exceptional politician to whom the following remarks do not apply stands at a disadvantage in winning elections and wielding influence.) First, a political career would generally have been less appealing in the first place to a skeptic about government than to a man who saw great opportunities in it for doing good. Opportunities for also gaining personal success in that endeavor are greater for a politician, as for a bureaucrat, if government is big and growing than if it is kept small. Secondly, winning elections on a platform of *restricting* government activities depends on a greater degree of sophisticated understanding among voters than they are likely to have (although hope on this score is now emerging). . . .

Our amateur psychologizing about politicians should pay some attention to the members of legislators' staffs. With government expansion and legislative burdens making increasing demands on their employers' time and ability to absorb information, staff members have growing influence. They further their own careers by helping their employers gain prominence. Bright ideas help. Although a few ideas may focus on repealing laws and abolishing agencies, activism generally offers more scope for brightness, as well as for maintaining political alliances, especially in an intellectual atmosphere predisposed to activism.

The Bureaucrat

The bureaucrat, like the politician, may well see his mission in life as doing good through the agency of government. He is likely, though, except at the highest levels, to be a specialist. (At the highest levels, he is likely to be mobile between government positions and to be judged more by his reputed abilities and performance in the short run than by the long-run consequences of how he runs any particular agency.) The specialist identifies with the mission of his bureau, appreciates the value of its services, but appreciates less clearly the alternative results obtainable from devoting the necessary money and resources to other purposes, public or private. Like most people, he wants to think that his job is important and demanding and that he is doing it well. With a bigger budget and a larger staff, he could serve the public still better. Fortunately for his ambitions, the legislators must depend largely on what he and his fellow experts tell them about the benefits and costs of his agency's activities. Because his job is specialized and complicated and because they have other tasks also, the legislators cannot monitor him closely. Furthermore, alliances tend to form among the agency, the members of the legislative committee monitoring it, and the constituency in the private sector that benefits from the agency's services or regulations.[26]

The Courts

Judges, like other government decisionmakers, are often in a position to take a narrow view, doing what seems good or benevolent in the particular case at hand without having to weigh costs against benefits carefully and without having to exercise adequate foresight about the long-run repercussions of a particular decision. Of course, judges are under an obligation to decide accord-

ing to the law, including precedent; but when legislation, administrative decrees, lawsuits, and court decisions have vastly proliferated, the judge—cued by the litigants' attorneys—has all the more decisions to hunt among for the precedent that will rationalize the decision he wants to make.

Nathan Glazer describes several factors contributing to a tide of judicial activism. Powerful new interests are at work, including public-advocacy law centers supported by government or foundations. "Law—for the purpose of the correction of presumed evils, for changing government practices, for overruling legislatures, executives, and administrators, for the purpose indeed of replacing democratic procedures with the authoritarian decisions of judges—became enormously popular." Second, the courts must work out the logic of positions once taken and cannot easily withdraw from their implications. New decisions create precedents whose applications and extensions cannot be fully foreseen; case law evolves with a momentum of its own. Examples concern the concepts of "standing" to sue, of due process, and of equal protection. Third, expansion of government activity provides all the more subject matter for court cases. The "facts" relevant to court decisions become all the more numerous and complex. Social science becomes relevant; and as it changes, so may the law. The judges acquire all the more opportunities for second-guessing not only ordinary citizens but also the legislative and executive branches of government.[27] In short, the courts well illustrate the main theme of this paper: the fragmentation, on the governmental scene, of cost-benefit calculation, decisions, and responsibility. . . .

EFFECTS ON POLICY

Policy Drift

The fragmentation of decisions over time contributes to an unintended drift of the character of the whole economic and political system. Especially under a two-party system, platform-builders and campaigners often avoid drawing issues in a clear-cut way.[28] A candidate opposed to protective tariffs would not call for complete free trade for fear of losing some protectionist voters who would support him on other issues. He realizes that many a voter will choose the lesser evil rather than "waste his vote" on a third party even if one happened to mirror his own set of views more accurately. Political straddling, together with the jumbling together of unrelated issues (and even the candidates' personalities) in every election, water down the issue of interventionism versus the free market into an uninspiring choice between parties leaning just a little more one way or a little more the other. . . . The kinds of choices that voters and politicians consider feasible (and, similarly, the positions they consider unrealistically extreme) are conditioned by how policy has been drifting. Resistance to drift weakens when not only politicians but even scholars make a fetish of recommending only policies they consider politically "realistic."[29] Under such circumstances, discussion does not adequately consider long-run repercussions and long-run compatibilities and clashes among various goals and measures. Major choices, such as ones affecting the general character of the economic and social system, may get made by default as the cumulative result of piecemeal decisions whose combined tendencies were not realized when they were made.

Fragmentation Bad and Good

Closely related to dispersion of decisionmaking among persons and over time is dispersion of responsibility. Things that would be considered morally reprehensible if done by a single decision maker escape moral condemnation when done by government, since it is not apparent where the responsibility lies. Examples are our inflation mess, the quasi repudiation of government debt, the taxation of phantom earnings and phantom capital gains, even when the taxpayer has suffered a real loss and even when he has suffered it on bonds of the government itself, and the government's continued pushing of its savings bonds.

Fragmentation of decisionmaking is not to be condemned *tout court*. In many cases, keeping decisions close to the affected level will improve the cost-benefit confrontation. Furthermore, it helps preserve freedom. In fact, this is one of the chief arguments for the market as opposed to government control.[30]

Crowding Out

Another disadvantage of routine reliance on government to suppress all bad and promote all good is that it tends to freeze out alternative solutions to the problems tackled. It can hamper diverse initiatives and experimentation. It can crowd out private activity by taxing away funds that people would otherwise spend themselves on satisfying their wants, by transferring real resources from the private to the public sector, by creating or threatening subsidized competition with private approaches, and by stifling imagination with the thought

that the problem in question is already being taken care of. It is instructive to ponder what the state of affairs in education, health and retirement programs, housing, transportation, the mails, and other fields would be today if government had not gotten so heavily involved as it has in fact. One frequent advantage of private over government financing is that it can take better account of how strongly people desire an activity on the whole and in its various possible forms. Far from the importance of an activity arguing for its being taken over by the government, one should think that its importance argues against its being dominated by one big supplier. . . .

An advocate of limited government cannot specify just what nongovernmental solution to a problem might have been found if it had not been crowded out. An economist sympathetic to the market can explain how entrepreneurs have incentives to seek unfilled wants and ways of filling them, but he cannot predict what unfilled wants are going to be filled, and how and when.[31] Hence his position seems complacent; it reeks of the ivory tower. In contrast, the interventionist position looks concrete, active, practical, and down-to-earth.

Here I am in danger of being misunderstood. While I deplore regulating voluntary transactions that are not immoral and that adults are undertaking with their eyes open, the case is different with hidden safety or health hazards or with the imposition of costs onto innocent third parties. I have qualms about cold-turkey deregulation in such cases. Yet over the long run, phasing out government regulation could open the way for entrepreneurial discovery of alternatives that we can hardly imagine in advance. Such alternatives might, for example, include inspection and certification by specialist firms, as well as regulations imposed by insurance companies as a condition of insurance. My emphasis, however, is not on predicting alternative approaches but on their unpredictability and on how central control can forestall their discovery.[32]

Still Broader Costs of Regulation

Costs (and conceivably benefits) of regulatory measures include effects on the whole social, political, and economic climate and on people's attitudes. One example of what I have in mind concerns how even the vaguest hints about discriminatory enforcement of myriad regulations can be used to encourage "voluntary" compliance with the wage and price controls decreed by the president, without legal authority, in October 1978.[33] Another hard-to-fathom cost is the danger (already alluded to in the section on "The Courts") of undermining the rule of law and the law's objectivity, predictability, and worthiness of respect. . . .

The issue of regulation falls under the broader question of whether policy should serve principle or expediency, the latter meaning to act on the supposed merits of each individual case, narrowly considered. Elements of an answer to that question argue for framing policy with prime attention, instead, to the general framework of rules within which persons and companies can pursue their own goals. (In philosophical terminology, the argument favors rules-utilitarianism over act-utilitarianism.)

Some types of regulation are even open to objection on ethical grounds. Notions of human rights properly belong in the discussion, including rights of people to make open-and-above-board voluntary transactions with each other and to use and deal in their own property.[34] It is a questionable view to accord equal respect to people's use of their own property and forcible interference with that use. That view sets aside the question of who has a right to do what in favor of the question of which expected pattern of property use and resource allocation appeals more to politicians and other outside observers.

POLICY IMPLICATIONS

What implications follow from my argument, if it is broadly correct? Most generally, it recommends alertness to activist bias, and an appropriate constitutional attitude. Proposals have been made for a regulatory budget: included in the annual limit to each regulatory agency's expenses would be not only its own cash outlays but also the estimated costs that compliance with its regulations would impose on the private sector. Admittedly, implementing such a proposal would run into practical difficulties, but it is mainly its spirit that concerns us here. . . .

A constitutional amendment might require that enactment of new regulatory measures be coupled with repeal of others of comparable scope (perhaps as judged by numbers of regulators involved, or number of persons or dollar volume of activities in the private sector directly affected.) Perhaps it would be necessary to settle for some vaguer and more nearly only hortatory restraint. Anyway, good intentions would not be enough to justify a new regulation; the proposed measure would have to be shown to be not merely desirable but exceptionally so, desirable even against the

background of an already overgrown government. The objective is a framework of constraints and opinion in which different government activities are seen to be in rivalry with one another, each costing the sacrifice of others. Ideally, advocates of each new regulatory measure would accept the obligation of showing it to be so desirable as to be worth the sacrifice of specified existing regulations.

Opponents sometimes charge that a budget limit would undemocratically tie the hands of democratic government, and a similar objection would no doubt be made to constitutional restrictions on regulation. Yet the purpose of either limit is not to undercut democracy but to make it more effective by remedying a flaw that has so far kept the people from controlling the overall consequences of piecemeal decisions. A budget limit or a regulatory limit no more subverts democracy than the First Amendment does by setting limits to what Congress may do. Without that amendment, popular majorities might have placed many particular restrictions on freedom of speech, but our Founding Fathers rolled all these issues up together instead of letting each one be decided by a separate majority vote.[35]

Just as proponents of tax cuts or budget limits face the supposedly embarrassing demand that they draw up lists of specific expenditure cuts, so proponents of limits to regulation might encounter a similar demand. This one might well be easier to comply with than the demand about spending cuts. Either demand, however, is unreasonable. It in effect invites the limitationists to shut up unless they exhibit detailed knowledge of government (and private) activities that they cannot realistically be expected to have. It tacitly denies that the principle of specialization and division of labor applies in public policymaking as in other areas of life. It tacitly supposes that general knowledge—namely, knowledge of bias in the current system—is worthless unless accompanied by detailed further knowledge on the part of the same persons. Yet the very purpose of an overall limit is to bring the detailed knowledge of its possessors to bear in coping with that bias.

SUMMARY

The private sector is routinely made the target of regulation because of externalities, meaning cases in which the persons who decide on some activity or its scale decide wrongly because they do not themselves bear or take full account of all of its costs and benefits.[36] How ironic, then, routinely to expect a solution from government! Government is the prototypical sector in which decision makers do *not* take accurate account of all the costs as well as all the benefits of each activity. The fragmentation of decisionmaking and responsibility goes part way toward explaining this condition, along with the kinds of opportunities and incentives that bureaucrats, politicians, legislative staff members, judges, and citizens have.

It is difficult to compare even the relatively direct and obvious costs and benefits of an individual government policy action. It is practically impossible to assess the indirect and long-run consequences of individual actions and of their aggregate, including their effects on the drift of policy and on the character of the economic and social system. The aggregate of activities all appearing individually desirable may itself turn out quite undesirable. Hence the importance of frankly allowing considerations of political philosophy into policy discussions. Broad principles should count, including a principle of skepticism about government activity. Even when no strong and obvious disadvantages are apparent, there is presumption (though a defeasible one) against each new government function. The pragmatic, "realistic" approach of considering each individual function separately and narrowly, on its own supposed merits, is fatally flawed.

Our Founding Fathers accepted the concept of human rights that government should not violate. That concept need not be based on mysticism. It follows from a version of rules-utilitarianism (as distinguished from act-utilitarianism). As John Stuart Mill argued (in *Utilitarianism,* Chapter 5, writing when the word "justice" had not yet been stretched into uselessness for all but emotive purposes), unswervingly to put respect for justice ahead of what might be called narrow expediency is a rule of topmost utility (or expediency in a broad and deep sense). I believe it can be shown that respect for and basing policy on certain rights and values, like justice, accords with human nature and with the sort of society in which people have good chances for cooperating effectively as they pursue happiness in their own specific ways. Ludwig von Mises and Henry Hazlitt, following David Hume, have persuasively argued that social cooperation is such an indispensible means to people's pursuit of their own diverse specific goals that it deserves recognition practically as a goal in its own right.[37] Considerations like these merit respect again in appraisals of government regulation.

ENDNOTES

1. As F. A. Hayek notes, "we are not fully free to pick and choose whatever combination of features we wish our society to possess, or to . . . build a desirable social order like a mosaic by selecting whatever particular parts we like best. . . ." Yet this idea "seems to be intolerable to modern man." The suggestion draws scorn that unwanted developments may necessarily stem from earlier decisions. "I am myself now old enough," Hayek continued, "to have been told more than once by my elders that certain consequences of their policy which I foresaw would never occur, and later, when they did appear, to have been told by younger men that these had been inevitable and quite independent of what in fact was done." *Rules and Order,* vol. 1 of *Law, Legislation and Liberty* (Chicago: University of Chicago Press, 1973), pp. 59–60.

2. Obviously, I have in mind F. A. Hayek, "The Use of Knowledge in Society," *American Economic Review* 35 (September 1945): 519–530.

   Of course, externalities, transactions costs, and all that keep the price system from operating with all imaginable perfection. But what is a fringe "imperfection" of the market economy is a central characteristic of governmental decisionmaking.

3. Samuel Brittan, in *The Political Economy of Inflation,* ed. Fred Hirsch and John H. Goldthorpe (Cambridge: Harvard University Press, 1978), pp. 165–166.

4. See, in part, Milton Friedman, *Capitalism and Freedom* (Chicago: University of Chicago Press, 1962), p. 32. In the technical jargon, government activities have external diseconomies.

5. One presentation of the diagnosis appears in William F. Rickenbacker and Lewis K. Uhler, *A Taxpayer's Guide to Survival: Constitutional Tax-Limitation* (Briarcliff Manor, N.Y.: National Tax-Limitation Committee, 1977), chap. 1.

6. See "Single-Issue Politics," *Newsweek,* 6 November 1978, pp. 48–60, and, on congressmen's feelings of insecurity, see Thomas E. Mann, *Unsafe at Any Margin* (Washington: American Enterprise Institute, 1978).

7. Stephen J. Sansweet, "Proposition 13's Impact on the Arts," *Wall Street Journal,* 14 July 1978, p. 11.

8. Roy A. Beaver, letter to *Wall Street Journal,* 26 July 1978, p. 12.

9. Kenneth N. Waltz makes an analogous point, which illuminates this one, in his *Theory of International Politics* (Reading, Mass. And Menlo Park, Calif.: Addison-Wesley Publishing Company, 1979). Almost regardless of the internal character of its regime, we can say much about how a country behaves in the arena of international politics in view of the situation confronting it—in particular, according to whether or not it is a dominant power and, if it is,

whether it is one of several or one of only two dominant powers.

10. The concept of monitoring as a public good is due, I believe, to Roland McKean.

11. The weakness of personal incentives to seek collective rather than individual benefits is a leading theme of Mancur Olson, Jr., *The Logic of Collective Action* (Cambridge: Harvard University Press, 1965). The free-ride motivation of the average voter also characterizes the individual member of a special-interest group. It operates, though, to a lesser degree. The group member belongs to a smaller group with a more intense and concentrated interest than the average voter does; his own interest is less diluted by being shared with others. Furthermore, as Olson notes, an organized interest group may be able to command the support of its members by supplying services of value to them individually, such as business information and other trade-association services, in addition to its collectively desired lobbying function.

12. "Rational ignorance" is a leading theme of Anthony Downs, *An Economic Theory of Democracy* (New York: Harper, 1957).

13. Here I am falling into temptation—into amateur psychologizing—and what follows should perhaps be discounted.

14. His articles on "Scientism and the Study of Society," *Economica* (August 1942, February 1943, and February 1944) are reprinted in *The Counter-Revolution of Science* (Glencoe: Free Press, 1952), pt. 1.

15. See below in the section on "crowding out."

16. George Stigler quotes a pair of rather typical passages on the defects of a private market economy that could readily be overcome by "a socialist economy" (Oskar Lange) or by "the State" (A. C. Pigou). Then he substitutes "Almighty Jehovah" and "his Serene Omnipotence" for the words here in quotation marks—with amusing and telling effect. See Stigler, *The Citizen and the State* (Chicago: University of Chicago Press, 1975), pp. 112–113. The assumption illustrated is now being undermined by the application of methodological individualism to the study of government.

17. "Minorities Rule" is the title of the reprinted version, in *American Democracy,* ed. Leonard J. Fein (New York: Holt, Rinehart and Winston, 1964), pp. 125–130, of Robert A. Dahl, *A Preface to Democratic Theory* (Chicago: University of Chicago Press, 1963), pp. 124–134.

18. Herbert Stein, "The Real Reasons for a Tax Cut," *Wall Street Journal,* 18 July 1978, p. 20.

19. Stigler, *The Citizen and the State,* p. 188.

20. " . . . the people's representatives seem to be enchanted with the notion that they are not doing their job unless they are manufacturing laws." James McClellan, "The Tyranny of Legalism" (a review of Bruno Leoni, *Freedom and the Law*), *University Bookman* (Spring 1974), p. 66.

21. Benjamin Constant, *Cours de Politique Constitutionnelle* (1818–20), 1, 10, as quoted in Bertrand de Jouvenel, *On Power* (New York: Viking, 1949), p. 384, and also de Jouvenel himself, p. 10.

22. Relevant here is Amitai Etzioni, "The Grand Shaman," *Psychology Today* 6 (November 1972): pp. 88–92, 142–143. Headed "Got a problem . . . ? . . . call or write The Grand Shaman," the article notes people's propensity to look to the federal government for solutions to all sorts of problems. Its main concern, however, is the empty, symbolic character of many ostensible solutions. Speeches are made, conferences held, commissions appointed, bills passed, agencies established, funds appropriated, and programs launched, often doing little of substance to treat the problems involved.

23. Richard A. Posner, "Theories of Economic Regulation," *Bell Journal of Economics and Management Science* 5 (Autumn 1974): 339–340.

24. Robert Bork in *Taxpayers' Revolt: Are Constitutional Limits Desirable?* American Enterprise Institute Round Table, July 1978 (Washington: American Enterprise Institute, 1978), p. 13.

25. See Jacques Ellul, *The Political Illusion,* trans. Konrad Kellen (New York: Knopf, 1967), pp. 150–151: "The politician is generally not competent with regard to the problems that are his to solve, particularly if, as it is now inevitable, he has become a specialist in political affairs. . . . The political leader must be a politician by trade, which means to be a clever technician in the capture and defense of positions . . . desire for power clearly has priority . . . because he cannot undertake just and desirable reforms or guard the common good unless he *first* obtains power and keeps it. . . . The two forms of politics . . . demand radically different personal qualities and contrary preoccupations. To be a clever maneuverer in arriving at the summit is no qualification for perceiving the common good, making decisions, being politically enlightened, or mastering economic problems. Conversely, to have the moral qualities and intellectual competence to be capable of genuine thought and of eventually putting a genuine political program into operation in no way ensures having the equipment to reach the top."

26. William A. Niskanen argues that bureaucrats strive to maximize their budgets. See *Bureaucracy and Representative Government* (Chicago: Aldine-Atherton, 1971). Years earlier, Ludwig von Mises had stressed the contrast between a profit-seeking firm and a bureau. In a firm, the higher executives can monitor the performance of their subordinates by financial accounting and the test of profit and loss. Monitoring is more complicated in a nonprofit organization. Especially in one that gets its funds from budget appropriations rather than by selling goods or serv-

ices to willing customers, the financial tests are necessarily weakened, and detailed "bureaucratic" rules and regulations must take their place as best they can. *Bureaucracy* (London: Hodge, 1945).

27. Nathan Glazer, "Towards an Imperial Judiciary?" *The Public Interest* 41 (Fall 1975): 104–123, quotation from p. 123. (I have rearranged and interpreted Glazer's points.) Glazer cites numerous specific examples of judicial activism.

28. An early explanation was provided by Harold Hotelling in an article basically dealing with economic matters: "Stability in Competition," *Economic Journal* 39 (March 1929): 41–57.

29. On the harmfulness and even immorality of such "realism," see Clarence E. Philbrook, " 'Realism' in Policy Espousal," *American Economic Review* 43 (December 1953): 846–859.

30. "The system of direct regulation cannot allow flexibility in the application to individual cases because favoritism cannot be distinguished from flexibility and diversity of conditions cannot be distinguished from caprice. The price system, however, possesses this remarkable power: if we make an activity expensive in order to reduce its practice, those who are most attached to the practice may still continue it. It is the system which excludes from an industry not those who arrived last but those who prize least the right to work in that industry. It is the system which builds roads by hiring men with an aptitude for road-building, not by the corvée of compulsory labor." Stigler, *The Citizen and the State,* p. 36.

The recent gasoline shortage and proposals to deal with it by rationing or by making everybody forgo driving one day a week, or the nonsystem of rationing by inconvenience, all illustrate Stigler's points about regulation versus the market. Regulation cannot take into account the detailed personal knowledge that people have about their own needs and wants and circumstances.

31. See Hayek, *Rules and Order,* especially the section headed "Freedom can be preserved only by following principles and is destroyed by following expediency," pp. 56–59. Hayek reminds us that the benefits of civilization rest on using more knowledge than can be deployed in any deliberately concerted effort. "Since the value of freedom rests on opportunities it provides for unforeseen and unpredictable actions, we will rarely know what we lose through a particular restriction of freedom." Any restriction will aim at some foreseeable particular benefit, while what it forecloses will usually remain unknown and disregarded. Deciding each issue on its own apparent merits means overestimating the advantages of central direction.

32. Israel M. Kirzner explains how regulation can impede the process of discovery. His concern, however, is not so much with alternative solutions to problems taken under the gov-

ernment's wing as, rather, with discovery of new and better goods and services and production methods. Furthermore, regulation diverts entrepreneurs' energies from seeking discoveries of these constructive kinds into coping with or circumventing the regulations themselves. See *The Perils of Regulation: A Market-Process Approach,* Law and Economics Center Occasional Paper (Coral Gables: Law and Economics Center of the University of Miami, 1979), especially chap. 4.

33. Referring to this program, one Federal Reserve economist has written as follows: "Violators are explicitly threatened with bad publicity and loss of government contracts. Implicitly, possible violators must be aware of potential retaliation by regulatory agencies not formally incorporated in the wage-price control program. . . . Due to the magnitude of discretionary authority possessed by the Internal Revenue Service, Environmental Protection Agency, Federal Trade Commission, Occupational Safety and Health Administration, etc., a large potential for retaliation confronts any business." Roy H. Webb, "Wage-Price Restraint and Macroeconomic Disequilibrium," Federal Reserve Bank of Richmond, *Economic Review* 65, no. 3, (May/June 1979): 14n.

34. See Tibor R. Machan, "Some Normative Considerations of Deregulation," *Journal of Social and Political Studies* 3 (Winter 1979): 363–377.

35. Milton Friedman, *Policy Review* 5 (Summer 1978): 8–10.

36. Externalities are due, anyway, not to the very logic of the market system but to difficulties and costs of fully applying that system, including property rights, to the cases in question.

37. See Ludwig von Mises, *Human Action* (New Haven: Yale University Press, 1949), and *Theory and History* (New Haven: Yale University Press, 1957), esp. pp. 57–58, and Henry Hazlitt, *The Foundations of Morality* (Princeton: Van Nostrand, 1964). An emphasis on social cooperation as a near-ultimate criterion, if not the use of the term, traces back at least as far as Thomas Hobbes.

QUESTIONS ON YEAGER

1. What sort of assumptions does Yeager make about the motivations of the politician, the bureaucrat, and the lobbyist? Do you think Yeager is correct? Is it impossible for the politician to act for the public interest?

2. Are there structural or ideological biases that might work against government regulation? What sort of regulations, if any, might serve the public good?

3. Why does Yeager say the voter is "rationally ignorant"? Do you agree? Are there reasons for voting that Yeager has not discussed?

The Limits of Business Self-Regulation

Ian Maitland

Ian Maitland is Professor at the Carlson School of Management, University of Minnesota. He is the author of The Causes of Industrial Disorder *(1983) and other scholarly articles on business ethics.*

In a liberal democracy, there are limits to the extent to which socially responsible behavior can be ordered by law. Beyond a certain point, the costs of expanding the apparatus of state control become prohibitive—in terms of abridged liberties, bureaucratic hypertrophy, and sheer inefficiency. This fact probably accounts for the lasting appeal of the concept of self-regulation—the idea that we would be better off if we could rely on the promptings of a corporate "conscience" to regulate corporate behavior instead of the heavy hand of government regulation.

To its advocates, the virtues of self-regulation—or "corporate social responsibility"—seem self-evident. It promises simultaneously to allay business fears of further government encroachment and to restore the public's faith in business. What is more, it asks of business only that it behave in its own enlightened self-interest. While this entails a radical break with the way managers have conceived of their role in the past, it does not make any impossible or self-contradictory demands that an imaginative manager cannot adapt to. In any case, such things as the new awareness of the fragility of the physical environment, the quantum leap in the power of large corporations, and a New American Ideology, all demand no less.

The period from the mid-1950s to the mid-1970s saw a stream of proposals for the moral reconstruction of the corporation. The principal obstacle to self-regulation was diagnosed as managers' single-minded preoccupation with profit maximization. This, in turn, was attributed to intellectual shortcomings—managers' insularity, their failure to keep up with changing values, their inability to see their role in a system-wide perspective, and their attachment to an outmoded ideology which defined the public interest as the unintended outcome of the pursuit of selfish interests. Also implicated were the organizational structure and culture of the modern corporation which supposedly embodied and perpetuated this orientation to profit. The advocates of self-regulation saw their task as being the proselytizing and scolding of managers into a broader definition of their role and the drawing up of blueprints for the socially responsible corporation.

This most recent wave of enthusiasm for self-regulation has largely receded, leaving behind it few enduring achievements. By and large, the exhortations appear to have fallen on deaf ears, or at best to have had only a marginal impact on corporate conduct. The primacy of profit maximization remains unchallenged and we continue to rely—and will do so for the foreseeable future—on legal compulsion administered by the state to regulate the undesirable consequences of economic activity.

If the marriage between the corporation and self-regulation was made in heaven, why has it not been consummated? The failure of self-regulation to live up to its promise is attributable to factors that have, for the most part, been overlooked by its advocates. In their attempts to make over managers' value systems and restructure the modern corporation, they have largely neglected the very real limits on managers' discretion that result from the operation of a market economy. As a consequence of these limits, managers are largely *unable* to consider their firms' impact on society or to subordinate profit-maximization to social objectives, no matter how well-intentioned they are.

A GAME THEORETIC ANALYSIS OF SELF-REGULATION

The crux of this argument is the recognition that an individual firm's interests as a competitor in the marketplace often diverge from its interests as a part of the wider society (or, for that matter, as a part of the business community). In this latter role, the firm is likely to welcome a cleaner environment, but as a competitor in the marketplace it has an interest in minimizing its own pollution abatement costs. It may philosophically favor a free market, but it will probably lobby in favor of protection for itself. This observation is a commonplace one, but its implications are rarely fully explored.

The firm's interests as part of a broader group typically take the form of collective or public goods. Using a rational choice model of behavior, Mancur Olson has demonstrated that it is not in the interest of a group member (let us say, the firm) to contribute to the costs of providing such goods.[1] Public goods (e.g., a cleaner environment or the free market) are goods that are available to all firms irrespective of whether or not they have contributed to their upkeep or refrained from abusing them. Since their availability is not contingent on a firm having contributed, each firm has a rational incentive to free-ride, i.e., to leave the costs of providing them to other firms.

However, if each firm succumbs to this temptation, as it must if it acts in its own rational self-interest, then the public good will not be provided at all. Thus, even when they are in agreement, "rational, self-interested individuals will not act to achieve their common or group interests."[2] In a rational world, Olson concludes, "it is certain that a collective good will *not* be provided unless there is coercion or some outside inducement."[3]

The typical objectives of business self-regulation and responsible corporate behavior—such as a cleaner environment—are public goods. Olson's theory therefore provides a basis for explaining why business self-regulation appears so hard to achieve.

Russell Hardin has pointed out that the logic underlying Olson's theory of collective action is identical to that of an n-person prisoner's dilemma (PD).[4] The strategy of not contributing toward the cost of a public good dominates the strategy of paying for it, in the sense that no matter what other firms do, any particular firm will be better off if it does not contribute.

. . . Ford Runge (following A.K. Sen) has argued that what appears to be a prisoner's dilemma proves, on closer inspection, to be an "assurance problem" (AP).[5] According to this theory, the group member (i.e., firm) does not withhold its contribution to a public good based on a rational calculation of the costs and benefits involved (as with the PD) but rather does so because it is unable to obtain the necessary assurance that other firms will contribute their fair share. In other words, the AP substitutes the more lenient assumption that firms prefer equal or fair shares for the PD's assumption that they invariably try to maximize their individual net gain. Under the AP, we can expect firms to regulate their own behavior in some larger interest so long as they are confident that other firms are doing the same.

But in a market economy, where decision making is highly dispersed, the prediction of other firms' behavior becomes problematic. As a consequence, no individual firm can be sure that it is not placing itself at a competitive disadvantage by unwittingly interpreting its own obligations more strictly than its competitors do theirs. In these circumstances, all firms are likely to undertake less self-regulation than they would in principle be willing (indeed, eager) to accept.

In spite of their differences, both the PD and the AP involve problems of collective action. In the case of the PD, the problem is that it is always in the rational interest of each firm to put its own individual interests ahead of its collective interests. In the case of the AP, the problem is that of coordinating firms' expectations regarding fair shares.

The sub-optimal supply of business self-regulation can be explained largely in terms of the barriers to collective action by firms. There are three levels of self-regulation: the firm level (corporate social responsibility); the industry level (industry self-regulation); and the level of the economy (business-wide self-regulation). It is only at the third level that the necessary collective action is likely to be of a socially benign variety.

THREE LEVELS OF SELF-REGULATION

Corporate Social Responsibility

Contemporary advocates of corporate social responsibility acknowledge the difficulties of implementing it, but they go on to proclaim its inevitability anyway. In their view, it has to work because nothing else will; at best, the law elicits grudging and literal compliance with certain minimal standards when what is needed is corporations' spontaneous and whole-hearted identification with the *goals* of the law.[6] As Christopher Stone says, there are clear advantages to "encouraging people to act in socially responsible ways because they believe it the 'right thing' to do, rather than because (and thus, perhaps, only to the extent that) they are ordered to do so."[7]

Advocates of social responsibility have offered a number of prescriptions for curing firms' fixation on profit maximization. The weakness of these proposals lies in their assumption that social responsibility can be produced by manipulating the corporation. They overlook the extent to which the firm's behavior is a function of market imperatives rather than of managers' values or corporate structure. . . .

This point is . . . illustrated by cases where competitive pressures have prevented firms from acting responsibly even where it would be in their economic interest to do so. Robert Leone has described how aerosol spray manufacturers were reluctant to abandon the use of fluorocarbon propellants (which were suspected of depleting the ozone layer in the stratosphere) even though the alternative technology was cheaper. The problem was that "any individual company that voluntarily abandoned the use of such propellants ran the risk of a sizeable loss of market share as long as competitors still offered aerosol versions of their products [which the public values for their convenience]."[8] In situations of this kind it is not unusual for responsible firms, aware of their own helplessness, to solicit regulation in order to prevent themselves being taken advantage of by competitors who do not share their scruples about despoiling the environment or injuring the industry's reputation. Thus aerosol manufacturers did not oppose the ban on fluoro-carbons in spite of the tenuous scientific evidence of their dangers. Similarly, following the Tylenol poisonings, the pharmaceutical industry sought and obtained from the FDA a uniform national rule on tamper-resistant packaging, because no individual firm had wanted to unilaterally incur the expense of such packaging.[9] The list of examples is endless.

In a market economy, firms are usually *unable* to act in their own collective interests because "responsible" conduct risks placing the firms that practice it at a competitive disadvantage unless other firms follow suit. Where there is no well-defined standard that enjoys general acceptance, it will take some sort of tacit or overt coordination by firms to supply one. Even if that coordination survives the attentions of the Antitrust Division and the FTC, compliance will still be problematic because of the free-rider problem. Arrow has pointed out that a "code [of behavior] may be of value to . . . all firms if all firms maintain it, and yet it will be to the advantage of any one firm to cheat—in fact the more so, the more other firms are sticking to it."[10] We are therefore faced with the paradox that the voluntary compliance of the majority of firms may depend on the coercive imposition of the code of behavior on the minority of free riders. Thus, although it is fashionable to view voluntarism and coercion as opposites—and to prefer the former for being more humane and, ultimately, effective—they are more properly seen as interdependent.[11]

Industry Self-Regulation

If responsible corporate conduct must ultimately be backed by coercion, there remains the question of who is to administer the coercion. Is self-regulation by a trade association or other industry body a practical alternative to government regulation? The classic solution to the public goods dilemma is "mutual coercion, mutually agreed upon."[12] The possibility of "permitting businesses to coerce themselves" has been raised by Thomas Schelling who adds that such an approach "could appeal to firms which are prepared to incur costs but only on condition that their competitors do also."[13]

The record of industry self-regulation in the United States suggests that it does indeed commonly arise in response to the public goods problem. David A. Garvin explains the development of self-regulation in the advertising industry in this way.[14] Michael Porter has noted that self-regulation may be of particular importance to an emerging industry which is trying to secure consumer acceptance of its products. At this stage of its

life cycle, an industry's reputation could be irretrievably injured by the actions of a single producer.[15] Thus the intense self-regulation in the microwave industry is understandable in terms of the industry's need to "overcome the inherent suspicion with which many people view 'new' technology like microwave ovens."[16] Nevertheless, industry self-regulation remains the exception in the United States. This is so because it is a two-edged sword: the powers to prevent trade abuses are the same powers that would be needed to restrain trade.

Because of the potential anti-competitive implications of industry self-regulation, its scope has been strictly limited. Anti-trust laws have significantly circumscribed the powers of trade associations. Legal decisions have proscribed industry-wide attempts to eliminate inferior products or impose ethical codes of conduct. Major oil firms were frustrated by the anti-trust statutes when they tried to establish an information system to rate the quality of oil tankers in an attempt to reduce the incidence of oil spills from substandard vessels.[17] Airlines have had to petition the civil Aeronautics Board for anti-trust immunity so that they could discuss ways of coordinating their schedules in order to reduce peak-hour overcrowding at major airports.[18]

In short, industry or trade associations appear to hold out little promise of being transformed into vehicles for industry self-regulation. The fear is too entrenched that industry self-regulation, however plausible its initial rationale, will eventually degenerate into industry protectionism.

Business Self-Regulation

If self-regulation at the level of the individual firm is of limited usefulness because of the free-rider problem, and if industry self-regulation is ruled out by anti-trust considerations, we are left with self-regulation on a business-wide basis, presumably administered by a confederation or peak organization. An "encompassing" business organization of this sort would be less vulnerable to the anti-trust objections that can be levelled at industry associations. This is so because the diversity of its membership would inhibit such an organization from aligning itself with the sectional interests of particular firms or industries. Because it would embrace, for example, both producers and consumers of steel, it would be unable to support policies specifically favoring the steel industry (such as a cartel or tariffs) without antagonizing other parts of its membership that would be injured by such policies. A business peak organization would thus be constrained to adopt a pro-competitive posture.[19]

How might a peak organization contribute to resolving the assurance problem and the prisoner's dilemma? In the case of the AP, we saw that the principal impediment to cooperation is the difficulty of predicting others' behavior—without which coordination is impossible. By defining a code of responsible corporate conduct—and/or making authoritative rulings in particular cases—a peak organization might substantially remove this difficulty. In particular, if it is equipped to *monitor* compliance with the code, it could provide cooperating firms with the necessary assurance that they were not shouldering an unfair burden.

The point here is not that a peak organization would necessarily be more competent to make ethical judgments or that its code would be ethically superior; it is that the code would be a *common* one that would enable firms to coordinate their behavior. As we have seen, where there is a multiplicity of standards, there is effectively no standard at all, because no firm can be confident that its competitors are playing by the same rules.

A common external code would also help defuse two contentious issues in top management's relations with the firm's stockholders. First, managers would be at least partly relieved of the task of making subjective (and often thankless) judgments about the firm's obligations to various stakeholders—a task for which they are generally not equipped by training, by aptitude, or by inclination. Second, such a code would permit them to heed society's demands that the firm behave responsibly while at the same time protecting them from the charge that their generosity at the stockholders' expense was jeopardizing the firm's competitive position.[20]

So far we have assumed that each firm *wants* to cooperate (i.e., to contribute to the realization of the public good, in this case by acting responsibly) provided other firms do the same. As long as there is some means of coordinating their behavior, then firms can be counted on to cooperate. What happens if we allow for the likelihood that, while most firms may be disposed to comply with the code, some number of opportunistic firms will choose to defect?

A code of conduct—even if only morally binding—can be expected to exert a powerful constraining influence on the behavior of would-be defectors. Such a code would embody "good practice" and so would serve as a standard against which corporate behavior could be judged in individual cases. Consequently, firms which violated the code would be isolated and the spotlight of public indignation would be turned on them. In the cases where moral suasion failed, the code would still offer certain advantages (at least from business's standpoint).

First, an adverse ruling by the peak organization would serve to distance the business community as a whole from the actions of a deviant firm and so would counter the impression that business was winking at corporate abuses.[21] Second, the standards defined by the peak organization might become the basis for subsequent legislation or regulatory rulemaking. By setting the agenda in this fashion, the peak organization might forestall more extreme or onerous proposals.

However, the defection of even a handful of firms (if it involved repeated or gross violation of the code) would undermine the social contract on which the consent of the majority was based. Their continued compliance would likely be conditional on the code being effectively policed. Therefore, it seems inconceivable that business self-regulation could be based on moral suasion alone. . . .

Thus, if we modify the AP to reflect the real-world probability that some number of opportunistic firms will disregard the code, the case for investing the peak organization with some powers of compulsion becomes unanswerable. The case is stronger still if we accept the axiom of the PD that firms will invariably defect when it is in their narrow self-interest to do so. Some form of sovereign to enforce the terms of the social contract then becomes indispensable. . . .

THE CONSEQUENCES OF PEAK ORGANIZATION

Peak (or "encompassing") organizations are not merely larger special interest organizations. By virtue of the breadth and heterogeneity of their membership, they are transformed into a qualitatively different phenomenon. Indeed, peak organizations are likely to exert pressure on the behavior of their members in the direction of the public interest.

In the interests of its own stability, any organization must resist efforts by parts of its membership to obtain private benefits at the expense of other parts. It follows that the more inclusive or encompassing the organization, the larger the fraction of society it represents, and so the higher the probability that it will oppose self-serving behavior (by sections of its membership) that inflicts external costs on the rest of society. . . .

The officers of business peak organizations in Germany, Japan, and Sweden have a quasi-public conception of their role that is far removed from the American interest group model. According to Andrew Shonfield, Germany's two business *Spitzenverbände* "have typically seen themselves as performing an important public role, as guardians of the long-term interests of the nation's industries."[22] The same finding is reported by an American scholar who evidently has difficulty in taking at face value the claims made by leaders of the BDI (Confederation of German Industry): "To avoid giving an impression that it is an interest group with base, selfish and narrow aims, the BDI constantly identifies its own goals, with those of the entire nation."[23] Finally, David Bresnick recently studied the role of the national confederation of employers and trade unions of six countries in the formation and implementation of youth employment policies. In Germany, these policies were largely made and administered by the confederations themselves. In Bresnick's words, "The system in Germany has evolved with minimal government regulation and maximum protection of the interests of the young, while promoting the interests of the corporations, trade unions and the society in general. It has reduced the government role to one of occasional intervenor. It has taken the government out of the business of tax collector and achieved a degree of social compliance that is extraordinary."[24]

A similar account is given by Ezra Vogel of the role of the Japanese business peak organization, *Keidanren.*[25] Keidanren concentrates on issues of interest to the business community as a whole and "cannot be partial to any single group or any industrial sector." Vogel reports that Japanese business leaders are surprised at "the extent to which American businessmen thought only of their own company and were unprepared to consider business problems from a broader perspective." In Japan, this "higher level of aggregation of interests within the business community tends to ensure that the highest level politicians also think in comparably broad terms."[26] . . .

While the data on . . . German and Japanese peak organizations are too unsystematic to constitute a strict test concerning the consequences of peak organizations, they do shed a revealing light on the role such an organization might play in the U.S. In particular, in administering a system of self-regulation, a peak organization would be in a position to take into account a broader range of interests than is catered for by our present structures of interest representation. Also, a peak organization might promote more harmonious business-government relations without entailing the cooptation or capture of either one by the other.

PROSPECTS

What are the prospects of [a] system of business self-regulation administered by a peak organization taking root in the U.S.? What incentives would an American peak organization be able to rely on to secure firms' compliance with its standards and rulings? We have seen that, by itself, recognition of the mutuality of gains to be had from a peak organization cannot guarantee such compliance. In order to overcome the free-rider problem, the would-be peak organization must be able to offer firms private benefits or "selective incentives" that are unavailable outside the organization but that are sufficiently attractive to induce firms to comply.[27]

Students of organizations have identified an array of incentives—both positive and negative—that have been used to attract and hold members. These include: selective access to information (e.g., about government actions, technical developments, and commercial practices) under the organization's control; regulation of jurisdictional disputes between members; predatory price-cutting; boycotts; withdrawal of credit; public disparagement; fines; social status; and conviviality. . . . Finally, purposive incentives—"intangible rewards that derive from the sense of satisfaction of having contributed to the attainment of a worthwhile cause"—have provided at least a transient basis for organization. . . .

The difficulties encountered by trade associations that try to influence their members' behavior are compounded in the case of a would-be peak organization. A peak organization has access to fewer selective benefits with which to maintain members' allegiance, and its goals are even further removed from the immediate concerns of most firms. Moreover, these goals tend to be public goods (e.g., maintaining the private enterprise system or avoiding higher taxes). Wilson notes that "no single businessman has an incentive to contribute to the attainment of what all would receive if the organized political efforts are successful." In these circumstances, "the creation and maintenance of an association such as the [U.S.] Chamber, which seeks to represent all business in general and no business in particular, has been a considerable achievement."[28]

The Chamber, of course, seeks only to speak for business's collective interests. It is not difficult to imagine how much more precarious its existence would be if it also tried to set and enforce standards of conduct. It follows that if trade associations have generally been ineffective except when their powers have been underwritten by the government, a peak organization is *a fortiori* likely to be dependent on government support. And, in fact, in Western Europe, it appears that "many of the peak associations . . . reached their hegemonic status with major contributions from the more or less official recognition of key government agencies."[29]

What form would such public support have to take in the U.S.? It might involve waiving anti-trust laws in the case of the peak organization, e.g., by permitting it to punish free-riding behavior by imposing fines or administering boycotts. Government might grant it certain prerogatives—e.g., privileged access to key policy deliberations or agency rule-making, which it might in turn use to obtain leverage over recalcitrant firms. The government might require—as in Japan[30]—that every firm be a registered member of the peak organization. All these actions would serve to strengthen the peak organization vis-à-vis its members.

However, the chances are slight that actions of this kind could be taken in the U.S. In the first place, as Salisbury says, "American political culture is so rooted in individualist assumptions that [interest] groups have no integral place."[31] In contrast with Europe, associations have not been officially incorporated into the process of policy formation; bureaucrats in the U.S. deal directly with constituent units (individual firms, hospitals, universities, etc.) not with associations.[32] Given the dubious legitimacy of interest organizations in general, it seems improbable that semi-official status or privileged access would be granted to a peak organization.

A second obstacle is the structure of American government. The fragmentation of power in the American system—federalism, separation of powers, legislators nominated and elected from single-member districts—has created multiple points of access for interests that want to influence the policy process. Wilson has persuasively argued that a country's interest group structure is largely a reflection of its political structure. Thus a centralized, executive-led government is likely to generate strong national interest associations and, conversely, "the greater decentralization and dispersion of political authority in the United States helps explain the greater variety of politically active American voluntary associations."[33] In the American context, then, it is virtually inconceivable that a peak organization could secure a monopolistic or privileged role in public policymaking in even a few key areas; but without superior access of this sort it is deprived of one of the few resources available to influence its members' behavior. . . .

CONCLUSION

. . . This article has examined the ways it might be possible for firms to coordinate their behavior (both in their own larger interests and the public interest) while at the same time minimizing the risk that this coordination would be exploited for anti-social purposes. Such a benign outcome could be obtained by permitting collective action to be administered by a business-wide peak organization. At this level of coordination, a competitive market economy could coexist with effective self-regulation. However, the United States—given its distinctive political institutions—is not likely to provide a congenial soil for such an organization to take root.

ENDNOTES

1. Mancur Olson, *The Logic of Collective Action* (Cambridge, MA: Harvard University Press, 1965).
2. Ibid., p. 2.
3. Ibid., p. 44.
4. Russell Hardin, "Collective Action as an Agreeable n-Prisoner's Dilemma," *Behavioral Science,* vol. 16 (1971), pp. 472–79.
5. C. Ford Runge, "Institutions and the Free Rider: The Assurance Problem in Collective Action," *Journal of Politics,* vol. 46 (1984), pp. 154–81.
6. Cf. Henry Mintzberg, "The Case for Corporate Social Responsibility," *Journal of Business Strategy,* vol. 14 (1983), pp. 3–15.
7. Christopher Stone, *Where the Law Ends* (New York, NY: Harper Torchbooks, 1975), p. 112.
8. Robert A. Leone, "Competition and the Regulatory Boom," in Dorothy Tella, ed., *Government Regulation of Business: Its Growth, Impact, and Future* (Washington, D.C.: Chamber of Commerce of the United States, 1979), p. 34.
9. Susan Bartlett Foote, "Corporate Responsibility in a Changing Legal Environment," *California Management Review,* vol. 26 (1984), pp. 217–28.
10. Kenneth J. Arrow, "Social Responsibility and Economic Efficiency," *Public Policy,* vol. 21 (1973), p. 315.
11. See Thomas Schelling on "the false dichotomy of voluntarism and coercion," in "Command and Control," in James W. McKie, ed., *Social Responsibility and the Business Predicament* (Washington, D.C.: Brookings, 1974), p. 103.
12. The phrase is from Garrett Hardin's "The Tragedy of the Commons," *Science,* vol. 162 (1968), p. 1247.
13. Schelling, op. cit., p. 103.
14. David Garvin, "Can Industry Self-Regulation Work?" *California Management Review,* vol. 25 (1983), p. 42.
15. Michael Porter, *Competitive Strategy* (New York, NY: Free Press, 1980), p. 230.
16. Thomas P. Grumbly, "Self-Regulation: Private Vice and Public Virtue Revisited," in Eugene Bardach and Robert Kagan, eds., *Social Regulation: Strategies for Reform* (San Francisco, CA: Institute for Contemporary Studies, 1982), p. 97.
17. Garvin, op. cit., p. 155, 156.

18. Christopher Conte, "Transport Agency's Dole Vows to Restrict Traffic at 6 Busy Airports if Carriers Don't," *Wall Street Journal,* August 16, 1984, p. 10.

19. Mancur Olson, *The Rise and Decline of Nations* (New Haven, CT: Yale University Press, 1982), pp. 47–48.

20. These objections lie at the heart of the complaint that the doctrine of corporate social responsibility provides no operational guidelines to assist managers in making responsible choices. The most sophisticated (but, I think, ultimately unsuccessful) attempt to supply an objective, external standard (located in what they call the public policy process) is Lee Preston and James Post, *Private Management and Public Policy* (Englewood Cliffs, NJ: Prentice Hall, 1975).

21. See on this point the remarks of Walter A. Haas, Jr., of Levi Strauss quoted in Leonard Silk and David Vogel, *Ethics and Profits* (New York, NY: Simon & Schuster, 1976), pp. 25–27.

22. Andrew Shonfield, *Modern Capitalism,* (New York and London: Oxford University Press, 1965), p. 245.

23. Gerard Baunthal, *The Federation of German Industries in Politics* (Ithaca, NY: Cornell University Press, 1965), pp. 56–57.

24. David Bresnick, "The Youth Employment Policy Dance: Interest Groups in the Formulation and Implementation of Public Policy," paper presented at the American Political Science Association meetings in Denver, September 2–5, 1982, p. 33.

25. Ezra Vogel, *Japan as Number 1* (New York, NY: Harper Colophon, 1979), chapter 5.

26. Ibid.

27. This is, of course, the essence of the argument in Olson's *Logic,* op. cit. This section draws heavily on James Q. Wilson, *Political Organizations,* op. cit.: Robert H. Salisbury, "Why No Corporatism in America?," in Philippe Schmitter and Gerhard Lehmbruch, *Trends Toward Corporatist Intermediation* (Beverly Hills: Sage, 1979); and Philippe Schmitter and Donald Brand, "Organizing Capitalists in the United States: The Advantages and Disadvantages of Exceptionalism," presented at a workshop at the International Institute of Management, Berlin, November 14–16, 1979.

28. James Q. Wilson, *Political Organizations* (New York, NY: Basic Books, 1973), pp. 153, 161.

29. Salisbury, op. cit., p. 215. See also Wilson, op. cit., p. 82.

30. Vogel, *Japan as Number 1,* op. cit., p. 112.

31. Salisbury, op. cit. p. 222.

32. Schmitter and Brand, op. cit., p. 71.

33. Wilson, op. cit., p. 83; see generally chapter 5.

QUESTIONS ON MAITLAND

1. Does Maitland assume that profit maximization and good conduct may diverge? In what ways does market competition ensure good conduct? In what ways does market competition encourage bad conduct? Of what sorts?

2. How do you understand the idea of "peak organizations"? Is there any risk that the development of these organizations would concentrate power (economic or governmental) unnecessarily?

3. What are some of the "public goods" (or types of responsible behavior) that Maitland believes a peak organization could seek to maintain? Why can't these be maintained through other means?

FOR FURTHER READING

Ayres, Ian. *Responsive Regulation: Transcending the Deregulation Debate.* New York: Oxford University Press, 1992.

Black, Duncan. *The Theory of Committees and Elections.* Cambridge: Cambridge University Press, 1958.

Breyer, Stephen. *Regulation and Its Reform.* Cambridge: Harvard University Press, 1982.

Buchanan, Allen. *Ethics, Efficiency, and the Market.* Totowa, N.J.: Rowman & Littlefield, 1988.

Coase, Ronald W. "The Problem of Social Cost," *Journal of Law and Economics* 3 (October 1960): 1–44.

Cowen, Tyler, ed. *The Theory of Market Failure: A Critical Examination.* Fairfax, Va: George Mason University, 1988.

Downs, Anthony. *An Economic Theory of Democracy.* New York: Harper and Bros., 1957.

Epstein, Richard. *Simple Rules for a Complex World.* Cambridge: Harvard University Press, 1995.

Friedman, David D., *Law's Order: What Economics Has to Do with Law and Why It Matters.* Princeton, N.J.: Princeton University Press, 2000.

Gwartney, James D., and Richard E. Wagner. "Public Choice and the Conduct of Representative Government," in *Public Choice and Constitutional Economics,* edited by Gwartney and Wagner. Greenwich, Conn.: JAI Press, 1998.

Klein, Daniel B. "Trust for Hire: Voluntary Remedies for Quality and Safety," in *Reputation: Studies in the Voluntary Elicitation of Good Conduct,* edited by Klein. Ann Arbor: University of Michigan Press, 1996.

Kolko, Gabriel. *The Triumph of Conservatism: A Reinterpretation of American History, 1900–1916.* New York: The Free Press, 1963.

Libecap, Gary, and Claudia Goldin, eds. *The Regulated Economy: A Historical Approach to Political Economy.* Chicago: University of Chicago Press, 1994.

McCraw, Thomas K. "Regulation in America: A Review Article." *Business History Review* 49 (Summer 1975): 159–83.

Okun, Arthur. *Equality and Efficiency.* Washington, D.C.: The Brookings Institution, 1975.

Olson, Mancur. *The Logic of Collective Action: Public Goods and the Theory of Groups.* Cambridge: Harvard University Press, 1965.

Peltzman, Sam. "Toward a General Theory of Regulation." *Journal of Law and Economics* 19 (August 1976): 211–48.

Schmidtz, David. *The Limits of Government: An Essay on the Public Goods Argument.* Boulder, Colo.: Westview Press, 1991.

Schultze, Charles. *The Public Use of Private Interest.* Washington, D.C.: Brookings Institution, 1977.

Scott, James. *Seeing Like a State: How Certain Schemes to Improve the Human Condition Have Failed.* New Haven, Conn.: Yale University Press, 1998.

Spulber, Daniel F. *Regulation and Markets.* Cambridge: M.I.T. Press, 1989.

Stigler, George J. *The Citizen and the State: Essays on Regulation.* Chicago: University of Chicago Press, 1975.

The Moral Conditions of Commerce

Your corn is ripe today; mine will be so tomorrow. 'Tis profitable for us both, that I shou'd labour with you today, and that you should aid me tomorrow. I have no kindness for you, and know you have as little for me. . . . Hence I learn to do a service to another, without bearing him any real kindness; because I foresee, that he will return my service, in expectation of another of the same kind, and in order to maintain the same correspondence of good offices with me or with others.

David Hume[1]

Self-discipline, a sense of justice, honesty, fairness, chivalry, moderation, public spirit, respect for human dignity, firm ethical norms—all of these are things which people must possess before they go to market and compete with each other. These are the indispensable supports which preserve both market and competition from degeneration. Family, church, genuine communities, and tradition are their sources.

Wilhelm Röpke[2]

[A]lthough property rights and other modern economic institutions were necessary for the creation of modern businesses, we are often unaware that the latter rest on a bedrock of social and cultural habits that are too often taken for granted. Modern institutions are a necessary but not a sufficient condition for modern prosperity and the social well-being that it undergirds; they have to be combined with certain traditional social and ethical habits if they are to work properly. Contracts allow strangers with no basis for trust to work with one another, but the process works far more efficiently when the trust exists.

Francis Fuyukama[3]

Now trust has a very important pragmatic value, if nothing else. Trust is an important lubricant of a social system. It is extremely efficient; it saves a lot of trouble to have a fair degree of reliance on other people's

---

1. *A Treatise of Human Nature* [1739–1740], edited by L. H. Selby-Bigge, revised by P. H. Nidditch (Oxford: Clarendon Press, 1978), Book III.ii.v (pp. 520, 521), with revised spelling.

2. *A Humane Economy: The Social Framework of the Free Market* [1957] (Wilmington, Del.: ISI Books, 1998), 125.

3. *Trust: The Social Virtues and the Creation of Prosperity* (New York: The Free Press, 1995), 140.

word. Unfortunately this is not a commodity which can be bought very easily. If you have to buy it, you already have some doubts about what you've bought. Trust and similar values, loyalty or truth-telling, are examples of what the economist would call 'externalities.' They are goods, they are commodities; they have real, practical, economic value; they increase the efficiency of the system, enable you to produce more goods or more of whatever values you hold in high esteem. But they are not commodities for which trade on the open market is technically possible or even meaningful.

Kenneth J. Arrow[4]

Since the rise of commerce in the eighteenth century, the relation between markets and morals has often been a subject of debate. Though often wide-ranging and diffuse, these debates have often focused on two questions: (1) Apart from the legal institutions of property, contract, and commercial law, are there any moral or cultural prerequisites for the successful operation of markets and business? And (2) does the long-term operation of markets and business have beneficial effects on either morality or the general culture (including the fine arts)? These queries are related in that each pivots on a causal question concerning either the antecedents of markets or their effects; here we shall investigate whether there are certain moral or cultural conditions of markets. For now, we set aside an inquiry into the *effects* of markets (Section C) and instead examine whether or not there are moral or cultural norms or qualities that are either necessary for the successful operation of markets or that render the operation of markets more efficient or more desirable.

THE RELATION BETWEEN THE DESCRIPTIVE AND THE NORMATIVE

Our focus therefore is whether or not, or to what extent, the effective functioning of markets and commerce *presupposes* certain moral norms or characteristics. This question is a descriptive and causal question rather than a purely normative one; in other words, we are concerned with whether the characteristics of successful markets require that market participants adhere to certain extralegal norms or moral traits. However, that this is a descriptive matter does not mean that it is without normative moral implications. Consider, if only summarily, two arguments that illustrate the possible moral implications:

If successful markets require certain normative conditions, and

If we want to participate in successful markets, and

If the relevant normative conditions are either permissible or compatible with other acceptable moral norms,

Then we ought to cultivate the relevant normative traits or norms.

One might construct a similar, but negative, argument along the following lines:

If successful markets require certain normative conditions, and

If the relevant normative conditions are not permissible or are incompatible with other acceptable moral norms,

Then any feature (or aspect) of the market that requires these norms would be unacceptable *unless* the benefits of these market features were to outweigh the unacceptable norms on which these features depended.

Of course, these conclusions—whether of the positive or the negative argument—would seem to assume that to some degree the qualities and practices of a society are within our control.[5] Sometimes we make this assumption simply because we observe that across the ages, and across the world, differing societies emphasize different practices. That fact alone does not tell us whether or not our practices are within our control, for many of the norms and patterns of *any* society are more

4. *The Limits of Organization* (New York: Norton, 1974), 23.

5. Adam Smith warned against the "man of system" who "seems to imagine that he can arrange the different members of a great society with as much ease as the hand arranges the different pieces upon a chess-board. He does not consider that the pieces upon the chess-board have no other principle of motion besides that which the hand impresses upon them; but that, in the great chess-board of human society, every single piece has a principle of motion of its own, altogether different from that which the legislature might chuse to impress upon it." *The Theory of Moral Sentiments* [1759], edited by D. D. Raphael and A. L. Macfie (Indianapolis: Liberty Classics, 1982), VI.ii.2.17 (p. 234).

the result of historical contingencies, as much the unintended consequences of human action, than they are the results of deliberation and foresight. Of course, that many important social patterns are unintended need not entail that rational deliberation is fruitless. Rather, it is all the more important that we have some recognition of how historical contingency can affect our intentional actions, and of whether certain economic practices and institutions presuppose a certain moral or psychological makeup. We glimpse some of the interesting complexity of these questions in the readings in this section.

Is Law Sufficient?

Why might someone suppose that nothing other than a legal framework is necessary for markets? A legal framework includes laws that define property rights, that articulate the parameters of contracts, and that establish a basis for commerce. In economic theory it is typically assumed that the participants in markets are rational individuals who, in "buying low and selling high," act only in such a way as to maximize their long-term self-interest. On this view, all that is needed for the successful operation of markets is that the participants act rationally and that the legal framework is known, predictable, and securely enforced. In this way, rational actors not only have reliable expectations about the law, but they can also have reliable expectations about what other individuals will most probably do (or refrain from doing).

Obviously, the overall structure and patterns of the society would be determined by rational individuals as they interact together against a particular framework of law and public policy. The content (or aim) and extent of these laws may have enormous effects on commercial activity. Whether as laws, regulations, or policies of taxation, legal rules not only permit business activity but may also serve to stifle certain kinds of commerce, to drive certain exchanges underground, to raise the cost of doing business, to encourage (or discourage) certain types of firms, to require certain hiring practices, to specify modes of production, and to encourage development in one geographical area over another. Within these laws, regulations, and policies, all that the economic theorist need presuppose is that individuals are rational maximizers; any additional reference to religious or moral values, cultural traditions, or habits and dispositions is essentially irrelevant.

However even if legal rules are necessary for markets, it has also been argued that legal rules and human ra-

tionality are not sufficient for the operation of markets. For what is left out of the purely economic account is the plain fact that actual economic systems are "embedded" in deeper social, cultural, and moral contexts and that these contexts may affect, for better or worse, economic systems.[6] An alternative to the economic account is sometimes undertaken in terms of how a society's "culture" functions as an essential ingredient in the society's economic development.[7] However, the discussion is also carried out in the vocabulary of "social capital," a phrase that refers to a subset of moral norms, social expectations, and habitual modes of conduct (expressing and exemplifying honesty, trust, and self-restraint), which are often taken to be born of reciprocal and interlocking networks of voluntary social interaction.[8] For our purposes, we shall simply consider whether certain social or moral norms or traits may have a better fit with certain economic systems. For example, it may be that the successful operation of markets requires that the individual participants act according to certain moral norms or traits. What might these traits be? And how might we investigate this topic?

A MORAL BASIS FOR COMMERCE?

Conditions for Successful Markets

Are there nonlegal conditions for the successful operation of markets? This question opens two distinct inquiries, one about what is meant by a "successful" market, the other about the sense in which such conditions may operate as a cause.

To broach the first question, there is no unanimity on what is to count as a successful market. To some this might mean a market in which efficiency or productivity are maximized. How might one link certain underlying moral norms with the maximization of efficiency?

6. Mark Granovetter, "Economic Action and Social Structure: The Problem of Embeddedness," *American Journal of Sociology* 91 (1985): 481–510.

7. For example, see Lawrence E. Harrison and Samuel P. Huntington, eds., *Culture Matters: How Values Shape Human Progress* (New York: Basic Books, 2000.)

8. See, for example, James S. Coleman, "Social Capital in the Creation of Human Capital," *American Journal of Sociology,* Supplement 94 (1988): S95–S120; Coleman; "The Creation and Destruction of Social Capital: Implications for the Law," *Journal of Law, Ethics, and Public Policy* 3 (1988): 375–404; Francis Fukuyama, *The Great Disruption: Human Nature and the Reconstitution of Social Order* (New York: The Free Press, 1999); and Robert D. Putnam, *Bowling Alone: The Collapse and Revival of American Community* (New York: Simon and Schuster, 2000).

For example, if we assume that, in conjunction with the standard legal framework of a market, individuals share a basic trust among one another, value innovation, and exhibit a common disposition to work hard, then all things being equal, that society might prove more productive than a similar society that suffers generalized distrust, discourages hard work, and is suspicious of innovation and new ideas. On the other hand, one might be less interested in *maximizing* efficiency than in whether or not a market exhibits certain types or manners of human relations. On this view a successful market might be one in which individuals exhibit certain qualities of civility, friendliness, and kindness, some of which inhibit certain types of trades and may reduce wealth overall. Finally, one might even argue that no market can survive only on a legal framework because the interaction of purely rational individuals (rational maximizers) would eliminate the sort of trust that is essential to almost all commercial transactions. Without such trust, individuals would require both enormous layers of safeguards (to insure that they are not being cheated) and a rigorous governmental regime to search out, discover, and punish cheaters.

Moral Norms: Internal or External

It is one thing to discuss the sort of market that is to be achieved, and it is another to consider the moral and cultural *causes* or antecedents of that market. Here, too, there is variation and debate. We can distinguish an internal and an external account of the norms requisite to markets. A norm internal to a market would arise via the interaction of rational individuals within a legal framework permitting commerce and exchange; a norm external to a market could not reasonably arise via the interaction of individuals within a market setting but requires cultural or historical conditions in addition to the legal framework presupposed by market. Let us consider these in turn.

Internal Norms

As noted above, economic theory typically assumes that efficient markets ensue from certain legal conditions (including freedom of entry and exit) as well as rationality on the part of the participants. Some theorists would argue that if certain moral norms or traits are required in order to achieve market success, then these norms emerge as a result of individuals interacting in rational ways. On this view, even if markets require certain norms, these norms will develop over time within, or internal to, the market framework itself. The market does not need to be supplemented by a moral or cultural base from outside; rather the market is self-sufficient and via interaction and exchange the requisite norms and traits will emerge. For example, the desire for ongoing trade will encourage individuals to treat one another in respectful and honest ways. It is the very possibility of iterated exchange that encourages individuals to develop and adhere to certain norms of honesty, reliability, and fair dealing. Bernard Mandeville, for example, regards the individual as a creature of egoistic appetites, and it is out of these appetites that individuals come to develop other-regarding norms, norms whose real motives are egoistic (private vices) but whose effect is to benefit all (public benefits). This view is also illustrated in David Hume's statement (see the quotation at the commencement of the section) that individuals can "learn" to be serviceable to one another simply because each recognizes a value in their mutual commerce.

External Norms

Against this view are those who hold that some set of moral norms or moral traits, necessary for the successful operation of markets, cannot arise via interaction within a market but must be generated (or sustained) by institutions or conditions that are distinct from, or external to, the forces of market interaction. Since this external account is an alternative to the internal account of economic theory, one might infer that the externalist must hold that the relevant moral norms are in some sense nonrational. Although the externalist may have to agree that our adherence to the relevant norms is nonrational, at least in the sense that the norms could not be *maintained* among a group of rational maximizers, that does entail that the norms could never *emerge* among such a group. Perhaps they could emerge but could not be sustained.

Those who maintain some version of an external view may appeal to moral or to religious norms. Some argue that the moral traditions of a society must include certain norms without which markets will not survive or will not be successful. Others have suggested that particular religious values are necessary for the emergence or sustenance of market institutions. Those who argue that there must be external foundations often begin with the invocation of Max Weber, the great sociologist who argued that capitalism emerged at least in part because of a certain religious view, namely, Protestant Calvinism. On this view, the norms of a religion prove effective in generating the types of behaviors that render business and markets most effective.

Some Essential Norms

In all of these arguments, whether internal or external, what sort of norms or characteristics are thought to be essential? We might categorize these norms or traits in terms of whether their primary benefit is to self or to others. Thus, the norms or traits that are necessary to the success of the individual might include those that emphasize work, initiative, industry, effort, and self-control. Other norms, whose primary benefit may be to others (but which may also be necessary to the success of the individual), would include traits such as honesty, civility, fairness (or fair dealing), and cooperativeness. Some, if not all, of these traits may prove to increase efficiency overall, just as they may also serve to bring a certain moral tone to the enterprise of commerce and to human relations more generally. For example, dispositions toward industry (industrious action), as well as other attitudes toward work may serve to increase the overall productivity of a society. It is worth pointing out, for example, that the fact that some individuals must, or do, work hard does not entail that these individuals share a "work ethic." Such an ethic, manifested in conduct, implies a certain view about the status of work, the value of industriousness, or about how labor is to be carried out (working methodically and with dispatch, for example). Similarly, attitudes about honesty, fair dealing, frugality, and innovation—all of which may influence overall productivity as well as individual success—should be manifested in action as well as in words if one is to describe these as exemplifying a "work ethic."

More recent arguments assert that the disposition to cooperate with nonkin is crucial to the success of economies and to the ability of persons to form enterprises of a large size. Within extended families, there is an underlying element of trust and understanding which permits unified action towards organizational goals. The expansion of an enterprise beyond the family requires trust among individuals who may not share common histories, memories, or goals. Francis Fukuyma has argued that "spontaneous sociability,"[9] or the capacity to form cooperative associations beyond family and kin, has proved strongest in the United States, Japan, and Germany, societies in which family life is strong and in which organizations operate between the family and state (such as volunteer groups, religious institutions, clubs, and neighborhoods). This sort of cooperation emerges out of a sense of trust that exists among the members of a society, a trust that may spring from the experience of individuals in voluntary social groups intermediary between family and government. Where such trust is lacking (either due to the domination of the state over spontaneous groups or due to traditional assumptions that draw sharp distinctions between kin and nonkin), it is difficult for individuals to combine into large organizations, including large commercial organizations that must be staffed by individuals who are not one's own kin.

MORAL CONDITIONS AS CAUSAL CONDITIONS

A Question of Social Causation

That certain norms or traits might be conditions for markets is a thesis which concerns *cause* and *effect:* If conditions X and Y are present, then effect Z will hold; conversely, if effect Z holds, then conditions X and Y must be present. Although we often think of causality as operating only in the biological or physical sphere, questions of causation also occur with regard to social and economic phenomena. However, social and economic phenomena are typically so complex—the variables in operation are so many and often of such differing types—that any inquiry is difficult (much more difficult than making assertions that sound correct or which hew to intellectual fashion). Indeed, in assessing social causes and effects we should not expect the level of precision and particularity that we might achieve in the physical or biological sciences. Rather, our conclusions may be both general and abstract assessments of what may happen (or did happen) under certain general and abstract circumstances.

Causal Argument

Because of this complexity, we should at least equip ourselves with some sense of what a causal inquiry demands. A causal argument is an *inductive* rather than a deductive argument. A deductive argument is an argument in which one's acceptance of the premises entails that one must accept the conclusion. An inductive argument is, on the other hand, probabilistic. In an inductive argument the conclusion goes beyond what is stated in the premises, and so we must judge inductive validity in terms of whether the probability of the conclusion is commensurate with all that we know about the premises.

If one posits a conclusion as to when one thing is the cause of another, one must take care to distinguish two senses of "cause." To say that a is the cause of b involves not only that a occurs prior to b but that when-

---

9. Francis Fukuyma, *Trust: The Social Virtues and the Creation of Prosperity* (New York: The Free Press, 1995), 27.

ever *a* occurs, then *b* must occur. In this sense, *a* is sufficient for the occurrence of *b*. However, causation often is taken to imply only that *a* is necessary for the occurrence of *b*. In the readings that follow, it will be important to consider what sort of causal claim is being made about the market or its conditions. (Is the writer claiming that certain traits generate or bring about certain types of markets? Is the writer claiming that certain traits or norms are necessary for maximizing efficiency? Or is the writer claiming that certain norms are necessary if a market is to have a certain moral character?)

The first reading, by Bernard Mandeville, contends that our egoistic appetites are necessary for generating and sustaining large and productive markets. Max Weber contends that it is not egoism that is crucial but a certain perspective on work, leisure, and saving, a perspective which, in the Western world, was advocated by a certain form of Protestantism. F. A. Hayek contends that markets require a reorientation from an ethic of the small group to an ethic of large and anonymous societies. In so doing he distinguishes the rules or norms of small groups from those of spontaneous orders made up of individuals pursuing a variety of aims. In the final selection, Jane Jacobs offers a dialogue in which one of the participants discusses the interlocking norms of commerce.

THE READINGS

Bernard Mandeville   In the preface to his poem "The Grumbling Hive," Mandeville indicates that the purpose of his writing is to point out how some of our "vilest and most hateful Qualities" are necessary for creating a large and bustling commercial society. Not only are these qualities necessary for commercial exchange, they also serve as the underlying motivation for our other-regarding behavior, including norms of sociability. (In Mandeville's view, a vicious action is any action motivated not by other-regarding reason but by an appetite or passion.) Mandeville is not claiming that *all* vices help to bring about something good; rather he is saying that vice is at the root of a happy, large, and productive society, and that this occurs because certain vices are permitted and others are restrained ("So Vice is beneficial found, When it's by Justice lopt and bound"). The poem illustrates Mandeville's views through the metaphor of a happy, large, and luxurious hive of bees, a hive governed by the rule of law, a veritable "Nursery/Of Sciences and Industry." Within this hive all who want work find it, and all contrive to supply the wants of the other bees in order to satisfy their own. The bees seek to hide their vices by behaving in ways that seem to accord with virtue ("And Virtue, who from Politicks/Had learn'd a Thousand Cunning Tricks,/Was, by their happy Influence,/Made Friends with Vice"), even as they are still motivated only by selfish appetites. In the midst of this plenty, complaints arise about the vices of the bees, and so the god Jove rids the hive of vice, restoring true virtue. Once this is done, individuals resume the practice of true virtue, setting aside selfish appetites and desires. As a result, however, "All Arts and Crafts neglected lie;/Content, the Bane of Industry." The few bees who remain in the hive fly into a tree "Blest with Content and Honesty."

Max Weber   Weber wishes to explain the historical concept of the "spirit of capitalism," and to do so he first characterizes the thought of Benjamin Franklin, for whom work is a virtue, a "calling" to a certain sphere of activity. This view of work, as well as a view about the accumulation of money, should not be understood as expressive of some unique greed; capitalism did not invent greed or unscrupulous conduct in moneymaking. The spirit of modern capitalism, which demands an "attitude which seeks profit rationally and systematically," has its origins in the Protestant idea of a "calling," an idea expressed in the work of the leader of the Protestant Reformation, Martin Luther. However, to illustrate the Protestant view, Weber appeals to sermons of the Presbyterian Richard Baxter, who contends that God wills for everyone a life of productive activity in service to the glory of God. Not a burdensome means but an end in itself, labor is the evidence of one's saving grace. The result of the Puritan idea of a calling meant condemnation of the spontaneous, the irrational, the impulsive, and the luxurious. One was allowed to accumulate wealth and to use it in ways that properly served the practical needs of humanity. Although the result of the combination of methodical labor and limited consumption was the accumulation of enormous capital, the ideals of Puritanism tended to diminish with the acquisition of wealth, leaving in its wake a set of bourgeois virtues.

F. A. Hayek   Hayek draws a distinction between small groups defined by a common purpose and the nonpurposive order of the extended or Great Society. In Hayek's view capitalism has grown alongside the realization that human beings could live together peacefully without sharing the same purposes or ends. A market operates without our having to agree on particular ends and allows individuals to contribute to the good of others without knowing these persons or having any particular affection for them. Without a common end or goal the market is united only through economic relations. However, Hayek contends that human beings have inherited from their distant past certain tribal instincts for loyalty to and identification with groups devoted to concrete purposes. These instincts come into conflict with the sort of rules that unite market societies, for the rules of spontaneous market orders are abstract rules that "demarcate the domain of the means that each is allowed to use for his purposes." These rules, which may seem artificial, not only extend the range of people with whom we interact but weaken any altruistic duties to aim at the concrete good of others. In the market we are guided not by concrete knowledge but by prices, and this may entail that we are doing the most good when we serve unknown aims by pursuing our market tasks (rather than seeking to benefit known people).

Jane Jacobs This selection is an excerpt from a larger fictional dialogue between five characters. Armbruster is a retired publisher who has invited five friends to a discussion concerning the "breakdowns of honesty." Jasper, a fifty-year-old crime novelist, is one of Armbruster's most successful authors. Kate is a thirty-year-old professor. Ben, around age 43, is an environmentalist and author of *Numbered Days for the Planet*. Quincy is a high-ranking executive at a New York Bank, and Hortense, the niece of Armbruster, is a lawyer in her early forties. In this excerpt Kate has presented to the group her findings about the current state of our commonplace morality. She has discovered two moral syndromes, each of which is a list of moral precepts that underlie certain kinds of work. In this discussion, Kate presents her findings concerning the moral precepts underlying the world of commerce. In her view, the fifteen precepts form a coherent whole that serves as the moral and social basis for the everyday work of commerce. These precepts also divide into closely related "clusters." One cluster advises one to shun force, adhere to voluntary agreements, be honest, collaborate with strangers, maintain competition, and respect contracts. A second cluster focuses on inventiveness, efficiency, the promotion of convenience, and the need for dissent. A final cluster includes investment for productive purposes, industriousness, and thrifty-mindedness. Kate concludes with a discussion of the precept of optimism and suggests that the values underlying business are similar to those underlying science.

The Grumbling Hive

Bernard Mandeville

Bernard Mandeville (1670–1733) was born in Rotterdam, Holland, but lived most of his adult life in England. The poem "The Grumbling Hive" first appeared in 1714 and was several times reissued with additional commentary and essays. The final two-volume work, The Fable of the Bees: Or Private Vices, Publick Benefits *appeared in 1732.*

THE PREFACE

Laws and Government are to the Political Bodies of Civil Societies, what the Vital Spirits and Life it self are to the Natural Bodies of Animated Creatures; and as those that study the Anatomy of Dead Carcases may see, that the chief Organs and nicest Springs more immediately required to continue the Motion of our Machine, are not hard Bones, strong Muscles and Nerves, nor the smooth white Skin that so beautifully covers them, but small trifling Films and little Pipes that are either overlook'd, or else seem inconsiderable to Vulgar Eyes; so they that examine into the Nature of Man, abstract from Art and Education, may observe, that what renders him a Sociable Animal, consists not in his desire of Company, Good-nature, Pity, Affability, and other Graces of a fair Outside; but that his vilest and most hateful Qualities are the most necessary Accomplishments to fit him for the largest, and, according to the World, the happiest and most flourishing Societies. . . .

What Country soever in the Universe is to be understood by the Bee-Hive represented here, it is evident from what is said of the Laws and Constitution of it, the Glory, Wealth, Power and Industry of its Inhabitants, that it must be a large, rich and warlike Nation, that is happily govern'd by a limited Monarchy. The Satyr therefore to be met with in the following Lines upon the several Professions and Callings, and almost every Degree and Station of People, was not made to injure and point to particular Persons, but only to shew the Vileness of the Ingredients that all together compose the wholesome Mixture of a well-order'd Society; in order to extol the wonderful Power of Political Wisdom, by the help of which so beautiful a Machine is rais'd from the most contemptible Branches. For the main Design of the Fable, (as it is briefly explain'd in the Moral) is to shew the Impossibility of enjoying all the most elegant Comforts of Life that are to be met with in an industrious, wealthy and powerful Nation, and at the same time be bless'd with all the Virtue and Innocence that can be wish'd for in a Golden Age; from thence to expose the Unreasonableness and Folly of those, that desirous of being an opulent and flourishing People, and wonderfully greedy after all the Benefits they can receive as such, are yet always murmuring at and exclaiming against those Vices and Inconveniences, that from the Beginning of the World to this present Day, have been inseparable from all Kingdoms and States that ever were fam'd for Strength, Riches, and Politeness, at the same time.

To do this, I first slightly touch upon some of the Faults and Corruptions the several Professions and Callings are generally charged with. After that I shew that those very Vices of every particular Person by skilful Management, were made subservient to the Grandeur and worldly Happiness of the whole. Lastly, by setting forth what of necessity must be the consequence of general Honesty and Virtue, and National Temperance, Innocence and Content, I demonstrate that if Mankind could be cured of the Failings they are Naturally guilty of, they would cease to be capable of being rais'd into such vast, potent and polite Societies, as they have been under the several great Commonwealths and Monarchies that have flourish'd since the Creation.

If you ask me, why I have done all this, *cui bono?* and what Good these Notions will produce? truly, besides the Reader's Diversion, I believe none at all; but if I was ask'd, what Naturally ought to be expected from 'em, I wou'd answer, That in the first Place the People, who continually find fault with others, by reading them, would be taught to look at home, and examining their own Consciences, be made asham'd of always railing at what they are more or less guilty of themselves; and that in the next, those who are so fond of the Ease and Comforts, and reap all the Benefits that are the Consequence of a great and flourishing Nation, would learn more patiently to submit to those Inconveniences, which no Government upon Earth can remedy, when they should see the Impossibility of enjoying any great share of the first, without partaking likewise of the latter. . . .

When I assert, that Vices are inseparable from great and potent Societies, and that it is impossible their Wealth and Grandeur should subsist without, I do not say that the particular Members of them who are guilty of any should not be continually reprov'd, or not be punish'd for them when they grow into Crimes.

There are, I believe, few People in *London,* of those that are at any time forc'd to go a-foot, but what could wish the Streets of it much cleaner than generally they are; while they regard nothing but their own Clothes and private Conveniency: but when once they come to consider, that what offends them is the result of the Plenty, great Traffick and Opulency of that mighty City, if they have any Concern in its Welfare, they will hardly ever wish to see the Streets of it less dirty. For if we mind the Materials of all Sorts that must supply such an infinite number of Trades and Handicrafts, as are always going forward; the vast quantity of Victuals, Drink and Fewel that are daily consum'd in it, the Waste and Superfluities that must be produced from them; the multitudes of Horses and other Cattle that are always dawbing the Streets, the Carts, Coaches and more heavy Carriages that are perpetually wearing and breaking the Pavement of them, and above all the numberless swarms of People that are continually harassing and trampling through every part of them: If, I say, we mind all these, we shall find that every Moment must produce new Filth; and considering how far distant the great Streets are from the River side, what Cost and Care soever be bestow'd to remove the Nastiness almost as fast as 'tis made, it is impossible *London* should be more cleanly before it is less flourishing. Now would I ask if a good Citizen, in consideration of what has been said, might not assert, that dirty Streets are a necessary Evil inseparable from the Felicity of *London,* without being the least hindrance to the cleaning of Shoes, or sweeping of Streets, and consequently without any Prejudice either to the *Blackguard* or the *Scavingers.*

But if, without any regard to the Interest or Happiness of the City, the Question was put, What Place I thought most pleasant to walk in? No body can doubt but, before the stinking Streets of *London,* I would esteem a fragrant Garden, or a shady Grove in the Country. In the same manner, if laying aside all worldly Greatness and Vain-Glory, I should be ask'd where I thought it was most probable that Men might enjoy true Happiness, I would prefer a small peaceable Society, in which Men, neither envy'd nor esteem'd by Neighbours, should be contented to live upon the Natural Product of the Spot they inhabit, to a vast Multitude abounding in Wealth and Power, that should always be conquering others by their Arms Abroad, and debauching themselves by Foreign Luxury at Home.

Thus much I had said to the Reader in the First Edition; and have added nothing by way of Preface in the Second. But since that, a violent Out-cry has been made against the Book, exactly answering the Expectation I always had of the Justice, the Wisdom, the Charity, and Fair-dealing of those whose Good-will I despair'd of. It has been presented by the Grand-Jury, and condemn'd by thousands who never saw a word of it. It has been preach'd against before my Lord Mayor; and an utter

Refutation of it is daily expected from a Reverend Divine, who has call'd me Names in the Advertisements, and threatned to answer me in two Months time for above five Months together. What I have to say for my self, the Reader will see in my Vindication at the End of the Book, where he will likewise find the Grand-Jury's Presentment, and a Letter to the Right Honourable Lord *C.* which is very Rhetorical beyond Argument or Connexion. The Author shews a fine Talent for Invectives, and great Sagacity in discovering Atheism, where others can find none. He is zealous against wicked Books, points at the Fable of the Bees, and is very angry with the Author: he bestows four strong Epithets on the Enormity of his Guilt, and by several elegant Innuendo's to the Multitude, as the Danger there is in suffering such Authors to live, and the Vengeance of Heaven upon a whole Nation, very charitably recommends him to their Care.

Considering the length of this Epistle, and that it is not wholly levell'd at me only, I thought at first to have made some Extracts from it of what related to my self; but finding, on a nearer Enquiry, that what concern'd me was so blended and interwoven with what did not, I was oblig'd to trouble the Reader with it entire, not without Hopes that, prolix as it is, the Extravagancy of it will be entertaining to those who have perused the Treatise it condemns with so much Horror.

[1] **THE GRUMBLING HIVE:**
OR, KNAVES *TURN'D HONEST*

A Spacious Hive well stockt with Bees,
That liv'd in Luxury and Ease;
And yet as fam'd for Laws and Arms,
As yielding large and early Swarms:
Was counted the great Nursery
Of Sciences and Industry.
No Bees had better Government,
More Fickleness, or less Content:
They were not Slaves to Tyranny,
Nor rul'd by wild *Democracy;*
[2] But Kings, that could not wrong, because
Their Power was circumscrib'd by Laws.

THESE Insects liv'd like Men, and all
Our Actions they perform'd in small:
They did whatever's done in Town,
And what belongs to Sword or Gown:
Tho' th' Artful Works, by nimble Slight
Of minute Limbs, 'scap'd Human Sight;
Yet we've no Engines, Labourers,
Ships, Castles, Arms, Artificers,

Craft, Science, Shop, or Instrument,
But they had an Equivalent:
Which, since their Language is unknown,
Must be call'd, as we do our own.
As grant, that among other Things,
They wanted Dice, yet they had Kings;
And those had Guards; from whence we may
Justly conclude, they had some Play;
Unless a Regiment be shewn
Of Soldiers, that make use of none.

VAST Numbers throng'd the fruitful Hive;   [3]
Yet those vast Numbers made 'em thrive;
Millions endeavouring to supply
Each other's Lust and Vanity;
While other Millions were employ'd,
To see their Handy-works destroy'd;
They furnish'd half the Universe;
Yet had more Work than Labourers.
Some with vast Stocks, and little Pains,
Jump'd into Business of great Gains;
And some were damn'd to Sythes and Spades,
And all those hard laborious Trades;
Where willing Wretches daily sweat,
And wear out Strength and Limbs to eat:
While others follow'd Mysteries,
To which few Folks bind 'Prentices;
That want no Stock, but that of Brass,
And may set up without a Cross;
As Sharpers, Parasites, Pimps, Players,
Pick-pockets, Coiners, Quacks, South-sayers,
And all those, that in Enmity,   [4]
With downright Working, cunningly
Convert to their own Use the Labour
Of their good-natur'd heedless Neighbour.
These were call'd Knaves, but bar the Name,
The grave Industrious were the same:
All Trades and Places knew some Cheat,
No Calling was without Deceit.

THE Lawyers, of whose Art the Basis
Was raising Feuds and splitting Cases,
Oppos'd all Registers, that Cheats
Might make more Work with dipt Estates;
As wer't unlawful, that one's own,
Without a Law-Suit, should be known.
They kept off Hearings wilfully,
To finger the refreshing Fee;
And to defend a wicked Cause,
Examin'd and survey'd the Laws,
As Burglars Shops and Houses do,
To find out where they'd best break through.

[5] PHYSICIANS valu'd Fame and Wealth
Above the drooping Patient's Health,
Or their own Skill: The greatest Part
Study'd, instead of Rules of Art,
Grave pensive Looks and dull Behaviour,
To gain th' Apothecary's Favour;
The Praise of Midwives, Priests, and all
That serv'd at Birth or Funeral.
To bear with th' ever-talking Tribe,
And hear my Lady's Aunt prescribe;
With formal Smile, and kind How d'ye,
To fawn on all the Family;
And, which of all the greatest Curse is,
T' endure th' Impertinence of Nurses.

AMONG the many Priests of *Jove,*
Hir'd to draw Blessings from Above,
Some few were Learn'd and Eloquent,
But thousands Hot and Ignorant:
Yet all pass'd Muster that could hide
Their Sloth, Lust, Avarice and Pride;
[6] For which they were as fam'd as Tailors
For Cabbage, or for Brandy Sailors:
Some, meagre-look'd, and meanly clad,
Would mystically pray for Bread,
Meaning by that an ample Store,
Yet lit'rally received no more;
And, while these holy Drudges starv'd,
The lazy Ones, for which they serv'd,
Indulg'd their Ease, with all the Graces
Of Health and Plenty in their Faces.

THE Soldiers, that were forc'd to fight,
If they surviv'd, got Honour by't;
Tho' some, that shunn'd the bloody Fray,
Had Limbs shot off, that ran away:
Some valiant Gen'rals fought the Foe;
Others took Bribes to let them go:
Some ventur'd always where 'twas warm,
Lost now a Leg, and then an Arm;
Till quite disabled, and put by,
They liv'd on half their Salary;
[7] While others never came in Play,
And staid at Home for double Pay.

THEIR Kings were serv'd, but Knavishly,
Cheated by their own Ministry;
Many, that for their Welfare slaved,
Robbing the very Crown they saved:
Pensions were small, and they liv'd high,
Yet boasted of their Honesty.
Calling, whene'er they strain'd their Right,

The slipp'ry Trick a Perquisite;
And when Folks understood their Cant,
They chang'd that for Emolument;
Unwilling to be short or plain,
In any thing concerning Gain;
For there was not a Bee but would
Get more, I won't say, than he should;
But than he dar'd to let them know,
That pay'd for't; as your Gamesters do,
That, tho' at fair Play, ne'er will own
Before the Losers what they've won.

BUT who can all their Frauds repeat? [8]
The very Stuff, which in the Street
They sold for Dirt t'enrich the Ground,
Was often by the Buyers found
Sophisticated with a quarter
Of good-for-nothing Stones and Mortar;
Tho' *Flail* had little Cause to mutter,
Who sold the other Salt for Butter.

JUSTICE her self, fam'd for fair Dealing,
By Blindness had not lost her Feeling;
Her Left Hand, which the Scales should hold,
Had often dropt 'em, brib'd with Gold;
And, tho' she seem'd Impartial,
Where Punishment was corporal,
Pretended to a reg'lar Course,
In Murther, and all Crimes of Force;
Tho' some, first pillory'd for Cheating,
Were hang'd in Hemp of their own beating;
Yet, it was thought, the Sword she bore
Check'd but the Desp'rate and the Poor;
That, urg'd by meer Necessity, [9]
Were ty'd up to the wretched Tree
For Crimes, which not deserv'd that Fate,
But to secure the Rich and Great.

THUS every Part was full of Vice,
Yet the whole Mass a Paradise;
Flatter'd in Peace, and fear'd in Wars,
They were th' Esteem of Foreigners,
And lavish of their Wealth and Lives,
The Balance of all other Hives.
Such were the Blessings of that State;
Their Crimes conspir'd to make them Great:
And Virtue, who from Politicks
Had learn'd a Thousand Cunning Tricks,
Was, by their happy Influence,
Made Friends with Vice: And ever since,
The worst of all the Multitude
Did something for the Common Good.

[10]
THIS was the State's Craft, that maintain'd
The Whole of which each Part complain'd:
This, as in Musick Harmony,
Made Jarrings in the main agree;
Parties directly opposite,
Assist each other, as 'twere for Spight;
And Temp'rance with Sobriety,
Serve Drunkenness and Gluttony.

THE Root of Evil, Avarice,
That damn'd ill-natur'd baneful Vice,
Was Slave to Prodigality,
That noble Sin; whilst Luxury
Employ'd a Million of the Poor,
And odious Pride a Million more:
Envy it self, and Vanity,
Were Ministers of Industry;
Their darling Folly, Fickleness,
In Diet, Furniture and Dress,
That strange ridic'lous Vice, was made
The very Wheel that turn'd the Trade.

[11]
Their Laws and Clothes were equally
Objects of Mutability;
For, what was well done for a time,
In half a Year became a Crime;
Yet while they alter'd thus their Laws,
Still finding and correcting Flaws,
They mended by Inconstancy
Faults, which no Prudence could foresee.

THUS Vice nurs'd Ingenuity,
Which join'd with Time and Industry,
Had carry'd Life's Conveniencies,
It's real Pleasures, Comforts, Ease,
To such a Height, the very Poor
Liv'd better than the Rich before,
And nothing could be added more.

How Vain is Mortal Happiness!
Had they but known the Bounds of Bliss;
And that Perfection here below
Is more than Gods can well bestow;

[12]
The Grumbling Brutes had been content
With Ministers and Government.
But they, at every ill Success,
Like Creatures lost without Redress,
Curs'd Politicians, Armies, Fleets;
While every one cry'd, *Damn the Cheats,*
And would, tho' conscious of his own,
In others barb'rously bear none.

ONE, that had got a Princely Store,
By cheating Master, King and Poor,

Dar'd cry aloud, *The Land must sink
For all its Fraud;* And whom d'ye think
The Sermonizing Rascal chid?
A Glover that sold Lamb for Kid.

The least thing was not done amiss,
Or cross'd the Publick Business;
But all the Rogues cry'd brazenly,
Good Gods, Had we but Honesty!
Merc'ry smil'd at th' Impudence,   [13]
And others call'd it want of Sense,
Always to rail at what they lov'd:
But *Jove* with Indignation mov'd,
At last in Anger swore, *He'd rid
The bawling Hive of Fraud;* and did.
The very Moment it departs,
And Honesty fills all their Hearts;
There shews 'em, like th' Instructive Tree,
Those Crimes which they're asham'd to see;
Which now in Silence they confess,
By blushing at their Ugliness:
Like Children, that would hide their Faults,
And by their Colour own their Thoughts:
Imag'ning, when they're look'd upon,
That others see what they have done.

BUT, Oh ye Gods! What Consternation,
How vast and sudden was th' Alteration!
In half an Hour, the Nation round,
Meat fell a Peny in the Pound.
The Mask Hypocrisy's flung down,   [14]
From the great Statesman to the Clown:
And some in borrow'd Looks well known,
Appear'd like Strangers in their own.
The Bar was silent from that Day;
For now the willing Debtors pay,
Ev'n what's by Creditors forgot;
Who quitted them that had it not.
Those, that were in the Wrong, stood mute,
And dropt the patch'd vexatious Suit:
On which since nothing less can thrive,
Than Lawyers in an honest Hive,
All, except those that got enough,
With Inkhorns by their sides troop'd off.

JUSTICE hang'd some, set others free;
And after Goal delivery,
Her Presence being no more requir'd,
With all her Train and Pomp retir'd.
First march'd some Smiths with Locks and Grates,
Fetters, and Doors with Iron Plates:
Next Goalers, Turnkeys and Assistants: [15]

Before the Goddess, at some distance,
Her chief and faithful Minister,
'Squire CATCH, the Law's great Finisher,
Bore not th' imaginary Sword,
But his own Tools, an Ax and Cord:
Then on a Cloud the Hood-wink'd Fair,
JUSTICE her self was push'd by Air:
About her Chariot, and behind,
Were Serjeants, Bums of every kind,
Tip-staffs, and all those Officers,
That squeeze a Living out of Tears.

THO' Physick liv'd, while Folks were ill,
None would prescribe, but Bees of skill,
Which through the Hive dispers'd so wide,
That none of them had need to ride;
Wav'd vain Disputes, and strove to free
The Patients of their Misery;
Left Drugs in cheating Countries grown,
And us'd the Product of their own;
[16]   Knowing the Gods sent no Disease
To Nations without Remedies.

THEIR Clergy rous'd from Laziness,
Laid not their Charge on Journey-Bees;
But serv'd themselves, exempt from Vice,
The Gods with Pray'r and Sacrifice;
All those, that were unfit, or knew
Their Service might be spar'd, withdrew:
Nor was there Business for so many,
(If th' Honest stand in need of any,)
Few only with the High-Priest staid,
To whom the rest Obedience paid:
Himself employ'd in Holy Cares,
Resign'd to others State-Affairs.
He chas'd no Starv'ling from his Door,
Nor pinch'd the Wages of the Poor;
But at his House the Hungry's fed,
The Hireling finds unmeasur'd Bread,
The needy Trav'ler Board and Bed.

[17]   AMONG the King's great Ministers,
And all th' inferior Officers
The Change was great; for frugally
They now liv'd on their Salary:
That a poor Bee should ten times come
To ask his Due, a trifling Sum,
And by some well-hir'd Clerk be made
To give a Crown, or ne'er be paid,
Would now be call'd a downright Cheat,
Tho' formerly a Perquisite.,
All Places manag'd first by Three,

Who watch'd each other's Knavery,
And often for a Fellow-feeling,
Promoted one another's stealing,
Are happily supply'd by One,
By which some thousands more are gone.

No Honour now could be content,
To live and owe for what was spent;
Liv'ries in Brokers Shops are hung,
They part with Coaches for a Song;
Sell stately Horses by whole Sets;   [18]
And Country-Houses, to pay Debts.

VAIN Cost is shunn'd as much as Fraud;
They have no Forces kept Abroad;
Laugh at th' Esteem of Foreigners,
And empty Glory got by Wars;
They fight, but for their Country's sake,
When Right or Liberty's at Stake.

Now mind the glorious Hive, and see
How Honesty and Trade agree.
The Shew is gone, it thins apace;
And looks with quite another Face.
For 'twas not only that They went,
By whom vast Sums were Yearly spent;
But Multitudes that liv'd on them,
Were daily forc'd to do the same.
In vain to other Trades they'd fly;
All were o'er-stock'd accordingly.

THE Price of Land and Houses falls;   [19]
Mirac'lous Palaces, whose Walls,
Like those of *Thebes,* were rais'd by Play,
Are to be let; while the once gay,
Well-seated Houshold Gods would be
More pleas'd to expire in Flames, than see
The mean Inscription on the Door
Smile at the lofty ones they bore.
The building Trade is quite destroy'd,
Artificers are not employ'd;
No Limner for his Art is fam'd,
Stone-cutters, Carvers are not nam'd.

THOSE, that remain'd, grown temp'rate, strive,
Not how to spend, but how to live,
And, when they paid their Tavern Score,
Resolv'd to enter it no more:
No Vintner's Jilt in all the Hive
Could wear now Cloth of Gold, and thrive;
Nor *Torcol* such vast Sums advance,
For *Burgundy* and *Ortelans;*
The Courtier's gone, that with his Miss   [20]

Supp'd at his House on *Christmas* Peas;
Spending as much in two Hours stay,
As keeps a Troop of Horse a Day.

THE haughty *Chloe,* to live Great,
Had made her Husband rob the State:
But now she sells her Furniture,
Which th' *Indies* had been ransack'd for;
Contracts th' expensive Bill of Fare,
And wears her strong Suit a whole Year:
The slight and fickle Age is past;
And Clothes, as well as Fashions, last.
Weavers, that join'd rich Silk with Plate,
And all the Trades subordinate,
Are gone. Still Peace and Plenty reign,
And every Thing is cheap, tho' plain:
Kind Nature, free from Gard'ners Force,
Allows all Fruits in her own Course;
But Rarities cannot be had,
Where Pains to get them are not paid.

[21]
As Pride and Luxury decrease,
So by degrees they leave the Seas.
Not Merchants now, but Companies
Remove whole Manufactories.
All Arts and Crafts neglected lie;
Content, the Bane of Industry,
Makes 'em admire their homely Store,
And neither seek nor covet more.

SO few in the vast Hive remain,
The hundredth Part they can't maintain
Against th' Insults of numerous Foes;
Whom yet they valiantly oppose:
'Till some well-fenc'd Retreat is found,
And here they die or stand their Ground.
No Hireling in their Army's known;
But bravely fighting for their own,
Their Courage and Integrity
At last were crown'd with Victory.
   They triumph'd not without their Cost,
For many Thousand Bees were lost.
[22]
Hard'ned with Toils and Exercise,
They counted Ease it self a Vice;
Which so improv'd their Temperance;
That, to avoid Extravagance,
They flew into a hollow Tree,
Blest with Content and Honesty.

[23] **THE MORAL**

*THEN leave Complaints: Fools only strive
To make a Great an Honest Hive*

*T' enjoy the World's Conveniences,
Be fam'd in War, yet live in Ease,
Without great Vices, is a vain*
EUTOPIA *seated in the Brain.
Fraud, Luxury and Pride must live,
While we the Benefits receive:
Hunger's a dreadful Plague, no doubt,
Yet who digests or thrives without?
Do we not owe the Growth of Wine
To the dry shabby crooked Vine?
Which, while its Shoots neglected stood,
Chok'd other Plants, and ran to Wood;
But blest us with its noble Fruit,
As soon as it was ty'd and cut:
So Vice is beneficial found,* [24]
*When it's by Justice lopt and bound;
Nay, where the People would be great,
As necessary to the State,
As Hunger is to make 'em eat.
Bare Virtue can't make Nations live
In Splendor; they, that would revive
A Golden Age, must be as free,
For Acorns, as for Honesty.*

QUESTIONS ON MANDEVILLE

1. Explain the relation between private vice and public benefit. How does vice bring about commercial benefits? How does vice bring about norms of sociability?

2. Is Mandeville a psychological egoist (see the discussion of egoism in Section AV)? Or does he hold out the possibility that humans can act nonegoistically?

3. Do you agree with Mandeville's assessment of the need for vice? Or can virtuous individuals construct a bustling society?

Asceticism and the Spirit of Capitalism

Max Weber

Max Weber (1864–1920) was a Professor at Freiburg, Heidelberg, and Munich and is one of the early fathers of the discipline of sociology. His classic work, The Protestant Ethic and the Spirit of Capitalism, *an inquiry into the psychological conditions of capitalism, was first published as two articles in 1904 and 1905.*

In order to understand the connection between the fundamental religious ideas of ascetic Protestantism and its maxims for everyday economic conduct, it is necessary to examine with especial care such writings as have evidently been derived from ministerial practice. For in a time in which the beyond meant everything, when the social position of the Christian depended upon his admission to the communion, the clergyman, through his ministry, Church discipline, and preaching, exercised an influence (as a glance at collections of *consilia, casus conscientiæ,* etc., shows) which we modern men are entirely unable to picture. In such a time the religious forces which express themselves through such channels are the decisive influences in the formation of national character.

For the purposes of this chapter, though by no means for all purposes, we can treat ascetic Protestantism as a single whole. But since that side of English Puritanism which was derived from Calvinism gives the most consistent religious basis for the idea of the calling, we shall, following our previous method, place one of its representatives at the centre of the discussion. Richard Baxter stands out above many other writers on Puritan ethics, both because of his eminently practical and realistic attitude, and, at the same time, because of the universal recognition accorded to his works, which have gone through many new editions and translations. He was a Presbyterian and an apologist of the Westminster Synod, but at the same time, like so many of the best spirits of his time, gradually grew away from the dogmas of pure Calvinism. At heart he opposed Cromwell's usurpation as he would any revolution. He was unfavourable to the sects and the fanatical enthusiasm of the saints, but was very broad-minded about external peculiarities and objective towards his opponents. He sought his field of labour most especially in the practical promotion of the moral life through the Church. In the pursuit of this end, as one of the most successful ministers known to history, he placed his services at the disposal of the Parliamentary Government, of Cromwell, and of the Restoration,[1] until he retired from office under the last, before St. Bartholomew's day. His *Christian Directory* is the most complete compendium of Puritan ethics, and is continually adjusted to the practical experiences of his own ministerial activity. In comparison we shall make use of Spener's *Theologische Bedenken,* as representative of German Pietism, Barclay's *Apology* for the Quakers, and some other representatives of ascetic ethics,[2] which, however, in the interest of space, will be limited as far as possible.[3]

Now, in glancing at Baxter's *Saints' Everlasting Rest,* or his *Christian Directory,* or similar works of others,[4] one is struck at first glance by the emphasis placed, in the discussion of wealth[5] and its acquisition, on the ebionitic elements of the New Testament.[6] Wealth as such is a great danger; its temptations never end, and its pursuit[7] is not only senseless as compared with the dominating importance of the Kingdom of God, but it is morally suspect. Here asceticism seems to have turned much more sharply against the acquisition of earthly goods than it did in Calvin, who saw no hindrance to the effectiveness of the clergy in their wealth, but rather a thoroughly desirable enhancement of their prestige. Hence he permitted them to employ their means profitably. Examples of the condemnation of the pursuit of money and goods may be gathered without end from Puritan writings, and may be contrasted with the late mediæval ethical literature, which was much more open-minded on this point.

Moreover, these doubts were meant with perfect seriousness; only it is necessary to examine them somewhat more closely in order to understand their true ethical significance and implications. The real moral objection is to relaxation in the security of possession,[8] the enjoyment of wealth with the consequence of idleness and the temptations of the flesh, above all of distraction from the pursuit of a righteous life. In fact, it is only because possession involves this danger of relaxation that it is objectionable at all. For the saints' everlasting rest is in the next world; on earth man must, to be certain of his state of grace, "do the works of him who sent him, as long as it is yet day." Not leisure and enjoyment, but only activity serves to increase the glory of God, according to the definite manifestations of His will.[9]

Waste of time is thus the first and in principle the deadliest of sins. The span of human life is infinitely short and precious to make sure of one's own election. Loss of time through sociability, idle talk,[10] luxury,[11] even more sleep than is necessary for health,[12] six to at most eight hours, is worthy of absolute moral condemnation.[13] It does not yet hold, with Franklin, that time is money, but the proposition is true in a certain spiritual sense. It is infinitely valuable because every hour lost is lost to labour for the glory of God.[14] Thus inactive contemplation is also valueless, or even directly reprehensible if it is at the expense of one's daily work.[15] For it is less pleasing to God than the active performance of His will in a calling.[16] Besides, Sunday is provided for that, and, according to Baxter, it is always those who are not diligent in their callings who have no time for God when the occasion demands it.[17]

Accordingly, Baxter's principal work is dominated by the continually repeated, often almost passionate preaching of hard, continuous bodily or mental labour.[18] It is due to a combination of two different motives.[19] Labour is, on the one hand, an approved ascetic technique, as it always has been[20] in the Western Church, in sharp contrast not only to the Orient but to almost all monastic rules the world over.[21] It is in particular the specific defence against all those temptations which Puritanism united under the name of the unclean life, whose rôle for it was by no means small. The sexual asceticism of Puritanism differs only in degree, not in fundamental principle, from that of monasticism; and on account of the Puritan conception of marriage, its practical influence is more far-reaching than that of the latter. For sexual intercourse is permitted, even within marriage, only as the means willed by God for the increase of His glory according to the commandment, "Be fruitful and multiply."[22] Along with a moderate vegetable diet and cold baths, the same prescription is given for all sexual temptations as is used against religious doubts and a sense of moral unworthiness: "Work hard in your calling."[23] But the most important thing was that even beyond that labour came to be considered in itself[24] the end of life, ordained as such by God. St. Paul's "He who will not work shall not eat" holds unconditionally for everyone.[25] Unwillingness to work is symptomatic of the lack of grace.[26] . . .

Even the wealthy shall not eat without working, for even though they do not need to labour to support their own needs, there is God's commandment which they, like the poor, must obey.[27] For everyone without exception God's Providence has prepared a calling, which he should profess and in which he should labour. And this calling is not, as it was for the Lutheran,[28] a fate to which he must submit and which he must make the best of, but God's commandment to the individual to work for the divine glory. This seemingly subtle difference had far-reaching psychological consequences, and became connected with a further development of the providential interpretation of the economic order which had begun in scholasticism. . . .

Baxter expresses himself in terms which more than once directly recall Adam Smith's well-known apotheosis of the division of labour.[29] The specialization of occupations leads, since it makes the development of skill possible, to a quantitative and qualitative improvement in production, and thus serves the common good, which is identical with the good of the greatest possible number. So far, the motivation is purely utilitarian, and is closely related to the customary view-point of much of the secular literature of the time.[30]

But the characteristic Puritan element appears when Baxter sets at the head of his discussion the statement that "outside of a well-marked calling the accomplishments of a man are only casual and irregular, and

he spends more time in idleness than at work," and when he concludes it as follows: "and he [the specialized worker] will carry out his work in order while another remains in constant confusion, and his business knows neither time nor place[31] . . . therefore is a certain calling the best for everyone." Irregular work, which the ordinary labourer is often forced to accept, is often unavoidable, but always an unwelcome state of transition. A man without a calling thus lacks the systematic, methodical character which is, as we have seen, demanded by worldly asceticism.

The Quaker ethic also holds that a man's life in his calling is an exercise in ascetic virtue, a proof of his state of grace through his conscientiousness, which is expressed in the care[32] and method with which he pursues his calling. What God demands is not labour in itself, but rational labour in a calling. In the Puritan concept of the calling the emphasis is always placed on this methodical character of worldly asceticism, not, as with Luther, on the acceptance of the lot which God has irretrievably assigned to man.[33] . . .

It is true that the usefulness of a calling, and thus its favour in the sight of God, is measured primarily in moral terms, and thus in terms of the importance of the goods produced in it for the community. But a further, and, above all, in practice the most important, criterion is found in private profitableness.[34] For if that God, whose hand the Puritan sees in all the occurrences of life, shows one of His elect a chance of profit, he must do it with a purpose. Hence the faithful Christian must follow the call by taking advantage of the opportunity.[35] "If God show you a way in which you may lawfully get more than in another way (without wrong to your soul or to any other), if you refuse this, and choose the less gainful way, you cross one of the ends of your calling, and you refuse to be God's steward, and to accept His gifts and use them for Him when He requireth it: you may labour to be rich for God, though not for the flesh and sin."[36]

Wealth is thus bad ethically only in so far as it is a temptation to idleness and sinful enjoyment of life, and its acquisition is bad only when it is with the purpose of later living merrily and without care. But as a performance of duty in a calling it is not only morally permissible, but actually enjoined.[37] The parable of the servant who was rejected because he did not increase the talent which was entrusted to him seemed to say so directly.[38] To wish to be poor was, it was often argued, the same as wishing to be unhealthy;[39] it is objectionable as a glorification of works and derogatory to the glory of God. Especially begging, on the part of one able to work, is not only the sin of slothfulness, but a violation of the duty of brotherly love according to the Apostle's own word.[40]

The emphasis on the ascetic importance of a fixed calling provided an ethical justification of the modern specialized division of labour. In a similar way the providential interpretation of profit-making justified the activities of the business man.[41] The superior indulgence of the *seigneur* and the parvenu ostentation of the *nouveau riche* are equally detestable to asceticism. But, on the other hand, it has the highest ethical appreciation of the sober, middle-class, self-made man.[42] "God blesseth His trade" is a stock remark about those good men[43] who had successfully followed the divine hints. The whole power of the God of the Old Testament, who rewards His people for their obedience in this life,[44] necessarily exercised a similar influence on the Puritan who, following Baxter's advice, compared his own state of grace with that of the heroes of the Bible,[45] and in the process interpreted the statements of the Scriptures as the articles of a book of statutes. . . .

Let us now try to clarify the points in which the Puritan idea of the calling and the premium it placed upon ascetic conduct was bound directly to influence the development of a capitalistic way of life. As we have seen, this asceticism turned with all its force against one thing: the spontaneous enjoyment of life and all it had to offer. This is perhaps most characteristically brought out in the struggle over the *Book of Sports*[46] which James I and Charles I made into law expressly as a means of counteracting Puritanism, and which the latter ordered to be read from all the pulpits. The fanatical opposition of the Puritans to the ordinances of the King, permitting certain popular amusements on Sunday outside of Church hours by law, was not only explained by the disturbance of the Sabbath rest, but also by resentment against the intentional diversion from the ordered life of the saint, which it caused. And, on his side, the King's threats of severe punishment for every attack on the legality of those sports were motivated by his purpose of breaking the anti-authoritarian ascetic tendency of Puritanism, which was so dangerous to the State. The feudal and monarchical forces protected the pleasure seekers against the rising middle-class morality and the anti-authoritarian ascetic conventicles, just as to-day capitalistic society tends to protect those willing to work against the class morality of the proletariat and the anti-authoritarian trade union.

As against this the Puritans upheld their decisive characteristic, the principle of ascetic conduct. For otherwise the Puritan aversion to sport, even for the Quakers, was by no means simply one of principle. Sport was accepted if it served a rational purpose, that of recreation necessary for physical efficiency. But as a means for the spontaneous expression of undisciplined impulses, it was under suspicion; and in so far as it became purely a means of enjoyment, or awakened pride, raw instincts or the irrational gambling instinct, it was of course strictly condemned. Impulsive enjoyment of life, which leads away both from work in a calling and from religion, was as such the enemy of rational asceticism, whether in the form of seigneurial sports, or the enjoyment of the dance-hall or the public-house of the common man.[47]

Its attitude was thus suspicious and often hostile to the aspects of culture without any immediate religious value. It is not, however, true that the ideals of Puritanism implied a solemn, narrow-minded contempt of culture. Quite the contrary is the case at least for science, with the exception of the hatred of Scholasticism. Moreover, the great men of the Puritan movement were thoroughly steeped in the culture of the Renaissance. The sermons of the Presbyterian divines abound with classical allusions,[48] and even the Radicals, although they objected to it, were not ashamed to display that kind of learning in theological polemics. Perhaps no country was ever so full of graduates as New England in the first generation of its existence. The satire of their opponents, such as, for instance, Butler's *Hudibras,* also attacks primarily the pedantry and highly trained dialectics of the Puritans. This is partially due to the religious valuation of knowledge which followed from their attitude to the Catholic *fides implicita.*

But the situation is quite different when one looks at non-scientific literature,[49] and especially the fine arts. Here asceticism descended like a frost on the life of "Merrie old England." And not only worldly merriment felt its effect. The Puritan's ferocious hatred of everything which smacked of superstition, of all survivals of magical or sacramental salvation, applied to the Christmas festivities and the May Pole[50] and all spontaneous religious art. That there was room in Holland for a great, often uncouthly realistic art[51] proves only how far from completely the authoritarian moral discipline of that country was able to counteract the influence of the court and the regents (a class of *rentiers*), and also the joy in life of the parvenu bourgeoisie, after the short supremacy of the Calvinistic theocracy had been transformed into a moderate national Church, and with it Calvinism had perceptibly lost in its power of ascetic influence.[52]

The theatre was obnoxious to the Puritans,[53] and with the strict exclusion of the erotic and of nudity from the realm of toleration, a radical view of either literature or art could not exist. The conceptions of idle talk, of superfluities,[54] and of vain ostentation, all designations of an irrational attitude without objective purpose, thus not ascetic, and especially not serving the glory of God, but of man, were always at hand to serve in deciding in favour of sober utility as against any artistic tendencies. This was especially true in the case of decoration of the person, for instance clothing.[55] That powerful tendency toward uniformity of life, which to-day so immensely aids the capitalistic interest in the standardization of production,[56] had its ideal foundations in the repudiation of all idolatry of the flesh.[57]

Of course we must not forget that Puritanism included a world of contradictions, and that the instinctive sense of eternal greatness in art was certainly stronger among its leaders than in the atmosphere of the Cavaliers.[58] Moreover, a unique genius like Rembrandt, however little his conduct may have been acceptable to God in the eyes of the Puritans, was very strongly influenced in the character of his work by his religious environment.[59] But that does not alter the picture as a whole. In so far as the development of the Puritan tradition could, and in part did, lead to a powerful spiritualization of personality, it was a decided benefit to literature. But for the most part that benefit only accrued to later generations. . . .

This worldly Protestant asceticism, as we may recapitulate up to this point, acted powerfully against the spontaneous enjoyment of possessions; it restricted consumption, especially of luxuries. On the other hand, it had the psychological effect of freeing the acquisition of goods from the inhibitions of traditionalistic ethics. It broke the bonds of the impulse of acquisition in that it not only legalized it, but (in the sense discussed) looked upon it as directly willed by God. The campaign against the temptations of the flesh, and the dependence on external things, was, as besides the Puritans the great Quaker apologist Barclay expressly says, not a struggle against the rational acquisition, but against the irrational use of wealth.

But this irrational use was exemplified in the outward forms of luxury which their code condemned as idolatry of the flesh,[60] however natural they had appeared to the feudal mind. On the other hand, they approved the rational and utilitarian uses of wealth which were willed by God for the needs of the individual and the community. They did not wish to impose mortification[61] on the man of wealth, but the use of his means for necessary and practical things. The idea of comfort characteristically limits the extent of ethically permissible expenditures. It is naturally no accident that the de-

velopment of a manner of living consistent with that idea may be observed earliest and most clearly among the most consistent representatives of this whole attitude toward life. Over against the glitter and ostentation of feudal magnificence which, resting on an unsound economic basis, prefers a sordid elegance to a sober simplicity, they set the clean and solid comfort of the middle-class home as an ideal.[62]

On the side of the production of private wealth, asceticism condemned both dishonesty and impulsive avarice. What was condemned as covetousness, Mammonism, etc., was the pursuit of riches for their own sake. For wealth in itself was a temptation. But here asceticism was the power "which ever seeks the good but ever creates evil"[63]; what was evil in its sense was possession and its temptations. For, in conformity with the Old Testament and in analogy to the ethical valuation of good works, asceticism looked upon the pursuit of wealth as an end in itself as highly reprehensible; but the attainment of it as a fruit of labour in a calling was a sign of God's blessing. And even more important: the religious valuation of restless, continuous, systematic work in a worldly calling, as the highest means to asceticism, and at the same time the surest and most evident proof of rebirth and genuine faith, must have been the most powerful conceivable lever for the expansion of that attitude toward life which we have here called the spirit of capitalism.[64]

When the limitation of consumption is combined with this release of acquisitive activity, the inevitable practical result is obvious: accumulation of capital through ascetic compulsion to save.[65] The restraints which were imposed upon the consumption of wealth naturally served to increase it by making possible the productive investment of capital. How strong this influence was is not, unfortunately, susceptible of exact statistical demonstration. In New England the connection is so evident that it did not escape the eye of so discerning a historian as Doyle.[66] But also in Holland, which was really only dominated by strict Calvinism for seven years, the greater simplicity of life in the more seriously religious circles, in combination with great wealth, led to an excessive propensity to accumulation.[67] . . .

As far as the influence of the Puritan outlook extended, under all circumstances—and this is, of course, much more important than the mere encouragement of capital accumulation—it favoured the development of a rational bourgeois economic life; it was the most important, and above all the only consistent influence in the development of that life. It stood at the cradle of the modern economic man.

To be sure, these Puritanical ideals tended to give way under excessive pressure from the temptations of wealth, as the Puritans themselves knew very well. With great regularity we find the most genuine adherents of Puritanism among the classes which were rising from a lowly status,[68] the small bourgeois and farmers, while the *beati possidentes,* even among Quakers, are often found tending to repudiate the old ideals.[69] It was the same fate which again and again befell the predecessor of this worldly asceticism, the monastic asceticism of the Middle Ages. In the latter case, when rational economic activity had worked out its full effects by strict regulation of conduct and limitation of consumption, the wealth accumulated either succumbed directly to the nobility, as in the time before the Reformation, or monastic discipline threatened to break down, and one of the numerous reformations became necessary.

In fact the whole history of monasticism is in a certain sense the history of a continual struggle with the problem of the secularizing influence of wealth. The same is true on a grand scale of the worldly asceticism of Puritanism. The great revival of Methodism, which preceded the expansion of English industry toward the end of the eighteenth century, may well be compared with such a monastic reform. We may hence quote here a passage[70] from John Wesley himself which might well serve as a motto for everything which has been said above. For it shows that the leaders of these ascetic movements understood the seemingly paradoxical relationships which we have here analysed perfectly well, and in the same sense that we have given them.[71] He wrote:

I fear, wherever riches have increased, the essence of religion has decreased in the same proportion. Therefore I do not see how it is possible, in the nature of things, for any revival of true religion to continue long. For religion must necessarily produce both industry and frugality, and these cannot but produce riches. But as riches increase, so will pride, anger, and love of the world in all its branches. How then is it possible that Methodism, that is, a religion of the heart, though it flourishes now as a green bay tree, should continue in this state? For the Methodists in every place grow diligent and frugal; consequently they increase in goods. Hence they proportionately increase in pride, in anger, in the desire of the flesh, the desire of the eyes, and the pride of life. So, although the form of religion remains, the spirit is swiftly vanishing away. Is there no way to prevent this—this continual decay of pure religion? We ought not to prevent people from being diligent and frugal; *we must exhort all Christians to gain all they can, and to save all they can; that is, in effect, to grow rich.*[72]

There follows the advice that those who gain all they can and save all they can should also give all they can, so that they will grow in grace and lay up a treasure in heaven. It is clear that Wesley here expresses, even in detail, just what we have been trying to point out.[73] . . .

A specifically bourgeois economic ethic had grown up. With the consciousness of standing in the fullness of God's grace and being visibly blessed by Him, the bourgeois business man, as long as he remained within the bounds of formal correctness, as long as his moral conduct was spotless and the use to which he put his wealth was not objectionable, could follow his pecuniary interests as he would and feel that he was fulfilling a duty in doing so. The power of religious asceticism provided him in addition with sober, conscientious, and unusually industrious workmen, who clung to their work as to a life purpose willed by God.[74]

Finally, it gave him the comforting assurance that the unequal distribution of the goods of this world was a special dispensation of Divine Providence, which in these differences, as in particular grace, pursued secret ends unknown to men.[75] Calvin himself had made the much-quoted statement that only when the people, i.e. the mass of labourers and craftsmen, were poor did they remain obedient to God.[76] In the Netherlands (Pieter de la Court and others), that had been secularized to the effect that the mass of men only labour when necessity forces them to do so. This formulation of a leading idea of capitalistic economy later entered into the current theories of the productivity of low wages. Here also, with the dying out of the religious root, the utilitarian interpretation crept in unnoticed, in the line of development which we have again and again observed.

Mediæval ethics not only tolerated begging but actually glorified it in the mendicant orders. Even secular beggars, since they gave the person of means opportunity for good works through giving alms, were sometimes considered an estate and treated as such. Even the Anglican social ethic of the Stuarts was very close to this attitude. It remained for Puritan Asceticism to take part in the severe English Poor Relief Legislation which fundamentally changed the situation. And it could do that, because the Protestant sects and the strict Puritan communities actually did not know any begging in their own midst.[77] . . .

Now naturally the whole ascetic literature of almost all denominations is saturated with the idea that faithful labour, even at low wages, on the part of those whom life offers no other opportunities, is highly pleasing to God. In this respect Protestant Asceticism added in itself nothing new. But it not only deepened this idea most powerfully, it also created the force which was alone decisive for its effectiveness: the psychological sanction of it through the conception of this labour as a calling, as the best, often in the last analysis the only means of attaining certainty of grace.[78] And on the other hand it legalized the exploitation of this specific willingness to work, in that it also interpreted the employer's business activity as a calling.[79] It is obvious how powerfully the exclusive search for the Kingdom of God only through the fulfilment of duty in the calling, and the strict asceticism which Church discipline naturally imposed, especially on the propertyless classes, was bound to affect the productivity of labour in the capitalistic sense of the word. The treatment of labour as a calling became as characteristic of the modern worker as the corresponding attitude toward acquisition of the business man. . . .

One of the fundamental elements of the spirit of modern capitalism, and not only of that but of all modern culture: rational conduct on the basis of the idea of the calling, was born—that is what this discussion has sought to demonstrate—from the spirit of Christian asceticism. One has only to re-read the passage from Franklin, quoted at the beginning of this essay, in order to see that the essential elements of the attitude which was there called the spirit of capitalism are the same as what we have just shown to be the content of the Puritan worldly asceticism,[80] only without the religious basis, which by Franklin's time had died away. The idea that modern labour has an ascetic character is of course not new. Limitation to specialized work, with a renunciation of the Faustian universality of man which it involves, is a condition of any valuable work in the modern world; hence deeds and renunciation inevitably condition each other today. This fundamentally ascetic trait of middle-class life, if it attempts to be a way of life at all, and not simply the absence of any, was what Goethe wanted to teach, at the height of his wisdom, in the *Wanderjahren,* and in the end which he gave to the life of his *Faust.*[81] For him the realization meant a renunciation, a departure from an age of full and beautiful humanity, which can no more be repeated in the course of our cultural development than can the flower of the Athenian culture of antiquity.

The Puritan wanted to work in a calling; we are forced to do so. For when asceticism was carried out of monastic cells into everyday life, and began to dominate worldly morality, it did its part in building the tremendous cosmos of the modern economic order. This order is now bound to the technical and economic conditions of machine production which to-day determine the lives of all the individuals who are born into this mechanism, not only those directly concerned with economic acquisition, with irresistible force. Perhaps it will so determine them until the last ton of fossilized coal is burnt. In Baxter's view the care for external goods should only lie on the shoulders of the "saint like a light cloak, which can be thrown aside at any moment."[82] But fate decreed that the cloak should become an iron cage.

Since asceticism undertook to remodel the world and to work out its ideals in the world, material goods have gained an increasing and finally an inexorable power over the lives of men as at no previous period in history. To-day the spirit of religious asceticism—whether finally, who knows?—has escaped from the cage. But victorious capitalism, since it rests on mechanical foundations, needs its support no longer. The rosy blush of its laughing heir, the Enlightenment, seems also to be irretrievably fading, and the idea of duty in one's calling prowls about in our lives like the ghost of dead religious beliefs. Where the fulfilment of the calling cannot directly be related to the highest spiritual and cultural values, or when, on the other hand, it need not be felt simply as economic compulsion, the individual generally abandons the attempt to justify it at all. In the field of its highest development, in the United States, the pursuit of wealth, stripped of its religious and ethical meaning, tends to become associated with purely mundane passions, which often actually give it the character of sport.[83]

No one knows who will live in this cage in the future, or whether at the end of this tremendous development entirely new prophets will arise, or there will be a great rebirth of old ideas and ideals, or, if neither, mechanized petrification, embellished with a sort of convulsive self-importance. For of the last stage of this cultural development, it might well be truly said: "Specialists without spirit, sensualists without heart; this nullity imagines that it has attained a level of civilization never before achieved." . . .

The modern man is in general, even with the best will, unable to give religious ideas a significance for culture and national character which they deserve. But it is, of course, not my aim to substitute for a one-sided materialistic an equally one-sided spiritualistic causal interpretation of culture and of history. Each is equally possible,[84] but each, if it does not serve as the preparation, but as the conclusion of an investigation, accomplishes equally little in the interest of historical truth.[85]

ENDNOTES

1. See the excellent sketch of his character in Edward Dowden, *Puritan and Anglican* (London, 1900). A passable introduction to Baxter's theology, after he had abandoned a strict belief in the double decree, is given in the introduction to the various extracts from his works printed in the *Works of the Puritan Divines* (by Jenkyn). His attempt to combine universal redemption and personal election satisfied no one. For us it is important only that he even then held to personal election, i.e. to the most important point for ethics in the doctrine of predestination. On the other hand, his weakening of the forensic view of redemption is important as being suggestive of baptism.

2. Tracts and sermons by Thomas Adams, John Howe, Matthew Henry, J. Janeway, Stuart Charnock, Baxter, Bunyan, have been collected in the ten volumes of the *Works of the Puritan Divines* (London, 1845–8), though the choice is often somewhat arbitrary. Editions of the works of Bailey, Sedgwick, and Hoornbeek have already been referred to.

3. We could just as well have included Voet and other continental representatives of worldly asceticism. Brentano's view that the whole development was purely Anglo-Saxon is quite wrong. My choice is motivated mainly (though not exclusively) by the wish to present the ascetic movement as much as possible in the second half of the seventeenth century, immediately before the change to utilitarianism. It has unfortunately been impossible, within the limits of this sketch, to enter upon the fascinating task of presenting the characteristics of ascetic Protestantism through the medium of the biographical literature; the Quakers would in this connection be particularly important, since they are relatively little known in Germany.

4. For one might just as well take the writings of Gisbert Voet, the proceedings of the Huguenot Synods, or the Dutch Baptist literature. Sombart and Brentano have unfortunately taken just the ebionitic parts of Baxter, which I myself have strongly emphasized, to confront me with the undoubted capitalistic backwardness of his doctrines. But (1) one must know this whole literature thoroughly in order to use it correctly, and (2) not overlook the fact that I have attempted to show how, in spite of its anti-mammonistic doctrines, the spirit of this ascetic religion nevertheless, just as in the monastic communities, gave birth to economic rationalism because it placed a premium on what was most important for it: the fundamentally ascetic rational motives. That fact alone is under discussion and is the point of this whole essay.

5. Similarly in Calvin, who was certainly no champion of bourgeois wealth (see the sharp attacks on Venice and Antwerp in *Jes. Opp.*, III, 140a, 308a).

6. *Saints' Everlasting Rest*, chaps. x, xii. Compare Bailey (*Praxis Pietatis*, p. 182) or Matthew Henry (*The Worth of the Soul, Works of the Puritan Divines*, p. 319). "Those that

are eager in pursuit of worldly wealth despise their Soul, not only because the Soul is neglected and the body preferred before it, but because it is employed in these pursuits" (Psa. cxxvii, 2). On the same page, however, is the remark to be cited below about the sinfulness of all waste of time, especially in recreations. Similarly in almost the whole religious literature of English-Dutch Puritanism. See, for instance, Hoornbeek's (*Theologia practica*, Utrecht, 1663, L, X, ch. 18, 18) Phillipics against *avaritia*. This writer is also affected by sentimental pietistic influences. See the praise of *tranquillitas animi* which is much more pleasing to God than the *sollicitudo* of this world. Also Bailey, referring to the well-known passage in Scripture, is of the opinion that "A rich man is not easily saved" (*Praxis pietatis*, Leipzig, 1724, p. 182). The Methodist catechisms also warn against "gathering treasure on this earth." For Pietism this is quite obvious, as also for the Quakers. Compare Barclay (*Apology for the True Christian Divinity*, London, 1701, p. 517), ". . . and therefore beware of such temptations as to use their callings as an engine to be richer."

7. For not wealth alone, but also the impulsive pursuit of it (or what passed as such) was condemned with similar severity. In the Netherlands the South Holland Synod of 1574 declared, in reply to a question, that money-lenders should not be admitted to communion even though the business was permitted by law; and the Deventer Provincial Synod of 1598 (Art. 24) extended this to the employees of money-lenders. The Synod of Gorichem in 1606 prescribed severe and humiliating conditions under which the wives of usurers might be admitted, and the question was discussed as late as 1644 and 1657 whether Lombards should be admitted to communion (this against Brentano, who cites his own Catholic ancestors, although foreign traders and bankers have existed in the whole European and Asiatic world for thousands of years). Gisbert Voet (*Disp. Theol.*, IV, 1667, *de usuris*, p. 665) still wanted to exclude the Trapezites (Lombards, Piedmontese). The same was true of the Huguenot Synods. This type of capitalistic classes were not the typical representatives of the philosophy or the type of conduct with which we are concerned. They were also not new as compared with antiquity or the Middle Ages.

8. Developed in detail in the tenth chapter of the *Saints' Everlasting Rest*. He who should seek to rest in the shelter of possessions which God gives, God strikes even in this life. A self-satisfied enjoyment of wealth already gained is almost always a symptom of moral degradation. If we had everything which we could have in this world, would that be all we hoped for? Complete satisfaction of desires is not attainable on earth because God's will has decreed it should not be so.

9. *Christian Directory*, I, pp. 375–6. "It is for action that God maintaineth us and our activities; work is the moral as well

as the natural end of power. . . . It is action that God is most served and honoured by. . . . The public welfare or the good of the many is to be valued above our own." Here is the connecting-point for the transition from the will of God to the purely utilitarian view-point of the later liberal theory. On the religious sources of Utilitarianism, see below in the text and above, chap. iv, note 145.

10. The commandment of silence has been, starting from the Biblical threat of punishment for every useless word, especially since the Cluny monks, a favourite ascetic means of education in self-control. Baxter also speaks in detail of the sinfulness of unnecessary words. Its place in his character has been pointed out by Sanford, *Studies and Reflections of the Great Rebellion,* pp. 90 ff.

What contemporaries felt as the deep melancholy and moroseness of the Puritans was the result of breaking down the spontaneity of the *status naturalis,* and the condemnation of thoughtless speech was in the service of this end. When Washington Irving (*Bracebridge Hall,* chap. xxx) seeks the reason for it partly in the calculating spirit of capitalism and partly in the effect of political freedom, which promotes a sense of responsibility, it may be remarked that it does not apply to the Latin peoples. For England the situation was probably that: (1) Puritanism enabled its adherents to create free institutions and still become a world power; and (2) it transformed that calculating spirit (what Sombart calls *Rechenhaftigkeit*), which is in truth essential to capitalism, from a mere means to economy into a principle of general conduct.

11. *Op. cit.,* I, p. 111.

12. *Op. cit.,* I, p. 383 f.

13. Similarly on the preciousness of time, see Barclay, *op. cit.,* p. 14.

14. Baxter, *op. cit.,* I, p. 79. "Keep up a high esteem of time and be every day more careful that you lose none of your time, than you are that you lose none of your gold and silver. And if vain recreation, dressings, feastings, idle talk, unprofitable company, or sleep be any of them temptations to rob you of any of your time, accordingly heighten your watchfulness." "Those that are prodigal of their time despise their own souls," says Matthew Henry (*Worth of the Soul, Works of the Puritan Divines,* p. 315). Here also Protestant asceticism follows a well-beaten track. We are accustomed to think it characteristic of the modern man that he has no time, and for instance, like Goethe in the *Wanderjahren,* to measure the degree of capitalistic development by the fact that the clocks strike every quarter-hour. So also Sombart in his *Kapitalismus.* We ought not, however, to forget that the first people to live (in the Middle Ages) with careful measurement of time were the monks, and that the church bells were meant above all to meet their needs.

15. Compare Baxter's discussion of the calling, *op. cit.,* I, pp. 108 ff. Especially the following passage: "Question:

But may I not cast off the world that I may only think of my salvation? Answer: You may cast off all such excess of worldly cares or business as unnecessarily hinder you in spiritual things. But you may not cast off all bodily employment and mental labour in which you may serve the common good. Everyone as a member of Church or Commonwealth must employ their parts to the utmost for the good of the Church and the Commonwealth. To neglect this and say: I will pray and meditate, is as if your servant should refuse his greatest work and tie himself to some lesser, easier part. And God hath commanded you some way or other to labour for your daily bread and not to live as drones of the sweat of others only." God's commandment to Adam, "In the sweat of thy brow," and Paul's declaration, "He who will not work shall not eat," are also quoted. It has always been known of the Quakers that even the most well-to-do of them have had their sons learn a calling, for ethical and not, as Alberti recommends, for utilitarian reasons.

16. Here are points where Pietism, on account of its emotional character, takes a different view. Spener, although he emphasizes in characteristic Lutheran fashion that labour in a calling is worship of God (*Theologische Bedenken,* III, p. 445), nevertheless holds that the restlessness of business affairs distracts one from God, a most characteristic difference from Puritanism.

17. I, *op. cit.,* p. 242. "It's they that are lazy in their callings that can find no time for holy duties." Hence the idea that the cities, the seat of the middle class with its rational business activities, are the seats of ascetic virtue. Thus Baxter says of his hand-loom weavers in Kidderminister: "And their constant converse and traffic with London doth much to promote civility and piety among tradesmen . . ." in his autobiography (*Works of the Puritan Divines,* p. 38). That the proximity of the capital should promote virtue would astonish modern clergymen, at least in Germany. But Pietism also inclined to similar views. Thus Spener, speaking of a young colleague, writes: "At least it appears that among the great multitudes in the cities, though the majority is quite depraved, there are nevertheless a number of good people who can accomplish much, while in villages often hardly anything good can be found in a whole community" (*Theologische Bedenken,* I, 66, p. 303). In other words, the peasant is little suited to rational ascetic conduct. Its ethical glorification is very modern. We cannot here enter into the significance of this and similar statements for the question of the relation of asceticism to social classes.

18. Take, for instance, the following passages (*op. cit.,* p. 336 f.): "Be wholly taken up in diligent business of your lawful callings when you are not exercised in the more immediate service of God." "Labour hard in your callings." "See that you have a calling which will find you employment for all the time which God's immediate service spareth."

19. That the peculiar ethical valuation of labour and its dignity was not originally a Christian idea nor even peculiar to Christianity has recently again been strongly emphasized by Harnack (*Mitt. des Ev.-Soz. Kongr.,* 14. Folge, 1905, Nos. 3, 4, p. 48).

20. Similarly in Pietism (Spener, *Theologische Bedenken,* Halle, 1712, III, pp. 429–30). The characteristic Pietist version is that loyalty to a calling which is imposed upon us by the fall serves to annihilate one's own selfish will. Labour in the calling is, as a service of love to one's neighbour, a duty of gratitude for God's grace (a Lutheran idea), and hence it is not pleasing to God that it should be performed reluctantly (*op. cit.,* III, p. 272). The Christian should thus "prove himself as industrious in his labour as a worldly man" (III, p. 278). That is obviously less drastic than the Puritan version.

21. The significance of this important difference, which has been evident ever since the Benedictine rules, can only be shown by a much wider investigation.

22. "A sober procreation of children" is its purpose according to Baxter. Similarly Spener, at the same time with concessions to the coarse Lutheran attitude, which makes the avoidance of immorality, which is otherwise unavoidable, an accessory aim. Concupiscence as an accompaniment of sexual intercourse is sinful even in marriage. For instance, in Spener's view it is a result of the fall which transformed such a natural, divinely ordained process into something inevitably accompanied by sinful sensations, which is hence shameful. Also in the opinion of various Pietistic groups the highest form of Christian marriage is that with the preservation of virginity, the next highest that in which sexual intercourse is only indulged in for the procreation of children, and so on down to those which are contracted for purely erotic or external reasons and which are, from an ethical standpoint, concubinage. On these lower levels a marriage entered into for purely economic reasons is preferred (because after all it is inspired by rational motives) to one with erotic foundations. We may here neglect the Herrnhut theory and practice of marriage. Rationalistic philosophy (Christian Wolff) adopted the ascetic theory in the form that what was designed as a means to an end, concupiscence and its satisfaction, should not be made an end in itself.

The transition to a pure, hygienically oriented utilitarianism had already taken place in Franklin, who took approximately the ethical standpoint of modern physicians, who understand by chastity the restriction of sexual intercourse to the amount desirable for health, and who have, as is well known, even given theoretical advice as to how that should be accomplished. As soon as these matters have become the object of purely rational consideration the same development has everywhere taken place. The Puritan and the hygienic sex-rationalist generally tread very different paths, but here they understand each other perfectly. In a lecture, a zealous adherent of hygienic prostitution—it was a question of the regulation of brothels and prostitutes—defended the moral legitimacy of extra-marital intercourse (which was looked upon as hygienically useful) by referring to its poetic justification in the case of Faust and Margaret. To treat Margaret as a prostitute and to fail to distinguish the powerful sway of human passions from sexual intercourse for hygienic reasons, both are thoroughly congenial to the Puritan standpoint. Similar, for instance, is the typical specialist's view, occasionally put forward by very distinguished physicians, that a question which extends so far into the subtlest problems of personality and of culture as that of sexual abstinence should be dealt with exclusively in the forum of the physician (as an expert). For the Puritan the expert was the moral theorist, now he is the medical man; but the claim of competence to dispose of the questions which seem to us somewhat narrow-minded is, with opposite signs of course, the same in both cases.

But with all its prudery, the powerful idealism of the Puritan attitude can show positive accomplishments, even from the point of view of race conservation in a purely hygienic sense, while modern sex hygiene, on account of the appeal to unprejudicedness which it is forced to make, is in danger of destroying the basis of all its success. How, with the rationalistic interpretation of sexual relations among peoples influenced by Puritanism, a certain refinement and spiritual and ethical penetration of marital relationships, with a blossoming of matrimonial chivalry, has grown up, in contrast to the patriarchal sentimentality (*Brodem*), which is typical of Germany even in the circles of the intellectual aristocracy, must necessarily remain outside this discussion. Baptist influences have played a part in the emancipation of woman; the protection of her freedom of conscience, and the extension of the idea of the universal priesthood to her were here also the first breaches in patriarchal ideas.

23. This recurs again and again in Baxter. The Biblical basis is regularly either the passages in Proverbs, which we already know from Franklin (xxii, 29), or those in praise of labour (xxxi. 16). Cf. *op. cit.,* I, pp. 377, 382, etc.

24. Even Zinzendorf says at one point: "One does not only work in order to live, but one lives for the sake of one's work, and if there is no more work to do one suffers or goes to sleep" (Plitt, *Zinzendorf's Theologie,* Gotha, 1869, I, p. 428).

25. Also a symbol of the Mormons closes (after quotations) with the words: "But a lazy or indolent man cannot be a Christian and be saved. He is destined to be struck down and cast from the hive." But in this case it was primarily the grandiose discipline, half-way between monastery and factory, which placed the individual before the dilemma of labour or annihilation and, of course in connection with religious enthusiasm and only possible through it, brought forth the astonishing economic achievements of this sect.

26. Hence (*op. cit.,* I, p. 380) its symptoms are carefully analysed. Sloth and idleness are such deadly sins because

they have a cumulative character. They are even regarded by Baxter as "destroyers of grace" (*op. cit.,* I, pp. 279–80). That is, they are the antitheses of the methodical life.

27. Similarly Spener (*op. cit.,* III, pp. 338, 425), who for this reason opposes the tendency to early retirement as morally objectionable, and, in refuting an objection to the taking of interest, that the enjoyment of interest leads to laziness, emphasizes that anyone who was in a position to live upon interest would still be obligated to work by God's commandment.

28. Including Pietism. Whenever a question of change of calling arises, Spener takes the attitude that after a certain calling has once been entered upon, it is a duty of obedience to Providence to remain and acquiesce in it.

29. Baxter, *op. cit.,* I, p. 377.

30. But this does not mean that the Puritan view-point was historically derived from the latter. On the contrary, it is an expression of the genuinely Calvinistic idea that the cosmos of the world serves the glory of God. The utilitarian turn, that the economic cosmos should serve the good of the many, the common good, etc., was a consequence of the idea that any other interpretation of it would lead to aristocratic idolatry of the flesh, or at least did not serve the glory of God, but only fleshly cultural ends. But God's will, as it is expressed (chap. iv, note 34) in the purposeful arrangements of the economic cosmos, can, so far as secular ends are in question at all, only be embodied in the good of the community, in impersonal usefulness. Utilitarianism is thus, as has already been pointed out, the result of the impersonal character of brotherly love and the repudiation of all glorification of this world by the exclusiveness of the Puritan *in majorem Dei gloriam.*

How completely this idea, that all idolatry of the flesh is inconsistent with the glory of God and hence unconditionally bad, dominated ascetic Protestantism is clearly shown by the doubts and hesitation which it cost even Spener, who certainly was not infected with democracy, to maintain the use of titles as *a'διάφορον* against numerous objections. He finally comforted himself with the reflection that even in the Bible the Prætor Festus was given the title of κρα'τιστος by the Apostles. The political side of the question does not arise in this connection.

31. "The inconstant man is a stranger in his own house," says Thomas Adams (*Works of the Puritan Divines,* p. 77).

32. On this, see especially George Fox's remarks in the *Friends' Library* (ed. W. & T. Evans, Philadelphia, 1837), I, p. 130.

33. Above all, this sort of religious ethic cannot be regarded as a reflex of economic conditions. The specialization of occupations had, if anything, gone further in mediæval Italy than in the England of that period.

34. Such ideas are not to be found, at least in the writings, of the leading Continental Pietists. Spener's attitude vacillates between the Lutheran (that of satisfaction of needs) and Mercantilist arguments for the usefulness of the prosperity of commerce, etc. (*op. cit.,* III, pp. 330, 332; I, p. 418: "the cultivation of tobacco brings money into the country and is thus useful, hence not sinful." Compare also III, pp. 426–7, 429, 434). But he does not neglect to point out that, as the example of the Quakers and the Mennonites shows, one can make profit and yet remain pious; in fact, that even especially high profits, as we shall point out later, may be the direct result of pious uprightness (*op. cit.,* p. 435).

35. These views of Baxter are not a reflection of the economic environment in which he lived. On the contrary, his autobiography shows that the success of his home missionary work was partly due to the fact that the Kidderminster tradesmen were not rich, but only earned food and raiment, and that the master craftsmen had to live from hand to mouth just as their employees did. "It is the poor who receive the glad tidings of the Gospel." Thomas Adams remarks on the pursuit of gain: "He [the knowing man] knows . . . that money may make a man richer, not better, and thereupon chooseth rather to sleep with a good conscience than a full purse . . . therefore desires no more wealth than an honest man may bear away" (*Works of the Puritan Divines,* LI). But he does want that much, and that means that every formally honest gain is legitimate.

36. Thus Baxter, *op. cit.,* I, chap. x, I, 9 (par. 24); I, p. 378, 2. In Prov. xxiii. 4: "Weary thyself not to be rich" means only "riches for our fleshly ends must not ultimately be intended." Possession in the feudal-seigneurial form of its use is what is odious (cf. the remark, *op. cit.,* I, p. 380, on the "debauched part of the gentry"), not possession in itself. Milton, in the first *Defensio pro populo Anglicano,* held the well-known theory that only the middle class can maintain virtue. That middle class here means bourgeoisie as against the aristocracy is shown by the statement that both luxury and necessity are unfavourable to virtue.

37. This is most important. We may again add the general remark: we are here naturally not so much concerned with what concepts the theological moralists developed in their ethical theories, but, rather, what was the effective morality in the life of believers—that is, how the religious background of economic ethics affected practice. In the casuistic literature of Catholicism, especially the Jesuit, one can occasionally read discussions which—for instance on the question of the justification of interest, into which we do not enter here—sound like those of many Protestant casuists, or even seem to go farther in permitting or tolerating things. The Puritans have since often enough been reproached that their ethic is at bottom the same as that of the Jesuits. Just as the Calvinists often cite Catholic moralists, not only Thomas Aquinas, Bernhard of Clairvaux, Bonaventura, etc., but also contemporaries, the Catholic casuists also took notice of heretical ethics. We cannot discuss all that here.

But quite apart from the decisive fact of the religious sanction of the ascetic life for the layman, there is the fundamental difference, even in theory, that these latitudinarian ideas within Catholicism were the products of peculiarly lax ethical theories, not sanctioned by the authority of the Church, but opposed by the most serious and strictest disciples of it. On the other hand, the Protestant idea of the calling in effect placed the most serious enthusiasts for asceticism in the service of capitalistic acquisition. What in the one case might under certain conditions be allowed, appeared in the other as a positive moral good. The fundamental differences of the two ethics, very important in practice, have been finally crystallized, even for modern times, by the Jansenist controversy and the Bull *Unigenitus.*

38. "You may labour in that manner as tendeth most to your success and lawful gain. You are bound to improve all your talents." There follows the passage cited above in the text. A direct parallel between the pursuit of wealth in the Kingdom of Heaven and the pursuit of success in an earthly calling is found in Janeway, *Heaven upon Earth* (*Works of the Puritan Divines,* p. 275).

39. Even in the Lutheran Confession of Duke Christopher of Württemberg, which was submitted to the Council of Trent, objection is made to the oath of poverty. He who is poor in his station should bear it, but if he swore to remain so it would be the same as if he swore to remain sick or to maintain a bad reputation.

40. Thus in Baxter and also in Duke Christopher's confession. Compare further passages like: ". . . the vagrant rogues whose lives are nothing but an exorbitant course; the main begging," etc. (Thomas Adams, *Works of the Puritan Divines,* p. 259). Even Calvin had strictly forbidden begging, and the Dutch Synods campaigned against licences to beg. During the epoch of the Stuarts, especially Laud's regime under Charles I, which had systematically developed the principle of public poor relief and provision of work for the unemployed, the Puritan battle-cry was: "Giving alms is no charity" (title of Defoe's later well-known work). Towards the end of the seventeenth century they began the deterrent system of workhouses for the unemployed (compare Leonard, *Early History of English Poor Relief,* Cambridge, 1900, and H. Levy, *Die Grundlagen des ökonomischen Liberalismus in der Geschichte der englischen Volkswirtschaft,* Jena, 1912, pp. 69 ff.).

41. The President of the Baptist Union of Great Britain and Ireland, G. White, said emphatically in his inaugural address before the assembly in London in 1903 (*Baptist Handbook,* 1904, p. 104): "The best men on the roll of our Puritan Churches were men of affairs, who believed that religion should permeate the whole of life."

42. Here also lies the characteristic difference from all feudal view-points. For the latter only the descendants of the parvenu (political or social) can reap the benefit of his success in a recognized station (characteristically expressed in the Spanish *Hidalgo* = *hijo d'algo* = *filius de aliquo* where the *aliquid* means an inherited property). However rapidly these differences are to-day fading out in the rapid change and Europeanization of the American national character, nevertheless the precisely opposite bourgeois attitude which glorifies business success and earnings as a symptom of mental achievement, but has no respect for mere inherited wealth, is still sometimes represented there. On the other hand, in Europe (as James Bryce once remarked) in effect almost every social honour is now purchasable for money, so long as the buyer has not himself stood behind the counter, and carries out the necessary metamorphosis of his property (formation of trusts, etc.). Against the aristocracy of blood, see for instance Thomas Adams, *Works of the Puritan Divines,* p. 216.

43. That was, for instance, already true of the founder of the Familist sect, Hendrik Nicklaes, who was a merchant (Barclay, *Inner Life of the Religious Societies of the Commonwealth,* p. 34).

44. This is, for instance, definitely true for Hoornbeek, since Matt. v. 5 and I Tim. iv. 8 also made purely worldly promises to the saints (*op. cit.,* I, p. 193). Everything is the work of God's Providence, but in particular He takes care of His own. *Op. cit.,* p. 192: "Super alios autem summa cura et modis singularissimis versatur Dei providentia circa fideles." There follows a discussion of how one can know that a stroke of luck comes not from the *communis providentia,* but from that special care. Bailey also (*op. cit.,* p. 191) explains success in worldly labours by reference to Providence. That prosperity is often the reward of a godly life is a common expression in Quaker writings (for example see such an expression as late as 1848 in *Selection from the Christian Advices,* issued by the General Meeting of the Society of Friends, London, sixth edition, 1851, p. 209). We shall return to the connection with the Quaker ethics.

45. Thomas Adams's analysis of the quarrel of Jacob and Esau may serve as an example of this attention to the patriarchs, which is equally characteristic of the Puritan view of life (*Works of the Puritan Divines,* p. 235): "His [Esau's] folly may be argued from the base estimation of the birthright" [the passage is also important for the development of the idea of the birthright, of which more later] "that he would so lightly pass from it and on so easy condition as a pottage." But then it was perfidious that he would not recognize the sale, charging he had been cheated. He is, in other words, "a cunning hunter, a man of the fields"; a man of irrational, barbarous life; while Jacob, "a plain man, dwelling in tents," represents the "man of grace."

The sense of an inner relationship to Judaism, which is expressed even in the well-known work of Roosevelt, Köhler (*Die Niederl. ref. Kirche,* Erlangen, 1856) found widespread among the peasants in Holland. But, on the other hand, Puritanism was fully conscious of its differences from Hebrew ethics in practical affairs, as Prynne's attack on the Jews (apropos of Cromwell's proposals for toleration) plainly shows.

46. Printed in Gardiner's *Constitutional Documents*. One may compare this struggle against anti-authoritarian asceticism with Louis XIV's persecution of Port Royal and the Jansenists.

47. Calvin's own standpoint was in this respect distinctly less drastic, at least in so far as the finer aristocratic forms of the enjoyment of life were concerned. The only limitation is the Bible. Whoever adheres to it and has a good conscience, need not observe his every impulse to enjoy life with anxiety. The discussion in Chapter X of the *Instit. Christ* (for instance, "nec fugere ea quoque possumus quæ videntur oblectatione magis quam necessitate inservire") might in itself have opened the way to a very lax practice. Along with increasing anxiety over the *certitudo salutis* the most important circumstance for the later disciples was, however, as we shall point out in another place, that in the era of the *ecclesia militans* it was the small bourgeoisie who were the principal representatives of Calvinistic ethics.

48. Thomas Adams (*Works of the Puritan Divines*, p. 3) begins a sermon on the "three divine sisters" ("but love is the greatest of these") with the remark that even Paris gave the golden apple to Aphrodite!

49. Novels and the like should not be read; they are "wastetimes" (Baxter, *Christian Directory*, 1, p. 51). The decline of lyric poetry and folk-music, as well as the drama, after the Elizabethan age in England is well known. In the pictorial arts Puritanism perhaps did not find very much to suppress. But very striking is the decline from what seemed to be a promising musical beginning (England's part in the history of music was by no means unimportant) to that absolute musical vacuum which we find typical of the Anglo-Saxon peoples later, and even to-day. Except for the negro churches, and the professional singers whom the Churches now engage as attractions (Trinity Church in Boston in 1904 for $8,000 annually), in America one also hears as community singing in general only a noise which is intolerable to German ears (partly analogous things in Holland also).

50. Just the same in Holland, as the reports of the Synods show. (See the resolutions on the Maypole in the Reitmaas Collection, VI, 78, 139.)

51. That the "Renaissance of the Old Testament" and the Pietistic orientation to certain Christian attitudes hostile to beauty in art, which in the last analysis go back to Isaiah and the 22nd Psalm, must have contributed to making ugliness more of a possible object for art, and that the Puritan repudiation of idolatry of the flesh played a part, seems likely. But in detail everything seems uncertain. In the Roman Church quite different demagogic motives led to outwardly similar effects, but, however, with quite different artistic results. Standing before Rembrandt's *Saul and David* (in the Mauritshuis), one seems directly to feel the powerful influence of Puritan emotions. The excellent analysis of Dutch cultural influences in Carl Neumann's *Rembrandt* probably gives everything that for the time being we can know about how far ascetic Protestantism may be credited with a positive fructifying influence on art.

52. The most complex causes, into which we cannot go here, were responsible for the relatively smaller extent to which the Calvinistic ethic penetrated practical life there. The ascetic spirit began to weaken in Holland as early as the beginning of the seventeenth century (the English Congregationalists who fled to Holland in 1608 were disturbed by the lack of respect for the Sabbath there), but especially under the Stadtholder Frederick Henry. Moreover, Dutch Puritanism had in general much less expansive power than English. The reasons for it lay in part in the political constitution (particularistic confederation of towns and provinces) and in the far smaller degree of military force (the War of Independence was soon fought principally with the money of Amsterdam and mercenary armies. English preachers illustrated the Babylonian confusion of tongues by reference to the Dutch Army). Thus the burden of the war of religion was to a large extent passed on to others, but at the same time a part of their political power was lost. On the other hand, Cromwell's army, even though it was partly conscripted, felt that it was an army of citizens. It was, to be sure, all the more characteristic that just this army adopted the abolition of conscription in its programme, because one could fight justly only for the glory of God in a cause hallowed by conscience, but not at the whim of a sovereign. The constitution of the British Army, so immoral to traditional German ideas, had its historical origin in very moral motives, and was an attainment of soldiers who had never been beaten. Only after the Restoration was it placed in the service of the interests of the Crown.

The Dutch *schutterijen*, the champions of Calvinism in the period of the Great War, only half a generation after the Synod of Dordrecht, do not look in the least ascetic in the pictures of Hals. Protests of the Synods against their conduct occur frequently. The Dutch concept of *Deftigkeit* is a mixture of bourgeois-rational honesty and patrician consciousness of status. The division of church pews according to classes in the Dutch churches shows the aristocratic character of this religion even to-day. The continuance of the town economy hampered industry. It prospered almost alone through refugees, and hence only sporadically. Nevertheless, the worldly asceticism of Calvinism and Pietism was an important influence in Holland in the same direction as elsewhere. Also in the sense to be referred to presently of ascetic compulsion to save, as Groen van Prinsterer shows in the passage cited below, note 67.

Moreover, the almost complete lack of *belles lettres* in Calvinistic Holland is of course no accident (see for instance Busken-Huet, *Het Land van Rembrandt*). The significance of Dutch religion as ascetic compulsion to save appears clearly even in the eighteenth century in the writings of Albertus Haller. For the characteristic peculiarities of the Dutch attitude toward art and its motives, compare for example the autobiographical remarks of Constantine Huyghens (written in 1629–31) in *Oud Holland*, 1891. The work of Groen van Prinsterer, *La Hollande et l'influence de Calvin*, 1864, already referred to, offers nothing important for our problems. The New Netherlands colony in America was socially a half-feudal settlement of *patroons*, merchants who advanced capital, and, unlike New England, it was difficult to persuade small people to settle there.

53. We may recall that the Puritan town government closed the theatre at Stratford-on-Avon while Shakespeare was still alive and residing there in his last years. Shakespeare's hatred and contempt of the Puritans appear on every occasion. As late as 1777 the City of Birmingham refused to license a theatre because it was conducive to slothfulness, and hence unfavourable to trade (Ashley, *Birmingham Trade and Commerce*, 1913).

54. Here also it was of decisive importance that for the Puritan there was only the alternative of divine will or earthly vanity. Hence for him there could be no *adiaphora*. As we have already pointed out, Calvin's own view was different in this respect. What one eats, wears, etc., as long as there is no enslavement of the soul to earthly desire as a result, is indifferent. Freedom from the world should be expressed, as for the Jesuits, in indifference, which for Calvin meant an indifferent, uncovetous use of whatever goods the earth offered (pp. 409 ff. of the original edition of the *Instit. Christ*).

55. The Quaker attitude in this respect is well known. But as early as the beginning of the seventeenth century the heaviest storms shook the pious congregation of exiles in Amsterdam for a decade over the fashionable hats and dresses of a preacher's wife (charmingly described in Dexter's *Congregationalism of the Last Three Hundred Years*). Sanford (*op. cit.*) has pointed out that the present-day male hair-cut is that of the ridiculous Roundheads, and the equally ridiculous (for the time) male clothing of the Puritans is at least in principle fundamentally the same as that of to-day.

56. On this point again see Veblen's *Theory of Business Enterprise*.

57. Again and again we come back to this attitude. It explains statements like the following: "Every penny which is paid upon yourselves and children and friends must be done as by God's own appointment and to serve and please Him. Watch narrowly, or else that thievish, carnal self will leave God nothing" (Baxter, *op. cit.*, I, p. 108). This is decisive; what is expended for personal ends is withdrawn from the service of God's glory.

58. Quite rightly it is customary to recall (Dowden, *op. cit.*) that Cromwell saved Raphael's drawings and Mantegna's *Triumph of Cæsar* from destruction, while Charles II tried to sell them. Moreover, the society of the Restoration was distinctly cool or even hostile to English national literature. In fact the influence of Versailles was all-powerful at courts everywhere. A detailed analysis of the influence of the unfavourable atmosphere for the spontaneous enjoyment of everyday life on the spirit of the higher types of Puritan, and the men who went through the schooling of Puritanism, is a task which cannot be undertaken within the limits of this sketch. Washington Irving *(Bracebridge Hall)* formulates it in the usual English terms thus: "It [he says political freedom, we should say Puritanism] evinces less play of the fancy, but more power of the imagination." It is only necessary to think of the place of the Scotch in science, literature, and technical invention, as well as in the business life of Great Britain, to be convinced that this remark approaches the truth, even though put somewhat too narrowly. We cannot speak here of its significance for the development of technique and the empirical sciences. The relation itself is always appearing in everyday life. For the Quakers, for instance, the recreations which are permissible (according to Barclay) are: visiting of friends, reading of historical works, mathematical and physical experiments, gardening, discussion of business and other occurrences in the world, etc. The reason is that pointed out above.

59. Already very finely analysed in Carl Neumann's *Rembrandt*, which should be compared with the above remarks in general.

60. This is, as must continually be emphasized, the final decisive religious motive (along with the purely ascetic desire to mortify the flesh). It is especially clear in the Quakers.

61. Baxter (*Saints' Everlasting Rest*, p. 12) repudiates this with precisely the same reasoning as the Jesuits: the body must have what it needs, otherwise one becomes a slave to it.

62. This ideal is clearly present, especially for Quakerism, in the first period of its development, as has already been shown in important points by Weingarten in his *Englische Revolutionskirchen*. Also Barclay's thorough discussion (*op. cit.*, pp. 519 ff., 533) shows it very clearly. To be avoided are: (1) Worldly vanity; thus all ostentation, frivolity, and use of things having no practical purpose, or which are valuable only for their scarcity (i.e. for vanity's sake). (2) Any unconscientious use of wealth, such as excessive expenditure for not very urgent needs above necessary provision for the real needs of life and for the future. The Quaker was, so to speak, a living law of marginal utility. "Moderate use of the creature" is definitely permissible, but in particular one might pay attention to the quality and durability of materials so long as it did not lead to vanity. On all

this compare *Morgenblatt für gebildete Leser,* 1846, pp. 216 ff. Especially on comfort and solidity among the Quakers, compare Schneckenburger, *Vorlesungen,* pp. 96 f.

63. Adapted by Weber from Faust, Act I. Goethe there depicts Mephistopheles as "Die Kraft, die stets das Böse will, und stets das Gute schafft."—TRANSLATOR'S NOTE.

64. It has already been remarked that we cannot here enter into the question of the class relations of these religious movements (see the essays on the *Wirtschaftsethik der Weltreligionen*). In order to see, however, that for example Baxter, of whom we make so much use in this study, did not see things solely as a bourgeois of his time, it will suffice to recall that even for him in the order of the religious value of callings, after the learned professions comes the husband-man, and only then mariners, clothiers, booksellers, tailors, etc. Also, under mariners (characteristically enough) he probably thinks at least as often of fishermen as of shipowners. In this regard several things in the *Talmud* are in a different class. Compare, for instance, in Wünsche, *Babyl. Talmud,* II, pp. 20, 21, the sayings of Rabbi Eleasar, which though not unchallenged, all contend in effect that business is better than agriculture. In between see II, 2, p. 68, on the wise investment of capital: one-third in land, one-third in merchandise, and one-third in cash.

For those to whom no causal explanation is adequate without an economic (or materialistic as it is unfortunately still called) interpretation, it may be remarked that I consider the influence of economic development on the fate of religious ideas to be very important and shall later attempt to show how in our case the process of mutual adaptation of the two took place. On the other hand, those religious ideas themselves simply cannot be deduced from economic circumstances. They are in themselves, that is beyond doubt, the most powerful plastic elements of national character, and contain a law of development and a compelling force entirely their own. Moreover, the most important differences, so far as non-religious factors play a part, are, as with Lutheranism and Calvinism, the result of political circumstances, not economic.

65. That is what Eduard Bernstein means to express when he says, in the essay referred to above (*Geschichte des Sozialismus,* Stuttgart, 1895, pp. 625, 681), "Asceticism is a bourgeois virtue." His discussion is the first which has suggested these important relationships. But the connection is a much wider one than he suspected. For not only the accumulation of capital, but the ascetic rationalization of the whole of economic life was involved.

For the American Colonies, the difference between the Puritan North, where, on account of the ascetic compulsion to save, capital in search of investment was always available, from the conditions in the South has already been clearly brought out by Doyle.

66. Doyle, *The English in America,* II, chap. i. The existence of iron-works (1643), weaving for the market (1659), and

also the high development of the handicrafts in New England in the first generation after the foundation of the colonies are, from a purely economic view-point, astounding. They are in striking contrast to the conditions in the South, as well as the non-Calvinistic Rhode Island with its complete freedom of conscience. There, in spite of the excellent harbour, the report of the Governor and Council of 1686 said: "The great obstruction concerning trade is the want of merchants and men of considerable estates amongst us" (Arnold, *History of the State of Rhode Island,* p. 490). It can in fact hardly be doubted that the compulsion continually to reinvest savings, which the Puritan curtailment of consumption exercised, played a part. In addition there was the part of Church discipline which cannot be discussed here.

67. That, however, these circles rapidly diminished in the Netherlands is shown by Busken-Huet's discussion (*op. cit.,* II, chaps. iii and iv). Nevertheless, Groen van Prinsterer says (*Handb. der Gesch. van het Vaderland,* third edition, par. 303, note, p. 254), "De Nederlanders verkoopen veel en verbruiken weinig," even of the time after the Peace of Westphalia.

68. This is noted by Petty (*Pol. Arith.*), and all the contemporary sources without exception speak in particular of the Puritan sectarians, Baptists, Quakers, Mennonites, etc., as belonging partly to a propertyless class, partly to one of small capitalists, and contrast them both with the great merchant aristocracy and the financial adventurers. But it was from just this small capitalist class, and not from the great financial magnates, monopolists, Government contractors, lenders to the King, colonial entrepreneurs, promoters, etc., that there originated what was characteristic of Occidental capitalism: the middle-class organization of industrial labour on the basis of private property (see Unwin, *Industrial Organization in the Sixteenth and Seventeenth Centuries,* London, 1914, pp. 196 ff.). To see that this difference was fully known even to contemporaries, compare Parker's *Discourse Concerning Puritans* of 1641, where the contrast to promoters and courtiers is also emphasized.

69. On the way in which this was expressed in the politics of Pennsylvania in the eighteenth century, especially during the War of Independence, see Sharpless, *A Quaker Experiment in Government,* Philadelphia, 1902.

70. Quoted in Southey, *Life of Wesley,* chap. xxix (second American edition, II, p. 308). For the reference, which I did not know, I am indebted to a letter from Professor Ashley (1913). Ernst Troeltsch, to whom I communicated it for the purpose, has already made use of it.

71. The reading of this passage may be recommended to all those who consider themselves to-day better informed on these matters than the leaders and contemporaries of the movements themselves. As we see, they knew very well

what they were doing and what dangers they faced. It is really inexcusable to contest so lightly, as some of my critics have done, facts which are quite beyond dispute, and have hitherto never been disputed by anyone. All I have done is to investigate their underlying motives somewhat more carefully. No one in the seventeenth century doubted the existence of these relationships (compare Manley, *Usury of 6 per Cent. Examined,* 1669, p. 137). Besides the modern writers already noted, poets like Heine and Keats, as well as historians like Macaulay, Cunningham, Rogers, or an essayist such as Matthew Arnold, have assumed them as obvious. From the most recent literature see Ashley, *Birmingham Industry and Commerce* (1913). He has also expressed his complete agreement with me in correspondence.

72. Weber's italics.

73. That exactly the same things were obvious to the Puritans of the classical era cannot perhaps be more clearly shown than by the fact that in Bunyan Mr. Money-Love argues that one may become religious in order to get rich, for instance to attract customers. For why one has become religious makes no difference (see p. 114, Tauchnitz edition).

74. Baxter, *op. cit.,* II, p. 16, warns against the employment of "heavy, flegmatic, sluggish, fleshly, slothful persons" as servants, and recommends preference for godly servants, not only because ungodly servants would be mere eye-servants, but above all because "a truly godly servant will do all your service in obedience to God, as if God Himself had bid him do it." Others, on the other hand, are inclined "to make no great matter of conscience of it." However, the criterion of saintliness of the workman is not for him the external confession of faith, but the "conscience to do their duty." It appears here that the interests of God and of the employers are curiously harmonious. Spener also (*Theologische Bedenken,* III, p. 272), who otherwise strongly urges taking time to think of God, assumes it to be obvious that workers must be satisfied with the extreme minimum of leisure time (even on Sundays). English writers have rightly called the Protestant immigrants the pioneers of skilled labour. See also proofs in H. Levy, *Die Grundlagen des ökonomischen Liberalismus in der Geschichte der englischen Volkswirtschaft,* p. 53.

75. The analogy between the unjust (according to human standards) predestination of only a few and the equally unjust, but equally divinely ordained, distribution of wealth, was too obvious to be escaped. See for example Hoornbeek, *op. cit.,* I, p. 153. Furthermore, as for Baxter, *op. cit.,* I, p. 380, poverty is very often a symptom of sinful slothfulness.

76. Thomas Adams (*Works of the Puritan Divines,* p. 158) thinks that God probably allows so many people to remain poor because He knows that they would not be able to withstand the temptations that go with wealth. For wealth all too often draws men away from religion.

77. See above, note 40, and the study of H. Levy referred to there. The same is noted in all the discussions (thus by Manley for the Huguenots).

78. Baxter's activity in Kidderminster, a community absolutely debauched when he arrived, which was almost unique in the history of the ministry for its success, is at the same time a typical example of how asceticism educated the masses to labour, or, in Marxian terms, to the production of surplus value, and thereby for the first time made their employment in the capitalistic labour relation (putting-out industry, weaving, etc.) possible at all. That is very generally the causal relationship. From Baxter's own view-point he accepted the employment of his charges in capitalistic production for the sake of his religious and ethical interests, From the standpoint of the development of capitalism these latter were brought into the service of the development of the spirit of capitalism.

79. Furthermore, one may well doubt to what extent the joy of the mediæval craftsman in his creation, which is so commonly appealed to, was effective as a psychological motive force. Nevertheless, there is undoubtedly something in that thesis. But in any case asceticism certainly deprived all labour of this worldly attractiveness, to-day for ever destroyed by capitalism, and oriented it to the beyond. Labour in a calling as such is willed by God. The impersonality of present-day labour, what, from the standpoint of the individual, is its joyless lack of meaning, still has a religious justification here. Capitalism at the time of its development needed labourers who were available for economic exploitation for conscience' sake. To-day it is in the saddle, and hence able to force people to labour without transcendental sanctions.

80. That those other elements, which have here not yet been traced to their religious roots, especially the idea that honesty is the best policy (Franklin's discussion of credit), are also of Puritan origin, must be proved in a somewhat different connection (see the following essay [not translated here]). Here I shall limit myself to repeating the following remark of J. A. Rowntree (*Quakerism, Past and Present,* pp. 95–6), to which E. Bernstein has called my attention: "Is it merely a coincidence, or is it a consequence, that the lofty profession of spirituality made by the Friends has gone hand in hand with shrewdness and tact in the transaction of mundane affairs? Real piety favours the success of a trader by insuring his integrity and fostering habits of prudence and forethought, important items in obtaining that standing and credit in the commercial world, which are requisites for the steady accumulation of wealth" (see the following essay). "Honest as a Huguenot" was as proverbial in the seventeenth century as the respect for law of the Dutch which Sir W. Temple admired, and, a century later, that of the English as compared with those Continental peoples that had not been through this ethical schooling.

81. Well analysed in Bielschowsky's *Goethe*, II, chap. xviii. For the development of the scientific cosmos Windelband, at the end of his *Blütezeit der deutschen Philosophie* (Vol. II of the *Gesch. d. Neueren Philosophie*), has expressed a similar idea.

82. *Saints' Everlasting Rest*, chap. xii.

83. "Couldn't the old man be satisfied with his $75,000 a year and rest? No! The frontage of the store must be widened to 400 feet. Why? That beats everything, he says. In the evening when his wife and daughter read together, he wants to go to bed. Sundays he looks at the clock every five minutes to see when the day will be over—what a futile life!" In these terms the son-in-law (who had emigrated from Germany) of the leading dry-goods man of an Ohio city expressed his judgment of the latter, a judgment which would undoubtedly have seemed simply incomprehensible to the old man. A symptom of German lack of energy.

84. For the above sketch has deliberately taken up only the relations in which an influence of religious ideas on the material culture is really beyond doubt. It would have been easy to proceed beyond that to a regular construction which logically deduced everything characteristic of modern culture from Protestant rationalism. But that sort of thing may be left to the type of dilettante who believes in the unity of the group mind and its reducibility to a single formula. Let it be remarked only that the period of capitalistic development lying before that which we have studied was everywhere in part determined by religious influences, both hindering and helping. Of what sort these were belongs in another chapter. Furthermore, whether, of the broader problems sketched above, one or another can be dealt with in the limits of this Journal [the essay first appeared in the *Archiv für Sozialwissenschaft und Sozialpolitik*—TRANSLATOR'S NOTE] is not certain in view of the problems to which it is devoted. On the other hand, to write heavy tomes, as thick as they would have to be in this case, and dependent on the work of others (theologians and historians), I have no great inclination (I have left these sentences unchanged).

    For the tension between ideals and reality in early capitalistic times before the Reformation, see now Strieder, *Studien zur Geschichte der kapit. Organizationsformen*, 1914, Book II. (Also as against the work of Keller, cited above, which was utilized by Sombart.)

85. I should have thought that this sentence and the remarks and notes immediately preceding it would have sufficed to prevent any misunderstanding of what this study was meant to accomplish, and I find no occasion for adding anything. Instead of following up with an immediate continuation in terms of the above programme, I have, partly for fortuitous reasons, especially the appearance of Troeltsch's *Die Soziallehren der christlichen Kirchen und Gruppen*, which disposed of many things I should have had to investigate in a way in which I, not being a theologian,

could not have done it; but partly also in order to correct the isolation of this study and to place it in relation to the whole of cultural development, determined, first, to write down some comparative studies of the general historical relationship of religion and society. These follow. Before them is placed only a short essay in order to clear up the concept of sect used above, and at the same time to show the significance of the Puritan conception of the Church for the capitalistic spirit of modern times.

QUESTIONS ON WEBER

1. How do you understand the "spirit of capitalism"? How is this related to the idea of a "calling"? Do you believe that there are any signs of a "spirit of capitalism" which prevails in the present culture?

2. How did the Protestant ethic suggest that labor has an inherent value? Is there an inherent good in productive activity and work?

3. Toward the close of his account, Weber states that capitalism is "victorious" and no longer needs the "support" of religious asceticism. Is this true? Does capitalism require a certain asceticism, and must that asceticism be religious?

4. State exactly the causal relation between the Protestant Ethic, the spirit of capitalism, and capitalism. How does one set of ideas bring about the resulting phenomenon? Can you think of any exceptions to this causal claim?

———————

The Market Order and Abstract Rules

F. A. Hayek

F. A. Hayek (1899–1993), a recipient of the Nobel Prize in Economics (1974), is the author of numerous works in economics in addition to works in social and political philosophy, including The Road to Serfdom *(1944),* The Constitution of Liberty *(1960), and* Law, Legislation, and Liberty *(1979). This excerpt is from volume 2 of* Law, Legislation, and Liberty.

THE MARKET ORDER OR CATALLAXY

The Nature of the Market Order

In chapter 2 we have discussed the general character of all spontaneous orders. It is necessary now to examine more fully the special attributes possessed by the order of the market and the nature of the benefits we owe to it. This order serves our ends not merely, as all order does, by guiding us in our actions and by bringing about a certain correspondence between the expectations of the different persons, but also, in a sense which we must now make more precise, by increasing the prospects or chances of every one of a greater command over the various goods (i.e. commodities and services) than we are able to secure in any other way. We shall see, however, that this manner of co-ordinating individual actions will secure a high degree of coincidence of expectations and an effective utilization of the knowledge and skills of the several members only at the price of a constant disappointment of some expectations.

For a proper understanding of the character of this order it is essential that we free ourselves of the misleading associations suggested by its usual description as an 'economy.' An economy, in the strict sense of the word in which a household, a farm, or an enterprise can be called economies, consists of a complex of activities by which a given set of means is allocated in accordance with a unitary plan among the competing ends according to their relative importance. The market order serves no such single order of ends. What is commonly called a social or national economy is in this sense not a single economy but a network of many interlaced economies.[1] Its order shares, as we shall see, with the order of an economy proper some formal characteristics but not the most important one: its activities are not governed by a single scale or hierarchy of ends. The belief that the economic activities of the individual members of society are or ought to be part of one economy in the strict sense of this term, and that what is commonly described as the economy of a country or a society ought to be ordered and judged by the same criteria as an economy proper, is a chief source of error in this field. But, whenever we speak of the economy of a country, or of the world, we are employing a term which suggests that these systems ought to be run on socialist lines and directed according to a single plan so as to serve a unitary system of ends.

While an economy proper is an organization in the technical sense in which we have defined that term, that is, a deliberate arrangement of the use of the means which are known to some single agency, the cosmos of the market neither is nor could be governed by such a single scale of ends; it serves the multiplicity of separate and incommensurable ends of all its separate members.

The confusion which has been created by the ambiguity of the word economy is so serious that for our present purposes it seems necessary to confine its use strictly to the original meaning in which it describes a complex of deliberately co-ordinated actions serving a single scale of ends, and to adopt another term to describe the system of numerous interrelated economies which constitute the market order. Since the name 'catallactics' has long ago been suggested for the science which deals with the market order[2] and has more recently been revived,[3] it would seem appropriate to adopt a corresponding term for the market order itself. The term 'catallactics' was derived from the Greek verb *katallattein* (or *katallassein*) which meant, significantly, not only 'to exchange' but also 'to admit into the community' and 'to change from enemy into friend.'[4] From it the adjective 'catallactic' has been derived to serve in the place of 'economic' to describe the kind of phenomena with which the science of catallactics deals. The ancient Greeks knew neither this term nor had a corresponding noun; if they had formed one it would probably have been *katallaxia*. From this we can form an English term *catallaxy* which we shall use to describe the order brought about by the mutual adjustment of many individual economies in a market. A catallaxy is thus the special kind of spontaneous order produced by the market through people acting within the rules of the law of property, tort and contract.

A Free Society Is a Pluralistic Society Without a Common Hierarchy of Particular Ends

It is often made a reproach to the Great Society and its market order that it lacks an agreed ranking of ends. This, however, is in fact its great merit which makes individual freedom and all it values possible. The Great Society arose through the discovery that men can live together in peace and mutually benefiting each other without agreeing on the particular aims which they severally pursue. The discovery that by substituting abstract rules of conduct for obligatory concrete ends made it possible to extend the order of peace beyond the small groups pursuing the same ends, because it enabled each individual to gain from the skill and knowledge of others whom he need not even know and whose aims could be wholly different from his own.[5]

The decisive step which made such peaceful collaboration possible in the absence of concrete common purposes was the adoption of barter or exchange. It was the simple recognition that different persons had different uses for the same things, and that often each of two individuals would benefit if he obtained something the other had, in return for his giving the other what he needed. All that was required to bring this about was that rules be recognized which determined what belonged to each, and how such property could be transferred by consent.[6] There was no need for the parties to agree on the purposes which this transaction served. It is indeed characteristic of such acts of exchange that they serve different and independent purposes of each partner in the transaction, and that they thus assist the parties as means for different ends. The parties are in fact the more likely to benefit from exchange the more their needs differ. While within an organization the several members will assist each other to the extent that they are made to aim at the same purposes, in a catallaxy they are induced to contribute to the needs of others without caring or even knowing about them.

In the Great Society we all in fact contribute not only to the satisfaction of needs of which we do not know, but sometimes even to the achievement of ends of which we would disapprove if we knew about them. We cannot help this because we do not know for what purposes the goods or services which we supply to others will be used by them. That we assist in the realization of other people's aims without sharing them or even knowing them, and solely in order to achieve our own aims, is the source of strength of the Great Society. So long as collaboration presupposes common purposes, people with different aims are necessarily enemies who may fight each other for the same means; only the introduction of barter made it possible for the different individuals to be of use to each other without agreeing on the ultimate ends.

When this effect of exchange of making people mutually benefit each other without intending to do so was first clearly recognized,[7] too much stress was laid on the resulting division of labour and on the fact that it was their 'selfish' aims which led the different persons to render services to each other. This is much too narrow a view of the matter. Division of labour is extensively practised also within organizations; and the advantages of the spontaneous order do not depend on people being selfish in the ordinary sense of this word. The important point about the catallaxy is that it reconciles different knowledge and different purposes which, whether the individuals be selfish or not, will greatly differ from one person to another. It is because in the catallaxy men, while following their own interests, whether wholly egotistical or highly altruistic, will further the aims of many others, most of whom they will never know, that it is as an overall order so superior to any deliberate organization: in the Great Society the different members benefit from each other's efforts not only in spite of but often even because of their several aims being different.[8]

Many people regard it as revolting that the Great Society has no common concrete purposes or, as we may say, that it is merely means-connected and not

ends-connected. It is indeed true that the chief common purpose of all its members is the purely instrumental one of securing the formation of an abstract order which has no specific purposes but will enhance for all the prospects of achieving their respective purposes. The prevailing moral tradition, much of which still derives from the end-connected tribal society, makes people often regard this circumstance as a moral defect of the Great Society which ought to be remedied. Yet it was the very restriction of coercion to the observance of the negative rules of just conduct that made possible the integration into a peaceful order of individuals and groups which pursued different ends; and it is the absence of prescribed common ends which makes a society of free men all that it has come to mean to us.

Though the conception that a common scale of particular values is a good thing which ought, if necessary, to be enforced, is deeply founded in the history of the human race, its intellectual defence today is based mainly on the erroneous belief that such a common scale of ends is necessary for the integration of the individual activities into an order, and a necessary condition of peace. This error is, however, the greatest obstacle to the achievement of those very ends. A Great Society has nothing to do with, and is in fact irreconcilable with 'solidarity' in the true sense of unitedness in the pursuit of known common goals.[9] If we all occasionally feel that it is a good thing to have a common purpose with our fellows, and enjoy a sense of elation when we can act as members of a group aiming at common ends, this is an instinct which we have inherited from tribal society and which no doubt often still stands us in good stead whenever it is important that in a small group we should act in concert to meet a sudden emergency. It shows itself conspicuously when sometimes even the outbreak of war is felt as satisfying a craving for such a common purpose; and it manifests itself most clearly in modern times in the two greatest threats to a free civilization: nationalism and socialism.[10]

Most of the knowledge on which we rely in the pursuit of our ends is the unintended by-product of others exploring the world in different directions from those we pursue ourselves because they are impelled by different aims; it would never have become available to us if only those ends were pursued which we regarded as desirable. To make it a condition for the membership of a society that one approved of, and deliberately supported, the concrete ends which one's fellow members serve, would eliminate the chief factor which makes for the advancement of such a society. Where agreement on concrete objects is a necessary condition of order and peace, and dissent a danger to the order of the society, where approval and censure depend on the concrete ends which particular actions serve, the forces for intellectual progress would be much confined. However much the existence of agreement on ends may in many respects smooth the course of life, the possibility of disagreement, or at least the lack of compulsion to agree on particular ends, is the basis of the kind of civilization which has grown up since the Greeks developed independent thought of the individual as the most effective method of advancement of the human mind.[11]

Though Not a Single Economy, the Great Society Is Still Held Together Mainly by What Vulgarly Are Called Economic Relations

The misconception that the market order is an economy in the strict sense of the term is usually found combined with the denial that the Great Society is held together by what are loosely called economic relations. These two views are frequently held by the same persons because it is certainly true that those deliberate organizations which are properly called economies are based on an agreement on common ends which in turn mostly are non-economic; while it is the great advantage of the spontaneous order of the market that it is merely means-connected and that, therefore, it makes agreement on ends unnecessary and a reconciliation of divergent purposes possible. What are commonly called economic relations are indeed relations determined by the fact that the use of all means is affected by the striving for those many different purposes. It is in this wide sense of the term 'economic' that the interdependence or coherence of the parts of the Great Society is purely economic.[12]

The suggestion that in this wide sense the only ties which hold the whole of a Great Society together are purely 'economic' (more precisely 'catallactic') arouse great emotional resistance. Yet the fact can hardly be denied; nor the fact that, in a society of the dimensions and complexity of a modern country or of the world, it can hardly be otherwise. Most people are still reluctant to accept the fact that it should be the disdained 'cash-nexus' which holds the Great Society together, that the great ideal of the unity of mankind should in the last resort depend on the relations between the parts being governed by the striving for the better satisfaction of their material needs.

It is of course true that within the overall framework of the Great Society there exist numerous networks of other relations that are in no sense economic.

But this does not alter the fact that it is the market order which makes peaceful reconciliation of the divergent purposes possible—and possible by a process which redounds to the benefit of all. That interdependence of all men, which is now in everybody's mouth and which tends to make all mankind One World, not only is the effect of the market order but could not have been brought about by any other means. What today connects the life of any European or American with what happens in Australia, Japan or Zaire are repercussions transmitted by the network of market relations. This is clearly seen when we reflect how little, for instance, all the technological possibilities of transportation and communication would matter if the conditions of production were the same in all the different parts of the world.

The benefits from the knowledge which others possess, including all the advances of science, reach us through channels provided and directed by the market mechanism. Even the degree to which we can participate in the aesthetic or moral strivings of men in other parts of the world we owe to the economic nexus. It is true that on the whole this dependence of every man on the actions of so many others is not a physical but what we call an economic fact. It is therefore a misunderstanding, caused by the misleading terms used, if the economists are sometimes accused of 'pan-economism,' a tendency to see everything from the economic angle, or, worse, wanting to make 'economic purposes' prevail over all others.[13] The truth is that catallactics is the science which describes the only overall order that comprehends nearly all mankind, and that the economist is therefore entitled to insist that conduciveness to that order be accepted as a standard by which all particular institutions are judged.

It is, however, a misunderstanding to represent this as an effort to make 'economic ends' prevail over others. There are, in the last resort, no economic ends. The economic efforts of the individuals as well as the services which the market order renders to them, consist in an allocation of means for the competing ultimate purposes which are always non-economic. The task of all economic activity is to reconcile the competing ends by deciding for which of them the limited means are to be used. The market order reconciles the claims of the different non-economic ends by the only known process that benefits all—without, however, assuring that the more important comes before the less important, for the simple reason that there can exist in such a system no single ordering of needs. What it tends to bring about is merely a state of affairs in which no need is served at the cost of withdrawing a greater amount of means from the use for other needs than is necessary to satisfy it. The market is the only known method by which this can be achieved without an agreement on the relative importance of the different ultimate ends, and solely on the basis of a principle of reciprocity through which the opportunities of any person are likely to be greater than they would otherwise be. . . .

THE DISCIPLINE OF ABSTRACT RULES AND THE EMOTIONS OF THE TRIBAL SOCIETY

The Pursuit of Unattainable Goals May Prevent the Achievement of the Possible

. . . We live at present under the governance of two different and irreconcilable conceptions of what is right; and after a period of ascendancy of conceptions which have made the vision of an Open Society possible, we are relapsing rapidly into the conceptions of the tribal society from which we had been slowly emerging. We had hoped that with the defeat of the European dictators we had banished the threat of the totalitarian state; but all we have achieved was to put down the first flare-up of a reaction which is slowly spreading everywhere. Socialism is simply a re-assertion of that tribal ethics whose gradual weakening had made an approach to the Great Society possible. The submergence of classical liberalism under the inseparable forces of socialism and nationalism is the consequence of a revival of those tribal sentiments.

Most people are still unwilling to face the most alarming lesson of modern history: that the greatest crimes of our time have been committed by governments that had the enthusiastic support of millions of people who were guided by moral impulses. It is simply not true that Hitler or Mussolini, Lenin or Stalin, appealed only to the worst instincts of their people: they also appealed to some of the feelings which also dominate contemporary democracies. Whatever disillusionment the more mature supporters of these movements may have experienced as they came to see the effects of the policies they had supported, there can be no doubt that the rank and file of the communist, national-socialist or fascist movements contained many men and women inspired by ideals not very different from those of some of the most influential social philosophers in the Western countries. Some of them certainly believed that they were engaged in the creation of a just society in which the needs of the most deserving or 'socially most valuable' would be better cared for. They were led by a desire for a visible common purpose which is our inheritance from

the tribal society and which we still find breaking through everywhere.

The Causes of the Revival of the Organizational Thinking of the Tribe

One reason why in recent times we have seen a strong revival of organizational thinking and a decline in the understanding of the operation of the market order is that an ever growing proportion of the members of society work as members of large organizations and find their horizon of comprehension limited to what is required by the internal structure of such organizations. While the peasant and the independent craftsman, the merchant and the journeyman, were familiar with the market and, even if they did not understand its operation, had come to accept its dictates as the natural course of things, the growth of big enterprise and of the great administrative bureaucracies has brought it about that an ever increasing part of the people spend their whole working life as members of large organizations, and are led to think wholly in terms of the requirements of the organizational form of life. Even though in the pre-industrial society the great majority also spent most of their lives within the familial organization which was the unit of all economic activity,[14] the heads of the households saw society as a network of family units connected by the markets.

Today organizational thinking increasingly dominates the activities of many of the most powerful and influential figures of modern society, the organizers themselves.[15] The modern improvements in the technique of organization, and the consequent increase of the range of particular tasks which can be performed by means of large-scale organization far beyond what was possible before, have created the belief that there are no limits to what organization can achieve. Most people are no longer aware of the extent to which the more comprehensive order of society on which depends the very success of the organizations within it is due to ordering forces of an altogether different kind.

The other main reason for the growing dominance of organizational thinking is that the success of the deliberate creation of new rules for purposive organizations has in many respects been so great, that men no longer recognize that the more comprehensive order within which the organizations operate rests on a different type of rules which have not been invented with a definite foreseen purpose in mind, but are the product of a process of trial and error in the course of which more experience has been accumulated than any living person is aware of.

The Immoral Consequences of Morally Inspired Efforts

. . . The values which still survive from the small end-connected groups whose coherence depended upon them, are, however, not only different from, but often incompatible with, the values which make possible the peaceful coexistence of large numbers in the Open Society. The belief that while we pursue the new ideal of this Great Society in which all human beings are regarded as equal, we can also preserve the different ideals of the small closed society, is an illusion. To attempt it leads to the destruction of the Great Society.

The possibility of men living together in peace and to their mutual advantage without having to agree on common concrete aims, and bound only by abstract rules of conduct,[16] was perhaps the greatest discovery mankind ever made. The 'capitalist' system which grew out of this discovery no doubt did not fully satisfy the ideals of liberalism, because it grew up while legislators and governments did not really understand the *modus operandi* of the market, and largely in spite of the policies actually pursued.[17] Capitalism as it exists today in consequence undeniably has many remediable defects that an intelligent policy of freedom ought to correct. A system which relies on the spontaneous ordering forces of the market, once it has reached a certain level of wealth, is also by no means incompatible with government providing, outside the market, some security against severe deprivation. But the attempt to secure to each what he is thought to deserve, by imposing upon all a system of common concrete ends towards which their efforts are directed by authority, as socialism aims to do, would be a retrograde step that would deprive us of the utilization of the knowledge and aspirations of millions, and thereby of the advantages of a free civilization. Socialism is not based merely on a different system of ultimate values from that of liberalism, which one would have to respect even if one disagreed; it is based on an intellectual error which makes its adherents blind to its consequences. This must be plainly said because the emphasis on the alleged difference of the ultimate values has become the common excuse of the socialists for shirking the real intellectual issue. The pretended difference of the underlying value judgments has become a protective cloak used to conceal the faulty reasoning underlying the socialist schemes. . . .

The Revolt Against the Discipline of Abstract Rules

The rise of the ideal of impersonal justice based on formal rules has been achieved in a continuous struggle against those feelings of personal loyalty which provide the basis of the tribal society but which in the Great Society must not be allowed to influence the use of the coercive powers of government. The gradual extension of a common order of peace from the small group to ever larger communities has involved constant clashes between the demands of sectional justice based on common visible purposes and the requirements of a universal justice equally applicable to the stranger and to the member of the group.[18] This has caused a constant conflict between emotions deeply ingrained in human nature through millennia of tribal existence and the demands of abstract principles whose significance nobody fully grasped. Human emotions are attached to concrete objects, and the emotions of justice in particular are still very much connected with the visible needs of the group to which each person belongs—the needs of the trade or profession, of the clan or the village, the town or the country to which each belongs. Only a mental reconstruction of the overall order of the Great Society enables us to comprehend that the deliberate aim at concrete common purposes, which to most people still appears as more meritorious and superior to blind obedience to abstract rules, would destroy that larger order in which all human beings count alike.

As we have already seen, much that will be truly social in the small end-connected group because it is conducive to the coherence of the working order of that society, will be anti-social from the point of view of the Great Society. The demand for 'social justice' is indeed an expression of revolt of the tribal spirit against the abstract requirements of the coherence of the Great Society with no such visible common purpose. It is only by extending the rules of just conduct to the relations with all other men, and at the same time depriving of their obligatory character those rules which cannot be universally applied, that we can approach a universal order of peace which might integrate all mankind into a single society.

While in the tribal society the condition of internal peace is the devotion of all members to some common visible purposes, and therefore to the will of somebody who can decide what at any moment these purposes are to be and how they are to be achieved, the Open Society of free men becomes possible only when the individuals are constrained only to obey the abstract rules that demarcate the domain of the means that each is allowed to use for his purposes. So long as any particular ends, which in a society of any size must always be the ends of some particular persons or group, are regarded as a justification of coercion, there must always arise conflicts between groups with different interests. Indeed, so long as particular purposes are the foundation of political organization, those whose purposes are different are inevitably enemies; and it is true that in such a society politics necessarily is dominated by the friend-enemy relation.[19] Rules of just conduct can become the same for all only when particular ends are not regarded as justification for coercion (apart from such special passing circumstances as war, rebellion or natural catastrophes).

The Morals of the Open and of the Closed Society

The process we are describing is closely associated with, and indeed a necessary consequence of, the circumstance that in an extensive market order the producers are led to serve people without knowing of their individual needs. Such an order which relies on people working with the effect of satisfying the wants of people of whom they do not know presupposes and requires somewhat different moral views, from one in which people serve visible needs. The indirect guidance by an expected monetary return, operating as an indicator of the requirements of others, demanded new moral conceptions which do not prescribe particular aims but rather general rules limiting the range of permitted actions.

It did become part of the ethos of the Open Society that it was better to invest one's fortune in instruments making it possible to produce more at smaller costs than to distribute it among the poor, or to cater for the needs of thousands of unknown people rather than to provide for the needs of a few known neighbours. These views, of course, did not develop because those who first acted upon them understood that they thus conferred greater benefits on their fellows, but because the groups and societies which acted in this way prospered more than others; it became in consequence gradually the recognized moral duty of the 'calling' to do so. In its purest form this ethos regards it as the prime duty to pursue a self-chosen end as effectively as possible without paying attention to the role it plays in the complex network of human activities. It is the view which is now commonly but somewhat misleading described as the Calvinist ethic—misleading because it prevailed already in the mercantile towns of medieval Italy and was taught by the Spanish Jesuits at about the same time as by Calvin.

We still esteem doing good only if it is done to benefit specific known needs of known people, and regard

it as really better to help one starving man we know than to relieve the acute need of a hundred men we do not know; but in fact we generally are doing most good by pursuing gain. It was somewhat misleading, and did his cause harm, when Adam Smith gave the impression as if the significant difference were that between the egoistic striving for gain and the altruistic endeavour to meet known needs. The aim for which the successful entrepreneur wants to use his profits may well be to provide a hospital or an art gallery for his home town. But quite apart from the question of what he wants to do with his profits after he has earned them, he is led to benefit more people by aiming at the largest gain than he could if he concentrated on the satisfaction of the needs of known persons. He is led by the invisible hand of the market to bring the succour of modern conveniences to the poorest homes he does not even know.[20]

It is true, however, that the moral views underlying the Open Society were long confined to small groups in a few urban localities, and have come generally to govern law and opinion in the Western world so comparatively recently that they are often still felt to be artificial and unnatural in contrast to the intuitive, and in part perhaps even instinctive, sentiments inherited from the older tribal society. The moral sentiments which made the Open Society possible grew up in the towns, the commercial and trading centres, while the feelings of the large numbers were still governed by the parochial sentiments and the xenophobic and fighting attitudes governing the tribal group.[21] The rise of the Great Society is far too recent an event to have given man time to shed the results of a development of hundreds of thousands of years, and not to regard as artificial and inhuman those abstract rules of conduct which often conflict with the deeply ingrained instincts to let himself be guided in action by perceived needs.

The resistance against the new morals of the Open Society was strengthened also by the realization that it not only indefinitely enlarged the circle of other people in relation to whom one had to obey moral rules, but that this extension of the scope of the moral code necessarily brought with itself a reduction of its content. If the enforceable duties towards all are to be the same, the duties towards none can be greater than the duties towards all—except where special natural or contractual relations exist. There can be a general obligation to render assistance in case of need towards a circumscribed group of fellowmen, but not towards men in general. The moral progress by which we have moved towards the Open Society, that is, the extension of the obligation to treat alike, not only the members of our tribe but persons of ever wider circles and ultimately all men, had to be bought at the price of an attenuation of the enforceable duty to aim deliberately at the well-being of the other members of the same group. When we can no longer know the others or the circumstances under which they live, such a duty becomes a psychological and intellectual impossibility. Yet the disappearance of these specific duties leaves an emotional void by depriving men both of satisfying tasks and the assurance of support in case of need.[22]

It would therefore not be really surprising if the first attempt of man to emerge from the tribal into an open society should fail because man is not yet ready to shed moral views developed for the tribal society; or, as Ortega y Gasset wrote of classical liberalism, . . . it is not to be wondered that 'humanity should soon appear anxious to get rid of . . . so noble an attitude, so paradoxical, so refined, so anti-natural . . . a discipline too difficult and complex to take firm root on earth.' At a time when the great majority are employed in organizations and have little opportunity to learn the morals of the market, their intuitive craving for a more humane and personal morals corresponding to their inherited instincts is quite likely to destroy the Open Society. . . .

The advance of justice continued until recent times as a progressive ascendancy of the general rules of just conduct applying to our relations to any fellow member of society over the special rules serving the needs of particular groups. It is true that this development in some measure stopped at national frontiers; but most nations were of such a size that it still brought about a progressive replacement of the rules of the purpose-connected organization by the rules of the spontaneous order of an Open Society.

The main resistance to this development was due to its requiring a predominance of abstract rational principles over those emotions that are evoked by the particular and the concrete, or the predominance of conclusions derived from abstract rules, whose significance was little understood, over the spontaneous response to the perception of concrete effects which touched the lives and conditions of those familiar to us. This does not mean that those rules of conduct which refer to special personal relations have lost their importance for the functioning of the Great Society. It merely means that, since in a society of free men the membership in such special groups will be voluntary, there must also be no power of enforcing the rules of such groups. It is in such a free society that a clear distinction between the moral rules which are not enforced and the rules of law which are enforced becomes so important. If the smaller groups are to be integrated into

the more comprehensive order of society at large, it must be through the free movement of individuals between groups into which they may be accepted if they submit to their rules. . . .

The Importance of Voluntary Associations

It would be a sad misunderstanding of the basic principles of a free society if it were concluded that, because they must deprive the small group of all coercive powers, they do not attach great value to voluntary action in the small groups. In restricting all coercion to the agencies of government and confining its employment to the enforcement of general rules, these principles aim at reducing all coercion as much as possible and leaving as much as possible to voluntary efforts. The mischievous idea that all public needs should be satisfied by compulsory organization and that all the means that the individuals are willing to devote to public purposes should be under the control of government, is wholly alien to the basic principles of a free society. The true liberal must on the contrary desire as many as possible of those 'particular societies within the state,' voluntary organizations between the individual and government, which the false individualism of Rousseau and the French Revolution wanted to suppress; but he wants to deprive them of all exclusive and compulsory powers. Liberalism is not individualistic in the 'everybody for himself' sense, though necessarily suspicious of the tendency of organizations to arrogate exclusive rights for their members.

We shall later (in chapter 15) have to consider more fully the problems raised by the consideration that such voluntary organizations, because their power is so much greater than that of any individual, may have to be restricted in their activities by law in ways in which the individual need not be restrained and, in particular, that they may have to be denied some of the rights to discriminate which for the individual are an important part of his freedom. What we wish to stress at this point, however, is not the necessary limits but rather the importance of the existence of numerous voluntary associations, not only for the particular purposes of those who share some common interest, but even for public purposes in the true sense. That government should have the monopoly of coercion is necessary in order to limit coercion; but this must not mean that government should have the exclusive right to pursue public purposes. In a truly free society, public affairs are not confined to the affairs of government (least of all of central government) and public spirit should not exhaust itself in an interest in government.[23]

It is one of the greatest weaknesses of our time that we lack the patience and faith to build up voluntary organizations for purposes which we value highly, and immediately ask the government to bring about by coercion (or with means raised by coercion) anything that appears as desirable to large numbers. Yet nothing can have a more deadening effect on real participation by the citizen than if government, instead of merely providing the essential framework for spontaneous growth, becomes monolithic and takes charge of the provision for all needs which can be provided for only by the common efforts of many. It is the great merit of the spontaneous order concerned only with means that it makes possible the existence of a large number of distinct and voluntary value communities serving such values as science, the arts, sports and the like. And it is a highly desirable development that in the modern world these groups tend to extend beyond national boundaries and that, e.g. a mountain climber in Switzerland may have more in common with a mountain climber in Japan than with the football fan in his own country; and that he may even belong to a common association with the former which is wholly independent of any political organization to which either belongs.

The present tendency of governments to bring all common interests of large groups under their control tends to destroy real public spirit; and as a result an increasing number of men and women are turning away from public life who in the past would have devoted much effort to public purposes. On the European continent the over-solicitude of governments has in the past largely prevented the development of voluntary organizations for public purposes and produced a tradition in which private efforts were often regarded as the gratuitous meddling of busybodies, and modern developments seem progressively to have produced a similar situation even in the Anglo-Saxon countries where at one time private efforts for public purposes were so characteristic a feature of social life.

ENDNOTES

1. Cf. Carl Menger, *Problems of Economics and Sociology* (Illinois, 1963), p. 93: "The *nation* as such is not a large subject that has needs, that works, practices economy, and consumes; and what is called 'national economy' is therefore not the economy of a nation in the true sense of the word. 'National economy' is not a phenomenon analogous to the singular economies in the nation to which also the economy of finance belongs. It is not a large singular economy; just as little as it is one opposed to or existing along with the singular economies in the nation. It is in its most general form of phenomena a peculiar complication of singular economies." Cf. also Appendix I to that work.

2. Richard Whately, *Introductory Lectures on Political Economy* (London, 1855), p. 4.

3. Especially by L. von Mises, *Human Action* (Yale, 1949), *passim*.

4. H. G. Liddell and R. A. Scott, *A Greek-English Dictionary* (London, new ed., 1940), s.v. *katallagden, katallage, katallagma, katallaktikos, katallasso (-tto), katallakterios* and *katallaxis*.

5. In the Greek terms we have used an economy proper is thus a *taxis* and a *teleocracy,* while the katallaxy is a *kosmos* and a *nomocracy.*

6. It was these rules to which David Hume and Adam Smith emphatically referred as 'rules of justice' and which Adam Smith meant when (*The Theory of Moral Sentiments,* part I, sect. ii, chap. iii) he spoke of justice as 'the main pillar of the whole edifice. If it is removed, the great, the immense fabric of human society, the fabric which to raise and support seems in this world, if I may say so, to have been the peculiar and darling care of Nature, must in a moment crumble into atoms.'

7. At the beginning of the eighteenth century, when Bernard Mandeville with his *Fable of the Bees* became its most influential expositor. But it seems to have been more widespread and is to be found, e.g., in the early Whig literature such as in Thomas Gordon, 'Cato's Letter' no. 63, dated 27 January 1721 (in the reprint in *The English Libertarian Heritage,* ed. David L. Jacobson, Indianapolis, 1965, pp. 138–9): 'Every Man's honest Industry and useful Talents, while they are employed for the Publick, will be employed for himself; and while he serves himself, he will serve the Publick; Publick and private Interest will secure each other; all will cheerfully give a Part to secure the Whole—and be brave to defend it.' It then found first expression in classical works (in both instances probably under the influence of Mandeville) in C. de S. de Montesquieu, *The Spirit of the Laws,* Book III, sect. 7 (trs. T. Nugent, New York, 1949), p. 35: 'Each individual advances the public good, while he only thinks of promoting his own interest,' and in David Hume, *Treatise* in *Works* II, p. 289: 'I learn to do a service to another, without bearing him any real kindness'; and *ibid.,* p. 291: 'advantage to the public, though it not be intended for that purpose'; cf. also *Essays, Works* III, p. 99: 'made it not the interest, even of bad men, to act for the public good.' It occurs later in Josiah Tucker, *Elements of Commerce* (London, 1756), in Adam Smith, *Theory of Moral Sentiments* (London, 1759), part IV, chapter I, where he speaks of men being 'led by an invisible hand . . . without intending it, without knowing it, [to] advance the interest of society,' and of course in its most famous formulation in Smith's *Wealth of Nations* (ed. Cannan, London, 1910), vol. I, p. 421: 'By directing that industry in such a manner as its produce may be of the

greatest value, he intends only his own gain, and he is in this, as in many other cases, led by an invisible hand to promote an end which was no part of his intention. Nor is it always the worse for the society that it was no part of it. By pursuing his own interest he frequently promotes that of the society more effectually than when he really intends to promote it.' Cf. also Edmund Burke, *Thoughts and Details of Scarcity* (1795), in *Works* (World's Classics ed.), vol. VI, p. 9: 'The benign and wise disposer of all things, who obliges men whether they will or not, in pursuing their own selfish interest, to connect the general good with their own individual success.'

8. Cf. Adam Smith, *Wealth of Nations,* I, p. 16: 'It is not from the benevolence of the butcher, the brewer, or the baker, that we expect our dinner, but from their regard to their own interest.'

9. It is in the insistence on social 'solidarity' that the constructivist approach to sociology of Auguste Comte, Emile Durkheim and Léon Duguit shows itself most clearly.

10. Both of which were characteristically regarded by John Stuart Mill as the only 'elevated' feelings left in modern man.

11. On the significance of the development of criticism by the ancient Greeks see particularly Karl R. Popper, *The Open Society and Its Enemies* (London and Princeton, 1947 and later), *passim.*

12. Cf. already A. L. C. Destutt de Tracy, *A Treatise on Political Economy* (Georgetown, 1817), pp. 6ff.: 'Society is purely and solely a continual series of exchanges. . . . *Commerce is the whole of society.*' Before the term 'society' came into general use, 'economy' was often used where we would now speak of 'society.' Cf. for instance John Wilkins, *Essay toward a Real Character and a Philosophical Language* (London, 1668) as quoted by H. R. Robbins, *A Short History of Linguistics* (London, 1967), pp. 114–15, who appears to use 'economical' as equivalent to 'interpersonal.' At that time 'economy' seems also to have been used generally to mean what we call here a spontaneous order, as such frequently recurring phrases as the 'economy of creation' and the like show.

13. The chief objections to the 'allocational' approach or the 'economicism' of much of current economic theory from very different angles comes, on the one side, from J. M. Buchanan, most recently restated in the essay 'Is Economics the Science of Choice' in E. Streissler (ed.), *Roads to Freedom* (London, 1969), and G. Myrdal, especially in *The Political Element in the Development of Economic Theory* (London, 1953) and *Beyond the Welfare State* (Yale, 1960). Cf. also Hans Peter, *Freiheit der Wirtschaft* (Cologne, 1953); Gerhard Weisser, 'Die Überwindung des Ökonomismus in der Wirtschaftswissenschaft' in *Grundfragen der Wirtschaftsordnung* (Berlin, 1954); and Hans Albert, *Ökonomische Theorie und Politische Ideologie* (Göttingen, 1954).

What is often inexactly though perhaps conveniently described as 'economic ends' are the most general and yet undifferentiated means such as money or general purchasing power which in the course of the ordinary process of earning a living are the immediate ends, because the particular purpose for which they will be used is not yet known. On the fact that there are strictly speaking no economic ends and for the clearest statement of economics seen as a theory of choice see L. C. Robbins, *The Nature and Significance of Economic Science* (London, 1930 and later).

14. Cf. Peter Laslett, *The World We Have Lost* (London and New York, 1965).

15. See W. H. Whyte, *The Organization Man* (New York, 1957).

16. In the present connection we revert to the term 'abstract rule' in order to stress that the rules of just conduct do not refer to specific purposes and that the resulting order is what Sir Karl Popper has called an 'abstract society.'

17. Cf. Adam Smith, *Wealth of Nations*, ed. Cannan, vol. II, p. 43: 'The natural effort of every individual to better his own condition, where suffered to exert itself with freedom and security, is so powerful a principle, that it is alone, and without any assistance, not only capable of carrying on the society to wealth and prosperity, but of surmounting a hundred impertinent obstructions with which the folly of human laws too often encumbers its operations; though the effect of these obstructions is always more or less either to encroach upon its freedom, or to diminish its security.'

18. J.-J. Rousseau has clearly seen that what in his sense of the 'general will' may be just for a particular group, may not be so for a more comprehensive society. Cf. *The Political Writings of J.-J. Rousseau,* ed. E. E. Vaughan (Cambridge, 1915), vol. I, p. 243: 'Pour les membres de l'association, c'est une volonté générale; pour la grande société, c'est une volonté particulière, qui très souvent se trouve droite au premier égard, et vicieuse au second.' But to the positivist interpretation of justice which identifies it with the commands of some legitimate authority, it comes inevitably to be thought that, as e.g. E. Forsthoff, *Lehrbuch des Verwaltungsrechts* (eighth ed., Munich, 1961, vol. I, p. 66) maintains, 'any question of a just order is a question of law.' But this 'orientation on the idea of justice,' as this view has been curiously called, is certainly not sufficient to turn a command into a rule of just conduct unless by that phrase is meant, not merely that the rule satisfies somebody's claim for just treatment, but that the rule satisfies the Kantian test of universal applicability.

19. This is the main thesis of Carl Schmitt, *Der Begriff des Politischen* (Berlin, 1932). Cf. the comment on it by J. Huizinga quoted on p. 71 of vol. I of the present work.

20. The constructivist prejudice which still makes so many socialists scoff at the 'miracle' that the unguided pursuit of their own interests by the individuals should produce a beneficial order is of course merely the reverse form of that dogmatism

which opposed Darwin on the ground that the existence of order in organic nature was proof of intelligent design.

21. Cf. H. B. Acton, *The Morals of Markets* (London, 1971).
22. Cf. Bertrand de Jouvenel, *Sovereignty* (London and Chicago, 1957), p. 136: 'We are thus driven to three conclusions. The first is that the small society, the milieu in which man is first found, retains for him an infinite attraction; the next, that he undoubtedly goes to it to renew his strength; but, the last, that any attempt to graft the same features on a large society is utopian and leads to tyranny'; to which the author adds in a footnote: 'In this respect Rousseau (*Rousseau Juge de Jean-Jaques,* Third Dialogue) displayed a wisdom which his disciples missed: 'His object could not be to recall populous countries and large states to their primitive simplicity, but only to check, if possible, the progress of those whom smallness and situation had preserved from the same headlong rush to the perfection of society and the deterioration of the species.'
23. Cf. Richard Cornuelle, *Reclaiming the American Dream* (New York, 1965).

QUESTIONS ON HAYEK

1. Hayek draws a distinction between the rules of the small group and those of the extended society. How does he characterize the rules of the small group and those of the extended society? Do you think this characterization is complete? Or correct?

2. Hayek claims that we have inherited from our past certain "tribal emotions" and that these are sometimes expressed by socialist movements. Do you think this is correct? Why does Hayek believe that this is a negative development? If these "tribal emotions" exist, are they of cultural or biological origin?

3. Why does Hayek claim that "tribal emotions" are unsuited to market societies? What role is left in market societies for voluntary groups which have concrete common purposes? Does Hayek ignore the value of these groups?

A Dialogue on the Moral Foundations of Commerce

Jane Jacobs

Jane Jacobs was born in Pennsylvania and now lives in Toronto. She is the author of The Death and Life of Great American Cities *(1961) and* Cities and the Wealth of Nations *(1984). This excerpt is from* Systems of Survival: A Dialogue on the Moral Foundations of Commerce and Politics *(1994).*

A PAIR OF CONTRADICTIONS

Relieved to see all four on the appointed morning, Armbruster expansively showed off his new coffee maker, which managed its own heating, and fiddled with his tape recorder while Kate passed out typed sheets.

"You can keep these in front of you for reference," she said. "I'll explain later why I call them syndromes." She paused as they glanced down the lists.

Moral Syndrome A
Shun force
Come to voluntary agreements
Be honest
Collaborate easily with strangers and aliens
Compete
Respect contracts
Use initiative and enterprise
Be open to inventiveness and novelty
Be efficient
Promote comfort and convenience
Dissent for the sake of the task
Invest for productive purposes
Be industrious
Be thrifty
Be optimistic

Moral Syndrome B
Shun trading
Exert prowess
Be obedient and disciplined
Adhere to tradition
Respect hierarchy
Be loyal
Take vengeance
Deceive for the sake of the task
Make rich use of leisure
Be ostentatious
Dispense largesse
Be exclusive
Show fortitude
Be fatalistic
Treasure honor

Jasper was first to speak. "This is mystifying. Why are you presenting us with two sets of morals? And look how they dispute each other! What are you up to? This makes no sense."

"I realize these lists aren't self-explanatory," said Kate. "But give me a chance to explain. . . ."

Maybe I'd better tell you how I went about this," said Kate. "First, I immured myself in the library, opening to closing. Read, read, read, and took notes."

"Read what?" asked Hortense.

"Hit and miss at first, but sharpened up as I went along. Biographies; business histories; scandals; sociology, although that was less help than I expected, except for some of the Europeans. I dipped into general history and, in spite of what you said, Armbruster, about ignoring tribesmen's spears, skimmed some cultural anthropology. Nights at home I clipped newspapers.

"I drew on three kinds of evidence. Whenever I ran across behavior that was extolled as admirable, I cast it in the form of a precept. If a businessman was praised because his handshake was as good as his bond, I cast it in the precept 'Respect contracts.' If another was admired for tenaciously carrying out a commercial idea successfully in the face of contrary conventional advice and discouragement from experts and bankers—Edwin Land, inventor and producer of the Polaroid camera, for instance—I cast that as 'Be open to inventiveness and novelty,' 'Use initiative and enterprise,' and 'Dissent for the sake of the task.' I should emphasize, though, that not one of these precepts is here because it turned up as a unique or even a rare instance. Every one showed up over and over, in varying contexts. If a soldier was extolled for redeeming the honor of his regiment by rallying it when it was about to retreat, I cast it as 'Treasure honor,' and so on.

"I did the same with behavior that was laid out as expected or proper, as in job-training manuals, and such useful sociology as I did find. These are the kinds of rules or tips cast in such precepts as 'Be industrious,' 'Be honest,' 'Be efficient,' 'Collaborate easily with strangers and aliens,' in Syndrome A, and 'Be obedient and disciplined,' 'Respect hierarchy,' 'Be loyal,' in Syndrome B. A lot of the universals show up too in what's expected or proper.

"My third type of evidence was behavior that was deemed scandalous, disgraceful, or criminal. I identified what was being transgressed, such as honesty; or if extortion, say, was the crime, I cast it as 'Shun force,' and 'Come to voluntary agreement.' If conflict of interest was the gist of a scandal, I cast it as 'Shun trading.' I also made note of what sorts of work or positions in life were associated with a given precept.'" . . .

KATE ON THE COMMERCIAL SYNDROME

The sequence of these precepts doesn't imply order of importance," Kate began. "I'm merely moving from the simpler to the more complex for my own expository convenience, and for yours as listeners. All the precepts are important, and all are connected.

"*Shun force,* to start with, is simple in principle but not always easily accomplished because commercial wealth is found in the midst of things. It's accessible to customers, suppliers, the public. It travels on common carriers. So it's tempting, and likely it always has been, to robbers, sacking armies, hijackers, and sneak thieves. Jasper told us the first night here how ruinous this vulnerability can be if it's not protected. So many pirates lurked off the coasts of medieval England that London merchants went to the expense of financing a fleet of fighting ships and gave it to the Crown. That's supposed to be the way the English navy started."

"Why give it to the Crown?" asked Jasper.

"Because 'Shun force' has a second meaning. It also forbids commercial people themselves to use force."

"You mean, if they did they'd be scared of each other?" asked Ben.

"Of course. They'd have good reason to be. The precept, in this second meaning, gives substance to the second item, *Come to voluntary agreements.* Even children know that this is what 'I'll trade you' means. When violence or intimidation enters a transaction, it's no longer trade. It's taking by force.

"*Be honest,* in its turn, gives substance to voluntary agreement. To be sure, as Armbruster pointed out with that Augean stables list of white-collar criminality, some commercial organizations practice dishonesty and some get away with it, too, much as some predators on commerce get away with violence. But by definition, dishonesty is kept down to supportable levels wherever commerce remains viable. My guess is that the earliest form of commercial fraud and cheating was with weights and measures. One oddity I ran across in the library was a translation of letters of recommendation addressed to the gods. Ancient Egyptians prepared or commissioned the letters for their tombs. One standard popular bit ran like this: 'I neither increase nor diminish the measure of grain, I am not one who shorts the palm's length'—that refers to the hand, a unit of measurement for dry goods, like cloth, for instance—'I am not one who shorts the field's measure, I put not pressure upon the beam of the balance, I tamper not with the tongue of the balance.' Evidence like that, along with the fact that the earliest forms of standardization imposed by governments seem to have been standardized weights, implies that the ancients took commercial dishonesty as seriously as we do, if not more so."

"Since we have engaged to stay for the day, can we get on to something less obvious than the stunning news that honesty is the best policy?" said Jasper.

"I don't know that it is that obvious after my stolen-software experience," said Armbruster. "But Jasper does have a point; you're laboring the obvious a bit."

"Sorry, I'll try to be brisker, but I have a point of my own to make before moving on. Notice that we now have basic reasons that commercial people need symbiotic help from guardians: to combat violent predators on commerce, of course, but also to mandate honesty and give the mandate teeth by ferreting out dishonesty in commercial life, investigating, exposing, disgracing, prosecuting, and punishing it—in short, suppressing it down to supportable levels even if the ideal of eliminating it completely isn't realistic, alas.

"The next precept, *Collaborate easily with strangers and aliens,* links tightly with honesty. Here's an account by a traveler in Asia Minor back at the time Greeks and Turks were furiously at war, the Greeks trying to free themselves from the Ottoman Empire. This is the headman of a backwater Turkish village speaking. 'We Turks have the land and we have the fruit trees but we have no capital and we don't know how to sell our fruit. Every spring the Greek merchants come to our village and together we make an estimate of our crop. They lend us the money to pay for collecting and packing the fruit and for our own needs. In the autumn we send the fruit to Smyrna or Panderma. It never happens that a Turk will sell his crop to any merchant but the one who lent him the money, and it never happens that the merchant fails to send back the balance of the sale price of our fruit. If we trust each other in this way, why can't . . . leaders trust each other too? . . . We are being ruined by these foolish wars.'

"In any commercial life more complicated than a hamlet market," Kate went on, "and it would have to be an isolated hamlet at that, commercial people are compelled to deal with strangers and almost-strangers as suppliers or customers, and often enough with aliens. This requires enormous trust, like Armbruster's trust in the stranger at the Hanover bank. But trust is feasible only where honesty is usual.

"Commercial people invent devices to facilitate trust among strangers, always have. Receipts are likely the oldest forms of business documents. Long ago receipts or bills of account were put into trade just as if they themselves were the valuables they represented; they were exchanged as if they were money. That was possible only because honesty could be presumed and commercial life was being operated on the premise that it is as disgraceful to defraud strangers and aliens as it is to cheat a friend.

"That premise is the foundation of the quality we call cosmopolitanism, from the Greek words *cosmos* and *polis,* meaning 'universal people.' The principal places in which strangers do business together are big commercial cities. The cosmopolitanism of these cities is no accident. It's an instance of functional necessity becoming a cultural trait. To make mundane, everyday deals with strangers and aliens, for no reason except that they're customers or suppliers, demands tolerance for people outside one's own background and personal preferences and, often enough, even respect for them as well. Cosmopolitanism spills over into other fields, such as the arts, but its roots are commercial." She paused to locate a note.

"Here, Mariam Slater, she's an anthropologist, wrote this about Nairobi as it was in 1960. 'Each ethnic group meets almost exclusively its own kind in private arks of family, club or place of worship. The visitor quickly learns to spin a tight cocoon in an atmosphere in which an Ismali does not speak to his Baluchi or Hindu neighbor except in the marketplace.' "

"I wouldn't tag that as a cosmopolitan spirit," said Hortense.

"No, it wasn't. But the point is that insofar as ethnic collaboration existed at all in Nairobi, its locus was specifically and only the marketplace. Here's something you'll like, Jasper," Kate continued. "Cosmopolitanism and insularity are contrasts, but not a tidy, discrete pair. They're two poles, rather, with shadings and degrees and mixtures all the way from one pole to the other.

"Those shadings and degrees are in great part a reflection of permanence and impermanence of relationships. That's an interesting subtlety expounded by Norbert Elias, a great German sociologist who exhaustively studied the old French royal courts. He contrasted the permanent court relationships—until the French Revolution swept them away—with the impermanent relationships that the French bourgeoisie were taking in their stride during the same period. He said of the courtiers that each stood 'by and large in a lifelong relationship with every other member of his society . . . inescapably dependent on each other as friends, enemies or relatively neutral parties. They must therefore observe extreme caution at each encounter with each other. Prudence or reserve are dominant features. . . . Because every relationship in this society is necessarily permanent, a single unconsidered utterance can have a permanent effect.' That's the insularity pole. The same observations hold true of humble insular societies, too, where family grudges and feuds are tenacious, sometimes handed along for generations, or where being born on the wrong side of the tracks can be the most important element in a person's identity for life.

"Elias contrasts the court life with the relatively free-and-easy bourgeoisie, who 'usually deal with each other over far more specific and short-lived purposes. . . . The relationship comes quickly to an end if the material opportunities each offers to the other no longer seem favorable enough. . . . Permanent relationships are confined to private life.' That's the cosmopolitan pole. Realities give most of us in commercial cities something between the two. When trust among strangers and aliens breaks down in large commercial cities, insularity is no practical substitute for the loss. Many people flee such places if they can. It's serious; it's nothing less than the failure of commercial civilization, where trust among strangers and aliens is vital.

"Now I'm moving along to the precept *Compete*. Its most obvious direct link is with voluntary agreement, which presupposes choice. Effective choice demands competition. Choice is impossible, and voluntary agreement a sham, if one of the parties to the agreement holds a monopoly. I hope you're noticing, Jasper, how every precept in this syndrome links directly with other precepts, and indirectly with all of them. That's the clustering and overlapping I mentioned earlier. I emphasize, this isn't just a linear set of rules and values. Taken singly, the precepts are banal. But you can't reject them singly without devastating the syndrome as a whole.

"Competition also links with honesty and shunning force, because of the sheer costs of dishonesty and force. The sign on the door of my neighborhood supermarket says, SHOPLIFTING COSTS US ALL. That's true. The costs of shoplifting have to be figured into prices. I won't go on about that because we touched on it sufficiently, I think, while we were flailing around our first evening."

"But that must mean that, taken as a whole, a country with high crime and dishonesty rates suffers in international commercial competition," said Hortense thoughtfully.

"To be sure," said Kate, "although that wouldn't necessarily be the most important competitive factor. Probably not, but it figures in. I'll get back to more about competition later." Armbruster made a note.

"*Respect contracts* gives substance to voluntary agreement. That's obvious. But in my hasty dip into law, I gathered that contracts and contractual law somehow create individual rights; however, I'm still hazy about it."

"I can help clarify that," said Hortense.

"Please. I'm out of my depth."

"People doing commercial work need contracts, whether they're written or not," said Hortense. "They need assurance the courts will enforce contracts if need be—another honesty safeguard requiring guardian help—and will do so justly. 'Justly' means according to what the contract says."

"Not always," said Jasper. "Make a contract with a killer to murder somebody, or an arsonist to burn down a building, and it will not be enforceable by a court. Far from."

"Of course," said Hortense. "Actions in conflict with recognized public policy are not protected by contracts or the courts. That was a point Shakespeare made in *The Merchant of Venice*. To us, the chief oddity of the contract between Shylock and Antonio is that anyone would think for a moment of taking to court a contract demanding the forfeit of flesh from a defaulter.

"To get back to enforcement of an intrinsically legal contract: among other things, 'justly' means that nobody's rank or status permits him to terminate a lease on whim, evade a legitimate debt, welsh on a promise to deliver, withhold agreed-on wages, and so on. What the contract says is of the essence; the social status of the parties to it is irrelevant.

"Now picture this," she went on enthusiastically. "Picture a society where commercial need for contracts is growing but the law doesn't take that into account. Commercial contractual law is missing. In early medieval Europe, that was the situation. The established law courts—the courts of the guardians—were shaped by feudal law, which is the rule of rank, hierarchical law. So for a long time, hundreds of years, commercial people were pretty much on their own legally. They not only invented the kinds of contracts they needed; they also set up binding arbitration courts. You could say they were inventing their own guardians, to fill a gap. They built up precedents and the whole contraption was known as the Custom of Merchants.

"Admiralty law started the same way. Originally it was the rules and rulings sailors, shipowners, and merchants invented to deal with salvage rights, insurance on cargoes, liability for losses, and so on. Admiralty law's a delight. You can smell the salt air and feel the stormy waves. Matters like the tides and the seaworthiness of vessels skirting reefs come into adjudications. Admiralty lawyers travel a lot and know distant ports firsthand. I really wish that's what I'd gone into, but it's not welcoming to women.

"Eventually, admiralty and contractual law were absorbed into rulers' formal legal systems. Consulates have a similar history; they were first set up by merchants in cosmopolitan trading cities as a kind of home away from home, to give help when it was needed. It's now thought the Jews invented them and then other ethnic groups of foreign merchants took up the idea too. Eventually, states took them over."

"States aren't inventive, like commercial people," said Kate. "But I thought Rome had commercial law."

"It did. So did the Greeks. But you must understand that all ancient concepts of rights were connected to status. Rights were thought of as the by-products of duties, and duties were attached to status. For instance, the head of a Greek or Roman household had duties owed to that status; therefore he also had rights not possessed by other household members, nor by men who didn't head households. It was the same with other aspects of status, such as military rank, religious authority, slave ownership, citizenship, whatever. So, as biological, individual, natural creatures, people in ancient Greece and Rome had no rights. That was the feudal European concept, too. It's also the Confucian concept. The Roman commercial law you mentioned, Kate, was available only to people whose duties required it. Incidentally, it was called the Law of Foreigners, even when Romans themselves were using it. It omitted a lot of rigmarole and ritual attaching to noncommercial law. But it didn't introduce individual rights as we understand them in the tradition of commercial law we've inherited."

"I thought individual rights were natural rights," said Ben.

"That's the sort of fiction we call myth," said Hortense. "Useful symbolically. But as a practical matter, society confers or withholds rights. The medieval European Custom of Merchants let the genie of individual rights out of the bottle—or opened the Pandora's box of their nuisances and evils, as people who deplore individual rights would have it.

"The contractual law we inherited from those medieval merchants contained radical conceptions. Not only did it apply alike to all individuals, no matter who they were or what their social status might be, but it was available to individuals for no other reason than that they were individuals, making contracts. That second notion is so inseparable from our contractual law that we even have the fiction that a corporation is a person. That's so corporations, like individuals, can make contracts and carry on commercial life under protection of civil law. To realize how radical the Custom of Merchants was, we only need to think about some of the battles to extend the jurisdiction of contractual law.

"For instance, slaves lack rights as individuals. After slaves in the United States were freed, the Fourteenth Amendment to the Constitution theoretically gave them access to all the rights of individuals available under contractual law. But by custom, hierarchical law, the rule of rank, still prevailed, so freedmen and their descendants seldom enjoyed the benefits of contractual law. Every time a black homeowner was driven from his legally purchased house in a white neighborhood he was being treated as if hierarchical law, derived from social status, prevailed. Every time effective barriers were thrown up against black-owned businesses, and they were, more often than not, or against employment of qualified blacks, or they were excluded from labor unions and apprenticeships controlled by unions, it was as if contractual law did not exist for African Americans. As someone has said, even buying a loaf of bread is a contract. So is being served a meal in a restaurant. A bus ticket is a contract, but if you have to stand instead of sit because of your color, that's the rule of rank, not contract. So many of what we call civil rights are actually rights to make contracts as equals.

"A generation ago," Hortense continued indignantly, "large numbers of American women began to create businesses of their own. To their outrage and disbelief, many discovered they were blocked from signing commercial leases or borrowing commercial funds on their own responsibility. Banks and landlords demanded a male cosigner, usually a husband or father. By custom, sexism was excluding women from individual rights under contractual law. Another variety of sexism has often denied homosexuals the benefits of contractual law; those battles still continue.

"Neither rulers nor philosophers invented individual rights. Nor did nature invent them. Not Rousseau or Thomas Paine or Thomas Jefferson, much less the barons who extorted Magna Carta from King John on grounds of the rights their rank entitled them to. The strange idea of rights unconnected to status was what medieval serfs referred to when they said, 'City air makes free.' By getting to the city and subscribing to its extraordinary customs, they wiggled out of hierarchical law and into contractual law. I don't need to tell you individual rights still frighten many governments. They also frighten economic oligarchies. It's no wonder the very idea had to emerge outside of government—and even then as a by-product of other practical purposes."

"If you're still worried that your pair of syndromes is old hat, Kate, relax," said Armbruster. "You definitely won't find equal contractual law or individual rights in Plato."

Kate picked up a new sheaf of notes. "Contractual law allows ordinary people to *Use initiative and enterprise*—makes it feasible as a practical matter. Initiative and enterprise are highly esteemed in commercial life, as well they should be. Wherever commerce flourishes over extended time, new products and services keep entering trade. And so do new ways of producing, distributing, and communicating. These all require initiative and enterprise.

"We're into a big cluster of precepts now: *Be open to inventiveness and novelty. Be efficient. Promote comfort and convenience,* and *Dissent for the sake of the task.*

"All of these link directly and tightly with competition, which I said I'd get back to. Commercial life affords so many ways to compete. A company can build a successful commercial position upon efficient ways of producing. It can develop entirely new things to purvey, or significantly improve old things. Competing for customers—whether they are other producers or ultimate consumers—often entails promoting convenience and comfort for them.

"Elias, the sociologist of court life I mentioned earlier, notes that in prerevolutionary French cities the homes of established tradesmen, artisans, and merchants looked modest. But they incorporated more comforts and conveniences than the grand and ostentatious residences of aristocrats. Comforts and conveniences are quintessential bourgeois preoccupations, both for themselves and for customers. That preoccupation may perhaps provide the principal motor driving commercial life. It's the reason, for instance, that I have use of a clothes-washing machine, where the elves do the work for me, and the comfort of a hot shower.

"Ben, surely you recognize how many comforts and conveniences have become necessities, even for the ascetic likes of you: refrigeration, operating-room anesthetics, telephones, copying machines, computers, faxes, modems . . . or jumping back in time, how about printed books instead of scanty, expensive manuscripts, clocks and watches instead of hourglasses and sundials, warm gloves instead of chilblains—"

"You're cheating," Ben broke in. "You're pretending to be a cool observer but you're a special pleader. What about aerosol cans, what about forests felled for junky comic books full of violence, what about sealed windows that force energy-wasting air-conditioning in even the best weather, what about gas-guzzling cars, what about tobacco, what about wasteful, ostentatious packaging?"

"Touché," said Kate. "I got carried away because commercial preoccupation with comfort and conveniences down through the years means we aren't living lives of drudgery shivering in the rain with a hoe or beating out the laundry on a rock.

"The whole cluster of precepts I last mentioned demand *Dissent for the sake of the task.* We're so brainwashed into thinking of dissent only in political or philosophical terms. But consider that every single improvement in efficiency of production or distribution requires dissent from the way things were previously done. So does every new kind of material used in production. So does every innovative product—even the deplorable ones. Innumerable practical acts of dissent. Like individual rights, this is radical stuff—subversive of things as they are.

"Furthermore," Kate went on, "when this commercial type of dissent is successful, it is often quickly and obviously so. That can seldom be said of purely intellectual, spiritual, or ideological dissent, which is apt to be influential—when it's influential at all—on posterity rather than contemporaries. Dissent of both kinds takes wrong turnings. But when intellectual or ideological dissents are impractical, it can take breakdown after generations of turmoil, hardship, and conflict to demonstrate that fact.

"Now we come to another cluster: *Invest for productive purposes, Be industrious,* and *Be thrifty.* These are tightly linked with dissent, because changes in the way things are done commercially, and especially additions of new products or services into trade, demand productive investment. To be sure, just continuing in traditional ways requires some productive investment too, because tools wear out. But mere replacement costs are as nothing compared with the time, risk, and effort devoted to experimenting, and the costs of changed production or distribution, or communication equipment. Making productive investments requires a surplus over current consumption—in other words, it requires thrift. And producing surpluses requires industriousness.

"Nobody wins esteem in commercial life by being an able-bodied idler or freeloader. Pity, maybe; moral esteem, no. But I think the harshness of the bourgeois attitude toward idlers goes deeper than the connection of industriousness with thrift and investment. It may be rooted in the fact that trade and production are viable only when people apply themselves in continuous effort, not sporadic fits and starts."

"Isn't that true of successful effort of any sort?" asked Armbruster.

"By no means," said Kate, "as we'll see when we look at the guardian moral syndrome." Armbruster made a note.

"Those three precepts, to be industrious, thrifty, and invest productively, compose a famous trio. Marx called them exploitation of the workers, profiteering, and unjust ownership of the means of production. Max Weber called them the Protestant work ethic, an unsatisfactory term, as he himself granted, because it's parochial and misleading."

"It's past lunchtime," said Armbruster. "You've touched on all your precepts except *Be optimistic*. That shouldn't be complicated."

"Not complicated, but superficially paradoxical. I think it's connected with fear of violence and dread of insecurity generally. Business people are forever trying to protect themselves from nasty surprises. They try to penetrate the future with forecasts, surveys, and voracious consumption of news. Newspapers began with what we now call their business sections. The earliest seems to have been a newsletter put out by the Fuggers, a German banking and mercantile family, to keep themselves and their clients well informed. The foundations of the family's banking enterprise, incidentally, were laid down by an early-fifteenth-century artisan, a weaver, who expanded from weaving into merchant trading and from trading into banking.

"Commercial people then and now take security measures with insurance policies, pledges of collateral, letters of credit from customers and bills of lading from suppliers, and so on. All that paperwork! The earliest writing, on clay tablets, seems to have been notations of how many jars of wine and cruets of oil were on hand, and seals laying out who they came from or what belonged to whom. So writing done by ordinary people for everyday life seems to have started with commercial accounting.

"Offhand, you'd expect obsession with security to be associated with pessimism, withdrawal, and fear of the future, maybe chronic, bitter suspicion of it. Certainly not anything as cheerful as optimism. But look at it this way. People who take practical steps to forestall surprise and misfortunes are, by definition, optimists. They aren't resigned to misfortune, they aren't fatalistic. Furthermore, the precautions are often successful. So they lead commercial people to assume that after a mistake or an unpreventable disaster there'll likely be a second chance or a third. It's not necessarily true. Commercial life is full of failures. But because the insurance money comes in, or the courts order redress, the second chances do work out often enough to sustain a comforting belief in the paper forts."

"Outrageous complacency," said Ben. "Meantime, the planet—"

"I'm with you about environmental complacency," Kate interrupted him. "But face the fact that commercial optimism, and the courage it gives to forge on, are much

esteemed, and then think about the implications of that fact for strategies of environmental protection. As a generalization, people with a commercial cast of mind find it almost impossible to believe they're headed willynilly into irreversible environmental disaster. They can't believe there's no way out. It doesn't ring true emotionally. Instead, what does grab commercial people, emotionally as well as practically, is ingenious ways to forestall disaster. That's why business papers these days are full of reports about recycling discarded tires into rubberized road pavements; de-inking newsprint to save pulpwood, and somebody's even newer invention that doesn't require de-inking; possible methods of storing solar heat so that electricity could be generated even in the dark; retaining tropical forests by emphasizing nut production and using them as sources of pharmaceutical and medical research—that sort of thing.

"When ingenuity is the approach to conserving resources and repairing past mistakes, at least you have commercial life and its powerful force of optimism working with you. You don't, simply by crying gloom and doom. Of course the ingenuities, unless they're merely wishful, demand initiative, invention, dissent, industriousness, thrift, productive investment, and the spurs of competition—in fact, the whole moral syndrome."

"Let's keep talking during lunch," said Armbruster. "I've a question for you right off, just wait a minute."

He restarted his coffee maker and put out plates and a pitcher of cider while Ben unwrapped a parcel of sprouts and dates, Hortense found a spoon for her yogurt, Kate pulled two peanut butter sandwiches from among news clippings in a manila envelope, and Jasper, to the accompaniment of oh's and ah's from the others, opened an elegant lacquered box of sushi and a small bottle of sake.

"Early on," said Armbruster, seating himself with an apple and a generous slice of Gouda, "you told us science belongs to this commercial syndrome, but you haven't referred to science since, except in some glancing references to technology. What did you have in mind when you said that?"

"We're always saying 'the arts and sciences,' at least in the university we are, as if they were twins. But they have different parentage and differ in many other important ways as well. For instance, the arts can flourish magnificently in cultures and subcultures with little commerce to speak of. They often have. Science, on the contrary, develops only feebly in a culture until trade and production have already been developing vigorously. Oh, I don't mean that science is absent in noncommercial societies, or that an impulse toward it isn't ancient, maybe even universal. Or at least as universal as curiosity. All the same, scientific investigation proliferates and scientific knowledge ramifies and accumulates as a sequel to flourishing commercial life."

"Does that mean we can expect the Japanese to become leaders in science?" asked Hortense.

"I think so," said Kate. "And probably Koreans, too."

"But why the connection?" Armbruster pressed.

"It's partly circumstantial. Trade, production, and the technologies they use stimulate all manner of scientific curiosity; simultaneously, inventive commercial life provides diversifying tools for pursuing the curiosity.

"But more important, science needs the same values and precepts as commerce. Honesty is the bedrock of science. Moral rules for research are: don't lie, don't deceive or cheat under any circumstances; if you're making reasoned guesses, say so and lay out your reasons.

"Voluntary agreement is the agreement that counts among scientists. Forced agreement to findings or conclusions is worse than useless. Science thrives on dissent for the sake of the task. Any theory is thus only provisionally true in science. It's understood that theories can't be proved; they can only be disproved. An accepted theory is merely one not yet proved false—and the possibility always exists that it may be.

"T. H. Huxley, Darwin's great defender, said, 'Science and her methods gave me a resting place independent of authority and tradition.' Obedience, adherence to tradition, and subservience to authority aren't morally esteemed in science. Instead, science is open to novelty. It's inventive. It demands initiative and enterprise. It is an unremittingly industrious occupation. Scientists believe, perhaps excessively, in investment for production of information at the expense of current consumption.

"As for thrift—it's interesting that a major tenet is what's called 'parsimony of explanation,' meaning the leanest and simplest explanation—the thriftiest—that accounts for the data is preferred over more extravagant, elaborate, or convoluted explanations. Of course that isn't literal thrift but it shows a cast of mind that values economy of means, and this cast of mind also rules good technology.

"Science requires and values easy collaboration with strangers and aliens—that's how scientists pool what they learn and build on one another's work. Like trade, this collaboration hops, skips, and jumps without regard to confinements of territory. In pre-modern Japan, men with an interest in science who dared associate on their own initiative with the occasional alien geographer or navigator who penetrated the realm—or even read and studied alien

scientific thought and findings—were sometimes driven to suicide by social disapproval or were hunted down by the police. Cold war hawks here persecuted scientists suspected of associating with Communists. Exclusiveness and secrecy were even more treasured by the Soviet government, which didn't help Soviet science.

"Guardian values and rules, in their entirety, are so contradictory to the rules and values of science that it's worrying to see guardian assumptions creeping in as an accompaniment to government-dispensed research grants, which are now far and away the biggest sources for scientific research. Researchers sniff out what subjects and approaches will please the guardians and tailor their own interests accordingly. Worse, they neglect unexpected puzzles they encounter if delving into them won't be on the beam. This is serious because pursuing unexpected side issues has proved fruitful. The unanticipated discovery of penicillin's lethal effects on bacteria is a famous instance. Also, the value guardian grant-givers place on hierarchy becomes reflected in research laboratories themselves. He who can bring in the grants is king. Sometimes the guardian values are so blatant as to be stunning." . . .

. . . "The underlying trouble here is that guardian controllers of research funds either are not aware that the commercial moral syndrome guides science or, if they are aware, give short shrift to the integrity of that syndrome. It isn't the guardian syndrome they themselves work by, with its contradictory values of obedience, hierarchy, loyalty, and exclusiveness; also deceptiveness for the sake of the task, which in the case of the Department of Health and Human Services seems to include protecting the department's political, public relations, or other interests. Could be an interest in answers they've already settled upon and want the research to verify. That's all that a lot of people think science is good for."

"I've a question," said Jasper. "How does religion come into your commercial syndrome? You did mention the Protestant work ethic."

"She said it was an empty catchword," said Ben.

"No, no, not empty," said Kate. "What happened seems to me similar to what Hortense told us about medieval commercial practices' taking root and flourishing outside established law, then later being assimilated as civil law by the courts. In this case they were eventually assimilated into religious doctrines. You must realize, first, that in medieval Europe the Christian church forbade usury. It was a sin."

"Usury is loan-sharking," said Ben. "Good thing to be down on, I'd say."

"That's our meaning of usury, but to medieval Christians usury meant lending money in return for interest, no matter what the rate. Gradually a few loopholes were condoned, the major one being that if a loan was put at serious risk—say, to finance a chancy venture like a trading voyage with its hazards of shipwreck and pirates—then interest could be justifiable as recompense for the risk of total loss. Other religions have forbidden lending at interest; to this day that remains Islamic doctrine, although in practice ample loopholes now exist, mainly under the concept that loans represent 'buying into' an enterprise, with interest rationalized as a share of its profits.

"In sixteenth-century Europe, some religious reformers, followers of Calvin especially, dissented from the church view of usury, as they did from many other points of church doctrine. Calvinism—the Dutch Reformed church and the Presbyterian church and its offshoots, including Congregationalism, the variety of Presbyterianism the Puritans brought to America—held that lending at interest was not only morally respectable but praiseworthy in the eyes of God.

"Furthermore, they held that wealth was the consequence of godly industry, thrift, and productive investment. Previously, possession of wealth had been theologically accounted for as a gift from God for His own inscrutable purposes, or alternatively as the Devil's doing.

"Thousands of Calvinist sermons and tracts drummed those reform ideas into Protestant flocks and extolled the benefits of wealth from productive investment, thrift, and industriousness, provided that some of the proceeds were given charitably for the work of the church and that the sin of avarice was avoided. A clergyman named Baxter strikes me as a champion killjoy but his published sermons were popular. He exhorted the righteous to 'keep up a high esteem of time and be every day more careful that you lose none of your time than you are that you lose none of your gold and silver. And if your recreations, dressings, feastings, idle talk, unprofitable company or sleep be any of them temptations to rob you of your time, accordingly heighten your watchfulness.'

"But the Calvinist divines had more congenial tidings, too. While they condemned waste of wealth on vainglory, luxury, and profligacy, they approved the use of riches for comfort. They urged a decent comfort of the home as praiseworthy. And all the Protestants weren't insanely extreme about industriousness. The ruling bodies of the Dutch Reformed and French Huguenot branches of Calvinism condemned excessive labor on grounds it robbed time and energy from the service of God. From time to time they even backtracked on the advisability of usury. Not all Protestant movements were as radical as the Calvinists, either. Luther and his followers didn't condone lending at interest."

"You're a long time getting around to Weber," said Jasper.

"Weber was trying to explain the remarkable success of northwestern Europe in commerce and industry. He proposed giving credit to what he called the Protestant work ethic. But here we get into knotty problems of cause and effect. Weber's critics soon pointed out that no place was more enthusiastically Calvinist than Scotland, where Presbyterianism had been enthroned as the state religion, and no population was more willing to endure sermonizing than the Scots. Yet Scotland remained poor and for the most part backward in commerce and industry. Critics also pointed out that Geneva, where Calvin had been based, was already—before his time—probably the most bourgeois city in Europe. The Dutch cities where Calvinism took root quickly and firmly had also anticipated Calvinists in their actual commercial practices. In sum, Weber's critics suggested he'd got things backward: that commercial ways shaped Calvinism, not the reverse. Weber himself then wavered on this point of cause and effect, which is a credit to his science-minded respect for dissent and to his own honesty.

"What happened, as I said, seems to be that religious reformers were catching up with existing commercial morality and legitimizing it. But that's not to say that Protestantism had no significant influence on commercial behavior, Scotland notwithstanding. Wherever commercial precepts and practices were strong, religious approval must have further reinforced them.

"Moreover, religion also concentrated on trying to prevent commercial greed from getting out of hand. The sin of avarice was expounded and excoriated. And once the Calvinists accepted commercial behavior as one facet of divine order, this influenced secular conceptions about the nobleness of mundane work and enterprise. For instance"—she dug among her notes—"Emerson said this: 'A man coins himself unto his labor, turns his day, his strength, his thought, his affections into some product which remains as the visible sign of his power.' Notice the commercial turn of phrase 'A man coins himself,' and along with it the spiritual tone of 'calling' and dedication. It's a far cry from saying bourgeois values are base or business is a racket."

"Let me give you a quote now," said Ben.

The golf links lie so near the mill
That almost every day
The laboring children can look out
And see the men at play.

"How does child labor fit into this amazingly high-minded picture of yours? Or a guy condemned to turn the same five bolts over and over all his life on an assembly line?"

"One way they fit in is that both are now obsolete in commercially advanced societies," said Kate. "But your question does touch on an interesting paradox. The very industriousness of commercial life—of course, along with attention to productive investment, thrift, efficiency, comfort and convenience, dissent from traditional ways of doing things, and the rest of the moral syndrome—eats away at grinding drudgery. Commercial life creates novel and enterprising ways of evading it, not only on assembly lines and in mills but in homes, too, and on farms."

"You have given more thought to these precepts than I expected when you dropped them on us," said Jasper. "But your fixation on a pair of moral syndromes still troubles me. So arbitrary. If there are two independent sets of precepts, then why not three? Or for that matter, why not four, or seven?"

QUESTIONS ON JACOBS

1. Kate says that she has not mentioned virtues such as cooperation, courage, and perseverance because they are esteemed "across the board, in all kinds of work." Do you agree with Kate? Or do these virtues manifest themselves differently in different contexts? For example, is commercial courage different from the courage of a guardian?

2. How did Kate devise her two syndromes? Do you think her method is sound? Are there precepts that you think she has left out of the commercial syndrome?

3. Is the commercial syndrome, as explained by Kate, a coherent whole? Explain the coherence of these precepts (or the coherence of each specific cluster of precepts).

FOR FURTHER READING

Banfield, Edward. *The Moral Basis of a Backward Society.* Glencoe, Ill.: The Free Press, 1958.

Coleman, James S. "Social Capital in the Creation of Human Capital," *American Journal of Sociology* 94 (1988): S95–S120.

Fukuyama, Francis. *The Great Disruption: Human Nature and the Recognition of Social Order.* New York: The Free Press, 1999.

———. *Trust: The Social Virtues and the Creation of Prosperity.* New York: The Free Press, 1995.

Gambetta, Diego, ed. *Trust: Making and Breaking Cooperative Relations.* Oxford: Blackwell, 1987.

Gellner, Ernest. *Conditions and Liberty: Civil Society and Its Rivals.* London: Hamish Hamilton, 1994.

Harrison, Lawrence E., and Samuel P. Huntington, eds. *Culture Matters: How Values Shape Human Progress.* New York: Basic Books, 2000.

Hirschman, Albert O. *The Passions and the Interests: Political Arguments for Capitalism Before Its Triumph.* Princeton, N.J.: Princeton University Press, 1977.

Hollis, Martin. *Trust Within Reason.* Cambridge: Cambridge University Press, 1998.

Jacobs, Jane. *Systems of Survival: A Dialogue on the Moral Foundations of Commerce and Politics.* New York: Vintage, 1992.

Lal, Deepak. *Unintended Consequences: The Impact of Factor Endowments, Culture, and Politics on Long Run Economic Performance.* Cambridge: M.I.T. Press, 1998.

Knight, Frank. "The Ethics of Competition," *Quarterly Journal of Economics* 37 (1923).

Novak, Michael. *The Catholic Ethic and the Spirit of Capitalism.* New York: The Free Press, 1993.

Putnam, Robert D., with Robert Leonardi and Raffaella Y. Nanetti. *Making Democracy Work: Civic Traditions in Modern Italy.* Princeton, N.J.: Princeton University Press, 1993.

Putnam, Robert D. *Bowling Alone: The Collapse and Revival of American Community.* New York: Simon and Schuster, 2000.

Röpke, Wilhelm. *A Humane Economy: The Social Framework of the Free Market.* Wilmington, Del.: ISI Books, 1998.

Sacks, Jonathan. "Wealth and Poverty: A Jewish Analysis," in *Tradition in an Untraditional Age.* London: Vallentine Mitchell, 1990.

Sen, Amartya. "Rational Fools: A Critique of the Behavioral Foundations of Economic Theory," *Philosophy and Public Affairs* 6 (1977): 317–44.

Yeager, Leland B. *Ethics as Social Science: The Moral Philosophy of Social Cooperation.* Cheltenham, U.K.: Edward Elgar, 2001.

Ethical Theory

It is clear that the virtue we must examine is human virtue, since we are also seeking the human good and human happiness. And by human virtue we mean virtue of the soul, not of the body, since we say that happiness is an activity of the soul.

Aristotle[1]

I think it is more than a verbal point to say that what should be aimed at is goodness, and not freedom or right action, although right action, and freedom in the sense of humility, are the natural products of attention to the Good. Of course, right action is important in itself, with an importance which is not difficult to understand. But it should provide the starting-point of reflection and not its conclusion. . . . However, the aim of morality cannot be simply action. Without some more positive conception of the soul as a substantial and continually developing mechanism of attachments, the purification and reorientation of which must be the task of morals, 'freedom' is readily corrupted into self-assertion and 'right action' into some sort of ad hoc *utilitarianism.*

Iris Murdoch[2]

Human beings are not like exactly similar bottles of whisky each marked 'for export only' or some device indicating a common destination or end. Men do not share a fixed nature, nor, therefore, are there any ends which they must necessarily pursue in fulfillment of such nature. There is no end set for the human race by an abstraction called 'human nature.' There are only ends which individuals choose, or are forced by circumstances to accept. Men are not created for a purpose as a piano is built to produce certain sounds. Or if they are we have no idea of the purpose.

Margaret MacDonald[3]

1. *Nicomachean Ethics,* translated by Terence Irwin (Indianapolis, Ind.: Hackett Publishing, 1985), 1102a15.

2. *The Sovereignty of Good* (New York: Schocken Books, 1971), 70–71.

3. "Natural Rights," *Proceedings of the Aristotelian Society,* xlvii (1946–47), 236–38.

For a moral law states categorically what ought to be done, whether it pleases us or not. It is, therefore, not a case of satisfying an inclination. If it were, there would be no moral law, but every one might act according to his own feeling.

Immanuel Kant[4]

Nature has placed mankind under the governance of two sovereign masters, pain *and* pleasure. *It is for them alone to point out what we ought to do, as well as to determine what we shall do. On the one hand the standard of right and wrong, on the other the chain of causes and effects, are fastened to their throne. They govern us in all we do, in all we say, in all we think: every effort we can make to throw off our subjection, will serve but to demonstrate and confirm it. In words a man may pretend to abjure their empire: but in reality he will remain subject to it all the while. The* principle of utility *recognizes this subjection, and assumes it for the foundation of that system, the object of which is to rear the fabric of felicity by the hands of reason and of law. Systems which attempt to question it, deal in sounds instead of senses, in caprice instead of reason, in darkness instead of light.*

Jeremy Bentham[5]

A normative evaluation of the market seeks to evaluate market rules, practices, or traits by appeal to some standard or principle of value. These standards may, in turn, be subject to a reasonable evaluation, justification, or defense, all of which can be found in moral (or ethical) theories. An ethical theory not only provides a theoretical justification of important moral principles, concepts, and ideas but also serves as a guide to action and provides a substantively developed basis for moral evaluation. In other words, an ethical theory provides a more or less theoretical account of how one *should* live (or what one *should* do), and it is in this sense that ethical theory relates to economic systems generally, as well as to particular market practices or to human propensities, habits, or practices.

If an economic system concerns itself with the creation and distribution of scarce goods and services, then an ethical theory should provide some guidance as to how one *ought* to evaluate that system or to alter its framework, practices, or conditions of operation. Thus, if a market presupposes laws and institutions that establish a set of permissions, prohibitions, and requirements, then an ethical theory should provide some guidance, even if abstract and general, about the legitimacy of that framework and about the sort of actions or traits that the participants should perform or exhibit. Which prohibitions or requirements *ought* to be established, adhered to, or altered? And of the actions or qualities that we are permitted to do or express, which of these are moral obligations or virtues?

Some of the prohibitions, requirements, and permissions can be discussed in terms of philosophical ideas concerning justice (Section AII). However, philosophical considerations of justice typically take place with reference to a larger ethical system. It is to these larger ethical systems that we direct our attention in this section. Moreover, since justice is but one aspect of morality, our ethical reflections must extend beyond questions of justice to encompass other ideas of good and bad, right and wrong.

ETHICAL THEORY

Kinds of Ethical Theory

Philosophical reflection on moral matters has often taken the form of normative ethical theory, but there are other modes of intellectual inquiry into ethical matters

---

4. "The Supreme Principle of Morality," in *Lectures on Ethics* [1775–1780], translated by Louis Infield (Indianapolis, Ind.: Hackett Publishing, 1963), 37.

5. *An Introduction to the Principles of Morals and Legislation* [1789], edited by J. H. Burns and H. L. A. Hart (London: The Athlone Press, 1970), chapter I.1 (p. 11).

and it is wise to differentiate these. One can distinguish three types of inquiry: descriptive theory, normative ethical theory, and metaethics. The *descriptive* (or sociological or anthropological) inquiry attempts to provide a factual account of some group or society's ethical outlook. What principles does a society use to justify or evaluate certain actions or traits? What mode of moral reasoning or persuasion is utilized? What areas of social life exhibit which sorts of moral norms? These sorts of questions invoke sociological, anthropological, and historical assessments and shall not be our concern in this section. (In Section AIV, on the foundations of markets, we make use of a more sociological approach.) Another type of inquiry is *metaethical* theory. This type of theory focuses less on what one *should* do than on the logic of moral reasoning, the meaning of moral terms, and on whether we can have moral knowledge that is *objective* (rather than *relative*). Although we shall not concentrate on metaethical questions, we shall discuss, briefly, the topic of relativism.

Apart from the purely descriptive and the metaethical, there is the mode of ethical inquiry that is concerned with guiding conduct: normative ethical theory (or moral theory). A moral or ethical theory is foundational and practical in that it seeks to defend or justify certain moral principles that can be used to help an individual (or society) to determine how a person (or a society) ought to act or what sort of person one ought to be. Such a theory should not only elucidate important concepts and principles, but it should justify these by offering grounds or reasons for accepting and employing them in one's life or society. If one puts into practice an ethical theory, then that theory should not only provide guidance in those situations that call for a (moral) response, but it should provide a more basic foundation or grounding by which one can deliberate further about what to do or be. For example, in a society's legal and political framework the principles elucidated should provide guidance as to what is to be permitted, prohibited, or required; at the level of individual choice, the theory should prove useful in deliberating about what one should do or what sort of person one should be.

The Purpose of Normative Ethics

Of course, anyone who comes to the study of business ethics and ethical theory already possesses an ethical outlook, so what does the study of ethical theory provide? A normative ethical theory is neither a summation of moral opinions or judgments nor an opportunity for moralizing or preaching; it is, rather, a reasoned exploration and justification of ethical principles. Thus, the study of any single ethical theory may provide a critical perspective by which to evaluate one's own outlook. That does not entail that one should reject one's outlook if it clashes with an ethical theory. The purpose of studying ethics is not to change one's ethical opinions (even if that does happen as a result of the study), but to deepen one's appreciation of the importance of the ethical, to point out how difficult and complex certain ethical questions are, and to provide, via the examination of specific theories, a single coherent outlook that may complement one's own views, provide a means for self-criticism, or supply a theoretical vision useful for further reflection.

ETHICAL RELATIVISM AND MORAL DIFFERENCES

It is obvious that our everyday moral beliefs—including beliefs about our obligations, duties, or virtues—spring from a variety of sources. The inheritance of particular cultures, religions, and traditions, our moral beliefs are leavened with the sparks of reading and reflection, and seasoned, sometimes quite heavily, with the attitudes, vocabulary, and impulses of popular culture. That these beliefs, or the beliefs of persons of other epochs or cultures, may originate from a variety of sources (local, cultural, or historical) does not demonstrate, however, that all questions of right or wrong are *relative* to a particular culture or origin. Whatever the historical or cultural origin of one's moral beliefs or moral principles, it could still be the case that these are not just relative to a culture but are, in fact, true beliefs or principles that should hold for everyone. Indeed, beyond the varied sources of one's current beliefs, it is possible to seek a more rigorous and reflective grounding, as is done in theoretical or philosophical accounts of morality. In so doing, one may find that some of one's current beliefs accord well with some aspects of a particular moral theory; in other cases one may discover that some of one's beliefs are inconsistent with a moral theory.

Ethical Relativism

Of course, one might object that even a moral theory is nothing but a product of a particular time and place; a moral theory, like our everyday moral beliefs, is not, and cannot be, anything other than an inescapably cultural perspective. That an ethical outlook, whether that of everyday moral beliefs or that of theory, cannot be justified in any objective manner but is dependent on a society or culture is the claim of the ethical relativist: Moral beliefs and theoretical principles cannot be justified independent of society or culture. This claim is often formulated in distinct ways, and it is important to distinguish ethical relativism from a similar but distinct doctrine about differences in moral beliefs.

The Claim of Moral Differences

The claim that different societies—across the ages and across the globe—have held divergent ethical beliefs is not equivalent to a claim of ethical relativism; rather, an assertion of divergent ethical beliefs is just what it claims and no more: an empirical or descriptive assertion about moral differences across the ages and across societies.

> *Moral Differences:* As a matter of fact, different societies in different epochs or locations have different moral outlooks concerning good and bad, right and wrong.

This claim may or may not be true, but it is not *obviously* true, and one should be cautious about embracing it too readily. Whether or not there are deep divisions in our moral principles is a controversial question, and it should not be decided without some analysis and thought.

Consider, first, that the claim of moral difference draws no distinction between underlying moral *principles* and derivative moral *judgments*. Yet even if our moral judgments differ, our principles may not necessarily differ. For the same principle might lead to distinct judgments if the judgments were issued by individuals with distinct nonmoral beliefs. Two societies may share the same prohibition on killing the innocent ("It is wrong to kill innocent persons"), but the societies may differ in their beliefs about personhood or in their beliefs about the criteria of innocence. And it is these differences that may lead to distinct moral judgments about similar types of situations. It would not be surprising that individuals living in different societies, different climates, or in different epochs would have differing nonmoral beliefs. Because of these differing beliefs, and not because of differing principles, these individuals *may* issue divergent judgments.

Indeed, it seems worthwhile to consider that all societies may share some general principles concerning honesty, peaceful interaction, property, and childrearing, if only because *no* society would long survive if it did not establish some such principles. This is not to say that there are *no* differences among societies, for surely such there are and it is important to distinguish whether these differences reflect divergencies of culture, beliefs, or moral principles. Nor is it to deny that the fundamental institutions of a society may have significant consequences for our moral beliefs and practices, not to mention other cultural practices. Nonetheless, this is to affirm that the claim that societies differ in moral beliefs is not obviously true. However, even if the claim were true, and there were deep divergencies in moral principles across the ages and the world, this claim would still not be equivalent to the claim of ethical relativism, nor does it *imply* ethical relativism.[6]

Relativism and Moral Differences: Distinctions

To understand these two points, let us consider a formulation of the doctrine of ethical relativism.

> *Ethical Relativism:* There are no moral norms, principles, and judgments that are justifiably true for all human beings; moral norms, principles, and judgments are true only within the particular society that has adopted these norms, principles, or judgments.

This doctrine espouses the idea that no single universal morality can be shown to hold for all human beings simply as human beings; rather all judgments, principles (and so on) are dependent on, or *relative* to, a particular social, ethnic, religious or cultural outlook, and these are inescapably particular. Although the doctrine of relativism may be true, it is not *equivalent* to the claim of moral differences, nor does the descriptive claim *entail* the claim of ethical relativism. The descriptive statement about moral differences would not, even if true, entail a statement that there is no one objective morality that applies, justifiably, to all human beings. One could agree that there are differences across or between societies or epochs but nonetheless hold that some or all societies have misguided moral principles and that the correct moral principles still hold for everyone, even those who are currently misguided. That the claim of moral differences does not *entail* the truth of the thesis of ethical relativism does not prove that relativism is untrue, only that it cannot be *shown* to be true by asserting a claim of moral differences. Whether ethical relativism

6. What does it mean to say that "A implies B" (or "A entails B")? Briefly, if A implies B, then if one accepts A, one must also accept B. On the other hand, if A does not imply B, then one could accept A without accepting B. Note that if A does not imply B, that does not prove that B is not true. B could well be true even if A does not establish that B is true.

can be formulated so that it is true is a question we set aside for now.

Of course, even if ethical relativism were true, that would not mean that the study of ethics is pointless. Whether or not one is a relativist or objectivist about morals, the study of normative ethics (and its applications in business) can help deepen one's moral awareness, provide a critical perspective on one's own ethics and that of one's society, and grant one a more thorough grasp of some of the finer aspirations of humanity.

NORMATIVE ETHICAL THEORIES: AN OVERVIEW

Doing *versus* Being; Rules *versus* Virtues

In Western philosophy, there have been a variety of moral theories—some articulated by ancient Greeks, others by medieval philosophers, and some by modern and contemporary philosophers. Each theory may bear similarities or divergences to some other theory. However, as an introduction to some of these theories, we will begin with a standard method of categorization, one that is not without the distorting flaws of oversimplification but which nonetheless offers some insight. This categorization builds on a distinction between the *characteristics* of persons and the *actions* of persons, between *being* a certain kind of person and *doing* or performing certain kinds of actions.

A particular normative ethical theory may focus either on acts and rules (what one is to *do* or by what rule one should act) or on some ideal of the person (what sort of person one should *be*). The first kind of theory focuses primarily on what a person should do, and from this account moves, only secondarily, to the consideration of those qualities of character necessary for performing such actions. Conversely, the second type of theory focuses primarily on what sort of person one should *be,* and then moves, secondarily, to the matter of what one ought to *do* in some specific kind of situation. By emphasizing traits of character, this theory suggests that appropriate actions arise only from persons who have the right sort of character and judgment. In the readings that follow, Aristotle's thought exemplifies that mode of theory which emphasizes the characteristics of a person. Kant and Mill, writing in the modern period (late eighteenth- and early nineteenth-centuries), emphasize right actions. It is to these modern theories that we turn first.

Nonconsequentialism and Kant

Although Kant and Mill focus on right action their theories differ in how each responds to this question: What makes a right act *right?* The two general responses to this question can be summarized as follows:

> *Nonconsequentialism:* An act is right simply because that act has some inherent quality.

> *Consequentialism:* An act is right simply because of the consequences that that act brings into effect.

One of the most prominent nonconsequentialist theories[7] is that of Kant, who contends that an action is right because that action exhibits the quality of rationality and is performed out of respect for duty, moral duty being determinable by a supreme standard of morality: universalizability. (Because of his emphasis on acting from duty, Kant's theory is referred to as a *deontological* theory, for *deon* is the Greek term for duty.) Insofar as each person is rational, then so is each person obligated by the same duties. Moreover, the very rationality of persons entails a second formulation of the supreme standard of morality, one that is, Kant suggests, equivalent to that of universalizability: that we should never treat other individuals solely as a means to our ends, but always as ends in themselves.

Consequentialism and Utilitarianism

On the other hand, one might contend, as the consequentialist does, that the rightness of some action or practice is not a function of some inherent quality of the action but depends, instead, on whether or not the action generates some consequence or state of affairs that is essentially distinct from the action. For example, if one believes that consequences are relevant to our moral judgments, then one might contend that what makes an action right is that it tends to ameliorate conflicts or that it generates happiness among those affected by the action. Perhaps the most famous species of consequentialism is that of utilitarianism. As J. S. Mill argues, the rightness or wrongness of an action is a function not of the inherent nature of the act but of the kind of consequences that the act tends to bring about. The doctrine of utilitarianism may be formulated as follows:

---

7. Another nonconsequentialist theory, that of the divine command theory, holds that an act is right because it expresses God's command.

Utilitarianism: An action (or a rule) is morally right if and only if that action (or rule) can be reasonably expected to produce at least as great a balance of good (utility) over evil as any other action (or rule) that is a relevant option.

Understood properly, the doctrine of utilitarianism includes a theory of obligation (specifying that an act is obligatory if and only if that act will maximize utility) and a theory of value (specifying what is to count as good).

The first explicit account of utilitarianism was offered, in the late eighteenth-century, by Jeremy Bentham (1748–1832), who identified utility with quantities of pleasure, understood by Bentham to be the only intrinsic good.[8] Bentham's account of utility was challenged by John Stuart Mill, who argued that the quality, not merely the quantity, of pleasure must be taken into account in determining the utility of an action or rule. For Mill, utility must be equated with happiness, and human happiness is dependent on the satisfaction of "higher pleasures," those pleasures that involve the use of the higher or rational faculties of the human being. The hedonistic utilitarianism of Bentham and Mill has more recently been countered by both a nonhedonistic explanation of utility as including a plurality of goods (such as love, beauty, knowledge, and friendship) and by an account in which utility is understood in terms of individual "preferences." On this last view, one should seek to perform that action (or adhere to that rule) which has the greatest chance of satisfying the maximum number of preferences.

In addition to this debate concerning the utilitarian theory of value, there is, within utilitarianism, another issue of contention. To what is the principle of utility to be applied? What is to be subjected to the calculus of utility? Are we to apply the principle of utility to the particular actions we might take at a specific time and place? Or should we apply the principle to the possible rules in accordance with which we might act? The *act-utilitarian* argues that one should apply the principle of utility to one's particular actions. Thus, in any scenario of decision one should ask which of one's possible ac-

tions has the greatest probability of increasing good over evil. Although in many situations one may rely on "rules of thumb" that have proven to advance utility, one should not adhere to rules in any blind fashion. On the other hand, a *rule-utilitarian* contends that one should not apply the principle of utility to particular actions; rather, one should act in conformity to *rules* which, if generally followed, would maximize utility. Given the set of possible rules to which individuals might generally adhere, one should act in accordance with that rule the general adherence to which would maximize utility.

Theories of Virtue

Unlike the Kantian or the utilitarian theories, another and more ancient mode of normative theory—exemplified in the thought of classical Greek philosophers such as Plato and Aristotle—focuses less on what one is to *do* than on what one is to *be*. Instead of asking, "What are my duties? What ought I do in this sort of situation?" one should ask, "How should my life be as a whole? What sort of life—what sort of character—should I possess?" The point here is to ask about the shape of one's life or character and, from a response to this question, find responses to the questions concerning what one should do. This will involve an appeal to traits or qualities of character—virtues—constitutive of a life lived well. Because a theory of virtue is grounded in appeals to character, rather than in principles or rules of action, it does not contain formalized procedures for responding to ethical questions or solving ethical dilemmas. Indeed, one important implication of such a theory is precisely that rule-following (even if necessary in a complex society) is not a sufficient substitute for character and moral judgment.

The Challenge of Egoism

Perhaps at this point, it might be suggested that there is no need for ethical theory because most theories state that we are sometimes obliged to act against what we believe to be our own interest and that any such action is impossible. No persons can be motivated to act against what they perceive to be their own self-interest. If this is so, then there is no genuinely other-regarding action. That all action is, deep down, self-regarding and egoistic is the contention of the *psychological egoist*.

> *Psychological Egoism:* Human beings are so constituted that each is motivated to advance only his or her own perceived self-interest.

---

8. To measure the quantity of pleasure one must consider seven variables: "To a number of persons, with reference to each of whom the value of a pleasure or pain is considered, it will be greater or less, according to seven circumstances: to wit . . . 1. Its *intensity.* 2. Its *duration.* 3. Its *certainty* or *uncertainty.* 4. Its *propinquity* or *remoteness.* 5. Its *fecundity.* 6. *Its purity.* And one other; to wit: Its *extent;* that is, the number of persons to whom it *extends.*" *An Introduction to the Principles of Morals and Legislation,* chapter IV.4 (p. 39).

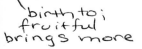
birth to;
fruitful
brings more

Although some persons are attracted to this thesis, it is not obviously true. As stated, the claim purports to be a factual or empirical statement about human motives (or intentions). The thesis makes a *universal* claim about all of the motives (or intentions) of all human beings, so it would seem to be easy to come up with an example of an action that was not motivated by an agent's perceived self-interest. Indeed, there seem to be any number of cases in which human beings are motivated to act in defiance of their perceived self-interest (for example, one person risks his life to save the life of another person). Thus, as an empirical statement the thesis is subject to refutation, whether one recalls an actual example of an other-regarding action or one draws up a hypothetical scenario that is clearly within the realm of possible actions. Once these instances are brought forth, then the original thesis of psychological egoism is either shown to be false or it must be amended in some way. If the thesis is amended, then one must be careful that the thesis is not so altered that it ceases to be an empirical thesis and becomes an *analytical* claim. (An analytical statement is one in which the very meaning of the predicate of the statement is contained within the meaning of the subject: for example, "All bachelors are unmarried males" is an analytically true statement, but it is not an empirical one.) However, the claim of psychological egoism *cannot* be analytical, for all such statements are either necessarily true (or necessarily false) and there is nothing necessarily true (or false) about the claim of psychological egoism.

As an alternative to psychological egoism, one might opt for a normative thesis about egoism. The normative theory is usually referred to as *ethical egoism,* a doctrine, which, like utilitarianism, is *consequentialist;* unlike utilitarianism, however, ethical egoism states that one should seek to advance only those consequences that are beneficial for oneself.

> *Ethical Egoism:* Each person ought to seek to advance only his or her own reasonable self-interest.

On this version of ethical egoism, each and every person is to seek to maximize what is in his or her rational self-interest. In emphasizing one's rational (or long-term) self-interest, this formulation of egoism would disallow acting merely to satisfy one's immediate pleasure or whim. In addition, this principle permits one to aid others but only if such aid does not conflict with one's rational self-interest.

Although ethical egoism has not received as many defenders as utilitarianism or Kantianism, it has been defended most prominently by the novelist and philosopher Ayn Rand (1905–1982). In fact, Rand argues that her particular kind of egoism is the only moral view compatible with capitalism, though it is not obvious either that this is true of her theory alone or of any other theory of ethical egoism. (See section BI for a discussion of and readings on self-interest and the market.) Indeed, some utilitarians and Kantians have considered their theories to be compatible with and supportive of commerce and markets, just as some utilitarians and Kantians have argued against market institutions. Obviously, the application of moral theories to particular situations is exceedingly complex. To consider this matter more fully, let us consider how different theories may lead to the same judgments, how judgments may be used to test a theory, and how moral theories might or might not relate to commerce and markets.

Moral Theory and Moral Judgments

Distinct moral theories, with divergent principles, need not always entail different moral judgments. In other words, divergent theoretical principles often lead to the same moral judgments. For example, a nonconsequentialist theory, such as that of Kant, may imply certain judgments about honesty in business that are no different from those derived from a utilitarian theory. However, there are other cases in which moral theories lead to divergent judgments. For example, if one has a duty to be honest, then one should, if one is a Kantian, adhere to this duty (and adhere to it *because* it is one's duty), despite any probability that dishonesty might allow one to reap great rewards or to benefit everyone as a whole. On the other hand, an act-utilitarian might determine that in certain particular instances, happiness would be maximized if an individual were to lie or otherwise distort the truth.

In fact, the sort of moral judgments that proceed from the principles of a moral theory provide one means of testing the acceptability of that theory. If the application of an ethical theory would imply moral judgments which, on reflection, are unacceptable, then one has a good reason for rejecting the theory or, at the least, altering the theory in some coherent manner so it does not entail judgments that are clearly unacceptable. In fact, this is one of the reasons that led to the development of rule-utilitarianism. The decisions reached by the act-utilitarian would often conflict with deeply held moral judgments, judgments that seemed more acceptable than the act-utilitarian theory which denied them. An alternative, therefore, was to apply the principle of utility to rules rather than acts. Whereas an act-utilitarian might reason that on certain occasions honesty might not be the best (utilitarian) policy, the rule-utilitarian reasons that the rule of honesty, if generally adhered to, is the best policy because it serves to maximize utility. For this reason, the rule-utilitarian contends that the norm of honesty should be observed even in those instances in which the act-utilitarian might find a justification for dishonesty.

Moral Theory and Commerce

How do normative ethical theories relate to business and markets? There is no obvious or direct route from one particular theory to this or that economic system. The issues here are complex, and a complete moral understanding of an economic system, especially one as complex as a market, may demand that one investigate certain non-moral views about how markets function. Nonetheless, there is real value in considering how one might evaluate or judge certain aspects of the market if one were an Aristotelian, a Kantian, or a utilitarian.

In so doing, one should take into account the legal foundations of the system and consider how these foundations are compatible or incompatible with fundamental principles of the moral theory. In addition, one could employ a moral theory to evaluate specific rules (or systems of rules), policies, and practices, whether these apply to all businesses (or persons or organizations) or whether these are relevant to a particular industry or a particular firm. Finally, there is the question of whether there are certain traits of character (virtues or vices) that are typical of markets or that are required if one is to live well *and* prosper.

None of this tells us whether one particular theory is more acceptable than any other or more likely to support or devalue the institutions and practices of commerce. Many have held that theories of virtue are more applicable to small societies with common aims than to large modern societies with divergent ends and purposes. Indeed, the theories of virtue long associated with the ancient Greeks have, in much of the modern era, been displaced by theories of rules and principles. Some have contended that this divergence reflects larger differences in the societies, differences that relate as much to philosophical outlooks as to sociological and economic ones. For one's traits or virtues are the very qualities that allow a person to live well within a community, a community which, for the ancient Greeks, had a common end by which to determine what would constitute excellent living. In the modern era, the rise of commerce and economic liberalism—which sought to define a sphere of liberty outside of the prerogatives of the state—replaced the idea of a substantive end for society with the idea of free and equal spheres of action. Some have argued that without a common end, the very idea of virtue has lost its resonating power to the idea of rules, adherence to which allows individuals to pursue their disparate and plural ends. Despite this claim, it is not obvious that virtues have no place in commercial life, and we shall see, in Section B, how some of the traditional virtues may still have a significant place in the lives of market participants.

In the readings that follow, we begin with the first systematic theory of the moral life, that of Aristotle, who commences his thought with the classical assumption that there is an end or goal of the good (and moral) life, and that by acquiring clarity about this end we acquire knowledge about the sort of qualities we should develop. In the eighteenth century, the work of Kant illustrates the modern concern with moral duties as universalizable rules applicable to all persons or rational beings (and not only those with particular ends or purposes). Kant's theory is a nonconsequentialist one, but that of J. S. Mill is consequentialist: The rightness of an action is determined by whether or not it maximizes utility.

THE READINGS

Aristotle Aristotle develops an account of the good (*telos*) for human beings, contending that happiness (or *eudaimonia*, living well) is the final and complete good and that virtue constitutes the essence of happiness. Happiness, it turns out, is not a feeling but a manner of activity, a unified mode of living well. Thus, the final good is a happy life, and this involves having a settled character in which one pursues actions and holds desires that are appropriate to one's circumstances and to one's nature as a rational being. The good of something is its *function performed well,* and so the final good of the human being will be the excellent performance of reason, an excellence which presupposes qualities or virtues that dispose an individual to perform well its (human) function. Human excellence and virtue can be understood more fully by considering the three capacities of the soul: the vegetative, the appetitive, and the rational. The irrational part of the soul contains the vegetative element, irrelevant to ethics, and the appetitive. The latter, however, seems to share in reason insofar as it can obey and listen to reason. Similarly, the rational part of the soul could be said to have a twofold property: one part listens to reason and one part exercises reason. The difference between listening to (or adhering to) reason and exercising reason leads to two classes of virtues: the moral and the intellectual. Aristotle opens Book II by noting that each type is developed in different ways. Intellectual virtue is acquired by teaching, but moral virtue arises "as a result of habit." What, then, is a virtue? A state of character concerned with "passions and actions," a virtue is a *mean* between excess and defect (of either emotions or actions). Aristotle elaborates on various virtues of character, and in Book VI he returns to the intellectual virtues, noting that moral choice demands both correct desire and good reasoning. Practical wisdom, or deliberating well about the good life, involves more than deliberation about universals (such as courage or benevolence), for it is concerned with action or practice "and practice is concerned with particulars" (Book VI, 7), but such knowledge of particulars comes only with experience.

Immanuel Kant   Kant not only maintains that morality is rational but that the very rightness of an act lies in its rational character and not in the consequences that ensue from the performance of the act. For Kant, the only thing which is good in itself, good without qualification, is a *good will*. A good will is a will that chooses morally right actions, and an act is morally right only if it is done "from duty" (where acting "from duty" is distinct from acting *in conformity* with duty). The moral importance of an act done from duty is found not in reference to the consequences that might ensue from the act but in the nature of the maxim that describes the aim, means, and circumstances of the act. The reading selection describes how this is so. Having distinguished how the will might be moved either objectively or subjectively—a distinction that generates the idea of two types of imperatives, the categorical and the hypothetical—Kant contends that our duties are not determined by any subjective desire or by any hypothetical imperative but by reason. Kant seeks to determine our duties by considering whether an intentional act, as described by a *maxim* (a general rule that characterizes the action), could be *universalized*. The idea of universalization connects with rationality in the following manner: An act is done from duty if and only if it is in accordance with a maxim M, and the act is performed because the agent believes (truly) that M is a *rational* maxim. But an agent's maxim is *rational* if and only if the agent can will that M be a universal law. There are two ways in which a maxim M could *fail* to be universalizable:

There is some sort of contradiction in everyone's *acting* on the maxim;

There would be some sort of contradiction in the agent's *willing* that the maxim be generally followed.

So an act is right if it is done from duty and that means, therefore, that the act is performed on the basis of a maxim M, that the agent can will that M be a universal law, and that the agent acts on M because the agent believes that M is universalizable. A supreme principle of morality (the Categorical Imperative) can thus be formulated as a standard of right action: *"Act only on that maxim whereby thou canst at the same time will that it should become a universal law."* How can one be motivated to act from duty when duty is determined not by particular substantive desire but by the (purely formal) Categorical Imperative? Kant answers this question by considering whether there might be something whose end might not be external to itself but which might be *in itself* an end—something whose very nature is an *end in itself.* A rational being is an end in itself and, as such, need posit no end other than its rationality if it is to be motivated by the categorical imperative: it is the very rationality of the imperative that effects the will. This solution leads Kant to offer a second formulation of the Categorical Imperative: *"So act as to treat humanity, whether in thine own person or in that of any other, in every case as an end withal, never as means only."*

John Stuart Mill   Utilitarianism is the normative theory that an act is morally right if and only if the act maximizes utility (or accords with a rule which, if generally followed, would maximize utility). Stated in this manner the doctrine of utilitarianism includes both a theory of right action and a theory of value. The former states that rightness entails maximizing utility, the latter contends that those things which have "utility," or some intrinsic value, are certain types of states (such as pleasure or the satisfaction of preferences). Mill's account of utilitarianism is one of the most popular and readable. In the selection below, chapter two of *Utilitarianism,* Mill offers a summary statement of his doctrine: "the Greatest Happiness Principle, holds that actions are right in proportion as they tend to promote happiness, wrong as they tend to produce the reverse of happiness. By happiness is intended pleasure, and the absence of pain. . . ." Subsequent to this statement Mill discusses more fully how his account of value differs from that of his predecessor, Jeremy Bentham. Unlike Bentham, who did not distinguish *qualities* of pleasure, Mill believes that *pleasure* has a higher and a lower form, a distinction that is not without controversy. After developing his account of the higher and lower pleasures, Mill proceeds to consider some objections to the general doctrine of utilitarianism. In so doing, Mill points out how utilitarianism is not a doctrine of selfishness but one which, he believes, expresses the Golden Rule. Mill also replies to those who might contend that utilitarianism is too exacting or that it renders us "cold and unsympathising." Finally, Mill considers how the utilitarian may rely upon past actions and history to help determine what course of action might maximize happiness.

Nicomachean Ethics*

Aristotle

One of the most important philosophers of all time, Aristotle (384–322 B.C.), the son of a physician, was a polymath who wrote on a variety of subjects, including biology, psychology, metaphysics, rhetoric, logic, and physics. His Nicomachean Ethics *was the first systematic treatment of moral matters.*

BOOK I

1

Every art and every inquiry, and similarly every action and pursuit, is thought to aim at some good; and for this reason the good has rightly been declared to be that at which all things aim. But a certain difference is found among ends; some are activities, others are products apart from the activities that produce them. Where there are ends apart from the actions, it is the nature of the products to be better than the activities. Now, as there are many actions, arts, and sciences, their ends also are many; the end of the medical art is health, that of ship-building a vessel, that of strategy victory, that of economics wealth. But where such arts fall under a single capacity—as bridle-making and the other arts concerned with the equipment of horses fall under the art of riding, and this and every military action under strategy, in the same way other arts fall under yet others—in all of these the ends of the master arts are to be preferred to all the subordinate ends; for it is for the sake of the former that the latter are pursued. It makes no difference whether the activities themselves are the ends of the actions, or something else apart from the activities, as in the case of the sciences just mentioned.

2

If, then, there is some end of the things we do, which we desire for its own sake (everything else being desired for the sake of this), and if we do not choose everything for the sake of something else (for at that rate the process would go on to infinity, so that our desire would be empty and vain), clearly this must be the good and the chief good. Will not the knowledge of it, then, have a great influence on life? Shall we not, like archers who have a mark to aim at, be more likely to hit upon what is right? If so, we must try, in outline at least, to determine what it is, and of which of the sciences or capacities it is the object. It would seem to belong to the most authoritative art and that which is most truly the master art. And politics appears to be of this nature; for it is this that ordains which of the sciences should be studied in a state, and which each class of citizens should learn and up to what point they should learn them; and we see even the most highly esteemed of capacities to fall under this, e.g. strategy, economics, rhetoric; now, since politics uses the rest of the sciences, and since, again, it legislates as to what we are to do and what we are to abstain from, the end of this science must include those of the others, so that this end must be the good for man. For even if the end is the same for a single man and for a state, that of the state seems at all events something greater and more complete whether to attain or to preserve; though it is worth while to attain the end merely for one man, it is finer and more godlike to attain it for a nation or for city-states. These, then, are the ends at which our inquiry aims, since it is political science, in one sense of that term.

3

Our discussion will be adequate if it has as much clearness as the subject-matter admits of, for precision is not to be sought for alike in all discussions, any more than in all the products of the crafts. Now fine and just actions, which political science investigates, admit of much variety and fluctuation of opinion, so that they may be thought to exist only by convention, and not by nature. And goods also give rise to a similar fluctuation because they bring harm to many people; for before now men have been undone by reason of their wealth, and others by reason of their courage. We must be content, then, in speaking of such subjects and with such premises to indicate the truth roughly and in outline, and in speaking about things which are only for the most part true and with premises of the same kind to reach conclusions that are no better. In the same spirit,

*Translated by W. D. Ross.

therefore, should each type of statement be *received;* for it is the mark of an educated man to look for precision in each class of things just so far as the nature of the subject admits; it is evidently equally foolish to accept probable reasoning from a mathematician and to demand from a rhetorician scientific proofs.

Now each man judges well the things he knows, and of these he is a good judge. And so the man who has been educated in a subject is a good judge of that subject, and the man who has received an all-round education is a good judge in general. Hence a young man is not a proper hearer of lectures on political science; for he is inexperienced in the actions that occur in life, but its discussions start from these and are about these; and, further, since he tends to follow his passions, his study will be vain and unprofitable, because the end aimed at is not knowledge but action. And it makes no difference whether he is young in years or youthful in character; the defect does not depend on time, but on his living, and pursuing each successive object, as passion directs. For to such persons, as to the incontinent, knowledge brings no profit; but to those who desire and act in accordance with a rational principle knowledge about such matters will be of great benefit.

These remarks about the student, the sort of treatment to be expected, and the purpose of the inquiry, may be taken as our preface.

4

Let us resume our inquiry and state, in view of the fact that all knowledge and every pursuit aims at some good, what it is that we say political science aims at and what is the highest of all goods achievable by action. Verbally there is very general agreement; for both the general run of men and people of superior refinement say that it is happiness, and identify living well and doing well with being happy; but with regard to what happiness is they differ, and the many do not give the same account as the wise. For the former think it is some plain and obvious thing, like pleasure, wealth, or honour; they differ, however, from one another—and often even the same man identifies it with different things, with health when he is ill, with wealth when he is poor; but, conscious of their ignorance, they admire those who proclaim some great ideal that is above their comprehension. Now some thought that apart from these many goods there is another which is self-subsistent and causes the goodness of all these as well. To examine all the opinions that have been held were perhaps somewhat fruitless; enough to examine those that are most prevalent or that seem to be arguable.

Let us not fail to notice, however, that there is a difference between arguments from and those to the first principles. For Plato, too, was right in raising this question and asking, as he used to do, 'are we on the way from or to the first principles?' There is a difference, as there is in a race-course between the course from the judges to the turning-point and the way back. For, while we must begin with what is known, things are objects of knowledge in two senses—some to us, some without qualification. Presumably, then, *we* must begin with things known to *us*. Hence any one who is to listen intelligently to lectures about what is noble and just, and generally, about the subjects of political science must have been brought up in good habits. For the fact is the starting-point, and if this is sufficiently plain to him, he will not at the start need the reason as well; and the man who has been well brought up has or can easily get starting-points. And as for him who neither has nor can get them, let him hear the words of Hesiod:

> Far best is he who knows all things himself;
>
> Good, he that hearkens when men counsel right;
>
> But he who neither knows, nor lays to heart
>
> Another's wisdom, is a useless wight.

5

Let us, however, resume our discussion from the point at which we digressed. To judge from the lives that men lead, most men, and men of the most vulgar type, seem (not without some ground) to identify the good, or happiness, with pleasure; which is the reason why they love the life of enjoyment. For there are, we may say, three prominent types of life—that just mentioned, the political, and thirdly the contemplative life. Now the mass of mankind are evidently quite slavish in their tastes, preferring a life suitable to beasts, but they get some ground for their view from the fact that many of those in high places share the tastes of Sardanapallus. A consideration of the prominent types of life shows that people of superior refinement and of active disposition identify happiness with honour; for this is, roughly speaking, the end of the political life. But it seems too superficial to be what we are looking for, since it is thought to depend on those who bestow honour rather than on him who receives it, but the good we divine to be something proper to a man and not easily taken from him. Further, men seem to pursue honour in order that they may be assured of their goodness; at least it is by men of practical wisdom that they seek to be honoured, and among those who know them, and on the ground of their virtue; clearly, then, according to them, at any rate, virtue is better. And perhaps one might even suppose this to be, rather than honour, the end of the political life. But even this appears somewhat incomplete; for possession of virtue seems actually compatible with being asleep, or with lifelong inactivity, and, further, with the greatest sufferings and misfortunes; but a man who was living so no one would call happy, unless he were maintaining a thesis at all costs. But enough of this; for the subject has been sufficiently treated even in the current discussions. Third comes the contemplative life, which we shall consider later.

The life of money-making is one undertaken under compulsion, and wealth is evidently not the good we are seeking; for it is merely useful and for the sake of something else. And so one might rather take the aforenamed objects to be ends; for they are loved for themselves. But it is evident that not even these are ends; yet many arguments have been thrown away in support of them. Let us leave this subject, then.

6 . . .

7

Let us again return to the good we are seeking, and ask what it can be. It seems different in different actions and arts; it is different in medicine, in strategy, and in the other arts likewise. What then is the good of each? Surely that for whose sake everything else is done. In medicine this is health, in strategy victory, in architecture a house, in any other sphere something else, and in every action and pursuit the end; for it is for the sake of this that all men do whatever else they do. Therefore, if there is an end for all that we do, this will be the good achievable by action, and if there are more than one, these will be the goods achievable by action.

So the argument has by a different course reached the same point; but we must try to state this even more clearly. Since there are evidently more than one end, and we choose some of these (e.g. wealth, flutes, and in general instruments) for the sake of something else, clearly not all ends are final ends; but the chief good is evidently something final. Therefore, if there is only one final end, this will be what we are seeking, and if there are more than one, the most final of these will be what we are seeking. Now we call that which is in itself worthy of pursuit more final than that which is worthy of pursuit for the sake of something else, and that which is never

desirable for the sake of something else more final than the things that are desirable both in themselves and for the sake of that other thing, and therefore we call final without qualification that which is always desirable in itself and never for the sake of something else.

Now such a thing happiness, above all else, is held to be; for this we choose always for self and never for the sake of something else, but honour, pleasure, reason, and every virtue we choose indeed for themselves (for if nothing resulted from them we should still choose each of them), but we choose them also for the sake of happiness, judging that by means of them we shall be happy. Happiness, on the other hand, no one chooses for the sake of these, nor, in general, for anything other than itself.

From the point of view of self-sufficiency the same result seems to follow; for the final good is thought to be self-sufficient. Now by self-sufficient we do not mean that which is sufficient for a man by himself, for one who lives a solitary life, but also for parents, children, wife, and in general for his friends and fellow citizens, since man is born for citizenship. But some limit must be set to this; for if we extend our requirement to ancestors and descendants and friends' friends we are in for an infinite series. Let us examine this question, however, on another occasion; the self-sufficient we now define as that which when isolated makes life desirable and lacking in nothing; and such we think happiness to be; and further we think it most desirable of all things, without being counted as one good thing among others—if it were so counted it would clearly be made more desirable by the addition of even the least of goods; for that which is added becomes an excess of goods, and of goods the greater is always more desirable. Happiness, then, is something final and self-sufficient, and is the end of action.

Presumably, however, to say that happiness is the chief good seems a platitude, and a clearer account of what it is still desired. This might perhaps be given, if we could first ascertain the function of man. For just as for a flute-player, a sculptor, or an artist, and, in general, for all things that have a function or activity, the good and the 'well' is thought to reside in the function, so would it seem to be for man, if he has a function. Have the carpenter, then, and the tanner certain functions or activities, and has man none? Is he born without a function? Or as eye, hand, foot, and in general each of the parts evidently has a function, may one lay it down that man similarly has a function apart from all these? What then can this be? Life seems to be common even to plants, but we are seeking what is peculiar to man. Let us exclude, therefore, the life of nutrition and growth.

Next there would be a life of perception, but *it* also seems to be common even to the horse, the ox, and every animal. There remains, then, an active life of the element that has a rational principle; of this, one part has such a principle in the sense of being obedient to one, the other in the sense of possessing one and exercising thought. And, as 'life of the rational element' also has two meanings, we must state that life in the sense of activity is what we mean; for this seems to be the more proper sense of the term. Now if the function of man is an activity of soul which follows or implies a rational principle, and if we say 'so-and-so' and 'a good so-and-so' have a function which is the same in kind, e.g. a lyre, and a good lyre-player, and so without qualification in all cases, eminence in respect of goodness being added to the name of the function (for the function of a lyre-player is to play the lyre, and that of a good lyre-player is to do so well): if this is the case, [and we state the function of man to be a certain kind of life, and this to be an activity or actions of the soul implying a rational principle, and the function of a good man to be the good and noble performance of these, and if any action is well performed when it is performed in accordance with the appropriate excellence: if this is the case,] human good turns out to be activity of soul in accordance with virtue, and if there are more than one virtue, in accordance with the best and most complete.

But we must add 'in a complete life.' For one swallow does not make a summer, nor does one day; and so too one day, or a short time, does not make a man blessed and happy.

Let this serve as an outline of the good; for we must presumably first sketch it roughly, and then later fill in the details. But it would seem that any one is capable of carrying on and articulating what has once been well outlined, and that time is a good discoverer or partner in such a work; to which facts the advances of the arts are due; for any one can add what is lacking. And we must also remember what has been said before, and not look for precision in all things alike, but in each class of things such precision as accords with the subject-matter, and so much as is appropriate to the inquiry. For a carpenter and a geometer investigate the right angle in different ways; the former does so in so far as the right angle is useful for his work, while the latter inquires what it is or what sort of thing it is; for he is a spectator of the truth. We must act in the same way, then, in all other matters as well, that our main task may not be subordinated to minor questions. Nor must we demand the cause in all matters alike; it is enough in some cases that

the *fact* be well established, as in the case of the first principles; the fact is the primary thing or first principle. Now of first principles we see some by induction, some by perception, some by a certain habituation, and others too in other ways. But each set of principles we must try to investigate in the natural way, and we must take pains to state them definitely, since they have a great influence on what follows. For the beginning is thought to be more than half of the whole, and many of the questions we ask are cleared up by it.

8

We must consider it, however, in the light not only of our conclusion and our premises, but also of what is commonly said about it; for with a true view all the data harmonize, but with a false one the facts soon clash. Now goods have been divided into three classes, and some are described as external, others as relating to soul or to body; we call those that relate to soul most properly and truly goods, and psychical actions and activities we class as relating to soul. Therefore our account must be sound, at least according to this view, which is an old one and agreed on by philosophers. It is correct also in that we identify the end with certain actions and activities; for thus it falls among goods of the soul and not among external goods. Another belief which harmonizes with our account is that the happy man lives well and does well; for we have practically defined happiness as a sort of good life and good action. The characteristics that are looked for in happiness seem also, all of them, to belong to what we have defined happiness as being. For some identify happiness with virtue, some with practical wisdom, others with a kind of philosophic wisdom, others with these, or one of these, accompanied by pleasure or not without pleasure; while others include also external prosperity. Now some of these views have been held by many men and men of old, others by a few eminent persons; and it is not probable that either of these should be entirely mistaken, but rather that they should be right in at least some one respect or even in most respects.

With those who identify happiness with virtue or some one virtue our account is in harmony; for to virtue belongs virtuous activity. But it makes, perhaps, no small difference whether we place the chief good in possession or in use, in state of mind or in activity. For the state of mind may exist without producing any good result, as in a man who is asleep or in some other way quite inactive, but the activity cannot; for one who has the activity will of necessity be acting, and acting well. And as in the

Olympic Games it is not the most beautiful and the strongest that are crowned but those who compete (for it is some of these that are victorious), so those who act win, and rightly win, the noble and good things in life.

Their life is also in itself pleasant. For pleasure is a state of *soul*, and to each man that which he is said to be a lover of is pleasant; e.g. not only is a horse pleasant to the lover of horses, and a spectacle to the lover of sights, but also in the same way just acts are pleasant to the lover of justice and in general virtuous acts to the lover of virtue. Now for most men their pleasures are in conflict with one another because these are not by nature pleasant, but the lovers of what is noble find pleasant the things that are by nature pleasant; and virtuous actions are such, so that these are pleasant for such men as well as in their own nature. Their life, therefore, has no further need of pleasure as a sort of adventitious charm, but has its pleasure in itself. For, besides what we have said, the man who does not rejoice in noble actions is not even good; since no one would call a man just who did not enjoy acting justly, nor any man liberal who did not enjoy liberal actions; and similarly in all other cases. If this is so, virtuous actions must be in themselves pleasant. But they are also *good* and *noble*, and have each of these attributes in the highest degree, since the good man judges well about these attributes; his judgement is such as we have described. Happiness then is the best, noblest, and most pleasant thing in the world, and these attributes are not severed as in the inscription at Delos—

Most noble is that which is justest, and best is health;

But pleasantest is it to win what we love.

For all these properties belong to the best activities; and these, or one—the best—of these, we identify with happiness.

Yet evidently, as we said, it needs the external goods as well; for it is impossible, or not easy, to do noble acts without the proper equipment. In many actions we use friends and riches and political power as instruments; and there are some things the lack of which takes the lustre from happiness, as good birth, goodly children, beauty; for the man who is very ugly in appearance or ill-born or solitary and childless is not very likely to be happy, and perhaps a man would be still less likely if he had thoroughly bad children or friends or had lost good children or friends by death. As we said, then, happiness seems to need this sort of prosperity in addition; for which reason some identify happiness with good fortune, though others identify it with virtue.

9

For this reason also the question is asked, whether happiness is to be acquired by learning or by habituation or some other sort of training, or comes in virtue of some divine providence or again by chance. Now if there is *any* gift of the gods to men, it is reasonable that happiness should be god-given, and most surely god-given of all human things inasmuch as it is the best. But this question would perhaps be more appropriate to another inquiry; happiness seems, however, even if it is not god-sent but comes as a result of virtue and some process of learning or training, to be among the most godlike things; for that which is the prize and end of virtue seems to be the best thing in the world, and something godlike and blessed.

It will also on this view be very generally shared; for all who are not maimed as regards their potentiality for virtue may win it by a certain kind of study and care. But if it is better to be happy thus than by chance, it is reasonable that the facts should be so, since everything that depends on the action of nature is by nature as good as it can be, and similarly everything that depends on art or any rational cause, and especially if it depends on the best of all causes. To entrust to chance what is greatest and most noble would be a very defective arrangement.

The answer to the question we are asking is plain also from the definition of happiness; for it has been said to be a virtuous activity of soul, of a certain kind. Of the remaining goods, some must necessarily pre-exist as conditions of happiness, and others are naturally co-operative and useful as instruments. And this will be found to agree with what we said at the outset; for we stated the end of political science to be the best end, and political science spends most of its pains on making the citizens to be of a certain character, viz. good and capable of noble acts.

It is natural, then, that we call neither ox nor horse nor any other of the animals happy; for none of them is capable of sharing in such activity. For this reason also a boy is not happy; for he is not yet capable of such acts, owing to his age; and boys who are called happy are being congratulated by reason of the hopes we have for them. For there is required, as we said, not only complete virtue but also a complete life, since many changes occur in life, and all manner of chances, and the most prosperous may fall into great misfortunes in old age, as is told of Priam in the Trojan Cycle; and one who has experienced such chances and has ended wretchedly no one calls happy.

10 . . . **11** . . . **12** . . .

13

Since happiness is an activity of soul in accordance with perfect virtue, we must consider the nature of virtue; for perhaps we shall thus see better the nature of happiness. The true student of politics, too, is thought to have studied virtue above all things; for he wishes to make his fellow citizens good and obedient to the laws. As an example of this we have the lawgivers of the Cretans and the Spartans, and any others of the kind that there may have been. And if this inquiry belongs to political science, clearly the pursuit of it will be in accordance with our original plan. But clearly the virtue we must study is human virtue; for the good we were seeking was human good and the happiness human happiness. By human virtue we mean not that of the body but that of the soul; and happiness also we call an activity of soul. But if this is so, clearly the student of politics must know somehow the facts about soul, as the man who is to heal the eyes or the body as a whole must know about the eyes or the body; and all the more since politics is more prized and better than medicine; but even among doctors the best educated spend much labour on acquiring knowledge of the body. The student of politics, then, must study the soul, and must study it with these objects in view, and do so just to the extent which is sufficient for the questions we are discussing; for further precision is perhaps something more laborious than our purposes require.

Some things are said about it, adequately enough, even in the discussions outside our school, and we must use these; e.g. that one element in the soul is irrational and one has a rational principle. Whether these are separated as the parts of the body or of anything divisible are, or are distinct by definition but by nature inseparable, like convex and concave in the circumference of a circle, does not affect the present question.

Of the irrational element one division seems to be widely distributed, and vegetative in its nature, I mean that which causes nutrition and growth; for it is this kind of power of the soul that one must assign to all nurslings and to embryos, and this same power to fullgrown creatures; this is more reasonable than to assign some different power to them. Now the excellence of this seems to be common to all species and not specifically human; for this part or faculty seems to function most in sleep, while goodness and badness are least manifest in sleep (whence comes the saying that the happy are not better off than the wretched for half their lives; and this happens naturally enough, since sleep is an inactivity of the soul in that respect in which it is called good or bad), unless perhaps to a small extent some of the movements actually penetrate to the soul, and in this respect the dreams of good men are better than those of ordinary people. Enough of this subject, however; let us leave the nutritive faculty alone, since it has by its nature no share in human excellence.

There seems to be also another irrational element in the soul—one which in a sense, however, shares in a rational principle. For we praise the rational principle of the continent man and of the incontinent, and the part of their soul that has such a principle, since it urges them aright and towards the best objects; but there is found in them also another element naturally opposed to the rational principle, which fights against and resists that principle. For exactly as paralysed limbs when we intend to move them to the right turn on the contrary to the left, so is it with the soul; the impulses of incontinent people move in contrary directions. But while in the body we see that which moves astray, in the soul we do not. No doubt, however, we must none the less suppose that in the soul too there is something contrary to the rational principle, resisting and opposing it. In what sense it is distinct from the other elements does not concern us. Now even this seems to have a share in a rational principle, as we said; at any rate in the continent man it obeys the rational principle and presumably in the temperate and brave man it is still more obedient; for in him it speaks, on all matters, with the same voice as the rational principle.

Therefore the irrational element also appears to be two-fold. For the vegetative element in no way shares in a rational principle, but the appetitive and in general the desiring element in a sense shares in it, in so far as it listens to and obeys it; this is the sense in which we speak of 'taking account' of one's father or one's friends, not that in which we speak of 'accounting for a mathematical property.' That the irrational element is in some sense persuaded by a rational principle is indicated also by the giving of advice and by all reproof and exhortation. And if this element also must be said to have a rational principle, that which has a rational principle (as well as that which has not) will be twofold, one subdivision having it in the strict sense and in itself, and the other having a tendency to obey as one does one's father.

Virtue too is distinguished into kinds in accordance with this difference; for we say that some of the virtues are intellectual and others moral, philosophic wisdom and understanding and practical wisdom being intellectual, liberality and temperance moral. For in speaking about a man's character we do not say that he is wise or has understanding but that he is good-tempered or temperate; yet we praise the wise man also with respect to his state of mind; and of states of mind we call those which merit praise virtues.

BOOK II

1

Virtue, then, being of two kinds, intellectual and moral, intellectual virtue in the main owes both its birth and its growth to teaching (for which reason it requires experience and time), while moral virtue comes about as a result of habit, whence also its name *(ethike)* is one that is formed by a slight variation from the word *ethos* (habit). From this it is also plain that none of the moral virtues arises in us by nature; for nothing that exists by nature can form a habit contrary to its nature. For instance the stone which by nature moves downwards cannot be habituated to move upwards, not even if one tries to train it by throwing it up ten thousand times; nor can fire be habituated to move downwards, nor can anything else that by nature behaves in one way be trained to behave in another. Neither by nature, then, nor contrary to nature do the virtues arise in us; rather we are adapted by nature to receive them, and are made perfect by habit.

Again, of all the things that come to us by nature we first acquire the potentiality and later exhibit the activity (this is plain in the case of the senses; for it was not by often seeing or often hearing that we got these senses, but on the contrary we had them before we used them, and did not come to have them by using them); but the virtues we get by first exercising them, as also happens in the case of the arts as well. For the things we have to learn before we can do them, we learn by doing them, e.g. men become builders by building and lyre-players by playing the lyre; so too we become just by doing just acts, temperate by doing temperate acts, brave by doing brave acts.

This is confirmed by what happens in states; for legislators make the citizens good by forming habits in them, and this is the wish of every legislator, and those who do not effect it miss their mark, and it is in this that a good constitution differs from a bad one.

Again, it is from the same causes and by the same means that every virtue is both produced and destroyed, and similarly every art; for it is from playing the lyre that both good and bad lyre-players are produced. And the corresponding statement is true of builders and of all the rest; men will be good or bad builders as a result of building well or badly. For if this were not so, there would have been no need of a teacher, but all men would have been born good or bad at their craft. This, then, is the case with the virtues also; by doing the acts that we do in our transactions with other men we become just or unjust, and by doing the acts that we do in the presence of danger, and being habituated to feel fear or confidence, we become brave or cowardly. The same is true

of appetites and feelings of anger; some men become temperate and good-tempered, others self-indulgent and irascible, by behaving in one way or the other in the appropriate circumstances. Thus, in one word, states of character arise out of like activities. This is why the activities we exhibit must be of a certain kind; it is because the states of character correspond to the differences between these. It makes no small difference, then, whether we form habits of one kind or of another from our very youth; it makes a very great difference, or rather *all* the difference.

2

Since, then, the present inquiry does not aim at theoretical knowledge like the others (for we are inquiring not in order to know what virtue is, but in order to become good, since otherwise our inquiry would have been of no use), we must examine the nature of actions, namely how we ought to do them; for these determine also the nature of the states of character that are produced, as we have said. Now, that we must act according to the right rule is a common principle and must be assumed—it will be discussed later, i.e. both what the right rule is, and how it is related to the other virtues. But this must be agreed upon beforehand, that the whole account of matters of conduct must be given in outline and not precisely, as we said at the very beginning that the accounts we demand must be in accordance with the subject-matter; matters concerned with conduct and questions of what is good for us have no fixity, any more than matters of health. The general account being of this nature, the account of particular cases is yet more lacking in exactness; for they do not fall under any art or precept but the agents themselves must in each case consider what is appropriate to the occasion, as happens also in the art of medicine or of navigation.

But though our present account is of this nature we must give what help we can. First, then, let us consider this, that it is the nature of such things to be destroyed by defect and excess, as we see in the case of strength and of health (for to gain light on things imperceptible we must use the evidence of sensible things); both excessive and defective exercise destroys the strength, and similarly drink or food which is above or below a certain amount destroys the health, while that which is proportionate both produces and increases and preserves it. So too is it, then, in the case of temperance and courage and the other virtues. For the man who flies from and fears everything and does not stand his ground against anything becomes a coward, and the man who fears nothing at all but goes to meet every danger becomes rash; and similarly the man who indulges in every pleasure and abstains from none becomes self-indulgent, while the man who shuns every pleasure, as boors do, becomes in a way insensible; temperance and courage, then, are destroyed by excess and defect, and preserved by the mean.

But not only are the sources and causes of their origination and growth the same as those of their destruction, but also the sphere of their actualization will be the same; for this is also true of the things which are more evident to sense, e.g. of strength; it is produced by taking much food and undergoing much exertion, and it is the strong man that will be most able to do these things. So too is it with the virtues; by abstaining from pleasures we become temperate, and it is when we have become so that we are most able to abstain from them; and similarly too in the case of courage; for by being habituated to despise things that are terrible and to stand our ground against them we become brave, and it is when we have become so that we shall be most able to stand our ground against them.

3

We must take as a sign of states of character the pleasure or pain that ensues on acts; for the man who abstains from bodily pleasures and delights in this very fact is temperate, while the man who is annoyed at it is self-indulgent, and he who stands his ground against things that are terrible and delights in this or at least is not pained is brave, while the man who is pained is a coward. For moral excellence is concerned with pleasures and pains; it is on account of the pleasure that we do bad things, and on account of the pain that we abstain from noble ones. Hence we ought to have been brought up in a particular way from our very youth, as Plato says, so as both to delight in and to be pained by the things that we ought; for this is the right education.

Again, if the virtues are concerned with actions and passions, and every passion and every action is accompanied by pleasure and pain, for this reason also virtue will be concerned with pleasures and pains. This is indicated also by the fact that punishment is inflicted by these means; for it is a kind of cure, and it is the nature of cures to be effected by contraries.

Again, as we said but lately, every state of soul has a nature relative to and concerned with the kind of things by which it tends to be made worse or better; but it is by reason of pleasures and pains that men become bad, by pursuing and avoiding these—either the pleas-

ures and pains they ought not or when they ought not or as they ought not, or by going wrong in one of the other similar ways that may be distinguished. Hence men even define the virtues as certain states of impassivity and rest; not well, however, because they speak absolutely, and do not say 'as one ought' and 'as one ought not' and 'when one ought or ought not,' and the other things that may be added. We assume, then, that this kind of excellence tends to do what is best with regard to pleasures and pains, and vice does the contrary.

The following facts also may show us that virtue and vice are concerned with these same things. There being three objects of choice and three of avoidance, the noble, the advantageous, the pleasant, and their contraries, the base, the injurious, the painful, about all of these the good man tends to go right and the bad man to go wrong, and especially about pleasure; for this is common to the animals, and also it accompanies all objects of choice; for even the noble and the advantageous appear pleasant.

Again, it has grown up with us all from our infancy; this is why it is difficult to rub off this passion, engrained as it is in our life. And we measure even our actions, some of us more and others less, by the rule of pleasure and pain. For this reason, then, our whole inquiry must be about these; for to feel delight and pain rightly or wrongly has no small effect on our actions.

Again, it is harder to fight with pleasure than with anger, to use Heraclitus' phrase, but both art and virtue are always concerned with what is harder; for even the good is better when it is harder. Therefore for this reason also the whole concern both of virtue and of political science is with pleasures and pains; for the man who uses these well will be good, he who uses them badly bad.

That virtue, then, is concerned with pleasures and pains, and that by the acts from which it arises it is both increased and, if they are done differently, destroyed, and that the acts from which it arose are those in which it actualizes itself—let this be taken as said.

4

The question might be asked, what we mean by saying that we must become just by doing just acts, and temperate by doing temperate acts; for if men do just and temperate acts, they are already just and temperate, exactly as, if they do what is in accordance with the laws of grammar and of music, they are grammarians and musicians.

Or is this not true even of the arts? It is possible to do something that is in accordance with the laws of grammar, either by chance or at the suggestion of another. A man will be a grammarian, then, only when he has both done something grammatical and done it grammatically; and this means doing it in accordance with the grammatical knowledge in himself.

Again, the case of the arts and that of the virtues are not similar; for the products of the arts have their goodness in themselves, so that it is enough that they should have a certain character, but if the acts that are in accordance with the virtues have themselves a certain character it does not follow that they are done justly or temperately. The agent also must be in a certain condition when he does them; in the first place he must have knowledge, secondly he must choose the acts, and choose them for their own sakes, and thirdly his action must proceed from a firm and unchangeable character. These are not reckoned in as conditions of the possession of the arts, except the bare knowledge; but as a condition of the possession of the virtues knowledge has little or no weight, while the other conditions count not for a little but for everything, i.e. the very conditions which result from often doing just and temperate acts.

Actions, then, are called just and temperate when they are such as the just or the temperate man would do; but it is not the man who does these that is just and temperate, but the man who also does them *as* just and temperate men do them. It is well said, then, that it is by doing just acts that the just man is produced, and by doing temperate acts the temperate man; without doing these no one would have even a prospect of becoming good.

But most people do not do these, but take refuge in theory and think they are being philosophers and will become good in this way, behaving somewhat like patients who listen attentively to their doctors, but do none of the things they are ordered to do. As the latter will not be made well in body by such a course of treatment, the former will not be made well in soul by such a course of philosophy.

5

Next we must consider what virtue is. Since things that are found in the soul are of three kinds—passions, faculties, states of character, virtue must be one of these. By passions I mean appetite, anger, fear, confidence, envy, joy, friendly feeling, hatred, longing, emulation, pity, and in general the feelings that are accompanied by pleasure or pain; by faculties the things in virtue of which we are said to be capable of feeling these, e.g. of becoming angry or being pained or feeling pity; by states of character the things in virtue of which we stand well or badly with reference to the passions, e.g. with reference to anger we stand badly if we feel it violently or too weakly, and well if we feel it moderately; and similarly with reference to the other passions.

Now neither the virtues nor the vices are *passions,* because we are not called good or bad on the ground of our passions, but are so called on the ground of our virtues and our vices, and because we are neither praised nor blamed for our passions (for the man who feels fear or anger is not praised, nor is the man who simply feels anger blamed, but the man who feels it in a certain way), but for our virtues and our vices we *are* praised or blamed.

Again, we feel anger and fear without choice, but the virtues are modes of choice or involve choice. Further, in respect of the passions we are said to be moved, but in respect of the virtues and the vices we are said not to be moved but to be disposed in a particular way.

For these reasons also they are not *faculties;* for we are neither called good nor bad, nor praised nor blamed, for the simple capacity of feeling the passions; again, we have the faculties by nature, but we are not made good or bad by nature; we have spoken of this before.

If, then, the virtues are neither passions nor faculties, all that remains is that they should be *states of character.*

Thus we have stated what virtue is in respect of its genus.

6

We must, however, not only describe virtue as a state of character, but also say what sort of state it is. We may remark, then, that every virtue or excellence both brings into good condition the thing of which it is the excellence and makes the work of that thing be done well; e.g. the excellence of the eye makes both the eye and its work good; for it is by the excellence of the eye that we see well. Similarly the excellence of the horse makes a horse both good in itself and good at running and at carrying its rider and at awaiting the attack of the enemy. Therefore, if this is true in every case, the virtue of man also will be the state of character which makes a man good and which makes him do his own work well.

How this is to happen we have stated already, but it will be made plain also by the following consideration of the specific nature of virtue. In everything that is continuous and divisible it is possible to take more, less, or an equal amount, and that either in terms of the thing itself or relatively to us; and the equal is an intermediate between excess and defect. By the intermediate in the object I mean that which is equidistant from each of the extremes, which is one and the same for all men; by the intermediate relatively to us that which is neither too much nor too little—and this is not one, nor the same for all. For instance, if ten is many and two is few, six is the intermediate, taken in terms of the object; for it exceeds and is exceeded by an equal amount; this is intermediate according to arithmetical proportion. But the intermediate relatively to us is not to be taken so; if ten pounds are too much for a particular person to eat and two too little, it does not follow that the trainer will order six pounds; for this also is perhaps too much for the person who is to take it, or too little—too little for Milo, too much for the beginner in athletic exercises. The same is true of running and wrestling. Thus a master of any art avoids excess and defect, but seeks the intermediate and chooses this—the intermediate not in the object but relatively to us.

If it is thus, then, that every art does its work well—by looking to the intermediate and judging its works by this standard (so that we often say of good works of art that it is not possible either to take away or to add anything, implying that excess and defect destroy the goodness of works of art, while the mean preserves it; and good artists, as we say, look to this in their work), and if, further, virtue is more exact and better than any art, as nature also is, then virtue must have the quality of aiming at the intermediate. I mean moral virtue; for it is this that is concerned with passions and actions, and in these there is excess, defect, and the intermediate. For instance, both fear and confidence and appetite and anger and pity and in general pleasure and pain may be felt both too much and too little, and in both cases not well; but to feel them at the right times, with reference to the right objects, towards the right people, with the right motive, and in the right way, is what is both intermediate and best, and this is characteristic of virtue. Similarly with regard to actions also there is excess, defect, and the intermediate. Now virtue is concerned with passions and actions, in which excess is a form of failure, and so is defect, while the intermediate is praised and is a form of success; and being praised and being successful are both characteristics of virtue. Therefore virtue is a kind of mean, since, as we have seen, it aims at what is intermediate.

Again, it is possible to fail in many ways (for evil belongs to the class of the unlimited, as the Pythagoreans conjectured, and good to that of the limited), while to succeed is possible only in one way (for which reason also one is easy and the other difficult—to miss the mark easy, to hit it difficult); for these reasons also, then, excess and defect are characteristic of vice, and the mean of virtue;

For men are good in but one way, but bad in many.

Virtue, then, is a state of character concerned with choice, lying in a mean, i.e. the mean relative to us, this being determined by a rational principle, and by that principle by which the man of practical wisdom would determine it. Now it is a mean between two vices, that which depends on excess and that which depends on defect; and again it is a mean because the vices respectively fall short of or exceed what is right in both passions and actions, while virtue both finds and chooses that which is intermediate. Hence in respect of its substance and the definition which states its essence virtue is a mean, with regard to what is best and right an extreme.

But not every action nor every passion admits of a mean; for some have names that already imply badness, e.g. spite, shamelessness, envy, and in the case of actions adultery, theft, murder; for all of these and suchlike things imply by their names that they are themselves bad, and not the excesses or deficiencies of them. It is not possible, then, ever to be right with regard to them; one must always be wrong. Nor does goodness or badness with regard to such things depend on committing adultery with the right woman, at the right time, and in the right way, but simply to do any of them is to go wrong. It would be equally absurd, then, to expect that in unjust, cowardly, and voluptuous action there should be a mean, an excess, and a deficiency; for at that rate there would be a mean of excess and of deficiency, an excess of excess, and a deficiency of deficiency. But as there is no excess and deficiency of temperance and courage because what is intermediate is in a sense an extreme, so too of the actions we have mentioned there is no mean nor any excess and deficiency, but however they are done they are wrong; for in general there is neither a mean of excess and deficiency, nor excess and deficiency of a mean.

7

We must, however, not only make this general statement, but also apply it to the individual facts. For among statements about conduct those which are general apply more widely, but those which are particular are more genuine, since conduct has to do with individual cases, and our statements must harmonize with the facts in these cases. We may take these cases from our table. With regard to feelings of fear and confidence courage is the mean; of the people who exceed, he who exceeds in fearlessness has no name (many of the states have no name), while the man who exceeds in confidence is rash, and he who exceeds in fear and falls short in confidence is a coward. With regard to pleasures and pains—not all of them, and not so much with regard to the pains—the mean is temperance, the excess self-indulgence. Persons deficient with regard to the pleasures are not often found; hence such persons also have received no name. But let us call them 'insensible.'

With regard to giving and taking of money the mean is liberality, the excess and the defect prodigality and meanness. In these actions people exceed and fall short in contrary ways; the prodigal exceeds in spending and falls short in taking, while the mean man exceeds in taking and falls short in spending. (At present we are giving a mere outline or summary, and are satisfied with this; later these states will be more exactly determined.) With regard to money there are also other dispositions—a mean, magnificence (for the magnificent man differs from the liberal man; the former deals with large sums, the latter with small ones), an excess, tastelessness and vulgarity, and a deficiency, niggardliness; these differ from the states opposed to liberality, and the mode of their difference will be stated later.

With regard to honour and dishonour the mean is proper pride, the excess is known as a sort of 'empty vanity,' and the deficiency is undue humility; and as we said liberality was related to magnificence, differing from it by dealing with small sums, so there is a state similarly related to proper pride, being concerned with small honours while that is concerned with great. For it is possible to desire honour as one ought, and more than one ought, and less, and the man who exceeds in his desires is called ambitious, the man who falls short unambitious, while the intermediate person has no name. The dispositions also are nameless, except that that of the ambitious man is called ambition. Hence the people who are at the extremes lay claim to the middle place; and we ourselves sometimes call the intermediate person ambitious and sometimes unambitious, and sometimes praise the ambitious man and sometimes the unambitious. The reason of our doing this will be stated in what follows; but now let us speak of the remaining states according to the method which has been indicated.

With regard to anger also there is an excess, a deficiency, and a mean. Although they can scarcely be said to have names, yet since we call the intermediate person good-tempered let us call the mean good temper; of the persons at the extremes let the one who exceeds be called irascible, and his vice irascibility, and the man who falls short an inirascible sort of person, and the deficiency inirascibility.

There are also three other means, which have a certain likeness to one another, but differ from one another: for they are all concerned with intercourse in words and actions, but differ in that one is concerned with truth in this sphere, the other two with pleasantness; and of this one kind is exhibited in giving amusement, the other in all the circumstances of life. We must therefore speak of these too, that we may the better see that in all things the mean is praiseworthy, and the extremes neither praiseworthy nor right, but worthy of blame. Now most of these states also have no names, but we must try, as in the other cases, to invent names ourselves so that we may be clear and easy to follow. With regard to truth, then, the intermediate is a truthful sort of person and the mean may be called truthfulness, while the pretence which exaggerates is boastfulness and the person characterized by it a boaster, and that which understates is mock modesty and the person characterized by it mock-modest. With regard to pleasantness in the giving of amusement the intermediate person is ready-witted and the disposition ready wit, the excess is buffoonery and the person characterized by it a buffoon, while the man who falls short is a sort of boor and his state is boorishness. With regard to the remaining kind of pleasantness, that which is exhibited in life in general, the man who is pleasant in the right way is friendly and the mean is friendliness, while the man who exceeds is an obsequious person if he has no end in view, a flatterer if he is aiming at his own advantage, and the man who falls short and is unpleasant in all circumstances is a quarrelsome and surly sort of person.

There are also means in the passions and concerned with the passions; since shame is not a virtue, and yet praise is extended to the modest man. For even in these matters one man is said to be intermediate, and another to exceed, as for instance the bashful man who is ashamed of everything; while he who falls short or is not ashamed of anything at all is shameless, and the intermediate person is modest. Righteous indignation is a mean between envy and spite, and these states are concerned with the pain and pleasure that are felt at the fortunes of our neighbours; the man who is characterized by righteous indignation is pained at undeserved good fortune, the envious man, going beyond him, is pained at all good fortune, and the spiteful man falls so far short of being pained that he even rejoices. But these states there will be an opportunity of describing elsewhere; with regard to justice, since it has not one simple meaning, we shall, after describing the other states, distinguish its two kinds and say how each of them is a mean; and similarly we shall treat also of the rational virtues.

8

There are three kinds of disposition, then, two of them vices, involving excess and deficiency respectively, and one a virtue, viz. the mean, and all are in a sense opposed to all; for the extreme states are contrary both to the intermediate state and to each other, and the intermediate to the extremes; as the equal is greater relatively to the less, less relatively to the greater, so the middle states are excessive relatively to the deficiencies, deficient relatively to the excesses, both in passions and in actions. For the brave man appears rash relatively to the coward, and cowardly relatively to the rash man; and similarly the temperate man appears self-indulgent relatively to the insensible man, insensible relatively to the self-indulgent, and the liberal man prodigal relatively to the mean man, mean relatively to the prodigal. Hence also the people at the extremes push the intermediate man each over to the other, and the brave man is called rash by the coward, cowardly by the rash man, and correspondingly in the other cases.

These states being thus opposed to one another, the greatest contrariety is that of the extremes to each other, rather than to the intermediate; for these are further from each other than from the intermediate, as the great is further from the small and the small from the great than both are from the equal. Again, to the intermediate some extremes show a certain likeness, as that of rashness to courage and that of prodigality to liberality; but the extremes show the greatest unlikeness to each other; now contraries are defined as the things that are furthest from each other, so that things that are further apart are more contrary.

To the mean in some cases the deficiency, in some the excess is more opposed; e.g., it is not rashness, which is an excess, but cowardice, which is a deficiency, that is more opposed to courage, and not insensibility, which is a deficiency, but self-indulgence, which is an excess, that is more opposed to temperance. This happens from two reasons, one being drawn from the thing itself; for because one extreme is nearer and liker to the intermediate, we oppose not this but rather its contrary to the intermediate. E.g. since rashness is thought liker and nearer to courage, and cowardice more unlike, we oppose rather the latter to courage; for things that are further from the intermediate are thought more contrary to it. This, then, is one cause, drawn from the thing itself; another is drawn from ourselves; for the things to which we ourselves more naturally tend seem more contrary to the intermediate. For instance, we ourselves tend more naturally to pleasures, and hence are more

easily carried away towards self-indulgence than towards propriety. We describe as contrary to the mean, then, rather the directions in which we more often go to great lengths; and therefore self-indulgence, which is an excess, is the more contrary to temperance.

9

That moral virtue is a mean, then, and in what sense it is so, and that it is a mean between two vices, the one involving excess, the other deficiency, and that it is such because its character is to aim at what is intermediate in passions and in actions, has been sufficiently stated. Hence also it is no easy task to be good. For in everything it is no easy task to find the middle, e.g. to find the middle of a circle is not for every one but for him who knows; so, too, any one can get angry—that is easy—or give or spend money; but to do this to the right person, to the right extent, at the right time, with the right motive, and in the right way, *that* is not for every one, nor is it easy; wherefore goodness is both rare and laudable and noble.

Hence he who aims at the intermediate must first depart from what is the more contrary to it, as Calypso advises—

Hold the ship out beyond that surf and spray.

For of the extremes one is more erroneous, one less so; therefore, since to hit the mean is hard in the extreme, we must as a second best, as people say, take the least of the evils; and this will be done best in the way we describe.

But we must consider the things towards which we ourselves also are easily carried away; for some of us tend to one thing, some to another; and this will be recognizable from the pleasure and the pain we feel. We must drag ourselves away to the contrary extreme; for we shall get into the intermediate state by drawing well away from error, as people do in straightening sticks that are bent.

Now in everything the pleasant or pleasure is most to be guarded against; for we do not judge it impartially. We ought, then, to feel towards pleasure as the elders of the people felt towards Helen, and in all circumstances repeat their saying; for if we dismiss pleasure thus we are less likely to go astray. It is by doing this, then, (to sum the matter up) that we shall best be able to hit the mean.

But this is no doubt difficult, and especially in individual cases; for it is not easy to determine both how and with whom and on what provocation and how long one should be angry; for we too sometimes praise those who fall short and call them good-tempered, but sometimes we praise those who get angry and call them manly. The man, however, who deviates little from goodness is not blamed, whether he do so in the direction of the more or of the less, but only the man who deviates more widely; for *he* does not fail to be noticed. But up to what point and to what extent a man must deviate before he becomes blameworthy it is not easy to determine by reasoning, any more than anything else that is perceived by the senses; such things depend on particular facts, and the decision rests with perception. So much, then, is plain, that the intermediate state is in all things to be praised, but that we must incline sometimes towards the excess, sometimes towards the deficiency; for so shall we most easily hit the mean and what is right.

BOOK VI

1

Since we have previously said that one ought to choose that which is intermediate, not the excess nor the defect, and that the intermediate is determined by the dictates of the right rule, let us discuss the nature of these dictates. In all the states of character we have mentioned, as in all other matters, there is a mark to which the man who has the rule looks, and heightens or relaxes his activity accordingly, and there is a standard which determines the mean states which we say are intermediate between excess and defect, being in accordance with the right rule. But such a statement, though true, is by no means clear; for not only here but in all other pursuits which are objects of knowledge it is indeed true to say that we must not exert ourselves nor relax our efforts too much nor too little, but to an intermediate extent and as the right rule dictates; but if a man had only this knowledge he would be none the wiser, e.g. we should not know what sort of medicines to apply to our body if some one were to say 'all those which the medical art prescribes, and which agree with the practice of one who possesses the art.' Hence it is necessary with regard to the states of the soul also not only that this true statement should be made, but also that it should be determined what is the right rule and what is the standard that fixes it.

We divided the virtues of the soul and said that some are virtues of character and others of intellect. Now we have discussed in detail the moral virtues; with regard to the others let us express our view as follows, beginning with some remarks about the soul. We said before that there are two parts of the soul—that which

grasps a rule or rational principle, and the irrational; let us now draw a similar distinction within the part which grasps a rational principle. And let it be assumed that there are two parts which grasp a rational principle—one by which we contemplate the kind of things whose originative causes are invariable, and one by which we contemplate variable things; for where objects differ in kind the part of the soul answering to each of the two is different in kind, since it is in virtue of a certain likeness and kinship with their objects that they have the knowledge they have. Let one of these parts be called the scientific and the other the calculative; for to deliberate and to calculate are the same thing, but no one deliberates about the invariable. Therefore the calculative is one part of the faculty which grasps a rational principle. We must, then, learn what is the best state of each of these two parts; for this is the virtue of each.

2

The virtue of a thing is relative to its proper work. Now there are three things in the soul which control action and truth—sensation, reason, desire.

Of these sensation originates no action; this is plain from the fact that the lower animals have sensation but no share in action.

What affirmation and negation are in thinking, pursuit and avoidance are in desire; so that since moral virtue is a state of character concerned with choice, and choice is deliberate desire, therefore both the reasoning must be true and the desire right, if the choice is to be good, and the latter must pursue just what the former asserts. Now this kind of intellect and of truth is practical; of the intellect which is contemplative, not practical nor productive, the good and the bad state are truth and falsity respectively (for this is the work of everything intellectual); while of the part which is practical and intellectual the good state is truth in agreement with right desire.

The origin of action—its efficient, not its final cause—is choice, and that of choice is desire and reasoning with a view to an end. This is why choice cannot exist either without reason and intellect or without a moral state; for good action and its opposite cannot exist without a combination of intellect and character. Intellect itself, however, moves nothing, but only the intellect which aims at an end and is practical; for this rules the productive intellect, as well, since every one who makes makes for an end, and that which is made is not an end in the unqualified sense (but only an end in a particular relation, and the end of a particular operation)—only that which is *done* is that; for good action is an end, and desire aims at this. Hence choice is either desiderative reason or ratiocinative desire, and such an origin of action is a man. (It is to be noted that nothing that is past is an object of choice, e.g. no one chooses to have sacked Troy; for no one *deliberates* about the past, but about what is future and capable of being otherwise, while what is past is not capable of not having taken place; hence Agathon is right in saying

> For this alone is lacking even to God,

> To make undone things that have once been done.)

The work of both the intellectual parts, then, is truth. Therefore the states that are most strictly those in respect of which each of these parts will reach truth are the virtues of the two parts.

3

Let us begin, then, from the beginning, and discuss these states once more. Let it be assumed that the states by virtue of which the soul possesses truth by way of affirmation or denial are five in number, i.e. art, scientific knowledge, practical wisdom, philosophic wisdom, intuitive reason; we do not include judgement and opinion because in these we may be mistaken. . . .

4 . . .

5

Regarding *practical wisdom* we shall get at the truth by considering who are the persons we credit with it. Now it is thought to be the mark of a man of practical wisdom to be able to deliberate well about what is good and expedient for himself, not in some particular respect, e.g. about what sorts of thing conduce to health or to strength, but about what sorts of thing conduce to the good life in general. This is shown by the fact that we credit men with practical wisdom in some particular respect when they have calculated well with a view to some good end which is one of those that are not the object of any art. It follows that in the general sense also the man who is capable of deliberating has practical wisdom. Now no one deliberates about things that are invariable, nor about things that it is impossible for him to do. Therefore, since scientific knowledge involves demonstration, but there is no demonstration of things whose first principles are variable (for all such things might actually be otherwise), and since it is impossible to deliberate about things that are of necessity, practical wisdom cannot be scientific knowledge nor art; not sci-

ence because that which can be done is capable of being otherwise, not art because action and making are different kinds of thing. The remaining alternative, then, is that it is a true and reasoned state of capacity to act with regard to the things that are good or bad for man. For while making has an end other than itself, action cannot; for good action itself is its end. It is for this reason that we think Pericles and men like him have practical wisdom, viz. because they can see what is good for themselves and what is good for men in general; we consider that those can do this who are good at managing households or states. (This is why we call temperance (*sophrosune*) by this name; we imply that it preserves one's practical wisdom (*sozousa tan phronsin*). Now what it preserves is a judgement of the kind we have described. For it is not any and every judgement that pleasant and painful objects destroy and pervert, e.g. the judgement that the triangle has or has not its angles equal to two right angles, but only judgements about what is to be done. For the originating causes of the things that are done consist in the end at which they are aimed; but the man who has been ruined by pleasure or pain forthwith fails to see any such originating cause—to see that for the sake of this or because of this he ought to choose and do whatever he chooses and does; for vice is destructive of the originating cause of action.

Practical wisdom, then, must be a reasoned and true state of capacity to act with regard to human goods. But further, while there is such a thing as excellence in art, there is no such thing as excellence in practical wisdom; and in art he who errs willingly is preferable, but in practical wisdom, as in the virtues, he is the reverse. Plainly, then, practical wisdom is a virtue and not an art. There being two parts of the soul that can follow a course of reasoning, it must be the virtue of one of the two, i.e. of that part which forms opinions; for opinion is about the variable and so is practical wisdom. But yet it is not only a reasoned state; this is shown by the fact that a state of that sort may be forgotten but practical wisdom cannot.

6 . . .

7

. . . Practical wisdom on the other hand is concerned with things human and things about which it is possible to deliberate; for we say this is above all the work of the man of practical wisdom, to deliberate well, but no one deliberates about things invariable, nor about things which have not an end, and that a good that can be brought about by action. The man who is without qualification good at deliberating is the man who is capable of aiming in accordance with calculation at the best for man of things attainable by action. Nor is practical wisdom concerned with universals only—it must also recognize the particulars; for it is practical, and practice is concerned with particulars. This is why some who do not know, and especially those who have experience, are more practical than others who know; for if a man knew that light meats are digestible and wholesome, but did not know which sorts of meat are light, he would not produce health, but the man who knows that chicken is wholesome is more likely to produce health.

Now practical wisdom is concerned with action; therefore one should have both forms of it, or the latter in preference to the former. But of practical as of philosophic wisdom there must be a controlling kind.

8

Political wisdom and practical wisdom are the same state of mind, but their essence is not the same. Of the wisdom concerned with the city, the practical wisdom which plays a controlling part is legislative wisdom, while that which is related to this as particulars to their universal is known by the general name 'political wisdom'; this has to do with action and deliberation, for a decree is a thing to be carried out in the form of an individual act. This is why the exponents of this art are alone said to 'take part in politics'; for these alone 'do things' as manual labourers 'do things.'

Practical wisdom also is identified especially with that form of it which is concerned with a man himself—with the individual; and this is known by the general name 'practical wisdom'; of the other kinds one is called household management, another legislation, the third politics, and of the latter one part is called deliberative and the other judicial. Now knowing what is good for oneself will be one kind of knowledge, but it is very different from the other kinds; and the man who knows and concerns himself with his own interests is thought to have practical wisdom, while politicians are thought to be busybodies; hence the words of Euripides,

> But how could I be wise, who might at ease,
>
> Numbered among the army's multitude,
>
> Have had an equal share?
>
> For those who aim too high and do too much.

Those who think thus seek their own good, and consider that one ought to do so. From this opinion, then, has come the view that such men have practical wisdom; yet perhaps one's own good cannot exist without household management, nor without a form of government. Further, how one should order one's own affairs is not clear and needs inquiry.

What has been said is confirmed by the fact that while young men become geometricians and mathematicians and wise in matters like these, it is thought that a young man of practical wisdom cannot be found. The cause is that such wisdom is concerned not only with universals but with particulars, which become familiar from experience, but a young man has no experience, for it is length of time that gives experience; indeed one might ask this question too, why a boy may become a mathematician, but not a philosopher or a physicist. Is it because the objects of mathematics exist by abstraction, while the first principles of these other subjects come from experience, and because young men have no conviction about the latter but merely use the proper language, while the essence of mathematical objects is plain enough to them?

Further, error in deliberation may be either about the universal or about the particular; we may fail to know either that all water that weighs heavy is bad, or that this particular water weighs heavy.

That practical wisdom is not scientific knowledge is evident; for it is, as has been said, concerned with the ultimate particular fact, since the thing to be done is of this nature. It is opposed, then, to intuitive reason; for intuitive reason is of the limiting premises, for which no reason can be given, while practical wisdom is concerned with the ultimate particular, which is the object not of scientific knowledge but of perception—not the perception of qualities peculiar to one sense but a perception akin to that by which we perceive that the particular figure before us is a triangle; for in that direction as well as in that of the major premiss there will be a limit. But this is rather perception than practical wisdom, though it is another kind of perception than that of the qualities peculiar to each sense.

9

There is a difference between inquiry and deliberation; for deliberation is inquiry into a particular kind of thing. We must grasp the nature of excellence in deliberation as well whether it is a form of scientific knowledge, or opinion, or skill in conjecture, or some other kind of thing. *Scientific knowledge* it is not; for men do not inquire about the things they know about, but good deliberation is a kind of deliberation, and he who deliberates inquires and calculates. Nor is it *skill in conjecture;* for this both involves no reasoning and is something that is quick in its operation, while men deliberate a long time, and they say that one should carry out quickly the conclusions of one's deliberation, but should deliberate slowly. Again, *readiness of mind* is different from excellence in deliberation; it is a sort of skill in conjecture. Nor again is excellence in deliberation *opinion* of any sort. But since the man who deliberates badly makes a mistake, while he who deliberates well does so correctly, excellence in deliberation is clearly a kind of correctness, but neither of knowledge nor of opinion; for there is no such thing as correctness of knowledge (since there is no such thing as error of knowledge), and correctness of opinion is truth; and at the same time everything that is an object of opinion is already determined. But again excellence in deliberation involves reasoning. The remaining alternative, then, is that it is *correctness of thinking;* for this is not yet assertion, since, while even opinion is not inquiry but has reached the stage of assertion, the man who is deliberating, whether he does so well or ill, is searching for something and calculating.

But excellence in deliberation is a certain correctness of deliberation; hence we must first inquire what deliberation is and what it is about. And, there being more than one kind of correctness, plainly excellence in deliberation is not any and every kind; for (1) the incontinent man and the bad man, if he is clever, will reach as a result of his calculation what he sets before himself, so that he will have deliberated correctly, but he will have got for himself a great evil. Now to have deliberated well is thought to be a good thing; for it is this kind of correctness of deliberation that is excellence in deliberation, viz. that which tends to attain what is good. But (2) it is possible to attain even good by a false syllogism, and to attain what one ought to do but not by the right means, the middle term being false; so that this too is not yet excellence in deliberation this state in virtue of which one attains what one ought but not by the right means. Again (3) it is possible to attain it by long deliberation while another man attains it quickly. Therefore in the former case we have not yet got excellence in deliberation, which is rightness with regard to the expedient-rightness in respect both of the end, the manner, and the time. (4) Further it is possible to have deliberated well either in the unqualified sense or with reference to a particular end. Excellence in deliberation in the unqualified sense, then, is that which succeeds with reference to what is the end in the unqualified sense, and excellence in deliberation in a particular sense is that which succeeds relatively to a particular end. If, then, it is characteristic of men of practical wisdom to have deliberated well, excellence in deliberation

will be correctness with regard to what conduces to the end of which practical wisdom is the true apprehension.

10

Understanding, also, and goodness of understanding, in virtue of which men are said to be men of understanding or of good understanding, are neither entirely the same as opinion or scientific knowledge (for at that rate all men would have been men of understanding), nor are they one of the particular sciences, such as medicine, the science of things connected with health, or geometry, the science of spatial magnitudes. For understanding is neither about things that are always and are unchangeable, nor about any and every one of the things that come into being, but about things which may become subjects of questioning and deliberation. Hence it is about the same objects as practical wisdom; but understanding and practical wisdom are not the same. For practical wisdom issues commands, since its end is what ought to be done or not to be done; but understanding only judges. (Understanding is identical with goodness of understanding, men of understanding with men of good understanding.) Now understanding is neither the having nor the acquiring of practical wisdom; but as learning is called understanding when it means the exercise of the faculty of knowledge, so 'understanding' is applicable to the exercise of the faculty of opinion for the purpose of judging of what some one else says about matters with which practical wisdom is concerned—and of judging soundly; for 'well' and 'soundly' are the same thing. And from this has come the use of the name 'understanding' in virtue of which men are said to be 'of good understanding,' viz. from the application of the word to the grasping of scientific truth; for we often call such grasping understanding.

11

What is called judgement, in virtue of which men are said to 'be sympathetic judges' and to 'have judgement,' is the right discrimination of the equitable. This is shown by the fact that we say the equitable man is above all others a man of sympathetic judgement, and identify equity with sympathetic judgement about certain facts. And sympathetic judgement is judgement which discriminates what is equitable and does so correctly; and correct judgement is that which judges what is true.

Now all the states we have considered converge, as might be expected, to the same point; for when we speak of judgement and understanding and practical wisdom and intuitive reason we credit the same people with possessing judgement and having reached years of reason and with having practical wisdom and understanding. For all these faculties deal with ultimates, i.e. with particulars; and being a man of understanding and of good or sympathetic judgement consists in being able to judge about the things with which practical wisdom is concerned; for the equities are common to all good men in relation to other men. Now all things which have to be done are included among particulars or ultimates; for not only must the man of practical wisdom know particular facts, but understanding and judgement are also concerned with things to be done, and these are ultimates. And intuitive reason is concerned with the ultimates in both directions; for both the first terms and the last are objects of intuitive reason and not of argument, and the intuitive reason which is presupposed by demonstrations grasps the unchangeable and first terms, while the intuitive reason involved in practical reasonings grasps the last and variable fact, i.e. the minor premiss. For these variable facts are the starting-points for the apprehension of the end, since the universals are reached from the particulars; of these therefore we must have perception, and this perception is intuitive reason.

This is why these states are thought to be natural endowments—why, while no one is thought to be a philosopher by nature, people are thought to have by nature judgement, understanding, and intuitive reason. This is shown by the fact that we think our powers correspond to our time of life, and that a particular age brings with it intuitive reason and judgement; this implies that nature is the cause. [Hence intuitive reason is both beginning and end; for demonstrations are from these and about these.] Therefore we ought to attend to the undemonstrated sayings and opinions of experienced and older people or of people of practical wisdom not less than to demonstrations; for because experience has given them an eye they see aright.

We have stated, then, what practical and philosophic wisdom are, and with what each of them is concerned, and we have said that each is the virtue of a different part of the soul.

12

Difficulties might be raised as to the utility of these qualities of mind. For (1) philosophic wisdom will contemplate none of the things that will make a man happy (for it is not concerned with any coming into being), and though practical wisdom has *this* merit, for what purpose do we need it? Practical wisdom is the quality of mind concerned with things just and noble and good for

man, but these are the things which it is the mark of a *good* man to do, and we are none the more able to act for *knowing* them if the virtues are states of *character,* just as we are none the better able to act for knowing the things that are healthy and sound, in the sense not of producing but of issuing from the state of health; for we are none the more able to act for having the art of medicine or of gymnastics. But (2) if we are to say that a man should have practical wisdom not for the sake of knowing moral truths but for the sake of becoming good, practical wisdom will be of no use to those who are good; again it is of no use to those who have not virtue; for it will make no difference whether they have practical wisdom themselves or obey others who have it, and it would be enough for us to do what we do in the case of health; though we wish to become healthy, yet we do not learn the art of medicine. (3) Besides this, it would be thought strange if practical wisdom, being inferior to philosophic wisdom, is to be put in authority over it, as seems to be implied by the fact that the art which produces anything rules and issues commands about that thing.

These, then, are the questions we must discuss; so far we have only stated the difficulties.

(1) Now first let us say that in themselves these states must be worthy of choice because they are the virtues of the two parts of the soul respectively, even if neither of them produce anything.

(2) Secondly, they do produce something, not as the art of medicine produces health, however, but as health produces health; so does philosophic wisdom produce happiness; for, being a part of virtue entire, by being possessed and by actualizing itself it makes a man happy.

(3) Again, the work of man is achieved only in accordance with practical wisdom as well as with moral virtue; for virtue makes us aim at the right mark, and practical wisdom makes us take the right means. (Of the fourth part of the soul—the nutritive—there is no such virtue; for there is nothing which it is in its power to do or not to do.)

(4) With regard to our being none the more able to do because of our practical wisdom what is noble and just, let us begin a little further back, starting with the following principle. As we say that some people who do just acts are not necessarily just, i.e. those who do the acts ordained by the laws either unwillingly or owing to ignorance or for some other reason and not for the sake of the acts themselves (though, to be sure, they do what they should and all the things that the good man ought), so is it, it seems, that in order to be good one must be in a certain state when one does the several acts, i.e. one

must do them as a result of choice and for the sake of the acts themselves. Now virtue makes the choice right, but the question of the things which should naturally be done to carry out our choice belongs not to virtue but to another faculty. We must devote our attention to these matters and give a clearer statement about them. There is a faculty which is called cleverness; and this is such as to be able to do the things that tend towards the mark we have set before ourselves, and to hit it. Now if the mark be noble, the cleverness is laudable, but if the mark be bad, the cleverness is mere smartness; hence we call even men of practical wisdom clever or smart. Practical wisdom is not the faculty, but it does not exist without this faculty. And this eye of the soul acquires its formed state not without the aid of virtue, as has been said and is plain; for the syllogisms which deal with acts to be done are things which involve a starting-point, viz. 'since the end, i.e. what is best, is of such and such a nature,' whatever it may be (let it for the sake of argument be what we please); and this is not evident except to the good man; for wickedness perverts us and causes us to be deceived about the starting-points of action. Therefore it is evident that it is impossible to be practically wise without being good.

13

We must therefore consider virtue also once more; for virtue too is similarly related; as practical wisdom is to cleverness—not the same, but like it—so is natural virtue to virtue in the strict sense. For all men think that each type of character belongs to its possessors in some sense by nature; for from the very moment of birth we are just or fitted for self control or brave or have the other moral qualities; but yet we seek something else as that which is good in the strict sense—we seek for the presence of such qualities in another way. For both children and brutes have the natural dispositions to these qualities, but without reason these are evidently hurtful. Only we seem to see this much, that, while one may be led astray by them, as a strong body which moves without sight may stumble badly because of its lack of sight, still, if a man once acquires reason, that makes a difference in action; and his state, while still like what it was, will then be virtue in the strict sense. Therefore, as in the part of us which forms opinions there are two types, cleverness and practical wisdom, so too in the moral part there are two types, natural virtue and virtue in the strict sense, and of these the latter involves practical wisdom. This is why some say that all the virtues are forms of practical wisdom, and why Socrates in one respect was on the right track while in another he went astray; in thinking that all the virtues were forms of practical wisdom he was wrong, but in saying they implied practical wisdom he was right. This is confirmed by the fact that even now all men, when they define virtue, after naming the state of character and its objects add 'that (state) which is in accordance with the right rule'; now the right rule is that which is in accordance with practical wisdom. All men, then, seem somehow to divine that this kind of state is virtue, viz. that which is in accordance with practical wisdom. But we must go a little further. For it is not merely the state in accordance with the right rule, but the state that implies the *presence* of the right rule, that is virtue; and practical wisdom is a right rule about such matters. Socrates, then, thought the virtues were rules or rational principles (for he thought they were, all of them, forms of scientific knowledge), while we think they *involve* a rational principle.

It is clear, then, from what has been said, that it is not possible to be good in the strict sense without practical wisdom, nor practically wise without moral virtue. But in this way we may also refute the dialectical argument whereby it might be contended that the virtues exist in separation from each other; the same man, it might be said, is not best equipped by nature for all the virtues, so that he will have already acquired one when he has not yet acquired another. This is possible in respect of the natural virtues, but not in respect of those in respect of which a man is called without qualification good; for with the presence of the one quality, practical wisdom, will be given all the virtues. And it is plain that, even if it were of no practical value, we should have needed it because it is the virtue of the part of us in question; plain too that the choice will not be right without practical wisdom any more than without virtue; for the one determines the end and the other makes us do the things that lead to the end.

But again it is not *supreme* over philosophic wisdom, i.e. over the superior part of us, any more than the art of medicine is over health; for it does not use it but provides for its coming into being; it issues orders, then, for its sake, but not to it. Further, to maintain its supremacy would be like saying that the art of politics rules the gods because it issues orders about all the affairs of the state.

QUESTIONS ON ARISTOTLE

1. Review Aristotle's account of activity and the aims of activity (in paragraph 1 of Book I) and then consider the activity of work or labor. Is labor an activity whose good is its product? Or is the activity of work good in itself?

2. How does the idea of a "final end" relate to virtue? What is Aristotle's conception of happiness, and how does it differ from the contemporary conception? What is Aristotle's definition of virtue? Relate this definition to (a) the idea of an activity as an end and (b) the idea of happiness.

3. How does Aristotle characterize the soul? What are the two types of reason? In what sense is moral virtue acquired by habit? How can a practice that involves deliberation be acquired by a nonreflective habit?

4. In what way is practical wisdom concerned with universals and particulars? In what sense does the moral life require perception and awareness? Is there any sense in which business skills require perception and awareness? Is this sort of perception the same as moral perception, or related to moral perception?

5. How might Aristotle's virtues relate to commerce? Consider in particular the virtues of generosity, courage, temperance, and truthfulness. Are there other virtues, left unmentioned in Aristotle, that bear a special relevance to business?

Fundamental Principles of the Metaphysic of Morals*

Immanuel Kant

Immanuel Kant (1724–1804) lived throughout his life in Königsberg, East Prussia (now Kaliningrad, Russia). One of the greatest philosophers to have lived, Kant also proved to be a remarkably popular and effective teacher at the University of Königsberg, where he held a post from 1755. His Critique of Pure Reason *(1781) sought to delineate the possibility and limits of knowledge. The excerpt below is from the second chapter of the* Foundations of the Metaphysic of Morals *(1785), a work that offers a provisional account that Kant developed further in his* Critique of Practical Reason *(1788).*

TRANSITION FROM POPULAR MORAL PHILOSOPHY TO THE METAPHYSIC OF MORALS

If we have hitherto drawn our notion of duty from the common use of our practical reason, it is by no means to

*Translated by Thomas Kingsmill Abbott.

be inferred that we have treated it as an empirical notion. On the contrary, if we attend to the experience of men's conduct, we meet frequent and, as we ourselves allow, just complaints that one cannot find a single certain example of the disposition to act from pure duty. Although many things are done in *conformity* with what *duty* prescribes, it is nevertheless always doubtful whether they are done strictly *from duty,* so as to have a moral worth. Hence there have at all times been philosophers who have altogether denied that this disposition actually exists at all in human actions, and have ascribed everything to a more or less refined self-love. Not that they have on that account questioned the soundness of the conception of morality; on the contrary, they spoke with sincere regret of the frailty and corruption of human nature, which, though noble enough to take its rule an idea so worthy of respect, is yet weak to follow it and employs reason which ought to give it the law only for the purpose of providing for the interest of the inclinations, whether singly or at the best in the greatest possible harmony with one another.

In fact, it is absolutely impossible to make out by experience with complete certainty a single case in which the maxim of an action, however right in itself, rested simply on moral grounds and on the conception of duty. Sometimes it happens that with the sharpest self-examination we can find nothing beside the moral principle of duty which could have been powerful enough to move us to this or that action and to so great a sacrifice; yet we cannot from this infer with certainty that it was not really some secret impulse of self-love, under the false appearance of duty, that was the actual determining cause of the will. We like them to flatter ourselves by falsely taking credit for a more noble motive; whereas in fact we can never, even by the strictest examination, get completely behind the secret springs of action; since, when the question is of moral worth, it is not with the actions which we see that we are concerned, but with those inward principles of them which we do not see.

Moreover, we cannot better serve the wishes of those who ridicule all morality as a mere chimera of human imagination overstepping itself from vanity, than by conceding to them that notions of duty must be drawn only from experience (as from indolence, people are ready to think is also the case with all other notions); for this is to prepare for them a certain triumph. I am willing to admit out of love of humanity that even most of our actions are correct, but if we look closer at them we everywhere come upon the dear self which is always prominent, and it is this they have in view and not the strict command of duty which would often require self-denial. Without being an enemy of virtue, a cool observer, one that does not mistake the wish for good, however lively, for its reality, may sometimes doubt whether true virtue is actually found anywhere in the world, and this especially as years increase and the judgement is partly made wiser by experience and partly, also, more acute in observation. This being so, nothing can secure us from falling away altogether from our ideas of duty, or maintain in the soul a well-grounded respect for its law, but the clear conviction that although there should never have been actions which really sprang from such pure sources, yet whether this or that takes place is not at all the question; but that reason of itself, independent on all experience, ordains what ought to take place, that accordingly actions of which perhaps the world has hitherto never given an example, the feasibility even of which might be very much doubted by one who founds everything on experience, are nevertheless inflexibly commanded by reason; that, *e.g.,* even though there might never yet have been a sincere friend, yet not a whit the less is pure sincerity in friendship required of every man, because, prior to all experience, this duty is involved as duty in the idea of a reason determining the will by *a priori* principles.

When we add further that, unless we deny that the notion of morality has any truth or reference to any possible object, we must admit that its law must be valid, not merely for men but for all *rational creatures generally,* not merely under certain contingent conditions or with exceptions but *with absolute necessity,* then it is clear that no experience could enable us to infer even the possibility of such apodeictic laws. For with what right could we bring into unbounded respect as a universal precept for every rational nature that which perhaps holds only under the contingent conditions of humanity? Or how could laws of the determination of *our* will be regarded as laws of the determination of the will of rational beings generally, and for us only as such, if they were merely empirical and did not take their origin wholly *a priori* from pure but practical reason?

Nor could anything be more fatal to morality than that we should wish to derive it from examples. For every example of it that is set before me must be first itself tested by principles of morality, whether it is worthy to serve as an original example, *i.e.,* as a pattern; but by no means can it authoritatively furnish the conception of morality. Even the Holy One of the Gospels must first be compared with our ideal of moral perfection before we can recognise Him as such; and so He says of Himself, "Why call ye Me [whom you see] good; none

is good [the model of good] but God only [whom ye do not see]?" But whence have we the conception of God as the supreme good? Simply from the *idea* of moral perfection, which reason frames *a priori* and connects inseparably with the notion of a free will. Imitation finds no place at all in morality, and examples serve only for encouragement, *i.e.,* they put beyond doubt the feasibility of what the law commands, they make visible that which the practical rule expresses more generally, but they can never authorize us to set aside the true original which lies in reason and to guide ourselves by examples.

If then there is no genuine supreme principle of morality but what must rest simply on pure reason, independent of all experience, I think it is not necessary even to put the question whether it is good to exhibit these concepts in their generality *(in abstracto)* as they are established *a priori* along with the principles belonging to them, if our knowledge is to be distinguished from the *vulgar* and to be called philosophical.

In our times indeed this might perhaps be necessary; for if we collected votes whether pure rational knowledge separated from everything empirical, that is to say, metaphysic of morals, or whether popular practical philosophy is to be preferred, it is easy to guess which side would preponderate.

This descending to popular notions is certainly very commendable, if the ascent to the principles of pure reason has first taken place and been satisfactorily accomplished. This implies that we first *found* Ethics on Metaphysics, and then, when it is firmly established, procure a *hearing* for it by giving it a popular character. But it is quite absurd to try to be popular in the first inquiry, on which the soundness of the principles depends. It is not only that this proceeding can never lay claim to the very rare merit of a true *philosophical popularity,* since there is no art in being intelligible if one renounces all thoroughness of insight; but also it produces a disgusting medley of compiled observations and half-reasoned principles. Shallow pates enjoy this because it can be used for every-day chat, but the sagacious find in it only confusion, and being unsatisfied and unable to help themselves, they turn away their eyes, while philosophers, who see quite well through this delusion, are little listened to when they call men off for a time from this pretended popularity, in order that they might be rightfully popular after they have attained a definite insight.

We need only look at the attempts of moralists in that favourite fashion, and we shall find at one time the special constitution of human nature (including, however, the idea of a rational nature generally), at one time perfection, at another happiness, here moral sense, there fear of God. A little of this, and a little of that, in marvellous mixture, without its occurring to them to ask whether the principles of morality are to be sought in the knowledge of human nature at all (which we can have only from experience); or, if this is not so, if these principles are to be found altogether *a priori,* free from everything empirical, in pure rational concepts only and nowhere else, not even in the smallest degree; then rather to adopt the method of making this a separate inquiry, as pure practical philosophy, or (if one may use a name so decried) as metaphysic of morals,[1] to bring it by itself to completeness, and to require the public, which wishes for popular treatment, to await the issue of this undertaking. . . .

From what has been said, it is clear that all moral conceptions have their seat and origin completely *a priori* in the reason, and that, moreover, in the commonest reason just as truly as in that which is in the highest degree speculative; that they cannot be obtained by abstraction from any empirical, and therefore merely contingent, knowledge; that it is just this purity of their origin that makes them worthy to serve as our supreme practical principle, and that just in proportion as we add anything empirical, we detract from their genuine influence and from the absolute value of actions; that it is not only of the greatest necessity, in a purely speculative point of view, but is also of the greatest practical importance, to derive these notions and laws from pure reason, to present them pure and unmixed, and even to determine the compass of this practical or pure rational knowledge, *i.e.,* to determine the whole faculty of pure practical reason; and, in doing so, we must not make its principles dependent on the particular nature of human reason, though in speculative philosophy this may be permitted, or may even at times be necessary; but since moral laws ought to hold good for every rational creature, we must derive them from the general concept of a rational being. In this way, although for its *application* to man morality has need of anthropology, yet, in the first instance, we must treat it independently as pure philosophy, *i.e.,* as metaphysic, complete in itself (a thing which in such distinct branches of science is easily done); knowing well that unless we are in possession of this, it would not only be vain to determine the moral element of duty in right actions for purposes of speculative criticism, but it would be impossible to base morals on their genuine principles, even for common practical purposes, especially of moral instruction, so as to produce pure moral dispositions, and to engraft them on men's minds to the promotion of the greatest possible good in the world.

But in order that in this study we may not merely advance by the natural steps from the common moral judgement (in this case very worthy of respect) to the philosophical, as has been already done, but also from a popular philosophy, which goes no further than it can reach by groping with the help of examples, to metaphysic (which does allow itself to be checked by anything empirical and, as it must measure the whole extent of this kind of rational knowledge, goes as far as ideal conceptions, where even examples fail us), we must follow and clearly describe the practical faculty of reason, from the general rules of its determination to the point where the notion of duty springs from it.

Everything in nature works according to laws. Rational beings alone have the faculty of acting according *to the conception* of laws, that is according to principles, *i.e.,* have a *will.* Since the deduction of actions from principles requires reason, the will is nothing but practical reason. If *reason* infallibly determines the will, then the actions of such a being which are recognised as objectively necessary are subjectively necessary also, *i.e.,* the will is a faculty to choose *that only* which reason independent of inclination recognises as practically necessary, *i.e.,* as good. But if reason of itself does not sufficiently determine the will, if the latter is subject also to subjective conditions (particular impulses) which do not always coincide with the objective conditions; in a word, if the will does not *in itself* completely accord with reason (which is actually the case with men), then the actions which objectively are recognised as necessary are subjectively contingent, and the determination of such a will according to objective laws is *obligation,* that is to say, the relation of the objective laws to a will that is not thoroughly good is conceived as the determination of the will of a rational being by principles of reason, but which the will from its nature does not of necessity follow.

The conception of an objective principle, in so far as it is obligatory for a will, is called a command (of reason), and the formula of the command is called an imperative.

All imperatives are expressed by the word *ought* [or *shall*], and thereby indicate the relation of an objective law of reason to a will, which from its subjective constitution is not necessarily determined by it (an obligation). They say that something would be good to do or to forbear, but they say it to a will which does not always do a thing because it is conceived to be good to do it. That is practically *good,* however, which determines the will by means of the conceptions of reason, and consequently not from subjective causes, but objectively, that is on principles which are valid for every rational being as such. It is distinguished from the *pleasant,* as that which influences the will only by means of sensation from merely subjective causes, valid only for the sense of this or that one, and not as a principle of reason, which holds for every one.[2]

A perfectly good will would therefore be equally subject to objective laws (viz., laws of good), but could not be conceived as *obliged* thereby to act lawfully, because of itself from its subjective constitution it can only be determined by the conception of good. Therefore no imperatives hold for the Divine will, or in general for a *holy* will; *ought* is here out of place, because the volition is already of itself necessarily in unison with the law. Therefore imperatives are only formulae to express the relation of objective laws of all volition to the subjective imperfection of the will of this or that rational being, *e.g.,* the human will.

Now all *imperatives* command either *hypothetically* or *categorically.* The former represent the practical necessity of a possible action as means to something else that is willed (or at least which one might possibly will). The categorical imperative would be that which represented an action as necessary of itself without reference to another end, *i.e.,* as objectively necessary.

Since every practical law represents a possible action as good and, on this account, for a subject who is practically determinable by reason, necessary, all imperatives are formulae determining an action which is necessary according to the principle of a will good in some respects. If now the action is good only as a means *to something else,* then the imperative is *hypothetical;* if it is conceived as good *in itself* and consequently as being necessarily the principle of a will which of itself conforms to reason, then it is *categorical. . . .*

There is *one* end, however, which may be assumed to be actually such to all rational beings (so far as imperatives apply to them, viz., as dependent beings), and, therefore, one purpose which they not merely *may* have, but which we may with certainty assume that they all actually *have* by a natural necessity, and this is *happiness.* The hypothetical imperative which expresses the practical necessity of an action as means to the advancement of happiness is assertorial. We are not to present it as necessary for an uncertain and merely possible purpose, but for a purpose which we may presuppose with certainty and *a priori* in every man, because it belongs to his being. Now skill in the choice of means to his own greatest well-being may be called *prudence,*[3] in the narrowest sense. And thus the imperative which refers to the choice of means to one's own happiness, *i.e.,* the precept of prudence, is still always *hypothetical;* the ac-

tion is not commanded absolutely, but only as means to another purpose.

Finally, there is an imperative which commands a certain conduct immediately, without having as its condition any other purpose to be attained by it. This imperative is categorical. It concerns not the matter of the action, or its intended result, but its form and the principle of which it is itself a result; and what is essentially good in it consists in the mental disposition, let the consequence be what it may. This imperative may be called that of Morality.

. . . For it is *law* only that involves the conception of an *unconditional* and objective necessity, which is consequently universally valid; and commands are laws which must be obeyed, that is, must be followed, even in opposition to inclination. *Counsels,* indeed, involve necessity, but one which can only hold under a contingent subjective condition, viz., they depend on whether this or that man reckons this or that as part of his happiness; the categorical imperative, on the contrary, is not limited by any condition, and as being absolutely, although practically, necessary, may be quite properly called a command. We might also call the first kind of imperatives *technical* (belonging to art), the second *pragmatic* (to welfare), the third *moral* (belonging to free conduct generally, that is, to morals). . . .

Now arises the question, how are all these imperatives possible? This question does not seek to know how we can conceive the accomplishment of the action which the imperative ordains, but merely how we can conceive the obligation of the will which the imperative expresses. . . .

[T]he question how the imperative of *morality* is possible, is undoubtedly one, the only one, demanding a solution, as this is not at all hypothetical, and the objective necessity which it presents cannot rest on any hypothesis, as is the case with the hypothetical imperatives. Only here we must never leave out of consideration that we *cannot* make out *by any example,* in other words empirically, whether there is such an imperative at all, but it is rather to be feared that all those which seem to be categorical may yet be at bottom hypothetical. For instance, when the precept is: "Thou shalt not promise deceitfully"; and it is assumed that the necessity of this is not a mere counsel to avoid some other evil, so that it should mean: "Thou shalt not make a lying promise, lest if it become known thou shouldst destroy thy credit," but that an action of this kind must be regarded as evil in itself, so that the imperative of the prohibition is categorical; then we cannot show with certainty in any example that the will was determined merely by the law, without any other spring of action, although it may appear to be so. For it is always possible that fear of disgrace, perhaps also obscure dread of other dangers, may have a secret influence on the will. Who can prove by experience the nonexistence of a cause when all that experience tells us is that we do not perceive it? But in such a case the so-called moral imperative, which as such appears to be categorical and unconditional, would in reality be only a pragmatic precept, drawing our attention to our own interests and merely teaching us to take these into consideration.

We shall therefore have to investigate *a priori* the possibility of a categorical imperative, as we have not in this case the advantage of its reality being given in experience, so that [the elucidation of] its possibility should be requisite only for its explanation, not for its establishment. In the meantime it may be discerned beforehand that the categorical imperative alone has the purport of a practical law; all the rest may indeed be called *principles* of the will but not laws, since whatever is only necessary for the attainment of some arbitrary purpose may be considered as in itself contingent, and we can at any time be free from the precept if we give up the purpose; on the contrary, the unconditional command leaves the will no liberty to choose the opposite; consequently it alone carries with it that necessity which we require in a law.

Secondly, in the case of this categorical imperative or law of morality, the difficulty (of discerning its possibility) is a very profound one. It is an *a priori* synthetical practical proposition;[4] and as there is so much difficulty in discerning the possibility of speculative propositions of this kind, it may readily be supposed that the difficulty will be no less with the practical.

In this problem we will first inquire whether the mere conception of a categorical imperative may not perhaps supply us also with the formula of it, containing the proposition which alone can be a categorical imperative; for even if we know the tenor of such an absolute command, yet how it is possible will require further special and laborious study, which we postpone to the last section.

When I conceive a hypothetical imperative, in general I do not know beforehand what it will contain until I am given the condition. But when I conceive a categorical imperative, I know at once what it contains. For as the imperative contains besides the law only the necessity that the maxims[5] shall conform to this law, while the law contains no conditions restricting it, there remains nothing but the general statement that the maxim of the action should conform to a universal law, and it is this conformity alone that the imperative properly represents as necessary.

There is therefore but one categorical imperative, namely, this: *Act only on that maxim whereby thou canst at the same time will that it should become a universal law.*

Now if all imperatives of duty can be deduced from this one imperative as from their principle, then, although it should remain undecided what is called duty is not merely a vain notion, yet at least we shall be able to show what we understand by it and what this notion means.

Since the universality of the law according to which effects are produced constitutes what is properly called *nature* in the most general sense (as to form), that is the existence of things so far as it is determined by general laws, the imperative of duty may be expressed thus: *Act as if the maxim of thy action were to become by thy will a universal law of nature.*

We will now enumerate a few duties, adopting the usual division of them into duties to ourselves and ourselves and to others, and into perfect and imperfect duties.[6]

1. A man reduced to despair by a series of misfortunes feels wearied of life, but is still so far in possession of his reason that he can ask himself whether it would not be contrary to his duty to himself to take his own life. Now he inquires whether the maxim of his action could become a universal law of nature. His maxim is: "From self-love I adopt it as a principle to shorten my life when its longer duration is likely to bring more evil than satisfaction." It is asked then simply whether this principle founded on self-love can become a universal law of nature. Now we see at once that a system of nature of which it should be a law to destroy life by means of the very feeling whose special nature it is to impel to the improvement of life would contradict itself and, therefore, could not exist as a system of nature; hence that maxim cannot possibly exist as a universal law of nature and, consequently, would be wholly inconsistent with the supreme principle of all duty.

2. Another finds himself forced by necessity to borrow money. He knows that he will not be able to repay it, but sees also that nothing will be lent to him unless he promises stoutly to repay it in a definite time. He desires to make this promise, but he has still so much conscience as to ask himself: "Is it not unlawful and inconsistent with duty to get out of a difficulty in this way?" Suppose, however, that he resolves to do so; then the maxim of his action would be expressed thus: "When I think myself in want of money, I will borrow money and promise to repay it, although I know that I never can do so." Now this principle of self-love or of one's own advantage may perhaps be consistent with my whole future welfare; but the

question now is, "Is it right?" I change then the suggestion of self-love into a universal law, and state the question thus: "How would it be if my maxim were a universal law?" Then I see at once that it could never hold as a universal law of nature, but would necessarily contradict itself. For supposing it to be a universal law that everyone when he thinks himself in a difficulty should be able to promise whatever he pleases, with the purpose of not keeping his promise, the promise itself would become impossible, as well as the end that one might have in view in it, since no one would consider that anything was promised to him, but would ridicule all such statements as vain pretences.

3. A third finds in himself a talent which with the help of some culture might make him a useful man in many respects. But he finds himself in comfortable circumstances and prefers to indulge in pleasure rather than to take pains in enlarging and improving his happy natural capacities. He asks, however, whether his maxim of neglect of his natural gifts, besides agreeing with his inclination to indulgence, agrees also with what is called duty. He sees then that a system of nature could indeed subsist with such a universal law although men (like the South Sea islanders) should let their talents rest and resolve to devote their lives merely to idleness, amusement, and propagation of their species—in a word, to enjoyment; but he cannot possibly *will* that this should be a universal law of nature, or be implanted in us as such by a natural instinct. For, as a rational being, he necessarily wills that his faculties be developed, since they serve him and have been given him, for all sorts of possible purposes.

4. A fourth, who is in prosperity, while he sees that others have to contend with great wretchedness and that he could help them, thinks: "What concern is it of mine? Let everyone be as happy as Heaven pleases, or as he can make himself; I will take nothing from him nor even envy him, only I do not wish to contribute anything to his welfare or to his assistance in distress!" Now no doubt if such a mode of thinking were a universal law, the human race might very well subsist, and doubtless even better than in a state in which everyone talks of sympathy and good-will, or even takes care occasionally to put it into practice, but, on the other side, also cheats when he can, betrays the rights of men, or otherwise violates them. But although it is possible that a universal law of nature might exist in accordance with that maxim, it is impossible to *will* that such a principle should have the universal validity of a law of nature. For a will which resolved this would contradict itself, inasmuch as many cases might occur in which one would

have need of the love and sympathy of others, and in which, by such a law of nature, sprung from his own will, he would deprive himself of all hope of the aid he desires.

These are a few of the many actual duties, or at least what we regard as such, which obviously fall into two classes on the one principle that we have laid down. We must be *able to will* that a maxim of our action should be a universal law. This is the canon of the moral appreciation of the action generally. Some actions are of such a character that their maxim cannot without contradiction be even *conceived* as a universal law of nature, far from it being possible that we should *will* that it *should* be so. In others this intrinsic impossibility is not found, but still it is impossible to *will* that their maxim should be raised to the universality of a law of nature, since such a will would contradict itself. It is easily seen that the former violate strict or rigorous (inflexible) duty; the latter only laxer (meritorious) duty. Thus it has been completely shown how all duties depend as regards the nature of the obligation (not the object of the action) on the same principle.

If now we attend to ourselves on occasion of any transgression of duty, we shall find that we in fact do not will that our maxim should be a universal law, for that is impossible for us; on the contrary, we will that the opposite should remain a universal law, only we assume the liberty of making an *exception* in our own favour or (just for this time only) in favour of our inclination. Consequently if we considered all cases from one and the same point of view, namely, that of reason, we should find a contradiction in our own will, namely, that a certain principle should be objectively necessary as a universal law, and yet subjectively should not be universal, but admit of exceptions. As, however, we at one moment regard our action from the point of view of a will wholly conformed to reason, and then again look at the same action from the point of view of a will affected by inclination, there is not really any contradiction, but an antagonism of inclination to the precept of reason, whereby the universality of the principle is changed into a mere generality, so that the practical principle of reason shall meet the maxim half way. Now, although this cannot be justified in our own impartial judgement, yet it proves that we do really recognise the validity of the categorical imperative and (with all respect for it) only allow ourselves a few exceptions, which we think unimportant and forced from us.

We have thus established at least this much, that if duty is a conception which is to have any import and real legislative authority for our actions, it can only be expressed in categorical and not at all in hypothetical imperatives. We have also, which is of great importance, exhibited clearly and definitely for every practical application the content of the categorical imperative, which must contain the principle of all duty if there is such a thing at all. We have not yet, however, advanced so far as to prove *a priori* that there actually is such an imperative, that there is a practical law which commands absolutely of itself and without any other impulse, and that the following of this law is duty.

With the view of attaining to this, it is of extreme importance to remember that we must not allow ourselves to think of deducing the reality of this principle from the *particular attributes of human nature.* For duty is to be a practical, unconditional necessity of action; it must therefore hold for all rational beings (to whom an imperative can apply at all), and *for this reason only* be also a law for all human wills. On the contrary, whatever is deduced from the particular natural characteristics of humanity, from certain feelings and propensions, nay, even, if possible, from any particular tendency proper to human reason, and which need not necessarily hold for the will of every rational being; this may indeed supply us with a maxim, but not with a law; with a subjective principle on which we may have a propension and inclination to act, but not with an objective principle on which we should be *enjoined* to act, even though all our propensions, inclinations, and natural dispositions were opposed to it. In fact, the sublimity and intrinsic dignity of the command in duty are so much the more evident, the less the subjective impulses favour it and the more they oppose it, without being able in the slightest degree to weaken the obligation of the law or to diminish its validity.

Here then we see philosophy brought to a critical position, since it has to be firmly fixed, notwithstanding that it has nothing to support it in heaven or earth. Here it must show its purity as absolute director of its own laws, not the herald of those which are whispered to it by an implanted sense or who knows what tutelary nature. Although these may be better than nothing, yet they can never afford principles dictated by reason, which must have their source wholly *a priori* and thence their commanding authority, expecting everything from the supremacy of the law and the due respect for it, nothing from inclination, or else condemning the man to self-contempt and inward abhorrence.

Thus every empirical element is not only quite incapable of being an aid to the principle of morality, but is even highly prejudicial to the purity of morals; for the proper and inestimable worth of an absolutely good will consists just in this, that the principle of action is free from all influence of contingent grounds, which alone experience can furnish. We cannot too much or too often repeat our warning against this lax and even mean habit of thought which seeks for its principle amongst empirical motives and laws; for human reason in its weariness is glad to rest on this pillow, and in a dream of sweet illusions (in which, instead of Juno, it embraces a cloud) it substitutes for morality a bastard patched up from limbs of various derivation, which looks like anything one chooses to see in it, only not like virtue to one who has once beheld her in her true form.[7]

The question then is this: "Is it a necessary law *for all rational beings* that they should always judge of their actions by maxims of which they can themselves will that they should serve as universal laws?" If it is so, then it must be connected (altogether *a priori*) with the very conception of the will of a rational being generally. But in order to discover this connexion we must, however reluctantly, take a step into metaphysic, although into a domain of it which is distinct from speculative philosophy, namely, the metaphysic of morals. In a practical philosophy, where it is not the reasons of what *happens* that we have to ascertain, but the laws of what *ought to happen,* even although it never does, i.e., objective practical laws, there it is not necessary to inquire into the reasons why anything pleases or displeases, how the pleasure of mere sensation differs from taste, and whether the latter is distinct from a general satisfaction of reason; on what the feeling of pleasure or pain rests, and how from it desires and inclinations arise, and from these again maxims by the co-operation of reason: for all this belongs to an empirical psychology, which would constitute the second part of physics, if we regard physics as the *philosophy* of nature, so far as it is based on *empirical laws.* But here we are concerned with objective practical laws and, consequently, with the relation of the will to itself so far as it is determined by reason alone, in which case whatever has reference to anything empirical is necessarily excluded; since if *reason of itself alone* determines the conduct (and it is the possibility of this that we are now investigating), it must necessarily do so *a priori.*

The will is conceived as a faculty of determining oneself to action *in accordance with the conception of certain laws.* And such a faculty can be found only in rational beings. Now that which serves the will as the objective ground of its self-determination is the *end,* and if this is assigned by reason alone, it must hold for all rational beings. On the other hand, that which merely contains the ground of possibility of the action of which the effect is the end, this is called the *means.* The subjective ground of the desire is the *spring,* the objective ground of the volition is the *motive;* hence the distinction between subjective ends which rest on springs, and objective ends which depend on motives valid for every rational being. Practical principles are *formal* when they abstract from all subjective ends; they are *material* when they assume these, and therefore particular springs of action. The ends which a rational being proposes to himself at pleasure as *effects* of his actions (material ends) are all only relative, for it is only their relation to the particular desires of the subject that gives them their worth, which therefore cannot furnish principles universal and necessary for all rational beings and for every volition, that is to say practical laws. Hence all these relative ends can give rise only to hypothetical imperatives.

Supposing, however, that there were something *whose existence* has *in itself* an absolute worth, something which, being *an end in itself,* could be a source of definite laws; then in this and this alone would lie the source of a possible categorical imperative, *i.e.,* a practical law.

Now I say: man and generally any rational being *exists* as an end in himself, *not merely as a means* to be arbitrarily used by this or that will, but in all his actions, whether they concern himself or other rational beings, must be always regarded at the same time as an end. All objects of the inclinations have only a conditional worth, for if the inclinations and the wants founded on them did not exist, then their object would be without value. But the inclinations, themselves being sources of want, are so far from having an absolute worth for which they should be desired that, on the contrary, it must be the universal wish of every rational being to be wholly free from them. Thus the worth of any object which is *to be acquired* by our action is always conditional. Beings whose existence depends not on our will but on nature's, have nevertheless, if they are irrational beings, only a relative value as means, and are therefore called *things;* rational beings, on the contrary, are called *persons,* because their very nature points them out as ends in themselves, that is as something which must not be used merely as means, and so far therefore restricts freedom of action (and is an object of respect). These, therefore, are not merely subjective ends whose existence has a worth *for us* as an effect of our action, but *objective ends,* that is, things whose existence is an end in itself; an end moreover for which no other can be substituted, which they should subserve *merely* as means, for otherwise nothing whatever would possess *absolute worth;* but if all worth were conditioned and therefore contingent, then there would be no supreme practical principle of reason whatever.

If then there is a supreme practical principle or, in respect of the human will, a categorical imperative, it must be one which, being drawn from the conception of that which is necessarily an end for everyone because it is *an end in itself,* constitutes an *objective* principle of will, and can therefore serve as a universal practical law. The foundation of this principle is: *rational nature exists as an end in itself.* Man necessarily conceives his own existence as being so; so far then this is a *subjective* principle of human actions. But every other rational being regards its existence similarly, just on the same rational principle that holds for me: so that it is at the same time an objective principle, from which as a supreme practical law all laws of the will must be capable of being deduced. Accordingly the practical imperative will be as follows: *So act as to treat humanity, whether in thine own person or in that of any other, in every case as an end withal, never as means only.* . . .

ENDNOTES

1. Just as pure mathematics are distinguished from applied, pure logic from applied, so if we choose we may also distinguish pure philosophy of morals (metaphysic) from applied (viz. applied to human nature). By this designation we are also at once reminded that moral principles are not based on properties of human nature, but must subsist *a priori* of themselves, while from such principles practical rules must be capable of being deduced for every rational nature, and accodingly for that of man.

2. The dependence of the desires on sensations is called inclination, and this accordingly always indicates a *want.* The dependence of a contingently determinable will on principles of reason is called an *interest.* This, therefore, is found only in the case of a dependent will which does not always of itself conform to reason; in the Divine will we cannot conceive any interest. But the human will can also *take an interest* in a thing without therefore acting *from interest.* The former signifies the *practical* interest in the action, the latter the *pathological* in the object of the action. The former indicates only dependence of the will on principles of reason in themselves; the second, dependence on principles of reason for the sake of inclination, reason supplying only the practical rules how the requirement of the inclination may be satisfied. In the first case the action interests me; in the second the object of the action (because it is pleasant to me). We have seen in the first section that in an action done from duty we must look not to the interest in the object, but only to that in the action itself, and in its rational principle (viz. the law).

3. The word *prudence* is take in two senses: in the one it may bear the name of knowledge of the world, in the other that of

private prudence. The former is a man's ability to influence others so as to use them for his own purposes. The latter is the sagacity to combine all these purposes for his own lasting benefit. This latter is properly that to which the value even of the former is reduced, and when a man is prudent in the former sense, but not in the latter, we might better say of him that he is clever and cunning, but, on the whole, imprudent.

4. I connect the act with the will without presupposing any condition resulting from any inclination, but *a priori,* and therefore necessarily (though only objectively, *i.e.* assuming the idea of a reason possessing full power over all subjective motives). This is accordingly a practical proposition which does not deduce the willing of an action by mere analysis from another already presupposed (for we have not such a perfect will), but connects it immediately with the conception of the will of a rational being, as something not contained in it.

5. A maxim is a subjective principle of action, and must be distinguished from the *objective principle,* namely, practical law. The former contains the practical rule set by reason according to the conditions of the subject (often its ignorance or its inclinations), so that it is the principle on which the subject *acts;* but the law is the objective principle valid for every rational being, and is the principle on which it *ought to act* that is an imperative.

6. It must be noted here that I reserve the division of duties for a future *metaphysic of morals;* so that I give it here only as an arbitrary one (in order to arrange my examples). For the rest, I understand by a perfect duty one that admits no exception in favour of inclination and then I have not merely external but also internal perfect duties. This is contrary to the use of the word adopted in the schools; but I do not intend to justify there, as it is all one for my purpose whether it is admitted or not.

7. To behold virtue in her proper form is nothing else but to contemplate morality stripped of all admixture of sensible things and of every spurious ornament of reward or self-love. How much she then eclipses everything else that appears charming to the affections, every one may readily perceive with the least exertion of his reason, if it be not wholly spoiled for abstraction.

QUESTIONS ON KANT

1. Give an example in which someone acts *from duty* and another example in which a person acts *in conformity* with duty. Why is it important to act *from* duty? Are there any instances in which an action *from* duty might be less moral than an action motivated by some feeling or emotion?

2. Kant offers four examples of the application of the categorical imperative. Explain how Kant employs the categorical imperative in each of these. Do you find his application of universalizability to be successful?

3. Do you think that the categorical imperative proves to be a sufficient test of moral obligation? Or is it but a necessary condition of moral obligation?

4. Consider the second formulation of the categorical imperative. Explain in your own words what it means to treat someone as "a means only." How do you distinguish between treating someone as a "means" and treating someone as a "means only"? Does economic life require us to treat others as "means" to our ends? Does it also require that we treat others as a "means only"?

5. Are there instances in which a businessperson (or a firm) should act from principle (or out of duty) regardless of the consequences? Explain with examples.

What Utilitarianism Is

John Stuart Mill

J. S. Mill (1806–1873) was born in London and received an intensive education from his father, learning Greek at the age of three, logic by the age of twelve. A logician (System of Logic, *1843), economist* (Principles of Political Economy, *1848), and philosopher, Mill is the author of the celebrated* On Liberty *(1859) as well as the work* Utilitarianism *(1861), from which this selection is drawn.*

A passing remark is all that needs be given to the ignorant blunder of supposing that those who stand up for utility as the test of right and wrong, use the term in that restricted and merely colloquial sense in which utility is opposed to pleasure. An apology is due to the philosophical opponents of utilitarianism, for even the momentary appearance of confounding them with any one capable of so absurd a misconception; which is the more extraordinary, inasmuch as the contrary accusation, of referring everything to pleasure, and that too in its grossest form, is another of the common charges against utilitarianism: and, as has been pointedly remarked by an able writer, the same sort of persons, and often the very same persons, denounce the theory "as impracticably dry when the word utility precedes the word pleasure, and as too practically voluptuous when the word pleasure precedes the word utility." Those who know anything about the matter are aware that every writer, from Epicurus to Bentham, who maintained the theory of utility, meant by it, not something to be contradistinguished from pleasure, but pleasure itself, together with exemption from pain; and instead of opposing the useful to the agreeable or the ornamental, have always declared that the useful means these, among other things. Yet the common herd, including the herd of writers, not only in newspapers and periodicals, but in books of weight and pretension, are perpetually falling into this shallow mistake. Having caught up the word utilitarian, while knowing nothing whatever about it but its sound, they habitually express by it the rejection, or the neglect, of pleasure in some of its forms; of beauty, of ornament, or of amusement. Nor is the term thus ignorantly misapplied solely in disparagement, but occasionally in compliment; as though it implied superiority to frivolity and the mere pleasures of the moment. And this perverted use is the only one in which the word is popularly known, and the one from which the new generation are acquiring their sole notion of its meaning. Those who introduced the word, but who had for many years discontinued it as a distinctive appellation, may well feel themselves called upon to resume it, if by doing so they can hope to contribute anything towards rescuing it from this utter degradation.[1]

The creed which accepts as the foundation of morals, Utility, or the Greatest Happiness Principle, holds that actions are right in proportion as they tend to promote happiness, wrong as they tend to produce the reverse of happiness. By happiness is intended pleasure, and the absence of pain; by unhappiness, pain, and the privation of pleasure. To give a clear view of the moral standard set up by the theory, much more requires to be said; in particular, what things it includes in the ideas of pain and pleasure; and to what extent this is left an open question. But these supplementary explanations do not affect the theory of life on which this theory of morality is grounded—namely, that pleasure, and freedom from pain, are the only things desirable as ends; and that all desirable things (which are as numerous in the utilitarian as in any other scheme) are desirable either for the pleasure inherent in themselves, or as means to the promotion of pleasure and the prevention of pain.

Now, such a theory of life excites in many minds, and among them in some of the most estimable in feeling and purpose, inveterate dislike. To suppose that life has (as they express it) no higher end than pleasure—no better and nobler object of desire and pursuit—they designate as utterly mean and grovelling; as a doctrine worthy only of swine, to whom the followers of Epicurus

were, at a very early period, contemptuously likened; and modern holders of the doctrine are occasionally made the subject of equally polite comparisons by its German, French, and English assailants.

When thus attacked, the Epicureans have always answered, that it is not they, but their accusers, who represent human nature in a degrading light; since the accusation supposes human beings to be capable of no pleasures except those of which swine are capable. If this supposition were true, the charge could not be gainsaid, but would then be no longer an imputation; for if the sources of pleasure were precisely the same to human beings and to swine, the rule of life which is good enough for the one would be good enough for the other. The comparison of the Epicurean life to that of beasts is felt as degrading, precisely because a beast's pleasures do not satisfy a human being's conceptions of happiness. Human beings have faculties more elevated than the animal appetites, and when once made conscious of them, do not regard anything as happiness which does not include their gratification. I do not, indeed, consider the Epicureans to have been by any means faultless in drawing out their scheme of consequences from the utilitarian principle. To do this in any sufficient manner, many Stoic, as well as Christian elements require to be included. But there is no known Epicurean theory of life which does not assign to the pleasures of the intellect, of the feelings and imagination, and of the moral sentiments, a much higher value as pleasures than to those of mere sensation. It must be admitted, however, that utilitarian writers in general have placed the superiority of mental over bodily pleasures chiefly in the greater permanency, safety, uncostliness, etc., of the former—that is, in their circumstantial advantages rather than in their intrinsic nature. And on all these points utilitarians have fully proved their case; but they might have taken the other, and, as it may be called, higher ground, with entire consistency. It is quite compatible with the principle of utility to recognise the fact, that some kinds of pleasure are more desirable and more valuable than others. It would be absurd that while, in estimating all other things, quality is considered as well as quantity, the estimation of pleasures should be supposed to depend on quantity alone.

If I am asked, what I mean by difference of quality in pleasures, or what makes one pleasure more valuable than another, merely as a pleasure, except its being greater in amount, there is but one possible answer. Of two pleasures, if there be one to which all or almost all who have experience of both give a decided preference, irrespective of any feeling of moral obligation to prefer it, that is the more desirable pleasure. If one of the two is, by those who are competently acquainted with both, placed so far above the other that they prefer it, even though knowing it to be attended with a greater amount of discontent, and would not resign it for any quantity of the other pleasure which their nature is capable of, we are justified in ascribing to the preferred enjoyment a superiority in quality, so far outweighing quantity as to render it, in comparison, of small account.

Now it is an unquestionable fact that those who are equally acquainted with, and equally capable of appreciating and enjoying, both, do give a most marked preference to the manner of existence which employs their higher faculties. Few human creatures would consent to be changed into any of the lower animals, for a promise of the fullest allowance of a beast's pleasures; no intelligent human being would consent to be a fool, no instructed person would be an ignoramus, no person of feeling and conscience would be selfish and base, even though they should be persuaded that the fool, the dunce, or the rascal is better satisfied with his lot than they are with theirs. They would not resign what they possess more than he for the most complete satisfaction of all the desires which they have in common with him. If they ever fancy they would, it is only in cases of unhappiness so extreme, that to escape from it they would exchange their lot for almost any other, however undesirable in their own eyes. A being of higher faculties requires more to make him happy, is capable probably of more acute suffering, and certainly accessible to it at more points, than one of an inferior type; but in spite of these liabilities, he can never really wish to sink into what he feels to be a lower grade of existence. We may give what explanation we please of this unwillingness; we may attribute it to pride, a name which is given indiscriminately to some of the most and to some of the least estimable feelings of which mankind are capable: we may refer it to the love of liberty and personal independence, an appeal to which was with the Stoics one of the most effective means for the inculcation of it; to the love of power, or to the love of excitement, both of which do really enter into and contribute to it: but its most appropriate appellation is a sense of dignity, which all human beings possess in one form or other, and in some, though by no means in exact, proportion to their higher faculties, and which is so essential a part of the happiness of those in whom it is strong, that nothing which conflicts with it could be, otherwise than momentarily, an object of desire to them.

Whoever supposes that this preference takes place at a sacrifice of happiness—that the superior being, in anything like equal circumstances, is not happier than the inferior—confounds the two very different ideas, of happiness, and content. It is indisputable that the being whose capacities of enjoyment are low, has the greatest chance of having them fully satisfied; and a highly endowed being will always feel that any happiness which he can look for, as the world is constituted, is imperfect. But he can learn to bear its imperfections, if they are at all bearable; and they will not make him envy the being who is indeed unconscious of the imperfections, but only because he feels not at all the good which those imperfections qualify. It is better to be a human being dissatisfied than a pig satisfied; better to be Socrates dissatisfied than a fool satisfied. And if the fool, or the pig, are of a different opinion, it is because they only know their own side of the question. The other party to the comparison knows both sides.

It may be objected, that many who are capable of the higher pleasures, occasionally, under the influence of temptation, postpone them to the lower. But this is quite compatible with a full appreciation of the intrinsic superiority of the higher. Men often, from infirmity of character, make their election for the nearer good, though they know it to be the less valuable; and this no less when the choice is between two bodily pleasures, than when it is between bodily and mental. They pursue sensual indulgences to the injury of health, though perfectly aware that health is the greater good.

It may be further objected, that many who begin with youthful enthusiasm for everything noble, as they advance in years sink into indolence and selfishness. But I do not believe that those who undergo this very common change, voluntarily choose the lower description of pleasures in preference to the higher. I believe that before they devote themselves exclusively to the one, they have already become incapable of the other. Capacity for the nobler feelings is in most natures a very tender plant, easily killed, not only by hostile influences, but by mere want of sustenance; and in the majority of young persons it speedily dies away if the occupations to which their position in life has devoted them, and the society into which it has thrown them, are not favourable to keeping that higher capacity in exercise. Men lose their high aspirations as they lose their intellectual tastes, because they have not time or opportunity for indulging them; and they addict themselves to inferior pleasures, not because they deliberately prefer them, but because they are either the only ones to which they have access, or the only ones which they are any longer capable of enjoying. It may be questioned whether any one who has remained equally susceptible to both classes of pleasures, ever knowingly and calmly preferred the lower; though many, in all ages, have broken down in an ineffectual attempt to combine both.

From this verdict of the only competent judges, I apprehend there can be no appeal. On a question which is the best worth having of two pleasures, or which of two modes of existence is the most grateful to the feelings, apart from its moral attributes and from its consequences, the judgment of those who are qualified by knowledge of both, or, if they differ, that of the majority among them, must be admitted as final. And there needs be the less hesitation to accept this judgment respecting the quality of pleasures, since there is no other tribunal to be referred to even on the question of quantity. What means are there of determining which is the acutest of two pains, or the intensest of two pleasurable sensations, except the general suffrage of those who are familiar with both? Neither pains nor pleasures are homogeneous, and pain is always heterogeneous with pleasure. What is there to decide whether a particular pleasure is worth purchasing at the cost of a particular pain, except the feelings and judgment of the experienced? When, therefore, those feelings and judgment declare the pleasures derived from the higher faculties to be preferable in kind, apart from the question of intensity, to those of which the animal nature, disjoined from the higher faculties, is susceptible, they are entitled on this subject to the same regard.

I have dwelt on this point, as being a necessary part of a perfectly just conception of Utility or Happiness, considered as the directive rule of human conduct. But it is by no means an indispensable condition to the acceptance of the utilitarian standard; for that standard is not the agent's own greatest happiness, but the greatest amount of happiness altogether; and if it may possibly be doubted whether a noble character is always the happier for its nobleness, there can be no doubt that it makes other people happier, and that the world in general is immensely a gainer by it. Utilitarianism, therefore, could only attain its end by the general cultivation of nobleness of character, even if each individual were only benefited by the nobleness of others, and his own, so far as happiness is concerned, were a sheer deduction from the benefit. But the bare enunciation of such an absurdity as this last, renders refutation superfluous.

According to the Greatest Happiness Principle, as above explained, the ultimate end, with reference to and for the sake of which all other things are desirable (whether we are considering our own good or that of other people), is an existence exempt as far as possible from pain, and as rich as possible in enjoyments, both in point of quantity and quality; the test of quality, and the rule for measuring it against quantity, being the preference felt by those who in their opportunities of experience, to which must be added their habits of self-consciousness and self-observation, are best furnished with the means of comparison. This, being, according to the utilitarian opinion, the end of human action, is necessarily also the standard of morality; which may accordingly be defined, the rules and precepts for human conduct, by the observance of which an existence such as has been described might be, to the greatest extent possible, secured to all mankind; and not to them only, but, so far as the nature of things admits, to the whole sentient creation.

Against this doctrine, however, arises another class of objectors, who say that happiness, in any form, cannot be the rational purpose of human life and action; because, in the first place, it is unattainable: and they contemptuously ask, what right hast thou to be happy?—a question which Mr. Carlyle clenches by the addition, What right, a short time ago, hadst thou even *to be*? Next, they say, that men can do *without* happiness; that all noble human beings have felt this, and could not have become noble but by learning the lesson of *Entsagen*, or renunciation; which lesson, thoroughly learnt and submitted to, they affirm to be the beginning and necessary condition of all virtue.

The first of these objections would go to the root of the matter were it well founded; for if no happiness is to be had at all by human beings, the attainment of it cannot be the end of morality, or of any rational conduct. Though, even in that case, something might still be said for the utilitarian theory; since utility includes not solely the pursuit of happiness, but the prevention or mitigation of unhappiness; and if the former aim be chimerical, there will be all the greater scope and more imperative need for the latter, so long at least as mankind think fit to live, and do not take refuge in the simultaneous act of suicide recommended under certain conditions by Novalis. When, however, it is thus positively asserted to be impossible that human life should be happy, the assertion, if not something like a verbal quibble, is at least an exaggeration. If by happiness be meant a continuity of highly pleasurable excitement, it is evident enough that this is impossible. A state of exalted pleasure lasts only moments, or in some cases, and with some intermissions, hours or days, and is the occasional brilliant flash of enjoyment, not its permanent and steady flame. Of this the philosophers who have taught that happiness is the end of life were as fully aware as those who taunt them. The happiness which they meant was not a life of rapture; but moments of such, in an existence made up of few and transitory pains, many and various pleasures, with a decided predominance of the active over the passive, and having as the foundation of the whole, not to expect more from life than it is capable of bestowing. A life thus composed, to those who have been fortunate enough to obtain it, has always appeared worthy of the name of happiness. And such an existence is even now the lot of many, during some considerable portion of their lives. The present wretched education, and wretched social arrangements, are the only real hindrance to its being attainable by almost all.

The objectors perhaps may doubt whether human beings, if taught to consider happiness as the end of life, would be satisfied with such a moderate share of it. But great numbers of mankind have been satisfied with much less. The main constituents of a satisfied life appear to be two, either of which by itself is often found sufficient for the purpose: tranquillity, and excitement. With much tranquillity, many find that they can be content with very little pleasure: with much excitement, many can reconcile themselves to a considerable quantity of pain. There is assuredly no inherent impossibility in enabling even the mass of mankind to unite both; since the two are so far from being incompatible that they are in natural alliance, the prolongation of either being a preparation for, and exciting a wish for, the other. It is only those in whom indolence amounts to a vice, that do not desire excitement after an interval of repose: it is only those in whom the need of excitement is a disease, that feel the tranquillity which follows excitement dull and insipid, instead of pleasurable in direct proportion to the excitement which preceded it. When people who are tolerably fortunate in their outward lot do not find in life sufficient enjoyment to make it valuable to them, the cause generally is, caring for nobody but themselves. To those who have neither public nor private affections, the excitements of life are much curtailed, and in any case dwindle in value as the time approaches when all selfish interests must be terminated by death: while those who leave after them objects of personal affection, and especially those who have also cultivated a fellow-feeling with the collective interests of mankind, retain as lively an interest in life on the eve of death as in the vigour of youth and health. Next to selfishness, the principal cause which makes life unsatisfactory is want of mental cultivation. A cultivated mind—I do not mean that of a philosopher, but any mind to which the fountains of knowledge have been opened, and which has been taught, in any tolerable degree, to exercise its faculties—finds sources of inexhaustible interest in all that surrounds it; in the objects of nature, the achievements of art, the imaginations of poetry, the incidents of history, the ways of mankind, past and present, and their prospects in the future. It is possible, indeed, to become indifferent to all this, and that too without having exhausted a thousandth part of it; but only when one has had from the beginning no moral or human interest in these things, and has sought in them only the gratification of curiosity.

Now there is absolutely no reason in the nature of things why an amount of mental culture sufficient to give an intelligent interest in these objects of contemplation, should not be the inheritance of every one born in a civilised country. As little is there an inherent necessity that any human being should be a selfish egotist, devoid of every feeling or care but those which centre in his own miserable individuality. Something far superior to this is sufficiently common even now, to give ample earnest of what the human species may be made. Genuine private affections and a sincere interest in the public good, are possible, though in unequal degrees, to every rightly brought up human being. In a world in which there is so much to interest, so much to enjoy, and so much also to correct and improve, every one who has this moderate amount of moral and intellectual requisites is capable of an existence which may be called enviable; and unless such a person, through bad laws, or subjection to the will of others, is denied the liberty to use the sources of happiness within his reach, he will not fail to find this enviable existence, if he escape the positive evils of life, the great sources of physical and mental suffering—such as indigence, disease, and the unkindness, worthlessness, or premature loss of objects of affection. The main stress of the problem lies, therefore, in the contest with these calamities, from which it is a rare good fortune entirely to escape; which, as things now are, cannot be obviated, and often cannot be in any material degree mitigated. Yet no one whose opinion deserves a moment's consideration can doubt that most of the great positive evils of the world are in themselves removable, and will, if human affairs continue to improve, be in the end reduced within narrow limits. Poverty, in any sense implying suffering, may be completely extinguished by the wisdom of society, combined with the good sense and providence of individuals. Even that most intractable of enemies, disease, may be indefinitely reduced in dimensions by good physical and moral education, and proper control of noxious influences; while the progress of science holds out a promise for the future of still more direct conquests over this detestable foe. And every advance in that direction relieves us from some, not only of the chances which cut short our own lives, but, what concerns us still more, which deprive us of those in whom our happiness is wrapt up. As for vicissitudes of fortune, and other disappointments connected with worldly circumstances, these are principally the effect either of gross imprudence, of ill-regulated desires, or of bad or imperfect social institutions.

All the grand sources, in short, of human suffering are in a great degree, many of them almost entirely, conquerable by human care and effort; and though their removal is grievously slow—though a long succession of generations will perish in the breach before the conquest is completed, and this world becomes all that, if will and knowledge were not wanting, it might easily be made—yet every mind sufficiently intelligent and generous to bear a part, however small and unconspicuous, in the endeavour, will draw a noble enjoyment from the contest itself, which he would not for any bribe in the form of selfish indulgence consent to be without.

And this leads to the true estimation of what is said by the objectors concerning the possibility, and the obligation, of learning to do without happiness. Unquestionably it is possible to do without happiness; it is done involuntarily by nineteen-twentieths of mankind, even in those parts of our present world which are least deep in barbarism; and it often has to be done voluntarily by the hero or the martyr, for the sake of something which he prizes more than his individual happiness. But this something, what is it, unless the happiness of others or some of the requisites of happiness? It is noble to be capable of resigning entirely one's own portion of happiness, or chances of it: but, after all, this self-sacrifice must be for some end; it is not its own end; and if we are told that its end is not happiness, but virtue, which is better than happiness, I ask, would the sacrifice be made if the hero or martyr did not believe that it would earn for others immunity from similar sacrifices? Would it be made if he thought that his renunciation of happiness for himself would produce no fruit for any of his fellow creatures, but to make their lot like his, and place them also in the condition of persons who have renounced happiness? All honour to those who can abnegate for themselves the personal enjoyment of life, when by such renunciation they contribute worthily to increase the amount of happiness in the world; but he who does it, or professes to do it, for any other purpose, is no more deserving of admiration than the ascetic mounted on his pillar. He may be an inspiriting proof of what men can do, but assuredly not an example of what they should.

Though it is only in a very imperfect state of the world's arrangements that any one can best serve the happiness of others by the absolute sacrifice of his own, yet so long as the world is in that imperfect state, I fully acknowledge that the readiness to make such a sacrifice is the highest virtue which can be found in man. I will add, that in this condition the world, paradoxical as the assertion may be, the conscious ability to do without happiness gives the best prospect of realising, such happiness as is attainable. For nothing except that consciousness can raise a person above the chances of life, by making him feel that, let fate and fortune do their worst, they have not power to subdue him: which, once felt, frees him from excess of anxiety concerning the evils of life, and enables him, like many a Stoic in the worst times of the Roman Empire, to cultivate in tranquillity the sources of satisfaction accessible to him, without concerning himself about the uncertainty of their duration, any more than about their inevitable end.

Meanwhile, let utilitarians never cease to claim the morality of self-devotion as a possession which belongs by as good a right to them, as either to the Stoic or to the Transcendentalist. The utilitarian morality does recognise in human beings the power of sacrificing their own greatest good for the good of others. It only refuses to admit that the sacrifice is itself a good. A sacrifice which does not increase, or tend to increase, the sum total of happiness, it considers as wasted. The only self-renunciation which it applauds, is devotion to the happiness, or to some of the means of happiness, of others; either of mankind collectively, or of individuals within the limits imposed by the collective interests of mankind.

I must again repeat, what the assailants of utilitarianism seldom have the justice to acknowledge, that the happiness which forms the utilitarian standard of what is right in conduct, is not the agent's own happiness, but that of all concerned. As between his own happiness and that of others, utilitarianism requires him to be as strictly impartial as a disinterested and benevolent spectator. In the golden rule of Jesus of Nazareth, we read the complete spirit of the ethics of utility. To do as you would be done by, and to love your neighbour as yourself, constitute the ideal perfection of utilitarian morality. As the means of making the nearest approach to this ideal, utility would enjoin, first, that laws and social arrangements should place the happiness, or (as speaking practically it may be called) the interest, of every individual, as nearly as possible in harmony with the interest of the whole; and secondly, that education and opinion, which have so vast a power over human character, should so use that power as to establish in the mind of every individual an indissoluble association between his own happiness and the good of the whole; especially between his own happiness and the practice of such modes of conduct, negative and positive, as regard for the universal happiness prescribes; so that not only he may be unable to conceive the possibility of happiness to himself, consistently with conduct opposed to the general good, but also that a direct impulse to promote the general good may be in every individual one of the habitual motives of action, and the sentiments connected therewith may fill a large and prominent place in every human being's sentient existence. If the impugners of the utilitarian morality represented it to their own minds in this, its true character, I know not what recommendation possessed by any other morality they could possibly affirm to be wanting to it; what more beautiful or more exalted developments of human nature any other ethical system can be supposed to foster, or what springs of action, not accessible to the utilitarian, such systems rely on for giving effect to their mandates.

The objectors to utilitarianism cannot always be charged with representing it in a discreditable light. On the contrary, those among them who entertain anything like a just idea of its disinterested character, sometimes find fault with its standard as being too high for humanity. They say it is exacting too much to require that people shall always act from the inducement of promoting the general interests of society. But this is to mistake the very meaning of a standard of morals, and confound the rule of action with the motive of it. It is the business of ethics to tell us what are our duties, or by what test we may know them; but no system of ethics requires that the sole motive of all we do shall be a feeling of duty; on the contrary, ninety-nine hundredths of all our actions are done from other motives, and rightly so done, if the rule of duty does not condemn them. It is the more unjust to utilitarianism that this particular misapprehension should be made a ground of objection to it, inasmuch as utilitarian moralists have gone beyond almost all others in affirming that the motive has nothing to do with the morality of the action, though much with the worth of the agent. He who saves a fellow creature from drowning does what is morally right, whether his motive be duty, or the hope of being paid for his trouble; he who betrays the friend that trusts him, is guilty of a crime, even if his object be to serve another friend to whom he is under greater obligations.

But to speak only of actions done from the motive of duty, and in direct obedience to principle: it is a misapprehension of the utilitarian mode of thought, to conceive it as implying that people should fix their minds upon so wide a generality as the world, or society at large. The great majority of good actions are intended not for the benefit of the world, but for that of individuals, of which the good of the world is made up; and the thoughts of the most virtuous man need not on these occasions travel beyond the particular persons concerned, except so far as is necessary to assure himself that in benefiting them he is not violating the rights, that is, the legitimate and authorised expectations, of any one else. The multiplication of happiness is, according to the utilitarian ethics, the object of virtue: the occasions on which any person (except one in a thousand) has it in his power to do this on an extended scale, in other words to be a public benefactor, are but exceptional; and on these occasions alone is he called on to consider public utility; in every other case, private utility, the interest or happiness of some few persons, is all he has to attend to. Those alone the influence of whose actions extends to society in general, need concern themselves habitually about so large an object. In the case of abstinences indeed—of things which people forbear to do from moral considerations, though the consequences in the particular case might be beneficial—it would be unworthy of an intelligent agent not to be consciously aware that the action is of a class which, if practised generally, would be generally injurious, and that this is the ground of the obligation to abstain from it. The amount of regard for the public interest implied in this recognition, is no greater than is demanded by every system of morals, for they all enjoin to abstain from whatever is manifestly pernicious to society.

The same considerations dispose of another reproach against the doctrine of utility, founded on a still grosser misconception of the purpose of a standard of morality, and of the very meaning of the words right and wrong. It is often affirmed that utilitarianism renders men cold and unsympathising; that it chills their moral feelings towards individuals; that it makes them regard only the dry and hard consideration of the consequences of actions, not taking into their moral estimate the qualities from which those actions emanate. If the assertion means that they do not allow their judgment respecting the rightness or wrongness of an action to be influenced by their opinion of the qualities of the person who does it, this is a complaint not against utilitarianism, but against having any standard of morality at all; for certainly no known ethical standard decides an action to be good or bad because it is done by a good or a bad man, still less because done by an amiable, a brave, or a benevolent man, or the contrary. These considerations are relevant, not to the estimation of actions, but of persons; and there is nothing in the utilitarian theory inconsistent with the fact that there are other things which interest us in persons besides the rightness and wrongness of their actions. The Stoics, indeed, with the paradoxical misuse of language which was part of their system, and by which they strove to raise themselves above all concern about anything but virtue, were fond of saying that he who has that has everything; that he, and only he, is rich, is beautiful, is a king. But no claim of this description is made for the virtuous man by the utilitarian doctrine. Utilitarians are quite aware that there are other desirable possessions and qualities besides virtue, and are perfectly willing to allow to all of them their full worth. They are also aware that a right action does not necessarily indicate a virtuous character, and that actions which are blamable, often proceed from qualities entitled to praise. When this is apparent in any particular case, it modifies their estimation, not certainly of the act, but of the agent. I grant that they are, notwithstanding, of opinion, that in the long run the best proof of a good character is good actions; and resolutely refuse to consider any mental disposition as good, of which the predominant tendency is to produce bad conduct. This makes them unpopular with many people; but it is an unpopularity which they must share with every one who regards the distinction between right and wrong in a serious light; and the reproach is not one which a conscientious utilitarian need be anxious to repel.

If no more be meant by the objection than that many utilitarians look on the morality of actions, as measured by the utilitarian standard, with too exclusive a regard, and do not lay sufficient stress upon the other beauties of character which go towards making a human being lovable or admirable, this may be admitted. Utilitarians who have cultivated their moral feelings, but not their sympathies nor their artistic perceptions, do fall into this mistake; and so do all other moralists under the same conditions. What can be said in excuse for other moralists is equally available for them, namely, that, if there is to be any error, it is better that it should be on that side. As a matter of fact, we may affirm that among utilitarians as among adherents of other systems, there is every imaginable degree of rigidity and of laxity in the application of their standard: some are even puritanically rigorous, while others are as indulgent as can possibly be desired by sinner or by sentimentalist. But on the whole, a doctrine which brings prominently forward the interest that mankind have in the repression and prevention of conduct which violates the moral law, is likely to be inferior to no other in turning the sanctions of opinion against such violations. It is true, the question, What does violate the moral law? is one on which those who recognise different standards of morality are likely now and then to differ. But difference of opinion on moral questions was not first introduced into the world by utilitarianism, while that doctrine does supply, if not always an easy, at all events a tangible and intelligible, mode of deciding such differences.

It may not be superfluous to notice a few more of the common misapprehensions of utilitarian ethics, even those which are so obvious and gross that it might appear impossible for any person of candour and intelligence to fall into them; since persons, even of considerable mental endowments, often give themselves so little trouble to understand the bearings of any opinion against which they entertain a prejudice, and men are in general so little conscious of this voluntary ignorance as a defect, that the vulgarest misunderstandings of ethical doctrines are continually met with in the deliberate writings of persons of the greatest pretensions both to high principle and to philosophy. We not uncommonly hear the doctrine of utility inveighed against as a *godless* doctrine. If it be necessary to say anything at all against so mere an assumption, we may say that the question depends upon what idea we have formed of the moral character of the Deity. If it be a true belief that God desires, above all things, the happiness of his creatures, and that this was his purpose in their creation, utility is not only not a godless doctrine, but more profoundly religious than any other. If it be meant that utilitarianism does not recognise the revealed will of God as the supreme law of morals, I answer, that a utilitarian who believes in the perfect goodness and wisdom of *God,* necessarily believes that whatever God has thought fit to reveal on the subject of morals, must fulfil the requirements of utility in a supreme degree. But others besides utilitarians have been of opinion that the Christian revelation was intended, and is fitted, to inform the hearts and minds of mankind with a spirit which should enable them to find for themselves what is right, and incline them to do it when found, rather than to tell them, except in a very general way, what it is; and that we need a doctrine of ethics, carefully followed out, to *interpret* to us the will of God. Whether this opinion is correct or not, it is superfluous here to discuss; since whatever aid religion, either natural or revealed, can afford to ethical investigation, is as open to the utilitarian moralist as to any other. He can use it as the testimony of God to the usefulness or hurtfulness of any given course of action, by as good a right as others can use it for the indication of a transcendental law, having no connection with usefulness or with happiness.

Again, Utility is often summarily stigmatised as an immoral doctrine by giving it the name of Expediency, and taking advantage of the popular use of that term to contrast it with Principle. But the Expedient, in the sense in which it is opposed to the Right, generally means that which is expedient for the particular interest of the agent himself; as when a minister sacrifices the interests of his country to keep himself in place. When it means anything better than this, it means that which is expedient for some immediate object, some temporary purpose, but which violates a rule whose observance is expedient in a much higher degree. The Expedient, in this sense, instead of being the same thing with the useful, is a branch of the hurtful. Thus, it would often be expedient, for the purpose of getting over some momentary embarrassment, or attaining some object immediately useful to ourselves or others, to tell a lie. But inasmuch as the cultivation in ourselves of a sensitive feeling on the subject of veracity, is one of the most useful, and the enfeeblement of that feeling one of the most hurtful, things to which our conduct can be instrumental; and inasmuch as any, even unintentional, deviation from truth, does that much towards weakening the trustworthiness of human assertion, which is not only the principal support of all present social well-being, but the insufficiency of which does more than any one thing that can be named to keep back civilisation, virtue, everything on which human happiness on the largest scale depends; we feel that the violation, for a present advantage, of a rule of such transcendant expediency, is not expedient, and that he who, for the sake of a convenience to himself or to some other individual, does what depends on him to deprive mankind of the good, and inflict upon them the evil, involved in the greater or less reliance which they can place in each other's word, acts the part of one of their worst enemies. Yet that even this rule, sacred as it is, admits of possible exceptions, is acknowledged by all moralists; the chief of which is when the withholding of some fact (as of information from a malefactor, or of bad news from a person dangerously ill) would save an individual (especially an individual other than oneself) from great and unmerited evil, and when the withholding can only be effected by denial. But in order that the exception may not extend itself beyond the need, and may have the least possible effect in weakening reliance on veracity, it ought to be recognised, and, if possible, its limits defined; and if the principle of utility is good for anything, it must be good for weighing these conflicting utilities against one another, and marking out the region within which one or the other preponderates.

Again, defenders of utility often find themselves called upon to reply to such objections as this—that there is not time, previous to action, for calculating and weighing the effects of any line of conduct on the general happiness. This is exactly as if any one were to say that it is impossible to guide our conduct by Christianity, because there is not time, on every occasion on which anything has to be done, to read through the Old and New Testaments. The answer to the objection is, that there has been ample time, namely, the whole past duration of the human species. During all that time, mankind have been learning by experience the tendencies of actions; on which experience all the prudence, as well as all the morality of life, are dependent. People talk as if the commencement of this course of experience had hitherto been put off, and as if, at the moment when some man feels tempted to meddle with the property or life of another, he had to begin considering for the first time whether murder and theft are injurious to human happiness. Even then I do not think that he would find the question very puzzling; but, at all events, the matter is now done to his hand.

It is truly a whimsical supposition that, if mankind were agreed in considering utility to be the test of morality, they would remain without any agreement as to what is useful, and would take no measures for having their notions on the subject taught to the young, and enforced by law and opinion. There is no difficulty in proving any ethical standard whatever to work ill, if we suppose universal idiocy to be conjoined with it; but on any hypothesis short of that, mankind must by this time have acquired positive beliefs as to the effects of some actions on their happiness; and the beliefs which have thus come down are the rules of morality for the multitude, and for the philosopher until he has succeeded in finding better. That philosophers might easily do this, even now, on many subjects; that the received code of ethics is by no means of divine right; and that mankind have still much to learn as to the effects of actions on the general happiness, I admit, or rather, earnestly maintain. The corollaries from the principle of utility, like the precepts of every practical art, admit of indefinite improvement, and, in a progressive state of the human mind, their improvement is perpetually going on.

But to consider the rules of morality as improvable, is one thing; to pass over the intermediate generalisations entirely, and endeavour to test each individual action directly by the first principle, is another. It is a strange notion that the acknowledgment of a first principle is inconsistent with the admission of secondary ones. To inform a traveller respecting the place of his ultimate destination, is not to forbid the use of landmarks and direction-posts on the way. The proposition that happiness is the end and aim of morality, does not mean that no road ought to be laid down to that goal, or that persons going thither should not be advised to take one direction rather than another. Men really ought to leave off talking a kind of nonsense on this subject, which they would neither talk nor listen to on other matters of practical concernment. Nobody argues that the art of navigation is not founded on astronomy, because sailors cannot wait to calculate the Nautical Almanack. Being rational creatures, they go to sea with it ready calculated; and all rational creatures go out upon the sea of life with their minds made up on the common questions of right and wrong, as well as on many of the far more difficult questions of wise and foolish. And this, as long as foresight is a human quality, it is to be presumed they will continue to do. Whatever we adopt as the fundamental principle of morality, we require subordinate principles to apply it by; the impossibility of doing without them, being common to all systems, can afford no argument against any one in particular; but gravely to argue as if no such secondary principles could be had, and as if mankind had remained till now, and always must remain, without drawing any general conclusions from the experience of human life, is as high a pitch, I think, as absurdity has ever reached in philosophical controversy.

The remainder of the stock arguments against utilitarianism mostly consist in laying to its charge the common infirmities of human nature, and the general difficulties which embarrass conscientious persons in shaping their course through life. We are told that a utilitarian will be apt to make his own particular case an exception to moral rules, and, when under temptation, will see a utility in the breach of a rule, greater than he will see in its observance. But is utility the only creed which is able to furnish us with excuses for evil doing, and means of cheating our own conscience? They are afforded in abundance by all doctrines which recognise as a fact in morals the existence of conflicting considerations; which all doctrines do, that have been believed by sane persons. It is not the fault of any creed, but of the complicated nature of human affairs, that rules of conduct cannot be so framed as to require no exceptions, and that hardly any kind of action can safely be laid down as either always obligatory or always condemnable. There is no ethical creed which does not temper the rigidity of its laws, by giving a certain latitude, under the moral responsibility of the agent, for accommodation to peculiarities of circumstances; and under every creed, at the opening thus made, self-deception and dishonest casuistry get in. There exists no moral system under which there do not arise unequivocal cases of conflicting obligation. These are the real difficulties, the knotty points both in the theory of ethics, and in the conscientious guidance of personal conduct. They are overcome practically, with greater or with less success, according to the intellect and virtue of the individual; but it can hardly be pretended that any one will be the less qualified for dealing with them, from possessing an ultimate standard to which conflicting rights and duties can be referred. If utility is the ultimate source of moral obligations, utility may be invoked to decide between them when their demands are incompatible. Though the application of the standard may be difficult, it is better than none at all: while in other systems, the moral laws all claiming independent authority, there is no common umpire entitled to interfere between them; their claims to precedence one over another rest on little better than sophistry, and unless determined, as they generally are, by the unacknowledged influence of considerations of utility, afford a free scope for the action of personal desires and partialities. We must remember that only in these cases of conflict between secondary principles is it requisite that first principles should be appealed to. There is no case of moral obligation in which some secondary principle is not involved; and if only one, there can seldom be any real doubt which one it is, in the mind of any person by whom the principle itself is recognised.

ENDNOTE

1. The author of this essay has reason for believing himself to be the first person who brought the word utilitarian into use. He did not invent it, but adopted it from a passing expression in Mr. Galt's *Annals of the Parish.* After using it as a designation for several years, he and others abandoned it from a growing dislike to anything resembling a badge or watchword of sectarian distinction. But as a name for one single opinion, not a set of opinions—to denote the recognition of utility as a standard, not any particular way of applying it—the term supplies a want in the language, and offers, in many cases, a convenient mode of avoiding tiresome circumlocution.

QUESTIONS ON MILL

1. How does Mill distinguish between the higher and the lower pleasures? Is this distinction convincing?

2. In what way or ways do you think that utilitarianism challenges traditional conceptions of morality? Does utilitarianism demand more of us than does traditional morality?

3. Can you think of any counterexamples to the doctrine of utilitarianism? In other words, do you think that utilitarianism might, on some occasions, demand that one should perform an act which, though justified by utility, might still seem deeply immoral or unjust?

4. How might utilitarianism relate to markets and commerce? For example, does the claim that we should maximize utility entail that we should maximize economic productivity? Is the maximization of profit within a firm the same as maximizing utility?

5. Suppose that you are seeking a new assistant manager for your company, and you have narrowed the applicants to four individuals. As it happens, these individuals are similar in almost all of the aspects relevant to job performance: skills, experience, knowledge, motivation, interests, and educational backgrounds. However, in your final interviews with these individuals you have learned that one is a virtue ethicist, one an act-utilitarian, one a rule-utilitarian, and the fourth a Kantian. Given that these candidates are equal in so many aspects, how will their ethical outlooks affect your evaluation of them? Whom would you most desire to hire? Whom would you least wish to hire?

FOR FURTHER READING

General Introductions to Ethical Theory

Frankena, William K. *Ethics* Englewood Cliffs, N.J.: Prentice Hall, 1973.

Mackie, J. L. *Ethics.* Harmondsworth: Penguin, 1977.

Rachels, James. *The Elements of Moral Philosophy.* New York: McGraw-Hill, 1999.

Raphael, D. D. *Moral Philosophy.* Oxford: Oxford University Press, 1994.

Warnock, G. J. *The Object of Morality.* London: Methuen, 1971.

Scholarly Works with Special Relevance to Aristotle, Kant, or Mill

Anscombe, G. E. M. "Modern Moral Philosophy." *Philosophy* 33 (January 1958).

Baron, Marcia. *Kantian Ethics Almost Without Apology.* Ithaca: Cornell University Press, 1995.

Becker, Lawrence. "The Neglect of Virtue." *Ethics* 85 (1975): 110–22.

Brandt, Richard B. *Morality, Utilitarianism, and Rights.* New York: Cambridge University Press, 1992.

Broadie, Sarah. *Ethics with Aristotle.* New York: Oxford University Press, 1991.

Hardie, W. F. R. *Aristotle's Ethical Theory.* Oxford: Clarendon Press, 1968.

Herman, Barbara. *The Practice of Moral Judgment.* Cambridge: Harvard University Press, 1993.

Korsgaard, Christine M. "Kant." *Encyclopedia of Ethics,* Vol. 1, edited by Lawrence C. Becker and Charlotte B. Becker. New York: Garland Press, 1992.

Louden, Robert. "On Some Vices of Virtue Ethics." *American Philosophical Quarterly* 21 (1984): 227–36.

MacIntyre, Alasdair. *After Virtue.* Notre Dame: University of Notre Dame Press, 1981.

Maitland, Ian H. "Virtuous Markets: The Markets as School of the Virtues." *Business Ethics Quarterly* 7 (1997): 17–31

Murdoch, Iris. *The Sovereignty of Good.* New York: Schocken Books, 1971.

O'Neill, Onora. "Kantian Ethics." In *A Companion to Ethics,* edited by Peter Singer. Oxford: Basil Blackwell, 1991.

Plamenatz, John. *The English Utilitarians.* Oxford: Blackwell, 1958.

Rorty, Amelie O. ed. *Essays on Aristotle's Ethics.* Berkeley: University of California Press, 1980.

Ross, W. D. *The Right and the Good.* Oxford: Oxford University Press, 1930.

Scheffler, Samuel. *Consequentialism and Its Critics.* New York: Oxford University Press, 1988.

Sen, Amartya, and Bernard Williams, eds. *Utilitarianism and Beyond.* Cambridge: Cambridge University Press, 1982.

Smart, J. J. C., and Bernard Williams, eds. *Utilitarianism: For and Against.* Cambridge: Cambridge University Press, 1973.

Sullivan, Roger. *Immanuel Kant's Moral Theory.* New York: Cambridge University Press, 1989.

Wallace, James D. *Virtues and Vices.* Ithaca, N.Y.: Cornell University Press, 1978.

Other Normative Ethical Theories

Natural Law Theories

Aquinas, *Summa Theologiae,* I–II (esp. questions 90–97), available in William P. Baumgarth and Richard J. Regan, S. J., eds., Saint Thomas Aquinas, *On Law, Morality and Politics.* Indianapolis, Ind.: Hackett, 1988.

Finnis, John. *Natural Law and Natural Rights.* Oxford: Clarendon Press, 1982.

Simon, Yves. *The Tradition of Natural Law.* New York: Fordham University Press, 1965.

Sympathy and Sentiment

Hume, David. *A Treatise of Human Nature* [1739–40]. 2d ed. Edited by L. A. Selby-Bigge. Revised by P. H. Niddituh. Oxford: Clarendon Press, 1978. (esp. Book III.i & ii).

———. *An Enquiry Concerning the Principles of Morals* [1751]. 3d ed. Edited by L. A. Selby-Bigge. Revised by P. H. Nidditch. Oxford: Clarendon Press, 1975 (esp. Section I).

Wilson, James Q. *The Moral Sense.* New York: The Free Press, 1993.

The Impartial Spectator

Smith, Adam. *The Theory of Moral Sentiments* [1759]. Edited by D. D. Raphael and A. L. Macfie. Indianapolis, Ind.: Liberty Classics, 1982.

Ethical Egoism

Rand, Ayn. *The Virtue of Selfishness: A New Concept of Egoism.* New York: New American Library, 1965.

Stirner, Max. *The Ego and Its Own* [1845]. Translated by Steven Byington. London: Rebel Press, 1982.

Recent Challenges

Feminist Revisions

Baier, Annette. "What Do Women Want in a Moral Theory?" *Nous* 19 (1985): 53–63.

Card, Claudia. *Feminist Ethics.* Lawrence: University Press of Kansas, 1991.

Gilligan, Carol. *In a Different Voice: Psychological Theory and Women's Development.* Cambridge: Harvard University Press, 1982.

Kittay, Eva Feder, and Diana Meyers, eds. *Women and Moral Theory.* Totowa, N.J.: Rowman & Littlefield, 1987.

Morality and Evolution

Maienschein, Jane, and Michael Ruse, eds. *Biology and the Foundation of Ethics.* Cambridge: Cambridge University Press, 1999.

Midgley, Mary. *The Ethical Primate: Humans, Freedom, and Morality.* London: Routledge, 1994.

Singer, Peter. *The Expanding Circle: Ethics and Sociobiology.* Oxford: Oxford University Press, 1983.

Wilson, E. O. *Sociobiology: The New Synthesis.* Cambridge: Belknap Press of Harvard University, 1975.

Wright, Robert. *The Moral Animal: Evolutionary Psychology and Everyday Life.* New York: Pantheon, 1994.

Against Moral Theory

Gass, William. "The Case of the Obliging Stranger." *Philosophical Review* LXVI (1957): 193–204.

Oakeshott, Michael. "The Tower of Babel." In *Rationalism in Politics and Other Essays.* Edited by Timothy Fuller. Indianapolis, Ind.: Liberty Classics, 1991.

Vice and Virtue in the Conduct of Business

Character and Commerce

[I]t is moral virtue that is concerned with emotions and actions, and it is in emotions and actions that excess, deficiency, and the median are found. Thus we can experience fear, confidence, desire, anger, pity, and generally any kind of pleasure and pain either too much or too little, and in either case not properly. But to experience all this at the right time, toward the right objects, toward the right people, for the right reason, and in the right manner—that is the median and the best course, the course that is a mark of virtue.

Aristotle[1]

'Get money,' someone says, 'so that we may have some.' If I can get it while keeping self-respect and trustworthiness and high-mindedness, show me the way and I will get it. But if you demand that I lose the good things that are mine so that you may acquire things that are not good, see for yourselves how unfair and inconsiderate you are. Which do you want more, money or a self-respecting and trustworthy friend?

Epictetus[2]

GENERAL CONSIDERATIONS

It is often thought that business conduct requires that one act in a self-interested way, seeking only to "buy low and sell high." However, it is not at all obvious that commercial conduct must be construed in some narrowly self-interested way or that commercial life has no connection to moral character or virtue. If it is important to consider whether or not certain moral norms or virtues provide an important condition for successful commerce (Section AIV), and if it is important to examine whether commerce has beneficial or negative moral consequences (Section CI), then it should be of

equal importance to consider how virtues (or vices) might be expressed or applied in the everyday practice of commerce or in market societies more generally. In other words, how do virtues relate to the day-to-day conduct of persons in business, whether they be managers, professionals, colleagues, employees, or customers? Are certain virtues incompatible with or difficult to reconcile with business? Or are there commercial virtues to which we should lend greater attention than we do? To begin our consideration of these questions, we will consider the relation between virtue and character and then consider more generally the way in which virtues may relate to commercial life.

---

1. *Nicomachean Ethics*, translated by Martin Ostwald (Englewood Cliffs, N.J.: Prentice Hall, 1962), II.6.106b15–23.

2. *The Handbook (The Encheiridion)*[1st–2nd century, A.D.], translated by Nicholas P. White (Indianapolis, Ind.: Hackett Publishing, 1983), § 24.

Character and Personality

We often describe a person in terms of physical appearance, occupation, or personality. However, if we describe someone in terms of that person's *character,* then we have offered a description that is not only more deeply attuned to who the person is but offers an account of normative import as well as predictive value. To speak of a person's character is to speak about who the person is in some fundamental way. Knowledge of character allows one to know something about how the person typically thinks, feels, and acts.

There is a relation between personality and character, if not some overlap, but there are also differences. If we know that a person is gregarious or quiet, serious or light-hearted, shy or assertive, then we know something about how that person typically thinks, feels, and acts. The set of traits that mark one's personality often includes inimitable aspects or features that are more deeply individualized than the more general and less personal traits which are taken as defining one's character, especially *moral* character. Although character may be less personal, it is nonetheless more *fundamental* than personality, more resistant to alteration. Finally, character has a normative if not moral aspect, a fact notable in that we tend to describe the qualities of character in terms of praise or blame; however, the qualities of one's personality, even if describable as good or bad, are not subject to the same sort of praise and blame. Of course, we need not assume that one's character must be understood in moral terms alone, even though character does seem to have normative implications. For example, that a person is *methodical* need not be understood as a moral trait, even though, for example, a person in business ought to be methodical.

Character and Virtue

Another way of understanding the moral significance of character lies in the way in which character comprises moral qualities or traits, including virtues and vices. This is not to say that character is equivalent to a set of virtues or traits. Having traits is essential to character—that is why these are traits *of* character—but one's character as a whole would seem to be more than just a set of isolated traits. At the very least one's character involves a stable unity of traits, desires, commitments, and actions. It is in this sense we might remark that an individual is a person of *character.* A person's character tells us something about how that person would act in certain circumstances, and these

actions arise from dispositions, among which are those we call virtues or vices.

Very generally, a virtue is a trait or quality of character that disposes an agent to act appropriately (or to express the appropriate emotion) and to desire to act in this way (or to express the requisite emotion). To be virtuous thus involves knowledge of what is appropriate, a settled inclination, tendency, or disposition to act (or feel) appropriately, and a motive or desire internal to the virtue itself. Roughly speaking, a motive or desire is *internal* to a virtue when one wants to manifest (or practice) the virtue for its own sake and not solely for some reason extraneous to the nature of the virtue. The person who is honest wishes to be honest for its own sake, *not* as a means of winning friends, gaining esteem, or making money. Though a virtuous disposition is cultivated and practiced for its own sake, a virtue is, nonetheless, of peculiar value to the human being. Thus, it could also be said that a virtue, unlike a vice, is a disposition that is beneficial (or valuable) and praiseworthy; a vice is a disposition that is not valuable and not praiseworthy. It is for this reason that virtues are related to living well.

Virtue and Living Well

Aristotle's view was that in order to have any conception of virtue or character, one must first delineate what it is to live well. Aristotle argued (see Section AV) that the end of a good human life is happiness or *eudaimonia,* which means living well. To live well presupposed that one was disposed to certain actions and emotions appropriate to a human being. Despite the variation in what many people believe about living well, Aristotle also held that there were certain universal traits that were the conditions of living well, and these conditions had to do precisely with certain passions or emotions (such as fear), as well as certain actions, such as generosity. Although happiness is the end of human action, one must take into account that this end should not be understood as something beyond the manner and content of the activity; rather the very manner and content of a happy life, of living well, is constituted by virtue.

Aristotle on Virtue

To live well is to live happily, but happiness for Aristotle is not so much the outcome of one's activities as it is the manner in which one lives. The appropriate ends and manner of living are determined by the kind of creature one is, and, as Aristotle contends, the human being is rational. So living well involves the excellent performance of one's characteristic reason. But if we are to do, perform, or live well, then we must have certain qualities or virtues that dispose us to feel and act in the appropriate ways and toward the appropriate ends. Just as an excellent harpist must possess certain qualities like tone recognition, grace, nimble fingers, and so forth (and just as an excellent surgeon must have certain qualities such as knowledge, dexterity, and a methodical calm), so does a human life lived well require certain traits of character.

Aristotle defined virtue in this way:

> Virtue, then, is a state of character concerned with choice, lying in a mean, i.e. the mean relative to us, this being determined by a rational principle, and by that principle by which the man of practical wisdom would determine it.

Virtue is acquired by habituation, and that is how virtue becomes part of one's very *character.* Insofar as virtue is acquired by habit it becomes part of one's very identity and disposes one to the right emotions and actions in the appropriate circumstances. Aristotle construed this disposition in terms of a *mean,* thus indicating that each virtue is a disposition to hit the mean, or the appropriate, in emotion and in action. But in what sense is an emotion or action appropriate? What are we to aim at? For Aristotle, virtue disposes one to appropriate conduct in seven distinct ways:

1. that we experience the emotion or perform the action at the right time,
2. for the right length,
3. in the right circumstances,
4. to or for the right persons,
5. in the right manner,
6. to the right degree,
7. for the right end or purpose.

Virtue consists in a *choice.* To be virtuous one must choose the act for its own sake; the act must be chosen because it is understood to be a virtuous act. The point is not, however, that we make some overtly conscious decision but that our choice is voluntary. Thus it is important to recognize, as Aristotle does, that even though our character is acquired via habituation, we are responsible for our character and thus we are responsible for those actions or emotions that flow from, or are expressions of, our character. A person's character runs deep, and Aristotle believed that our character was formed over time. It was not for nothing that the poet John Dryden wrote, "Ill habits gather by unseen degrees—As brooks make rivers, rivers run to seas."[3]

3. *The Worship of Æsculapius,* Book xv, Line 155.

Virtue is voluntary but it also expresses *reason,* either in that virtuous conduct *conforms* to reason or that it is the result of our *exercise* of reason. The exercise of reason involves deliberation about the means to our ends as well as thoughtful consideration of what our ends should be. To reason well, then, one must not only have some rational recognition of certain goods, such as those general goods of truth, generosity, or pride, but one must also be able to consider how and when to manifest these so that they are integrated fully into one's whole life. This will involve, among other things, reasoning about the seven characteristics noted above. For example, a virtuous person does not go about trying to be honest: "My goal for today is to be honest." Rather, one sets out to do things (to achieve goals) in an honest way, or in a generous way, a just way, and so on. To conduct oneself well will involve a sort of reasoning in which one balances certain ends with the ends of living well. And this should mean that reason, for Aristotle, is not a mere calculation: If you want X, then do Y. In fact, the appeal to the seven characteristics is also an appeal to the very particulars of moral decision making. So even if reason requires that one balance and weigh distinct goods, it will also involve moral perception. The virtuous person must perceive (or recognize) that this is a situation that calls for action or that this is a situation in which something should be done. In this sense reason involves recognition, attention, and discrimination, and these demand that we move beyond self-involvement and self-concern.

VIRTUE AND SOCIETY

Moral Circumstances

Are there any universal circumstances which affect what is to count as a virtue? It seems obvious enough that human beings have certain physical needs, among which are food, clothing, and shelter; human beings require a certain insulation from physical harm, be it from the vicissitudes of nature, from animals, or from other human beings. Along with these physical requirements we have a variety of wants and desires, whose means of satisfaction are in short supply. It is not just that the means of satisfying these wants and desires cannot be found, in nature, ready to use or that they must be produced and manufactured; it is also the case that resources are scarce. Not all of our desires and wants can be satisfied at one time or at all—some may conflict, and some may not be at all attainable. Even if we consider the human being alone, we might consider that "there is absolutely no reason to assume that the needs, wants, and interests of any one individual will just naturally form what might be called a consistent set, or coherent programme."[4] Moreover each of us may have but a limited sympathy in that we tend to seek our own satisfactions and those of our family, prior to seeking the satisfactions of others. In addition, we have a limited knowledge and are motivated more often by beliefs about local circumstances and the short-term than by beliefs about distant circumstances or the long-term.

Social Conditions and Virtue: Some Examples

The realization of our needs and desires is precisely what an economic system should provide. Even though some moral circumstances are universal, economic systems and social conditions may differ. Similarly, certain virtues may be universal in type but their particular tokens may vary according to the economic and social conditions of a society or epoch. Indeed, certain qualities may be emphasized more in one system or society than in another. This need not entail relativism—the idea that moral principles and standards cannot be known to be true or false independent of cultural beliefs. For even if the dispositions that allow us to live well may differ according to the conditions in which we find ourselves, it may still be true that certain dispositions (virtues) are appropriate and others not. Thus Aristotle espouses the virtues of courage, liberality, magnificence, good temper, truthfulness, wit, friendliness, and justice, as well as pride. For medieval Christians, however, pride is not a virtue but a spiritual vice that gives rise to other vices.

Within a commercial society certain virtues may serve more ably than others. For example, it is not surprising that in the eighteenth century, the philosopher David Hume (1711–1776) sought to articulate qualities of "common life" and in so doing distinguished between qualities of character useful to others or to the self, and qualities agreeable to others or to the self. Benevolence, generosity, courage, honesty, loyalty are, according to Hume, useful to the public; industry and frugality, as well as honesty and fidelity, are useful to the agent as are discretion, caution, enterprise, assiduity, economy, good sense, prudence, discernment, temperance, sobriety, patience, constancy, perseverance, forethought, and considerateness, among others. A quality immediately agreeable to the self is cheerfulness; qualities agreeable to others include good manners and politeness, as well as wit, ingenuity, and decency. These virtues of common life, Hume insisted, are radically distinct from the "monkish virtues" of "celibacy, fasting, penance, mortification, self-denial, humility, silence, solitude," all of which are "everywhere rejected by men of sense, but because they serve to no manner of purpose; neither advance a man's fortune in the world, nor render him a more valuable member of society."[5] Even more utilitarian than Hume was Benjamin Franklin (1706–1790), who listed thirteen virtues: temperance, silence, order, resolution, frugality, industry, sincerity, justice, moderation, cleanliness, tranquility, chastity, and humility. A more contemporary list of market virtues is offered by Samuel Smiles and Deirdre McCloskey in the readings of this section.

Commercial Virtues

It seems clear enough that there are a variety of virtues and traits that have been articulated and defended over the centuries and that there are distinct ways of categorizing these qualities. There may be a core of universal social virtues just because every society must inculcate certain traits such as honesty, generosity, politeness, or friendliness. Even if universal, the particular tokens may vary from society to society and may have different rankings across societies (for example, some societies emphasize politeness more than others). If we recall that a virtue enables one to live well, then it may be that there are virtues particularly appropriate to a society in which one must live by commercial production and exchange. (Perhaps some of these virtues would be seen as qualities that are not moral. However, the distinction between the moral and the nonmoral was not always as strong as it is today.) One might consider a virtue in terms of whether it is a general trait, such as honesty, which is applicable to human beings in general, or whether the virtue is a quality relevant to a particular economic or social system. Thus one could contend that honesty, integrity, loyalty, generosity, courage, and humility are traits worthy of any human being, regardless of social circumstance or economic system. Even so, one might consider that any of these virtues might have particular applications within the institutionalized practices of a time and place. Courage might be manifested differently within a market system than within a socialist system; the demands on one's honesty and integrity might be distinct depending on whether one were tempted by the lure of money or by the lure of social prominence or political power.

---

4. G. J. Warnock, *The Object of Morality* (London: Methuen, 1971), 19.

5. *An Enquiry Concerning the Principles of Morals,* edited by L. A. Selby-Bigge, revised by P. H. Nidditch (Oxford: Clarendon Press, 1975), 270. The qualities of common life are listed in Section VI, part I, pp. 242–43.

VIRTUES, ROLES, AND RULES

Virtues and Roles

Within any institution, business, or organization, certain obligations may arise from the very nature of one's position. Some of these obligations may be contractually defined, but others orginate from one's position or function within the business. Thus, the role of the manager is different from that of an owner, the tasks of an employee are distinct from that of an executive. Given these different roles, the manifestation of a virtue may differ as that virtue is practiced by an owner of a firm, a manager, or an employee. It seems true enough that honesty is crucial for anyone, whether it involve the honesty of the salesperson, or that of a manager to employees, or that of the employee who refrains from stealing, giving false information, or illegally copying computer software, for example. And yet one might want to consider how virtues may take on particular manifestations as they are practiced by owners or entrepreneurs, managers or professionals, skilled artisans, laborers, or salespersons. Thus, for any person participating in a market system, it is important to be industrious, persevering, diligent, and self-disciplined. Yet the self-discipline of the manager may be different from that of the young and inexperienced employee, just as the perseverance required to learn a new job may differ from the perseverance required to embark upon the establishment of a new enterprise.

Leadership

For the owner, manager, or executive, the quality of leadership is of particular importance, and this involves, preeminently, leadership by example. Exemplary conduct not only allows others to learn but also serves as inspiration and motivation. The manager who leads by example may thereby show others how to produce quality work; how to treat suppliers, customers, and colleagues; and, more generally, how to shun the slapdash and the slipshod. For example, George Washington said, "Whenever you reprove another be unblameable yourself, for example is more prevalent than precepts."[6] True leadership is in large part something that is earned by the acceptance of responsibility. For the owner of a business firm, responsibility arises from the commitment of resources and from the obligations of contract; for the manager, responsibility arises from the obligations of one's role within the firm or company.

Rules and Codes

It might be suggested that there is no reason to appeal to the idea of virtue in business. Business positions are defined in terms of rules, and if these rules are not sufficient, then the firm should enact codes to help insure that individuals not only fulfill the tasks of business but do so in a moral fashion. Many large corporations have adopted "ethics statements" or "codes of ethics" which either articulate the values a business seeks to practice or delineate certain general principles or standards of behavior. Thus the Boeing Company not only offers an ethical statement affirming integrity but also stipulates that a manager must be a person who "has a record of excellent performance with the highest ethical standards."[7] Some codes articulate general principles concerning respect for colleagues, suppliers, stockholders, and customers; others emphasize adherence to standards of honesty and integrity; and some stress the need to strive for quality in all that is done, to comply with applicable laws or regulations, and to avoid any conflicts of interest.

It should be clear that the appeal to virtue does not obviate a code of ethics. However, it should also be plain that a code of ethics is not sufficient to ensure that businesses will succeed or that they will do so in an ethical fashion. This is so for three reasons: the complexity of rules, the necessity of moral perception, and the matter of motivation. It might be possible to imagine a business scenario in which individuals acted only by appealing to some set of rules, a business code by which to determine what to do and when. Of course, if one is to rely *wholly* on rules to guide one's behavior, then not only must the rules be many, but they must also be specific to each possible type of circumstance or problem. However, this sort of scenario seems dubious because it presumes that we can devise a sufficient number of rules and that these rules would be so carefully delineated that they would be appropriate to each relevant situation. As Aristotle suggested, ethics simply may not be formulable in precise rules, for ethics, unlike mathematics, is acquired by experience and habituation and not by learning rules and principles. The complexity of the moral life is ex-

---

6. *Rules of Civility, The 110 Precepts that Guided Our First President in War and Peace,* edited by Richard Brookhiser (New York: The Free Press, 1997), § 48.

7. The statement of the Boeing Company, as well as those of some eighty diverse businesses, can be found in Patrick E. Murphy, *Eighty Exemplary Ethics Statements* (Notre Dame, Ind.: University of Notre Dame Press, 1998), 25–26.

pressed more pithily by the nineteenth-century novelist, George Eliot (1819–1880), in *Adam Bede:*

> . . . and I know there's a deal in a man's inward life as you can't measure by the square, and say, 'do this and that'll follow,' and 'do that and this'll follow.'[8]

A second reason why a code of ethics is not sufficient is that, despite our imagined scenario, our conduct *cannot* be guided solely by rules. Even if rules and principles are important—as they are—we can abide by a rule only if (a) we recognize or perceive that *this* is a situation in which a certain rule should be applied, and (b) we understand how to apply the relevant rule. Both (a) and (b) are not themselves rule-guided but are dependent on perception and understanding of the sort not articulable into precise rules.

The final reason that business conduct is not guided by rules is that the mere appeal to a code of ethics does not tell us whether we would have a *motive* for abiding by a particular rule. A person of virtue, however, does have a disposition to respond in a particular manner, with the right motive, in the right circumstances, and so on. If there is no appeal to virtue, then in the case of ethical decisions one would have to rely upon some means of reward or punishment. Even if this is possible, it is not clear that it is preferable to reliance upon virtue.

Virtue and Self-Interest

Of course, it might be charged that the appeal to virtue fails to recognize that within the business sphere, all that really matters is the pursuit of self-interest. If individuals are to pursue their self-interests, and if that is the motive of commercial interaction, then there is little place at all for virtuous behavior. However, it is not at all obvious that self-interest is the single or prime motive of those engaged in commercial exchange; nor is it obvious that other qualities of character are not relevant to the practice of business or to the world of commercial work. In the subsequent portions of this section, we will examine the idea of selfishness and self-interest, consider whether or not generosity or liberality has a role within commerce, explore the idea of prudential action, and take up the often neglected ideas of manners and courtesy.

THE READINGS

Samuel Smiles   Smiles seeks to provide moral advice to young persons who are just beginning their lives of work. The qualities that Smiles discusses are those

8. *Adam Bede* (Harmondsworth: Penguin, 1980), 227.

which, he claims, are necessary for any "important undertaking." Contending that there is no inconsistency between "brilliance" and business, Smiles emphasizes first the importance of self-reliance. He then proceeds to specify other qualities required for success, including "attention, application, accuracy, method, punctuality, and dispatch . . .," as well as "sound discretion, quick perception, and firmness in the execution of [one's] plans." Finally, although Smiles agrees that honesty is "the best policy" for business, he also holds that honesty is good in itself: "And even though a man should for a time be unsuccessful, still he must be honest: better lose all and save character, for character is itself a fortune. . . ."

Robert Solomon   Solomon describes six characteristics of the Aristotelian approach to business ethics, beginning with a description of the idea of community as the precondition for human development. Solomon proceeds to describe how excellence (or virtue) is the heart of business ethics, and notes how one's specific role or position in a firm complicates ethical choice. A fourth characteristic refers to the idea that business is not isolated from the whole of our lives; the fifth establishes the need to aspire to an elevated level of noble and honorable conduct; and the sixth reveals how good judgment includes both moral perception and a nonmechanical mode of deliberation and decision. Solomon then notes that the Aristotelian approach is "antigreed" but not antibusiness, for the idea of happiness presupposes financial success even if it is not *reducible* to such success. For Solomon, the Aristotelian approach requires a conception of self that includes reference to the community, a point that is explored in relation to qualities of loyalty, honor, and shame, all of which relate to the virtue of integrity and all of which relate to the larger community or enterprise.

Deirdre McCloskey   McCloskey points out that for too long, we have understood the virtues according to either of two traditions, the classical and the Christian (or peasant). However, these conceptualizations are not appropriate for commercial societies, so she suggests another conceptualization of virtue more attuned to a bourgeois business society. Too often it has been assumed that there are no virtues relevant to the conditions of bourgeois society, only greed; however, businesspeople, entrepreneurs, and the commercial middle class exhibit qualities of conduct that are worthy of theoretical articulation and social cultivation and esteem. Common   classes of virtues exist in distinct manners across divergent conditions and epochs, and McCloskey offers a schema summarizing the similar types of virtues existing in aristocratic, peasant, and bourgeois societies. McCloskey suggests that we should cultivate rather than denigrate bourgeois qualities, noting that the market promotes the virtues of honesty and tolerance. She closes with critical remarks about intellectuals who have all too often steadfastly refused to understand the bourgeois life of commerce.

Business Qualities

Samuel Smiles

Samuel Smiles (1812–1904) was born in Haddington, Scotland, one of eleven children in a fatherless family. An editor of The Leeds Times, *later a railway administrator, Smiles wrote a number of works including a three-volume history,* Lives of the Engineers *(1861–1862) as well as* Character *(1871),* Thrift *(1875), and* Duty *(1880). The work from which this excerpt is taken,* Self-Help, with Illustrations of Character and Conduct *(1859), had its beginnings in lectures Smiles gave to workers in Leeds.*

> "Seest thou a man diligent in his business? he shall stand before kings"—*Proverbs of Solomon*

> "That man is but of the lower part of the world that is not brought up to business and affairs."—*Owen Feltham*

Hazlitt, in one of his clever essays,* represents the man of business as a mean sort of person put in a go-cart, yoked to a trade or profession; alleging that all he has to do is not to go out of the beaten track, but merely to let his affairs take their own course. "The great requisite," he says, "for the prosperous management of ordinary business is the want of imagination, or of any ideas but those of custom and interest on the narrowest scale." But nothing could be more one-sided, and in effect untrue, than such a definition. Of course, there are narrow-minded men of business, as there are narrow-minded scientific men, literary men, and legislators; but there are also business men of large and comprehensive minds, capable of action on the very largest scale. As Burke said in his speech on the India Bill, he knew statesmen who were peddlers, and merchants who acted in the spirit of statesmen.

If we take into account the qualities necessary for the successful conduct of any important undertaking—that it requires special aptitude, promptitude of action

*"On Thought and Action."

on emergencies, capacity for organizing the labors often of large numbers of men, great tact and knowledge of human nature, constant self-culture, and growing experience in the practical affairs of life, it must, we think, be obvious that the school of business is by no means so narrow as some writers would have us believe. Mr. Helps has gone much nearer the truth when he said that consummate men of business are as rare almost as great poets—rarer, perhaps, than veritable saints and martyrs. Indeed, of no other pursuit can it so emphatically be said as of this, that "business makes men."

But it has also been a favorite fallacy with dunces in all times, that men of genius are unfitted for business pursuits. Yet Shakespeare was a successful manager of a theatre, perhaps priding himself more upon his practical qualities in that capacity than on his writing of plays and poetry. Pope was of opinion that Shakespeare's principal object in cultivating literature was to secure an honest independence. Indeed, he seems to have been altogether indifferent to literary reputation. It is not known that he superintended the publication of a single play, or even sanctioned the printing of one; and the chronology of his writings is still a mystery. It is certain, however, that he prospered in his business, and realized sufficient to enable him to retire upon a competency to his native town of Stratford-upon-Avon.

Chaucer was in early life a soldier, and afterward an effective Commissioner of Customs, and Inspector of Woods and Crown Lands. Spenser was Secretary to the Lord Deputy of Ireland, and is said to have been very shrewd and attentive in matters of business. Milton, originally a schoolmaster, was afterward elevated to the post of Secretary to the Council of State during the Commonwealth; and the extant Order-book of the Council, as well as many of Milton's letters which are preserved, give abundant evidence of his activity and usefulness in that office. Sir Isaac Newton proved himself a most efficient Master of the Mint, the new coinage of 1694 having been carried on under his immediate personal superintendence. Cowper prided himself upon his business punctuality, though he confessed that he "never knew a poet except himself who was punctual in any thing." But against this we may set the lives of Wordsworth and Scott—the former a distributer of stamps, the latter a clerk to the Court of Sessions—both of whom, though great poets, were, eminently punctual and practical men of business. David Ricardo, amid the occupations of his daily business as a London banker, in conducting which he acquired an ample fortune, was able to concentrate his mind upon his favorite subject—on which he was enabled to throw great light—

the principles of political economy; for he united in himself the sagacious commercial man and the profound philosopher. We have abundant illustrations, even in our own day, of the fact that the highest intellectual power is not incompatible with the active and efficient performance of routine duties. Grote, the great historian of Greece, like Ricardo, is a London banker. And it is not long since John Stuart Mill, one of our greatest living thinkers, retired from the Examiner's department of the East India Company, carrying with him the admiration and esteem of his fellow-officers, not on account of his high views of philosophy, but because of the high standard of efficiency which he had established in his office, and the thoroughly satisfactory manner in which he had conducted the business of his department.

The path of success in business is invariably the path of common sense. Notwithstanding all that is said about "lucky hits," the best kind of success in every man's life is not that which comes by accident. The only "good time coming" we are justified in hoping for is that which we are capable of making for ourselves. The fable of the labors of Hercules is indeed the type of all human doing and success. Every youth should early be made to feel that if he would get through the world usefully and happily, he must rely mainly upon himself and his own independent energies. The late Lord Melbourne embodied a piece of useful advice in a letter which he wrote to Lord John Russell, in reply to an application for a provision for one of Moore the poet's sons: "My dear John," he said, "I return you Moore's letter. I shall be ready to do what you like about it when we have the means. I think whatever is done should be done for Moore himself. This is more distinct, direct, and intelligible. Making a small provision for young men is hardly justifiable, and it is, of all things, the most prejudicial to themselves. They think what they have much larger than it really is, and they make no exertion. The young should never hear any language but this: 'You have your own way to make, and it depends upon your own exertions whether you starve or not.' Believe me, etc., Melbourne."

It is not good for human nature to have the road of life made too easy. Better to be under the necessity of working hard and faring meanly, than to have every thing done ready to our hand and a pillow of down to repose upon. Indeed, to start in life with comparatively small means seems so necessary as a stimulus to work, that it may almost be set down as one of the conditions essential to success in life. Hence an eminent judge, when asked what contributed most to success at the bar, replied, "Some succeed by great talent, some by high connections, some by miracle, but the majority by commencing without a shilling." So is it a common saying at Manchester, that the men who are the most successful in business there are those who begin the world in their shirtsleeves; whereas those who begin with fortunes generally lose them. Necessity is always the first stimulus to industry, and those who conduct it with prudence, perseverance, and energy will rarely fail. Viewed in this light, the necessity of labor is not a chastisement, but a blessing—the very root and spring of all that we call progress in individuals and civilization in nations. It may, indeed, be questioned whether a heavier curse could be imposed on man than the complete gratification of all his wishes without effort on his part, leaving nothing for his hopes, desires, or struggles. The feeling that life is destitute of any motive or necessity for action must be, of all others, the most distressing and the most insupportable to a rational being. The Marquis de Spinola asking Sir Horace Vere what his brother died of, Sir Horace replied, "He died, sir, of having nothing to do." "Alas!" said Spinola, "that is enough to kill any general of us all."

Those who fail in life are very apt to assume the tone of injured innocence, and conclude too hastily that every body excepting themselves has had a hand in their personal misfortunes. A literary man lately published a book, in which he described his numerous failures in business, naïvely admitting, at the same time, that he was ignorant of the multiplication table, probably because he would not take the trouble to learn it. But, instead of attributing his failures to himself, this eminent man sat down deliberately to cast all the blame upon the money-worshiping spirit of the age. Lamartine also did not hesitate to profess his profound contempt for arithmetic; but, had it been less, probably we should not have witnessed the unseemly spectacle of the admirers of that distinguished personage engaged in collecting subscriptions for his support in his old age.

There is a Russian proverb which says that Misfortune is next door to Stupidity; and it will generally be found that men who are constantly lamenting their ill luck are only reaping the consequences of their own neglect, mismanagement, improvidence, or want of application. Dr. Johnson, who came up to London with a single guinea in his pocket, and who once accurately described himself in his signature to a letter addressed to a noble lord as *Impransus,* or Dinnerless, has honestly said, "All the complaints which are made of the world are unjust; I never knew a man of merit neglected; it was generally by his own fault that he failed of success."

The dictionary definition of Business shows how large a part of practical life arranges itself under this head. It is "Employment; an affair; serious engagement;

something to be transacted; something required to be done." Every human being has duties to be performed, and, therefore, has need of cultivating the capacity for doing them, whether the sphere of action be the management of a household, the conduct of a trade or profession, or the government of a nation.

Attention, application, accuracy, method, punctuality, and dispatch are the principal qualities required for the efficient conduct of business of any sort. These, at first sight, may appear to be small matters, and yet they are of essential importance to human happiness, wellbeing, and usefulness. They are little things, it is true; but human life is made up of comparative trifles. It is the repetition of little acts which constitute not only the sum of human character, but which determine the character of nations; and where men or nations have broken down, it will almost invariably be found that neglect of little things was the rock on which they split.

It is related of a well-known Manchester manufacturer that, on retiring from business, he purchased a large estate from a noble lord, and it was part of the arrangement that he was to take the house, with all its furniture, precisely as it stood. On taking possession, however, he found that a cabinet which was in the inventory had been removed; and, on applying to the former owner about it, the latter said, "Well, I certainly did order it to be removed, but I hardly thought you would have cared for so trifling a matter in so large a purchase." "My lord," was the characteristic reply, "if I had not all my life attended to trifles, I should not have been able to purchase this estate; and, excuse me for saying so, perhaps if your lordship had cared more about trifles, you might not have had occasion to sell it."

The examples we have already given of great workers in various branches of industry, art, and science, render it unnecessary farther to enforce the importance of persevering application in any department of life. It is the result of every-day experience, that steady attention to matters of detail lies at the root of human progress; and that diligence, above all, is the mother of good luck. Accuracy is also of much importance, and an invariable mark of good training in a man: accuracy in observation, accuracy in speech, accuracy in the transaction of affairs. What is done in business must be well done; for it is better to accomplish perfectly a small amount of work, than to half-do ten times as much. A wise man used to say, "Stay a little, that we may make an end the sooner."

Too little attention, however, is paid to this highly important quality of accuracy. As a man eminent in practical science lately observed to us, "It is astonishing how few people I have met with in the course of my ex-

perience who can *define a fact* accurately." Yet, in business affairs, it is the manner in which even small matters are transacted that often decides men for or against you. With virtue, capacity, and good conduct in other respects, the person who is habitually inaccurate can not be trusted; his work has to be gone over again; and he thus causes an infinity of annoyance, vexation, and trouble. Truer words were never uttered than those spoken by Mr. Dargan, the Irish railway contractor, at a public meeting in Dublin: "I have heard a great deal," he said, "about the independence that we were to get from this, that, and the other source, yet I have always been deeply impressed with the conviction that our industrial independence depends upon ourselves. *Simple industry and careful exactness* would be the making of Ireland. We have, it is true, made a step, but perseverance is indispensably necessary for eventual success."

It was one of the characteristic qualities of Charles James Fox that he was thoroughly painstaking in all that he did. When appointed secretary of state, being piqued at some observation as to his bad writing, he actually took a writing-master, and wrote copies like a schoolboy until he had sufficiently improved himself. Though a corpulent man, he was wonderfully active at picking up cut tennis-balls, and when asked how he contrived to do so, he playfully replied, "Because I am a very painstaking man." The same accuracy in trifling matters was displayed by him in things of greater importance; and he acquired his reputation, like the painter, "by neglecting nothing."

Method is essential, and enables a larger amount of work to be got through with satisfaction. "Method," said Cecil (afterward Lord Burleigh), "is like packing things in a box; a good packer will get in half as much again as a bad one." Cecil's dispatch of business was extraordinary, his maxim being, "The shortest way to do many things is to do only one thing at once;" and he never left a thing undone with a view of recurring to it at a period of more leisure. When business pressed, he rather chose to encroach on his hours of meals and rest than omit any part of his work. De Witt's maxim was like Cecil's: "One thing at a time." "If," said he, "I have any necessary dispatches to make, I think of nothing else till they are finished; if any domestic affairs require my attention, I give myself wholly up to them till they are set in order." Dispatch comes with practice. A French minister, who was alike remarkable for his dispatch of business and his constant attendance at places of amusement, being asked how he contrived to combine both objects, replied, "Simply by never postponing till tomorrow what should be done to-day." Lord Brougham has said that a certain English statesman reversed the process, and that his maxim was, never to transact to-day what could be postponed till to-morrow. Unhappily, such is the practice of many besides that minister, already almost forgotten: the practice is that of the indolent and the unsuccessful. Such men, too, are apt to rely upon agents, who are not always to be relied upon. Important affairs must be attended to in person. "If you want your business done," says the proverb, "go and do it; if you don't want it done, send some one else." An indolent country gentleman had a freehold estate producing about five hundred a year. Becoming involved in debt, he sold half of the estate, and let the remainder to an industrious farmer for twenty years. About the end of the term the farmer called to pay his rent, and asked the owner whether he would sell the farm. "Will *you* buy it?" asked the owner, surprised. "Yes, if we can agree about the price." "That is exceedingly strange," observed the gentleman; "pray tell me how it happens that, while I could not live upon twice as much land for which I paid no rent, you are regularly paying me two hundred a year for your farm, and are able, in a few years, to purchase it." "The reason is plain," was the reply; "you sat still, and said *Go;* I got up, and said *Come:* you lay in bed and enjoyed your estate; I rose in the morning, and minded my business."

Sir Walter Scott, writing to a youth who had obtained a situation and asked him for his advice, gave him in reply this sound counsel: "Beware of stumbling over a propensity which easily besets you from not having your time fully employed—I mean what the women call *dawdling.* Your motto must be *Hoc age.* Do instantly whatever is to be done, and take the hours of recreation after business, never before it. When a regiment is under march, the rear is often thrown into confusion because the front do not move steadily and without interruption. It is the same with business. If that, which is first in hand is not instantly, steadily, and regularly dispatched, other things accumulate behind, till affairs begin to press all at once, and no human brain can stand the confusion."

Promptitude in action may be stimulated by a due consideration of the value of time. An Italian philosopher was accustomed to call time his estate—an estate which produces nothing of value without cultivation, but, duly improved, never fails to recompense the labors of the diligent worker. Allowed to lie waste, the product will be only noxious weeds and vicious growths of all kinds. One of the minor uses of steady employment is that it keeps one out of mischief, for truly an idle brain is the devil's workshop, and a lazy man the devil's bolster. To be occupied is to be possessed as by a tenant, whereas to be idle is to be empty; and when the doors of the imagination are opened, temptation finds a ready access, and evil thoughts come trooping in. It is observed at sea that men are never so much disposed to grumble and mutiny as when least employed. Hence an old captain, when there was nothing else to do, would issue the order to "scour the anchor."

Men of business are accustomed to quote the maxim that time is money, but it is much more; the proper improvement of it is self-culture, self-improvement, and growth of character. An hour wasted daily on trifles or in indolence would, if devoted to self-improvement, make an ignorant man wise in a few years, and, employed in good works, would make his life fruitful, and death a harvest of worthy deeds. Fifteen minutes a day devoted to self-improvement will be felt at the end of the year. Good thoughts and carefully gathered experience take up no room, and are carried about with us as companions every where, without cost or encumbrance. An economical use of time is the true mode of securing leisure: it enables us to get through business and carry it forward, instead of being driven by it. On the other hand, the miscalculation of time involves us in perpetual hurry, confusion, and difficulties, and life becomes a mere shuffle of expedients, usually followed by disaster. Nelson once said, "I owe all my success in life to having been always a quarter of an hour before my time."

Some take no thought of the value of money until they have come to an end of it, and many do the same with their time. The hours are allowed to flow by unemployed, and then, when life is fast waning, they bethink themselves of the duty of making a wiser use of it. But the habit of listlessness and idleness may already have become confirmed, and they are unable to break the bonds with which they have permitted themselves to become bound. Lost wealth may be replaced by industry, lost knowledge by study, lost health by temperance or medicine, but lost time is gone forever.

A proper consideration of the value of time will also inspire habits of punctuality. "Punctuality," said Louis XIV., "is the politeness of kings." It is also the duty of gentlemen, and the necessity of men of business. Nothing begets confidence in a man sooner than the practice of this virtue, and nothing shakes confidence sooner than the want of it. He who holds to his appointment, and does not keep you waiting for him, shows that he has regard for your time as well as for his own. Thus punctuality is one of the modes by which we testify our personal respect for those whom we are called upon to meet in the business of life. It is also conscientiousness in a measure; for an appointment is a contract, express or implied, and he who does not keep it breaks faith, as well as dishonestly uses other people's time, and thus inevitably loses character. We naturally come to the conclusion that the person who is careless about time will be careless about business, and that he is not the one to be trusted with the transaction of matters of importance. When Washington's secretary excused himself for the lateness of his attendance, and laid the blame upon his watch, his master quietly said, "Then you must get another watch, or I another secretary."

The unpunctual man is a general disturber of others' peace and serenity. Every body with whom he has to do is thrown from time to time into a state of fever; he is systematically late—regular only in his irregularity. He conducts his dawdling upon a system; always arrives at his appointment after time; gets to the railway station after the train has started; and posts his letter when the box has closed. Business is thus thrown into confusion, and every body concerned is put out of temper. It will generally be found that the men who are thus habitually behind time are as habitually behind success, and the world generally casts them aside to swell the ranks of the grumblers and the railers against fortune. The late Mr. Tegg, the publisher, who rose from a very humble position in life, once said of himself that he "had lodged with beggars, and had the honor of presentation to royalty," and that he attributed his success in life mainly to three things—punctuality as to time, self-reliance, and integrity in word and deed.

It is astonishing how much an energetic man of business can accomplish by methodical working, and by the careful economy of his time. It would even appear as if, the more business he had, the more leisure he had for other affairs. It is said of Lord Brougham that when he was in the full career of his profession, presiding in the House of Lords and the Court of Chancery, he found time to be at the head of some eight or ten public associations, one of which was the Society for the Diffusion of Useful Knowledge, and that he was most punctual in his attendances, always contriving to be in the chair when the hour of meeting had arrived.

In addition to these ordinary working qualities, the business man of the highest class requires sound discretion, quick perception, and firmness in the execution of his plans. Business tact is also important; and, though this is partly the gift of nature, it is yet capable of being cultivated and developed by observation and experience. Men of this quality are quick to see the right mode of action, and, if they have decision of purpose, are prompt to carry out their undertakings to a successful issue. Such men give a new life to industry; they put their character into every work that they enter upon, and are among the most powerful agents in the progress of society in all times.

It will be observed from what we have said that the successful conduct of business consists in a great measure in assiduous attention to matters of detail—in short, to what is ordinarily called Routine, and sometimes Red-Tapeism. Accuracy, discipline, punctuality, method, payment of debts, organization, all are routine. No doubt a blind, stupid routine causes hinderance to business, but a wise routine greatly facilitates it, while it is the only check to rashness and incapacity on the part of individuals where the business of large departments has to be conducted. In the case of a business in the hands of a single person, such as that of a merchant or manufacturer, there will be greater promptitude in action, and less need for the interposition of checks, because no one has to be consulted but the master himself; and he is stimulated by self-interest to watch closely all the outgoings and incomings of his concern. But where self-interest is less active, and where a large business, as of a corporation or a government, is managed by *employés,* routine necessarily becomes complicated by checks; for, though the large majority of men are honest, it is absolutely necessary that provision should be made against the possible rogue or the jobber. . . .

The truth of the good old maxim, that "Honesty is the best policy," is upheld by the daily experience of life, uprightness and integrity being found as successful in business as in every thing else. As Hugh Miller's worthy uncle used to advise him, "In all your dealings give your neighbor the cast of the bauk—'good measure, heaped up, and running over'—and you will not lose by it in the end." A well-known brewer of beer attributed his success to the liberality with which he used his malt. Going up to the vat and tasting it, he would say, "Still rather poor, my lads; give it another cast of the malt." The brewer put his character into his beer, and it proved generous accordingly, obtaining a reputation in England, India, and the colonies, which laid the foundation of a large fortune. Integrity of word and deed ought to be the very corner-stone of all business transactions. To the tradesman, the merchant, and manufacturer, it should be what honor is to the soldier, and charity to the Christian. In the humblest calling there will always be found scope for the exercise of this uprightness of character. Hugh Miller speaks of the honest mason with whom he served his apprenticeship, who *"put his conscience into every stone that he laid."* So the true mechanic will pride himself upon the thoroughness and solidity of his work, and the high-minded contractor upon the honesty of performance of his contract in every particular. The upright manufacturer will find not only honor and reputation, but substantial success, in the genuineness of the article which he produces, and the merchant in the honesty of what he sells, and that it really is what it seems to be. Baron Dupin, speaking of the general probity of Englishmen, which he held to be a principal cause of their success, observed, "We may succeed for a time by fraud, by surprise, by violence, but we can succeed permanently only by means directly opposite. It is not alone the courage, the intelligence, the activity of the merchant and manufacturer which maintain the superiority of their productions and the character of their country; it is far more their wisdom, their economy, and, above all, their probity. If ever in the British Islands the useful citizen should lose these virtues, we may be sure that, for England as for every other country, the vessels of a degenerate commerce, repulsed from every shore, would speedily disappear from those seas whose surface they now cover with the treasures of the universe, bartered for the treasures of the industry of the three kingdoms."

It must be admitted that Trade tries character perhaps more severely than any other pursuit in life. It puts to the severest tests honesty, self-denial, justice, and truthfulness; and men of business who pass through such trials unstained are perhaps worthy of as great honor as soldiers who prove their courage amid the fire and perils of battle. And, to the credit of the multitudes of men engaged in the various departments of trade, we think it must be admitted that, on the whole, they pass through their trials nobly. If we reflect but for a moment on the vast amount of wealth daily intrusted even to subordinate persons, who themselves probably earn but a bare competency—the loose cash which is constantly passing through the hands of shopmen, agents, brokers, and clerks in banking-houses—and note how comparatively few are the breaches of trust which occur amid all this temptation, it will probably be admitted that this steady daily honesty of conduct is most honorable to human nature, if it do not even tempt us to be proud of it. The same trust and confidence reposed by men of business in each other, as implied by the system of Credit, which is mainly based upon the principle of honor, would be surprising if it were not so much a matter of ordinary practice in business transactions. Dr. Chalmers has well said, that the implicit trust with which merchants are accustomed to confide in distant agents, separated from them perhaps by half the globe—often consigning vast wealth to men, recommended only by their character, whom perhaps they never saw—is probably the finest act of homage of one human being to another.

Although common honesty is still happily in the ascendant among common people, and the general business community of England is still sound at heart, putting their honest character into their respective callings, there are unhappily, as there have been in all times, but too many instances of flagrant dishonesty and fraud, exhibited by the unscrupulous, the over-speculative, and the intensely selfish, in their haste to be rich. There are tradesmen who adulterate, contractors who "scamp," manufacturers who give us shoddy instead of wool, "dressing" instead of cotton, cast-iron tools instead of steel, needles without eyes, razors made only "to sell," and swindled fabrics in many shapes. But these we must hold to be the exceptional cases, of low-minded and grasping men, who, though they may gain wealth which they probably can not enjoy, will never gain an honest character, nor secure that without which wealth is nothing—a satisfied conscience. "The rogue cozened not me, but his own conscience," said Bishop Latimer of a cutler who made him pay twopence for a knife not worth a penny. Money earned by screwing, cheating, and overreaching may for a time dazzle the eyes of the unthinking, but the bubbles blown by unscrupulous rogues, when full-blown, usually glitter only to burst. The Sadleirs, Dean Pauls, and Redpaths, for the most part, come to a sad end even in this world; and though the successful swindles of others may not be "found out," and the gains of their roguery may remain with them, it will be as a curse and not as a blessing. To such the words of the apostle strongly apply: "Your gold and silver is cankered; and the rust of them shall be a witness against you, and shall eat your flesh as it were fire."

It is possible that the scrupulously honest man may not grow rich so fast as the unscrupulous and dishonest one; but the success will be of a truer kind, earned without fraud or injustice. And even though a man should for a time be unsuccessful, still he must be honest: better lose all and save character, for character is itself a fortune; and if the high-principled man will but hold on his way courageously, success will surely come—nor will the highest reward of all be withheld from him. Wordsworth well describes the "Happy Warrior" as he

> "Who comprehends his trust, and to the same
> Keeps faithful with a singleness of aim;
> And therefore does not stoop nor lie in wait
> For wealth, or honor, or for worldly state;
> Whom they must follow, on whose head must fall,
> Like showers of manna if they come at all."

As an example of the high-minded mercantile man, trained in upright habits of business, and distinguished for justice, truthfulness, and honesty of dealing in all things, the career of the well-known David Barclay, grandson of Robert Barclay, of Ury, the author of the celebrated "Apology for the Quakers," may be briefly referred to. For many years he was the head of an extensive house in Cheapside, chiefly engaged in the American trade; but, like Granville Sharp, he entertained so strong an opinion against the war with our American colonies that he determined to retire altogether from the trade. While a merchant, he was as much distinguished by his talents, knowledge, integrity, and power, as he afterward was by his patriotism and munificent philanthropy. He was a mirror of truthfulness and honesty; and, as became the good Christian and true gentleman, his word was always held to be as good as his bond. His position and his high character induced the ministers of the day on many occasions to seek his advice; and, when examined before the House of Commons on the subject of the American dispute, his views were so clearly expressed, and his advice was so strongly justified by the reasons stated by him, that Lord North publicly acknowledged that he had derived more information from David Barclay than from all others east of Temple Bar. On retiring from business, it was not to rest in luxurious ease, but to enter upon new labors of usefulness for others. With ample means, he felt that he still owed to society the duty of a great example. He founded a house of industry near his residence at Walthamstow, which he supported at a large cost for several years, until at length he succeeded in rendering it a source of comfort as well as independence to the well-disposed families of the poor in that neighborhood. When an estate in Jamaica fell to him, he determined, though at a cost of some £10,000, at once to give liberty to the whole of the slaves on the property. He sent out an agent, who hired a ship, and he had the little slave community transported to one of the free American states, where they settled down and prospered. Mr. Barclay had been assured that the negroes were too ignorant and too barbarous for freedom, and it was thus that he determined practically to demonstrate the fallacy of the assertion. In dealing with his accumulated savings, he made himself the executor of his own will, and instead of leaving a large fortune to be divided among his relatives at his death, he extended to them his munificent aid during his life, watched and aided them in their respective careers, and thus not only laid the foundation, but lived to see the maturity, of some of the largest and most prosperous business concerns in the metropolis. We believe that to this day some of our most eminent merchants, such as the Gurneys, Hanburys, and Buxtons,

are proud to acknowledge with gratitude the obligations they owe to David Barclay for the means of their first introduction to life, and for the benefits of his counsel and countenance in the early stages of their career. Such a man stands as a mark of the mercantile honesty and integrity of his country, and is a model and example for men of business in all time to come.

QUESTIONS ON SMILES

1. List the various "business qualities" described by Smiles. Are all of these qualities, as noted by Smiles, *moral* qualities? Are these qualities *virtues?* Explain.

2. In what ways is Smiles' account of business qualities similar to Aristotle's account of virtue?

3. Are the qualities noted by Smiles *peculiar* to commerce, or are they, as Smiles says, relevant to any "important undertaking"? Are there other qualities, not noted by Smiles, that are essential to commerce?

An Aristotelian Approach to Business Ethics

Robert C. Solomon

Robert C. Solomon is the Quincy Lee Centennial Professor of Business and Philosophy at the University of Texas at Austin. The author of numerous articles, his books include The Passions *(1976);* Love: Emotion, Myth, and Metaphor *(1981);* Above the Bottom Line: An Introduction to Business Ethics *(with Kristine R. Hansen, 1983); and* The Joy of Philosophy *(1999). The excerpt below appeared in Thomas J. Donaldson and R. Edward Freeman, editors,* Business as a Humanity *(1994).*

FROM POLIS TO PHRONESIS

So what is the Aristotelian approach to business ethics? What are its primary ingredients? A deontological approach to the subject would highlight such terms as "rational principles," "consistency," "obligation," and "duties." A utilitarian approach would rather emphasize "interests," "preferences," "consequences," and "help and harm." Libertarians would no doubt emphasize the notion of "rights." So, too, the Aristotelian approach has its distinctive vocabulary and characteristics. I want to list a half dozen of them, which I will describe here only briefly. (I think that the point will soon become obvious—if it isn't already.)

Community (*polis*). The Aristotelian approach begins with the idea that we are all members of an organized group, with something of a history and established practices governing everything from eating and working to worshiping. To be sure, communities in the contemporary "Western" world are anything but homogeneous or harmonious, but the claim I am making here is more metaphysical than nostalgic, and that is that what we call "the individual" is him- or herself socially constituted and socially situated. The philosophical myth that has grown almost cancerous in many business circles, the neo-Hobbesian view that "it's a jungle out there" and "it's every man [*sic*] for himself," is the direct denial of the Aristotelian view that we are all first and foremost members of a community and that our self-interest is for the most part identical to the larger interests of the group. As the Greeks used to say, "To live the good life, one must live in a great city." To my business students today, who are all too likely to choose a job on the basis of salary and start-up bonus alone, I always say, "To live a decent life, choose the right company." In business ethics the corporation is one's community, but, of course, the corporation is itself a part of a larger community—as diverse as that may be—without which it would have no identity, serve no purpose, and sell no products. Quite the contrary of the cynical business "wisdom" that preaches "every man [*sic*] for himself," the truth is that every business activity, from the small-time hustler to the giant corporation, presupposes and itself incorporates a community, a polis in which the virtues of mutual trust and cooperation are taken for granted (even in their intentional breach).

Excellence. The Greek *arete* is often translated as either "virtue" or "excellence," and, unlike the rather modest and self-effacing notion of virtue that we inherited from our Victorian ancestors (indeed, even Kant used the term), the dual translation by itself makes a striking point. It is not enough to do no wrong. "Knowingly do no harm" [*primum non nocere*] is *not* the end of business ethics (as Peter Drucker suggests).[1] The hardly original slogan I sometimes use to sell what I do, "ethics and excellence," is not just a tag-along with Peters and Waterman. Virtue is doing one's best, excelling, not merely (from top to bottom) "keeping one's nose clean" and "toeing the line." The virtues that constitute business ethics are, above all, the virtues of doing business, and these should not be conceived of as if business ethics were nothing other than the general application of

moral principles to one specific context (among others), primarily as an inhibiting force or a set of side constraints, rather than the underlying set of rules and expectations that make the practice of business possible in the first place. The word "quality," though much overused in advertising, defines the bottom line of business competition far better than "profits," which readily follow. The virtues of self-respect and integrity, far from being antagonistic to long-term success, form its very precondition. (Which is not to say, of course, that slimeballs don't succeed; it is just to point out that they are, nevertheless, still slimeballs.)

Position. Much has been written (e.g., by Norman Bowie, in his good little book *Business Ethics*) on the importance of "role morality" and on "my Position and its duties."[2] It is the situatedness of corporate roles that lends them their particular ethical poignancy, the fact that an employee or an executive is not just a person who happens to be in a place and is constrained by no more than the usual ethical prohibitions. To work for a company is to accept a set of particular obligations, to assume a prima facie loyalty to one's employer, to adopt a certain standard of excellence and conscientiousness that is largely defined by the job itself. There may be general ethical rules and guidelines that cut across most positions, but, as these get more general and more broadly applicable, they also become all but useless in concrete ethical dilemmas. Robert Townsend's cute claim that if a company needs an ethical code, use the Ten Commandments, is not only irreverent but ultimately irrelevant.[3] The Aristotelian approach to business ethics presumes concrete situations and particular people and their place in organizations. There is little point to an ethics that tries to transcend all such particularities and embrace the chairman of the board as well as a middle manager, a secretary, and a factory worker. All ethics is contextual, and one of the problems with all of those grand theories is that they try to transcend context and end up with vacuity.

Holism. It more or less follows from what I've said that one of the problems of traditional business thinking is our tendency to isolate our business or professional roles from the rest of our lives, a process that Marx, following Friedrich Schiller, described as "alienation." The good life may have many facets, but they are facets and not mere components, much less isolated aspects of a fragmented existence. We hear more and more in managerial circles that a manager's primary and ultimate concern is *people*. It's gotten trite, but as I watch our more ambitious students and talk with more and more semisuccessful but "trapped" middle managers and executives, I become more and more convinced that the tunnel vision of business life encouraged by the too narrow business curriculum and the daily rhetoric of the corporate community is damaging and counterproductive. Good employees are good people, and to pretend that the virtues of business stand isolated from the virtues of the rest of our lives—and this is not for a moment to deny the particularity of either our business roles or our lives—is to set up that familiar tragedy in which a pressured employee violates his or her "personal values" because, from a purely business point of view, he or she "didn't really have any choice."

Nobility. This is a word, like "honor"—its close kin—that seems all but archaic in the modern business world, part of an elitist world that we have all (happily) left behind. These are concepts that we greet with suspicion, for example, when Richard Nixon, on two very separate occasions, declared "peace with honor" as he retreated from Vietnam and "the nobility of work" when he declared a wage-and-price freeze during one of his several economic crises. But hypocrisy and abuse aside, these are concepts that did not die out with the passing of the Greek polis and the French aristocracy in flight from the revolution. It is our overly individualistic thinking that keeps us from appreciating the importance of a sense of honor, which presupposes our embeddedness in a community, and the significance of a notion of nobility that refers not to a social class and the rituals and pretensions thereof but to a certain mode of behavior and self-respect, a sense of "being above" not other people but certain forms of selfish and otherwise vulgar behavior. There is indeed the "nobility of work," but this phrase, which makes a serious effort to counter residual prejudices against work, has as much to do with ethics as that self-serving defense of the Protestant ethic that would pretend that lousy jobs are just as desirable as good jobs.[4]

Judgment (phronesis). Against the view that ethics consists primarily of general principles that get applied to particular situations, Aristotle thought that it was "good judgment," or *phronesis,* that was of the greatest importance in ethics. Good judgment (which centered on perception, rather than on the abstract formulation and interpretation of general principles) was the product of a good upbringing, a proper education. It was always situated, perhaps something like Joseph Fletcher's still much referred to notion of a "situation ethics," and took into careful account the particularity of the persons and circumstances involved. But I think the real importance of *phronesis* is not just its priority to ethical deliberation and ratiocination; it has rather to do with the inevitable conflicts of both concerns and principles that define almost every ethical dilemma. Justice, for example, may sound as if it were a monolithic, hierarchically layered, and almost mechanical process (especially in the writings of some philosophers). As I have argued elsewhere, however, there are a dozen or more different considerations that enter into most deliberations about justice, including not only rights and prior obligations and the public good but questions of merit (which themselves break down into a variety of sometimes conflicting categories) and responsibility and risk.[5] I won't go into this here, but the point is that there is *no* (nonarbitrary) mechanical decision procedure for resolving most disputes about justice; what is required, in each and every case, is the ability to balance and weigh competing concerns and come to a "fair" conclusion. But what's fair is not the outcome of one or several preordained principles of justice; it is (as they say) a judgment call, always disputable but nevertheless well or badly made. I have often thought that encouraging abstract ethical theory actually discourages and distracts us from the need to make judgments. I have actually heard one of my colleagues say (without qualms) that, since he's been studying ethical theory, he no longer has any sense of ethics. If this sounds implausible, I urge you to remember your last department or boardroom meeting and the inverse relationship between the high moral tone of the conversation and the ridiculousness of the proposals and decisions that followed. . . .

The Aristotelian approach is not antibusiness and certainly not antisuccess but only anti-*pleonexia,* antigreed. Aristotle's central ethical concept is "happiness" (more accurately, *eudaimonia,* perhaps better translated as "flourishing" or "doing well"). "Happiness," therefore, has what we would call "success" built into it, and success in a consumer society necessarily entails a certain level of financial success. Let's remember, however, that we "consume" art and music, books and ideas, as well as cars and kitchenware, and the dollar costs of such consumption may not be considerable at all. What Aristotle's conception excludes is mediocrity and isolation—especially the mean-spirited competition that too many people in business abstractly confuse with free enterprise. Moreover, it is not enough to be a subjectively contented or even blithe failure; it is what one actually accomplishes, with and for others as well as by and for oneself, that counts.

It would be a crass vulgarization to suppose that doing well is to be understood, in our society, as just a matter of "making it." Most Americans, when not engaged in business conversation, would rather readily admit that the only bottom line that counts is how happy we are, as individuals, as families, as employees, as a people. Happiness may include success, but it is not wholly defined by success, and while an excellent company will almost always do well in the market, it is not doing well that makes them excellent. Tom Peters's incessant insistence on the "satisfied customer" and the "contented employee" highlights an extremely important Aristotelian measure. The rather banal equation between happiness and having fun too readily blinds us to the idea that our work ought to be satisfying and rewarding (only occasionally "fun"). The familiar image of the harried manager, on the other hand, is a symptom of something very wrong, in a career, in a company, in the market itself. Happiness (for us as well as for Aristotle) is a holistic concept, and it is one's character, not one's bottom line, that is the ultimate determinant and beneficiary of happiness. This is equally true, I want to insist, for giant corporations as it is for the individuals who work for them. . . .

The virtue of the Aristotelian approach to business ethics, I have argued, is its focus on the character of the individual and not just on impersonal policies and abstract principles and theories. A related virtue, however, points us in just the opposite direction, toward the enlargement of the self as a thoroughly social self and not an isolated Hobbesian or Lockean self whose place in society is up for negotiation. The Aristotelian approach must be understood in terms of a certain concept of self, an expanded self that is constituted by and identifies itself with the larger community or society. The self is, as I have argued elsewhere, first of all a matter of emotions, and so one might suspect that a special set of emotions will be particularly concerned with this enlarged sense of self. Too often it is assumed without argument or discussion that the emotions are merely personal, whether this means that they are merely subjective, exclusively of concern to the emotee, or merely physical and of no real importance. But emotions can be "about" all sorts of things and of varied significance to both the individual and the society. Some emotions are not only "about" society (as their "object") but involve society in the very identity of their subject. They are emotions that would be unintelligible without this larger sense of self. I should like to end this brief essay, therefore, with an even more brief outline of a few of the emotional virtues that it is the aim of the Aristotelian approach to business to cultivate.

Of particular interest here is a mixed set of emotions that, with the rise of radical individualism and the loss of a sense of Aristotelian virtue, the emphasis on policies and principles and the neglect of the person, has all but dropped out of business ethics. They include *loyalty, honor,* and a sense of *shame.* (Guilt is quite different from shame and is not part of the set.) All three emotions tie into the central notion of *integrity,* the first two by way of definition, the latter in the breach. Loyalty is a kind of integrity, not within oneself (conceived of as a self-sufficient, integral whole), but rather with oneself conceived as a part of a larger self, a group, a community, an organization or institution. As Josiah Royce wrote in his *Philosophy of Loyalty,* "Loyalty has its domestic, its religious, its commercial, its professional forms, and many other forms as well. The essence of it, whatever forms it may take, is . . . this: Since no man can find a plan of life by merely looking within his own chaotic nature, he has to look without, to the world of social conventions, deeds and causes."[6] Business ethics too often ignores loyalty in favor of the more abstract and universal concepts of rights. It is as if to say that, so long as we respect contracts, we need not be concerned with a superfluous and perhaps childish emotion like loyalty. Of course, loyalty (like patriotism, one special variant of it) can be a refuge from responsibility or a forum for venal self-righteousness, but it does not follow—as many people seem to think it does—that it is an emotion that has lost its place in the corporate world and that one's loyalties should always be first and foremost to oneself, to one's conscience, or to some set of "higher" standards. Every employer wants the loyalty of the employees, of course, but the objection to such loyalty is that the employees will thereby lose sight of their own best interests and perhaps find themselves bound to plans or policies that they find unethical or even illegal. The argument here, however, is not against loyalty but rather in support of the need for critical self-awareness of one's loyalties. It is not an argument against loyalty any more than the dangers of love are an argument against love. (Loyalty would not be wrongly conceived as a variety of love, appropriate to groups and institutions as well as to individuals.) Against the recent "work-for-hire" approach to employer-employee relations, I want to argue that an Aristotelian emphasis on loyalty—and that means loyalty in both directions—has a lot to offer to business ethics that too often gets dismissed with the usual stories of uncritical loyalty and gross corporate malfeasance.[7]

Honor is a second grand emotion of the Aristotelian self, an essential ingredient in integrity (some people would equate the two) and another emotion that is an endangered species in radical individualist thinking. Honor, when we use the term at all, usually means pride—a very different emotion—or even vanity, a very different and hardly flattering emotion indeed. As Hume argued in his *Treatise,* pride has mainly to do with a sense of personal accomplishment. Its focus is typically the individual self, but through loyalty and affiliation it can be expanded to encompass one's community and corporation. Pride, however, tends to be too personal and too concerned with accomplishment. Honor, by contrast, need not involve accomplishment at all (although it certainly may and often does), and it makes very little sense as a purely personal notion. (That is why, when people say that they are defending their honor but are obviously nursing their pride, we find such behavior not only foolish but pretentious as well.) Honor requires a sense of belonging, a sense of membership, a sense of self that incorporates one's corporate identity. It also involves living up to the expectations of the corporation, whether these are spelled out as a code of honor or set of moral rules or are simply implicit in the practices and goals of the group. (It is not obeying moral rules that makes a person honorable, however; it is obeying the rules because they are the rules of his or her corporation—very un-Kantian). A person's honor, in other words, is never his or her honor alone. It is the honor of the community or corporation that he or she represents, and standing up for honor necessarily entails defending it as a representative of that community or corporation. In business ethics, this sense of honor helps clarify both the role of the individual employee or executive in the corporation and, even more important, the role of both the individual and the corporation in society. (Tragedy in business ethics, one might add, does not usually consist of a conflict of interests but rather a conflicting sense of honor, a sense of being torn between one membership and another—as an employee of the company, as the friend of one's immediate supervisor or as the member of the greater community.)

Honor should not be thought of as a set of personal constraints defined by membership in a group. The notion of constraints is appropriate rather to a group of which one is not a member or, perhaps, is a member only by chance or because one was a member even though one now desperately wants to extricate oneself. One's sense of honor is, if not voluntary, at least personally acceptable, part and parcel of one's sense of self. It is, in this sense, a species of merit, but this is very different from any sense of desert or what one has achieved. Merit in the context of honor has to do with who one is—namely, a member of the group in good standing—and not particularly with anything that one has done (or not done) except insofar as such acts are part of one's membership in the group. So, too, there is

a natural affinity between honor and self-esteem; one's self-esteem depends on one's sense of honor (though not vice versa), and one's standing in the group becomes the criterion of self-esteem. One cannot be much of a member if one can be humiliated in the group and nevertheless have a solid sense of self-worth. So, too, the contemporary idea that one's main objective after public humiliation is to "get over it" makes impossible any sense of honor—which presupposes that one doesn't just "get over it." One might note that one symptom of our collective loss of honor is the fact that no one seems to believe in the concept of a "ruined life" anymore. One just moves to another town or gets another job or sets up another company and "starts over." In practical terms, what this means is that the business community is notoriously poor in sanctioning its own rules and punishing even the most flagrant offenders of those rules. Business failure is neither adequate nor sufficiently dependable as a measure or a punishment for unethical business practices. It is a person's sense of honor that must be put into play, and for those who don't understand or who scoff at this notion the old tribal practice of exile (federal minimum security prisons will do) serves an extremely necessary function in the survival of the business community.

The opposite of honor is *shame.* Aristotle lists, with some discomfort, shame as one of the virtues, not because it is good to be ashamed but rather because, as in that Ethiopian proverb, "where there is no shame, there is no honor." Thus, John Rawls is not entirely wrong when he insists that shame is the opposite of self-esteem, since honor can be the criterion for self-esteem. Not all societies are honor societies, however, and not everyone's self-esteem is tied to a sense of honor. Shame is not, as Rawls says, failing to live up to one's potential; it is, much more specifically, failing to live up to the standards of the group through which one gains one's self-identity and one's standards. Shame is, in other words, a loss of integrity, a breach of the commitments or principles one accepts and knows that one should accept.[8] Of course, in the Aristotelian approach to business ethics, failing to live up to one's potential may well be equivalent to failing to live up to the standards of the group, perhaps because one has made a commitment that cannot be kept or set a goal that cannot be met. But personal achievement and failure as such are not essential and often not relevant to honor and shame. What one fails to *be* is acceptable to the group and, accordingly, acceptable in terms of one's own essential sense of identity. To feel shame (not quite the same as "being ashamed") is quite literally to fail oneself, but only in the context of one's larger self.

It is in this sense that shame is contrasted to guilt, for it is guilt, not shame, that defines the appropriate attitude in our nonhonor society. Shame is always defined in a group context; guilt is borne by one alone. It is not surprising that the Scriptures talk mainly of sin and guilt when discussing an individual's wrongdoing before God. Guilt is an emotion that permeates the personal self, but other people, one's peers, play no clear role in its workings. We feel guilty, not shamed, for failing to live up to our own goals and standards. We feel guilty, not shamed, for breaking the rules or committing a moral infelicity. Guilt is appropriate to isolated individuals; shame is possible only in groups. Guilt ties in nicely with the traditional concept of the individual soul; shame is essentially a tribal emotion. It has often been said (by Nietzsche and Freud most famously) that there is too much guilt in our society. I would like to suggest that, while this is probably true, there isn't nearly enough shame. Indeed, the payoff for public humiliation in current-day America seems to be a fat book advance and profitable public appearances, not repentence, apology, and retribution. We may have more guilt than we ought to have, but part of the reason may be that we don't have enough room for honor—or shame.

What all of this amounts to is the idea that business ethics is at once more personal and more social than it is usually thought to be. It is not enough to teach principles and policies, much less the theories of the great, dead, mostly white male philosophers. Business ethics requires the cultivation of the civic virtues, not something possible in an isolated business ethics course—on this, at least, the critics are correct—but nevertheless, as Aristotle himself surely would have argued, something absolutely necessary for the health and well-being of the business world itself. What business ethics does and what business ethics courses do is not to "teach" ethics to business students and managers. Instead, they remind us all that there are standards and virtues at issue in business without which an enterprise (no matter how "free") will not and does not deserve to survive. . . .

ENDNOTES

1. Peter Drucker, *Management* (New York: Harper and Row, 1974), chap. 28.
2. Norman Bowie, *Business Ethics* (Englewood Cliffs, N.J.: Prentice-Hall, 1982), pp. 1–16.
3. Robert Townsend, *Up the Organization* (New York: Alfred A. Knopf, 1970), p. 147. See also Townsend, *Further Up the Organization* (New York: Alfred A. Knopf, 1984), p. 176.
4. See Joanne B. Ciulla, "Honest Work," in *Above the Bottom Line,* 2d ed., edited by Robert C. Solomon (New York: Harcourt Brace, 1994).
5. Robert C. Solomon, *A Passion for Justice* (New York: Addison-Wesley, 1989), esp. chap. 4.
6. Josiah Royce, *The Philosophy of Loyalty* (New York: Macmillan, 1908); quoted in Bowie, *Business Ethics,* p. 14.
7. For a good philosophical discussion of loyalty, see Andrew Oldenquist, "Loyalties," *Journal of Philosophy* 79, no. 4 (April 1982): 173ff.
8. By far, the best discussion of integrity and its violations I know is Lynne McFall, "Integrity," *Ethics* 98 (October 1987): 5–20.

QUESTIONS ON SOLOMON

1. Solomon claims that the "Aristotelian approach . . . presumes concrete situations and particular people. . . ." How does this assumption affect moral judgment? If one adopts the Aristotelian view, then is there any point to rules of business conduct or business codes ("Codes of Ethics")?

2. If the human self, like the virtues, makes reference to a larger community, then how is one to discern the features of a good community? Is business, the commercial life, essential to good communities?

3. How are the qualities of honor and shame related to a larger community? In what ways could one's honor involve the honor of a corporation? In what ways might the honor of a business firm or corporation involve the honor of the wider community?

Bourgeois Virtue

Deirdre N. McCloskey

Deirdre N. McCloskey is University Professor of the Human Sciences at the University of Illinois at Chicago where she teaches history and economics. The author of numerous scholarly articles, her books include The Rhetoric of Economics *(1985),* If You're So Smart: The Narrative of Economic Expertise *(1990),* The Vices of Economists; the Virtues of the Bourgeoisie *(1997), and* Crossing: A Memoir *(1999).*

We have two ways of talking about the virtues, and we seem stuck on them. One way is patrician, which concerns what John Casey calls "pagan" virtues. The four classical pagan virtues are those of Odysseus: prudence, temperance, justice, and courage. The aristocrat is honorable, great-hearted in hospitality, quick to anger.

"You wine sack, with a dog's eyes, with a deer's heart," says Achilles—exhibiting more courage than prudence, temperance, or justice—"Never / once have you taken courage in your heart to arm with your people."

The other way of virtue-talk is plebeian, the way of St. Paul. The peasant suffers yet endures. "Let every soul be subject unto the higher powers. For there is no power but of God. . . . Owe no man any thing, but to love one another." Faith, hope, and charity, these three, but the greatest is charity. It is a "slave morality," bending to the aristocratic virtues that Nietzsche and other Hellenizers prized.

The two vocabularies of the virtues are spoken in the camp and common. Achilles struts through the camp in his Hephaestian armor, exercising a noble wrath. Jesus stands barefoot on the Mount, preaching to the least of the commoners.

And yet we live mostly now in the town, we bourgeois, or else we are moving to townly occupations as fast as we can manage, trading the old cow for a car. The aristocracy is gone, though some intellectuals wish not. And the prediction that the proletariat at the other end would become the universal class has proven to be mistaken.

Jobs for the two older classes are disappearing. Half of the employment in rich countries is white-collar, and the percentage is rising. The very soldiers in capitalist democracies are shufflers of paper. The production of things has become steadily cheaper. A barber or a professor was not much more productive in 1990 than in 1800, or, for that matter, in 400 B.C. It still takes fifteen minutes with a pair of scissors to do a short back and sides and fifty minutes with a piece of chalk to convey the notion of comparative advantage. But the farmer since 1800 has become more productive in the United States by a factor of 36. We cannot eat 36 times more food, though some of us try, and so the farmer's share in employment has fallen towards nil. A piece of cotton cloth that sold for 40 shillings in the 1780s sold for 5 shillings in the 1850s, and nowadays, using the same values of money, for a few pence. The cheapness led spinning out of the home, then weaving, canning, the making of men's and women's clothing, and food preparation. Stanley Lebergott recently calculated that the time involved in food preparation during the years from 1900 to 1965 fell from 44 hours a week to 10. Calculating power itself—adding, multiplying, and carrying—that sold for $400 in 1970 sold for $4 in 1990. Workers on the American manufacturing line peaked at about a fifth of the total labor force after World War II and the percentage has been falling ever since, although only slowly at first. Fifty years from now a maker of things on an assembly line will be as rare as a farmer. The only jobs left will be hamburger flipping on the one side and bourgeois occupations on the other.

It is usual to praise a pagan or a Christian virtue and then to complain how much we moderns lack it. Shamefully we bourgeois are neither saints nor heroes. The age is one of mere iron—or aluminum, or plastic—not pagan gold or Christian silver. The townsfolk are useful, maybe necessary, but not *virtuous*. "Why, the very idea! Bourgeois *virtue?*" The bourgeois virtues have been reduced to the single vice of greed.

The intelligentsia thunders at the middle class but offers no advice on how to be good within it. The only way to become a good bourgeois, according to Flaubert and Sinclair Lewis and Paolo Pasolini, is to stop being one. Not having an ideal of bourgeois virtue, or devaluing the ideal by comparison with Christian and aristocratic virtue, leaves us unable to talk about virtue at all. We bourgeois are left without reasons for ethical standards. We are left with What's Profitable: "Yet a great deal of money is made here. Good day, sir."

Ethics courses in business and medical schools exhibit the dilemma. Some time ago the Harvard Business School was given $20 million to study ethics in the old way—all the ethics that money could buy. Harvard Medical School has waxed ethical, too. The professors staffing the courses believe that ethical questions are matters of crisis. What are the ethics of insider trading? Would Jesus have signed on? What about the transplantation of organs? How would Kant have felt about that one? Yet neither aristocratic nor peasant virtue can offer much minute-by-minute help in how to be a good bourgeois.

Ethics has turned recently from universal theories to the particular virtues, as in Alasdair MacIntyre's *After Virtue: A Study in Moral Theory,* or John Casey's *Pagan Virtue: An Essay in Ethics.* It has also turned to narratives in aid of the virtues—for example, Albert Jonsen and Stephen Toulmin's *The Abuse of Casuistry: A History of Moral Reasoning* or Wayne Booth's *The Company We Keep: An Ethics of Fiction.* Feminist thinking on the matter, such as that found in Carol Gilligan's *In a Different Voice,* or Nel Noddings's *Caring: A Feminine Approach to Ethics and Moral Education,* has questioned the presumption of universal ethics, in particular the worship of masculine virtues. As Bernard Williams puts it, in the new approach—as new as Aristotle—"morality is seen as something whose real existence must consist in personal experience and social institutions, not in sets of propositions." It is local knowledge, not universal, located in the camp or common or town.

Consider the virtues of the three classes, matched to their character. The "character" might be in the eyes of others, or in its own eyes, or, less commonly, in fact.

The Classes and the Virtues

Aristocrat Patrician	Peasant Plebeian	Bourgeois Mercantile
pagan	Christian	secular
Achilles	St. Francis	Benjamin Franklin
pride of being	pride of service	pride of action
honor	duty	integrity
forthrightness	candor	honesty
loyalty	solidarity	trustworthiness
courage	fortitude	enterprise
wit	jocularity	humor
courtesy	reverence	respect
propriety	humility	modesty
magnanimity	benevolence	consideration
justice	fairness	responsibility
foresight	wisdom	prudence
moderation	frugality	thrift
love	charity	affection
grace	dignity	self-possession
subjective	objective	conjective

The point is not to elevate bourgeois virtue over the others in some universal sense. The point is to sidestep universal senses. In some personal and social circumstances, courage is a virtue. (In others, it is a vice.) So is humility. (Likewise.) But when the class left out by the virtue-talk is half the population, on its way to being all the population, the vocabulary of the virtues is not doing its job. As Richard Rorty puts it, "detailed descriptions of particular varieties of pain and humiliation (in, e.g., novels and ethnographies), rather than philosophical or religious treatises, were the modern intellectual's principal contributions to moral progress." Chinua Achebè's *Things Fall Apart* or the writings of Borges inspire me to act ethically toward Nigerians or Argentineans more than does any amount of philosophizing about universal good. A modern society needs poetry and history and movies about bourgeois virtue: integrity, honesty, trustworthiness, enterprise, humor, respect, modesty, consideration, responsibility, prudence, thrift, affection, self-possession.

So far society has gotten poetry and history and movies about the older virtues, looking back on many-tower'd Camelot and sweet Auburn, loveliest village of the plain. The result has been mostly bad, as in the nationalist wars down to 1914 and the ideological wars that followed.

Hellenism, for example, made war into a contest of aristocratic virtues, Hector and Achilles armed with cordite and barbed wire. In his autobiography of 1928, the German classicist Ulrich von Wilamowitz-Moellendorff speaks fondly of a Scottish colleague, who "was a gentleman in the full sense of the word. . . . [He was] proud of his great nation and of the British Empire, as was proper, but also as a true patriot ready to give free play to the patriotism and pride of another. United in this frame of mind as good friends," he continues, dreaming of Ilium and immortal fame, "we sent our sons to meet each other in the field." Wilamowitz's son Tycho attained in the trenches of the Great War "an early death on the field of honour," honorably gassed, perhaps, or suffocated in his bunker, or run over by a truck.

Romantic Teutonism, on the other hand, invented a primitive community of equals exhibiting the peasant virtues. The theory is still credited by non-historians. Prince Kropotkin, writing to the Russians in 1901 from the safety of a bourgeois nation, declared that communism would be "nearer to the folkmote self-government than representative government can ever be," and promised that "owing to the immense productivity of human labor which has been reached nowadays [and how reached, my dear Prince?] . . . a very high degree of well-being can easily be obtained in a few years by communist work." Ah yes, a few years of communist work.

We are all bourgeois now (for some decades about 80 percent of Americans have identified themselves as "middle class," a consciousness that may of course be false). The ideals of nationalism or socialism do not suit our lives. Those of townspeople, the bourgeoisie, do.

I am suggesting, in other words, that we stop sneering at the bourgeoisie, stop being ashamed of being middle class, and stop defining a participant in an economy as an amoral brute. The bad talk creates a reality. Adam Smith knew that a capitalist society such as eighteenth-century Edinburgh could not flourish without the virtues of trustworthiness or bourgeois pride, supported by talk. Smith's other book, *The Theory of Moral Sentiments,* which scarcely any economist reads, was about love, not greed; esteem, not venality. Yet even many economists have learned by now that moral sentiment must ground a market. (Some go on trying to solve the Hobbes Problem, well into its fourth century of irresolution—namely: Can a mob of unsocialized brutes be proven on a blackboard to create in the end a civil society? The problem lacks point if people are already French or American.)

The growth of the market, I would argue, promotes virtue, not vice. Most intellectuals since 1848 have thought the opposite: that it erodes virtue. "It was a fundamental principle of the Gradgrind philosophy that everything was to be paid for. . . . Gratitude was to be abolished, and the virtues springing from it were not to be. Every inch of the existence of mankind, from birth to death, was to be a bargain across a counter." As James Boyd White puts it in his otherwise admirable *Justice As Translation,* bourgeois growth is bad because it is "the expansion of the exchange system by the conversion of what is outside it into its terms. It is a kind of steam shovel chewing away at the natural and social world."

And yet we all take happily what the market gives—polite, accommodating, energetic, enterprising, risk-taking, trustworthy people; not bad people. In the Bulgaria of old (I am informed by Poles who claimed to have seen it), the department stores had a policeman on every floor, not to prevent theft but to stop the customers from attacking the arrogant and incompetent clerks selling goods that fell apart at the moment of sale. The way a salesperson in an American store greets customers startles foreigners: "How can I help you?" It is an instance in miniature of bourgeois virtue.

Even an ethics of greed for the almighty dollar, to take the caricature at its face value, is not the worst. For example, an ethics of greed is better than an ethics of slaughter, whether by patrician sword or plebeian pike. Commercial greed must work by mutual agreement, not by violence. "There are few ways in which a man can be more innocently employed than in getting money," said Dr. Johnson. The disdain for modest greed is ethically naïve, because it fails to acknowledge that the greed prospers in a market economy only by satisfying the customer.

Donald Trump offends. But for all the envy he has provoked, he is not a thief. He didn't get his millions from aristocratic cattle raids, acclaimed in bardic glory. He made, as he put it in his first book, deals. The deals were voluntary. He didn't use a .38 or a broadsword to get people to agree. He bought the Commodore Hotel low and sold it high because Penn Central, Hyatt Hotels, and the New York City Board of Estimate—and behind them the voters and hotel guests—put the old place at a low value and the new place, trumped up, at a high value. Trump earned a suitably fat profit for seeing that a hotel in a low-value use could be moved into a high-value use. An omniscient central planner would have ordered the same move. Market capitalism should be defended as the most altruistic of systems, each capitalist working, working, working to help a customer, for pay. Trump does good by doing well.

And even from a strictly individual view, the bourgeois virtues, though not those of Achilles or Jesus, are not ethical zeros. Albert Hirschman (who speaks precisely of "bourgeois virtues") recounts the career from Montesquieu to Marx of the phrase "doux commerce," quoting for instance William Robertson in 1769: that sweet commerce "tends to wear off those prejudices which maintain distinctions and animosity between nations. It softens and polishes the manners of men." In his play at the dawn of bourgeois power, George Lillo has his ideal of the London merchant, Thorowgood, assert that "as the name of merchant never degrades the gentleman, so by no means does it exclude him." Thorowgood on leaving the office instructs his assistant to "look carefully over the files to see whether there are any tradesmen's bills unpaid." The aristocrat can sneer at the goody-goodness of the bourgeois; but after all, in seriousness, is it not a matter of virtue to pay one's tailor? What kind of person accepts the wares of tradesmen and refuses to give something in return, though promised? No merchant he.

The honesty of a society of merchants goes beyond what would be strictly self-interested in a society of rats, as in that much maligned model of the mercantile society, the small midwestern city. A reputation for fair dealing is necessary for a roofer whose trade is limited to a town with a population of fifty thousand. One bad roof and he is finished in Iowa City, and so he practices virtue with care. By now he would not put on a bad roof even if he could get away with it, and he behaves like a growing child internalizing virtues once forced on him. A woman at a cocktail party who told the story of her bad roof (redone for free, at the roofer's instigation) refused to tell his name. A rat would have ruined the businessman to improve the story. After all, the woman's own reputation wasn't at stake.

A potent source of bourgeois virtue and a check on bourgeois vice is the premium that a bourgeois society puts on discourse. The bourgeois must talk. The aristocrat gives a speech, the peasant tells a tale. But the bourgeois must in the bulk of his transactions talk to an equal. It is wrong to imagine, as modern economics does, that the market is a field of silence. "I will buy with you, sell with you, talk with you, walk with you, and so following. . . . What news on the Rialto?"

For one thing, talk defines business reputation, as at the Iowa City cocktail party. A market economy looks forward and therefore depends on trust. The persuasive talk that establishes trust is necessary for doing much business, and that is why co-religionists or co-ethnics deal so profitably with each other. Avner Greif has explored the business dealings of Mediterranean Jews in the Middle Ages, accumulating evidence for a reputational conversation. In 1055 one Abun ben Zedaka of Jerusalem, for example, "was accused (though not charged in court) of embezzling the money of a Maghribi trader. When word of this accusation reached other Maghribi traders, merchants as far away as Sicily canceled their agency relations with him." Reputational gossip, Greif notes, was cheap, "a by-product of the commercial activity [itself] and passed along with other commercial correspondence." A letter from Palermo to an Alexandrian merchant who had disappointed the writer said, "Had I listened to what people say, I never would have entered into a partnership with you." With such information, cheating was profitless within the community.

Old Believers in Russia during the eighteenth and nineteenth centuries held a similar position, as Alexander Gerschenkron once pointed out. The Old Believers refused to adopt the late-seventeenth-century reforms in the Russian church, and were in other ways far from progressive. Yet because of their peculiarity they were able to establish a speech community within the larger society. Old Believers on the northern River Vyg, for example, were able in the early eighteenth century to become major grain merchants to the new St. Petersburg "by utilizing their connections with the other Old Believers' communities in the southern parts of the country." Sir William Petty observed at the time that "trade is not fixed to any species of religion as such, but rather to the heterodox part of the whole." Any distinction will do. Quakers were great merchants in eighteenth-century England. The overseas Chinese, segregated from the rest of the population (and therefore able to talk inexpensively with one another about breaches of contract among their own), are more successful in trade than their cousins at home.

The aristocrat does not deign to bargain. Hector tries, and Achilles answers: "Argue me no agreements. I cannot forgive you. / As there are no trustworthy oaths between men and lions, / Nor wolves and lambs have spirit that can be brought into agreement." The Duke of Ferrara speaks of his last, late duchess there upon the wall, "Even had you skill / In speech—(which I have not)—to make your will / Quite clear to such an one. . . ./ —E'en then would be some stooping; and I choose / Never to stoop." The aristocrat never stoops; the peasant stoops silently to harvest the grain or to run the machine; the bourgeois stoops metaphorically to make his will quite clear, and to know the will and reason of the other. The aristocrat's speech is declamation, and his proofs are like commands, which is perhaps why Plato the aristocrat and some Western intellectuals after him loved them so. The proof of the irrationality of the square root of 2 convinces (*vincere,* to conquer). The bourgeois by contrast must persuade, sweetly (*suadeo,* from the same root as English *sweet*).

The bourgeois goes at persuasion with a will. About a quarter of national income is earned from merely bourgeois and feminine persuasion: not orders or information but persuasion. One thinks immediately of advertising, but in fact advertising is a tiny part of the total—1.5 percent of national income. Take instead the detailed categories of work and make a guess as to the percentage of the time in each job spent on persuasion. Out of the 115 million civilian workers it seems reasonable to assign 100 percent of the time of the 760,000 lawyers and judges to persuasion; and likewise all the public relations specialists and actors and directors. Perhaps 75 percent of the time of the 14.2 million executive, administrative, and managerial employees is spent on persuasion, and a similar share of the time of the 4.8 million teachers and the 11.2 million salespeople (excluding cashiers). Half of the effort of police, writers, and health workers, one might guess, is spent on persuasion. And so forth. The result is 28.2 million person-years, a quarter of the labor force, persuading.

The result can be checked against other measures. John Wallis and Douglass North measure 50 percent of national income as transaction costs, the costs of persuasion being part of these. Not all of the half of American workers who are white-collar talk for a living, but in an extended sense many do, and for that matter, so do many blue-collar workers, persuading each other to handle the cargo just so, and pink-collar workers dealing all day with talking customers and cooks. Of the talkers a good percentage are persuaders. The secretary shepherding a document through the company bureaucracy is called on to exercise sweet talk and veiled threats. The bureaucrats and professionals who constitute most of the white-collar workforce are not themselves merchants, but they do a merchant's business inside and outside their companies.

Note the persuasion exercised the next time you buy a suit. Specialty clothing stores charge more than discount stores not staffed with rhetoricians. The differential pays for the persuasion: "It's you, my dear" or "The fish tie makes a statement." As Adam Smith said in his lectures on jurisprudence, "everyone is practising oratory . . . [and therefore] they acquire a certain dexterity and address in managing their affairs, or in other words in managing of men; and this is altogether the practise of every man in most ordinary affairs. . . the constant employment or trade of every man." Not constant, perhaps, but in Smith's time a substantial percentage and in modern times fully 25 percent.

Is the persuasive talk of the bourgeoisie then "empty," mere comforting chatter with no further economic significance? It can't be. If that was all it was, the economy would be engaging in an expensive activity to no purpose. By shutting up we could pick up a $20 bill (or more exactly a $1,500,000,000,000 bill). A quarter of national income is a lot to pay for economically functionless warm and fuzzies. The fact would not square with the most modest claims of economics. The businesspeople circling La Guardia on a rainy Monday night could have stayed home. The crisis meeting in the plant cafeteria between the managers and the workers would lack point.

Adam Smith, as usual, put the matter well. The division of labor is the "consequence of a certain propensity . . . to truck, barter, and exchange . . . [I cannot pause here to consider] whether this propensity be one of those original principles in human nature, of which no further account can be given; or whether, as seems more probable, it be the necessary consequence of the faculties of reason *and speech.*" *The Wealth of Nations* did not again mention the faculty of speech in a foundational role, though Smith, who began his career as teacher of rhetoric, did remark frequently on how businesspeople and politicians talked together. In *The Theory of Moral Sentiments,* he called speech "the characteristic faculty of human nature."

Half of Smith's formula, the faculty of reason, became in time the characteristic obsession of economists. Smith himself did not much pursue it. Economic Man, rationally seeking, is not a Smithian character. It was later economists, especially Paul Samuelson during the 1940s, who reduced economics to the reasoning of a constrained maximizer, Seeking Man, *Homo petens.* Samuelson's seeking has a peasant cast to it: the maximization of known utility under known constraints sounds more like Piers Plowman than Robinson Crusoe. The utilitarian reduction of all the virtues to one maxim and makes all virtues into prudence. The windup mice of modern economic theory know nothing of humor, affection, integrity, and self-possession. Smith's notion of *Homo loquans,* Speaking Man, squares better with the varied virtues of the bourgeoisie.

The high share of persuasion provides a scene for bourgeois virtue. One must establish a relationship of trust with someone in order to persuade him. *Ethos,* the character that a speaker claims, is the master argument.

So the world of the bourgeoisie is jammed with institutions for making relationships and declaring character, from credit bureaus to business schools. The aristocracy and the peasantry got their characters ready-made by status, and, in any case, they did not need to persuade. Thomas Buddenbrook bitterly scolds his unbusinesslike brother, a harbinger of bohemianism in the family: "In a company consisting of business as well as professional men, you make the remark, for everyone to hear, that, when one really considers it, every businessman is a swindler—you, a businessman yourself, belonging to a firm that strains every nerve and muscle to preserve its perfect integrity and spotless reputation."

The bourgeoisie works with its mouth, and it depends on word of mouth. Tom Buddenbrook, in the 1850s, thinks of his grandfather who during the Napoleonic Wars made the family's fortune out of talk: "He drove in a four-horse coach to Southern Germany, as commissary to the Prussian army—an old man in pumps, with his head powdered. And there he played his charms and his talents and made an astonishing amount of money." Tom himself most enjoys "trade he came by through his own personal efforts. Sometimes, entirely by accident, perhaps on a walk with the family, he would go into a mill for a chat with the miller, who would feel himself much honoured by the visit; and quite *en passant,* in the best of moods, he could conclude a good bargain." At the crisis of 1848, the Assembly in the novel is trapped by a mob in the town hall. "The natural instinct towards industry, common to all these good burghers, began to assert itself: they ventured to bargain a little, to pick up a little business here and there." Charming the generals, chatting with the miller, picking up a little business here and there. What news on the Rialto?

On the other hand, idle talk is not bourgeois. Idle, artistic, romantic talk is a habit of the bohemians sprung from the bourgeoisie, adumbrated in Christian Buddenbrook, of whom Tom the bourgeois says, "There is such a lack of modesty in so much communicativeness. . . . Control, equilibrium, is, at least for me, the important thing. There will always be men who are justified in this interest in themselves, this detailed observation of their own emotions, . . . poets," or novelists, like the Mann brothers, Thomas and Heinrich.

Now of course the sweet talk among the bourgeoisie can be parodied, and it has been since 1848 to the point of tedium. In *Buddenbrooks:* "Everybody puts his best foot forward before strangers. We all take care to say what will be pleasant to hear." The intellectuals sneer at the vulgarity of business talk ("Run it up the flagpole and see if anyone salutes"), "the clumsy but comfortable idioms which seemed to embody to [the burghers] the business efficiency and the easy well-being of their community."

Bourgeois friendship is false in aristocratic or peasant terms. Tom's father recalls his own business experiments as a young man: "My journey to England had for its chief purpose to look out for connections there for my undertakings. To this end I went as far as Scotland, and made many valuable acquaintances." These acquaintances of which one hears so much in a bourgeois society are hardly friends on the aristocratic model of Achilles and Patroclus. The acquaintances could turn, exhibiting "all the sudden coldness, the reserve, the mistrust at the banks, with 'friends,' and among firms abroad which such an event, such a weakening of working capital, was sure to bring in its train." Yet even such acquaintanceship—even if not Aristotle's notion of true friendship—is a virtue.

The virtues of the bourgeois are those necessary for town life, for commerce and self-government. The virtue of tolerance, for example, can be viewed as bourgeois. Its correlations in European history, such as between Spain and Holland, suggest so. The experience of uncertainty in trading creates a skepticism about certitude—the arrogant and theoretical certitude of the aristocrat or the humble and routine certitude of the peasant. As Arjo Klamer has pointed out, "the dogma of doubt" is bourgeois, an attitude suited to the vagaries of the marketplace.

Bourgeois charity, again, if not the "charity," meaning love, of the English bibles, runs contrary to the caricature of greed. More than the peasant or aristocrat, the bourgeois gives to the poor—as in the ghettos of Eastern Europe or in the small towns of America. Acts of charity follow the bourgeois norm of reciprocity. The American Gospel of Wealth, founding hospitals, colleges, and libraries wherever little fortunes were made, is a bourgeois notion, paying back what was taken in profit. Walter Annenberg gives $500 million to schools in one jolt and we are not astonished. Middle-class people in the nineteenth century habitually gave a biblical tenth of their incomes to charity. The intrusion of the state into charity killed the impulse, remaking charity into a *taille* imposed on grumbling peasants: I gave at the office.

And yet the intelligentsia detests this splendid bourgeoisie. The detestation is not new. Anciently the poet prefers his Sabine valley to troublesome riches, even while accepting large gifts in cash or land from Maecenas and Augustus. The disdain for moneygrub-

bing has always been a literary theme, and it merged smoothly into Christian virtue. But over the past century and a half, hostility to the money grubbing class has become frantic. After a brief flirtation with pro-bourgeois attitudes in the eighteenth and early nineteenth centuries—Daniel Defoe's heroes are not aristocrats; Voltaire admired the English bourgeois virtues; Jane Austen, late, admired at least the marriage market—literature sinks into a sustained sneer. The novel begins as the epic of the bourgeoisie but becomes with Balzac and Dickens an anti-epic, a *Dunciad* of the middle classes. German romantics and French statists and English evangelicals in the early nineteenth century were bourgeois by origin, but did not like it, not one bit.

As Shaw observed in 1912:

> The first half of the XIX century considered itself the greatest of all centuries. The second discovered that it was the wickedest of all centuries. The first half despised and pitied the Middle Ages. . . . The second half saw no hope for mankind except in the recovery of the faith, the art, the humanity of the Middle Ages. . . . For that was how men felt, and how some of them spoke, in the early days of the Great Conversion, which produced, first, such books as the *Latter Day Pamphlets* of Carlyle, Dickens' *Hard Times*, . . . and later on the Socialist movement . . . which has succeeded in convincing even those who most abhor the name of Socialism that the condition of the civilized world is deplorable.

The Great Conversion took decades to spread beyond a handful of avant-garde clerks. Meanwhile popular literature from the Horatio Alger stories to Dale Carnegie and the *Reader's Digest* continued to reflect on bourgeois virtues. And yet the clerks won in the end. High culture does.

The treason of the clerks since the middle of the nineteenth century has been a treason against their fathers, who were uniformly bourgeois. Overwhelmingly the French men of letters who barked at the bourgeoisie were the sons of lawyers and mill owners. So too were German men of letters, for instance, Marx and Engels. The American progressives, advocating a secularized but nonetheless Christian ideal for public policy, were the sons and daughters of Protestant ministers, bourgeois all.

It is a puzzle. In his astonishing *Bohemian versus Bourgeois: French Society and the French Man of Letters in the Nineteenth Century,* published in 1964, César Graña asked, "What is it in the spiritual scene of modern society that may account for such intellectual touchiness, willfulness, and bitterness" among the intelligentsia against the bourgeoisie? His answer was what has since been called the "aporia of the Enlightenment project"—namely, the conflict between freedom and rationalism in modern life. The bourgeoisie is seen by intellectuals such as Dickens, Weber, and Freud as the embodiment of rationality.

Graña was probably correct. Impatience with calculation is the mark of romance, especially in parody. Don Quixote's idiocies in aid of chivalry are uncalculated but noble. Mr. Gradgrind becomes a Member of Parliament, "one of the respected members for ounce weights and measures, one of the representatives of the multiplication table, one of the deaf honorable gentlemen, . . . one of the dead honorable gentlemen, to every other consideration."

But the intellectuals were mistaken about the growth of rationality. They mistook bourgeois life, the way a rebellious son mistakes the life of his father. The life of the bourgeoisie is not routine but creative. What has raised income per head in the rich countries by a factor of twelve since the eighteenth century is originality backed by commercial courage, not science. Dickens was mistaken to think that Facts alone are wanted in the life of manufacturing. Manufacturing depends on enterprise and single-mindedness, far from the coolly rational. Weber was mistaken to think that the modern state embodies principles of rationality in bureaucracy. Anyone who thinks that a large modern bureaucracy runs "like an army" cannot have experienced either a large modern bureaucracy or an army. Freud was mistaken to claim that modern life compels a choice between the reality principle and eroticism. A businessperson without an erotic drive, suitably sublimated, achieves nothing.

The lack of insight by the intelligentsia into business life is odd. It reminds one, I repeat, of an adolescent boy sneering at his father: remarkable how the old chap matured between my seventeenth and twenty-first birthdays. The European novel contains hardly a single rounded and accurate portrait of a businessman (Thomas Buddenbrook is a notable exception). The businessman is almost always a cardboard fool, unless he proves in the end, to evince aristocratic or Christian virtues. Intellectuals in the West have had a tin ear for business and its values. Thus Arthur Hugh Clough in 1862 said in "The Latest Decalogue": "Thou shalt have one God only; who / Would be at the expense of two?" and so on in the vein of a clever lad sneering at the commercial success that put him through Rugby School in Oxford (Clough's father was a cotton merchant), down to "Thou shalt not steal; an empty feat, / When it's so lucrative to cheat. / . . . Thou shalt not covet, but tradition / Approves all forms of competition."

Economics, as the science of business, has been similarly spurned, leading to more adolescent sneering at what the lad does not quite grasp. (Lad, not lass: portraits of bourgeois women in literature are numerous and accurate; it is bourgeois men on the job whom novelists, male or female, have failed to grasp.) Early in the nineteenth century such writers as Macaulay or Manzoni read and understood economics and applied it intelligently. Manzoni's novel *The Betrothed* (whose last edition was 1840) contains an entire chapter on the unhappy effects of imposing price controls during a famine. But later the intellectuals construed economics as the faculty of Reason, arrayed against the Freedom they loved, a misunderstanding encouraged by the chatter about "iron laws" among classical economists. Or else they portrayed businesspeople as con men (thus Twain and Howells).

By the late nineteenth century economics had dropped out of the conversation entirely. No intellectual since 1890 has been ashamed to be ignorant about the economy or economics. Lawyers and physicists sound off about economics without having cracked a book. Historians study Marx as though he were not a minor Ricardian. Biologists passionate about economic ecology could not pass the first hour exam in Econ. 101. It is a rare English professor—David Lodge, for example, in *Nice Work*—who can see the businessperson as anything other than The Other, or The Enemy.

It is supposed not to be relevant that the intellectuals who are nostalgic for aristocratic or peasant virtues do not know what they are talking about, whether it is the bourgeois work they spurn or the manual labor they deplore. Marx never visited a factory. The longshoreman and writer Eric Hoffer, who was in a position to have opinions on the matter, once observed that Marx, the son of a lawyer and a grandson and nephew of rabbis, "never did a day's work in his life, and knew as much about the proletariat as I do about chorus girls."

A change is overdue. To admire the bourgeois virtues is not to buy into admiration for selfishness. Capitalism needs encouragement—it being the hope for the poor of the world and being in any case what we have. But capitalism need not be hedonistic or monadic and certainly not unethical. An aristocratic, country-club capitalism, well satisfied with itself, or a peasant, grasping capitalism, hating itself, are both lacking in virtue. And neither works in town. They lead to monopoly and economic failure, alienation and revolution. We need a capitalism that nurtures communities of good townsfolk, in South Central Los Angeles as much as in Iowa City. We encourage it by talking seriously about the bourgeois virtues.

One can think of people and countries to stand as models. Benjamin Franklin and America lead the pack. Graña recounts the venom against Franklin in the writings of D. H. Lawrence, Stendhal, and Baudelaire: "a knave in Franklin's style," writes Baudelaire, was part of "the rising bourgeoisie come to replace the faltering aristocracy," which otherwise a new aristocracy of intellectuals would resupply. It is natural to think of millionaires in imagining an ideal bourgeois, Henry Ford, for example, or Sam Walton of Walmart. But it is not necessary: Macaulay, Whitman, Lincoln, Twain, Frost, Orwell were bourgeois and in their best moods unashamed of it. Being ashamed of being bourgeois has for a long time amounted to being ashamed of America. Scratch a pro-American and you find a pro-bourgeois. The sneerers at Franklin, such as Baudelaire and Lawrence, were antidemocrats and anti-Americans. Dickens came to detest the United States as much as he came to detest businessmen.

A myth of recency has made the virtues arising from towns seem those of a shameful parvenu, such as Franklin and America. In economic history dependent on Marx, such as Max Weber's *General Economic History* or Karl Polanyi's *The Great Transformation,* the market is seen as a novelty. "Market economy," claimed Polanyi with little evidence, "is an institutional structure which, as we all too easily forget, has been present at no time except our own." From this Marxist historical mistake arose the fairy tales of lost paradises for aristocrats or peasants and a reason for ignoring the bourgeois virtues.

It has taken a century of professional history to correct the mistake. The late David Herlihy put it this way in 1971: "Research has all but wiped from the ledgers the supposed gulf once considered fundamental, between a medieval manorial economy and the capitalism of the modern period." Medieval men bought and sold everything from grain to bishoprics. The Vikings were traders, too. Greece and Rome were business empires. The city of Jericho dates to 8000 B.C. The emerging truth is that we have lived in a world market for centuries, a market run by the bourgeoisie. Time to recognize the fact and to cultivate a bourgeois virtue.

QUESTIONS ON MCCLOSKEY

1. Review the table of virtues outlined by McCloskey (p. 261) and focus on the virtues of "pride of being," "pride of service," and "pride of action." How is "pride of action" manifested in commerce? How might "pride of service" be significant in peasant societies?

2. Refer again to the table of virtues (p. 261) and consider the traits of "courage," "fortitude," and "enterprise." How do you understand the conceptual distinctions among these three related terms? What is the virtue of *enterprise?* How is it distinct from fortitude? Why might enterprise be important in commercial conditions?

3. With reference to the table of virtues, think about the traits associated with the "subjective," the "objective," and the "conjective." How might the subjective be related to creativity, the objective to duty, and the conjective to conjecture and risk?

4. McCloskey seems to assume that virtues and qualities of character are related to social conditions and circumstances. Are you convinced that the virtues of commercial societies are distinct from those of non-commercial societies?

———————

Selfishness

The idea of a really good man living in a private dream world seems unacceptable. Of course a good man may be infinitely eccentric, but he must know certain things about his surroundings, most obviously the existence of other people and their claims. The chief enemy of excellence in morality (and also in art) is personal fantasy: the tissue of self-aggrandizing and consoling wishes and dreams which prevents one from seeing what is there outside one.

Iris Murdoch[9]

The first principle of Economics is that every agent is actuated only by self-interest.

Francis Y. Edgeworth[10]

In order to realize what all this means for the efficiency of the capitalist engine of production we need only recall that the family and the family home used to be the typically bourgeois kind of profit motive. Economists have not always given due weight to this fact. When we look more closely at their idea of the self-interest of entrepreneurs and capitalists, we cannot fail to discover that the results it was supposed to produce are really not at all what one would expect from the rational self-interest of the detached individual or the childless couple who no longer look at the world through the windows of a family home. Consciously or unconsciously they analyzed the behavior of a man whose views and motives are shaped by such a home and who means to work and to save primarily for wife and children.

Joseph Schumpeter[11]

SELFISHNESS AND ECONOMIC MOTIVES

One of the most common complaints about businesspersons is that they act only for themselves. Of course some of those who level this charge might say the same thing of everyone, thus making a claim of *psycho-logical egoism,* namely, that each and every person is always motivated only by perceived self-interest. However, most who describe businesspersons as "out only for themselves" assume, often without evidence, that business life—unlike academic life or journalism—occurs within a sphere of society in which selfish be-

9. *The Sovereignty of Good* (New York: Schocken Books, 1971), 59.

10. *Mathematical Psychics: An Essay on the Application of Mathematics to the Moral Sciences* (London: C. Kegan Paul & Company, 1881), 16.

11. *Capitalism, Socialism and Democracy,* 3d ed. (New York: Harper and Brothers, 1942), 160 (emphases omitted).

havior is permitted, allowed, and encouraged. Against this sort of charge, it is worth remembering that the mere *prevalence* of selfishness—delightfully captured in Ambrose Bierce's definition of the egotist as "a person of low taste, more interested in himself than in me"[12]—does not entail the thesis of psychological egoism; nor does it entail that the commercial sphere encourages selfishness at the expense of other-regarding behavior.

Selfishness and Self-Interest

We should distinguish between the person who acts in his or her self-interest and the person who is selfish. The selfish person acts in his or her self-interest and does so at the expense of others or without sufficient regard for the interests of others. But one who acts in his or her self-interest need not be acting selfishly simply because the person who acts out of self-interest may, in fact, have taken account of the interests of others. For example, a person who visits the physician need not be engaged in a selfish action, even if it is in that person's interest to attend to a broken ankle. Alongside the distinction between self-interested motives and those that are selfish, there remains the category of motives that are other-regarding (or benevolent). Indeed, Philip Wicksteed, in the second reading that follows, suggests that two individuals engaged reciprocally in an economic transaction may each be motivated by benevolent concerns, even though neither person is concerned directly with the good of the other party to the exchange.

That economic behavior is motivated by some interest of the agent is lent support by the theoretical use, within economics, of a postulate of rational maximization; according to this basic assumption, each person seeks to acquire the goods that he or she values most highly. Even if it is true that agents will act in order to achieve their highest value or strongest interest, that alone does not imply that the agents are acting selfishly, for an agent's strongest interest might be in helping others, caring for his or her family, or in earning money to contribute to a social or political cause. Moreover, that an economic agent acts in self-interest, or that an agent acts selfishly, does not imply that the agent *ought* to act only in self-interest or that the agent *ought* to act selfishly. The doctrine of *ethical egoism,* as noted in Section AV, stipulates that each person ought to seek to advance only his or her own reasonable self-interest. In one of the readings to follow, Ayn Rand suggests that ethical egoism is the only normative ethic compatible with capitalism. Although Rand's version of egoism should not be confused with rapacious or criminal selfishness, it remains true that most persons not only reject the doctrine of ethical egoism, they also reject the view that commerce requires that one advance only one's own self-interest.

At this juncture, it is worthwhile pointing out that when Adam Smith (1723–1790) utilized the terms of "self-love" and "self-interest," he did not mean to imply that individuals acting within the market were motivated only by some narrow selfishness. Smith writes, famously, that the person of commerce,

> . . . will be more likely to prevail if he can interest their self-love in his favour, and shew them that it is for their own advantage to do for him what he requires of them. . . . It is not from the benevolence of the butcher, the brewer or the baker that we expect our dinner, but from their regard to their own interest. We address ourselves, not to their humanity, but to their self-love, and never talk to them of our own necessities but of their advantages.[13]

Despite Smith's language, we should not assume that he sought to reduce all of commerce to a motive of self-love; indeed, as Smith endeavors to reject the egoism espoused by Bernard Mandeville (see Section AIV), he also points out (1) that we cannot rely merely on the benevolence of others to supply us with our needs and desires and (2) that the interests that motivate us are often the interests of our family and friends, as well as the more narrow interests of self.

THE READINGS

Ayn Rand In the first of these excerpts from Rand's best-known and popular novel (*Atlas Shrugged*), Francisco d'Anconia contends that money serves as an instrument and symbol of productive trade and human reason. In making these points d'Anconia describes how money expresses one's values and how force and coercion are the only alternatives to production via reason, effort, and exchange. The love of money is not the root of evil but a recognition of the value of effort and achievement. Those who do not live by trade and production are "looters," who live off of the productivity of others. In the second excerpt, d'Anconia focuses on how the moral code of altruism has condemned the person of achievement and independence, inducing guilt in businessmen whose very qualities were left unacknowledged and undefended even as they were necessary to existence. The final excerpt selects from the courtroom

---

12. *The Devil's Dictionary* (Cleveland: World Publishing, 1941), 81.

13. *An Inquiry into the Nature and Causes of the Wealth of Nations* [1776], edited by R. H. Campbell, A. S. Skinner, and W. B. Todd (Indianapolis, Ind.: Liberty Classics, 1981), I.ii.2 (pp. 26–27).

testimony of the businessman Hank Rearden. Rearden defends the outlook of the ethical egoist, asserting that he works for nothing but his own profit, just as those who buy from him do so for their own benefit.

Philip Wicksteed   Wicksteed begins by distinguishing between "economic conditions," "economic motive," "economic relation," and "economic forces." Of particular importance are the concepts of motive and relation. The phrase "economic motive" is often used confusedly. Some have used the phrase to refer to a motive to acquire material wealth, but the idea that there is an isolable motive to possess wealth seems dubious. Nor should we assume that no altruistic motive could enter into one's economic motive, for it seems quite possible that one might enter into an exchange for altruistic purposes. The phrase "economic relation" can be more precisely defined in terms of a trade or exchange in which we give up something we own for something that someone else has or does, thereby furthering another's purpose by furthering our own. An economic relation is a "non-tuistic" relation in which each party to the trade does not take into account the interest of the other trader, considering this other person as a means to an end, even though *this* end need not be egoistic. Thus, economic relations ensure that persons of divergent purposes can nonetheless interact and cooperate, but there is no reason to assume that their motives are egoistic. Wicksteed points out that it would be absurd to think that a housewife is acting in an egoistic manner when she is buying potatoes for her family or that she is altruistic only when serving the potatoes to her family. Economic relations expand our freedom and opportunity without requiring that others agree in our purposes.

Atlas Shrugged

Ayn Rand

Ayn Rand (1905–1982) was born in St. Petersburg, Russia. In 1925, she received permission to leave the Soviet Union, and she never returned. She is the author of numerous essays and several novels articulating a philosophy of rational egoism, which she terms "objectivism." The novels include We the Living *(1936),* The Fountainhead *(1943), and* Atlas Shrugged *(1957), from which these passages appear.*

. . . "So you think that money is the root of all evil?" said Francisco d'Anconia. "Have you ever asked what is the root of money? Money is a tool of exchange, which can't exist unless there are goods produced and men able to produce them. Money is the material shape, of the principle that men who wish to deal with one another must deal by trade and give value for value. Money is not the tool of the moochers, who claim your product by tears, or of the looters, who take it from you by force. Money is made possible only by the men who produce. Is this what you consider evil?

"When you accept money in payment for your effort, you do so only on the conviction that you will exchange it for the product of the effort of others. It is not the moochers or the looters who give value to money. Not an ocean of tears nor all the guns in the world can transform those pieces of paper in your wallet into the bread you will need to survive tomorrow. Those pieces of paper, which should have been gold, are a token of honor—your claim upon the energy of the men who produce. Your wallet is your statement of hope that somewhere in the world around you there are men who will not default on that moral principle which is the root of money. Is this what you consider evil?

"Have you ever looked for the root of production? Take a look at an electric generator and dare tell yourself that it was created by the muscular effort of unthinking brutes. Try to grow a seed of wheat without the knowledge left to you by men who had to discover it for the first time. Try to obtain your food by means of nothing but physical motions—and you'll learn that man's mind is the root of all the goods produced and of all the wealth that has ever existed on earth.

"But you say that money is made by the strong at the expense of the weak? What strength do you mean? It is not the strength of guns or muscles. Wealth is the product of man's capacity to think. Then is money made by the man who invents a motor at the expense of those who did not invent it? Is money made by the intelligent at the expense of the fools? By the able at the expense of the incompetent? By the ambitious at the expense of the lazy? Money is *made*—before it can be looted or mooched—made by the effort of every honest man, each to the extent of his ability. An honest man is one who knows that he can't consume more than he has produced.

"To trade by means of money is the code of the men of good will. Money rests on the axiom that every man is the owner of his mind and his effort. Money allows no power to prescribe the value of your effort except the voluntary choice of the man who is willing to trade you his effort in return. Money permits you to obtain for your goods and your labor that which they are worth to the men who buy them, but no more. Money permits no deals except those to mutual benefit by the unforced judgment of the traders. Money demands of you the recognition that men must work for their own benefit, not for their own injury, for their gain, not their loss—the recognition that they are not beasts of burden, born to carry the weight of your misery—that you must offer them values, not wounds—that the common bond among men is not the exchange of suffering, but the exchange of *goods*. Money demands that you sell, not your weakness to men's stupidity, but your talent to their reason; it demands that you buy, not the shoddiest they offer, but the best that your money can find. And when men live by trade—with reason, not force, as their final arbiter—it is the best product that wins, the best performance, the man of best judgment and highest ability—and the degree of a man's productiveness is the degree of his reward. This is the code of existence whose tool and symbol is money. Is this what you consider evil?

"But money is only a tool. It will take you wherever you wish, but it will not replace you as the driver. It will give you the means for the satisfaction of your desires, but it will not provide you with desires. Money is the scourge of the men who attempt to reverse the law of causality—the men who seek to replace the mind by seizing the products of the mind.

"Money will not purchase happiness for the man who has no concept of what he wants: money will not give him a code of values, if he's evaded the knowledge of what to value, and it will not provide him with a purpose, if he's evaded the choice of what to seek. Money will not buy intelligence for the fool, or admiration for the coward, or respect for the incompetent. The man who attempts to purchase the brains of his superiors to serve him, with his money replacing his judgment, ends up by becoming the victim of his inferiors. The men of intelligence desert him, but the cheats and the frauds come flocking to him, drawn by a law which he has not discovered: that no man may be smaller than his money. Is this the reason why you call it evil?

"Only the man who does not need it, is fit to inherit wealth—the man who would make his own fortune no matter where he started. If an heir is equal to his money, it serves him; if not, it destroys him. But you look on and you cry that money corrupted him. Did it? Or did he corrupt his money? Do not envy a worthless heir; his wealth is not yours and you would have done no better with it. Do not think that it should have been distributed among you; loading the world with fifty parasites instead of one, would not bring back the dead virtue which was the fortune. Money is a living power that dies without its root. Money will not serve the mind that cannot match it. Is this the reason why you call it evil?

"Money is your means of survival. The verdict you pronounce upon the source of your livelihood is the ver-dict you pronounce upon your life. If the source is corrupt, you have damned your own existence. Did you get your money by fraud? By pandering to men's vices or men's stupidity? By catering to fools, in the hope of getting more than your ability deserves? By lowering your standards? By doing work you despise for purchasers you scorn? If so, then your money will not give you a moment's or a penny's worth of joy. Then all the things you buy will become, not a tribute to you, but a reproach; not an achievement, but a reminder of shame. Then you'll scream that money is evil. Evil, because it would not pinch-hit for your self-respect? Evil, because it would not let you enjoy your depravity? Is this the root of your hatred of money?

"Money will always remain an effect and refuse to replace you as the cause. Money is the product of virtue, but it will not give you virtue and it will not redeem your vices. Money will not give you the unearned, neither in matter nor in spirit. Is this the root of your hatred of money?

"Or did you say it's the *love* of money that's the root of all evil? To love a thing is to know and love its nature. To love money is to know and love the fact that money is the creation of the best power within you, and your passkey to trade your effort for the effort of the best among men. It's the person who would sell his soul for a nickel, who is loudest in proclaiming his hatred of money—and he has good reason to hate it. The lovers of money are willing to work for it. They know they are able to deserve it.

"Let me give you a tip on a clue to men's characters: the man who damns money has obtained it dishonorably; the man who respects it has earned it.

"Run for your life from any man who tells you that money is evil. That sentence is the leper's bell of an approaching looter. So long as men live together on earth and need means to deal with one another—their only substitute, if they abandon money, is the muzzle of a gun.

"But money demands of you the highest virtues, if you wish to make it or to keep it. Men who have no courage, pride or self-esteem, men who have no moral sense of their right to their money and are not willing to defend it as they defend their life, men who apologize for being rich—will not remain rich for long. They are the natural bait for the swarms of looters that stay under rocks for centuries, but come crawling out at the first smell of a man who begs to be forgiven for the guilt of owning wealth. They will hasten to relieve him of the guilt—and of his life, as he deserves.

"Then you will see the rise of the men of the double standard—the men who live by force, yet count on those who live by trade to create the value of their looted money—the men who are the hitchhikers of virtue. In a moral society, these are the criminals, and the statutes are written to protect you against them. But when a society establishes criminals-by-right and looters-by-law—men who use force to seize the wealth of *disarmed* victims—then money becomes its creators' avenger. Such looters believe it safe to rob defenseless men, once they've passed a law to disarm them. But their loot becomes the magnet for other looters, who get it from them as they got it. Then the race goes, not to the ablest at production, but to those most ruthless at brutality. When force is the standard, the murderer wins over the pickpocket. And then that society vanishes, in a spread of ruins and slaughter.

"Do you wish to know whether that day is coming? Watch money. Money is the barometer of a society's virtue. When you see that trading is done, not by consent, but by compulsion—when you see that in order to produce, you need to obtain permission from men who produce nothing—when you see that money is flowing to those who deal, not in goods, but in favors—when you see that men get richer by graft and by pull than by work, and your laws don't protect you against them, but protect them against you—when you see corruption being rewarded and honesty becoming a self-sacrifice—you may know that your society is doomed. Money is so noble a medium that it does not compete with guns and it does not make terms with brutality. It will not permit a country to survive as half-property, half-loot.

"Whenever destroyers appear among men, they start by destroying money, for money is men's protection and the base of a moral existence. Destroyers seize gold and leave to its owners a counterfeit pile of paper. This kills all objective standards and delivers men into the arbitrary power of an arbitrary setter of values. Gold was an objective value, an equivalent of wealth produced. Paper is a mortgage on wealth that does not exist, backed by a gun aimed at those who are expected to produce it. Paper is a check drawn by legal looters upon an account which is not theirs: upon the virtue of the victims. Watch for the day when it bounces, marked: 'Account overdrawn.'

"When you have made evil the means of survival, do not expect men to remain good. Do not expect them to stay moral and lose their lives for the purpose of becoming the fodder of the immoral. Do not expect them to produce, when production is punished and looting rewarded. Do not ask, 'Who is destroying the world?' You are.

"You stand in the midst of the greatest achievements of the greatest productive civilization and you wonder why it's crumbling around you, while you're damning its life-blood—money. You look upon money

as the savages did before you, and you wonder why the jungle is creeping back to the edge of your cities. Throughout men's history, money was always seized by looters of one brand or another, whose names changed, but whose method remained the same: to seize wealth by force and to keep the producers bound, demeaned, defamed, deprived of honor. That phrase about the evil of money, which you mouth with such righteous recklessness, comes from a time when wealth was produced by the labor of slaves—slaves who repeated the motions once discovered by somebody's mind and left unimproved for centuries. So long as production was ruled by force, and wealth was obtained by conquest, there was little to conquer. Yet through all the centuries of stagnation and starvation, men exalted the looters, as aristocrats of the sword, as aristocrats of birth, as aristocrats of the bureau, and despised the producers, as slaves, as traders, as shopkeepers—as industrialists.

"To the glory of mankind, there was, for the first and only time in history, a *country of money*—and I have no higher, more reverent tribute to pay to America, for this means: a country of reason, justice, freedom, production, achievement. For the first time, man's mind and money were set free, and there were no fortunes-by-conquest, but only fortunes-by-work, and instead of swordsmen and slaves, there appeared the real maker of wealth, the greatest worker, the highest type of human being—the self-made man—the American industrialist.

"If you ask me to name the proudest distinction of Americans, I would choose—because it contains all the others—the fact that they were the people who created the phrase 'to *make* money.' No other language or nation had ever used these words before; men had always thought of wealth as a static quantity—to be seized, begged, inherited, shared, looted or obtained as a favor. Americans were the first to understand that wealth has to be created. The words 'to make money' hold the essence of human morality.

"Yet these were the words for which Americans were denounced by the rotted cultures of the looters' continents. Now the looters' credo has brought you to regard your proudest achievements as a hallmark of shame, your prosperity as guilt, your greatest men, the industrialists, as blackguards, and your magnificent factories as the product and property of muscular labor, the labor of whip-driven slaves, like the pyramids of Egypt. The rotter who simpers that he sees no difference between the power of the dollar and the power of the whip, ought to learn the difference on his own hide—as, I think, he will.

"Until and unless you discover that money is the root of all good, you ask for your own destruction. When money ceases to be the tool by which men deal with one another, then men become the tools of men. Blood, whips and guns—or dollars. Take your choice—there is no other—and your time is running out." . . .

"You, who would not submit to the hardships of nature, but set out to conquer it and placed it in the service of your joy and your comfort—to what have you submitted at the hands of men? You, who know from your work that one bears punishment only for being wrong—what have you been willing to bear and for what reason? All your life, you have heard yourself denounced, not for your faults, but for your greatest virtues. You have been hated, not for your mistakes, but for your achievements. You have been scorned for all those qualities of character which are your highest pride. You have been called selfish for the courage of acting on your own judgment and bearing sole responsibility for your own life. You have been called arrogant for your independent mind. You have been called cruel for your unyielding integrity. You have been called anti-social for the vision that made you venture upon undiscovered roads. You have been called ruthless for the strength and self-discipline of your drive to your purpose. You have been called greedy for the magnificence of your power to create wealth. You, who've expended an inconceivable flow of energy, have been called a parasite. You, who've created abundance where there had been nothing but wastelands and helpless, starving men before you, have been called a robber. You, who've kept them all alive, have been called an exploiter. You, the purest and most moral man among them, have been sneered at as a 'vulgar materialist.' Have you stopped to ask them: by what right?—by what code?—by what standard? No, you have borne it all and kept silent. You bowed to their code and you never upheld your own. You knew what exacting morality was needed to produce a single metal nail, but you let them brand you as immoral. You knew that man needs the strictest code of values to deal with nature, but you thought that you needed no such code to deal with men. You left the deadliest weapon in the hands of your enemies, a weapon you never suspected or understood. Their moral code is their weapon. Ask yourself how deeply and in how many terrible ways you have accepted it. Ask yourself what it is that a code of moral values does to a man's life, and why he can't exist without it, and what happens to him if he accepts the wrong standard, by which the evil is the good. Shall I tell you why you're drawn to me, even though you think you ought to damn me? It's because I'm the first man who has given you what the whole world owes you and what you should have demanded of all men before you dealt with them: a moral sanction." . . .

"You're guilty of a great sin, Mr. Rearden, much guiltier than they tell you, but not in the way they preach. The worst guilt is to accept an undeserved guilt—and that is what you have been doing all your life. You have been paying blackmail, not for your vices, but for your virtues. You have been willing to carry the load of an unearned punishment—and to let it grow the heavier the greater the virtues you practiced. But your virtues were those which keep men alive. Your own moral code—the one you lived by, but never stated, acknowledged or defended—was the code that preserves man's existence. If you were punished for it, what was the nature of those who punished you? Yours was the code of life. What, then, is theirs? What standard of value lies at its root? What is its ultimate purpose? Do you think that what you're facing is merely a conspiracy to seize your wealth? You, who know the source of wealth, should know it's much more and much worse than that. Did you ask me to name man's motive power? Man's motive power is his moral code. Ask yourself where their code is leading you and what it offers you as your final goal. A viler evil than to murder a man, is to sell him suicide as an act of virtue. A viler evil than to throw a man into a sacrificial furnace, is to demand that he leap in, of his own will, and that he build the furnace, besides. By their own statement, it is *they* who need you and have nothing to offer you in return. By their own statement, you must support them because they cannot survive without you. Consider the obscenity of offering their impotence and their need—their need of *you*—as a justification for your torture. Are you willing to accept it? Do you care to purchase—at the price of your great endurance, at the price of your agony—the satisfaction of the needs of your own destroyers?"

"No!"

"Mr. Rearden," said Francisco, his voice solemnly calm, "if you saw Atlas, the giant who holds the world on his shoulders, if you saw that he stood, blood running down his chest, his knees buckling, his arms trembling but still trying to hold the world aloft with the last of his strength, and the greater his effort the heavier the world bore down upon his shoulders—what would you tell him to do?"

"I . . . don't know. What . . . could he do? What would *you* tell him?"

"To shrug." . . .

The eldest judge leaned forward across the table and his voice became suavely derisive: "You speak as if you were fighting for some sort of principle, Mr. Rearden, but what you're actually fighting for is only your property, isn't it?"

"Yes, of course. I am fighting for my property. Do you know the kind of principle *that* represents?"

"You pose as a champion of freedom, but it's only the freedom to make money that you're after."

"Yes, of course. All I want is the freedom to make money. Do you know what that freedom implies?"

"Surely, Mr. Rearden, you wouldn't want your attitude to be misunderstood. You wouldn't want to give support to the widespread impression that you are a man devoid of social conscience, who feels no concern for the welfare of his fellows and works for nothing but his own profit."

"I work for nothing but my own profit. I earn it."

There was a gasp, not of indignation, but of astonishment, in the crowd behind him and silence from the judges he faced. He went on calmly:

"No, I do not want my attitude to be misunderstood. I shall be glad to state it for the record. I am in full agreement with the facts of everything said about me in the newspapers—with the facts, but not with the evaluation. I work for nothing but my own profit—which I make by selling a product they need to men who are willing and able to buy it. I do not produce it for their benefit at the expense of mine, and they do not buy it for my benefit at the expense of theirs; I do not sacrifice my interests to them nor do they sacrifice theirs to me; we deal as equals by mutual consent to mutual advantage—and I am proud of every penny that I have earned in this manner. I am rich and I am proud of every penny I own. I made my money by my own effort, in free exchange and through the voluntary consent of every man I dealt with—the voluntary consent of those who employed me when I started, the voluntary consent of those who work for me now, the voluntary consent of those who buy my product. I shall answer all the questions you are afraid to ask me openly. Do I wish to pay my workers more than their services are worth to me? I do not. Do I wish to sell my product for less than my customers are willing to pay me? I do not. Do I wish to sell it at a loss or give it away? I do not. If this is evil, do whatever you please about me, according to whatever standards you hold. These are mine. I am earning my own living, as every honest man must. I refuse to accept as guilt the fact of my own existence and the fact, that I must work in order to support it. I refuse to accept as guilt the fact that I am able to do it and do it well. I refuse to accept as guilt the fact that I am able to do it better than most people—the fact that my work is of greater value than the work of my neighbors

and that more men are willing to pay me. I refuse to apologize for my ability—I refuse to apologize for my success—I refuse to apologize for my money. If this is evil, make the most of it. If this is what the public finds harmful to its interests, let the public destroy me. This is my code—and I will accept no other. I could say to you that I have done more good for my fellow men than you can ever hope to accomplish—but I will not say it, because I do not seek the good of others as a sanction for my right to exist, nor do I recognize the good of others as a justification for their seizure of my property or their destruction of my life. I will not say that the good of others was the purpose of my work—my own good was my purpose, and I despise the man who surrenders his. I could say to you that you do not serve the public good—that nobody's good can be achieved at the price of human sacrifices—that when you violate the rights of one man, you have violated the rights of all, and a public of rightless creatures is doomed to destruction. I could say to you that you will and can achieve nothing but universal devastation—as any looter must, when he runs out of victims. I could say it, but I won't. It is not your particular policy that I challenge, but your moral premise. If it were true that men could achieve their good by means of turning some men into sacrificial animals, and I were asked to immolate myself for the sake of creatures who wanted to survive at the price of my blood, if I were asked to serve the interests of society apart from, above and against my own—I would refuse. I would reject it as the most contemptible evil, I would fight it with every power I possess, I would fight the whole of mankind, if one minute were all I could last before I were murdered, I would fight in the full confidence of the justice of my battle and of a living being's right to exist. Let there be no misunderstanding about me. If it is now the belief of my fellow men, who call themselves the public, that their good requires victims, then I say: The public good be damned, I will have no part of it!"

The crowd burst into applause.

QUESTIONS ON RAND

1. How does Rand justify the love of money? Who would count among the looters of civilization? Is there a difference between law and looting?

2. According to Rand, how do most individuals view the successful individual? What is the content of the moral code that has condemned business? What virtues are necessary for success in business?

3. Rand believes it is morally justifiable to work "for nothing but my own profit." Is the pursuit of profit necessarily egoistic? Or is the egoistic pursuit of profit the only morally coherent means of pursuing profit?

Business and the Economic Nexus

Philip Wicksteed

Philip H. Wicksteed (1844–1927) was born in Leeds, England, and followed his father into the Unitarian ministry, leaving the pulpit only in 1897. His intellectual interests and writings ranged from classics, literature, and theology, to philosophy and economics. Among his noneconomic writings are Dante and Aquinas *(1913) and* Dogma and Philosophy *(1920); his economic treatises include* An Essay on the Coordination of the Laws of Distribution *(1894),* The Alphabet of Economic Science *(1888) as well as the two-volume work,* The Common Sense of Political Economy *(1910), from which this excerpt is taken.*

. . . To begin with, we have seen that the broadest conception of Economics includes all dealings with exchangeable things, but does not extend beyond them. Thus when we speak of the "economic conditions" realised by any community we think of the general command of exchangeable things they enjoy, and we call these conditions good or bad, favourable or unfavourable, according to the extent and perhaps the nature of this command. And since material things are those that first occur to our minds when we think of exchanges, there is a marked tendency (sometimes conscious and deliberate, sometimes unconscious or even counter to deliberate purpose and definition) to treat "economic" as equivalent to "material" conditions. Broadly speaking, when we hear that in any community the "economic conditions" are satisfactory we think of the people as well fed, well clothed, well housed, and more vaguely as being in the enjoyment of decent and reasonable "comforts." And note that though all this depends upon the command of things that are exchangeable, it does not follow that the things are all of them actually exchanged. If a man lives largely on the potatoes he grows on his own patch, they affect, and help to constitute, the economic conditions under which he lives just as much as if he had bought them. In the use of the phrase "economic conditions," therefore, we start from a fairly intelligible basis, though it is obvious on consideration that the word in this connection can have no scientific precision. The transition from material comforts to aesthetic enjoyment, for example, is continuous and imperceptible. Clothes, crockery, counterpanes, furniture, are all valued for the comfort they afford, the pleasure they give to the eye, and the social distinctions that are attached to them. So we cannot purge our conception of the economic conditions under which a man lives from all aesthetic and kindred elements; the interpenetration is too close and intimate. And if we take a broader view and include all exchangeable things in our purview we shall have to include literature, art, education, spiritual enjoyment and edification, and much more, just so far as books, pictures, concerts, and the teachings and the ministrations of religion, come into the circle of exchange and can therefore be commanded by money. The use of the word "economic" in this connection, then, though fairly well understood, eminently convenient, and not seriously or generally misleading, is entirely without precision, and though useful in description it should be avoided in argument.

But when we pass from the phrase "economic conditions" to the phrase "the economic motive" the case becomes very different. Here we are in the presence of one of the most dangerous and indeed disastrous confusions that obstruct the progress of Economics. Many writers have thought that the Economist, as such, must not only limit his consideration to certain actions and conditions which concern exchangeable and mainly material things, but must also shut out of consideration all *motives* that are not "economic." And the economic motive is generally defined as the "desire to possess wealth." The widest definition of wealth, in this connection, would make it include all exchangeable things, but nothing else. Now since we have already seen that no ultimate object of desire can ever be the direct subject of exchange at all, we perceive at once that to regard the "economic" man (as he is often called) as actuated solely by the desire to possess wealth is to think of him as only desiring to collect tools and never desiring to do or to make anything with them. More than this, we have seen that the very law that regulates and balances one against the other a man's selections amongst exchangeable things, also regulates and balances his choice between wealth and leisure, for instance; that is, between acquiring a larger command of exchangeable things and cultivating a finer enjoyment of those he already commands, or between command of exchangeable things and immunity from painful exertions. It is therefore impossible to examine the action of the "desire for wealth" without at the same time relating it to the desire for ease or the desire for enjoyment. And this conclusion is so inevitable that it has generally been found necessary to associate "love of ease" with "desire for wealth" under the economic motive. And yet this does not help us. A man may be just as strenuous in the pursuit of knowledge or of fame, or in his obedience to an artistic impulse, as in the pursuit of wealth. "The demands of vanity may be as imperious as those of hunger," so that all the motives and passions that actuate the human breast may either stimulate or restrain the desire to possess wealth. How, then, can we isolate that desire as a "motive"?

Yet it is not unusual expressly to exclude all altruistic motives from the field of economic study and to say, or to imply, that in his economic relations a man is purely self-regarding. We are asked then, first to recognise no other motive than "the desire to possess wealth," and then, by way of extra precaution, expressly to exclude altruistic motives. But this additional demand is not only arbitrary, but, so far from fortifying the other, it expressly contradicts it; for a man may clearly desire wealth from altruistic motives, so that if I am to exclude altruistic motives I must insist on going behind the "desire to possess wealth" and knowing why the man desires it, so as to be able to exclude all (economically) improper motives. This is not treating the "desire to possess wealth" as itself the "motive" at all. . . .

The phrase "economic relation" places us on much firmer ground; for it may be applied with perfect precision and appropriateness to a great class of relations which we have already been led to examine. We will here recapitulate and expand the conclusions we have reached with respect to them. Every man has certain purposes, impulses, and desires. They may be of a merely instinctive and elementary nature, or they may be deliberate and far-reaching; they may be self-regarding or social; they may be spiritual or material; but whatever they are it is impossible for him to give effect to them by his own unaided action upon the forces and substances of nature. No man, standing naked upon the face of the earth, can feed, clothe, or house his body, or secure an entrance for his mind into the regions of intellectual, imaginative, and emotional enjoyment; nor (suppose he has altruistic impulses) can he, thus unaided, minister to like needs or develop like possibilities in others. Neither can he accomplish these things by the direct application of his own faculties supported by all the material supplies and instruments he possesses or can possess; nor yet, except under very special circumstances, simply by enlisting the co-operation directly inspired by sympathy with him or with his purposes. But by direct and indirect processes of exchange, by the social alchemy of which money is the symbol, the things I have and the things I can are transmuted into the things I want and the things I would. By these processes I can convert my acquaintance with the nature of different kinds of wood, and my skill in handling certain tools, or my knowledge of the higher mathematics, or my capacity for firing men's imaginations or for chastening or stimulating their religious emotions, into food and clothing, into books and pictures, into the rapid transport of my own person through distant lands, into dinners for hungry children, into May festivities for listless villagers, into the collation of Syriac manuscripts, or into any of the thousand other things that I want to have, to experience, or to get done: and all this independently of any interest in these desires of mine, or any knowledge of them, on the part of very many of the persons who assist me to accomplish them. Even when such an interest exists it may be insufficient (if unsupported by other considerations) to make my sympathisers qualify themselves for the work, and set to it for mere love of the thing to be done. Why, then, do they co-operate with me at all? Not primarily, or not solely, because they are interested in my purposes, but because they have certain purposes of their own; and just as I find that I can only secure the accomplishment of my purposes by securing their co-operation, so they find that they can only accomplish theirs by securing the co-operation of yet others, and they find that I am in a position, directly or indirectly, to place this co-operation at their disposal.

A vast range, therefore, of our relations with others enters into a system of mutual adjustment by which we further each other's purposes simply as an indirect way of furthering our own. All such relations may be fitly called "economic." The range of activity they cover is "business," and in the last chapter we have already incidentally opened our investigation into the causes that lead to it. It often happens that a man's individual faculties or possessions are not so well suited for the accomplishment of his own purposes as they are for those of another, and the great principle of division of labour, the conception of which is sufficiently widely spread to obviate the necessity of any elementary exposition, reenforces the natural diversity of capacities and increases the economy of the indirect furtherance of many of our purposes as against their direct furtherance. . . . By the system of "economic relations," then, I understand that system which enables me to throw in at some point of the circle of exchange the powers and possessions I directly command, and draw out other possessions and the command of other powers whether at the same point or at some other. And I define my relation with any other man as "economic" when I enter into it for this purpose of transmuting, either at one or at two or at more removes, what I have and can into what I want and would.

Lastly, "economic forces" or "the economic force" may suitably be used to indicate the resultant pressure of all the conditions, material and psychological, that urge men to enter into economic relations with each other. Could "motive" be used, in accordance with its etymological significance, simply as equivalent to a driving force of any kind, there need to be no objection to the use, in this sense, of the phrase "economic motive." But since it easily suggests a deliberately selected end or goal and has been expressly applied, in connection with economics, to the ethical distinction between egoism and altruism, it will be far safer to avoid it altogether. I shall therefore speak of "economic relations" and "economic forces," but not of "economic motives." And by economic forces I shall mean anything and everything which tends to bring men into economic relations. . . .

We have now, it is to be hoped, reached an adequately clear and precise conception of the meaning of "the economic relation," of "economic forces," and of "economic conditions," in this latter sense of the considerations which determine a change of flow in the economic activities. But the misconceptions and confusions that surround this subject are so obstinate, and reassert themselves so persistently, that it will be well to fortify ourselves against them; and I shall therefore endeavour in this chapter to make good certain propositions, some of which have already been provisionally established in an explicit manner, and only need elaboration and confirmation; all of which are implicitly contained in the conclusions we have reached; none of which, except perhaps the last, seem to be uniformly or adequately recognised in the current, treatment of Political Economy. These propositions [include]:

That the economic relation is entered into at the prompting of the whole range of human purposes and impulses, and rests in no exclusive or specific way on an egoistic or self-regarding basis. . . .

It is often said or implied that the housewife, for example, is actuated by a different set of motives in her economic transactions in the market and her noneconomic transactions at home; but this is obviously not so. The buying potatoes and cabbages in the market and helping them at table are integral portions of the same process, and the housewife is considering the wants of her family when she is making her purchases just as much as when she is distributing them. She is herself one of the family, and her personal and particular tastes and wants are consulted more or less consciously, and carry more or less weight, according to her disposition, her powers of imagination, and her state of mind at the moment; but her purchases are effected and her distributions made with reference to one and the same set of wants. It would be transparently absurd to say that she is only thinking of herself in the market-place, and thinking chiefly of others in the home; or that her motives are entirely egoistic when she is buying the potatoes, and preponderatingly or exclusively altruistic when she is helping them. And as it will be generally admitted that she conducts her marketing in the main on business principles, it follows that the difference between what we are to consider a business transaction and what we are not so to consider is not determined by the selfishness or unselfishness, the egoism or altruism, of the inspiring motive. In like manner, when Paul of Tarsus abode with Aquila and Priscilla in Corinth and wrought with them at his craft of tent-making we shall hardly say that he was inspired by egoistic motives. It is, indeed, likely enough that he was not inspired by any conscious desire to further the purposes (pastoral, military, or what not) of the men for whom he was making or mending tents, but it is very certain that he was impelled to practise his craft by his desire not to be a burden to the Churches, and that his economic life was to his mind absolutely integral to his evangelising mission.

And, indeed, in any complex industrial civilisation every man (unless he is subsidised, which only throws the process one step further back) must obviously be dependent for the accomplishment of his purposes on the indirect process of doing something, or allowing something, in furtherance of the purposes of others, on condition of securing from them the command of services and commodities which will directly minister to his own purposes. The economic relation, then, or business nexus, is necessary alike for carrying on the life of the peasant and the prince, of the saint and the sinner, of the apostle and the shepherd, of the most altruistic and the most egoistic of men.

And if it be not true of any single individual, neither can we expect it to be true of any small group of individuals, whether domestic or other, that the faculties and resources which they collectively command can directly supply their collective wants or fulfil their collective purposes. The group of men who unite to propagate a set of religious doctrines or to call attention to a social or national wrong, or to secure a sanitary or dietary reform, or to preach any gospel or advertise any fad, may have in their own ranks the capacity to expound the truth they believe themselves to possess and the means and willingness to study and to write, but you may be sure that they will want "subscriptions." That is to say, they will want the means of procuring specified services from persons outside their ranks. They will wish to get persons to print or to distribute literature, or to allow them to occupy a room for a few hours in the week or to store their properties there; and the persons whose services, or the temporary use of whose possessions, they require for the accomplishment of their purpose will be persons who may be selfish or unselfish, but amongst whose purposes, good or bad, the promulgation of the particular thing in question does not take such a place as to induce them to render the services or encounter the sacrifices in question merely for love of the cause on its own merits. Even if Mr. X lends a room and Miss Y does all the clerkage for love of the cause, yet the stationery is manufactured by persons who are paid for their work and have no knowledge of the "cause," and the circulars are impartially delivered by the same postman who hands in the rival appeals of the enemy, and is himself probably unconcerned alike as to the bane and the antidote, but is intent on keeping his home together, or propagating in his leisure hours some political, social, or religious gospel of his own. Or even if the circulars themselves are printed by an enthusiastic apostle, for love, the type was founded by one of the heathen, whose co-operation in the cause was necessary, and had to be obtained for a consideration. All these profane persons have purposes of their own, which may or may not be as disinterested as those of the Society which deals with them, but which are at any rate different; and it is only if they are put in command of services which will promote their own purposes that they will be willing to render the specific services required to further the purposes of the Society. And seeing that the Society itself is only willing thus to further their purposes on condition that they further its own, there is no room for charges of selfishness on either side, but great room for satisfaction and congratulation on both. It would be ridiculous to say that the enthusiasts who give the printer an order for ten thousand copies of their most effective tract are actuated by purely "egoistic" motives, and if we choose to imagine the case that the printer, on his side, is getting weary of his trade, but keeps on in order to be able to make handsome subsidies to a certain "cause" in which he in his turn is interested, it would be equally ridiculous to say that his motives were "egoistic." Yet the relation on both sides might be purely economic. Each might enter upon it altogether in furtherance of his own purposes, and in no degree from sympathy in the other's.

Our complex system of economic relations puts us in command of the co-operation necessary to accomplish our purposes, independently of a complete coincidence between our purposes and our own faculties, and independently also of our being able to command the effective sympathy of persons possessing all the necessary faculties that we lack. A right understanding of the nature of the business or economic nexus, therefore, ought to dispel for ever the animosity with which Political Economy has often been attacked as a degrading study, and the uneasiness with which its own representatives have often defended their science against the charge. In principle the study of business relations is the study of the machinery by which men are liberated, over a large area of life, from the limitations which a failure of correspondence between their faculties and their purposes would otherwise impose upon them. The things they have and can are not the things they want and would; but by the machinery of exchange they can be transmuted into them. The economic relation, then, liberates them from the limitations imposed by the nature of their own direct resources. And this liberation comes about by the very act that brings a corresponding liberation to those with whom they deal. "It is twice bless'd. It blesseth him that gives, and him that takes." Surely the study of such a relation needs no apology, and there seems to be no room to bring against it the charge of being intrinsically sordid and degrading. The conditions under which business is actually conducted (like other conditions under which we live) may be far from ideal, but the business or economic relation, as such, does not seem to be open to the faintest suspicion of a taint, even when regarded from the loftiest æsthetic or ethical position.

And yet the ground on which this stubborn prejudice rests is obvious enough, and the example of the apostolic tent-maker has already suggested it. We have seen that although Paul was certainly not thinking of himself or of his own advantage when he was making tents in Corinth, yet neither was he necessarily or even probably thinking, in any disinterested or enthusiastic manner, of the advantage of those for whom he was working and whose wants he was immediately supplying. In his attitude towards himself and "others" at large, a man may be either selfish or unselfish without affecting the economic nature of any given relation, such as that of Paul to his customers; but as soon as he is moved by a direct and disinterested desire to further the purposes or consult the interests of those particular "others" for whom he is working at the moment, then in proportion as this desire becomes an ultimate object to him (so that he is directly fulfilling one of his own purposes in supplying these wants) the transaction on his side ceases to be purely economic. No doubt Paul took conscientious pains with his tent-making. So far as this was with a view to business it was done in obedience to an economic force. So far as it was an expression of his own personality or of his independent sympathy with his employers it was not. If you and I are conducting a transaction which on my side is purely economic, I am furthering your purposes, partly or wholly perhaps for my own sake, perhaps entirely for the sake of others, but certainly not for your sake. What makes it an economic transaction is that I am not considering you except as a link in the chain, or considering your desires except as the means by which I may gratify those of some one else—not necessarily myself. The economic relation does not exclude from my mind every one but me, it potentially includes every one but you. You it does indeed exclude, and therefore it emphasises, though it does not narrow or tighten, the limitations of the altruism of the man who enters into it; for it calls our attention to the fact that, however wide his sympathies may be, they do not urge him to any particular effort or sacrifice for the sake of the person with whom he is dealing at the moment. An economic relation may be entered upon equally well from egoistic or altruistic motives; but as long as it remains purely economic, it must remind us that no man's altruism is undiscriminating to the extent of lavishing itself upon all persons or all purposes at all times. Short of this, clearly the most altruistic person may enter into a relation with another man, the purpose of which is to further the good of those who are other than himself, and also other than the person with whom he is dealing. In that case his action is altruistic because it is inspired by a desire for the good of some one other than himself, and the relation is economic because it is entered into for the sake of some one other than his correspondent.

It is impossible at this point to refrain from . . . reflecting how seldom the economic motive can maintain itself in isolation; and by what insensible degrees I may pass from regarding you solely as a means to my ends into taking some measure of interest, for your sake, in what I am doing for you; but our present concern is not to shew how the economic relation allies itself with others, but to form a sharply defined conception of the nature of that economic relation itself; and to this we must return.

The distinction that we have drawn between the selfish motive, which considers me alone, and the economic motive, which may consider any one but you, is well illustrated by the case of trustees. Trustees who have no personal interest whatever in the administration of the estates to which they give time and thought will often drive harder bargains—that is to say, will more rigidly exclude all thought or consideration of the advantage of the person with whom they are dealing—in their capac-

ity as trustees than they would do in their private capacity. Thus we see that the very reason why a man feels absolutely precluded from in any way considering the interests of the person with whom he is transacting business may be precisely the fact that his motive in doing business at all is absolutely and entirely unselfish. The reason why, in this instance, there is no room for "you" in my consideration is just because "I" am myself already excluded from my own consideration. If I counted myself I should find room for you just so far as "I" take an interest in "you," but if I do not admit myself I cannot bring in your interests as part of my own programme. The "others" for whom I act are others than you, more completely and irrevocably other than I myself should be; for though I might myself adopt as mine some of your purposes, I cannot affiliate those purposes of yours upon these "others" for whom I am acting. The transaction then becomes more rigidly " economic," just because my motive in entering upon it is altruistic. . . .

The same principles apply to the analysis of the transactions of the housewife with which we started. When she is in the market she is actively and consciously thinking of exactly the same people and exactly the same wants which she is thinking of when she applies and distributes her purchases at home. But when she is sitting at the table she is in the presence of, and is dealing with, no other persons than those whose wants she is considering. When she is in the kitchen or the storeroom giving orders to her servants, she is in the presence of persons whose individual wants are more or less an object of direct interest to her according to circumstances and according to her disposition, and whose tastes and susceptibilities she will be wise to consider for her own sake if not for theirs. Whereas when she is in the market she is dealing with people in whose welfare she has not necessarily any direct concern, and part of whose business it is to consult her tastes and susceptibilities with sedulous care. The economic nature of the transaction therefore emphasises, though it does not impose, the limitations of her altruism. The difference between an administrative act which is also a business transaction and an administrative act which is not, is not that she is thinking of a different set of persons or is actuated by a different set of motives in one case and in the other, but that in one case she is dealing with one set of persons and considering the wants of another set, in the other she is considering the wants of the very people with whom she is at the moment dealing. She is herself one of the people for whom she is providing, yet she is probably, in the main, "unselfish" enough in her dealings in the market-place—that is to say, she is thinking chiefly of "others than herself"—but she is not thinking equally of every one that is not herself. The mere fact that a person is other than herself does not at once awake her keen interest in him, and it may well happen that the persons with whom she is dealing at the moment are amongst those of whom she is thinking little or not at all.

Both in the market-place and the home, then, her main object of consideration is a group of persons of whom she is one, and in which the stall-keepers in the market-place are not included. She is just as selfish and just as unselfish in one case as in the other. But though the members of her household are included in the group of people of whom she is thinking in the market-place, it does not follow that no one else is. You can draw no such line. We have seen that her purchases in the market may be restricted not only by the pressure of other domestic claims, but by the determination to make certain contributions to charitable or religious institutions, or by any other object whatever in which she is interested, however wide or however narrow its application, however near or however remote it may be from the centre of the domestic circle. It is by the nature of the general motives which inspire her life, the general adjustment of her resources, the general principles on which she administers one part of her husband's income, and the general trend of her influence upon the expenditure of the rest and upon his methods of earning the whole, by the pressure of her character and energy in guiding and stimulating not only his impulses, but those of his and her acquaintances, and any portion of the public to which she has direct or indirect access, by speech, by example, or by written word; above all, it is by her way of looking at things and feeling them, by her mental attitude towards life and her general sense of values, that the degree of her selfishness or unselfishness, her egoism or altruism, is to be determined; and she is actuated by selfish or unselfish, by public-spirited or private-spirited motives, by a broad or a narrow selfishness, by a stupid appetite for martyrdom or a large sense of the significance of life for herself and others, according to her character, not according to the particular act that she is performing. The reason why she does not spend more in the market-place may be because she considers others besides her family; the reason why she eats some of the new potatoes herself may be because she considers herself; the reason why she does not eat more may be because she considers others as well as herself; but probably she is not thinking at all, but feels the collective or conjunct self from which neither she nor any other individual member could be withdrawn without impoverishment to the whole collective life, and into which so much as the idea of self-sacrifice could not be introduced without destroying its vital processes. Self-sacrifice would be no less fatal than self-assertion, and altruism and egoism are alike lost in the communal sense

of which she is the organ., If she has occasionally to rebuke the egoism and appeal to the altruism of the little barbarians around her, it is because their communal sense is undeveloped; and she is well aware of the danger of turning them from barbarians into prigs if she develops altruism when it is the communal sense that needs development. Her normal function is by her own unconscious communal sense unconsciously to develop theirs.

But the boundaries of this communal sense are neither stable nor rigidly fixed. Individuals or groups within the family separate themselves (more or less completely, and in few or many relations of life) from the parent stem, and arrangements with them partake of the nature of business. The pressure of the communal sense rises and falls incessantly in the infinite variety of the relations of any community, and the formal limits of the family neither impose a barrier over which the altruistic impulses cannot pass outward; nor form a preserve into which egoistic motives can make no incursions; and wherever altruism and egoism can be rightly spoken of—that is to say, wherever there is a conscious distinction between what I do for my own sake and what I do for the sake of others—it is clear that the note of a business transaction between A and B is not that A's *ego* alone is consciously in his mind, but that, however many the *alteri* are, B is not one of them; and B, in like manner, whether he is thinking only of his own *ego* or of innumerable *alteri,* is not thinking of A.

The proposal to exclude "benevolent" or "altruistic" motives from consideration in the study of Economics is therefore wholly irrelevant and beside the mark. A man's purposes may, of course, be selfish, but however unselfish they are he requires the co-operation of others who are not interested, or who are inadequately interested in them, in order to accomplish them. We enter into business relations with others, not because our purposes are selfish, but because those with whom we deal are relatively indifferent to them, but are (like us) keenly interested in purposes of their own, to which we in our turn are relatively indifferent. "Business," then, is primarily a vast network of organisations by which any person or combination of persons can direct their resources and their powers to the accomplishment of their purposes, without the necessity of a direct relation, hard and often impossible to secure, between the objects sought and the faculties and materials directly at command.

There is surely nothing degrading or revolting to our higher sense in this fact of our mutually furthering each other's purposes because we are interested in our own. There is no taint or presumption of selfishness in the matter at all. The economic nexus indefinitely expands our freedom of combination and movement; for it enables us to form one set of groups linked by community of purpose, without having to find the "double coincidence" which would otherwise be necessary. This economy and liberty will be equally valued by altruistic and by egoistic groups or individuals, and it would be just as true, and just as false, to say that the business motive ignores egoistic as to say that it ignores altruistic impulses. The specific characteristic of an economic relation is not its "egoism," but its "non-tuism."

It may be urged, however, that since, as a rule, "ego" and "tu" fill the whole canvas, not only to the spectator, but to the actors also; that is to say, since a man, when he is doing business, is generally only thinking of his own bargain, and how to deal with his correspondent, and not of any one else at all, the exclusion of "tu" is tantamount to the solitary survival of "ego." So that, after all, "altruism" has no place in business, and "non-tuism" is equivalent to "egoism." And, indeed, it may be true enough that, as a rule, the average man of business is not likely to be thinking of any "others" at all in the act of bargaining, but even so the term "egoism" is misapplied, for neither is he thinking of himself! He is thinking of the matter in hand, the bargain or the transaction, much as a man thinks of the next move in a game of chess or of how to unravel the construction of a sentence in the Greek text he is reading. He wants to make a good bargain or do a good piece of business, and he is directly thinking of nothing else. All manner of considerations of loyalty, of humanity, of reputation, and so forth, are no doubt present to his mind in solution, so to speak, as restraining influences; and they may easily be precipitated and emerge into consciousness at any moment of vacillation or reflection; but in making his bargain the business man is not usually thinking of these things, and when he thinks of them they act chiefly as restraints. Neither is he thinking of the ultimate purposes to which he will apply the resources that he gains. He is not thinking either of missions to the heathen or of famine funds, or of his pew rent, or of his political association. But neither is he thinking of his wife and family, nor yet of himself and the champagne suppers he may enjoy with his bachelor friends, nor of a season ticket for concerts, nor of opportunities for increasing his knowledge of Chinese or mathematics, nor of free expenditure during his next holiday on the Continent, nor of a week at Monte Carlo, nor of anything else whatever except his bargain. He is exactly in the position of a man who is playing a game of chess or cricket. He is considering nothing except his game. It would be absurd to call a man selfish for protecting his king in a game of chess, or to say that he was actuated by purely egoistic motives in so doing. It would be equally absurd to call a cricketer selfish for protecting his wicket, or to say that in making runs he was actuated by egoistic motives qualified by a secondary concern for his eleven. The fact is that he has no conscious motive whatever, and is wholly intent on the complex feat of taking the ball. If you want to know whether he is selfish or unselfish you must consider the whole organisation of his life, the place which chess-playing or cricket takes in it, and the alternatives which they open or close. At the moment the categories of egoism and altruism are irrelevant.

And yet this analogy of the game will further explain the obstinacy with which the phrase and the idea reassert themselves, that, in matters of business, a man is solely actuated by the desire for "his own advantage." It is just because we look upon two men engaged in driving a hard bargain (a very small part of the life of a man of business by the way) much as we look upon two men who are playing a game. Each is intent upon victory, that is, upon raising his score against the other's, and in this sense the man who has driven a close or a hard bargain is certainly intent on securing an advantage, and we call it "his" advantage, because he is struggling to gain it, though it may in the final instance be the advantage of a client or a ward in which he has either an indirect share only or no share at all. Once more, then, if *ego* and *tu* are engaged in any transaction, whether egoism or altruism furnishes my inspiring motive, or whether my thoughts at the moment are wholly impersonal, the economic nature of the action on my side remains undisturbed. It is only when tuism to some degree actuates my conduct that it ceases to be wholly economic. It is idle, therefore, to consider "egoism" as a characteristic mark of the economic life. . . .

QUESTIONS ON WICKSTEED

1. What are economic relations? Why does Wicksteed think that these relations are inevitable in any complex civilization? How do economic relations serve the purposes of each of the parties to the relation?

2. How can the motives of those engaged in economic relations be altruistic? Why does Wicksteed state that "it would be just as true, and just as false, to say that the business motive ignores egoistic as to say that it ignores altruistic motives"?

3. What is "non-tuism"? How is non-tuism distinguishable from selfishness? Is there a sense in which even an economic relation *ought* to take into account some of the interests of the other party to trade? How much of their interests should count?

Prudence

Although the economic agent need not be assumed to be narrowly self-interested or selfish, it is nonetheless true that we engage in commercial production and trade in order, primarily, to secure and improve our material conditions. Prudence is the virtue concerned with rational planning and foresight to secure the goods necessary for living and to attempt to forestall the misfortunes that so often arise. And yet this virtue, if it is a virtue, is not regarded highly at all, even though it has a noble history. Why is this?

Prudence: Noble and Ordinary

The virtue of prudence was considered to be one of the cardinal virtues and was understood by Plato to refer to wisdom or sound judgment, and by Aristotle to refer to *phronesis,* or practical wisdom. The term itself, which derives from the Latin *prudential,* a contraction of the term "providence" (*providentia*), is indicative of the ideas of thought, foresight, and proper planning. However, the classical view of prudence understood that prudential concern and prudential reasoning were not dis-

---

14. *The Complete English Tradesman* [1889], two volumes (New York: Burt Franklin, 1970), vol. 1, 88.

15. "Prudence," *Essays: First Series* [1841], in *The Collected Works of Ralph Waldo Emerson,* vol. II (Cambridge: Belknap Press of Harvard University, 1979), 132.

tinct from moral reasoning but were the very essence of moral reasoning. Thus it was that for Aristotle, practical wisdom involves perception and deliberation about the goods of life. In the modern period, especially with the deontological theory of Immanuel Kant (1724–1804), a distinction has been invoked between moral and prudential reasoning, leaving prudence as a virtue with little importance or moral esteem. Adam Smith (1723–1790) also distinguishes between higher and lower forms of prudence, the lower sort being concerned with economic action, material security, and reputation. The higher form of prudence is directed to "greater and nobler purposes" and is more closely akin to the wisdom of Plato or the practical wisdom of one of Aristotle's wise rulers. It is in the wake of this transition, noted by Smith, that we explore a scaled-down version of prudence, one that is less Aristotelian than modern, one that focuses on securing and improving one's material state.

Prudence and Self-Interest

Smith maintains that prudence is one of the lesser virtues, but he also believes that it is crucial for economic growth. Thus a growing economy for Smith does not rely on self-interest but on "The uniform, constant, and uninterrupted effort of every man to better his condition, the principle from which publick and national, as well as private opulence is originally derived, is frequently powerful enough to maintain the natural progress of things toward improvement, in spite both of the extravagance of government, and of the greatest errors of administration."[16] Although prudence is often taken to mean the pursuit of self-interest, one must distinguish, on the one hand, between deliberate caution and effective planning for an end and, on the other hand, the pursuit of one's self-interest (or the pursuit of self-interest to the detriment of others). The pursuit of self-interest need not entail prudence, nor does prudence entail the pursuit of narrowly self-interested or selfish ends.

Prudence and Business

In commercial life more generally, prudence may involve the balancing of ends with risks and circumstances, and this requires foresight, knowledge, and planning. For ex-

ample, prudence is often invoked in commercial and financial planning. A long-range plan of investment must take appropriate account of facts and risks in relation to the needs and objectives of the investor. Prudence is measured less by success than by the manner in which the planner relates circumstances, risk, and objectives. The financial planner exercises prudence insofar as he or she attends to (or diligently investigates) the features and risks of an investment, and determines how appropriate that investment is for a person of specific circumstances and objectives. The appropriateness of a particular investment may depend, therefore, on the diversity of the person's portfolio as well as on the liquidity of the investment.

Prudence, Self-Control, and Thrift

Prudence often requires the exercise of other companion virtues, in particular, those of thrift and self-control. Prudence requires that one put work before leisure, the long run before the short, and that one be able to organize one's time. However, if one is to do this, then one must exercise self-discipline. For Aristotle, the virtue of self-control (or temperance) is concerned with the physical pleasures of sight, sound, and taste, but he also discusses how moral strength is a consequence of self-control (*Nicomachean Ethics* VII. 1–10). The self-controlled person is one who possesses the virtues and responds appropriately without any inner struggle. Thus did Adam Smith believe that self-command was an essential element to all virtues, "from it all the other virtues seem to derive their principal luster."[17]

To be self-controlled is also to live within one's means, to avoid extravagance. However, the idea of planning for the future also entails the importance of thrift. Thus did Andrew Carnegie (1835–1919), the industrialist and philanthropist, contend that thrift is the first duty because it is at "the bottom of all improvement."[18] The ultimate effect of thrift is not to create great fortunes but—by each individual saving for his or her own future—to provide the basis, from the savings of millions, for large investment on the part of prudential financial institutions, such as banks and lending agencies. What remains at issue is how prudence, thrift, and commerce can be reconciled with the virtue of generosity. We leave that question for the next section.

---

16. *An Inquiry into the Nature and Causes of the Wealth of Nations* [1776], edited by R. H. Campbell, A. S. Skinner, and W. B. Todd (Indianapolis, Ind.: Liberty Classics, 1976), Book II.iii (p. 343).

17. *The Theory of Moral Sentiments* [1759], edited by D. D. Raphael and A. L. Macfie (Indianapolis, Ind.: Liberty Classics, 1976), VI.iii.11 (p. 241).

18. "Thrift as a Duty," *The Empire of Business* (New York: Doubleday, 1902), 96.

THE READINGS

Adam Smith   Smith contends that prudence involves the "care and foresight" necessary to secure and increase the goods of living, even as our desire to secure these goods is also influenced by the desire to earn the respectful admiration of others. To delineate the idea of prudence, Smith offers a portrait of a prudent person. The first object of the prudent person is security, and so this person is cautious, earnest, unostentatious, modest, sincere, inoffensive, industrious, frugal, and in general, actuated by self-command. The prudent person does not seek out new or surprising avenues of endeavor, does not meddle in the business of others, and shys from political disputes. This virtue says Smith is not one of the "most ennobling" and can be distinguished from a higher form of prudence "directed to greater and nobler purposes."

H. J. N. Horsburgh   Horsburgh contends that prudence utilizes rational foresight and self-control in order to protect the agent from those significant sorts of misfortunes that might occur to any individual over the whole of life. That an action may be prudent does not depend on the results but on whether one exercised reasonable foresight. Prudence differs from practical wisdom in that prudence focuses on avoiding great ills (that might accrue to any agent, including poverty, sickness, and so on) and thus counsels caution, whereas practical wisdom may allow for greater risk at distinct stages of life. The prudent person is self-regarding, but this does not come at the expense of the interests of others. Most people do not have whole-hearted approval of prudence, and this is revealed, says Horsburgh, in how we appraise prudence and prudent actions. Prudence may conflict with moral greatness because it seems to be inconsistent with a deep attachment to any vocation or duty that may engender risk or hardship. Finally, Horsburgh contends that prudence cannot be considered a specific virtue because its scope of application is too great, and if it comes to dominate one's life, it may do so at the expense of moral action.

Of Prudence

Adam Smith

Adam Smith (1723–1790) was born in Kirkcaldy, Scotland, and taught at Glasgow University, lecturing on jurisprudence, rhetoric, moral philosophy, and political economy. Known primarily for his work in political economy, An Inquiry into the Nature and Causes of the Wealth of Nations *(1776), Smith was a thinker of extraordinary breadth, publishing* The Theory of Moral Sentiments *(1759) at the age of 36, and writing other essays on science and literature. This selection is from Part VI.i of the* Moral Sentiments.

The preservation and healthful state of the body seem to be the objects which Nature first recommends to the care of every individual. The appetites of hunger and thirst, the agreeable or disagreeable sensations of pleasure and pain, of heat and cold, etc. may be considered as lessons delivered by the voice of Nature herself, directing him what he ought to chuse, and what he ought to avoid, for this purpose. The first lessons which he is taught by those to whom his childhood is entrusted, tend, the greater part of them, to the *same* purpose. Their principal object is to teach him how to keep out of harm's way.

As he grows up, he soon learns that some care and foresight are necessary for providing the means of gratifying those natural appetites, of procuring pleasure and avoiding pain, of procuring the agreeable and avoiding the disagreeable temperature of heat and cold. In the proper direction of this care and foresight consists the art of preserving and increasing what is called his external fortune.

Though it is in order to supply the necessities and conveniences of the body, that the advantages of external fortune are originally recommended to us, yet we cannot live long in the world without perceiving that the respect of our equals, our credit and rank in the society we live in, depend very much upon the degree in which we possess, or are supposed to possess, those advantages. The desire of becoming the proper objects of this respect, of deserving and obtaining this credit and rank among our equals, is, perhaps, the strongest of all our desires, and our anxiety to obtain the advantages of fortune is accordingly much more excited and irritated by this desire, than by that of supplying all the necessities and conveniencies of the body, which are always very easily supplied.

Our rank and credit among our equals, too, depend very much upon, what, perhaps, a virtuous man would wish them to depend entirely, our character and conduct, or upon the confidence, esteem, and good-will, which these naturally excite in the people we live with.

The care of the health, of the fortune, of the rank and reputation of the individual, the objects upon which his comfort and happiness in this life are supposed principally to depend, is considered as the proper business of that virtue which is commonly called Prudence.

We suffer more, it has already been observed, when we fall from a better to a worse situation, than we ever enjoy when we rise from a worse to a better. Security, therefore, is the first and the principal object of prudence. It is averse to expose our health, our fortune, our rank, or reputation, to any sort of hazard. It is rather cautious than enterprising, and more anxious to preserve the advantages which we already possess, than forward to prompt us to the acquisition of still greater advantages. The methods of improving our fortune, which it principally recommends to us, are those which expose to no loss or hazard; real knowledge and skill in our trade or profession, assiduity and industry in the exercise of it, frugality, and even some degree of parsimony, in all our expences.

The prudent man always studies seriously and earnestly to understand whatever he professes to understand, and not merely to persuade other people that he understands it; and though his talents may not always be very brilliant, they are always perfectly genuine. He neither endeavours to impose upon you by the cunning devices of an artful impostor, nor by the arrogant airs of an assuming pedant, nor by the confident assertions of a superficial and imprudent pretender. He is not ostentatious even of the abilities which he really possesses. His conversation is simple and modest, and he is averse to all the quackish arts by which other people so frequently thrust themselves into public notice and reputation. For reputation in his profession he is naturally disposed to rely a good deal upon the solidity of his knowledge and abilities; and he does not always think of cultivating the favour of those little clubs and cabals, who, in the superior arts and sciences, so often erect themselves into the supreme judges of merit; and who make it their business to celebrate the talents and virtues of one another, and to decry whatever can come into competition with them. If he ever connects himself with any society of this kind, it is merely in self-defence, not with a view to impose upon the public, but to hinder the public from being imposed upon, to his disadvantage, by the clamours, the whispers, or the intrigues, either of that particular society, or of some other of the same kind.

The prudent man is always sincere, and feels horror at the very thought of exposing himself to the disgrace which attends upon the detection of falsehood. But though always sincere, he is not always frank and open; and though he never tells any thing but the truth, he does not always think himself bound, when not properly called upon, to tell the whole truth. As he is cautious in his actions, so he is reserved in his speech; and never rashly or unnecessarily obtrudes his opinion concerning either things or persons.

The prudent man, though not always distinguished by the most exquisite sensibility, is always very capable of friendship. But his friendship is not that ardent and passionate, but too often transitory affection, which appears so delicious to the generosity of youth and inexperience. It is a sedate, but steady and faithful attachment to a few well-tried and well-chosen companions; in the choice of whom he is not guided by the giddy admiration of shining accomplishments, but by the sober esteem of modesty, discretion, and good conduct. But though capable of friendship, he is not always much disposed to general sociality. He rarely frequents, and more rarely figures in those convivial societies which are distinguished for the jollity and gaiety of their conversation. Their way of life might too often interfere with the regularity of his temperance, might interrupt the steadiness of his industry, or break in upon the strictness of his frugality.

But though his conversation may not always be very sprightly or diverting, it is always perfectly inoffensive. He hates the thought of being guilty of any petulance or rudeness. He never assumes impertinently over any body, and, upon all common occasions, is willing to place himself rather below than above his equals. Both in his conduct and conversation, he is an exact observer of decency, and respects with an almost religious scrupulosity, all the established decorums and ceremonials of society. And, in this respect, he sets a much better example than has frequently been done by men of much more splendid talents and virtues; who, in all ages, from that of Socrates and Aristippus, down to that of Dr. Swift and Voltaire, and from that of Philip and Alexander the Great, down to that of the great Czar Peter of Moscovy, have too often distinguished themselves by the most improper and even insolent contempt of all the ordinary decorums of life and conversation, and who have thereby set the most pernicious example to those who wish to resemble them, and who too often content themselves with imitating their follies, without even attempting to attain their perfections.

In the steadiness of his industry and frugality, in his steadily sacrificing the ease and enjoyment of the present moment for the probable expectation of the still greater ease and enjoyment of a more distant but more lasting period of time, the prudent man is always both supported and rewarded by the entire approbation of the impartial spectator, and of the representative of the impartial spectator, the man within the breast. The impartial spectator does not feel himself worn out by the present labour of those whose conduct he surveys; nor does he feel himself and what is likely to be their future situation, are very nearly the same: he sees them nearly at the same distance, and is affected by them very nearly in the same manner. He knows, however, that to the persons principally concerned, they are very far from being the same, and that they naturally affect *them* in a very different manner. He cannot therefore but approve, and even applaud, that proper exertion of self-command, which enables them to act as if their present and their future situation affected them nearly in the same manner in which they affect him.

The man who lives within his income, is naturally contented with his situation, which, by continual, though small accumulations, is growing better and better every day. He is enabled gradually to relax, both in the rigour of his parsimony and in the severity of his application; and he feels with double satisfaction this gradual increase of ease and enjoyment, from having felt before the hardship which attended the want of them. He has no anxiety to change so comfortable a situation, and does not go in quest of new enterprises and adventures, which might endanger, but could not well increase, the secure tranquillity which he actually enjoys. If he enters into any new projects or enterprises, they are likely to be well concerted and well prepared. He can never be hurried or drove into them by any necessity, but has always time and leisure to deliberate soberly and coolly concerning what are likely to be their consequences.

The prudent man is not willing to subject himself to any responsibility which his duty does not impose upon him. He is not a bustler in business where he has no concern; is not a meddler in other people's affairs; is not a professed counsellor or adviser, who obtrudes his advice where nobody is asking it. He confines himself, as much as his duty will permit, to his own affairs, and has no taste for that foolish importance which many people wish to derive from appearing to have some influence in the management of those of other people. He is averse to enter into any party disputes, hates faction, and is not always very forward to listen to the voice even of noble and great ambition. When distinctly called upon, he will not decline the service of his country, but he will not cabal in order to force himself into it; and would be much better pleased that the public business were well managed by some other person, than that he himself should have the trouble, and incur the responsibility, of managing it. In the bottom of his heart he would prefer the undisturbed enjoyment of secure tranquillity, not only to all the vain splendour of successful ambition, but to the real and solid glory of performing the greatest and most magnanimous actions.

Prudence, in short, when directed merely to the care of the health, of the fortune, and of the rank and reputation of the individual, though it is regarded as a most respectable and even, in some degree, as an amiable and agreeable quality, yet it never is considered as one, either of the most endearing, or of the most ennobling of the virtues. It commands a certain cold esteem, but seems not entitled to any very ardent love or admiration.

Wise and judicious conduct, when directed to greater and nobler purposes than the care of the health, the fortune, the rank and reputation of the individual, is frequently and very properly called prudence. We talk of the prudence of the great general, of the great statesman, of the great legislator. Prudence is, in all these cases, combined with many greater and more splendid virtues, with valour, with extensive and strong benevolence, with a sacred regard to the rules of justice, and all these supported by a proper degree of self-command. This superior prudence, when carried to the highest degree of perfection, necessarily supposes the art, the talent, and the habit or disposition of acting with the most perfect propriety in every possible circumstance and situation. It necessarily supposes the utmost perfection of all the intellectual and of all the moral virtues. It is the best head joined to the best heart. It is the most perfect wisdom combined with the most perfect virtue. It constitutes very nearly the character of the Academical or Peripatetic sage, as the inferior prudence does that of the Epicurean.

QUESTIONS ON SMITH

1. Explain some of the characteristics of the prudent person. How do these characteristics relate to the desire to improve one's economic condition or one's position in society?

2. Does Smith's account of prudence reveal something about the *other* virtues of the prudent person? Is the prudent man also a just person? A trustworthy person? Is the prudent person merely out for self-interest?

3. What is the moral status of prudence? Why should prudence merit only a "cold esteem"?

Prudence

H. J. N. Horsburgh

H. J. N. Horsburgh was born in Darjeeling, India, the son of a clergyman. He was a Professor of Philosophy at the University of Victoria, British Columbia, and he is the author of Mahatma Gandhi *(1972) and* Non-violence and Aggression: A Study of Gandhi's Moral

Equivalent of War *(1968). This essay was originally written in response to an essay by J. D. Mabbott ("Prudence,"* Proceedings of the Aristotelian Society, *1962).*

In my view, a prudent action or policy is one that involves distinctively human powers of rational foresight and self-control, and that can be expected to protect the agent, either in the relatively distant future or over a protracted period that may date from the action's performance, from a considerable misfortune or disaster of a kind that might overtake any agent.

It will be difficult to justify the whole of this statement. But I shall try to do so.

We seldom describe an action as prudent if it can be justified by its expected results in the immediate future. This is because immediate threats can usually be met without the exercise of distinctively human powers of self-control or rational foresight. For example, looking up and down a street before crossing it does not deserve to be described as prudent. But saving for one's retirement or being vaccinated against poliomyelitis fully merits such a description, since, in different ways, they both involve rational foresight and at least a measure of self-control. It should also be noted that the propriety of describing actions as prudent does not depend on whether the expectations by which they would be justified prove to be correct but upon whether they are reasonable. The man who is playing the markets is not called shrewd unless his predictions are actually fulfilled even if they appeared to be soundly based at the time he made them. But we do not await the results of actions or policies before describing them as prudent. . . .

. . . All cautious actions are not prudent but all prudent actions are cautious, not only in being undertaken with care but also in being actively concerned to anticipate, evade, or ward off something that seriously threatens the future well-being of the agent. It is partly because self-interested behaviour, unlike that which we call prudent, may be quite unmindful of danger, that it has much less to do with the securing of general means to future satisfactions. It is also important to emphasise that prudence is concerned solely with the avoidance of major ills and disasters. On Mr. Mabbott's view, a man who often moved from one town to another would show prudence if he bought a radio that could be used with either A.C. or D.C. mains. But I question whether we should describe such an action as prudent since it does not greatly matter whether one has a radio and it is only an inconvenience to have bought one that one cannot always use.

At first hearing it is an odd proviso that a prudent action should be one that can be expected to protect the agent from a misfortune of a kind that might overtake any agent. But it seems to me that such a requirement is needed if we are to mark the difference between prudent actions and other members of the class of actions which are in some way conducive to the satisfaction of some or all of our desires, or if we are to take account of the fact that there are eventualities much dreaded by agents the avoidance of which would not count as prudent. . . . The special concern of prudence seems to be the avoidance of such evils as poverty, ill-health, disablement, loneliness, deep frustration, etc., etc.—evils that can befall us all and which are universally recognised to be major obstacles to the achievement of happiness. We all have a wish to avoid these evils in virtue of our common nature as human beings; and I wish to maintain that when we are considering actions or men and women from the standpoint of prudence we are concerned to stress what people have in common rather than the desires or inclinations which serve to differentiate one individual from another. Serviceable, expedient, politic and prudent actions are all conducive, in one way or another, to the fulfillment of the agent's desires. But whereas serviceable, politic and expedient actions are alike in being conducive to the satisfaction of any of one's desires, regardless of whether they are of kinds that activate few or many other people, prudent actions are conducive to the satisfaction of only those of one's desires which are of kinds that would be assumed to characterise any human being. Consider, for example, the case of a junior minister of high ambition who performs a special service for the prime-minister. His action is politic, but I do not think that we should call it prudent, since, from the standpoint of prudence, failure to reach cabinet rank does not count as a major adversity. On the other hand, the frustration or personal bitterness that might be engendered by such failure does count as a considerable misfortune. But the voice of prudence would counsel actions calculated to restrain high ambition rather than actions likely to satisfy it. For high ambition is a recipe for unhappiness since only in exceptional cases can it attain even partial fulfilment, and it cannot be prudent to act in a way calculated to satisfy a desire that it is imprudent not to curb. Similarly, the fact that one wants a short life and a merry one, or values high accomplishment more than safety, does not make it less imprudent to drink excessively or to take unnecessary risks. Therefore, when we are judging whether actions are prudent we abstract as far as possible from individual differences, ignoring the peculiar desires or scales of values of those whose actions are being scrutinised.

Prudent actions may or may not be performed for prudential reasons. But one would not describe an agent as prudent unless one believed, not only that he acted prudently, but that he did so in order to secure his own future happiness. Furthermore, one would expect him to be actively concerned about the whole remaining course of his life. Thus, the prudent man, *par excellence,* is the man who seeks to take care of his whole future, warding off all serious reverses of fortune to the limit of his capacity. . . .

As I have already said, the ideally prudent man seeks to safeguard his whole future. Such an undertaking seems to presuppose a general conception of the course of the individual's life as falling naturally into stages distinguished from one another by their dominant needs and desires, and hence, by the activities appropriate to them. The enjoyment of each stage is threatened by the great evils of human life. But different evils are specially menacing at different stages, so that the ideally prudent man, looking down the years, must prepare either to meet or to evade several vistas of human problems. Such an interpretation of prudence draws it into relation with the accepted conception—well-charted in some communities and more nebulous in others—of the practically wise life, *i.e.,* the kind of life which, taken as a whole, is likely to yield the biggest dividend of happiness. And this point of view enables us to offer a further explanation of our reluctance to attribute prudence to those who seriously impoverish their present lives out of exaggerated concern for the future. For, although impoverishment of the present and neglect of the future are errors that we often contrast, from the standpoint of accepted practical wisdom they illustrate the same error, namely, failure to give each stage of life neither more nor less than its due.

But if there are similarities between prudence and accepted practical wisdom, there are also important differences arising out of the concentration of the former upon the avoidance of major ills. The most obvious of these is to be found in their contrasting attitudes to dangerous play and experiment in the lives of the very young. The sowing of wild oats is usually accorded a place in the practically wise life but is quite alien to the life of prudence. Accepted practical wisdom distrusts, or even frowns upon, old heads set upon young shoulders, whereas prudence thinks that any pair of shoulders are the better for bearing such a head.

It is clear from what has already been said that . . . I should want to insist on there being some differences between the lives of prudence and enlightened self-interest. Most of these differences are sufficiently obvious. But it is worth pointing out that enlightened self-interest is closer to selfishness than prudence can be said

to be. This is because self-interested behaviour, however enlightened, is expected to further one's interests partly at the expense of other people's, whereas prudent behaviour, although self-regarding, is not expected to produce conflicts of interest. For example, my refusal to smoke may do nothing to safeguard your health, but the benefits I hope to derive from it are not gained, in the least degree, at your expense; and this is entirely typical of prudence. I think that it is this difference, more than any other, which accounts for the fact that when we say "*X* is acting prudently" we are sometimes expressing moral approval whereas when we say "*X* is acting self-interestedly" the note of moral approval is altogether absent however enlightened we may judge *X* to be. . . .

Somewhat surprised by Mr. Mabbott's unqualified approval of prudence I have asked a number of friends and acquaintances to define their attitude towards it. These enquiries suggest that it has few whole-hearted admirers. Most people seem to be either lukewarm in its support or to view it with positive hostility; and this lack of enthusiasm seems to be what one would expect since even Christian teaching, as represented by the parables, is ambiguous on this subject. What follows is to be thought of as, in some ways, complementary to Mr. Mabbott's vigorous defence of prudence. It is meant to account for these widely held attitudes of luke-warmness and hostility.

But before I proceed with this task I should like to justify it by providing some illustrations of the coolness to which I refer. First, such an attitude seems to be implied by our greater readiness to praise prudent actions than prudent people; for our inclinations move in the reverse direction when a quality elicits whole-hearted admiration. For example, eager as we are to praise courageous actions we are still more eager to praise courageous people. Again, even those who do not question that prudence is a virtue are most unlikely to use the word 'prudent' when describing those whom—in the moral sense—they most admire. Here it must be remembered that even a full description of somebody is far from being exhaustive since it normally includes only those characteristics which are either possessed to a conspicuous degree or which are more marked than any other characteristics. It is true that those whom we most admire will often act prudently, since to act otherwise is frequently sheer folly or wickedness; but such behaviour will not be so habitual as to make prudence one of their fundamental or salient characteristics. Finally, while one can say with warmth of approval, "What courage!" "What generosity!" or even "What self-control!" the expression "What prudence!" smacks of derision rather than of intense approbation.

I think it is clear from these illustrations that many people, when they call someone prudent, not only mean to praise him, but also to indicate that he does not belong to a very exalted moral class.

But this does not follow in any simple way from the meaning of the word 'prudent.' No quality obviously outstrips prudence in the way that nobility eclipses mere agreeableness. And it is not part of what is meant by prudence that it characterises the morally limited in the way that it is part of what is ordinarily meant by obedience that if it is a virtue at all it is a virtue of inferiors. The connexion between prudence and moral limitedness is felt to be less simple than this. And, in any case, it is at least questionable whether a quality that is a moral virtue in one man can be other than a moral virtue in another. So although it may usually be the duty of a servant to obey his master, obedience is not a moral virtue at all, whether it be found in servants or in masters.

Nevertheless, it is widely believed that although many people would be the better for being more prudent than they are, prudence is a quality that in some way limits the moral potentiality of those who possess it, setting a ceiling to their development. But how is this to be interpreted? There seem to be at least two ways in which a characteristic might limit achievement. First, a quality may be such that its possession is valuable in combination with, but harmful in the absence of, certain other qualities. For example, a speaker must regard natural fluency as an asset. But a man who lacks this talent may become a good speaker when its possession would have turned him into a perfect rattle. Secondly, a quality may be such as to favour mushroom growth up to but not beyond a certain level, its eventual result being to limit the development of the qualities to which it gave initial encouragement, or to prevent the development of other qualities that are also essential to high achievement. For example, complete fearlessness might be said to make for the rapid development of certain valuable qualities. But it is arguable that it also rules out the proper appreciation of danger and that such appreciation is essential to the development of courage and other important qualities. Prudence does not seem to be limiting in the first sense, since this requires that a quality should always be harmful unless accompanied by certain other qualities and that it should only limit those who lack these other qualities; and, on the view that I am maintaining, the development of prudence represents an advance in some but an inevitable limiting of any. Thus, if no other qual-

ities were mentioned, one would be more favourably disposed towards a man described as prudent than towards a man described as imprudent; but imprudence is just consistent with moral greatness and prudence is not. I am claiming, therefore, that prudence is morally limiting in the second sense.

But why should this be so? The short answer is that while it is only common sense to think of one's own future from time to time, doing what one can to protect oneself from poverty, disease, etc., when there is no more pressing business to attend to, to be so actively concerned with the avoidance of great personal misfortune for this to be a fundamental or salient characteristic, is to be unwilling to make departures from prudent schemes of life either as soon or as often as any marked fidelity to principles is bound to require. A longer answer is to be found by looking more closely at the lives of those whom we most admire. Almost invariably such people seem to possess one or other or both of the following characteristics: a sense of having a vocation that must be fulfilled however much suffering it brings down on themselves, or an extraordinary responsiveness to duty that makes them willing to down one mode of life and take up another without regard to the pain or hardship or loss of security that the substitution will cause them. Both these characteristics are utterly at odds with prudence; and the lives of those in whom they are to be found could as readily be confined within the boundaries of prudence as headlong passion within the channels of convention.

The attitude of those who are positively hostile to prudence might also be justified on the basis of what has already been said. For it might be contended that to aim at any life short of the best is to deserve a moral anathema; and few of us believe that the prudent life represents the summit of moral aspiration. But I shall leave aside such questions since it is very doubtful whether the severest critics of prudence would justify their attitude solely or even mainly on the ground that prudence represents too low a target. They are more likely to contend that it is the wrong target altogether; and consequently, that it is a positive affront to morality.

I suspect that this hostility is sometimes based upon gross carelessness or confusion. For example, one might condemn prudence on the basis of the contrast that we make between prudential reasons and moral reasons, arguing that since prudential reasons are not moral they must necessarily be immoral.

But there are more solid grounds for hostility to prudence. They rest on the fact that even if one approves of prudence its scope is such that it cannot be termed a specific virtue. Compare it with courage, for example. One can live courageously, and can even adopt a courageous way of life. But the injunction, "Be courageous!" gives one so little guidance in many of one's activities that one is bound to feel the need for additional injunctions. Prudence, on the other hand, is like the blind man's stick: in spite of its inferiority to some other guides it can be used to test one's every step. In other words, "Be prudent!" rivals "Be good!" in its breadth of application—and its rivalry is the more dangerous for its being the easier to interpret. It is this which gives point to the contrast between moral reasons and prudential reasons, and at the same time serves to justify the hostility of which I have spoken. It may be that there are limits to the legitimate cultivation of any virtue, and that we can be too generous, too magnanimous, etc.—although, for my own part, I question whether this is true. But prudential reasons can do more than encroach upon ground that should be reserved for moral reasons; they can entirely usurp the place of morality. Therefore, the quality of prudence, if it comes to dominate a man's character, is a very desperate threat to morality.

I think I have said enough to show that I am in sympathy with all the attitudes which Mr. Mabbott and I have distinguished—though not with all the defences which have been made of them. I sometimes approve of prudent actions and policies; and approve of them because they are prudent. On the other hand, I not only think that it is morally limiting to be the kind of person whom we describe as prudent, I positively disapprove of those whose lives and characters have largely been shaped by prudence.

QUESTIONS ON HORSBURGH

1. How does Horsburgh characterize or define prudence? How does Horsburgh distinguish self-interested behavior from prudential behavior?

2. Horsburgh states that prudence must be concerned with avoiding only "major ills and disasters" that might overtake anyone, but he also claims that prudence "can be used to test one's every step." If one employs "prudence" to test "every step," then is one still concerned with "major ills" or has one's prudence become obsessive?

3. Why would the prudential person be unlikely to have great ambitions? How is prudence morally limiting? Can one imagine a prudent person who aspires to and achieves moral greatness (in spite of the hardship or risk)?

———————————

Generosity

Alas! My poor money, my poor money, my dear friend! they have deprived me of you, and, now that you are taken away from me, I have lost my support, my consolation, my joy; all is finished, I have no longer any concern with the world: without you, it is impossible for me to live. All is over, I cannot do anything more, I am dying, I am dead, I am buried. Is there no one who will bring me back to life by giving me back my dear money, or by telling me who has taken it? . . . I will hang the whole world; and if I do not find my money, I will then hang myself.

Molière[19]

[T]he very Existence of the Civil Society . . . is entirely built upon the Variety of our Wants, so the whole Superstructure is made up of the reciprocal Services, which Men do to each other. How to get these Services perform'd by others, when we have Occasion for them, is the grand and almost constant Sollicitude in Life of every individual Person. To expect, that others should serve us for nothing, is unreasonable; therefore all Commerce, that Men can have together, must be a continual bartering of one thing for another.

Bernard Mandeville[20]

[T]here is no such thing as an 'economic end.' Economy is simply a process of applying means to whatever ends a person may adopt. An individual can aim at any ends he pleases, 'selfish' or 'altruistic.' Other psychic factors being equal, it is to everyone's self-interest to maximize his monetary income on the market. But this maximum income can then be used for 'selfish' or for 'altruistic' ends. . . . A successful businessman can use his money to buy a yacht or to build a home for destitute orphans. The choice rests with him.

Murray Rothbard[21]

19. As spoken by Harpargon in *The Miser* [1668], in *The Plays of Molière,* vol. VI, translated by A. R. Waller (Edinburgh: John Grant, 1907), Act IV, Scene VII.

20. *The Fable of the Bees,* vol. II [1728], edited by F. B. Kaye (Indianapolis, Ind.: Liberty Classics, 1988), 349.

21. "Antimarket Ethics: A Praxeological Critique," in *Power and Market: Government and the Economy* (Menlo Park, Calif.: Institute for Humane Studies, 1970), 166.

LIBERALITY AND GENEROSITY

Market Exchange and Giving

To interact within a market is to engage in economic exchange. The items exchanged are not equivalent in value but differ in value. If I give you A for B, then you and I value differently the goods A and B. As parties to this exchange, each of us is seeking the highest reward attainable at the time. Market exchange is reciprocal, and in this manner it differs from acts of generosity not predicated on some reciprocating act or from acts of gift giving in which one person bestows some desirable object on another person. It was Adam Smith's view that since we could not rely solely on the benevolence of others to supply us with goods to satisfy our needs and desires, we would have to interest others in reciprocal trades.[22] If commercial exchange involves a reciprocity that is distinct from a generous action, then it is necessary to ask whether generosity is incompatible with business. One response to this question suggests that generosity is compatible with business insofar as one uses commerce as the *means* of funding one's generous giving (as it arises in one's noncommercial life). Another response suggests that, in fact, generosity can *complement* (or accompany) commercial activity in important ways.

Generosity as Complement and as Aim

Generosity can often complement our commercial exchanges in that a generous action may accompany an exchange. How might this be possible? The Roman Stoic, Cicero, points out that generosity may involve the giving of one's time and labor or the giving of money and that "that sort of bounty, which consists in doing kindnesses by our labour and industry, is more virtuous and creditable, can oblige more people, and has more ways of doing it than that other has."[23] In business life, one may often have the opportunity to help a colleague or a customer by assisting in some task. This labor need not be part of one's "job description" and need not be remunerated, for it is this very lack of reciprocity that renders one's efforts generous. Thus, if one is truly gener-

ous then one's virtuous disposition may supervene on one's economic transactions in such a way that as one relates to customer, colleague, or employee, one may give more of oneself—in effort, time, attention, and consideration—than the person who is not generous. On the other hand, one might think of one's business life as the very means by which one can practice generosity. On this view, one's generosity may take the form of the giving of wealth, but since wealth must first be produced if one is to bestow it, its production may require business effort and acumen.

Aristotelian Liberality and the Vice of Greed

We often think of generosity as concerned only with giving. Aristotle, however, speaks of generosity as the virtue of *liberality,* a virtue concerned with the proper use of wealth, both in giving *and* receiving. Liberality has its corresponding vices, prodigality and illiberality, and these may be understood in terms of excess or deficiency. Thus we can see how the illiberal person might be considered to be excessive in the sense of being greedy; this person takes from others more than is appropriate. That the greedy person is illiberal does not entail the doing of an injustice; it is only that the person takes excessively from those who are willing to give of their time and effort. On the other hand, an illiberal person may not give enough to others; this is the stingy person, the miser who overvalues money and fails to use it properly, either for self or society.

THE READINGS

Aristotle   For Aristotle a virtue is a characteristic that involves choice and consists in a mean (relative to the agent) determined by reason. In this selection, Aristotle describes the virtue of liberality as a mean concerning wealth—material goods that are measureable in money. Liberality is primarily concerned with giving, but it may also concern itself with the receipt of goods from others. Liberality does not depend on giving a specific amount but involves giving in the right manner, to the right person, at the right time, with the right motive, in the right amount, and doing so with pleasure. The extremes of this virtue are the deficiency of meanness (stinginess) and that of excess, prodigality (extravagance).

Tibor Machan   Generous conduct involves a spontaneous disposition to act benevolently toward others without any direct personal gain. Generosity does not arise from a sense of duty, nor does it expect any return of fa-

---

22. The work of the French sociologist Marcel Mauss (1872–1950) is one of the first to examine the manner in which social relationships could be structured not by exchange but by the giving of gifts, a term with a wider reference than the usage of our day. *The Gift: Forms and Functions of Exchange in Archaic Societies,* translated by Ian Cunnison (New York: Norton, 1967).

23. *The Offices* in *Offices, Essays, and Letters* (New York: E.P. Dutton, 1949), Book II, xv (p. 95).

vor. There are three types of contexts—private, social, and political—in which one might express one's generosity; in this excerpt Machan focuses on generosity in the social and political spheres. Our acts of generosity must occur within a framework of certain basic rights to life, liberty, and property. Basic rights must be negative rather than positive, Machan argues, and it is only negative rights that grant one a sovereignty without which no generosity would be possible. In certain forms of communal living it would be unlikely that generosity would be considered a virtue at all.

Liberality*

Aristotle

One of the most important philosophers of all time, Aristotle (384–322 B.C.), the son of a physician, was a polymath who wrote on a variety of subjects including biology, psychology, metaphysics, rhetoric, logic, and physics. His Nicomachean Ethics *was the first systematic treatment of moral matters.*

BOOK IV

1

Let us speak next of liberality. It seems to be the mean with regard to wealth; for the liberal man is praised not in respect of military matters, nor of those in respect of which the temperate man is praised, nor of judicial decisions, but with regard to the giving and taking of wealth, and especially in respect of giving. Now by 'wealth' we mean all the things whose value is measured by money. Further, prodigality and meanness are excesses and defects with regard to wealth; and meanness we always impute to those who care more than they ought for wealth, but we sometimes apply the word 'prodigality' in a complex sense; for we call those men prodigals who are incontinent and spend money on self-indulgence. Hence also they are thought the poorest characters; for they combine more vices than one. Therefore the application of the word to them is not its proper use; for a 'prodigal' means a man who has a single evil quality, that of wasting his substance; since a prodigal is one who is being ruined by his own fault, and the wasting of substance is thought to be a sort of ruining of oneself, life being held to depend on possession of substance.

This, then, is the sense in which we take the word 'prodigality.' Now the things that have a use may be used either well or badly; and riches is a useful thing; and everything is used best by the man who has the virtue concerned with it; riches, therefore, will be used best by the man who has the virtue concerned with wealth; and this is the liberal man. Now spending and giving seem to be the using of wealth; taking and keeping rather the possession of it. Hence it is more the mark of the liberal man to give to the right people than to take from the right sources and not to take from the wrong. For it is more characteristic of virtue to do good than to have good done to one, and more characteristic to do what is noble than not to do what is base; and it is not hard to see that giving implies doing good and doing what is noble, and taking implies having good done to one or not acting basely. And gratitude is felt towards him who gives, not towards him who does not take, and praise also is bestowed more on him. It is easier, also, not to take than to give; for men are apter to give away their own too little than to take what is another's. Givers, too, are called liberal; but those who do not take are not praised for liberality but rather for justice; while those who take are hardly praised at all. And the liberal are almost the most loved of all virtuous characters, since they are useful; and this depends on their giving.

Now virtuous actions are noble and done for the sake of the noble. Therefore the liberal man, like other virtuous men, will give for the sake of the noble, and rightly; for he will give to the right people, the right amounts, and at the right time, with all the other qualifications that accompany right giving; and that too with pleasure or without pain; for that which is virtuous is pleasant or free from pain—least of all will it be painful. But he who gives to the wrong people or not for the sake of the noble but for some other cause, will be called not liberal but by some other name. Nor is he liberal who gives with pain; for he would prefer the wealth to the noble act, and this is not characteristic of a liberal man. But no more will the liberal man take from wrong sources; for such taking is not characteristic of the man who sets no store by wealth. Nor will he be a ready asker; for it is not characteristic of a man who confers benefits to accept them lightly. But he will take from the right sources, e.g. from his own possessions, not as something noble but as a necessity, that he may have something to give. Nor will he neglect his own property, since he wishes by means of this to help others. And he will refrain from giving to anybody and everybody, that he may have something to give to the right people, at the right time, and where it is noble to do so. It is highly characteristic of a liberal man also to go to excess in giving, so that he leaves too little for himself; for it is the

* Translated by W.D. Ross

nature of a liberal man not to look to himself. The term 'liberality' is used relatively to a man's substance; for liberality resides not in the multitude of the gifts but in the state of character of the giver, and this is relative to the giver's substance. There is therefore nothing to prevent the man who gives less from being the more liberal man, if he has less to give those are thought to be more liberal who have not made their wealth but inherited it; for in the first place they have no experience of want, and secondly all men are fonder of their own productions, as are parents and poets. It is not easy for the liberal man to be rich, since he is not apt either at taking or at keeping, but at giving away, and does not value wealth for its own sake but as a means to giving. Hence comes the charge that is brought against fortune, that those who deserve riches most get it least. But it is not unreasonable that it should turn out so; for he cannot have wealth, any more than anything else, if he does not take pains to have it. Yet he will not give to the wrong people nor at the wrong time, and so on; for he would no longer be acting in accordance with liberality, and if he spent on these objects he would have nothing to spend on the right objects. For, as has been said, he is liberal who spends according to his substance and on the right objects; and he who exceeds is prodigal. Hence we do not call despots prodigal; for it is thought not easy for them to give and spend beyond the amount of their possessions. Liberality, then, being a mean with regard to giving and taking of wealth, the liberal man will both give and spend the right amounts and on the right objects, alike in small things and in great, and that with pleasure; he will also take the right amounts and from the right sources. For, the virtue being a mean with regard to both, he will do both as he ought; since this sort of taking accompanies proper giving, and that which is not of this sort is contrary to it, and accordingly the giving and taking that accompany each other are present together in the same man, while the contrary kinds evidently are not. But if he happens to spend in a manner contrary to what is right and noble, he will be pained, but moderately and as he ought; for it is the mark of virtue both to be pleased and to be pained at the right objects and in the right way. Further, the liberal man is easy to deal with in money matters; for he can be got the better of, since he sets no store by money, and is more annoyed if he has not spent something that he ought than pained if he has spent something that he ought not, and does not agree with the saying of Simonides.

The prodigal errs in these respects also; for he is neither pleased nor pained at the right things or in the right way; this will be more evident as we go on. We have said

that prodigality and meanness are excesses and deficiencies, and in two things, in giving and in taking; for we include spending under giving. Now prodigality exceeds in giving and not taking, while meanness falls short in giving, and exceeds in taking, except in small things.

The characteristics of prodigality are not often combined; for it is not easy to give to all if you take from none; private persons soon exhaust their substance with giving, and it is to these that the name of prodigals is applied—though a man of this sort would seem to be in no small degree better than a mean man. For he is easily cured both by age and by poverty, and thus he may move towards the middle state. For he has the characteristics of the liberal man, since he both gives and refrains from taking, though he does neither of these in the right manner or well. Therefore if he were brought to do so by habituation or in some other way, he would be liberal; for he will then give to the right people, and will not take from the wrong sources. This is why he is thought to have not a bad character; it is not the mark of a wicked or ignoble man to go to excess in giving and not taking, but only of a foolish one. The man who is prodigal in this way is thought much better than the mean man both for the aforesaid reasons and because he benefits many while the other benefits no one, not even himself.

But most prodigal people, as has been said, also take from the wrong sources, and are in this respect mean. They become apt to take because they wish to spend and cannot do this easily; for their possessions soon run short. Thus they are forced to provide means from some other source. At the same time, because they care nothing for honour, they take recklessly and from any source; for they have an appetite for giving, and they do not mind how or from what source. Hence also their giving is not liberal; for it is not noble, nor does it aim at nobility, nor is it done in the right way; sometimes they make rich those who should be poor, and will give nothing to people of respectable character, and much to flatterers or those who provide them with some other pleasure. Hence also most of them are self-indulgent; for they spend lightly and waste money on their indulgences, and incline towards pleasures because they do not live with a view to what is noble.

The prodigal man, then, turns into what we have described if he is left untutored, but if he is treated with care he will arrive at the intermediate and right state. But meanness is both incurable (for old age and every disability is thought to make men mean) and more innate in men than prodigality; for most men are fonder of getting money than of giving. It also extends widely, and is multiform, since there seem to be many kinds of meanness.

For it consists in two things, deficiency in giving and excess in taking, and is not found complete in all men but is sometimes divided; some men go to excess in taking, others fall short in giving. Those who are called by such names as 'miserly,' 'close,' 'stingy,' all fall short in giving, but do not covet the possessions of others nor wish to get them. In some this is due to a sort of honesty and avoidance of what is disgraceful (for some seem, or at least profess, to hoard their money for this reason, that they may not some day be forced to do something disgraceful; to this class belong the cheese-parer and every one of the sort; he is so called from his excess of unwillingness to give anything); while others again keep their hands off the property of others from fear, on the ground that it is not easy, if one takes the property of others oneself, to avoid having one's own taken by them; they are therefore content neither to take nor to give.

Others again exceed in respect of taking by taking anything and from any source, e.g. those who ply sordid trades, pimps and all such people, and those who lend small sums and at high rates. For all of these take more than they ought and from wrong sources. What is common to them is evidently sordid love of gain; they all put up with a bad name for the sake of gain, and little gain at that. For those who make great gains but from wrong sources, and not the right gains, e.g. despots when they sack cities and spoil temples, we do not call mean but rather wicked, impious, and unjust. But the gamester and the footpad [and the highwayman] belong to the class of the mean, since they have a sordid love of gain. For it is for gain that both of them ply their craft and endure the disgrace of it, and the one faces the greatest dangers for the sake of the booty, while the other makes gain from his friends, to whom he ought to be giving. Both, then, since they are willing to make gain from wrong sources, are sordid lovers of gain; therefore all such forms of taking are mean.

And it is natural that meanness is described as the contrary of liberality; for not only is it a greater evil than prodigality, but men err more often in this direction than in the way of prodigality as we have described it.

So much, then, for liberality and the opposed vices.

QUESTIONS ON ARISTOTLE

1. How does liberality involve a mean relative to the agent? What is the excess of liberality? What is the deficiency? Why is the deficiency a "deficiency in giving and an excess in taking"?

2. Does the virtue of liberality presuppose that one hold property? How does the virtue of liberality differ from the demands of justice?

3. Aristotle writes that "the liberal man is easy to deal with in money matters; for he can be got the better of. . . ." Why does Aristotle say this? In what way does Aristotle understand liberality to be manifested in business? How might liberality manifest itself in trade? In relations with co-workers? In the evaluation of personnel?

Dimensions of Generosity

Tibor R. Machan

Tibor R. Machan was smuggled out of Hungary in 1953 and emigrated to the United States three years later. He is Distinguished Fellow and Professor at the Leatherby Center for Entrepreneurship and Business Ethics, Chapman University, California, and the author of Human Rights and Human Liberties *(1975),* Individuals and Their Rights *(1989),* Capitalism and Individualism: Reframing the Argument for the Free Society *(1990), and* Classical Individualism *(1999), among other works. This excerpt is from* Generosity: Virtue in Civil Society *(1998).*

GENEROSITY, A BENEVOLENT VIRTUE

Ordinary Generosity

Generous persons were originally understood to be ones whose basic nature was sound. Later the meaning of the term "generous" evolved and came to mean, roughly, a disposition or inclination to act benevolently toward some other persons. Still, the original meaning left its imprint.

We tend to take it that generous people are benevolent because of their character, not as a matter of deliberation or calculation. As a character trait, generosity inclines one to do good for others. It can manifest itself in small or large measures: "As he began to shave, he thought to turn off the running water in his hotel bathroom since the pressure during morning hours nearly vanished. If he restricted the flow somewhat in his sink, the rest of the guests would have a better chance at getting water to come out of their faucets." "When she heard that those folks wanted to get themselves on their feet, following their narrow escape from their wretched homeland, she went to her desk and wrote out and sent them a sizable check."

No direct personal gain is involved in generous conduct. A generous person doesn't think, "If I am good to them, I'll get this or that for my trouble." Generosity, when viewed under a microscope, is a member of the family of benevolent moral principles. One may be "benevolent" in a variety of ways, among them by being generous, charitable, kind, compassionate, or thoughtful. But what distinguishes generosity from, for example, kindness or compassion is not always clear. The terms are often used interchangeably, although kindness is more of an attitude, and an attitude need not issue in action. Compassion tends to presuppose the beneficiary is pitiable, heartbreaking, deserving of special care. When we are urged to be compassionate, it is toward those who are in trouble.

Generosity involves spontaneously doing good things—giving gifts, providing help or advice, showing tolerance or special consideration—for others, who may or may not be in trouble. The acts are spontaneous in that they flow from one's character, not from calculation or even deliberation. Character, in turn, is a gradually evolved collection of traits that we acquire through our rearing and, later, through perseverance, commitment, and resistance to laxness—all sustained through a kind of low-key reflection on how or who we ought to be.

Charity, in contrast, is benevolence arising from a sense of duty. One would be charitable by extending oneself toward others as a result of the realization that one has the duty to do something for them. A duty is an action that is morally prescribed, a matter of a rule or law that one must explicitly know before one can follow it. Generosity is more of a morally commendable trait, leading as it does to spontaneous acts. Those distinctions are not always observed in ordinary reflection and usage, but there are examples of our use of the terms that clearly suggest what is noted above.

When one talks of a generous person, one usually has in mind someone who does good for others as a matter of course, without hesitation. There is nothing forced or self-disciplined about it. One is not resisting greed when one is being generous. Charity, in contrast, involves telling oneself to give others what one ought to give them, because one has the explicit belief that one ought to give to them. Charity is deliberative, not spontaneous.

One might object that generosity flows from the discipline one has once exercised, just as good, smooth driving follows early training that was rigorous and re-

quired considerable direct mental focus. That is a good point, but it characterizes the way someone might *become* generous, not generosity itself. It misses an important aspect of generosity by ascribing to a given action a quality that has not yet been absorbed within the agent. Generosity, in contrast, is such a quality—absorbed and ready to go into action effortlessly, as it were, on all appropriate occasions. Charitable conduct may involve deliberate discipline or concentration, but generosity does not. It is a character trait, an aspect of a person and not a form of behavior a person imposes on himself.

Yet one's generosity is extended as a result of a generalized—perhaps even automatized or self-programmed—outlook or disposition one has toward (some) other people in one's life. Generosity involves giving of oneself or what one has to those one finds precious or to persons or causes one thinks highly of or feels close to. Generosity flows from a generalized valuation of some other people or their goals.

Lack of generosity is a moral vice. That vice must, as must all moral vices, in principle be possible for the opposite, the moral virtue, to amount to something morally praiseworthy. Those who want to prohibit all vices—say, by transforming law enforcement agencies into a kind of massive vice squad—fail to appreciate that if vice is banned, unambiguous virtue becomes impossible: there will be no possibility of crediting people for making right choices.

In any case, *generosity is not self-sacrificial* in the way charity and even compassion can be. Nor is it calculating: there is no quid pro quo involved in generous acts. They involve giving without the expectation of anything like a return of favors. Of course, the virtue of generosity does involve a type of benefiting oneself, but only in the broadest possible sense. As David Schmidtz observes, "There are reasons to embrace and nurture our concern for others, reasons that have to do with what is conducive to our own health, survival, and growth."[1]

That self-benefiting comes from one's being a morally good person. In other words, being morally good is to one's benefit. That follows if moral virtues serve a person's project of living a good human life. Some moral theorists see no benefit to a person from that kind of life. But others do, and they have the best of the debate—what else could a good human life amount to than one that is good for the agent in a most fundamental respect? A good human life is the one thing valuable in and of itself, without reference to any other end or goal. But I will discuss that more extensively shortly.

To explore further the matter of the spontaneous element of generosity, we should consider that a generous person is not fighting to restrain some stingy inclination, needing to withstand the temptation of avarice. One is not generous for having restrained oneself from spending too much of one's money on a shopping spree and disciplined oneself to send care packages to starving Sudanese children. Rather, a generous person is acting, as it were, from second nature. Generous conduct is for such a person a matter of course. Generous people do not perform select good deeds or resist doing specific bad deeds. Rather, routinely in the course of their lives, they are giving, considerate, and expansive.

Generosity (as a moral virtue) would, then, be a benevolent trait that, although cultivated for oneself, would have become an unselfconscious way of conducting one's life. Under appropriate circumstances and without much effort, conduct helpful (but not by right due) to others would flow from generous persons. When one is generous, one does not do for others what is due them by right. Positive-rights theorists might argue the contrary, but they are mistaken: Obligatory giving requires too much distributional calculation or, alternatively, rote conduct to amount to generosity. If my help is due someone—as it is, for example, my children—I am not being generous in giving it. If people are due respect for their human dignity—so that I ought not to intrude on their "moral space"—that again is not a matter of generosity. Such behavior involves knowing and acting on one's obligations toward others. . . .

DIMENSIONS OF GENEROSITY: PRIVATE, SOCIAL, AND POLITICAL

Contexts of Generosity

. . . [W]e will look at the various contexts of generosity that are open to most people and examine just how that virtue manifests itself in those contexts. While there are many special contexts we could focus on—for example, relations among colleagues in a given profession or at a given institution (firm, university, division, department, team)—I plan to concentrate on three broad areas: the private, the social, and the political. By private I mean the sphere that touches on one's personal, romantic, family, and fraternal concerns—the intimate dimension of one's life. Of course, those are already encumbered by social elements. Yet what distinguishes them as private is that the people one relates to in those contexts are concerned with one's personal life, with oneself as an individual—not as doctor, teacher, taxicab driver, athlete, artist, or trading partner—and one's own concern with those persons is not confined to the "utilitarian" dimensions of life.

By social I mean the vast sphere of relationships one can have with others in one or another of the vast manifestations of humanity—persons in their roles as teachers, coaches, airline attendants, butchers, priests, postal service employees, dental hygienists, service station attendants, psychiatrists, trumpet players, veterinarians, publishers, philosophers, biologists, economists, news reporters, and so forth. Those are all individuals we might relate to and with whom situations might arise in which generosity could play a role. It is instructive to inquire just how the generosity of a person would manifest itself in that broader social context.

There is also the political dimension of our lives, one that pertains to the upholding of the principles of our legal community. Here we are concerned mainly with whether the basic framework of our society is adequately taken care of, administered, and maintained. What, if any, bearing does generosity have on this dimension of our lives? And how does politics bear on the prospect of generosity within a human community?

I will take a close look at each of these areas with an eye to seeing how generosity is affected by or related to it.

Generosity in Private

It is possible for one to be generous in a variety of types of circumstances. Although public discussions tend to center on generosity that reaches beyond the borders of one's private life—that is, organized "charity" and philanthropy—that does not make generosity in the private context morally irrelevant.[2] No pundits sing praises of the generosity of one's aunt or sister; yet in the actual lives of people, that is just the sort of manifestation of generosity that is of vital importance. And while not everyone gains a public reputation for his moral character, including his generosity, the actual moral quality of the lives of those who engage in private generosity could be every bit as noble as that of the lives of some prominently praised public figure.

Furthermore, it is also in private that generosity can often misfire. While from the viewpoint of other people one's generosity to a fault might not be a severe failure, as far as one's personal responsibilities are concerned, it clearly can be. If a husband becomes too enamored of stray dogs and neglects his wife, or a father extends himself too far to reach out toward a special cause such as wildlife preservation and thus neglects his duties to his children, that could be generosity gone astray. . . .

Generosity in the Social Fabric

People take part in numerous projects that may not seem to be of direct personal significance to them. They champion the arts, sciences, wildlife, historical preservation, antique cars, old movies, intramural sports, the moral education of the young, promulgation of religious beliefs, and so forth. Although when looked at from the perspective of a life span, the success of those causes may be to their benefit, contributing to their advancement will not usually provide an immediate payoff. Rather, one is disposed, as a matter of one's character, to see to it that certain causes are furthered and those who make their success likely are given support.

Here is where generosity as a distinctive part of one's social life manifests itself. When one provides support, help, or assistance so as to promote the sort of causes in the above list, neither with the expectation of some direct benefit or self-satisfaction ("I did it so as to feel good about myself") nor to fulfill an obligation or duty ("It is required of me to support the environmental movement"), one manifests generosity on the social front.

It is, moreover, a moral failure, not a legal or political one, to stand apart from all such social involvements, unless one is facing dire straits.

Speaking generally, it is a mistake of our time to ignore the social dimension of human life or, more accurately, to conflate it with the political or legal. Thus, those who speak of the social responsibility of, say, corporations often mean not what corporations ought to do about their social surroundings but what the law should make them do or what public policy should be enacted to get them to do. The same holds for lamentations about people's lack of generosity, charity, kindness, or compassion—many such lamentations immediately entail calling upon the government to get us all to be more generous, charitable, and the like. Unlike moral responsibilities vis-à-vis various aspects of our society—religion, science, athletics, education, and the like—legal obligations involve imperatives that can be enforced coercively. And those are necessarily limited in a society of free and responsible persons. Moral virtues such as generosity, courage, and prudence must be practiced voluntarily—one is not *obligated to others* to act on them. They are binding on one as a matter of one's own choice to live a full human life, not because failing to act on them would invade another's moral space or sphere of jurisdiction.[3]

We have moral responsibilities to others, not because those who might benefit are entitled, but because those of our choice to live human lives within the company of others. And if we fulfill those responsibilities simply out of fear of coercion, we do not deserve any moral credit. In the terms made famous by Immanuel Kant, we cease to be "ends in ourselves," to be autonomous, sovereign persons, if moral virtues are dictated to us.

Generosity, as are other moral virtues, is due from us because we have a commitment to ourselves to live fully human lives. But it is not due from us because others have a right to it. Those who insist that this is the justification of moral generosity unjustifiably politicize all of human life. They propose to make all of human life a matter of regimentation from above, with little room left for life's greatest task, the achievement of the moral life of a responsible human being through our own free choice.

Politics and Generosity

Rights as Social Guidelines   Individuals have rights to life, liberty, and property—which is to say that in society no one may murder, kidnap, assault, steal from, or extort from another person.[4] Those are negative rights—they impose on others the enforceable obligation not to act in certain ways, not to invade other people's private domains. (The operative term here is "private," meaning that some way of distinguishing "mine" from "thine" needs to be at work here, and the theory of natural private-property rights serves this purpose.) Positive rights, in turn, are supposed to spell out duties to provide some service to the rightsholder. But positive rights are not basic rights. They arise from the explicit or implicit consent of individuals—for example, from contracts or from reproduction. To appreciate the difference, one might consider that it is no virtue not to kill, assault, rape, or extort from others—it goes without saying that we need to abstain from such actions—whereas providing help to one in need would normally qualify as a morally virtuous act. The reason is that prohibitions of such conduct are a social prerequisite for people to act morally, to achieve a morally good life. If we could be subjected with impunity to murder, assault, kidnapping, robbery, and their various nuanced implications, we would in effect have no life of our own to live. We would be at the mercy of others' decisions; we would need permission to act (just as we do once something is treated as a public matter).

So, positive rights transform what are cases of moral virtue into cases of coerced obligation for which no moral credit is to be earned. They are also impossible to secure equally for all, without the protection of the rights of some people trampling the rights of others. Unfairness, then, is built into the very idea of positive basic rights.

It is not in order here to defend the claim that basic human individual rights are negative. I have argued that elsewhere.[5] But a few points need to be offered to explain the position, since there is in our time considerable sympathy for the view that basic rights ought really to include some positive rights, for example, rights to health care, social security, housing, nutrition, and education.

Even if those benefits might warrant public provision, they are not basic rights. They cannot be basic because they beg the question of what kind of impositions, if any, may be placed upon others in one's interaction with them. If we may force others to educate our children, to feed us, to provide us with health care, why not with their one eye when we are blind, their one kidney when both ours are damaged, their entire life if we need it badly enough? And if we are entitled to their support, when are they entitled to ours, and who has priority in all this?

Such positive rights constrain, arbitrarily, the jurisdiction of individuals in the sphere of choosing or neglecting to choose to do what is right, and they introduce a state of perpetual war within societies that aim to provide them protection.[6] Negative basic rights—which is to say the rights not to be killed, assaulted, and so forth—amount to placing borders around individuals as human beings, within which they are the sovereign judges in charge of what is to be done. Forbidding others to violate such rights does not amount to dictating to them how to live and treats them as the kind of beings they are, human. It is for this reason they were dubbed "natural" rights in the first place, because they pertain to the conditions required in society for living a properly human life.

The reason basic rights are negative is that their function is to provide adult persons with a sphere of moral jurisdiction and to alert others who want to benefit from social life to the scope of that sphere: if you live among people and want, as you properly should, to reap the benefits of such a life, certain basic principles need to be heeded. Basic negative rights, prohibitions of certain acts toward others, are those conditions. The basic rights of others are due them because of their moral nature, because they have moral tasks in life that they must fulfill. Intruding on their sphere of moral jurisdiction amounts to thwarting their moral agency. And basic

rights spell out where the conduct of others would or would not amount to intrusion. That is why the "border" analogy is useful, even if it runs the risk of giving too materialist an image of a person's sphere of moral authority. Moral agents require borders around them so as to know what their responsibilities are and where others must ultimately leave decisions up to them. . . .

Rights and Generosity

How does all this apply to our topic, generosity? We must note, first of all, how respect for rights is not in the same moral category as the practice of virtues. When another is owed something by right, granting what is owed is not a matter of generosity, not a matter of practicing one of several virtues. It is not that kind of good deed but another, namely, respect without conditions for the other as a person.

When one acts without violation of other people's rights, there are several options. One may discover that to be generous is not the best option—not the most rational way to act under the circumstances. Instead, one should be prudent or tolerant or courageous or honest—or, again, some proper combination of all of those. Within the hierarchy of the virtues, one or another may dominate in any specific situation. When it comes to treating others simply as human beings who are fellow members of political communities—which is what is spelled out by reference to their fundamental rights as human beings—there is no such hierarchy. In other words, basic human rights are political imperatives to fully respect the sovereignty of all adult members of one's human community, so there is no option as to which of those rights need to be protected most vigilantly. This is where the issue of compossibility, including mutual respectability and protectability, comes in. For them all to be such, they must form a compossible set. . . .

Put generally, generosity requires a kind of community life in which one's sovereignty is acknowledged—that is, where individuals have jurisdiction over themselves and their belongings. Of course, individual sovereignty does not have to be officially acknowledged, so long as it does receive some recognition by oneself and one's fellows, explicitly or even tacitly. (That is why, even in collectivist societies, people will be able to distinguish generous, courageous, and prudent conduct and individuals, even though that is rendered more difficult by the attempt to abolish privacy, the sphere wherein moral decisions are initiated. In short, the law denies but reality reaffirms the sphere of individual moral responsibility.) The point is that moral sovereignty[7] must be a fact taken to be such by the relevant parties—those who could act on or in defiance of it. As David Levine puts it, "When I have a right over some object or activity, this means that I determine the activity and the manner of the object's disposal. In this sense, my right endows me with power."[8] That power is what renders me an effective moral agent whose conduct can be right or wrong, depending on how the right is exercised (i.e., how the power is deployed).[9]

Now, if moral sovereignty were impossible for us, we would be unable to practice any virtue, least of all generosity. We would then probably be related to our society and to humanity as a whole in the way our arms and eyes are related to us, not as individuals with moral responsibilities of our own. Or we would be like the lower animals, like lobsters, that are not collectivist but cannibalistic. We could possess no moral virtues at all, since morality can exist only where the possibility of and the capacity for making some choices are present. One does not praise one's arm for a good discus throw, except figuratively. One's eyes are not given moral credit for having correctly detected disease, even if the eyes played a role in that detection. In short, if we were part of a collective whole, we could not be regarded as moral agents and our good traits could not be moral virtues.

Let us consider a person who is not a sovereign but who *belongs* to a tribe, community, or state.[10] He has nothing of his own to give or contribute for the benefit of another. If we were simply elements of a larger whole—as is arguably advanced in Marx's understanding of communism—or elements of the "organic body" of humanity, there would be no opportunity for any of us to choose to give or to cultivate a giving character. We would have nothing of our own, and we would have no personal jurisdiction. . . .

The "Generous" Commonwealth

Strictly speaking, only individuals can choose to be morally virtuous, including generous. It may, however, make sense to speak of a generous community, corporation, or family, provided it is kept in mind that such generosity comes from the persons who make up the groups in question. This is no different from the realization that when we speak of the Soviet invasion of Hungary, we in fact have in mind the thousands of Soviet soldiers, their officers, and ultimately the Soviet dictatorship's leaders.

In line with such an outlook, if the moral sovereignty of human individuals did not exist, generosity would not be possible. Of course, a kind of replacement might manifest itself in rebellion against the general so-

cial structure, as when under communism someone must courageously break the rule of communal ownership. (As Robert Heilbroner so perceptively notes,[11] under communism everyone's labor belongs to the community as a whole, so even lending another a hand could strictly be considered impermissible—one would require the permission of the community, so only the community as a whole might conceivably be considered generous, never an individual.)

Even in voluntary communes, special benevolent outreach toward one person might be viewed with suspicion since it might tend to undermine the disciplined prior obligation of all to the whole. Of course, many groups lack a precise form, so people treat each other in mixed fashion—as friends, compatriots, associates, neighbors, and so forth—and there are numerous moral dimensions that can be manifest, some of which appear to contradict the others. A family is a communal arrangement, but generosity is clearly possible between its members.

In any case, whatever the merits of the kind of communal living in which members are treated as belonging to the whole unit, generosity is unlikely to be a virtue under such a system. It is incompatible with any kind of actual, strictly maintained collectivism—that is, a system under which the sovereignty of the individual is effectively rejected in favor of total or substantial subservience to some common purpose—whether freely accepted or imposed, except, perhaps, if the initial choice to join such a collective is itself motivated by generosity.

Without effective individual sovereignty, there would be nothing about which one could make a decision. And that would preclude most virtues, since they all presuppose the moral initiative of the individual person who possesses or lacks them. No room would be left for generosity—the choice to benefit others with one's skills or belongings, or with anything else of one's own. The decision to join a collective farm may, however, involve the generous contribution of one's skills. However, in the opinions of some thinkers, as noted above, one does not even own those and the decision to devote them to some task or another must be left to the collective and not to oneself.

Both direct, personal generosity and indirect, institutional generosity presuppose human communities in which a significant degree of personal sovereignty exists. Such communities would also have to include a significant degree of respect for a system of stable, private-property rights, and that system would have to be extensive enough to permit the development of habits of ownership of valued skills, items, time, and so forth on the part of individuals. Only with such a stable system of private-property rights can generosity be expected to be a part of the character of members of the community. Without such a system, lack of generosity generates not so much particularized guilt as lack of self-esteem on the part of those who are not allowed to be generous.

ENDNOTES

1. David Schmidtz, "Reasons for Altruism," *Social Philosophy and Policy* 10 (Winter 1993): 56. Schmidtz considers why one might act altruistically, not as a matter of psychology or sociology, but as a matter of having one's own good reasons for so acting. Whereas I am discussing generosity, Schmidtz is concerned with what he refers to as altruistic acts, namely, being charitable, behaving compassionately, and the like. Those kinds of behavior may or may not be altruistic—in the sense of placing the well-being of others before all else.

   Altruism is the term Auguste Comte coined to designate an ethical system whereby others are placed at the head of the list of each person's priorities. It is misleading to designate benevolent conduct as altruistic. Doing so begs the question of whether only altruists—those who accept and practice the system of ethics in which being concerned with the well-being of others is one's primary duty in life—can be generous, kind, or compassionate.

2. Earlier I made the point that charity is different from generosity because the former is seen as our duty and is taken to involve giving aid to those who need not deserve it at all, simply because they are in need. Organized charities, however, are not in conformity with this traditional meaning of the term. A charitable trust, for example, may have as its beneficiary artists, educators, scientists, as well as orphans, political refugees, and disaster survivors. Here I use this common sense of the term, not its more technical meaning in formal (duty) ethics.

3. An interesting clue to the difference may be found in the fact that generous conduct is something for which gratitude is naturally expressed, whereas conduct that respects rights—not murdering, assaulting, raping, stealing from and kidnapping people—invites no thanks.

4. John Locke uses the term "property" to encompass all of the above: "Lives, Liberties and Estates, which I call by the general name *property*." John Locke, *Two Treatises of Government,* ed. Peter Laslett (Cambridge: Cambridge University Press, 1988), II, p. 350.

5. See Tibor R. Machan, "Moral Myths and Basic Positive Rights," *Tulane Studies in Philosophy* (1985): 35–41.

6. It is no accident that the greatest source of political conflict in our time is the division of entitlements: Who gets the limited resources that are deemed to be public property and thus something to which all of us have a positive right? Should resources go to AIDS research, the arts, education, public housing, environmental protection, scientific research and development, or other things? A framework of negative rights provides a principled guide to what one is entitled to; roughly, what is the result of one's choices and actions that do not encroach on the choices and actions of others. Nearly all public scandals now have to do with unabashed attempts to influence political leaders about who gets the "public wealth." For more on this, see Tibor R. Machan, *Private Rights and Public Illusions* (New Brunswick, N.J.: Transaction Books, 1995).

7. By moral sovereignty I do not mean that one is the source of the truths of morality, only that one must be the source of decisions concerning whether one will do the right or wrong thing. Suppose Joe compels me with a gun to share my house with someone else. Even if that action of sharing is the morally proper one for me to take, I did not make the decision to behave that way. I cannot gain moral credit for my behavior, or be blamed for its absence, since I was deprived of my role as the cause of it. I was deprived of my moral sovereignty.

   There is another argument that I have not developed, namely, that property is often deserved by the good deeds of those who have produced it—that is, property can be the result of prudent conduct. Therefore, to eliminate private ownership of property is to sever a proper or even a just connection, namely, between an act that is good and its results. If Jones's act is good and it brings about Jones's possession of X, Jones's possession of X is prima facie good. The institution of private-property rights acknowledges the wrong of taking X from Jones. See Tibor R. Machan, *Capitalism and Individualism* (New York: St. Martin's, 1990), pp. 83–84.

8. David Levine, *Needs, Rights and the Market* (London: Lynne Rienner, 1988), p. 29.

9. This fact was noted about rights throughout the history of political philosophy. William of Ockham identifies natural rights as "the power to conform to right reason, without an agreement or compact." Quoted from *Opus Nonaginta Dierum,* in M. P. Golding, "The Concept of Rights: A Historical Sketch," *Bioethics and Human Rights,* ed. E. B. Bandman (Boston: Little, Brown, 1978), p. 48.

10. The term "belonging" is used by Charles Taylor in his essay attacking liberalism. See "Atomism" in Charles Taylor, *Philosophy and the Human Sciences* (Cambridge: Cambridge University Press, 1985), pp. 188–210.

11. It is acknowledged by some scholars that Karl Marx's idea that the major means of production are collectively owned implies that everyone's labor belongs to the community as a whole, given that labor is the primary means of production according to Marx's theory. See, for example, Robert Heilbroner, *Marxism: For and Against* (New York: W. W. Norton, 1980), pp. 156–57.

QUESTIONS ON MACHAN

1. What are the criteria of a generous act? How is generosity distinct from charity? Under what types of circumstances can one be generous?

2. How does Machan distinguish between negative and positive rights? How do negative rights provide a sovereign sphere in which one may act? Why does Machan believe that basic rights cannot be positive rights? Do you agree?

3. What is the relation between generosity and personal sovereignty? Why does Machan assert that generosity requires sovereignty over oneself and one's belongings? Does generosity within a family require sovereignty over one's belongings?

Manners

The gentle mind by gentle deeds is known. For a man by nothing is so well betrayed, as by his manners.

Edmund Spenser [24]

Manners are of more importance than laws. Upon them, in a great measure, the laws depend. The law touches us but here and there, and now and then. Manners are what vex or soothe, corrupt or purify, exalt or debase, barbarize or refine us, by a constant, steady, uniform, insensible operation, like that of the air we breathe in. They give their whole form and color to our lives. According to their quality, they aid morals, they supply them, or they totally destroy them.

Edmund Burke [25]

But let it be how and which way it will, whether mercer or draper, or what trade you please, the man that stands behind the counter must be all courtesy, civility, and good manners; he must not be affronted, or any way moved, by any manner of usage, whether owing to casualty or design; if he sees himself ill-used, he must wink, and not appear to see it, nor any way show dislike or distaste; if he does, he reproaches, not only himself, but his shop, and puts an ill name upon the general usage of customers in it; and it is not to be imagined how, in this gossiping, tea-drinking age, the scandal will run, even among people who have had no knowledge of the person first complaining.

Daniel Defoe [26]

COURTESY AND MANNERS

The prudent businessperson may be a generous person, but generosity is a virtue that focuses on the giving of labor or wealth to others. Such benevolence presupposes that one takes into account the good of others, as agents worthy of consideration. Another way in which we take into account the dignity and worth of others is through our manner of conduct. The idea of manners has been long neglected by philosophers and seems to suffer a similar neglect in our ordinary lives. However, manners may not only be good business practice, but they may also be qualities worthy of cultivation for their own sake.

24. *The Faerie Queen* [1596], in *The Works of Edmund Spenser,* edited by Edwin Greenlaw, Charles Grosvenor Osgood, Frederick Morgan Padelford, and Ray Heffner (Baltimore, Md.: Johns Hopkins Press, 1938), Book 6, canto 3, stanza 1.

25. *Letter 1* [1796] of *Letters on a Regicide Peace,* in *Select Works of Edmund Burke,* vol. 3 (Indianapolis, Ind.: Liberty Fund, 1999), 126.

26. *The Complete English Tradesman* [1726], vol. 1 (New York: Burt Franklin, 1970), 62.

What Are Manners?

In its broadest sense, the idea of manners incorporates a number of terms with different connotations: civility, politeness, courtesy, etiquette. The idea of civility would seem to entail self-restraint and deference toward others, proclivities which serve to recognize our separate identities, projects, and ideals, and ensure that we treat others who differ from us with dignity and respect. Politeness has the connotation of agreeability. The polite person engenders ease and security in those with whom he or she is in contact. Politeness and courtesy would seem to be closely related, perhaps interchangeable, though the idea of courtesy seems to imply a modicum of individual consideration that is not present in politeness. Etiquette is a matter of following rules that establish acceptable modes of address and attire, as well as appropriate norms for the table. In what follows, we will refer to manners as inclusive of all of these concepts.

Class and Insincerity

It might be charged, however, that manners are but a means of division utilized by persons of powerful social or economic classes to mark their differences from others less fortunate. It is not obvious that this is the function of manners, certainly not the *sole* function. Even if certain refined modes of behavior have often been identified with a particular class, this historical origin does not, however, tell us whether we *ought* to practice manners. After all, manners can elevate behavior from the ordinary and the vulgar. The person who acts with a natural courtesy and politeness adds grace, sophistication, and refinement to every endeavor. Indeed, the bearing of the well-mannered individual is altogether different from the comportment of persons who bump and bruise their way through society, ignoring others, talking loudly, interrupting peremptorily, acting imperiously, and, in general, exhibiting an aggressively self-centered view of the world that would seem to allot no place for the claims and activities of others.

It would seem, then, that the well-mannered person must exercise some self-discipline and self-control. Manners are, of course, inculcated largely within the home and family, and it is there that we first learn to restrain our desires and to conduct ourselves in certain approved modes of behavior. Such self-restraint may require that we exhibit behavior that does not correspond to our actual feelings. This leads some to believe that we ought *not* to pay much attention to manners because manners concern appearances alone, and the attention to appearances serves to inhibit the expression of our true selves. Of course, even if manners are nothing but appearances and do inhibit the expressions of our (true) selves, that does

not settle the question of whether we should practice manners, for it may be that such appearances serve important moral purposes, just as it may be that our true selves should be inhibited in certain circumstances.

Manners and Commerce

There would seem to be no doubt that manners are essential to a certain smoothness of social relation. Thus F. A. Hayek points out "That the existence of common conventions and traditions among a group of people will enable them to work together smoothly and efficiently with much less formal organization and compulsion than a group without such common background, is, of course, a commonplace."[27] Bernard Mandeville (see Section AIV) thought that manners did serve to cover up our more ugly appetites and that certain forms of courtesy and politeness were encouraged by commercial interactions. In his account of the courteous and agreeable conversation entered into by a seller and a customer, Mandeville relates how the seller of silk, who wishes to sell as much as he can at a reasonable price, endeavors to be as polite as possible.

> Here facing her [the customer], with a profound Reverence and modish Phrase he [the seller] begs the favour of knowing her Commands. Let her say and dislike what she pleases, she can never be directly contradicted: she deals with a Man in whom consummate Patience is one of the Mysteries of his Trade, and whatever trouble she creates, she is sure to hear nothing but the most obliging Language, and has always before her a cheerful Countenance, where Joy and Respect seem to be blended with Good-humour, and altogether make up an Artificial Serenity more engaging than untaught Nature is able to produce.[28]

To the contrary, others have noticed that as society has commercialized, manners have come to be seen as less essential than the bottom line: "Reliance on technical competence reduces dependence on personal goodwill, inherent grace, gestures of respect. . . ."[29] The essay by Engelhardt also suggests that within the realm of commerce our manners become more formal and less meaningful. Whether or not manners are encouraged or discouraged within commerce, there may be reasons to cultivate them, and these are discussed in the two reading selections that close this section.

27. "Individualism: True and False," *Individualism and Economic Order* (Chicago: University of Chicago Press, 1948), 23–24.

28. "A Search into the Nature of Society" [1723], in *The Fable of the Bees,* vol. 1, edited by F. B. Kaye (Indianapolis, Ind.: Liberty Classics, 1988), 351.

29. Bryan Wilson, Foreword to *Gentility Recalled: 'Mere' Manners and the Making of Social Order,* edited by Digby Anderson (London: Social Affairs Unit, 1996), 18.

THE READINGS

Sarah Buss   Buss contends that the virtue of courtesy involves respecting the dignity of other persons, and for that reason courtesy is a moral obligation. If we treat someone with respect, then we acknowledge the intrinsic dignity of the person, and this involves more than merely not interfering with a person's pursuit of some goal or project. Buss recognizes three features distinguishing morals from manners, but she contends there is a moral function that can be performed only by manners. Recognizing, with Hume, that manners may render one more agreeable, Buss contends that manners have a moral consequence independent of any such agreeability. Manners help us to conceive of human beings as the very beings to whom we bear moral relations, thus helping to ensure social harmony and justice more generally. However, manners also affirm in a direct, rather than an indirect, way the special dignity of the human being.

H. Tristram Engelhardt   Both morals and manners are more difficult to practice in the postmodern age, for we no longer possess a common conception of life or proper behavior. Historically, manners serve multiple purposes and are deeply woven into the culture and its values; unlike morals, which have a universal and transcendant claim on us, manners are instrumental and do not exert their claims universally. In the contemporary world, manners have been brought into question because we no longer possess a shared moral conception (and so we disagree about how to show respect and courtesy to others) and because it is charged that manners are elitist. Society is composed of distinct communities of identity held together by a "thin" culture of strangers who do not share a common outlook. This thin agreement, which forms the basis for manners in markets and democracies, is not grounded in any thick view of human life and society, but consists of a "polished courtesy without substance," and is often hostile to the manners of more substantive communities.

Appearing Respectful: The Moral Significance of Manners

Sarah Buss

Sarah Buss is Assistant Professor of Philosophy at the University of Iowa and the author of essays on moral philosophy and the theory of action. The complete version of this essay appeared in Ethics *(July 1999).*

Moral philosophers constantly remind us how very important it is to treat one another with respect. After all, we are persons; and persons have a special dignity. Persons are ends in themselves—and must be acknowledged as such.

Experts on manners have a strikingly similar drum beat. They tell us how very important it is to treat one another respectfully. We must not offend the dignity of others if we can possibly avoid doing so. We must treat other people with as much consideration as possible.

When the same words are used in very different contexts, they often mean very different things. Nonetheless, it seems to me that the "respect" and "dignity" of such importance in moral philosophy are the very same "respect" and "dignity" of such importance in manners. Systems of manners play an essential role in our moral life. What's more, playing this role is the essential function of good manners.[1]

This, at any rate, is the two-part thesis I hope to defend in the pages that follow. I will not argue that it applies to each particular rule in a code of etiquette. Rather, I will focus on the virtue that is essential to good manners: the virtue we call "courtesy." Codes of etiquette tell us how to set the fork, the knife, and the spoon. But the most important lessons in manners are the lessons in how to avoid being discourteous, impolite, rude, inconsiderate, offensive, insulting. I will argue that someone who flouts these lessons behaves in a manner that is immoral as well as impolite. And if a system of manners encourages such immorality, then it can be criticized from the point of view of manners itself: it is a code of bad manners as well as a code of bad morals.

To most people uncorrupted by philosophy this will probably not be a surprising thesis: in appraising one another's behavior we are not committed to a clear division of labor between rules of manners and rules of morality. Many philosophers, however, seem to take it for granted that manners lie outside the scope of morality. They assume that doing one's moral duty is one thing, being polite quite another. In defending the moral function of manners I will at the same time be challenging the assumption that in order to treat other persons as ends in themselves, it suffices to pursue one's own ends in a way that permits them to pursue theirs. I will, that is, be making the case for a more inclusive conception of the moral duty to treat other persons with respect.[2]

To treat someone "with respect" is to treat her in a way that acknowledges her intrinsic value, or "dignity."[3] This is a value she has no matter what her deeds and accomplishments may be; it is tied to what she *is*, not to what she *has done*. Many of us believe that what makes someone valuable in this respect is not that she is a duchess, or some member of a privileged class, but that she is a person, capable of evaluating her situation for herself and setting her own goals accordingly. On this view, the obligation to acknowledge the intrinsic value of everyone who is intrinsically valuable is the obligation to acknowledge the intrinsic value of everyone.

But how is this acknowledgment accomplished? There is widespread agreement that we acknowledge the intrinsic value of persons by permitting them to constrain our decisions in a special way: in deciding what to do, we accommodate ourselves to the fact that other persons have their own interests and concerns, their own ends. Of course, philosophers disagree about just what the necessary accommodation requires. My point about manners, however, is that whatever we must do in order to accommodate our ends to the ends of others, we must do something more in order to acknowledge the intrinsic value of others. Acknowledging a person's intrinsic value—treating her with respect—also requires that one treat her politely (considerately, respectfully). If we treat someone rudely, then we fail to treat her with respect—even if we do not prevent her from pursuing her most fundamental goals. Having defended this claim, I will consider what it implies about one of our own most basic rules of polite behavior.

* * *

If I am to have any hope of convincing anyone that good manners are an essential aspect of a morally decent life, I must confront those features of manners that seem to distinguish them from morals. Though there are surely many such features, I will focus on the three which, to my mind, are the most significant.

First, then, one of the primary objectives of systems of manners is to encourage us to make ourselves *agreeable*. This feature is closely related to the second: insofar as one's aim is good manners, acting from a good will is less important than *appearing* to be good willed. As Miss Manners succinctly puts it: "Manners involve the appearance of things, rather than the total reality."[4] Finally, everyone seems to agree that what counts as good manners in one culture does not necessarily count as good manners in another culture; when the subject is manners, relativism is an uncontroversial thesis.

Despite these obvious respects in which rules of manners differ from moral commands, I want to argue that a moral life would be severely impoverished without good manners. What's more, I want to argue that it would be impoverished because good manners have an important moral function—a function only they can perform. It is, I believe, a striking fact that people who are

boorish or sulky or obnoxious or otherwise *disagreeable* are *morally* deficient precisely because they make so little effort to please. Why should this be? The simplest answer is that we believe that, all else being equal, people have a basic moral obligation to make themselves agreeable to others. This seems to have been Hume's view in the *Enquiry*. A quick glance at his discussion, however, suggests that this answer is, at best, incomplete. Making oneself agreeable to others is not only an end in itself; it is also, and more importantly, a means to treating them with respect.

According to Hume, the primary difference between rules of polite behavior and laws of justice is the sphere to which they apply: "As the mutual shocks, in *society*, and the oppositions of interest and self-love have constrained mankind to establish the laws of *justice*, in order to preserve the advantages of mutual assistance and protection: in like manner, the eternal contrarieties, in *company*, of men's pride and self-conceit, have introduced the rules of Good Manners or Politeness, in order to facilitate the intercourse of minds, and an undisturbed commerse and conversation."[5]

Hume lists some of the ways in which expressions of pride and self-conceit are constrained by good manners: "Among well-bred people, a mutual deference is affected; contempt of others disguised; authority concealed; attention given to each in his turn; and an easy stream of conversation maintained, without vehemence, without interruption, without eagerness for victory, and without any airs of superiority."[6]

Notice the priority Hume gives here to *appearances*: he speaks of "affecting" mutual deference, of "disguising" contempt, of avoiding "airs." This suggests another, more important, difference between the rules of manners and the laws of justice: whereas the latter impose limits on an individual's doing things that *suggest* she *would* pursue her self-interest at the expense of others if given half a chance. The point of good manners is to create a certain appearance, to show others that one does not care overly much for one's own dear self.[7]

Hume is right to stress that the best way to accomplish this goal is to be considerate of others. He is also right that the things people do to show consideration are often "immediately agreeable," and that this is what makes them suitable modes of showing consideration. Nonetheless, it seems to me that Hume's account of good manners is seriously inadequate; for it fails to do justice to the fact that good manners have a value independent of the pleasure they directly inspire. More particularly, Hume underestimates the contribution that good manners make to good morals; and (more importantly) he fails to appreciate the extent to which both this contribution and the more immediate pleasure we experience when we are treated politely reflect the fundamental moral purpose of polite behavior. I will take up each of these points in turn.

Try to consider, for a moment, what it would be like to live in a society in which there were no conventions of politeness. As Hume suggests, there would be much less social harmony: people would find one another's company far less tolerable; they would not be so favorably disposed toward one another; they would be far more likely to get on one another's nerves. It seems to me, moreover, that such social disharmony could not fail to adversely affect people's willingness to regulate their behavior according to certain principles of justice, and this for at least three reasons. First, people who feel anger and resentment toward one another are far less inclined to go out of their way to avoid harming one another. Second, people so ill equipped to be agreeable to one another are likely to keep at a distance from one another; and people thus alienated are less likely to care about one another's well-being. . . . Finally, and most importantly, people who have never developed the habit of treating one another with courtesy are not constantly encouraged to take it for granted that people *deserve* to be so treated; that is, they are not conditioned to regard people as having a special dignity that imposes limitations on what it is reasonable for other people to do.

The importance of such conditioning has recently been called to our attention in a thought-provoking article by Cora Diamond. In "Eating Meat and Eating People," Diamond suggests that our conventions of courtesy influence our assumptions about the moral status of human beings. The countless little rituals we enact to show one another consideration are, she argues, the means whereby we "build our notion of human beings."[8] They are "the ways in which we mark what human life is,"[9] and, as such, they "belong to the source of moral life."[10] From our earliest childhood, we learn that *Homo sapiens* is the sort of animal whose death it is appropriate to mark with a funeral, the sort of animal it is inappropriate to eat, the sort of animal it is inappropriate to kill for convenience or sport. These lessons contrast sharply with our lessons about nonhuman animals: as children we "see insect pests killed, or spiders or snakes merely because they are distasteful; [we] hear about the killing of dangerous animals or of superfluous puppies and kittens, and are encouraged early to fish or collect butterflies—and so on."[11]

Again, the point is that human and nonhuman animals "are not given for our thought independently of such a mass of ways of thinking about and responding

to them."[12] Though Diamond does not herself stress the extent to which conventions of polite behavior figure among these ways of responding, she certainly means to include them. Indeed, she notes the moral significance of the fact that human beings are the only animals whose company we accept at the dinner table.[13]

Good manners, then, not only inspire good morals. They do so by constructing a conception of human beings as objects of moral concern. To learn that human beings are the sort of animal to whom one must say "please," "thank you," "excuse me," and "good morning," that one ought not to interrupt them when they are speaking, that one ought not to avoid eye contact and yet ought not to stare, that one ought not to crowd them and yet ought not to be standoffish, to learn all this and much more is to learn that human beings deserve to be treated with respect, that they are respectworthy, that is, that they have a dignity not shared by those whom one does not bother to treat with such deference and care.

It is a small step from noting *that* manners play a key role in our moral education to understanding *why* they are so well suited to playing this role. With this step, we arrive at the second, more fundamental, moral function of polite behavior: polite behavior not only has important moral *consequences;* it has an essentially moral *point.* Though Hume did not fully appreciate this point, he did remark upon it. Thus, consider the following observation in his discussion of "qualities immediately agreeable to others": "Many of the forms of breeding are arbitrary and casual; but the thing expressed by them is still the same. A Spaniard goes out of his own house before his guest, to signify that he leaves him master of all. In other countries, the landlord walks out last, as a common mark of deference and regard."[14]

I would like to make three comments about this brief passage. First, Hume calls attention to the *expressive* function of manners: by behaving politely, we are, in effect, "saying" something to one another. Second, by Hume's own account, the message expressed is that we defer to another person because we hold him in regard. Third, Hume's insistence to the contrary notwithstanding, such expressive behavior is *not immediately* agreeable. The pleasure it inspires is *mediated* by the guest's appreciation of what is expressed. If this guest were ignorant of the symbolic significance of his host's behavior, his host would be powerless to please him with this behavior. Indeed, if the guest were a Spaniard in one of those "other countries," he might even experience considerable *dis*pleasure.

Hume's remarks thus suggest that the reason why manners play such an important role in moral education is simply because they enable people to acknowledge one another's special dignity. This is their most basic purpose. An act of politeness may be intrinsically agreeable to others; and if it is intrinsically agreeable to others, this may be why it came to be regarded as a "mark of deference." What *makes* it a mark of deference, however, is *not* that it is agreeable. Rather, it is a mark of deference because this is the expressive function that has been assigned to it. Though there is an obvious sense in which the point of behaving politely is to be agreeable, the point of being agreeable in this way is to acknowledge the dignity of others. Indeed, it is often only if this more basic point is appreciated that the behavior is capable of giving pleasure.

But why should we care so much about whether someone acknowledges our dignity? Why should we find it so disagreeable when someone fails to exhibit some mark of deference? The answer, I wish to suggest, is simply that we believe we are worthy of respect, we believe that because we are respectworthy we deserve to be *treated with respect,* and we believe that being treated with *courtesy*—being *treated respectfully*—is a very important way—indeed, a necessary condition for the possibility—of being treated with respect.[15]

To treat people with respect is to act in a way that acknowledges their dignity, and to act this way *because* they have dignity. Moral philosophers have investigated the various ways we can make this acknowledgment *indirectly.* Very roughly: we indirectly acknowledge a person as respectworthy whenever we treat his interests and goals as constraints on our own most basic aims. There is, however, more to treating someone with respect than accommodating our ends to his. It is also essential that we more *directly* acknowledge that he is worthy of this accommodation; and in order to satisfy this requirement, we must treat him *politely.* When we treat one another politely, we are directly expressing respect for one another in the only way possible. We are, in effect, saying: "I respect you," "I acknowledge your dignity."[16]

The only way possible? Is there really no other means of acknowledging people directly? Instead of speaking the more subtle language of good manners, one could, of course, pepper one's conversation with the explicit assurance: "You are worthy of respect." As far as I can tell, however, this would not be an alternative method of direct acknowledgment. For if the phrase really did function to directly acknowledge people's respectworthiness, it would, in effect, be a stand-in for "please," "thank you," and so on. When you wanted someone to pass you the salt, you would say, "Pass the salt, you are worthy of respect"; and when someone passed you the salt, you and

she would tell each other, "You are worthy of respect," "You are worthy of respect." This would be rather odd, to be sure, but not deeply different from the more specialized tokens of politeness with which we are familiar. Perhaps subtle alterations in tone of voice could pick up much of the slack. In any case, the practice would not be an alternative to being polite but just an alternative way of being polite. Nor would things be different for any other apparent alternative mode of direct acknowledgment: either it, too, would just be a different means of being polite, or it would not be a means of direct acknowledgment, after all.

Still, one might wonder whether treating people with respect really requires directly acknowledging their respectworthiness. I doubt whether this is the sort of thing that can be proved. Nonetheless, I hope to build on my discussion of Hume to show that a conception of treating people with respect which includes treating them politely is more compelling than the alternative conception, according to which treating people with respect is one thing, and behaving respectfully is another.

First, then, once we see polite behavior as essential to acknowledging the dignity of others, we can better understand the moral consequences of treating people rudely. I have already noted that when people treat one another rudely, they are less likely to accommodate their actions to others, or even to believe that they ought to. It is difficult to see why this would be so, if treating people rudely were not at odds with acknowledging their intrinsic value, their dignity, their worthiness of being treated with respect.

So, too, unless good manners are essential to acknowledging another's dignity, it is difficult to see why treating someone politely so often plays an essential role in enabling her to pursue her own ends. As John Rawls reminds us, when a person doubts that others regard her as respectworthy, she tends to doubt that her "plan of life" is "worth carrying out," and that she has what it takes to carry out any life plan of value.[17] But why does rude behavior have the power to create doubts of this sort? Because, I submit, good manners are essential to acknowledging the intrinsic value of anyone who deserves to be treated with respect. It is precisely because treating people with courtesy is a direct way of acknowledging their dignity that treating them rudely can undermine their belief in their own intrinsic worth.

Additional support for the moral importance of direct acknowledgment comes from cases of nonmoral acknowledgment. Consider, for example, what is required to acknowledge that someone (A) is an expert on some topic (X). When doing a research project on X, one ought to look up A's papers. But surely this indirect acknowledgment is not sufficient. If, for example, when one is discussing X with A (and others), one repeatedly interrupts A's attempts to explain something about X or responds to her comments with a sniff of the nose, a roll of the eyes, or a "That's what *you* say," then one has failed to acknowledge her expertise (or has not acknowledged it enough, which comes to the same thing where giving people their due is concerned). Similarly, one does not adequately acknowledge A's skill at doing X if one hires her to do X, and yet in her presence enthusiastically praises the ability of others (and only others) to do X, gives them (and only them) awards for doing X, and so on.

To my mind, the most compelling reason for thinking that good manners have an essentially moral function and that this function is essential to treating persons with respect is that this is what is revealed by a simple exercise of the imagination. Consider what things would be like if there were a human community in which no human being violated the Kantian Categorical Imperative or had the least worry that others would do so. Would courtesy be pointless under these ideal conditions? Would polite behavior have no moral value? Would this imaginary kingdom be a "kingdom of ends," in which the intrinsic value of each is acknowledged by all? The answer, it seems to me, is clearly "no." Even if every citizen of the realm enabled every other citizen to exercise his capacity for rational choice, it would still be possible for these people to fail to treat one another with respect. For they would still be capable of hurting one another's feelings, offending one another's dignity, treating one another discourteously, inconsiderately, impolitely.

In short, even if I were confident that everyone in my community respected my right to choose and act "autonomously," someone could still fail to treat me with respect if she stared off into the middle distance, or carefully examined her fingernails, whenever I tried to engage her in conversation. Someone can value me as a person without valuing my opinions. She can acknowledge my dignity as a person even if she condemns my opinions and actions on moral grounds. But she fails to treat me with respect if she makes no effort to hide her disinterest in, or contempt for, my feelings. When she treats me this way, she implies that my concerns, my feelings, my point of view do not matter, that is, that I have no intrinsic value, after all.[18]

Whereas acknowledging people *indirectly* involves considering how they feel about certain things, people, and projects, acknowledging people *directly* involves considering how they feel about having their feelings ig-

nored. Prominent among this second group of feelings are shame and humiliation. When our words and deeds tell someone that it does not matter whether we hurt her feelings, we offend against her dignity by directly offending *her*.

But couldn't there be a "kingdom of ends" in which no behavior counted as rude? If this were a kingdom in which all behavior counted as polite, then it would not be a counterexample to the moral importance of direct acknowledgment. But what if it were a world in which no behavior counted as polite? In trying to imagine such a world, the best I can come up with is the "world" of many small children: though small children can easily provoke one another to tears, they generally do not take offense as readily as most adults; they say harsh things to each other, or ignore each other, without seeming to notice that there is anything amiss. The "world" of small children is not, however, a counterexample to the moral importance of direct acknowledgment. For it is, essentially, a child's world, and so it is not populated by full-fledged moral agents. Good manners matter less to the inhabitants of this world because these little people have not yet figured out what they and their comrades are really worth, and because, as a consequence, they do not yet treat one another with respect.

Not only are good manners essential to treating people with respect, but this is the essential point of good manners. In making this claim, I do not mean to be saying anything about the origin of rules of courtesy. Like our moral code, our code of manners may have originated as a way to encourage peaceful coexistence among people, or as a way for the powerful to maintain control over the resentful weak, or as a way for the resentful weak to claim power for themselves. Even if one or more of these stories is true, and even if the code continues to serve its original purpose, we can still ask: what does the code mean now? what do its rules signify to those who accept its authority? If, as seems obvious, the essential point of these rules is to instruct people on how to treat each other respectfully, and if, as I have argued, treating people respectfully is essential to treating them with respect, then the essential point of good manners is a moral point: to enable us to treat one another with respect. . . .

ENDNOTES

1. Notice that this thesis is perfectly compatible with the view that the most important function of manners is to maintain social stability and order. After all, it may well be that

maintaining social stability and order is the most important function of morality! In claiming that treating people with respect is the point of manners, I mean to be focusing attention on the fundamental *internal* aim of manners. This aim is compatible with, and may even contribute to, other desirable or undesirable goals—just as the internal aim of religious rituals (very roughly: to promote the worship of God) is compatible with and contributes to many other desirable and undesirable goals.

2. David Brink expresses a widely shared view when he claims that requirements of etiquette differ from moral requirements because "their inescapability is not grounded in facts about rational agents as such." "Perhaps," Brink speculates, "rational agents . . . need not live under the rule of etiquette at all" (David O. Brink, "Kantian Rationalism: Inescapability, Authority, and Supremacy," in *Ethics and Practical Reason,* ed. Garrett Cullity and Berys Gaut [Oxford: Clarendon, 1997], pp. 255–91, p. 281). If, as seems to be the case, Brink means to include rules of manners among the rules of etiquette, then the burden of my article is to show that he is wrong about etiquette, at least where the rational agents at issue are anything remotely like us. In defending a broader conception of our duty to treat people with respect, I will, in effect, be defending a broader conception of the right to be treated with respect. According to Joseph Raz, "one can, and people often do, show disrespect to others, including disrespect which amounts to denying their status as persons, by acts which do not violate rights" (Joseph Raz, *The Morality of Freedom* [Oxford: Clarendon, 1986], p. 191). Similarly, Judith Jarvis Thomson speculates that respect for persons may be "something other than respect for their rights. Then the work would remain to be done of saying what it is, and how this or that in morality issues from it" (Judith Jarvis Thomson, *The Realm of Rights* [Cambridge, Mass.: Harvard University Press, 1990], p. 211). To my mind, however, to divide disrespectful acts into those that violate a person's rights and those that merely "deny his status as a person" is to obscure the intimate connection between respecting a person's rights and acknowledging his moral status. At the very least, this sort of taxonomy encourages the false belief that we have fulfilled our duty to treat others as ends in themselves as long as we have enabled them to pursue their own morally permissible ends. (Though I agree with Raz that respect for persons should not be confused with respect for their rights, I am persuaded by Cora Diamond's suggestion that a person has rights only *because* she has moral standing. See Cora Diamond, "Eating Meat and Eating People," in Diamond's *The Realistic Spirit: Wittgenstein, Philosophy, and the Mind* [Cambridge, Mass.: MIT Press, 1991]. Raz is wrong, I think, to insist that moral rights are "based on" our interests and not, ultimately, on the independent fact that we are persons, ends in ourselves (Raz, p. 189). The moral significance of a person's *interests* depends on the fact that *she* has moral significance; our respect for a person's rights is based on the fact that we respect the person herself. (For more on this point, see Sarah Buss, "Respect for Persons," unpublished manuscript.)

3. According to Kant, "The respect which I bear others or which another can claim from me . . . is the acknowledgment of the dignity (*dignitas*) of another man, i.e., a worth which has no price, no equivalent for which the object of valuation (*aestimii*) could be exchanged" (Immanuel Kant, *The Metaphysics of Morals, Part II: The Metaphysical Principles of Virtue,* in *Ethical Philosophy,* trans. James W. Ellington [Indianapolis: Hackett, 1983], p. 127). There are passages in which Kant suggests that in order to acknowledge a person's dignity, it is not enough to accommodate our ends to hers. Thus, he writes, "Holding up to ridicule real faults or faults attributed as real with the intention of depriving a person of his deserved respect, and the propensity to do this, may be called bitter derision (*spiritus causticus*). . . . [It is] a severe violation of the duty to respect other men" (p. 132). (I thank an editor of this journal for calling my attention to this passage.) At the same time, however, Kant seems to reject my interpretation of the relation between morals and manners insofar as he claims that "I am not bound to venerate others (regarded merely as men), i.e., to show them positive reverence. The only respect which I am bound to by nature is that for the law generally (*reverere legem*)" (p. 133).

4. Judith Martin, *Miss Manners' Guide to Excruciatingly Correct Behavior* (New York: Warner Books, 1983), p. 13. There are actually two points here, each of which Miss Manners stresses on many occasions. First, as Phillippa Foot points out, "moral judgment concerns itself with a man's reasons for acting as well as with what he does. Law and etiquette require only that certain things are done or left undone" (Phillippa Foot, "Morality as a System of Hypothetical Imperatives," *Philosophical Review* 81 [1972]: 305–16, p. 312). Second, "in manners, as distinct from morals . . . the only recognized act is one that has been witnessed" (Martin, p. 249). In an interesting article, Julia Driver challenges the view that the stress on appearance distinguishes etiquette from morality. Appearing to be virtuous, she argues, can be essential to really being virtuous (see her "Caesar's Wife: On the Moral Significance of Appearing Good," *Journal of Philosophy* 89 [1992]: 331–43).

5. David Hume, *An Enquiry concerning the Principles of Morals,* in *Enquiries concerning Human Understanding and concerning the Principles of Morals,* 3d ed. (Oxford: Oxford University Press, 1979), sec. 8, pp. 169–346, p. 261.

6. Ibid.

7. It may well be, of course, that a person will have a better chance of creating this appearance if she really does care about the others. I owe this point to Jonathan Adler.

8. Diamond, p. 324.

9. Ibid., p. 325.

10. Ibid., p. 326. A difficulty for this account of the moral status of human beings is that it does not seem to allow for the possibility of a moral critique of the practices which contribute to the conception of what it is to be human. My own view is that our practices are not the only thing to which we can appeal to defend our views about what we owe one another. I take this for granted at the end of the article, when I call into question the requirement that people "mind their own business."

11. Ibid., p. 330.

12. Ibid., p. 331.

13. Ibid., p. 324. ("We are around the table and they are on it.")

14. Hume, p. 262.

15. Note that this answer is compatible with the fact that the pain we experience in being treated rudely is often, in part, the pain of being shunned, rejected, treated as an outsider. I will refer later to the capacity of manners to define in-groups. For now, it suffices to stress that the reason why it is so painful to be treated as an outsider is that this is one way of being treated as though one has less intrinsic worth than the insiders.

16. Note that an acknowledgment of dignity can be both direct and indirect. Thus, e.g., asking permission to smoke is both a way of saying, "You are worthy of respect," and a way of adjusting one's ends to the ends of others.

17. John Rawls, *A Theory of Justice* (Cambridge, Mass.: Harvard University Press, 1971), p. 440.

18. As Henry Richardson has reminded me, international negotiations provide a vivid example of how important good manners are in this regard.

QUESTIONS ON BUSS

1. Why does Buss contend that manners contribute to good morals? In what sense do manners serve to directly acknowledge the dignity of others?

2. If manners serve to directly acknowledge the intrinsic value of others, then what is it that we are acknowledging? How can our manners have a meaning unless we have some agreement on the value of a human being and the nature of human dignity?

3. What types of manners does Buss's treatment seem to refer to? Is the ideal of treating people with respect an idea appropriate for a society of strangers?

Why Do It? Because That's What We Do: Manners in the Ruins of Community

H. Tristram Engelhardt, Jr.

H. Tristram Engelhardt, Jr. is Professor of Philosophy at Rice University and Professor in the Department of Medicine, Baylor College of Medicine. He is the author of The Foundations of Bioethics *(1986),* Bioethics and Secular Humanism *(1991),* The Foundations of Christian Bioethics *(2000), and has edited numerous other works. This essay appeared in* Gentility Recalled: Mere Manners and the Making of Social Order *(1996).*

RELATIONSHIP OF MORALS AND MANNERS IN THE ORDERED SOCIETY

Morals and good manners are not the same. Yet they are not that different. Both are concerned with values and behaviour. Both good manners and morals are challenged by our failure to share (or our recognition that we no longer share) a common understanding of life's meaning or the character of proper behaviour. In their particularity, our traditional canons of good manners are a further sign of our divisions. Our manners are euro-centric (i.e., ours are the manners of Europeans). Rather than this being a point in favour of manners (did not Europe fashion our contemporary world culture?), this particularity is perceived by many as discrediting our traditional elements of courtesy. Though good manners should be an expression of mutual respect and social solidarity, our manners are often received as anti-manners. Rather than sustaining social solidarity, they disclose fundamental disagreements regarding our cultural identity and our values.

Against this background, what can one make of good manners? How can one sustain good manners if one can identify them? This chapter will explore the nature of manners and their bond to intact moral traditions. A distinction will be drawn between the manners that bind those joined in a thick understanding of proper conduct (here referred to as friends, those with whom one has a thick binding of commitment in culture and manners) and those that foster collaboration with strangers. Finally, some closing reflections will be advanced regarding the future of manners in an age when traditions are in disarray and decay.

MANNERS, VALUES AND SOCIAL BONDS IN CIVIL SOCIETY

Manners are embedded in a complex social fabric richly framed with values and directed towards particular visions of human flourishing. Manners express a particular set of values; endorse particular exemplars of proper deportment; are sustained by and reinforce a particular social nexus; while often, in addition, affirming a particular metaphysics, a particular understanding of the deep structure of reality, as well as its meaning. Manners have an axiological dimension. They guide deportment. They are integral to particular social structures. They can intimate truths. As scientific theories distinguish between noise and information, good manners do so by identifying considerate and inconsiderate conduct out of a universe of behaviour, much of which is inconsiderate. Good manners interpret and transform social reality. They provide social orientation. They direct personal energies and guide behaviour.

The term manners is richly ambiguous. It identifies a number of social phenomena associated through various family resemblances. 'Manners' has connections with the Latin *manuarius,* belonging to the hand, itself a term derived from *manus*. This derivation suggests that manners are ways of getting things in hand, of rendering them manageable, tractable. Manners provide ways of mastering a situation through showing respect towards others, supporting common values and endorsing social solidarity. The term has meanings that range from a form of expression to a customary mode of acting, including usage, form, and fashion. Manners identify as well the subject of morality itself. Manners concern the ways in which individuals should behave, deport themselves, and conduct themselves with others. As such, manners are not just modes of behaviour, but properly good manners, polished courtesy, canons of civility. In this chapter, the focus is on manners as polite behaviour. Manners are that deportment indicative of good breeding expressed in appropriate forms of politeness and courtesy.

MANNERS, THOUGH NOT MORALS, ARE AN IMPORTANT CIVILIZING FORCE

There are many values important to the good life, which are not in and of themselves moral values. Judgments regarding the sublimity of a scene in nature, the beauty of a painting, the excellence of a wine, all involve values, though not moral values. So, too, judgments regarding manners involve non-moral assessments of the excellence and grace of deportment. Manners also have moral significance. They are embedded in moral understandings. But their peculiar focus is on a non-moral sphere of values. The Romans' *humanissimus vir* was a man of excellence, who realized both intellectual virtues as well as refinement of taste, even when his pagan moral virtues may have been in decay. So, too, a lady or gentleman appropriately incarnates excellences of deportment, which are not only moral.

Manners can support both civility and morals even in the conduct of immoral actions. Manners like hypocrisy can pay a tribute to background moral understandings. For example, though one may very well condemn duelling as immoral, one can understand the good manners by which a gentleman should conduct a duel. Armies at war have ceased hostilities for a common Christmas celebration and shown courtesy and civility to each other without even considering how Christians ought appropriately to resolve disputes, or the comparative justice of the two sides in battle. Manners affirm framing traditions, moral commitments, and metaphysical understandings, even when individuals and groups fail to realize the moral virtues endorsed by those traditions and their morals. They provide minimal rules of considerate behaviour even when one is violating moral rules.

COMMUNITY DEPENDENT ON SHARED VALUES WHICH MANNERS HELP TO MAINTAIN

Good manners betoken a community, however thin. In a homogeneous culture united in common traditions and strong in its moral practices, there is no gulf between morals and manners. Where throne and altar are united in a coherent moral vision, proper deportment reflects a vision of how things ought to be, of how one should act, of how one should be moral, and of how one should show courtesy. But even within thick and coherent world views, there are contrasts between the rules of morality and courtesy. In Christendom, the contrast of morals and manners reflects the circumstance that morals have transcendent significance. Manners have at best instrumental, facilitatory, or local character. All should have good morals, the claims of morality are universal, and the content of morality is binding on all. Though moral understandings may be nurtured by particular communities with particular histories, their moral claims as moral claims are directed to all. Manners, on the other hand, are conventional and in their particularity local. The canons of courtesy in Japan are not those observed by the best families in the American South. Still, though manners may be conventional in character, when they are well-ordered, they support the underlying morality.

MANNERS AND MORALS IN INTACT MORAL COMMUNITIES

Manners tend to be set within larger moral concerns. Consider a contrast between morals and conventional courtesies in a highly traditional community: Orthodox Christianity. All Orthodox Christians are bound in a common morality, though manners differ, depending on whether one is Finnish or Japanese, Texan or Lebanese. There is nothing clearly wrong in the circumstance that Japanese tend to bow to each other as they stand in line for confession and that they rarely embrace each other, delivering a brace of kisses. The bowing appears not only innocent, but even praiseworthy as an expression of humility and respect. Still, what of their reticence to kiss in greeting? Perhaps, since the Apostles greeted each other with a kiss, so, too, should the Japanese. If Texans can learn such manners, why cannot the Japanese? Yet, the matter is not as essential as are the Commandments, the canons, and the teachings of ecumenical and regional councils. Still, there is something out of place in meeting Christians who simply exchange bows or handshakes, rather than a kiss.[1] As distant as are Ethiopia and Alaska, India and the Czech Republic, to be Orthodox is still to be orthodox. All should feel the same desire to return to the Fathers, to live in their vision, and to see things as they received manners from the Apostles. Christianity is a way of life that should as far as possible be maintained along with its received usages. If one meets as brothers, one should meet in a kiss.[2]

This very particular example illustrates how a world-wide community can be united in a common morality, yet divided in manners. It shows as well how a moral community can reshape manners. It brings into question a diversity of manners, a diversity of respectful greetings, leads to a re-examination of differences, and redirects them within a tradition towards a common moral vision. A tradition carries practices with it as well as the bases for revising practices. In this case, the mode of recognizing a brother in the Faith can be regarded as not merely a matter of convention, but as having moral significance. Manners and morality are bound together even where there is a disparity of customs and a diversity of manners. Because manners are embedded within the larger and more substantial context of a moral vi-

sion, manners can be obliged to express the background moral vision. Although manners are not as central to the good life as are good morals, they support the good life.

The term morals can identify behaviour essential to determining praiseworthiness and blameworthiness, worthiness of happiness and unworthiness of happiness. Manners, in contrast, concern behaviour important in determining social adeptness. A man can be of good heart but innocently thoughtless, vulgar of expression, and lacking in social graces. He can be of good morals but bad manners. He can be of good morals but not understand the canons of courtesy. Still, there is an obligation to have good manners so as appropriately to discharge obligations (e.g., adequately to express thanks) and to show respect. Insofar as courtesy supports the moral life, courtesy is morally obligatory. In communities that are united around a common understanding of what is important, manners and morals tend to form parts of a whole.

LOSS OF SHARED CULTURAL VALUES POSES A THREAT TO SHARED MANNERS

Unlike the Orthodox, when we meet in a secular pluralist society, we have significant disagreements about how to be respectful or show courtesy, because we have significant disagreements about the nature of morality and the good life. Alasdair MacIntyre's description of our culture as no longer in possession of a common vision of virtue suggests as well a world without a common notion of manners.[3] We meet in the ruins of previously intact social practices, among the shards of once well-functioning understandings of the human condition. Even the 'we' by which we describe ourselves has fragmented and become problematic. Though never have more people used European languages as their first or second idiom of expression, employed legal systems influenced by European-American jurisprudence, and been influenced by European-American economic and cultural styles (e.g., from fast food to styles of dress), there is a reluctance to speak confidently from the perspective of European-American manners and morals. Indeed, confidence in European manners is for many a mark of an execrable cultural imperialism, rather than the celebration of cultural vigour and success. Though cultural differences have never been as muted as in our age of mass communication and mass marketing, though there has never been such a singularity of cultural perspective for world history and culture (e.g., the United Nations and the International Court of Justice, which have some claim to being the assemblages of our planet, are the creations of Euro-American culture), there is ever more talk of moral diversity and cultural pluralism. Indeed, the systematic study of cultural differences along with their toleration is an innovation of European-American culture. Despite all of this, eurocentrism is a criticism rather than a ground of support for our manners.

Not only are our understandings of manners brought into question because of their special bond to the European roots of our cultures, not only does this bond invite the recognition of cultural differences, but in addition the notion of courtesy has an elitist valence. Manners are properly not the canons of common, vulgar behaviour. Courtesy is courtly politeness. Good manners express the rules of refined deportment, those of the court which sets the standard. Manners and courtesy are how the best people behave (or how they should behave) to each other. Manners are how those who have cultivated proper deportment show each other proper regard. Good manners acknowledge and aspire to an ideal of deportment, not the usual (i.e., common or vulgar) patterns of behaviour. In their normative, not merely descriptive character, as well as because of their association with aristocracies and with those who rule, good manners are suspect. . . .

POLITICAL CORRECTNESS SUBLIMATES TRADITIONAL MANNERS TO A 'THIN WORLD CULTURE'

Manners in their particularity separate. They announce commitments, including moral understandings, that collide with the commitments of others. One can only show consideration through particular forms and conventions. It is this particularity that vexes. For a gentleman to open a door for a lady or to kiss her hand can be regarded as sexist. For a Texan lady to walk to the right of the gentleman so that, should the occasion necessitate, he might more easily draw his revolver from his shoulder holster in defence can be regarded as an expression of false consciousness. To inquire whether one is dining according to the Spanish or the French court before opening a potato may be received as elitist. To date one's letters AD 1995, rather than 1995, can be appreciated as religiously insensitive ('1995 CE' can demonstrate a special delicacy). To say 'God bless' to a sneeze may evoke puzzlement. To require coat and tie at one's club can suggest a eurocentric sexism. And, *miserabile factu,* to fly the Stainless Banner on Confederate Memo-

rial Day in remembrance of fallen heroes will likely be decried as racist.

While a certain thin world culture has emerged, still primarily framed in terms of European concerns, manners and morals have been politicized as our polities have broken into numerous and competing self-consciously diverse moral communities. In the face of this diversity, to act according to traditional manners can be received as a reactionary political manifesto. This is the character of post-modernity. A once officially homogeneous Christian culture has fragmented such that even reference to the West as Christendom is not merely appreciated as inaccurate but impolite, indeed, 'insensitive' and offensive. There is no longer a universal moral narrative, nor the secular resources for reclaiming a universal vision of proper deportment.[4]

We live in an age in which the received manners and morals of our culture are in disarray and under attack. We confront diverse and often mutually hostile visions of appropriate behaviour. Moreover, our traditional understandings of proper behaviour are frequently regarded as improper (i.e., as being sexist, elitist, eurocentric, etc.). In response to this challenge, canons of courtesy have been framed to share without the offence occasioned by particularity (e.g., Christmas greetings become best wishes for a generic winter festival, Easter greetings become best wishes for a nameless spring festival, etc.). It is with such vacuous understandings of courtesy that we communicate in the ruins of a once intact Western European morality and canon of manners.

ESTABLISHING MANNERS BETWEEN STRANGERS

What are the good manners that can bind a feminist and a Southern gentleman, a proletarian and a titled lady? What common courtesy governs when individuals do not share a moral vision or a common understanding of the good life? How can individuals share manners when they confront each other across conflicting moral understandings and competing political visions? This daunting task of providing canons of appropriate politeness in such circumstances defines the project of civility in most secular pluralist societies. To establish such canons of courtesy, one must speak to the authority of their governance. But how does one do this, given our foundational controversies regarding the proper character of manners? How does one decide whose manners are normative—those of the feminist or the Southern gentleman, the proletarian or the titled lady?

As with moral controversies, controversies regarding good manners can be solved by appeals: to force; to faith; to rational argument; or to agreement (including agreement peaceably not to agree).[5] Force may be an effective short-term means of suppressing controversies in manners. One can impose a particular understanding of courtesy. But this will not by itself provide either intellectual or moral satisfaction. This is not to say that one cannot show good manners in war or in a combat to the death. Individuals entering into a duel can find themselves united in common understandings of appropriate manners, even if they have resolved to conclude a controversy through force. Indeed, going to the field of honour to resolve a controversy presupposes a common sense of honour and with it common standards of appropriate deportment. Such standards guide those involved, even when they acknowledge that these activities are immoral. In order with others to distinguish honourable from dishonourable uses of force, one must already share a common vision of courtesy.

RATIONALITY NOT SUFFICIENT FOR MANNERS BETWEEN STRANGERS

The appeal to a particular vision of proper conduct presupposes faith in this vision. Such a commitment can arise from being born into as well as later converting to a particular vision of appropriate behaviour. As with matters of religion and morals, if one deports oneself well according to a particular set of manners, others may adopt those practices. They may appreciate an excellence to which they ought to aspire. Though such conversions may resolve some controversies regarding appropriate manners by bringing some individuals into concord, the general incivility of the world, as well as the class of contrary visions of appropriate canons of courtesy, suggests that an appeal to conversion will not generally be sufficient for the difficulties at hand.

An attempt to resolve controversies regarding proper canons of courtesy through rational argument will not succeed unless one already shares a common background understanding of values. One cannot compare the consequences of particular canons of deportment unless one already understands how to assess such consequences. How does one, for example, compare the consequences of frankness in speech with the solidarity and support conveyed by the polite euphemisms that protect against hurt feelings? Such comparisons can

only proceed if one already understands how to rank or compare different interests and goals. Yet those in dispute often fail to share common visions of what is at stake, much less how to resolve the controversies at hand. If one shares sufficient background premises, rules of evidence, rules of inference, then sound rational argument can give guidance regarding the canons of courtesy one should embrace. But the more this is lacking, the more one will meet as strangers disunited in manners and behaviour.

PROBLEM OF REGAINING MANNERS IN A POST-MODERN SOCIETY WITHOUT SHARED VALUES

Those who meet in the conflicts of post-modernity are often separated by incommensurable visions of proper human conduct and human flourishing. They meet as strangers, as persons whose morals and manners are alien to each other. To be strangers, they need not be so alien as to be incomprehensible to each other. It is enough if the others, who appear as strangers, assemble the important elements of the good life and proper manners in substantially wrong ways. One can understand them and in understanding disagree and perceive a deep gulf of manners and sensibilities. Yet one does not share enough in common to resolve controversies by sound rational argument. In intact moral communities with functioning traditions, one can have the friendship of common understandings of courtesy. Outside of one's community of shared manners and morals, one meets those who find one's courtesies alien, strange, if not profoundly misguided. The 'other' appears not only strange but often hostile: a person denying one's manners as well as the values and social structures for which they stand.

COMMON CAUSE, AND SHARED MANNERS, REQUIRE APPEAL TO THE AUTHORITY OF THE PARTICIPANTS

How does one resolve controversies regarding courtesy with those strange to one's commitments? If one does not share a common vision of courtesy, and if one wishes to resolve controversies with an authority other than force, then one can appeal to the authority of common agreement. Insofar as one acts together in agreement, one possesses authority drawn from mutual consent. Insofar as individuals peaceably withdraw to their own communities, the very practice of resolving controversies by common agreement, not force, restrains one from interfering. Authority grounded in the sparseness of consent frames contracts, the market, and the foundations of limited democracies. The authority of such practices is derived from an appeal neither to God nor to rational argument, but to the agreement of those who participate. In such circumstances, common projects can be undertaken with authority, but they will in principle be limited by the limited character of the agreements of those who entered into such undertakings. Forbearance rights and limited welfare rights will be recognized, but they will not be grounded in a thick vision of human flourishing. Rather, their legitimacy will be derived from what it means to acknowledge persons as the source of authoritative consent.[6] Courtesy will not derive its authority from tradition or from a content-full moral view, but from the tacit consent to various practices that develop in social interaction.

MANNERS FOR COSMOPOLITANS: SHARED VALUES REPLACED BY BUREAUCRACY

Against this thin morality, which is background to the market and limited democracies, what can one say of manners? What role can courtesy play? When one meets as moral strangers in the marketplace, as well as in the public assemblies of limited democracies, there will often be advantages in preserving peace and supporting the limited exchange of views required for the functioning of limited projects. Rules of procedure, rules of order, bureaucratic safeguards, and the courtesies associated with due process will tend to frame the canons of civil deportment for such circumstances. A bureaucratic courtesy emerges in which dates appear as 1995, as neither AD 1995 nor 1995 CE. There is a language of studied politeness neither aristocratic nor proletarian (toilets are for men or women, not for ladies or gentlemen). Women are Ms. never Mrs. or Miss unless they insist on what some would insist is an anachronism. There is a polished attention to avoid a clash of cultures and moralities occasioned by a clash of contrary courtesies.

Canons of effective advertising will often underlie the canons of common courtesy.[7] After all, expressions of gratitude, solicitude, and interest can function to reinforce market transactions. Many may trade more willingly if they not only are treated honestly, but are also offered products and services within frameworks of civility and respect. Given our divergent notions of civility and respect, expressions of courtesy must be as vac-

uous and general in character as possible. One avoids wishing a Merry Christmas or Happy Easter but announces instead one's best wishes for the holidays. Any offence may impose market costs. The result is a practised general politeness without particular tradition or history. In such a world there are no Christian gentlemen, only good gentlepersons.

BANKRUPTCY OF COSMOPOLITAN MANNERS WHEN DIVORCED FROM TRADITION

A courtesy that aspires to be polite to everyone is polished courtesy without substance.[8] Indeed, because of its commitment to generality, cosmopolitan manners runs the risk of encouraging a hostility to those courtesies designed to communicate tradition and substance. The courtesy that attempts to be polite to everyone is ideally a courtesy of nowhere and no time. It is in its very nature hostile to traditions. This genre of manners is embedded in what Alasdair MacIntyre characterizes as a cosmopolitan culture articulated in an international language of modernity. In a post-modern world sharing no substantive moral narrative or vision, the remaining aspiration of modernity is to a civility that can bind moral strangers and be expressed in a language without particular commitments.

> The social and cultural condition of those who speak that kind of language [is] a certain type of rootless cosmopolitanism, the condition of those who aspiring to be at home anywhere—except that is, of course, in what they regard as the backward, outmoded, undeveloped cultures of traditions—are therefore in an important way citizens of nowhere. . . . It is the fate toward which modernity moves precisely insofar as it successfully modernizes itself and others by emancipating itself from social, cultural, and linguistic particularity and so from tradition.[9]

The manners of cosmopolitans are sufficiently vacuous as to betoken only the most general respect for the other. It is a courtesy that expresses respect without giving any content to respect.

Substantive understandings of courtesy break the generality of cosmopolitan aspirations. It is for this reason that, from the perspective of cosmopolitans, substantive practices and traditions of courtesy run the risk of being insensitive, indeed, politically incorrect. Substantive understandings of manners can only bind those with whom one shares traditions, customs, and, ideally, content-full moral principles. Such manners are the forms of courtesy that reveal the other either as a stranger to one's traditions, or as a friend to one's commitments in manners, if not in morals. Such substantive understandings run the risk of appearing not just insensitive but fanatical, because they recall individuals to particular communities and traditions. From the perspective of the cosmopolitan, the politeness that binds moral friends within substantive moral traditions will often be experienced as an enemy of peace in a world too often rent by moral particularity and the misunderstandings and conflicts they can engender.

MANNERS TOWARD STRANGERS: TRADITIONALLY SEEN AS A MORAL IMPERATIVE

From the perspective of moral friends, especially those who share traditional moral understandings and manners, the manners that bind moral strangers are unavoidable. They are also occasions of moral compromise. Even if one lives one's life among the Amish or Hassidim, one must enter the market with those hostile to one's moral commitments and communicate through manners which avoid reference to the matters one takes to be most important. This is morally tolerable, as long as one distinguishes between the manners one shares with strangers and those one shares with friends. Most importantly, one must not confuse the manners of moral strangers with the manners of moral friends. One must not mistakenly conclude that the courtesy that guides in the marketplace or in the *agora* of secular pluralist democracies should be the manners that should bind in the important friendships that unite around substantive traditions. The cost of such a mistake is the loss of substance and tradition in the manners of one's life.

IN THE RUINS, WITHIN THE MARKET, BEHIND THE WALLS

In many respects, our situation is like that of our forebears a millennium and a half ago, as the Empire in the West fell into chaos. Those who could retreated to their villas, which became fortifications in Britain and in Gaul against a tide of chaos and pillage. If all could not be saved, at least remnants of civilization could be preserved. Even if civility was temporarily in retreat, there was still the hope that it could be sustained behind the walls of particular communities bent on preserving what was important. . . .

MANNERS ULTIMATELY ONLY POSSIBLE WITH THE PRESERVATION OF A CIVILIZED MORAL SOCIETY

. . . Our life of manners is bifurcated. We must distinguish the context in which they can still thrive from the context in which they are given no place. If we confuse the two contexts, we will endanger the civility and manners of our surviving traditions. Those who enter the market or the general transactions of a limited democracy participate in a vacuous fabric of courtesies aimed at showing respect, gratitude and solidarity without promoting contention. On the other hand, those who belong to content-full traditions have rich notions of proper deportment, which to some will be offensive. Such thick understandings of courtesy will be affirmed within the bounds of particular communities. Manners are no longer whole and of one piece. There are the manners through which one collaborates with strangers. There are manners that bind friends in common understandings of the good life. Courtesy has become contextual and freighted with controversy.

ENDNOTES

1. As an example of how manners can be antimanners, the author of this chapter encountered after a lapse of years an old friend, a Jesuit priest. Moved with joy, he proceeded to kiss the Jesuit on both cheeks as one would a long-lost Orthodox brother. To the amusement of friends and bystanders, this greeting (perhaps because of recent scandals regarding certain acts of carnality on the part of Roman clerics) was received with some shock and disorientation.

2. Here the author reports the puzzlement of a secular friend who, without knowledge about the background of the behaviour, observed the author as an Indian nurse who looked not at all to be his kin, discovered he was Orthodox and responded with the exclamation, 'my brother!' which was followed by mutual heartfelt kisses on both cheeks and the author's exclamation 'my sister!' For one Calvinist observer, this act of courtesy between members of one spiritual family seemed out of place and unseemly.

3. Alasdair MacIntyre, *After Virtue,* Notre Dame, Ind: University of Notre Dame Press, 1981.

4. In this essay, I use the term post-modernity to underscore our failure to share, and our recognition that we no longer share, a universal moral narrative or common cultural perspective. Here I follow one suggestion of Lyotard: 'In contemporary society and culture—postindustrial society, postmodern culture—the question of the legitimation of knowledge is formulated in different terms. The grand narrative has lost its credibility, regardless of what mode of unification it uses,

regardless of whether it is a speculative narrative or a narrative of emancipation.' Jean-François Lyotard, *The Postmodern Condition*, (trans. G. Bennington and B. Massumi), Manchester: Manchester University Press, 1984, p 37.

5. This account of moral strangers, moral friends, and the character of moral discourse in a world fractured by diverse moral visions is developed at greater length in *The Foundations of Bioethics*, 2nd ed., New York: Oxford, 1996.

6. Ibid.

7. H.T. Engelhardt Jr. and M.A. Rie, 'Selling Virtue: Ethics as a Profit Maximising Strategy in Health Care Delivery,' *Journal of Health and Social Policy*, 4, 1992, pp. 27–35.

8. See H.T. Engelhardt Jr., 'The Yuppie as a Prophet of a Secular Tradition for Health Care,' in *Bioethics and Secular Humanism: The Search for a Common Morality*, London: SCM Press, 1991, pp. 33–40.

9. Alasdair MacIntyre, *Whose Justice? Which Rationality?*, Notre Dame, Ind.: University of Notre Dame Press, 1988, p. 388.

QUESTIONS ON ENGELHARDT

1. What functions do manners serve in society, in particular those manners that depend on a thick understanding of life? What function is served by the manners of markets and democracies? Can markets function well with a thicker conception of manners and morals?

2. In what sense is it true, that the thinness of manners derives from the lack of any substantive and deep moral commitments? Is Engelhardt correct in asserting that Western societies lack a common conception of life and morals? Do you agree with his claim that we have "significant disagreements about how to be respectful or show courtesy, because we have significant disagreements about the nature of morality and the good life"?

3. What are some examples of the manners of the market? the manners of thicker communities? In what sense is it true that the manners of contemporary society offer a courtesy that "expresses respect without giving any content to respect"?

FOR FURTHER READING

Character and Commerce

Action, H. B. *The Morals of Markets and Related Essays*. Edited by David Gordon and Jeremy Shearmur. Indianapolis, Ind.: Liberty Fund, 1993.

Anderson, Digby, ed. *The Loss of Virtue: Moral Confusion and Social Disorder in Britain and America*. London: Social Affairs Unit, 1992.

Casey, John. *Pagan Virtues: An Essay in Ethics*. Oxford: Clarendon Press, 1990.

Ciulla, Joanne. *The Ethics of Leadership*. Belmont, Calif.: Wadsworth, 2002.

Harris, George W. *Dignity and Vulnerability: Strength and Quality of Character*. Berkeley: University of California Press, 1997.

Hood, John M. *The Heroic Enterprise: Business and The Common Good*. New York: The Free Press, 1996.

Hunt, Lester. *Character and Culture*. Totowa, N.J.: Rowman and Littlefield, 1997.

Kruschwitz, Robert C., and Robert C. Roberts, eds. *The Virtues: Contemporary Essays on Moral Character*. Belmont, Calif.: Wadsworth, 1987.

Kupperman, Joel J. *Character*. New York: Oxford University Press, 1991.

Machan, Tibor, and James Chesler. *The Business of Commerce: Examining an Honorable Profession*. Stanford: Hoover Institution Press, 1999.

MacIntyre, Alasdair. *After Virtue*. Notre Dame, Ind.: University of Notre Dame Press, 1981.

Maitland, Ian. "Virtuous Markets: The Markets as School of the Virtues." *Business Ethics Quarterly* 7 (1997): 17–33.

May, William F. "The Virtues in a Professional Setting." *Soundings* 67 (Fall 1984).

McCloskey, Deirdre N. *The Vices of the Economists; the Virtues of the Bourgeoisie*. Amsterdam: Amsterdam University Press, 1996.

McKenzie, Richard B. "The Economic Dimensions of Ethical Behavior." *Ethics* 87 (April 1977): 208–21.

Mueller, John. *Capitalism, Democracy, and Ralph's Pretty Good Grocery*. Princeton, N.J.: Princeton University Press, 1999.

Paul, Ellen Frankel, Fred D. Miller, Jr., and Jeffrey Paul, eds. *Virtue and Vice*. Cambridge: Cambridge University Press, 1998.

Pincoffs, Edmund. *Quandaries and Virtues*. Lawrence, Kans.: University Press of Kansas, 1986.

Schwartz, Joel. *Fighting Poverty with Virtue: Moral Reform and America's Urban Poor, 1825–2000*. Bloomington: Indiana University Press, 2000.

Wallace, James D. *Virtues and Vices*. Ithaca, N.Y.: Cornell University Press, 1978.

Selfishness and Economic Motives

Heil, John, ed. *Rationality, Morality, and Self-interest.* Lanham, Md.: Rowman & Littlefield, 1993.

Milo, Ronald D., ed. *Egoism and Altruism.* Belmont, Calif.: Wadsworth, 1973.

Paul, Ellen Frankel, Fred D. Miller, Jr., and Jeffrey Paul, eds. *Altruism.* Cambridge: Cambridge University Press, 1993.

———. *Self-Interest.* Cambridge: Cambridge University Press, 1997.

Rand, Ayn. *The Virtue of Selfishness.* New York: New American Library, 1964.

Schmidtz, David. *Rational Choice and Moral Agency.* Princeton, N.J.: Princeton University Press, 1995.

Sen, Amartya. *On Ethics and Economics.* Oxford: Basil Blackwell, 1987.

Stirner, Max. *The Ego and Its Own* [1845], translated by Steven Byington. London: Rebel Press, 1982.

Prudence

Bricker, Philip. "Prudence." *Journal of Philosophy* 77 (July 1980): 381–400.

Broughton, Janet. "The Possibility of Prudence." *Philosophical Studies* 43 (March 1983): 253–66.

Den Uyl, Douglas J. *The Virtue of Prudence.* New York: Peter Lang, 1991.

Kekes, John. *Moral Wisdom and Good Lives.* Ithaca, N.Y.: Cornell University Press, 1995.

Kraut, Richard. "The Rationality of Prudence." *Philosophical Review* 81 (July 1972): 351–59.

Longman, Phillip. *The Return of Thrift.* New York: The Free Press, 1996.

Mabbott, J. D. "Prudence." *Proceedings of the Aristotelian Society, Supplementary Volume* 36 (1962): 51–64.

Pieper, Josef. *Prudence.* New York: Pantheon, 1959.

Rotenstreich, Nathan. "Prudence and Folly." *American Philosophical Quarterly* 22 (April 1984): 93–104.

Zagzebski, Linda Trinkaus. *Virtues of the Mind: An Inquiry into the Nature of Virtue and the Ethical Foundations of Knowledge.* New York: Cambridge University Press, 1996.

Generosity

Arrow, Kenneth. "Gifts and Exchanges." *Philosophy and Public Affairs* 1 (1972): 343–62.

Hunt, Lester. "Generosity and the Diversity of the Virtues." In *The Virtues: Contemporary Essays on Moral Character,* edited by Robert B. Kruschwitz and Robert C. Roberts. Belmont, Calif.: Wadsworth, 1987.

Schrift, Alan, ed. *The Logic of the Gift: Toward an Ethic of Generosity.* New York: Routledge, 1997.

Titmuss, Richard. *The Gift Relationship.* New York: Pantheon, 1971.

Wallace. "Generosity." In *Virtues and Vices.* Ithaca, N.Y.: Cornell University Press, 1978.

Courtesy and Manners

Ackerman, Felicia. "A Man by Nothing Is so Well Betrayed as by His Manners? Politeness as a Virtue." *Midwest Studies in Philosophy* 13 (1988): 250–58.

Brookhiser, Richard. *Rules of Civility: The 110 Precepts That Guided Our First President in War and Peace.* New York: The Free Press, 1997.

Buss, Sarah. "Appearing Respectful: The Moral Significance of Manners." *Ethics* 109 (July 1999): 795–826.

Caudwell, Mark. *A Short History of Rudeness.* Picador, 1999.

Elias, Norbert. *The Civilizing Process: The History of Manners and State Formation and Civilization* [1939], translated by Edmund Jephcott. Oxford: Blackwell, 1994.

Kingwell, Mark. "Is It Rational to Be Polite?" *The Journal of Philosophy* 90 (August 1993): 387–404.

Martin, Judith. *Miss Manners' Guide to Excruciatingly Correct Behavior.* New York: Warner Books, 1983.

Honesty and Integrity in Business

Honesty

It is true, not to tell a thing, is not properly to conceal it; but not to tell that which people are concerned to know, merely for the sake of some advantage to yourself, I think is: and there is nobody but knows what kind of concealing this is, and who they are that make a custom of it; I am sure not your plain, sincere, ingenuous, honest, and good sort of people; but rather your shifting, sly, cunning, deceitful, roguish, crafty, foxish, juggling kind of fellows.

Cicero[1]

Tricks and Treachery are the Practice of Fools, that have not Wit enough to be honest.

Benjamin Franklin[2]

But he had borrowed from the terrible usurer, Falsehood, and the loan had mounted and mounted with the years, till he belonged to the usurer, body and soul.

George Eliot[3]

Whether honesty is considered as an *obligation* (or duty) to tell the truth or whether it is considered as a *virtue* of character by which individuals may express a range of behavior in a variety of circumstances, the importance of honesty cannot be underestimated. Indeed, honesty may not only be intrinsically good but it may also serve as a condition for the very existence of any society in which individuals can interact and communicate effectively. If one could not trust that others would tell the truth, then communication would be pointless, and without communication there would, in fact, be no society at all. It would seem therefore that honesty is a condition of *any* society, and in this sense honesty serves a social function, one which is particularly important in a commercial society in which communication is important and in which trust is the precondition for working together, making contracts, holding to promises and agreements, and exchanging goods and services. It is the

---

1. *The Offices* [44 B.C.] in *Offices, Essays, and Letters,* translated by Thomas Cockman (London: J. M. Dent, 1909), book III, xiii.

2. *Poor Richard, 1740. An Almanack for the Year of Christ 1740,* entry of May, in *The Papers of Benjamin Franklin,* vol. 2, edited by Leonard W. Labaree and Whitfield J. Bell, Jr. (New Haven: Yale University Press, 1960), 250.

3. *Romula* [1862–63] (London: T. Nelson & Sons, 1900), chapter 39 (p. 349).

honest person who not only eschews deceit but avoids those individuals who might demand, suggest, or counsel dishonesty, and steers clear of those situations that might require some sort of chicanery.

Honesty and Dishonesty

The honest person tells the truth and is for this reason a trustworthy person. However, this plain statement does not reveal all of the complex nuances involved in being an honest person. An individual may be honest even as the person does not tell the *whole* truth. Indeed, the honest individual may exaggerate certain aspects of the truth, playing up, or emphasizing, certain features (overstatement, magnification, hyperbole) and playing down, or deemphasizing, other features (understatement, self-effacement). On the other hand, silence itself may prove dishonest, especially if one's silence would cause a false belief in an individual who has a claim on one's being truthful. Yet despite these complexities, the honest person would seem to be one who does not intentionally state or write falsehoods with the aim of getting another person to believe the falsehoods. Thus a person of *honest character* seeks to minimize exaggeration and overstatement, especially when such would give another person a false impression. For the person who is *characteristically* honest not only eschews the intentional falsehood but also seeks to avoid any utterance or deed that might *cause* another person to arrive at a false belief. Thus, honesty may not be a matter only of words but of actions and deeds. The characteristically honest person can be trusted to adhere to a contract or promise, or to do that which was legitimately expected, given the circumstances and context (as in the case of a salesperson or sales agent). Similarly, the honest person can be trusted to apply or use knowledge appropriately (as in the case of a professional or a person with special expertise).

Of course, the opposite of honesty is dishonesty, the intentional effort to deceive wrongfully another person. Typically, a deception is *wrongful* when it seeks to take advantage of someone's trust or when the deception affects someone who had a claim or right to be told the truth; deception can, therefore, involve not only outright lying but the withholding of relevant information. In commerce, as in politics, journalism, or academe, there are a variety of ways to be dishonest. The relevant forms of dishonesty may be practiced by the businessperson, the employee, or the customer and these may include conniving, lying, dissembling, scheming, tricking, cheating, swindling, withholding relevant information,

or manipulation. There are, in addition, the borderline cases of overstatement, exaggeration, and bluffing. What is important to acknowledge in these last cases is how easily a person's overstatement may become a misrepresentation that deceives or how an understatement may serve to disguise or put a false construction upon some product, service, or skill, thereby misleading a colleague, employer, or customer.

Honesty as the Best Policy

Even though there are a variety of ways of being dishonest in life and in commerce, the person suspected of dishonesty will not be trusted and will not be a desirable partner in trade. It is in this sense that dishonesty may place one at a competitive disadvantage, for individuals prefer to deal with the honest person, not the dishonest (see Sections AIV and CI). That honesty is a good business policy is a reasonable claim even if, as Franklin notes, fools may not have wit enough to recognize this. However, even if honesty is the best business policy, the person of honest character believes honesty to be an intrinsic good regardless of its implications for one's business or professional life. In other words, the truly honest person practices honesty not because it is the means to an end but because it is a good in itself. If one wishes to hold that honesty is nothing more than a means or instrument of business success, then honesty would be justified in terms of its consequences.

The Sensible Knave

In the eighteenth century, David Hume (1711–1776) offered the challenge of the "sensible knave" who agrees that honesty is the best policy but who chooses to violate honesty when he thinks it reasonable. Hume writes of how

> . . . a sensible knave, in particular incidents, may think that an act of iniquity or infidelity will make a considerable addition to his fortune, without causing any considerable breach in the social union. . . . That *honesty is the best policy,* may be a good general rule, but is liable to many exceptions; and he, it may perhaps be thought, conducts himself with most wisdom, who observes the general rule, and takes advantage of all the exceptions.[4]

Hume admits that there is no reply to the sensible knave except one that appeals to character. For even if the

---

4. *Enquiry Concerning the Principles of Morals* [1751], 3d ed., edited by L. A. Selby-Bigge, revised by P. H. Nidditch (Oxford: Clarendon Press, 1975), 282–83.

knave is able to consistently cheat—which seems doubt-ful—it is Hume's view that such cheating involves the sac-rifice of one's character "for the acquisition of worthless toys and gewgaws."[5] For Hume, it is the very ideal of char-acter, and the peace of mind which accompanies it, that serves to prevent one from becoming the sensible knave.

Honesty and Games

It is sometimes argued, however, that character must be set aside if one is to succeed in business, for business is a sort of game within which the common rules of hon-esty are relaxed. Thus, it might be suggested that within society there are distinct spheres of action in some of which there are mutual agreements to abide by certain rules that allow us to interact in ways which might be forbidden in other spheres. For example, in ordinary life we cannot throw someone to the ground, but in the game of football the act of throwing someone to the ground is legitimate under certain conditions. Games have well-defined boundaries, rules that serve to define or consti-tute the activities of the game itself (and define any roles one may take within the game), as well as other regula-tive rules that determine the more specific aspects of game activities or the particular manner in which a game role is to be acted out. Some argue, as does Carr in the reading below,[6] that business or commerce is a game in that it is a separate sphere of society whose rules not only permit but encourage deviations from more general stan-dards of honesty. The claim rests on the analogy between business (or markets) and games, an analogy that should be considered carefully. However, even if business is some sort of game it is not obvious that everyone in busi-ness must play *this* game in order to engage in market ex-changes or that the suggested rules are constitutive of or essential to business. To consider these matters more fully, let us examine three reading selections. That of Sissela Bok probes the general importance of honesty, the others focus on honesty in the practice of business.

THE READINGS

Daniel Defoe   Defoe begins by emphasizing the in-trinsic difference between honesty and deception, a dif-ference that is not altered by the conditions of trade. Nonetheless some "latitudes" must be granted to the tradesman, the first of which is that the tradesman must be able to ask for a higher price than he is actually will-ing to take. The second instance in which some latitude ought to be allowed is in the case of a promise to repay a creditor. Defoe recognizes the solemnity of a promise but notes that the tradesman intends the promise to be contingent on the tradesman's receiving, via business transactions, the money by which to repay the debt. De-foe contends that all promises are conditional, but in the case of business the person who demands the money will not permit anything less than an absolute promise. This case is, Defoe remarks, distinct from the case of the person who makes a promise with the intention of breaking it. In the second section Defoe takes up the matter of false and flattering speech utilized by sales-persons to render more pleasant the transaction. At-tempting to mock the egregious examples of this speech, Defoe offers a script of the language rendered plain, thereby showing that both buyer and seller are accusing the other of lying as each tries to get the better deal from the other. Defoe concludes that there is an appropriate medium according to which the shopkeeper speaks well of his goods, without lying, and does so with politeness but not extravagant flattery.

Sissela Bok   Deceit is analogous to violence in that it coerces people into acting against their wills, but deceit functions on our beliefs as well as our acts, distorting in-formation about reality and shifting power to the liar. To bring into perspective the significance of honesty, Bok considers the perspective of the deceived and the de-ceiver. The wrong felt by those who are deceived·stems from the fact that their choice was not their own, re-gardless of whether the lies were trivial rather than large. On the other hand, the perspective of the liar re-veals different concerns, for the liar may assume to be using well the power that the lie gives even as the liar also wishes *not* to be deceived. Some of those who pre-varicate seek to carve out an exception for themselves from the rules of honesty; others excuse their lying as a means of survival in a society in which others lie. The liar is affected by his lies in that he knows his integrity has suffered, and he views his victims with particular caution. Even though trivial lies may not affect one's in-tegrity they run the risk of doing so, especially since few lies are solitary, and the ease with which one can lie de-creases credibility. If deception spreads throughout the society, there is a diminished sense of trust necessary for social cooperation and interaction.

---

5. Ibid., p.283.

6. The economist Frank Knight has also argued that competition, in so far as it demands ability, effort, and luck, should be understood as a game in which the best of human ideals are rarely realized. Frank Knight, "The Ethics of Competition" [1923], in *The Ethics of Compe-tition and Other Essays* (Freeport, N.Y.: Books for Libraries, 1969).

Albert Z. Carr   In this famous, if not notorious, article, Albert Carr contends that that there is a conflict between private (noncommercial) morality and the morality of business. Offering a variety of examples of business behavior that would be condemnable outside of a business context, Carr seems to suggest several distinct theses: (a) that business is a sphere with characteristic practices; (b) that these practices are analogous to the ethics of games (such as poker); (c) that if one were to abide by these (commercial) practices in a nonbusiness sphere, then one's actions would be condemned; and (d) that, kept within the confines of commerce, the practices of business are not condemned but are expected and encouraged.

Of Honesty and Veracity in Dealing

Daniel Defoe

Daniel Defoe (1660–1731) was born in London and by the age of 23 was a successful hosiery merchant. After going bankrupt in 1692, he involved himself in politics and journalism, subsequently turning to fiction writing. His works include Robinson Crusoe *(1719),* Moll Flanders *(1722), and other novels. He also completed a three-volume travel book,* Tour Through the Whole Island of Great Britain *(1724–27), as well as the work from which this excerpt is taken,* The Complete English Tradesman *(1726).*

There is a specific difference between honesty and knavery, which can never be altered by trade, or any other thing; nor can that integrity of mind which describes, and is peculiar to, a man of honesty, be ever abated to a tradesman; the rectitude of his soul must be the same; and he must not only intend or mean honestly and justly, but he must act so, and that in all his dealings; he must neither cheat nor defraud, overreach nor circumvent, his neighbour, or anybody he deals with; nor must he design to do so, or lay any plots or snares to that purpose in his dealing; as is frequent in the general conduct of too many, who yet would take it very ill to have any one tax their integrity.

But, after all this is premised, there are some latitudes which a tradesman is and must be allowed, and which, by the custom and usage of trade, he may give himself a liberty in, which cannot be allowed in other cases; some of which are,

1. The liberty of asking more than he will take. I know some people have condemned this practice as dis-

honest: and the quakers, for a time, strictly stood to their point in the contrary practice, resolving to ask no more than they would take, upon any occasion whatsoever, and choosing rather to lose the selling of their goods, though they could afford sometimes to take what was offered, rather than abate a farthing of the price they had asked; but time, and the necessities of trade, have brought them a good deal off of that severity; and they by degrees came to ask, and abate, just as other honest tradesmen do, though not perhaps as those do who give themselves too great a liberty that way.

Indeed it is the buyers that make this custom necessary; for they, especially those who buy for immediate use, will first pretend positively to tie themselves up to a limited price, and bid them a little and a little more, till they come so near the price, that the sellers cannot find in their hearts to refuse it, and then they are tempted to take it, notwithstanding their first words to the contrary. It is common indeed for the tradesmen to say, they cannot abate anything, when yet they do and can afford it; but the tradesman should indeed not be understood strictly and literally to his words, but as he means it; that is to say, that he cannot reasonably abate; and that he cannot abate, without underselling the market, or underrating the value of his goods; and there he may say true: and so the meaning is honest, that he cannot abate; and yet, rather than not take your money, he may at last resolve to do it, in hopes of getting a better price for the remainder, or being willing to abate his ordinary gain, rather than disoblige the customer; or being perhaps afraid he should not sell off the quantity in tolerable time, having possibly a large stock by him, the disposing of some of which will enhance the value of the rest.

In these cases I cannot say a shopkeeper should be tied down to the literal meaning of his words in the price he asks; or that he is guilty of lying in not adhering stiffly to the letter of his first demand; though at the same time I would have every tradesman take as little liberty that way as may be. And if the buyers would expect the tradesman should keep strictly to his demand, they should not stand and haggle, and screw the shopkeeper down, bidding from one penny to another, to a trifle within his price, so as it were to push him to the extremity either to turn away his customer for a sixpence, or some such trifle, or to break his word; as if he would say, I will force you to speak falsely, or turn me away for a trifle.

In such cases, if indeed there is a breach, the sin is the buyer's; at least he puts himself in the devil's stead, and makes himself both tempter and accuser; nor can I say that the seller is, in that case, so much to blame as the buyer; for the latter as often says, I won't give a farthing more, and yet advances; as the former says, I can't abate a farthing, and yet complies. These are, as I call them, trading-lies; and it were to be wished they could be avoided on both sides; and the honest tradesman does avoid them as much as possible; but yet must not, in all cases, be tied up to the strict literal sense of the expression.

2. Another trading license is that of appointing and promising payments of money; which men in business are often forced to make, and too often obliged to break. Let us state this case as clearly as we can.

The credit usually given by one tradesman to another, as particularly by the merchant to the wholesale-man, and by the wholesale-man to the retailer, is such, that, without tying the buyer up to a particular day of payment, they go on buying and selling, and the buyer pays money upon account, as his convenience admits, and as the seller is content to take it; this occasions the merchants, or the wholesale-men, to go about, as they call it, a dunning among their dealers, and which is generally the work of every Saturday. When the merchant comes to his customer, the wholesale-man, or warehouse-keeper, for money, he puts him off, very probably, from week to week, making each time promises of payment, which he is forced to break; but at last, after several disappointments, he makes shift to pay him.

The occasion of this is, the wholesale-man sells the merchant's goods to several retailers; and, if they paid him in time, he would be able to keep his word; but they disappointing him, he is forced, in his turn, to disappoint the merchant; but all the while it is presumed, if he be an honest man, he never makes a promise but he intends otherwise; and has reasonable, and very probable grounds, for hoping he shall be enabled so to do.

The merchant, in his turn, except his circumstances are very good, is obliged to put off the Blackwel-hall factor, or the packer, or the clothier, or whomever he deals with, in proportion; and thus promises go round for payment; and those promises are kept or broken as money comes in, or as disappointments happen; and all this while here is no breach of honesty or parole, no lying or supposition of it, among the tradesman, either on one side or other.

But let us come to the morality of it. To break a solemn promise is a very bad thing, that is certain; there is no coming off of it; and here the first fault might be enlarged upon, viz., of making the promise, which, say the strict objectors, they should not do. But the tradesman's answer is this; all those promises ought to be taken as they are made, namely, with a contingent dependence upon the circumstances of trade, such as promises made them by others who owe them money, or the supposition of a week's trade bringing in money by retail, as usual both of which are liable to fail, or at least to fall short; and this the person who calls for the money knows, and takes the promise with those attending casualties, which, if they fail, he knows the shopkeeper, or whoever he is, must fail him too.

The case is plain; if the man had the money in cash, he need not make a promise or appointment for a further day; for that promise is no more or less than a capitulation for a week's forbearance, on his assurance, that, if possible, he will not fail to pay him at that time. It is objected, that the words, if possible, should then be mentioned; which would solve the morality of the case. To this I must answer that I think it needless, unless the man, to whom the promise was made, could be supposed to believe the promise was to be performed, whether it was possible or no; which no reasonable man can be supposed to do. . . .

It is objected to this, that then I should not make my promises absolute, but conditional. To this I say, that the promises, as is above observed, are really not absolute, but conditional, in the very nature of them, and are understood so when they are made; or else they that hear them do not understand them as all human appointments ought to be understood. I do confess it would be better not to make an absolute promise at all, but to express the condition or reserve with the promise, and say, I will if I can; or, I will if people are just to me, and perform their promises to me.

But the importunity of the person who demands the payment will not permit it; nothing short of a positive promise will satisfy; they never believe the person intends to perform, if he makes the least reserve or condition in his promise, though at the same time they know that even the nature and the reason of the promise strongly imply the condition; and the importunity of the creditor occasions the breach which he reproaches the debtor with the immorality of.

Custom, indeed, has driven us beyond the limits of our morals in many things, which trade makes necessary, and which we can now very rarely avoid; so that if we must pretend to go back to the literal sense of the command, if our yea must be yea, and our nay, nay, why, then, it is impossible for tradesmen to be Christians, and we must unhinge all business, act upon new principles in trade, and go on by new rules; in short, we must shut up shop, and leave of trade, and so in many things we must leave off living; for as conversation is called life, we must leave off to converse. All the ordinary communication of life is now full of lying; and what with table-lies, salutation-lies, and trading-lies, there is no such thing as every man speaking truth with his neighbour. . . .

This necessarily brings me to observe here, and it is a little for the ease of the tradesman's mind, in such severe cases, that there is a distinction to be made in this case, between wilful premeditated lying, and the necessity men may be driven to by their disappointments and other accidents of their circumstances, to break such promises as they had made with a honest intention of performing them.

He that breaks a promise, however solemnly made, may be a honest man; but he that makes a promise with a design to break it, or with no resolution of performing it, cannot be so. Nay, to carry it further, he that makes a promise and does not do his endeavour to perform it, or to put himself into a condition to perform it, cannot be a honest man. A promise once made supposes the person willing to perform it, if it were in his power, and has a binding influence upon the person who made it, so far as his power extends; or that he can, within the reach of any reasonable ability, perform the conditions; but if it is not in his power to perform it, as in this affair of payment of money is often the case, the man cannot be condemned as dishonest.

It must, however, be acknowledged, that it is a very mortifying thing to a honest tradesman to be obliged to break his word; and therefore where men can possibly avoid it, they should not make their promises of payment so positive, but rather conditional, and thereby avoid both the immorality and the discredit of breaking their word; nor will any tradesman, I hope, harden himself in a careless forwardness to promise, without endeavouring or intending to perform, from anything said in this chapter; for be the excuse for it as good as it will, as to the point of strict honesty, he can have but small regard to his own peace of mind, or to his own credit in trade, who will not avoid it as much as possible.

. . . I come next to the setting out their goods to the buyer, by the help of the tongue. And here I must confess our shop rhetoric is a strange kind of speech; it is to be understood, in a manner, by itself: it is to be taken in such a latitude as requires as many flourishes to excuse it, as it contains in itself.

The end of it, in short, is corrupt, and it is made up of a mass of impertinent flattery to the buyer, filled with hypocrisy, compliment, self-praises, falsehood, and, in short, a complication of wickedness: it is a corrupt means to a vicious end; and I cannot see anything in it but what a wise man laughs at, a good man abhors, and any man of honesty avoids as much as possible.

The shopkeeper ought indeed to have a good tongue, but he should not make a common whore of it,

and employ it to the wicked purpose of imposing upon all that come to deal with him. There is a modest license which trade allows to all; but this cannot excuse a wilful lie behind the counter, any more than in any other place; and I recommend it to all honest tradesmen to consider what a scandal it is upon trade to suppose that a tradesman cannot live without lying.

Indeed, I must say, that much of it is owing to the buyers: they begin the work, and give the occasion; and perhaps it was for that reason that Solomon reproved the buyers rather than the sellers, when he says, *It is naught, it is naught, says the buyer; but when he goes away, then he boasteth;* Prov. xx. 14: and it is the less to be wondered at, when the one undervalues the goods, that the other as much overvalues them.

It was a kind of a step to the cure of this vice in trade, that there was an old office erected in the city of London for searching and viewing all the goods which were sold in bulk, and could not be searched into by the buyer. This was called garbling; and the garbler having viewed the goods, and caused all damaged and unsound goods to be taken out, used to set his seal upon the cask, or bags, which held the rest; and then they were vouched to be marketable; so that when the merchant and shopkeeper met to deal, there was no room for any words about the goodness of the ware; there was the garbler's seal to vouch that they were marketable and good; and if they were otherwise, the garbler was answerable.

This respected some particular sorts of goods only, and chiefly spices and drugs, and dye-stuffs, and the like. It were well if some other method than that of a voluble tongue could be found out to ascertain the goodness and value of goods between the shopkeeper and the retail buyer, that such a flux of falsehoods and untruths might be avoided, as we see every day made use of to run up and run down everything that is bought or sold, and that without any effect too; for, take it one time with another, all the shopkeeper's protestations don't make the buyer like the goods at all the better; nor does the buyer's depreciating them make the shopkeeper sell the cheaper.

It would be worth while to consider a little the language that passes between the tradesman and his customer over the counter, and put it into plain homespun English, as the meaning of it really imports: we would not take that usage if it were put into plain words; it would set all the shopkeepers and their customers together by the ears; and we should have fighting and quarrelling, instead of bowing and courtseying, in every shop. Let us hear how it would sound between them. A lady, we'll suppose, comes into a mercer's shop to buy some silks; or to the laceman's to buy some silver laces, or the like; and when she pitches upon a piece which she likes, she begins thus:—

La. I like that colour and that figure well enough; but I don't like the silk, there's no substance in it.

Mer. Indeed, madam, your ladyship lies; 'tis a very substantial silk.

La. No, no, you lie. Indeed, sir, 'tis good for nothing; 'twill do no service.

Mer. Pray, madam, feel how heavy 'tis; the very weight of it may satisfy you that you lie, indeed, madam.

La. Come, come, show me a better: I am sure you have better, and tell me no lie.

Mer. Indeed, madam, your ladyship lies. I may show you more pieces, but I cannot show you a better: there is not a better piece of silk, of that sort, in London, madam.

La. Let me see that piece of crimson, there.

Mer. Here it is, madam.

La. No, that won't do neither; 'tis not a good colour.

Mer. Indeed, madam, you lie; 'tis as fine a colour as can be dyed.

La. O fie: you lie, indeed, sir; why it is not in grain.

Mer. Your ladyship lies, upon my word, madam; 'tis in grain, indeed; and as fine as can be dyed.

I might make this dialogue much longer; but here is enough to set the mercer and the lady both in a flame, if it were but spoken out in plain language, as above; and yet what is all the shop-dialect less or more than this? The meaning is plain; it is nothing but you lie, and you lie, wrapped up in silk and satin, and delivered dressed finely up in better clothes than perhaps it might come dressed in between a carman and a porter.

I am not for making my discourse a satire upon the shopkeepers or upon their customers; if I were, I could give a long detail of the arts and tricks made use of behind the counter to wheedle and persuade the buyer, and manage the selling part among shopkeepers; but this is rather a work for a ballad or a song. My business is to tell the complete tradesman how to act a wiser part, to talk to his customers like a man of sense and business, and not like a mountebank; to let him see that there is a way of managing behind a counter, that, let the customer be man or woman, impertinent or not, he may behave himself so as to avoid all those impertinences, falsehoods, and foolish and wicked excursions which I complain of.

There is a happy medium in these things: the shopkeeper, far from being rude to his customers, on one hand, or sullen and silent on the other; may speak handsomely and modestly of his goods what they deserve, and no other; may with truth, and good manners too, set

forth his goods as they ought to be set forth, and neither be wanting to the commodity he sells, or run out into a ridiculous extravagance of words, which have neither truth of fact, or honesty of design in them.

Nor is this middle way of management at all less likely to succeed, if the customers have any share of sense in them, or the goods he shows any merit to recommend them.

Let the tradesman then try the honest part, and stand by that, keeping a stock of fashionable and valuable goods in his shop to show; and, I dare say he will run no venture, nor need he fear customers. If anything calls for the help of rattling words, it must be mean, unfashionable, and ordinary goods, together with weak and silly buyers; and let the buyers that chance to read this, remember, that whenever they find the shopkeeper begins his fine speeches, they ought to suppose he has trash to bring out, and believes he has fools to show it to.

QUESTIONS ON DEFOE

1. Defoe seems to hold that honesty is essential to being a good human being and to successful trade, and yet he also contends that the conditions of trade allow for a certain "latitude" in honesty. What are these circumstances? How wide is this latitude? Do you think that this is justified? Does Defoe provide a justification for this? Does bargaining over price require that we send misleading messages to one another?

2. Why does Defoe assert that certain lapses from honesty are the fault of the buyer? Do you agree? In what sense does business ethics extend to the consumer and customer as well as to the merchant and producer?

3. The second instance in which the tradesman may have a certain latitude is that of promise-keeping. In what sense is a promise conditional? Do you think that this is correct?

4. How does Defoe offer criticisms of the kind of language employed in trade? Is the language of trade necessarily dishonest?

Truthfulness, Deceit, and Trust

Sissela Bok

Sissela Bok was born in Stockholm and is a Distinguished Fellow at the Harvard Center for Population and Development Studies, having previously been a Professor of Philosophy at Brandeis University. She is the author of numerous works on practical ethical problems, including Secrets: On the Ethics of Concealment and Revelation *(1983). This excerpt is from* Lying: Moral Choice in Public and Private Life *(1978).*

LYING AND CHOICE

Deceit and violence—these are the two forms of deliberate assault on human beings.[1] Both can coerce people into acting against their will. Most harm that can befall victims through violence can come to them also through deceit. But deceit controls more subtly, for it works on belief as well as action. Even Othello, whom few would have dared to try to subdue by force, could be brought to destroy himself and Desdemona through falsehood.

The knowledge of this coercive element in deception, and of our vulnerability to it, underlies our sense of the *centrality* of truthfulness. Of course, deception—again like violence—can be used also in self-defense, even for sheer survival. Its use can also be quite trivial, as in white lies. Yet its potential for coercion and for destruction is such that society could scarcely function without some degree of truthfulness in speech and action.*

Imagine a society, no matter how ideal in other respects, where word and gesture could never be counted upon. Questions asked, answers given, information exchanged—all would be worthless. Were all statements randomly truthful or deceptive, action and choice would be undermined from the outset. There must be a minimal degree of trust in communication for language and action to be more than stabs in the dark. This is why some level of truthfulness has always been seen as essential to human society, no matter how deficient the observance of other moral principles. Even the devils themselves, as Samuel Johnson said, do not lie to one another, since the society of Hell could not subsist without truth any more than others.[2]

A society, then, whose members were unable to distinguish truthful messages from deceptive ones, would collapse. But even before such a general collapse, individual choice and survival would be imperiled. The search for food and shelter could depend on no expectations from others. A warning that a well was poisoned or a plea for help in an accident would come to be ignored unless independent confirmation could be found.

All our choices depend on our estimates of what is the case; these estimates must in turn often rely on information from others. Lies distort this information and therefore our situation as we perceive it, as well as our choices. A lie, in Hartmann's words, "injures the deceived person in his life; it leads him astray."[3]

To the extent that knowledge gives power, to that extent do lies affect the distribution of power; they add to that of the liar, and diminish that of the deceived, altering his choices at different levels.[4] A lie, first, may misinform, so as to obscure some *objective*, something the deceived person wanted to do or obtain. It may make the objective seem unattainable or no longer desirable. It may even create a new one, as when Iago deceived Othello into wanting to kill Desdemona.

Lies may also eliminate or obscure relevant *alternatives*, as when a traveler is falsely told a bridge has collapsed. At times, lies foster the belief that there are more alternatives than is really the case; at other times, a lie may lead to the unnecessary loss of confidence in the best alternative. Similarly, the estimates of *costs and benefits* of any action can be endlessly varied through successful deception. The immense toll of life and human welfare from the United States' intervention in Vietnam came at least in part from the deception (mingled with self-deception) by those who channeled overly optimistic information to the decision-makers.

Finally, the degree of *uncertainty* in how we look at our choices can be manipulated through deception. Deception can make a situation falsely uncertain as well as falsely certain. It can affect the objectives seen, the alternatives believed possible, the estimates made of risks and benefits. Such a manipulation of the dimension of certainty is one of the main ways to gain power over the choices of those deceived. And just as deception can initiate actions a person would otherwise never have chosen, so it can prevent action by obscuring the necessity for choice. This is the essence of camouflage and of the cover-up—the creation of apparent normality to avert suspicion.

Everyone depends on deception to get out of a scrape, to save face, to avoid hurting the feelings of others. Some use it much more consciously to manipulate and gain ascendancy. Yet all are intimately aware of the threat lies can pose, the suffering they can bring. This two-sided experience which we all share makes the singleness with which either side is advocated in action all the more puzzling. Why are such radically different evaluations given to the effects of deception, depending on whether the point of view is that of the liar or the one lied to?

---

*But truthful statements, though they are not meant to deceive, can, of course, themselves be coercive and destructive; they can be used as weapons, to wound and do violence.

THE PERSPECTIVE OF THE DECEIVED

Those who learn that they have been lied to in an important matter—say, the identity of their parents, the affection of their spouse, or the integrity of their government—are resentful, disappointed, and suspicious. They feel wronged; they are wary of new overtures. And they look back on their past beliefs and actions in the new light of the discovered lies. They see that they were manipulated, that the deceit made them unable to make choices for themselves according to the most adequate information available, unable to act as they would have wanted to act had they known all along.

It is true, of course, that personal, informed choice is not the only kind available to them. They may *decide* to abandon choosing for themselves and let others decide for them—as guardians, financial advisors, or political representatives. They may even decide to abandon choice based upon information of a conventional nature altogether and trust instead to the stars or to throws of the dice or to soothsayers.

But such alternatives ought to be personally chosen and not surreptitiously imposed by lies or other forms of manipulation. Most of us would resist loss of control over which choices we want to delegate to others and which ones we want to make ourselves, aided by the best information we can obtain. We resist because experience has taught us the consequences when others choose to deceive us, even "for our own good." Of course, we know that many lies are trivial. But since we, when lied to, have no way to judge which lies are the trivial ones, and since we have no confidence that liars will restrict themselves to just such trivial lies, the perspective of the deceived leads us to be wary of *all* deception.

Nor is this perspective restricted to those who are actually deceived in any given situation. Though only a single person may be deceived, many others may be harmed as a result. If a mayor is deceived about the need for new taxes, the entire city will bear the consequences. Accordingly, the perspective of the deceived is shared by all those who feel the consequences of a lie, whether or not they are themselves lied to. When, for instance, the American public and world opinion were falsely led to believe that bombing in Cambodia had not begun, the Cambodians themselves bore the heaviest consequences, though they can hardly be said to have been deceived about the bombing itself. . . .

Deception, then, can be coercive. When it succeeds, it can give power to the deceiver—power that all who suffer the consequences of lies would not wish to abdicate. From this perspective, it is clearly unreasonable to assert that people should be able to lie with impunity whenever they want to do so. It would be unreasonable, as well, to assert such a right even in the more restricted circumstances where the liars claim a good reason for lying. This is especially true because lying so often accompanies every *other* form of wrongdoing, from murder and bribery to tax fraud and theft. In refusing to condone such a right to decide when to lie and when not to, we are therefore trying to protect ourselves against lies which help to execute or cover up all other wrongful acts.

For this reason, the perspective of the deceived supports the statement by Aristotle:

> Falsehood is in itself mean and culpable, and truth noble and full of praise.[5]

There is an initial imbalance in the evaluation of truth-telling and lying. Lying requires a *reason,* while truth-telling does not. It must be excused; reasons must be produced, in any one case, to show why a particular lie is not "mean and culpable."

THE PERSPECTIVE OF THE LIAR

Those who adopt the perspective of would-be-liars, on the other hand, have different concerns. For them, the choice is often a difficult one. They may believe, with Machiavelli, that "great things" have been done by those who have "little regard for good faith." They may trust that they can make wise use of the power that lies bring. And they may have confidence in their own ability to distinguish the times when good reasons support their decision to lie.

Liars share with those they deceive the desire not to *be* deceived. As a result, their choice to lie is one which they would like to reserve for themselves while insisting that others be honest. They would prefer, in other words, a "free-rider" status, giving them the benefits of lying without the risks of being lied to. Some think of this free-rider status as for them alone. Others extend it to their friends, social group, or profession. This category of persons can be narrow or broad; but it does require as a necessary backdrop the ordinary assumptions about the honesty of most persons. The free rider trades upon being an exception, and could not exist in a world where everybody chose to exercise the same prerogatives.

At times, liars operate as if they believed that such a free-rider status is theirs and that it excuses them. At other times, on the contrary, it is the very fact that others *do* lie that excuses their deceptive stance in their own eyes. It is crucial to see the distinction between the free-loading liar and the liar whose deception is a strategy for survival in a corrupt society.*

All want to avoid being deceived by *others* as much as possible. But many would like to be able to weigh the advantages and disadvantages in a more nuanced way whenever they are themselves in the position of choosing whether or not to deceive. They may invoke special reasons to lie—such as the need to protect confidentiality or to spare someone's feelings. They are then much more willing, in particular, to exonerate a well-intentioned lie on their own part; dupes tend to be less sanguine about the good intentions of those who deceive them.

But in this benevolent self-evaluation by the liar of the lies he might tell, certain kinds of disadvantage and harm are almost always overlooked. Liars usually weigh only the immediate harm to others from the lie against the benefits they want to achieve. The flaw in such an outlook is that it ignores or underestimates two additional kinds of harm—the harm that lying does to the liars themselves and the harm done to the general level of trust and social cooperation. Both are cumulative; both are hard to reverse.

How is the liar affected by his own lies? The very fact that he *knows* he has lied, first of all, affects him. He may regard the lie as an inroad on his integrity; he certainly looks at those he has lied to with a new caution. And if they find out that he has lied, he knows that his credibility and the respect for his word have been damaged. When Adlai Stevenson had to go before the United Nations in 1961 to tell falsehoods about the United States' role in the Bay of Pigs invasion, he changed the course of his life. He may not have known beforehand that the message he was asked to convey was untrue; but merely to carry the burden of being the means of such deceit must have been difficult. To lose the confidence of his peers in such a public way was harder still.

Granted that a public lie on an important matter, once revealed, hurts the speaker, must we therefore conclude that *every* lie has this effect? What of those who tell a few white lies once in a while? Does lying hurt them in the same way? It is hard to defend such a notion. No one trivial lie undermines the liar's integrity. But the problem for liars is that they tend to see *most* of their lies in this benevolent light and thus vastly underestimate the risks they run. While no one lie always carries harm for the liar, then, there is *risk* of such harm in most.

These risks are increased by the fact that so few lies are solitary ones. It is easy, a wit observed, to tell a lie, but hard to tell only one. The first lie "must be thatched with another or it will rain through." More and more lies may come to be needed; the liar always has more mending to do. And the strains on him become greater each time—many have noted that it takes an excellent memory to keep one's untruths in good repair and disentangled.[6] The sheer energy the liar has to devote to shoring them up is energy the honest man can dispose of freely.

After the first lies, moreover, others can come more easily. Psychological barriers wear down; lies seem more necessary, less reprehensible; the ability to make moral distinctions can coarsen; the liar's perception of his chances of being caught may warp. These changes can affect his behavior in subtle ways; even if he is not found out he will then be less trusted than those of unquestioned honesty. And it is inevitable that more frequent lies *do* increase the chance that some will be discovered. At that time, even if the liar has no personal sense of loss of integrity* from his deceitful practices, he will surely regret the damage to his credibility which their discovery brings about. Paradoxically, once his word is no longer trusted, he will be left with greatly *decreased* power—even though a lie often does bring at least a short-term gain in power over those deceived.

Even if the liar cares little about the risks to others from his deception, therefore, all these risks to himself argue in favor of at least weighing any decision to lie quite seriously. Yet such risks rarely enter his calculations. Bias skews all judgment, but never more so than in the search for good reasons to deceive. Not only does it combine with ignorance and uncertainty so that liars are apt to overestimate their own good will, high motives, and chances to escape detection; it leads also to overconfidence in their own imperviousness to the personal entanglements, worries, and loss of integrity which might so easily beset them.[7]

The liar's self-bestowed free-rider status, then, can be as corrupting as all other unchecked exercises of

---

*While different, the two are closely linked. If enough persons adopt the free-rider strategy for lying, the time will come when all will feel pressed to lie to survive.

*The word "integrity" comes from the same roots which have formed "intact" and "untouched." It is used especially often in relation to truthfulness and fair dealing and reflects, I believe, the view that by lying one hurts oneself. The notion of the self-destructive aspects of doing wrong is part of many traditions. See, for example, the *Book of Mencius:* "Every man has within himself these four beginnings [of humanity, righteousness, decorum, wisdom]. The man who considers himself incapable of exercising them is destroying himself." See Merle Severy, ed., *Great Religions of the World* (Washington, D.C.: National Geographic Society, 1971), p. 167; and W.A.C.H. Dobson trans., *Mencius* (Toronto: University of Toronto Press, 1963), p. 132.

power. There are, in fact, very few "free rides" to be had through lying. I hope to examine, in this book, those exceptional circumstances where harm to self and others from lying is less likely, and procedures which can isolate and contain them. But the chance of harm to liars can rarely be ruled out altogether.

Bias causes liars often to ignore the second type of harm as well. For even if they make the effort to estimate the consequences to *individuals*—themselves and others—of their lies, they often fail to consider the many ways in which deception can spread and give rise to practices very damaging to human communities. These practices clearly do not affect only isolated individuals. The veneer of social trust is often thin. As lies spread—by imitation, or in retaliation, or to forestall suspected deception—trust is damaged. Yet trust is a social good to be protected just as much as the air we breathe or the water we drink. When it is damaged, the community as a whole suffers; and when it is destroyed, societies falter and collapse.

We live at a time when the harm done to trust can be seen first-hand. Confidence in public officials and in professionals has been seriously eroded. This, in turn, is a most natural response to the uncovering of practices of deceit for high-sounding aims such as "national security" or the "adversary system of justice." It will take time to rebuild confidence in government pronouncements that the CIA did not participate in a Latin American coup, or that new figures show an economic upturn around the corner. The practices engendering such distrust were entered upon, not just by the officials now so familiar to us, but by countless others, high and low, in the government and outside it, each time for a reason that seemed overriding.

Take the example of a government official hoping to see Congress enact a crucial piece of antipoverty legislation. Should he lie to a Congressman he believes unable to understand the importance and urgency of the legislation, yet powerful enough to block its passage? Should he tell him that, unless the proposed bill is enacted, the government will push for a much more extensive measure?

In answering, shift the focus from this case taken in isolation to the vast practices of which it forms a part. What is the effect on colleagues and subordinates who witness the deception so often resulting from such a choice? What is the effect on the members of Congress as they inevitably learn of a proportion of these lies? And what is the effect on the electorate as it learns of these and similar practices? Then shift back to the narrower world of the official troubled about the legislation he believes in, and hoping by a small deception to change a crucial vote.

It is the fear of the harm lies bring that explains statements such as the following from Revelations (22.15), which might otherwise seem strangely out of proportion:

> These others must stay outside [the Heavenly City]: dogs, medicine-men, and fornicators, and murderers, and idolaters, and everyone of false life and false speech.[8]

It is the deep-seated concern of the multitude which speaks here; there could be few contrasts greater than that between this statement and the self-confident, individualistic view by Machiavelli:

> Men are so simple and so ready to obey present necessities, that one who deceives will always find those who allow themselves to be deceived.

. . .

ENDNOTES

1. See quotation on p. 43 [*Lying: Moral Choice in Public and Private Life*], where Dante characterizes force and fraud as the two forms of malice aiming at injustice. See also Northrop Frye, *The Secular Scripture: A Study of the Structure of Romance* (Cambridge, Mass.: Harvard University Press, 1976), chap. 3.
2. Samuel Johnson, *The Adventurer* 50 (28 April 1753), in *Selected Essays from The Rambler, Adventurer, and Idler*, ed. W. J. Bate (New Haven and London: Yale University Press, 1968).
3. Nicolai Hartmann, *Ethics,* 2: 282.
4. The discussion that follows draws upon the framework provided by decision theory for thinking about choice and decision-making. This framework includes the *objectives* as they are seen by the decision maker, the *alternatives* available for reaching them, an estimate of *costs and benefits* associated with both, and a *choice rule* for weighing these.
5. Aristotle, *Nicomachean Ethics,* trans. H. Rackham (London: William Heinemann, and Cambridge, Mass.: Harvard University Press, 1934), bk. 4, chap. 7. For a discussion of Aristotle's concept of "truth," see Paul Wilpert, "Zum Aristotelischen Wahrheitsbegriff," *Phil. Jahrbuch der Görresgesellschaft,* Band 53, 1940, pp. 3–16.
6. See Michel de Montaigne, "Des Menteurs," in *Essais*, vol. 1, chap. 9 (pp. 30–35); and *What Luther Says: An Anthology,* comp. Ewald M. Plass (St. Louis, Mo.: Concordia Press, 1959), p. 871.
7. For a discussion of bias and "opportunistically distorted beliefs," see Gunnar Myrdal, *Objectivity in Social Research* (New York: Pantheon, 1968).
8. "Dogs" is taken to mean "heathens" or "sodomites"; and John Noonan, Jr., argues, in *The Morality of Abortion* (Cambridge, Mass.: Harvard University Press, 1970), p. 9,

that the word *pharmakoi*, here translated as "medicine-men," referred to those who procured abortions and prescribed abortifacient drugs.

QUESTIONS ON BOK

1. How does a lie shift power to the liar and away from the victim? How might lies shift power to the salesperson? Can lies shift power to the customer or client?

2. In what sense do liars see their lies in so benevolent a light that they "underestimate the risks they run"? What are these risks? How might these risks occur in commerce?

3. Consider the distinction between the liar as a "free rider" and the liar as a strategist who is trying to survive in a corrupt society. Is one type preferable to the other? In what areas of commercial life are you more likely to find one of these?

Is Business Bluffing Ethical?

Albert Z. Carr

Albert Z. Carr (1902–1971) served as an economic advisor in the White House from 1944 to 1946, as a consultant to President Truman, from 1948 to 1952, and as an officer in several private companies during the 1950s. Among his books are A Matter of Life and Death: How the Conflicts of our Century Arose *(1967) and* Business as a Game *(1968). This essay originally appeared in* Harvard Business Review *(1968).*

A respected businessman with whom I discussed the theme of this article remarked with some heat, "You mean to say you're going to encourage men to bluff? Why, bluffing is nothing more than a form of lying! You're advising them to lie!"

I agreed that the basis of private morality is a respect for truth and that the closer a businessman comes to the truth, the more he deserves respect. At the same time, I suggested that most bluffing in business might be regarded simply as game strategy—much like bluffing in poker, which does not reflect on the morality of the bluffer.

I quoted Henry Taylor, the British statesman who pointed out that "falsehood ceases to be falsehood when it is understood on all sides that the truth is not

expected to be spoken"—an exact description of bluffing in poker, diplomacy, and business. I cited the analogy of the criminal court, where the criminal is not expected to tell the truth when he pleads "not guilty." Everyone from the judge down takes it for granted that the job of the defendant's attorney is to get his client off, not to reveal the truth; and this is considered ethical practice. I mentioned Representative Omar Burleson, the Democrat from Texas, who was quoted as saying, in regard to the ethics of Congress, "Ethics is a barrel of worms"[1]—a pungent summing up of the problem of deciding who is ethical in politics.

I reminded my friend that millions of businessmen feel constrained every day to say *yes* to their bosses when they secretly believe *no* and that this is generally accepted as permissible strategy when the alternative might be the loss of a job. The essential point, I said, is that the ethics of business are game ethics, different from the ethics of religion.

He remained unconvinced. Referring to the company of which he is president, he declared: "Maybe that's good enough for some businessmen, but I can tell you that we pride ourselves on our ethics. In 30 years not one customer has ever questioned my word or asked to check our figures. We're loyal to our customers and fair to our suppliers. I regard my handshake on a deal as a contract. I've never entered into price-fixing schemes with my competitors. I've never allowed my salesmen to spread injurious rumors about other companies. Our union contract is the best in our industry. And, if I do say so myself, our ethical standards are of the highest!"

He really was saying, without realizing it, that he was living up to the ethical standards of the business game—which are a far cry from those of private life. Like a gentlemanly poker player, he did not play in cahoots with others at the table, try to smear their reputations, or hold back chips he owed them.

But this same fine man, at that very time, was allowing one of his products to be advertised in a way that made it sound a great deal better than it actually was. Another item in his product line was notorious among dealers for its "built-in obsolescence." He was holding back from the market a much-improved product because he did not want it to interfere with sales of the inferior item it would have replaced. He had joined with certain of his competitors in hiring a lobbyist to push a state legislature, by methods that he preferred not to know too much about, into amending a bill then being enacted.

In his view these things had nothing to do with ethics; they were merely normal business practice. He himself undoubtedly avoided outright falsehoods—never lied in so many words. But the entire organization that he ruled was deeply involved in numerous strategies of deception.

PRESSURE TO DECEIVE

Most executives from time to time are almost compelled, in the interests of their companies or themselves, to practice some form of deception when negotiating with customers, dealers, labor unions, government officials, or even other departments of their companies. By conscious misstatements, concealment of pertinent facts, or exaggeration—in short, by bluffing—they seek to persuade others to agree with them. I think it is fair to say that if the individual executive refuses to bluff from time to time—if he feels obligated to tell the truth, the whole truth, and nothing but the truth—he is ignoring opportunities permitted under the rules and is at a heavy disadvantage in his business dealings.

But here and there a businessman is unable to reconcile himself to the bluff in which he plays a part. His conscience, perhaps spurred by religious idealism, troubles him. He feels guilty; he may develop an ulcer or a nervous tic. Before any executive can make profitable use of the strategy of the bluff, he needs to make sure that in bluffing he will not lose self-respect or become emotionally disturbed. If he is to reconcile personal integrity and high standards of honesty with the practical requirements of business, he must feel that his bluffs are ethically justified. The justification rests on the fact that business, as practiced by individuals as well as by corporations, has the impersonal character of a game—a game that demands both special strategy and an understanding of its special ethics.

The game is played at all levels of corporate life, from the highest to the lowest. At the very instant that a man decides to enter business, he may be forced into a game situation, as is shown by the recent experience of a Cornell honor graduate who applied for a job with a large company:

> This applicant was given a psychological test which included the statement, "Of the following magazines, check any that you have read either regularly or from time to time, and double-check those which interest you most. *Reader's Digest, Time, Fortune, Saturday Evening Post, The New Republic, Life, Look, Ramparts, Newsweek, Business Week, U.S. News & World Report, The Nation, Playboy, Esquire, Harper's, Sports Illustrated.*"

His tastes in reading were broad, and at one time or another he had read almost all of these magazines. He was a subscriber to *The New Republic,* an enthusiast for *Ramparts,* and an avid student of the pictures in *Playboy.* He was not sure whether his interest in *Playboy* would be held against him, but he had a shrewd suspicion that if he confessed to an interest in *Ramparts* and *The New Republic,* he would be thought a liberal, a radical, or at least an intellectual, and his chances of getting the job, which he needed, would greatly diminish. He therefore checked five of the more conservative magazines. Apparently it was a sound decision, for he got the job.

He had made a game player's decision, consistent with business ethics.

A similar case is that of a magazine space salesman who, owing to a merger, suddenly found himself out of a job:

> This man was 58, and, in spite of a good record, his chance of getting a job elsewhere in a business where youth is favored in hiring practice was not good. He was a vigorous, healthy man, and only a considerable amount of gray in his hair suggested his age. Before beginning his job search he touched up his hair with a black dye to confine the gray to his temples. He knew that the truth about his age might well come out in time, but he calculated that he could deal with that situation when it arose. He and his wife decided that he could easily pass for 45, and he so stated his age on his résumé.

This was a lie; yet within the accepted rules of the business game, no moral culpability attaches to it.

THE POKER ANALOGY

We can learn a good deal about the nature of business by comparing it with poker. While both have a large element of chance, in the long run the winner is the man who plays with steady skill. In both games ultimate victory requires intimate knowledge of the rules, insight into the psychology of the other players, a bold front, a considerable amount of self-discipline, and the ability to respond swiftly and effectively to opportunities provided by chance.

No one expects poker to be played on the ethical principles preached in churches. In poker it is right and proper to bluff a friend out of the rewards of being dealt a good hand. A player feels no more than a slight twinge of sympathy, if that, when—with nothing better than a single ace in his hand—he strips a heavy loser, who holds a pair, of the rest of his chips. It was up to the other fellow to protect himself. In the words of an excellent poker player, former

President Harry Truman, "If you can't stand the heat, stay out of the kitchen." If one shows mercy to a loser in poker, it is a personal gesture, divorced from the rules of the game.

Poker has its special ethics, and here I am not referring to rules against cheating. The man who keeps an ace up his sleeve or who marks the cards is more than unethical; he is a crook, and can be punished as such— kicked out of the game or, in the Old West, shot.

In contrast to the cheat, the unethical poker player is one who, while abiding by the letter of the rules, finds ways to put the other players at an unfair disadvantage. Perhaps he unnerves them with loud talk. Or he tries to get them drunk. Or he plays in cahoots with someone else at the table. Ethical poker players frown on such tactics.

Poker's own brand of ethics is different from the ethical ideals of civilized human relationships. The game calls for distrust of the other fellow. It ignores the claim of friendship. Cunning deception and conceal- ment of one's strength and intentions, not kindness and openheartedness, are vital in poker. No one thinks any the worse of poker on that account. And no one should think any the worse of the game of business because its standards of right and wrong differ from the prevailing traditions of morality in our society. . . .

'WE DON'T MAKE THE LAWS'

Wherever we turn in business, we can perceive the sharp distinction between its ethical standards and those of the churches. Newspapers abound with sen- sational stories growing out of this distinction:

> We read one day that Senator Philip A. Hart of Michigan has attacked food processors for deceptive packaging of numerous products.[2]
> The next day there is a Congressional to-do over Ralph Nader's book, *Unsafe At Any Speed,* which demon- strates that automobile companies for years have neglected the safety of car-owning families.[3]
> Then another Senator, Lee Metcalf of Montana, and journalist Vic Reinemer show in their book, *Overcharge,* the methods by which utility companies elude regulating government bodies to extract unduly large payments from users of electricity.[4]

These are merely dramatic instances of a prevailing condition; there is hardly a major industry at which a sim- ilar attack could not be aimed. Critics of business regard such behavior as unethical, but the companies concerned know that they are merely playing the business game.

Among the most respected of our business insti- tutions are the insurance companies. A group of in- surance executives meeting recently in New England was startled when their guest speaker, social critic Daniel Patrick Moynihan, roundly berated them for "unethical" practices. They had been guilty, Moyni- han alleged, of using outdated actuarial tables to ob- tain unfairly high premiums. They habitually delayed the hearings of lawsuits against them in order to tire out the plaintiffs and win cheap settlements. In their employment policies they used ingenious devices to discriminate against certain minority groups.[5]

It was difficult for the audience to deny the validity of these charges. But these men were business game play- ers. Their reaction to Moynihan's attack was much the same as that of the automobile manufacturers to Nader, of the utilities to Senator Metcalf, and of the food processors to Senator Hart. If the laws governing their businesses change, or if public opinion becomes clamorous, they will make the necessary adjustments. But morally they have in their view done nothing wrong. As long as they comply with the letter of the law, they are within their rights to operate their businesses as they see fit.

The small business is in the same position as the great corporation in this respect. For example:

> In 1967 a key manufacturer was accused of providing mas- ter keys for automobiles to mail-order customers, although it was obvious that some of the purchasers might be auto- mobile thieves. His defense was plain and straightforward. If there was nothing in the law to prevent him from selling his keys to anyone who ordered them, it was not up to him to inquire as to his customers' motives. Why was it any worse, he insisted, for him to sell car keys by mail, than for mail-order houses to sell guns that might be used for mur- der? Until the law was changed, the key manufacturer could regard himself as being just as ethical as any other businessman by the rules of the business game.[6]

Violations of the ethical ideals of society are common in business, but, they are not necessarily vi- olations of business principles. Each year the Federal Trade Commission orders hundreds of companies, many of them of the first magnitude, to "cease and de- sist" from practices which, judged by ordinary stan- dards, are of questionable morality but which are stoutly defended by the companies concerned.

In one case, a firm manufacturing a well-known mouthwash was accused of using a cheap form of al- cohol possibly deleterious to health. The company's chief executive, after testifying in Washington, made this comment privately:

"We broke no law. We're in a highly competitive industry. If we're going to stay in business, we have to look for profit wherever the law permits. We don't make the laws. We obey them. Then why do we have to put up with this 'holier than thou' talk about ethics? It's sheer hypocrisy. We're not in business to promote ethics. Look at the cigarette companies, for God's sake! If the ethics aren't embodied in the laws by the men who made them, you can't expect businessmen to fill the lack. Why, a sudden submission to Christian ethics by businessmen would bring about the greatest economic upheaval in history!"

It may be noted that the government failed to prove its case against him.

CAST ILLUSIONS ASIDE

. . . The illusion that business can afford to be guided by ethics as conceived in private life is often fostered by speeches and articles containing such phrases as, "It pays to be ethical," or "Sound ethics is good business." Actually this is not an ethical position at all; it is a self-serving calculation in disguise. The speaker is really saying that in the long run a company can make more money if it does not antagonize competitors, suppliers, employees, and customers by squeezing them too hard. He is saying that oversharp policies reduce ultimate gains. That is true, but it has nothing to do with ethics. The underlying attitude is much like that in the familiar story of the shopkeeper who finds an extra $20 bill in the cash register, debates with himself the ethical problem—should he tell his partner?—and finally decides to share the money because the gesture will give him an edge over the s.o.b. the next time they quarrel.

I think it is fair to sum up the prevailing attitude of businessmen on ethics as follows:

We live in what is probably the most competitive of the world's civilized societies. Our customs encourage a high degree of aggression in the individual's striving for success. Business is our main area of competition, and it has been ritualized into a game of strategy. The basic rules of the game have been set by the government, which attempts to detect and punish business frauds. But as long as a company does not transgress the rules of the game set by law, it has the legal right to shape its strategy without reference to anything but its profits. If it takes a long-term view of its profits, it will preserve amicable relations, so far as

possible, with those with whom it deals. A wise businessman will not seek advantage to the point where he generates dangerous hostility among employees, competitors, customers, government, or the public at large. But decisions in this area are, in the final test, decisions of strategy, not of ethics. . . .

FOR OFFICE USE ONLY

. . . If a man plans to take a seat in the business game, he owes it to himself to master the principles by which the game is played, including its special ethical outlook. He can then hardly fail to recognize that an occasional bluff may well be justified in terms of the game's ethics and warranted in terms of economic necessity. Once he clears his mind on this point, he is in a good position to match his strategy against that of the other players. He can then determine objectively whether a bluff in a given situation has a good chance of succeeding and can decide when and how to bluff, without a feeling of ethical transgression.

To be a winner, a man must play to win. This does not mean that he must be ruthless, cruel, harsh, or treacherous. On the contrary, the better his reputation for integrity, honesty, and decency, the better his chances of victory will be in the long run. But from time to time every businessman, like every poker player, is offered a choice between certain loss or bluffing within the legal rules of the game. If he is not resigned to losing, if he wants to rise in his company and industry, then in such a crisis he will bluff—and bluff hard.

Every now and then one meets a successful businessman who has conveniently forgotten the small or large deceptions that he practiced on his way to fortune. "God gave me my money," old John D. Rockefeller once piously told a Sunday school class. It would be a rare tycoon in our time who would risk the horse laugh with which such a remark would be greeted.

In the last third of the twentieth century even children are aware that if a man has become prosperous in business, he has sometimes departed from the strict truth in order to overcome obstacles or has practiced the more subtle deceptions of the half-truth or the misleading omission. Whatever the form of the bluff, it is an integral part of the game, and the executive who does not master its techniques is not likely to accumulate much money or power.

ENDNOTES

1. *The New York Times,* March 9, 1967.
2. *The New York Times,* November 21, 1996.
3. New York, Grossman Publishers, Inc., 1965.
4. New York, David McKay Company, Inc., 1967.
5. *The New York Times,* January 17, 1967.
6. Cited by Ralph Nader in "Business Crime," *The New Republic,* July 1, 1967, p. 7.

QUESTIONS ON CARR

1. Is Carr offering a descriptive or a normative thesis about business? In other words, is he describing how business is in fact conducted? Or is he asserting that this is how business *ought* to be conducted?

2. Are there, in fact, different spheres of moral practice (for example, the commercial and the private)? Are Carr's examples convincing? Are each of the business practices mentioned by Carr accepted as morally right or morally permissible *within* business? Do these examples *prove* his point?

3. Carr claims that the ethics of business are analogous to game ethics. What are some of the similarities noted by Carr? Is business analogous only to the game of poker or to other games? What sort of practices would be permitted (or prohibited) according to game ethics? Are there analogous practices in the world of business?

4. Assuming that there are, as a matter of fact, differing moral practices in business and nonbusiness spheres, are the practices, as described by Carr, *essential* or *necessary* to successful commerce? Are certain practices essential to competition?

———————

Sales and Advertising

As a society becomes increasingly affluent, wants are increasingly created by the process by which they are satisfied. This may operate passively. Increases in consumption, the counterpart of increases in product, act by suggestion or emulation to create wants. Expectation rises with attainment. Or producers may proceed actively to create wants through advertising and salesmanship. Wants thus come to depend on output.

John Kenneth Galbraith[7]

One should hardly have to tell academicians that information is a valuable resource: knowledge is *power. And yet it occupies a slum dwelling in the town of economics. Mostly it is ignored: the best technology is assumed to be known; the relationship of commodities to consumer preferences is a datum. And one of the information-producing industries, advertising, is treated with a hostility that economists normally reserve for tariffs or monopolists.*

George Stigler[8]

You can tell the ideals of a nation by its advertisements.

Norman Douglas[9]

You don't understand: Willy was a salesman. And for a salesman, there is no rock bottom to the life. He don't put a bolt to a nut, he don't tell you the law or give you medicine. He's a man way out there in the blue, riding on a smile and a shoeshine. And when they start not smiling back—that's an earthquake. And then you get yourself a couple of spots on your hat, and you're finished. Nobody dast blame this man. A salesman is got to dream, boy. It comes with the territory.

Arthur Miller[10]

---

7. "The Dependence Effect" in *The Affluent Society,* 3d. ed. (Boston, Mass.: Houghton Mifflin, 1976), 131.

8. "The Economics of Information," in *The Essence of Stigler* (Stanford, Conn.: Hoover Institution Press, 1986), 46.

9. *South Wind* (New York: Random House, Modern Library, 1925), 77.

10. As spoken by Charley in Arthur Miller, *Death of a Salesman* (New York: Viking Press, 1949), 138 ("Requiem").

A transaction between a business firm (or salesperson) and a consumer occurs because each expects the exchange to be beneficial; if this were not the case then there would be no transaction. There are at least two conditions essential to such exchange: The two parties must be informed about the nature of the exchange, and each party must freely choose to engage in the exchange. One of the chief means by which businesses seek to alert and inform consumers and to encourage commerce is via advertising.

Advertising

Advertising is the means by which one party seeks to inform and encourage another party to purchase some product or service, or to participate in some event. In this discussion, we will focus on *consumer* advertising, even though *trade* advertising (or business-to-business advertising involving communication to wholesalers or from manufacturers to businesses) is a significant activity in itself. Advertising is used in both direct and indirect ways. Direct advertising seeks to sell a specific product or service. Indirect advertising focuses on improving consumer attitudes about a firm in the expectation that this will motivate consumers to patronize the company or business. Thus, a business might seek to generate in consumers an attitude of *trust* in the expectation that consumer trust is an essential condition of customer patronage.

Unlike other forms of speech, advertising is regulated by the Federal Trade Commission (FTC) established in 1941. The FTC requires that all visual ads, or product demonstrations, be accurate. This regulatory agency may also stipulate that advertisers make public corrections for any misleading ad, issue regulations for entire industries (for example, regulations on the advertising of tobacco products, on the disclosure of food contents, health hazards, and so on), and initiate action against an advertiser if it can be shown that the advertisement *tends* to deceive (even if no one was deceived).

There is, of course, controversy about any limitation on free speech and interesting questions arise concerning the regulation of the economic speech found in advertising. What are the criteria by which to distinguish the economic speech of advertising from other forms of persuasive speech? Might limitations on commercial speech provide a precedent for regulating speech in other spheres of society? These issues, and many others, we must set aside in order to consider some of the ethical issues in advertising.

Deceptive Advertising

Because advertising involves alerting or informing consumers of some product or service, one of the first issues

of advertising ethics concerns the question of *deceptive* advertising. Although a clearly deceptive practice involves an interference with one's free choice, it is not always clear what sorts of advertising practices are deceptive. Advertisers often emphasize the positive and downplay or omit the negative, but it is not obvious that this is sufficient for deception. One might argue that if freedom of speech is a right, then advertisers should be able to say what they want. On this view, an advertiser could make any sort of claim, provided that the claim was not fraudulent. What renders a fraudulent claim impermissible is that it is akin to outright coercion: An act of fraud makes of the victim an unwilling participant. If we are to distinguish fraud from other types of persuasion, then we would have to inquire into issues of intention and effect: (a) whether the advertiser intended to defraud, and (b) whether consumers were in fact defrauded. However, even if we agree that advertising should not be fraudulent, that alone does not entail that advertising must involve rational persuasion. Advertising often appeals to nonrational hopes, desires, or expectations, but do these appeals violate one's autonomy? Must all of one's choices be grounded in some rational choice?

Manipulation

Some have argued that the plethora of advertising not only *creates* consumer desires but that it renders null any hope of rational consumer choice. In the 1950s, Vance Packard warned[11] of the menace of advertisers who manipulate our desires so that our choices are not really *ours* but *theirs*. Perhaps advertisements play upon some desires or fears related to sex or death for example, or perhaps some advertisements utilize some allegedly subliminal means to alter our desires or to suggest desires that we might not otherwise have. John Kenneth Galbraith attacked corporate advertising because, he claimed, it produced the very wants that corporations sought to satisfy, contending that "One cannot defend production as satisfying wants if that production creates the wants."[12] As Galbraith pointed out, the forces of advertising and salesmanship creates these wants, and because these wants are created they are not real or urgent. This is the argument of the "dependence effect." F. A. Hayek stated, to the contrary, that Galbraith was guilty of a *non sequitur*: "Surely an individual's want for literature is not original with himself in the sense that he would experience it if

11. *The Hidden Persuaders* (New York: D. McKay, 1957).

12. *The Affluent Society,* 3d ed., 126–27.

literature were not produced. Does this then mean that the production of literature cannot be defended as satisfying a want because it is only the production which provokes the demand?"[13]

The underlying concern is that our choices (or desires) be autonomous. However, that an individual's choice is autonomous need not entail that the choice is rational or that it resulted from rational persuasion. Indeed, it is not clear that we should want all of our persuasion to be rational even if in certain circumstances rational persuasion is the only sort of persuasion that will do. Rational persuasion uses argument and reason to convince and avoids extraneous appeals to emotion, force, or authority. There are countless influences on our decisions, and many of these are nonrational. However, we do not, for that reason, conclude that these decisions are not autonomous decisions. In fact, it might seem excessively rationalistic, if not naive, to suppose that all instances of persuasion should be instances of rational persuasion. Although we should not persuade in ways that might interfere with an individual's autonomy (including the use of emotional pressure, outright deception, or coercive threats), some forms of nonrational persuasion would clearly seem permissible, so long as they avoid any undue influence on a person's capacity to choose. Thus, the mere fact that one is persuaded by nonrational means is not evidence either of wrongdoing on the part of the persuader or of an interference with the person persuaded.

Sales and Selling

The ethical issues raised in advertising, including those of deception and manipulation, are similar to those raised in sales. The old saying, *caveat emptor* ("let the buyer beware"), is hardly true of most economic trades, but it is nonetheless true enough of some—so true that a pall has been cast over many business transactions, at least in the popular mind. However, let us suppose that all exchanges occur along a continuum that runs from complete ignorance of a product to complete information. The sort of trades that occur under conditions of buyer ignorance are precisely those for which it is true that the buyer should beware. Such exchanges might be permissible *so long as* each participant was cognizant that he or she should be aware as a buyer. Nonetheless the extreme of *caveat emptor* does not seem to be the ethical ideal, even if both parties are voluntarily agree-

ing to the exchange and each may examine, presumably, the article to be exchanged. The alternative to *caveat emptor* is that of information disclosure, informing the party to the exchange of any relevant information concerning the article or service and doing so in an accessible and comprehensible manner.

These very general considerations need to be considered in light of particular cases, as is done in the following reading from Holley. There are various categories by which to consider the wrongs that may occur in selling. One may lie, deceive, withhold information, or bluff. In addition, there are questions concerning appropriate modes of persuasion. Nonetheless, it would seem that a salesperson of good character, such as the type delineated in the reading by Jones, should be able to give reasons for the purchase of a good or service, and these should be truthful and useful relative to the values of the customer. Should, however, these reasons be the whole truth about the article or service? Must the honest salesperson give, in addition to reasons for buying the article, an account of any of the article's disadvantages? Should the salesperson inform the customer of alternative products or services that can be obtained more inexpensively? To consider these questions more fully, let us consider some readings on sales and advertising.

THE READINGS

John G. Jones   Jones seeks to give practical advice to the salesperson and contends that selling requires that one be a person of good character. Jones examines several characteristics relevant to success in sales, beginning first with those qualities related to the salesperson's knowledge of the product and customer. In addition, the salesperson should be an individual of ambition and application, observant and tactful, the latter characteristic essential if the salesperson is to adapt to changing circumstances. The quality of courage forms the basis for self-control, enabling the salesperson to hew to the demands of good character even under difficult circumstances. The virtue of honesty has ramifications beyond those of truthful speech and requires that actions, as well as words, reflect a commitment to truth. Finally, the salesperson should have confidence in himself, his company, and the article he is proposing to sell, and should exhibit enthusiasm in action and loyalty to both company and customers.

David M. Holley   Holley investigates sales practices within a teleological view of the market. If the market is to provide an efficient means for meeting needs and desires, then market exchanges must be voluntary and this

---

13. "The *Non Sequitur* of the 'Dependence Effect,'" in Hayek, *Studies in Philosophy, Politics, and Economies* (Chicago: University of Chicago Press, 1967), 314–15.

requires that each party meet three conditions: knowledge, noncompulsion, and rationality. No salesperson should undermine any of these conditions. For each condition Holley delineates several distinct scenarios, not all of which have obvious solutions or are without controversy. The knowledge condition is exemplified by cases involving misinformation and withholding information; the condition of noncompulsion is set forth in cases in which an exchange is initiated without the consumer being aware of it; the condition of rationality is illustrated with cases involving appeals to one's emotions or insecurities.

Israel Kirzner Kirzner provides a robust defense of advertising against criticisms that it is wasteful, offensive, deceptive, or serves to modify and change our desires. He begins by asking us to imagine a perfectly free market in which every participant is honest, government intervention is at a minimum, and there is freedom of entry and exit for all persons and firms. Although there is price competition in this market there is also nonprice competition in the form of quality competition. Within this market, any distinction between production costs and selling costs is arbitrary, argues Kirzner, because without being informed of a product, via advertising, the consumer would not desire the product at all. Advertising is often loud and garish because the point is not merely to provide information but to call one's attention to the product. Is advertising deceitful? If it is, then this is less a reflection on advertising than on ourselves. Advertisers do seek to alter our tastes and desires, but other organizations and institutions endeavor the same.

Robert L. Arrington Commencing with a summary of six examples of advertising puffery and exaggeration, Arrington asks whether these examples show that advertising involves the manipulation of the customer or whether it provides an efficient means of informing consumers. In response Arrington considers four ideas related to autonomy: autonomous desire, rational desire, free choice, and manipulation. It is not the case, says Arrington, that advertising *per se* interferes with autonomy and freedom, even if it might in some particular cases. In the case of autonomous desires, Arrington points out that what is essential to an autonomous desire is that it is a desire that one wishes to maintain. Thus, even if advertising produces many of our desires, if we accept these desires (or desire to have these desires), then they are autonomous desires. Nor is it obvious that advertising leads us to form irrational desires, because a rational desire or choice is one that is based on having the relevant information by which one can know how to satisfy some other prior desires. A voluntary choice may be understood as one for which the agent has a reason or one for which the agent could have acted otherwise; to examine whether a consumer has acted in some unfree and compulsive manner, we would have to examine each case. In the case of manipulation, Arrington suggests that there are three criteria according to which one person could be said to control the behavior of another, but these render it doubtful that advertising controls our choices.

Character and Caliber in Salesmanship

John G. Jones

John G. Jones (1869–1956) was born in Wales and came to the United States at the age of nineteen. He was a sales manager for the Alexander Hamilton Institute and a lecturer on salesmanship at the New York University School of Commerce, Accounts, and Finance. He is the author of Salesmanship and Sales Management *(1918), from which this excerpt is taken.*

DEVELOPMENT OF CHARACTER AND CALIBER

Part of Character and Caliber in Salesmanship While there is a science of salesmanship, and while we can obtain from the experience of other successful salesmen rules and suggestions for getting in to see a prospect and for holding his attention and interest, the only real way to get in to see a man, after all is said and done, is to look and act like the kind of man who ought to be allowed to come in. The only real way to hold a man's attention and interest and to gain his confidence, is to be a man of sufficiently large caliber to command the attention and interest of the prospect, and to be a man of such a character as to compel his respect and admiration. In other words, the way to increase one's selling ability is to increase one's caliber and strengthen one's character.

Thought, Study and Work Curiously enough, only one of the qualifications essential to good salesmanship has to do directly with the goods to be sold; the others have to do with the salesman himself. The professional back-slapper type of salesman has given place to the keen analyst and close student of human nature. It is not surprising, therefore, that the qualities of the successful salesmen of today closely resemble those which mark successful men in general. The salesman, however, must possess to a higher degree than most men, a pleasing personality and a keen sympathy for others so that he may establish in a short time that confidence and esteem, the cultivation of which men in other walks may leave to time.

Any list of the qualifications essential to salesmanship must be more or less arbitrary. Probably no two sales managers would give exactly the same answer if they were asked what qualities they look for in salesmen. A close study of various answers to this question, however, reveals the fact that the differences are largely matters of definition. The list here given is the product of the experience of many successful salesmen and sales managers. . . .

Preparedness   Two salesmen were talking together in the lobby of a large hotel. One of them, who had been selling paint successfully for one concern for fifteen years, confided to the other that he had not done a stroke of business on the trip he was then making, and announced his intention of going back to his headquarters in Cleveland and resigning. The other, who was a salesman of the new school, having ascertained that this man's paint concern was an old establishment, but little known, began to ply the older man with questions as to what points of superiority his paints had over others, how they compared in price with better known paints, and what reasons there were, in his opinion, for a person to buy his paint in preference to the more widely advertised brands. The paint salesman was unable to answer any one of these questions! He did not know! He had just been dropping around on the dealers in that section for the last fifteen years, selling them paint, and now he suddenly found himself unable to sell them any more. That was all he knew. Before the conversation ended he had made a note of the questions that the younger man had asked, and had decided to go back to his concern, not to resign, but to get the answers to those questions; then, he resolved, he would take another swing around the circuit. That man was unprepared.

Senator Beveridge, who was once a salesman, says that being prepared is the secret of most successes in this world; that fate seldom sides with the unequipped. To succeed in selling anything, the salesman must prepare himself by first acquiring a knowledge of the principles of his craft, and then mastering the details of his proposition. He must have his selling points marshalled and under full control. He must be prepared to answer any questions that may arise. The fact that a salesman has had a good preparation does not mean that his study should cease when he begins to work, any more than one would expect a good lawyer to stop reading law after starting practice. Knowledge of goods and of selling points does not come by intuition or inspiration, but by study and application. . . .

The question very often put to buyers: "What kind of salesman secures your friendship and your business?" invariably brings the response: "The man who knows his business and tells me something new about it, and who brings me new ideas about mine." This answer seems to be especially applicable in the case of highly competitive lines and would seem to indicate the way to success for the salesmen who must compete with others on an even basis as regards price, quality and service. There are any number of men soliciting orders for printing, but there are comparatively few among them who know enough about printing to furnish the buyer with fresh ideas or to originate plans for him. The printing buyer, nine times out of ten, does not know as much as he should about printing and therefore welcomes the man who can increase his information. He shows his appreciation by giving such a man his business, sometimes even paying a higher price than he ordinarily would pay. The engraving salesman who knows his business and can correctly interpret the buyer's ideas in regard to the finished cut is as successful as he is rare.

But the salesman's information should include more than this. He should know what raw materials enter into the product he is selling, the history of those raw materials and the processes that they go thru. The retail lace salesman can arouse in the prospect a very keen interest if he will but read up on laces. The grocery salesman who can talk about growing and canning processes is a man who will interest the dealer. The clothing salesman who knows something about long and short staple wool, the processes in the making of fine worsteds, dyeing in the piece and in the thread, and the small details that make for quality in a garment, can interest the buyer and, incidentally, point out some of the superior qualities of the garment that he is selling. . . .

Ambition Some men dream of success and others will frankly admit that they are ambitious, but the men who will go forth in earnest and struggle unceasingly to satisfy their ambition are few and far between. This kind of ambition is a prime requisite of salesmanship. Salesmen should take ambition for their running mate; they should be imbued with a steadfast purpose of achieving something worth while. The salesman's ambition to make a record is often the means of his discovering new methods of increasing sales, new avenues of approach and new uses for the product. Complacency, on the other hand, never increased business. When a salesman's self-satisfaction becomes indifference and indolence he is on the road to dismal failure.

The spur of ambition should continually urge the salesman forward. Did he have a large volume of sales today? Make tomorrow's better. Did he secure some particularly large single orders? How can he make the next ones larger? Has he discovered a new class of prospects for his goods? Are there any that he has missed? Most men achieve little because they attempt little. On the other hand, the more one accomplishes the more one becomes capable of accomplishing. In order to increase his capacity, therefore, a man need only combine ambition with application.

Application As the term is here used, application includes the determination to carry things thru—a capacity for hard work, stick-to-it-iveness, perseverance, energy. The difference between success and failure in any line is found largely in the degree of application. There is, perhaps, no profession where this is more apparent than in salesmanship. A man of fair intelligence and great energy will succeed in the selling field, whereas a man of brilliant mind and little energy is likely to fail miserably.

Observation A salesman arrives in a town. He should have his eyes open and begin his observations immediately. He climbs on a bus, and is driven to his hotel. By the time he reaches it he should have observed something that will enable him to say a good word about the town. He immediately gets out his sample case and walks up the street to his first prospect. From the moment he gets into his prospect's place of business, or in the case of a retail salesman, the moment the prospect approaches the counter, various signs that he should read are in evidence; he should train his powers of observation to see and interpret them. He should be able to make a quick mental note of the surroundings, of the prospect's appearance and of the conditions in which he finds him. He should be able to determine whether the circumstances are auspicious for a favorable approach. He should observe the tone of his prospect's voice, the expression of his eye and his general bearing, for these things will indicate to the salesman his method of procedure. A rapid estimate of this kind will enable the salesman to adjust himself to the situation without delay. Above all, he should be quick to note when the prospect has reached a favorable decision, and strive to close the sale. This power of quick observation can be acquired and developed by practice.

Tact Such observation as has just been mentioned is closely associated with another important quality—tact. . . .

Tact is defined as the ready power of appreciating and doing what is required by circumstances. It is really the outward expression of intuition. It is the attribute that enables a man to deal with others without friction, to adapt himself to circumstances and to do the right thing in the right place. The tactful salesman humors his customers' opinions when they are not antagonistic; he governs his manner and speech to suit the peculiarities of the man with whom he is dealing. He bases his selling talks on his knowledge of his customer's likes and dislikes. He avoids such topics of conversation with his customer as politics and religion. Tact, in short, is a sort of sixth sense—a combination of wisdom and good judgment—which enables the salesman at a glance to size up the man and the situation in which he finds him and to take the right steps to secure an immediate order and establish future cordial relations.

A great sales manager has said that there are three kinds of salesmen: Men who always say the right thing at the right time and know their reasons for doing so—they are big, steady producers; men who occasionally say the right thing at the right time, but who have no definite reason for saying it—they are spasmodic producers; men who never say the right thing at the right time because they have neither intuition nor tact—the few sales they make are made by main strength.

Some fortunate people are born with tact highly developed; others have it, but allow it to fall into disuse; still more must acquire it; and there are a few who are neither born with it nor acquire it. Lack of tact, however, is largely a matter of thoughtlessness and selfishness—of being so self-centered as to be unable to get the other person's point of view.

Tact should be cultivated, for it is as essential to success as knowledge. As a matter of fact, without tact a great deal of knowledge goes for nothing. A simple, practical and effective rule for developing tact and the personal magnetism that goes with it, is for the salesman to strive to do or say something in each interview that will leave the prospect feeling better for having met him and influence him to give the salesman a warm, friendly reception when he comes again.

Concentration   The sun's rays do not burn until they are brought to a focus. The success of the salesman results not so much from effort as from an intelligent direction of effort, which, in turn, presupposes concentration—concentration on the acquiring of desirable habits; concentration on the planning of the work; concentration on the goods to be sold, and concentration on each individual sale. This is a quality that must be acquired by constant practice. David Graham Phillips, a close student of human nature, said:

> Most of us cannot concentrate at all; any slight distraction suffices to disrupt and destroy the whole train of thought. A good many can concentrate for a few hours, for a week or so, for two or three months; but there comes a small achievement and they are satisfied; or a small discouragement, and they are disheartened. Only to the rare few is given the power to concentrate steadily, year in and year out, thru good and evil events or reports.

Concentration, or singleness of purpose, is a distinguishing characteristic of success in selling or in any other field. . . .

Courage   It takes courage to be honest under all circumstances; to apply the whip of ambition relentlessly; to look the tenth man in the face with a smile after having been turned down by the preceding nine—not with a smile that ends at the teeth, but with one that extends right to the heart; to persist in the face of difficulty; to refrain from overindulgence; to force oneself to work at top speed; and to refuse to let one's mentality slumber during working hours. Courage, in this connection, is synonymous with a determined will—a will that is akin to audacity, that is fearless to the verge of recklessness, that will not yield to seemingly insurmountable difficulties.

Want of courage—fear—mars the first moment of the salesman's interview; makes the voice shake, when it should be round and full; causes the mouth to droop at the corners, when it should be smiling; and robs the handshake of its grip. Fear of the prospect will cause the salesman instinctively to dislike him, prevent him from carrying out carefully laid plans and greatly weaken the close. Most young salesmen have this fear at the start. They can be successful only in so far as they overcome it; and just as soon as they overcome it entirely—provided they have the necessary qualifications—they will join the ranks of the big producers. No salesman should allow a lack of courage to stand between him and big business success.

Honesty   As a business proposition, it pays a man to be honest—with himself first of all, and then with his firm and his customers. Modern business has raised the standard of business ethics and has made honesty both popular and profitable. The salesman, in asking himself whether or not he is an honest man—and we should always remember that the only true answer to that question must come from within—should bear in mind that there are various grades of dishonesty. Of course, it takes a desperate man actually to appropriate his concern's funds; and a small man to pad an expense account. But that man is dishonest as well who knowingly oversells a customer; who makes loose promises to secure an order; who fails to correct a misunderstanding for fear of jeopardizing an order; who fails to get a sample room when he knows that his negligence will hurt the interests of his house; who waits over a train or two to have the company of a fellow salesman to the next stop—or so as not to break up a congenial card party; who carries a side line; or who spends his spare time in such a manner as to give his house below-par service. A salesman cannot do any of these things and retain his self-respect and the confidence and esteem of his concern and his customers.

There are some salesmen who are known as "one-trippers." Their first trip to a territory results in a fine volume of business, but eventually there comes a cancelation because of overselling, a protest that the salesman's promise of an exclusive agency was not kept, and complaints everywhere of shady dealings. The salesman is not in a position, under such circumstances, to go over the territory again, and the chances of future business for the concern are doubtful. These offenses are not tolerated by the right kind of employers—

and any other sort cannot buy the services of self-respecting men.

The truly honest salesman gives his house the best that is in him, tells nothing but the truth about his goods, never oversells, and can go over his territory again and again, gathering an increasing host of friends for himself and his concern on each trip. He is a "repeater."

Above all, no one should sell a proposition that is not strictly honest in every particular. The demand for able salesmen to sell honest propositions so far exceeds the supply that there is no reason for a man's soiling his hands with a dishonest business. A man cannot sell a proposition in which he does not believe and at the same time respect himself and hold the esteem of his fellow men. Furthermore, dishonest success must always be counted a failure. A salesman's honor is his best selling asset.

Confidence   A salesman should have confidence in himself, in his house and in his proposition. Before a sale can be made, the prospect must be imbued with confidence in all three. To inspire that confidence in others the salesman must first possess it himself. His success will be in direct proportion to his estimate of his own ability, his belief in the firm that he represents, and his faith in his goods.

A man who makes a conscientious study of his own physical, moral and mental characteristics, with a firm determination to correct his faults and to increase his efficiency, and who is at all successful in carrying out that determination, acquires a justifiable confidence in himself that will enable him to take up any proposition with reasonable assurance of his ability to carry it thru to success.

Careful distinction should be made, however, between confidence and conceit. Conceit is rooted in ignorance and a misapprehension of facts. Conceit thinks it can, but it really cannot. Confidence is intelligent faith based on facts. Confidence believes it can and the results demonstrate the truth of that belief. There is little hope for the salesman who does not believe in himself. The salesman who is easily discouraged when he is turned aside will never win. Half the strength of the giant is in the conviction that he is a giant.

Confidence in the proposition is not an easy thing to maintain. The salesman usually starts out with absolute confidence in his line as his principal selling asset. But soon, perhaps, a glance into a competitor's sample room reveals virtues in the competing line that he does not see in his own; a few buyers inform him of the superiority and lower prices of still other lines—and before long we find him writing in to the house about the shortcomings of his line and the superiority of those whose competition he has to fight. Or, if he is a specialty salesman, a few of his prospects begin to ridicule the idea that his proposition is a necessity for them, and his confidence begins to weaken—ever so little at first, but eventually sufficiently to make him despondent and send him out half-whipped every day. . . .

Confidence in the house that employs him is an immensely valuable asset to the salesman—confidence in his firm's financial condition, in its ability to keep its promises, in the character and the ideals of the men at the head, and in its desire to deal honestly with everybody. Thoro[ugh] confidence increases the salesman's respect and liking for his employer, promotes his general satisfaction and contentment, gives him assurance of solid backing, and adds dignity to his work. Furthermore, if he realizes that his firm is composed of men who have put out his line and put their money and reputations behind it, he will realize, despite the opposing claims of other lines, that his goods are right.

Enthusiasm   Enthusiasm is confidence in action; all great achievements in the world's history have been due to enthusiasm and without it little of importance has been accomplished. In the salesman it is the white heat that fuses all the other essential qualities into one effective whole. Enthusiasm needs only direction to turn it into success; and no matter how big the setback may have been, any ground can be regained if enthusiasm is not lost. Enthusiasm is the life of the interview. The salesman who is truly enthusiastic talks as if he meant what he said because he does mean every word. He is working for the love of the game. He would rather be selling those goods than doing anything else. He is fired with an intense desire to impart his ardor to others. Enthusiasm makes a salesman "talk shop" whenever there is the slightest chance of effecting a sale. It enables him to forget disappointments and failures and to start afresh with renewed determination to succeed. . . .

Loyalty   Closely associated with honesty, confidence and enthusiasm is a fourth requisite of good salesmanship, a higher product, which develops when men are associated in groups. This essential is loyalty. The salesman should be loyal to both his house and his customers; as he stands between the two, he should look after the best interests of both. Loyalty involves something more than this, however.

A certain concern which is today firmly and successfully established had to ask its salesmen, during the early days of its existence, to be satisfied with little or no compensation for a period of almost six months. In other words, it asked them to stay on the firing line selling goods, and practically support themselves without the company's aid. Eighty per cent of the men stayed and worked without any loss of confidence or enthusiasm even under these conditions. That was an example of loyalty at its best. The twenty per cent who quit were doubtless honest and probably had confidence in the goods and were enthusiastic, but their loyalty was not equal to the severe test to which it was put. It would seem, then, that there is something which distinguishes loyalty from the other essential qualities. Loyalty begets loyalty, and the salesman who is loyal to his house and to his customers will find that they are also loyal to him.

Optimism   There are two kinds of optimists—the man who absolutely refuses to recognize that anything is wrong in the world; and the man who recognizes that lots of things are wrong, but who has a cheerful faith that they will be made right and that he can be a power toward that end. The first, ostrich-like, hides his head from surrounding dangers and tries to believe they do not exist—he is a false optimist. The second is a true optimist.

Lack of ambition, indifference, laziness and satisfaction with ease and quiet are not optimism. To sit still and be content to see other men forge ahead—that is false optimism. To recognize that effort alone can bring improvement, that progress is attained only thru struggle, and to throw oneself into the struggle, and to glory in it—that is real optimism. . . .

Voice   If the salesman has a strident voice and a harsh manner the prospect will probably be prejudiced against him, while a man of fine sensibilities will certainly be repelled. A clear, full, soothing voice will do much to predispose the prospect in favor of the salesman. No man who must speak a great deal should neglect the cultivation of his voice. He should be particularly careful to keep it, if possible, in a pleasantly low range.

There are many methods for training and cultivating the voice. One that is known to produce satisfactory results is to read poems aloud. Another is to take lessons from a vocal instructor. The salesman should be particularly careful to cultivate a sympathetic tone of voice. . . .

Appearance   It goes without saying that a salesman should always be well dressed and well groomed. Slovenliness prejudices a prospect against him and his proposition. His clothing should be fresh pressed and his linen spotless. His shoes should be of the best, with straight heels, and should be kept well shined. The salesman must be careful of his teeth, his hair and his finger nails, and he should never appear before a prospect with a day's growth of beard on his face.

The keynote of the salesman's dress should be unobtrusiveness. Any exaggeration in his costume is detrimental to his obtaining the best results. Just as the finest French plate-glass is the kind that is entirely unobtrusive to the eye, so the best dressed man is he whose apparel attracts no attention to itself.

Personality   Personality is that indefinable something which makes the presence of one man welcome and the presence of another unwelcome. Combined with sympathy, and the ability to see the other fellow's point of view, it is the prime factor in the quick creation of confidence. Personality is that quality which definitely characterizes a person and distinguishes him from another, not by his nature, or by the way his features are molded, but by his expression, his manner and his actions. Personality includes poise, that elusive characteristic which is more than mere calm or assurance, and which enables its possessor to appear to advantage, and to be at ease under any circumstances.

Personality, as such, cannot be acquired apart from those elements of which it is composed. Personality is the sum total of one's mentality, education, habits of thought and experience. . . .

QUESTIONS ON JONES

1. In the first paragraph, Jones writes that "the only real way to get in to see a man . . . is to look and act like the kind of man who ought to be allowed to come in." What does Jones mean by this claim? What sort of person "ought to be allowed . . . in"? Do the qualities discussed by Jones support this claim?

2. Which of the qualities elucidated by Jones are *intrinsically good* qualities? And which are *instrumental* qualities, relevant to successful selling in a commercial society? Are all of these qualities traits of moral character?

3. Consider the account of honesty. How does Jones show that the trait of honesty extends beyond honesty of word alone? Do you think it is dishonest to spend one's "spare time in such a manner as to give his house below-par service?" Why or why not?

A Moral Evaluation of Sales Practices

David M. Holley

David M. Holley is Professor of Philosophy at the University of Southern Mississippi. The author of essays in the philosophy of religion and in applied ethics, Holley has also written Self-Interest and Beyond *(1999).*

. . . In this paper I will attempt to develop a framework for evaluating the morality of various sales practices. Although I recognize that much of the sales force in companies is occupied exclusively or primarily with sales to other businesses, my discussion will focus on sales to the individual consumer. Most of what I say should apply to any type of sales activity, but the moral issues arise most clearly in cases where a consumer may or may not be very sophisticated in evaluating and responding to a sales presentation. My approach will be to consider first the context of sales activities, a market system of production and distribution. Since such a system is generally justified on teleological grounds, I describe several conditions for its successful achievement of key goals. Immoral sales practices are analyzed as attempts to undermine these conditions.

I

The primary justification for a market system is that it provides an efficient procedure for meeting people's needs and desires for goods and services.[1] This appeal to economic benefits can be elaborated in great detail, but at root it involves the claim that people will efficiently serve each other's needs if they are allowed to engage in voluntary exchanges. Because individuals have different resources or may organize to produce desired goods and services, they may through exchange achieve mutually beneficial results. At the simplest

level, suppose one person has a product, say a television set, but would rather have five hundred dollars. Another has five hundred dollars but would rather have the television set. By making the exchange, both achieve a desired goal.

A crucial feature of this argument is the condition that exchange be voluntary. Assuming that individuals know best how to benefit themselves and that they will act to achieve such benefits, voluntary exchange can be expected to serve both parties. On the other hand, if the exchanges are not made voluntarily, we have no basis for expecting mutually beneficial results. To the extent that mutual benefit does not occur, the system will lack efficiency as a means for the satisfaction of needs and desires. Hence, this justification presupposes that conditions necessary for the occurrence of voluntary exchange are ordinarily met. What are these conditions? For simplicity's sake, let us deal only with the kind of exchange involving a payment of money for some product or service. We can call the one providing the product the seller and the one making the money payment the buyer. I would suggest that voluntary exchange occurs only if the following conditions are met:

1. Both buyer and seller understand what they are giving up and what they are receiving in return.

2. Neither buyer nor seller is compelled to enter into the exchange as a result of coercion, severely restricted alternatives, or other constraints on the ability to choose.

3. Both buyer and seller are able at the time of exchange to make a rational judgement about its costs and benefits.

I will refer to these three conditions as the knowledge, non-compulsion, and rationality conditions, respectively.[2] . . .

. . . If the parties are uninformed, it is possible that an exchange might accidentally turn out to benefit them. But given the lack of information, they would not be in a position to make a rational judgment about their benefit, and we cannot reasonably expect beneficial results as a matter of course in such circumstances. Similarly, if the exchange is made under compulsion, then the judgment of personal benefit is not the basis of the exchange. It is possible for someone to be forced or manipulated into an arrangement which is in fact beneficial. But there is little reason to think that typical or likely.[3]

It should be clear that all three conditions are subject to degrees of fulfillment. For example, the parties may understand certain things about the exchange, but not others. Let us posit a theoretical situation in which both parties are fully informed, fully rational, and enter into the exchange entirely of their own volition. I will call this an *ideal exchange.* In actual practice there is virtually always some divergence from the ideal. Knowledge can be more or less adequate. Individuals can be subject to various irrational influences. There can be borderline cases of external constraints. Nevertheless, we can often judge when a particular exchange was adequately informed, rational, and free from compulsion. Even when conditions are not ideal, we may still have an *acceptable exchange.*

With these concepts in mind, let us consider the obligations of sales personnel. I would suggest that the primary duty of salespeople to customers is not to undermine the conditions of acceptable exchange. It is possible by act or omission to create a situation in which the customer is not sufficiently knowledgeable about what the exchange involves. It is also possible to influence the customer in ways which short-circuit the rational decision-making process. To behave in such ways is to undermine the conditions which are presupposed in teleological justifications of the market system. Of course, an isolated act is not sufficient to destroy the benefits of the system. But the moral acceptability of the system may become questionable if the conditions of acceptable exchange are widely abused. The individual who attempts to gain personally by undermining these conditions does that which, if commonly practiced, would produce a very different system from the one which supposedly provides moral legitimacy to that individual's activities. . . .

II

If a mutually beneficial exchange is to be expected, the parties involved must be adequately informed about what they are giving up and what they are receiving. In most cases this should create no great problem for the seller,[4] but what about the buyer? How is she to obtain the information needed? One answer is that the buyer is responsible for doing whatever investigation is necessary to acquire the information. The medieval principle of *caveat emptor* encouraged buyers to take responsibility for examining a purchase thoroughly to determine whether it had any hidden flaws. If the buyer failed to find defects, that meant that due caution had not been exercised.

If it were always relatively easy to discover defects by examination, then this principle might be an efficient method of guaranteeing mutual satisfaction. Sometimes, however, even lengthy investigation does not disclose what the buyer wants to know. With products of great complexity, the expertise needed for an adequate examination may be beyond what could reasonably be expected of most consumers. Even relatively simple products can have hidden flaws which most people would not discover until after the purchase, and the responsibility for closely examining every purchase would involve a considerable amount of a highly treasured modern commodity, the buyer's time. Furthermore, many exchange situations in our context involve products that cannot be examined in this way—goods that will be delivered at a later time or sent through the mail, for example. Finally, even if we assume that most buyers, by exercising enough caution, can protect their interests, the system of caveat emptor would take advantage of those least able to watch out for themselves. It would in effect justify mistreatment of a few for a rather questionable benefit.

In practice, the buyer almost always relies on the seller for some information, and if mutually beneficial exchanges are to be expected, the information needs to meet certain standards of both quality and quantity. With regard to quality, the information provided should not be deceptive. This would include not only direct lies, but truths which are intended to mislead the buyer. Consider the following:

1.1 An aluminum siding salesperson tells customers that they will receive "bargain factory prices" for letting their homes be used as models in a new advertising campaign. Prospective customers will be brought to view the houses and a commission of $100 will be paid for each sale that results. In fact the price paid is well above market rates, the workmanship and materials are substandard, and no one is ever brought by to see the houses.[5]

1.2 A used car salesperson turns back the odometer reading on automobiles by an average of 25,000 to 30,000 miles per car. If customers ask whether the reading is correct, the salesperson replies that it is illegal to alter odometer readings.

1.3 A salesperson at a piano store tells an interested customer that the "special sale" will only be good through this evening. She neglects to mention that another "special sale" will begin the next day.

1.4 A telephone salesperson tells people who answer the phone that they have been selected to receive a free gift, a brand new freezer. All they have to do is buy a year's subscription to a food plan.

1.5 A salesperson for a diet system proclaims that under this revolutionary new plan the pounds will melt right off. The system is described as a scientific advance that makes dieting easy. In fact, the system is a low-calorie diet composed of foods and liquids that are packaged under the company name, but are no different from standard grocery store items.

The possibilities are endless, and whether or not a lie is involved, each illustrates an attempt to get a customer to believe something which is false in order to make the sale. It might be pointed out that these kinds of practices would not deceive a sophisticated consumer. Perhaps so, but whether they are always successful deceptions is not the issue. They are attempts to mislead the customer, and given that the customer must often rely on information which is furnished by the salesperson attempts to use misinformation as a basis for customer judgment rather than allowing that judgment to be based on accurate beliefs. Furthermore, if these kinds of practices were not successful fairly often, they would probably not be used.

In the aluminum siding case, the customer is led to believe that there will be a discount in exchange for a kind of service, allowing the house to be viewed by prospective customers. This leaves the impression both that the job will be of high quality and that the price paid will be offset by commissions. The car salesperson alters the product in order to suggest false information about the extent of its use. With such information, the customer is not able to judge accurately the value of the car. The misleading reply to inquiries is not substantially different from a direct lie. The piano salesperson deceives the customer about how long the product will be obtainable at a discount price. In this way, the nature of the exchange is obscured.

The diet system case raises questions about how to distinguish legitimate "puffery" from deception. Obviously, the matter will depend to some extent on how gullible we conceive the customer to be. As described, the case surely involves an attempt to get the customer to believe that dieting will be easier under this system and that what is being promoted is the result of some new scientific discovery. If there were no prospect that a customer would be likely to believe this, we would probably not think the technique deceptive. But in fact a number of individuals are deceived by claims of this type.

Some writers have defended the use of deceptive practices in business contexts on the grounds that there are specific rules applying to these contexts which differ from the standards appropriate in other contexts. It is argued, for example, that deception is standard practice, understood by all participants as something to be expected and, therefore, harmless, or that it is a means of self-defense justified by pressures of the competitive context.[6] To the extent that claims about widespread practice are true, people who know what is going on may be able to minimize personal losses, but that is hardly a justification of the practice. If I know that many people have installed devices in their cars which can come out and puncture the tires of the car next to them, that may help to keep me from falling victim, but it does not make the practice harmless. Even if no one is victimized, it becomes necessary to take extra precautions, introducing a significant disutility into driving conditions. Analogously, widespread deception in business debases the currency of language, making business communication less efficient and more cumbersome.

More importantly, however, people are victimized by deceptive practices, and the fact that some may be shrewd enough to see through clouds of misinformation does not alter the deceptive intent. Whatever may be said with regard to appropriate behavior among people who "know the rules," it is clear that many buyers are not aware of having entered into some special domain where deception is allowed. Even if this is naive, it does not provide a moral justification for subverting those individuals' capacity for making a reasoned choice.

Only a few people would defend the moral justifiability of deceptive sales practices. However, there may be room for much more disagreement with regard to how much information a salesperson is obligated to provide. In rejecting the principle of *caveat emptor,* I have suggested that there are pragmatic reasons for expecting the seller to communicate some information about the product. But how much? When is it morally culpable to withhold information? Consider the following cases:

2.1 An auto dealer has bought a number of cars from another state. Although they appear to be new or slightly used, these cars have been involved in a major flood and were sold by the previous dealer at a discount rate. The salesperson knows the history of the cars and does not mention it to the customers.

2.2 A salesperson for an encyclopedia company never mentions the total price of a set unless he has to. Instead he emphasizes the low monthly payment involved.

2.3 A real estate agent knows that one reason the couple owning a house listed by her company would like to move is that the neighbors are fond of loud parties, and neighborhood children have committed minor acts of vandalism. She makes no mention of this to prospective customers.

2.4 An admissions office for a private college speaks enthusiastically about the advantages of the school. No mention is made of the fact that the school is not accredited.

2.5 A prospective retirement home resident is under the impression that a particular retirement home is affiliated with a certain church. He makes it known that this is one of the features he finds attractive about the home. Though the belief is false, the recruiters make no attempt to correct the misunderstanding.

In all of these cases the prospective buyer lacks some piece of knowledge which might be relevant to the decision to buy. The conditions for ideal exchange are not met. Perhaps, however, there can be an acceptable exchange. Whether or not this is the case depends on whether the buyer has adequate information to decide if the purchase would be beneficial. In the case of the flood-damaged auto, there is information which is relevant to evaluating the worth of the car which the customer could not be expected to know unless informed by the seller. If this information is not revealed, the buyer would not have adequate knowledge to make a reasonable judgment. To determine exactly how much information needs to be provided is not always clear cut. We must in general rely on our assessments of what a reasonable person would want to know. As a practical guide, a salesperson might consider, "what would I want to know if I were considering buying this product?"

Surely a reasonable person would want to know the total price of a product. Hence, the encyclopedia salesperson who omits this data is not providing adequate information. The salesperson may object that this information could be inferred from other information about the monthly payment, length of term, and interest rate. But if the intention is not to have the customer act without knowing the full price, then why shouldn't it be provided directly? The admissions officer's failure to mention that the school was unaccredited also seems unacceptable when we consider what a reasonable person would want to know. There are some people who would consider it a plus since they are suspicious about accrediting agencies

imposing some alien standards (e.g., standards which conflict with religious views). But regardless of how one evaluates the fact, most people would judge it to be important for making a decision.

The real estate case is more puzzling. Most real estate agents would not reveal the kind of information described, and would not feel they had violated any moral duties in failing to reveal it. Clearly, many prospective customers would want to be informed about such problems. However, in most cases failing to know these facts would not be of crucial importance. We have a case of borderline information. It would be known by all parties to an ideal exchange, but we can have an acceptable exchange even if the buyer is unaware of it. Failure to inform the customer of these facts is not like failing to inform the customer that the house is on the sight of a hazardous waste dump or that a major freeway will soon be adjacent to the property.

It is possible to alter the case in such a way that the information should be revealed or at least the buyer should be redirected. Suppose the buyer makes it clear that his primary goal is to live in a quiet neighborhood where he will be undisturbed. The "borderline" information now becomes more central to the customer's decision. Notice that thinking in these terms moves us away from the general standard of what a reasonable person would want to know to the more specific standard of what is relevant, given the criteria of this individual. In most cases, however, I think that a salesperson would be justified in operating under general "reasonable person" standards until particular deviations become important.[7]

The case of the prospective retirement home resident is a good example of how the particular criteria of the customer might assume great importance. If the recruiters, knowing what they know about this man's religious preferences, allow him to make his decision on the basis of a false assumption, they will have failed to support the conditions of acceptable exchange. It doesn't really matter that the misunderstanding was not caused by the salespeople. Their allowing it to be part of the basis for a decision borders on deception. If the misunderstanding was not on a matter of central importance to the individual's evaluation, they might have had no obligation to correct it. But the case described is not of that sort.

Besides providing non-deceptive and relatively complete information, salespeople may be obligated to make sure that their communications are understandable. Sales presentations containing technical information which is likely to be misunderstood are morally questionable. However, it would be unrealistic to expect all presentations to be immune to misunderstanding. The salesperson is probably justified in developing presentations that would be intelligible to the average consumer of the product he or she is selling, and making adjustments in cases where it is clear that misunderstanding has occurred.

III

The condition of uncompelled exchange distinguishes business dealings from other kinds of exchanges. . . .

In the standard business arrangement, neither party is forced to enter negotiations. A threat of harm would transform the situation to something other than a purely business arrangement. Coercion is not the only kind of compulsion, however. Suppose that there is only one producer of food to which I have access. I arrange to buy food from this producer, but given my great need for food and the absence of alternatives, the seller is able to dictate the terms. In one sense I choose to make the deal, but the voluntariness of my choice is limited by the absence of alternatives. . . .

Ordinarily, the individual salesperson will not have the power to take away the buyer's alternatives. However, a clever salesperson can sometimes make it seem as if options are very limited, and can use the customer's ignorance to produce the same effect. For example, imagine an individual who begins to look for a particular item at a local store. The salesperson extolls the line carried by his store, warns of the deficiencies of alternative brands, and warns about the dishonesty of competitors in contrast to his store's reliability. With a convincing presentation, a customer might easily perceive the options to be very limited. Whether or not the technique is questionable may depend upon the accuracy of the perception. If the salesperson is attempting to take away a legitimate alternative, that is an attempt to undermine the customer's voluntary choice.

Another way the condition of uncompelled choice might be subverted is by involving a customer in a purchase without allowing her to notice what is happening. This would include opening techniques that disguise the purpose of the encounter so there can be no immediate refusal. The customer is led to believe that the interview is about a contest or a survey or an opportunity to make money. Not until the end does it become apparent that this is an attempt to sell something, and occasionally if the presentation is

smooth enough, some buyers can be virtually unaware that they have bought anything. Obviously, there can be degrees of revelation, and not every approach which involves initial disguise of certain elements which might provoke an immediate rejection is morally questionable. But there are enough clear cases in which the intention is to get around, as much as possible, the voluntary choice of the customer. Consider the following examples:

> 3.1 A seller of children's books gains entrance to houses by claiming to be conducting an educational survey. He does indeed ask several "survey" questions, but uses these to qualify potential customers for his product.

> 3.2 A salesperson alludes to recent accidents involving explosions of furnaces and, leaving the impression of having some official government status, offers to do a free safety inspection. She almost always discovers a "major problem" and offers to sell a replacement furnace.

> 3.3 A man receives a number of unsolicited books and magazines through the mail. Then he is sent a bill and later letters warning damage to his credit rating if he does not pay.

These are examples of the many variations on attempts to involve customers in exchanges without letting them know what is happening. The first two cases involve deceptions about the purpose of the encounter. Though they resemble cases discussed earlier which involved deception about the nature or price of a product, here the salesperson uses misinformation as a means of limiting the customer's range of choice. The customer does not consciously choose to listen to a sales presentation, but finds that this is what is happening. Some psychological research suggests that when people do something which appears to commit them to a course of action, even without consciously choosing to do so, they will tend to act as if such a choice had been made in order to minimize cognitive dissonance. Hence, if a salesperson successfully involves the customer in considering a purchase, the customer may feel committed to give serious thought to the matter. The third case is an attempt to get the customer to believe that an obligation has been incurred. In variations on this technique, merchandise is mailed to a deceased person to make relatives believe that some payment is owed. In each case, an effort is made to force the consumer to choose from an excessively limited range of options.

IV

. . . How can a salesperson subvert the rationality condition? Perhaps the most common way is to appeal to emotional reactions which cloud an individual's perception of relevant considerations. Consider the following cases:

4.1 A man's wife has recently died in a tragic accident. The funeral director plays upon the man's love for his wife and to some extent his guilt about her death to get him to purchase a very expensive funeral.

4.2 A socially insecure young woman has bought a series of dance lessons from a local studio. During the lessons, an attractive male instructor constantly compliments her on her poise and natural ability, and tries to persuade her to sign up for more lessons.[8]

4.3 A life insurance salesperson emphasizes to a prospect the importance of providing for his family in the event of his death. The salesperson tells several stories about people who put off this kind of preparation.

4.4 A dress salesperson typically remarks to customers about how fashionable they look in a certain dress. Her stock comments also include pointing out that a dress is slimming or sexy or "looks great on you."

4.5 A furniture salesperson regularly tells customers that a piece of furniture is the last one in stock and that another customer recently showed great interest in it. He sometimes adds that it may not be possible to get any more like it from the factory.

These cases remind us that emotions can be important motivators. It is not surprising that salespeople appeal to them in attempting to get the customer to make a purchase. In certain cases the appeal seems perfectly legitimate. When the life insurance salesperson tries to arouse the customer's fear and urges preparation, it may be a legitimate way to get the customer to consider something which is worth considering. Of course, the fact that the fear is aroused by one who sells life insurance may obscure to the customer the range of alternative possibilities in preparing financially for the future. But the fact that an emotion is aroused need not make the appeal morally objectionable.

If the appeal of the dress salesperson seems more questionable, this is probably because we are not as convinced of the objective importance of appearing fashionable, or perhaps because repeated observations of this kind are often insincere. But if we assume that the salesperson is giving an honest opinion about how the dress looks on a customer, it may provide some input for the individual who has a desire to achieve a particular effect. The fact that such remarks appeal to one's vanity or ambition does not in itself make the appeal unacceptable.

The furniture salesperson's warnings are clearly calculated to create some anxiety about the prospect of losing the chance to buy a particular item unless immediate action is taken. If the warnings are factually based, they would not be irrelevant to the decision to buy. Clearly, one might act impulsively or hastily when under the spell of such thoughts, but the salesperson cannot be faulted for pointing out relevant considerations.

The case of the funeral director is somewhat different. Here there is a real question of what benefit is to be gained by choosing a more expensive funeral package. For most people, minimizing what is spent on the funeral would be a rational choice, but at a time of emotional vulnerability it can be made to look as if this means depriving the loved one or the family of some great benefit. Even if the funeral director makes nothing but true statements, they can be put into a form designed to arouse emotions which will lessen the possibility of a rational decision being reached.

The dance studio case is similar in that a weakness is being played upon. The woman's insecurity makes her vulnerable to flattery and attention, and this creates the kind of situation where others can take advantage of her. Perhaps the dance lessons fulfill some need, but the appeal to her vanity easily becomes a tool to manipulate her into doing what the instructor wants.[9]

The key to distinguishing between legitimate and illegitimate emotional appeals lies in whether the appeal clouds one's ability to make a decision based on genuine satisfaction of needs and desires. Our judgment about whether this happens in a particular case will depend in part on whether we think the purchase likely to benefit the customer. The more questionable the benefits, the more an emotional appeal looks like manipulation rather than persuasion. When questionable benefits are combined with some special vulnerability on the part of the consumer, the use of the emotional appeal appears even more suspect. . . .

V

I have attempted to provide a framework for evaluating the morality of a number of different types of sales practices. The framework is based upon conditions for mutually beneficial exchange and ultimately for an efficient satisfaction of economic needs and desires. An inevitable question is whether this kind of evaluation is of any practical importance. . . .

. . . If we set before ourselves the ideal of a knowledgeable, unforced, and rational decision on the part of a customer, it is not difficult to see how some types of practices would interfere with this process. We must, of course, be careful not to set the standards too high. A customer may be partially but adequately informed to judge a purchase's potential benefits. A decision may be affected by nonrational and even irrational factors and yet still be rational enough in terms of being plausibly related to the individual's desires and needs. There may be borderline cases in which it is not clear whether acting in a particular way would be morally required or simply overscrupulous, but that is not an objection to this approach, only a recognition of a feature of morality itself. . . .

People in business who support the market system and benefit from it have a responsibility for minimizing abuses which undermine the system's moral legitimacy. To argue that the realities of the marketplace are such that we must inevitably expect violations of moral norms is in effect to give an argument against the market system. Whether the argument would be strong enough to call for replacement of the system depends on the merits of the alternatives. In any event, those who have a stake in the market system have an interest in protecting it against abuses.

ENDNOTES

1. The classic statement of the argument from economic benefits is found in Adam Smith, *The Wealth of Nations* (1776) (London: Methuen and Co. Ltd., 1930). Modern proponents of this argument include Ludwig von Mises, Friedrich Hayek, and Milton Friedman. Sometimes arguments for economic benefits are mixed with arguments appealing to the desirability of maximizing freedom. The appeal to freedom is occasionally made using the language of rights. Though I do not explore the matter here, I believe that justifications of market activity other than the one I mention also presuppose what I call conditions of voluntary exchange. The primary reason for wanting to maximize freedom or to give it the status of a right is to enable individuals to exercise some control over their destiny. Hence, economic freedom would be desirable only in so far as it was consistent with the ability of the parties involved to make voluntary choices.

2. One very clear analysis of voluntariness making use of these conditions may be found in John Hosper's *Human Conduct: Problems of Ethics,* 2nd ed. (New York: Harcourt Brace Jovanovich, Inc., 1982), pp. 385–388. Alan Gewirth gives an account of voluntary action which excludes direct compulsion, internal causes (including ignorance) which "decisively contribute" to the behavior beyond the individual's control, and indirect compulsion (coercion). He understands voluntariness to include the ability to control behavior by "unforced and informed choice." Though he does not explicitly state a rationality condition, he implies one when he says, "When there is such control, the person chooses on the basis of informed reasons he has for acting as he does. Among other things, he knows what action he is performing, for what purpose, its proximate outcome, and his recipients . . . informed reasons are coherently interrelated with other desires and choices." *Reason and Morality* (Chicago: The University of Chicago Press, 1978), p. 31.

3. I will refer to the three conditions indifferently as conditions for voluntary exchange or conditions for mutually beneficial exchange. By the latter designation I do not mean to suggest that they are either necessary or sufficient conditions for the occurrence of mutual benefit, but that they are conditions for the reasonable expectation of mutual benefit.

4. There are cases, however, in which the buyer knows more about a product than the seller. For example, suppose Cornell has found out that land Fredonia owns contains minerals which make it twice as valuable as Fredonia thinks. The symmetry of my conditions would lead me to conclude that Cornell should give Fredonia the relevant information unless perhaps Fredonia's failure to know was the result of some culpable negligence.

5. This case is described in Warren Magnuson and Jean Carper, *The Dark Side of the Marketplace* (Englewood Cliffs, N.J.: Prentice Hall, 1968), pp. 3–4.

6. Albert Carr, "Is Business Bluffing Ethical?" *Harvard Business Review* 46 (January–February, 1968), pp. 143–53. See also Thomas L. Carson, Richard E. Wokutch, and Kent F. Murrmann, "Bluffing in Labor Negotiations: Legal and Ethical Issues," *Journal of Business Ethics* 1 (1982), pp. 13–22.

7. My reference to a reasonable person standard should not be confused with the issue facing the FTC of whether to evaluate advertising by the reasonable consumer or ignorant consumer standard as described in Ivan Preston, "Reasonable Consumer or Ignorant Consumer: How the FTC Decides," in Tom Beauchamp and Norman Bowie, *Ethical Theory and Business,* 2nd ed. (Englewood Cliffs, N.J.: Prentice Hall, 1983), pp. 348–357. There the primary issue deals with whom the government should protect from claims which might be misunderstood. My concern here is with determining what amount of information is necessary for informed judgment. In general, I suggest

that a salesperson should begin with the assumption that information a reasonable consumer would regard as important needs to be revealed and that when special interests and concerns of the consumer come to light those concerns may make further revelations necessary. This approach parallels the one taken by Tom Beauchamp and James Childress regarding the information that a physician needs to provide to obtain informed consent. See their *Principles of Biomedical Ethics*, 2nd ed. (New York: Oxford University Press, 1983), pp. 74–79.

8. This is adapted from a court case quoted in David Braybrooke, *Ethics in the World of Business* (Totona, N.J.: Rowman and Allenheld, 1983), pp. 68 ff.

9. One reader commented on this example that ". . . the woman's insecurity in the dance studio scenario is very real to her, and if dance lessons help ameliorate it, the benefits could be substantial; even if false compliments are given." While not denying the potential importance of psychological benefits, I want to claim that the situation described is one where the capacity to make a rational judgment about benefit might be undermined. In the court case from which the example is adapted, a woman spent over thirty thousand dollars in a sixteen month period for dance lessons.

QUESTIONS ON HOLLEY

1. Holley suggests that a practical guide for the salesperson is to consider the question "what would I want to know if I were considering buying this product?" Is this a good practical guide? Or does this demand too much of the salesperson?

2. Think about the case (2.1) of the auto that had been in the flood. Suppose that the flood had done no damage to the car but that mentioning the matter might give customers an unwarranted negative impression. Should it be mentioned?

3. Consider the case (2.2) of the encyclopedia salesperson. Is this a matter of withholding information, or is it a case of emphasizing certain features more than others? Is there a relevant difference?

———————

Advertising

Israel Kirzner

Israel Kirzner is Professor of Economics at New York University. A preeminent economist of the "Austrian School," Kirzner is the author of numerous articles and essays on markets, competition, and entrepreneurship, *including* Competition and Entrepreneurship *(1973),* Perception, Opportunity and Profit *(1979),* Discovery and the Capitalist Process *(1985),* Discovery, Capitalism, and Distributive Justice *(1989), and* Essays on Capital and Interest *(1996), among other works. This essay originally appeared in* The Freeman.

Advertising has been badly treated by many scholars who should know better. Not only Marxists and liberals, but even conservatives have given advertising a bad press. Let us examine some of the criticisms.

First, many advertising messages are said to be offensive—by esthetic or ethical and moral standards. Unfettered, unhampered, laissez-faire capitalism, it is contended, would propagate such messages in a way that could very well demoralize and offend the tastes and morals of members of society.

Second, advertising, it is argued, is deceitful, fraudulent, full of lies. Misinformation is spread by advertising, in print, on the airwaves, and this does harm to the members of society; for that reason advertising should be controlled, limited, taxed away.

Third, it is argued that where advertising is not deceitful, it is at best persuasive. That is, it attempts to change people's tastes. It attempts not to fulfill the desires of man but to change his desires to fit that which has been produced. The claim of the market economist has always been that the free market generates the flow of production along the lines that satisfy consumer tastes; their tastes determine what shall be produced—briefly, consumer sovereignty. On the contrary, the critics of advertising argue, capitalism has developed into a system where producers produce and then mold men's minds to buy that which has been produced. Rather than production being governed by consumer sovereignty, quite the reverse: the consumer is governed by producer sovereignty.

A fourth criticism has been that advertising propagates monopoly and is antithetical to competition. In a competitive economy, it is pointed out, there would be no advertising; each seller would sell as much as he would like to sell without having to convince consumers to buy that which they would not otherwise have bought. So, advertising is made possible by imperfections in the market. More seriously, it is contended, advertising leads toward monopoly by building up a wall of good will, a protective wall of loyalty among consumers which renders a particular product immune to outside competition. Competing products, which do not share in the fruits of the advertising campaign, find themselves on the outside. This barrier to entry may gradually lead a particular producer to control a share of the market which is rendered invulnerable to the winds of outside competition.

Finally—and this in a way sums up all of these criticisms—advertising is condemned as wasteful. The consumer pays a price for a product which covers a very large sum of money spent on advertising. Advertising does not change the commodity that has been purchased; it could have been produced and sold at a much lower price without the advertising. In other words, resources are being used and paid for by the consumer without his receiving anything that he could not have received in their absence. . . .

THE FREE ECONOMY AND HOW IT FUNCTIONS

. . . Let me imagine a world, a free market, in which there are no deceitful men at all. All the messages beamed to consumers and prospective consumers would be, as far as the advertisers themselves believe, the strict truth. We will consider later the implications of the fact that men are imperfect and that men succumb to the temptation in selling something to say a little bit less, a little bit more, than the exact truth. In the meantime, let us talk about a world of honest men, men who do not try to deceive.

Further, let us imagine a pure market economy with government intervention kept to the absolute minimum—the night watchman role. The government stands to the sidelines and ensures the protection of private property rights, the enforcement of contracts freely entered into. Everyone then proceeds to play the game of the free market economy with producers producing that which they believe can be sold to the consumers at the highest possible money price. Entrepreneur producers, who detect where resources are currently being used in less than optimum fashion, take these resources and transfer them to other uses in the economy where they will serve consumer wants which the entrepreneurs believe are more urgently desired, as measured by the amounts of money consumers are willing to pay for various products.

We will assume that there is freedom of entry into all industries. No entrepreneur has sole control over any resource that is uniquely necessary for the production of a given product. No government licenses are required in order to enter into the practice of a given profession or to introduce a particular product. All entrepreneurs are free to produce what they believe to be profitable. All resource owners are free to sell their resources, whether labor, natural resources, capital goods. They are free to sell or rent these resources to the highest bidder. In this way the agitation of the market gradually shuffles resources around until they begin to be used to produce those products which consumers value most highly. Consumers arrange their spending to buy the commodities they believe to be most urgently needed by themselves. And the market flows on in the way that we understand it.

OPEN COMPETITION

We say this is a free market, a laissez-faire, competitive system. But we do not mean a *perfectly* competitive market, as this notion has been developed by the neoclassical economists. In a perfectly competitive market, each seller faces a demand curve which is perfectly horizontal. That is to say, each seller believes that he can sell as much as he would like to sell without having to lower the price. Each buyer faces a perfectly horizontal supply curve and each buyer believes that he can buy as much as he would like to buy of anything without having to offer a higher price. In such a world of "perfect competition," we have what we call an "equilibrium" situation, that is a situation where all things have already been fully adjusted to one another. All activities, all decisions have been fully coordinated by the market so that there are no disappointments. No participant in the economy discovers that he could have done something better. No participant in the economy discovers that he has made plans to do something which it turns out he cannot do.

In this model of the perfectly competitive economy, there would in fact be *no* competition in the sense in which the layman, or the businessman, understands the term. The term "competition" to the businessman, the layman, means an activity designed to outstrip one's competitors, a rivalrous activity designed to get ahead of one's colleagues, or those with whom one is competing. In a world of equilibrium, a world of "perfect competition," there would be no room for further rivalry. There would be no reason to attempt to do something better than is currently being done. There would, in fact, be no competition in the everyday sense of the term.

When we describe the laissez-faire economy as competitive, we mean something quite different. We mean an economy in which there is complete freedom of entry: if anyone believes that he can produce something that can serve consumers' wants more faithfully, he can try to do it. If anyone believes that the current producers are producing at a price which is too high, then he is free to try to produce and sell at a lower price. This is what competition means. It does not mean that the market has already attained the "equilibrium" situation, which goes under the very embarrassing technical name of "perfectly competitive economy."

NON-PRICE COMPETITION

Now, economists and others understand generally that competition means price competition: offering to sell at a lower price than your competitors are asking, or offering to buy at a higher price than your competitors are bidding. Entrepreneurs will offer higher prices than others are offering for scarce labor. They will offer to sell a product at lower prices than the competing store is asking. This is what price competition means. This is the most obvious form in which competition manifests itself.

However, we must remember that there is another kind of competition, sometimes called "nonprice competition," sometimes called "quality competition." Competition takes the form not only of producing the identical product which your competitors are producing and selling it at a lower price, not only in buying the identical resource which your competitors are buying and offering a higher price. Competition means sometimes offering a better product, or perhaps an inferior product, a product which is more in line with what the entrepreneur believes consumers are in fact desirous of purchasing. It means producing a different model of a product, a different quality, putting it in a different package, selling it in a store with a different kind of lighting, selling it along with an offer of free parking, selling through salesmen who smile more genuinely, more sincerely. It means competing in many, many ways besides the pure price which is asked of the consumer in monetary terms.

With freedom of entry, every entrepreneur is free to choose the exact package, the exact opportunity which he will lay before the public. Each opportunity, each package has many dimensions. He can choose the specifications for his package by changing many, many of these variables. The precise opportunity that he will lay before the public will be that which, in his opinion, is more urgently desired by the consumer as compared with that which happens to be produced by others. So long as there's freedom of entry, the fact that my product is different from his does not mean that I am a monopolist. . . .

Professor [Edward H.] Chamberlin popularized a distinction which was not original with him but which owes its present widely circulated popularity primarily to his work. That is a distinction between "production costs" and "selling costs." In his book of almost forty years ago, *The Theory of Monopolistic Competition,* Chamberlin argued that there are two kinds of costs which manufacturers, producers, sellers, suppliers incur. First, they incur the fabrication costs, the costs of producing what it is they want to sell. Second, they incur additional expenditures that do not produce the product or change it or improve it, but merely get it sold. Advertising, of course, is the most

obvious example which Chamberlin cited. But "selling costs" of all kinds were considered by him to be sharply different from "production costs." In his original formulation, Chamberlin argued that "production costs" are costs incurred to produce the product for a given Demand Curve while "selling costs" simply shift the Demand Curve over to the right. That is to say, the same product is now purchased in greater quantities at a given price but the product is the same.

A FALSE DISTINCTION

The fallacy in the distinction between production costs and selling costs is fairly easy to notice. In fact, it is impossible for the outside observer—except as he resorts to arbitrary judgments of value—to distinguish between expenditures which do, and expenditures which do not, alter the product. We know as economists that a product is not an objective quantity of steel or paper. A product is that which is perceived, understood, desired by a consumer. If there are two products otherwise similar to the outside eye which happen to be considered to be different products by the consumer, then to the economist these *are* different products.

Ludwig von Mises gives the example, which cannot be improved upon, of eating in a restaurant. A man has a choice of two restaurants, serving identical meals, identical food. But in one restaurant they haven't swept the floor for six weeks. The meals are the same. The food is the same. How shall we describe the money spent by the other restaurant in sweeping the floor? "Production costs" or "selling costs?" Does sweeping change the food? No. Surely, then, it could be argued that this is strictly a "selling cost." It is like advertising. The food remains the same; but, because you have a man sweeping out the floor, more people come to this restaurant than to that. But this is nonsense. What you buy when you enter a restaurant is not the food alone. What you buy is a meal, served in certain surroundings. If the surroundings are more desirable, it's a different meal, it's a different package. That which has been spent to change the package is as much production cost as the salary paid to the cook; no difference.

Another example that I recall was the case of the coal being run out of Newcastle and traveling along the railroad toward London. Every mile that coal travels nearer the London drawing room, the Demand Curve shifts over to the right. How shall we describe that transportation cost? "Production cost" or "selling cost?" Of course, it's "production cost." In fact, it's "selling cost" too. All "production costs" are "selling costs." All costs of production are incurred in order to produce something which will be more desirable than the raw materials. . . .

Clearly then, the distinction between a so-called "selling cost" and "production cost" is quite arbitrary. It depends entirely on the value judgments of the outside observer. The outside observer can say that this particular selling effort does not change the product, but in that situation he is arrogating to himself the prerogative of pronouncing what is and what is not a product. That is something which violates our fundamental notions of individual consumer freedom: that a consumer's needs are defined by no one else other than himself. This may seem quite a detour from advertising and yet it is all relevant to the question of what role advertising has to play.

THE PROVISION OF INFORMATION

Let us consider how some of these notions apply to the matter of information. One of the standard defenses for advertising is that it provides a service which consumers value: the provision of knowledge, the provision of information. People buy books. People go to college. People enroll in all kinds of courses. Advertising is simply another way of providing information. To be sure, it would seem that the information provided by suppliers comes from a tainted source, but don't forget that we are imagining for the meantime a world without deceitful people.

We can even relax that assumption for a moment. It may be cheaper for the consumer to get his information from the supplier or the producer than from an outside source. In other words, if you, a consumer, have the choice of acquiring information about a particular product—either more cheaply from the producer or more expensively from an outside, "objective" source—you may decide that, on balance, you're likely to get a better deal, penny-for-penny, information-wise, by reading the information of the producer, scanning it perhaps with some skepticism, but nonetheless relying on that rather than buying it from an outside source. Technically, this involves what is known as the problem of transactions costs. It may be more economical for the information to be packaged together with the product, or at least to be produced jointly with the product, than to have the information produced and communicated by an outside source. This is a possibility not to be ignored.

Advertising provides information, and this goes a long way to explain the role which advertising and other kinds of selling efforts must play. Does this not seem to contradict the point just made, that there is no distinction between "production costs" and "selling costs"? Surely, information about a product is distinct from the product. Surely the costs incurred to provide information are a different kind of costs than the costs incurred

to produce the product. The answer is clearly, no. Information is produced; it is desired; it is a product; it is purchased jointly with the product itself; it is a part of the package; and it is something which consumers value. Its provision is not something performed on the outside that makes people consume something which they would not have consumed before. It is something for which people are willing to pay; it is a service.

You can distinguish different parts of a service. You can distinguish between four wheels and a car. But the four wheels are complementary commodities. That is to say, the usefulness of the one is virtually nil without the availability of the other. The car and gasoline are two separate products, to be sure, and yet they are purchased jointly, perhaps from different producers, different suppliers, but they are nonetheless parts of a total package, a total product. If it happens that the information is produced and sold jointly with the product itself, then we have no reason to question the characteristics of the costs of providing information as true "production costs," not producing necessarily the physical commodity about which information is produced, but producing information which is independently desired by consumers, independently but jointly demanded, complementarily used together with the "product" itself. In other words, the service of providing information is the service of providing something which is needed just as importantly as the "product" itself.

WHY THE SHOUTING?

There is another aspect of advertising which is often overlooked. Information is exceedingly important. But, surely, it is argued, information can be provided without the characteristics of advertising that we know, without the color, without the emotion, without the offensive aspects of advertising. Surely information can be provided in simple straight-forward terms. The address of this and this store is this and this place. These and these qualities of commodities are available at these and these prices. Why do illustrated advertising messages have to be projected? Why do all kinds of obviously uninformative matter have to be introduced into advertising messages? This is what renders the information aspects of advertising so suspect. The Marxists simply laugh it away. They say it is ridiculous to contend that advertising provides any kind of genuine information. If one rests the defense of advertising on its informative role, then one has a lot of explaining to do. One has to explain why information that could be provided in clear cut straightforward terms is provided in such garish and loud forms, in the way that we know it.

The answer, I think, is that advertising does much more than provide information which the consumer wishes to have. This is something which is often overlooked, even by economists. Supposing I set up a gas station. I buy gasoline and I have it poured into my cellar, my tanks. I have a pump carefully hidden behind some bushes, and cars that come down the road can buy gas if they know that I'm here. But I don't go to the effort to let them know I'm here. I don't put out a sign. Well, gas without information is like a car without gas. Information is a service required complementarily with the gas.

CUSTOMERS WANT TO KNOW WHERE TO FIND THE PRODUCT

Supposing, then, I take a piece of paper, type very neatly in capital letters, "GAS," and stick it on my door. Cars speed down the road in need of gas, but they don't stop to read my sign. What is missing here? Information is missing. Don't people want information? Yes. They would like to know where the gas station is, but it's a well kept secret. Now, people *are* looking for that information. It's my task as an entrepreneur not only to have gas available but to have it in a form which is known to consumers. It is my task to supply gas-which-is-known-about, not to provide gas *and* information.

I have not only to produce opportunities which are available to consumers; I have to make consumers aware of these opportunities. This is a point which is often overlooked. An opportunity which is not known, an opportunity to which a consumer is not fully awakened, is simply not an opportunity. I am not fulfilling my entrepreneurial task unless I project to the consumer the awareness of the opportunity. How do I do that? I do that, not with a little sign on my door, but with a big neon sign, saying GAS; and better than that I chalk up the price; and better than that I make sure that the price is lower than the price at nearby stations; and I do all the other things that are necessary to *make* the consumer *fully* aware of the opportunity that I am in fact prepared to put before him. In other words, the final package consists not only of abstract academic information but in having the final product placed in front of the consumer in such a form that he cannot miss it. . . .

THE GROWTH OF ADVERTISING

Advertising has grown. Compare the volume of advertising today with the volume of 100 years ago and it has grown tremendously. More! Consider the price of a commodity that you buy in a drug store or in a supermarket. Find out what portion of that price can be attributed to advertising costs and it turns out that a much larger percentage of the final cost to the consumer can be attributed to advertising today than could have been attributed 50 years ago, 70 years ago, 100 years ago. Why is this? Why has advertising expenditure grown in proportion to total value of output? Why has advertising expenditure grown in proportion to the price of a finished commodity? Why has advertising apparently grown more offensive, more loud, more shrill? It's fairly easy to understand.

I give, as example, the lobby walls of a college building that I know very well. At one time this was a handsome lobby with walls of thick marble; you could walk from one end of the building to the other and the walls would be clear. Some years ago an enterprising entrepreneur decided to use some free advertising space. He pasted up a sign. It was the only sign on the wall; everybody looked at it, saw the message. I don't remember what the message was or whether it was torn down, but I do remember that soon afterward those walls were full of signs. As you walked down the passage, you could read all kinds of messages, all kinds of student activities, non-student activities. It was fairly easy to learn about what was going on simply by reading the signs.

At first, the signs did not have to be big. But as advertisers saw the opportunity, the free space gradually filled up. The Ricardian rent theory came into play; all the free land was in use. And as the free land or space was taken, of course, it became more and more important to get up early to paste up your sign. That was the "rent," the high price, getting up early. But more than that, it became necessary now to arouse all kinds of interest in me in order to get me to read these signs. In other words, the variety and multiplicity of messages make it harder and harder to get a hearing.

THE PRICE OF AFFLUENCE

We live in a world which is often described as an "affluent society." An affluent society is one in which there are many, many opportunities placed before consumers. The consumer enters a supermarket and if he is to make a sensible, intelligent decision he is going to have to spend several hours calculating very carefully, reading, rereading everything that's on the packages and doing a complete research job before feeding all the information into the computer and waiting for the optimum package to be read off. It's a tough job to be a consumer. And the multiplicity of opportunities makes it necessary for advertisers, for producers, to project more and more provocative messages if they want to be heard. This is a cost of affluence. It is a cost, certainly; something that we'd much rather do without, if we could; but we can't.

The number of commodities that have been produced is so great that in order for any one particular product to be brought to the attention of the consumer a large volume of advertising is necessary. And we can expect to get more and more. Is it part of production costs? Very definitely, yes. It is completely arbitrary for anyone to argue that, whether or not the consumer knows it, the commodity is there anyway, so that when he pays the price which includes the advertising communication he is paying *more* than is necessary for the opportunity made available. For an opportunity to be made available, it must be in a form which it is impossible to miss. And this is what advertising is all about.

One more word about the offensiveness of advertising. Ultimately in a free market, consumers tend to get what they want. The kinds of products produced will reflect the desires of the consumer. A society which wants moral objects will get moral objects. A society which wants immoral objects will tend to get immoral objects. Advertised communication is part of the total package produced and made available to consumers. The kind of advertising we get, sad to say, is what we deserve. The kind of advertising we get reflects the kind of people that we are. No doubt, a different kind of advertising would be better, more moral, more ethical in many respects; but I'm afraid we have no one to blame but ourselves, as in all cases where one deplores that which is produced by a market society.

A final word about deceit. Of course, deceitful advertising is to be condemned on both moral and economic grounds. But we have to put it in perspective. Let me read from one very eminent economist who writes as follows:

> The formation of wants is a complex process. No doubt wants are modified by Madison Avenue. They are modified by Washington, by the university faculties and by churches. And it is not at all clear that Madison Avenue has the advantage when it comes to false claims and exaggerations.[1]

TAKE WITH A GRAIN OF SALT

In other words, we live in a world where you have to be careful what you read, to whom you listen, whom to believe. And it's true of everything, every aspect of life. If one were to believe everything projected at him, he would be in a sorry state.

It is very easy to pick out the wrong messages to believe. Now, this doesn't in any way condone or justify deceitful messages of any kind. We have to recognize, however, while particular producers may have a short-run interest in projecting a message to consumers of doubtful veracity, that so long as there's freedom of competition the consumer has his choice not only of which product to buy but who to believe. And notice what is the alternative in this world of imperfect human beings. The alternative, of course, is government control—still by imperfect human beings. So there is no way to render oneself invulnerable to the possibility of false, fraudulent, deceitful messages.

It would be nice to live in a world where no deceitful men were present. It would be cheaper. You could believe any message received. You wouldn't have to check out the credentials of every advertiser. But this is not the world in which we live. You check out the credit standing of individuals, the character of people with whom you deal; and this is an unavoidable, necessary cost. To blame advertising for the imperfections and weaknesses of mankind is unfair. Advertising would exist under any type of free market system. Advertising would be less deceitful if men were less deceitful. It would be more ethical, less offensive, if men were less offensive and more ethical. But advertising itself is an intergral, inescapable aspect of the market economy.

ENDNOTE

1. H. Demsetz, "The Technostructure, Forty-Six Years Later." (*Yale Law Journal,* 1968), p. 810.

QUESTIONS ON KIRZNER

1. How does Kirzner's idea of a pure market economy differ from the model of the perfectly competitive economy? Why does he state that the model of perfect competition is actually a model in which there would be *no* competition?

2. How does Kirzner seek to rebut the distinction between production costs and selling costs? How does this rebuttal rely on the idea of "subjectivity"? How does this rebuttal support his case for advertising?

3. Why is advertising often loud, garish, or overstated? Do you think that advertising reflects consumer desires? In what sense might this be true? In what sense might it be false?

4. Kirzner develops his explanation against a background of a free and competitive market. Does his account provide any reasons against the regulation of advertising?

Advertising and Behavior Control

Robert L. Arrington

Robert L. Arrington is Professor of Philosophy and Director of Wittgenstein Studies at Georgia State University. His books include Rationalism, Realism, and Relativism *(1989),* Western Ethics *(1997), as well as edited works and numerous essays.*

Consider the following advertisements:

1. "A woman in *Distinction Foundations* is so beautiful that all other women want to kill her."

2. Pongo Peach color for Revlon comes "from east of the sun . . . west of the moon where each tomorrow dawns." It is "succulent on your lips" and "sizzling on your finger tips (and on your toes goodness knows.)" Let it be your "adventure in paradise."

3. "Musk by English Leather—The Civilized Way to Roar."

4. "Increase the value of your holdings. Old Charter Bourbon Whiskey—The Final Step Up."

5. Last Call Smirnoff Style: "They'd never really miss us, and it's kind of late already, and it's quite a long way, and I could build a fire, and you're looking very beautiful, and we could have another martini, and it's awfully nice just being home . . . you think?"

6. A Christmas Prayer. "Let us pray that the blessing of peace be ours—the peace to build and grow, to live in harmony and sympathy with others, and to plan for the future with confidence." New York Life Insurance Company.

These are instances of what is called puffery—the practice by a seller of making exaggerated, highly fanciful or suggestive claims about a product or service. Puffery, within ill-defined limits, is legal. It is considered a legitimate, necessary, and very successful tool of the advertising industry. Puffery is not just bragging; it is bragging carefully designed to achieve a very definite effect. Using the techniques of so-called motivational research, advertising firms first identify our often hidden needs (for security, conformity, oral stimulation) and our desires (for power, sexual dominance and dalliance, adventure) and then they design ads which respond to these needs and desires. By associating a product, for which we may have little or no direct need or desire, with symbols reflecting the fulfillment of these other, often subterranean interests, the advertisement can quickly generate large numbers of consumers eager to purchase the product advertised. What woman in the sexual race of life could resist a foundation which would turn other women envious to the point of homicide? Who can turn down an adventure in paradise, east of the sun where tomorrow dawns? Who doesn't want to be civilized and thoroughly libidinous at the same time? Be at the pinnacle of success—drink Old Charter. Or stay at home and dally a bit—with Smirnoff. And let us pray for a secure and predictable future, provided for by New York Life, God willing. It doesn't take very much motivational research to see the point of these sales pitches. Others are perhaps a little less obvious. The need to feel secure in one's home at night can be used to sell window air conditioners, which drown out small noises and provide a friendly, dependable companion. The fact that baking a cake is symbolic of giving birth to a baby used to prompt advertisements for cake mixes which glamorized the "creative" housewife. And other strategies, for example involving cigar symbolism, are a bit too crude to mention, but are nevertheless very effective.

Don't such uses of puffery amount to manipulation, exploitation, or downright control? In his very popular book *The Hidden Persuaders,* Vance Packard points out that a number of people in the advertising world have frankly admitted as much:

> As early as 1941 Dr. Dichter (an influential advertising consultant) was exhorting ad agencies to recognize themselves for what they actually were—"one of the most advanced laboratories in psychology." He said the successful ad agency "manipulates human motivations and desires and develops a need for goods with which the public has at one time been unfamiliar—perhaps even undesirous of purchasing." The following year *Advertising Agency* carried an ad man's statement that psychology not only holds promise for understanding people but "ultimately for controlling their behavior."[1]

Such statements lead Packard to remark: "With all this interest in manipulating the customer's subconscious, the old slogan 'let the buyer beware' began taking on a new and more profound meaning."[2] . . .

A look at some other advertising techniques may reinforce the suspicion that Madison Avenue controls us like so many puppets. T.V. watchers surely have noticed that some of the more repugnant ads are shown over and over again, *ad nauseum*. My favorite, or most hated, is the one about A-1 Steak Sauce which goes something like this: Now, ladies and gentlemen, what is hamburger? It has succeeded in destroying my taste for hamburger, but it has surely drilled the name of A-1 Sauce into my head. And that is the point of it. Its very repetitiousness has generated what ad theorists call *information*. In this case it is indirect information, information derived not from the content of what is said but from the fact that it is said so often and so vividly that it sticks in one's mind—i.e., the information yield has increased.

And not only do I always remember A-1 Sauce when I go to the grocers, I tend to assume that any product advertised so often has to be good—and so I usually buy a bottle of the stuff.

Still another technique: On a recent show of the television program "Hard Choices" it was demonstrated how subliminal suggestion can be used to control customers. In a New Orleans department store, messages to the effect that shoplifting is wrong, illegal, and subject to punishment were blended into the Muzak background music and masked so as not to be consciously audible. The store reported a dramatic drop in shoplifting. The program host conjectured whether a logical extension of this technique would be to broadcast subliminal advertising messages to the effect that the store's $15.99 sweater special is the "bargain of a lifetime." Actually, this application of subliminal suggestion to advertising has already taken place. Years ago in New Jersey a cinema was reported to have flashed subthreshold ice cream ads onto the screen during regular showings of the film—and yes, the concession stand did a landslide business.[3]

Puffery, indirect information transfer, subliminal advertising—are these techniques of manipulation and control whose success shows that many of us have forfeited our autonomy and become a community, or herd, of packaged souls?[4] The business world and the advertising industry certainly reject this interpretation of their efforts. *Business Week,* for example, dismissed the charge that the science of behavior, as utilized by advertising, is engaged in human engineering and manipulation. It editorialized to the effect that "it is hard to find anything very sinister about a science whose principle conclusion is that you get along with people by giving them what they want."[5] The theme is familiar: businesses just give the consumer what he/she wants; if they didn't they wouldn't stay in business very long. Proof that the consumer wants the products advertised is given by the fact that he buys them, and indeed often returns to buy them again and again.

The techniques of advertising we are discussing have had their more intellectual defenders as well. For example, Theodore Levitt, Professor of Business Administration at the Harvard Business School, has defended the practice of puffery and the use of techniques depending on motivational research.[6] What would be the consequences, he asks us, of deleting all exaggerated claims and fanciful associations from advertisements? We would be left with literal descriptions of the empirical characteristics of products and their functions. Cosmetics would be presented as facial and bodily lotions—and powders which produce certain odor and color changes; they

would no longer offer hope or adventure. In addition to the fact that these products would not then sell as well, they would not, according to Levitt, please us as much either. For it is hope and adventure we want when we buy them. We want automobiles not just for transportation, but the feelings of power and status they give us. . . .

Phillip Nelson, a Professor of Economics at SUNY–Binghamton, has developed an interesting defense of indirect information advertising.[7] He argues that even when the message (the direct information) is not credible, the fact that the brand is advertised, and advertised frequently, is valuable indirect information for the consumer. The reason for this is that the brands advertised most are more likely to be better buys—losers won't be advertised a lot, for it simply wouldn't pay to do so. Thus even if the advertising claims made for a widely advertised product are empty, the consumer reaps the benefit of the indirect information which shows the product to be a good buy. . . .

I don't know of any attempt to defend the use of subliminal suggestion in advertising, but I can imagine one form such an attempt might take. Advertising information, even if perceived below the level of conscious awareness, must appeal to some desire on the part of the audience if it is to trigger a purchasing response. Just as the admonition not to shoplift speaks directly to the superego, the sexual virtues of TR-7's, Pongo Peach, and Betty Crocker cake mix present themselves directly to the id, by-passing the pesky reality principle of the ego. With a little help from our advertising friends, we may remove a few of the discontents of civilization and perhaps even enter into the paradise of polymorphous perversity.[8]

The defense of advertising which suggests that advertising simply is information which allows us to purchase what we want, has in turn been challenged. Does business, largely through its advertising efforts, really make available to the consumer what he/she desires and demands? John Kenneth Galbraith has denied that the matter is as straightforward as this.[9] In his opinion the desires to which business is supposed to respond, far from being original to the consumer, are often themselves created by business. The producers make both the product and the desire for it, and the "central function" of advertising is "to create desires." Galbraith coins the term "The Dependence Effect" to designate the way wants depend on the same process by which they are satisfied. . . .

The central issue which emerges between the above critics and defenders of advertising is this: do the advertising techniques we have discussed involve a violation of human autonomy and a manipulation and control of consumer behavior, *or* do they simply provide an efficient and cost-effective means of giving the consumer information on the basis of which he or she makes a free choice. Is advertising information, or creation of desire?

To answer this question we need a better conceptual grasp of what is involved in the notion of autonomy. This is a complex, multifaceted concept, and we need to approach it through the more determinate notions of (a) autonomous desire, (b) rational desire and choice, (c) free choice, and (d) control or manipulation. In what follows I shall offer some tentative and very incomplete analyses of these concepts and apply the results to the case of advertising.

(a) Autonomous Desire   Imagine that I am watching T.V. and see an ad for Grecian Formula 16. The thought occurs to me that if I purchase some and apply it to my beard, I will soon look younger—in fact I might even be myself again. Suddenly want to be myself! I want to be young again! So I rush out and buy a bottle. This is our question: was the desire to be younger manufactured by the commercial, or was it "original to me" and truly mine? Was it autonomous or not?

F. A. von Hayek has argued plausibly that we should not equate nonautonomous desires, desires which are not original to me or truly mine, with those which are culturally induced.[10] If we did equate the two, he points out, then the desires for music, art, and knowledge could not properly be attributed to a person as original to him, for these are surely induced culturally. The only desires a person would really have as his own in this case would be the purely physical ones for food, shelter, sex, etc. But if we reject the equation of the nonautonomous and the culturally induced, as von Hayek would have us do, then the mere fact that my desire to be young again is caused by the T.V. commercial—surely an instrument of popular culture transmission—does not in and of itself show that this is not my own, autonomous desire. Moreover, even if I never before felt the need to look young, it doesn't follow that this new desire is any less mine. I haven't always liked 1969 Aloxe Corton Burgundy or the music of Satie, but when the desires for these things first hit me, they were truly mine.

This shows that there is something wrong in setting up the issue over advertising and behavior control as a question whether our desires are truly ours *or* are created in us by advertisements. Induced and autonomous desires do not separate into two mutually exclusive classes. To obtain a better understanding of autonomous and nonautonomous desires, let us consider some cases of a desire which a person does not *acknowledge* to be his own even though he *feels* it. The kleptomaniac has a desire to steal which in many instances he repudiates, seeking by treatment to rid himself of it. And if I were suddenly overtaken by a desire to attend an REO concert, I would immediately disown this desire, claiming possession or momentary madness. These are examples of desires which one might have but with which one would not identify. They are experienced as foreign to one's character or personality. Often a person will have what Harry Frankfurt calls a second-order desire, that is to say, a desire *not* to have another desire.[11] In such cases, the first-order desire is thought of as being nonautonomous, imposed on one. When on the contrary a person has a second-order desire to maintain and fulfill a first-order desire, then the first-order desire is truly his own, autonomous, original to him. So there is in fact a distinction between desires which are the agent's own and those which are not, but this is not the same as the distinction between desires which are innate to the agent and those which are externally induced.

If we apply the autonomous/nonautonomous distinction derived from Frankfurt to the desires brought about by advertising, does this show that advertising is responsible for creating desires which are not truly the agent's own? Not necessarily, and indeed not often. There may be some desires I feel which I have picked up from advertising and which I disown—for instance, my desire for A-1 Steak Sauce. If I act on these desires it can be said that I have been led by advertising to act in a way foreign to my nature. In these cases my autonomy has been violated. But most of the desires induced by advertising I fully accept, and hence most of these desires are autonomous. The most vivid demonstration of this is that I often return to purchase the same product over and over again, without regret or remorse. And when I don't, it is more likely that the desire has just faded than that I have repudiated it. Hence, while advertising may violate my autonomy by leading me to act on desires which are not truly mine, this seems to be the exceptional case.

Note that this conclusion applies equally well to the case of subliminal advertising. This may generate subconscious desires which lead to purchases, and the act of purchasing these goods may be inconsistent with other conscious desires I have, in which case I might repudiate my behavior and by implication the subconscious cause of it. But my subconscious desires may not be inconsistent in this way with my conscious ones; my id may be cooperative and benign rather than hostile and malign.[12] Here again, then, advertising may or may not produce desires which are "not truly mine.". . .

(b) Rational Desire and Choice . . . [A] possible criticism of advertising is that it leads us to act on irrational desires or to make irrational choices. It might be said that our autonomy has been violated by the fact that we are prevented from following our rational wills or that we have been denied the "positive freedom" to develop our true, rational selves. It might be claimed that the desires induced in us by advertising are false desires in that they do not reflect our essential, i.e., rational, essence.

The problem faced by this line of criticism is that of determining what is to count as rational desire or rational choice. If we require that the desire or choice be the product of an awareness of *all* the facts about the product, then surely every one of us is always moved by irrational desires and makes nothing but irrational choices. How could we know all the facts about a product? If it be required only that we possess all of the *available* knowledge about the product advertised, then we still have to face the problem that not all available knowledge is *relevant* to a rational choice. If I am purchasing a car, certain engineering features will be, and others won't be, relevant, *given what I want in a car.* My prior desires determine the relevance of information. Normally a rational desire or choice is thought to be one based upon relevant information, and information is relevant if it shows how other, prior desires may be satisfied. It can plausibly be claimed that it is such prior desires that advertising agencies acknowledge, and that the agencies often provide the type of information that is relevant in light of these desires. To the extent that this is true, advertising does not inhibit our rational wills or our autonomy as rational creatures.

It may be urged that much of the puffery engaged in by advertising does not provide relevant information at all but rather makes claims which are not factually true. If someone buys Pongo Peach in anticipation of an adventure in paradise, or Old Charter in expectation of increasing the value of his holdings, then he/she is expecting purely imaginary benefits. In no literal sense will the one product provide adventure and the other increased capital. A purchasing decision based on anticipation of imaginary benefits is not, it might be said, a rational decision, and a desire for imaginary benefits is not a rational desire.

In rejoinder it needs to be pointed out that we often wish to purchase subjective effects which in being subjective are nevertheless real enough. The feeling of adventure or of enhanced social prestige and value are examples of subjective effects promised by advertising. Surely many (most?) advertisements directly promise subjective effects which their patrons actually desire (and obtain when they purchase the product), and thus the ads provide relevant information for rational choice. Moreover, advertisements often provide accurate indirect information on the basis of which a person who wants a certain subjective effect rationally chooses a product. The mechanism involved here is as follows.

To the extent that a consumer takes an advertised product to offer a subjective effect and the product does not, it is unlikely that it will be purchased again. If this happens in a number of cases, the product will be taken off the market. So here the market regulates itself, providing the mechanism whereby misleading advertisements are withdrawn and misled customers are no longer misled. At the same time, a successful bit of puffery, being one which leads to large and repeated sales, produces satisfied customers and more advertising of the product. The indirect information provided by such large-scale advertising efforts provides a measure of verification to the consumer who is looking for certain kinds of subjective effect. For example, if I want to feel well dressed and in fashion, and I consider buying an Izod Alligator shirt which is advertised in all of the magazines and newspapers, then the fact that other people buy it and that this leads to repeated advertisements shows me that the desired subjective effect is real enough and that I indeed will be well dressed and in fashion if I purchase the shirt. The indirect information may lead to a rational decision to purchase a product because the information testifies to the subjective effect that the product brings about.[13]

Some philosophers will be unhappy with the conclusion of this section, largely because they have a concept of true, rational, or ideal desire which is not the same as the one used here. A Marxist, for instance, may urge that any desire felt by alienated man in a capitalistic society is foreign to his true nature. Or an existentialist may claim that the desires of inauthentic men are themselves inauthentic. Such concepts are based upon general theories of human nature which are unsubstantiated and perhaps incapable of substantiation. Moreover, each of these theories is committed to a concept of an ideal desire which is normatively debatable and which is distinct from the ordinary concept of a rational desire as one based upon relevant information. But it is in the terms of the ordinary concept that we express our concern that advertising may limit our autonomy in the sense of leading us to act on irrational desires, and if we operate with this concept we are driven again to the conclusion that advertising may lead, but probably most often does not lead, to an infringement of autonomy.

(c) Free Choice   It might be said that some desires are so strong or so covert that a person cannot resist them, and that when he acts on such desires he is not acting freely or voluntarily but is rather the victim of irresistible impulse or an unconscious drive. Perhaps those who condemn advertising feel that it produces this kind of desire in us and consequently reduces our autonomy.

This raises a very difficult issue. How do we distinguish between an impulse we *do* not resist and one we *could* not resist, between freely giving in to a desire and succumbing to one? I have argued elsewhere that the way to get at this issue is in terms of the notion of acting for a reason.[14] A person acts or chooses freely if he does so for a reason, that is, if he can adduce considerations which justify in his mind the act in question. Many of our actions are in fact free because this condition frequently holds. Often, however, a person will act from habit, or whim, or impulse, and on these occasions he does not have a reason in mind. Nevertheless he often acts voluntarily in these instances, i.e., he could have acted otherwise. And this is because if there *had been* a reason for acting otherwise of which he was aware, he would in fact have done so. Thus acting from habit or impulse is not necessarily to act in an involuntary manner. If, however, a person is aware of a good reason to do *x* and still follows his impulse to do *y,* then he can be said to be impelled by irresistible impulse and hence to act involuntarily. Many kleptomaniacs can be said to act involuntarily, for in spite of their knowledge that they likely will be caught and their awareness that the goods they steal have little utilitarian value to them, they nevertheless steal. Here their "out of character" desires have the upper hand, and we have a case of compulsive behavior.

Applying these notions of voluntary and compulsive behavior to the case of behavior prompted by advertising, can we say that consumers influenced by advertising act compulsively? The unexciting answer is: sometimes they do, sometimes not. I may have an overwhelming, T.V. induced urge to own a Mazda Rx-7 and all the while realize that I can't afford one without severely reducing my family's caloric intake to a dangerous level. If, aware of this good reason not to purchase the car, I nevertheless do so, this shows that I have been the victim of T.V. compulsion. But if I have the urge, as

I assure you I do, and don't act on it, or if in some other possible world I could afford an Rx-7, then I have not been the subject of undue influence by Mazda advertising. Some Mazda Rx-7 purchasers act compulsively; others do not. The Mazda advertising effort *in general* cannot be condemned, then, for impairing its customers' autonomy in the sense of limiting free or voluntary choice. Of course the question remains what should be done about the fact that advertising may and does *occasionally* limit free choice. We shall return to this question later.

In the case of subliminal advertising we may find an individual whose subconscious desires are activated by advertising into doing something his calculating, reasoning ego does not approve. This would be a case of compulsion. But most of us have a benevolent subconsciousness which does not overwhelm our ego and its reasons for action. And therefore most of us can respond to subliminal advertising without thereby risking our autonomy. To be sure, if some advertising firm developed a subliminal technique which drove all of us to purchase Lear jets, thereby reducing our caloric intake to the zero point, then we would have a case of advertising which could properly be censured for infringing our right to autonomy. We should acknowledge that this is possible, but at the same time we should recognize that it is not an inherent result of subliminal advertising.

(d) Control or Manipulation   Briefly let us consider the matter of control and manipulation. Under what conditions do these activities occur? In a recent paper on "Forms and Limits of Control" I suggested the following criteria.[15]

A person *C* controls the behavior of another person *P* if

1. *C* intends *P* to act in a certain way *A;*

2. *C*'s intention is causally effective in bringing about *A;* and

3. *C* intends to ensure that all of the necessary conditions of *A* are satisfied.

These criteria may be elaborated as follows. To control another person it is not enough that one's actions produce certain behavior on the part of that person; additionally one must intend that this happen. Hence control is the intentional production of behavior. Moreover, it is not enough just to have the intention; the intention must give rise to the conditions which bring about the intended effect. Finally, the controller must intend to establish by his actions any otherwise unsatisfied necessary conditions for the production of the intended effect. The controller is not just influencing the outcome, not just having input; he is as it were guaranteeing that the sufficient conditions for the intended effect are satisfied.

Let us apply these criteria of control to the case of advertising and see what happens. Conditions (1) and (3) are crucial. Does the Mazda manufacturing company or its advertising agency intend that I buy an Rx-7? Do they intend that a certain number of people buy the car? *Prima facie* it seems more appropriate to say that they *hope* a certain number of people will buy it, and hoping and intending are not the same. But the difficult term here is "intend." Some philosophers have argued that to intend *A* it is necessary only to desire that *A* happen and to believe that it will. If this is correct, and if marketing analysis gives the Mazda agency a reasonable belief that a certain segment of the population will buy its product, then, assuming on its part the desire that this happen, we have the conditions necessary for saying that the agency intends that a certain segment purchase the car. If I am a member of this segment of the population, would it then follow that the agency intends that I purchase an Rx-7? Or is control referentially opaque? Obviously we have some questions here which need further exploration.

Let us turn to the third condition of control, the requirement that the controller intend to activate or bring about any otherwise unsatisfied necessary conditions for the production of the intended effect. It is in terms of this condition that we are able to distinguish brainwashing from liberal education. The brainwasher arranges all of the necessary conditions for belief. On the other hand, teachers (at least those of liberal persuasion) seek only to influence their students—to provide them with information and enlightenment which they may absorb *if they wish*. We do not normally think of teachers as controlling their students, for the students' performances depend as well on their own interests and inclinations.

Now the advertiser—does he control, or merely influence, his audience? Does he intend to ensure that all of the necessary conditions for purchasing behavior are met, or does he offer information and symbols which are intended to have an effect only *if* the potential purchaser has certain desires? Undeniably advertising induces some desires, and it does this intentionally; but more often than not it intends to induce a desire for a particular object, *given* that the purchaser already has other desires. Given a desire for youth, or power, or adventure, or ravishing beauty, we are led to desire Grecian Formula 16, Mazda Rx-7's, Pongo Peach, and Distinctive Foundations. In this light, the advertiser is influencing

us by appealing to independent desires we already have. He is not creating those basic desires. Hence it seems appropriate to deny that he intends to produce all of the necessary conditions for our purchases, and appropriate to deny that he controls us.[16]

Let me summarize my argument. The critics of advertising see it as having a pernicious effect on the autonomy of consumers, as controlling their lives and manufacturing their very souls. The defense claims that advertising only offers information and in effect allows industry to provide consumers with what they want. After developing some of the philosophical dimensions of this dispute, I have come down tentatively in favor of the advertisers. Advertising may, but certainly does not always or even frequently, control behavior, produce compulsive behavior, or create wants which are not rational or are not truly those of the consumer. Admittedly it may in individual cases do all of these things, but it is innocent of the charge of intrinsically or necessarily doing them or even, I think, of often doing so. This limited potentiality, to be sure, leads to the question whether advertising should be abolished or severely curtailed or regulated because of its potential to harm a few poor souls in the above ways. This is a very difficult question, and I do not pretend to have the answer. I only hope that the above discussion, in showing some of the kinds of harm that can be done by advertising and by indicating the likely limits of this harm, will put us in a better position to grapple with the question.

ENDNOTES

1. Vance Packard, *The Hidden Persuaders* (Pocket Books, New York, 1958), 20–21.

2. Ibid., 21.

3. For provocative discussions of subliminal advertising, see W. B. Key, *Subliminal Seduction* (The New American Library, New York, 1973), and W. B. Key, *Media Sexploitation* (Prentice-Hall, Inc., Englewood Cliffs, N.J., 1976).

4. I would like to emphasize that in what follows I am discussing these techniques of advertising from the standpoint of the issue of control and not from that of deception. For a good and recent discussion of the many dimensions of possible deception in advertising, see Alex C. Michalos, "Advertising: Its Logic, Ethics, and Economics" in J. A. Blair and R. H. Johnson (eds.), *Informal Logic: The First International Symposium* (Edgepress, Pt. Reyes, Calif., 1980).

5. Quoted by Packard, op. cit., 220.

6. Theodore Levitt, "The Morality (?) of Advertising," *Harvard Business Review* 48 (1970), 84–92.

7. Phillip Nelson, "Advertising and Ethics," in Richard T. De George and Joseph A. Pichler (eds.), *Ethics, Free Enterprise,*

and Public Policy (Oxford University Press, New York, 1978), 187–198.

8. For a discussion of polymorphous perversity, see Norman O. Brown, *Life Against Death* (Random House, New York, 1969), chapter III.

9. John Kenneth Galbraith, *The Affluent Society;* reprinted in Tom L. Beauchamp and Norman E. Bowie (eds.), *Ethical Theory and Business* (Prentice-Hall, Englewood Cliffs, 1979), 496–501.

10. F. A. von Hayek, "The *Non Sequitur* of the 'Dependence Effect,' " *Southern Economic Journal* (1961); reprinted in Beauchamp and Bowie (eds.), op. cit., 508–512.

11. Harry Frankfurt, "Freedom of the Will and the Concept of a Person," *Journal of Philosophy* LXVIII (1971), 5–20.

12. For a discussion of the difference between a malign and a benign subconscious mind, see P.H. Nowell-Smith, "Psychoanalysis and Moral Language," *The Rationalist Annual* (1954); reprinted in P. Edwards and A. Pap (eds.), *A Modern Introduction to Philosophy,* Revised Edition (The Free Press, New York, 1965), 86–93.

13. Michalos argues that in emphasizing a brand name—such as Bayer Aspirin—advertisers are illogically attempting to distinguish the indistinguishable by casting a trivial feature of a product as a significant one which separates it from other brands of the same product. The brand name is said to be trivial or unimportant "from the point of view of the effectiveness of the product or that for the sake of which the product is purchased" (op. cit., 107). This claim ignores the role of indirect information in advertising. For example, consumers want an aspirin *they can trust* (trustworthiness being part of "that for the sake of which the product is purchased"), and the indirect information conveyed by the widespread advertising effort for Bayer aspirin shows that this product is judged trustworthy by many other purchasers. Hence the emphasis on the name is not at all irrelevant but rather is a significant feature of the product from the consumer's standpoint, and attending to the name is not at all an illogical or irrational response on the part of the consumer.

14. Robert L. Arrington, "Practical Reason, Responsibility and the Psychopath," *Journal for the Theory of Social Behavior* 9 (1979), 71–89.

15. Robert L. Arrington, "Forms and Limits of Control," delivered at the annual meeting of the Southern Society for Philosophy and Psychology, Birmingham, Alabama, 1980.

16. Michalos distinguishes between appealing to people's tastes and molding those tastes (op. cit., 104), and he seems to agree with my claim that it is morally permissible for advertisers to persuade us to consume some article *if* it suits our tastes (105). However, he also implies that advertisers mold tastes as well as appeal to them. It is unclear what evidence is given for this claim, and it is unclear what is meant by *tastes*. If the latter are thought of as basic desires and wants, then I would agree that advertisers are controlling their customers to the extent that they intentionally mold tastes. But if by molding tastes is meant generating a desire for the particular object they promote, advertisers in doing so may well be appealing to more basic desires, in which case they should not be thought of as controlling the consumer.

QUESTIONS ON ARRINGTON

1. How does Arrington understand the idea of rational choice? Does this account address the question of whether a desire is irrational?

2. How is an autonomous desire to be distinguished from a nonautonomous desire? Is the case of the A1 Steak Sauce a convincing case of the violation of one's autonomy? Why should we assume that an individual accepts most of the desires induced by advertising?

3. Are there ways, not mentioned by Arrington, in which advertising might manipulate our desires or choices? Can you apply Arrington's analysis to political advertisements or speeches?

Integrity, Loyalty, and Whistleblowing

Nothing more completely baffles one who is full of trick and duplicity, than straightforward and simple integrity in another.

Charles Caleb Colton[14]

The verdict you pronounce upon the source of your livelihood is the verdict you pronounce upon your life. If the source is corrupt, you have damned your own existence. Did you get your money by fraud? By pandering to men's vices or men's stupidity? By catering to fools, in the hope of getting more than your ability deserves? By lowering your standards? By doing work you despise for purchasers you scorn? If so, then your money will not give you a moment's or a penny's worth of joy. Then all the things you buy will become, not a tribute to you, but a reproach; not an achievement, but a reminder of shame.

Ayn Rand[15]

It is easier for a man to be loyal to his club than to his planet; the by-laws are shorter, and he is personally acquainted with the other members.

E. B. White[16]

We often think of integrity in terms of honesty and keeping one's word. However, the very idea of moral character suggests a type of integrity that is broader and more basic. The virtues of a good person intimate a unified manner of living and a more or less unified set of ideals; such a unity can be sundered by any variety of wrong choices or bad habits, but a good person should want to keep this unity intact. The Latin term *integri* (as whole) captures this idea, and it is in the sense of an integrated whole that we will use the term "integrity" in this discussion. The idea of integrity, as Gabriele Taylor points out below, implies deep commitments, if not loyalties. However, it may nonetheless happen that one's integrity comes into conflict with one's loyalty to a business enterprise, an eventuality that often arises in cases of "whistleblowing."

Integrity in Business

How might integrity relate to business? Consider some of these examples. An executive has embarked on a bold

---

14. *Lacon: or, Many things in few words addressed to those who think* (New York: E. Bliss and E. White, 1822–23).

15. *Atlas Shrugged* (New York: New American Library, 1957), 389.

16. *One Man's Meat* (New York: Harper & Brothers, 1938) 277.

new advertising campaign, but after a few months he senses that the program may not be succeeding in winning new customers or maintaining the allegiance of old customers. Nonetheless this executive demands, at the risk of his own business reputation, that the evidence about the success of the strategy be presented honestly, fully, and without delay. In another instance, an accountant is asked by a client to adjust her audit so that shareholders will not so easily see how poor the financial condition of the company is. The accountant, however, remains true to her professional commitment and refuses to fiddle with the numbers. In yet other instances, a firm might refuse to trade with a corrupt government or a totalitarian regime. Or consider the fictional case of Alexander Powers,[17] a railway supervisor who has pledged to consider all of his actions in light of his Christian religious principles. Powers discovers that the company he works for is violating the Interstate Commerce Acts, and he believes not only that this is wrong but that if he reports these violations then he will be fired. However, Powers is committed to doing what is right and so he reports the violations to the authorities and resigns his position.

Integrity, Loyalty, and Human Relationships

Our interactions within society occur within numerous and varied networks of trust, devotion, and identification, just as our own conduct may occur with an eye toward a particular project or goal. We can conceive of integrity at least *in part* in terms of holding to our commitments, some of which may be to ideals, others of which may be to persons, institutions, or organizations. Commitment to a certain person, ideal, or institution may be understood in terms of loyalty. Josiah Royce refers to loyalty as "the willing and practical and thoroughgoing devotion of a person to a cause,"[18] that extends beyond the self; on the other hand, we often think of loyalty as an interpersonal relation by which one individual is devoted to another.

It is not just any sort of relation that creates the conditions for loyalty. The philosopher John Ladd contends that loyalty can arise only if persons are members of a specific group, with a common background and interests, and if these persons have differentiated roles within this group.[19] These conditions would most certainly allow for

loyalty within a family, or within a religious or political community (or organization). Indeed, these conditions seem to allow for loyalty to operate within commercial firms and businesses. However, some ethicists, such as Ronald Duska (see the following reading), suggest that there are conditions for loyalty distinct from those just noted, and that these preclude loyalty from having any place within the organizations and firms that operate within the market.

An Economic Argument

Indeed, one might argue that in either professional or commercial interaction, one is to seek the best price for the relevant quality of item or service and that one is, therefore, to shift one's custom, from one trader to another, in the quickest and most efficient manner. It is, on this account, the very fact that individuals respond to price signals rather than to their affections, sentiments, or loyalities that generates the efficiency of markets. Thus, the extent to which one remains loyal to a firm, colleague, or product raises the psychological costs of leaving and is, therefore, inefficient.

What this sort of explanation fails to take into account, however, is that loyalty itself may enter into one's calculation of the value of goods, services, or labor. For example, consider two employees who work at company C, the first of whom feels a special loyalty to the firm, the second of whom does not. Each of these employees is equally productive and equally desirable to another company, D, that wishes to hire one or both of them. Assume that the only relevant difference between these two employees lies in the loyalty felt by the first employee. If company D wishes to hire the first employee, it will have to offer more than if it wishes to hire the second employee, for if an employee feels loyalty to a firm, then that employee may be less reluctant to move to another firm for the same salary as another employee who feels no loyalty. However, what must be underscored here is that the first employee is not acting in any inefficient manner, for this employee simply places a higher value on working at C than does the second employee. The value that the first employee feels is manifested in that employee's loyalty.

Whistleblowing and Loyalty

Loyalty is not an unalloyed good, for one may devote oneself to a bad cause, person, or institution, or one's devotion may become unthinking and blind.

> Blind adherence to any object of loyalty—whether friend, lover, or nation—converts loyalty into idolatry.

---

17. This is one of the cases developed by Charles Sheldon in *In His Steps* [1935] (New York: Grosset and Dunlap, 1966). See, in particular, chapters 5 and 8.

18. *The Philosophy of Loyalty* (New York: MacMillan, 1915), 17.

19. "Loyalty," *Encyclopedia of Philosophy,* vol. 5 (New York: MacMillan, 1967), 97.

There is a moral danger in thinking that any concrete person or entity could become the ultimate source of right and wrong, but the moral danger is no greater in the case of patriotism than it is in friendship, erotic or filial love, or political commitment.[20]

The employee who does feel loyalty to a company (institution or organization) may find his loyalty tested if he discovers that the company is engaged in unlawful or immoral behavior or manufacturing, for example, producing, or selling some good that contains an otherwise unknown risk or health hazard. In these instances, an employee may not only have to reconsider his loyalty to the company but do so in light of his own integrity, specifically the sort of commitments to the welfare of others (or to moral principles) which, in light of a rational accounting of the evidence, force the employee to reach a decision that may test not only his integrity but his courage and judgment. If the employee cannot find redress within the company, then, it may be argued, the employee may "blow the whistle" so as to call attention to the specific risk or harm that threatens the welfare of others, providing thereby a probable means of preventing that harm. Thus the whistleblower is not someone who anonymously leaks information but one who places himself at risk (of dismissal, public scorn, or resentment) in order to alert the public to some specific harm or danger.

Conditions for Whistleblowing

One risk of encouraging whistleblowing is that such encouragement may also embolden the surly or disgruntled employee to blow the whistle falsely. However, a series of false accusations, designed to punish a company or organization, may not only put an entire firm at risk but it may besmirch the reputations of specific individuals and discourage us from taking seriously the real cases which should warrant our attention, many of which involve engineers who have disclosed specific risks to public safety. It is for these reasons that some have argued[21] that one must meet certain specific conditions if whistleblowing is *permissible,* still further conditions if it is to be *obligatory.* This view is discussed and challenged in the selection by Mike Martin, who suggests that the decision to "blow the whistle" should

not be made in accordance with some rules or conditions but should be taken in light of the circumstances and context; the best judgment that can be made is that which is made by a person of virtuous character, not one who is merely adhering to certain rules or conditions. To consider these matters more fully, let us turn to the readings on integrity, loyalty, and "blowing the whistle."

THE READINGS

Gabriele Taylor The common-sense notion of integrity has to do with honesty, but this view does not get at the fundamental idea of integrity: that of a whole and integrated life. If one is to live one's life as an integrated whole, then one must have commitments and one must adhere to them. To illustrate the idea of integrity more fully, Taylor describes different ways in which a person could *lack* integrity. She explains how hypocrisy, shallow sincerity, weakness of will, and self-deception all exhibit a failure either to have commitments or to hold to the commitments one has. From this account, Taylor adumbrates three conditions for integrity: that one is rational, that one lives under the "due influence of the past," and that one's commitments are constitutive of one's view of the world. Given this account of integrity, Taylor addresses the issue of how integrity might relate to other virtues and values, affirming that the person of integrity is likely to be the sort of person who is committed to the right sorts of values. Moreover, the person of integrity will not regard the world from some neutral point of view, nor will the person who is committed to certain values even consider certain options or reasons as relevant.

Josiah Royce For Royce, the basic moral principle is that of loyalty to loyalty. But what is loyalty? Royce encourages us to consider the conflict between a social will and self-will, between the individual subject and the general will of society. This conflict is solved if individual conformity to the more general will also allows for the exaltation of the self. Loyalty looks outward for its plan or purpose but inward for its motive, thus uniting free self-expression with a larger social goal. Loyalty is a freely chosen attachment to some larger social purpose or goal and may appear in a variety of spheres, including the commercial. Loyalty provides a "unity of purpose" that "centralizes your powers" and provides "unity and peace" in life. The central problem of modern life is that we do not find causes that are rational and worthy of our devotion. However, the right cause serves to give us our duties and to unify our ideals and goals.

---

20. George Fletcher, *Loyalty: An Essay on the Morality of Relationships* (New York: Oxford University Press, 1993), 6.

21. The most notable case is that of Richard De George in *Business Ethics* (New York: MacMillan, 1986), 231–38. The work of De George is discussed in the reading by Mike Martin.

Ronald Duska   In this excerpt Duska suggests that it is peculiar that so many consider it to be a moral issue as to whether or not whistleblowing is justified. For Duska, the reason so many consider whistleblowing to require some elaborate justification is that it may be viewed as an act of disloyalty to one's employer or company. However, whistleblowing is not disloyal because no employee has a duty of loyalty to a profit-seeking enterprise. Loyalty is grounded on a relation that presupposes trust and confidence. Such relations would allow loyalty to any group that is formed for reciprocal enrichment of the members, but this reciprocal requirement precludes a corporation (which produces goods for profit) from being the sort of group to which one can be loyal. Thus, the corporate whistleblower has no reason to consider loyalty in deliberating whether or not to "blow the whistle."

Michael W. Martin   After reviewing three actual cases of whistleblowing by engineers, Martin describes three general approaches to the problem of whistleblowing. The third approach is illuminated by a set of five conditions (delineated by Richard De George) that are sufficient to render whistleblowing obligatory. This third approach, in Martin's view, sets out a general rule for all occasions, but Martin argues that any set of general rules or conditions for whistleblowing cannot be adequate for ethical decision making because such decisions must take into account the context and circumstances, including the burdens that might be placed on the whistleblower. Even if there is a *prima facie* duty to blow the whistle, this duty must be weighed against the personal life and responsibilities of the whistleblower. Martin proceeds to discuss three types of arguments that might be used to challenge his contextual approach. Having rejected these arguments, Martin explains how the contextual approach places a special reliance on good judgment, itself a product of character and virtue. The virtues that are most significant for engineers are self-direction, teamwork, and public spirit. The ideals that motivate some whistleblowers entail responsibilities, and these may go beyond the requirements accepted by many others. The person who is so committed *must* act, because failure to do so would violate the individual's integrity.

Integrity

Gabriele Taylor

Gabriele Taylor is Professor Emerita of Philosophy at St. Anne's College, Oxford University. Along with es-

says in moral philosophy, she is the author of Pride, Shame, and Guilt: Emotions of Self Assessment *(1985).*

The aim of this paper is to tie together and explain the various elements of the extremely complex concept of integrity. Its complexity is so great that I cannot do justice to it; to do so would require at least a much more detailed working out of individual points, where these touch on central problems in both Moral Philosophy and the Philosophy of Mind. My account will therefore be somewhat schematic but will catch, I hope, what is the essence of integrity.

There are different ways of characterizing the person of integrity. Such a person is usually thought of as being honest, upright and loyal. Sometimes this is understood simply in terms of certain types of behaviour which conform to the socially accepted code of morality: he keeps his promises, he does not cheat at cards or in business; he does not tell lies. Sometimes it is thought that what matters is not so much adherence to an accepted code, but rather that the person of integrity should do what he himself thinks right, regardless of whether this coincides with the more conventional view. He will be true to the standards he has come to accept, stick to the principles he has evolved. The focus of his honesty and loyalty will be these principles themselves, and how he behaves in a social context will depend on their nature. We may dislike his principles, but we admire him at least for having the courage of his convictions. While on the first interpretation 'integrity' appears to be a label for a selected set of moral virtues, on the second interpretation it seems rather a label for a special application of these virtues, viz. honesty about and loyalty to one's own principles.

But the notion of integrity may also be approached not by picking out such moral qualities as are normally associated with it, but by thinking of the person possessing integrity as being the person who 'keeps his inmost self intact,' whose life is 'of a piece,' whose self is whole and integrated. My claim is that it is this view of integrity which is the fundamental one. The person of integrity keeps his self intact, and the person who lacks integrity is corrupt in the sense that his self is disintegrated. An account of integrity so interpreted will explain the somewhat elusive role it plays in our moral discourse, and will account for the different sorts of demands we make on the person of integrity. It will explain, among other things, why such a person will by and large possess the moral qualities cited earlier. The lack of such qualities can, on the whole, be taken as showing lack of integrity. On the other hand, the possession of them is not enough for possession of integrity. When we ascribe integrity to him who behaves in socially acceptable ways, or to him who sticks to his principles however adverse the circumstances, then we do so on the assumption that he who behaves in these sorts of ways is he who keeps his self intact. To some considerable extent this must remain an assumption, for whatever content may be given to the notion of keeping one's self intact, it is unlikely to yield conditions which are sufficiently accessible grounds for the ascription of integrity.

Lack of Integrity   I shall start with what I take to be an intuitively acceptable general characterization: the person possessing integrity is true to his commitments. The ambiguity of 'his commitment' reflects the different approaches to integrity outlined earlier. Where this is interpreted as referring not to what conventionally might count as his commitment but to what the agent is supposed to feel himself committed to, the proposal is misleading. It suggests that the person of integrity must fulfil two independent conditions: he must have commitments, and he must be true to them. But these are not independent of one another, for to be committed at all requires at least to some extent being true to one's commitments. It follows that 'being true to' does not in this case function as an ordinary relation between a person and his commitments, and that an elucidation of it cannot be divorced from an explanation of 'being committed to.' Given the nature of integrity such difficulties are inherent in any general characterization. I shall not attempt to meet them head on, but consider rather different types of lack of integrity, suggested by my characterization.

1. A person cannot be committed to some project or way of life if he only pretends to others that he is so committed. The hypocrite pretends to live by certain standards when in fact he does not. In the clearest case he consciously and calculatingly exploits for his own ends the fact that certain types of behaviour are seen by others as constituting or implying certain commitments and that therefore he will be seen by others to be acting as he does because he is so committed. But his reason for acting on relevant occasions is not that doing such-and-such will bring about the state of affairs required by his commitment; it is that this is how the person so committed would act on this occasion. As what matters to him is how he appears to others he will act on this reason only when he thinks doing so necessary for making the appropriate impression.

2. A person cannot be committed to some project if he only says so, even if he is not insincere in saying so. He is the shallowly sincere.[1] He may be the person whose undertakings are prompted by impulse and momentary enthusiasm, but are as quickly forgotten. Or he may be the person who believes himself to be uttering his sincere convictions although at other times and in different company he with equal sincerity utters 'convictions' which are quite different and incompatible with the earlier ones. He takes on the colour of his surroundings. To be committed to some view or project does not of course mean that one must inflexibly and forever hold just this view or pursue just this aim. It would be a grave flaw in any account of integrity if it implied that a person of integrity is incapable of change and development. But although he can of course come to see that he has been misguided, that he has attached too much importance to this and too little to that, he cannot change his commitments just when he feels so inclined. He must see a reason for changing them, otherwise he does not count as having been committed at all. Unlike the hypocrite, the shallowly sincere occasionally acts on the sorts of reasons required for being committed to some project, but he does not act on them with any consistency, and where he does not act on them he does not do so for sufficient reason. Again unlike the hypocrite, he is not insincere. But given this, he shows a total lack of self-knowledge: the evidence that he will not behave as in a moment of spontaneous sympathy he thinks he will, or the evidence that his deepest convictions are not what at the time he presents them as being, is there for all to see. But he is blind to this evidence.

3. Neither the hypocrite nor the shallowly sincere is true to his commitments because neither can be said to be relevantly committed at all. By contrast, it might be said of the weak-willed that although he has commitments he is not always true to them. He lets others manipulate him into positions in which he does not really want to be, and finds himself accepting as true what he knows or suspects he really wants to reject. He does not set out to deceive, it merely so happens that he deceives. He is the moral coward who does not act in accordance with his commitments when it is difficult for him to do so. On those occasions he acts on reasons which in his own view are insufficient reasons for acting; in his own view he has overriding reasons for acting otherwise. Like the shallowly sincere he does not act on the required sorts of reasons consistently enough; unlike him, he is aware of his failure.

4. A person is not committed to some project if he self-deceptively takes himself to be so committed. The

case of self-deception is the most important and indeed fundamental case of lack of integrity: it combines the features of the other cases, and it shows more clearly than they do the interrelation between these features. It is therefore worthwhile to give this case some detailed attention. I start with an example of self-deception taken from George Eliot's *Middlemarch*.

Mr Casaubon believes, or appears to believe, that scholarship and all this implies is of great value, and his life is, or appears to be, built around this value. He appears to be a man wholly committed to scholarship, and so indeed he is seen by his neighbours. As he appears to his neighbours so Mr Casaubon appears to himself, he sees himself as the truly devoted scholar. But in order to maintain this identification he has to take certain steps: he isolates himself from other scholars in his field both physically and in the sense that he does not make himself acquainted with their work. He refuses to learn German and so lets himself remain ignorant of work already done in this field. He looks for constant support in keeping his self-image going: his marriage to Dorothea is to serve just this purpose. In short, Mr Casaubon quite systematically takes steps which are to prevent him from ever having to abolish this image of himself and the life he leads.

If Mr Casaubon is to be committed to a scholarly life then this should be reflected in his reasons for acting (on the relevant occasions). They should very roughly be of the sort that doing so-and-so will in some way contribute towards the production of a work of scholarship. But this is only what he takes them to be, or what he has managed to persuade himself they are. The reasons which actually cause him to act in the way he does are quite otherwise, and are not consistent with the assumption that he is committed to the scholarly life. Acting on reasons related to being scholarly does not produce the type of behaviour displayed by him. From his behaviour we must understand him to mean by 'being scholarly': working away in isolation and ignoring relevant evidence. But 'being scholarly' means nothing of the kind, and Mr Casaubon himself would of course not offer this description. His dealing with the value is therefore corrupt. He thinks of himself as being committed to it, but in his handling what he values has ceased to be what he believes himself to be committed to.

Mr Casaubon is no doubt true to his commitments in a conventional sense. It is unthinkable that he would cheat his tradesmen or break his promises. In this respect he behaves towards others as a man of integrity is expected to behave. Nevertheless, he deceives others. The deception of others is a necessary consequence of his self-deception: he identifies with a certain type of person, and it must be as this type of person that he presents himself in a social context. Otherwise he could hardly be said to think of himself as that sort of person. But as this identification is a false identification he must misrepresent himself to others and so deceive them about what he is really like. I take Mr Casaubon to represent at any rate the central case of self-deception. Like all the other characters who are not true to their commitments he deceives others; like the shallowly sincere he is blind to relevant evidence, and like the weak-willed he acts on reasons which, given what he believes to be his commitment, he himself would regard as insufficient reasons for action were he to think clearly about the matter. In the self-deceived all these characteristics are interdependent, and their interdependence is not fortuitous. They are all, I shall suggest, the consequence of the self's disintegration.

THE POSSESSION OF INTEGRITY

If we now turn from the lack to the possession of integrity then the discussion of the last section seems to have got us little further. Of course, the person of integrity will not behave in the ways outlined, but it would be rash to deduce from this that therefore he will always behave in certain other ways, always tell the truth, keep his promises etc. Such a move would neither yield a characterization of the person of integrity which is entirely correct, nor would it be at all explanatory of the demands we in fact make of such a person. It would leave us where we started. However, the points arising from the last section provide us at least with a new beginning: the person of integrity will be rational in a number of related ways. He will not ignore relevant evidence, he will be consistent in his behaviour, he will not act on reasons which, given the circumstances, are insufficient reasons for action.

My claim is that the person possessing integrity is the person who keeps his self intact. The first condition for doing so is that he be rational in the ways outlined. But this gives us no more than the bare bones of the notion; in our ascriptions of integrity we refer to more than just some essence of rationality. At the very least we want to say that the person of integrity is not inconsistent in ways that somehow matter.

The inconsistencies we think important are connected, in one way or another, with a person's identity.

Mr Casaubon illustrates one such link: Mr Casaubon does not keep his self intact. He identifies and yet does not identify with a certain type of person. One identification is governed by wishful thinking, the other emerges in his behaviour and reactions. His behaviour is not that of a scholar, yet it is prompted by his thinking himself a scholar. The trouble with Mr Casaubon is not that he does not behave as scholars do. Many people don't and are none the worse for that. Rather, his behaviour is distorted scholar-behaviour. It is precisely because in his wishful thought he identifies himself as he does that his identity as revealed in his behaviour is what it is, and is inconsistent with what in his wishful thought he identifies himself with. The reasons on which in fact he acts are therefore not the kinds of reasons he can accept while he clings to the wishful picture of himself. His own view of his behaviour on relevant occasions must then be distorted and he will be incapable of properly assessing available evidence. He is unable to do so because what would then be revealed would totally undermine what he wishfully clings to. . . .

To keep one's self intact does then at least entail that one must be free of the specific kind of inconsistency just discussed. And there are further conditions related to this one which will serve to make the notion of a self which is intact somewhat more precise. One of these is the condition that a person who keeps his self intact will be under 'due' influence of his past. The phrase is Richard Wollheim's and the point relies on his discussion of persons and their lives.[2] The argument behind this condition rests on the plausible assumption that prominent among the criteria for personal identity are memory conditions. In particular, that we have experiential memory is essential to being a person at all. Not only should we without such memory lack a sense of our own identity altogether; it also contributes towards the self as it is and will be, for memories affect a person's present thoughts, feelings and attitudes. Conversely, the self has not remained static over time, and the person's way of now remembering an earlier experience will contribute to the memory something of the present self. There is thus a two-way process which links different experiences to each other and because of which they are all one person's experiences and constitute his life.

There are a number of ways in which this two-way process may go wrong, and a number of ways, therefore, in which the unity of the person's life may to a greater or lesser extent be interfered with. It could be the case, for example, that one particular memory resists modification over time and continues to flourish at the expense of other memories and of the impact of present experience. The person concerned would then be obsessed by this memory. Or a memory of some important event may be very short-lived and not be allowed to affect present experiences at all. In one case the present self does not acknowledge a present and future self whose experiences go beyond that of the past self, in the other it refuses to acknowledge the past self that had certain experiences. Either way the person concerned will not be under due influence of his past. . . .

A further condition for keeping one's self intact can be extracted when we consider that a person's commitments may well have far-reaching implications in different areas of his life, so that there is also this dimension in which his life may be of a piece or, alternatively, fall apart. An example used by Bernard Williams in a similar context illustrates this case.[3] George is a chemist who can find no job other than one which involves him in research relating to chemical and biological warfare. He is poor and has family responsibilities. He is also strongly opposed to biological warfare. If George under these circumstances were to accept the job his life would fall apart. His opposition to biological warfare cannot possibly be an isolated commitment, it must be related to more general views about how to treat people, and such views will find expression in other areas of his life, e.g. in the upbringing of his children. But if so then, should he accept the job, he will either be unable to express what he believes consistently in all areas of his life, or he will maintain consistency by shaping his views to fit the implications of being engaged in research into biological warfare. It is difficult to see how he could maintain either course without engaging in some form of self-deception.

The self-deceived does not keep his self intact: nor do the three other characters introduced in the last section. The shallowly sincere is quite obviously very similar to the self-deceived. The weak-willed will under certain circumstances deny the implications of his commitments so that there will be inconsistency between different aspects of his life. The same is true of the hypocrite. In his case, as in that of the self-deceived, we have two inconsistent identifications one of which is expressed in past, or present behaviour and is not acknowledged by the agent.[4] Lack of self-integration is therefore at least a common feature of the most typical instances of lack of integrity.

INTEGRITY AND MORAL VALUES

The account I have given of 'keeping one's self intact' explains the rather peculiar status allotted to integrity. We are inclined to think of possession of integrity as being possession of a virtue, but it is quite unlike possessing any of the other virtues that come to mind, like e.g. courage or generosity. One indication of this is that only in the case of integrity can ascription of it not be expressed in adjectival form. Those who have generosity are generous, those who have courage are brave, but what are those who possess integrity? On my account the gap would appropriately be filled by 'is integrated' or 'is intact,' but in contrast to 'he is brave' etc. this would convey no specific information about the agent and would be of no practical use. This lack of informativeness reflects the fact that from the conditions to be fulfilled by the person who keeps himself intact nothing whatever can be deduced about any particular kind of behaviour on the part of that person. . . .

I hope to show in the remainder of this paper that, on the contrary, my view of integrity fits and explains many of our intuitions and the major demands we make on the person of integrity. In particular, nothing forces us to think of a Macbeth type character as possessing integrity, for although various types of inconsistency rule out integrity, the kind of consistency of behaviour he displays is not sufficient for its ascription. On the other hand, I cannot show that ruthless pursuing of one's own ends is incompatible with integrity. We like to think that the whole or integrated person is also the wholly good person, but to some extent at least this thought remains an assumption.[5]

A central demand in our ascriptions of integrity seems to be that the person of integrity be honest in various ways, and that deception of others is sufficient for the lack of it. We do, however, seem to allow quite systematic pieces of deception without regarding the deceiver as a hypocrite. Beethoven's Leonora, for example, finds herself involved in quite serious deception of people who treat her as a friend. But we should cite her nonetheless as a case of integrity rather than the lack of it. We should do so because we take her to be fulfilling demands which are more basic to integrity than the demand not to deceive.

1. Leonora does not of course deceive lightly, she thinks she does so for a sufficient reason: to see justice done, to have her husband freed. But that she herself should think the reason sufficient is not enough; we should be much more reluctant to regard someone as having integrity if he did so for his own gain, irrespective of whether he regards his reasons as sufficient. We think of Leonora that she is right in some objective sense, but doubt this in the case of the egoist. We demand of a person of integrity that he get his values right. This becomes plain whenever integrity is publicly discussed, e.g. when there is a major spy revelation. The sentiment often expressed on such occasions is that the spy is in a muddle about his values, that he just cannot be right if for instance he thinks that loyalty to friends is more important than loyalty to one's country. The concern is not just that the spy is simply telling a lie about his motives, but is rather that he cannot have got at the truth, whatever he himself may think. 'Getting one's values right' may mean here: there is an objective scale of virtues where 'loyalty to country' occurs in a higher position than 'loyalty to friends,' and sometimes of course this is just what the spy's critic has in mind. Similarly, we may think that Leonora is right just because she acts from noble motives and not from selfish ones. This kind of objective appeal to values I do not intend either to justify or to show to be central to the possession of integrity. But implied by this appeal to objectivity is another which is centrally relevant. The spy is thought to be so wrong in his assessment of loyalties because he does not get his values right in the light of the evidence there is. He is thought to refuse to reflect and so to be misguided. The implication of this is that on some level he was not sincere when he thought his action expressed what he valued most, that he was deceiving himself. If only he had been prepared to sort things out he would have seen the error of his ways. Interpreted in this way the demand that a person of integrity must get his values right evidently fits the notion that he keeps his self intact; if he keeps his self intact then he will in this sense get his values right. It is because we take Leonora to be sound in this respect that we allow her possession of integrity. We are inclined to regard acting from altruistic motives a better indication of not being muddled in this respect than acting from self-interested ones. So indeed it may be, but we have here not enough grounds for excluding *a priori* the possible case of someone who deceives for personal gain and yet does not lose integrity.

2. For Leonora there was no doubt that she had to act as she did although her course of action might involve her in harming others to some extent. It was inconceivable to her that she might stand by and leave her husband to his fate. Such an attitude is typical of the person of integrity: there are certain things he cannot bring himself to do, and certain other things he feels he must do, irrespective of the consequences. It is because of this feature

that the charge of self-indulgence is sometimes levelled against him who acts with integrity, for, it is thought, he may not be able to bring himself to do what in fact it would be right to do, or conversely, he may feel himself obliged to engage in what is the more harmful of the alternative courses of action open to him. So integrity comes to be regarded as a specific form of weakness. . . .

Yet there is truth in the point that integrity has to do with the relation between a person and his actions. On my account, the modal terms in 'he has to act in certain ways and cannot act in certain other ways' derive their force from the fact that were the person to act otherwise he would fall apart. If he cannot bring himself to do something, or if he just must do something else, then this implies a commitment on his part which covers much more than merely the particular action he is now concerned with. There is to the 'must' or 'cannot' a background consisting of the various implications of some one commitment or of interrelated commitments. . . . George [is] the sort of person who will not work for war, and such identifications cannot mean merely that on some one particular occasion they will act in a certain way. Their commitments will rather be constitutive of their view of the world and the life to lead. One implication of this is that he who is so committed will not consider the 'facts' of a situation from a detached and neutral point of view and weigh the consequences of alternative courses of action against each other. He will already see the situation in a certain light, and because he views it in that light certain features will strike him as constituting categorical demands for action or abstention, and other features will not present themselves as possible reasons for action at all.[6] It is therefore true that, as Williams says (*op. cit.,* p. 89), even if from some abstract point of view one state of affairs is better than another, it does not follow that he should regard it as his business to bring it about. It is in this sense that integrity has to do with actions which are peculiarly one's own. This has nothing whatever to do with acting self-indulgently. . . . George, rather than putting his integrity above the well-being of his family, may on the contrary be particularly concerned with their well-being for he may believe, and with good reason believe, that unless he stands firm his own corruption cannot but spread to his family as well. The self-indulgent man will act *in order to* keep his self intact, and it is hard to see how a person of integrity can act for this reason. As an agent's commitment, 'keeping one's self intact' must be a higher order commitment, for by itself it cannot be a commitment with which the agent could identify; by itself it is totally vacuous. It would therefore occupy a peculiar position

vis-à-vis his other commitments and be isolated from them. Consequently, it could hardly form part of a consistent perspective on life, and so would conflict with the conditions set out for the integrated self.

3. Earlier I rejected the suggestion that the reason why we think of Leonora as a person of integrity is that she is prompted by other-regarding and noble motives; the reason was rather that because she acted from such motives we assume that she gets her values right in the relevant sense. This seems to leave the link between integrity and morality more tenuous than perhaps it should be, for we tend to think that the wicked cannot be candidates for integrity, that it and moral goodness go together. On my account it does not follow that he who has integrity is necessarily virtuous, if by this is understood that he acts out of consideration for others. On the other hand, it follows that he will lack the defects of confusion and weakness which make a person a burden to himself and others. He will have the admirable quality of moral courage, and because he is consistent, the socially desirable one of reliability. He will also be immune to corruption. He will not be tempted to act in certain ways, because to be tempted implies that certain features of a situation will present themselves to the agent as reasons for action to be weighed against reasons for acting otherwise. But the person who is committed in the way described will not even consider such reasons. It is easy to see how this point leads to the conviction that the person of integrity has his own defence against chaos and so is a person the different aspects of whose life (or soul) are in harmony. And so, perhaps, he is the happy person. Further, the demands of consistency extend over the reasons for action generated by his commitments. If he is committed to freedom or scholarship then this provides him with a reason for bringing freedom or scholarship about, and not just with a reason for seeing to it that *he* is free or becomes a scholar. He cannot be committed to just his own advancement without thinking that others should be similarly committed, for it is hard to see on what grounds he could consistently and without ignoring relevant evidence deny that what in his view is a good for him is also a good for others. He would have to regard self-advancement as a human good and accept the implications of its general practice. Finally, the person of integrity will not deceive others, or can deceive others only for sufficient reason, where 'sufficient reason' is constrained by all the conditions he must fulfil in order to keep his self intact. This rules out at least the more common forms of moral wickedness which consist in deceitfully manipulating others for one's own ends.

The person who keeps his self intact has emerged, I think, as having those qualities on which in our ordinary judgments we base ascriptions of integrity. We expect him to have strength of will and to be honest in various ways; we do not demand that he be generous or charitable. Whether or not he has these latter characteristics will depend on the nature of his commitments. I have not ruled out the possibility that all the conditions I have given may be fulfilled by someone who ruthlessly and without regard for the well-being of others pursues his own aim, even if in doing so he behaves in ways we regard as morally wrong. Not every immoral action need be a sign of the agent's corruption. I am inclined to think, however, that the ruthless egoist will not in fact possess integrity. 'Being truly committed to some project' has no doubt more implications than I have been able to draw out. A person fulfilling the conditions of lack of confusion and lack of self-deception cannot, for instance, be in the grip of some obsession, and the ruthless egoist may well turn out to be just that. And it may be that the person of integrity has further virtues based on features of my characterization which I have not explored. As he will be free from confusion he will get his commitments right, and so he will get right his identity in terms of these commitments. In this sense he can be said to have self-knowledge. And this seems to imply that should the occasion arise he will be capable of self-criticism, and so perhaps he cannot be wholly self-complacent and self-righteous. If this is true then it may well be that this line of investigation will yield yet further constraints on the person possessing integrity.

himself as being, on the other he refuses to accept this behaviour as expressing what he really is. But this difference does not alter the similarity of their falling apart.

5. This is not to say that nothing more can be done in this area. But the types of arguments needed here go beyond the scope of this paper. For the kind of enquiry I have in mind see Richard Wollheim's "The Good Self and the Bad Self," *Proceedings of the British Academy,* 1975.

6. See John McDowell, "Are Moral Requirements Hypothetical Imperatives?" *Aristotelian Society, Supplementary Volume LII.* 1978, pp. 13–29.

QUESTIONS ON TAYLOR

1. Summarize Taylor's account of integrity. Can you think of particular examples, famous or not, for each of the four instances of a *lack* of integrity?

2. How might integrity play a role in business decision making or in everyday commerce more generally? Specifically devise examples which show how rationality (i.e., considering the evidence) or being true to one's commitments might affect the conduct of a business owner, manager, employee, or customer.

3. Should an account of integrity seek to link integrity more closely to moral virtue? Should a person's commitments be moral rather than wicked?

4. Must the person of integrity be immune from temptation? Why does Taylor assert that the person of integrity will not deceive or manipulate others?

ENDNOTES

1. The term is Fingarette's, *Self-Deception* (Routledge & Kegan Paul, 1977), pp. 51–2.

2. "On Persons and Their Lives" in *Explaining Emotions,* ed. A. Oksenberg Rorty (University of California Press, 1980), sections v and vii. See also "Memory, Experiential Memory and Personal Identity," in *Perception and Identity, Essays presented to A. J. Ayer,* ed. G. F. Macdonald (Macmillan, 1979), sections IX and X.

3. J. J. C. Smart and Bernard Williams, *Utilitarianism For and Against* (Cambridge University Press, 1973), p. 89. Williams uses the case to make a different point.

4. They differ of course in the sense in which they disown this identity. The hypocrite who deliberately presents a certain persona to the world is not prevented by wishful thought from acknowledging it. It is rather that while on the one hand he takes responsibility for his behaviour in that he wants to be given credit for being the person he presents

Loyalty

Josiah Royce

Josiah Royce (1855–1916) was a Professor of Philosophy at Harvard University and one of America's most notable philosophers. Among his numerous works are The Religious Aspect of Philosophy *(1885),* The Spirit of Modern Philosophy *(1892),* Studies of Good and Evil *(1898),* The World and the Individual *(1900–1901), and* The Philosophy of Loyalty *(1908), from which this excerpt is taken.*

. . . Suppose a being whose social conformity has been sufficient to enable him to learn many skilful social arts,—arts of speech, of prowess in contest, of influence over other men. Suppose that these arts have at the same time awakened this man's pride, his self-confidence, his disposition to assert himself. Such a man will have in him a good deal of what you can well call social will. He will be no mere anarchist. He will have been trained into much obedience. He will be no natural enemy of society, unless, indeed, fortune has given him extraordinary opportunities to win his way without scruples. On the other hand, this man must acquire a good deal of self-will. He becomes fond of success, of mastery, of his own demands. To be sure, he can find within himself no one naturally sovereign will. He can so far find only a general determination to define some way of his own, and to have his own way. Hence the conflicts of social will and self-will are inevitable, circular, endless, so long as this is the whole story of the man's life. By merely consulting convention, on the one hand, and his disposition to be somebody, on the other hand, this man can never find any one final and consistent plan of life, nor reach any one definition of his duty.

But now suppose that there appears in this man's life some one of the greater social passions, such as patriotism well exemplifies. Let his country be in danger. Let his elemental passion for conflict hereupon fuse with his brotherly love for his own countrymen into that fascinating and blood-thirsty form of humane but furious ecstasy, which is called the war-spirit. The mood in question may or may not be justified by the passing circumstances. For that I now care not. At its best the war-spirit is no very clear or rational state of anybody's mind. But one reason why men may love this spirit is that when it comes, it seems at once to define a plan of life,—a plan which solves the conflicts of self-will and conformity. This plan has two features: (1) it is through and through a social plan, obedient to the general will of one's country, submissive; (2) it is through and through an exaltation of the self, of the inner man, who now feels glorified through his sacrifice, dignified in his self-surrender, glad to be his country's servant and martyr,—yet sure that through this very readiness for self-destruction he wins the rank of hero.

Well, if the man whose case we are supposing gets possessed by some such passion as this, he wins for the moment the consciousness of what I call loyalty. This loyalty no longer knows anything about the old circular conflicts of self-will and of conformity. The self, at such moments, looks indeed *outwards* for its plan of life. "The country needs me," it says. It looks, meanwhile, *inwards* for the inspiring justification of this plan. "Honor, the hero's crown, the soldier's death, the patriot's devotion—these," it says, "are my will. I am not giving up this will of mine. It is my pride, my glory, my self-assertion, to be ready at my country's call." And now there is no conflict of outer and inner.

How wise or how enduring or how practical such a passion may prove, I do not yet consider. What I point out is that this war-spirit, for the time at least, makes self-sacrifice seem to be self-expression, makes obedience to the country's call seem to be the proudest sort of display of one's own powers. Honor now means submission, and to obey means to have one's way. Power and service are at one. Conformity is no longer opposed to having one's own will. One has no will but that of the country.

As a mere fact of human nature, then, there are social passions which actually tend to do at once two things: (1) to intensify our self-consciousness, to make us more than ever determined to express our own will and more than ever sure of our own rights, of our own strength, of our dignity, of our power, of our value; (2) to make obvious to us that this our will has no purpose but to do the will of some fascinating social power. This social power is the cause to which we are loyal.

Loyalty, then, fixes our attention upon some one cause, bids us look without ourselves to see what this unified cause is, shows us thus some one plan of action, and then says to us, "In this cause is your life, your will, your opportunity, your fulfilment."

Thus loyalty, viewed merely as a personal attitude, solves the paradox of our ordinary existence, by showing us outside of ourselves the cause which is to be served, and inside of ourselves the will which delights to do this service, and which is not thwarted but enriched and expressed in such service.

I have used patriotism and the war-spirit merely as a first and familiar illustration of loyalty. But now, as we shall later see, there is no necessary connection between loyalty and war; and there are many other forms of loyalty besides the patriotic forms. Loyalty has its domestic, its religious, its commercial, its professional forms, and many other forms as well. The essence of it, whatever forms it may take, is, as I conceive the matter, this: Since no man can find a plan of life by merely looking within his own chaotic nature, he has to look without, to the world of social conventions, deeds, and causes. Now, a loyal man is one who has found, and who sees, neither mere individual fellow-men to be loved or hated, nor mere conventions, nor customs, nor laws to be obeyed, but some social cause, or some system of causes, so rich, so well knit, and, to him, so fascinating, and withal so kindly in its appeal to his natural self-will, that he says to his cause: "Thy will is mine and mine is thine. In thee I do not lose but find myself, living intensely in proportion as I live for thee." If one could find such a cause, and hold it for his lifetime before his mind, clearly observing it, passionately loving it, and yet calmly understanding it, and steadily and practically serving it, he would have one plan of life, and this plan of life would be his own plan, his own will set before him, expressing all that his self-will has ever sought. Yet this plan would also be a plan of obedience, because it would mean living for the cause.

Now, in all ages of civilized life there have been people who have won in some form a consciousness of loyalty, and who have held to such a consciousness through life. Such people may or may not have been right in their choice of a cause. But at least they have exemplified through their loyalty one feature of a rational moral life. They have known what it was to have unity of purpose.

And again, the loyal have known what it was to be free from moral doubts and scruples. Their cause has been their conscience. It has told them what to do. They have listened and obeyed, not because of what they took to be blind convention, not because of a fear of external authority, not even because of what seemed to themselves any purely private and personal intuition, but because, when they have looked first outwards at their cause, and then inwards at themselves, they have found themselves worthless in their own eyes, except when viewed as active, as confidently devoted, as willing instruments of their cause. Their cause has forbidden them to doubt; it has said: "You are mine, you cannot do otherwise." And they have said to the cause: "I am, even of my own will, thine. I have no will except thy will. Take me, use me, control me, and even thereby fulfil me and exalt me." That is again the speech of the devoted patriots, soldiers, mothers, and martyrs of our race. They have had the grace of this willing, this active loyalty.

Now, people loyal in this sense have surely existed in the world, and, as you all know, the loyal still exist amongst us. And I beg you not to object to me, at this point, that such devoted people have often been loyal to very bad causes; or that different people have been loyal to causes which were in deadly war with one another, so that loyal people must often have been falsely guided. I beg you, above all, not to interpose here the objection that our modern doubters concerning moral problems simply cannot at present see to what one cause they ought to be loyal, so that just herein, just in our inability to see a fitting and central object of loyalty, lies the root of our modern moral confusion and distraction. All those possible objections are indeed perfectly fair considerations. I shall deal with them in due time; and I am just as earnestly aware of them as you can be. But just now we are getting our first glimpse of our future phi-

losophy of loyalty. All that you can say of the defects of loyalty leaves still untouched the one great fact that, if you want to find a way of living which surmounts doubts, and centralizes your powers, it must be some such a way as all the loyal in common have trodden, since first loyalty was known amongst men. What form of loyalty is the right one, we are hereafter to see. But unless you can find some sort of loyalty, you cannot find unity and peace in your active living. You must find, then, a cause that is really worthy of the sort of devotion that the soldiers, rushing cheerfully to certain death, have felt for their clan or for their country, and that the martyrs have shown on behalf of their faith. This cause must be indeed rational, worthy, and no object of a false devotion. But once found, it must become your conscience, must tell you the truth about your duty, and must unify, as from without and from above, your motives, your special ideals, and your plans. You ought, I say, to find such a cause, if indeed there be any ought at all. And this is my first hint of our moral code.

But you repeat, perhaps in bewilderment, your question: "Where, in our distracted modern world, in this time when cause wars with cause, and when all old moral standards are remorselessly criticised and doubted, are we to find such a cause—a cause, all-embracing, definite, rationally compelling, supreme, certain, and fit to centralize life? What cause is there that for us would rationally justify a martyr's devotion?" I reply: "A perfectly simple consideration, derived from a study of the very spirit of loyalty itself, as this spirit is manifested by all the loyal, will soon furnish to us the unmistakable answer to this question." For the moment we have won our first distant glimpse of what I mean by the general nature of loyalty, and by our common need of loyalty.

QUESTIONS ON ROYCE

1. How does Royce define loyalty? Do you think there is any need to unite the self to some larger social goal? Is this a philosophical need, a natural need, or no need at all?

2. What are some instances, situations, or relationships in which loyalty is important? Do you think loyalty is possible in commerce?

3. Even if it is true that "no man can find a plan of life by merely looking within his own chaotic nature," does this entail that one's plan of life comes from a social cause? Should we suppose that a single individual will discover *one* unifying cause, or might one have plural, if not conflicting, loyalties?

4. How might Royce's conception of loyalty be applied to commercial life? If one is loyal to one's firm then what duties might that loyalty imply? And how might this commercial loyalty serve to unify one's ideals and plans? Should commercial life be the central unifying force of one's life and loyalty?

Whistleblowing and Employee Loyalty

Ronald F. Duska

Ronald F. Duska is the Charles F. Lamont Post Chair of Ethics and the Professions, The American College. He has published numerous essays in business ethics and ethical theory and is co-author or editor of numerous books, including Business Ethics *(1990, with Norman E. Bowie).*

. . . Discussions of whistleblowing generally revolve around four topics: (1) attempts to define whistleblowing more precisely; (2) debates about whether and when whistleblowing is permissible; (3) debates about whether and when one has an obligation to blow the whistle; and (4) appropriate mechanisms for institutionalizing whistleblowing.

In this paper I want to focus on the second problem, because I find it somewhat disconcerting that there is a problem at all. When I first looked into the ethics of whistleblowing it seemed to me that whistleblowing was a good thing, and yet I found in the literature claim after claim that it was in need of defense, that there was something wrong with it, namely that it was an act of disloyalty.

If whistleblowing was a disloyal act, it deserved disapproval, and ultimately any action of whistleblowing needed justification. This disturbed me. It was as if the act of a good Samaritan was being condemned as an act of interference, as if the prevention of a suicide needed to be justified. My moral position in favor of whistleblowing was being challenged. The tables were turned and the burden of proof had shifted. My position was the one in question. Suddenly instead of the company being the bad guy and the whistleblower the good guy, which is what I thought, the whistleblower was the bad guy. Why? Because he was disloyal. What I discovered was that in most of the literature it was taken as axiomatic that whistleblowing was an act of disloyalty. My moral intuitions told me that axiom was mistaken. Nevertheless, since it is accepted by a large segment of the ethical community it deserves investigation.

In his book *Business Ethics,* Norman Bowie, who presents what I think is one of the finest presentations of the ethics of whistleblowing, claims that "whistleblowing . . . violate[s] a *prima facie* duty of loyalty to one's employer." According to Bowie, there is a duty of loyalty which prohibits one from reporting his employer or company. Bowie, of course, recognizes that this is only a *prima facie* duty, i.e., one that can be overridden by a higher duty to the public good. Nevertheless, the axiom that whistleblowing is disloyal is Bowie's starting point.

Bowie is not alone. Sissela Bok, another fine ethicist, sees whistleblowing as an instance of disloyalty.

> The whistleblower hopes to stop the game; but since he is neither referee nor coach, and since he blows the whistle on his own team, his act is seen as a *violation of loyalty* [italics mine]. In holding his position, he has assumed certain obligations to his colleagues and clients. He may even have subscribed to a loyalty oath or a promise of confidentiality. . . . Loyalty to colleagues and to clients comes to be pitted against loyalty to the public interest, to those who may be injured unless the revelation is made.[1]

Bowie and Bok end up defending whistleblowing in certain contexts, so I don't necessarily disagree with their conclusions. However, I fail to see how one has an obligation of loyalty to one's company, so I disagree with their perception of the problem, and their starting point. The difference in perception is important because those who think employees have an obligation of loyalty to a company fail to take into account a relevant moral difference between persons and corporations and between corporations and other kinds of groups where loyalty is appropriate. I want to argue that one does not have an obligation of loyalty to a company, even a *prima facie* one, because companies are not the kind of things which are proper objects of loyalty. I then want to show that to make them objects of loyalty gives them a moral status they do not deserve and in raising their status, one lowers the status of the individuals who work for the companies.

But why aren't corporations the kind of things which can be objects of loyalty? . . .

Loyalty is ordinarily construed as a state of being constant and faithful in a relation implying trust or confidence, as a wife to husband, friend to friend, parent to child, lord to vassal, etc. According to John Ladd "it is not founded on just *any* casual relationship, but on a specific kind of relationship or tie. The ties that bind the persons together provide the basis of loyalty."[2] But all sorts of ties bind people together to make groups. I am a member of a group of fans if I go to a ball game. I am a member of a group if I merely walk down the street. I am in a sense tied to them, but don't owe them loyalty. I don't owe loyalty to just anyone I encounter. Rather I owe loyalty to persons with whom I have special relationships. I owe it to my children, my spouse, my parents, my friends and certain groups, those groups which are formed for the mutual enrichment of the members. It is important to recognize that in any relationship which demands loyalty the relationship works both ways and involves mutual enrichment. Loyalty is incompatible with self-interest, because it is something that necessarily requires we go beyond self-interest. My loyalty to my friend, for example, requires I put aside my interests some of the time. It is because of this reciprocal requirement which demands surrendering self-interest that a corporation is not a proper object of loyalty.

A business or corporation does two things in the free enterprise system. It produces a good or service and makes a profit. The making of a profit, however, is the primary function of a business as a business. For if the production of the good or service was not profitable the business would be out of business. Since non-profitable goods or services are discontinued, the providing of a service or the making of a product is not done for its own sake, but from a business perspective is a means to an end, the making of profit. People bound together in a business are not bound together for mutual fulfillment and support, but to divide labor so the business makes a profit. Since profit is paramount if you do not produce in a company or if there are cheaper laborers around, a company feels justified in firing you for the sake of better production. Throughout history companies in a pinch feel no obligation of loyalty. Compare that to a family. While we can jokingly refer to a family as "somewhere they have to take you in no matter what," you cannot refer to a company in that way. "You can't buy loyalty" is true. Loyalty depends on ties that demand self-sacrifice with no expectation of reward, e.g., the ties of loyalty that bind a family together. Business functions on the basis of enlightened self-interest. I am devoted to a company not because it is like a parent to me. It is not, and attempts of some companies to create "one big happy family" ought to be looked on with suspicion. I am not "devoted" to it at all, or should not be. I *work* for it because it pays me. I am not in a family to get paid, but I am in a company to get paid. . . .

The cold hard truth is that the goal of profit is what gives birth to a company and forms that particular group. Money is what ties the group together. But in such a commercialized venture, with such a goal there is

no loyalty, or at least none need be expected. An employer will release an employee and an employee will walk away from an employer when it is profitable to do so. That's business. It is perfectly permissible. Contrast that with the ties between a lord and his vassal. A lord could not in good conscience wash his hands of his vassal, nor could a vassal in good conscience abandon his lord. What bound them was mutual enrichment, not profit. . . .

To think we owe a company or corporation loyalty requires us to think of that company as a person or as a group with a goal of human enrichment. If we think of it in this way we can be loyal. But this is just the wrong way to think. A company is not a person. A company is an instrument, and an instrument with a specific purpose, the making of profit. To treat an instrument as an end in itself, like a person, may not be as bad as treating an end as an instrument, but it does give the instrument a moral status it does not deserve, and by elevating the instrument we lower the end. All things, instruments and ends, become alike. . . .

If my analysis is correct, the issue of the permissibility of whistleblowing is not a real issue, since there is no obligation of loyalty to a company. Whistleblowing is not only permissible but expected when a company is harming society. The issue is not one of disloyalty to the company, but the question of whether the whistleblower has an obligation to society if blowing the whistle will bring him retaliation. . . .

ENDNOTES

1. Sissela Bok, "Whistleblowing and Professional Responsibilities," *New York University Education Quarterly,* vol. II, 4 (1980), 3.
2. John Ladd, "Loyalty," *The Encyclopedia of Philosophy,* vol. 5, 97.

QUESTIONS ON DUSKA

1. According to Duska, what are the conditions of loyalty? Are these conditions necessary or sufficient for loyalty? Are there any other conditions required if one is to have an obligation of loyalty? Do you agree that loyalty demands that certain conditions be present if one is to be loyal?

2. Why are the conditions of loyalty *not* present in companies or corporations? Are they present in *any* business firms, including small proprietorships? Note that Duska writes that we owe loyalty to "those groups

which are formed for the mutual enrichment of its members." Why isn't this a description of some types of businesses, including, for example, investment clubs or mutual funds?

3. Duska admits that if one thinks of a company as a group with the goal of human enrichment, then one could be loyal to the company. However, he then states that "this is just the wrong way to think." Why is this "the wrong way to think?" Is there only one goal of business firms? *Must* there be but one goal?

Whistleblowing

Professionalism, Personal Life, and Shared Responsibility

Michael W. Martin

Michael W. Martin is Professor of Philosophy at Chapman University, California. He is the author of many essays and books, including Self-Deception and Morality *(1986),* Ethics in Engineering *(1996, with Roland Schinzinger),* Love's Virtues *(1996), and* Everyday Morality *(2001).*

. . . Whistleblowing occurs in all professions, and most of what I say will have general relevance to professional ethics. Only in engineering ethics, however, has whistleblowing been something of a preoccupation. The reason is clear. Engineers work on projects that affect the safety of large numbers of people. As professionals, they live by codes of ethics which ascribe to them a paramount obligation to protect the safety, health, and welfare of the public, an obligation that sometimes implies whistleblowing. As employees of corporations, however, their obligation is to respect the authority of managers who sometimes give insufficient attention to safety matters, and who also severely punish whistleblowers. As a result, there are inevitable conflicts between professional obligations to employers and the public, as well as conflicts between professional and personal life.

I want to take a fresh look at whistleblowing in order to draw attention to some neglected issues concerning the moral relevance of personal life to understanding professional responsibilities. Specifically, the issues concern: personal rights and responsibilities in deciding how to meet professional obligations; increased personal burdens when others involved in collective endeavors fail to meet their responsibilities; the role of the virtues, especially personal integrity, as they bear on "living with oneself"; and personal commitments to moral ideals beyond minimum requirements.

DEFINITION AND CASES

By "whistleblowing" I have in mind the actions of employees (or former employees) who identify what they believe to be a significant moral problem concerning their corporation (or corporations they deal with), who convey information about the problem outside approved organizational channels or against pressure from supervisors or colleagues not to do so, with the intention of drawing attention to the problem (whatever further motives they may have).[1] Examples of serious moral problems include felonies, immoral treatment of clients or employees (such as sexual harassment), misuse of public funds, and—my focus here—technological products that are unacceptably dangerous to the public.

I will focus on cases where whistleblowers identify themselves. While anonymous whistleblowing is a legitimate option in some situations, acknowledging one's identity and credentials is usually necessary in order to be taken seriously; in any case, corporations typically have resources to hunt down "leaks" in order to identify whistleblowers.[2] I will discuss both external whistleblowing, where information is passed outside the corporation (for example, to government officials, the press, professional societies), and internal whistleblowing, where information is passed to higher management against corporate policy or one's supervisor's directives.

Let me bring to mind three well-known cases.

(1) In 1972 Dan Applegate wrote a memo to his supervisor, the vice-president of Convair Corporation, telling him in no uncertain terms that the cargo door for the DC-10 airplane was unsafe, making it "inevitable that, in the twenty years ahead of us, DC-10 cargo doors will come open and I would expect this to usually result in the loss of the airplane."[3] As a subcontractor for McDonnell Douglas, Convair had designed the cargo door and the DC-10 fuselage. Applegate was Director of Product Engineering at Convair and the senior engineer in charge of the design. His supervisor did not challenge his technical judgment in the matter, but told him that nothing could be done because of the likely costs to Convair in admitting responsibility for a design error that would need to be fixed by grounding DC-10's. Two years later, the cargo door on a Turkish DC-10 flying near Paris opened in flight, decompressurizing the cargo

area so as to collapse the passenger floor—along which run the controls for the aircraft. All 346 people on board died, a record casualty figure at that time for a single-plane crash. Tens of millions of dollars were paid out in civil suits, but no one was charged with criminal or even unprofessional conduct.

(2) Frank Camps was a principal design engineer for the Pinto.[4] Under pressure from management he participated in coaxing the Pinto windshield through government tests by reporting only the rare successful test and by using a Band-Aid fix design that resulted in increased hazard to the gas tank. In 1973, undergoing a crisis of conscience in response to reports of exploding gas tanks, he engaged in internal whistleblowing, writing the first of many memos to top management stating his view that Ford was violating federal safety standards. It took six years before his concerns were finally incorporated into the 1979 model Pinto, after nearly a million Pintos with unsafe windshields and gas tanks were put on the road. Shortly after writing his memos he was given lowered performance evaluations, then demoted several times. He resigned in 1978 when it became clear his prospects for advancement at Ford were ended. He filed a law suit based in part on age discrimination, in part on trying to prevent Ford from making him a scapegoat for problems with the Pinto, and in part on trying to draw further attention to the dangers in the Pinto.

(3) On January 27, 1986, Roger Boisjoly and other senior engineers at Morton Thiokol firmly recommended that space shuttle *Challenger* not be launched.[5] The temperature at the launch site was substantially below the known safety range for the O-ring seals in the joints of the solid rocket boosters. Top management overrode the recommendation. Early in the launch, the *Challenger* boosters exploded, killing the seven crew members, to the terrified eyes of millions who watched because schoolteacher Christa McAuliffe was aboard. A month later Boisjoly was called to testify before the Rogers Commission. Against the wishes of management, he offered documents to support his interpretation of the events leading to the disaster—and to rebut the interpretation given by his boss. Over the next months Boisjoly was made to feel increasingly alienated from his coworkers until finally he had to take an extended sick leave. Later, when he desired to find a new job he found himself confronted with companies unwilling to take a chance on a known whistleblower.

As the last two cases suggest, there can be double horrors surrounding whistleblowing: the public horror of lost lives, and the personal horror of responsible whistleblowers who lose their careers. Most whistle-

blowers undergo serious penalties for "committing the truth." One recent study suggests that two out of three of them suffer harassment, lowered performance evaluations, demotions, punitive transfers, loss of jobs, or blacklisting that can effectively end a career.[6] Horror stories about whistleblowers are not the exception; they are the rule.

THREE APPROACHES TO WHISTLEBLOWING ETHICS

The literature on whistleblowing is large and growing. Here I mention three general approaches. The first is to condemn whistleblowers as disloyal troublemakers who "rat" on their companies and undermine teamwork based on the hierarchy of authority within the corporation. Admittedly, whistleblowers' views about safety concerns are sometimes correct, but final decisions about safety belong to management, not engineers. When management errs, the corporation will eventually pick up the costs in law suits and adverse publicity. Members of the public are part of the technological enterprise which both benefits them and exposes them to risks; when things go wrong they (or their surviving family) can always sue.

I once dismissed this attitude as callous, as sheer corporate egoism that misconstrues loyalty to a corporation as an absolute (unexceptionless) moral principle. *If,* however—and it is a big "if"—the public accepts this attitude, as revealed in how it expresses its will through legitimate political processes, then so be it. As will become clear later, I take public responsibilities seriously. If the public refuses to protect whistleblowers, it tacitly accepts the added risks from not having available important safety information. I hope the public will protect the jobs of whistleblowers; more on this later.

A second approach, insightfully defended by Michael Davis,[7] is to regard whistleblowing as a tragedy to be avoided. On occasion whistleblowing may be a necessary evil or even admirable, but it is always bad news all around. It is proof of organizational trouble and management failure; it threatens the careers of managers on whom the whistle is blown; it disrupts collegiality by making colleagues feel resentment toward the whistleblower, and it damages the important informal network of friends at the workplace; it shows the whistleblower lost faith in the organization and its authority, and hence is more likely to be a troublemaker in the future; and it almost always brings severe penalties to whistleblowers who are viewed by employers and colleagues as unfit employees.

I wholeheartedly support efforts to avoid the need for whistleblowing. There are many things that can be done to improve organizations to make whistleblowing unnecessary. Top management can—and must—set a moral tone, and then implement policies that encourage safety concerns (and other bad news) to be communicated freely. Specifically, managers can keep doors open, allowing engineers to convey their concerns without retribution. Corporations can have in-house ombudspersons and appeal boards, and even a vice-president for corporate ethics. For their part, engineers can learn to be more assertive and effective in making their safety concerns known, learning how to build support from their colleagues. (Could Dan Applegate have pushed harder than he did, or did he just write a memo and drop the matter?) Professional societies should explore the possibility of creating confidential appeal groups where engineers can have their claims heard.

Nevertheless, this second approach is not enough. There will always be corporations and managers willing to cut corners on safety in the pursuit of short-term profit, and there will always be a need for justified whistleblowing. Labelling whistleblowing as a tragedy to be avoided whenever possible should not deflect attention from issues concerning justified whistleblowing. . . .

A third approach is to affirm unequivocally the obligation of engineers (and other professionals) to whistleblow in certain circumstances, and to treat this obligation as paramount—as overriding all other considerations, whatever the sacrifice involved in meeting it. Richard De George gave the classical statement of this view.[8] External whistleblowing, he argued, is obligatory when five conditions are met (by an engineer or other corporate employee):

1. "Serious and considerable harm to the public" is involved;

2. one reports the harm and expresses moral concern to one's immediate superior;

3. one exhausts other channels within the corporation;

4. one has available "documented evidence that would convince a reasonable, impartial observer that one's view of the situation is correct"; and

5. one has "good reasons to believe that by going public the necessary changes will be brought about" to prevent the harm.

De George says that whistleblowing is morally *permissible* when conditions 1–3 are met, and is morally *obligatory* when 1–5 are met.

As critics have pointed out, conditions (4) and (5) seem far too strong. Where serious safety is at stake, there is some obligation to whistleblow even when there are only grounds for hope (not necessarily belief) that whistleblowing will significantly improve matters, and even when one's documentation is substantial but less than convincing to every rational person.[9] Indeed, often whistleblowing is intended to prompt authorities to garner otherwise-unavailable evidence through investigations.

Moreover, having a reasonable degree of documentation is a requirement even for permissible whistleblowing—lest one make insupportable allegations that unjustifiably harm the reputations of individuals and corporations. So too is having a reasonable hope for success—lest one waste everyone's time and energy.[10] Hence, De George's sharp separation of requirements for permissibility and obligation begins to collapse. There may be an obligation to whistleblow when 1–3 are met and the person has some reasonable degree of documentation and reasonable hope for success in bringing about necessary changes.

My main criticism of this third approach, however, is more fundamental. I want to call into question the whole attempt to offer a general rule that tells us when whistleblowing is mandatory, *tout court*. Final judgments about obligations to whistleblow must be made contextually, not as a matter of general rule. And they must take into account the burdens imposed on whistleblowers.[11]

THE MORAL RELEVANCE OF PERSONAL LIFE TO PROFESSIONAL DUTY

In my view, there is a strong *prima facie* obligation to whistleblow when one has good reason to believe there is a serious moral problem, has exhausted normal organizational channels (except in emergencies when time precludes that), has available a reasonable amount of documentation, and has reasonable hope of solving the problem by blowing the whistle. Nevertheless, however strong, the obligation is—only *prima facie*: It can sometimes have exceptions when it conflicts with other important considerations. Moreover, the considerations which need to be weighed include not only *prima facie* obligations to one's employer, but also considerations about one's personal life. Before they make all-things-considered judgments about whether to whistleblow, engineers may and should consider their responsibilities to their family, other personal obligations which depend on having an income, and their rights to pursue their careers.

Engineers are people, as well as professionals. They have personal obligations to their families, as well as sundry other obligations in personal life which can be met only if they have an income. They also have personal rights to pursue careers. These personal obligations and rights are moral ones, and they legitimately interact with professional obligations in ways that sometimes make it permissible for engineers not to whistleblow, even when they have a *prima facie* obligation to do so. Precisely how these considerations are weighed depends on the particular situation. And here as elsewhere, we must allow room for morally reasonable people to weigh moral factors differently.

In adopting this contextual approach to balancing personal and professional obligations, I am being heretical. Few discussions of whistleblowing take personal considerations seriously, as being morally significant, rather than a matter of nonmoral, prudential concern for self-interest. But responsibilities to family and to others outside the workplace, as well as the right to pursue one's career, are moral considerations, not just prudential ones. Hence further argument is needed to dismiss them as irrelevant or always secondary in this context. I will consider three such arguments.

(i) The *Prevent-Harm Argument* says that morality requires us to prevent harm and in doing so to treat others' interests equally and impartially with our own. This assumption is often associated with utilitarianism, the view that we should always produce the most good for the most people. Strictly, at issue here is "negative utilitarianism," which says we should always act to minimize total harm, treating everyone's interests as equally important with our own. The idea is that even though engineers and their families must suffer, their suffering is outweighed by the lives saved through whistleblowing. Without committing himself to utilirarianism, De George uses a variation of the impartiality requirement to defend his criteria for obligatory whistleblowing: "It is not implausible to claim both that we are morally obliged to prevent harm to others at relatively little expense to ourselves, and that we are morally obliged to prevent great harm to a great many others, even at considerable expense to ourselves."[12]

The demand for strict impartiality in ethics has been under sustained attack during the past two decades, and from many directions.[13] Without attempting to review all those arguments, I can indicate how they block any straightforward move from impartiality to absolute (exceptionless) whistleblowing obligations, thereby undermining the Prevent-Harm Argument. One argument is that a universal requirement of strict impartiality (as opposed to a limited requirement restricted to certain contexts) is self-demeaning. It undermines our ability to give our lives meaning through special projects, careers, and relationships that require the resources which strict impartiality would demand we give away to others. The general moral right to autonomy—the right to pursue our lives in a search for meaning and happiness—implies a right to give considerable emphasis to our personal needs and those of our family.

As an analogy, consider the life-and-death issues surrounding world hunger and scarce medical resources.[14] It can be argued that all of us share a general responsibility (of mutual aid) for dealing with the tragedy of tens of thousands of people who die each day from malnutrition and lack of medical care. As citizens paying taxes that can be used toward this end, and also as philanthropists who voluntarily recognize a responsibility to give to relief organizations, each of us has a *prima facie* obligation to help. But there are limits. Right now, you and I could dramatically lower our lifestyles in order to help save lives by making greater sacrifices. We could even donate one of our kidneys to save a life. Yet we have a right not to do that, a right to give ourselves and our families considerable priority in how we use our resources. Similarly, engineers' rights to pursue their meaning-giving careers, and the projects and relationships made possible by those careers, have relevance in understanding the degree of sacrifice required by a *prima facie* whistleblowing obligation.

(ii) The *Avoid-Harm Argument* proceeds from the obligation not to cause harm to others. It then points out that engineers are in a position to cause or avoid harm on an unusual scale. As a result, according to Kenneth Alpern, the ordinary moral obligation of due care in avoiding harm to others implies that engineers must "be ready to make greater personal sacrifices than can normally be demanded of other individuals."[15] In particular, according to Gene James, whistleblowing is required when it falls under the general obligation to "prevent unnecessary harm to others" and "to not cause avoidable harm to others," where "harm" means violating their rights.[16]

Of course there is a general obligation not to cause harm. That obligation, however, is so abstract that it tells us little about exactly how much effort and sacrifice is required of us, especially where many people share responsibility for avoiding harm. I have an obligation not to harm others by polluting the environment, but it does not follow that I must stop driving my car at the cost of my job and the opportunities it makes possible for my family. That would be an unfair burden. These abstract difficulties multiply as we turn to the context of engineering practice which involves collective responsibility for technological products.

Engineers work as members of authority-structured teams which sometimes involve hundreds of other professionals who share responsibility for inherently-risky technological projects.[17] Engineers are not the only team-members who have responsibilities to create safe products. Their managers have exactly the same general responsibilities. In fact, they have greater accountability insofar as they are charged with the authority to make final decisions about projects. . . .

Dan Applegate and Roger Boisjoly acted responsibly in making unequivocal safety recommendations; their managers failed to act responsibly. Hence their moral dilemmas about whether to whistleblow arose because of unjustified decisions by their superiors. It is fair to ask engineers to pick up the moral slack for managers' irresponsible decisions—as long as we afford them legal protection to prevent their being harassed, fired, and blacklisted. Otherwise, we impose an unfair burden. Government and the general public share responsibility for safety in engineering. They set the rules that business plays by. It is hypocrisy for us to insist that engineers have an obligation to whistleblow to protect us, and then to fail to protect them when they act on the obligation.

(iii) The *Professional-Status Argument* asserts that engineers have special responsibilities as professionals, specified in codes of ethics, which go beyond the general responsibilities incumbent on everyone to prevent and avoid harm, and which override all personal considerations. Most engineering codes hint at a whistleblowing obligation with wording similar to that of the code of the National Society of Professional Engineers (NSPE):

> Engineers shall at all times recognize that their primary obligation is to protect the safety, health, property and welfare of the public. If their professional judgment is over-ruled under circumstances where the safety, health, property or welfare of the public are endangered, they shall notify their employer or client and such other authority as may be appropriate.[18]

The phrase "as may be appropriate" is ambiguous. Does it mean "when morally justified," or does it mean "as necessary in order to protect the public safety, health, and welfare." The latter interpretation is the most common one, and it clearly implies whistleblowing in some situations, no matter what the personal cost.

I agree that the obligation to protect public safety is an essential professional obligation that deserves emphasis in engineers' work. It is not clear, however, that it is paramount in the technical philosophical sense of overriding all other professional obligations in all situations. In any case, I reject the general assumption that

codified professional duties are all that are morally relevant in making whistleblowing decisions. It is quite true that professional considerations require setting aside personal interests in many situations. But it is also true that personal considerations have enormous and legitimate importance in professional life, such as in choosing careers and areas of specialization, choosing and changing jobs, and deciding how far to go in sacrificing family life in pursuing a job and a career.

Spouses have a right to participate in professional decisions such as those involving whistleblowing.[19] At the very least, I would be worried about professionals who do not see the moral importance of consulting their spouses before deciding to engage in acts of whistleblowing that will seriously affect them and their children. I would be equally worried about critics who condemn engineers for failing to whistleblow without knowing anything about their personal situation.[20]

Where does all this leave us on the issue of engineers' obligations? It is clear there is a minimum standard which engineers must meet. They have strong obligations not to break the law and not to approve projects which are immoral according to standard practice. They also have a *prima facie* obligation to whistleblow in certain situations. Just how strong the whistleblowing responsibility is, all things considered, remains unclear—as long as there are inadequate legal protections.

What is clear is that whistleblowing responsibilities must be understood contextually, weighed against personal rights and responsibilities, and assessed in light of the public's responsibilities to protect whistleblowers. We must look at each situation. Sometimes the penalties for whistleblowing may not be as great as is usually the case, perhaps because some protective laws have been passed, and sometimes family responsibilities and rights to pursue a career may not be seriously affected. But our all-things-considered judgments about whistleblowing are not a matter of a general absolute principle that always overrides every other consideration.

Yes, the public has a right to be warned by whistleblowers of dangers—assuming the public is willing to bear its responsibility for passing laws protecting whistleblowers. In order to play their role in respecting that right, engineers should have a legally-backed *right of conscience* to take responsible action in safety matters beyond the corporate walls.[21] As legal protections are increased, as has begun to happen during the past decade,[22] then the relative weight of personal life to professional duty changes. Engineers will be able to whistleblow more often without the kind of suffering to which they have been exposed, and thus the *prima facie* obligation to whistleblow will be less frequently overridden by personal responsibilities.

CHARACTER, INTEGRITY, AND PERSONAL IDEALS

Isn't there a danger that denying the existence of absolute, all-things-considered, principles for whistleblowers will further discourage whistleblowing in the public interest? After all, even if we grant my claims about the moral relevance of personal rights and responsibilities, there remains the general tendency for self-interest to unduly bias moral decisions. Until adequate legal protection is secured, won't this contextual approach result in fewer whistleblowers who act from a sense of responsibility? I think not.

If all-things-considered judgments about whistleblowing are not a matter of general rule, they are still a matter of good moral judgment. Good judgment takes into account rules whenever they provide helpful guidance, but essentially it is a product of good character—a character defined by virtues. Character is a further area in which personal aspects of morality bear on engineering ethics, and in the space remaining I want to comment on it.

Virtues are those desirable traits that reveal themselves in all aspects of personality—in attitudes, emotions, desires, and conduct. They are not private merit badges. (To view them as such is the egoistic distortion of self-righteousness.[23]) Instead, virtues are desirable ways of relating to other people, to communities, and to social practices such as engineering. Which virtues are most important for engineers to cultivate?

Here are some of the most significant virtues, sorted into three general categories.[24]

(1) *Virtues of self-direction* are those which enable us to guide our lives. They include the *intellectual virtues* which characterize technical expertise: mastery of one's discipline, ability to communicate, skills in reasoning, imagination, ability to discern dangers, a disposition to minimize risk, and humility (understood as a reasonable perspective on one's abilities). They also include *integrity virtues* which promote coherence among one's attitudes, commitments, and conduct based on a core of moral concern. They include honesty, courage, conscientiousness, self-respect, and fidelity to promises and commitments—those in both personal and professional life. And *wisdom* is practical good judgment in making responsible decisions. This good moral judgment, grounded in the experience of concerned and accountable engineers, is essential in balancing the aspirations embedded in the next two sets of virtues.

(2) *Team-work virtues* include (a) loyalty: concern for the good of the organization for which one works;

(b) collegiality: respect for one's colleagues and a commitment to work with them in shared projects; and (c) cooperativeness: the willingness to make reasonable compromises. Reasonable compromises can be integrity-preserving in that they enable us to meet our responsibilities to maintain relationships in circumstances where there is moral complexity and disagreement, factual uncertainty, and the need to maintain ongoing cooperative activities—exactly the circumstances of engineering practice.[25] Unreasonable compromises are compromising in the pejorative sense: they betray our moral principles and violate our integrity. Only good judgment, not general rules, enables engineers to draw a reasonable line between these two types of compromise.

(3) *Public-spirited virtues* are those aimed at the good of others, both clients and the general public affected by one's work. *Justice virtues* concern fair play. One is respect for persons: the disposition to respect people's rights and autonomy, in particular, the rights not to be injured in ways one does not consent to.

Public-spiritedness can be shown in different degrees, as can all the virtues. This helps us understand the sense of responsibility to protect the public that often motivates whistleblowers. Just as professional ethics has tended to ignore the moral relevance of personal life to professional responsibilities, it has tended to think of professional responsibilities solely in terms of *role responsibilities*—those minimal obligations which all practitioners take on when they enter a given profession. While role responsibilities are sufficiently important to deserve this emphasis, they are not the whole of professional ethics. There are also *ideals* which evoke higher aspirations than the minimum responsibilities.[26] These ideals are important to understanding the committed conduct of whistleblowers.

Depth of commitment to the public good is a familiar theme in whistleblowers' accounts of their ordeals. The depth is manifested in how they connect their self-respect and personal integrity to their commitments to the good of others. Roger Boisjoly, for example, has said that if he had it all to do over again he would make the same decisions because otherwise he "couldn't live with any self respect."[27] Similarly, Frank Camps says he acted from a sense of personal integrity.[28]

Boisjoly, Camps, and whistleblowers like them also report that they acted from a sense of responsibility. In my view, they probably acted beyond the minimum standard that all engineers are required to meet, given the absence of protective laws and the severity of the personal suffering they had to undergo. Does it follow that they are simply confused about how much was required of them? J.O. Urmson once suggested that moral heroes who claim to be meeting their duties are either muddled in their thinking or excessively modest about their moral zealousness, which has carried them beyond the call of duty.[29]

Urmson, like most post-Kantian philosophers, assumed that obligations are universal, and hence that there could not be personal obligations that only certain individuals have. I hold a different view.[30] There is such a thing as voluntarily assuming a responsibility and doing so because of commitments to (valid) ideals, to a degree beyond what is required of everyone. Sometimes the commitment is shown in career choice and guided by religious ideals: think of Albert Schweitzer or Mother Teresa of Calcutta. Sometimes it is shown in professional life in an unusual degree of *pro bono publico* work. And sometimes it is shown in whistleblowing decisions.

According to this line of thought, whistleblowing done at enormous personal cost, motivated by moral concern for the public good, and exercising good moral judgment is both (a) supererogatory—beyond the general call of duty incumbent on everyone, and (b) appropriately motivated by a sense of responsibility. Such whistleblowers act from a sense that they *must* do what they are doing.[31] Failure to act would constitute a betrayal of the ideal to which they are committed, and also a betrayal of their integrity as a person committed to that ideal.

Here, then, is a further way in which personal life is relevant to professional life. Earlier I drew attention to the importance of personal rights and responsibilities, and to the unfair personal burdens when others involved in collective enterprises fail to meet their responsibilities. Equally important, we need to appreciate the role of personal integrity grounded in supererogatory commitments to ideals. The topic of being able to live with oneself should not be dismissed as a vagary of individual psychology. It concerns the ideals to which we commit ourselves, beyond the minimum standard incumbent on everyone. This appreciation of personal integrity and commitments to ideals is compatible with a primary emphasis on laws that make it possible for professionals to serve the public good without having to make heroic self-sacrifices.

ENDNOTES

1. Cf. Mike W. Martin and Roland Schinzinger, *Ethics in Engineering,* 2d ed. (New York: McGraw-Hill, 1989), p. 213 ff.
2. See Frederick Elliston, "Anonymous Whistleblowing," *Business & Professional Ethics Journal* Vol. 1, No. 2 (Winter 1982): 39–58.
3. Paul Eddy, Elaine Potter, Bruce Page, *Destination Disaster* (New York: Quandrangle, 1976), p. 185.
4. Frank Camps, "Warning an Auto Company About an Unsafe Design," in Alan F. Westin (ed.), *Whistle-Blowing!* (New York: McGraw-Hill, 1981), pp. 119–129.
5. Roger M. Boisjoly, "The Challenger Disaster: Moral Responsibility and the Working Engineer," in Deborah G. Johnson (ed.), *Ethical Issues in Engineering* (Englewood Cliffs, NJ: Prentice Hall, 1991), pp. 6–14.
6. See, e.g., Myron P. Glazer and Penina Migdal Glazer, *The Whistleblowers* (New York: Basic Books, 1989).
7. Michael Davis, "Avoiding the Tragedy of Whistleblowing," *Business & Professional Ethics Journal* Vol. 8, No. 4, (Winter, 1989): 3–19. Davis also draws attention to the potentially negative aspects of laws, as does Sissela Bok in "Whistleblowing and Professional Responsibilities," in D. Callahan and S. Bok (eds.), *Ethics Teaching in Higher Education* (New York: Plenum), pp. 277–295. Those aspects, which include violating corporate privacy, undermining trust and collegiality, and lowering economic efficiency, are serious. But I am convinced that well-framed laws to protect whistleblowers can take them into account. The laws should protect only whistleblowing that meets the conditions for the *prima facie* obligation I state at the beginning of section 3 [The Moral Relevance of Personal Life to Professional Duty, p. 381].
8. The quotes are from Richard T. De George's most recent statement of his view in *Business Ethics,* 3d ed. (New York: Macmillan Publishing, 1990), pp. 208–212. They parallel his view as first stated in "Ethical Responsibilities of Engineers in Large Organizations," *Business & Professional Ethics Journal* Vol. 1, No. 1 (Fall 1981): 1–14. As an example of a far higher demand on engineers see Kenneth D. Alpern, "Moral Responsibility for Engineers," *Business & Professional Ethics Journal* Vol. 2, No. 2 (Winter 1983): 39–47.
9. Gene G. James, "Whistle Blowing: Its Moral Justification," in W. Michael Hoffman and Jennifer Mills Moore (eds.), *Business Ethics,* 2d ed. (New York: McGraw-Hill, 1990), pp. 332–344.
10. David Theo Goldberg, "Tuning in to Whistle Blowing," *Business & Professional Ethics Journal* Vol. 7, No. 2 (Summer, 1988): 85–94.
11. As his reason for conditions (4) and (5), De George cites the fate of whistleblowers who put themselves at great risk: "If there is little likelihood of his success, there is no moral obligation for the engineer to go public. For the harm he or she personally incurs is not offset by the good such action achieves." ("Ethical Responsibilities of Engineers in Large Organizations," p. 7.) Like myself, then, he sees the personal suffering of whistleblowers as morally relevant to understanding professional responsibilities, even though, as I go on to argue, he invokes that relevance in the wrong way.

12. De George, *Business Ethics,* p. 124.

13. See especially Bernard Williams, "A Critique of Utilitarianism" in *Utilitarianism for and Against* (Cambridge: Cambridge University Press, 1973) and "Persons, Character, and Morality," in *Moral Luck* (New York: Cambridge University Press, 1981). For samples of more recent discussions see the special edition of *Ethics* 101 (July 1991), devoted to "Impartiality and Ethical Theory."

14. Cf. John Arthur, "Rights and Duty to Bring Aid," in William Aiken and Hugh La Follette (eds.) *World Hunger and Moral Obligation* (Englewood Cliffs, NJ: Prentice-Hall, 1977).

15. Alpern, "Moral Responsibilities for Engineers," p. 39.

16. James, "Whistle Blowing: Its Moral Justification," pp. 334–335.

17. See Martin and Schinzinger, *Ethics in Engineering,* chapter 3. The emphasis on engineers adopting a wide view of their activities does not imply that they are culpable for all the moral failures of colleagues and managers.

18. National Society of Professional Engineers, Code of Ethics.

19. Cf. Thomas M. Devine and Donald G. Aplin, "Whistleblower Protection—The Gap Between the Law and Reality," *Howard Law Journal* 31 (1988), p. 236.

20. I am glad that the NSPE and other professional codes say what they do in support of responsible whistleblowing, as long as it is understood that professional codes only state professional, not personal and all-things-considered obligations. Codes provide a backing for morally concerned engineers, and they make available to engineers the moral support of an entire profession. At the same time, professional societies need to do far more than most of them have done to support the efforts of conscientious whistleblowers. Beyond moral and political support, and beyond recognition awards, they need to provide economic support, in the form of legal funds and job-placement.

21. I defend this right in "Rights of Conscience Inside the Technological Corporation," *Conceptus-Studien, 4: Wissen and Gewissen* (Vienna: VWGO, 1986): 179–191.

22. Alan F. Westin offers helpful suggestions about laws protecting whistleblowers in *Whistle-Blowing!* For a recent overview of the still fragmented and insufficient legal protection of whistleblowers see Rosemary Chalk, "Making the World Safe for Whistle-Blowers," *Technology Review* 91 (January 1988): 48–57; and James C. Petersen and Dan Farrell, *Whistleblowing: Ethical and Legal Issues in Expressing Dissent* (Dubuque, Iowa: Kendall/Hunt, 1986).

23. Cf. Edmund L. Pincoffs, *Quandaries and Virtues* (Lawrence, KS: University Press of Kansas, 1986), pp. 112–114.

24. Important discussions of the role of virtues in professional ethics include: John Kultgen, *Ethics and Professionalism* (Philadelphia: University of Pennsylvania Press, 1988); Albert Flores (ed.), *Professional Ideals* (Belmont, CA: Wadsworth, 1988); and Michael D. Bayles, *Professional Ethics,* 2d edition (Belmont, CA: Wadsworth, 1989). John Kekes insightfully discusses the virtues of self-direction in *The Examined Life* (Lewisburg: Bucknell University Press, 1988).

25. Martin Benjamin, *Splitting the Difference* (Lawrence, KS: University Press of Kansas), 1990.

26. On the distinction between moral rules and ideals see Bernard Gert, *Morality* (New York: Oxford University Press, 1988), pp. 160–178.

27. Roger Boisjoly, ibid., p. 14.

28. Frank Camps, ibid., p. 128.

29. J. O. Urmson, "Saints and Heroes," in A. I. Melden (ed.), *Essays in Moral Philosophy* (Seattle: University of Washington Press, 1958), pp. 198–216.

30. Cf. A. I. Melden, "Saints and Supererogation," in *Philosophy and Life: Essays on John Wisdom* (The Hague: Martinus Nijhoff, 1984), pp. 61–81.

31. Harry Frankfurt insightfully discusses this felt "must" as a sign of deep caring and commitment in *The Importance of What We Care About* (New York: Cambridge University Press, 1988), pp. 86–88.

QUESTIONS ON MARTIN

1. Reconsider the summation of De George's account of whistleblowing. What are the three conditions that render an act of whistleblowing permissible? What are the additional two conditions that render whistleblowing obligatory? Do you agree with De George's approach? In what ways does Martin criticize the conditions and the general approach?

2. What are some of the personal values and responsibilities that may weigh against a *prima facie* obligation to blow the whistle? How strongly do you consider these? How strongly should these be considered if the lives of other persons are at stake?

3. Martin's contextual approach relies upon an account of the virtues. Are the virtues he delineates relevant only to engineering, or do they apply to other areas of enterprise? How would these virtues help one make a wise decision? What role does character play in making a good decision about whether to blow the whistle?

FOR FURTHER READING

Honesty

Baier, Annette. "Trust and Antitrust." *Ethics* 96 (1986): 231–60.

Campbell, Jeremy. *The Liar's Tale: A History of Falsehood.* New York: Norton, 2001.

Fried, Charles. *Right and Wrong.* Cambridge: Harvard University Press, 1978.

Gert, Bernard. "Don't Deceive, Keep Your Promise, Don't Cheat." In *Morality: A New Justification of the Moral Rules.* New York: Oxford University Press, 1988.

Klein, Daniel, ed. *Reputation: Studies in the Voluntary Elicitation of Good Conduct.* Ann Arbor: University of Michigan Press, 1997.

Luhmann, Niklas, *Trust: A Mechanism for the Reduction of Social Complexity.* In Luhmann, *Trust and Power,* edited by Tom Burns and Gianfranco Poggi, translated by Howard David, John Raffan, and Kathryn Rooney. New York: Wiley, 1980.

Advertising and Sales

Beauchamp, Tom L. "Manipulative Advertising," *Business and Professional Ethics Journal* 3 (Spring/Summer 1984): 1–22.

Benn, Stanley I. "Freedom and Persuasion." *Australasian Journal of Philosophy* 45 (December 1967): 259–75.

Ebejer, James M., and Michael J. Morden, "Paternalism in the Marketplace: Should a Salesman Be His Buyer's Keeper?" *Journal of Business Ethics* 7 (1988): 337–39.

Lacznick, Gene R., and Patrick E. Murphy, eds. *Marketing Ethics.* Lexington, Mass.: Lexington, Books, 1993.

Machan, Tibor R. "Advertising: The Whole or Only Some of the Truth?" *Public Affairs Quarterly* 1 (October 1987): 59–71.

Oakes, G. "The Sales Process and the Paradoxes of Trust," *Journal of Business Ethics* 9 (August 1990): 671–79.

Phillips, Barbara J. "In Defense of Advertising: A Social Perspective," *Journal of Business Ethics* 16 (1997): 109–18.

Integrity, Loyalty, and Whistleblowing

Baron, Marcia. *The Moral Status of Loyalty.* Dubuque, Ia.: Kendall/Hunt, 1984.

Bok, Sissela. "Whistleblowing and Leaking." In *Secrets: On the Ethics of Concealment and Revelation.* New York: Pantheon, 1982.

Carter, Stephen L. *Integrity.* New York: Basic Books, 1996.

De George, Richard T. *Business Ethics,* 5th ed. Upper Saddle River, N.J.: Prentice Hall, 1999.

Drucker, Peter F. *Management: Tasks, Responsibilities, Practices.* New York: Harper and Row, 1974.

Ewin, R. E. "Corporate Loyalty: Its Objects and Its Grounds." *Journal of Business Ethics* 12 (May 1993): 387–96.

Fiedler, John H. "Organizational Loyalty." *Business and Professional Ethics Journal* 11 (Spring 1992): 71–90.

Fletcher, George. *Loyalty: An Essay on the Morality of Relationships.* New York: Oxford University Press, 1993.

Gaita, Raymond. "Integrity." *The Aristotelian Society,* Supplementary volume 55 (1981): 163–76.

Halfon, Mark S. *Integrity: A Philosophical Integrity.* Philadelphia, Pa.: Temple University Press, 1989.

Hanson, Karen. "The Demands of Loyalty." *Idealistic Studies* 16 (April 1986): 195–204.

Hirschman, Albert O. *Exit, Voice, and Loyalty: Response to Decline in Firms, Organizations and States.* Cambridge: Harvard University Press, 1970.

Maccoby, Michael. "Integrity: A Fictional Dialogue." In *Executive Integrity: The Search for High Human Values in Organizational Life,* edited by Suresh Srivastva and Associates. San Francisco, Calif.: Jossey-Bass, 1988.

Montefiore, Alan, and David Vines, eds. *Integrity in the Public and Private Domains.* London: Routledge, 1999.

Oldenquist, Andrew. "Loyalties." *Journal of Philosophy* 79 (1982): 173–93.

Pettit, Philip. "The Paradox of Loyalty." *American Philosophical Quarterly* 163 (April 1988): 163–71.

Shapiro, Ian, and Robert Adams, eds. *Integrity and Conscience.* New York: New York University Press, 1998.

Responsibility, Action, and the Conduct of Business

Individual Responsibility

And he also who had the two talents came forward saying, 'Master, you delivered to me two talents; here I have made two talents more.' His master said to him, 'Well done, good and faithful servant; you have been faithful over a little, I will set you over much.'

Matthew 25:22–23

My heart goes out to the man who does his work when the 'boss' is away, as well as when he is at home. And the man who, when given a letter for Garcia, quietly takes the missive, without asking any idiotic questions, and with no lurking intention of chucking it into the nearest sewer, or of doing aught else but deliver it, never gets 'laid off,' nor has to go on a strike for higher wages. Civilization is one long anxious search for just such individuals. Anything such a man asks shall be granted. He is wanted in every city, town and village—in every office, shop, store and factory. The world cries out for such; he is needed and needed badly—the man who can 'Carry a Message to Garcia.'

Elbert Hubbard[1]

There are many who find a good alibi far more attractive than an achievement. For an achievement does not settle anything permanently. We still have to prove our worth anew each day: we have to prove that we are as good today as we were yesterday. But when we have a valid alibi for not achieving anything we are fixed, so to speak, for life. Moreover, when we have an alibi for not writing a book, painting a picture and so on, we have an alibi for not writing the greatest book and not painting the greatest picture. Small wonder that the effort expended and the punishment endured in obtaining a good alibi often exceed the effort and grief requisite for the attainment of a most marked achievement.

Eric Hoffer[2]

---

1. "A Message to Garcia," in *A Message to Garcia and Other Essays* (New York: Thomas Y. Crowell, 1916), 22–23.
2. *The Passionate State of Mind and Other Aphorisms* (New York: Harper and Row, 1954), §241.

One of the most important things that can be said of an individual is that the person is "responsible." Such a person can be trusted to act in certain appropriate ways, for the responsible person's manner of conduct exemplifies seriousness of purpose, attention, and effort. A responsible person, therefore, manifests a *sense* of responsibility, a disposition or tendency that is not only valuable for that individual but for society as well. As Elbert Hubbard describes this person, "He is wanted in every city, town, and village. . . ." In this first section of BIII, let us consider the idea of responsibility as well as the corollary concept of a responsible person.

Responsibility

The notion of "responsibility" is often employed in divergent ways. There are at least five types of responsibility worth noting: causal, legal, moral, capacity, and role responsibility.[3] *Causal responsibility* refers to how a person's action or omission brings about, or causes, some effect or event. A second type of responsibility is that of *legal liability,* a form of responsibility determined by legal rules; legal liability may or may not entail causal responsibility or moral responsibility. *Moral responsibility,* which presupposes causal responsibility, refers to whether one is morally blameworthy for some act or omission. To ascribe moral responsibility to a person also presumes that the person has *capacity responsibility,* which includes the capacity to understand, to reason, and to control one's actions. A fifth type of responsibility, *role responsibility,* is of special significance to persons in organizations, including those of commerce and business, and it is, therefore, our concern here.

Role Responsibility and the Responsible Person

The contractual arrangement or agreement by which one comes to assume a task or role requires that one perform certain duties, whether these are defined by the contract itself or by the fact that the agreement may presuppose that one practices a certain profession or skill or has a certain type of knowledge. Thus, within any organization—whether or not commercial—a person may come to occupy a particular position with specific duties and tasks related to the aim of the organization. (Of course, in addition to these duties, one will have the re-

sponsibility to adhere to moral, legal, or customary expectations, not all of which will be explicitly defined). Thus, as noted in the quotation from Hubbard, it is the responsibility of the messenger to get "a message to Garcia." However, even if a messenger delivers the message, thereby fulfilling a particular responsibility, it might still be the case that the messenger is not a *responsible person* (or one who is fulfilling the role in a responsible way). How might this be so?

We might observe first that the failure to be responsible—morally, legally, or in terms of one's role—may occur either via the omission of an action (one's failure to perform some action) or by performing the requisite action in the wrong manner or in the most minimal way. It is this second type of failure that reveals how it is possible to draw a distinction between the performance of certain defined responsibilities and being a responsible person. One individual might meet his or her responsibilities by performing that which is required, even as the person's performance did not manifest the sense of responsibility emblematic of the responsible person.

With regard to a specific role or task, an individual is responsible just insofar as he or she not only performs the duties but does so with a certain attitude of thoughtfulness, seriousness, and effort: "A responsible person is one who is disposed to take his duties seriously; to think about them, and to make serious efforts to fulfil them."[4] Responsible conduct is intentional conduct and is as much a matter of the *manner* of one's actions as of the *ends*.

Responsibility and Virtue

Thus role responsibility may generate questions of moral responsibility simply because the failure to perform certain actions in the appropriate way is morally blameworthy. Though we don't often speak of responsibility as a virtue, we do think of individuals as responsible and hold them morally accountable for their failure to be responsible in the relevant circumstances. If responsibility is not itself a virtue, it is very close to one for it serves to characterize a certain disposition of action and awareness. As the philosopher J. R. Lucas considers the matter, if I am responsible,

> I shall think about what I am doing, rather than act thoughtlessly or on impulse, and act for reasons that are faceable rather than ones I should be ashamed to avow. Equally, I shall give thought to the situation generally, keep an eye out for anything that needs to

3. These are drawn from H. L. A. Hart's account in *Punishment and Responsibility: Essays in the Philosophy of Law* (Oxford: Oxford University Press, 1968), 211–12. Hart portrays the moral and the legal as *one* form of liability responsibility, but I distinguish these for the purposes of clarity.

4. Hart, *Punishment and Responsibility,* 213.

be done, and take care that nothing in my sphere of responsibility that needs to be done is left undone, and that if anything goes amiss I shall be ready to put things right again. That is what it is to be a responsible person.[5]

If responsibility is not itself a virtue, is there a sense in which it encompasses other virtues? The responsible person—whether manager, owner, executive, colleague, or employee—is not only one who is eager to fulfill the duties and tasks of a role (one who is, as the saying goes, "willing to work"), but also one whose conduct exhibits good judgment and self-control. As Aristotle points out, the person of good judgment, or practical wisdom (see Section AV), is not only one who deliberates well but one who correctly perceives, and is attentive to, the particulars of circumstance and is, therefore, one who recognizes the sorts of situations or contingencies that call for a certain kind and manner of action. Thus even if responsibility is not the same as practical wisdom it would seem to be included within it, at least in the sense that the responsible person is one who, as Lucas points out, "keep[s] an eye out for anything that needs to be done" and performs the requisite action with a certain readiness and alacrity. In order to do this, the responsible person must also possess a virtue that is essential to practical wisdom, namely, the virtue of self-control. For the responsible person is reliable in the sense that the person can be counted on not to be corrupted by pleasure or pain or by the allurements of vice, even if vice may masquerade as the "quick fix" or as the "job done but not done well."

It should be clear that one is responsible not simply by performing the explicit duties of one's role. Many duties may be general rather than specific and these will require a seriousness of attention and effort if they are to be performed well. Given that a business firm or corporation is comprised of relationships and hierarchies, one's role within the firm may include tasks and duties of varying levels of specificity. Even if some professional codes (such as those of accountants, physicians, or lawyers) or some codes of ethics help to structure various roles—delineating certain obligations, duties, or limits to which persons must conform—responsibility is not exhausted by conformity to rules. For explicit rules, codes, or duties cannot delineate the varying circumstances of business life and cannot specify when or how the duty becomes incumbent or the manner in which it is to be performed. Moreover, it is precisely because a person is responsible that the person *responds* to tasks

5. *Responsibility* (Oxford: Clarendon Press, 1995), 11.

and situations that are not, strictly speaking, part of the person's duties. Thus, the responsible person is the thoughtful person who not only performs the requisite duties but does so readily and in terms of the individual's relation to others within the enterprise, the aims of the business, and the requirements of ethics.

THE READINGS

John Lachs According to Lachs, there is a growing lack of responsibility: Employees are unmotivated and seek to perform only the most narrow and minimal job requirements. Rejecting two economic explanations of this phenomenon, Lachs also rejects any explanation that locates the cause of irresponsibility in some "malfunction" of society. Lachs states that any large-scale society will have a certain level of "mediation," by which one agent performs an action on behalf of another. This generates three negative consequences: a growing manipulation of people; an increasing passivity as we surrender to functional roles; and psychic distance from our actions. Within corporations there are mediated chains that create significant distance between the worker and his or her actions, as well as between the worker and the relations that comprise the company. Although mediation cannot be avoided, psychic distance can be reduced in certain ways, perhaps by introducing employees and managers to the various ways in which their particular corporation functions (so that each person understands his role within the whole and begins to regard the corporation as his own) or by introducing some elements of democratic decision making into the firm.

Michael Hardimon Hardimon seeks to give an account of our ordinary understanding of the obligations we have insofar as we have certain institutional roles, including those defined by occupation. Although Hardimon agrees that contractual role obligations are acquired by "signing on" to perform the role in question, he contends that this account does not adequately delineate what it is to "sign on" to a role. Some argue that "signing on" means nothing more than making a promise to fulfill the given duties; however, Hardimon points out that roles are a package of duties that are institutionally and socially fixed. These are not made up by contract but are enduring structures that are also subject to interpretation by individuals. A more sophisticated account of promising may try to incorporate these ideas, but it seems doubtful that there is any promise at work in the fact of a role obligation. Alternatively, the preferable interpretation includes both the idea of the voluntary acceptance of one's role as well as one's identification with that role. Hardimon explains how the person who identifies with a role understands the norms of the role to function as reasons for action.

"I Only Work Here"
Mediation and Responsibility

John Lachs

Born in Hungary, John Lachs is the Centennial Professor of Philosophy at Vanderbilt University. The author of numerous essays, he has edited two collections of the unpublished essays of George Santayana and has authored, among his other books, Intermediate Man *(1981),* The Relevance of Philosophy to Life *(1995) and, with Michael Hodges,* Thinking in the Ruins: Wittgenstein and Santayana on Contingency *(2000).*

The countries of Eastern Europe are said to be notorious for worker irresponsibility. There, production is inefficient, the performance of duties on a job is perfunctory, the quality of service is inferior. Few of the workers display interest in their work; fewer still take any pride in what they do. Travelers report that censure from supervisors is greeted with sullenness, complaints from customers with a shrug of the shoulders or a quiet curse. On being called on the carpet, the standard defense for incompetence or for anything that goes awry is the declaration "I only work here. Why pick on me?"

"I only work here" implies that I do not make the rules and do not wish to be responsible for them. It suggests that I have little notion of the interconnectedness of things and desire to restrict my operation to the narrowest limits of my job. This is one of the meanings, in fact, of the word "job." A job, in this sense, is contrasted with a position or a profession; it is simply a task to be performed for pay in as mechanical a fashion as possible. Individuals who hold down jobs in this sense make sure that there is little personal involvement in their work. To them, work is something that must be done for a living. Their conception of it is expressed accurately by the description a telephone company employee once gave me. "It is as if I took a deep breath at 8:15 in the morning and went under water," he said. "I surface about 5:00 in the afternoon and breathe a sigh of relief."

Jobs, in the current sense, are narrow roles in which virtually each operation to be performed requires explicit instructions. It is as if the human beings who perform these roles were denuded of activity and waited like machine parts to be caused to act. Since the cause of the action, the purpose, the motive, all come from the outside, it is not altogether surprising that people fail to feel responsible for failures. Machines, after all, are mere instruments, and no one could rightly blame the tires for crushing a man when the driver of the car is drunk.

There is something reassuring about the thought that such irresponsibility is rampant in Eastern Europe. The natural corollary is the supposition that it cannot happen here. Yet employers and customers alike are keenly aware that something quite like this is a widespread and growing reality in our own country, as well. I hear businessmen complain vigorously about the difficulty of obtaining the services of people who are willing to work. And what they mean by "someone willing to work" is someone who is self-motivated. That, in turn, involves the readiness to assume responsibility for getting things done, along with the corresponding responsibility for failure when that occurs. . . .

I believe that it is possible to develop concepts that help to explain the source of the irresponsibility in the face of which we manage and in the teeth of which we must live. Before I talk about the concepts that are adequate to do the job, however, I want to reject some other explanations. . . .

Inequality, injustice, and want are not major sources of negligence. By the same token, material wealth does little to render people more conscientious. On the contrary, the more we think of prosperity as our birthright, the less we understand its relation to a responsible role in the productive process. The result is that people demand to have all manner of good things, while with a clear conscience they offer little or nothing in return. I must dismiss, therefore, the sometimes exaggerated claim of unions that if only workers were treated better, earned more money, and received greater fringe benefits, they would take greater interest in their work and assume responsibility for doing well what must be accomplished.

Management frequently responds to the union claim by the classic capitalist argument that it is not higher wages that create responsibility in a corporation but actual ownership. There is some truth to this idea. Generally, we tend to be more responsible in handling things that belong to us than in dealing with objects or situations where success or failure makes little difference. But the interpretation of ownership and its embodiment in the form of holding shares, both of which are integral parts of this analysis, are inadequate. I shall try to show that economic ownership must be only a part of a larger appropriation by workers of the activities of the corporation as their own. The fundamental notion of ownership is not economic, therefore. It is personal and psychological, and requires an understanding of the organic interconnectedness of the operations that constitute a company. To own five shares out of fifty million outstanding makes little difference by itself. The very idea that the paper certificate one gets from the transfer agent in fact makes one a part owner of a company is difficult to conceive. The effectiveness of the thought that I am an owner of the company is a direct function of the understanding I have of the company and of the strength of my belief that its operations are somehow mine. If this understanding and this belief are lacking, the thought that we are owners becomes empty: its only content is the expectation of the dividend.

I want, then, to reject the notion that the primary source of our troubles is economic. In fact, I want to repudiate any thought that would identify the problem as due to some malfunction of society. Our intellectual history is a record of violent disagreements about what special structure or feature of modern industrial civilization is the primary cause of the depersonalized, irresponsible, alienated state in which we live. It is time to undercut this interminable debate by what I think is a radical departure. My argument is that no special structure is responsible for where we are. Although there may be malfunctions in our society, these cannot adequately account for our maladies. The narrow job orientation of employees, the social irresponsibility of employers, the general disaffection and depersonalization we all experience are natural costs of large-scale human society. When I say natural costs, I do not mean costs that cannot be minimized. My point is just that any society in which there is large-scale mediation will unavoidably tend to render individuals passive, ignorant, and irresponsible.

Mediation is a universal phenomenon, although it is rarely called by that name. It is simply the performance of an action by some agent on behalf of another. If you ask me to bring you a glass of water and I do, the action is mediated. It is mediated because I did it for you. Had I not done it, you would have had to do it yourself; in some sense, therefore, I performed an action that was or was to be yours. The same is true when there is no specific request for the performance of the act. I never ask the people at the generating plant to make me

some electricity, yet they do it on my behalf. If they did not provide the power to turn on my lights, I would have to do it myself or make some alternative arrangement. That they are working on my behalf is amply demonstrated by the fact that I pay them.

The contracts with distant people to perform actions on my behalf can be more open-ended and informal even than this. When Frank Sinatra cuts a new record, nothing is further from his thoughts than that some obscure philosopher in Tennessee will use it to express his love. Yet Sinatra's singing captured on disk can fulfill just that function, and it is not too farfetched to say that the series of acts of which it consists were performed for (among others) me. In this way, actions that range from the trivial to the most momentous, from the specifically contracted all the way to the generally available, are all mediated—that is, performed by one on behalf of and frequently for the benefit of others. Almost all the actions necessary for life, for satisfaction, and for self-expression are mediated in industrial society.

Mediation has four major consequences. The first is impressively beneficial. It is, simply put, to make civilization possible. For the division of labor is simply a form of mediation, and mediation—at its best—is just cooperative effort. If each person had to do everything for himself, the world would fall apart into a string of isolated and, I hasten to add, starving hermits. What anthropologists call the benefits of culture are simply the record of past acts done on our behalf (or at least turned to our benefit) by people who act as our agents. Teachers and engineers, businessmen and bulldozer operators all do their jobs, perhaps unmindful of what these mean to *me*. Yet they enable me and others to do what we want and to live in the way we will.

We all know the benefits of mediation. I omit a full discussion of them not because I think them insignificant but precisely because they are uncontroversial and evident. We are so blinded by the good, in fact, that we altogether overlook the cost. If I dwell on the costs, therefore, it is not to minimize the benefits, only to present a more balanced picture.

The three remaining major effects of mediation are all costs. The first is the growing manipulation of people. This is natural, given the fact that in mediation others perform my acts for me. Since I want only the act and its desired consequences, my interest is in bringing it about quickly, certainly, and at the least possible cost. The person who is to perform it becomes an instrument of my will; my interest in him is limited to the role he performs. He is not a person, or at least not a person primarily, in my eyes. He is a means to the end I desire, and I must be sure that I know what to say, do, or promise to elicit the desired response. When such manipulation becomes necessary on a large scale, virtually everyone begins to feel used and retaliates by using others. Obviously, people do not become things simply because of this. But the more we use people, the more we adopt toward them the attitude we normally have only toward inanimate physical objects. Depersonalization consists in the disregard of our subjective, emotional inner life in favor of exclusive focus on eliciting desirable behaviors.

The second deleterious result of mediation is our growing sense of passivity. Roles in social institutions are defined functionally: their usefulness and justification derive largely from the body of mediated acts they demand. The more others look to us for the satisfaction of their desires, the more our actions must be reliable, predictable, sane. The natural tendency is to surrender oneself to one's role. If we do what the rules require without thought and without fail, we will have fulfilled, we believe, all our responsibilities.

Not surprisingly, the more we make ourselves parts of an extended chain of mediation and the more we identify with our roles, the more we surrender any claim to be the causes of our actions. A sense of passivity then descends on us like dusk; in reflective moments, we begin to feel that even the actions we physically perform are not really our own. And there is some truth to this frustrating suspicion. It is not that the industrial world leaves us passive or lazy. On the contrary, we are busier than ever, doing for others what they cannot or will not do for themselves. It is just that the motives for our acts lie not within us; what we do is not a natural consequence of our dispositions or choices. It is as if there were only one decision to make: to take the job or not. Once that choice is behind us, our actions are largely determined by the requirements of the post. Typically, there is not much leeway left for personal discretion: what is to be done, when, and how are all prescribed externally. We thus feel pulled and shoved but inactive; it is difficult to think of ourselves *doing* anything without direct experience of the union of motive and execution.

An experience of impotence usually accompanies this sense of passivity. In mediated chains, the physical agent typically feels that the act is not his. He is, after all, caused to do it by his position in the chain. His own acts, in turn, are performed on his behalf by others far away. The longer the chain of intermediaries between himself and his distant act, the less he is in control of it. Even the most powerful man at the center of a large corporation time and again must taste this impotence. When things go awry, he suddenly comes face to face with his inability to control what his employees do. Often the most elaborate measures are inadequate to stop the slippage between command and execution. Even tightly organized social structures have an element of drift and, on the whole, the larger the structure the more difficult it is to regulate the behavior of its parts.

The third and perhaps most serious cost of mediation is what I call "psychic distance." As others perform my action, they and they alone come in contact with the circumstances that make it appropriate. Direct experience of the act resides in them alone; they see the immediate consequences, though sometimes even they do not see them all. The individual on whose behalf such actions are undertaken knows little about them; soon he may not even know that they occur. The result is a vast impoverishment of our personal experience and an immense, growing blindness to what we do. . . .

The psychic distance of which I speak is the direct result of the lack of direct experience. It shows itself in our unwillingness or even inability to appropriate actions that are clearly ours. It is reinforced by the fact that intermediate men hide from us both the immediate and the long-range consequences of our acts. Without firsthand acquaintance with his actions, even the best of men moves in a moral vacuum; the abstract recognition of evil is neither a reliable guide nor an adequate motive. If we keep in mind the psychic distance between the agent and his act, along with its source in impoverished personal experience, we shall not be surprised at the immense and largely unintentional cruelty of men of good will. The mindless indifference of what is sometimes called "the system" is in reality our indifference. It springs from our inability to appropriate acts as our own and thus assume responsibility for them—along with our bland perceptual life sheltered from encounter with evil. We do not know the suffering that is caused and cannot believe that *we* are the ones who cause it.

Our psychic distance from our deeds renders us ignorant of the conditions of our existence and the outcome of our acts. It fosters what seems to come naturally to most men anyway: blindness to the interconnection of all things, but especially of our acts and happiness. The distance we feel from our actions is proportionate to our ignorance of them; our ignorance, in turn, is largely a measure of the length of the chain of intermediaries between the original agent and his acts. The greater our ignorance, the more difficult it becomes to view the action as ours. And the less we are able to appropriate the act, the less inclined—in fact, the less able—we are to assume responsibility for it.

A tragic case demonstrating slippage of control, the danger of psychic distance, and the resultant problems of responsibility occurred during the Second World War in the Philippines when the Japanese General Tomoyuki Yamashita ordered his troops to do what was necessary to stop guerrilla activity.[1] It may be reasonable to believe, as he argued at his subsequent war crimes trial, that he did not mean for the troops to commit illegal atrocities and would have stopped them had he known what they were doing. The fact is that in spite of all the paraphernalia of modern communication, he was not in effective control of his troops, just as American commanders—with even better equipment—were apparently not in effective control at the time of the My Lai massacre. The loss of control is a direct consequence of mediation; its magnitude varies with the number of intermediaries involved (the chain of command) and the distance, both physical and psychological, at which policies ordered are executed. . . .

Evidently, there are very few instances of irresponsibility due to psychic distance in corporate life which are this dramatic. Yet the same concepts which render the Yamashita case intelligible can be used to shed light on the causes and cures of employee irresponsibility. The mediated chains of which corporations consist naturally create a momentous psychic distance between individuals in the chains and those acts which are performed on their behalf and without which the corporation could not survive. In ordinary terms, this means simply that just about everybody in a large company is ignorant of the detailed interconnectedness of its operations. The nescience is particularly pronounced among those who serve on a relatively low level: most of the decision making, integration, and social impact of the company are typically beyond their horizon. But there is a corresponding ignorance among the decision makers. These may well understand the outlines or principles of the manner in which the corporation produces and markets goods. Yet they have little knowledge of the actual experience of production. They have no just sense of the toll menial jobs exact or of the debilitating effects of routine. The daily boredom of managers escapes them, as does the way in which narrow role and stressful home combine to create lives without content and prospect.

The acts of all these agents constitute a single whole: they are so interconnected that it is not inappropriate to read each as being performed on behalf of many or all the people in the company. Yet this interconnectedness is not understood. The worker does not grasp the rationale behind management decisions and thus views them as alien; management, in turn, sees worker demands as self-serving and unacceptable. The result is the same: each person in the chain finds the perfect excuse by disappearing in his job. Each can convince himself that he is a victim of circumstance, an insignificant cog in the machine. How can anyone be held responsible if he is not an autonomous source of activity, if agency—so to speak—merely flows through him the way it flows through each link in a steel chain?

Responsibility is inconsistent with anonymity. Yet links in a chain of mediation have no names and no personality. All that is caught of the man is the role he plays, the job he performs: he is salesman, mail clerk, concentration camp guard, or sergeant assigned to command an execution squad. And paradoxically, the more we fade into our jobs and disappear in them, the less we identify with them, the less they express us, the less they satisfy. If my job is to serve as a shield from moral accountability, I must be utterly uninvolved with it: it must always appear that I am a cool, impersonal agent intent on doing what I must. In this way, job activity is mated to personal passivity, and our institutional obligations become the blanket excuse we offer to those who would hold us humanly and morally responsible. "It is nothing personal, you know," one can hear the Lord High Executioner whisper to his victim or the manager to the employees he is about to fire. "It is just my job to do this," we all say. "Who am I to question the wisdom of it all?" To the skeptical, we might add, "I owe an obligation to the company that pays my way," and then hasten to the ultimate disclaimer, "and in any case, if I did not do it, they would simply get someone else."

The high note of obligation to the company is, of course, a sham. For most, the duty extends no further than the narrowest limits of the job. Irresponsibility beyond the corporation and irresponsibility within it are of the same fabric. The same absorption of the man into his job that protects from responsibility to customers and the society beyond also protects from any but the narrowest accountability within the corporate structure. In this way, "I only work here" is in natural alliance with "that isn't my job." Both forms of irresponsibility have their origin in the psychic distance that is a natural outcome of mediation. Both suggest an inability to appropriate actions performed on our behalf, an unawareness of the nature and consequences of our acts, a very real ignorance of the interconnectedness of our lives.

If this analysis of the causes of employee irresponsibility is accurate, the cure should not be difficult to find. It is obvious that mediation cannot be abandoned. To hanker for smallness is to express a romantic dream.

In any case, to give up the large-scale mediated structures of our industrial society would entail a cost so staggering that it outstrips the ability of our imagination to measure it. The only hope is to reduce the psychic distance that attends mediation. In an unconscious way, some of this is already being accomplished for potential managers. Training programs in banks and other institutions take young people through the entire hierarchy from the mail room to the board room. The trainees learn to do each job and actually do many of them for a stretch of time. The avowed purpose of doing this is laudable: someone who will soon be in a management position has every reason to learn the way in which his corporation operates. The important thing to realize is that such exposure yields not only factual knowledge. A possibly unintended benefit is that by understanding the nature of each operation and the interconnectedness of them all, the manager begins to think of the corporation as *his*.

By saying that he views the entire company as his, I do not mean he supposes that he owns it. The true meaning of ownership is not the formal one we have enshrined in the law. It is something far more personal and immediate, which in the social or corporate context involves at least three abilities. The first is to see the complex operations of others as conditions of our own activity; the second is to think of their work as beneficial to us and as being done on our behalf; the third is to view the whole that their work and ours compose, as an expression of our creative life.

It is this vision of the whole and a just appraisal of our part in it that we must promote, if irresponsibility is to be overcome. The mail clerk needs this no less than the president. It is not that by understanding how he contributes, the mail clerk will think his job more lofty or exalted. It is just that he may begin to take due pride in the fact that it is as indispensable as the decision-making of the chairman of the board. He may also develop a better grasp of how the consequences of his acts may hinder or endanger the entire enterprise. And if he understands that, it may suddenly dawn on him that in hurting the whole he is—in however roundabout a fashion, yet very really—hurting himself.

Mere understanding is not enough. Lectures on how the corporation works never suffice to overcome psychic distance. Immediate exposure to what others do and how is essential in rendering our abstract knowledge vivid and effective. But in addition to this increase in immediacy, we need also to give employees the genuine sense that they are participants, nay partners, in a joint enterprise. This requires the introduction of an element of grassroots democracy into the corporation. For employees to feel that the corporation is somehow *theirs* (even though legally they do not own it), they must sense that what it does is to some little extent the result of their decisions. Obviously, whenever large numbers are involved, the influence of any one individual must remain minuscule. Yet the very fact that on some important issues each employee is offered a say increases the likelihood that he will be able to appropriate the course of action that emerges as his own. People do not want to be told the lie that their decision in the corporation or in the state can be decisive. They know that their view is but one of many, and what frustrates them is not that what they want fails to come about but that they rarely get a serious hearing. It is the serious hearing that should always be provided, along with realistic information about the presence and strength of many conflicting views.

One might think that such autonomy within business organizations would be exceptionally costly. This is both true and false. Admittedly, time would have to be devoted to educating employees and to canvassing their opinions. But whatever loss this might involve would be more than made up for by increased readiness to assume responsibility, increased enthusiasm, and increased productivity. This is the lesson of the failure of collective farms in Eastern Europe. Their productivity proved to be a disaster compared to what happened on the small plots the state left to individuals and families. In their home gardens, the peasants worked efficiently and well; they saw what they did as somehow their very own. By contrast, they could never view the collective farms as extensions of their personalities, as in any important sense belonging to them. The result was the inefficiency that comes from not caring, the surly negligence typical of those who are made to do things and thus feel put upon.

We can avoid this fate and improve productivity by making corporations psychologically the property of all who work in them. Making them shareholders will not necessarily give workers the sense that they have a stake in its welfare. Teaching them how the corporation works and asking them to participate in running it frequently will. The choice is between full participation and continued growing irresponsibility.

ENDNOTE

1. The two most instructive documents on the Yamashita case are A. Frank Reel, *The Case of General Yamashita* (New York: Octagon Books, 1971), and Courtney Whitney, *The Case of General Yamashita: A Memorandum* (Supreme Commander for the Allied Powers. Government Section, 1949).

QUESTIONS ON LACHS

1. Lachs writes that "the more we think of prosperity as our birthright, the less we understand its relation to a responsible role in the productive process." What does he mean by this statement? In what sense might this be increasingly true of the United States?

2. What is "mediation" and why does it affect any complex society? What are some of the benefits of mediation? What are some of its costs? Why should it be the case, as Lachs claims, that "the more we use people, the more we adopt toward them the attitude we normally have only toward inanimate physical objects"? Is there a difference between using people as a means and using them *only* as a means?

3. Summarize Lachs' account of the problem of psychic distance within a corporation. Is psychic distance a result of mediation? How does psychic distance engender anonymity?

4. Why can't mediation be abandoned? How can psychic distance be reduced? What is the concept of ownership (involving three abilities) that Lachs believes helps to remedy the problem of distance?

Role Obligations

Michael O. Hardimon

Michael O. Hardimon is Professor of Philosophy at the University of California at San Diego. His areas of research include nineteenth-century German philosophy and social and political philosophy. He is the author of Hegel's Social Philosophy *(1994). This excerpt is taken from a longer essay that originally appeared in* The Journal of Philosophy *(1994).*

The subject of this paper is role obligations, the sort of obligations we have (or take ourselves to have) as occupants of social roles: as citizens, family members, teachers, and so forth. Contemporary moral philosophers have, by and large, neglected these obligations, regarding them as marginal at best.[1] I argue that the view that role obligations are marginal is mistaken, that they are central to morality and should be taken seriously. Role obligations are especially interesting because they illustrate the existence and importance of a dimension of the moral life largely unnoticed by the ethical mainstream:

the dimension that is lived through social institutions— the dimension Hegel called *Sittlichkeit.* This dimension is in fact the real target of this paper. I focus on role obligations as a way of bringing it into plain view. My underlying aim is to enable us to appreciate the importance of the institutional dimension of the moral life.

PRELIMINARY REMARKS

Not every status is a role. The statuses of human being or person, for example, are not roles. To speak of the obligations we have as human beings or persons as *role* obligations is a confusion. Still, the range of things that can properly be called roles is remarkably heterogeneous and wide. The social roles I shall focus on are *institutional roles,* ones that are institutionally defined. More specifically, my focus shall be on political, familial, and occupational roles. Accordingly, I shall follow the common practice of using the term 'role' to refer to constellations of institutionally specified rights and duties organized around an institutionally specified social function.[2] Purely biological relations, considered merely as such, are not roles in my sense of the term. Thus, we need to distinguish between, for example, the *biological relation* of sister, which is defined by biology, and the *institutional role* of sister, which is institutionally defined. Standing in a particular biological relationship may be a necessary and sufficient condition of occupying a given institutional role, but it is the institution—not biology—that specifies who may occupy the role; and it is the institution—not biology—that specifies the rights and duties that individuals have as occupants of that role.[3] I focus on institutional roles because they are the kind of roles that illustrate the existence of the institutional dimension of the moral life.[4] It is by entering such roles that we enter this dimension and by fulfilling the obligations associated with such roles that we participate in its arrangements.

As I shall understand the term, a 'role obligation' is a moral requirement, which attaches to an institutional role, whose content is fixed by the function of the role, and whose normative force flows from the role. To say that a role obligation "attaches to an institutional role" is to say that it applies to an individual in her capacity as an occupant of that role: as a sister, as a citizen, or as a bus driver, for example. . . . It might also be useful to contrast my account of role obligations with that of Ronald Dworkin. He regards role obligations as a species of "associative obligations," which he defines as "special responsibilities social practice attaches to membership in some biological or social group" (*op.*

cit., p. 196). Whether people actually have morally binding associative obligations is a matter about which I wish to remain agnostic. But, in any case, role obligations, as I understand them, are not usefully thought of as a species of associative obligation. Role obligations are defined in terms of institutions, not groups, and attach to institutionally specified roles rather than membership in groups. Membership in an ethnic group might conceivably confer an associative obligation in Dworkin's sense of the term, but it would not generate a role obligation in mine. Being a member of an ethnic group is not a role.

According to one common philosophical usage, any public system of rules counts as an institution. My use of the term is narrower than this. The state and the family are institutions; so are associations such as firms, schools, trade unions, and professions. Promising, however, on my account, is not an institution but a practice. An institution includes rules that define offices and positions, which can be occupied by different individuals at different times. Hospitals, for example, retain their identity across changes of health-care professionals, patients, and staff. Institutions are ongoing, self-reproducing structures, each with a life of its own, so to speak. Since it sounds odd to refer to individual (nuclear) families as institutions, it should be pointed out that familial roles (husband, wife, father, mother, son, daughter, sister, brother, and so forth), being institutionally defined, are genuine institutional roles. For ease of reference we can speak of individual families as institutionally defined groups. Whether they are properly characterized as institutions is not a matter that needs to be settled here. . . .

In what follows, I shall present my account of role obligations as a challenge to the standard view of role obligations, or, more precisely, to the picture of the subject it conveys. The standard view can be formulated in three propositions:

1. Role obligations are of two kinds, "contractual" and "noncontractual."

2. Contractual role obligations are acquired by signing on for the roles from which they derive.

3. Noncontractual role obligations are extremely problematic, if they exist at all.

My attitude toward the standard view is complex. On the one hand, I believe that there is a clear sense in which it is correct. On the other hand, I believe that it conveys a picture of role obligations (and the moral life) which is misleading and distorted. Moral philosophy needs a new way of thinking about role obligations which can free us from the problems associated with the standard view while preserving its kernel of truth. . . .

CONTRACTUAL ROLE OBLIGATIONS

The standard view's claim that contractual role obligations are acquired by signing on for the roles from which they derive is largely correct. It is true that contractual role obligations are acquired by signing on for the roles from which they derive. But what does "signing on for" amount to? What is it that we sign on for, when we "sign on for" a social role? Proponents of the standard view provide no answer to these questions. This is an important respect in which their approach is defective. Considering some of the familiar ways in which these questions can be answered will enable us to move beyond the problems associated with the standard view while retaining its kernel of truth.

According to one popular interpretation, which I shall call the *promising account,* what "signing on for" amounts to is making a promise. In signing on for a role, we promise to carry out the duties of the role, the tasks that the role requires. Morally speaking, there is nothing more to a role obligation than a promise to perform these tasks. Role obligations are just a special case of promises.

This account has the clear advantage of bringing the voluntary aspect of contractual role obligations into clear focus, explaining it in terms of a familiar and well-accepted moral notion. Many will also be attracted by the account's individualism, for it maintains that the fact that an individual occupies a social role is never in and of itself a morally significant fact. What matters morally is that, in signing on for a role, one has promised to do something. Unfortunately, the promising account has a clear disadvantage, for there is one especially salient fact about contractual role obligations which it overlooks: the fact that what one signs on for in signing on for a contractual social role is a package of duties, fixed by the institution of which the role is a part.[5]

Roles, contractual and noncontractual alike, are institutionally defined clusters of rights and duties. Even if, as is often the case, the duties attaching to roles are loosely defined,[6] it is still true that the duties are specified by the institutions from which they derive: what one signs on for is a *socially specified* cluster of duties. In this respect, the language of contract is misleading, for it wrongly suggests that "contractual" social roles are a species of individually negotiated contracts. Superstar lawyers may be able to name their own price, but what it is to be a lawyer is something no lawyer can settle.

Social roles are not things that we, as individuals, make up, but enduring, socially defined structures that we, as individuals, enter.

Several caveats are in order. To say that social roles are *enduring* is not to say that they cannot change, for roles do change along with the social institutions of which they are a part. Human history is, among other things, the story of the transformation of social roles. Nor is there any incompatibility between saying that social roles are enduring and recognizing that they can be changed and that we can change them. To say that roles are *socially* defined is to say that they are defined by us, that we, as a society, have defined and continue to define them in a particular way. Like the matter of how our social world is to be organized, the question concerning how our social roles are to be defined is ultimately up to us. Recognizing the reality of social structures need not involve a denial of responsibility. It should, on the contrary, expand our sense of responsibility. It raises the question: Are these structures, which we maintain and reproduce through the exercise of our roles, structures we want to affirm?

It is also important to remember that role concepts are interpretive. How the clusters of duties associated with contractual social roles are to be understood is no less a matter of interpretation than how the clusters of duties associated with noncontractual role obligations are to be understood. Different individuals occupying the same contractual role may reasonably disagree about the contents of their roles. They may act in good faith on the basis of their conflicting interpretations, exercising the very same roles in very different ways. It is also possible for reasonable individuals to interpret their social roles in unconventional ways. Furthermore, taking on a social role is, at least ideally, largely a matter of finding an interpretation that fits one's own temperament and character. There are different ways of being a flight attendant, oncologist, and police officer. Part of what it is to become a good flight attendant, oncologist, or police officer is to find a way of carrying out the responsibilities of these roles which suits one's particularities.[7] All this being said, it remains true that individuals cannot custom tailor the obligations they undertake in entering contractual social roles.[8] To the extent that a role contains options, those options are fixed by the role. To sign on for a role is to sign on for the whole package, properly understood.

Sophisticated proponents of the promising account can, of course, incorporate these points. They can say that what one promises to do in signing on for a social role is to promise to carry out the cluster of duties associated with that role, and they can allow that the contents of these duties are institutionally specified. At the same time, they can insist that the normative force of contractual role obligations consists wholly in the promises people make. This move allows them to retain the intuition that, in and of itself, the fact that a given individual occupies a social role can never be a morally significant fact. Let us call the position that results from making this move the *sophisticated promising account.* What are we to make of this view?

One obvious attraction is that it recognizes the role played by institutions in the specification of the content of role-related duties. But is it really true that what we do when we sign on for a contractual role is to make a promise to carry out its duties? To whom do we make the promise? Ourselves? The other participants in the relevant institution? The community at large? It seems to me that, although the voluntary acceptance associated with contractual role obligations belongs to the same normative genus as promising, it belongs to a different normative species. It would seem more accurate to say that what we do when we sign on for a social role is to agree to carry out its tasks. Nonetheless, the basic idea—common to both the naive and sophisticated versions of the promising account—seems correct, namely, that choice and voluntary acceptance—actual choice and actual acceptance—are essential factors in contractual role obligation. I shall call the view that interprets signing on as voluntary acceptance, the *voluntary acceptance view.* This approach seems especially appealing because it connects the idea of contractual role obligation to the basic normative notion of consent: what we do in voluntarily accepting social roles is to consent to undertake them. . . .

Voluntary acceptance may be tacit. People can come to accept their roles without ever having said or otherwise made explicit that they have done so. The idea of tacit acceptance may be greeted with skepticism. Since what counts as tacit acceptance is contextually defined, there may be no general answer to the question concerning how we are to determine when someone has tacitly accepted a given role. Presumably, there will be cases in which it is objectively unclear whether a given person has or has not accepted a particular role. Nonetheless, it seems plausible to say that once someone has traded her Birkenstocks for Bass Weejuns, her jeans for khakis; once someone has begun to refer to sore throats as 'pharyngitis,' treat patients, and use the medical "we"; once someone has completed medical school, made her first reservation in the name of doctor so-and-so, and had the letters 'MD' imprinted on her checks—that person has signed on for the role of doctor.[9] She has voluntarily accepted it. There is such a thing as tacit voluntary acceptance of social roles. The phenomenon is both common and familiar.

Replacing the promising account with the voluntary acceptance account and making the necessary qualifications brings us much closer to an adequate understanding of contractual role obligation than we had before. But even if these modifications are made, there is still another absolutely vital factor that this account leaves out, namely, the idea of *role identification,* the idea of identifying with a role or conceiving of oneself as an occupant of a role.

For present purposes, I want to say that to *identify with a role* is

i.   to occupy the role;

ii. to recognize that one occupies the role;

iii. to conceive of oneself as someone for whom the norms of the role function as reasons.

The point of the first condition is straightforward. One cannot (sanely) conceive of oneself as someone for whom the norms of a role give reasons unless one actually occupies that role. The motivation for the second condition is equally clear. In order to conceive of oneself as someone for whom the norms of a role give reasons, one must recognize that one occupies that role. It is the third condition that does the real work. The key component of the idea of identifying with a role is that of conceiving of oneself as someone for whom the norms, that is, the evaluative standards associated with a role, its rights, duties, virtues, ideals, and supererogations, have reason-giving force.[10]

Here is the idea. If you identify with a role, its norms will function for you as reasons. If you are a judge who identifies with the role of judge, the fact that *this* is something judges do (in the normative sense) will give you a reason for doing it. And conversely, if you regard the fact that this is something judges do as giving you a reason to do it, you conceive of yourself as a judge. Were you to say—"I recognize that this is something judges do and I recognize that I am a judge (that I occupy this legally specified position), but why should *I* do that?"—you would not conceive of yourself as a judge, as someone for whom the norms of the role provide reasons. I do not mean to suggest that people who identify with their roles generally form the thought "I am someone for whom the norms of the role give reasons" in some explicit way. My claim is rather that in regarding the norms of their roles as providing reasons for them, people do at least implicitly conceive of themselves in this way. To regard a given consideration as a reason for acting is to conceive of oneself as the sort of person for whom that consideration is a reason. The process of coming to identify with a social role is at once a process of coming to regard certain considerations as reasons and a process of coming to conceive of oneself as a person of a certain kind.

It is worth pointing out that, being philosophically "modest" or "thin," this conception of role identification avoids many of the difficulties associated with similar notions. For example, it is possible to identify with a role in my sense of the term without regarding the role as essential to "who one is" or taking the role to be an essential component of one's "true self." In this respect, the idea of role identification is metaphysically unobjectionable. It is also possible to identify with a role and recognize that one is more than the occupant of that particular role and more than the occupant of all the roles one is in.[11] One can identify with a role and still regard oneself as a "self" who can step back from and assess that role. Role identification need not result in what Gerald Cohen[12] has called "engulfment," the loss of the self within the role. Moreover, it is possible to identify with a role while recognizing that one is free not to identify with the role and that one is responsible for identifying with the role: role identification need not be a form of bad faith.[13] And it is also possible to identify with a role without hiding, denying, or suppressing one's humanity—without turning it into a "mask" in John T. Noonan, Jr.'s[14] sense of the term. Nor does role identification prevent one from recognizing that one has duties that are independent of one's role, duties that apply to people generally. So the idea of role identification is not morally objectionable.

It is also worth emphasizing that role identification and voluntary acceptance are distinct. This point can be illustrated by the following example. Let us imagine a person with strong anarchist leanings who has successfully completed his medical training. Such a person might voluntarily accept the cluster of duties associated with the role of doctor and yet refuse to identify with this role. He would recognize that he has the knowledge and skills of a doctor and that he has the title of doctor, but adamantly refuse to identify with the role of doctor. Although scrupulous in fulfilling the duties of his role, his reason for performing these tasks would invariably be that he had agreed to perform them. He would never do anything just because he is a doctor. He might acknowledge that he had special responsibilities to others because he possessed certain skills, but he would deny that he had any responsibilities to others qua doctor, qua occupant of that role. Such a person would, I think, be odd, but imagining this possibility makes it possible to distinguish identification from the idea of voluntary acceptance. The fact that we are forced to consider such an extreme case in order to imagine voluntary acceptance and role identification coming apart is testimony to how closely they go together in real life. It also brings out how familiar the phenomenon of role identification really is.

So what does the idea of role identification add to the idea of voluntary acceptance? The first and most obvious thing it adds is the idea of identifying with a role. The fact that people can and do identify with their social roles in the sense I have defined is an important but largely unnoticed feature of the moral life. A second thing it contributes is the idea of self-transformation. In coming to identify with a social role, one's moral self-conception is transformed. One comes to conceive of oneself as an occupant of a role, a member of the social world, and a participant in the moral life that is lived through institutions. The third thing that the idea of role identification adds to the idea of voluntary acceptance is an important source of motivation. When people identify with their roles they acquire reasons for carrying out the duties distinct from those deriving from the fact that they have signed on for them. One such reason is that they occupy these roles. If, for example, I identify with the role of teacher, the fact that I am a teacher gives me a reason for grading a set of papers when I am tired and it is late at night. The fact that I signed on for the role of teacher gives me one reason for carrying out its tasks. The fact that I am a teacher gives me another. . . .

There are of course circumstances in which people should not identify with their roles, such as when their roles are morally impermissible, dehumanizing, or degrading. And, correspondingly, there are circumstances in which it is inappropriate to expect people to identify with their roles. We should not, for example, expect an underpaid and exploited department store worker to identify with the role of salesclerk. It goes without saying that we should never regard people solely in terms of their roles. As Bernard Williams[15] has put it, we owe each person "an effort at identification." Instead of viewing others as the "surface" to which a "certain label" applies, we should make an effort to see the world, including the label, from their point of view. But there is nothing in the idea of role identification that would prevent us from recognizing this point.

The central defect of the voluntary acceptance view, then, consists in its failure to recognize the phenomenon of role identification. Because it lacks this notion, it conveys a distorted picture of our relation to our roles. It suggests, for example, that the only reason doctors do the things that doctors do is that they have promised or agreed to do those things—that they never do them simply because they are doctors. It also suggests, more generally, that people are indifferent to the norms associated with their roles and that the only thing they care about, morally speaking, is keeping their promises or agreements. This picture is far too individualistic, far too voluntaristic to be true. The fact of the matter is that people do identify with their social roles and are motivated by the fact that they identify with their social roles. This is not to say that people do not care about the fact that they have signed on for their roles or that they are unconcerned with breaking faith. Nor is it to say that people never view their roles in such a radically individualistic and voluntaristic way. Nor, again, is it to deny that there are many people who are alienated from their roles and the social world. But, as an account of the ordinary understanding of our relation to our roles, the voluntary acceptance account fails. If we want to do justice to the full complexity of contractual role obligation and the nature of moral life, we must recognize the phenomenon of role identification. . . .

ENDNOTES

1. That the topic of role obligations has been neglected is a commonplace among critics of the ethical mainstream. See, for example, Bernard Williams, *Ethics and the Limits of Philosophy* (Cambridge: Harvard, 1985), pp. 7–8; Michael Sandel, *Liberalism and the Limits of Justice* (New York: Cambridge, 1982), p. 179; Alasdair MacIntyre, *After Virtue* (Notre Dame: University Press, 1981); Lawrence Blum, *Friendship, Altruism, and Morality* (New York: Routledge, 1980); and Christina Hoff Sommers, "Filial Morality," this JOURNAL, LXXXIII, 8 (August 1986): 439–55. An especially telling example of the mainstream's tendency to marginalize role obligations is provided by Thomas Nagel, who recognizes "that most people would acknowledge a noncontractual obligation to show special concern" for at least some of those to whom they are closely related, but says that he mentions them "only for completeness"; *The View from Nowhere* (New York: Oxford, 1986), p. 165. One notable exception to this general pattern is to be found in Ronald Dworkin, *Law's Empire* (Cambridge: Harvard, 1986), p. 196.

2. See, e.g., R. S. Downie, *Roles and Values* (New York: Methuen, 1971), pp. 127–8.

3. It may also be useful to distinguish between *nominal* and *real* occupancy of institutional roles. Thus, two (biologi-

cal) brothers separated at birth nominally occupy the (institutionally defined) role of brother, but their occupancy of this role is not real since they were not raised within the same family.

4. Social roles can be divided into institutional and noninstitutional roles. I do not think that social roles as such form a unified subject matter. I do, however, think that *institutional* roles form a unified subject matter. Their unity derives from the unity of the institutional dimension of the moral life.

5. The idea that what individuals sign on for in signing on for a social role is a *package* of duties is taken from Daniels's "Duty to Treat or Right to Refuse," *Hasting Center Report* (March–April 1991), p. 43.

6. One of the striking transformations in the ethical life that is lived within institutions which has taken place within at least the last hundred years is that social roles have become less determinately structured and more open-ended. Nowadays, the packages of rights and duties associated with social roles contain more options, more room for negotiation than they did in times past.

7. It is sometimes suggested that worries about alienation can be adequately addressed simply by saying that people should choose roles that fit their temperaments. See, for example, Michael Quinlan, "Ethics in the Public Service," in *Governance,* VI, 4 (October): 538–44; here p. 540. But this view overlooks the problem that the social world may fail to offer social roles suitable to the temperaments of its members. See, e.g., Goethe's *The Sorrows of Young Werther.*

8. The phrase 'individuals cannot custom tailor the obligations' is borrowed from Daniels, "Duty to Treat or Right to Refuse," p. 43.

9. These examples are borrowed from Elisabeth Rosenthal's "How Doctors Learn to Think They're Doctors," *The New York Times* (November 28, 1993), sect. 4, pp. 1, 4.

10. One can recognize that one occupies a social role without conceiving of oneself as someone for whom the norms of the role function as reasons. This will presumably occur in cases in which a person occupies a role whose norms he regards as illegitimate or reflectively unacceptable. A soldier who naively volunteered for the Nazi *Wehrmacht* and later came to appreciate the horrors of National Socialism might recognize that he occupied the role of soldier without regarding the norms of that role as having reason-giving force.

11. See Virginia Held, *Rights and Goods* (Chicago: University Press, 1984).

12. "Beliefs and Roles," *Proceedings of the Aristotelian Society,* LXVII (1966–67): 17–34; here p. 34.

13. Jean-Paul Sartre, *Being and Nothingness,* Hazel E. Barnes, trans. (New York: Washington Square, [1943] 1966), pp. 101–3.

14. *Persons and Masks of the Law* (New York: Farrar, Straus & Giroux, 1976), p. 21.

15. "The Idea of Equality," in *Problems of the Self* (New York: Cambridge, 1973), p. 236.

QUESTIONS ON HARDIMON

1. What does it mean to identify with a role? Can one identify with distinct roles, and, if so, might these roles ever conflict? Do you think that role identification is limited to certain types of positions or jobs?

2. Hardimon claims that the voluntary acceptance of a role and identification with that role are distinct even though they go together closely in most instances. How does identification relate to reasons and to motivation? Is there a problem in business life of people failing to identify with their roles?

3. In the previous article, John Lachs contends that "the more we identify with our roles, the more we surrender any claim to be the causes of our actions," further increasing our passivity. Is it possible to identify with one's role in such a way that the self is lost? Do you think that this is a hazard for the account of role identification given by Hardimon?

Corporate Responsibility

There are few ways in which a man can be more innocently employed than in getting money.

Samuel Johnson[6]

'But you were always a good man of business, Jacob,' faltered Scrooge, who now began to apply this to himself. 'Business!' cried the ghost, wringing its hands again. 'Mankind was my business. The common welfare was my business; charity, mercy, forbearance, and benevolence, were, all, my business. The dealings of my trade were but a drop of water in the comprehensive ocean of my business!'

Charles Dickens[7]

When you see that trading is done, not by consent, but by compulsion—when you see that in order to produce, you need to obtain permission from men who produce nothing—when you see that money is flowing to those who deal, not in goods, but in favors—when you see that men get richer by graft and by pull than by work, and your laws don't protect you against them, but protect them against you—when you see corruption being rewarded and honesty becoming a self-sacrifice—you may know that your society is doomed.

Ayn Rand[8]

Within a society and within a business firm it is essential for individuals to act responsibly and to be responsible. Is there also a sense in which corporations or businesses, as economic organizations, must be responsible? For many, an answer to this question turns on the nature of the corporation and on whether there is any meaningful sense in which a corporation could be responsible. It seems clear enough that individuals can bear moral responsibility, but is there any sense in which a corporation can do so? Some have argued that we can ascribe, in a meaningful manner, moral responsibilities to organizations, especially if we locate the responsibility in the hands of the managers.[9] However, on this view it would seem that the ascription of

6. As recounted in James Boswell, *The Life of Samuel Johnson* [1791], edited by Christopher Hibbert (Harmondsworth: Penguin, 1986), 177.

7. *A Christmas Carol* [1843], in *The Works of Charles Dickens,* vol. xviii (London: Chapman & Hall, n.d) chapter 1 (p. 26).

8. *Atlas Shrugged* (New York: New American Library, 1957), 390.

9. Kenneth E. Goodpaster and John B. Matthews, "Can a Corporation Have a Conscience?" *Harvard Business Review* (January–February, 1982). An alternative view can be found in Manuel G. Velasquez, "Why Corporations Are Not Morally Responsible for Anything They Do," *Business and Professional Ethics Journal* 2 (Spring 1983): 1–18.

responsibility still rests with individuals within the corporation. If a corporation can be responsible at least in the sense that its managers or executives can be held responsible, then do these managers or executives have any role responsibilities requiring that they direct the corporation (or that they use corporate funds) for any purpose other than an economic aim, such as profit maximization? Such a question raises the issue of whether a business, or its managers, has a responsibility to society—a social responsibility.

Social Responsibility and Ethics

Many persons may assume that ethical business practices entail social responsibility; in other words, if one is to conduct one's business in an ethical manner, then one must exercise some social responsibility. However, it is not at all obvious that one's *moral obligations* entail certain social responsibilities, at least as these are typically understood. Nor is it obvious that *business ethics* entail any specific social responsibilities. Even if social responsibility is a *topic* within the academic study of business ethics, it is not a foregone conclusion that ethics, in general, or the ethics necessary for conducting business, properly generate social responsibilities.

After all, even if a business functions only to maximize profit, the business must still adhere to certain legal and ethical obligations. Consider that a firm might seek to maximize profit within the legal constraints that frame a market, constraints that allow individuals to buy and sell, establish firms, and to make and enforce contracts. Such a framework prohibits violence, fraud, and coercion; so presumably, a profit-making enterprise would not be engaged in such morally impermissible activities. In this sense the pursuit of profit takes place against a basic legal (and moral) framework. However, the pursuit of profit also seems to occur within certain other everyday moral considerations or constraints, including those of honesty, integrity, prudence, and generosity. In this sense much of the pursuit of profit may be compatible with one's moral obligations. If these moral and legal obligations were all that is typically meant by "social responsibility," then there would be little left to debate. However, the appeals to social responsibility often range beyond the moral or legal obligations just noted.

What Is a Social Responsibility?

The concept of "social responsibility" is typically invoked to refer to acts (or omissions of actions) which vary quite widely. Some of these are not obviously moral or legal obligations; others are, at best, the sort of imperfect obligation the performance of which may rest upon the discretion of the agent; others assume their normativity only if one accepts certain political or social propositions (none of which should be assumed to be incontestable). Some typical examples of socially responsible actions or programs would include the donation of corporate funds to aid the poor, feed the hungry, encourage literacy, or to subsidize art galleries or music concerts. Other examples might include that a business refrain from establishing factories in countries with oppressive governments or that a firm take the lead in reducing pollution. These modes of action are distinct from refraining from fraud, violence, or misrepresentation. Moreover, these types of action are also distinct from treating one's employees with respect and fairness, whether in promotion, salary, or working conditions.

This does not mean that *all* social responsibilities are distinct from moral obligations or that *no* moral obligation can be understood as involving a responsibility to society. However, some of the demands raised by the calls for social responsibility are often demands which are distinct from the moral demands placed on everyone. Indeed, if social responsibilities were nothing but moral obligations, then surely there would be no controversy about them. Thus, as one prominent business ethicist writes,

> The growing literature on the social obligations of corporations includes a grab bag of obligations, some of them moral and some not. The social obligations that some people would like to have corporations undertake include taking care of the poor, rebuilding inner cities, fighting illicit drug traffic, giving to charity, endowing universities, and funding cultural programs. None of these is a moral obligation of corporations.[10]

Permission or Obligation?

Even if many social responsibilities may not be *moral* obligations, that does not tell us whether or not it is either permissible for corporations to exercise some social responsibility or whether it would be a good, but not obligatory, thing for corporations to do so. In this regard, we might want to reflect on the aims or ends of a business firm or corporation. Even if there is an economic argument for firms to seek to maximize their profits, that does not mean that it would be impermissible or morally wrong for a firm to pursue other goals alongside that of profit making. That a market provides

10. Richard De George, *Business Ethics,* 4th ed. (Englewood Cliffs, N.J.: Prentice Hall, 1990), 199.

the conditions under which businesses compete for profit, thereby producing the goods and services that consumers most want, should not entail that it would be *impermissible* or morally wrong for an owner of a firm to seek a minimum level of profit while pursuing other goals for the firm. Similarly, it might be argued that just as a firm or corporation may permissibly pursue goals other than profit maximization, so may a firm freely pursue, within the constraints of the market framework, nothing other than profit maximization. Even if profit maximization is permissible, some have argued that firms ought to pursue socially responsible aims; others (such as R. Edward Freeman) have argued that these should be required: The laws of corporations should be revised so that corporations must take into account the views and interests of stakeholders. There is, however, another aspect of corporate responsibility that has received very little attention but which lies at the very core of commerce and competition among firms.

Rent-Seeking and Responsibility

Whether or not a firm is a pure profit maximizer, commerce takes place within a legal framework that allows for free competition and for entry and exit into a market. Even within a democracy, however, it is possible for organizations and businesses to seek laws, regulations, or administrative actions that have the effect of favoring one firm (or industry) over another, thereby allowing a firm to gain at the expense of other firms (or at the expense of taxpayers). A firm that benefits from this favorable treatment thus has its income raised to a level higher than that which would have been achieved if the market had been left more competitive. This phenomena is labeled by economists as "rent-seeking"—a relatively new concept in economics.[11] Rent-seeking involves the efforts of businesses, individuals, or groups to obtain, via law or administrative action, either some sort of monopoly status or an increase in their incomes beyond what could be achieved in a competitive market. Most rent-seeking oc-

curs when hired lobbyists secure from the government some rule or regulation that advantages an industry or disadvantages a competitor, including, for example, import quotas that raise the price of foreign goods, government bailouts of companies or industries, special tax breaks, or restrictive regulations. Other examples would include the subsidies given by municipalities, in the form of stadium facilities, to privately owned professional sports teams.

To illustrate the idea of rent-seeking more fully, imagine a business that faces economic competition from overseas. In order to compete more effectively, the firm could revise its production techniques, a restructuring that would incur a significant short-run cost. However, it occurs to the managers of the firm that there is a less expensive way of gaining a competitive advantage: Have legislators enact a tariff against the competing products from overseas. With higher tariffs in place, the foreign competition will be at a disadvantage. Although the business firm had a legal right to lobby for higher tariffs, and even though such lobbying occurs all the time in the capitals of most nations, it is another question as to whether rent-seeking should be regarded as an unsavory act antithetical to good business practice.

Economically, rent-seeking produces a restriction on trade and is therefore unproductive or inefficient in at least two senses. The restriction itself is inefficient, and the very *pursuit* of the rent diverts resources from productive uses. Where there are rent-seekers so are there lobbyists for "rent-avoidance," namely, those who lobby to protect themselves against some rule or policy that will put them at a disadvantage. (In many developing countries rent-seeking takes the form of bribes to skirt regulations or to gain permission to do business at all. Not only are these and other rent-seeking practices unproductive, but they also serve to undermine the very idea of the rule of law.) Rent-seeking is itself a morally neutral concept. The question is, should a business refrain from seeking these sorts of privileges? One may grant that certain interventions may render the market less efficient (perhaps protecting industries from becoming stronger), but that doesn't answer the moral question of whether there is an obligation, in commerce, to seek to compete via the forces of the market rather than through political favors. The selection from DeBow offers some tentative answers to this question.

THE READINGS

Milton Friedman   Friedman offers a reply to those who argue that business has a social responsibility. Contending that the executive is the employee of the owners

---

11. The term was first employed by Anne O. Krueger, "The Political Economy of the Rent-Seeking Society," *The American Economic Review* 64 (1976): 291–303. The major theorist of rent-seeking is Gordon Tullock. See, *The Economics of Special Privilege and Rent Seeking* (Boston: Kluwer Academic Publishing, 1989) or *Rent Seeking* (Aldershot, England: Edward Elgar, 1993). Without a doubt, Adam Smith was also aware of how merchants, companies, and guilds might seek to use the power of legislation to affect the prices of their goods. See, for example, sections I.vii.26–28 or I.x.c.25 of *An Inquiry into the Nature and Causes of the Wealth of Nations* [1776], edited by R. H. Campbell, A. S. Skinner, and W. B. Todd (Indianapolis: Liberty Classics, 1979).

(stockholders), Friedman insists that the executive should conduct the business in accordance with the desires of the owners and that this will typically mean that the executive is to "make as much money as possible while conforming to the basic rules of the society, both those embodied in law and those embodied in ethical custom." Friedman offers two main arguments against social responsibility, one based on principle and one based on consequences. The first argument suggests that an executive who spends funds on projects deemed socially responsible is, in effect, levying a tax, thereby appropriating a function that belongs to government. The second argument focuses on whether or not an executive would *know* what could be done or how to do it. Finally, Friedman seems to employ a third type of argument, suggesting that the very appeal to social responsibility undermines the foundations of a free society by encouraging the view that persons do not have a right to pursue their interests, including profit-making, unless they are also contributing to some recognized social purpose.

R. Edward Freeman   Against the traditional view that a manager has a fiduciary duty only to stockholders, Freeman contends that managers have duties to all of those who have a stake in the corporation. He first notes how the law has already begun to constrain or circumscribe the manager's duty to pursue the interests of the shareholders, obliging the manager to attend to consumers, employees, and the community at large. According to Freeman, the corporation bears responsibility to stakeholders, the groups "who are vital to the survival and success of the corporation." Along with management itself, these groups include the owners, suppliers, employees, customers, and the local community, and these groups have a right to participate in decisions that affect them. The task of management is to safeguard the corporation while balancing the claims of the stakeholders. Stakeholder theory redefines the very purpose of a business firm, even as the overall theory may take on a variety of different forms or "normative cores," one of which is "pragmatic liberalism." In the last section of the essay, Freeman develops the contractualist core at the heart of a stakeholder theory of pragmatic liberalism.

Michael E. DeBow   DeBow considers the neglected question of whether it is right for a business to seek to realize higher profits by using for its advantage some government policy, regulation, law, or subsidy. This sort of pursuit, referred to as "rent-seeking," may generate three possible ethical problems: waste, exploitation of

public ignorance, and regressive effects on income. Having summarized these problems, DeBow recounts three arguments *in favor* of rent-seeking: that certain rent-seeking laws may have public benefits, thereby rendering rent-seeking socially responsible; that rent-protection or rent-avoidance may be justifiable under certain circumstances; and that rent-seeking may be a manager's duty. Although the first and third arguments seem dubious, the second is more defensible.

The Social Responsibility of Business Is to Increase Its Profits

Milton Friedman

Milton Friedman was born in New Jersey, receiving his undergraduate degree from Rutgers University. The 1976 Nobel Laureate in economics, Friedman is noted for his work on consumption theory and in monetary economics. A Professor Emeritus of Economics at the University of Chicago, Friedman is the author of A Theory of the Consumption Function *(1957),* A Monetary History of the United States, 1867–1960, *cowritten with Anna Schwartz (1963), and the popular work,* Free to Choose: A Personal Statement *(1980), cowritten with his wife, Rose Friedman. This essay originally appeared in the* New York Times Magazine *(1970).*

When I hear businessmen speak eloquently about the "social responsibilities of business in a free-enterprise system," I am reminded of the wonderful line about the Frenchman who discovered at the age of 70 that he had been speaking prose all his life. The businessmen believe that they are defending free enterprise when they declaim that business is not concerned "merely" with profit but also with promoting desirable "social" ends; that business has a "social conscience" and takes seriously its responsibilities for providing employment, eliminating discrimination, avoiding pollution and whatever else may be the catchwords of the contemporary crop of reformers. In fact they are—or would be if they or anyone else took them seriously—preaching pure and unadulterated socialism. Businessmen who talk this way are unwitting puppets of the intellectual forces that have been undermining the basis of a free society these past decades.

The discussions of the "social responsibilities of business" are notable for their analytical looseness and lack of rigor. What does it mean to say that "business" has responsibilities? Only people can have responsibilities. A corporation is an artificial person and in this sense may have artificial responsibilities, but "business" as a whole cannot be said to have responsibilities, even in this vague sense. The first step toward clarity in examining the doctrine of the social responsibility of business is to ask precisely what it implies for whom.

Presumably, the individuals who are to be responsible are businessmen, which means individual proprietors or corporate executives. Most of the discussion of social responsibility is directed at corporations, so in what follows I shall mostly neglect the individual proprietor and speak of corporate executives.

In a free-enterprise, private-property system, a corporate executive is an employe of the owners of the business. He has direct responsibility to his employers. That responsibility is to conduct the business in accordance with their desires, which generally will be to make as much money as possible while conforming to the basic rules of the society, both those embodied in law and those embodied in ethical custom. Of course, in some cases his employers may have a different objective. A group of persons might establish a corporation for an eleemosynary purpose—for example, a hospital or a school. The manager of such a corporation will not have money profit as his objective but the rendering of certain services.

In either case, the key point is that, in his capacity as a corporate executive, the manager is the agent of the individuals who own the corporation or establish the eleemosynary institution, and his primary responsibility is to them.

Needless to say, this does not mean that it is easy to judge how well he is performing his task. But at least the criterion of performance is straightforward, and the persons among whom a voluntary contractual arrangement exists are clearly defined.

Of course, the corporate executive is also a person in his own right. As a person, he may have many other responsibilities that he recognizes or assumes voluntarily—to his family, his conscience, his feelings of charity, his church, his clubs, his city, his country. He may feel impelled by these responsibilities to devote part of his income to causes he regards as worthy, to refuse to work for particular corporations, even to leave his job, for example, to join his country's armed forces. If we wish, we may refer to some of these responsibilities as "social responsibilities." But in these respects he is acting as a principal, not an agent; he is spending his own money or time or energy, not the money of his employers or the time or energy he has contracted to devote to their purposes. If these are "social responsibilities," they are the social responsibilities of individuals, not of business.

What does it mean to say that the corporate executive has a "social responsibility" in his capacity as businessman? If this statement is not pure rhetoric, it must mean that he is to act in some way that is not in the interest of his employers. For example, that he is to refrain from increasing the price of the product in order to contribute to the social objective of preventing inflation, even though a price increase would be in the best interests of the corporation. Or that he is to make expenditures on reducing pollution beyond the amount that is in the best interests of the corporation or that is required by law in order to contribute to the social objective of improving the environment. Or that, at the expense of corporate profits, he is to hire "hardcore" unemployed instead of better-qualified available workmen to contribute to the social objective of reducing poverty.

In each of these cases, the corporate executive would be spending someone else's money for a general social interest. Insofar as his actions in accord with his "social responsibility" reduce returns to stockholders, he is spending their money. Insofar as his actions raise the price to customers, he is spending the customers' money. Insofar as his actions lower the wages of some employes, he is spending their money.

The stockholders or the customers or the employes could separately spend their own money on the particular action if they wished to do so. The executive is exercising a distinct "social responsibility," rather than serving as an agent of the stockholders or the customers or the employes, only if he spends the money in a different way than they would have spent it.

But if he does this, he is in effect imposing taxes, on the one hand, and deciding how the tax proceeds shall be spent, on the other.

This process raises political questions on two levels: principle and consequences. On the level of political principle, the imposition of taxes and the expenditure of tax proceeds are governmental functions. We have established elaborate constitutional, parliamentary and judicial provisions to control these functions, to assure that taxes are imposed so far as possible in accordance with the preferences and desires of the public—after all, "taxation without representation" was one of the battle cries of the American Revolution. We have a system of checks and balances to separate the legislative function of imposing taxes and enacting expenditures from the executive function of collecting taxes and administering expenditure programs, and from the judicial function of mediating disputes and interpreting the law.

Here the businessman—self-selected or appointed directly or indirectly by stockholders—is to be simultaneously legislator, executive and jurist. He is to decide whom to tax by how much and for what purpose, and he is to spend the proceeds—all this guided only by general exhortations from on high to restrain inflation, improve the environment, fight poverty and so on and on.

The whole justification for permitting the corporate executive to be selected by the stockholders is that the executive is an agent serving the interests of his principal. This justification disappears when the corporate executive imposes taxes and spends the proceeds for "social" purposes. He becomes in effect a public employe, a civil servant, even though he remains in name an employe of a private enterprise. On grounds of political principle, it is intolerable that such civil servants—insofar as their actions in the name of social responsibility are real and not just window-dressing—should be selected as they are now. If they are to be civil servants, then they must be selected through a political process. If they are to impose taxes and make expenditures to foster "social" objectives, then political machinery must be set up to guide the assessment of taxes and to determine through a political process the objectives to be served.

This is the basic reason why the doctrine of "social responsibility" involves the acceptance of the socialist view that political mechanisms, not market mechanisms, are the appropriate way to determine the allocation of scarce resources to alternative uses.

On the grounds of consequences, can the corporate executive in fact discharge his alleged "social responsibilities"? On the one hand, suppose he could get away with spending the stockholders' or customers' or employes' money. How is he to know how to spend it? He is told that he must contribute to fighting inflation. How is he to know what action of his will contribute to that end? He is presumably an expert in running his company—in producing a product or selling it or financing it. But nothing about his selection makes him an expert on inflation. Will his holding down the price of his product reduce inflationary pressure? Or, by leaving more spending power in the hands of his customers, simply divert it elsewhere? Or, by forcing him to produce less because of the lower price, will it simply contribute to shortages? Even if he could answer these questions, how much cost is he justified in imposing on his stockholders, customers and employes for this social pur-

pose? What is his appropriate share, and what is the appropriate share of others?

And, whether he wants to or not, can he get away with spending his stockholders,' customers' or employes' money? Will not the stockholders fire him? (Either the present ones or those who take over when his actions in the name of social responsibility have reduced the corporation's profits and the price of its stock.) His customers and his employes can desert him for other producers and employers less scrupulous in exercising their social responsibilities.

This facet of "social responsibility" doctrine is brought into sharp relief when the doctrine is used to justify wage restraint by trade unions. The conflict of interest is naked and clear when union officials are asked to subordinate the interest of their members to some more general social purpose. If the union officials try to enforce wage restraint, the consequence is likely to be wildcat strikes, rank-and-file revolts and the emergence of strong competitors for their jobs. We thus have the ironic phenomenon that union leaders—at least in the U.S.—have objected to Government interference with the market far more consistently and courageously than have business leaders.

The difficulty of exercising "social responsibility" illustrates, of course, the great virtue of private competitive enterprise—it forces people to be responsible for their own actions and makes it difficult for them to "exploit" other people for either selfish or unselfish purposes. They can do good—but only at their own expense.

Many a reader who has followed the argument this far may be tempted to remonstrate that it is all well and good to speak of government's having the responsibility to impose taxes and determine expenditures for such "social" purposes as controlling pollution or training the hard-core unemployed, but that the problems are too urgent to wait on the slow course of political processes, that the exercise of social responsibility by businessmen is a quicker and surer way to solve pressing current problems.

Aside from the question of fact—I share Adam Smith's skepticism about the benefits that can be expected from "those who affected to trade for the public good"—this argument must be rejected on grounds of principle. What it amounts to is an assertion that those who favor the taxes and expenditures in question have failed to persuade a majority of their fellow citizens to be of like mind and that they are seeking to attain by undemocratic procedures what they cannot attain by democratic procedures. In a free society, it is hard for "good" people to do "good," but that is a small price to pay for making it hard for "evil" people to do "evil," especially since one man's good is another's evil.

I have, for simplicity, concentrated on the special case of the corporate executive, except only for the brief digression on trade unions. But precisely the same argument applies to the newer phenomenon of calling upon stockholders to require corporations to exercise social responsibility (the recent G.M. crusade, for example). In most of these cases, what is in effect involved is some stockholders trying to get other stockholders (or customers or employes) to contribute against their will to "social" causes favored by the activists. Insofar as they succeed, they are again imposing taxes and spending the proceeds.

The situation of the individual proprietor is somewhat different. If he acts to reduce the returns of his enterprise in order to exercise his "social responsibility," he is spending his own money, not someone else's. If he wishes to spend his money on such purposes, that is his right, and I cannot see that there is any objection to his doing so. In the process, he, too, may impose costs on employes and customers. However, because he is far less likely than a large corporation or union to have monopolistic power, any such side effects will tend to be minor.

Of course, in practice the doctrine of social responsibility is frequently a cloak for actions that are justified on other grounds rather than a reason for those actions.

To illustrate, it may well be in the long-run interest of a corporation that is a major employer in a small community to devote resources to providing amenities to that community or to improving its government. That may make it easier to attract desirable employes, it may reduce the wage bill or lessen losses from pilferage and sabotage or have other worthwhile effects. Or it may be that, given the laws about the deductibility of corporate charitable contributions, the stockholders can contribute more to charities they favor by having the corporation make the gift than by doing it themselves, since they can in that way contribute an amount that would otherwise have been paid as corporate taxes.

In each of these—and many similar—cases, there is a strong temptation to rationalize these actions as an exercise of "social responsibility." In the present climate of opinion, with its widespread aversion to "capitalism," "profits," the "soulless corporation" and so on, this is one way for a corporation to generate goodwill as a by-product of expenditures that are entirely justified in its own self-interest.

It would be inconsistent of me to call on corporate executives to refrain from this hypocritical window-dressing because it harms the foundations of a free society. That would be to call on them to exercise a "social re-sponsibility"! If our institutions, and the attitudes of the public make it in their self-interest to cloak their actions in this way, I cannot summon much indignation to denounce them. At the same time, I can express admiration for those individual proprietors or owners of closely held corporations or stockholders of more broadly held corporations who disdain such tactics as approaching fraud.

Whether blameworthy or not, the use of the cloak of social responsibility, and the nonsense spoken in its name by influential and prestigious businessmen, does clearly harm the foundations of a free society. I have been impressed time and again by the schizophrenic character of many businessmen. They are capable of being extremely far-sighted and clear-headed in matters that are internal to their businesses. They are incredibly short-sighted and muddle-headed in matters that are outside their businesses but affect the possible survival of business in general. This short-sightedness is strikingly exemplified in the calls from many businessmen for wage and price guidelines or controls or incomes policies. There is nothing that could do more in a brief period to destroy a market system and replace it by a centrally controlled system than effective governmental control of prices and wages.

The short-sightedness is also exemplified in speeches by businessmen on social responsibility. This may gain them kudos in the short run. But it helps to strengthen the already too prevalent view that the pursuit of profits is wicked and immoral and must be curbed and controlled by external forces. Once this view is adopted, the external forces that curb the market will not be the social consciences, however highly developed, of the pontificating executives; it will be the iron fist of Government bureaucrats. Here, as with price and wage controls, businessmen seem to me to reveal a suicidal impulse.

The political principle that underlies the market mechanism is unanimity. In an ideal free market resting on private property, no individual can coerce any other, all cooperation is voluntary, all parties to such cooperation benefit or they need not participate. There are no "social" values, no "social" responsibilities in any sense other than the shared values and responsibilities of individuals. Society is a collection of individuals and of the various groups they voluntarily form.

The political principle that underlies the political mechanism is conformity. The individual must serve a more general social interest—whether that be determined by a church or a dictator or a majority. The individual may have a vote and a say in what is to be done, but if he is overruled, he must conform. It is appropriate for some to require others to contribute to a general social purpose whether they wish to or not.

Unfortunately, unanimity is not always feasible. There are some respects in which conformity appears unavoidable, so I do not see how one can avoid the use of the political mechanism altogether.

But the doctrine of "social responsibility" taken seriously would extend the scope of the political mechanism to every human activity. It does not differ in philosophy from the most explicitly collectivist doctrine. It differs only by professing to believe that collectivist ends can be attained without collectivist means. That is why, in my book *Capitalism and Freedom,* I have called it a "fundamentally subversive doctrine" in a free society, and have said that in such a society, "there is one and only one social responsibility of business—to use its resources and engage in activities designed to increase its profits so long as it stays within the rules of the game, which is to say, engages in open and free competition without deception or fraud."

QUESTIONS ON FRIEDMAN

1. What is Friedman's argument from principle? Does this argument contend that the problem of social responsibility is that the executive is appropriating a government function? That the executive has not been properly selected to administer such a function? Or is the problem simply that the executive has broken his fiduciary duty to the stockholders?

2. What are the distinguishing features of taxation? How does Friedman relate taxation to the issue of social responsibility? If the shares of a corporation can be bought and sold easily and freely, and if owners can readily discover whether or not corporate funds are being expended on projects deemed socially responsible, then why should any disbursement of funds on some socially responsible goal be understood as a "tax"?

3. Friedman seems to draw an implicit distinction between moral responsibility and social responsibility. Thus he says that the executive may have to conform to the basic rules of the society, whether "embodied in law" or in "ethical custom," but he makes no mention of ethical custom in any discussion of social responsibility. Is there a distinction between one's moral responsibilities and some putative social responsibility?

4. Friedman concludes by suggesting that if we take seriously the doctrine of social responsibility then we

"extend the political mechanism to every human activity." If an artist wishes to pursue his or her creative interests, must that artist also paint at least some pictures that are socially responsible? How might this differ from demanding that a business must be socially responsible if it is to be permitted to pursue profit?

A Stakeholder Theory of the Modern Corporation

R. Edward Freeman

R. Edward Freeman is Elis and Signe Olsson Professor of Business Administration at the Darden School of Business, University of Virginia. He is the author of several books in management and business ethics, including Strategic Management: A Stakeholder Approach *(1984). He is a coeditor (with Patricia Werhane) of* The Blackwell Encyclopedic Dictionary of Business Ethics *(1997).*

INTRODUCTION

Corporations have ceased to be merely legal devices through which the private business transactions of individuals may be carried on. Though still much used for this purpose, the corporate form has acquired a larger significance. The corporation has, in fact, become both a method of property tenure and a means of organizing economic life. Grown to tremendous proportions, there may be said to have evolved a "corporate system"—which has attracted to itself a combination of attributes and powers, and has attained a degree of prominence entitling it to be dealt with as a major social institution.[1]

Despite these prophetic words of Berle and Means (1932), scholars and managers alike continue to hold sacred the view that managers bear a special relationship to the stockholders in the firm. Since stockholders own shares in the firm, they have certain rights and privileges, which must be granted to them by management, as well as by others. Sanctions, in the form of "the law of corporations," and other protective mechanisms in the form of social custom, accepted management practice, myth, and ritual, are thought to reinforce the assumption of the primacy of the stockholder.

The purpose of this paper is to pose several challenges to this assumption, from within the framework of managerial capitalism, and to suggest the bare bones of an alternative theory, *a stakeholder theory of the modern corporation.* I do not seek the demise of the modern corporation, either intellectually or in fact. Rather, I seek its transformation. In the words of Neurath, we shall attempt to "rebuild the ship, plank by plank, while it remains afloat."[2]

My thesis is that I can revitalize the concept of managerial capitalism by replacing the notion that managers have a duty to stockholders with the concept that managers bear a fiduciary relationship to stakeholders. Stakeholders are those groups who have a stake in or claim on the firm. Specifically I include suppliers, customers, employees, stockholders, and the local community, as well as management in its role as agent for these groups. I argue that the legal, economic, political, and moral challenges to the currently received theory of the firm, as a nexus of contracts among the owners of the factors of production and customers, require us to revise this concept. That is, each of these stakeholder groups has a right not to be treated as a means to some end, and therefore must participate in determining the future direction of the firm in which they have a stake.

The crux of my argument is that we must reconceptualize the firm around the following question: For whose benefit and at whose expense should the firm be managed? I shall set forth such a reconceptualization in the form of a *stakeholder theory of the firm.* I shall then critically examine the stakeholder view and its implications for the future of the capitalist system.

THE ATTACK ON MANAGERIAL CAPITALISM

The Legal Argument

The basic idea of managerial capitalism is that in return for controlling the firm, management vigorously pursues the interests of stockholders. Central to the managerial view of the firm is the idea that management can pursue market transactions with suppliers and customers in an unconstrained manner.

The law of corporations gives a less clearcut answer to the question: In whose interest and for whose benefit should the modern corporation be governed? While it says that the corporations should be run primarily in the interests of the stockholders in the firm, it says further that the corporation exists "in contemplation of the law" and has personality as a "legal person," limited liability for its actions, and immortality, since its existence transcends that of its members. Therefore, direc-

tors and other officers of the firm have a fiduciary obligation to stockholders in the sense that the "affairs of the corporation" must be conducted in the interest of the stockholders. And stockholders can theoretically bring suit against those directors and managers for doing otherwise. But since the corporation is a legal person, existing in contemplation of the law, managers of the corporation are constrained by law.

Until recently, this was no constraint at all. In this century, however, the law has evolved to effectively constrain the pursuit of stockholder interests at the expense of other claimants on the firm. It has, in effect, required that the claims of customers, suppliers, local communities, and employees be taken into consideration, though in general they are subordinated to the claims of stockholders.

For instance, the doctrine of "privity of contract," as articulated in *Winterbottom v. Wright* in 1842, has been eroded by recent developments in products liability law. Indeed, *Greenman v. Yuba Power* gives the manufacturer strict liability for damage caused by its products, even though the seller has exercised all possible care in the preparation and sale of the product and the consumer has not bought the product from nor entered into any contractual arrangement with the manufacturer. Caveat emptor has been replaced, in large part, with caveat venditor.[3] The Consumer Product Safety Commission has the power to enact product recalls, and in 1980 one U.S. automobile company recalled more cars than it built. Some industries are required to provide information to customers about a product's ingredients, whether or not the customers want and are willing to pay for this information.[4]

The same argument is applicable to management's dealings with employees. The National Labor Relations Act gave employees the right to unionize and to bargain in good faith. It set up the National Labor Relations Board to enforce these rights with management. The Equal Pay Act of 1963 and Title VII of the Civil Rights Act of 1964 constrain management from discrimination in hiring practices; these have been followed with the Age Discrimination in Employment Act of 1967.[5] The emergence of a body of administrative case law arising from labor-management disputes and the historic settling of discrimination claims with large employers such as AT&T have caused the emergence of a body of practice in the corporation that is consistent with the legal guarantee of the rights of the employees. . . .

The law has also protected the interests of local communities. The Clean Air Act and Clean Water Act have constrained management from "spoiling the commons." In an historic case, *Marsh v. Alabama,* the Supreme Court ruled that a company-owned town was subject to the provisions of the U.S. Constitution, thereby guaranteeing the rights of local citizens and negating the "property rights" of the firm. Some states and municipalities have gone further and passed laws preventing firms from moving plants or limiting when and how plants can be closed. In sum, there is much current legal activity in this area to constrain management's pursuit of stockholders' interests at the expense of the local communities in which the firm operates.

I have argued that the result of such changes in the legal system can be viewed as giving some rights to those groups that have a claim on the firm, for example, customers, suppliers, employees, local communities, stockholders, and management. It raises the question, at the core of a theory of the firm: In whose interest and for whose benefit should the firm be managed? The answer proposed by managerial capitalism is clearly "the stockholders," but I have argued that the law has been progressively circumscribing this answer.

The Economic Argument

In its pure ideological form managerial capitalism seeks to maximize the interests of stockholders. In its perennial criticism of government regulation, management espouses the "invisible hand" doctrine. It contends that it creates the greatest good for the greatest number, and therefore government need not intervene. However, we know that externalities, moral hazards, and monopoly power exist in fact, whether or not they exist in theory. Further, some of the legal apparatus mentioned above has evolved to deal with just these issues.

The problem of the "tragedy of the commons" or the free-rider problem pervades the concept of public goods such as water and air. No one has an incentive to incur the cost of clean-up or the cost of nonpollution, since the marginal gain of one firm's action is small. Every firm reasons this way, and the result is pollution of water and air. Since the industrial revolution, firms have sought to internalize the benefits and externalize the costs of their actions. The cost must be borne by all, through taxation and regulation; hence we have the emergence of the environmental regulations of the 1970s. . . .

Finally, we see the avoidance of competitive behavior on the part of firms, each seeking to monopolize a small portion of the market and not compete with one another. In a number of industries, oligopolies have emerged, and while there is questionable evidence that oligopolies are not the most efficient corporate form in some industries, suffice it to say that the potential for

abuse of market power has again led to regulation of managerial activity. In the classic case, AT&T, arguably one of the great technological and managerial achievements of the century, was broken up into eight separate companies to prevent its abuse of monopoly power.

Externalities, moral hazards, and monopoly power have led to more external control on managerial capitalism. There are de facto constraints, due to these economic facts of life, on the ability of management to act in the interests of stockholders.

A STAKEHOLDER THEORY OF THE FIRM

The Stakeholder Concept

Corporations have stakeholders, that is, groups and individuals who benefit from or are harmed by, and whose rights are violated or respected by, corporate actions. The concept of stakeholders is a generalization of the notion of stockholders, who themselves have some special claim on the firm. Just as stockholders have a right to demand certain actions by management, so do other stakeholders have a right to make claims. The exact nature of these claims is a difficult question that I shall address, but the logic is identical to that of the stockholder theory. Stakes require action of a certain sort, and conflicting stakes require methods of resolution.

Freeman and Reed (1983)[6] distinguish two senses of *stakeholder*. The "narrow definition" includes those groups who are vital to the survival and success of the corporation. The "wide-definition" includes any group or individual who can affect or is affected by the corporation. I shall begin with a modest aim: to articulate a stakeholder theory using the narrow definition.

Stakeholders in the Modern Corporation

Figure 1 depicts the stakeholders in a typical large corporation. The stakes of each are reciprocal, since each can affect the other in terms of harms and benefits as well as rights and duties. The stakes of each are not univocal and would vary by particular corporation. I merely set forth some general notions that seem to be common to many large firms.

Owners have financial stake in the corporation in the form of stocks, bonds, and so on, and they expect some kind of financial return from them. Either they have given money directly to the firm, or they have some historical claim made through a series of morally justified exchanges. The firm affects their livelihood or, if a substantial portion of their retirement income is in

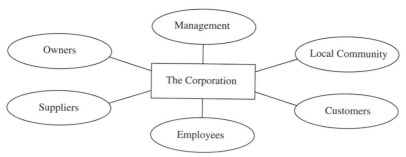

FIGURE 1 A stakeholder model of the corporation.

stocks or bonds, their ability to care for themselves when they can no longer work. Of course, the stakes of owners will differ by type of owner, preferences for money, moral preferences, and so on, as well as by type of firm. The owners of AT&T are quite different from the owners of Ford Motor Company, with stock of the former company being widely dispersed among 3 million stockholders and that of the latter being held by a small family group as well as by a large group of public stockholders.

Employees have their jobs and usually their livelihood at stake; they often have specialized skills for which there is usually no perfectly elastic market. In return for their labor, they expect security, wages, benefits, and meaningful work. In return for their loyalty, the corporation is expected to provide for them and carry them through difficult times. Employees are expected to follow the instructions of management most of the time, to speak favorably about the company, and to be responsible citizens in the local communities in which the company operates. Where they are used as means to an end, they must participate in decisions affecting such use. The evidence that such policies and values as described here lead to productive company-employee relationships is compelling. It is equally compelling to realize that the opportunities for "bad faith" on the part of both management and employees are enormous. "Mock participation" in quality circles, singing the company song, and wearing the company uniform solely to please management all lead to distrust and unproductive work.

Suppliers, interpreted in a stakeholder sense, are vital to the success of the firm, for raw materials will determine the final product's quality and price. In turn the firm is a customer of the supplier and is therefore vital to the success and survival of the supplier. When the firm treats the supplier as a valued member of the stakeholder network, rather than simply as a source of materials, the supplier will respond when the firm is in need. Chrysler traditionally had very close ties to its suppliers, even to the extent that led some to suspect the transfer of illegal payments. And when Chrysler was on the brink of disaster, the suppliers responded with price cuts, accepting late payments, financing, and so on. Supplier and company can rise and fall together. Of course, again, the particular supplier relationships will depend on a number of variables such as the number of suppliers and whether the supplies are finished goods or raw materials.

Customers exchange resources for the products of the firm and in return receive the benefits of the products. Customers provide the lifeblood of the firm in the form of revenue. Given the level of reinvestment of earnings in large corporations, customers indirectly pay for the development of new products and services. Peters and Waterman (1982)[7] have argued that being close to the customer leads to success with other stakeholders and that a distinguishing characteristic of some companies that have performed well is their emphasis on the customer. By paying attention to customers' needs, management automatically addresses the needs of suppliers and owners. Moreover, it seems that the ethic of customer service carries over to the community. Almost without fail the "excellent companies" in Peters and Waterman's study have good reputations in the community. I would argue that Peters and Waterman have found multiple applications of Kant's dictum, "Treat persons as ends unto themselves," and it should come as no surprise that persons respond to such respectful treatment, be they customers, suppliers, owners, employees, or members of the local community. The real surprise is the novelty of the application of Kant's rule in a theory of good management practice.

The local community grants the firm the right to build facilities and, in turn, it benefits from the tax base and economic and social contributions of the firm. In return for the provision of local services, the firm is expected to be a good citizen, as is any person, either "natural or artificial." The firm cannot expose the community to unreasonable hazards in the form of pollution, toxic waste, and so on. If for some reason the firm must leave a community, it is expected to work with local leaders to make the transition as smoothly as possible. Of course, the firm does not have perfect knowledge, but when it discovers some danger or runs afoul of new competition, it is expected to inform the local community and to work with the community to overcome any problem. When the firm mismanages its relationship with the local community, it is in the same position as a citizen who commits a crime. It has violated the implicit social contract with the community and should expect to be distrusted and ostracized. It should not be surprised when punitive measures are invoked.

I have not included "competitors" as stakeholders in the narrow sense, since strictly speaking they are not necessary for the survival and success of the firm; the stakeholder theory works equally well in monopoly contexts. However, competitors and government would be the first to be included in an extension of this basic theory. It is simply not true that the interests of competitors in an industry are always in conflict. There is no reason why trade associations and other multi-organizational groups cannot band together to solve common problems that have little to do with how to restrain trade. Implementation of stakeholder management principles, in the long run, mitigates the need for industrial policy and an increasing role for government intervention and regulation.

The Role of Management

Management plays a special role, for it too has a stake in the modern corporation. On the one hand, management's stake is like that of employees, with some kind of explicit or implicit employment contract. But, on the other hand, management has a duty of safeguarding the welfare of the abstract entity that is the corporation. In short, management, especially top management, must look after the health of the corporation, and this involves balancing the multiple claims of conflicting stakeholders. Owners want higher financial returns, while customers want more money spent on research and development. Employees want higher wages and better benefits, while the local community wants better parks and day-care facilities.

The task of management in today's corporation is akin to that of King Solomon. The stakeholder theory does not give primacy to one stakeholder group over another, though there will surely be times when one group will benefit at the expense of others. In general, however, management must keep the relationships among stakeholders in balance. When these relationships become imbalanced, the survival of the firm is in jeopardy.

When wages are too high and product quality is too low, customers leave, suppliers suffer, and owners sell their stocks and bonds, depressing the stock price and making it difficult to raise new capital at favorable rates. Note, however, that the reason for paying returns to owners is not that they "own" the firm, but that their support is necessary for the survival of the firm, and that they have a legitimate claim on the firm. Similar reasoning applies in turn to each stakeholder group.

A stakeholder theory of the firm must redefine the purpose of the firm. The stockholder theory claims that the purpose of the firm is to maximize the welfare of the stockholders, perhaps subject to some moral or social constraints, either because such maximization leads to the greatest good or because of property rights. The purpose of the firm is quite different in my view.

"The stakeholder theory" can be unpacked into a number of stakeholder theories, each of which has a "normative core," inextricably linked to the way that corporations should be governed and the way that managers should act. So, attempts to more fully define, or more carefully define, a stakeholder theory are misguided. Following Donaldson and Preston, I want to insist that the normative, descriptive, instrumental, and metaphorical (my addition to their framework) uses of 'stakeholder' are tied together in particular political constructions to yield a number of possible "stakeholder theories." "Stakeholder theory" is thus a genre of stories about how we could live. Let me be more specific.

A "normative core" of a theory is a set of sentences that includes among others, sentences like:

1.   Corporations ought to be governed . . .

2.   Managers ought to act to . . .

where we need arguments or further narratives which include business and moral terms to fill in the blanks. This normative core is not always reducible to a fundamental ground like the theory of property, but certain normative cores are consistent with modern understandings of property. Certain elaborations of the theory of private property plus the other institutions of political liberalism give rise to particular normative cores. But there are other institutions, other political conceptions of how society ought to be structured, so that there are different possible normative cores.

EXHIBIT 1 A Reasonable Pluralism

	A. Corporations ought to be governed . . .	B. Managers ought to act . . .	C. The background disciplines of "value creation" are . . .
Doctrine of Fair Contracts	. . . in accordance with the six principles.	. . . in the interests of stakeholders.	—business theories —theories that explain stakeholder behavior
Feminist Standpoint Theory	. . . in accordance with the principles of caring/connection and relationships.	. . . to maintain and care for relationships and networks of stakeholders.	—business theories —feminist theory —social science understanding of networks
Ecological Principles	. . . in accordance with the principle of caring for the earth.	. . . to care for the earth.	—business theories —ecology —other

So, one normative core of a stakeholder theory might be a feminist standpoint one, rethinking how we would restructure "value-creating activity" along principles of caring and connection.[8] Another would be an ecological (or several ecological) normative cores. Mark Starik has argued that the very idea of a stakeholder theory of the *firm* ignores certain ecological necessities.[9] Exhibit 1 is suggestive of how these theories could be developed.

In the next section I shall sketch the normative core based on pragmatic liberalism. But, any normative core must address the questions in columns A or B, or explain why these questions may be irrelevant, as in the ecological view. In addition, each "theory," and I use the word hesitantly, must place the normative core within a more full-fledged account of how we could understand value-creating activity differently (column C). The only way to get on with this task is to see the stakeholder idea as a metaphor. The attempt to prescribe one and only one "normative core" and construct "a stakeholder theory" is at best a disguised attempt to smuggle a normative core past the unsophisticated noses of other unsuspecting academics who are just happy to see the end of the stockholder orthodoxy.

If we begin with the view that we can understand value-creation activity as a contractual process among those parties affected, and if for simplicity's sake we initially designate those parties as financiers, customers, suppliers, employees, and communities, then we can construct a normative core that reflects the liberal notions of autonomy, solidarity, and fairness as articulated by John Rawls, Richard Rorty, and others.[10] Notice that building these moral notions into the foundations of how we understand value creation and contracting re-quires that we eschew separating the "business" part of the process from the "ethical" part, and that we start with the presumption of equality among the contractors, rather than the presumption in favor of financier rights.

The normative core for this redesigned contractual theory will capture the liberal idea of fairness if it ensures a basic equality among stakeholders in terms of their moral rights as these are realized in the firm, and if it recognizes that inequalities among stakeholders are justified if they raise the level of the least well-off stakeholder. The liberal ideal of autonomy is captured by the realization that each stakeholder must be free to enter agreements that create value for themselves, and solidarity is realized by the recognition of the mutuality of stakeholder interests.

One way to understand fairness in this context is to claim *a la* Rawls that a contract is fair if parties to the contract would agree to it in ignorance of their actual stakes. Thus, a contract is like a fair bet, if each party is willing to turn the tables and accept the other side. What would a fair contract among corporate stakeholders look like? If we can articulate this ideal, a sort of corporate constitution, we could then ask whether actual corporations measure up to this standard, and we also begin to design corporate structures which are consistent with this Doctrine of Fair Contracts.

Imagine if you will, representative stakeholders trying to decide on "the rules of the game." Each is rational in a straightforward sense, looking out for its own self-interest. At least *ex ante*, stakeholders are the relevant parties since they will be materially affected. Stakeholders know how economic activity is organized and could be organized. They know general facts about the way the corporate world works. They know that in the real world there are or could be transaction costs, externalities, and positive costs of contracting. Suppose they are uncertain about what other social institutions exist, but they know the range of those institutions. They do not know if government exists to pick up the tab for any externalities, or if they will exist in the nightwatchman state of libertarian theory. They know success and failure stories of businesses around the world. In short, they are behind a Rawls-like veil of ignorance, and they do not know what stake each will have when the veil is lifted. What groundrules would they choose to guide them?

The first groundrule is "The Principle of Entry and Exit." Any contract that is the corporation must have clearly defined entry, exit, and renegotiation conditions, or at least it must have methods or processes for so defining these conditions. The logic is straightforward: each stakeholder must be able to determine when an agreement exists and has a chance of fulfillment. This is not to imply that contracts cannot contain contingent claims or other methods for resolving uncertainty, but rather that it must contain methods for determining whether or not it is valid.

The second groundrule I shall call "The Principle of Governance," and it says that the procedure for changing the rules of the game must be agreed upon by unanimous consent. Think about the consequences of a majority of stakeholders systematically "selling out" a minority. Each stakeholder, in ignorance of its actual role, would seek to avoid such a situation. In reality this principle translates into each stakeholder never giving up its right to participate in the governance of the corporation, or perhaps into the existence of stakeholder governing boards.

The third groundrule I shall call "The Principle of Externalities," and it says that if a contract between A and B imposes a cost on C, then C has the option to become a party to the contract, and the terms are renegotiated. Once again the rationality of this condition is clear. Each stakeholder will want insurance that it does not become C.

The fourth groundrule is "The Principle of Contracting Costs," and it says that all parties to the contract must share in the cost of contracting. Once again the logic is straightforward. Any one stakeholder can get stuck.

A fifth groundrule is "The Agency Principle" that says that any agent must serve the interests of all stakeholders. It must adjudicate conflicts within the bounds of the other principals. Once again the logic is clear. Agents for any one group would have a privileged place.

A sixth and final groundrule we might call, "The Principle of Limited Immortality." The corporation shall be managed as if it can continue to serve the interests of stakeholders through time. Stakeholders are uncertain about the future but, subject to exit conditions, they realize that the continued existence of the corporation is in their interest. Therefore, it would be rational to hire managers who are fiduciaries to their interest and the interest of the collective. If it turns out the "collective interest" is the empty set, then this principle simply collapses into the Agency Principle.

Thus, the Doctrine of Fair Contracts consists of these six groundrules or principles:

1. The Principle of Entry and Exit

2. The Principle of Governance

3. The Principle of Externalities

4. The Principle of Contracting Costs

5. The Agency Principle

6. The Principle of Limited Immortality

Think of these groundrules as a doctrine which would guide actual stakeholders in devising a corporate constitution or charter. Think of management as having the duty to act in accordance with some specific constitution or charter.

Obviously, if the Doctrine of Fair Contracts and its accompanying background narratives are to effect real change, there must be requisite changes in the enabling laws of the land. I propose the following three principles to serve as constitutive elements of attempts to reform the law of corporations.

The Stakeholder Enabling Principle

Corporations shall be managed in the interests of its stakeholders, defined as employees, financiers, customers, employees, and communities.

The Principle of Director Responsibility

Directors of the corporation shall have a duty of care to use reasonable judgment to define and direct the affairs of the corporation in accordance with the Stakeholder Enabling Principle.

The Principle of Stakeholder Recourse

Stakeholders may bring an action against the directors for failure to perform the required duty of care.

Obviously, there is more work to be done to spell out these principles in terms of model legislation. As they stand, they try to capture the intuitions that drive the liberal ideals. It is equally plain that corporate constitutions which meet a test like the doctrine of fair contracts are meant to enable directors and executives to manage the corporation in conjunction with these same liberal ideals.

ENDNOTES

1. Cf. A. Berle and G. Means, *The Modern Corporation and Private Property* (New York: Commerce Clearing House, 1932), 1. For a reassessment of Berle and Means' argument after 50 years, see *Journal of Law and Economics* 26 (June 1983), especially G. Stigler and C. Friedland, "The Literature of Economics: The Case of Berle and Means," 237–68; D. North, "Comment on Stigler and Friedland," 269–72; and G. Means, "Corporate Power in the Marketplace," 467–85.

2. The metaphor of rebuilding the ship while afloat is attributed to Neurath by W. Quine, *Word and Object* (Cambridge: Harvard University Press, 1960), and W. Quine and J. Ullian, *The Web of Belief* (New York: Random House, 1978). The point is that to keep the ship afloat during repairs we must replace a plank with one that will do a better job. Our argument is that stakeholder capitalism can so replace the current version of managerial capitalism.

3. See R. Charan and E. Freeman, "Planning for the Business Environment of the 1980s," *The Journal of Business Strategy* 1 (1980): 9–19, especially p. 15 for a brief account of the major developments in products liability law.

4. See S. Breyer, *Regulation and Its Reform* (Cambridge: Harvard University Press, 1983), 133, for an analysis of food additives.

5. See I. Millstein and S. Katsh, *The Limits of Corporate Power* (New York: Macmillan, 1981), Chapter 4.

6. See E. Freeman and D. Reed, "Stockholders and Stakeholders: A New Perspective on Corporate Governance," in C. Huizinga, ed., *Corporate Governance: A Definitive Exploration of the Issues* (Los Angeles: UCLA Extension Press, 1983).

7. See T. Peters and R. Waterman, *In Search of Excellence* (New York: Harper and Row, 1982).

8. See, for instance, A. Wicks, D. Gilbert, and E. Freeman, "A Feminist Reinterpretation of the Stakeholder Concept," *Business Ethics Quarterly,* Vol. 4, No. 4, October 1994; and E. Freeman and J. Liedtka, "Corporate Social Responsibility: A Critical Approach," *Business Horizons,* Vol. 34, No. 4, July–August 1991, pp. 92–98.

9. At the Toronto workshop Mark Starik sketched how a theory would look if we took the environment to be a stakeholder. This fruitful line of work is one example of my main point about pluralism.

10. J. Rawls, *Political Liberalism,* New York: Columbia University Press, 1993; and R. Rorty, "The Priority of Democracy to Philosophy" in *Reading Rorty: Critical Responses to Philosophy and the Mirror of Nature (and Beyond),* ed. Alan R. Malachowski, Cambridge, MA: Blackwell, 1990.

QUESTIONS ON FREEMAN

1. Freeman argues that the law has been progressively constraining the manager's duty to the shareholder while widening the duties to other parties. Does this *fact* provide a *reason* for institutionalizing such constraint through a theory of the stakeholder?

2. Freeman asserts that "The stakeholder theory does not give primacy to one stakeholder group over another. . . ." However, the owners of a corporation have risked their capital on the enterprise. Why should those who have *not* risked their capital have an equal stake in an enterprise with those who have? Why doesn't this treat the owners of the corporation merely as a means? Explain.

3. Who exactly are the stakeholders in a firm? Is the largest supplier to a firm a more important stakeholder than a small supplier? Does a senior employee have a greater stake than a new employee? Who represents the customers to the firm?

4. Why does Freeman contend that stakeholder theory is a metaphor? What is it a metaphor *for*? How might there be distinct normative cores of stakeholder theories? Does the stakeholder theory substitute political decision making for economic decision making? Should the stakeholder theory be applied to other organizations in society besides corporations?

The Ethics of Rent-Seeking?

A New Perspective on Corporate Social Responsibility

Michael E. DeBow

Michael E. DeBow is Professor of Law at the Cumberland School of Law, Samford University, and Professor of Health Care Organization and Policy at the School of Public Health, University of Alabama–Birmingham. His articles have appeared in various law reviews and scholarly journals. The complete version of this essay appeared in the Journal of Law and Commerce *(1992).*

Much ink has been spilled on the subjects of business ethics and corporate social responsibility.[1] Remarkably, however, the question that will concern us here has received almost no attention. It is this: "Is it ethical for a business—or an industry, or a union, or other private group—to seek the aid of government, with its formidable coercive powers, in order to benefit itself at the expense of the public at large?"

This question is rooted in the increasingly accepted dictum that interest groups with political clout "use the political process effectively to increase their incomes."[2] Clearly, much interest group political activity is devoted to the pursuit of governmentally-supplied advantages. In the United States, government favors can take the form of tax breaks, poorly monitored government contracts (especially in the defense budget), "pork barrel" construction projects (including water projects and highway construction), direct government subsidies (as in agricultural production and loans to college students), protection from foreign competitors (the tariff system and the non-tariff barriers erected by trade laws such as the "anti-dumping" statutes), and barriers to the entry (or competitiveness)[3] of would-be domestic competitors—to name only a few.

Concern over the private manipulation of the political process has a long lineage. As the late George Stigler, the 1982 Nobel laureate in economics, noted:

> The explanation of public policies we have recently learned to give is that they are usually designed by particular groups in a society for their own benefit. That is scarcely news: James Madison found the central task of government to be the control and attenuation of factions (see *The Federalist* No. 10).[4]

Indeed, a concern over the manipulation of political processes for private gain inherent in mercantilism was one of the primary concerns that led Adam Smith to write *The Wealth of Nations* and *The Theory of Moral Sentiments*.[5]

Today, economists call the pursuit of governmentally-conferred benefits by private interest groups "rent-seeking."[6] The amount of rent-seeking in the American economy, and the social costs it imposes, is substantial. Economist Gordon Tullock, one of the key figures in the development of rent-seeking theory, argues that "anyone who spends any time in Washington quickly realizes that there is a major industry engaged in just this kind of activity."[7]

The rent-seeking industry has expanded dramatically during this century,[8] and has likely had a negative effect on economic growth.[9] One recent study estimates that today 10 to 20 percent of GNP in industrialized countries is "lost" through "overregulation, excessive redistributive lawyering, and inefficient conflict resolution."[10] In the United States at this time, there is little reason to believe that the amount of rent-seeking behavior will shrink; rather, it appears likely to continue to expand, as the role of government expands.

In spite of the significance of rent-seeking behavior,[11] there has been little discussion of the ethical dimensions of these activities, or of the social responsibility (or lack thereof) manifested by corporate and other groups that engage in it. . . .

The analysis in this article is framed by Gordon Tullock's statement that he finds it "implausible" that "people regard rent-seeking as immoral and that as a result, a great many people are simply unwilling to engage in it. I can think of no good way of proving or disproving this. Public expressions in this area are mixed and confused, and feelings are difficult to deduce."[12] Thus, although Tullock "do[es] not necessarily see [rent-seeking] as morally commendable," he "see[s] no signs that moral considerations have much effect here."[13] . . .

This Article focuses on rent-seeking by business owners, managers and labor, and the possible gains from discussing this phenomenon in business and law classrooms and research publications. . . .

Should rent-seeking be treated as a violation of ethical norms, or not? This article offers a starting point for addressing this question. . . .

Part I more fully describes the theory of rent-seeking, notes the positive ("what is") objections to rent-seeking behavior, and outlines a tentative normative ("what ought to be") analysis of the ethical questions raised by rent-seeking behavior. Part II explores possible justifications for some forms of rent-seeking behavior. Part III offers a tentative explanation of why these questions have received scant attention from legal and business scholars. Part IV offers some suggestions for further research and discussion.

I. THREE (ETHICAL?) PROBLEMS WITH RENT-SEEKING[14]

The theory of rent-seeking suggests that the practice 1) is itself wasteful and, if successful, further promotes the waste of society's resources; 2) exploits the "rational ignorance" of the public as voters and consumers in order to invoke government coercion; and 3) if successful, redistributes wealth, often in a regressive fashion. In light of these factors, I will take the position that a benchmark ethical constraint on business (and labor) should be a prohibition on calling on the coercive power of the government to help "shake down" the public.

A. Waste

The theory of rent-seeking identifies two ways in which such activity leads a society to waste its resources. First, *successful* rent-seeking leads to the adoption of policies that reduce economic efficiency by misallocating productive resources. Second, *successful or unsuccessful* rent-seeking requires the commitment of resources to the process of rent-seeking itself that could have been deployed elsewhere in the economy in a more productive use.

The first point, that successful rent-seeking results in a misallocation of resources and a concomitant decline in social well-being, is analogous to the criticism of price-fixing conspiracies among otherwise competing firms.[15] To see this more clearly, consider the now-classic example of rent-seeking: a firm (or an industry) striving to convince the government to impose a tariff on competing imports.[16]

If successful, the rent-seeking firm will see the market price of the good sold in the U.S.—both domestically produced and imported—increase, with a resulting decrease in the total quantity purchased by U.S. consumers. As a result of the higher market price and the disruption of competing imports, the domestic firm earns higher profits.

The increased profits flowing to the firm as a result of the trade restriction is simply a transfer to the firm and could, theoretically, be taxed away. It does not represent a net loss to society. I will defer consideration of the redistributive effects of rent-seeking to section I.C., below.

For the present time, I will focus on the resource misallocation attributable to the tariff, which *is* a net loss to society. This loss, known technically as a "dead-weight loss," represents consumer well-being foregone because of the misallocation of productive resources—both human and financial—engendered by the tariff. This loss occurs because prices charged in the protected market distort the signals sent to firms—both domestic and foreign—and, thereby, jam the price mechanism.

In the domestic industry, the tariff causes more resources to be used than would be used in the absence of the tariff. This pulls resources from alternative uses in other industries which would be, by definition, more valuable to consumers than their use in the protected industry, *sans* protection. The reverse happens in the foreign firms that would export less to the U.S. after the tariff: fewer resources are used there, with the resources released being redirected to their next highest alternative uses which are, by definition, less valuable to consumers than their use in the industry in question. The deadweight loss is the hidden cost of rejecting the benefits of "free trade."[17] . . .

Protectionism is thus a "negative sum game," in which the losers lose more than the winners gain. The idea that tariffs and other import barriers are negative sum policies that diminish a nation's overall economic well-being—an idea first popularized by Adam Smith—is one of the oldest and most widely accepted propositions among economists.[18] Most other forms of rent-conferring government policies can be classified as negative sum or, at best, zero sum (in which the winners' gains equal the losers' losses), for reasons that we will consider in section II.A.

Deadweight losses, however, are not the only "social costs" generated by corporate rent-seeking. In addition, rent-seeking—even if it is *unsuccessful*—results in a loss to society in the form of the rent-seeking costs incurred by the rent-seeking parties, as well as the costs of defensive measures undertaken by parties who would "lose" if the rent-seeking parties "win."[19] These costs can take many forms, including the making of legal campaign contributions, the employment of lobbying and public relations experts, the conduct of litigation, and so on. As public choice economist Robert Tollison explains, rent-seeking involves the expenditure of

> real resources to capture a pure transfer. Since expenditures to take a dollar from A and give it to B produce nothing, they are wasted from the point of view of the economy at large; they are zero-sum at best and are probably negative sum. A lawyer, for example, employed to transfer a dollar from A to B has an opportunity cost in terms of the lawyer output he or she could have produced alternatively. This opportunity cost is the social cost of rent-seeking.[20]

The opportunity costs of rent-seeking are often referred to as "Tullock costs," after Gordon Tullock.

Rent-seeking thus generates two kinds of social waste: 1) the resource misallocation due to the government's rent-conferring interference in the market (the deadweight loss); and 2) the diversion of resources towards rent-seeking and away from alternative uses that would, in a world without payoffs to rent-seeking, be more productive (the Tullock costs).

In most cases—and this point includes a number of forms of government intervention in addition to tariffs and other trade policies—we would expect these two costs generated by the rent-seeking behavior to outweigh the benefits actually received by the rent-seeking parties. Distributional concerns entirely aside, then, rent-seeking typically generates a net loss to society; it is a negative sum game in which the public at large gives up more than the rent-seekers gain.

Is this kind of waste ethically defensible? Consider Judge Richard Posner's claim that the conservation of scarce resources is one element of a common definition of "justice." He argues that

> when people describe as unjust convicting a person without a trial, taking property without just compensation, or failing to make a negligent automobile driver answer in damages to the victim of his negligence, this means nothing more pretentious than that the conduct wastes resources.... *And with a little reflection, it will come as no surprise that in a world of scarce resources waste should be regarded as immoral.*[21]

Posner's observations may provide one starting place for a discussion of the ethical dimensions of the waste involved in rent-seeking behavior.

B. Government Coercion and Rational Ignorance

If rent-seeking is (normally) a wasteful, negative sum game, why do we observe so much government activity that can be characterized as rent-conferring?

The answer appears to lie in the asymmetrical distribution of the costs of, and benefits from, rent-seeking activity. That is, successful rent-seeking firms—and their managers, employees, stockholders, and so on—enjoy higher profits (and wages, etc.). At the same time, the cost of the government policy which confers the rent—a tariff, for example—is borne by a much larger number of consumers (and would-be consumers) in the form of higher prices and decreased availability. The benefits from successful rent-seeking are concentrated, while the costs are dispersed. As a result, potential beneficiaries of rent-seeking have a greater incentive to engage in such behavior than individuals, as voters or as consumers, have to try to understand and have an effect on the political process. Because the cost to the average voter of following complex government processes tends to outweigh the benefits to that individual of studying those processes—especially in view of the exceedingly low probability that any single individual will have any effect whatever on those processes—government activity will tend to favor rent-seekers.[22]

This is morally questionable, on the grounds that such government policies tend to limit the realm of personal freedom in order to force the desired results. For example, individuals who continue to purchase products in a market "protected" from foreign competition are, in part, coerced into paying higher prices reflecting the tariff. And, short of emigration, individuals have no real choice about whether to pay higher

taxes reflecting subsidies and tax breaks, and so on. The substitution of governmentally-coerced behavior for freely chosen behavior appears to me *prima facie* undesirable.[23]

C. Redistribution and Regressivity

The standard case made by economists against rent-seeking tends to concentrate on deadweight and rent-seeking costs, and says little or nothing about another, arguably undesirable, result: the resulting income reallocation to the favored groups. Most economists demur from arguments over the correctness, or incorrectness, of a particular distribution (or redistribution) of income.[24] No such restraint is shown by other categories of academicians, and I see no reason why business and law school faculty members cannot at least raise the question of the propriety of transferring rents to favored groups via the political process.

Although the transfer to successful rent-seeking firms in the form of higher profits (net of rent-seeking costs) is not a social loss, it should be clear that the price increases involved—in effect, a form of indirect taxation, levied through government action to support the rent-seeking firm—can be dramatic. For example, the size of the price increases in the U.S. due to protectionist laws has been estimated at $1,200 per family *annually,*[25] while the increased costs to British consumers of the European Economic Community's "common agricultural policy" has been reckoned at 730 pounds sterling per family of four *annually.*[26]

It is interesting to note that scholars who attempt to discuss the redistributive aspect of rent-seeking will discover that virtually all of the literature dealing with the ethical dimensions of income and wealth redistribution through governmental action addresses what we may call top-down redistribution. That is, the philosophical writings on redistribution tend to argue for, or against, the correctness of taking from the rich and giving to the poor.[27] This is somewhat ironic, since it is reasonably clear that government redistribution is not predominantly top-down.[28] Rather, redistribution tends to be horizontal—from one (typically) larger, non-poor group to another, smaller group of non-poor recipients.[29] This is particularly true of rent-conferring policies such as tariffs and other governmentally-created barriers to entry.

Indeed, we can expect that the effects of rent-seeking will often be regressive; that is, lower income consumers will pay a disproportionately larger share of the indirect tax, as compared to higher income consumers. For example, a recent study by the United States Association of Importers of Textiles estimated that the Multifiber Agreement (or "MFA"), the U.S.'s barrier to the importation of foreign clothes, textiles, and shoes, costs poor families 8.8 percent of their disposable income.[30] There are numerous other examples of regressive results, including occupational licensing and taxi regulation.[31] . . .

II. JUSTIFIABLE RENT-SEEKING?

It is, however, possible to imagine arguments on behalf of particular types of rent-seeking.

A. Positive-Sum Rent-Seeking

For example, it may be argued that rent-seeking can be "socially responsible" if a corporation balances costs and benefits, pleasures and pains, and only asks for help where it is justified on utilitarian grounds. For instance, manufacturers of pollution-abatement equipment may lobby for the passage of stricter environmental controls that *may,* on the whole, benefit society, while defense contractors may lobby for the funding of weapons systems that *may* produce benefits in excess of costs,[32] and so on. Both of these examples involve government actions to cure what are termed "market failures"—instances in which the unfettered operation of the marketplace yields less than desirable results. The environmental rent-seeking of the pollution controls manufacturers *may* produce a public policy that satisfactorily addresses a "negative externality" problem, while the defense contractor's rent-seeking *may* improve the government's provision of the "public good" of national defense.[33]

There is a serious problem with this line of argument, however. Once you accept the possibility of positive-sum rent-seeking, it becomes possible for any interest group to argue that *its* rent-seeking activity is socially responsible, even when it in fact will harm the public.[34] This is roughly what is done with arguments for tariffs, as industries' attempts to secure protection from foreign competition are defended as socially responsible because of the resulting protection of workers' jobs, their communities, and so on. While saving American jobs has a nice ring to it and has been pitched as socially responsible throughout American history,[35] the evidence cited in this article demonstrates that trade protection is a net drain on social well-being. Nonetheless, politicians attempt to capitalize on the desire for tariffs—as well as the attendant xenophobia. In this fashion the invocation of such catch phrases as "saving American jobs" and the "American standard of living" can

be used to recast rent-seeking (merely a search for a "level playing field," after all) from interest group politics into a social responsibility.

Further, we should not expect to see positive-sum rent-seeking very often, because positive-sum exchanges can typically be arranged voluntarily in the marketplace and thus do not usually require government involvement. It follows that the existence of a government policy should raise doubts as to whether the exchanges it promotes are primarily positive-sum, or merely rent-conferring and redistributive, in nature.

I submit that the slipperiness of the concept of positive-sum rent-seeking, and the possibility of arranging positive-sum transactions through markets rather than through government, justifies placing the burden of persuasion as to this claim on the rent-seekers. That is, a petition for government aid should be viewed as *prima facie* harmful to society as a whole—and thus unethical and socially irresponsible—unless the petitioner/rent-seeker can demonstrate that the policies it seeks to promote will in fact benefit society through the amelioration of a market failure, net of the costs of those policies. This is a much heavier burden of proof than rent-seeking firms and interest groups are now made to bear.

B. Rent-Protecting and Rent-Avoiding Behavior

One might also argue that a firm is not behaving unethically if it expends resources in order to convince government not to take an action that would expropriate a privately-created rent.[36] Such "rent-protecting" behavior is a form of rent-seeking, but may deserve greater tolerance because of its goal of protecting the incentives to private parties to generate innovations free of governmental expropriation.

A similar regard may be appropriate for "rent-avoiding" behavior, in which parties seek to defeat the rent-seeking activities of others that would adversely affect their own interests. This defensive activity, although wasteful in itself, may have a salutary effect on social welfare in lowering the probability that rent-seeking will prevail, thereby deterring the implementation of some rent-seeking strategies.[37]

In addition, a firm may be on somewhat defensible ethical grounds if it is seeking to ensure the continuation of a pre-existing piece of regulation that benefits it. Since the firm's stock price already capitalizes the value of the rents conferred, the argument would run, the reduction or elimination of the transfer would lower the price of the stock and harm many investors who bought the stock at a price reflecting the capitalized value of the rent.[38]

C. Rent-Seeking as a Managerial Duty?

Another perspective on rent-seeking involves a substantial irony. While economists tend to disfavor rent-seeking, what would they say to a corporate manager who finds herself in a situation where her firm's profit-maximizing strategy appears to be to engage in rent-seeking? If, in the famous words of Milton Friedman, the social responsibility of business is to increase its profits,[39] this would seem to entail a responsibility on the part of corporate managers to pursue rent-seeking opportunities when, in light of all the evidence available to them, such a pursuit will yield the highest return possible from the set of options available. Are managers in this situation compelled by their fiduciary duty to the corporation and its shareholders to engage in rent-seeking?

Consider the Ford Motor Company's 1980 firing of its chief economist, William Niskanen. Niskanen was dismissed because he did not agree that abandoning Ford's 75-year-old free trade position in order to seek import protection was the company's best option. Clearly, Niskanen's superiors thought that Ford profits were to be maximized through rent-seeking.

It is interesting, for our present purposes, to note that one of Niskanen's objections to Ford's rent-seeking strategy appears rooted in a moral objection. A *Wall Street Journal* column on this subject explained Niskanen's moral position: "[F]or members of the business community to turn to Washington for such favors would be morally wrong: 'A common commitment to refrain from seeking special favors,' [Niskanen] wrote in a memo 'serves the same economic function as a common commitment to refrain from stealing.' "[40]

For those who favor the marketplace over politics, rent-seeking is troublesome—at the least on the grounds that it misallocates and wastes resources. These same observers would tend to agree with Friedman's view of the proper goals for corporate managers. Ironically, this goal-orientation, applied in a situation in which rent-seeking is the profit-maximizing strategy, would lead observers without an ethical standard to guide them to argue that managers should engage in rent-seeking!

As these remarks indicate, an ethical analysis of rent-seeking may in some cases prove a complicated task. Nonetheless the task seems well worth undertaking. . . .

ENDNOTES

1. Useful introductions to these areas include David Vogel, *Business Ethics Past and Present*, PUB. INTEREST, Winter 1991, at 49; Christopher D. Stone, *Corporate Social Responsibility: What it Might Mean, If it Were Really to Matter*, 71 IOWA L. REV. 557 (1986); Jerry L. Mashaw, *Corporate Social Responsibility: Comments on the Legal and Economic Context of a Continuing Debate*, 3 YALE L. & POL'Y REV. 114 (1984); Peter F. Drucker, *What Is "Business Ethics"?*, PUB. INTEREST, Spring 1981, at 18; David Engel, *An Approach to Corporate Social Responsibility*, 32 STAN. L. REV. 1 (1979). For surveys of the broader field of which business ethics and corporate social responsibility are constituent parts, see Earl F. Cheit, *Coming of Middle Age in Business and Society*, CALIF. MGMT. REV., Winter 1991, at 71, and Lee E. Preston, *Business and Public Policy*, 12 J. MGMT. 261 (1986).

2. GEORGE J. STIGLER, MEMOIRS OF AN UNREGULATED ECONOMIST 120 (1988). Landmark contributions to the literature supporting this proposition include MANCUR OLSON, JR., THE LOGIC OF COLLECTIVE ACTION (1965); Gordon Tullock, *The Welfare Costs of Tariffs, Monopolies, and Theft*, 5 W. ECON. J. 224 (1967); and George J. Stigler, *The Theory of Economic Regulation*, 2 BELL J. ECON. & MGMT. SCI. 3 (1971).

3. For a fascinating account of one rent-seeking episode, see BRUCE A. ACKERMAN & WILLIAM HASSLER, CLEAN COAL/DIRTY AIR (1981). It describes the tactics used by high-sulfur coal producers in successfully lobbying for changes in environmental legislation to protect the use of high-sulfur coal. The result was a less effective, and more expensive, approach to air pollution abatement.

4. STIGLER, MEMOIRS OF AN UNREGULATED ECONOMIST, *supra* note 2, at 115.

5. For a recent exploration of this aspect of Smith's scholarship, see Jerry Evensky, *Ethics and the Classical Liberal Tradition in Economics*, 24 HIST. POL. ECON. 61, 71–74 (1992) (discussing connection between Smith's reaction to "mercantilist rent-seeking run amok" and his work on ethics).

6. More formally, rent-seeking is defined as the search for "a return in excess of a resource owner's opportunity cost [that is] contrived artificially through . . . government action." Robert D. Tollison, *Rent-Seeking: A Survey*, 35 KYKLOS 575, 575 (1982). For a survey of research on rent-seeking, see DENNIS C. MUELLER, PUBLIC CHOICE II 229–46 (rev. ed. 1989).

7. Gordon Tullock, *Rent-Seeking, in* 4 THE NEW PALGRAVE: A DICTIONARY OF ECONOMICS 147, 148 (John Eatwell et al. eds., 1987).

8. Gerald W. Scully, *Rent-Seeking in U.S. Government Budgets, 1900–88,* 70 PUB. CHOICE 99 (1991) (portion of government budgets characterized as waste from rent-seeking activity three times larger today than during the period 1900–1920). *See generally* TERRY ANDERSON & PETER J. HILL, THE BIRTH OF A TRANSFER SOCIETY (1980); JONATHAN R. T. HUGHES, THE GOVERNMENTAL HABIT

REDUX (2d ed. 1991); ROBERT HIGGS, CRISIS AND LEVIATHAN: CRITICAL EPISODES IN THE GROWTH OF AMERICAN GOVERNMENT (1987).

9. One recent study finds that a country's rate of economic growth varies directly with the number of college students majoring in engineering, and inversely with the number of students in law. Kevin M. Murphy, et al., *The Allocation of Talent: Implications for Growth,* 106 Q.J.ECON. 503 (1991). *But cf.* Frank B. Cross, *The First Thing We Do, Let's Kill All the Economists: An Empirical Evaluation of the Effect of Lawyers on the United States Economy and Political System,* 70 TEX. L. REV. 645, 670–71, 672–76 (1992) (criticizing methods used by Murphy, Shleifer & Vishny, and offering an alternative).

10. STEPHEN P. MAGEE ET AL., WILLIAM A. BROCK & LESLIE YOUNG, BLACK HOLE TARIFFS AND ENDOGENOUS POLICY THEORY: POLITICAL ECONOMY IN GENERAL EQUILIBRIUM 225 (1989). *But cf.* Cross, *supra* note 9, at 668–70, 672–76 (criticizing methods used by Magee, Brock & Young, and offering an alternative).

11. And in spite of a large literature on corporate political activity—PACs and so forth. *See* DAVID VOGEL, FLUCTUATING FORTUNES: THE POLITICAL POWER OF BUSINESS IN AMERICA (1989); Gerald D. Keim & Barry D. Baysinger, *The Efficacy of Business Political Activity: Competitive Considerations in a Principal-Agent Context,* 14 J. MGMT. 163 (1988); Preston, *supra* note 1; Edwin M. Epstein, *Business Political Activity: Research Approaches and Analytical Issues,* 2 RESEARCH IN CORP. SOC. PERFORMANCE & POL'Y 1 (1980).

12. GORDON TULLOCK. THE ECONOMICS OF SPECIAL PRIVILEGE AND RENT-SEEKING 6–7 (1989).

13. *Id.* at 44.

14. For more extensive explanations of the theory of rent-seeking, see Tullock, *supra* note 2; Anne O. Krueger, *The Political Economy of the Rent-Seeking Society,* 64 AM. ECON. REV. 291 (1974); Richard A. Posner, *The Social Costs of Monopoly and Regulation,* 83 J. POL. ECON. 807 (1975); and Jagdish N. Bhagwati, *Directly Unproductive, Profit-seeking (DUP) Activities,* 90 J. POL. ECON. 988 (1982).

15. This suggests the possibility that higher marginal rent-seeking costs may increase social welfare by reducing the amount of successful rent-seeking. Dwight R. Lee, *Marginal Lobbying Cost and the Optimal Amount of Rent-Seeking,* 45 PUB. CHOICE 207 (1985).

16. JAGDISH N. BHAGWATI, PROTECTIONISM (1988) is a masterful explanation of the politics of international trade restraints. For good, less technical discussions of the negative effects of trade restraints, see Robert W. McGee, *Trade Deficits and Economic Policy: A Law and Economics Analysis,* 11 J. L. & COM. 159 (1992), and JAMES BOVARD, THE FAIR TRADE FRAUD: HOW CONGRESS PILLAGES THE CONSUMER AND DECIMATES AMERICAN COMPETITIVENESS (1991).

17. In most instances the deadweight loss probably understates the long-run social loss, for two reasons. First, trade protectionism can prompt retaliation by other national governments, hurting the citizens of the first nation by lowering the amount of exports from that nation to the retaliating nations. Second, the erection of barriers to imports removes, to some degree, the spur of competition which would otherwise tend to keep the domestic firms "on their toes." This "slack" will harm consumers in the form of higher prices over time for the protected firms' products, and will exacerbate the resource misallocation due to the protectionist policy.

18. See the survey results reported in David Colander & Arjo Klamer, *The Making of an Economist,* J. ECON. PERSP., Fall 1987, at 95; and Bruno S. Frey, Werner W. Pommerehne, Friedrich Schneider & Guy Gilbert, *Consensus and Dissension Among Economists: An Empirical Inquiry,* 74 AM. ECON. REV. 986 (1984). For a recent dissent from this consensus, see Krugman, *Is Free Trade Passé?, infra* note 43.

19. For an analysis of the costs of defending against rent-seeking activity, see Fred S. McChesney, *Rent Extraction and Rent Creation in the Economic Theory of Regulation,* 16 J. LEGAL STUD., 101 (1987).

20. Robert D. Tollison, *Is the Theory of Rent-Seeking Here to Stay?,* in DEMOCRACY AND PUBLIC CHOICE: ESSAYS IN HONOR OF GORDON TULLOCK 143, 145 (Charles K. Rowley ed., 1987).

21. RICHARD A. POSNER, ECONOMIC ANALYSIS OF LAW 25 (3d ed. 1986) (emphasis added).

22. *See generally* William C. Mitchell, *Interest Groups: Economic Perspectives and Contributions,* 2 J. THEORETICAL POL. 85 (1990); Barry R. Weingast, Kenneth A. Shepsle & Christopher Johnsen, *The Political Economy of Benefits and Costs: A Neoclassical Approach to Distributive Politics,* 89 J. POL. ECON. 642 (1981).

23. On a related theme, Bertrand de Jouvenal has argued that the coercion inherent in egalitarian government policies that redistribute income are ultimately harmful to the polity.

[H]owever desirable the wearing down of income inequality, its achievement, through legislation which discriminates among citizens, tends to corrupt the political institutions. Even though such legislation results in a better society, its means of achievement through the support of a majority that benefits, as against a minority that submits unwillingly, injures the political spirit of the commonwealth. It is implied in the definition of the citizen that he lays no obligations upon fellow citizens which he does not himself assume.

DE JOUVENAL, The Ethics of Redistribution (1952), at 76–77.

If this argument has force with regard to egalitarian redistributions, it clearly has greater force with regard to legislation and other government actions which confer rents in a less than egalitarian fashion—as discussed in the next section of this article.

24. However, the title of Tullock's seminal article—*The Welfare Costs of Tariffs, Monopolies and Theft, supra* note 2— can be read as suggesting a possible moral objection to tariff- and rent-seeking, as can Robert Bork's characterization of rent-seeking as "predation through governmental processes" (the title of chapter 18 of ROBERT BORK'S THE ANTITRUST PARADOX (1978)).

25. BOVARD, *supra* note 22. The effectiveness of the United States' barriers to imports recently earned the country an official rebuke from the General Agreement on Tariffs and Trade, the multi-national organization dedicated to free trade. *See GATT Study Accuses U.S. Of of Increasing Protectionism,* N.Y. Times, Mar. 13, 1992, at C16.

26. *Of Corn and Cash,* THE ECONOMIST, Aug. 10, 1991, at 50.

27. Perhaps the most famous instance of this face-off is the debate between John Rawls and Robert Nozick. *Compare* JOHN RAWLS, A THEORY OF JUSTICE (1971) *with* ROBERT NOZICK, ANARCHY, STATE, AND UTOPIA (1974). *See also* de Jouvenal, *supra* note 23.

28. According to one estimate, "only one of every eight federal benefit dollars actually reaches Americans in poverty." Neil Howe & Phillip Longman, *The Next New Deal,* ATL. MONTHLY, Apr. 1992.

29. Howe & Longman is a scathing attack on the U.S. "welfare state" for "distributing most of its benefits to the well-off," *id.* at 88, primarily in the form of non-means-tested direct benefits and tax breaks. For a more theoretical explanation of how this might have come to pass, see George Stigler, *Director's Law of Public Income Redistribution,* 13 J.L. & ECON. 1 (1970), and sources cited *supra* note 2.

30. James Bovard, *Mismanaged Trade,* NAT'L REV., Aug. 12, 1991, at 40, 41. Bovard also notes that "[t]he MFA hits poor families far harder than rich families." *Id.* at 41.

31. *See generally* WALTER WILLIAMS, THE STATE AGAINST BLACKS (1982); Edmund W. Kitch, Marc Isaacson & Daniel Kasper, *The Regulation of Taxicabs in Chicago,* 14 J.L. & ECON. 285 (1971).

32. For an elaboration of this point, see Dwight R. Lee, *Public Goods, Politics, and Two Cheers for the Military–Industrial Complex, in* ARMS, POLITICS, AND THE ECONOMY: HISTORICAL AND CONTEMPORARY PERSPECTIVES 22 (Robert Higgs ed., 1990); and Dwight R. Lee, *The Politics and Pitfalls of Reducing Waste in the Military,* 1 DEFENCE ECON. 129 (1990).

33. I emphasize the word "may" in order to avoid the "nirvana fallacy," the mistaken leap from the identification of a market failure to the assumption that government policies can and will be adopted that efficiently "cure" the market failure. "Government failure" in the form of inadequate information or rent-seeking politics may so flaw the government's policies that the cure is no better, or even worse, than the disease.

A classic statement of the theory of market failure is Francis M. Bator, *The Anatomy of Market Failure,* 72 Q.J. ECON. 351 (1958), *in* THE THEORY OF MARKET FAILURE: A CRITICAL EXAMINATION 35–66 (Tyler Cowen ed., 1988). For an explanation of the nirvana fallacy, see Harold Demsetz, *Information and Efficiency: Another Viewpoint,* 12 J.L. & ECON. 1 (1969). For further discussion of government failure, see CHARLES WOLF, JR., MARKETS OR GOVERNMENTS: CHOOSING BETWEEN IMPERFECT ALTERNATIVES (1988), and Michael E. DeBow, *Markets, Government Intervention, and the Role of Information: An "Austrian School" Perspective, With an Application to Merger Regulation,* 14 GEO. MASON U.L. REV. 31 (1991).

34. Peter Drucker makes this point forcefully in Drucker, *supra* note 1.

35. Both Jefferson and Madison accepted tariffs as the best way to protect domestic industries, FRANK W. TAUSSIG, THE TARIFF HISTORY OF THE UNITED STATES 14 (8th ed. 1931), and the "first economic law passed by the nation's new Congress on July 4, 1789, was a protective tariff. . . ." J. Hughes, *supra* note 8, at 17. Thus, long before automobile companies sought "orderly marketing agreements," rent-seekers sought to protect domestic manufacturing interests.

MIT economist Paul Krugman has recently developed a line of argument, largely in the mercantilist tradition, in favor of what he calls "managed protectionism." Paul Krugman, *Is Free Trade Passé?,* J. ECON. PERSP., Fall 1987, at 131. For critical responses, see Douglas A. Irwin, *Challenges to Free Trade,* J. ECON. PERSP., Spring 1991, at 201; and Irwin M. Stelzer, *How to Save Free Trade— And Still Trade With Japan,* COMMENTARY, July 1990, at 15. For an overview of the debate, see Robert E. Baldwin, *Are Economists' Traditional Trade Policy Views Still Valid?,* 30 J. ECON. LITERATURE 804 (1992).

36. *See supra* note 19 and accompanying text.

37. *Id.*

38. Such a firm is in a "transitional gains trap." *See* Gordon Tullock, *The Transitional Gains Trap,* 6 BELL J. ECON. 671 (1975).

39. Milton Friedman, *The Social Responsibility of Business Is To Increase Its Profits,* N.Y. TIMES, Sept. 13, 1970, § 6 (Magazine), at 32.

40. Robert L. Simison, *Ford Fires an Economist,* WALL ST. J., July 30, 1980, at 18. Niskanen apparently had other, more pragmatic objections to the proposal, including Ford's international scope and substantial cross-border operations and Niskanen's own intuition that protectionism would eventually prove to be a Faustian bargain.

QUESTIONS ON DEBOW

1. What are two ways in which rent-seeking activities are wasteful? Are wasteful activities immoral?

2. How is there an "asymmetrical distribution" of the costs and benefits of rent-seeking? How does this result in legislation that favors the rent-seekers? Why should rent-seeking laws or regulations have regressive effects on consumers?

3. DeBow does *not* claim that rent-seeking is unfair. Is it? Does rent-seeking undermine the very legal and normative framework that is essential to a competitive market?

4. Are there policies or laws that favor one industry over another but are nonetheless justifiable for (other) moral or economic reasons?

———————

Industry, Work, and Ambition

Do you see a man skillful in his work? He will stand before kings.

Proverbs 22:29

For there is a perennial nobleness, and even sacredness, in Work. Were he never so benighted, forgetful of his high calling, there is always hope in a man that actually and earnestly works: in Idleness alone is there perpetual despair. Work, never so Mammonish, mean, is communication with Nature; the real desire to get Work done will itself lead one more and more to truth, to Nature's appointments and regulations, which are truth.

Thomas Carlyle[12]

[T]he savage lives in himself; the man accustomed to the ways of society is always outside himself and knows how to live only in the opinion of others. And it is, as it were, from their judgment alone that he draws the sentiment of his own existence.

Jean-Jacques Rousseau[13]

Success is counted sweetest
By those who ne'er succeed.
To comprehend a nectar
Requires sorest need.

Emily Dickinson[14]

Work is sometimes seen as a burdensome activity we must engage in if we are to survive or if we are to satisfy desires above and beyond our needs. Some take this even further, contending that work is an onerous activity that is not only exhausting but alienating. And yet work occupies much of our lives, not only helping to define us but for many becoming an end in itself. Given its importance, it is worthwhile to consider both the idea of

12. *Past and Present* [1843] (London: George Routledge and Sons, n.d.), Book Third, Chapter XI (p. 148).

13. *Discourse on the Origin and Foundations of Inequality* [1754], translated by Donald A. Cress (Indianapolis, Ind.: Hackett, 1987), Part Two (p. 81).

14. First stanza of "Success Is Counted Sweetest" [c.1859], *The Complete Poems of Emily Dickinson,* edited by Thomas H. Johnson (Boston, Mass.: Little, Brown and Company, 1960), 35.

work, as well as two virtues associated with it—industry and ambition.

The Idea of Work

For the ancient Greeks, work was an activity that could leave one without time or leisure to engage one's reason, thereby thwarting the exercise of one's most human capacity. It was for this reason that Aristotle believed that certain persons, fully engaged in a life of work or money-making, were not truly free persons and were not, therefore, suitable to be citizens and to deliberate well. For Aristotle the best type of state would not allow those engaged in menial labor to be citizens.[15] In the Bible, the book of Genesis tells how in the Garden of Eden, prior to the Fall, Adam was to keep the garden, but there is no mention of onerous labor; however, once Adam and Eve had sinned by eating of the tree of the knowledge of good and evil, God states that "In the sweat of thy face shalt thou eat bread. . . " (Genesis 3:19).

With the Protestant Reformation a revised view of work was articulated according to which each person is willed by God to a life of productive labor. One's work should be less a matter of burdensome toil than it is a calling and an end in itself (see the selection by Max Weber in Section AIV). Along with this idea arose an ethic of work according to which one's labor or vocation should exhibit a method and system involving the steady application of reason, as well as the setting aside of concerns unrelated to one's work. A work ethic demands a level of industriousness that is distinct from merely working hard. A person may work hard out of fear or duress, but the person of industry works with steadiness and application and does so not because of some immediate reward or punishment but because industrious activity is preferable to the lackadaisical or the slothful.

Why *should* one prefer industry to sloth? One prominent view is that the activity of labor, including industrious activity, allows one to exercise and realize one's capacities at the same time as it provides one a greater chance of financial security and the opportunity for genuine leisure. That work should be something which is good in itself is an ideal that has attracted many thinkers. In the nineteenth century, Karl Marx (1818–1883) viewed labor as the essential means of activity in the world, as the very essence of the conscious human being whose activity constructs a world out of nature. Labor, for Marx, should be the means by which one realizes one's human capacities. However, under the conditions of capitalism, Marx argues, labor has become nothing more than the means by which one becomes estranged or alienated from the product of one's efforts, as well as from oneself, one's colleagues and from one's own humanity.

Work and Ambition

If work is a large part of a person's life then it is not surprising that our work will have much to do with whether we are living well. But what is required for living well? Many persons believe the conditions would include wealth, reputation (honor), or power, though it is not obvious that these are either necessary or sufficient for a *life lived well*. Although we may recognize that wealth, for example, does not guarantee happiness, we are often ambitious to achieve it, hoping that it will better or improve our lives or the lives of those whom we love. Even if we ought to invest ourselves in our work, we all too often succumb to a form of careerism by which we desire advancement and prestige more than we care about investing ourselves in vocations that bestow meaning and value on self and others.

What is this desire for achievement or recognition that we refer to as ambition? The ambitious person has a strong desire for and actively seeks to achieve some goal judged by society to be excellent. The particular aim might vary depending on the society or on the epoch, but the more common goals of the ambitious have been fame, glory, honor, reknown, or money. Ambition, then, may include a variety of ends, achievable through distinct avenues—commerce, government, art, science, or entertainment. However, not all of these ends are the sorts of ends that should be pursued too intently, or at the expense of other goods. For example, there is a difference between wanting to achieve some goal and wanting to be *known* for achieving some goal. Too often, the ambitious person focuses on the latter at the expense of the former, though it is not at all obvious that fame or recognition is essential to leading a good life.

Distinct avenues of ambition may offer dissimiliar types of risk. In some cases, the ambitious person seeks to accumulate wealth (perhaps as a means of achieving fame); in other instances, ambition is the fuel of those who seek political power. The ancient Greek philosopher, Plato, worried that ambition for wealth or honor might easily turn into the love of money (or reputation) at the expense of virtue.[16] The person who quests after political power may seek to achieve at any cost, includ-

---

15. *Politics* III.5.11278a.

16. See *Republic,* Book VIII (5549b–551b).

ing human lives; this is a particular risk when ambition is allied to political power that is not limited by constitution, morality, or public opinion. It was not for nothing when Shakespeare warned us that ambition is the "sin" that "fell the angels."[17]

Even if one does not agree that ambition is a vice, it is, nonetheless, a quality about which we manifest some ambivalence. Despite the risks of ambition, we regard those who lack any ambition (the lazy, the insouciant, the spiritless) with some disdain, because we think that a good life should involve some desire for achievement. We are aware that ambition might, as in the case of political power, induce one to use others for one's own success. In other cases, ambition may manifest a vicious desire for superiority, and in instances less cruel, ambition may reveal a craving for the most shallow sort of recognition. Ambition, then, would seem to be a risky quality, even though it is one that has fueled the good works of many an industrialist, artist, or scientist, thereby encouraging individuals to work hard in endeavors whose final results have benefited innumerable individuals.

In his travels around America in the nineteenth century, Tocqueville (1805–1859) noted that "The first thing which strikes a traveler in the United States is the innumerable multitude of those who seek to emerge from their original condition; and the second is the rarity of lofty ambition to be observed in the midst of the universally ambitious stir of society."[18] Tocqueville traces this middling ambition to the influence of democratic equality, which allows everyone to entertain ideas of improvement even as their ideals are not so grand as those that might occur under an aristocracy. Perhaps there is some virtue in individuals entertaining ambitions of a less lofty variety, for as we have noted, ambition is a trait that carries hazards not only for the ambitious, who may be seeking solace in fame alone, but also for those who may be sacrificed to the demands of the ambitious. One virtue of commercial ambition, then, is that it channels ambitions into those avenues in which the realization of success not only satisfies the desires of the ambitious but also serves the needs of others (consumers).

---

17. "Cromwell, I charge thee, fling away ambition:/By that sin fell the angels; how can man then,/The image of his Maker, hope to win by 't?" William Shakespeare, *King Henry VIII,* Act III, Scene ii, in *The Complete Works of William Shakespeare,* edited by W. J. Craig (London: Oxford University Press, 1914).

18. Alexis de Tocqueville, *Democracy in America,* edited by Richard D. Hefner (New York: New American Library, 1956), Part Two, Book III, chapter 46 (p. 256).

THE READINGS

Benjamin Franklin In this preface to the 1758 edition of *Poor Richard's Almanac,* the character Father Abraham gives a speech before the opening of a *vendue* (or public sale). Responding to complaints that taxes are too high, Father Abraham points out that there is yet a greater tax that individuals inflict on themselves: the tax of idleness or sloth. Opposed to sloth is the virtue of industry; not only does industry provide a livelihood, but industry within a trade is source of honor. To succeed in a trade or business, one's industry must be exercised with care, and one mustn't leave one's affairs to the attention of others. In addition to industry, Franklin emphasizes the importance of frugality and the avoidance of luxury and "artificial wants," the desire for which is often fueled by pride. One should avoid going into debt, for debt brings dependency.

Dorothy Sayers Sayers seeks to revise our attitudes toward work so that we no longer view work as something done merely to get money but as "a way of life" undertaken for its own sake. From this basic understanding, which Sayers considers expressive of Christianity, she delineates several theses or propositions, the first of which is that work should be "the full expression of the worker's faculties." From this claim she draws four consequences: that work should be its own reward; that each should perform the work for which he is most fit; that we cultivate new attitudes toward leisure; and that we should become more interested in the kind and quality of work that we do. Sayers' second thesis is that the Church should recognize that one's secular vocation is sacred; her third is that "the worker's first duty is to *serve the work.*" One serves the community only if one first devotes oneself to doing one's job as it should be done.

Adam Smith Smith asks "to what purpose is all the toil and bustle of this world?" We are ambitious not so much to better our condition as to reap the attention and notice of others and to sympathize with their attention. For Smith, "sympathy" refers to the similarity of feeling between two individuals, a pleasurable similarity which is sought after by all persons. We tend to sympathize more easily with feelings of joy and happiness than with sorrow and, thus, it is not only easier to sympathize with the wealthy and powerful, but *we* wish to acquire wealth and power so that we might sympathize with the regard of *our* admirers. However, the rich and powerful exhibit certain traits of character that may have more to do with style and authority than with actual knowledge or true virtue. On the other hand, the person of a more humble rank must advance by means of his own virtue, labor, and mental capacities. Smith is ambivalent about ambition, noting that it is a cause of the corruption of morals, for most people seek fame and fortune, not wisdom or virtue. Not only do we tend to evaluate others by these same values but we tend to imitate the bad habits of the wealthy.

The Way to Wealth

Benjamin Franklin

Benjamin Franklin (1706–1790) was born in Boston, the fifteenth of seventeen children, and began working for his father, a candlemaker, at the age of ten, later becoming a printer and moving to Philadelphia. The owner of a newspaper; the author of Poor Richard's Almanac, *from which this excerpt is taken; the founder of the first public library; an inventor, scientist, and a diplomat, Franklin was a member of the Second Continental Congress, helping to draft the Declaration of Independence.*

PREFACE TO *POOR RICHARD IMPROVED*, 1758

. . . I stopped my horse lately where a great number of people were collected at a vendue of merchant goods. The hour of sale not being come, they were conversing on the badness of the times, and one of the company called to a plain clean old man, with white locks, "Pray, Father Abraham, what think you of the times? Won't these heavy taxes quite ruin the country? How shall we be ever able to pay them? What would you advise us to?" Father Abraham stood up, and replied, "If you'd have my advice, I'll give it you in short, for *A word to the wise is enough,* and *many words won't fill a bushel,* as Poor Richard says." They joined in desiring him to speak his mind, and gathering round him, he proceeded as follows:

"Friends," says he, and neighbors, "the taxes are indeed very heavy, and if those laid on by the government were the only ones we had to pay, we might more easily discharge them; but we have many others, and much more grievous to some of us. We are taxed twice as much by our idleness, three times as much by our pride, and four times as much by our folly; and from these taxes the commissioners cannot ease or deliver us by allowing an abatement. However, let us hearken to good advice, and something may be done for us; *God helps them that help themselves,* as Poor Richard says in his Almanac of 1733.

"It would be thought a hard government that should tax its people one-tenth part of their time, to be employed in its service. But idleness taxes many of us much more, if we reckon all that is spent in absolute sloth, or doing of nothing, with that which is spent in idle employments or amusements that amount to nothing. Sloth, by bringing on diseases, absolutely shortens life. *Sloth, like rust, consumes faster than labor wears; while the used key is always bright,* as Poor Richard says. *But dost thou love life, then do not squander time, for that's the stuff life is made of,* as Poor Richard says. How much more than is necessary do we spend in sleep, forgetting that *The sleeping fox catches no poultry,* and that *There will be sleeping enough in the grave,* as Poor Richard says.

"*If Time be of all things the most precious, wasting time must be,* as Poor Richard says, *the greatest prodigality;* since, as he elsewhere tells us, *Lost time is never found again; and what we call time enough, always proves little enough.* Let us then up and be doing, and doing to the purpose; so by diligence shall we do more with less perplexity. *Sloth makes all things difficult, but industry all easy,* as Poor Richard says; and *He that riseth late must trot all day, and shall scarce overtake his business at night,* while *Laziness travels so slowly that poverty soon overtakes him,* as we read in Poor Richard, who adds, *Drive thy Business, let not that drive thee;* and *Early to bed, and early to rise, makes a man healthy, wealthy, and wise.*

"So what signifies wishing and hoping for better times? We may make these times better, if we bestir ourselves. *Industry need not wish,* as Poor Richard says, *and he that lives upon hope will die fasting. There are no gains without pains; then help hands, for I have no lands,* or if I have, they are smartly taxed. And, as Poor Richard likewise observes, *He that hath a trade hath an estate; and he that hath a calling, hath an office of profit and honor;* but then the trade must be worked at, and the calling well followed, or neither the estate nor the office will enable us to pay our taxes. If we are industrious, we shall never starve; for, as Poor Richard says, *At the workingman's house hunger looks in, but dares not enter.* Nor will the bailiff or the constable enter, for *Industry pays debts, while despair encreaseth them,* says Poor Richard. What though you have found no treasure, nor has any rich relation left you a legacy, *Diligence is the mother of good luck,* as Poor Richard says, *and God gives all things to industry. Then plough deep, while sluggards sleep, and you shall have corn to sell and to keep,* says Poor Dick. Work while it is called today, for you know not how much you may be hindered tomorrow, which makes Poor Richard say, *One today is worth two tomorrows,* and farther, *Have you somewhat to do tomorrow, do it today.* If you were a servant, would you not be ashamed that a good master should catch you idle? Are you then your own master, *be ashamed to catch yourself idle,* as Poor Dick says. When there is so much to be done for yourself, your family, your country, and your gracious king, be up by peep of day; *Let not the sun look down and say, Inglorious here he lies.* Handle your tools without mittens; remember that *The cat in gloves catches no mice,* as Poor Richard says. 'Tis true there is much to be done, and perhaps you are weakhanded; but stick to it steadily, and you will see great effects, for *Constant dropping wears away stones,* and *by diligence and patience the mouse ate in two the cable;* and *Little strokes fell great oaks,* as Poor Richard says in his Almanac, the year I cannot just now remember.

"Methinks I hear some of you say, *'Must a man afford himself no leisure?'* I will tell thee, my friend, what Poor Richard says, *Employ thy time well, if thou meanest to gain leisure; and, since thou art not sure of a minute, throw not away an hour.* Leisure is time for doing something useful; this leisure the diligent man will obtain, but the lazy man never; so that, as Poor Richard says, *A life of leisure and a life of laziness are two things.* Do you imagine that sloth will afford you more comfort than labor? No, for as Poor Richard says, *Trouble springs from idleness, and grievous toil from needless ease. Many without labor would live by their wits only, but they break for want of stock.* Whereas industry gives comfort, and plenty, and respect: *Fly pleasures, and they'll follow you. The diligent spinner has a large shift; and now I have a sheep and a cow, everybody bids me good morrow;* all which is well said by Poor Richard.

"But with our industry, we must likewise be steady, settled, and careful, and oversee our own affairs with our own eyes, and not trust too much to others; for, as Poor Richard says

> I never saw an oft-removed tree,
> Nor yet an oft-removed family,
> That throve so well as those that settled be.

And again, *Three removes is as bad as a fire;* and again, *Keep thy shop, and thy shop will keep thee;* and again, *If you would have your business done, go; if not, send.* And again,

> He that by the plough would thrive,
> Himself must either hold or drive.

And again, *The eye of a master will do more work than both his hands;* and again, *Want of care does us more damage than want of knowledge;* and again, *Not to oversee workmen, is to leave them your purse open.* Trusting too much to others' care is the ruin of many; for, as the Almanac says, *In the affairs of this world, men are saved, not by faith, but by the want of it;* but a man's own care is profitable; for, saith Poor Dick, *Learning is to the studious, and riches to the careful, as well as power to the bold, and heaven to the virtuous,* and farther, *If you would have a faithful servant, and one that you like, serve yourself.* And again, he adviseth to circumspection and care, even in the smallest matters, because sometimes *A little neglect may breed great mischief;* adding, *for want of a nail the shoe was lost; for want of a shoe the horse was lost; and for want of a horse the rider was lost, being overtaken and slain by the enemy; all for want of care about a horse-shoe nail.*

"So much for industry, my friends, and attention to one's own business; but to these we must add frugality, if we would make our industry more certainly successful. A man may, if he knows not how to save as he gets, keep his nose all his life to the grindstone, and die not worth a groat at last. *A fat kitchen makes a lean will,* as Poor Richard says; and

> Many estates are spent in the getting,
> Since women for tea forsook spinning and knitting,
> And men for punch forsook hewing and splitting.

If you would be wealthy, says he, in another Almanac, *think of saving as well as of getting: The Indies have not made Spain rich, because her outgoes are greater than her incomes.*

"Away then with your expensive follies, and you will not then have so much cause to complain of hard times, heavy taxes, and chargeable families; for, as Poor Dick says,

> Women and wine, game and deceit,
> Make the wealth small and the wants great.

And farther, *What maintains one vice, would bring up two children.* You may think, perhaps, that a little tea, or a little punch now and then, diet a little more costly, clothes a little finer, and a little entertainment now and then, can be no great matter; but remember what Poor Richard says, *Many a little makes a mickle;* and farther, *Beware of little expenses; a small leak will sink a great ship;* and again, *Who dainties love, shall beggars prove;* and moreover, *Fools make feasts, and wise men eat them.*

"Here you are all got together at this vendue of fineries and knicknacks. You call them *goods;* but if you do not take care, they will prove evils to some of you. You expect they will be sold cheap, and perhaps they may for less than they cost; but if you have no occasion for them, they must be dear to you. Remember what Poor Richard says; *Buy what thou hast no need of, and ere long thou shalt sell thy necessaries.* And again, *At a great pennyworth pause a while.* He means that perhaps the cheapness is apparent only, and not real; or the bargain, by straitening thee in thy business, may do thee more harm than good. For in another place he says, *Many have been ruined by buying good pennyworths.* Again, Poor Richard says, *'tis foolish to lay out money in a purchase of repentance;* and yet this folly is practised every day at vendues, for want of minding the Almanac. *Wise Men,* as Poor Dick says, *learn by others' harms, fools scarcely by their own; but felix quem faciunt aliena pericula cautum.* Many a one, for the sake of finery on the back, have gone with a hungry belly, and half-starved their Families. *Silks and satins, scarlet and velvets,* as Poor Richard says, *put out the kitchen fire.*

"These are not the necessaries of life; they can scarcely be called the conveniences; and yet only because they look pretty, how many want to have them! The artificial wants of mankind thus become more numerous than the natural; and, as Poor Dick says, *for one poor person, there are an hundred indigent.* By these, and other extravagancies, the genteel are reduced to poverty and forced to borrow of those whom they formerly despised, but who through industry and frugality have maintained their standing; in which case it appears plainly that *A ploughman on his legs is higher than a gentleman on his knees,* as Poor Richard says. Perhaps they have had a small estate left them, which they knew not the getting of; they think, *'tis day, and will never be night;* that a little to be spent out of so much, is not worth minding; *A child and a fool,* as Poor Richard says, *imagine twenty shillings and twenty years can never be spent* but, *always taking out of the meal tub, and never putting in, soon comes to the bottom;* as Poor Dick says, *When the well's dry, they know the worth of water.* But this they might have known before, if they had taken his advice; *If you would know the value of money, go and try to borrow some; for, he that goes a borrowing goes a sorrowing;* and indeed so does he that lends to such people, when he goes to get it in again. Poor Dick farther advises, and says,

Fond pride of dress is sure a very curse;
E'er fancy you consult, consult your purse.

And again, *Pride is as loud a beggar as Want, and a great deal more saucy.* When you have bought one fine thing, you must buy ten more, that your appearance may be all of a piece; but Poor Dick says, *'Tis easier to suppress the first desire than to satisfy all that follow it.* And 'tis as truly folly for the poor to ape the rich, as for the frog to swell, in order to equal the ox.

Great Estates may venture more,
But little boats should keep near shore.

'Tis, however, a folly soon punished; for *Pride that dines on vanity, sups on contempt,* as Poor Richard says. And in another Place, *Pride breakfasted with Plenty, dined with Poverty, and supped with Infamy.* And after all, of what use is this pride of appearance, for which so much is risked, so much is suffered? It cannot promote health, or ease pain; it makes no increase of merit in the person; it creates envy, it hastens misfortune.

What is a butterfly? At best
He's but a caterpillar drest
The gaudy fop's his picture just,

as Poor Richard says.

"But what madness must it be to run in debt for these superfluities! We are offered, by the terms of this vendue, six months' credit; and that perhaps has induced some of us to attend it, because we cannot spare the ready money, and hope now to be fine without it. But, ah, think what you do when you run in debt; you give to another power over your liberty. If you cannot pay at the time, you will be ashamed to see your creditor; you will be in fear when you speak to him; you will make poor pitiful sneaking excuses, and by degrees come to lose your veracity, and sink into base downright lying; for, as Poor Richard says, *The second vice is lying, the first is running in debt.* And again, to the same purpose, *Lying rides upon Debt's Back.* Whereas a free-born Englishman ought not to be ashamed or afraid to see or speak to any man living. But poverty often deprives a man of all spirit and virtue:; *'Tis hard for an empty bag to stand upright,* as Poor Richard truly says. . . .

. . . When you have got your bargain, you may, perhaps, think little of payment; but *Creditors,* Poor Richard tells us, *have better memories than debtors;* and in another place says, *Creditors are a superstitious sect, great observers of set days and times.* The day comes round before you are aware, and the demand is made before you are prepared to satisfy it. Or if you bear your debt in mind, the term which at first seemed so long will, as it lessens, appear extremely short. Time will seem to have added wings to his heels as well as shoulders. *Those have a short Lent,* saith Poor Richard, *who owe money to be paid at Easter.* Then since, as he says, *The borrower is a slave to the lender, and the debtor to the creditor,* disdain the chain, preserve your freedom, and maintain your independency. Be industrious and free; be frugal and free. At present, perhaps, you may think yourself in thriving circumstances, and that you can bear a little extravagance without injury; but,

> For age and want, save while you may;
> No morning sun lasts a whole day,

as Poor Richard says. Gain may be temporary and uncertain, but ever, while you live, expense is constant and certain; and *'tis easier to build two chimneys than to keep one in fuel,* as Poor Richard says. So, *Rather go to bed supperless than rise in debt.*

> Get what you can, and what you get hold;
> 'Tis the stone that will turn all your lead into gold,

as Poor Richard says. And when you have got the philosopher's stone, sure you will no longer complain of bad times or the difficulty of paying taxes.

"This doctrine, my friends, is reason and wisdom; but after all, do not depend too much upon your own industry, and frugality and prudence, though excellent things, for they may all be blasted without the blessing of heaven; and therefore, ask that blessing humbly, and be not uncharitable to those that at present seem to want it, but comfort and help them. Remember, Job suffered, and was afterwards prosperous.

"And now to conclude, *Experience keeps a dear school, but fools will learn in no other, and scarce in that;* for it is true, *we may give advice, but we cannot give conduct,* as Poor Richard says. However, remember this, *They that won't be counselled, can't be helped,* as Poor Richard says: and farther that, *if you will not hear Reason, she'll surely rap your knuckles.*"

Thus the old gentleman ended his harangue. The people heard it, and approved the doctrine, and immediately practiced the contrary, just as if it had been a common sermon; for the vendue opened, and they began to buy extravagantly, notwithstanding his cautions and their own fear of taxes. I found the good man had thoroughly studied my Almanacs, and digested all I had dropped on these topics during the course of five and twenty years. The frequent mention he made of me must have tired anyone else, but my vanity was wonderfully delighted with it, though I was conscious that not a tenth part of the wisdom was my own, which he ascribed to me, but rather

the gleanings I had made of the sense of all ages and nations. However, I resolved to be the better for the echo of it; and though I had at first determined to buy stuff for a new coat, I went away resolved to wear my old one a little longer. Reader, if thou wilt do the same, thy profit will be as great as mine. I am, as ever, thine to serve thee,

Richard Saunders
July 7, 1757

QUESTIONS ON FRANKLIN

1. What is involved in being "industrious"? How does Franklin's account of industry relate to the idea of a trade or calling? Is industry a specific virtue? Does industry also include or require diligence, judicious responsibility, or self-control?

2. In what ways does Franklin's Preface contain a certain view of the good person or the good life? Is the good life, for Franklin, a *useful* life? Does Franklin's account indicate a certain utilitarian outlook?

3. How does Franklin's account contain an implicit defense of market institutions? How does it also appeal to democratic, rather than aristocratic, sensibilities?

Why Work?

Dorothy Sayers

*Dorothy Sayers (1893–1957) was born in Oxford, England, and was one of the first women to graduate from Oxford University. Working first for an advertising agency, she published the first of her many detective novels (*Whose Body?*) in 1923. Other novels include* Strong Poison *(1930) and* Murder Must Advertise *(1933), but she also wrote short stories, stage plays, articles, essays, and theological studies, including* The Mind of the Maker *(1941). In addition, she translated, from the Old French, the* Song of Roland, *and from Old Italian,* The Divine Comedy. *This excerpt—originally an address delivered at Eastbourne, England, April 23, 1942—is from* Creed or Chaos? *(1947).*

I have already, on a previous occasion,* spoken at some length on the subject of Work and Vocation. What I

---

*At Brighton, March 1941. The major part of the address was printed in *A Christian Basis for the Post-War World* (S.C.M. Press).

urged then was a thorough-going revolution in our whole attitude to work. I asked that it should be looked upon—not as a necessary drudgery to be undergone for the purpose of making money, but as a way of life in which the nature of man should find its proper exercise and delight and so fulfil itself to the glory of God. That it should, in fact, be thought of as a creative activity undertaken for the love of the work itself; and that man, made in God's image, should make things, as God makes them, for the sake of doing well a thing that is well worth doing.

It may well seem to you—as it does to some of my acquaintances—that I have a sort of obsession about this business of the right attitude to work. But I do insist upon it, because it seems to me that what becomes of civilization after this war is going to depend enormously on our being able to effect this revolution in our ideas about work. Unless we do change our whole way of thought about work, I do not think we shall ever escape from the appalling squirrel-cage of economic confusion in which we have been madly turning for the last three centuries or so, the cage in which we landed ourselves by acquiescing in a social system based upon Envy and Avarice. A society in which consumption has to be artificially stimulated in order to keep production going is a society founded on trash and waste, and such a society is a house built upon sand. . . .

. . . The habit of thinking about work as something one does to make money is so ingrained in us that we can scarcely imagine what a revolutionary change it would be to think about it instead in terms of the work done. It would mean taking the attitude of mind we reserve for our unpaid work—our hobbies, our leisure interests, the things we make and do for pleasure—and making *that* the standard of all our judgments about things and people. We should ask of an enterprise, not "will it pay?" but "is it good?"; of a man, not "what does he make?" but "what is his work worth?"; of goods, not "can we induce people to buy them?" but "are they useful things well made?"; of employment, not "how much a week?" but "will it exercise my faculties to the utmost?" And shareholders in—let us say—brewing companies, would astonish the directorate by arising at shareholders' meetings and demanding to know, not merely where the profits go or what dividends are to be paid, not even merely whether the workers' wages are sufficient and the conditions of labour satisfactory, but loudly, and with a proper sense of personal responsibility: What goes into the beer?

You will probably ask at once: How is this altered attitude going to make any difference to the question of employment? Because it sounds as though it would result in not more employment, but less. I am not an economist, and I can only point to a peculiarity of war economy that usually goes without notice in economic text-books. In war, production for wasteful consumption still goes on: but there is one great difference in the goods produced. None of them is valued for what it will fetch, but only for what it is worth in itself. The gun and the tank, the aeroplane and the warship have to be the best of their kind. A war consumer does not buy shoddy. He does not buy to sell again. He buys the thing that is good for its purpose, asking nothing of it but that it shall do the job it has to do. Once again, war forces the consumer into a right attitude to the work. And, whether by strange coincidence, or whether because of some universal law, so soon as nothing is demanded of the thing made but its own integral perfection, its own absolute value, the skill and labour of the worker are fully employed and likewise acquire an absolute value.

This is probably not the kind of answer that you will find in any theory of economics. But the professional economist is not really trained to answer, or even to ask himself questions about absolute values. The economist is inside the squirrel-cage and turning with it. Any question about absolute values belongs to the sphere, not of economics, but of religion. And it is very possible that we cannot deal with economics at all, unless we can see economy from outside the cage; that we cannot begin to settle the relative values without considering absolute values. And if so, this may give a very precise and practical meaning to the words: "Seek first the kingdom of God and righteousness, and all these things shall be added to you." . . . I am persuaded that the reason why the Churches are in so much difficulty about giving a lead in the economic sphere is because they are trying to fit a Christian standard of economics to a wholly false and pagan understanding of work.

What is the Christian understanding of work? . . . I should like to put before you two or three propositions arising out of the doctrinal position which I stated at the beginning: namely, that work is the natural exercise and function of man—the creature who is made in the image of his Creator. You will find that any one of them, if given in effect everyday practice, is so revolutionary (as compared with the habits of thinking into which we have fallen), as to make all political revolutions look like conformity.

The first, stated quite briefly, is that work is not, primarily, a thing one does to live, but the thing one lives to do. It is, or it should be, the full expression of the worker's faculties, the thing in which he finds spiritual, mental, and bodily satisfaction, and the medium in which he offers himself to God.

Now the consequences of this are not merely that the work should be performed under decent living and working conditions. That is a point we have begun to grasp, and it is a perfectly sound point. But we have tended to concentrate on it to the exclusion of other considerations far more revolutionary.

(*a*) There is, for instance, the question of profits and remuneration. We have all got it fixed in our heads that the proper end of work is to be paid for—to produce a return in profits or payment to the worker which fully or more than compensates the effort he puts into it. But if our proposition is true, this does not follow at all. So long as Society provides the worker with a sufficient return in real wealth to enable him to carry on the work properly, then he has his reward. For his work is the measure of his life, and his satisfaction is found in the fulfillment of his own nature, and in contemplation of the perfection of his work. That, in practice, there is this satisfaction, is shown by the mere fact that a man will put loving labour into some hobby which can never bring him in any economically adequate return. His satisfaction comes, in the god-like manner, from looking upon what he has made and finding it very good. He is no longer bargaining with his work, but serving it. It is only when work has to be looked on as a means to gain that it becomes hateful; for then, instead of a friend, it becomes an enemy from whom tolls and contributions have to be extracted. What most of us demand from society is that we should always get out of it a little *more* than the value of the labour we give to it. By this process, we persuade ourselves that society is always in our debt—a conviction that not only piles up actual financial burdens, but leaves us with a grudge against society.

(*b*) Here is the second consequence. At present we have no clear grasp of the principle that every man should do the work for which he is fitted by nature. The employer is obsessed by the notion that he must find cheap labour, and the worker by the notion that the best-paid job is the job for him. Only feebly, inadequately, and spasmodically do we ever attempt to tackle the problem from the other end, and inquire: What type of worker is suited to this type of work? People engaged in education see clearly that this *is* the right end to start from; but they are frustrated by economic pressure, and by the failure of parents on the one hand and employers on the other to grasp the fundamental importance of this approach. And that the trouble results far more from a failure of intelligence than from economic necessity is seen clearly under war conditions, when, though competitive economics are no longer a governing factor, the right men and women are still persistently thrust into the wrong jobs, through sheer inability on everybody's part to imagine a purely vocational approach to the business of fitting together the worker and his work.

(*c*) A third consequence is that, if we really believed this proposition and arranged our work and our standard of values accordingly, we should no longer think of work as something that we hastened to get through in order to enjoy our leisure; we should look on our leisure as the period of changed rhythm that refreshed us for the delightful purpose of getting on with our work. And, this being so, we should tolerate no regulations of any sort that prevented us from working as long and as well as our enjoyment of work demanded. We should resent any such restrictions as a monstrous interference with the liberty of the subject. How great an upheaval of our ideas that would mean I leave you to imagine. It would turn topsy-turvy all our notions about hours of work, rates of work, unfair competition, and all the rest of it. We should all find ourselves fighting, as now only artists and the members of certain professions fight, for precious time in which to get on with the job—instead of fighting for precious hours saved from the job.

(*d*) A fourth consequence is that we should fight tooth and nail, not for mere employment, but for the quality of the work that we had to do. We should clamour to be engaged on work that was worth doing, and in which we could take a pride. The worker would demand that the stuff he helped to turn out should be good stuff—he would no longer be content to take the cash and let the credit go. Like the shareholders in the brewery, he would feel a sense of personal responsibility, and clamour to know, and to control, what went into the beer he brewed. There would be protests and strikes—not only about pay and conditions, but about the quality of the work demanded and the honesty, beauty, and usefulness of the goods produced. The greatest insult which a commercial age has offered to the worker has been to rob him of all interest in the end-product of the work and to force him to dedicate his life to making badly things which were not worth making.

This first proposition chiefly concerns the worker as such. My second proposition directly concerns Christians as such, and it is this: It is the business of the Church to recognize that the secular vocation, as such, is sacred. Christian people, and particularly perhaps the Christian clergy, must get it firmly into their heads that when a man or woman is called to a particular job of secular work, that is as true a vocation as though he or she were called to specifically religious work. The

Church must concern herself not only with such questions as the just price and proper working conditions: she must concern herself with seeing that the work itself is such as a human being can perform without degradation—that no one is required by economic or any other considerations to devote himself to work that is contemptible, soul-destroying, or harmful. It is not right for her to acquiesce in the notion that a man's life is divided into the time he spends on his work and the time he spends in serving God. He must be able to serve God *in* his work, and the work itself must be accepted and respected as the medium of divine creation.

In nothing has the Church so lost her hold on reality as in her failure to understand and respect the secular vocation. She has allowed work and religion to become separate departments, and is astonished to find that, as a result, the secular work of the world is turned to purely selfish and destructive ends, and that the greater part of the world's intelligent workers have become irreligious, or at least, uninterested in religion. But is it astonishing? How can any one remain interested in a religion which seems to have no concern with nine-tenths of his life? The Church's approach to an intelligent carpenter is usually confined to exhorting him not to be drunk and disorderly in his leisure hours, and to come to church on Sundays. What the Church *should* be telling him is this: that the very first demand that his religion makes upon him is that he should make good tables. Church by all means, and decent forms of amusement, certainly—but what use is all that if in the very centre of his life and occupation he is insulting God with bad carpentry? No crooked table-legs or ill-fitting drawers ever, I dare swear, came out of the carpenter's shop at Nazareth. Nor, if they did, could anyone believe that they were made by the same hand that made heaven and earth. No piety in the worker will compensate for work that is not true to itself; for any work that is untrue to its own technique is a living lie. Yet in her own buildings, in her own ecclesiastical art and music, in her hymns and prayers, in her sermons and in her little books of devotion, the Church will tolerate, or permit a pious intention to excuse, work so ugly, so pretentious, so tawdry and twaddling, so insincere and insipid, so *bad* as to shock and horrify any decent draftsman. And why? Simply because she has lost all sense of the fact that the living and eternal truth is expressed in work only so far as that work is true in itself, to itself, to the standards of its own technique. She has forgotten that the secular vocation is sacred. Forgotten that a building must be good architecture before it can be a good church; that a painting must be well painted before it can be a good sacred picture; that work must be good work before it can call itself God's work. . . .

This brings me to my third proposition; and this may sound to you the most revolutionary of all. It is this: the worker's first duty is to *serve the work*. The popular "catch" phrase of today is that it is everybody's duty to serve the community. It is a well-sounding phrase, but there *is* a catch in it. It is the old catch about the two great commandments. "Love God—and your neighbour; on those two commandments hang all the Law and the Prophets." The catch in it, which nowadays the world has largely forgotten, is that the second commandment depends upon the first, and that without the first, it is a delusion and a snare. Much of our present trouble and disillusionment have come from putting the second commandment before the first. If we put our neighbour first, we are putting man above God, and that is what we have been doing ever since we began to worship humanity and make man the measure of all things. Whenever man is made the centre of things, he becomes the storm-centre of trouble—and that is precisely the catch about serving the community. It ought perhaps to make us suspicious of that phrase when we consider that it is the slogan of every commercial scoundrel and swindler who wants to make sharp business practice pass muster as social improvement. "Service" is the motto of the advertiser, of big business, and of fraudulent finance. And of others, too. Listen to this: "I expect the judicature to understand that the nation does not exist for their convenience, but that justice exists to serve the nation." That was Hitler yesterday—and that is what becomes of "service," when the community, and not the work, becomes its idol. There is, in fact, a paradox about working to serve the community, and it is this: that to aim directly at serving the community is to falsify the work; the only way to serve the community is to forget the community and serve the work. There are three very good reasons for this:

The first is, that you cannot do good work if you take your mind off the work to see how the community is taking it—any more than you can make a good drive from the tee if you take your eye off the ball. "Blessed are the single-hearted" (for that is the real meaning of the word we translate *"the pure in heart"*). If your heart is not wholly in the work, the work will not be good—and work that is not good serves neither God nor the community; it only serves Mammon.

The second reason is that the moment you think of serving other people, you begin to have a notion that other people owe you something for your pains; you begin to think that you have a claim on the community.

You will begin to bargain for reward, to angle for applause, and to harbour a grievance if you are not appreciated. But if your mind is set upon serving the work, then you know you have nothing to look for; the only reward the *work* can give you is the satisfaction of beholding its perfection. The work takes all and gives nothing but itself; and to serve the work is a labour of pure love.

And thirdly, if you set out to serve the community, you will probably end by merely fulfilling a public demand—and you may not even do that. A public demand is a changeable thing. Nine-tenths of the bad plays put on in theatres owe their badness to the fact that the playwright has aimed at pleasing the audience, instead of at producing a good and satisfactory play. Instead of doing the work as its own integrity demands that it should be done, he has falsified the play by putting in this or that which he thinks will appeal to the groundlings (who by that time have probably come to want something else), and the play fails by its insincerity. The work has been falsified to please the public—and in the end even the public is not pleased. As it is with works of art, so it is with all work. We are coming to the end of an era of civilization which began by pandering to public demand, and ended by frantically trying to create public demand for an output so false and meaningless that even a doped public revolted from the trash offered to it and plunged into war rather than swallow any more of it. The danger of "serving the community" is that one is part of the community, and that in serving it one may only be serving a kind of communal egotism. The only true way of serving the community is to be truly in sympathy with the community— to be one's self part of the community—and then to serve the work, without giving the community another thought. Then the work will endure, because it will be true to itself. It is the work that serves the community; the business of the worker is to serve the work. . . .

QUESTIONS ON SAYERS

1. What sorts of things do you understand to be "work"? (Does Sayers provide an account of the things we might call "work"?) How does Sayers characterize the proper attitude toward work? How does her view differ from one who contends that work is anything done for money?

2. Sayers contends that our hobbies and leisurely interests provide experience of rewarding and unpaid work. Do these provide examples of the sort of "spiritual, mental, and bodily satisfaction" described by Sayers?

3. Is a division of labor compatible with Sayers' three propositions? Are all kinds of work capable of being regarded as Sayers counsels?

4. What does it mean to "serve the work"? How can one serve the community only by first serving the work?

Of the Origin of Ambition

Adam Smith

Adam Smith (1723–1790) was born in Kirkcaldy, Scotland, and taught at Glasgow University, lecturing on jurisprudence, rhetoric, moral philosophy, and political economy. Known primarily for his work in political economy, An Inquiry into the Nature and Causes of the Wealth of Nations *(1776), Smith was a thinker of extraordinary breadth, publishing* The Theory of Moral Sentiments *(1759) at the age of 36, and writing other essays on science and literature.*

OF THE ORIGIN OF AMBITION, AND OF THE DISTINCTION OF RANKS

It is because mankind are disposed to sympathize more entirely with our joy than with our sorrow, that we make parade of our riches, and conceal our poverty. Nothing is so mortifying as to be obliged to expose our distress to the view of the public, and to feel, that though our situation is open to the eyes of all mankind, no mortal conceives for us the half of what we suffer. Nay, it is chiefly from this regard to the sentiments of mankind, that we pursue riches and avoid poverty. For to what purpose is all the toil and bustle of this world? what is the end of avarice and ambition, of the pursuit of wealth, of power, and preheminence? Is it to supply the necessities of nature? The wages of the meanest labourer can supply them. We see that they afford him food and clothing, the comfort of a house, and of a family. If we examined his economy with rigour, we should find that he spends a great part of them upon conveniencies, which may be regarded as superfluities, and that, upon extraordinary occasions, he can give something even to vanity and distinction. What then is the cause of our aversion to his situation, and why should those who have been educated in the higher ranks of life, regard it as worse than death, to be reduced to live, even without labour, upon the same simple fare with him, to dwell under the same lowly roof, and to be clothed in the same humble attire? Do they imagine that their stomach is better, or their sleep sounder in a palace than in a cottage? The contrary has been so often observed, and, indeed, is so very obvious, though it had never been observed, that there is nobody ignorant of it. From whence, then, arises that emulation which runs through all the different ranks of men, and what are the advantages which we propose by that great purpose of human life which we call bettering our condition? To be observed, to be attended to, to be taken notice of with sympathy, complacency, and approbation, are all the advantages which we can propose to derive from it. It is the vanity, not the ease, or the pleasure, which interests us. But vanity is always founded upon the belief of our being the object of attention and approbation. The rich man glories in his riches, because he feels that they naturally draw upon him the attention of the world, and that mankind are disposed to go along with him in all those agreeable emotions with which the advantages of his situation so readily inspire him. At the thought of this, his heart seems to swell and dilate itself within him, and he is fonder of his wealth, upon this account, than for all the other advantages it procures him. The poor man, on the contrary, is ashamed of his poverty. He feels that it either places him out of the sight of mankind, or, that if they take any notice of him, they have, however, scarce any fellow-feeling with the misery and distress which he suffers. He is mortified upon both accounts; for though to be overlooked, and to be disapproved of, are things entirely different, yet as obscurity covers us from the daylight of honour and approbation, to feel that we are taken no notice of, necessarily damps the most agreeable hope, and disappoints the most ardent desire, of human nature. The poor man goes out and comes in unheeded, and when in the midst of a crowd is in the same obscurity as if shut up in his own hovel. Those humble cares and painful attentions which occupy those in his situation, afford no amusement to the dissipated and the gay. They turn away their eyes from him, or if the extremity of his distress forces them to look at him, it is only to spurn so disagreeable an object from among them. The fortunate and the proud wonder at the insolence of human wretchedness, that it should dare to present itself before them, and with the loathsome aspect of its misery presume to disturb the serenity of their happiness. The man of rank and distinction, on the contrary, is observed by all the world. Every body is eager to look at him, and to conceive, at least by sympathy, that joy and exultation with which his circumstances naturally inspire him. His actions are the objects of the public care. Scarce a word, scarce a gesture, can fall from him that is altogether neglected. In a great assembly he is the person

upon whom all direct their eyes; it is upon him that their passions seem all to wait with expectation, in order to receive that movement and direction which he shall impress upon them; and if his behaviour is not altogether absurd, he has, every moment, an opportunity of interesting mankind, and of rendering himself the object of the observation and fellow-feeling of every body about him. It is this, which, notwithstanding the restraint it imposes, notwithstanding the loss of liberty with which it is attended, renders greatness the object of envy, and compensates, in the opinion of all those mortifications which must mankind, all that toil, all that anxiety, be undergone in the pursuit of it; and what is of yet more consequence, all that leisure, all that ease, all that careless security, which are forfeited for ever by the acquisition.

When we consider the condition of the great, in those delusive colours in which the imagination is apt to paint it, it seems to be almost the abstract idea of a perfect and happy state. It is the very state which, in all our waking dreams and idle reveries, we had sketched out to ourselves as the final object of all our desires. We feel, therefore, a peculiar sympathy with the satisfaction of those who are in it. We favour all their inclinations, and forward all their wishes. What pity, we think, that any thing should spoil and corrupt so agreeable a situation! We could even wish them immortal; and it seems hard to us, that death should at last put an end to such perfect enjoyment. . . . Every calamity that befals them, every injury that is done them, excites in the breast of the spectator ten times more compassion and resentment than he would have felt, had the same things happened to other men. . . . The traitor who conspires against the life of his monarch, is thought a greater monster than any other murderer. All the innocent blood that was shed in the civil wars, provoked less indignation than the death of Charles I. A stranger to human nature, who saw the indifference of men about the misery of their inferiors, and the regret and indignation which they feel for the misfortunes and sufferings of those above them, would be apt to imagine, that pain must be more agonizing, and the convulsions of death more terrible to persons of higher rank, than to those of meaner stations.

Upon this disposition of mankind, to go along with all the passions of the rich and the powerful, is founded the distinction of ranks, and the order of society. Our obsequiousness to our superiors more frequently arises from our admiration for the advantages of their situation, than from any private expectations of benefit from their good-will. Their benefits can extend but to a few. but their fortunes interest almost every body. We are eager to assist them in completing a system of happiness that approaches so near to perfection; and we desire to serve them for their own sake, without any other recompense but the vanity or the honour of obliging them. Neither is our deference to their inclinations founded chiefly, or altogether, upon a regard to the utility of such submission, and to the order of society, which is best supported by it. Even when the order of society seems to require that we should oppose them, we can hardly bring ourselves to do it. That kings are the servants of the people, to be obeyed, resisted, deposed, or punished, as the public conveniency may require, is the doctrine of reason and philosophy; but it is not the doctrine of Nature. Nature would teach us to submit to them for their own sake, to tremble and bow down before their exalted station, to regard their smile as a reward sufficient to compensate any services, and to dread their displeasure, though no other evil were to follow from it, as the severest of all mortifications. To treat them in any respect as men, to reason and dispute with them upon ordinary occasions, requires such resolution, that there are few men whose magnanimity can support them in it, unless they are likewise assisted by familiarity and acquaintance. The strongest motives, the most furious passions, fear, hatred, and resentment, are scarce sufficient to balance this natural disposition to respect them: and their conduct must, either justly or unjustly, have excited the highest degree of all those passions, before the bulk of the people can be brought to oppose them with violence, or to desire to see them either punished or deposed. . . .

Do the great seem insensible of the easy price at which they may acquire the public admiration; or do they seem to imagine that to them, as to other men, it must be the purchase either of sweat or of blood? By what important accomplishments is the young nobleman instructed to support the dignity of his rank, and to render himself worthy of that superiority over his fellow-citizens, to which the virtue of his ancestors had raised them? Is it by knowledge, by industry, by patience, by self-denial, or by virtue of any kind? As all his words, as all his motions are attended to, he learns an habitual regard to every circumstance of ordinary behaviour, and studies to perform all those small duties with the most exact propriety. As he is conscious how much he is observed, and how much mankind are disposed to favour all his inclinations, he acts, upon the most indifferent occasions, with that freedom and elevation which the thought of this naturally inspires. His air, his manner, his deportment, all mark that elegant and graceful sense of his own superiority, which those who are born to inferior stations can hardly ever arrive at. These are the arts by which he proposes to make mankind more easily submit to his authority, and to

govern their inclinations according to his own pleasure: and in this he is seldom disappointed. These arts, supported by rank and preheminence, are, upon ordinary occasions, sufficient to govern the world. Lewis XIV, during the greater part of his reign, was regarded, not only in France, but over all Europe, as the most perfect model of a great prince. But what were the talents and virtues by which he acquired this great reputation? Was it by the scrupulous and inflexible justice of all his undertakings, by the immense dangers and difficulties with which they were attended, or by the unwearied and unrelenting application with which he pursued them? Was it by his extensive knowledge, by his exquisite judgment, or by his heroic valour? It was by none of these qualities. But he was, first of all, the most powerful prince in Europe, and consequently held the highest rank among kings; and then, says his historian, "he surpassed all his courtiers in the gracefulness of his shape, and the majestic beauty of his features. The sound of his voice, noble and affecting, gained those hearts which his presence intimidated. He had a step and a deportment which could suit only him and his rank, and which would have been ridiculous in any other person. . . ." These frivolous accomplishments, supported by his rank, and, no doubt too, by a degree of other talents and virtues, which seems, however, not to have been much above mediocrity, established this prince in the esteem of his own age, and have drawn, even from posterity, a good deal of respect for his memory. Compared with these, in his own times, and in his own presence, no other virtue, it seems, appeared to have any merit. Knowledge, industry, valour, and beneficence, trembled, were abashed, and lost all dignity before them.

But it is not by accomplishments of this kind, that the man of inferior rank must hope to distinguish himself. Politeness is so much the virtue of the great, that it will do little honour to any body but themselves. . . . The most perfect modesty and plainness, joined to as much negligence as is consistent with the respect due to the company, ought to be the chief characteristics of the behaviour of a private man. If ever he hopes to distinguish himself, it must be by more important virtues. He must acquire dependants to balance the dependants of the great, and he has no other fund to pay them from, but the labour of his body, and the activity of his mind. He must cultivate these therefore: he must acquire superior knowledge in his profession, and superior industry in the exercise of it. He must be patient in labour, resolute in danger, and firm in distress. These talents he must bring into public view, by the difficulty, importance, and, at the same time, good judgment of his undertakings, and by the severe and unrelenting application with which he pursues them. Probity and prudence, generosity and frankness, must characterize his behaviour upon all ordinary occasions; and he must, at the same time, be forward to engage in all those situations, in which it requires the greatest talents and virtues to act with propriety, but in which the greatest applause is to be acquired by those who can acquit themselves with honour. With what impatience does the man of spirit and ambition, who is depressed by his situation, look round for some great opportunity to distinguish himself? No circumstances, which can afford this, appear to him undesirable. He even looks forward with satisfaction to the prospect of foreign war, or civil dissension; and, with secret transport and delight, sees through all the confusion and bloodshed which attend them, the probability of those wished-for occasions presenting themselves, in which he may draw upon himself the attention and admiration of mankind. The man of rank and distinction, on the contrary, whose whole glory consists in the propriety of his ordinary behaviour, who is contented with the humble renown which this can afford him, and has no talents to acquire any other, is unwilling to embarrass himself with what can be attended either with difficulty or distress. To figure at a ball is his great triumph, and to succeed in an intrigue of gallantry, his highest exploit. He has an aversion to all public confusions, not from the love of mankind, for the great never look upon their inferiors as their fellow-creatures; nor yet from want of courage, for in that he is seldom defective; but from a consciousness that he possesses none of the virtues which are required in such situations, and that the public attention will certainly be drawn away from him by others. He may be willing to expose himself to some little danger, and to make a campaign when it happens to be the fashion. But he shudders with horror at the thought of any situation which demands the continual and long exertion of patience, industry, fortitude, and application of thought. These virtues are hardly ever to be met with in men who are born to those high stations. In all governments accordingly, even in monarchies, the highest offices are generally possessed, and the whole detail of the administration conducted, by men who were educated in the middle and inferior ranks of life, who have been carried forward by their own industry and abilities, though loaded with the jealousy, and opposed by the resentment, of all those who were born their superiors, and to whom the great, after having regarded them first with contempt, and afterwards with envy, are at last contented to truckle with the same abject meanness with which they desire that the rest of mankind should behave to themselves. . . .

"Love," says my Lord Rochfaucault, "is commonly succeeded by ambition; but ambition is hardly ever succeeded by love." That passion, when once it has got entire possession of the breast, will admit neither a rival nor a successor. To those who have been accustomed to the possession, or even to the hope of public admiration, all other pleasures sicken and decay. Of all the discarded statesmen who for their own ease have studied to get the better of ambition, and to despise those honours which they could no longer arrive at, how few have been able to succeed? The greater part have spent their time in the most listless and insipid indolence, chagrined at the thoughts of their own insignificancy, incapable of being interested in the occupations of private life, without enjoyment, except when they talked of their former greatness, and without satisfaction, except when they were employed in some vain project to recover it. Are you in earnest resolved never to barter your liberty for the lordly servitude of a court, but to live free, fearless, and independent? There seems to be one way to continue in that virtuous resolution; and perhaps but one. Never enter the place from whence so few have been able to return; never come within the circle of ambition; nor ever bring yourself into comparison with those masters of the earth who have already engrossed the attention of half mankind before you.

Of such mighty importance does it appear to be, in the imaginations of men, to stand in that situation which sets them most in the view of general sympathy and attention. And thus, place, that great object which divides the wives of aldermen, is the end of half the labours of human life; and is the cause of all the tumult and bustle, all the rapine and injustice, which avarice and ambition have introduced into this world. People of sense, it is said, indeed despise place; that is, they despise sitting at the head of the table, and are indifferent who it is that is pointed out to the company by that frivolous circumstance, which the smallest advantage is capable of overbalancing. But rank, distinction pre-eminence, no man despises, unless he is either raised very much above, or sunk very much below, the ordinary standard of human nature; unless he is either so confirmed in wisdom and real philosophy, as to be satisfied that, while the propriety of his conduct renders him the just object of approbation, it is of little consequence though he be neither attended to, nor approved of; or so habituated to the idea of his own meanness, so sunk in slothful and sottish indifference, as entirely to have forgot the desire, and almost the very wish, for superiority.

As to become the natural object of the joyous congratulations and sympathetic attentions of mankind is, in this manner, the circumstance which gives to prosperity all its dazzling splendour; so nothing darkens so much the gloom of adversity as to feel that our misfortunes are the objects, not of the fellow-feeling, but of the contempt and aversion of our brethren. It is upon this account that the most dreadful calamities are not always those which it is most difficult to support. It is often more mortifying to appear in public under small disasters, than under great misfortunes. The first excite no sympathy; but the second, though they may excite none that approaches to the anguish of the sufferer, call forth, however, a very lively compassion. The sentiments of the spectators are, in this last case, less wide of those of the sufferer, and their imperfect fellow-feeling lends him some assistance in supporting his misery. Before a gay assembly, a gentleman would be more mortified to appear covered with filth and rags than with blood and wounds. This last situation would interest their pity; the other would provoke their laughter. The judge who orders a criminal to be set in the pillory, dishonours him more than if he had condemned him to the scaffold. The great prince, who, some years ago, caned a general officer at the head of his army, disgraced him irrecoverably. The punishment would have been much less had he shot him through the body. By the laws of honour, to strike with a cane dishonours, to strike with a sword does not, for an obvious reason. Those slighter punishments, when inflicted on a gentleman, to whom dishonour is the greatest of all evils, come to be regarded among a humane and generous people, as the most dreadful of any. With regard to persons of that rank, therefore, they are universally laid aside, and the law, while it takes their life upon many occasions, respects their honour upon almost all. To scourge a person of quality, or to set him in the pillory, upon account of any crime whatever, is a brutality of which no European government, except that of Russia, is capable.

A brave man is not rendered contemptible by being brought to the scaffold; he is, by being set in the pillory. His behaviour in the one situation may gain him universal esteem and admiration. No behaviour in the other can render him agreeable. The sympathy of the spectators supports him in the one case, and saves him from that shame, that consciousness that his misery is felt by himself only, which is of all sentiments the most unsupportable. There is no sympathy in the other; or, if there is any, it is not with his pain, which is a trifle, but with his consciousness of the want of sympathy with which this pain is attended. It is with his shame, not with his sorrow. Those who pity him, blush and hang down their heads for him. He droops in the same manner, and feels himself irrecoverably degraded by the punishment, though not by the crime. The man, on the contrary, who

dies with resolution, as he is naturally regarded with the erect aspect of esteem and approbation, so he wears himself the same undaunted countenance; and, if the crime does not deprive him of the respect of others, the punishment never will. He has no suspicion that his situation is the object of contempt or derision to any body, and he can, with propriety, assume the air, not only of perfect serenity, but of triumph and exultation. . . .

Human virtue is superior to pain, to poverty, to danger, and to death; nor does it even require its utmost efforts do despise them. But to have its misery exposed to insult and derision, to be led in triumph, to be set up for the hand of scorn to point at, is a situation in which its constancy is much more apt to fail. Compared with the contempt of mankind, all other external evils are easily supported.

OF THE CORRUPTION OF OUR MORAL SENTIMENTS, WHICH IS OCCASIONED BY THIS DISPOSITION TO ADMIRE THE RICH AND THE GREAT, AND TO DESPISE OR NEGLECT PERSONS OF POOR AND MEAN CONDITION

This disposition to admire, and almost to worship, the rich and the powerful, and to despise, or, at least, to neglect persons of poor and mean condition, though necessary both to establish and to maintain the distinction of ranks and the order of society, is, at the same time, the great and most universal cause of the corruption of our moral sentiments. That wealth and greatness are often regarded with the respect and admiration which are due only to wisdom and virtue; and that the contempt, of which vice and folly are the only proper objects, is often most unjustly bestowed upon poverty and weakness, has been the complaint of moralists in all ages.

We desire both to be respectable and to be respected. We dread both to be contemptible and to be contemned. But, upon coming into the world, we soon find that wisdom and virtue are by no means the sole objects of respect; nor vice and folly, of contempt. We frequently see the respectful attentions of the world more strongly directed towards the rich and the great, than towards the wise and the virtuous. We see frequently the vices and follies of the powerful much less despised than the poverty and weakness of the innocent. To deserve, to acquire, and to enjoy the respect and admiration of mankind, are the great objects of ambition and emulation. Two different roads are presented to us, equally leading to the attainment of this so much desired object; the one, by the study of wisdom and the practice of virtue; the other, by the acquisition of wealth and greatness. Two different characters are presented to our emulation; the one, of proud ambition and ostentatious avidity. the other, of humble modesty and equitable justice. Two different models, two different pictures, are held out to us, according to which we may fashion our own character and behaviour; the one more gaudy and glittering in its colouring; the other more correct and more exquisitely beautiful in its outline: the one forcing itself upon the notice of every wandering eye; the other, attracting the attention of scarce any body but the most studious and careful observer. They are the wise and the virtuous chiefly, a select, though, I am afraid, but a small party, who are the real and steady admirers of wisdom and virtue. The great mob of mankind are the admirers and worshippers, and, what may seem more extraordinary, most frequently the disinterested admirers and worshippers, of wealth and greatness.

The respect which we feel for wisdom and virtue is, no doubt, different from that which we conceive for wealth and greatness; and it requires no very nice discernment to distinguish the difference. But, notwithstanding this difference, those sentiments bear a very considerable resemblance to one another. In some particular features they are, no doubt, different, but, in the general air of the countenance, they seem to be so very nearly the same, that inattentive observers are very apt to mistake the one for the other.

In equal degrees of merit there is scarce any man who does not respect more the rich and the great, than the poor and the humble. With most men the presumption and vanity of the former are much more admired, than the real and solid merit of the latter. It is scarce agreeable to good morals, or even to good language, perhaps, to say, that mere wealth and greatness, abstracted from merit and virtue, deserve our respect. We must acknowledge, however, that they almost constantly obtain it; and that they may, therefore, be considered as, in some respects, the natural objects of it. Those exalted stations may, no doubt, be completely degraded by vice and folly. But the vice and folly must be very great, before they can operate this complete degradation. The profligacy of a man of fashion is looked upon with much less contempt and aversion, than that of a man of meaner condition. In the latter, a single transgression of the rules of temperance and propriety, is commonly more resented, than the constant and avowed contempt of them ever is in the former.

In the middling and inferior stations of life, the road to virtue and that to fortune, to such fortune, at least, as men in such stations can reasonably expect to acquire, are, happily in most cases, very nearly the same. In all the middling and inferior professions, real and solid professional abilities, joined to prudent, just, firm, and temperate conduct, can very seldom fail of success. Abilities will even sometimes prevail where the conduct is by no means correct. Either habitual imprudence, however, or injustice, or weakness, or profligacy, will always cloud, and sometimes depress altogether, the most splendid professional abilities. Men in the inferior and middling stations of life, besides, can never be great enough to be above the law, which must generally overawe them into some sort of respect for, at least, the more important rules of justice. The success of such people, too, almost always depends upon the favour and good opinion of their neighbours and equals; and without a tolerably regular conduct these can very seldom be obtained. The good old proverb, therefore, That honesty is the best policy, holds, in such situations, almost always perfectly true. In such situations, therefore, we may generally expect a considerable degree of virtue; and, fortunately for the good morals of society, these are the situations of by far the greater part of mankind.

In the superior stations of life the case is unhappily not always the same. In the courts of princes, in the drawing-rooms of the great, where success and preferment depend, not upon the esteem of intelligent and well-informed equals, but upon the fanciful and foolish favour of ignorant, presumptuous, and proud superiors; flattery and falsehood too often prevail over merit and abilities. In such societies the abilities to please, are more regarded than the abilities to serve. In quiet and peaceable times, when the storm is at a distance, the prince, or great man, wishes only to be amused, and is even apt to fancy that he has scarce any occasion for the service of any body, or that those who amuse him are sufficiently able to serve him. The external graces, the frivolous accomplishments of that impertinent and foolish thing called a man of fashion, are commonly more admired than the solid and masculine virtues of a warrior, a statesman, a philosopher, or a legislator. All the great and awful virtues, all the virtues which can fit, either for the council, the senate, or the field, are, by the insolent and insignificant flatterers, who commonly figure the most in such corrupted societies, held in the utmost contempt and derision. When the duke of Sully was called upon by Lewis the Thirteenth, to give his advice in some great emergency, he observed the favourites and courtiers whispering to one another, and smiling at his unfashionable appearance. "Whenever your majesty's father," said the old warrior and statesman, "did me the honour to consult me, he ordered the buffoons of the court to retire into the antechamber.". . .

QUESTIONS ON SMITH

1. What does Smith mean when he states that "it is chiefly from this regard to the sentiments of mankind, that we pursue riches and avoid poverty"? What fuels or motivates ambition? How does ambition relate to vanity? Does this mean that our achievements are meaningful only if they are recognized or seconded by others?

2. Does the realization of one's ambition actually improve one's life? Or does it merely bring one the pleasurable attention of others?

3. What are the sorts of qualities or attributes which Smith believes we tend to take notice of in others? How does Smith distinguish between the conditions of success for those in the "middling" stations of life and those in "superior" stations? Do you think that these distinct conditions, or something analogous to them, might still hold true in today's society?

Courage, Entrepreneurship, and Profit

Fortune befriends the bold.

Vergil[19]

And one should bear in mind that there is nothing more difficult to execute, nor more dubious of success, nor more dangerous to administer than to introduce a new system of things: for he who introduces it has all those who profit from the old system as his enemies, and he has only lukewarm allies in all those who might profit from the new system.

Niccolò Machiavelli[20]

It was shown that the appropriation of unpaid labour is the basis of the capitalist mode of production and of the exploitation of the worker that occurs under it; that even if the capitalist buys the labour power of his labourer at its full value as a commodity on the market, he yet extracts more value from it than he paid for; and that in the ultimate analysis this surplus value forms those sums of value from which are heaped up the constantly increasing masses of capital in the hands of the possessing classes.

Friedrich Engels[21]

Yet bare labor produces very little if not aided by the employment of the outcome of previous saving and accumulation of capital. The products are the outgrowth of a cooperation of labor with tools and other capital goods directed by provident entrepreneurial design. The savers, whose saving accumulated and maintains the capital, and the entrepreneurs, who channel the capital into those employments in which it best serves the consumers, are no less indispensable for the process of production than the toilers. It is nonsensical to impute the whole product to the purveyors of labor and to pass over in silence the contribution of the purveyors of capital and of entrepreneurial ideas. What brings forth usable goods is not physical effort as such, but physical effort aptly directed by the human mind toward a definite goal.

Ludwig von Mises[22]

19. *Æneid* [1st century, B.C.], translated by John Dryden, Book X, line 398, in *The Harvard Classics,* Vol. XIII (New York: P. F. Collier & Son, 1909–14).

20. *The Prince* [1512–1513] in *The Portable Machiavelli,* edited and translated by Peter Bondanella and Mark Musa (New York: Penguin Books, 1979), chapter 6 (p. 94).

21. *Socialism: Utopian and Scientific* [1880] in *The Marx-Engels Reader,* edited by Robert C. Tucker, 2d ed. (New York: W. W. Norton, 1978), Part II (p. 700).

22. *Human Action* [1949], Third revised edition (Chicago: Henry Regnery, 1963), 300–301.

442

In the long run, no organization can succeed if its costs outrun its revenues. In fact, the very idea of development—commercial or national—implies that the value of one's assets has increased. In commerce, if a firm's revenues exceed its costs, then the firm has attained a profit. In a world of constant change, various circumstances, and limited and imperfect knowledge, profit and loss serve to direct individuals and firms toward those areas in which goods and services are most highly valued; thus profit and loss serve as powerful signals that help individuals channel their resources and efforts toward mutually productive avenues.

However, profit has often been regarded with skepticism, as if the one who garnered the profit had, somehow, taken that which was not deserved, that which was rightfully someone else's. Others criticize profits as being the reward of greed or self-interest. However, it should not be assumed, without argument, that the quest for a profit is essentially distinguishable from the quest for a wage or salary. Nor is it obvious that the desire to receive a good salary, a high wage, or a decent profit need be understood only in terms of narrow selfishness (see section BI, Selfishness, p. 241). Is there, however, a sense in which profits are deserved? And do the very commercial activities that may garner profits require a kind of boldness that is analogous to courage?

The Idea of Profit

The owner of a business endeavors to make a profit. However, that one strives to make a profit is a more particular manner of stating that one seeks to make an exchange, or a series of exchanges, in which the value one receives is greater than the value one gives away. Thus, within the framework of a competitive market, exchange is a voluntary relation, and *profit* is what transpires to a business owner after the owner has bought materials, hired labor, and produced or delivered goods or services for an amount greater than the total cost. Profit is achieved only if the owner of the resources has chosen wisely both the goods to be produced and the means of production.

There is an important distinction between the remuneration of profit and that of a wage or salary. When a business owner hires labor, the owner contracts with individuals to work at determinate tasks (and for a defined time or period) in return for a contractually specified wage or salary. However, there is no contract for a profit, for its possibility depends on foresight, effort, alertness, and fortune itself. Thus the owner runs the risk that some or all of the goods will not sell or that the goods will not be produced at all.

The Marxist Critique of Profit

According to Karl Marx (1818–1883), profits are the result of surplus value created not by the owner but by the laborers. A capitalist secures a profit by making an initial purchase or investment of the means of production, raw materials and equipment, as well as labor itself. The laborers work on these commodities to manufacture new items. If the new commodities are sold for a higher amount than that at which the original commodities were purchased, then the owner reaps a profit.

How are these profits generated? Marx responds to this question by appealing to a theory of "surplus value," a theory which holds that the value of labor power is less than the value that is *created* by labor power in the course of a working day. The additional or surplus value that is created by labor is taken by the capitalist as profit. Thus, for Marx, the single and only source of profit is found in labor. The value of labor is equal to the number of hours required to produce the means of subsistence for keeping labor alive and able to work. However, if, say, six hours of labor are required to produce the means of subsistence, and labor toils for some twelve hours, then labor creates a surplus value that is a result of the additional labor. This surplus value is appropriated by the capitalist as profit.[23]

The key idea for Marx is that the capitalist makes no contribution to the productive process, that is the province of labor alone. However, it might be suggested that the very fact that the capitalist provides the means of production is one contribution, and this involves some action on the part of the capitalist such as forgoing spending or consumption in order to acquire the wealth to provide the capital. The capitalist also bears a risk that is not undertaken by those who work for a wage or salary, forms of remuneration that are guaranteed to workers prior to the capitalist having received any revenues from the sale of goods or services. Finally, the capitalist who manages an enterprise also contributes to the activity of production the crucial element of organization. Is there, however, another element at work in the creation of profits?

Profit and Entrepreneurship

Perhaps something else is at play in the generation of profit, namely, the activity of entrepreneurship. The function of the entrepreneur can be conceptually distinguished from

---

23. The account of the creation of surplus value can be found in *Capital*, vol. 1 Part III, chapter 7, section 2. An excellent account of Marx's theory can be found in David Conway, *A Farewell to Marx* (Harmondsworth: Penguin, 1987). The classic refutation of Marx's theory of exploitation is that of Eugen von Böhm-Bawerk, *Karl Marx and the Close of His System* [1896], edited by Paul M. Sweezy (London: Merlin Press, 1974).

that of the manager or the owner. For the activity of entrepreneurship involves the act of recognizing and discovering opportunities for profit, and this presupposes entrepreneurial alertness. Opportunities for profit-making exist whenever there are discrepancies between the price at which a good is being sold and the (higher) price at which people are willing to purchase the good. The entrepreneur recognizes this discrepancy (or *disequilibrium*) and purchases the good at the lower cost and then resells the good to others at the (higher) price. This sort of entrepreneurial activity—which Schumpeter describes as the "carrying out of new combinations"—may take place throughout a market and may include simple arbitrage, or it may involve recognizing how production could be redesigned, or how resources could be utilized to produce new goods. However, the role of the entrepreneur is essentially distinct from the activity of managing resources or owning them. It is also an activity that has been relatively unnoticed.[24]

The Marxist account makes no mention of entrepreneurship, but surprisingly neither does the standard model of perfect competition. In the world invoked by the standard model of perfect competition, the model employed by many economic theorists, there is a competitive *equilibrium* in which there is but one price for a given good, all of the relevant economic data is known by the market participants and does not change. A producer knows what to produce and must calculate how to produce these goods in the most efficient manner. On this view, production is nothing more than economizing and requires no alertness to price discrepancies or to the discovery of new goods or services. For if a capitalist already knows what is to be produced and how it is to be produced, then all that the capitalist need do is to find the least expensive means of production and pay individuals to produce the requisite product. However, why should we assume that market participants have perfect knowledge or that the data of consumer desires, preferences, resources, and so on will not change? Once we relax these assumptions, then one can see how there is a role for *entrepreneurship*.

Courage and Risk

It seems clear enough that the entrepreneur initiates change into a market, but it should also be considered that entrepreneurship, insofar as it involves risk and uncertainty, may require boldness, decisiveness, and courage. To introduce a new product, a new mode of production, a new method of advertising, or to move into a hitherto untapped market, is, in effect, to engage in a hypothesis of experiment in which the ultimate resolution is unknown and the possibility of failure is real. The entrepreneur must recognize this possibility of failure but must not discount it in some sort of foolish or rash manner. Neither can the entrepreneur permit the fear of failure to stymie any action. "Whenever you see a successful business, someone once made a courageous decision."[25] The bold or courageous entrepreneur must make a realistic assessment and, once the business venture has begun, be resolute in allowing the initiative to take its course, leading to success or to failure.

> The virtue of boldness is not simply in taking a risk, and it most certainly is not in wild, uninformed gambling on poorly conceived schemes. Rather, it is in the optimism to venture forth gallantly and make the enterprise or scheme work successfully. It is the abiding commitment to face whatever may come, no matter how terrible or tragic the problems may be.[26]

THE READINGS

Aristotle   Courage is the mean between feelings of fear and confidence. What we fear is something evil, not just any sort of evil but one of importance, against which "a man can show his prowess or . . . can die a noble death." Although Aristotle indicates at first that the courageous person is fearless in the face of death, he later points out that a courageous person endures fear in the proper way, for fear is a matter of degree. One could fail to be courageous by fearing the wrong thing, in the wrong manner or at the wrong time. An excess of confidence (a deficiency of fear) is recklessness; a deficiency in confidence (or an excess of fear) is cowardice. There are several instances in which one's actions might be confused with courage, including those occasions in which one acts under compulsion, through prolonged experience, by a spirited temper, under optimism, or out of ignorance.

Joseph Schumpeter   Against the established and routine conditions, habits, knowledge, and modes of production, the entrepreneur "carries out new business

---

24. A major exception is Schumpeter (see below) as well as Frank Knight, *Risk, Uncertainty and Profit* (Boston: Houghton Mifflin, 1921). The major current theorist of entrepreneurship is Israel M. Kirzner. See, for example, *Competition and Entrepreneurship* (Chicago: University of Chicago Press, 1973), as well as the selection ("Advertising") contained in Section BII (pp. 352–357).

25. Peter Drucker, as quoted in *Money Talks*, edited by Robert W. Kent (New York: Facts on File, 1985), 233.

26. Charles Watson, *Managing with Integrity: Insight from America's CEOs* (New York: Praeger, 1991), 166–67.

combinations." Although this activity may occur in conjunction with other business activities, the entrepreneurial function involves an exercise of leadership at three levels. The entrepreneur performs a difficult task that demands a greater conscious rationality than routinized conduct; entrepreneurial success depends on acting without the usual information or certainty. Second, the entrepreneur, however tempted to remain within the tried and habitual, nonetheless forges ahead by dint of effort and will. And, finally, the entrepreneur must face the negative reaction of the social environment.

Scott Arnold   Arnold seeks to show how an entrepreneur deserves any profits won through commercial competition. To do so, he wishes to give a *basal reason* that links the entrepreneur to an essential purpose of the institution of markets. This basal reason should conform to a principle of proportionality by which there is some fit between the basal reason and the object of desert. Profit is a proper reward for entrepreneurial activity because the market seeks to meet the "wants and needs" of consumers, and it is entrepreneurial alertness to some nonoptimal allocation of resources that improves the allocation of scarce goods and resources, thereby helping to meet the wants and needs of consumers. Entrepreneurs deserve profits precisely because profits unify personal responsiblity with control over productive resources.

John Christman   Christman focuses on the question of whether entrepreneurs deserve the profits they gain in a competitive market. Defining the entrepreneur as the "primary organizer of production" and as owner of the assets of a firm, Christman points out that under the economists' model of perfect competition, there would be no profits at all. However, in the actual world of commerce profits accrue to an entrepreneur when, in the face of consumer demand for some product, there are also barriers to the entry of competitors into the marketplace. Turning specifically to profit and desert, Christman contends that one *deserves* some reward X only if there is some fact about that person that provides a reason by which the person can claim X. The reward must be both appropriate and proportional to the conduct of the person. Christman then charges that Arnold incorrectly construes desert in consequentialist terms and that Arnold's justification of the reward of profit is not based on the essential function of the entrepreneur. More generally, Christman argues that the assumption of risk is not a sufficient ground for deserving profits, nor is it the case that an entrepreneur deserves profits for providing consumers with the goods they desire, for the magnitude of these profits results not from the entrepreneur but from barriers to entry into the market.

*Courage**

Aristotle

One of the most important philosophers of all time, Aristotle (384–322 B.C.), the son of a physician, was a polymath who wrote on a variety of subjects, including biology, psychology, metaphysics, rhetoric, logic, and physics. His Nicomachean Ethics *was the first systematic treatment of moral matters.*

BOOK III

6

That it [courage] is a mean with regard to feelings of fear and confidence has already been made evident; and plainly the things we fear are terrible things, and these are, to speak without qualification, evils; for which reason people even define fear as expectation of evil. Now we fear all evils, e.g. disgrace, poverty, disease, friendlessness, death, but the brave man is not thought to be concerned with all; for to fear some things is even right and noble, and it is base not to fear them—e.g. disgrace; he who fears this is good and modest, and he who does not is shameless. He is, however, by some people called brave, by a transference of the word to a new meaning; for he has in him something which is like the brave man, since the brave man also is a fearless person. Poverty and disease we perhaps ought not to fear, nor in general the things that do not proceed from vice and are not due to a man himself. But not even the man who is fearless of these is brave. Yet we apply the word to him also in virtue of a similarity; for some who in the dangers of war are cowards are liberal and are confident in face of the loss of money. Nor is a man a coward if he fears insult to his wife and children or envy or anything of the kind; nor brave if he is confident when he is about to be flogged. With what sort of terrible things, then, is the brave man concerned? Surely with the greatest; for no one is more likely than he to stand his ground against what is awe-inspiring. Now death is the most terrible of all things; for it is the end, and nothing is thought to be any longer either good or bad for the dead. But the brave man would not seem to be concerned even with death in *all* circumstances, e.g. at sea or in disease. In what circumstances, then? Surely in the noblest. Now such deaths are those in battle; for these take place in the greatest and noblest danger. And these are correspondingly honoured in city-states

* Translated by W.D. Ross.

and at the courts of monarchs. Properly, then, he will be called brave who is fearless in face of a noble death, and of all emergencies that involve death; and the emergencies of war are in the highest degree of this kind. Yet at sea also, and in disease, the brave man is fearless, but not in the same way as the seaman; for he has given up hope of safety, and is disliking the thought of death in this shape, while they are hopeful because of their experience. At the same time, we show courage in situations where there is the opportunity of showing prowess or where death is noble; but in these forms of death neither of these conditions is fulfilled.

7

What is terrible is not the same for all men; but we say there are things terrible even beyond human strength. These, then, are terrible to every one—at least to every sensible man; but the terrible things that are *not* beyond human strength differ in magnitude and degree, and so too do the things that inspire confidence. Now the brave man is as dauntless as man may be. Therefore, while he will fear even the things that are not beyond human strength, he will face them as he ought and as the rule directs, for honour's sake; for this is the end of virtue. But it is possible to fear these more, or less, and again to fear things that are not terrible as if they were. Of the faults that are committed one consists in fearing what one should not, another in fearing as we should not, another in fearing when we should not, and so on; and so too with respect to the things that inspire confidence. The man, then, who faces and who fears the right things and from the right motive, in the right way and from the right time, and who feels confidence under the corresponding conditions, is brave; for the brave man feels and acts according to the merits of the case and in whatever way the rule directs. Now the end of every activity is conformity to the corresponding state of character. This is true, therefore, of the brave man as well as of others. But courage is noble. Therefore the end also is noble; for each thing is defined by its end. Therefore it is for a noble end that the brave man endures and acts as courage directs.

Of those who go to excess he who exceeds in fearlessness has no name (we have said previously that many states of character have no names), but he would be a sort of madman or insensible person if he feared nothing, neither earthquakes nor the waves, as they say the Celts do not; while the man who exceeds in confidence about what really is terrible is rash. The rash man, however, is also thought to be boastful and only a pretender to courage; at

all events, as the brave man *is* with regard to what is terrible, so the rash man wishes to *appear;* and so he imitates him in situations where he can. Hence also most of them are a mixture of rashness and cowardice; for, while in these situations they display confidence, they do not hold their ground against what is really terrible. The man who exceeds in fear is a coward; for he fears both what he ought not and as he ought not, and all the similar characterizations attach to him. He is lacking also in confidence; but he is more conspicuous for his excess of fear in painful situations. The coward, then, is a despairing sort of person; for he fears everything. The brave man, on the other hand, has the opposite disposition; for confidence is the mark of a hopeful disposition. The coward, the rash man, and the brave man, then, are concerned with the same objects but are differently disposed towards them; for the first two exceed and fall short, while the third holds the middle, which is the right, position; and rash men are precipitate, and wish for dangers beforehand but draw back when they are in them, while brave men are keen in the moment of action, but quiet beforehand.

As we have said, then, courage is a mean with respect to things that inspire confidence or fear, in the circumstances that have been stated; and it chooses or endures things because it is noble to do so, or because it is base not to do so. But to die to escape from poverty or love or anything painful is not the mark of a brave man, but rather of a coward; for it is softness to fly from what is troublesome, and such a man endures death not because it is noble but to fly from evil.

8

Courage, then, is something of this sort, but the name is also applied to five other kinds.

(1) First comes the courage of the citizen-soldier; for this is most like true courage. Citizen-soldiers seem to face dangers because of the penalties imposed by the laws and the reproaches they would otherwise incur, and because of the honours they win by such action; and therefore those peoples seem to be bravest among whom cowards are held in dishonour and brave men in honour. This is the kind of courage that Homer depicts, e.g. in Diomede and in Hector:

> First will Polydamas be to heap reproach on me then; and
>> For Hector one day 'mid the Trojans shall utter his vaulting harangue: "Afraid was Tydeides, and fled from my face."

This kind of courage is most like to that which we described earlier, because it is due to virtue; for it is due to shame and to desire of a noble object (i.e. honour) and avoidance of disgrace, which is ignoble. One might rank in the same class even those who are compelled by their rulers; but they are inferior, inasmuch as they do what they do not from shame but from fear, and to avoid not what is disgraceful but what is painful; for their masters compel them, as Hector does:

> But if I shall spy any dastard that cowers far from the fight,
> Vainly will such an one hope to escape from the dogs.

And those who give them their posts, and beat them if they retreat, do the same, and so do those who draw them up with trenches or something of the sort behind them; all of these apply compulsion. But one ought to be brave not under compulsion but because it is noble to be so.

(2) Experience with regard to particular facts is also thought to be courage; this is indeed the reason why Socrates thought courage was knowledge. Other people exhibit this quality in other dangers, and professional soldiers exhibit it in the dangers of war; for there seem to be many empty alarms in war, of which these have had the most comprehensive experience; therefore, they seem brave, because the others do not know the nature of the facts. Again, their experience makes them most capable in attack and in defence, since they can use their arms and have the kind that are likely to be best both for attack and for defence; therefore they fight like armed men against unarmed or like trained athletes against amateurs; for in such contests too it is not the bravest men that fight best, but those who are strongest and have their bodies in the best condition. Professional soldiers turn cowards, however, when the danger puts too great a strain on them and they are inferior in numbers and equipment; for they are the first to fly, while citizen-forces die at their posts, as in fact happened at the temple of Hermes. For to the latter flight is disgraceful and death is preferable to safety on those terms; while the former from the very beginning faced the danger on the assumption that they were stronger, and when they know the facts they fly, fearing death more than disgrace; but the brave man is not that sort of person.

(3) Passion also is sometimes reckoned as courage; those who act from passion, like wild beasts rushing at those who have wounded them, are thought to be brave, because brave men also are passionate; for passion above all things is eager to rush on danger, and hence Homer's "put strength into his passion" and "aroused their spirit and passion" and "hard he breathed panting" and "his blood boiled." For all such expressions seem to indicate the stirring and onset of passion. Now brave men act for honour's sake, but passion aids them; while wild beasts act under the influence of pain; for they attack because they have been wounded or because they are afraid, since if they are in a forest they do not come near one. Thus they are not brave because, driven by pain and passion, they rush on danger without foreseeing any of the perils, since at that rate even asses would be brave when they are hungry; for blows will not drive them from their food; and lust also makes adulterers do many daring things. [Those creatures are not brave, then, which are driven on to danger by pain or passion.] The "courage" that is due to passion seems to be the most natural, and to be courage if choice and motive be added.

Men, then, as well as beasts, suffer pain when they are angry, and are pleased when they exact their revenge; those who fight for these reasons, however, are pugnacious but not brave; for they do not act for honour's sake nor as the rule directs, but from strength of feeling; they have, however, something akin to courage.

(4) Nor are sanguine people brave; for they are confident in danger only because they have conquered often and against many foes. Yet they closely resemble brave men, because both are confident; but brave men are confident for the reasons stated earlier, while these are so because they think they are the strongest and can suffer nothing. (Drunken men also behave in this way; they become sanguine). When their adventures do not succeed, however, they run away; but it was the mark of a brave man to face things that are, and seem, terrible for a man, because it is noble to do so and disgraceful not to do so. Hence also it is thought the mark of a braver man to be fearless and undisturbed in sudden alarms than to be so in those that are foreseen; for it must have proceeded more from a state of character, because less from preparation; acts that are foreseen may be chosen by calculation and rule, but sudden actions must be in accordance with one's state of character.

(5) People who are ignorant of the danger also appear brave, and they are not far removed from those of a sanguine temper, but are inferior inasmuch as they have no self-reliance while these have. Hence also the sanguine hold their ground for a time; but those who have been deceived about the facts fly if they know or suspect that these are different from what they supposed, as happened to the Argives when they fell in with the Spartans and took them for Sicyonians.

We have, then, described the character both of brave men and of those who are thought to be brave.

9

Though courage is concerned with feelings of confidence and of fear, it is not concerned with both alike, but more with the things that inspire fear; for he who is undisturbed in face of these and bears himself as he should towards these is more truly brave than the man who does so towards the things that inspire confidence. It is for facing what is painful, then, as has been said, that men are called brave. Hence also courage involves pain, and is justly praised; for it is harder to face what is painful than to abstain from what is pleasant. Yet the end which courage sets before it would seem to be pleasant, but to be concealed by the attending circumstances, as happens also in athletic contests; for the end at which boxers aim is pleasant—the crown and the honours—but the blows they take are distressing to flesh and blood, and painful, and so is their whole exertion; and because the blows and the exertions are many the end, which is but small, appears to have nothing pleasant in it. And so, if the case of courage is similar, death and wounds will be painful to the brave man and against his will, but he will face them because it is noble to do so or because it is base not to do so. And the more he is possessed of virtue in its entirety and the happier he is, the more he will be pained at the thought of death; for life is best worth living for such a man, and he is knowingly losing the greatest goods, and this is painful. But he is none the less brave, and perhaps all the more so, because he chooses noble deeds of war at that cost. It is not the case, then, with all the virtues that the exercise of them is pleasant, except in so far as it reaches its end. But it is quite possible that the best soldiers may be not men of this sort but those who are less brave but have no other good; for these are ready to face danger, and they sell their life for trifling gains.

So much, then, for courage; it is not difficult to grasp its nature in outline, at any rate, from what has been said.

QUESTIONS ON ARISTOTLE

1. Summarize Aristotle's account of courage as a mean between feelings of fear and confidence. In what sense could someone fear the wrong thing or fear something for the wrong end? How could someone fear in the wrong manner?

2. Aristotle contends that the courageous person is motivated by what is noble. Is there any room in commerce for courageous action?

3. How can courage be concerned with feelings of either confidence or fear? How is courage more concerned with "the things that inspire fear"? Which is more important in business, confidence or fear?

The Entrepreneur

Joseph A. Schumpeter

Joseph A. Schumpeter (1883–1950) was born in Triesch, Moravia (now part of the Czech Republic), and died in Connecticut, having served on the faculty of Harvard University, 1932–1950. An influential teacher, economist, and historian of economics, he is the author of numerous works including Capitalism, Socialism, and Democracy *(1942),* History of Economic Analysis *(1954), the two-volume work* Business Cycles *(1939), as well as* The Theory of Economic Development *(1912) from which this excerpt is taken.*

. . . The carrying out of new combinations we call "enterprise"; the individuals whose function it is to carry them out we call "entrepreneurs." These concepts are at once broader and narrower than the usual. Broader, because in the first place we call entrepreneurs not only those "independent" businessmen in an exchange economy who are usually so designated, but all who actually fulfil the function by which we define the concept, even if they are, as is becoming the rule, "dependent" employees of a company, like managers, members of boards of directors, and so forth, or even if their actual power to perform the entrepreneurial function has any other foundations, such as the control of a majority of shares. As it is the carrying out of new combinations that constitutes the entrepreneur, it is not necessary that he should be permanently connected with an individual firm; many "financiers," "promoters," and so forth are not, and still they may be entrepreneurs in our sense. On the other hand, our concept is narrower than the traditional one in that it does not include all heads of firms or managers or industrialists who merely may operate an established business, but only those who actually perform that function. Nevertheless I maintain that the above definition does no more than formulate with greater precision what the traditional doctrine really means to convey. . . .

. . . The entrepreneur of earlier times was not only as a rule the capitalist too, he was also often—as he still is to-day in the case of small concerns—his own technical expert, in so far as a professional specialist was not called in for special cases. Likewise he was (and is) often his own 1) buying and selling agent, the 2) head of his office, his own 3) personnel manager, and sometimes, even though as a rule he of course employed solicitors, his own 4) legal adviser in current affairs. And it was performing some or all of these functions that regularly filled his days. The carrying out of new combinations can no more be a *vocation* than the making and execution of strategical decisions, although it is this function and not his routine work that characterises the military leader. Therefore the entrepreneur's essential function must always appear mixed up with other kinds of activity, which as a rule must be much more conspicuous than the essential one. Hence the Marshallian definition of the entrepreneur, which simply treats the entrepreneurial function as "management" in the widest meaning, will naturally appeal to most of us. We do not accept it, simply because it does not bring out what we consider to be the salient point and the only one which specifically distinguishes entrepreneurial from other activities.

Nevertheless there are types—the course of events has evolved them by degrees—which exhibit the entrepreneurial function with particular purity. The "promoter," to be sure, belongs to them only with qualifications. For, neglecting the associations relative to social and moral status which are attached to this type, the promoter is frequently only an agent intervening on commission, who does the work of financial technique in floating the new enterprise. In this case he is not its creator nor the driving power in the process. However, he *may* be the latter also, and then he is something like an "entrepreneur by profession." But the modern type of "captain of industry"[1] corresponds more closely to what is meant here, especially if one recognises his identity on the one hand with, say, the commercial entrepreneur of twelfth-century Venice—or, among later types, with John Law—and on the other hand with the village potentate who combines with his agriculture and his cattle trade, say, a rural brewery, an hotel, and a store. But whatever the type, everyone is an entrepreneur only when he actually "carries out new combinations," and loses that character as soon as he has built up his business, when he settles down to running it as other people run their businesses. This is the rule, of course, and hence it is just as rare for anyone always to remain an entrepreneur throughout the decades of his active life as it is for a businessman never to have a moment in which he is an entrepreneur, to however modest a degree.

Because being an entrepreneur is not a profession and as a rule not a lasting condition, entrepreneurs do not form a social class in the technical sense, as, for example, landowners or capitalists or workmen do. Of course the entrepreneurial function will *lead* to certain class positions for the successful entrepreneur and his family. It can also put its stamp on an epoch of social history, can form a style of life, or systems of moral and aesthetic values; but in itself it signifies a class position no more than it presupposes one. And the class position which may be attained is not as such an entrepreneurial position, but is characterised as landowning or capitalist, according to how the proceeds of the enterprise are used. Inheritance of the pecuniary result and of personal qualities may then both keep up this position for more than one generation and make further enterprise easier for descendants, but the function of the entrepreneur itself cannot be inherited, as is shown well enough by the history of manufacturing families.[2]

But now the decisive question arises: why then is the carrying out of new combinations a special process and the object of a special kind of "function"? Every individual carries on his economic affairs as well as he can. To be sure, his own intentions are never realised with ideal perfection, but ultimately his behavior is moulded by the influence on him of the results of his conduct, so as to fit circumstances which do not as a rule change suddenly. If a business can never be absolutely perfect in any sense, yet it in time approaches a relative perfection having regard to the surrounding world, the social conditions, the knowledge of the time, and the horizon of each individual or each group. New possibilities are continuously being offered by the surrounding world, in particular new discoveries are continuously being added to the existing store of knowledge. Why should not the individual make just as much use of the new possibilities as of the old, and, according to the market position as he understands it, keep pigs instead of cows, or even choose a new crop rotation, if this can be seen to be more advantageous? And what kind of special new phenomena or problems, not to be found in the established circular flow, can arise there?

While in the accustomed circular flow every individual can act promptly and rationally because he is sure of his ground and is supported by the conduct, as adjusted to this circular flow, of all other individuals, who in turn expect the accustomed activity from him, he cannot simply do this when he is confronted by a new task. While in the accustomed channels his own ability and experience suffice for the normal individual, when confronted with innovations he needs guidance. While he swims with the stream in the circular flow which is familiar to him, he swims against the stream if he wishes to change its channel. What was formerly a help becomes a hindrance. What was a familiar datum becomes an unknown. Where the boundaries of routine stop, many people can go no further, and the rest can only do so in a highly variable manner. The assumption that conduct is prompt and rational is in all cases a fiction. But it proves to be sufficiently near to reality, if things have time to hammer logic into men. Where this has happened, and within the limits in which it has happened, one may rest content with this fiction and build theories upon it. . . .

. . . Therefore, too, the carrying out of new combinations is a special function, and the privilege of a type of people who are much less numerous than all those who have the "objective" possibility of doing it. Therefore, finally, entrepreneurs are a special type,[3] and their behavior a special problem, the motive power of a great number of significant phenomena. . . .

Let us now formulate precisely the characteristic feature of the conduct and type under discussion. The smallest daily action embodies a huge mental effort. Every schoolboy would have to be a mental giant, if he himself had to create all he knows and uses by his own individual activity. And every man would have to be a giant of wisdom and will, if he had in every case to create anew all the rules by which he guides his everyday conduct. This is true not only of those decisions and actions of individual and social life the principles of which are the product of tens of thousands of years, but also of those products of shorter periods and of a more special nature which constitute the particular instrument for performing vocational tasks. But precisely the things the performance of which according to this should involve a supreme effort, in general demand no special individual effort at all; those which should be especially difficult are in reality especially easy; what should demand superhuman capacity is accessible to the least gifted, given mental health. In particular within the ordinary routine there is no need for leadership. Of course it is still necessary to set people their tasks, to keep up discipline, and so forth; but this is easy and a function any normal person can learn to fulfil. Within the lines familiar to all, even the function of directing other people, though still necessary, is mere "work" like any other, comparable to the service of tending a machine. All people get to know, and are able to do, their daily tasks in the customary way and ordinarily perform them by themselves; the "director" has his routine as they have theirs; and his directive function serves merely to correct individual aberrations.

This is so because all knowledge and habit once acquired becomes as firmly rooted in ourselves as a railway embankment in the earth. It does not require to be continually renewed and consciously reproduced, but sinks into the strata of subconsciousness. It is normally transmitted almost without friction by inheritance, teaching, upbringing, pressure of environment. Everything we think, feel, or do often enough becomes automatic and our conscious life is unburdened of it. The enormous economy of force, in the race and the individual, here involved is not great enough, however, to make daily life a light burden and to prevent its demands from exhausting the average energy all the same. But it is great enough to make it possible to meet the ordinary claims. This holds good likewise for economic daily life. And from this it follows also for economic life that every step outside the boundary of routine has difficulties and involves a new element. It is this element that constitutes the phenomenon of leadership.

The nature of these difficulties may be focussed in the following three points. First, outside these accustomed channels the individual is without those data for his decisions and those rules of conduct which are usually very accurately known to him within them. Of course he must still foresee and estimate on the basis of his experience. But many things must remain uncertain, still others are only ascertainable within wide limits, some can perhaps only be "guessed." In particular this is true of those data which the individual strives to alter and of those which he wants to create. Now he must really to some extent do what tradition does for him in everyday life, viz. consciously plan his conduct in every particular. There will be much more conscious rationality in this than in customary action, which as such does not need to be reflected upon at all; but this plan must necessarily be open not only to errors greater in degree, but also to other kinds of errors than those occurring in customary action. What has been done already has the sharp-edged reality of all the things which we have seen and experienced; the new is only the figment of our imagination. Carrying out a new plan and acting according to a customary one are things as different as making a road and walking along it.

How different a thing this is becomes clearer if one bears in mind the impossibility of surveying exhaustively all the effects and counter-effects of the projected enterprise. Even as many of them as could in theory be ascertained if one had unlimited time and means must practically remain in the dark. As military action must be taken in a given strategic position even if all the data potentially procurable are not available, so also in economic life action must be taken without working out all the details of what is to be done. Here the success of everything depends upon intuition, the capacity of seeing things in a way which afterwards proves to be true, even though it cannot be established at the moment, and of grasping the essential fact, discarding the unessential, even though one can give no account of the principles by which this is done. Thorough preparatory work, and special knowledge, breadth of intellectual understanding, talent for logical analysis, may under certain circumstances be sources of failure. The more accurately, however, we learn to know the natural and social world, the more perfect our control of facts becomes; and the greater the extent, with time and progressive rationalisation, within which things can be simply calculated, and indeed quickly and reliably calculated, the more the significance of this function decreases. Therefore the importance of the entrepreneur type must diminish just as the importance of the military commander has already diminished. Nevertheless a part of the very essence of each type is bound up with this function.

As this first point lies in the task, so the second lies in the psyche of the businessman himself. It is not only objectively more difficult to do something new than what is familiar and tested by experience, but the individual feels reluctance to it and would do so even if the objective difficulties did not exist. This is so in all fields. The history of science is one great confirmation of the fact that we find it exceedingly difficult to adopt a new scientific point of view or method. Thought turns again and again into the accustomed track even if it has become unsuitable and the more suitable innovation in itself presents no particular difficulties. The very nature of fixed habits of thinking, their energy-saving function, is founded upon the fact that they have become subconscious, that they yield their results automatically and are proof against criticism and even against contradiction by individual facts. But precisely because of this they become drag-chains when they have outlived their usefulness. So it is also in the economic world. In the breast of one who wishes to do something new, the forces of habit rise up and bear witness against the embryonic project. A new and another kind of effort of will is therefore necessary in order to wrest, amidst the work and care of the daily round, scope and time for conceiving and working out the new combination and to bring oneself to look upon it as a real possibility and not merely as a day-dream. This mental freedom presupposes a great surplus force over the everyday demand and is something peculiar and by nature rare.

The third point consists in the reaction of the social environment against one who wishes to do something new. This reaction may manifest itself first of all in the existence of legal or political impediments. But neglecting this, any deviating conduct by a member of a social group is condemned, though in greatly varying degrees according as the social group is used to such conduct or not. Even a deviation from social custom in such things as dress or manners arouses opposition, and of course all the more so in the graver cases. This opposition is stronger in primitive stages of culture than in others, but it is never absent. Even mere astonishment at the deviation, even merely noticing it, exercises a pressure on the individual. The manifestation of condemnation may at once bring noticeable consequences in its train. It may even come to social ostracism and finally to physical prevention or to direct attack. Neither the fact that progressive differentiation weakens this opposition—especially as the most important cause of the weakening is the very development which we wish to explain—nor the further fact that the social opposition operates under certain circumstances and upon many individuals as a stimulus, changes anything in principle in the significance of it. Surmounting this opposition is always a special kind of task which does not exist in the customary course of life, a task which also requires a special kind of conduct. In matters economic this resistance manifests itself first of all in the groups threatened by the innovation, then in the difficulty in finding the necessary cooperation, finally in the difficulty in winning over consumers. Even though these elements are still effective to-day, despite the fact that a period of turbulent development has accustomed us to the appearance and the carrying out of innovations, they can be best studied in the beginnings of capitalism. But they are so obvious there that it would be time lost for our purposes to dwell upon them.

There is leadership *only* for these reasons—leadership, that is, as a special kind of function and in contrast to a mere difference in rank, which would exist in every social body, in the smallest as in the largest, and in combination with which it generally appears. The facts alluded to create a boundary beyond which the majority of people do not function promptly by themselves and require help from a minority. If social life had in all respects the relative immutability of, for example, the astronomical world, or if mutable this mutability were yet incapable of being influenced by human action, or finally if capable of being so influenced this type of action were yet equally open to everyone, then there would be no special function of leadership as distinguished from routine work.

The specific problem of leadership arises and the leader type appears only where new possibilities present themselves. . . . Our three points characterise the nature of the *function* as well as the *conduct* or behavior which constitutes the leader type. It is no part of his function to "find" or to "create" new possibilities. They are always present, abundantly accumulated by all sorts of people. Often they are also generally known and being discussed by scientific or literary writers. In other cases, there is nothing to discover about them, because they are quite obvious. To take an example from political life, it was not at all difficult to see how the social and political conditions of France at the time of Louis XVI could have been improved so as to avoid a breakdown of the *ancien régime.* Plenty of people as a matter of fact did see it. But nobody was in a position to *do* it. Now, it is this "doing the thing," without which possibilities are dead, of which the leader's function consists. This holds good of all kinds of leadership, ephemeral as well as more enduring ones. The former may serve as an instance. What is to be done in a casual emergency is as a rule quite simple. Most or all people may see it, yet they want someone to speak out, to lead, and to organise. Even leadership which influences merely by example, as artistic or scientific leadership, does not consist simply in finding or creating the new thing but in so impressing the social group with it as to draw it on in its wake. It is, therefore, more by will than by intellect that the leaders fulfil their function, more by "authority," "personal weight," and so forth than by original ideas.

Economic leadership in particular must hence be distinguished from "invention." As long as they are not carried into practice, inventions are economically irrelevant. And to carry any improvement into effect is a task entirely different from the inventing of it, and a task, moreover, requiring entirely different kinds of aptitudes. . . .

The entrepreneurial kind of leadership, as distinguished from other kinds of economic leadership such as we should expect to find in a primitive tribe or a communist society, is of course colored by the conditions peculiar to it. It has none of that glamour which characterises other kinds of leadership. It consists in fulfilling a very special task which only in rare cases appeals to the imagination of the public. For its success, keenness and vigor are not more essential than a certain narrowness which seizes the immediate chance and *nothing else.* "Personal weight" is, to be sure, not without importance. Yet the personality of the capitalistic entrepreneur need not, and generally does not, answer to the idea most of us have of what a "leader" looks like,

so much so that there is some difficulty in realizing that he comes within the sociological category of leader at all. He "leads" the means of production into new channels. But this he does, not by convincing people of the desirability of carrying out his plan or by creating confidence in his leading in the manner of a political leader—the only man he has to convince or to impress is the banker who is to finance him—but by buying them or their services, and then using them as he sees fit. He also leads in the sense that he draws other producers in his branch after him. But as they are his competitors, who first reduce and then annihilate his profit, this is, as it were, leadership against one's own will. Finally, he renders a service, the full appreciation of which takes a specialist's knowledge of the case. It is not so easily understood by the public at large as a politician's successful speech or a general's victory in the field, not to insist on the fact that he seems to act—and often harshly—in his individual interest alone. We shall understand, therefore, that we do not observe, in this case, the emergence of all those affective values which are the glory of all other kinds of social leadership. Add to this the precariousness of the economic position both of the individual entrepreneur and of entrepreneurs as a group, and the fact that when his economic success raises him socially he has no cultural tradition or attitude to fall back upon, but moves about in society as an upstart, whose ways are readily laughed at, and we shall understand why this type has never been popular, and why even scientific critique often makes short work of it.[4] . . .

ENDNOTES

1. Cf. for example the good description in Wiedenfeld, *Das Persönliche im modernen Unternehmertum.* Although it appeared in Schmoller's *Jahrbuch* in 1910 this work was not known to me when the first edition of this book was published.

2. On the nature of the entrepreneurial function also compare my statement in the article "Unternehmer" in the *Handwörterbuch der Staatswissenschaften.*

3. In the first place it is a question of a type of *conduct* and of a type of *person* in so far as this conduct is accessible in very unequal measure and to relatively few people, so that it constitutes their outstanding characteristic. . . . The conduct in question is peculiar in two ways. First, because it is directed towards something different and signifies doing something different from other conduct. One may indeed in this connection include it with the latter in a higher unity, but this does not alter the fact that a theoretically relevant difference exists between the two, and that only one of them is adequately described by traditional theory. Secondly, the type

of conduct in question not only differs from the other in its object, "innovation" being peculiar to it, but also in that it presupposes aptitudes differing *in kind* and not only in degree from those of mere rational economic behavior.

4. It may, therefore, not be superfluous to point out that our analysis of the rôle of the entrepreneur does not involve any "glorification" of the type, as some readers of the first edition of this book seemed to think. We do hold that entrepreneurs *have* an economic function as distinguished from, say, robbers. But we neither style every entrepreneur a genius or a benefactor to humanity, nor do we wish to express any opinion about the comparative merits of the social organisation in which he plays his rôle, or about the question whether what he does could not be effected more cheaply or efficiently in other ways.

QUESTIONS ON SCHUMPETER

1. How does Schumpeter define the function of the entrepreneur? How is the function of entrepreneurship often mixed with other economic functions? How does entrepreneurship require that one challenge the flow of routine and custom?

2. Schumpeter refers to the entrepreneur as exhibiting leadership. How is this leadership understood? Does this leadership involve courage?

3. What psychological characteristics do you associate with ownership? With managerial decision making? With entrepreneurship?

Why Profits Are Deserved

N. Scott Arnold

N. Scott Arnold is Professor of Philosophy at the University of Alabama, Birmingham. He is the author of Marx's Radical Critique of Capitalist Society *(1990) and* The Philosophy and Economics of Market Socialism, *(1994), and is a co-editor of* Philosophy Then and Now *(1998). A complete version of this essay can be found in* Ethics *(1987).*

. . . What I should like to do in this paper is to examine the category of profit in the light of contemporary distribution theory. Specifically, I want to argue that, in general, those who win profits in a market system deserve them. How considerations of desert fit into a theory of justice or ethical theory in general is far from clear.[1] However, it seems reasonable to suppose that, if some-

one deserves something, that is a prima facie reason why he ought to receive it. Thus if it can be shown that, in general, those who get profits deserve them, it will not follow that they ought to have them, all things considered. It would, however, be one reason in favor of that.

I shall begin by sketching a theory of the nature of profit in a market economy. Following that will be a general account of how desert claims are justified in institutional contexts. Finally, I shall apply these results to the question of whether profits are deserved.

I

As it was traditionally conceived, profit was the income that accrued to the owner of the firm after he paid off the work force and suppliers and set aside some funds for capital depreciation. In short, profits constituted the income of the capitalists. After the Marginalist Revolution of the 1870s it became evident that this picture obscured the fact that this income arose from two very different sources. These sources correspond to the two different roles that the owner of the firm plays. As a capitalist, he is a provider of capital goods for which he receives a return on his investment (over and above replacement costs). This role is functionally indistinguishable from that of a bondholder to whom interest is paid. The term "interest" took on a broader significance to include the return on investment to owners of capital. In a competitive economy, this rate of return tends toward equality as resources are shifted from less productive to more productive uses. The other source of income accruing to the owner of the firm is the result of his entrepreneurship. In the most dramatic cases, the entrepreneur is a great innovator and gambler. He conceives of a whole new product or service and brings together the needed factors of production. Entrepreneurship is not management; indeed, often entrepreneurs hire others to manage the firm. Entrepreneurship consists essentially of organizing production—deciding what to produce, when to produce it, and how much to produce at what price.[2] The gains, if any, that the entrepreneur reaps over and above the going rate of interest constitute what economists, following Frank Knight,[3] have called "pure profits" (hereafter just "profits"). . . .

. . . Suppose an entrepreneur figures out a way to drive down production costs (e.g., by adopting a certain technological or organizational innovation). The marginal value product of some of his factors of production will go up, since he is using less of them, let us suppose, to produce the product. However, he is paying the factor owners the going rate. The spread between cost and price is his profit. A similar situation arises when a new product is produced and marketed for which there is great demand. Obviously, these situations cannot last, since competitors will imitate successful entrepreneurs; as a result, factor prices will tend to be bid up and product prices will tend to be driven down. Thus there will be a tendency for profits to be wiped out as a new equilibrium is approached. In this sense, all (pure) profits are ephemeral.

This story can be complicated in various ways to reflect more completely the real world. . . . However, the main source of profits in the final analysis is the malallocation of factors of production. This malallocation results from the fact that technology, consumer tastes, and other ultimate determinants of value are in a constant state of flux. Since no one is omniscient, some factors of production are always being used in nonoptimal ways. The successful entrepreneur is the one who is alert to differences in the marginal value products of factors of production and is in a position to do something about it. As Israel Kirzner has said, "Profit opportunities arise when the prices of products on the product markets are not adjusted to the price of resource services on the factor markets."[4] Other potential entrepreneurs are unaware of these discrepancies; otherwise they would have been competed away. The successful entrepreneur, then, can be characterized as someone who exploits social ignorance about the malallocation of resources.

An ethical evaluation of profit does not follow directly from a positive theory of the nature of profit. However, the latter suggests the outlines of such an evaluation that is probably consonant with a broad spectrum of opinion on morality and the marketplace, to wit: that entrepreneurial profit (which is, at bottom, pure speculative gain) is, on its face, ethically dubious but on balance morally acceptable because of its crucial functional significance in the successful operation of a market system. Libertarians and hard-line socialists who eschew markets would object to this ethical evaluation, but my guess is that, for those in between, this evaluation is attractive if not explicitly articulated. In what follows I should like to challenge this view directly by arguing that entrepreneurial profits are actually deserved by those who capture them. . . .

II

To make this case, it will be necessary to develop a general account of what it is to deserve something. Desert, in its primary sense, is a three-place relation among persons, things deserved, and what Feinberg calls basal reasons, that is, some fact about the person which grounds or warrants the desert claim. A general account of desert must explain what determines the basal reason(s) for desert claims as well as what determines the objects of desert or things deserved. Let us consider basal reasons first.

Basal Reasons

In his *Treatise of Human Nature,* Hume distinguishes natural and artificial virtues. The former are those "habits of mind" toward which we naturally feel approval. The artificial virtues—primarily justice according to Hume—do not command this instinctive approval. The approval they occasion is the result of artifice or convention. In more contemporary terms, these virtues might be called 'institutional.' If we think of basal reasons that warrant (positive) desert claims as virtues, Hume's distinction suggests that there are two kinds of desert claims—institutional and noninstitutional. The latter directly reflect general moral assessments of a person's character. Thus it is in this sense that good people deserve to be happy (Kant's *Summum Bonum*) and wicked people deserve to be miserable. On the other hand, institutional deserts are logically connected to particular social institutions.[5] The basal reasons (artificial virtues) that ground desert claims are determined by the nature of the institution and need not have any independent significance. . . .

In an institutional setting, the basal reason for a desert claim is determined by the goals or purposes of the institution. Consider a championship sporting event such as the World Series in baseball. The basal reason—being the best team—warrants claims of desert. If it is asked *why* being the best team warrants a desert claim, it is necessary to look to the institution's goals or purposes. In this case, the relevant goal or purpose is to discover and give positive recognition to the best team. Of course, the institution has other goals, such as making money and providing entertainment. However, for any social institution in which desert claims can be made, there is a goal or set of goals that are essential in that the institution would of necessity cease to exist if it lacked those goals.[6] A World Series could exist even if it made no money. It could not exist if it was not intended to discover the best team in U.S. professional baseball. It is these essential goals that determine basal reasons for desert claims.

Notice that it is possible for a person or group to deserve something without being *entitled* to it (and vice versa).[7] Entitlements are rights generated by the rules of the institution. They specify certain performance criteria, the satisfaction of which entitles the person to claim various benefits; some of the latter are the objects of desert (e.g., victory, prizes). However, entitlement and desert may diverge. For example, in a footrace, the runner who crosses the finish line first (without violating certain side constraints) is entitled to claim victory and the prize. However, he might not have deserved victory if, say, the fastest runner unavoidably tripped. The latter deserved to win, though he is not entitled to claim victory or the prize. The reason he deserved to win is that the essential goal of the institution is to discover and give positive recognition to the fastest runner (among the competitors). The rules are designed to determine who that is in the most effective way. For footraces it is rare that the fastest runner (on that day) fails to win. The same is true of well-designed academic tests. In such tests, students who deserve A's (because they know the material best) will, for the most part, get them, and those who get A's will deserve them. . . .

Objects of Desert

The objects of desert or things deserved are also determined by the institution's essential goals, though in this case the determination is indirect instead of direct. To illustrate, consider contests. One of the things deserved in a contest is victory. Some of the entitlement rules specify conditions that must be met for someone to claim victory. These entitlement rules will be a subset of the rules which define the institution itself. Let us call them achievement rules since they specify what counts as a (positive or negative) achievement relative to the institution's essential goal. Of course, as noted above, these entitlement rules cannot guarantee that the entitled person will be the one who deserved the achievement; luck almost always can be a factor. But, and this is the crucial point, the rules are designed to bring desert and entitlement together. If the essential purpose of a contest is to determine who has the greatest skill of a certain sort, the achievement rules will be designed to find that out.

Achievement rules can be justified or criticized in relation to the institution's essential goal. If the achievement rules do not regularly bring it about that the most deserving persons are entitled to the achievement (and the consequent rewards or punishments, if any), the rules are defective. Who the most deserving persons are is determined by the basal reason, which in turn is determined by the institution's essential goal. If the rules only accidentally bring desert and entitlement together, then the institution is not what it appears to be.

Other objects of desert such as prizes and awards (or, negatively, punishments) are directly specified by another subset of the entitlement rules (e.g., the winner is entitled to a certain cash prize), which can be called 'reward rules.' The general character of the things deserved (as specified by these reward rules) is also determined by the institution's essential goals. Thus, Miss America deserves publicity and other things she would positively value (e.g., cash), since the essential purpose of the contest is to recognize, promote, and honor feminine virtues and excellences in America. A pie in the face resulting in public humiliation would be inappropriate given the essential goals of the institution. Nonessential goals and conventional elements can shape the exact nature of the (reward rules specifying the) things deserved. For example, a particular brand of goods may be awarded in exchange for promotional considerations. Nonetheless, what counts as appropriate or inappropriate will depend on what furthers the essential goal of the institution. This is why the reward rules guaranteeing publicity are appropriate whereas a rule guaranteeing a pie in the face would be inappropriate.

This suggests how reward rules can be criticized or justified, namely, by an appeal to the institution's essential goals. If part of the essential goal of the institution is to give positive recognition to a complex of characteristics, the reward rules can be criticized on the grounds that they are inappropriate for that goal. The rewards offered might be judged ugly or offensive or, what is perhaps more common, insufficiently attractive to motivate the best potential participants to participate in the institution (or, on the other side, to deter the most likely participants, as in the case of the law); the reward rules, like the achievement rules, can be justified (criticized) in terms of what promotes (impedes) the institution's essential goal. . . .

. . . Both achievement and reward rules can be criticized (or justified) on grounds of proportionality. If an institution fails to take this into account in its achievement and reward rules, then participants in the institution will not be getting their deserts. This proportionality principle, as it might be called, is a consequence of the root idea of desert, namely, that there should be a "fit" between the basal reason and the things deserved. The nature and degree of that "fit" is determined by the institution's essential goal. For example, if the essential purpose of the institution of academic testing is to reflect accurately (within limits) students' knowledge of certain material and mastery of certain skills, something like a standard A through F grading scale is appropriate (or more appropriate), whereas a pass/fail system is inappropriate (or less appropriate). On the other hand, professional licensing or certification exams are often graded on a pass/fail basis, since the essential purpose of such tests is to certify a minimum level of competence. The object of desert is this certification, so the "fit" between the basal reason and the object of desert is not a matter of more or less. More fine-grained distinctions about competencies based on such tests are probably neither feasible nor necessary. . . .

A more fundamental objection to this general account of institutional desert surfaces when one considers institutions which are, by their very nature, morally objectionable. For example, if a criminal society sets up a competition of some sort to recognize and honor criminal skills, there could be desert claims made within this institutional context. What possible moral significance could such claims have? Perhaps the institutional desert claims of the sort identified in this essay are not moral in character.

The objection proceeds too quickly; from the fact that someone deserves something, it does not follow that, all things considered, he ought to get it. As I suggested at the beginning of this essay, desert claims are best thought of as having prima facie significance. An analogy with promise keeping is illuminating: from the fact that A promises B to do *x,* one cannot conclude that A ought to do *x.* It is, however, one reason in favor of A's doing *x,* though that reason may be overridden by other moral considerations. Similarly, desert claims within evil institutions do, on the interpretation offered here, have some moral significance, but such claims are easily trumped by a consideration of the wickedness of the institution in question. The institution of the Mafia comes to mind in this connection. Our sentiments are decidedly mixed when we consider the assertion that a lieutenant who double-crossed the godfather got what he deserved.

These concerns point to the larger question of how social institutions themselves are to be morally justified. Obviously, an adequate answer to this question cannot be given here. Nonetheless, institutional desert claims retain significance, however the larger question is to be answered. Their significance is best appreciated from the point of view of the reformer as opposed to that of the revolutionary. If entitlements significantly and systematically diverge from deserts (the latter, as I have shown, can be identified independently of the entitlement rules), that fact can serve as grounds for criticizing and urging reform of the entitlement rules (though these need not be the only morally relevant grounds for criticizing the entitlement rules). For example, if, as I shall argue, entrepreneurs generally deserve their profits in a market system, entitlement rules (i.e., laws) that impose confiscatory taxes on these profits violate the deserts of

successful entrepreneurs; this is one reason why such taxes should not be imposed, even if this is not decisive or the only morally relevant consideration. On the other hand, the revolutionary wants to destroy existing institutions and replace them by different ones, perhaps because he believes that existing institutions do not adequately meet their essential goals. Both he and his supporters—as well as his critics—bear a heavy burden of proof; they must provide an account of how social institutions themselves are to be justified. By contrast, institutional desert claims are not justified at this fundamental level. Consequently, in the next section I shall make no attempt to justify "the market" as such. However, as I shall suggest at the end of this essay, this omission is not as serious as it might first appear.

III

It is now possible to consider the question of whether or not entrepreneurs deserve their profits in a market system. It is important to distinguish this question from a similar one about entitlements. Entitlements in the marketplace are determined by legal rules. The extent to which entrepreneurs are entitled to profits in a given market system can be discovered by reading the relevant part of the legal code. The question at issue here concerns desert. Furthermore, it is entrepreneurial profit that is at stake, not interest or rate of return on investment to capitalists qua capitalists.[8] Terms like 'capitalist' and 'entrepreneur' are functional, and it often happens that the two functions are exercised by one and the same individual. In this essay my concern is with the pure profits generated in the process of change in the structure of production. In what follows I should like to examine two attempts to justify the claim that, in general, entrepreneurs deserve their profits.

Profits as a Reward for Bearing Uncertainty

Although entrepreneurs need not be capitalists, they usually are. The entrepreneurial function consists in organizing (or reorganizing) productive resources. Typically, the entrepreneur will have to put some of his own assets (not to mention his reputation) on the line. Because a market system is in a constant state of flux, it is rare that anyone can genuinely know that a new or expanded venture will result in a better allocation of resources. The pervasive uncertainty of profit opportunities was thought by some earlier apologists for capitalism (e.g., J. B. Clark) to serve as a basal reason for a desert claim by entrepreneurs. That is, entrepreneurs deserve their profits as a reward for bearing uncertainty.

The main problem with this account of why entrepreneurs deserve their profits concerns what I have called the "proportionality principle." The basal reason—bearing uncertainty—is a magnitude, as is the thing deserved—profits. However, the proportionality principle will not in general hold. It might be thought that the more uncertain the investment, the larger will be the profits, if the venture pays off. Sometimes this is true, but there is no reason to think it will hold in general. The size of the profits that can be won depends ultimately on the existing malallocation of resources. If the entrepreneur is especially alert or if he uniquely possesses certain information, the uncertainty he faces might be small relative to his profits. Contrariwise, a small profit might be earned on a big gamble. If entrepreneurs in general deserve their profits, it is not because profits are a reward for bearing uncertainty.

Profits as a Reward for Entrepreneurial Creativity

A more promising approach suggests itself if we recall that the basal reason for a desert claim is determined by the essential purpose of the institution in question. The institution is the market in exchangeable goods and services. What is its essential purpose? . . .

To pin down the essential goal or purpose of a market system, consider what a market system *is*.[9] A market system is a production-distribution system which allocates, via voluntary exchange, (rights over) scarce goods and resources. The social point (essential goal) of this allocational system is to meet the wants and needs of the consumers that can be satisfied by scarce and exchangeable goods and services. This is true even if this allocation is not optimal and even if not all exchangeable goods and services are (or should be) allocated by market mechanisms.

To see what might count as a basal reason for a desert claim for entrepreneurs, consider what entrepreneurs actually do in a market system. Primarily, entrepreneurs are those who control productive resources (natural resources, labor, and capital). They decide which configurations of productive resources will exist and which will not. This entails making decisions about what to produce, how much to produce, what price to charge, and so on—or to set the broad parameters within which these decisions are to be made and to hire people to work out the details. (Deciding whom to hire is often the most critical task an entrepreneur executes.) Entrepreneurship is most visible in the waves of "creative destruction" described so eloquently by Schumpeter,[10] which are generated by, among other things, dramatic changes in tastes, discovery of new resources, and perhaps most importantly, advances in technology. Such developments create significant profit opportunities which entrepreneurs seek to exploit. However, in an enormously complex market economy, there will be many profit opportunities (some large, but many small) which can be exploited by those alert to inefficiencies in existing ways of doing business. This suggests that the basal reason for a desert claim on behalf of entrepreneurs is their alertness to an inoptimal allocation of resources. Entrepreneurial alertness uncovers malallocations of resources. But why do they deserve the profits they uncover rather than, say, a pat on the back and a letter of commendation?

The appropriateness or "fittingness" of (a rule) allowing entrepreneurs to keep the profits they have uncovered consists in the fact that this rule brings control over productive resources together with personal responsibility for results. This rule best promotes the essential goal of the market for three reasons:

> i) If an entrepreneur (a controller of productive forces) cannot keep the profits he discovers, the cost (i.e., his cost) of forgoing innovation and reallocating resources goes down dramatically. Conversely, if he is allowed to keep the profits, the cost of not correcting a perceived malallocation of resources can be quite high. (The cost of something is the value of the most favorable forgone opportunity, but it is the forgone opportunity for the person doing the choosing, i.e., those in control.)

> ii) Another consequence of allowing entrepreneurs to keep the profits is that it tends to give (proportionate) control over productive resources to those who have demonstrated a capacity to use such resources wisely (i.e., to meet effectively the wants and needs of the consumers). The successful entrepreneur retains control over the productive resources under his command and usually reinvests some of his profits in an attempt to capture more profits. It might be objected that it is rare for an entrepreneur to have more than one or perhaps a couple of good ideas in the course of his career. However, this objection is based on a misconception about who the entrepreneurs are. Not all—or even most—entrepreneurs are inventors with a little marketing skill. In a capitalist economy, they are the independent businessmen, the promoters, the managers of large corporations with significant stock holdings, the arbitrage experts in the stock market, the instigators of hostile takeovers, and so on—and to a lesser extent, anyone who owns any stock in a firm; in short, entrepreneurs are the ones who decide where and how capital should be invested. They shape the structure of production in virtue of their control over productive resources, and their ideas are continually tested in the market.

> iii) Finally, the winning of big profits by some serves as an effective signal to competitors to follow suit by making

appropriate changes—or suffer the consequences. In a market economy there is a tendency for all (pure) profits to be competed away as factor prices are bid up and product prices are driven down; except for monopoly profits, all profits are ephemeral. However, if entrepreneurs were not allowed to keep their profits, it is not at all clear that those in control would rearrange the structure of production in such a way that these profits—and the malallocation of resources they represent—would disappear.

Notice that this account of the entrepreneur's deserts satisfies the proportionality principle. The bigger an entrepreneur's profits, the more serious had been the malallocation of resources. Finally, it is worth pointing out that this justification of the reward rule about entrepreneurial profit is consequentialist but not (or not necessarily) utilitarian. The essential purpose of the market is to meet people's wants and needs for scarce and exchangeable goods and services; promoting this goal may or may not maximize utility. However, observing this rule would, for the most part, give entrepreneurs their just deserts. . . .

Thus far the profits that have been discussed are the positive ones; the other side of the coin is equally important. This account of the deserts of entrepreneurs can also be applied to entrepreneurial losses (negative profits). If an entrepreneur acts on a false belief that resources could be better allocated in a certain way, he will suffer losses. In general, this is as it should be since, in retrospect, it is clear that he has squandered social wealth and impeded the essential purpose of the market system. In addition, allowing entrepreneurs to suffer their losses satisfies the proportionality principle—if the losses are big, the entrepreneur has seriously misallocated resources. Finally there are two further socially useful consequences of allowing entrepreneurs to suffer their losses—it tends to remove control over resources from those who use them unwisely, and it serves as a warning to others to avoid similar mistakes.

To sum up, the crucial point is that bringing control of productive resources together with personal responsibility for results best serves the essential function of the market. For entrepreneurs are the ones in control, the ones most directly responsible for shaping the structure of production. Rewarding them with profits and punishing them with losses (for their entrepreneurial alertness or thickheadedness as the case may be) is the most appropriate way for the market to bestow praise and blame. Attenuating the link between control and responsibility, either by confiscating (wholly or in part) the profits of successful entrepreneurs or by, for example, taxing citizens to cover entrepreneurial losses, impedes the market's essential function. . . .

IV

This completes my defense of the claim that entrepreneurs, by and large, deserve the profits they uncover. (I say, 'by and large' since no system can guarantee that desert and entitlement will always correspond.) One surprising consequence of this analysis is that capital gains taxes are, prima facie, immoral. However, there seems to be something suspiciously conservative about this account of who deserves profits. Those who deserve profits are those in control of the forces of production, the entrepreneurs. But what justifies their being in control in the first place? After all, not all of the assets entrepreneurs use to capture profits are themselves deserved profits that have been previously won. If possession of these assets is not deserved, then, so the objection runs, perhaps any profits that are won are not deserved. Indeed, if entrepreneurial alertness (itself an asset) is a natural talent, it too seems to be undeserved. In short, the undeserved nature of the asset base calls into question the entrepreneur's claims of desert.

The problem with this objection is that it rests on the principle that the assets used to capture objects of desert must themselves be deserved. However, this principle seems false.[11] Natural athletic talent is not deserved, and yet it is a major asset used to win things deserved. The only relevant constraint on assets is that the user be entitled to use the assets. A boy who has an engineer build his soap box racer does not deserve to win the Soap Box Derby because the rules of the institution require that the boy not get that kind of help. The analysis of institutional desert defended in this essay shows that the justification of desert claims need not be so "deep." Provided that the entrepreneur is entitled to use his assets, the mere fact that he does not deserve those assets cannot be used to subvert a desert claim.

Although these considerations show that one kind of attack on the rewards (and penalties) of entrepreneurs is misguided, they do not really show that entrepreneurs should be entitled to the assets they use to capture profits. In short, what justifies the entitlement rules themselves? To a certain extent, this question lies beyond the scope of this essay; some of the entitlement rules define the institution, so to justify these rules is to justify the institution itself. This sort of question needs to be taken up at a deeper level of analysis than can be provided here. However, this account of who deserves profits in a market system does permit the following relevant observations: (*a*) As noted in Section II, considerations of desert are relevant to the justification or criticism of at least some of the entitlement rules, especially the achievement and reward rules. Since (as I have argued) deserts can be identified independently of entitlements, some of the entitlement rules can be justified or criticized on grounds of desert. (*b*) In a related vein, it should not be assumed that existing market systems perfectly apportion the objects of desert to those who deserve them, even aside from the usual vagaries due to luck. A case could be made for the claim that sometimes nonentrepreneurs deserve some profits. A worker who makes a suggestion which allows a firm to produce more efficiently, thereby allowing it to capture for a time some (pure) profits, would deserve some of those profits. In a capitalist system, such a worker sometimes gets some of these profits in the form of a bonus, but sometimes he does not, in which case he is not getting his deserts. However, he may not deserve all the profits his suggestion generates. Those in control may have exercised entrepreneurial alertness in hiring him over someone else[12] or in setting up a work environment more conducive to creative suggestions from employees. Finally, not all apparently good suggestions will produce benefits for the firm. It takes a special talent to separate the good ideas from the apparently plausible but ultimately unsuccessful ones. So, some employees are in part responsible for generating (positive) profits; their deserts are proportional. On the other hand, some employees are responsible for generating negative profits. They deserve to suffer some of the losses subsequently incurred. (*c*) Perhaps most important, the account of who deserves profits defended in this essay is completely general and is not restricted to capitalist market systems. This is significant in light of the fact that a new generation of socialist critics of capitalism believe that markets will have to be more or less widely employed if and when capitalism is abolished.[13] Under alternative institutional arrangements, however, the locus of entrepreneurship will shift. In a Yugoslav-type system, the workers in individual firms jointly exercise considerable entrepreneurship, since they decide some investment questions (or hire those who do—itself an entrepreneurial act) and receive consequent profits and losses. From the point of view of (institutional) desert, a particular market system can be justly criticized only if those who are responsible for changing the structure of production to capture profits are systematically prevented from getting those profits (or suffering the losses, as the case may be). Some market socialists have recognized the importance of tying responsibility for entrepreneurship to profit and loss. From the point of view of desert, this is appropriate.

In closing I would like to consider an objection to the general account of desert offered here and its application to market systems. Earlier I noted that desert claims could be made within the context of institutions which are, on balance, morally objectionable. Clearly such desert claims have, in the final analysis, little moral significance. Radical socialist criticisms of market systems would seem to call into question the moral significance of the claim that, in general, entrepreneurs deserve their profits.

It is true that if, morally speaking, the market system is on a par with the security organs of a secret police state, the desert claims of entrepreneurs would be of little ultimate significance. This turns out not to be a very serious problem. Though the abolition of all market relations used to be high on the socialist agenda (see Marx's *Critique of the Gotha Program*), twentieth-century experience with command economies has changed that agenda. Command economies, such as that of the Soviet Union, have structural problems that do not stem from wickedness and corruption.[14] The idea that complete central planning should entirely replace market structures is not on the agenda of socialists who think seriously about economics. The debate today, among those who deserve to be taken seriously, is not over whether or not markets should be abolished but over how extensive they should be and how they should be organized. The analysis given here provides part of an ethical perspective from which to view this debate.

ENDNOTES

1. Rawls, e.g., explicitly excludes considerations of desert from his theory. See John Rawls, *A Theory of Justice* (Cambridge, Mass.: Harvard University Press, 1971), pp. 104, 310–15.
2. For a more complete discussion of the role of the entrepreneur, see Israel Kirzner, *Competition and Entrepreneurship* (Chicago: University of Chicago Press, 1973), chap. 2.
3. Frank Knight, *Risk, Uncertainty, and Profit* (Chicago: University of Chicago Press, 1971).
4. Kirzner, p. 85.
5. By 'institution' I mean a social activity governed by more or less explicit rules, which has, as part of its purpose, the distribution of certain benefits and/or costs. (Some of these benefits and costs will be objects of desert.) This notion is broad enough to include what social scientists call 'social practices' but not so broad to include things such as languages. The notion is a bit fuzzy but, as subsequent

examples will indicate, clear enough for the purposes at hand. Which institutions have deserts attached to them and why are questions I shall not explicitly address in this essay.

6. Talk about the essential goal of an institution obviously depends on a favored description of that institution; how one justifies one such description as favored is far from clear. For the purposes of this essay, I shall assume that the sort of distinction I am calling attention to here can be made and leave it to metaphysicians to give an adequate account of it.

7. Feinberg discusses this distinction, though it is not clear that he would agree with my account of it. See Joel Feinberg, "Justice and Personal Desert," in *Doing and Deserving* (Princeton, N.J.: Princeton University Press, 1970), pp. 55–87. See also John Kleinig, "The Concept of Desert," *American Philosophical Quarterly* 8 (1971): 71–78, p. 74.

8. I have discussed elsewhere the morality of the capitalist's (qua capitalist) return on investment. See my "Capitalists and the Ethics of Contribution," *Canadian Journal of Philosophy* 15 (1985): 89–105.

9. See n, 6 above.

10. Joseph Schumpeter, *Capitalism, Socialism, and Democracy* (New York: Harper & Row 1976), pp. 81–87.

11. Robert Nozick has also argued against this principle. See his *Anarchy, State and Utopia* (New York: Basic Books, 1975), pp. 222, 223.

12. See Kirzner, chap. 2.

13. See, e.g., David Schweickart, *Capitalism or Worker Control?* (New York: Praeger Publishing Co., 1980); and Branko Horvat, *The Political Economy of Socialism* (Armonk, N.Y.: M. E. Sharpe, 1982).

14. For a good theoretical discussion of why central planning cannot replace markets without incurring gross inefficiencies, see Don Lavoie, "A Critique of the Standard Account of the Socialist Calculation Debate," *Journal of Libertarian Studies* 3 (1981): 41–87.

QUESTIONS ON ARNOLD

1. Summarize in your own words how the concept of desert is a three-place relation between a person, a thing deserved, and a basal reason which grounds the claim of desert. Why do entrepreneurs deserve their profits? Is there any sense in which workers could deserve some share of the profit?

2. How does Arnold understand the essential goal of a market? How does this goal relate to a basal reason for deserving profits? Does a market, in fact, have a clear function or goal?

3. Is Arnold's conception of desert one that relies on the consequences of allowing entrepreneurs to keep their profits? If I deserve something, do I deserve it *because* of the consequences?

Entrepreneurs, Profits, and Deserving Market Shares

John Christman

John Christman is Associate Professor of Philosophy at Pennsylvania State University. He is the author of The Myth of Property: Toward an Egalitarian Theory of Ownership *(1994). This excerpt is taken from the essay published in* Social Philosophy and Policy *(1988).*

INTRODUCTION

The question I wish to take up in this paper is whether competitive markets, as mechanisms that initiate the distribution of scarce goods, allocate those goods in accordance with what participants in those markets deserve. I want to argue that in general people do not in fact deserve what they get from market interactions, when "what they get" is determined by the competitive forces coming to bear on the market (the laws of supply and demand). This more general claim is meant to apply to all participants in the market (workers and their wages as well as capitalists and their profits). However, my strategy here is to focus on the particular case of the role of entrepreneurs, as I will define them, and whether they deserve the profits they reap in a competitive capitalist market. In particular, I will argue that the claim that entrepreneurs deserve their profits, when spelled out precisely, is indeed not plausible. Generalizing from this claim, I want to suggest how moral desert is inappropriate as a justification of market shares whenever competition determines the magnitude of those shares.

I should stress, though, the particularity of my central claim: it is that "(strictly speaking) entrepreneurs do not (strictly speaking) deserve their (strictly speaking) profits."[1] This is not to say that, for *other* reasons (for example, reasons of entitlement or utility), people should not receive the rewards doled out by a market. My claim is only that desert has nothing directly to do with it. . . .

I. ENTREPRENEURS AND PROFITS

The term "entrepreneur" has been used variously to refer to anyone from a robber baron to a small shop owner to a money lender. There seem to emerge, however, two components to these usages that also fit with some of the standard economic definitions.[2] These are that the entrepreneur is the primary organizer of production and that she is the person or persons who holds primary title to the capital assets of the firm. Both of these notions can be summarized by calling the entrepreneur, simply, the person who owns, or comes to own, the productive factors of a firm. . . .

An entrepreneur who owns the capital assets of the firm will have final say over how those assets are utilized. The entrepreneur is the *primary* organizer of production in that she holds ultimate organizational control even if she chooses to delegate managerial functions to representatives—i.e., she could hire consultants and managers. But in such a case, the entrepreneur still has the primary organizational control insofar as whomever she hires, she can also *fire,* if not tell what to do. So in this sense, the entrepreneur is the primary organizer of production. In short, the entrepreneur is the person who perceives a certain malallocation of resources, information, or technology, and exploits this situation by starting a firm.[3] Even if all the start-up capital was borrowed, even if managers and consultants were hired to carry out the organizational tasks, it is the entrepreneur who begins the process and thus is the focus of my inquiry.

Turning now to "profits." . . . Generally speaking, profit is the difference between the market price for a good and the total cost of its production. Hence, in imperfect markets, the price of production (where that includes wages, rents, interest on borrowed capital,[4] etc.) may differ from the price of the good produced yielded by the market. Pure profit is this difference, whether it is positive or negative (though here I simplify and only speak of positive profits).[5] . . .

Now under conditions of perfect competition—ideal markets—an equilibrium will be reached at which profits for all firms will be zero. This results from constantly emerging competitors entering any market sector where firms are enjoying positive profit, thus driving prices down until they do not exceed the costs of production. But in real world markets, positive profits emerge when there is not completely free and costless shifting of resources. This malallocation of resources (where that includes information, technology, or even credit) allows for the market price of a commodity to stabilize above the marginal costs of the production of that commodity. An entrepreneur exploits the opportunity to produce such a good at a cost lower than the price the market will yield and to do so before others do.

So profits only arise when there is a sufficient lack of competition from other potential producers of the good. What *determines* the margin of profit is the presence of effective barriers to the entrance into the market of other producers. This could be caused in any number of ways: monopolies of various kinds (on resources or technology), high transaction costs, lack of credit for start-up capital, lack of information about consumer demand, etc. None of these factors are things an entrepreneur brings about herself (we are supposing), but they are nevertheless crucial in the determination of the size of the profit returned to the firm (and thus to the entrepreneur).

This is not to deny the importance of consumer demand for the economic success of a firm. But an essential determinant of that success—what determines the margin of profit—is the relative competitive threat posed by other producers. So entrepreneurial profits are the result of *both* consumer demand and the presence or absence of competing firms. This point, as we shall see, is crucial to my argument.

We come now to the concept of moral desert. This notion has been given a much recognized structural analysis by Joel Feinberg along the following lines: "S deserves X in virtue of F, where S is a person, X some mode of treatment, and F some fact about S, [and] the values of F (the desert bases) are determined in part by the nature of the various X's in question."[6] So a person deserves some benefit or loss (simplifying the possibilities) when there is some fact about her that is generally accepted as providing a reason grounding such a claim. And the response in question is both appropriate for, and proportional to, the relevant characteristics of the desert bases.

In addition, the concept of desert is an essentially nonconsequentialist notion. The justification of a particular claim to deserve something cannot, by the logic of the term, make reference to the results or consequences of the person's getting the reward or punishment in question. This is not to say that consequences are barred from consideration at the level of evaluating the bases of the desert claim. We do say, for example, that the criminal *caused* harm and therefore deserves punishment. But it is inappropriate to justify the reward or punishment *itself* with regards to *its* consequences. We will see in Section IV the relevance of this fact. Also, for the purposes of this paper, I will view desert claims as *prima facie* moral claims, which provide a defeasible moral reason that the deserving person(s) should receive the thing or mode of treatment deserved. This is not to say that denying the appropriateness of a desert claim rules out various alternative justifications for the receipt of some treatment, but the desert claim can be separated out of the justification and tested for its independent plausibility.

The conditions of propriety and proportionality necessitate further attention, as they will be crucial in the arguments to follow. For a person to deserve, for example, a favorable mode of treatment like praise, there must be some fact about her that provides a basis for that praise. If she performed some difficult and noble act, for example, then we would say the praise is deserved. But what must also be true for it to hold that she deserves the particular bit of praise offered, is both that praise is an appropriate response to the behavior in question and that the amount of praise given is proportional to the goodness or nobility of the acts. If the condition of proportionality[7] is violated—when the response is too much or too little—we say that the person in question does not deserve *that*.[8]

Another way to put the proportionality condition is this: it must be the case that the magnitude of the benefit or harm deserved is *determined by* the moral evaluation of the factors upon which the desert claim is based. Proportionality does not mean merely an accidental correlation of one with the other, but a relation between the two where the person receives a certain mode of treatment *because* of the characteristics calling for that treatment. That is, S deserves X in virtue of F only when the nature of X—its magnitude and quality—is determined in strict accordance with the value or disvalue of F. . . .

II. A DEFENSE OF ENTREPRENEURIAL DESERT CLAIMS

In "Why Profits are Deserved,"[9] N. Scott Arnold defends the claim that the fact entrepreneurs do deserve their profits. Arnold's strategy for supporting this position is along these lines. He accepts, in general, the Feinberg-type analysis of "desert" I discussed, but he spells out an additional kind of desert claim which he calls "institutional." What he has in mind is a desert claim which may be valid based solely on its relation to an institutional setting of some sort. An example is a baseball game, where the best team deserves to win because it is part of the "essential goals" of the institution of baseball that higher quality teams should win. So to understand the meaning of these sorts of desert claims, one has to know the goals of the institution. Desert claims are distinguished from entitlements in that the latter are generated directly by the "achievement rules" of the institution, while the former are based on the essential goals of the institution.

Entrepreneurs, for Arnold, are those persons whose creativity and alertness to malallocations of the market enable them to pursue new production strategies to meet the demand created by that malallocation. Markets, on his view, are an institution which have a central directive of distributing scarce goods to consumers. The essential goal of a market, then, is to allocate resources as efficiently as possible. Entrepreneurs engage in activity which contributes directly to this goal by redirecting production and distribution in response to perceived malallocations.

Arnold lists three ways in which profits are the "appropriate reward" for the contributions made by entrepreneurs. First, when entrepreneurs are allowed to keep the profits that the market returns to them, this provides an incentive to continue to pursue the kinds of production that are the most responsive to existing need. As he puts it, "if he [the entrepreneur] is allowed to keep the profits, the cost of not correcting a perceived malallocation of resources is quite high."[10]

Second, allowing entrepreneurs to keep profits keeps valuable financial resources in the hands of those whose success indicates a talent for effective investment. Those who have gained profits must be doing something right, so keeping those profits allows them to keep doing it. Finally, "the winning of profits by some serves as an effective signal to competitors to follow suit by making appropriate changes"[11] in their production strategies to respond to the newfound demand. Again, keeping profits functions as an incentive, this time to others who would enter that particular successful market sector.

The argument, then, can be summarized this way. Desert claims made in an institutional setting derive their validity from the essential goals of that institution. The essential goal of a market is the effective distribution of scarce resources. For the reasons just listed, entrepreneurial activity contributes to this goal (when profits are kept), so the profits are "fitting" rewards for the activities in question. Hence, the profits are deserved.

My criticism of this argument will be along several lines. First, is it the case that institutional frameworks are necessary for the determination of the validity of desert claims? Take Arnold's baseball example. Is it only because there is a principle *internal* to the game of baseball (that the best team deserves to win) that the desert claim (by the best team) gets its *moral* force? I think it is obvious that the principle (if it is a principle) that underlies our intuition that the best baseball team deserves to win is *not* based on anything internal to the rules or spirit of baseball. The entire phenomenon of games, or of competition generally, carries with it the idea that the best team, or the team or player that effectively exerts the most honest effort, deserves to win. And since the entire phenomenon of competition cannot be considered an institution, the intuitions that ground these claims are not tied to any particular institution at all.

This leads to a more important objection. If there are indeed goals internal to institutions that can be the basis of a desert claim, the *moral* status of the claim will depend solely on the moral status of the acts sanctioned by those goals. Evil institutions with evil goals should not be the basis for the desert of positive rewards. Arnold reminds us that desert claims have only *prima facie* force. My point here is that this force is *moral* only if the moral evaluation of the acts upon which the desert claim is based correspond to the moral worth of the thing deserved, (e.g., if they are good, then the things deserved must be good), *independent* of the institutional goals which those acts may promote.

Arnold is sensitive to this objection. He mentions it by way of imagining the Mafia, which may contain certain "institutional" rules and goals which would provide a basis for desert on his analysis, even though such an institution's goals are themselves immoral. His response is to remind us that the claims of desert here are indeed only *prima facie,* and thus would be overridden in this kind of case by the other moral considerations that make the actions of the Mafia immoral. But this response won't do. Imagine, for example, that the Mafia's institutional achievement rules demand that a person kill another person in order to avenge a minor insult made against the godfather. Imagine also that the effective carrying out of this action successfully contributes to the institutional goals of the syndicate. It will not do to say that the henchman who does this job well deserves a reward, in the *morally relevant sense,* but that this desert claim has only *prima facie* force. It has no moral force *at all.* It is immoral to kill someone to avenge an insult, so doing so does not deserve praise or reward. To say that there is an "institution-relative" sense in which the person deserves this merely is to use the word "desert" in a nonmoral manner. It strikes me as straightforwardly false that a hitman of the sort described *morally* deserves praise, and a view that entails this is thereby defective.

Now Arnold could demand that the goals of the institution in fact be morally beneficial ones, thus ruling out examples of this sort. This would in fact avoid these obvious counterexamples, but it would then remove the claims being made from the class of desert claims. This leads to a second major objection to Arnold's account, namely that his defense is actually a *consequentialist* defense of a claim of desert. This, as we have said, is in-

appropriate, for desert is an "essentially backward looking concept."[12] For Arnold to say that the goals of the institution that determine desert claims must be morally good, amounts to saying that a person deserves something because of the good results that emanate from her getting that thing. This consequentialist analysis effectively undercuts his claim that receiving accrued profits is something an entrepreneur deserves. It might have good results if she gets them, but this doesn't mean she deserves them. We might say, for example, that if we gave in to the demands of a terrorist organization, it would have the good result of initiating the freedom of the hostages being held, but this would not by any means entail that the terrorist deserved the ransom.

This also is an objection that Arnold mentions, but again his response is unsatisfactory. What he says is that the account may indeed *be* consequentialist, but since it is not *utilitarian,* his argument survives as a valid strategy for justifying desert claims. But this misses the point of the objection, for desert is not just a nonutilitarian concept, it is a nonconsequentialist one as well. As I have pointed out, the idea of deserving something is "backward looking"; its justification cannot be based on the consequences of getting the thing deserved. . . .

Finally, a closer look at the three ways that the actions of entrepreneurs promote the goals of the market reveal the curious fact that the desert claim is not based on the primary entrepreneurial function of changing production strategies after all. For the phenomenon that contributes to the overall goals of the institution of the market is the *receiving* of the profits by the entrepreneurs. That is what provides the incentives for continued investment, keeps money in the hands of those that can use it, and spurs others to act similarly. On Arnold's analysis, the beneficial effect upon which the desert claim is based is not the original activities of the entrepreneur in picking creative new production strategies to meet demand, but it is actually the receipt of the profits that has the beneficial effect grounding the desert claim. What this indicates, I think, is that Arnold has presented the rudiments of an argument for entitlements (to profits) by entrepreneurs based on the incentive effects of that property rights structure. While such an argument might be made (it is one that is of course much discussed), it is not one that has anything to do with desert.

I wish now to zero in on the central reasons why I think entrepreneurs do not deserve their profits. In doing so, I will focus on the benefit that the entrepreneur delivers in developing and producing a new product (or an old one in a different way). And I will assume that it is *this* that would provide the direct basis for a claim of desert.

III. WHY ENTREPRENEURS DO NOT DESERVE THEIR PROFITS

. . . The first suggestion I will consider is that entrepreneurs deserve their profits because they have born an undue burden of risk in the development of productive factors and the starting of a firm. That is, the entrepreneur takes a less risk-averse stance toward capital (and time and even reputation) in facing the possibility that the goods she produces will not be met by sufficient demand for consumers. Hence, it is claimed that the bearing of this risk is the basis for the desert of profits which arise if the venture is indeed successful.

The objections to this line of argument, though, are straightforward.[13] First, taking a risk, by itself, would not qualify as grounds for a desert claim unless the point of the risk-taking is in some independent way praise- or blameworthy. This is so despite our proclivity to say "she got what she deserved" when someone loses on a foolhardy risk. We wouldn't say, however, that a mountain climber deserved to fall because of the high risk of doing so that she assumes.

What this shows, I think, is that risk taking is not itself sufficient ground for deserving anything. It depends completely on the *point* of a person's taking a risk. Risking one's life in battle is often thought of as grounds for praise or decoration, but this is true only when the intended outcome of the behavior is itself noble or worthwhile. Taking the same risks for some evil or selfish end, or just "for the hell of it," would not support a claim for deserving anything (except perhaps disdain or ridicule). Whatever is deserved is thus based on the moral quality of the agent's ends, not on the risk taken to achieve those ends. . . .

This, then, brings us to the second proposal. This claim is that the basis by virtue of which entrepreneurs deserve their profits is that a benefit is provided by the production and sale of a good for which there is sufficient consumer demand. After all, those who buy the product in question, at a price that results in a profit for the entrepreneur, must have wanted or even needed that product, since we assume that consumer actions are voluntary. This provision of a benefit, at the cost of the entrepreneur's time, effort, and creative and organizational skills, is the kind of activity which would ground the claim that the entrepreneur deserves any resulting profits returned to the firm. So the claim amounts to this:

> An entrepreneur, E, deserves some profit, P, by virtue of the fact, F, that E has provided a benefit to a set of individuals, and the relation between the values of F and P meets the propriety and proportionality conditions of desert claims.

As I will presently argue, my denial of this claim rests on the contention that the factors which determine the magnitude of the profit returned after a cycle of production and exchange necessarily run afoul of the proportionality requirement for all desert claims set out above. That is, while we are assuming for argument's sake that the entrepreneur performs a service to the community of people that purchase her product, and thus might deserve some positive response, the *profit* she earns cannot be that deserved response. This is because an essential part of what determines the magnitude of profit for the production cycle is the proximity and capacity of potential competitors, and this is independent of the factors upon which the desert claim is purportedly made.

Recall that one of the essential factors in the determination of market prices is the unmet demand for that good in that sector of the market. And what affects that unmet demand are the various barriers to entering the market that face other potential producers, whose competitive presence would drive prices below what could be offered by the original producer-entrepreneur. The profit returned, then, which is a function of the market price, is directly determined by these barriers: such things as monopolies on information or technology (including patents and copyrights) held by the entrepreneur, lack of attractive credit opportunities for new producers, other high transaction costs (like the cost of physical relocation), and the like. And, again, these are conditions that the entrepreneur did not herself create; and more importantly, they are not part of what we have described as the beneficial effects of entrepreneurial activities (the desert's base, F).

Frank Knight has put essentially the same point this way: "Nearly all supplies of goods and services . . . enjoy some degree of monopoly. Each has a monopoly with a certain *market area,* and competition is effective only at the boundary between market areas."[14] My point here is that the size and scope of that limited sectoral monopoly determines the size of the profit margin returned on the sale of the commodity produced. And the various factors listed above determining the profit margin are not part of the value of entrepreneurial activity (which is limited to meeting demand).

That value, after all, amounts to the provision of a beneficial good or service to a group of consumers willing to pay the market price for the commodity. This benefit is not affected by the *source* of the product (except insofar as this affects prices). So whether or not the good is provided by our original entrepreneur or some competitor, the benefit (i.e., the product's being consumed) remains the same. In fact, since the existence of competing producers effectively drives the price down, the benefit of the entire enterprise to individual consumers is increased when profits to producers decrease.

But my point does not rest on the claim that a positive rate of profit represents less of a benefit to consumers (goods at a price which in principle could be lower), but rather that the size of the profit is not *determined* by the magnitude of consumer benefit upon which the purported desert claim is made.

Imagine an analogous case of a criminal who deserves some punishment. For it to be the case that the criminal deserves the particular sentence given to her, its severity must be proportional to the harmfulness of her criminal acts. If, for example, prison sentences were randomly pulled out of a hat, we would not say that the prisoner deserved that punishment, for the severity of the sentence was not *determined* by the harmfulness of the crime. To make the analogy closer to the present case, imagine that the sentence was determined, not by chance, but by the availability of prison space in the area, or the numbers of guards employed by the facility. These factors are not related to the severity of the crime, so if they determine the punishment, then we would not say that the criminal deserves that particular sentence. "Desert" is a fundamentally nonconsequentialist moral notion: what is deserved can only be determined by the value or disvalue of the factors which are the basis for the desert claim. . . .

IV. DESERVING MARKET SHARES IN GENERAL

. . . To sum up, I have argued that in market economies where profits arise from disequilibrium conditions which determine the size of profits returned to entrepreneurs, those profits are not deserved. The basis of this claim is that a necessary condition for the validity of a claim of personal desert is that a proportionality obtains between the actions upon which the desert claim is based and the mode of treatment or object deserved, where the value of the former determines the latter. And I have argued that, in the case of entrepreneurial profit, this condition is not met because the rate of profit is determined by factors independent of the value of the activities grounding the desert claim. By this more exact argument, I have tried to lend support to the general claim that competitive markets do not allocate goods according to a principle of desert. This is so whenever the rewards allocated by the market are determined by the competitive forces of supply and demand, in ways sufficiently similar to the case of entrepreneurial profits.

The relevance of this, if nothing else, consists in dislodging another pillar in the already shaky moral foundations of free market capitalism.

ENDNOTES

1. My arguments here apply to all profits, positive or negative. So my full thesis should read: "entrepreneurs deserve neither their profits *nor* their losses"; more generally, the market simply does not distribute resources (including profits) according to what people deserve.
2. Cf. Paul Samuelson, *Economics* (New York: McGraw Hill, 1967), ch. 31; Frank Knight, *Risk, Uncertainty and Profit* (New York: Kelly and Millman, 1957), ch. 9; and Hal Varian, *Microeconomic Analysis* (New York: Norton Press, 1984), p. 6. For a revision of the "standard account," *cf.* Israel Kirzner, *Competition and Entrepreneurship* (Chicago: Chicago University Press, 1973), ch. 2.
3. I simplify here by only talking of starting a firm. An entrepreneur can redirect production in an already existing firm in a variety of ways. The arguments I make should apply in those cases as well, though.
4. This includes interest on capital that the entrepreneur "borrows" from herself.
5. *Cf.* Knight, *Risk,* p. 280, where he speaks of the "residual income" of entrepreneurs.
6. Feinberg, "Justice and Personal Desert" in *Doing and Deserving* (Princeton, N.J.: Princeton University Press, 1970), p. 61.
7. From this point on I drop consideration of propriety, since my argument rests on the proportionality condition alone.
8. This is distinct from saying that a person is (simply) undeserving. She may, for example, deserve praise, but not the particular praise offered, when it violates this condition.
9. N. Scott Arnold, "Why Profits Are Deserved," *Ethics,* vol. 97, no. 2 (January 1987), pp. 387–402.
10. Arnold, "Why Profits Are Deserved," p. 397.
11. *Ibid.*
12. Feinberg, "Justice," pp. 81ff, also makes this point.
13. Arnold, "Profits," p. 395, makes points similar to these.
14. Knight, *Risks,* p. xx.

QUESTIONS ON CHRISTMAN

1. Why does Christman claim that desert is not a consequentialist notion? Does an entrepreneur reap a profit because of what will happen or because of what has happened? How might Arnold reply to Christman's criticisms of his account?

2. Christman claims that an entrepreneur does not deserve any profit for providing goods and services to

consumers because the profit that accrues results not from the magnitude of the benefit to consumers but from there being "barriers to entering the market," and these are not created by the entrepreneur. What sort of barriers are these? If the entrepreneur has knowledge or information that others do not have, then is this a "barrier"? Why isn't this something for which the entrepreneur has responsibility?

3. To what extent is Christman's argument based on the relevance of the model of perfect competition? What are some of the assumptions of this model (see, for example, the introduction to Section AIII, pp. 107-08)? Is a model that is based on unreal conditions (for example, perfect knowledge) relevant to moral justification of real conduct? Why or why not?

4. If an entrepreneur does not deserve his profits, then does an entrepreneur deserve his losses? Should we even think of profits (and losses) in terms of moral desert? Might one have a right or claim to one's profits even if these are not morally deserved?

———————

Freedom of Contract and Affirmative Action

If I have given a true account of that freedom which forms the goal of social effort, we shall see that freedom of contract, freedom in all the forms of doing what one will with one's own, is valuable only as a means to an end. That end is what I call freedom in the positive sense: in other words, the liberation of the powers of all men equally for contributions to a common good.

T. H. Green[27]

Under a system of the widest possible liberty, each man thinks and acts according to his own judgment and his own sense of right. He labors as he will, making such free bargains as he chooses respecting the price and all other conditions that affect his labor; he is idle or industrious, he spends or he lays by, he remains poor, or he becomes rich, he turns his faculties to wise and good account, or he wastes possessions, time and happiness in folly. He is, be it for good or evil, the owner and possessor of his own self, and he has to bear the responsibility of that ownership and possession to the full. . . . [E]ven if you believed that you could make men wise and good by depriving them of liberty of action, you have no right to do so. Who has given you a commission to decide what your brother shall or shall not do? Who has given you charge of his life and his faculties and his happiness as well as of your own?

Auberon Herbert[28]

I used to envy the 'colorblindness' which some liberal, enlightened, white people were supposed to possess; raised as I was, where I was, I am and will to the end of my life be acutely, sometimes bitterly, aware of color. Every adult around me in my childhood, white or black, was aware of it; it was a sovereign consciousness, a hushed and compelling secret. But I no longer believe that 'colorblindness'—if it even exists—is the opposite of racism; I think it is, in this world, a form of naiveté and moral stupidity. It implies that I would look at a black woman and see her as white, thus engaging in white solipsism to the utter erasure of her particular reality.

Adrienne Rich[29]

27. "Liberal Legislation and Freedom of Contract" [1881], in *The Political Theory of T. H. Green,* edited by John R. Rodman (New York: Appleton-Century-Crofts, 1964), 53.

28. *The Right and Wrong of Compulsion By the State, and Other Essays* [1885], edited by Eric Mack (Indianapolis, Ind.: Liberty Classics, 1978), 124–125, 127.

29. "Disloyal to Civilization: Feminism, Racism, Gynephobia," in *On Lies, Secrets, and Silences: Selected Prose 1966–1978* (New York: W.W. Norton, 1979), 300.

Within the modern civil rights discourse, however, diversity . . . becomes yet another buzzword in the campaign for political conformity to a state-imposed ideal. Institutions that do not hire the right number of women or minorities are deemed to be not politically correct; therefore they should be exposed to government action, be it by private suit for discrimination, by enforcement actions from the EEOC, or by being hauled before accreditation committees. Unpacked, diversity today amounts to little more than a call for race-conscious and sex-conscious hiring, and in some circumstances even the more extreme position of proportionate representation by race and by sex. In the name of diversity all institutions have to follow the same policies or face the wrath of the state.

Richard Epstein[30]

The Contract at Will

In a market, individuals have certain freedoms to dispose of their property as they wish and to forge mutually agreeable contracts with one another. Freedom of contract, the power or right to initiate binding agreements among mutually agreeing parties, is an essential component of competitive markets. Of course legal rules may limit the kinds of contracts we can make. For example, minimum-wage laws preclude any contract in which a person is paid less than some mandated minimum; other laws may stipulate a maximum rate of interest that can be charged for a loan, thereby preventing certain loan agreements. From a libertarian perspective, these sorts of legal limitations are impermissible inhibitions on complete liberty of contract: Individuals should be permitted to make contracts in whatever form they wish so long as the contract does not violate the rights of any other parties. Similarly, according to the doctrine of the "contract at will," a contract of employment is legitimate so long as each party enters the contract voluntarily and no other party's rights are violated. Of course, if such a view is to succeed, some account must be given of what constitutes a voluntary contract or agreement. Presumably, voluntary agreement would rest on two conditions: (1) that each party has the requisite knowledge and understanding to make a contract (and that neither party has misrepresented or lied about matters relevant to the contract), and (2) that neither party exercises any physical coercion, or threatens such. The legal theorist Richard Epstein, a defender of the contract at will doctrine, summarizes the view as follows:

> An employee who knows that he can quit at will understands what it means to be fired at will, even though he may not like it after the fact. So long as it is accepted that the employer is the full owner of his capital and the employee is the full owner of his labor, the two are free to

exchange on whatever terms and conditions they see fit, within the limited constraints just noted. If the arrangement turns out to be disastrous to one side, that is his problem; and once cautioned, he probably will not make the same mistake a second time.[31]

Limits on Contracts

Against the idea of the contract at will are the various legal decisions that have altered and affected the employer's right to hire or fire whomever he or she may wish and on whatever terms may be agreed upon. Limitations on liberty of contract have been justified in a variety of ways. Some have argued that the contract at will places the employee in a subservient position to the employer (or that the contract itself is not fully voluntary); others have suggested that individuals not only have a right to a job but that any person has a right to retain a job once it has been secured. On this latter view (one version of which is found in the reading by Werhane and Radin), any attempt by an employer to release an employee must be rationally justified and performed in accordance with recognized principles of due process.

Limitations on contract also include laws that seek to provide protection against unsafe working conditions and job hazards, laws limiting the amount of hours that may be worked, and those laws or rules that place limits on who can be hired and under what conditions. The latter kinds of law seek to prevent arbitrary discrimination against persons on account of their race, gender, or sexual preference. The most notable and controversial of these laws or policies are those of affirmative action.

Affirmative Action

Over the past 150 years, there has been dramatic social and economic progress in the United States, Nonethe-

---

30. *Forbidden Grounds: The Case Against Employment Discrimination Laws* (Cambridge: Harvard University Press, 1992), 502.

31. "In Defense of the Contract at Will," *University of Chicago Law Review* 34 (1984).

less many argue that the state must take an active role in improving the economic and social condition of persons or groups who have suffered because of unjust or unfair social or legal practices. Affirmative action began during the presidential administrations of Presidents Kennedy and Johnson. The term was first used in an executive order (10295) of President Kennedy in 1961 that required contractors with the federal government to use "affirmative steps" to ensure that applicants are employed without regard to their race, creed, color, or national origin. (In 1965 President Johnson, in executive order 11246, urged "affirmative action" for minorities; this policy was extended to women in executive order 11375 of 1967.) A crucial piece of legislation in the movement toward a full policy of affirmative action was the Civil Rights Act of 1964. Title VI of that act prohibits discrimination (based on race, color, religion, sex, or national origin) in any public accommodation or in any program receiving federal funds. Title VII prohibits discrimination by any public or private employer (or union). Those who voted for the Civil Rights Act were not of the view that it would require an employer to seek to achieve a particular racial balance in the work force,[32] but over the years the concept of "discrimination" has received varying treatments from the courts. These court decisions have confirmed a variety of policies that, falling under the rubric of affirmative action, affect commercial and employment contracts.

Types of Affirmative Action

The most basic form of affirmative action is that which seeks to ensure that there are as many applicants as possible for a position or place, including minority applicants. Under this type of policy, special effort is made to ensure that minorities are aware of an opening or are in a position to apply. However, all applicants are treated the same and judged by the same criteria. By the 1970s this policy was not deemed sufficient, for if one had not hired a sufficient number of women or minorities, then one could easily come under suspicion of discrimination. The best way to avoid this was to actually hire a requisite number (or, in the case of academic institutions, to admit a certain number) of minority and female applicants. A stronger type of affirmative action involves a policy of taking into account the race or sex of the person under consideration and giving the requisite race or sex an extra (positive) weight. This form of affirmative action need not entail quotas or any "set-aside" of a specific number of places, though in practice if a company (or university) were practicing this form of affirmative action but *failed* to admit or hire a certain number of minorities or women, that company (or university) might come under suspicion of practicing discrimination. The third and strongest type of affirmative action involves setting aside, either in a business or in an academic institution, a certain number or percentage of places and then proceeding to fill these places with individuals of the requisite race or sex.

It is not always obvious which type of policy an organization is implementing. Many academic institutions claim to practice the first form of affirmative action even as they, in fact, practice the second form, if not the third. The same also holds true of some large corporations. One concomitant of the policy of affirmative action is that many individuals and representatives of organizations find it difficult to state clearly and publicly the actual criteria by which they are making personnel decisions. On the other hand, some persons and organizations have been more candid, as when the executive editor of the *New York Times* stated, "One of the first things I did was to stop the hiring of non-blacks and set up an unofficial little quota system."[33] One might suggest that any public policy, including that of affirmative action, should be upheld and applied in a *transparent* manner so that no person need misrepresent or disguise what is involved in implementing the policy and no citizen be deprived of information on the execution of actions required by law. That the implementation of a public policy be transparent is particularly important given the weighty justifications of affirmative action.

Types of Justifications

The justifications of affirmative action policies are typically either *forward looking* or *backward looking*. A forward-looking justification seeks to defend affirmative action by appealing to the consequences of the policy for minorities and women and for society at large. The backward-looking justification forwards the view that affirmative action is required as the best means of compensating individuals for some previous injustice.

What sort of questions must be answered if one is to forward either of these types of justifications? A

---

32. See for example the remarks of Senators Joseph Clark, Clifford Case, or Harrison Williams. Senator Hubert Humphrey stated: "Title VII does not require an employer to achieve any sort of racial balance in his work force by giving preferential treatment to any individual or group." 110 *Congressional Record* (1964) 12723.

33. Max Frankel, as quoted in Ken Auletta, "Opening up the Times," *The New Yorker* 69 (June 28, 1993): 60–61.

backward-looking justification of affirmative action requires that one not only identify the relevant individuals (or groups) that are to be compensated but that one demonstrate that these individuals have suffered an injustice deserving compensation and that affirmative action is the appropriate form of compensation. A forward-looking justification must be able to show that this particular social policy offers a better probability of ameliorating some specific problem than any competing alternative (including the alternative of doing nothing) and that the policy in question does not violate any important moral, political, or constitutional principles. These types of justification require that one be able to evaluate, honestly and dispassionately, the history of individuals and groups, as well as the probable consequences of implementing a particular policy of affirmative action. Thus, any such justification requires that the means of implementation be transparent. To examine these matters more carefully, we must consider the arguments in the readings that follow.

THE READINGS

Patricia Werhane and Tara J. Radin   Werhane and Radin examine the principle of Employment at Will (EAW) according to which an employee can be fired or released at any time and without any justification, unless there is some law or prior contract stipulating otherwise. In contrast to many employees in the private sector, those in the public sector have "guaranteed rights, including due process." Procedural due process requires that employers give good reasons for their actions, thereby protecting employees from "demotion, transfer, or firing without cause." The authors point out how developments have steadily whittled away at the doctrine of EAW, even as the principle of EAW remains. Werhane and Radin seek to refute five distinct arguments for the principle of EAW, and they suggest that the very distinction between the public and the private realm is the underlying reason by which due process is extended to public employees but not to private. However, they contend that this distinction is rather "fuzzy," if not eroded, when applied to "private" corporations or businesses, and this provides another reason why substantive due process ought to be extended to business firms and corporations.

Eric Mack   Mack offers a defense of freedom of contract utilizing the natural rights perspective first adumbrated by John Locke. Distinguishing between the historical doctrine (as delineated in law and by courts) and the philosophical theory, Mack contends that the former must be defended in terms of the latter, according

to which each individual may enter into an agreement or association with any other individual on any terms that are voluntary. This view is defended in terms of the ultimate value of each individual's life. Each individual possesses an equal and natural moral sovereignty; a sovereignty which entails rights to life, liberty, and justifiably acquired property. To coerce a person is to constrain "a person against his will in a way that involves some violation of his rights." Given this account of rights and coercion, our enforceable obligations include the obligation not to coerce one another, as well as any obligation born of some contractual relationship. No one has a right that a contract be extended on certain terms, and everyone has a right that no contract be imposed upon him. Mack seeks to rebut several objections to his account, including that of advocates of positive freedom, who argue that persons in dire circumstances are not acting freely, as well as those who suggest that certain contractual offers are coercive, or that contracts which reflect unequal bargaining positions are illegitimate.

Gertrude Ezorsky   Ezorsky begins by asserting the distinction between forward-looking and backward-looking justifications of affirmative action. From the backward-looking perspective, slavery is the chief injustice and this requires compensation, especially in light of the private and public practices that have continued and extended the original injustice. Ezorsky examines each of the arguments offered by those who argue that affirmative action is the inappropriate means of compensation either because it is counterproductive or because it compensates well-off blacks or those who have not suffered the most. She then tackles the reasoning forwarded by those who contend that affirmative action unfairly disadvantages whites, violating their right to equal treatment. Against this view she holds that in some cases (layoffs and hiring), there is some justification for providing a monetary reward to whites who might lose a position or fail to gain a promotion. Another criticism of affirmative action turns on the idea that it violates the rights of more qualified whites. However, Ezorsky contends that selection by merit is not, in fact, the common practice for most jobs, and thus affirmative-action hiring would not violate any accepted practice.

Louis Pojman   Beginning with definitions of "discrimination," "prejudice," "equal opportunity," and "affirmative action," Pojman distinguishes a weaker and a stronger version of affirmative action, the latter of which would involve "discrimination" and the use of racial and sexual criteria in hiring and admissions. After offering a brief history of the policy of affirmative action, Pojman explains and rejects seven arguments in favor of affirmative action, the strongest of which, he suggests, is the argument that turns on compensation and may justify certain weaker forms of affirmative action. In the last section of the essay, he canvasses seven arguments against affirmative action, including the contentions that affirmative action encourages mediocrity, that it shifts the burden of proof onto employers (who are assumed "guilty until proven innocent"), and that there is strong evidence against the claim that affirmative action programs have been successful.

Employer and Employee Rights in an Institutional Context

Patricia H. Werhane and Tara J. Radin

Patricia H. Werhane is the Ruffin Professor of Business Ethics at the Darden Graduate School of Business, University of Virginia. The author of several books, including Adam Smith and His Legacy for Modern Capitalism *(1991), as well as* Moral Imagination and Management Decision-Making *(1999), she is the coeditor, along with R. Edward Freeman, of the* Blackwell Encyclopedic Dictionary of Business Ethics *(1997). Tara J. Radin is Assistant Professor of Management and General Business at Hofstra University.*

In 1980, Howard Smith III was hired by the American Greetings Corporation as a materials handler at the plant in Osceola, Arkansas. He was promoted to forklift driver and held that job until 1989, when he became involved in a dispute with his shift leader. According to Smith, he had a dispute with his shift leader at work. After work he tried to discuss the matter, but according to Smith, the shift leader hit him. The next day Smith was fired.

Smith was an "at-will" employee. He did not belong to, nor was he protected by, any union or union agreement. He did not have any special legal protection, for there was no apparent question of age, gender, race, or handicap discrimination. And he was not alleging any type of problem with worker safety on the job. The American Greetings Employee Handbook stated that "We believe in working and thinking and planning to provide a stable and growing business, to give such service to our customers that we may provide maximum job security for our employees." It did not state that em-

ployees could not be fired without due process or reasonable cause. According to the common law principle of Employment at Will (EAW), Smith's job at American Greetings could, therefore, legitimately be terminated at any time without cause, by either Smith or his employer, as long as that termination did not violate any law, agreement, or public policy.

> Smith challenged his firing in the Arkansas court system as a "tort of outrage." A "tort of outrage" occurs when employer engages in "extreme or outrageous conduct" or intentionally inflicts terrible emotional stress. If such a tort is found to have occurred, the action, in this case, the dismissal, can be overturned.
>
> Smith's case went to the Supreme Court of Arkansas in 1991. In court the management of American Greetings argued that Smith was fired for provoking management into a fight. The Court held that the firing was not in violation of law or a public policy, that the employee handbook did not specify restrictions on at-will terminations, and that the alleged altercation between Smith and his shift leader "did not come close to meeting" criteria for a tort of outrage. Howard Smith lost his case and his job.[1]

The principle of EAW is a common-law doctrine that states that, in the absence of law or contract, employers have the right to hire, promote, demote, and fire whomever and whenever they please. In 1887, the principle was stated explicitly in a document by H. G. Wood entitled *Master and Servant*. According to Wood, "A general or indefinite hiring is prima facie a hiring at will."[2] Although the term "master-servant," a medieval expression, was once used to characterize employment relationships, it has been dropped from most of the recent literature on employment.[3]

In the United States, EAW has been interpreted as the rule that, when employees are not specifically covered by union agreement, legal statute, public policy, or contract, employers "may dismiss their employees at will . . . for good cause, for no cause, *or even for causes morally wrong,* without being thereby guilty of legal wrong."[4] At the same time, "at will" employees enjoy rights parallel to employer prerogatives, because employees may quit their jobs for any reason whatsoever (or no reason) without having to give any notice to their employers. "At will" employees range from part-time contract workers to CEOs, including all those workers and managers in the private sector of the economy not covered by agreements, statutes, or contracts. Today at least 60 percent of all employees in the private sector in the United States are "at-will" employees. These employees have no rights to due process or to appeal employment decisions, and the employer does not have any obligation to give reasons for demotions, transfers, or dismissals. Interestingly, while employees in the *private* sector of the economy tend to be regarded as "at-will" employees, *public*-sector employees have guaranteed rights, including due process, and are protected from demotion, transfer, or firing without cause.

Due process is a means by which a person can appeal a decision in order to get an explanation of that action and an opportunity to argue against it. Procedural due process is the right to a hearing, trial, grievance procedure, or appeal when a decision is made concerning oneself. Due process is also substantive. It is the demand for rationality and fairness: for good reasons for decisions. EAW has been widely interpreted as allowing employees to be demoted, transferred or dismissed without due process, that is, without having a hearing and without requirement of good reasons or "cause" for the employment decision. This is not to say that employers do not have reasons, usually good reasons, for their decisions. But there is no moral or legal obligation to state or defend them. EAW thus sidesteps the requirement of procedural and substantive due process in the workplace, but it does not preclude the institution of such procedures or the existence of good reasons for employment decisions.

EAW is still upheld in the state and federal courts of this country, as the Howard Smith case illustrates, although exceptions are made when violations of public policy and law are at issue. According to the *Wall Street Journal,* the court has decided in favor of the employees in 67 percent of the wrongful discharge suits that have taken place during the past three years. These suits were won not on the basis of a rejection of the principle of EAW but, rather, on the basis of breach of contract, lack of just cause for dismissal when a company policy was in place, or violations of public policy. The court has carved out the "public policy" exception so as not to encourage fraudulent or wrongful behavior on the part of employers, such as in cases where employees are asked to break a law or to violate state public policies, and in cases where employees are not allowed to exercise fundamental rights, such as the rights to vote, to serve on a jury, and to collect worker compensation. For example, in one case, the court reinstated an employee who was fired for reporting theft at his plant on the grounds that criminal conduct requires such reporting.[5] In another case, the court reinstated a physician who was fired from the Ortho Pharmaceutical Corporation for refusing to seek approval to test a certain drug on human subjects. The court held that safety clearly lies in the interest of public welfare, and employees are not to be fired for refusing to jeopardize public safety.[6]

During the last ten years, a number of positive trends have become apparent in employment practices and in state and federal court adjudications of employment disputes. Shortages of skilled managers, fear of legal repercussions, and a more genuine interest in employee rights claims and reciprocal obligations have resulted in a more careful spelling out of employment contracts, the development of elaborate grievance procedures, and in general less arbitrariness in employee treatment.[7] . . .

Interestingly, substantive due process, the notion that employers should give good reasons for their employment actions, previously dismissed as legal and philosophical nonsense, has also recently developed positive advocates. Some courts have found that it is a breach of contract to fire a long-term employee when there is not sufficient cause—under normal economic conditions even when the implied contract is only a verbal one. In California, for example, 50 percent of the implied contract cases (and there have been over 200) during the last five years have been decided in favor of the employee, again, without challenging EAW.[8] In light of this recognition of implicit contractual obligations between employees and employers, in some unprecedented court cases *employees* have been held liable for good faith breaches of contract, particularly in cases of quitting without notice in the middle of a project and/or taking technology or other ideas to another job.[9]

These are all positive developments. At the same time, there has been neither an across-the-board institution of due process procedures in all corporations nor any direct challenges to the *principle* (although there have been challenges to the practice) of EAW as a justifiable and legitimate approach to employment practices. Moreover, as a result of mergers, downsizing, and restructuring, hundreds of thousands of employees have been laid off summarily without being able to appeal those decisions.

"At-will" employees, then, have no rights to demand an appeal to such employment decisions except through the court system. In addition, no form of due process is a requirement preceding any of these actions. Moreover, unless public policy is violated, the law has traditionally protected employers from employee retaliation in such actions. It is true that the scope of what is defined as "public policy" has been enlarged so that "at-will" dismissals without good reason are greatly reduced. It is also true that many companies have grievance procedures in place for "at-will" employees. But such procedures are voluntary, procedural due process is not *required,* and companies need not give any reasons for their employment decisions.

In what follows we shall present a series of arguments defending the claim that the right to procedural and substantive due process should be extended to all employees in the private sector of the economy. . . .

EMPLOYMENT AT WILL

EAW is often justified for one or more of the following reasons:

1. The proprietary rights of employers guarantee that they may employ or dismiss whomever and whenever they wish.

2. EAW defends employee and employer rights equally, in particular the right to freedom of contract, because an employee voluntarily contracts to be hired and can quit at any time.

3. In choosing to take a job, an employee voluntarily commits herself to certain responsibilities and company loyalty, including the knowledge that she is an "at-will" employee.

4. Extending due process rights in the workplace often interferes with the efficiency and productivity of the business organization.

5. Legislation and/or regulation of employment relationships further undermine an already overregulated economy.

Let us examine each of these arguments in more detail. The principle of EAW is sometimes maintained purely on the basis of proprietary rights of employers and corporations. In dismissing or demoting employees, the employer is not denying rights to *persons*. Rather, the employer is simply excluding that person's *labor* from the organization.

This is not a bad argument. Nevertheless, accepting it necessitates consideration of the proprietary rights of employees as well. To understand what is meant by "proprietary rights of employees" it is useful to consider first what is meant by the term "labor." "Labor" is sometimes used collectively to refer to the workforce as a whole. It also refers to the activity of working. Other times it refers to the productivity or "fruits" of that activity. Productivity, labor in the third sense, might be thought of as a form of property or at least as something convertible into property, because the productivity of working is what is traded for remuneration in employee-employer work agreements. For example, suppose an advertising agency hires an expert known for her cre-

ativity in developing new commercials. This person trades her ideas, the product of her work (thinking), for pay. The ideas are not literally property, but they are tradable items because, when presented on paper or on television, they are sellable by their creator and generate income. But the activity of working (thinking in this case) cannot be sold or transferred.

Caution is necessary, though, in relating productivity to tangible property, because there is an obvious difference between productivity and material property. Productivity requires the past or present activity of working, and thus the presence of the person performing this activity. Person, property, labor, and productivity are all different in this important sense. A person can be distinguished from his possessions, a distinction that allows for the creation of legally fictional persons such as corporations or trusts that can "own" property. Persons cannot, however, be distinguished from their working, and this activity is necessary for creating productivity, a tradable product of one's working.

In dismissing an employee, a well-intentioned employer aims to rid the corporation of the costs of generating that employee's work products. In ordinary employment situations, however, terminating that cost entails terminating that employee. In those cases the justification for the "at-will" firing is presumably proprietary. But treating an employee "at will" is analogous to considering her a piece of property at the disposal of the employer or corporation. Arbitrary firings treat people as things. When I "fire" a robot, I do not have to give reasons, because a robot is not a rational being. It has no use for reasons. On the other hand, if I fire a person arbitrarily, I am making the assumption that she does not need reasons either. If I have hired people, then, in firing them, I should treat them as such, with respect, throughout the termination process. This does not preclude firing. It merely asks employers to give reasons for their actions, because reasons are appropriate when people are dealing with other people.

This reasoning leads to a second defense and critique of EAW. It is contended that EAW defends employee and employer rights equally. An employer's right to hire and fire "at will" is balanced by a worker's right to accept or reject employment. The institution of any employee right that restricts "at-will" hiring and firing would be unfair unless this restriction were balanced by a similar restriction controlling employee job choice in the workplace. Either program would do irreparable damage by preventing both employees and employers from continuing in voluntary employment arrangements. These arrangements are guaranteed by "freedom of contract," the right of persons or organizations to enter into any voluntary agreement with which all parties of the agreement are in accord.[10] Limiting EAW practices or requiring due process would negatively affect freedom of contract. Both are thus clearly coercive, because in either case persons and organizations are forced to accept behavioral restraints that place unnecessary constraints on voluntary employment agreements.[11]

This second line of reasoning defending EAW, like the first, presents some solid arguments. A basic presupposition upon which EAW is grounded is that of protecting equal freedoms of both employees and employers. The purpose of EAW is to provide a guaranteed balance of these freedoms. But arbitrary treatment of employees extends prerogatives to managers that are not equally available to employees, and such treatment may unduly interfere with a fired employee's prospects for future employment if that employee has no avenue for defense or appeal. This is also sometimes true when an employee quits without notice or good reason. Arbitrary treatment of employees *or* employers therefore violates the spirit of EAW—that of protecting the freedoms of both the employees and employers.

The third justification of EAW defends the voluntariness of employment contracts. If these are agreements between moral agents, however, such agreements imply reciprocal obligations between the parties in question for which both are accountable. It is obvious that, in an employment contract, people are rewarded for their performance. What is seldom noticed is that, if part of the employment contract is an expectation of loyalty, trust, and respect on the part of an employee, the employer must, in return, treat the employee with respect as well. The obligations required by employment agreements, if these are free and non-coercive agreements, must be equally obligatory and mutually restrictive on both parties. Otherwise one party cannot expect—morally expect—loyalty, trust, or respect from the other.

EAW is most often defended on practical grounds. From a utilitarian perspective, hiring and firing "at will" is deemed necessary in productive organizations to ensure maximum efficiency and productivity, the goals of such organizations. In the absence of EAW unproductive employees, workers who are no longer needed, and even troublemakers, would be able to keep their jobs. Even if a business *could* rid itself of undesirable employees, the lengthy procedure of due process required by an extension of employee rights would be costly and time-consuming, and would likely prove distracting to other employees. This would likely slow production

and, more likely than not, prove harmful to the morale of other employees.

This argument is defended by Ian Maitland, who contends,

> [I]f employers were generally to heed business ethicists and institute workplace due process in cases of dismissals and take the increased costs or reduced efficiency out of workers' paychecks—then they would expose themselves to the pirating of their workers by other employers who would give workers what they wanted instead of respecting their rights in the workplace. . . . In short, there is good reason for concluding that the prevalence of EAW does accurately reflect workers' preferences for wages over contractually guaranteed protections against unfair dismissal.[12]

Such an argument assumes (a) that due process increases costs and reduces efficiency, a contention that is not documented by the many corporations that have grievance procedures, and (b) that workers will generally give up some basic rights for other benefits, such as money. The latter is certainly sometimes true, but not always so, particularly when there are questions of unfair dismissals or job security. Maitland also assumes that an employee is on the same level and possesses the same power as her manager, so that an employee can choose her benefit package in which grievance procedures, whistleblowing protections, or other rights are included. Maitland implies that employers might include in that package of benefits their rights to practice the policy of unfair dismissals in return for increased pay. He also at least implicitly suggests that due process precludes dismissals and layoffs. But this is not true. Procedural due process demands a means of appeal, and substantive due process demands good reasons, both of which are requirements for other managerial decisions and judgments. Neither demands benevolence, lifetime employment, or prevents dismissals. In fact, having good reasons gives an employer a justification for getting rid of poor employees.

In summary, arbitrariness, although not prohibited by EAW, violates the managerial ideal of rationality and consistency. These are independent grounds for not abusing EAW. Even if EAW itself is justifiable, the practice of EAW, when interpreted as condoning arbitrary employment decisions, is not justifiable. Both procedural and substantive due process are consistent with, and a moral requirement of, EAW. The former is part of recognizing obligations implied by freedom of contract, and the latter, substantive due process, conforms with the ideal of managerial rationality that is implied by a consistent application of this common law principle.

EMPLOYMENT AT WILL, DUE PROCESS, AND THE PUBLIC/PRIVATE DISTINCTION

The strongest reasons for allowing abuses of EAW and for not instituting a full set of employee rights in the workplace, at least in the private sector of the economy, have to do with the nature of business in a free society. Businesses are privately owned voluntary organizations of all sizes from small entrepreneurships to large corporations. As such, they are not subject to the restrictions governing public and political institutions. Political procedures such as due process, needed to safeguard the public against the arbitrary exercise of power by the state, do not apply to private organizations. Guaranteeing such rights in the workplace would require restrictive legislation and regulation. Voluntary market arrangements, so vital to free enterprise and guaranteed by freedom of contract, would be sacrificed for the alleged public interest of employee claims.

In the law, courts traditionally have recognized the right of corporations to due process, although they have not required due process for employees in the private sector of the economy. The justification put forward for this is that since corporations are public entities acting in the public interest, they, like people, should be afforded the right to due process.

Due process is also guaranteed for permanent full-time workers in the public sector of the economy, that is, for workers in local, state and national government positions. The Fifth and Fourteenth Amendments protect liberty and property rights such that any alleged violations or deprivation of those rights may be challenged by some form of due process. According to recent Supreme Court decisions, when a state worker is a permanent employee, he has a property interest in his employment. Because a person's productivity contributes to the place of employment, a public worker is entitled to his job unless there is good reason to question it, such as poor work habits, habitual absences, and the like. Moreover, if a discharge would prevent him from obtaining other employment, which often is the case with state employees who, if fired, cannot find further government employment, that employee has a right to due process before being terminated.[13]

This justification for extending due process protections to public employees is grounded in the public employee's proprietary interest in his job. If that argument makes sense, it is curious that private employees do not have similar rights. The basis for this distinction stems from a tradition in Western thinking that distinguishes between the public and private spheres of life. The public sphere contains that part of a person's life that lies within the bounds of government regulation, whereas the private sphere contains that part of a person's life that lies outside those bounds. The argument is that the portion of a person's life that influences only that person should remain private and outside the purview of law and regulation, while the portion that influences the public welfare should be subject to the authority of the law.

Although interpersonal relationships on any level—personal, family, social, or employee-employer—are protected by statutes and common law, they are not constitutionally protected unless there is a violation of some citizen claim against the state. Because entrepreneurships and corporations are privately owned, and since employees are free to make or break employment contracts of their choice, employee-employer relationships, like family relationships, are treated as "private." In a family, even if there are no due process procedures, the state does not interfere, except when there is obvious harm or abuse. Similarly, employment relationships are considered private relationships contracted between free adults, and so long as no gross violations occur, positive constitutional guarantees such as due process are not enforceable. . . .

There are some questions, however, with the justification of the absence of due process with regard to the public/private distinction. Our economic system is allegedly based on private property, but it is unclear where "private" property and ownership end and "public" property and ownership begin. In the workplace, ownership and control is often divided. Corporate assets are held by an ever-changing group of individual and institutional shareholders. It is no longer true that owners exercise any real sense of control over their property and its management. Some do, but many do not. Moreover, such complex property relationships are spelled out and guaranteed by the state. This has prompted at least one thinker to argue that "private property" should be defined as "certain patterns of human interaction underwritten by public power."[14]

This fuzziness about the "privacy" of property becomes exacerbated by the way we use the term "public" in analyzing the status of businesses and in particular corporations. For example, we distinguish between privately owned business corporations and government-owned or -controlled public institutions. Among those companies that are not government owned, we distinguish between regulated "public" utilities whose stock is owned by private individuals and institutions; "publicly held" corporations whose stock is traded publicly, who are governed by special SEC regulations, and whose financial statements are public knowledge; and privately held corporations and entrepreneurships, companies and smaller businesses that are owned by an individual or group of individuals and not available for public stock purchase.

There are similarities between government-owned, public institutions and privately owned organizations. . . . While the goals of private and public institutions differ in that public institutions are allegedly supposed to place the public good ahead of profitability, the simultaneous call for businesses to become socially responsible and the demand for governmental organizations to become efficient and accountable further question the dichotomy between "public" and "private."

Many business situations reinforce the view that the traditional public/private dichotomy has been eroded, if not entirely, at least in large part. For example, in 1981, General Motors (GM) wanted to expand by building a plant in what is called the "Poletown" area of Detroit. Poletown is an old Detroit Polish neighborhood. The site was favorable because it was near transportation facilities and there was a good supply of labor. To build the plant, however, GM had to displace residents in a nine-block area. The Poletown Neighborhood Council objected, but the Supreme Court of Michigan decided in favor of GM and held that the state could condemn property for private use, with proper compensation to owners, when it was in the public good. What is particularly interesting about this case is that GM is not a government-owned corporation; its primary goal is *profitability,* not the common good. The Supreme Court nevertheless decided that it was in the *public* interest for Detroit to use its authority to allow a company to take over property despite the protesting of the property owners. In this case the public/private distinction was thoroughly scrambled.

The overlap between private enterprise and public interests is such that at least one legal scholar argues that "developments in the twentieth century have significantly undermined the 'privateness' of the modern business corporations, with the result that the traditional bases for distinguishing them from public corporations have largely disappeared."[15] Nevertheless, despite the blurring of the public and private in terms of property rights and the status and functions of corporations, the subject of employee rights appears to remain immune from conflation.

The expansion of employee protections to what we would consider just claims to due process gives to the state and the courts more opportunity to interfere with the private economy and might thus further skew what

is seen by some as a precarious but delicate balance between the private economic sector and public policy. We agree. But if the distinction between public and private institutions is no longer clear-cut, and the traditional separation of the public and private spheres is no longer in place, might it not then be better to recognize and extend constitutional guarantees so as to protect all citizens equally? If due process is crucial to political relationships between the individual and the state, why is it not central in relationships between employees and corporations since at least some of the companies in question are as large and powerful as small nations? Is it not in fact inconsistent with our democratic tradition *not* to mandate such rights?

The philosopher T. M. Scanlon summarizes our institutions about due process. Scanlon says,

> The requirement of due process is one of the conditions of the moral acceptability of those institutions that give some people power to control or intervene in the lives of others.[16]

The institution of due process in the workplace is a moral requirement consistent with rationality and consistency expected in management decision-making. It is not precluded by EAW, and it is compatible with the overlap between the public and private sectors of the economy. Convincing business of the moral necessity of due process, however, is a task yet to be completed.

ENDNOTES

1. *Howard Smith III* v. *American Greetings Corporation,* 304 Ark. 596; 804 S.W.2d 683.
2. H. G. Wood, *A Treatise on the Law of Master and Servant* (Albany, NY: John D. Parsons, Jr., 1877), p. 134.
3. Until the end of 1980 the *Index of Legal Periodicals* indexed employee-employer relationships under this rubric.
4. Lawrence E. Blades, "Employment at Will versus Individual Freedom: On Limiting the Abusive Exercise of Employer Power," *Columbia Law Review,* 67 (1967), p. 1405, quoted from *Payne* v. *Western,* 81 Tenn. 507 (1884), and *Hutton* v. *Watters,* 132 Tenn. 527, S.W. 134 (1915).
5. *Palmateer* v. *International Harvester Corporation,* 85 Ill. App. 2d 124 (1981).
6. *Pierce* v. *Ortho Pharmaceutical Corporation* 845 NJ 58 (NJ 1980), 417 A.2d 505. See also Brian Heshizer, "The New Common Law of Employment: Changes in the Concept of Employment at Will," *Labor Law Journal,* 36 (1985), pp. 95–107.
7. See David Ewing, *Justice on the Job: Resolving Grievances in the Nonunion Workplace* (Boston: Harvard Business School Press, 1989).

8. See R. M. Bastress, "A Synthesis and a Proposal for Reform of the Employment at Will Doctrine," *West Virginia Law Review,* 90 (1988), pp. 319–51.

9. See "Employees' Good Faith Duties," *Hastings Law Journal,* 39 (198). See also *Hudson* v. *Moore Business Forms,* 609 Supp. 467 (N.D. Cal. 1985).

10. See *Lockner* v. *New York,* 198 U.S. (1905), and Adina Schwartz, "Autonomy in the Workplace," in Tom Regan, ed., *Just Business* (New York: Random House, 1984), pp. 129–40.

11. Eric Mack, "Natural and Contractual Rights," *Ethics,* 87 (1977), pp. 153–59.

12. Ian Maitland, "Rights in the Workplace: A Nozickian Argument," in Lisa Newton and Maureen Ford, eds., *Taking Sides* (Guilford, CT: Dushkin Publishing Group), 1990, pp. 34–35.

13. Richard Wallace, "Union Waiver of Public Employees' Due Process Rights," *Industrial Relations Law Journal,* 8 (1986), pp. 583–87.

14. Morris Cohen, "Dialogue on Private Property," *Rutgers Law Review* 9 (1954), pp. 357. See also *Law and the Social Order* (1933) and Robert Hale, "Coercion and Distribution in a Supposedly Non-Coercive State," *Political Science Quarterly,* 38 (1923), pp. 470; John Brest, "State Action and Liberal Theory," *University of Pennsylvania Law Review* (1982), 1296–1329.

15. Gerald Frug, "The City As a Legal Concept," *Harvard Law Review,* 93 (1980), p. 1129.

16. T. M. Scanlon, "Due Process," in J. Roland Pennock and John W. Chapman, eds., *Nomos XVIII: Due Process* (New York: New York University Press, 1977), p. 94.

QUESTIONS ON WERHANE AND RADIN

1. Werhane and Radin assert that EAW allows for an arbitrary treatment of employees that "extends prerogatives to managers that are not equally available to employees." What are these prerogatives? (Are these mentioned by the authors?) Are there specific virtues that might inhibit arbitrary firings?

2. The authors claim that "Arbitrary firings treat people as things." Can you think of examples in which this would be the case? On the other hand, if an *employee* arbitrarily leaves an *employer,* then does this mean that the employee has treated the employer as a "thing"? Why or why not? If the employer *ought* to give reasons for dismissing an employee, then *ought* an employee have to give good reasons if the employee wishes to quit? Should these obligations be enforced by law?

3. Werhane and Radin assert that the claim that due process reduces efficiency "is not documented by the many corporations that have grievance procedures." Does this statement provide a counterargument to the efficiency consideration? Are there laws (or court decisions) that might give large corporations an incentive to enact these grievance procedures?

4. Are there other arguments, not canvassed by Werhane and Radin, for giving employers greater leeway in hiring and firing? For example, might an employer be more willing to take a chance on an employee if the employer knew that the employee might be released easily and without threat of lawsuits? Might the freedom to hire and fire allow for greater productivity overall as employees and employers move to positions that are best for each?

In Defense of Unbridled Freedom of Contract

Eric Mack

Eric Mack is Professor of Philosophy, Tulane University. His scholarly essays focus on the nature of rights and political philosophy more generally. He is the editor of a new edition of Auberon Herbert's The Right and Wrong of Compulsion by the State *(1978).*

I. INTRODUCTION

If one merely stumbled across the phrase, "freedom of contract," one's best guess would be that this phrase referred to a very general doctrine to the effect that each individual is to be free to join with any number of individuals in any form of association or exchange on any terms that are mutually agreed to. That is, no outside party may prohibit or restrict individuals in the types of relationships they establish among themselves by mutual consent. It would be a corollary of such a view that no individual should be required, against his consent, to partake of any relationship with others. According to this corollary, no outside party may impose any relationship or any terms within a relationship upon two or more other parties and no party to a relationship may coercively impose that relationship or any terms of that relationship upon another. Subsequently I shall expand, clarify, and defend this general doctrine. It will, for instance, be important to explain what is to count as *coercive* imposition.

But before pursuing this explication and defense we must note that the actual historical doctrine referred to by the phrase "freedom of contract" represents the implications of this general philosophical doctrine merely within a narrow range of cases. The general doctrine would clearly classify as improper all victimless crime legislation, all coercive restrictions on free market relationships, and even all involuntary taxation. In contrast, the narrower historical doctrine classified as improper restrictions by an outside party (specifically, the State) on the specific terms of employment within legally and socially accepted economic activities. The historical doctrine opposed outside restriction upon who might perform how arduous a task and it opposed restrictions upon what form of payment might be made for agreed upon tasks. Thus, the narrower historical doctrine was among the legal doctrines invoked against laws restricting employment in certain occupations to those of a certain age or sex, against laws restricting the number of hours for which a person could agree to work, and against laws requiring that employees be paid in legal tender (as opposed to company scrip).[1] So, while the advocates of the narrower historical doctrine of liberty of contract are considered to have been radical laissez-fairists, their views were timidly moderate from the perspective of the general philosophical doctrine. In this more modest version freedom of contract probably reached its highwater mark as constitutional doctrine in *Coppage v. Kansas* (decided in 1915). In this decision the Supreme Court majority held unconstitutional a Kansas statute which forbade employers from requiring that their employees agree not to join labor unions as a condition of their employment. The court held that in insisting upon this clause in its employment contracts an employer engages in no "actual or implied coercion or duress." Rather the employer is merely insisting "upon its right to prescribe terms upon which alone it would consent to a continuance of the relationship of employer and employee."[2] The opinions offered in *Coppage v. Kansas* will provide illustrations for many of the arguments and positions discussed in this paper. . . .

Philosophically, there is no satisfactory way to defend the narrower, more hesitant, historical view except by defending the general, unbridled, view of which it is a logical part. Furthermore, anything less than a defense of the unbridled view allows some limitations on freedom of contract which, in turn, will be employed as precedents for further limitations. For example, in *Coppage v. Kansas,* the dissenting opinion cites the prohibition on the sale of lottery tickets[3] as a legitimate and constitutional curtailment of liberty of contract and,

hence, as a sign that other legitimate curtailments are likely to be found. In order to stay off the slippery slope which descends toward the admission of more and more constraints as legitimate, the freedom of contract advocate must reject the legitimacy of any genuine curtailment.[4] It must be remembered, however, that the setting aside of those contracts or clauses of contracts which have resulted from rights violating activities such as threats, deceptions, and (in some cases) "undue influence" will not count as genuine curtailments of freedom of contract. For it is only in terms of a recognition of the rights that are violated by such threats and deceptions that the doctrine of freedom of contract is defined and advanced. Furthermore, an apparent contract may be set aside on the basis of the contractual incompetence of one or more of the parties to it. What is crucial for the advocate of freedom of contract is not that nothing having the appearance of a contract be set aside but, rather, that contracts not be set aside simply *on the basis of their substantive terms.*[5]

II. NATURAL RIGHTS VERSUS SOCIAL GOALS

The moral philosophical perspective from which this essay proceeds is essentially Lockean.[6] Among individuals there are no natural moral slaves and no natural moral masters. No one's purposes or goals take moral precedence over the purposes and goals of any other person in a way which would justify the complete or partial subordination of any individual to any other individual or to any group of individuals. For there is a moral equality among persons. But this moral equality does not merely consist of an equal presence in a morally empty universe—a universe in which no values are objective and in which acts of aggression and subjugation, while not right, are also not wrong. The moral equality of persons includes the equal ultimacy of the value of each person's life. Each individual's life is an ultimate value—to him whose life it is. For each person that which is of fundamental value and is the rational goal of his action and planning is the fulfillment of his best (available) plan of life, i.e., the most harmonious lifetime satisfaction of his desires, interests, and capacities. The value of the fulfillment of a rational life plan or of the elements contributing to such a plan is objective, but agent-relative or positional.[7] It is for him who stands in relationship to a fulfilled rational plan of life as its agent and subject that this fulfillment is ultimately valuable. It is objectively the case that the fulfillment of any given rational plan of life is ultimately valuable to someone (and quite possibly of nonultimate value to other individuals). But the someone for whom it is fundamentally desirable is the party in the position of living and undergoing that life.

This individualistic conception of the equally (but noncommeasurably) ultimate value of each person's respective harmonious fulfillment of his desires, interests, and capacities has crucial implications for how individuals must act (or refrain from acting) toward others. These implications constitute individuals' fundamental natural rights and obligations. In maintaining that each person's well-being is an ultimate value, *the* ultimate value with respect to *that* agent, one is not only maintaining that people constitute a multiplicity of points or even receptacles in which value can be achieved and lodged. For the "receptacles" themselves, i.e., these individuals, respectively occupy moral space not merely as depots for the storage of well-being but as embodied, active, choosing beings having the achievement of their well-being as their respective rational purposes. Given that each person has a specific and separate rational end of his own, his faculties and capacities for choice and action, and his choices and actions, are not like natural resources which are equally morally available to whomever desires to put them to use. Rather, the possession of a separate moral purpose removes each person as an embodied, active, choosing being from the domain of objects which simply exist as possible material for the use of this or that contingently determined individual.

Since a person is an active, choosing being and his faculties and capacities are, morally speaking, uniquely *for* his own well-being, his person and faculties are uniquely a means to this end. One cannot coherently affirm that the well-being of each is his separate and distinctive end without affirming also that some things stand distinctly as means to that end, and hence, as means not available to others. On the most fundamental level, it is the person himself, his existence as an embodied, living, purposive being, which stands as a means to the end which is his well-being and, hence, as material which is morally out of bounds for other people's exploitation.

Since each person is an end-in-himself in the sense that the most cohesive realization of his person, desires, and capacities is the distinctive rational ultimate value (for him), each person is a means to that separate ultimate value which is his successful life and, therefore, no person is a means for anyone else's life or purposes. This is our reading and explication of the Kantian slogan that because each is an end-in-himself, each has a moral immunity against being treated as a means.[8] A

person's moral sovereignty over himself involves claims, i.e., rights, to life and liberty, to property in his own body, and to other property permissibly acquired. There are correlative obligations in all others not to (non-consensually) deprive him of life, liberty, and legitimate property. These (natural) moral rights and obligations exist independent of and prior to any agreements among persons and independent of the social utility or positive legality of recognizing these rights and obligations. These rights and obligations, subject of course to modification through individuals' free relationships with one another, provide the basic extralegal standards for what forms of conduct may be legally prohibited and what forms of conduct must be legally permitted.

In a limited sense, then, there are natural sovereigns—each being a natural sovereign over himself. And persons are not ethereal beings. A person's sovereignty over himself involves a claim to his body and whatever other objects he acquires as instruments of his purposes without violating the like sovereignty of others. His sovereignty involves a claim, a right, to life and liberty, to property in his own body, and to other property permissibly acquired. And its right involves a correlative obligation in all others not to (non-consensually) deprive him of life, liberty, and legitimate property. Understanding "coercion" as constraining a person against his will in a way that involves some violation of his rights, we can speak generally of a right against coercion possessed by each person and an obligation upon all persons not to coerce. These are the (natural) moral rights and obligations of individuals which exist independent of and prior to any agreements among persons and independent of the social utility or positive legality of recognizing these rights and obligations.

In one important respect these are very modest rights and obligations. While each person has a right against all others not to be coerced this right will be satisfied simply by that person's being left alone. As long as an individual is not made to act in ways which do not accord with his purposes he is uncoerced and his right against coercion is being respected. Each person can fulfill his obligation not to coerce by merely leaving others alone. Hence, these natural rights and obligations are negative. That is, Smith's rights require only that Jones *not* coerce him. They require no positive act from Jones. Jones' obligation is fulfilled in *not* coercing others. He needn't perform any positive act in order to fulfill his natural obligations.

This view of natural rights and obligations should be accompanied by a full theory of property rights in external objects. Such a theory would present something like the following structure. A person comes to possess a property right to an object when, through noncoercive activities, he comes to be so related to that object as an instrument of his purposes that subsequently to deprive him of that object without his agreement is to deprive him also of something to which he already has an acknowledged right, *e.g.,* to control over the time, effort, and skill which he has invested in the newly acquired and transformed object. If I have labored on a previously unowned field in order to clear it for planting and then it is seized by others for their purposes, my actions have been disposed of for the purposes of others which I do not share. I and my activities have been treated as resources at the disposal of others. Such a seizure (unless it is done in accordance with previous contractual agreement or as an act of restitution for a previous unjustified seizure) presupposes that the laborer is naturally subservient to and owned by those who seize his product. Nozick points out:

> Seizing the results of someone's labor is equivalent to seizing hours from him and directing him to carry on various activities. If people force you to do certain work, or unrewarded work, for a certain period of time, they decide what you are to do and what purposes your work is to serve apart from your decisions. This process whereby they take this decision from you makes them a *part-owner* of you; it gives them a [legal, but morally unjustified] property right in you. Just as having such partial control and power of decision, by right, over an animal or inanimate object would be to have a property right in it.[9]

Such a seizure is coercive. The natural obligation not to coerce requires, then, that no individual ever be deprived of his legitimate property without his consent. . . .

Of course, in any human *society* individuals do more than merely leave each other alone. Almost all individuals receive all sorts of goods and services from other individuals. Yet any disposal of the time, activity or property of Jones requires Jones' agreement. He must willingly make or allow that disposal (and he may will or allow anything noncoercive). In order to insure the provision of goods and services by others, each of us seeks pledges from others that desired goods or services will be forthcoming. A pledge from Smith to Jones to provide a certain service generates a positive right in Jones to have that service performed and a positive obligation in Smith to perform that service. Characteristically, of course, such a pledge from Smith to Jones will be elicited in return for a rights-generating pledge from Jones to Smith, *e.g.,* a pledge to pay Smith a certain fee for his service. All the special (positive) rights that in-

dividuals have beyond the (general) negative right against coercion and all the special (positive) obligations that individuals have beyond the (general) negative obligation not to coerce are the products of contractual relationships. Each person, then, has a right to accept any contractual offer (except for payments to coerce others). But no one has a right to be made any particular offer.[10] So, Smith must elicit contractual offers from Jones by means of the goods or services Smith can counter-offer to Jones. And it is the fact that Jones has no right to any particular counter-offer by Smith which requires that Jones adjust his offers to Smith's preferences just as Smith adjusts his counter-offers to Jones. In emphasizing this symmetry of rights to withhold agreement to exchanges, the majority in *Coppage v. Kansas* asserted that,

> The right of a person to sell his labor upon such terms as he deems proper is, in its essence, the same as the right of the purchaser of labor to prescribe the conditions upon which he will accept such labor from the person offering to sell it.[11]

Strictly speaking, however, neither party has a (precontractual) right to an exchange on any particular terms. Each simply has a right not to have terms of exchange imposed upon him. The actual terms of exchange in a noncoerced agreement must, then, represent a mutual accommodation among the contracting parties.

These symmetrically ascribed rights are violated by, *e.g.,* minimum wage laws. Suppose employee Jones, who in the absence of minimum wage laws would contract to work for Smith for $2.50 per hour, becomes subject to a $3.00 per hour minimum wage law. There are two alternative cases: either Jones will no longer be employed or he will be offered and will accept a contract at $3.00 per hour. The first case was, it seems, largely ignored by the courts in freedom of contract cases. Yet it is when this alternative is realized that Jones' freedom of contract is most clearly and grievously violated. For in this case Jones would want to offer his services at $2.50 per hour and would be coercively prevented from doing so. Suppose, in contrast, that Jones remains employed at $3.00 per hour. Characteristically, courts invoking the freedom of contract doctrine would say that here too Jones has been denied his freedom of contract. Now although this is true—Jones was not free to accept $2.50 per hour and an increased risk of unemployment was coercively imposed upon him—it also seems a bit disingenuous. For in these circumstances the only act which Jones is coercively forbidden to do (*viz.,* offering to work at $2.50 per hour) is one which, by hypothesis, Jones does not want to do (at least after he knows that he will still be employed at $3.00 per hour).[12] The real victim in this instance is Smith who is coercively required to make an offer which he has a right not to make and which, except for being coerced not to make a lower offer, he would not make. The right not to make contractual offers, which includes the right not to make the more pleasing (to others) offers which would not be made in the absence of coercion, is just as central to freedom of contract as the right to tender and accept offers. . . .

The type of individualistic and pluralistic natural rights view I have sketched has been labeled a "moral side-constraint" view. For on this view, the only constraints on an individual's actions are constraints against employing certain means in the pursuit of one's goals—whatever those goals be. Individuals are morally constrained from taking paths to their goals which involve the violation of others' natural or contractual rights, *i.e.*, which involve coercion or default on promised actions. What a person must aim at with his life and time is in no way constrained (except in the trivial sense of being constrained from acting with the violation of moral side-constraints as his end). Such an approach in social and legal philosophy is to be contrasted with what I call the social goal approach. According to each version of the social goal approach there is some single, overall, social goal *e.g.*, utility maximization, equality, stability, etc. or some mixture of these, to which each person's life and effort should be devoted. Each person is so obligated to pursue this or that favored social goal that he may properly be coerced into doing whatever most accords with realizing that goal. Persons are to look at themselves and others as resources to be devoted to this common social project. If particular coercive acts are not conducive to the greatest realization of the favored goal, then they should not be done. . . . Many objections to principled defenses of freedom—including defenses of freedom of contract—proceed from one social goal theory or another. But, to put it briefly, none of these objections are sound since no social goal theory is true since the moral side-constraint view is true. There are moral constraints on how we must treat other individuals which do not leave room for our thinking of people as (even partial) unclaimed resources permissibly to be used for "our" or "society's" purposes. There is no collective social purpose and no specially ordained individual purposes which can justify the forceful subordination of individuals and their (noncoercive) life-plans.[13]

III. OBJECTIONS TO UNBRIDLED FREEDOM OF CONTRACT

. . . We may now consider four recurring objections to unbridled freedom of contract each of which adopts the language of freedom, noncoercion or just exchange.

According to one objection, belief in unbridled freedom of contract results from slipping into a faultily empty conception of freedom. It is claimed that noncoercion should be valued only insofar as it is a condition for freedom in the sense of persons having abilities and opportunities to do what they want (or what would make them happy, or what they should do). One historically important advocate of this conception of freedom, T. H. Green, gives as the initial characterization of such "positive freedom": "a positive power or capacity of doing or enjoying something worth doing or enjoying."[14] The further claim is that if the promotion of such freedom is the valued goal, then although we might *sometimes* allow freedom of contract as a means to this goal, we should also be prepared to interfere with the terms of a (potential) contract if that interference would maximize positive freedom. While some forcible intervention against Jones, *i.e.*, some deprivation of Jones' negative liberty, may carry with it some loss of positive freedom for Jones, we are to favor it if it also brings a greater gain of positive freedom, for, *e.g.*, Smith. Many thinkers have pointed out that the theory of positive freedom blurs the useful distinctions between a person's being free to do X, his having the opportunity to do X, his having the ability to do X, etc. At the very least the advocate of positive liberty must acknowledge that he really is promoting some ill-defined mixture of (negative) freedom, opportunity, capacity, etc. More importantly, he turns out to be just another version of a social goal theorist. For his theory will take one of two possible forms. He may advocate a utilitarianism of positive freedom, *i.e.*, that everyone should be seen as a social resource for maximizing the sum of positive freedom. As with all types of utilitarianism, this approach will require that individuals be deprived of their positive freedom when and to the extent that such deprivations yield larger gains in positive freedom for others. Whereas one individual's enjoyment of negative freedom (*i.e.*, of freedom from coercion as previously defined) never requires that any other person surrender his enjoyment of negative freedom, one individual's possession of the opportunities and abilities which make up positive freedom may well require that others be denied or deprived of opportunities and abilities which are necessary for *their* positive freedom. In shifting to positive freedom, then, one becomes entangled in determining the relative moral weights of alternative combinations of positive freedoms with the aim of favoring the most socially weighty combination. If one wants to obscure the fact that some persons' freedoms are thereby to be sacrificed for larger gains in other individuals' freedoms, one can insist that only the freedoms which are part of the socially best combination of freedoms are true freedoms. To avoid acknowledging the clash of positive freedoms, one may whittle down what counts as freedom by declaring that true positive freedom is only displayed in actions which serve or partake of some sanctioned social goal, *e.g.,* "the common good." . . .

Two objections to the general doctrine of freedom of contract stem from the claim that on some occasions such a freedom sanctions coercion. The first of these two objections focuses especially on "necessitous" persons. It is claimed that persons who are in dire circumstances are not really acting freely in forming the contractual ties which will remove them from those dire circumstances. Thus, to take one familiar example, imagine that Jones comes across Smith hanging from the edge of a cliff. If Jones has no positive obligation to save Smith, then he can refuse to save Smith unless Smith contractually obligates himself to transfer all his worldly possessions to Jones. Suppose that such an agreement is reached and Smith is saved. It might then be argued that the obligation to Jones should be set aside or moderated because Smith was not truly free when it was made. But this argument once again confuses lack of freedom in the sense of incapacity in the face of natural facts to do certain things (pull oneself up over the edge of the cliff) and lack of freedom in the sense of being coerced, *i.e.,* being non-consensually deprived by another of something to which one has a right. As Smith is hanging over the edge he is perfectly uncoerced—unless Jones is standing on his fingers. He is no more in a state of being coerced than he would be if no one else were within 100 miles of him. Similarly Smith is not being threatened with the violation of his right against coercion. Even his trip to the foot of the cliff, should it occur, will not be caused by Jones (unless Jones stamps on his fingers).[15] Hence, although he may be very eager to elicit Jones' help, what he agrees to do in return for that help is not agreed to *under duress.* Smith's eagerness for the agreement is a measure of the value (to him) of the service which Jones can perform for him. When we are inclined to say that Jones takes advantage of Smith we should at least recall that, in Smith's eyes, the service Jones renders him is more valuable than what Smith surrenders for this service.

A third objection to freedom of contract asserts that attractive offers coerce persons into entering contractual relationships. In the face of an alluring offer an individual is "threatened" with the loss of the (offered) benefit. There are many ways to answer this charge. We can begin by noting that an attractive offer induces Smith to do something he wouldn't otherwise do *by means of appealing* to other purposes and aims of Smith. Smith places only negative value on standing on his head until, in light of an offer of monetary payment, he sees that standing on his head will be a means to a dinner at Antoine's. Rather than subverting the direction of a person's actions by his own aims and purposes, such offers provide new avenues by which a person can pursue his own relatively highly valued aims and purposes. Furthermore, it is misleading to say that Smith acts under the threat of losing (not getting) the payment. For the payment is not something to which he has a right (prior to a contractual agreement). Assuming that there is no prior contract, nothing is inflicted upon Smith by his simply not being provided with that payment. Hence, holding out the prospect of his not getting that payment does not constitute a threat of inflicting something on Smith. The program of respecting each person's rights, of coercing no (peaceful) individuals, is in no way compromised by "seductive" offers or by individuals being moved by a desire not to miss a chance of being seduced. . . .

Finally there is an objection that is directed against the claim that all free contracts are just in that each party *ex ante* advances his interests by means of each of his contractual relationships, *i.e.,* within a given relationship no party ever benefits at the expense of another party. Against this endorsement of free contractual relationships, it is often claimed that justice in an exchange requires an equitable division (usually conceived of as an equal division) of the benefits of exchange and that in some cases unregulated terms of exchange result in inequitable (specifically, unequal) divisions of the benefits. That the terms of a given contract involve an unequal "distribution" of the benefits of that contractual exchange is itself traced to the unequal economic status, and hence, to the unequal "bargaining power" of the parties to that agreed upon exchange. Now the logical inference to draw from these claims would seem to be that bargaining parties should be made equal and then allowed utter freedom of contract. But such an inference is not usually drawn and understandably so. For a program of continually bringing people back to the egalitarian starting point which free contracts would disrupt would be equivalent to a program of continuous regulation of the terms of contractual relationships. The inference which is drawn is that certain specific restrictions (*e.g.*, minimum wage laws) should be continuously imposed upon all relevant contracts—restrictions which would rule out supposedly blatantly inequitable terms. There are many problems with this view. One major problem is the lack of any basis for the claim that justice requires equality (or any other specific proportion) of benefits. Each person gains from free exchange. Each party gets some good or service from the other which he would not have gotten except for their mutual agreement. On what conceivable basis can it be known that the sum of benefits ought to be equally divided? The more plausible view is that these benefits should be divided in accordance with the terms freely agreed to by the parties to the exchange. . . .

Finally, the whole idea of unequal bargaining power leading to inequitable divisions of benefits is, at best, obscure. For the "stronger" bargaining power is simply the party who is the position to satisfy what are seen as another party's vital or vitally felt needs. But if a bargain is struck, then those purportedly most vital needs will be satisfied.[16] So the powerfully positioned bargainer is just the one who, if an exchange is allowed, renders what appears to be the more vital service. All that stands in the way of seeing the exchange from *this* perspective is the supposition that the less well positioned party really has a prior right to the services or goods of the better endowed party. Given this supposition, the free contractual outcome will be seen as inequitable since it reflects the failure of the well-positioned to fulfill his supposed (pre-contractual) obligation toward the less-positioned person. But in the absence of any previous agreement to provide his services or goods no person, however well-positioned, has such obligations. Each has only the negative obligation not to coerce others. And this obligation is fulfilled by the well positioned party.

Let us return to the horrendous cliff-hanging example to put this defense of "unbridled" freedom of contract within a broader moral perspective. The point of focusing on such extreme examples is to engage the opponent of freedom of contract on his (intuitively) strongest ground. It is to grant that there are extreme cases and to indicate the reasons why, on principle, even in these instances, the theoretical case for freedom of contract still stands. The theoretical motivation of the defender of freedom of contract is to block exceptions to this freedom which might then serve as bases for further, and far more costly and counterproductive, *legally imposed* encroachments on the freedom of contract. The principled advocate of freedom of contract need no

more delight in Jones's exercise of his right to demand great payments from Smith than the principled advocate of freedom of speech need delight in the racist's exercise of his freedom of speech.

Indeed, in both cases, the advocate of the right in question may view its particular exercise as morally despicable, as profoundly contrary to the advocate's conception of worthy human life. It is sometimes claimed that the libertarian's individualistic (agent-relative) conception of value precludes even a *moral* condemnation of, for example, the person who only sees another's distress as an attractive bargaining situation. But such claims, I think, ultimately rest on the idea that it is contrary to an individual's well-being to empathetically appreciate the value of others' lives and purposes and to be moved by such sentiments as sympathy and generosity or on the idea that an insistence upon people's libertarian rights will harden people and make them less able to empathize with others and less likely to be moved by sympathy and generosity. I believe that both of these ideas are profoundly mistaken. They are, after all, the flip sides of the implausible ideas that collectivist moralities enhance people's appreciation of the value of others' separate lives and purposes and that collectivist politics enhances people's sympathies and generous impulses. So the individualist libertarian is far from precluded from condemning *as a matter of morality* mean-spirited exercises of the rights he asserts as a matter of political philosophy. But he does assert those rights, including the right of freedom of contract, as defining the legitimate legal framework within which individual ambitions and social cooperation may be pursued.

ENDNOTES

1. Roscoe Pound, "Liberty of Contract," *Yale Law Journal* (May 1909): 417.
2. *Coppage* v. *Kansas* 236 U.S. 8 (1915).
3. *Coppage* v. *Kansas* 28.
4. The dissenting judges in *Coppage* v. *Kansas* pose hard questions for the advocate of freedom of contract. They ask, e.g., whether it can "be successfully contended that the State may not, in the public interest, prohibit an agreement to forego [milita] enlistment as against public policy?" And they ask whether the State may not prohibit an agreement "to forego affiliation with a particular political party, or the support of a particular candidate for office?" (37). To reject such proposed genuine curtailments, the advocates of unbridled freedom of contract must argue that: there can be no legitimate "public policy" over and above the protection of individual rights (including the rights involved in

liberty of contract); no violations of some individuals' rights (i.e., prohibiting parties from agreeing not to enlist) can be justified in terms of these violations' being the means for protecting others' rights; engaging in political activities is (at most) on a par with other rightful activities and hence, as in the case of these other activities, one can permissibly sell one's abstention from it.

5. For an illuminating emphasis on the distinction between substantive and procedural defects and an insistence that contract may be set aside or prohibited only on the basis of procedural defects, see Richard Epstein, "Unconscionability: A Critical Reappraisal," *Journal of Law and Economics* (October 1975). The insistence that substantively contracts not be "unconscionable" is the form taken by most recent attacks on freedom of contract. See Epstein for references to this literature.

6. Since a full defense of the general freedom of contract perspective would be a task for several volumes, it is my intention here to sketch some of the features of this defense, and to note why the social philosophy that embodies the general doctrine of freedom of contract is more plausible than each of its fundamental competitors. If these competing social philosophies are rejected, then many possible objections to universal freedom of contract are rejected also. For instance, if utilitarianism is dismissed, then so too will be the objections to liberty of contract that are based on claims that this or that set of restrictions on freedom of contract would enhance social utility. Similarly, if egalitarianism is dismissed, then so too will be objections to liberty of contract based on the inequality of outcomes that freedom of contract in general or free contract in specific tend to yield. However, as we shall see, the most common objections to unbridled freedom of contract—objections directed at restricting this freedom in special cases, not at utterly abolishing it—appear to come from within the philosophical perspective that generates the (initial) universal doctrine. For this perspective centers on the value of realizing individualistic conceptions of liberty and justice and the most common objections to unbridled freedom of contract assert that, in special cases, such a freedom leads to or sanctifies coercion or injustice. From the point of view of these objections, there is something inconsistent in and unstable about unbridled freedom of contract. For, the view goes, if one really values liberty or justice, then in the name of these values one must avoid the mechanical application of the doctrine to all possible cases, whatever the special features of the case. We shall turn to these specific, apparently internal, objections to unbridled freedom of contract after briefly considering the philosophical foundations for freedom of contract and the character of competing philosophical perspectives. For the next several paragraphs, I draw on my essay, "The Ethics of Taxation: Rights Versus

Public Goods," in D. R. Lee, ed., *Taxation and the Deficit Economy* (San Francisco: Pacific Institute, 1986).

7. For a recent account of this conception of objective, albeit relational, value, see Amartya Sen's "Evaluator Relativity and Consequential Evaluation," *Philosophy and Public Affairs* (Spring 1983).

8. But this is not intended as an explication of what Kant himself actually meant.

9. Robert Nozick, *Anarchy, State, and Utopia* (New York: Basic Books, 1974), p. 172.

10. In *Coppage* v. *Kansas* this principle is exemplified in the majority view that: "Concerning the full right of the individual to join the union, he has no inherent right to do this and still remain in the employ of one who is unwilling to employ a union man, any more than the same individual has a right to join the union without the consent of that organization. Can it be doubted that a labor organization—a voluntary association of working men—has the inherent and constitutional right to deny membership to any man who will not agree that during such membership he will not accept or retain employment in company with non-union men? Or that a union man has the constitutional right to decline proffered employment unless the employer will agree not to employ any non-union man?" (19–20). Note that this opinion assigns a constitutional liberty to unions that is violated by current right-to-work constraints on unions.

11. *Coppage* v. *Kansas* 10. As noted in the text, this passage is potentially misleading. It should be read in conjunction with the passage in note 16.

12. Although one does not have to want to do something in order to have a right to do it, and one's wanting to do something certainly does not give one a right to do it, it is odd to attach great *importance* to a person's being forbidden a rightful act that, by the nature of the case, he would not perform anyway.

13. For the rejections of all the types of theories I have labelled "social goal" theories on the basis of a Lockean view of individual entitlements, see Chapter 7 ("Distributive Justice") in Nozick, *Anarchy, State, and Utopia*, and my essays, "Distribution versus Justice," in *Ethics* (January 1976), and "Liberty and Justice" in J. Arthur and B. Shaw, eds., *Justice and Economic Distribution* (Englewood Cliffs, NJ: Prentice-Hall, 1978).

14. T. H. Green, "Freedom of Contract," in J. R. Rodman, ed., *The Political Theory of T. H. Green* (New York: Appleton-Century-Crofts, 1964), p. 51.

15. See Eric Mack, "Bad Samaritanism and the Causation of Harm," *Philosophy and Public Affairs* (Summer 1980).

16. Thus, in *Coppage* v. *Kansas,* we find ". . . each party when contracting is inevitably more or less influenced by the question of whether he has much property, or little, or none; for the contract is made to the very end that each may gain something that he needs or desires more urgently than that which he proposes to give in exchange."

QUESTIONS ON MACK

1. How does Mack justify his defense of "unbridled" freedom of contract? How does his account of rights follow from the claim that each person's life is of equal ultimate value? If each person's life has an ultimate value, then why wouldn't that entail that each person should be guaranteed the conditions necessary for living that life?

2. Consider the case of Smith who, hanging from the edge of a cliff, agrees to transfer all of his possessions to Jones in return for Jones saving him. Why does Mack contend that such an agreement would not be coercive and would not be impermissible? What alternatives does Smith have to agreeing to the terms of Jones' contract? Mack states that Smith is not *under duress,* but can a person's will be constrained in ways that do not involve the violation of rights? And even if the contract is valid, is there still room for considering the actions of Jones to be morally wrong (though permissible)?

3. How would Mack's account of contract affect the contracts of business and commerce? How does Mack attempt to rebut the charge of "coercive offers"? Can you think of potential contracts which might be considered to be coercive offers?

Moral Perspectives on Affirmative Action

Gertrude Ezorsky

Gertrude Ezorsky is Professor Emerita of Philosophy at the City University of New York, Brooklyn College. She is the editor of Moral Rights in the Workplace *(1987) and* Philosophical Perspectives on Punishment *(1973). This excerpt is taken from* Racism and Justice: The Case for Affirmative Action *(1991).*

AA's [Affirmative Action's] benefits to blacks can be viewed from both a forward-looking and a backward-looking moral perspective.[1] From a forward-looking perspective, the purpose of AA is to reduce institutional racism, thereby moving blacks toward the goal of occupational integration. When that goal is achieved, millions of blacks will no longer be unfairly barred by the effects of their racist history from employment benefits.

Moreover, such integration will significantly dissipate invidious racist attitudes. As I have suggested earlier, individuals socialized in a world where blacks are assimilated throughout the hierarchy of employment will no longer readily assume that they belong at the bottom.

From a backward-looking perspective, blacks have a moral claim to compensation for past injury. The paramount injustice perpetrated against blacks—enslavement—requires such compensation. If the effects of that murderous institution had been dissipated over time, the claim to compensation now would certainly be weaker. From the post-Reconstruction period to the present, however, racist practices have continued to transmit and reinforce the consequences of slavery. Today blacks still predominate in those occupations that in a slave society would be reserved for slaves.

Such ongoing racism has not been the work only of private parties. The racism of government practices encouraged race discrimination by landlords who blocked the escape of blacks from ghettos, and by employers and unions who refused to hire, promote, or train them, as well as widespread communication of an insulting stereotype of blacks, derogatory to their ability and character. During the first two-thirds of this century, racism was in many respects official public policy. That policy included: legally compulsory segregation into inferior private and publicly owned facilities such as schools, which—as recognized in *Brown* v. *Board of Education of Topeka* (1954)—violated the constitutional rights of black children; court-upheld racially restrictive covenants in the transfer of private residences; antimiscegenation laws that resembled the prohibition of marriage by persons with venereal diseases; race discrimination in government practices such as public employment, voting registration procedures, federal assistance to business persons and farmers, and allocation of state and municipal services to black neighborhoods (e.g., police protection, sanitation, and educational resources); manifest racial bias in the courts; and pervasive police brutality against black people.

The practices of the Federal Housing Authority exemplified governmental racism. For decades after its inception in 1934, the FHA, which insured mortgage loans, enshrined racial segregation as public policy. The agency set itself up as the protector of all-white neighborhoods, especially in the suburbs. According to urban planner Charles Abrams, the FHA's racial policies could "well have been culled from the Nuremberg Laws."[2] Today white suburban youths continue to benefit from the past racist practices of this government agency. Not only will they inherit homes purchased with the FHA assistance, denied to blacks; they also enjoy racially privileged access to the expanding employment opportunities in all-white suburbs. In 1973, legal scholar Boris I. Bittker summed up governmental misconduct against blacks: "More than any other form of official misconduct, racial discrimination against blacks was systematic, unrelenting, authorized at the highest governmental levels, and practiced by large segments of the population."[3] The role of government in practicing, protecting, and providing sanction for racism by private parties suffices to demonstrate the moral legitimacy of legally required compensation to blacks. . . .

Are AA measures, such as preferential treatment in employment, an appropriate method of compensation for blacks? In fact, federal and state governments recognized the appropriateness of employment preference as an instrument of compensation to veterans long before the adoption of AA measures.[4] This court-sanctioned policy has affected the employment of millions of workers, and in some states where veteran preference is practiced, nonveterans have practically no chance to obtain the best positions.

What are the specific claims of those who find moral fault with such programs? First, concerning the compensatory rationale for AA, some analysts argue that compensation for blacks is counter-productive. Others claim that better-off blacks do not deserve the compensation of preferential treatment, especially where whites excluded by such preference are themselves disadvantaged. Second, AA trammels the rights of others—of employers who have a right to hire whomever they please, or of white candidates who are wrongfully excluded by preferential treatment. Finally, some critics suggest that blacks themselves may be morally injured by racial preference, which allegedly damages their self-respect.

COMPENSATION AS COUNTERPRODUCTIVE?

Shelby Steele, a professor of English, criticizes the compensatory claim for AA, according to which AA is "something 'owed,' as reparation": "Suffering can be endured and overcome, it cannot be repaid. To think otherwise is to prolong the suffering."[5] But if compensation should be withheld from blacks because suffering cannot be repaid, then for the same reason compensation should also be withheld from veterans, Holocaust survivors, and victims of industrial accidents. Members of these groups do not complain that compensation prolongs their "suffering"; on the contrary, they have often insisted on their right to such benefits. I see no reason for assuming that compensation per se injures its recipients.

AFFLUENT BLACKS AS UNDESERVING

The philosopher William Blackstone criticizes the compensatory rationale for preferential treatment for affluent blacks:

> There is no invariable connection between a person's being black . . . and suffering from past invidious discrimination. . . . There are many blacks and other minority group members who are highly advantaged, who are sons and daughters of well-educated, affluent lawyers, doctors and industrialists. A policy of reverse discrimination would mean that such highly advantaged individuals would receive preferential treatment over the sons and daughters of disadvantaged whites or disadvantaged members of other minorities. I submit that such a situation is not social justice.[6]

Blackstone offers two arguments: (1) Black persons born into better-off black families have not suffered discrimination; hence, he suggests, they do not deserve compensation. (2) Preference that benefits these blacks at the expense of disadvantaged nonblacks is unjust.

First, it is false that blacks born into better-off families have not been injured by discrimination. Because racist treatment of blacks in business and professions reduced family income, it hurt their sons and daughters. Among the racist injuries these black parents suffered were the racially discriminatory policies of federal agencies in allocation of business loans, low-interest mortgages, agrarian price supports, and government contracts.[7] They also were victimized by racist exclusion from practice in white law firms and hospitals and by legally imposed or encouraged residential and school segregation that impaired their education and isolated them from white business contacts. Because of such invidious discrimination, black professionals and entrepreneurs could do far less for their children than their white counterparts. Moreover, the sons and daughters of black lawyers, doctors, and business persons have themselves suffered the experience of living in a segregated, pervasively racist society.

Laurence Thomas, a black university professor of philosophy, attests to the humiliating distrust that he and other well-placed black academics endure today in public places.[8] Fears that affect blacks of all classes are described by Don Jackson, a black police sergeant who, while investigating reports of police racism in 1989, was stopped by white police officers, one of whom shoved Jackson's head through a window during the arrest.

> The feeling that no matter how hard you worked you could always be reduced to the status of a "field nigger" haunts the lives of black Americans at every economic stratum. . . . It has long been the role of the police to see that the plantation mentality is passed from one generation of blacks to an-

other. . . . The black American finds that the most prominent reminder of his second-class citizenship are the police. . . . A variety of stringent laws were enacted and enforced to stamp the imprint of inequality on the mind of the black American. . . . No one has enforced these rules with more zeal than the police. Operating free of constitutional limitations, the police have long been the greatest nemesis of blacks, irrespective of whether they are complying with the law or not. We have learned that there are cars we are not supposed to drive, streets we are not supposed to walk. We may still be stopped and asked "Where are you going, boy?" Whether we're in a Mercedes or a Volkswagon.[9]

Even if one assumes that the economically better-off blacks are less deserving of compensation, it hardly follows that they do not deserve any compensation. As Bernard Boxill observes in *Blacks and Social Justice:* "Because I have lost only one leg, I may be less deserving of compensation than another who has lost two legs, but it does not follow that I deserve no compensation."[10]

It is true that where preference has been extended to blacks—as with craft workers, professionals, blue- and white-collar employees, teachers, police, and firefighters—some excluded whites may be financially less well off than the blacks who gained. This shift fails to show that these blacks were not victimized by invidious discrimination for which they should be compensated. . . .

UNQUALIFIED BLACKS AS UNAFFECTED BY AA

Thomas Nagel, a philosopher who endorses preferential treatment, nevertheless faults the compensatory justification for such preference, claiming that blacks who benefit from it are probably not the ones who suffered most from discrimination; "those who don't have the qualifications even to be considered" do not gain from preferential policies.[11]

Of course, AA preference does not help blacks obtain very desirable employment if they lack the qualifications even to be considered for such positions. But preferential treatment in diverse areas of the public and private sector has benefited not only highly skilled persons but also poorly educated workers. It is also true that blacks who lack the qualifications even to be considered for *any* employment will not gain from AA preference. As I indicated in my critique of William J. Wilson, AA cannot help those so destroyed as to be incapable of any work or on-the-job training, who require other compensatory race-specific rehabilitation programs. But AA employment programs should not perform the function of these programs.[12] The claim that unemployable blacks are most deserving does not imply that employ-

able blacks fail to deserve any—or even a great deal of—compensation.

Granted, we do not know whether the particular blacks who benefit from preference at each level in the hierarchy of employment are the very same individuals who, absent a racist past, would have qualified at that level by customary standards. Justified group compensation, however, does not require satisfaction of such rigid criteria. Veterans who enjoy hiring, promotion, and seniority preference are surely not the very same individuals who, absent their military service, would have qualified for the positions they gained by such preference.

Unlike job preference for veterans, AA racial preference in employment contributes to eradication of a future evil. It is an instrument for ending occupational segregation of blacks, a legacy of their enslavement.

THE RIGHTS OF EMPLOYERS

According to libertarian philosophers, laws that require any type of AA in the workplace—indeed, those merely requiring passive nondiscrimination—violate the rights of private employers. The philosopher Robert Nozick suggests that the right of employers to hire is relevantly similar to the right of individuals to marry.[13] Just as individuals should be free to marry whomever they please, so private entrepreneurs should be free to employ whomever they please, and government should not interfere with employers in their hiring decisions.

But surely the freedom to choose one's spouse and the freedom to select one's employees are relevantly different. Individuals denied such freedom of choice in marriage are forced to give their bodies to their spouses. They are subject to rape—a destructive, brutal, and degrading intrusion. Marital choices belong to the deeply personal sphere where indeed government should keep out. State intervention in employment is another matter. To require that an auto plant hire some black machinists falls outside the sphere of the deeply personal; it is not, like rape, a destructive, brutal, and degrading personal intrusion. I conclude that the analogy between freedom to marry and freedom to hire fails.[14]

THE RIGHTS OF WHITE CANDIDATES

According to some philosophers, while the social goal of preferential treatment may be desirable, the moral cost is too high. The burden it imposes on adversely affected whites violates their right to equal treatment. They are unfairly singled out for sacrifice. Thomas Nagel states that "the most important argument against preferential treatment is that it subordinates the individual's right to equal treatment to broader social aims."[15]

Some proponents of preferential treatment reject the charge of unfairness because, as they see the matter, whites have either been responsible for immoral racist practices or have gained from them. According to this claim, all whites *deserve* to pay the cost of preferential treatment (hereafter, the desert claim).[16] I do not accept the desert claim; indeed, I suggest that the criticism of racial preference as unfair to adversely affected whites is not without merit. The relevant point is not that such preference be abandoned but rather that it be implemented differently.

According to the desert claim, whites either have been responsible for racism or have passively benefited from it. Let us examine the responsibility claim first.

Certainly no one has demonstrated that all whites, or even a majority, are responsible for racism. How then shall the culpable whites be identified? Many employers and unions have certainly engaged in either overt racism or avoidable neutral practices that obviously excluded blacks. Perhaps they should pay the cost of discrimination remedies by, for example, continuing to pay blacks laid off by race-neutral seniority? But, on the other hand, some employers and union officials were not responsible for racist injury to blacks, and they do not deserve to pay the cost of a remedy for racism.

Similar problems arise when we attempt to identify those who passively benefited from racist practices. Let us assume that such beneficiaries do bear a measure of culpability for racism. How can we mark them out?

The salient fact is that white workers have *both* gained and lost from racism. On the one hand, the benefits to white workers from racism—overt and institutional—are undeniable. As a group, they have been first in line for hiring, training, promotion, and desirable job assignment, but last in line for seniority-based layoff. As white, they have also benefited from housing discrimination in areas where jobs could be had and from the racist impact of selection based on personal connections, seniority, and qualifications. Indeed many white candidates fail to realize that their superior qualifications may be due to their having attended predominantly white schools.

On the other hand, white workers have also lost because of racism. As a divisive force, racism harms labor, both black and white. Since blacks have more reason to fear management reprisal, they are less unwilling to work under excessive strain or for lower wages. This attitude, although quite understandable, makes it more difficult for labor, white as well as black, to attain better working conditions. . . .

The willingness of blacks to accept lower wages and adverse working conditions reduces labor's bargaining power generally with management. . . .

On the whole, some white workers have lost and some have gained from racism. But to disentangle the two groups is a practical impossibility; the blameworthy cannot be marked off from the innocent.

COMPENSATING WHITES FOR BLACK PREFERENTIAL TREATMENT

In some situations compensation by innocent parties appears to be morally acceptable. For example, Germans born after World War II surely have no responsibility for the Holocaust, yet they pay taxes that fund reparations for Jewish victims. These Germans, however, pay a not exorbitant monetary assessment, but an individual white worker affected by preferential treatment loses a promotion or a job, surely a significant difference.

Someone must bear the cost of overcoming the evil of racism, but preferential treatment does seem to distribute that burden unfairly. Whites adversely affected by such treatment do appear *singled out* for sacrifice, while others—among whom are perpetrators of racism—pay nothing. The singling-out issue arises in two kinds of situations, in layoff and in hiring and advancement.

Layoff. If AA is to be effective, it must include measures that protect black employees from layoffs induced by poor business conditions. However, the sacrifice for white workers who are deprived of their jobs as a result of preferential retention of blacks is serious. Hence, wherever possible, alternatives to layoff which reduce the burden or spread it more equitably over the work force should be utilized. Among such alternatives are deferred salary arrangements (which in 1991 helped prevent teacher layoffs in New York City), payless holidays, early retirement incentives for older workers, and work-sharing. . . . Since the reduced work disbenefit is distributed equitably among all the employees of Smith and Co. through a reduced work week and partial unemployment insurance, neither blacks nor whites suffer disproportionate injury.

Where work-sharing or other measures that avoid or reduce layoffs is impossible, the adverse effect of seniority-based layoff on blacks can be decreased by a preferential treatment measure: At Smith and Co., 20 percent of the whites and 20 percent of the blacks would be laid off by seniority within their racial group; hence the layoff burden is shared equally by whites and blacks. Since blacks as a group are less senior than whites, however, some blacks who retain their jobs will be less senior than some whites who lose them.

The singling-out effect of such preferential treatment on white employees can be diminished by substantial monetary awards, funded by the federal government to supplement unemployment insurance. Such financial awards are important not only because many workers are far from affluent, but also because they would tend to minimize opposition to preferential retention.[17] . . .

Hiring and Promotion. Preferential treatment in hiring is exemplified when a basically qualified black is selected over a more qualified white; preferential treatment in promotion occurs when a less qualified black is promoted or, where seniority determines promotion, when a black is advanced over a more senior employee. Although failure to gain a position or promotion is less serious than losing one's current job, the disbenefit of such singling out for affected whites is still significant. Monetary compensation to those whites, . . . funded by a progressive tax, appears to be a reasonable measure. Compensation, however, is a problem, because there is an important difference between seniority cases and qualifications cases—whether they involve promotion, hiring, or layoff. When preference is accorded to less senior blacks, the identity of the adversely affected, more senior whites is evident. Determining which white workers would be entitled to the financial awards I have proposed is an easy matter.

In qualifications cases, however, it is often not easy to determine which candidate, absent preferential treatment for blacks, would have been selected from among all the applicants. Does the past history of the firm or department show a clear commitment to the best-qualified candidate? Or were some candidates selected because they pandered to supervisors or knew how to use their influential contacts or because their ability posed no threat to mediocre incumbents?

Also, unless the qualifications criteria are themselves clear and objective, it would be very difficult to prove that one is the best qualified among all the candidates.

Hence in qualification cases monetary awards to rejected whites are reasonable only if there is already in place a clear selection criterion, such as a test, a Ph.d, or a blind review of research that makes it evident who, absent racial preference, would have been selected from all the candidates. . . .

MERITOCRATIC CRITICS

Some AA critics, whom I shall call meritocrats, believe that justice in the workplace is exemplified by selection according to merit standards. Hence they claim that racial preference violates the rights of more qualified white candidates. Note the difference between the meritocratic argument and the singling-out criticism I have just discussed. The meritocratic claim implies that the rights of rejected, more qualified whites are violated only because they are better qualified. Hence the meritocratic argument, unlike the singling-out criticism, has no bearing on racial preference in seniority-based selection.

Before we appraise the meritocratic criticism, a digression from the issue of preferential treatment will be useful. The meritocratic view conflicts with AA only when operative standards of competence are reduced by AA preference; however, there is a widespread perception that (seniority aside), all AA measures conflict with merit criteria. Hence I will show at the outset that certain types of AA, including some apparently preferential measures, actually raise the level of job performance. I then appraise the meritocratic criticism where it does apply, that is, to cases where preferential treatment would reduce competence on the job.

As indicated earlier, according to the employment guidelines upheld in *Griggs* (but now weakened), qualification requirements having exclusionary racial impact must pinpoint abilities needed for job performance. When enforced, these guidelines created increased interest in ensuring that such job requirements really measure ability to do the job. Thus one of the most compelling reasons for concern that licensing examinations be effective competence measures has been enforcement of these guidelines. According to a survey reported in the *New York Times,* such enforcement has contributed to a "concerted effort" by "occupational and professional groups" to ensure that their certification tests are "job relevant."[18] In 1986 the executive officer of the American Psychological Association stated: "On the specific issues addressed in the Guidelines, . . . psychologists generally agree that the caliber of employment practices in organizations has improved dramatically since [their 1978] publication."[19]

As a consequence of AA programs, black children see more black persons as teachers, administrators, and professionals. Having such role models tends to improve the self-image, vocational aspirations, and learning ability of black students, thereby increasing the pool of qualified candidates available for training and employment, a development that is likely to raise merit standards.

Some AA measures, then, such as permitting only job-related testing, improve job-selection processes. But what, generally speaking, has been the effect of AA on work performance? According to economist

Jonathan S. Leonard, while productivity estimates based on direct tests are too imprecise for a compelling conclusion either way, such tests of the effect of AA in increasing employment opportunities for blacks show no significant evidence of a productivity decline.[20]

Let us return now to a consideration of the meritocratic critique that focuses solely on preferential treatment. Whatever the effect of AA measures in their entirety, it is true that racial preference for a less qualified black can, in specific situations, reduce effective job performance. According to meritocrats, such selection violates the rights of adversely affected white candidates. Thus the philosopher Alan Goldman states:

> Unless reverse discrimination violates some *presently accepted rule for hiring* it will not be seriously unjust in the current social context. . . . The *currently accepted* rule which I believe to be just is that of *hiring by competence.* . . . In addition to its vast utility, competence is some barometer of prior effort. Thus society, it seems, does have a right in the name of welfare and equal opportunity to impose a rule for hiring, and the general rule ought to be hiring the most competent. This means that those individuals who attain maximal competence for various positions acquire rights through their efforts to those positions. (emphases added)[21]

Let us assume that insofar as maximally qualified candidates have exerted effort to attain positions under an accepted and just rule, they have a prima facie right to such positions. But the fact is that, contrary to Goldman, hiring the most competent candidate is not the "currently accepted" rule in employment. Being the most qualified candidate is indeed one way to get the job, but employers' ignoring of merit standards and their explicit preference for specific groups are widespread. Merit criteria are either ignored or undermined in several ways.

In accordance with a traditional legal principle— employment "at will"—private U.S. employers have had the right to discharge their workers without a reasonable cause based on work performance. This principle gives employers the legal right to dismiss qualified employees merely for refusing to support political candidates of the employer's choice or for expressing unpopular views on the job or even in the privacy of their own homes. An employer right to arbitrary discharge without reasonable cause is hardly compatible with a merit system. Although the employer's right to discharge is now restricted by specific exceptions identified in union contracts and in federal and state laws (e.g., prohibiting race and sex discrimination), employment at will is still a significant legal principle in U.S. courts.[22]

Competent job performance has also been undermined by the widespread use of unvalidated employment tests and irrelevant subjective standards for hiring and promotion.

As I described earlier, federal and state governments have continuously given employment preference to veterans, thereby excluding large numbers of more qualified nonveterans.

Many employees obtain their vocational qualifications in colleges and professional schools. In some such institutions preference for admission has been extended to children of alumni. After Allan Bakke sued the University of California medical school, it was revealed that the dean had been permitted to select some admittees without reference to the usual screening process. As one writer noted, "The dean's 'special admissions program' was evidently devoted to the *realpolitik* of sustaining influential support for the school."[23]

Seniority-based selection for training, promotion, and retention in layoff is commonly practiced in both the private and public sector of the economy. Such selection is based on years of service, not evaluation of job performance. Adherence to meritocratic principles would in some situations require the abolition of seniority criteria for reward.

As emphasized earlier, reliance on personal connections is probably the most widely used recruitment method in American employment, a practice that often works against a merit system. An incumbent's graduate-school friend, the boss's nephew, or a political-patronage appointee is frequently not the most qualified person available for the job.

Note too that gaining promotion through social networks within the firm may have a corrupting effect on job performance as well as on moral character. The employee may see pandering to the right people as the best route to success.

Because traditionally accepted preference is so widespread, some blacks selected by AA preference may in fact replace less-qualified whites who would have been chosen by such traditional preference.

I conclude that merit selection is not, as Goldman claims, the currently accepted rule. Goldman states, however, that unless preferential treatment violates a currently accepted rule it is not "seriously unjust."[24] In that case, preferential treatment is not seriously unjust.

A different version of the meritocratic claim might be that although hiring the best candidate is not the currently accepted rule and because (as Goldman says) merit selection has social utility, such selection *ought* to be the rule, and thus preferential treatment should not be extended to blacks. According to this meritocratic claim, all practices that often conflict with merit standards, such as selection by seniority ranking, veteran status, and powerful personal connections, should be eliminated. In that case, why not begin the struggle for merit in American employment by calling for an end to these practices? Why start by excluding members of a largely poor and powerless group, such as black people?

Let us focus on the consequences simply of denying preference to basically qualified blacks. Let us assume that this denial would produce some gain in social utility, that is, efficiency. That benefit would, I suggest, weigh very little in the moral balance against the double accomplishment of preferential treatment: compensation to blacks for past wrongs against them and achieving what this nation has never known—occupational integration, racial justice in the workplace.

PREFERENTIAL TREATMENT AND BLACK SELF-RESPECT

Some commentators suggest that preferential treatment may be morally injurious to black persons. Thus Midge Decter and the economist Thomas Sowell worry that preference damages the self-respect of blacks.[25]

Does preference really injure the self-respect of those it benefits? Traditional preference extended to personal connections has occasioned no such visible injury to self-respect. Career counselors who advise job seekers to develop influential contacts, exhibit no fear that their clients will think less well of themselves; indeed, job candidates who secure powerful connections count themselves *fortunate.*

It might be objected that blacks (or any persons) who gain their positions through preferential treatment ought to respect themselves less. But this claim assumes that these blacks do not deserve such treatment. I believe that, because the overwhelming majority of blacks has been grievously wronged by racism, they deserve to be compensated for such injury and that black beneficiaries of employment preference—like veterans compensated by employment preference—have no good reason to feel unworthy.

Moreover, telling blacks—the descendants of slaves—that they ought to feel unworthy of their preferential positions can become self-fulfilling prophecy. Where are the black persons whose spirit and self-confidence have not already suffered because of the palpable barriers to attending white schools, living in white neighborhoods, and enjoying relations of friendship and intimacy with white people? Those

blacks who, despite all the obstacles of overt and institutional racism, have become basically qualified for their positions should be respected for that achievement. Justice Marshall reminds us that the history of blacks differs from that of other ethnic groups. It includes not only slavery but also its aftermath, in which as a people they were marked inferior by our laws, a mark that has endured.[26] Opportunities created by preferential treatment should symbolize an acknowledgment of such injustice and a commitment to create a future free of racism.

ENDNOTES

1. For moral justifications of AA-type benefits to blacks which are also both backward and forward looking but differ in some respects from mine, see Howard McGary, Jr., "Justice and Reparations," *Philosophical Forum* 9 (1977–78): 250–63; Bernard R. Boxill, *Blacks and Social Justice* (Totowa, N.J.: Rowman and Allanheld, 1984), chap. 7.
2. Quoted in Kenneth T. Jackson, *Crabgrass Frontier* (New York: Oxford University Press, 1985), p. 214.
3. Boris I. Bittker, *The Case for Black Reparations* (New York: Random House, 1973), p. 21. The summary of past injustices to blacks is based on Bittker, chap. 2.; Michael Reich, "The Economics of Racism," *The Capitalist System,* ed. Richard C. Edwards, Michael Reich, and Thomas E. Weisskopf (Englewood Cliffs, N.J.: Prentice-Hall, 1972); Jackson, pp. 213–14; *A Common Destiny: Blacks and American Society,* ed. Gerald David Jaynes and Robin M. Williams, Jr., for the Committee on the Status of Black Americans, Commission on Behavioral and Social Sciences and Education, National Research Council (Washington, D.C.: National Academy Press, 1989), p. 366.
4. Robert Fullinwider, "The Equal Opportunity Myth," in *Report from the Center for Philosophy and Public Policy* (College Park: University of Maryland, Fall, 1981).
5. Shelby Steele, "A Negative Vote on Affirmative Action," *New York Times Magazine,* May 13, 1990.
6. William T. Blackstone, "Reverse Discrimination and Compensatory Justice," in *Social Justice and Preferential Treatment,* ed. William T. Blackstone and Robert T. Heslep (Athens: University of Georgia Press, 1977), p. 67.
7. Bittker, pp. 16–17.
8. Laurence Thomas, *New York Times,* op-ed, August 13, 1990.
9. Don Jackson, *New York Times,* op-ed, January 23, 1989.
10. Boxill, p. 148.
11. Thomas Nagel, "A Defense of Affirmative Action," in *Report from the Center for Philosophy and Public Policy,* p. 7.
12. Nor should AA employment programs substitute for other compensatory programs to blacks, such as cash payments to the elderly, compensatory education programs in primary

and secondary ghetto schools, and preferential admissions with effective financial support to black students for college and professional schools.

13. "If the woman who later became my wife rejected another suitor . . . would the rejected less intelligent and less handsome suitor have a legitimate complaint about unfairness . . . (Against whom would the rejected suitor have a legitimate complaint? Against what?). . . . The major objection to speaking of everyone's having a right *to* various things such as *equality of opportunity*, life and so on, and enforcing this right, is that these 'rights' require a substructure of things and materials and actions; and *other* people may have rights and entitlements over these" (Robert Nozick, *Anarchy, State, and Utopia* [New York: Basic Books, 1974], pp. 237–38; first and third emphases in original, second added).

14. Libertarians deny the right of government to interfere with private employers not only in hiring but also in determining working conditions, as by enacting minimum-wage laws and so forth. Libertarians such as Robert Nozick, however, could consistently claim such employer entitlement only for those employers who have either acquired their enterprises through efforts that satisfy an acceptable principle of justice or who received them (e.g., by inheritance) from individuals whose original acquisition and transfer satisfy these principles. But I know of no plausible historical evidence to show that, generally speaking, American private enterprises have been acquired and transferred in accordance with such moral principles. Absent such evidence, a libertarian endorsement of any general moral entitlement by private entrepreneurs today, over employment conditions in their firms, lacks a libertarian justification.

15. Thomas Nagel, Introduction to *Equality and Preferential Treatment,* ed. Marshall Cohen, Thomas Nagel, and Thomas Scanlon (Princeton, N.J.: Princeton University Press, 1977), p. viii.

16. Steven S. Schwarzschild, "American History, Marked by Racism," *New Politics* I (1987): 56–58.

17. For determining the specifics of awards to more senior white workers who lose their jobs because of racial preference during layoff, the *Vulcan* decision is instructive: "The court also concludes that those firefighters who have or will forfeit their seniority rights as a result of the affirmative action plan . . . ought to be compensated [by] . . . the federal government. . . . The amount of such compensation must, however, be 'just.' It is not intended to be a lifetime pension. Those senior firefighters who are laid off as a result of the affirmative action plan shall be under a duty to mitigate damages, by seeking to obtain other employment. Any claim for compensation shall be reduced by the amount of salaries or any benefits received as a result of such layoff. Moreover, the period of compensation shall end upon the attainment of other employment, but absent exceptional circumstances, no later than one year from the date of layoff" (*Vulcan Pioneers* v. *New Jersey Department of Civil Service,* 34 Fair Empl. Prac. Cas. [BNA] 1247–48 [D.N.J. 1984]).

18. Nancy Rubin, "Consumer and Government Forces Pushing for Job Competency Tests," *New York Times,* November 11, 1979.

19. *Oversight Hearings on EEOC's Proposed Modification of Enforcement Regulations, Including Uniform Guidelines on Employee Selection Procedures,* Hearings before the Subcommittee on Employment Opportunities of the Committee on Education and Labor, House of Representatives (Washington, D.C.: U.S. Government Printing Office 1986), p. 211. Ronald Dworkin, a legal philosopher writing on the *Bakke* case, makes a similar point about racially preferential admissions to medical school. "If [merit] . . . means . . . that a medical school should choose candidates that it supposes will make the most useful doctors, then everything turns on the judgement of what factors make different doctors useful. . . . black skin may be a socially useful trait in particular circumstances." ("Why Bakke Has No Case," *New York Review of Books,* November 10, 1977: 13–14).

20. Jonathan S. Leonard, "The Impact of Affirmative Action Regulation and Equal Employment Law on Black Employment," *Journal of Economic Perspectives* 4 (1990): 61–62.

21. Alan Goldman, "Limits to the Justification of Reverse Discrimination," *Social Theory and Practice* 3 (1975): 289–91.

22. *Coppage* v. *Kansas,* 236 U.S. 441 (1914); Burton Hall, "Collective Bargaining and Workers' Liberty," in *Moral Rights in the Workplace,* ed. Gertrude Ezorsky (New York: State University of New York Press, 1987), pp. 161–65.

23. Allan P. Sindler, *Bakke, DeFunis, and Minority Admissions* (New York: Longman, 1978), p. 69n. This practice was ended in 1977.

24. See Goldman.

25. Midge Decter, *New York Times,* op-ed, July 6, 1980; Thomas Sowell, " 'Affirmative Action' Reconsidered," *Public Interest* no. 42 (1976): 64.

26. *Regents of University of California* v. *Bakke,* 438 U.S. 265 (1978) (Marshall, J., concurring in part and dissenting in part).

QUESTIONS ON EZORSKY

1. Ezorsky claims that blacks deserve compensation for the injustice of slavery, even as she contends that if the effects of slavery "had been dissipated over time, the claim to compensation now would certainly be weaker." Why should the dissipation of the effects, if occurring, weaken the claim to compensation?

2. Ezorsky claims that "it is false that blacks born into better-off families have not been injured by discrimination." How would you assess the evidence she provides for this claim? What is the evidence for her claim that "white workers have *both* gained and lost from racism"? Do these claims apply to everyone who falls within the relevant category?

3. How does Ezorsky argue against the claim that affirmative action violates the principle of hiring by merit? Is hiring by merit the acceptable practice within business? Should it be? If it is permissible *not* to hire by merit, then under what conditions could a meritorious individual have a grievance against an employer who hires a less-qualified person?

4. Which of the arguments against affirmative action do you think is the strongest? Why?

The Moral Status of Affirmative Action

Louis Pojman

Louis Pojman is Professor of Philosophy at the United States Military Academy, West Point. He is the author or editor of numerous articles, including essays in the philosophy of religion and social and political philosophy, and the editor or author of a variety of books, including Philosophy of Religion: An Anthology *(1986),* The Theory of Knowledge: Classical and Contemporary Readings *(1992), and* Moral Philosophy: A Reader *(1998). This essay was first published in* Public Affairs Quarterly *(1992).*

Hardly a week goes by but that the subject of Affirmative Action does not come up. Whether in the guise of reverse discrimination, preferential hiring, non-traditional casting, quotas, goals and time tables, minority scholarships, or race-norming, the issue confronts us as a terribly perplexing problem. . . .

There is something salutary as well as terribly tragic inherent in this problem. The salutary aspect is the fact that our society has shown itself committed to eliminating unjust discrimination. Even in the heart of Dixie there is a recognition of the injustice of racial discrimination. Both sides of the affirmative action debate have good will and appeal to moral principles. Both sides are attempting to bring about a better society; one which is color blind, but they differ profoundly on the morally proper means to accomplish that goal.

And this is just the tragedy of the situation: good people on both sides of the issue are ready to tear each other to pieces over a problem that has no easy or obvious solution. And so the voices become shrill and the rhetoric hyperbolic. . . .

In this paper I will confine myself primarily to Affirmative Action policies with regard to race, but much of what I say can be applied to the areas of gender and ethnic minorities.

DEFINITIONS

First let me define my terms:

Discrimination is simply judging one thing to differ from another on the basis of some criterion. "Discrimination" is essentially a good quality, having reference to our ability to make distinctions. As rational and moral agents we need to make proper distinctions. To be rational is to discriminate between good and bad arguments, and to think morally is to discriminate between reasons based on valid principles and those based on invalid ones. What needs to be distinguished is the difference between rational and moral discrimination, on the one hand, and irrational and immoral discrimination, on the other hand.

Prejudice is a discrimination based on irrelevant grounds. It may simply be an attitude which never surfaces in action, or it may cause prejudicial actions. A prejudicial discrimination in action is immoral if it denies someone a fair deal. So discrimination on the basis of race or sex where these are not relevant for job performance is unfair. Likewise, one may act prejudicially in applying a relevant criterion on insufficient grounds, as in the case where I apply the criterion of being a hard worker but then assume, on insufficient evidence, that the black man who applies for the job is not a hard worker.

There is a difference between *prejudice* and *bias*. Bias signifies a tendency towards one thing rather than another where the evidence is incomplete or based on non-moral factors. For example, you may have a bias towards blondes and I towards red-heads. But prejudice is an attitude (or action) where unfairness is present—where one *should* know or do better, as in the case where I give people jobs simply because they are red-heads. Bias implies ignorance or incomplete knowledge, whereas prejudice is deeper, involving a moral failure—usually a failure to pay attention to the evidence. But note that calling people racist or sexist without good evidence is also an act of prejudice. I call this form of prejudice "defamism," for it unfairly defames the victim. . . .

Equal Opportunity is offering everyone a fair chance at the best positions that society has at its disposal. Only native aptitude and effort should be decisive in the outcome, not factors of race, sex or special favors.

Affirmative Action is the effort to rectify the injustice of the past by special policies. Put this way, it is Janus-faced or ambiguous, having both a backward-looking and a forward-looking feature. The backward-looking feature is its attempt to correct and compensate for past injustice. This aspect of Affirmative Action is strictly deontological. The forward-looking feature is its implicit ideal of a society free from prejudice; this is both deontological and utilitarian.

When we look at a social problem from a backward-looking perspective we need to determine who has committed or benefited from a wrongful or prejudicial act and to determine who deserves compensation for that act.

When we look at a social problem from a forward-looking perspective we need to determine what a just society (one free from prejudice) would look like and how to obtain that kind of society. The forward-looking aspect of Affirmative Action is paradoxically race-conscious, since it uses race to bring about a society which is not race-conscious, which is color-blind (in the morally relevant sense of this term).

It is also useful to distinguish two versions of Affirmative Action. *Weak Affirmative Action* involves such measures as the elimination of segregation (namely the idea of "separate but equal"), widespread advertisement to groups not previously represented in certain privileged positions, special scholarships for the disadvantaged classes (e.g., all the poor), using under-representation or a history of past discrimination as a tie breaker when candidates are relatively equal, and the like.

Strong Affirmative Action involves more positive steps to eliminate past injustice, such as reverse discrimination, hiring candidates on the basis of race and gender in order to reach equal or near equal results, proportionate representation in each area of society.

A BRIEF HISTORY OF AFFIRMATIVE ACTION

1. After a long legacy of egregious racial discrimination the forces of civil justice came to a head during the decade of 1954–1964. In the 1954 U.S. Supreme Court decision, *Brown v. Board of Education,* racial segregation was declared inherently and unjustly discriminatory, a violation of the constitutional right to equal protection, and in 1964 Congress passed the Civil Rights Act which banned all forms of racial discrimination.

During this time the goal of the Civil Rights movement was equal opportunity. The thinking was that if only we could remove the hindrances to progress, invidious segregation, discriminatory laws, and irrational prejudice against blacks, we could free our country from the evils of past injustice and usher in a just society in which the grandchildren of the slave could play together and compete with the grandchildren of the slave owner. We were after a color-blind society in which every child had an equal chance to attain the highest positions based not on his skin color but on the quality of his credentials. In the early '60s when the idea of reverse discrimination was mentioned in civil rights groups, it was usually rejected as a new racism. The Executive Director of the NAACP, Roy Wilkins, stated this position unequivocally during congressional consideration of the 1964 civil rights law. "Our association has never been in favor of a quota system. We believe the quota system is unfair whether it is used for [blacks] or against [blacks] . . . [We] feel people ought to be hired because of their ability, irrespective of their color . . . We want equality, equality of opportunity and employment on the basis of ability."[1]

So the Civil Rights Act of 1964 was passed outlawing discrimination on the basis of race or sex.

Title VII, Section 703(a) Civil Rights Act of 1964: It shall be an unlawful practice for an employer—(1) to fail or refuse to hire or to discharge any individual or otherwise to discriminate against any individual with respect to his compensation, terms, conditions, or privileges of employment, because of such individual's race, color, sex, or national origin; or

(2) to limit, segregate, or classify his employees or applicants for employment in any way which would deprive or tend to deprive any individual of employment opportunities or otherwise adversely affect his status as an employee because of such individual's race, color, religion, sex, or national origin. [42 U.S.C.2000e-2(a)]

. . . Nothing contained in this title shall be interpreted to require any employer . . . to grant preferential treatment to any individual or to any group . . . on account of an imbalance which may exist with respect to the total numbers or percentage of persons of any race . . . employed by any employer . . . in comparison with the total or percentage of persons of such race . . . in any community, State, section, or other areas, or in the available work force in any community, State, section, or other area. [42 U.S.C.2000e-2(j)]

The Civil Rights Act of 1964 espouses a meritocratic philosophy, calling for equal opportunity and prohibits reverse discrimination as just another form of prejudice.

The Voting Rights Act (1965) was passed and Jim Crow laws throughout the South were overturned. . . .

2. But it was soon noticed that the elimination of discriminatory laws was not producing the fully integrated society that leaders of the Civil Rights movement had envisioned. Eager to improve the situation, in 1965 President Johnson went beyond equal opportunity to Affirmative Action. He issued the famous Executive Order 11246 in which the Department of Labor was enjoined to issue government contracts with construction companies on the basis of race. That is, it would engage in reverse discrimination in order to make up for the evils of the past. He explained the act in terms of the shackled runner analogy.

> Imagine a hundred yard dash in which one of the two runners has his legs shackled together. He has progressed 10 yds., while the unshackled runner has gone 50 yds. How do they rectify the situation? Do they merely remove the shackles and allow the race to proceed? Then they could say that "equal opportunity" now prevailed. But one of the runners would still be forty yards ahead of the other. Would it not be the better part of justice to allow the previously shackled runner to make-up the forty yard gap; or to start the race all over again? That would be affirmative action towards equality. (President Lyndon Johnson 1965 inaugurating the Affirmative Action Policy of Executive Order 11246).

In 1967 President Johnson issued Executive order 11375 extending Affirmative Action (henceforth "AA") to women. Note here that AA originates in the executive branch of government. Until the Kennedy-Hawkins Civil Rights Act of 1990, AA policy was never put to a vote or passed by Congress. Gradually, the benefits of AA were extended to Hispanics, native Americans, Asians, and handicapped people.[2]

The phrase "An Equal Opportunity/Affirmative Action Employer" ("AA/EO") began to appear as official public policy. But few noticed an ambiguity in the notion of "AA" which could lead to a contradiction in juxtaposing it with "EO," for there are two types of AA. At first AA was interpreted as, what I have called, "Weak Affirmative Action," in line with equal opportunity, signifying wider advertisement of positions, announcements that applications from blacks would be welcomed, active recruitment and hiring blacks (and women) over *equally* qualified men. While few liberals objected to these measures, some expressed fears of an impending slippery slope towards reverse discrimination.

However, except in professional sports—including those sponsored by universities—Weak Affirmative Action was not working, so in the late 60's and early 70's a stronger version of Affirmative Action was embarked upon—one aimed at equal results, quotas (or "goals"— a euphemism for "quotas"). In *Swann v. Charlotte-Mecklenburg* (1971), regarding the busing of children out of their neighborhood in order to promote integration, the Court, led by Justice Brennan, held that Affirmative Action was implied in *Brown* and was consistent with the Civil Right Act of 1964. The NAACP now began to support reverse discrimination.

Thus began the search for minimally qualified blacks in college recruitment, hiring, and the like. Competence and excellence began to recede into second place as the quest for racial, ethnic, and gender diversity became the dominant goals. The slogan "We have to become race conscious in order to eliminate race consciousness" became the paradoxical justification for reverse discrimination.

3. In 1968 the Department of Labor ordered employers to engage in utilization studies as part of its policy of eliminating discrimination in the work place. The office of Federal Contract Compliance of the U.S. Department of Labor (Executive Order 11246) stated that employers with a history of *underutilization* of minorities and women were required to institute programs that went beyond passive nondiscrimination through deliberate efforts to identify people of "affected classes" for the purpose of advancing their employment. Many employers found it wise to adopt policies of preferential hiring in order to preempt expensive government suits.

Employers were to engage in "utilization analysis" of their present work force in order to develop "specific and result-oriented procedures" to which the employer commits "*every good-faith effort*" in order to provide "relief for members of an '*affected class,*' who by virtue of *past discrimination* continue to suffer the present effects of that discrimination." This self-analysis is supposed to discover areas in which such affected classes are underused, considering their availability and skills. "*Goals and timetables* are to be developed to guide efforts to correct deficiencies in the employment of affected classes people in each level and segment of the work force." . . .

4. The Department of Labor issued guidelines in 1970 calling for hiring representatives of *underutilized* groups. "*Nondiscrimination* requires the elimination of all existing discriminatory conditions, whether purposeful or inadvertent . . . *Affirmative action* requires . . . the employer to make additional efforts to recruit, employ and promote qualified members of groups formerly excluded" (HEW Executive Order 22346, 1972). In December of 1971 Guidelines were issued to

eliminate underutilization of minorities, aiming at realignment of job force at every level of society.

5. In *Griggs v. Duke Power Company* (1971) the Supreme Court interpreted Title VII of the Civil Rights Act as forbidding use of aptitude tests and high school diplomas in hiring personnel. These tests were deemed presumptively discriminatory, employers having the burden of proving such tests relevant to performance. The notion of *sufficiency* replaced that of excellence or best qualified, as it was realized (though not explicitly stated) that the social goal of racial diversity required compromising the standards of competence.

6. In 1977, the EEOC called for and *expected* proportional representation of minorities in every area of work (including universities).

7. In 1978 the Supreme Court addressed the Bakke case. Alan Bakke had been denied admission to the University of California at Davis Medical School even though his test scores were higher than the 16 blacks who were admitted under the Affirmative Action quota program. He sued the University of California and the U.S. Supreme Court ruled (*University of California v. Bakke,* July 28, 1978) in a 5 to 4 vote that reverse discrimination and quotas are illegal except (as Justice Powell put it) when engaged in for purposes of promoting diversity (interpreted as a means to extend free speech under the First Amendment) and restoring a situation where an institution has had a history of prejudicial discrimination. . . .

. . . The Bakke case only shifted the rhetoric from "quota" language to "goals and time tables" and "diversity" language. In the '80s affirmative action was alive and well, with preferential hiring, minority scholarships, and "race norming" prevailing in all walks of life. No other white who has been excluded from admission to college because of his race has even won his case. In fact only a year later, Justice Brennan was to write in *U.S. Steel v. Weber* that prohibition of racial discrimination against "any individual" in Title VII of the Civil Rights Act did not apply to discrimination against whites.[3]

8. Perhaps the last step in the drive towards equal results took place in the institutionalization of grading applicants by group related standards, race norming. Race norming is widely practiced but most of the public is unaware of it, so let me explain it.

Imagine that four men come into a state employment office in order to apply for a job. One is black, one Hispanic, one Asian and one white. They take the standard test (a version of the General Aptitude Test Battery or VG-GATB). All get a composite score of 300. None of them will ever see that score. Instead the numbers will be fed into a computer and the applicants' percentile ranking emerges. The scores are group-weighted. Blacks are measured against blacks, whites against whites, Hispanics against Hispanics. Since blacks characteristically do less well than other groups, the effect is to favor blacks. For example, a score of 300 as an accountant will give the black a percentile score of 87, an Hispanic a percentile score of 74 and a white or oriental a score of 47. The black will get the job as the accountant. See [table 1]:

TABLE 1 Percentile Conversion Tables

Jobs are grouped into five broad families: Family I includes, for example, machinists, cabinet makers, and tool makers; Family II includes helpers in many types of agriculture, manufacturing, and so on; Family III includes professional jobs such as accountant, chemical engineer, nurse, editor; Family IV includes bus drivers, bookkeepers, carpet layers; Family V includes exterminators, butchers, file clerks. A raw score of 300 would convert to the following percentile rankings:

	I	II	III	IV	V
Black	79	59	87	83	73
Hispanic	62	41	74	67	55
Other	39	42	47	45	42

Sources: Virginia Employment Commission: U.S. Department of Labor. Employment and Training Administration, Validity Generalization Manual (Section A: Job Family Scoring).

This is known as race norming. Until an anonymous governmental employee recently blew the whistle, this practice was kept a secret in several state employment services. Prof. Linda Gottfredson of the University of Delaware, one of the social scientists to expose this practice, has since had her funding cut off. In a recent letter published in the *New York Times* she writes:

> One of America's best-kept open secrets is that the Employment Service of the Department of Labor has unabashedly promulgated quotas. In 1981 the service recommended that state employment agencies adopt a race-conscious battery to avoid adverse impact when referring job applicants to employers. . . . The score adjustments are not trivial. An unadjusted score that places a job applicant at the 15th percentile among whites would, after race-norming, typically place a black near the white 50th percentile. Likewise, unadjusted scores at the white 50th percentile would, after race-norming,

typically place a black near the 85th percentile for white job applicants. . . . [I]ts use by 40 states in the last decade belies the claim that *Griggs* did not lead to quotas.[4]

9. In the *Ward Cove, Richmond,* and *Martin* decisions of the mid-80's the Supreme Court limited preferential hiring practices, placing a greater burden of proof on the plaintiff, now required to prove that employers have discriminated. The Kennedy-Hawkins Civil Rights Act of 1990, which was passed by Congress last year, sought to reverse these decisions by requiring employers to justify statistical imbalances not only in the employment of racial minorities but also that of ethnic and religious minorities. Wherever under-representation of an "identified" group exists, the employer bears the burden of proving he is innocent of prejudicial behavior. . . .

Affirmative Action in the guise of underutilized or "affected groups" now extends to American Indians, Hispanics—Spaniards (including Spanish nobles) but not Portuguese, Asians, the handicapped, and in some places Irish and Italians. Estimates are that 75% of Americans may obtain AA status as minorities: everyone except the white non-handicapped male. It is a strange policy that affords special treatment to the children of Spanish nobles and illegal immigrants but not the children of the survivors of Russian pogroms or Nazi concentration camps. . . .

ARGUMENTS FOR AFFIRMATIVE ACTION

Let us now survey the main arguments typically cited in the debate over Affirmative Action. I will briefly discuss seven arguments on each side of the issue.

1. Need for Role Models

This argument is straightforward. We all have need of role models, and it helps to know that others like us can be successful. We learn and are encouraged to strive for excellence by emulating our heroes and role models.

However, it is doubtful whether role models of one's own racial or sexual type are necessary for success. One of my heroes was Gandhi, an Indian Hindu, another was my grade school science teacher, one Miss DeVoe, and another was Martin Luther King. More important than having role models of one's own type is having genuinely good people, of whatever race or gender, to emulate. Furthermore, even if it is of some help to people with low self-esteem to gain encouragement from seeing others of their particular kind in leadership roles, it is doubtful whether this need is a sufficient condition to justify preferential hiring or reverse discrimination. What good is a role model who is inferior to other professors or business personnel? Excellence will rise to the top in a system of fair opportunity. Natural development of role models will come more slowly and more surely. Proponents of preferential policies simply lack the patience to let history take its own course.

2. The Need of Breaking the Stereotypes

Society may simply need to know that there are talented blacks and women, so that it does not automatically assign them lesser respect or status. We need to have unjustified stereotype beliefs replaced with more accurate ones about the talents of blacks and women. So we need to engage in preferential hiring of qualified minorities even when they are not the most qualified.

Again, the response is that hiring the less qualified is neither fair to those better qualified who are passed over nor an effective way of removing inaccurate stereotypes. If competence is accepted as the criterion for hiring, then it is unjust to override it for purposes of social engineering. Furthermore, if blacks or women are known to hold high positions simply because of reverse discrimination, then they will still lack the respect due to those of their rank. In New York City there is a saying among doctors, "Never go to a black physician under 40," referring to the fact that AA has affected the medical system during the past fifteen years. The police use "Quota Cops" and "Welfare Sergeants" to refer to those hired without passing the standardized tests. (In 1985, 180 black and Hispanic policemen, who had failed a promotion test, were promoted anyway to the rank of sergeant.) The destruction of false stereotypes will come naturally as qualified blacks rise naturally in fair competition (or if it does not—then the stereotypes may be justified.) Reverse discrimination sends the message home that the stereotypes are deserved—otherwise, why do these minorities need so much extra help?

3. Equal Results Argument

Some philosophers and social scientists hold that human nature is roughly identical, so that on a fair playing field the same proportion from every race and gender and ethnic group would attain to the highest positions in every area of endeavor. It would follow that any inequality of results itself is evidence for inequality of opportunity. John Arthur, in discussing an intelligence test, Test 21, puts the case this way.

> History is important when considering governmental rules like Test 21 because low scores by blacks can be traced in large measure to the legacy of slavery and racism: segregation, poor

schooling, exclusion from trade unions, malnutrition, and poverty have all played their roles. Unless one assumes that blacks are naturally less able to pass the test, the conclusion must be that the results are themselves socially and legally constructed, not a mere given for which law and society can claim no responsibility.

The conclusion seems to be that genuine equality eventually requires equal results. Obviously blacks have been treated unequally throughout US history, and just as obviously the economic and psychological effects of that inequality linger to this day, showing up in lower income and poorer performance in school and on tests than whites achieve. Since we have no reason to believe that differences in performance can be explained by factors other than history, equal results are a good benchmark by which to measure progress made toward genuine equality.[5]

The result of a just society should be equal numbers in proportion to each group in the work force.

However, Arthur fails even to consider studies that suggest that there are innate differences between races, sexes, and groups. If there are genetic differences in intelligence and temperament within families, why should we not expect such differences between racial groups and the two genders? Why should the evidence for this be completely discounted? . . .

Furthermore, on Arthur's logic, we should take aggressive AA against Asians and Jews since they are over-represented in science, technology, and medicine. So that each group receives its fair share, we should ensure that 12% of the philosophers in the United States are Black, reduce the percentage of Jews from an estimated 15% to 2%—firing about 1,300 Jewish philosophers. The fact that Asians are producing 50% of Ph.D's in science and math and blacks less than 1% clearly shows, on this reasoning, that we are providing special secret advantages to Asians.

But why does society have to enter into this results game in the first place? Why do we have to decide whether all difference is environmental or genetic? Perhaps we should simply admit that we lack sufficient evidence to pronounce on these issues with any certainty—but if so, should we not be more modest in insisting on equal results? Here is a thought experiment. Take two families of different racial groups, Green and Blue. The Greens decide to have only two children, to spend all their resources on them, to give them the best education. The two Green kids respond well and end up with achievement test scores in the 99th percentile. The Blues fail to practice family planning. They have 15 children. They can only afford 2 children, but lack of ability or whatever prevents them from keeping their family down. Now they need help for their large family. Why does so-

ciety have to step in and help them? Society did not force them to have 15 children. Suppose that the achievement test scores of the 15 children fall below the 25th percentile. They cannot compete with the Greens. But now enters AA. It says that it is society's fault that the Blue children are not as able as the Greens and that the Greens must pay extra taxes to enable the Blues to compete. No restraints are put on the Blues regarding family size. This seems unfair to the Greens. Should the Green children be made to bear responsibility for the consequences of the Blues' voluntary behavior?

My point is simply that Arthur needs to cast his net wider and recognize that demographics and childbearing and -rearing practices are crucial factors in achievement. People have to take some responsibility for their actions. The equal results argument (or axiom) misses a greater part of the future.

4. The Compensation Argument

The argument goes like this: blacks have been wronged and severely harmed by whites. Therefore white society should compensate blacks for the injury caused them. Reverse discrimination in terms of preferential hiring, contracts, and scholarships is a fitting way to compensate for the racist wrongs.

This argument actually involves a distorted notion of compensation. Normally, we think of compensation as owed by a specific person A to another person B whom A has wronged in a specific way C. For example, if I have stolen your car and used it for a period of time to make business profits that would have gone to you, it is not enough that I return your car. I must pay you an amount reflecting your loss and my ability to pay. If I have only made $5,000 and only have $10,000 in assets, it would not be possible for you to collect $20,000 in damages—even though that is the amount of loss you have incurred.

Sometimes compensation is extended to groups of people who have been unjustly harmed by the greater society. For example, the United States government has compensated the Japanese-Americans who were interred during the Second World War, and the West German government has paid reparations to the survivors of Nazi concentration camps. But here a specific people have been identified who were wronged in an identifiable way by the government of the nation in question.

On the face of it the demand by blacks for compensation does not fit the usual pattern. Perhaps Southern states with Jim Crow laws could be accused of unjustly harming blacks, but it is hard to see that the United States government was involved in doing so.

Furthermore, it is not clear that all blacks were harmed in the same way or whether some were *unjustly* harmed or harmed more than poor whites and others (e.g. short people). Finally, even if identifiable blacks were harmed by identifiable social practices, it is not clear that most forms of Affirmative Action are appropriate to restore the situation. The usual practice of a financial payment seems more appropriate than giving a high level job to someone unqualified or only minimally qualified, who, speculatively, might have been better qualified had he not been subject to racial discrimination. If John is the star tailback of our college team with a promising professional future, and I accidentally (but culpably) drive my pick-up truck over his legs, and so cripple him, John may be due compensation, but he is not due the tailback spot on the football team.

Still, there may be something intuitively compelling about compensating members of an oppressed group who are minimally qualified. Suppose that the Hatfields and the McCoys are enemy clans and some youths from the Hatfields go over and steal diamonds and gold from the McCoys, distributing it within the Hatfield economy. Even though we do not know which Hatfield youths did the stealing, we would want to restore the wealth, as far as possible, to the McCoys. One way might be to tax the Hatfields, but another might be to give preferential treatment in terms of scholarships and training programs and hiring to the McCoys.[6]

This is perhaps the strongest argument for Affirmative Action, and it may well justify some weak versions of AA, but it is doubtful whether it is sufficient to justify strong versions with quotas and goals and time tables in skilled positions. There are at least two reasons for this. First, we have no way of knowing how many people of group G would have been at competence level L had the world been different. Secondly, the normal criterion of competence is a strong *prima facie* consideration when the most important positions are at stake. There are two reasons for this:

1. society has given people expectations that if they attain certain levels of excellence they will be awarded appropriately and

2. filling the most important positions with the best qualified is the best way to insure efficiency in job-related areas and in society in general.

These reasons are not absolutes. They can be overridden. But there is a strong presumption in their favor so that a burden of proof rests with those who would override them. . . .

5. Compensation from Those Who Innocently Benefited from Past Injustice

White males as innocent beneficiaries of unjust discrimination of blacks and women have no grounds for complaint when society seeks to rectify the tilted field. White males may be innocent of oppressing blacks and minorities (and women), but they have unjustly benefited from that oppression or discrimination. So it is perfectly proper that less qualified women and blacks be hired before them.

The operative principle is: He who knowingly and willingly benefits from a wrong must help pay for the wrong. Judith Jarvis Thomson puts it this way. "Many [white males] have been direct beneficiaries of policies which have down-graded blacks and women . . . and even those who did not directly benefit . . . had, at any rate, the advantage in the competition which comes of the confidence in one's full membership [in the community], and of one's right being recognized as a matter of course."[7] That is, white males obtain advantages in self respect and self-confidence deriving from a racist system which denies these to blacks and women.

Objection. As I noted in the previous section, compensation is normally individual and specific. If A harms B regarding x, B has a right to compensation from A in regards to x. If A steals B's car and wrecks it, A has an obligation to compensate B for the stolen car, but A's son has no obligation to compensate B. Furthermore, if A dies or disappears, B has no moral right to claim that society compensate him for the stolen car—though if he has insurance, he can make such a claim to the insurance company. Sometimes a wrong cannot be compensated, and we just have to make the best of an imperfect world.

Suppose my parents, divining that I would grow up to have an unsurpassable desire to be a basketball player, bought an expensive growth hormone for me. Unfortunately, a neighbor stole it and gave it to little Lew Alcindor, who gained the extra 18 inches—my 18 inches—and shot up to an enviable 7 feet 2 inches. Alias Kareem Abdul Jabbar, he excelled in basketball, as I would have done had I had my proper dose.

Do I have a right to the millions of dollars that Jabbar made as a professional basketball player—the unjustly innocent beneficiary of my growth hormone? I have a right to something from the neighbor who stole the hormone, and it might be kind of Jabbar to give me free tickets to the Laker basketball games, and perhaps I should be remembered in his will. As far as I can see, however, he does not *owe* me anything, either legally or morally.

Suppose further that Lew Alcindor and I are in high school together and we are both qualified to play basketball, only he is far better than I. Do I deserve to start in his position because I would have been as good as he is had someone not cheated me as a child? Again, I think not. But if being the lucky beneficiary of wrong-doing does not entail that Alcindor (or the coach) owes me anything in regards to basketball, why should it be a reason to engage in preferential hiring in academic positions or highly coveted jobs? If minimal qualifications are not adequate to override excellence in basketball, even when the minimality is a consequence of wrong-doing, why should they be adequate in other areas?

6. The Diversity Argument

It is important that we learn to live in a pluralistic world, learning to get along with those of other races and cultures, so we should have fully integrated schools and employment situations. Diversity is an important symbol and educative device. Thus preferential treatment is warranted to perform this role in society.

But, again, while we can admit the value of diversity, it hardly seems adequate to override considerations of merit and efficiency. Diversity for diversity's sake is moral promiscuity, since it obfuscates rational distinctions, and unless those hired are highly qualified the diversity factor threatens to become a fetish. At least at the higher levels of business and the professions, competence far outweighs considerations of diversity. I do not care whether the group of surgeons operating on me reflect racial or gender balance, but I do care that they are highly qualified. . . .

7. Anti-Meritocratic (Desert) Argument to Justify Reverse Discrimination: "No One Deserves His Talents"

According to this argument, the competent do not deserve their intelligence, their superior character, their industriousness, or their discipline; therefore they have no right to the best positions in society; therefore society is not unjust in giving these positions to less (but still minimally) qualified blacks and women. In one form this argument holds that since no one deserves anything, society may use any criteria it pleases to distribute goods. The criterion most often designated is social utility. Versions of this argument are found in the writings of John Arthur, John Rawls, Bernard Boxill, Michael Kinsley, Ronald Dworkin, and Richard Wasserstrom. Rawls writes, "No one deserves his place in the distribution of native endowments, any more than one deserves one's

initial starting place in society. The assertion that a man deserves the superior character that enables him to make the effort to cultivate his abilities is equally problematic; for his character depends in large part upon fortunate family and social circumstances for which he can claim no credit. The notion of desert seems not to apply to these cases."[8] Michael Kinsley is even more adamant:

> Opponents of affirmative action are hung up on a distinction that seems more profoundly irrelevant: treating individuals versus treating groups. What is the moral difference between dispensing favors to people on their "merits" as individuals and passing out society's benefits on the basis of group identification?
>
> Group identifications like race and sex are, of course, immutable. They have nothing to do with a person's moral worth. But the same is true of most of what comes under the label "merit." The tools you need for getting ahead in a meritocratic society—not all of them but most: talent, education, instilled cultural values such as ambition—are distributed just as arbitrarily as skin color. They are fate. The notion that people somehow "deserve" the advantages of these characteristics in a way they don't "deserve" the advantage of their race is powerful, but illogical.[9]

It will help to put the argument in outline form.

1.   Society may award jobs and positions as it sees fit as long as individuals have no claim to these positions.

2.   To have a claim to something means that one has earned it or deserves it.

3.   But no one has earned or deserves his intelligence, talent, education or cultural values which produce superior qualifications.

4.   If a person does not deserve what produces something, he does not deserve its products.

5.   Therefore better qualified people do not deserve their qualifications.

6.   Therefore, society may override their qualifications in awarding jobs and positions as it sees fit (for social utility or to compensate for previous wrongs).

So it is permissible if a minimally qualified black or woman is admitted to law or medical school ahead of a white male with excellent credentials or if a less qualified person from an "underutilized" group gets a professorship ahead of a far better qualified white male. Sufficiency and underutilization together outweigh excellence.

Objection Premise 4 is false. To see this, reflect that just because I do not deserve the money that I have been given as a gift (for instance) does not mean that I am not entitled to what I get with that money. If you and I both get a gift of $100 and I bury mine in the sand for 5 years while you invest yours wisely and double its value at the end of five years, I cannot complain that you should split the increase 50/50 since neither of us deserved the original gift. If we accept the notion of responsibility at all, we must hold that persons deserve the fruits of their labor and conscious choices. Of course, we might want to distinguish moral from legal desert and argue that, morally speaking, effort is more important than outcome, whereas, legally speaking, outcome may be more important. Nevertheless, there are good reasons in terms of efficiency, motivation, and rough justice for holding a strong *prima facie* principle of giving scarce high positions to those most competent. . . .

But there is no good reason to accept the argument against desert. We do act freely and, as such, we are responsible for our actions. We deserve the fruits of our labor, reward for our noble feats and punishment for our misbehavior.

We have considered seven arguments for Affirmative Action and have found no compelling case for Strong AA and only one plausible argument (a version of the compensation argument) for Weak AA. We must now turn to the arguments against Affirmative Action to see whether they fare any better.[10]

ARGUMENTS AGAINST AFFIRMATIVE ACTION

1. Affirmative Action Requires Discrimination Against a Different Group

Weak Affirmative Action weakly discriminates against new minorities, mostly innocent young white males, and Strong Affirmative Action strongly discriminates against these new minorities. As I argued [above], this discrimination is unwarranted, since, even if some compensation to blacks were indicated, it would be unfair to make innocent white males bear the whole brunt of the payments. In fact, it is poor white youth who become the new pariahs on the job market. The children of the wealthy have no trouble getting into the best private grammar schools and, on the basis of superior early education, into the best universities, graduate schools, managerial and professional positions. Affirmative Action simply shifts injustice, setting blacks and women against young white males, especially ethnic and poor white males. It does little to rectify the goal of providing equal opportunity to all. If the goal is a society where everyone has a fair chance, then it would be bet-

ter to concentrate on support for families and early education and decide the matter of university admissions and job hiring on the basis of traditional standards of competence.

2. Affirmative Action Perpetuates the Victimization Syndrome

Shelby Steele admits that Affirmative Action may seem "the meagerest recompense for centuries of unrelieved oppression" and that it helps promote diversity. At the same time, though, notes Steele, Affirmative Action reinforces the spirit of victimization by telling blacks that they can gain more by emphasizing their suffering, degradation and helplessness than by discipline and work. This message holds the danger of blacks becoming permanently handicapped by a need for special treatment. It also sends to society at large the message that blacks cannot make it on their own.

Leon Wieseltier sums up the problem this way.

> The memory of oppression is a pillar and a strut of the identity of every people oppressed. It is no ordinary marker of difference. It is unusually stiffening. It instructs the individual and the group about what to expect of the world, imparts an isolating sense of aptness. . . . Don't be fooled, it teaches, there is only repetition. For that reason, the collective memory of an oppressed people is not only a treasure but a trap.
>
> In the memory of oppression, oppression outlives itself. The scar does the work of the wound. That is the real tragedy: that injustice retains the power to distort long after it has ceased to be real. It is a posthumous victory for the oppressors, when pain becomes a tradition. And yet the atrocities of the past must never be forgotten. This is the unfairly difficult dilemma of the newly emancipated and the newly enfranchised: an honorable life is not possible if they remember too little and a normal life is not possible if they remember too much.[11]

With the eye of recollection, which does not "remember too much," Steele recommends a policy which offers "educational and economic development of disadvantaged people regardless of race and the eradication from our society—through close monitoring and severe sanctions—of racial and gender discrimination."[12]

3. Affirmative Action Encourages Mediocrity and Incompetence

Last Spring Jesse Jackson joined protesters at Harvard Law School in demanding that the Law School faculty hire black women. Jackson dismissed Dean of the Law School, Robert C. Clark's standard of choosing the best qualified person for the job as "Cultural anemia." "We cannot just define who is qualified in the most narrow vertical academic terms," he said. "Most people in the world are yellow, brown, black, poor, non-Christian and don't speak English, and they can't wait for some White males with archaic rules to appraise them."[13] It might be noted that if Jackson is correct about the depth of cultural decadence at Harvard, blacks might be well advised to form and support their own more vital law schools and leave places like Harvard to their archaism.

At several universities, the administration has forced departments to hire members of minorities even when far superior candidates were available. Shortly after obtaining my Ph.D. in the late '70s I was mistakenly identified as a black philosopher (I had a civil rights record and was once a black studies major) and was flown to a major university, only to be rejected for a more qualified candidate when it discovered that I was white.

Stories of the bad effects of Affirmative Action abound. The philosopher Sidney Hook writes that "At one Ivy League university, representatives of the Regional HEW demanded an explanation of why there were no women or minority students in the Graduate Department of Religious Studies. They were told that a reading of knowledge of Hebrew and Greek was presupposed. Whereupon the representatives of HEW advised orally:" Then end those old fashioned programs that require irrelevant languages. And start up programs on relevant things which minority group students can study without learning languages.[14]

Government programs of enforced preferential treatment tend to appeal to the lowest possible common denominator. Witness the 1974 HEW Revised Order No. 14 on Affirmative Action expectations for preferential hiring: "Neither minorities nor female employees should be required to possess higher qualifications than those of the lowest qualified incumbents."

Furthermore, no tests may be given to candidates unless it is *proved* to be relevant to the job.

> No standard or criteria which have, by intent or effect, worked to exclude women or minorities as a class can be utilized, unless the institution can demonstrate the necessity of such standard to the performance of the job in question.
>
> Whenever a validity study is called for . . . the user should include . . . an investigation of suitable alternative selection procedures and suitable alternative methods of using the selection procedure which have as little adverse impact as possible. . . . Whenever the user is shown an alternative selection procedure with evidence of less adverse impact and substantial evidence of validity for the same job in similar circumstances, the user should investigate it to determine the appropriateness of using or validating it in accord with these guidelines.[15] . . .

4. Affirmative Action Policies Unjustly Shift the Burden of Proof

Affirmative Action legislation tends to place the burden of proof on the employer who does not have an "adequate" representation of "underutilized" groups in his work force. He is guilty until proven innocent. I have already recounted how in the mid-eighties the Supreme Court shifted the burden of proof back onto the plaintiff, while Congress is now attempting to shift the burden back to the employer. Those in favor of deeming disproportional representation "guilty until proven innocent" argue that it is easy for employers to discriminate against minorities by various subterfuges, and I agree that steps should be taken to monitor against prejudicial treatment. But being prejudiced against employers is not the way to attain a just solution to discrimination. The principle: innocent until proven guilty, applies to employers as well as criminals. Indeed, it is clearly special pleading to reject this basic principle of Anglo-American law in this case of discrimination while adhering to it everywhere else.

5. An Argument from Merit

Traditionally, we have believed that the highest positions in society should be awarded to those who are best qualified. . . . Rewarding excellence both seems just to the individuals in the competition and makes for efficiency. Note that one of the most successful acts of integration, the recruitment of Jackie Robinson in the late '40s, was done in just this way, according to merit. If Robinson had been brought into the major league as a mediocre player or had batted .200 he would have been scorned and sent back to the minors where he belonged.

Merit is not an absolute value. There are times when it may be overridden for social goals, but there is a strong *prima facie* reason for awarding positions on its basis, and it should enjoy a weighty presumption in our social practices.

In a celebrated article Ronald Dworkin says that "Bakke had no case" because society did not owe Bakke anything. That may be, but then why does it owe anyone anything? Dworkin puts the matter in Utility terms, but if that is the case, society may owe Bakke a place at the University of California/Davis, for it seems a reasonable rule-utilitarian principle that achievement should be rewarded in society. We generally want the best to have the best positions, the best qualified candidate to win the political office, the most brilliant and competent scientist to be chosen for the most challenging research project, the best qualified pilots to become commercial pilots, only the best soldiers to become generals. . . .

But note, no one is calling for quotas or proportional representation of *underutilized* groups in the National Basketball Association where blacks make up 80% of the players. But if merit and merit alone reigns in sports, should it not be valued at least as much in education and industry?

6. The Slippery Slope

Even if Strong AA or Reverse Discrimination could meet the other objections, it would face a tough question: once you embark on this project, how do you limit it? Who should be excluded from reverse discrimination? Asians and Jews are over-represented, so if we give blacks positive quotas, should we place negative quotas to these other groups? Since white males, "WMs," are a minority which is suffering from reverse discrimination, will we need a New Affirmative Action policy in the 21st century to compensate for the discrimination against WMs in the late 20th century?

Furthermore, Affirmative Action has stigmatized the *young* white male. Assuming that we accept reverse discrimination, the fair way to make sacrifices would be to retire *older* white males who are more likely to have benefited from a favored status. Probably the least guilty of any harm to minority groups is the young white male—usually a liberal who has been required to bear the brunt of ages of past injustice. Justice Brennan's announcement that the Civil Rights Act did not apply to discrimination against white shows how the clearest language can be bent to serve the ideology of the moment.[16]

7. The Mounting Evidence Against the Success of Affirmative Action

Thomas Sowell of the Hoover Institute has shown in his book *Preferential Policies: An International Perspective* that preferential hiring almost never solves social problems. It generally builds in mediocrity or incompetence and causes deep resentment. It is a short term solution which lacks serious grounding in social realities.

For instance, Sowell cites some disturbing statistics on education. Although twice as many blacks as Asians students took the nationwide Scholastic Aptitude Test in 1983, approximately fifteen times as many Asian students scored above 700 (out of a possible 800) on the mathematics half of the SAT. The percentage of Asians who scored above 700 in math was also more than six times higher than the percentage of American Indians and more than ten times higher than that of Mexican Americans—as well as more than double the percentage of whites. As Sowell points out, in all countries studied, "intergroup performance disparities are huge" (108).

There are dozens of American colleges and universities where the median combined verbal SAT score and mathematics SAT score total 1200 or above. As of 1983 there were less than 600 black students in the entire US with combined SAT scores of 1200. This meant that, despite widespread attempts to get a black student "representation" comparable to the black percentage of the population (about 11%), there were not enough black students in the entire country for the Ivy League alone to have such a "representation" without going beyond this pool—even if the entire pool went to the eight Ivy League colleges.[17]

Often it is claimed that a cultural bias is the cause of the poor performance of blacks on SAT (or IQ tests), but Sowell shows that these test scores are actually a better predictor of college performances for blacks than for Asians and whites. He also shows the harmfulness of the effect on blacks of preferential acceptance. At the University of California, Berkeley, where the freshman class closely reflects the actual ethnic distribution of California high school students, more than 70% of blacks fail to graduate. All 312 black students entering Berkeley in 1987 were admitted under "Affirmative Action" criteria rather than by meeting standard academic criteria. So were 480 out of 507 Hispanic students. In 1986 the median SAT score for blacks at Berkeley was 952, for Mexican Americans 1014, for American Indians 1082 and for Asian Americans 1254. (The average SAT for all students was 1181.)

The result of this mismatching is that blacks who might do well if they went to a second tier or third tier school where their test scores would indicate they belong, actually are harmed by preferential treatment. They cannot compete in the institutions where high abilities are necessary.

Sowell also points out that Affirmative Action policies have mainly assisted the middle class black, those who have suffered least from discrimination. "Black couples in which both husband and wife are college-educated overtook white couples of the same description back in the early 1970s and continued to at least hold their own in the 1980s" (115).

Sowell's conclusion is that similar patterns of results obtained from India to the USA wherever preferential policies exist. "In education, preferential admissions policies have led to high attrition rates and substandard performances for those preferred students . . . who survived to graduate." In all countries the preferred tended to concentrate in less difficult subjects which lead to less remunerative careers. "In the employment market, both blacks and untouchables at the higher levels have advanced substantially while those at the lower levels show no such advancement and even some signs of retrogression. These patterns are also broadly consistent with patterns found in countries in which majorities have created preferences for themselves . . ." (116).

The tendency has been to focus at the high level end of education and employment rather than on the lower level of family structure and early education. But if we really want to help the worst off improve, we need to concentrate on the family and early education. It is foolish to expect equal results when we begin with grossly unequal starting points—and discriminating against young white males is no more just than discriminating against women, blacks or anyone else. . . .

ENDNOTES

1. Quoted in William Bradford Reynolds, "Affirmative Action is Unjust" in D. Bender and B. Leone (eds.), *Social Justice* (St. Paul, MN, 1984), p. 23.

2. Some of the material in this section is based on Nicholas Capaldi's *Out of Order: Affirmative Action and the Crisis of Doctrinaire Liberalism* (Buffalo, NY, 1985), chapters 1 and 2. Capaldi, using the shackled runner analogy, divides the history into three stages: a *platitude stage* "in which it is reaffirmed that the face is to be fair, and a fair race is one in which no one has either special disadvantages or special advantages (equal opportunity)"; a *remedial stage* in which victims of past discrimination are to be given special help in overcoming their disadvantages; and a *realignment stage* "in which all runners will be reassigned to those positions on the course that they would have had if the race had been fair from the beginning" (p. 18f).

3. See Lino A. Graglia, " 'Affirmative Action,' " the Constitution, and the 1964 Civil Rights Act," *Measure,* no. 92 (1991).

4. Linda Gottfredson, "Letters to the Editor," *New York Times,* Aug. 1, 1990 issue. Gender-norming is also a feature of the proponents of Affirmative Action. Michael Levin begins his book *Feminism and Freedom* (New Brunswick, 1987) with federal Court case *Beckman v. NYFD* in which 88 women who failed the New York City Fire Department's entrance exam in 1977 filed a class-action sex discrimination suit. The court found that the physical strength component of the test was not job-related, and thus a violation of Title VII of the Civil Rights Act, and ordered the city to hire 49 of the women. It further ordered the fire department to devise a special, less-demanding physical strength exam for women. Following EEOC guidelines if the passing rate for women is less than 80% of that of the passing rate of men, the test is presumed invalid.

5. John Arthur, *The Unfinished Constitution* (Belmont, CA, 1990), p. 238.

6. See Michael Levin, "Is Racial Discrimination Special?" *Policy Review,* Fall issue (1982).

7. Judith Jarvis Thomson, "Preferential Hiring" in Marshall Cohen, Thomas Nagel and Thomas Scanlon (eds.), *Equality and Preferential Treatment* (Princeton, 1977).

8. John Rawls, *A Theory of Justice* (Cambridge, 1971), p. 104; See Richard Wasserstrom "A Defense of Programs of Preferential Treatment," *National Forum* (Phi Kappa Phi Journal), vol. 58 (1978). See also Bernard Boxill, "The Morality of Preferential Hiring," *Philosophy and Public Affairs,* vol. 7 (1978).

9. Michael Kinsley, "Equal Lack of Opportunity," *Harper's,* June issue (1983).

10. There is one other argument which I have omitted. It is one from precedence and has been stated by Judith Jarvis Thomson in the article cited earlier:

"Suppose two candidates for a civil service job have equally good test scores, but there is only one job available. We could decide between them by coin-tossing. But in fact we do allow for declaring for *A* straightaway, where *A* is a veteran, and *B* is not. It may be that *B* is a non-veteran through no fault of his own . . . Yet the fact is that *B* is not a veteran and *A* is. On the assumption that the veteran has served his country, the country owes him something. And it is plain that giving him preference is not an unjust way in which part of that debt of gratitude can be paid" (p. 379f).

The two forms of preferential hiring are analogous. Veteran's preference is justified as a way of paying a debt of gratitude; preferential hiring is a way of paying a debt of compensation. In both cases innocent parties bear the burden of the community's debt, but it is justified.

My response to this argument is that veterans should not be hired in place of better qualified candidates, but that benefits like the GI scholarships are part of the contract with veterans who serve their country in the armed services. The notion of compensation only applies to individuals who have been injured by identifiable entities. So the analogy between veterans and minority groups seems weak.

11. Quoted in Jim Sleeper, *The Closest of Strangers* (New York, 1990), p. 209.

12. Shelby Steele, "A Negative vote on Affirmative Action," *New York Times,* May 13, 1990 issue.

13. *New York Times,* May 10, 1990 issue.

14. Nicholas Capaldi, *op. cit.,* p. 85.

15. Ibid.

16. The extreme form of this New Speak is incarnate in the Politically Correct Movement ("PC" ideology) where a new orthodoxy has emerged, condemning white, European culture and seeing African culture as the new savior of us all. Perhaps the clearest example of this is Paula Rothenberg's book *Racism and Sexism* (New York, 1987) which asserts that there is no such thing as black racism; only whites are capable of racism (p. 6). Ms. Rothenberg's book has been

scheduled as required reading for all freshmen at the University of Texas. See Joseph Salemi, "Lone Star Academic Politics," no. 87 (1990).

17. Thomas Sowell, *Preferential Policies: An International Perspective* (New York, 1990), p. 108.

QUESTIONS ON POJMAN

1. How does Pojman distinguish between "weak" and "strong" affirmative action? What is the compensation argument for affirmative action, and why might this argument justify some weak types of affirmative action? Do you agree? Why or why not?

2. In what way does affirmative action shift the "burden of proof" to the employer? Do you think that this is a correct way of describing the practice in question? Why or why not?

3. What are the reasons given for asserting that affirmative action is not a successful social policy? How would things be different *now* if there had been no affirmative action? How would things be different in *fifty years?*

4. Which of the arguments in favor of affirmative action is the strongest? Why?

FOR FURTHER READING

Individual Responsibility

Aristotle. *Nicomachean Ethics,* Book III.1–5.

Hart, H. L. A. *Punishment and Responsibility: Essays in the Philosophy of Law.* Oxford: Oxford University Press, 1968.

Lucas, J. R. *Responsibility.* Oxford: Clarendon Press, 1995.

Paul, Ellen Frankel, Fred D. Miller, Jr., and Jeffrey Paul, eds. *Responsibility.* Cambridge: Cambridge University Press, 1999.

Schmidtz, David, and Robert E. Goodin. *Social Welfare and Individual Responsibility.* Cambridge: Cambridge University Press, 1998.

Corporate Responsibility

Social Responsibility

Brenkert, George G. "Private Corporations and Public Welfare." *Public Affairs Quarterly* 6 (April 1992): 155–68.

Burck, Gilbert. "The Hazards of 'Corporate Responsibility.'" *Fortune Magazine* 87 (June 1973): 114–17, 214–18.

Den Uyl, Douglas J. *The New Crusaders: The Corporate Social Responsibility Debate.* Bowling Green, Ohio: Social Philosophy and Policy Center, 1984.

Frank, Robert H. "Can Socially Responsible Firms Survive in a Competitive Environment?" *Codes of Conduct: Behavioral Research into Business Ethics,* edited by David Messick and Ann Tenbrunsel. New York: Russell Sage Foundation, 1996.

Freeman, R. Edward. *Strategic Management: A Stakeholder Approach.* Marshfield, Mass.: Pitman, 1984.

Goldman, Alan H. "Business Ethics: Profits, Utilities, and Moral Rights." *Philosophy and Public Affairs* 9 (1980): 260–86.

Hessen, Robert. *In Defense of the Corporation* (Stanford, Conn.: Hoover Institution Press, 1979).

Levitt, Theodore. "The Dangers of Social Responsibility." *Harvard Business Review* 36 (September–October 1958): 44–50.

Miller, Fred D., and John Ahrens. "The Social Responsibility of Corporations." In *Commerce and Morality,* edited by Tibor Machan. Totowa, N.J.: Rowman and Littlefield, 1988.

Rasmussen, Douglas B. "Managerial Ethics." In *Commerce and Morality,* edited by Tibor R. Machan. Totowa, N.J.: Rowman and Littlefield, 1988.

Rent-Seeking

Aranson, Peter H. "The Democratic Order and Public Choice." In *Politics and Process: New Essays in Democratic Thought,* edited by Geoffrey Brennan and Loren Lomasky. Cambridge: Cambridge University Press, 1989, 97–148.

Buchanan, James M., Robert D. Tollison, and Gordon Tullock, eds. *Toward a Theory of the Rent-Seeking Society.* College Station: Texas A & M University Press, 1980.

DiLorenzo, Thomas J. "Property Rights, Information Costs, and the Economics of Rent-Seeking." *Journal of Theoretical and Institutional Economics* 144 (April 1988).

Krueger, Anne O. "The Political Economy of the Rent-Seeking Society." The American Economic Review 64 (1976): 291–303.

Pasour, E.C., Jr. "Rent-Seeking: Some Conceptual Problems and Implications." *Review of Austrian Economics* 1 (1986): 123–43.

Rose-Ackerman, Susan. *Corruption and Government: Causes, Consequences and Reform.* Cambridge: Cambridge University Press, 1978.

Rowley, Charles K., Robert D. Tollison, and Gordon Tullock, eds. *The Political Economy of Rent-Seeking.* Boston, Mass.: Kluwer Academic Publishers, 1988.

Sunstein, Cass. "Constitutions and Democracies: An Epilogue." In *Constitutionalism and Democracy,* edited by Jon Elster and Rune Slagstad. Cambridge: Cambridge University Press, 1988: 327–53.

Tullock, Gordon. *The Economics of Special Privilege and Rent-Seeking.* Boston, Mass.: Kluwer Academic Publishing, 1989.

———. *Rent-Seeking.* Aldershot, England: Edward Elgar, 1993.

Industry, Work and Ambition

Industry and Work

Ciulla, Joanne B. *The Working Life: The Promise and Betrayal of Modern Work.* New York: Times Books, 2000.

De Grazia, Sebastian. *Of Time, Work, and Leisure.* New York: Twentieth Century Fund, 1962.

Erikson, Kai, and Steven Peter Vallas, eds. *The Nature of Work: Sociological Perspectives.* New Haven, Conn.: Yale University Press, 1990.

Meilander, Gilbert C., ed. *Working: Its Meaning and Its Limits.* Notre Dame, Ind.: University of Notre Dame Press, 2000.

Robertson, Brian C. *There's No Place Like Work: How Business, Government, and Our Obsession with Work Have Driven Parents from Home.* Dallas, Tex.: Spence Publishing, 2000.

Thomas, Keith, ed. *The Oxford Book of Work.* New York: Oxford University Press, 1999.

Thoreau, Henry David. *Life Without Principle: Three Essays* [1863]. Norwood, Pa.: Norwood Editions, 1978.

Tilgher, Adriano. *Work: What It Has Meant to Men Through the Ages,* translated by Dorothy Canfield Fisher. New York: Harcourt, Brace, 1930.

Ambition

Braudy, Leo. *The Frenzy of Renown: Fame and Its History.* New York: Oxford University Press, 1986.

Cowen, Tyler. *What Price Fame?* Cambridge, Mass.: Harvard University Press, 2000.

Epstein, Joseph. *Ambition: The Secret Passion.* New York: E.P. Dutton, 1980.

Harré, Rom. *Social Being.* Totowa, N.J.: Rowman and Littlefield, 1980.

Hazlitt, William. "On the Qualifications Necessary to Success in Life," Essay XVIII of *The Plain Speaker.* In *The Collected Works of William Hazlitt,* edited by A. R. Waller and Arnold Glover, Vol. VII London: J. M. Dent, 1903, 195–209.

Hume, David. "Of the Love of Fame." In *Essays, Moral, Political, and Literary,* edited by Eugene F. Miller. Indianapolis, Ind.: Liberty Classics, 1985.

Montaigne, Michel de, "Of Glory." In *The Complete Works of Montaigne,* translated by Donald M. Frame. Stanford, Conn.: Stanford University Press, 1957.

Palma, A. B. "On Wanting to Be Somebody." *Philosophy* 63 (1988): 373–87.

Courage, Entrepreneurship, and Profit

Courage

Mackenzie, Compton, Sir. *On Moral Courage.* London: Collins, 1962.

Miller, William Ian. *The Mystery of Courage.* Cambridge: Harvard University Press,

Walton, Douglas N. *Courage: A Philosophical Investigation.* Berkeley: University of California, 1986.

Entrepreneurship and Profit

Acton, H. B. *The Morals of Markets and Other Essays.* Indianapolis: Liberty Fund, 1993.

Child, James W. "Profit: The Concept and Its Moral Features." In *Social Philosophy and Policy: Problems of Market Liberalism* 15 (Summer 1998).

Cowan, Robin, and Mario Rizzo, eds. *Profits and Morality.* Chicago: University of Chicago Press, 1995.

Flew, Antony. "The Profit Motive." *Ethics* 85 (1976): 312–22.

Hébert, Robert, and Albert Link. *The Entrepreneur: Mainstream Views and Radical Critiques.* New York: Praeger, 1982.

Kirzner, Israel. *Perception, Opportunity, and Profit.* Chicago: University of Chicago Press, 1979.

———. *Discovery and the Capitalist Process.* Chicago: University of Chicago Press, 1985.

Parker David, and Richard Stead. *Profit and Enterprise: The Political Economy of Profit.* New York: Harvester Wheatsheaf, 1991.

Rothbard, Murray N. *Man, Economy, and State,* 2 vols. Auburn, Ala.: Ludwig von Mises Institute, 1993, esp. pp. 463–501.

Schweickart, David. "Capitalism, Contribution, and Sacrifice." *The Philosophical Forum* 7 (Spring/ Summer 1976).

Freedom of Contract, and Affirmative Action

Contracts

Atiyah, Patrick. *The Rise and Fall of Freedom of Contract.* Oxford: Clarendon Press, 1979.

Fried, Charles. *Contract as Promise: A Theory of Contractual Obligation.* Cambridge: Harvard University Press, 1981.

Katz, Leo. "Responsibility and Consent: The Libertarian's Problem with Freedom of Contract." *Social Philosophy and Policy: Responsibility* 16 (Summer 1999).

Kronman, Anthony T. "Contract Law and Distributive Justice." *Yale Law Journal* 89 (January 1980): 472–97.

Trebilcock, Michael J. *The Limits of Freedom of Contract.* Cambridge: Harvard University Press, 1993.

Women: Social and Economic Issues

Blum, Linda M. *Between Feminism and Labor: The Significance of the Comparable Worth Movement.* Berkeley: University of California Press, 1991.

Conway, David. *Free-Market Feminism* (with commentaries by Brenda Almond, Miriam E. David, Janet Radcliffe Richards, and Christina Hoff Sommers). London: IEA Health and Welfare Unit, 1998.

Goldberg, Steven. *Why Men Rule: A Theory of Male Domination.* Chicago: Open Court, 1993.

Goldin, Claudia. *Understanding the Gender Gap: An Economic History of American Women.* New York: Oxford University Press, 1990.

Jacobsen, Joyce P. *The Economics of Gender,* 2d ed. New York: Blackwell, 1998.

Jagger, Alison, and Iris Young, eds. *A Companion to Feminist Philosophy.* Malden, Mass.: Blackwell, 1998.

Korany, J. A., James P. Sterba, and Rosemarie Tong, eds. *Feminist Philosophies: Problems, Theories, and Applications.* Hemel Hempstead, England: Harvester Wheatsheaf, 1993.

Levin, Michael. *Feminism and Freedom.* New Brunswick, N.J.: Transaction Books, 1987.

Mill, John Stuart. *The Subjection of Women* [1869], edited by Susan Moller Okin. Indianapolis, Ind.: Hackett, 1988.

McElroy, Wendy, ed. *Freedom, Feminism, and the State,* 2d ed. New York: Holmes and Meier, 1991.

Taylor, Joan Kennedy. *Reclaiming the Mainstream: Individualist Feminism Reconsidered.* Amherst, N.Y.: Prometheus Books, 1992.

Tong, Rosemarie. *Feminist Thought: A More Comprehensive Introduction.* Boulder, Colo.: Westview, 1998.

Walker, Deborah. "Feminism and Economics: Legislation or Markets?" In *Neither Victim nor Enemy,* edited by Rita J. Simon. Lanham, Md.: University Press of America, 1995.

Minorities: Social and Economic Issues

Gilroy, Paul. *Against Race: Imagining Political Culture Beyond the Color Line.* Cambridge: Belknap Press of Harvard University, 2000.

Hacker, Andrew. *Two Nations: Black and White, Separate, Hostile, Unequal.* New York: Scribner's, 1992.

McWhorter, John H. *Losing the Race: Self-Sabotage in Black America.* New York: The Free Press, 2000.

Sniderman, Paul, and Thomas Piazza. *The Scar of Race.* Cambridge: Belknap Press of Harvard University, 1993.

Sowell, Thomas. *Ethnic America: A History.* New York: Basic Books, 1981.

———. *Markets and Minorities.* New York: Basic Books, 1981.

———. *Race and Culture: A World View.* New York: Basic Books, 1994.

Steele, Shelby. *The Content of Our Character: A New Vision of Race in America.* New York. St. Martin's Press, 1990.

Takaki, Ronald T. *A Different Mirror: A History of Multicultural America.* Boston, Mass.: Little, Brown, & Co., 1993.

Takaki, Ronald, ed. *From Different Shores: Perspectives on Race and Ethnicity in America.* New York: Oxford University Press, 1994.

Thernstrom, Abigail, and Stephan Thernstrom. *America in Black and White: One Nation, Indivisible.* New York: Simon & Schuster, 1997.

Thernstrom, Abigail, and Stephan Thernstrom, eds. *Beyond the Color Line: New Perspectives on Race and Ethnicity.* Stanford, Conn.: Hoover Institution Press, 2000.

Preferential Treatment: Affirmative Action

Block, W. E., and M. A. Walker, eds. *Discrimination, Affirmative Action, and Equal Opportunity: An*

Economic and Social Perspective. Vancouver: Fraser Institute, 1982.

Bowen, William G., and Derek Bok. *The Shape of the River: Long-Term Consequences of Considering Race in College and University Admissions.* Princeton, N.J.: Princeton University Press, 1998.

Boxill, Bernard. *Blacks and Social Justice.* Totowa, N.J.: Rowman and Littlefield, 1992.

Brimelow, Peter, and L. Spencer. "When Quotas Replace Merit, Everybody Suffers." *Forbes Magazine* (15 February 1993): 80–100.

Cahn, Steven M. ed. *Affirmative Action and the University: A Philosophical Inquiry.* Philadelphia, Pa.: Temple University Press, 1993.

Cohen, Marshall, Thomas Nagel, and Thomas Scanlon, eds. *Equality and Preferential Treatment.* Princeton, N.J.: Princeton University Press, 1977.

Epstein, Richard. *Forbidden Grounds: The Case Against Employment Discrimination Laws.* Cambridge: Harvard University Press, 1992.

Hill, Thomas E., Jr. "The Message of Affirmative Action." *Social Philosophy and Policy* 8 (1991): 108–29.

Lynch, Frederick R. *The Diversity Machine: The Drive to Change the 'White Male Workplace.'* New Brunswick, N.J.: Transaction, 2000.

McGary, Howard. *Race and Social Justice.* Malden, Mass.: Blackwell, 1999.

Mosley, Albert G., and Nicholas Capaldi. *Affirmative Action: Social Justice or Unfair Preference?* Lanham, Md.: Rowman and Littlefield, 1996.

Nagel, Thomas. "Equal Treatment and Compensatory Discrimination." *Philosophy and Public Affairs* 2. (1973): 348–63.

Orfield, Gary and Edward Miller, eds. *Chilling Admissions: The Affirmative Action Crisis and the Search for Alternatives.* Cambridge, Mass.: Civil Rights Project, Education Publishing Group, 1988.

Sowell, Thomas. *Preferential Policies: An International Perspective.* New York: W. Morrow, 1990.

Yates, Steven. *Civil Wrongs: What Went Wrong with Affirmative Action.* San Francisco, Calif.: ICS Press, 1994.

The Consequences of Commerce

The Moral Effects of Commerce

And so, as time goes on, and they advance in the pursuit of wealth, the more they hold that in honor the less they honor virtue. May not the opposition of wealth and virtue be conceived as if each lay in the scale of a balance inclining opposite ways?

Plato[1]

Commerce has a special character which distinguishes it from all other professions. It affects the feelings of men so strongly that it makes him who was proud and haughty suddenly turn supple, bending and serviceable. Through commerce, man learns to deliberate, to be honest, to acquire manners, to be prudent and reserved in both talk and action. Sensing the necessity to be wise and honest in order to succeed, he flees vice, or at least his demeanor exhibits decency and seriousness so as not to arouse any adverse judgement on the part of present and future acquaintances; he would not dare make a spectacle of himself for fear of damaging his credit standing and thus society may well avoid a scandal which it might otherwise have to deplore.

Samuel Ricard[2]

True, it must be owned, we for the present, with our Mammon-Gospel, have come to strange conclusions. We call it a Society; and go about professing openly the totalest separation, isolation. Our life is not a mutual helpfulness; but rather, cloaked under due laws-of-war, named 'fair competition' and so forth, it is a mutual hostility. We have profoundly forgotten everywhere that Cash-payment *is not the sole relation of human beings; we think, nothing doubting, that* it *absolves and liquidates all engagements of man.*

Thomas Carlyle[3]

---

1. *Republic,* Book VIII, 550e, in *Plato: The Collected Dialogues*, edited by Edith Hamilton and Huntington Cairns (Princeton, N.J.: Princeton University Press, 1980.)

2. *Traité general du commerce* [C1704] (Amsterdam: Chez E. van Harrevelt et Soeters, 1781), 463. As quoted in Albert O. Hirschman, "Rival Views of Market Society," in *Rival Views of Market Society and Other Recent Essays* (Cambridge: Harvard University Press, 1992), 108.

3. *Past and Present* (London: George Routledge and Sons, n.d. [1843]), 114.

Innumerable times [competition] achieves what usually only love can do: the divination of the innermost wishes of the other, even before he himself becomes aware of them. Antagonistic tension with his competitor sharpens the business man's sensitivity to the tendencies of the public, even to the point of clairvoyance, in respect to future changes in the public's tastes, fashions, interests—not only the businessman's, but also the journalist's, artist's, bookseller's, parliamentarian's. Modern competition is described as the fight of all against all, but at the same time it is the fight for *all.*

George Simmel[4]

The legal framework of an economic system includes a structure of permissions, requirements, and prohibitions that delimit the manner in which individuals may interact and trade with one another. The economic system of the market establishes laws of property, contract, and exchange within which individuals produce and exchange goods and services. However, the effective operation of any market may require that the participants not only adhere to the rules of the legal framework but that they exhibit certain qualities or norms of conduct, psychology, or character (see Section AIV). If so, then the legal framework together with these normative conditions would constitute an economic and social order within which individuals interact. Might this order, or the interaction of agents within it, bring about certain consequences of a moral sort? In other words, are there ethical *effects* of market systems?

The conduct of an individual is intentional in that it is initiated with the aim of bringing about certain consequences. However, within a complex economic system, such as a market, individuals possess divergent goals and aims, but their interaction may bring about consequences that were not part of any individual's intention. In fact, as individuals interact some of their aims and goals will materialize, some will not occur at all, and other consequences will eventuate that are utterly unintended. Indeed, some of these unintended consequences may serve to alter the very moral norms that underlie and guide behavior, thereby transforming, for better or worse, the very moral character of the society.

It should not be surprising that the market, as a particular economic system, might generate consequences of an ethical sort, whether positive or negative. Some have argued that the market has destructive effects on traditional morality, encouraging self-interest and an impersonal attitude toward others. However, it has also been argued that participation in market activities serves to bolster certain moral qualities, including honesty, civility, and impartiality. A consideration of the moral effects of commerce is not only eminently worthy of interest but vital to an understanding of the market and to a more nuanced evaluation of it as an economic system. If we are to consider the extent to which the operation of the market tends, over time, to generate or cause certain normative moral effects, then let us begin by considering the nature of causal arguments.

THE MARKET AS CAUSE

A Causal Argument[5]

The focus of our investigation is whether or not, or to what extent, the market, or certain specific market rules, institutions or processes, may causally affect the content or nature of the moral qualities or norms by which individuals conduct themselves. Such effects could be either positive or negative. For example, the operation of the market, or some aspect thereof, might serve either to strengthen or to weaken qualities or norms thought to be morally important. In analyzing any such causal claim it is important to establish, first, that the phenomenon alleged to be the effect has actually occurred (and to what extent, manner, degree, and location). From considering whether the effect has occurred, one must turn to its alleged cause (or causes), presumably some aspect of the market or the market as an economic system. In most matters of social explanation, there are multiple elements of causation for any particular effect. That the causes of some effect may be multifaceted renders more difficult any attempt at understanding. Nonetheless, it is worthwhile to note two additional matters regarding causes.

4. *Conflict* [1908] *and the Web of Group Affiliations* [1922], translated by Kurt H. Wolff and Reinhard Bendix (New York: The Free Press, 1955), 62.

5. A similar discussion of causal argument may be found in the introduction of Section AIV.

Sufficient or Necessary?   It is important to recognize that a causal argument may seek to show either that some feature or phenomenon is a *sufficient* condition for some effect or that it is a *necessary* condition. If it is claimed that markets are sufficient for some effect, then that effect should be present in every instance of the market (or in every instance in which the relevant market phenomenon is present). On the other hand, if it is claimed that markets, or some aspect thereof, are necessary for some effect, then if that effect occurs without the presence of the relevant market phenomena, one may reasonably infer that markets are not *necessary* for the production of the effect.

Contingent or Essential?   In considering any causal argument linking some aspect of the market to some moral effect, one should also examine whether the causal aspect of the market is merely a temporary or contingent feature of a particular market or whether the causal aspect is an essential or necessary aspect of any market. For example, do certain regulatory rules favor large corporations at the expense of smaller businesses, perhaps thereby encouraging the survival of organizations with a greater propensity to impersonality? Are such rules necessary or essential to the operation of markets, or are these rules incidental features of a particular market in a particular time and place?

It should be clear that it is not easy to diagnose the causal links between markets and their effects. Social and economic causality is often difficult to establish if only because the relevant circumstances exhibit complexity. The alleged effects, as *moral* effects, are nondiscrete general tendencies that are difficult not only to define but to measure; in addition, the causal forces that, presumably produce such effects are often several, and these operate in complex ways.

POSITIVE AND NEGATIVE EFFECTS

Market Neutrality

It might be argued that market systems generate no ethical consequences whatsoever; in other words, the market is neutral with respect to the ethics of the society, just as the market might be neutral with respect to the goods and services that are bought and sold. For example, if the legal framework of the market does not favor one type of economic good or service over another, then the market is neutral with respect to the goods that are exchanged— not favoring sofas over chairs, or lanterns over lamps, but producing and distributing whatever goods buyers and sellers might agree to exchange. Indeed, the fact that a market framework would allow for the exchange of any goods at mutually agreeable terms is the sort of assumption that might lead one to conclude that the market is also neutral with regard to human motivation, moral qualities, and moral norms. However, that the market is neutral with respect to the goods and services exchanged need not entail that the ongoing exchange of goods and services has no effects on the moral norms of the society. A market neutral to morality would not privilege or encourage one set of values, preferences, or virtues over any other; a neutral market would neither improve or corrupt morality, nor would it alter those spheres of society not governed by market norms (including familial and religious spheres). So stated, the assertion of market neutrality seems dubious, for it does not seem likely that the operations of the market would have *no* effect on the normative moral values of the individuals who interact within a commercial society.

Permissions and Incentives   Most arguments to the effect that the market brings about certain moral effects, whether positive or negative, focus on the question of *permissions* and *incentives*. For example, it has sometimes been suggested that the market permits conduct that is self-interested if not selfish. Of course, the very laws that permit selfish behavior also permit other-regarding, and nonselfish, conduct. If it is argued that markets affect morality because the markets *permit* certain kinds of conduct, then perhaps it is not the market that is causing or bringing about the moral effect; rather, the market permission allows for some prior moral tendency to appear. (As to whether that tendency is part of human nature or was developed through some social or cultural process is a question which must be set aside for now.) On the other hand, the market may create *incentives* for behaving in certain manners. For example, does the market create incentives to do what is right or does it provide incentives to act *against* what one knows to be right? Some have held that the market provides strong incentives for individuals to adhere to certain moral norms, but others have charged that the market encourages forms of selfishness which, if left unchecked, tend to permeate spheres of society previously exempt from the norms of commerce.

Positive Effects

Those who hold the view that the market tends to improve morals have often noted the important way in which markets provide incentives to do good. On this view, the market is so structured that adherence to some traditional moral standard or virtue is encouraged, either because the *failure* to adhere to such conduct is penalized or because adherence is *rewarded* in the form of success in the competitive marketplace. (This is not to say that the rightness of an act is determined by what will succeed in the marketplace, only that the marketplace may encourage right actions.) It is the very competitive aspect of the market that ensures that those persons and firms that exhibit moral behavior will also acquire a reputation for good conduct (or fair dealing) and, other things being equal, gain an edge over competitors.

There are at least three areas in which it has been argued that the market provides incentives for doing good. In the first type of instance, the market encourages or supports certain virtues, whether these be required for individual achievement or necessary for pleasant interaction with others. It might be argued that the market rewards the industrious, the prudent, and the self-reliant and in this manner encourages these virtues. Similarly, if friendliness, politeness, and civility are virtues, then it might be argued that commercial success requires that one be friendly, polite, and respectful. This claim might seem surprising only because so many of us are well-accustomed to a certain level of politeness. In nations that have not been introduced to widespread commerce, there are consistent tales of poor service, rude clerks, and belligerent workers.[6] For example, if we assume that consumers prefer to interact with a businessperson who is civil, polite, and honest, then a businessperson's deviation from the social virtues of civility, honesty, and politeness would, all else equal, be penalized. Insofar as the practice of these virtues are good for business, then so are they strengthened. However, are practices that are "good for business" practices that are truly ethical?

There is an important distinction between, say, honest conduct performed for strategic reasons and honest conduct performed for moral reasons. That said, it is worth considering that when the market provides incentives for doing good, it may serve to habituate a person to *be* good. For example, Immanuel Kant draws the distinction between an action that conforms to duty and one done from duty (or out of respect for duty). In developing this distinction he offers the example of a "prudent merchant"[7] who refrains from cheating a child not because such cheating is wrong, but because doing so would be bad for business. In this case, Kant holds that the shopkeeper acts prudentially rather than morally. However, even if one initiates and reiterates an action out of some prudential motive, the reiteration of that act may habituate one to perform the act, and, over time, one's motive may become less prudential than moral. Suppose that a rude and dishonest person comes to recognize that civility, honesty, and politeness are good for business, and this person decides to adhere to these norms for purely strategic reasons. Although this person conforms to these norms for reasons other than their virtue, the steady adherence to norms of civility, for example, may so affect the person's habits that the person comes to adhere to these norms out of moral commitment rather than out of business strategy.[8]

A second manner in which markets might have positive moral effects for social interaction lies in the very nature of markets to promote respectful and peaceful interaction with persons of different origins, backgrounds, and outlooks. Commercial exchange is, by definition, nonviolent exchange, and the proliferation of commerce serves to reward those who are adept at initiating and completing mutually beneficial exchanges. The parties to such exchanges need not share any commonalities except that each wishes to make a trade; it makes no difference whether one knows the other party to the exchange or whether the parties share one another's outlook, race, religion, ethnicity, or politics. Those who are willing to trade with strangers, or others who differ from their group or clan, have opportunities for beneficial exchange that others do not, a fact that would seem to encourage us to trade with persons different from us. Even if one does not like a certain person because of the group to which he belongs, the possibility of productive trade gives one an incentive to treat the person with respect and to engage in peaceful commerce. In the process of trading with a person from a differing group, one may come to understand the other less in terms of group identity than in terms of skills, knowledge, and productive capacity. In this way, markets may tend to stimulate change, breaking down barriers of culture and group identity, thereby rendering us

---

6. "In China, store clerks were so predictably rude that the government banned 50 of their choicest phrases: [including] . . . 'Hey!' 'Didn't you hear me? What do you have ears for?' " "If you're not buying, what are you looking at?" Seth Faison, "Service with Some Bile," *The New York Times,* 22 October 1995, 4E.

7. The relevant text is not included in the selection in Section AV. Consult Kant's *Grounding for the Metaphysics of Morals,* translated by James W. Ellington, 3d ed. (Indianapolis, Ind.: Hackett, 1993), 10 (Section I, 397).

8. Aristotle emphasizes how virtues are learned through habituation. See the selection, in Section AV, from *Nicomachean Ethics* (esp. Book II. 1–4).

less reliant on traditional partialities such as those born of race, ethnicity, kinship, language, or religion.

Finally, there is a third way in which markets help to generate good conduct. Insofar as success in the market is a function of satisfying the wishes of buyers and consumers, then so does the market link its rewards to the idea of serving others. If one wishes to sell a product or service, then one must take into account the wants and desires of other persons. Even if a person is motivated only by selfish concerns, these concerns can be satisfied only by serving consumers, thereby satisfying some of the wants of others. It must be granted that this may not entail that one is considering the needs of those who are least well-off, only the needs and wishes of potential *consumers* (those able and willing to pay for one's goods or services.) Nonetheless, it is a strength of a system that it cannot only coax other-regarding behavior out of *good* persons, but it can also elicit this behavior from those, such as the selfish, who might otherwise act in ways that would prove nonbeneficial, if not harmful, to others.

Negative Effects

There are interesting and powerful considerations as to whether the market has negative moral effects or undermines ethical conduct more generally. It is sometimes argued that a market tends to bring about a version of morality distinct from the moral norms that would typically prevail in other, noncommercial, spheres of society. Either the market encourages or celebrates self-interested behavior at the expense of some traditional norms or virtues (such as benevolence), or the practice of commerce encourages impersonal attitudes, an unwarranted emphasis on efficiency, and, more generally, a rationalistic mentality that is inimical to the very foundations of morality. The charge that the ethics of markets are distinct from those of noncommercial spheres often comes with a corollary indictment: that market morality seeps into other realms of society previously immune to the lure of profit, efficiency calculations, and contract, thereby undermining or destroying traditional moral norms.

The theory that the market generates a new and distinct morality, like the argument that the market generates beneficial moral effects, often focuses on certain virtues, traits, or norms. For example, it is suggested that benevolence is not reinforced by the market but dis-

couraged. The person who makes the effort to act benevolently, especially when there is no economic reward for doing so, is at a competitive disadvantage to the person whose conduct is less benevolent. Similarly, the virtue of honesty may suffer under the strains of commerce. Under the lure of profit, individuals are motivated—whether as businesspeople, workers, or consumers—to shade the truth and lie, if these acts promise a reward of a larger monetary gain.

Comparative Assessments

In examining the effects of any institutions or economic systems (rules or policies), it is worth pointing out that even if the market has certain negative incentives, one's overall evaluation of the market should also take into account the incentive effects of possible alternatives. For if the market (or some aspect thereof) has certain incentive effects that are negative, an alternative institution may have the same or worse incentive effects. As in most matters of complexity, there is little to be gained by demanding perfection or by relying upon slogans or invective. Rather, one must weigh, as best one can, the advantages and disadvantages of an institution, keeping in mind that the elimination of one system, institution, or rule may only bring into being an alternative whose effects are worse. In other words, even if it were true that the market does have negative moral incentives, that alone would not demonstrate that the market should be abandoned, for an alternative system or institution may operate via a set of incentives that are more harmful yet. For example, if one replaces decentralized market decision making with a centralized institution in which decisions are made or influenced by those who are elected or appointed to power, then those who affect economic decisions may not be individuals skilled in satisfying the wants of consumers but persons adept at acquiring political power. The qualities and norms required for the attainment of political power may be no better than the qualities that the market allegedly effects.

Market Domination

Another sort of negative effect sometimes attributed to the market is that the ethics of markets tend to permeate and dominate other noncommercial spheres of life. (This point of view, prevalent in the nineteenth century, has received renewed interest in the current debates over globalization.) In the first volume of *Capital,* Karl Marx forwards one version of this claim, contending that capitalism tends to turn all objects and actions (including human labor itself) into a commodity to be bought and sold. In this way, it is argued, the morals of markets tend to permeate the noncommercial spheres of society, corrupting or undermining what had been noncommercial modes of interaction, thereby *commodifying* society. Thus, if markets tend to generate a strategic mode of thinking in which objects are considered as commodities to be bought and sold and persons are understood in terms of their specific marketable skills, then as markets acquire ever greater importance so do these modes of thought permeate other spheres of society, effectively destroying the nonmarket relations among and between family members, friends, and co-religionists.

POLITICAL EFFECTS OF MARKETS

That the market may have moral effects, for good or ill, suggests that markets may also have *political* effects, a thesis that has been argued as often as the thesis of moral effects. The readings that follow focus on moral rather than political consequences, but it is worth pointing out, briefly, how some have understood the market to generate noteworthy political consequences. One might ask, first, whether there are certain *virtues* requisite for certain kinds of government, and if the market makes it more or less difficult to realize these virtues. The virtues of courage, self-control, and responsibility are often taken to be important for citizens living in democratic and free states, so one might ask whether participation in markets encourages the cultivation of these virtues. [9] If markets increase the likelihood that individuals will be courageous and self-controlled, then markets might serve to generate some of the virtues that render freedom more likely, depotism less likely.

Markets and Democracy

Some have argued that markets have a causal relation to democracy. Although the idea of a market is, of course, conceptually distinct from the idea of a democracy, historically the rise of democracy has occurred in those nations in which industry and commerce were also emerging. The association between democracy

9. In the eighteenth century Adam Ferguson argued that the rise of a commercial society might encourage weakness and moral decline. See *An Essay on the History of Civil Society* [1767], edited by Fania Oz-Salzberger (Cambridge: Cambridge University Press, 1995), esp Part V.

and markets may be a historical coincidence, but it may also provide evidence of a causal link between markets and democratic political institutions. In which way might the causal link run, if there is one? Since there have been, and are, market economies in which there are no democratic political institutions, it seems unlikely that democracy is a necessary condition for markets or that markets are a sufficient condition for democracy. However, since there has been no modern democracy in which there were not significant market institutions, this may provide evidence that markets are necessary for democracy, but this is not conclusive.

In order to weigh these matters more fully, let us consider whether certain principles essential to the market are similar to (or necessary for) principles essential to democracy or to democratic institutions. For our purposes the term "democracy" refers to a method or system of government in which both the procedures for enacting, or altering, the rules governing political decisions and the persons who make these decisions are subject to some form of popular control in which all adults share some equal rights to vote freely (in accordance with principles of majority rule and periodic elections) and in which there is freedom for candidates to enter the electoral process. In order for these features to be realized, however, there must be freedom of the press, freedom of assembly and organization, and the freedom to run for office. It has been argued that the freedoms necessary for a democracy, such as freedom of speech (including the freedom to write and publish what one wishes) and association, require that one also have the freedom to own property (whether that be a printing press or a computer) and to exchange that property with others. Whether or not the freedoms and institutions of a democracy must be understood solely in terms of property rights, it is at least clear that certain democratic freedoms would be considerably less secure if these freedoms could be exercised only under the aegis of the government itself. For if a democratic government were to fund, supply, regulate, or organize either political assemblies or the press, then it would be highly unlikely that the government would grant full liberty to those who assemble *against* democracy, speak out *against* the majoritarian impulses, or write *against* the governing classes or the major political parties. However, if there are sources of power and authority distinct from that of the government, then these would provide conditions for independent thought and action. In this sense, a case can be made that some of the very principles that permit a market to emerge are also necessary for democracies to function well.[10] The institutions that vouchsafe the decentralized decision making and dispersed power (and property) essential to markets also permit the independent sources of authority and thought that are crucial for a robust democracy. This is not to say that every market-oriented society is a democracy (that would mean that markets were a *sufficient* condition of democracy); rather, this claim entails only that a functioning democracy requires some of the same institutions as a functioning market.

HISTORICAL PERSPECTIVE ON MORAL EFFECTS

From the seventeenth into the eighteenth centuries, the nations of western Europe (in particular Britain and Holland) witnessed the steady emergence of commerce and industry, a growth in technological innovation, and rising standards of living. Those who questioned the rise of commerce (and the concomitant opulence) often suggested, either through the written word or in public debate, that societies were held together less by economic relations than by the observance of the traditional virtues. For these individuals the state and society must be so ordered that individuals would seek not a private but the public interest. Often referred to as *republican,* these thinkers suggested that the criteria for judging political and economic systems ought to concern whether those systems had beneficial effects on qualities of mind and character. Having assumed that a society could function only if a sufficient number of individuals were virtuous, and alarmed by the rise of commerce and the concomitant growth of wealth, many feared that public spirit and virtue would diminish in the pursuit of business and the acquisition of worldly goods. (Some of those who advocated this position were not, themselves, in commerce but were the inheritors of great estates; for these persons, the pursuit of money was not only an encouragement to self-interest but was, more broadly, corrupting of civic and public morality generally.) Aware of the contrast—whether real or imagined—between virtue and liberty, Montesquieu seeks to support the new regime of commercial liberty, and writes in book 3 of *The Spirit of the Laws:* "The political Greeks, who lived under a popular government, knew no other support than virtue. The modern inhabitants of that country are entirely taken up with manufacture, commerce, finances, opulence, and luxury."[11]

Eighteenth Century: The Positive View

Arrayed against the republican view were thinkers such as Bernard Mandeville (1670–1733), who argued that vice, not virtue, was the mainspring of society. Others, such as Turgot (1727–1781), believe that the new age of commerce is not only morally superior to its predecessors but the last of a series of societal stages progressing from hunting, to agriculture, to a final stage of commerce.[12] Some, including Samuel Ricard (1637–1717), argue that a social order characterized by economic growth and commerce not only ensures happiness but improves morals, for commerce provides incentives for cooperative and other-regarding conduct. Among the virtues advanced by commerce, the eighteenth-century thinkers emphasize industry, honesty, impartiality, punctuality, friendliness, and thrift. In his *Lectures on Jurisprudence,* Adam Smith (1723–1790) distinguishes the age of commerce from that of "rude and barbarous" societies and maintains that honesty (probity) and punctuality—both of which first arise from a view to one's own advantage—characterize commercial societies.

> Whenever commerce is introduced into any country probity and punctuality always accompany it. These virtues in a rude and barbarous society are almost unknown. Of the nations of Europe, the Dutch, the most commercial, are the most faithful to their word. The English are more so than the Scotch, but much inferior to the Dutch, and in some remote parts of this country they are far less so than in the more commercial parts of it. This is not at all to be imputed to national character, as some pretend. . . . It is far more reducible to self-interest, that general principle which regulates the actions of every man, and which leads men to act in a certain manner from views of advantage, and is as deeply implanted in an Englishman as a Dutchman. A dealer is afraid of losing his character, and is scrupulous in performing every engagement. When a person makes perhaps 20 contracts in a day, he cannot gain so much by endeavouring to impose on his neighbours, as the very appearance of a cheat would make him lose. Where people seldom deal with one another, we find that they are somewhat disposed to cheat, because they can gain more by a smart trick than they can lose by the injury which it does their character.[13]

---

10. Milton Friedman makes this sort of argument in chapter 1 ("The Relation Between Economic Freedom and Political Freedom") of *Capitalism and Freedom* (Chicago: University of Chicago Press, 1962).

11. *The Spirit of the Laws,* translated by Thomas Nugent (London: G. Bell & Sons, 1914), Book 3, chapter 3.

12. See Mandeville's poem, "The Grumbling Hive," in Section AIV. For a selection from Turgot, see Section CII.

13. *Lectures on Jurisprudence* [1762–3, 1766], edited by R. L. Meek, D. D. Raphael, and P. G. Stein (Indianapolis, Ind.: Liberty Classics, 1982), 538–39.

Eighteenth Century: The Negative View

In the eighteenth century, the idea that commerce improved morals did not go unchallenged. For Jean-Jacques Rousseau (1712–1778), it seemed obvious that humankind had, as a negative consequence of the invention of property, perverted and corrupted the natural tendencies of the human being. Rousseau adumbrates these ideas in two essays, the first of which was written as a response to an essay contest of 1749, sponsored by the Academy of Dijon. Though the Academy expected a positive response to its contest question, "Has the restoration of the Arts and Sciences Tended to Purify Morals?," Rousseau's prize-winning essay, *Discourse on the Sciences and the Arts* (1750), offered the opposite. Rousseau charges that progress in science and the technological arts has resulted in the corruption of morals and encouraged hypocrisy: "One no longer asks whether a man has integrity, but whether he has talents; not whether a book is useful, but whether it is well written. Rewards are showered upon the wit, and virtue is left without honors."[14] This *Discourse* proved to be a foreshadowing of a second essay, one focusing on inequality and on the manner in which the natural tendencies of self-preservation and compassion had been corrupted into egoism by modern luxury, itself the consequence of one fateful step, or misstep—the development of property.[15]

Nineteenth Century: Community and Society

In the nineteenth century, with the continuing growth of industry and commerce, new criticisms of the market emerged, many of them reflective of the growing awareness of a shift from traditional closely knit communities to larger groups whose bonds were often constituted by economic relations. The sociologist Ferdinand Tönnies (1855–1936) distinguished between a traditional community, or *Gemeinschaft,* and a society, *Gesellschaft:*[16] A community manifests an ethic of solidarity in which individuals are related through kinship, history, and religion; in a society, on the other hand, individuals are related to one another more through their functional roles than by rooted connections. The distinction between *Gemeinschaft* and *Gesellschaft* reflects an awareness of significant changes within society, alterations which some nineteenth-century thinkers viewed rather negatively. With the rise of industry and commerce there emerged a new emphasis on specialization (the division of labor), contract, individualism, competition, and self-interest, all characteristics which were attributed to a *Gesellschaft* and not a *Gemeinschaft.*

Some of the first to articulate a concern were the literary romantics such as Thomas Carlyle (1795–1881) and John Ruskin (1819–1900). For social critics such as these, the market generates a self-interested ethic in which, as Carlyle contends, individuals are related to one another by "Cash-payment." The market permeates all spheres of society, effectively dominating, if not destroying, the moral relations by which family, religion, and society had developed. As land, labor, and art are converted into saleable commodities, so do human beings become alienated from others and from their own labor.

Nineteenth Century: Marx

The idea of alienation was developed more fully and forcefully by Karl Marx, for it was he who articulated most insistently the idea, first broached in the eighteenth century, that economic arrangements—the division of labor, classes, and, more generally, the productive forces and relations of production—serve as the underlying cause of ethics and culture. It is in this sense that, for Marx, the material conditions of production determine the legal, cultural, and moral ideas of an epoch. Obviously, then, a capitalist mode of production must have moral effects and, in Marx's view, the emergence of capitalism, though an *essential* step toward a future communist order, nonetheless destroys the traditional moral relations and obligations of family and society. The growth of industry and commerce not only destroys traditional crafts and small farming, but it institutes a dehumanizing system of wage labor. Indeed, for Marx the very capitalist division of labor generates a fateful division of classes into which individuals come to view one another less in terms of their whole person but in terms of their specific contribution to commerce.[17]

Nineteenth Century: A Positive View

Not all of the nineteenth-century philosophers viewed commerce with scepticism. The French political philosopher

---

14. *Discourse on the Sciences and the Arts* in *Jean-Jacques Rousseau: The Basic Political Writings,* translated by Donald Cress (Indianapolis: Hackett Publishing, 1983), 17.

15. *Discourse on the Origin of Inequality* in *Jean-Jacques Rousseau: The Basic Political Writings.*

16. *Community and Society* [1887], translated by Charles P. Loomis (East Lansing: Michigan State University Press), 1957.

17. See, for example, "Economic and Philosophic Manuscripts of 1844," in *The Marx-Engels Reader,* by Robert C. Tucker, ed., 2d ed. (New York: W. W. Norton, 1978), 77.

Benjamin Constant (1767–1830) contended that the age of commerce replaces the age of war, noting that "War and commerce are only two different means to achieve the same end, that of possessing what is desired. . . . War then comes before commerce. The former is all savage impulse, the latter civilized calculation. It is clear that the more the commercial tendency prevails, the weaker must the tendency to war become." The English philosopher Herbert Spencer (1820–1903) believed that history progressed toward ever greater individualism and freedom, including rights to property and free exchange. For Spencer, spontaneous and free association was preferable to coercion by the state.[18]

Twentieth Century

That markets may have positive or negative effects has not been ignored in the previous century. Toward the close of the nineteenth century the great sociologist Emile Durkheim (1858–1917) argues that the division of labor creates new ties and obligations. In the early twentieth century the sociologist Georg Simmel (1858–1918) suggests that commerce moves one to consider the needs of the customer in ways that one might not otherwise do. And the economist Frank Knight (1885–1972), though a defender of markets, nonetheless laments "as unfortunate the dominance of the business game over life, the virtual identification of social living with it [business]."[19]

It is one thing to say that the market has the effect of altering traditional morality. It is another to say that the alteration is such that the market effectively destroys the very qualities that it requires in order to function successfully. This view is put forth by Daniel Bell who, borrowing from Max Weber (see Section AIV), argues that the ascetic morality essential for the emergence of capitalism creates an economy that destroys its very conditions. Others, including those affiliated with the Frankfurt Institute for Social Research, such as Max Horkheimer (1895–1973), have argued that the very instrumental reason that is celebrated by capitalism serves to deprive us of any rational discussion of common ends. We are left, then, relating to one another under the command of state-man-

aged capitalism.[20] Many in the twentieth century have—like Bell, Knight, and Horkheimer—decried the effects of capitalism in destroying traditional morality and undermining the virtues, but it is not obvious that they are correct. For even if it is the case that traditional morality has been undermined (which itself is not obvious), there may be alternative versions as to the cause of its destruction.

ALTERNATIVE EXPLANATIONS

Enlightened Reason and the Rise of Secular Religion

It has often been suggested that as American society has changed from a more settled and rooted life to a more mobile, prosperous, and impersonal one, there has been a simultaneous demise of the moral qualities of moderation, modesty, honesty, humility, industry, responsibility, civility, and a concomitant rise in selfishness, dishonesty, and cheating, not to mention crime and a host of social ills. Are these effects—if true—to be attributed to the market? Or might there be alternative explanations?

Of those who believe that morality has languished, one explanation traces its demise less to burgeoning commerce than to an enlightened secularism. On this view, the modern world of the past two hundred years is essentially a secular world, shorn of the religious principles that once animated individual conduct and social norms throughout much of history. Since the "Age of Reason" in the eighteenth century, this argument goes, individuals have been taught to appeal not to traditional religious beliefs but to the power of individual reason. Reason, it was said, would liberate individuals from traditional social and religious beliefs (allegedly the cause of oppression and suffering), serve as the arbiter of good and bad, and usher in a new and rational age of enlightenment. However, some argue that the exaltation of reason at the expense of received religion (or traditional institutions) has resulted in an increasing secularization in which moral conviction is weakened, hedonism is celebrated, and family life disrupted. Such an explanation of moral degeneration often relies upon a utilitarian defense of religion, a defense which is not altogether new. In 1531 Machiavelli (1469–1527) wrote, "Princes or republics that wish to maintain themselves without corruption must, above all else, maintain free of corruption the ceremonies of their religion and must hold them constantly in veneration; for

18. For Constant, see *The Spirit of Conquest and Usurpation and Their Relation to European Civilization* [1814] in *Political Writings,* translated and edited by Biancamaria Fontana (Cambridge: Cambridge University Press, 1988), 52. The relevant works of Spencer include *Social Statics* (1851) and *The Man versus the State* (1884).

19. Emile Durkheim, *The Division of Labor in Society* [1893], translated by George Simpson (New York: The Free Press, 1933); George Simmel, *Conflict and the Web of Group Affiliations;* Frank Knight, "The Ethics of Competition," in *The Ethics of Competition and Other Essays* (Freeport, New York: Books for Libraries, 1969), 66.

20. See for example, Max Horkheimer, "The End of Reason," in *The Essential Frankfurt School Reader,* edited by Andrew Arato and Eike Gebhardt (New York: Urizen Books, 1978), 26–48.

there is no greater indication of the ruin of a country than to see its religious worship not respected."[21]

War and Centralization

In one of the readings to follow, Robert Nisbet, while allowing that commerce may have played a role, suggests an alternative explanation that lies in the twin phenomena of war and governmental centralization. The eruption of World War I in 1914 and the entry of the United States into that war in 1917 served not only to break down custom and tradition but also to inspire more government intervention into society and the marketplace. As the central state took on more and more tasks in the twentieth century, it shifted power to the national government and shrunk the authority and power of the states and local communities. Moreover, the expanding role of the government served to diminish the function and authority of the numerous voluntary social groups, mutual-aid societies, charitable associations, and business, labor, and professional organizations that serve to foster benevolence, friendship, responsibility, and to informally enforce and encourage norms of civility, honesty, and trust. These institutions and societies—intermediary between the state and citizen and neither governmental nor commercial—serve to encourage individuals to relate to each other in ways other than through commercial exchange, thereby creating networks of friendship and acquaintance that might help to counterbalance any tendencies of the market to valorize efficiency and rational self-interest over the bonds of neighborhood, community, and society. These intermediary institutions, so noted by Alexis de Tocqueville (1805–1859), in 1835, after his travels throughout America,[22] may exist in tandem with the market, but they may

be easily diminished by the expanding powers of the state.

The centralization of power has often been accompanied by a cleavage between elite opinion and the opinion of the larger population. Joseph Schumpeter argued that capitalism would create an elite of intellectuals who were radically opposed to it and who would seek to undermine it.[23] Others have argued that elites have attacked the morality of the larger masses in order to acquire power for themselves. Allied with central government, elites have attacked alternative sources of authority, be they religious, local, or traditional, and in so doing nonmarket sources of moral authority have been diminished, leaving in their wake nothing but the norms of buying and selling and the unopposed ideology of the elites.

THE READINGS

Montesquieu *The Spirit of the Laws* is Montesquieu's account of how the English system of government—as distinct from governments traditionally classified as republics, monarchies, and despotic regimes—permits a wide liberty, including the freedom of commerce. In the first section, Montesquieu offers an account of a republican democracy in which each citizen has a small amount of land; there equality and the virtue of frugality prove reinforcing. In such a democracy, the spirit of commerce may allow for great wealth while ensuring the virtues of "frugality, economy, moderation, work, wisdom, tranquillity, order, and rule." In the four chapters from Book 20, Montesquieu considers the conditions of free government and offers several considerations on *"doux commerce."* Commercial interaction "cures destructive prejudices" and creates "gentle mores." By creating mutual dependence, commerce also creates peace among the nations; but if individuals engage in commerce without any compensating attitudes, then everything comes to be affected by money. In the last chapter, Montesquieu discusses briefly how commerce may affect different sorts of states or "constitutions." In a monarchy, the aim of commerce is the acquisition of luxury goods, but in a government ruled by many, commerce serves the more ordinary ends of individuals.

David Hume Originally published in 1754 (with the title "Of Luxury") this essay opens with a consideration of luxury, a concept which had proven controversial in

---

21. *The Discourses,* translated and edited by Peter Bondanella and Mark Musa (Harmondsworth: Penguin, 1979), chapter XII.

22. "Americans of all ages, all conditions, and all dispositions, constantly form associations. They have not only commercial and manufacturing companies, in which all take part, but associations of a thousand other kinds—religious, moral, serious, futile, general or restricted, enormous or diminutive. The Americans make associations to give entertainments, to found seminaries, to build inns, to construct churches, to diffuse books, and to send missionaries to the antipodes; they found in this manner hospitals, prisons, and schools. If it be proposed to inculcate some truth, or to foster some feeling by the encouragement of a great example, they form a society. Wherever, at the head of some undertaking, you see the government in France, or a man of rank in England, in the United States you will be sure to find an association." Alexis de Tocqueville, *Democracy in America* (New York: New American Library, 1956), Part 2, Book II, chapter 29 (p. 198).

23. *Capitalism, Socialism, and Democracy,* 3d ed. (New York: Harper, 1950), esp. chapters 11–13. See also, Christopher Lasch, *The Revolt of the Elites and the Betrayal of Democracy* (New York: W. W. Norton, 1995).

the eighteenth century. Bernard Mandeville [see Section AIV] had argued that all luxury was an outgrowth of our most vile appetites, whose indulgence was essential to a bustling commercial society. Others, such as Rousseau, had argued that even the smallest luxury is the very source of moral corruption. Hume challenges both points of view, contending that commercial ages are the happiest and that luxury should be avoided only if it is not beneficial. Hume addresses this second point at the close of the essay, contending that gratification in itself is not vicious but becomes so only when it precludes acts of moral duty. As to the first point, Hume maintains that since happiness consists of action, pleasure, and indolence, the progress of industry and the arts ensures not only the enjoyment of an occupation, but the development of one's mental faculties. Second, Hume explains, progress in industry and technology tends to generate progress in the liberal spheres of learning and the fine arts. As the refined arts develop, then so do men become more sociable. It is in this way that *industry, knowledge,* and *humanity,* are linked together by an indissoluble chain." The application of knowledge to the "vulgar arts" of commerce and manufacture also allows knowledge to grow in other areas including that of law and public order. Finally, the progress in the arts tends to preserve liberty by creating a large middle class of independent property owners.

Karl Marx   One of the most noted, if not notorious, writings of nineteenth-century socialism, the *Manifesto* offers a view of history, an account of communist doctrine, and a call to action. In the first part, excerpted here, Marx and Engels attempt to describe how the essential catalyst of history is the conflict between classes. Prior to the emergence of "bourgeois" society, the classes were various, but in the modern era two classes have emerged, bourgeoisie and proletariat. The rise of the bourgeoisie and modern manufacture has had a "revolutionary" effect on the social relations that had previously held sway, breaking apart prior social bonds and substituting in their stead purely economic relations born of self-interest. In the course of this destruction, the bourgeoisie constantly revises the modes of production to increase profit and, in so doing, alters the stable relations of earlier epochs: "All that is solid melts into air." Industries that heretofore had a national character are now cosmopolitan, a new interdependence between nations emerges, and urban centers grow in size and power. The expansion of productive forces goes hand in hand with the expansion of the proletariat, for whom work has become routinized, dehumanizing,

and mechanical—ever more so as the division of labor is increased and factories of mass production replace workshops. As members of the lower middle class fall into the proletariat, the proletariat grows and so does their awareness of themselves as a class. As it gains numbers and acquires political awareness, the proletariat becomes a "revolutionary class," capable of representing the interests of humanity and ruling in the interests of all.

Daniel Bell   Bell divides society into three structures, the techno-economic, the political, and the cultural, asserting that it is the "discordances between these realms which are responsible for the various contradictions within society." The specific contradiction that Bell argues for is that between the economic and the cultural. The value system of America is defined by Bell in terms of the Protestant ethic and the Puritan temper, a combined ethic which is crumbling not only because of changes in the culture but because of the very techno-economic order. The market order undermines the very norms that were essential to its genesis; this constitutes the cultural contradiction of capitalism. American life was shaped by the small town whose core values are expressed in the Puritanism of Jonathan Edwards and the Protestantism of Benjamin Franklin. From the Puritans was derived an ascetic sexual morality, the need to avoid sin, and the idea of a rational moral law which obliged each person to lead an "exemplary life." From Franklin derived the idea of self-improvement and the need to live a virtuous and useful life, manifesting temperance, resolution, frugality, and industry. Certain developments within commerce prove crucial to the transformation of the culture: technological innovations (such as the automobile); the emergence of mass consumption and marketing; and the use of credit, which stimulated consumption and diminished the importance of thrift. As the Puritan and Protestant ethic is vanquished by the pursuit of pleasure, capitalism is left without any ethical basis. A hedonistic society that celebrates materialism and pleasure-seeking not only lacks fortitude but has lost a common purpose and a sense of shared fate.

Robert Nisbet   Like Bell, Nisbet believes that America has undergone profound changes in the twentieth century. Whereas Bell attributes these changes to market forces, Nisbet considers how war and government centralization may have served to effect such changes. Nisbet begins by recounting the profound effects the first world war had on America, a nation of small towns in which power had been effectively and constitutionally divided among the states and between the states and the federal government: World War I "gave dynamic impact to the processes of secularisation, [and] individualization." These effects occurred not only because of the war itself, which served to diminish the Puritan culture of America, introducing a new consumerism and hedonism, but also because of the manner in which the federal government grew in importance, beginning with the war administration of Woodrow Wilson. In the third section, Nisbet summarizes two alternative accounts of how the bonds of society—be they those of nation, marriage, religion, or work—have loosened. On one account, described in the previous sections, the culprit is war and political centralization; another account contends that capitalism itself is the cause. Nisbet proceeds to delineate how the demise of hard property ownership in land and buildings, in conjunction with the rise of soft property in stocks and bonds, allows for diminished responsibility and an increased impersonality, changes which had their beginning in World War I.

Of Laws in Relation to Commerce

Montesquieu

Born in France, Charles-Louis de Secondat, Baron de la Brède et de Montesquieu (1689–1755) served in the Parlement of Bordeaux, managed his family estates, and was a member of the Academy of Bordeaux, as well as a frequent visitor to the salons of Paris. The Persian Letters, *his account of French society and politics, were published anonymously in 1721 and* The Spirit of the Laws *in 1748.*

BOOK XX: OF LAWS IN RELATION TO COMMERCE, CONSIDERED IN ITS NATURE AND DISTINCTIONS

1. Of Commerce   The following subjects deserve to be treated in a more extensive manner than the nature of this work will permit. Fain would I glide down a gentle river, but I am carried away by a torrent.

Commerce is a cure for the most destructive prejudices; for it is almost a general rule that wherever we find agreeable manners, there commerce flourishes; and that wherever there is commerce, there we meet with agreeable manners.

Let us not be astonished, then, if our manners are now less savage than formerly. Commerce has everywhere diffused a knowledge of the manners of all nations: these are compared one with another, and from this comparison arise the greatest advantages.

Commercial laws, it may be said, improve manners for the same reason that they destroy them. They corrupt the purest morals.[1] This was the subject of Plato's complaints; and we every day see that they polish and refine the most barbarous.

2. Of the Spirit of Commerce   Peace is the natural effect of trade. Two nations who traffic with each other become reciprocally dependent; for if one has an interest in buying, the other has an interest in selling: and thus their union is founded on their mutual necessities.

But if the spirit of commerce unites nations, it does not in the same manner unite individuals. We see that in countries[2] where the people move only by the spirit of commerce, they make a traffic of all the humane, all the moral virtues; the most trifling things, those which humanity would demand, are there done, or there given, only for money.

The spirit of trade produces in the mind of a man a certain sense of exact justice, opposite, on the one hand, to robbery, and on the other to those moral virtues which forbid our always adhering rigidly to the rules of private interest, and suffer us to neglect this for the advantage of others.

The total privation of trade, on the contrary, produces robbery, which Aristotle ranks in the number of means of acquiring; yet it is not at all inconsistent with certain moral virtues. Hospitality, for instance, is most rare in trading countries, while it is found in the most admirable perfection among nations of vagabonds.

It is a sacrilege, says Tacitus, for a German to shut his door against any man whomsoever, whether known or unknown. He who has behaved with hospitality to a stranger goes to show him another house where this hospitality is also practised; and he is there received with the same humanity.[3] But when the Germans had founded kingdoms, hospitality had become burdensome. This appears by two laws of the code of the Burgundians;[4] one of which inflicted a penalty on every barbarian who presumed to show a stranger the house of a Roman; and the other decreed that whoever received a stranger should be indemnified by the inhabitants, every one being obliged to pay his proper proportion.

3. Of the Poverty of the People   There are two sorts of poor; those who are rendered such by the severity of government: these are, indeed, incapable of performing almost any great action, because their indigence is a consequence of their slavery. Others are poor, only because they either despise or know not the conveniences of life; and these are capable of accomplishing great things, because their poverty constitutes a part of their liberty.

4. Of Commerce in Different Governments   Trade has some relation to forms of government. In a monarchy, it is generally founded on luxury; and though it be also founded on real wants, yet the principal view with which it is carried on is to procure everything that can contribute to the pride, the pleasure, and the capricious whims of the nation. In republics, it is commonly founded on economy. Their merchants, having an eye to all the nations of the earth, bring from one what is wanted by another. It is thus that the republics of Tyre, Carthage, Athens, Marseilles, Florence, Venice, and Holland engaged in commerce.

This kind of traffic has a natural relation to a republican government: to monarchies it is only occasional. For as it is founded on the practice of gaining little, and even less than other nations, and of remedying this by gaining incessantly, it can hardly be carried on by a people swallowed up in luxury, who spend much, and see nothing but objects of grandeur.

Cicero was of this opinion, when he so justly said, "I do not like that the same people should be at once both the lords and factors of the whole earth."[5] For this would, indeed, be to suppose that every individual in the state, and the whole state collectively, had their heads constantly filled with grand views, and at the same time with small ones; which is a contradiction.

Not but that the most noble enterprises are completed also in those states which subsist by economical commerce: they have even an intrepidity not to be found in monarchies. And the reason is this:

One branch of commerce leads to another, the small to the moderate, the moderate to the great; thus he who has gratified his desire of gaining a little raises himself to a situation in which he is not less desirous of gaining a great deal.

Besides, the grand enterprises of merchants are always necessarily connected with the affairs of the public. But, in monarchies, these public affairs give as much distrust to the merchants as in free states they appear to give safety. Great enterprises, therefore, in commerce are not for monarchical, but for republican, governments.

In short, an opinion of greater certainty, as to the possession of property in these states, makes them undertake everything. They flatter themselves with the hopes of receiving great advantages from the smiles of fortune; and thinking themselves sure of what they have already acquired, they boldly expose it in order to acquire more; risking nothing, but as the means of obtaining.

I do not pretend to say that any monarchy is entirely excluded from an economical commerce; but of its own nature it has less tendency towards it: neither do I mean that the republics with which we are acquainted are absolutely deprived of the commerce of luxury; but it is less connected with their constitution.

With regard to a despotic state, there is no occasion to mention it. A general rule: A nation in slavery labours more to preserve than to acquire; a free nation, more to acquire than to preserve.

ENDNOTES

1. Cæsar said of the Gauls that they were spoiled by the neighborhood and commerce of Marseilles; insomuch that they who formerly always conquered the Germans had now become inferior to them.—*De Bello Gallico,* vi. 23.
2. Holland.
3. *Et qui modo hospes fuerat, monstrator hospitii.*—*De Moribus Germanorum,* 21. See Cæsar, *De Bello Gallico,* vi. 21.
4. [*Leges Burgundionum*] Tit. 38.
5. Cicero, *De Republica,* iv.

QUESTIONS ON MONTESQUIEU

1. Montesquieu writes that a good democracy is one in which there is widespread ownership of small amounts of land. How does this relate to the virtue of frugality? And how might frugality relate to other qualities mentioned by Montesquieu?

2. Montesquieu states that commerce corrupts "pure mores" but "polishes and softens barbarous mores." What does he mean by these claims? What is corrupted? What is polished or softened?

3. What are some of the consequences of the "spirit of commerce," whether on the national or on the individual level? Does Montesquieu believe that commerce is, comparatively speaking, more compatible with human nature?

Of Refinement in the Arts

David Hume

David Hume (1711–1776) was born in Scotland and educated at Edinburgh University. Though he never received an academic post, Hume is one of the most important philosophers, having written A Treatise of Human Nature *(1739),* Enquiry Concerning Human Understanding *(1748),* Enquiry Concerning the Principles of Morals *(1751), the monumental* History of England *(1754–1762), and the posthumously published* Dialogues Concerning Natural Religion *(1779).*

LUXURY is a word of an uncertain signification, and may be taken in a good as well as in a bad sense. In general, it means great refinement in the gratification of the senses; and any degree of it may be innocent or blameable, according to the age, or country, or condition of the person. The bounds between the virtue and the vice cannot here be exactly fixed, more than in other moral subjects. To imagine, that the gratifying of any sense, or the indulging of any delicacy in meat, drink, or apparel, is of itself a vice, can never enter into a head, that is not disordered by the frenzies of enthusiasm. I have, indeed, heard of a monk abroad, who, because the windows of his cell opened upon a noble prospect, made a *covenant with his eyes* never to turn that way, or receive so sensual a gratification. And such is the crime of drinking CHAMPAGNE or BURGUNDY, preferably to small beer or porter. These indulgences are only vices, when they are pursued at the expence of some virtue, as liberality or charity; in like manner as they are follies, when for them a man ruins his fortune, and reduces himself to want and beggary. Where they entrench upon no virtue, but leave ample subject whence to provide for friends, family and every proper object of generosity or compassion, they are entirely innocent, and have in every age been acknowledged such by almost all moralists. To be entirely occupied with the luxury of the table, for instance, without any relish for the pleasures of ambition, study, or conversation, is a mark of stupidity and is incompatible with any vigour of temper or genius. To confine one's expence entirely to such a gratification, without regard to friends or family, is an indication of a heart destitute of humanity or benevolence. But if a man reserve time sufficient for all laudable pursuits, and money sufficient for all generous purposes, he is free from every shadow of blame or reproach.

Since luxury may be considered either as innocent or blameable, one may be surprised at those preposterous opinions, which have been entertained concerning it; while men of libertine principles bestow praises even on vicious luxury, and represent it as highly advantageous to society; and on the other hand, men of severe morals blame even the most innocent luxury and represent it as the source of all the corruptions, disorders, and factions, incident to civil government. We shall here endeavour to correct both these extremes, by proving, *first*, that the ages of refinement are both the happiest and most virtuous; *secondly*, that wherever luxury ceases to be innocent, it also ceases to be beneficial; and when carried a degree too far, is a quality pernicious, though perhaps not the most pernicious, to political society.

To prove the first point, we need but consider the effects of refinement both on *private* and on *public* life. Human happiness, according to the most received notions, seems to consist in three ingredients; action, pleasure, and indolence: And though these ingredients ought to be mixed in different proportions, according to the particular disposition of the person; yet no one ingredient can be entirely wanting, without destroying, in some measure, the relish of the whole composition. Indolence or repose, indeed, seems not of itself to contribute much to our enjoyment; but, like sleep, is requisite as an indulgence to the weakness of human nature, which cannot support an uninterrupted course of business or pleasure. That quick march of the spirits, which takes a man from himself, and chiefly gives satisfaction, does in the end exhaust the mind, and requires some intervals of repose, which, though agreeable for a moment, yet, if prolonged, beget a languor and lethargy, that destroys all enjoyment. Education, custom, and example, have a mighty influence in turning the mind to any of these pursuits; and it must be owned, that, where they promote a relish for action and pleasure, they are so far favourable to human happiness. In times when industry and the arts flourish, men are kept in perpetual occupation, and enjoy, as their reward, the occupation itself, as well as those pleasures which are the fruit of their labour. The mind acquires new vigour; enlarges its powers and faculties; and by an assiduity in honest industry, both satisfies its natural appetites, and prevents the growth of unnatural ones, which commonly spring up, when nourished by ease and idleness. Banish those arts from society, you deprive men both of action and of pleasure; and leaving nothing but indolence in their place, you even destroy the relish of indolence, which never is agreeable, but when it succeeds to labour, and recruits the spirits, exhausted by too much application and fatigue.

Another advantage of industry and of refinements in the mechanical arts, is, that they commonly produce some refinements in the liberal; nor can one be carried to perfection, without being accompanied, in some degree, with the other. The same age, which produces great philosophers and politicians, renowned generals and poets, usually abounds with skilful weavers, and ship-carpenters. We cannot reasonably expect, that a piece of woollen cloth will be wrought to perfection in a nation, which is ignorant of astronomy, or where ethics are neglected. The spirit of the age affects all the arts; and the minds of men, being once roused from their lethargy, and put into a fermentation, turn themselves on all sides, and carry improvements into every art and science. Profound ignorance is totally banished, and men enjoy the privilege of rational creatures, to think as well as to act, to cultivate the pleasures of the mind as well as those of the body.

The more these refined arts advance, the more sociable men become: nor is it possible, that, when enriched with science, and possessed of a fund of conversation, they should be contented to remain in solitude, or live with their fellow-citizens in that distant manner, which is peculiar to ignorant and barbarous nations. They flock into cities; love to receive and communicate knowledge; to show their wit or their breeding; their taste in conversation or living, in clothes or furniture. Curiosity allures the wise; vanity the foolish; and pleasure both. Particular clubs and societies are every where formed: Both sexes meet in an easy and sociable manner; and the tempers of men, as well as their behaviour, refine apace. So that, beside the improvements which they receive from knowledge and the liberal arts, it is impossible but they must feel an encrease of humanity, from the very habit of conversing together, and contributing to each other's pleasure and entertainment. Thus *industry*, *knowledge*, and *humanity*, are linked together by an indissoluble chain, and are found, from experience as well as reason, to be peculiar to the more polished, and, what are commonly denominated, the more luxurious ages.

Nor are these advantages attended with disadvantages, that bear any proportion to them. The more men refine upon pleasure, the less will they indulge in excesses of any kind; because nothing is more destructive to true pleasure than such excesses. One may safely affirm, that the TARTARS are oftener guilty of beastly gluttony, when they feast on their dead horses, than EUROPEAN courtiers with all their refinements of cookery. And if libertine love, or even infidelity to the marriage-bed, be more frequent in polite ages, when it is often regarded only as a piece of gallantry; drunkenness, on the other hand, is much less common: A vice more odious, and more pernicious both to mind and body. . . .

But industry, knowledge, and humanity, are not advantageous in private life alone: They diffuse their beneficial influence on the *public*, and render the government as great and flourishing as they make individuals happy and prosperous. The encrease and consumption of all the commodities, which serve to the ornament and pleasure of life, are advantageous to society; because, at the same time that they multiply those innocent gratifications to individuals, they are a kind of *storehouse* of labour, which, in the exigencies of state, may be turned to the public service. In a nation, where there is no demand for such superfluities, men sink into indolence, lose all enjoyment of life, and are useless to the public, which cannot maintain or support its fleets and armies, from the industry of such slothful members.

The bounds of all the EUROPEAN kingdoms are, at present, nearly the same [as] they were two hundred years ago: But what a difference is there in the power and grandeur of those kingdoms? Which can be ascribed to nothing but the encrease of art and industry. When CHARLES VIII of FRANCE invaded ITALY, he carried with him about 20,000 men: Yet this armament so exhausted the nation, as we learn from GUICCIARDIN, that for some years it was not able to make so great an effort. The late king of FRANCE, in time of war, kept in pay above 400,000 men; though from MAZARINE'S death to his own, he was engaged in a course of wars that lasted near thirty years.

This industry is much promoted by the knowledge inseparable from ages of art and refinement; as, on the other hand, this knowledge enables the public to make the best advantage of the industry of its subjects. Laws, order, police, discipline; these can never be carried to any degree of perfection, before human reason has refined itself by exercise, and by an application to the more vulgar arts, at least, of commerce and manufacture. Can we expect, that a government will be well modelled by a people, who know not how to make a spinning-wheel, or to employ a loom to advantage? Not to mention, that all ignorant ages are infested with superstition, which throws the government off its bias, and disturbs men in the pursuit of their interest and happiness.

Knowledge in the arts of government naturally begets mildness and moderation, by instructing men in the advantages of humane maxims above rigour and severity, which drive subjects into rebellion, and make the return to submission impracticable, by cutting off all hopes of pardon. When the tempers of men are softened as well as their knowledge improved, this humanity appears still more conspicuous, and is the chief characteristic which distinguishes a civilized age from times of barbarity and ignorance. Factions are then less inveterate, revolutions less tragical, authority less severe, and seditions less frequent. Even foreign wars abate of their cruelty; and after the field of battle, where honour and interest steel men against compassion as well as fear, the combatants divest themselves of the brute, and resume the man.

Nor need we fear, that men, by losing their ferocity, will lose their martial spirit, or become less undaunted and vigorous in defence of their country or their liberty. The arts have no such effect in enervating either the mind or body. On the contrary, industry, their inseparable attendant, adds new force to both. And if anger, which is said to be the whetstone of courage, loses somewhat of its asperity, by politeness and refinement; a sense of honour, which is a stronger, more constant, and more governable principle, acquires fresh vigour by that elevation of genius which arises from knowledge and a good education. Add to this, that courage can neither have any duration, nor be of any use, when not accompanied with discipline and martial skill, which are seldom found among a barbarous people. . . . It is observable, that, as the old ROMANS, by applying themselves solely to war, were almost the only uncivilized people that ever possessed military discipline; so the modern ITALIANS are the only civilized people, among EUROPEANS, that ever wanted courage and a martial spirit. Those who would ascribe this effeminacy of the ITALIANS to their luxury, or politeness, or application to the arts, need but consider the FRENCH and ENGLISH, whose bravery is as uncontestable, as their love for the arts, and their assiduity in commerce. The ITALIAN historians give us a more satisfactory reason for this degeneracy of their countrymen. They shew us how the sword was dropped at once by all the ITALIAN sovereigns; while the VENETIAN aristocracy was jealous of its subjects, the FLORENTINE democracy applied itself entirely to commerce; ROME was governed by priests, and NAPLES by women. War then became the business of soldiers of fortune, who spared one another, and to the astonishment of the world, could engage a whole day in what they called a battle, and return at night to their camp, without the least bloodshed.

What has chiefly induced severe moralists to declaim against refinement in the arts, is the example of ancient ROME, which, joining, to its poverty and rusticity, virtue and public spirit, rose to such a surprizing height of grandeur and liberty; but having learned from its conquered provinces the ASIATIC luxury, fell into every kind of corruption; whence arose sedition and civil wars, attended at last with the total loss of liberty.

All the LATIN classics, whom we peruse in our infancy, are full of these sentiments, and universally ascribe the ruin of their state to the arts and riches imported from the East: Insomuch that SALLUST represents a taste for painting as a vice, no less than lewdness and drinking. And so popular were these sentiments, during the later ages of the republic, that this author abounds in praises of the old rigid ROMAN virtue, though himself the most egregious instance of modern luxury and corruption; speaks contemptuously of the GRECIAN eloquence, though the most elegant writer in the world; nay, employs preposterous digressions and declamations to this purpose, though a model of taste and correctness.

But it would be easy to prove, that these writers mistook the cause of the disorders in the ROMAN state, and ascribed to luxury and the arts, what really proceeded from an ill modelled government, and the unlimited extent of conquests. Refinement on the pleasures and conveniencies of life has no natural tendency to beget venality and corruption. The value, which all men put upon any particular pleasure, depends on comparison and experience; nor is a porter less greedy of money, which he spends on bacon and brandy, than a courtier, who purchases champagne and ortolans. Riches are valuable at all times, and to all men; because they always purchase pleasures, such as men are accustomed to, and desire: Nor can any thing restrain or regulate the love of money, but a sense of honour and virtue; which, if it be not nearly equal at all times, will naturally abound most in ages of knowledge and refinement.

Of all EUROPEAN kingdoms, POLAND seems the most defective in the arts of war as well as peace, mechanical as well as liberal; yet it is there that venality and corruption do most prevail. The nobles seem to have preserved their crown elective for no other purpose, than regularly to sell it to the highest bidder. This is almost the only species of commerce, with which that people are acquainted.

The liberties of ENGLAND, so far from decaying since the improvements in the arts, have never flourished so much as during that period. And though corruption may seem to encrease of late years; this is chiefly to be ascribed to our established liberty, when our princes have found the impossibility of governing without parliaments, or of terrifying parliaments by the phantom of prerogative. Not to mention, that this corruption or venality prevails much more among the electors than the elected; and therefore cannot justly be ascribed to any refinements in luxury.

If we consider the matter in a proper light, we shall find, that a progress in the arts is rather favourable to liberty, and has a natural tendency to preserve, if not produce a free government. In rude unpolished nations, where the arts are neglected, all labour is bestowed on the cultivation of the ground; and the whole society is divided into two classes, proprietors of land, and their vassals or tenants. The latter are necessarily dependent, and fitted for slavery and subjection; especially where they possess no riches, and are not valued for their knowledge in agriculture; as must always be the case where the arts are neglected. The former naturally erect themselves into petty tyrants; and must either submit to an absolute master, for the sake of peace and order; or if they will preserve their independency, like the ancient barons, they must fall into feuds and contests among themselves, and throw the whole society into such confusion, as is perhaps worse than the most despotic government. But where luxury nourishes commerce and industry, the peasants, by a proper cultivation of the land, become rich and independent; while the tradesmen and merchants acquire a share of the property, and draw authority and consideration to that middling rank of men, who are the best and firmest basis of public liberty. These submit not to slavery, like the peasants, from poverty and meanness of spirit; and having no hopes of tyrannizing over others, like the barons, they are not tempted, for the sake of that gratification, to submit to the tyranny of their sovereign. They covet equal laws, which may secure their property, and preserve them from monarchical, as well as aristocratical tyranny.

The lower house is the support of our popular government; and all the world acknowledges, that it owed its chief influence and consideration to the encrease of commerce, which threw such a balance of property into the hands of the commons. How inconsistent then is it to blame so violently a refinement in the arts, and to represent it as the bane of liberty and public spirit! . . .

We come now to the *second* position which we proposed to illustrate, to wit, that, as innocent luxury, or a refinement in the arts and conveniences of life, is advantageous to the public; so wherever luxury ceases to be innocent, it also ceases to be beneficial; and when carried a degree farther, begins to be a quality pernicious, though, perhaps, not the most pernicious, to political society.

Let us consider what we call vicious luxury. No gratification, however sensual, can of itself be esteemed vicious. A gratification is only vicious, when it engrosses all a man's expence, and leaves no ability for such acts of duty and generosity as are required by his situation and fortune. Suppose, that he correct the vice, and employ part of his expence in the education of his children, in the support of his friends, and in relieving the poor; would any prejudice result to society? On the contrary, the same con-

sumption would arise; and that labour, which, at present, is employed only in producing a slender gratification to one man, would relieve the necessitous, and bestow satisfaction on hundreds. The same care and toil that raise a dish of peas at CHRISTMAS, would give bread to a whole family during six months. To say, that, without a vicious luxury, the labour would not have been employed at all, is only to say, that there is some other defect in human nature, such as indolence, selfishness, inattention to others, for which luxury, in some measure, provides a remedy; as one poison may be an antidote to another. But virtue, like wholesome food, is better than poisons, however corrected.

Suppose the same number of men, that are at present in GREAT BRITAIN, with the same soil and climate; I ask, is it not possible for them to be happier, by the most perfect way of life that can be imagined, and by the greatest reformation that Omnipotence itself could work in their temper and disposition? To assert, that they cannot, appears evidently ridiculous. As the land is able to maintain more than all its present inhabitants, they could never, in such a UTOPIAN state, feel any other ills than those which arise from bodily sickness; and these are not the half of human miseries. All other ills spring from some vice, either in ourselves or others; and even many of our diseases proceed from the same origin. Remove the vices, and the ills follow. You must only take care to remove all the vices. If you remove part, you may render the matter worse. By banishing *vicious* luxury, without curing sloth and an indifference to others, you only diminish industry in the state, and add nothing to men's charity or their generosity. Let us, therefore, rest contented with asserting, that two opposite vices in a state may be more advantageous than either of them alone; but let us never pronounce vice in itself advantageous. Is it not very inconsistent for an author to assert in one page, that moral distinctions are inventions of politicians for public interest; and in the next page maintain, that vice is advantageous to the public? And indeed it seems upon any system of morality, little less than a contradiction in terms, to talk of a vice, which is in general beneficial to society.

I thought this reasoning necessary, in order to give some light to a philosophical question, which has been much disputed in ENGLAND. I call it a *philosophical* question, not a *political* one. For whatever may be the consequence of such a miraculous transformation of mankind, as would endow them with every species of virtue, and free them from every species of vice; this concerns not the magistrate, who aims only at possibilities. He cannot cure every vice by substituting a virtue in its place. Very often he can only cure one vice by another; and in that case, he ought to prefer what is least pernicious to society. Luxury, when excessive, is the source of many ills; but is in general preferable to sloth and idleness, which would commonly succeed in its place, and are more hurtful both to private persons and to the public. When sloth reigns, a mean uncultivated way of life prevails amongst individuals, without society, without enjoyment. And if the sovereign, in such a situation, demands the service of his subjects, the labour of the state suffices only to furnish the necessaries of life to the labourers, and can afford nothing to those who are employed in the public service.

QUESTIONS ON HUME

1. Hume contends that "ages of refinement" are "both the happiest and most virtuous." What does Hume mean by "refinement"? How does he argue that a refined age is (a) happy and (b) virtuous?

2. How might industry or the arts enlarge the "powers and faculties" of the mind? How might work and industry occupy the mind in a beneficial way? Explain how Hume views the interrelation between industry, knowledge, and humanity. Do these tend to advance in tandem?

3. Hume writes that a government cannot be "well-modelled" if its people are ignorant and its moral habits barbarous. He later adds that progress in the arts tends to produce free governments. On what basis does Hume make these claims? Do you think that markets and democracies have any relation to one another? For example, are markets a necessary condition for democracy?

4. Why does Hume write that the banishment of vicious luxury without any diminution of sloth or indifference would not generate benevolence and would diminish industry? Is he correct on this point?

Manifesto of the Communist Party

Karl Marx and Friedrich Engels

Karl Marx (1818–1883) received a Ph.D. from the University of Jena, writing a dissertation on the Greek philosophers Democritus and Epicurus. He met Friedrich Engels (1820–1895) in Paris, and they collaborated on several works, including the Manifesto (1848) and The German Ideology (1845–1846). Of their collaboration, Engels wrote that although he "had a certain independent share in laying the foundations of the theory . . . the greater part of its leading basic principles . . . belong to Marx."[24]

BOURGEOIS AND PROLETARIANS

The history of all hitherto existing societies is the history of class struggles.

Freeman and slave, patrician and plebeian, lord and serf, guild-master and journeyman, in a word, oppressor and oppressed, stood in constant opposition to one another, carried on an uninterrupted, now hidden, now open fight, a fight that each time ended, either in a revolutionary re-constitution of society at large, or in the common ruin of the contending classes.

In the earlier epochs of history, we find almost everywhere a complicated arrangement of society into various orders, a manifold gradation of social rank. In ancient Rome we have patricians, knights, plebeians, slaves; in the Middle Ages, feudal lords, vassals, guild-masters, journeymen, apprentices, serfs; in almost all of these classes, again, subordinate gradations.

The modern bourgeois society that has sprouted from the ruins of feudal society has not done away with clash antagonisms. It has but established new classes, new conditions of oppression, new forms of struggle in place of the old ones.

Our epoch, the epoch of the bourgeoisie, possesses, however, this distinctive feature: it has simplified the class antagonisms: Society as a whole is more and more splitting up into two great hostile camps, into two great classes, directly facing each other: Bourgeoisie and Proletariat.

From the serfs of the Middle Ages sprang the chartered burghers of the earliest towns. From these burgesses the first elements of the bourgeoisie were developed.

The discovery of America, the rounding of the Cape, opened up fresh ground for the rising bourgeoisie. The East-Indian and Chinese markets, the colonisation of America, trade with the colonies, the increase in the means of exchange and in commodities generally, gave to commerce, to navigation, to industry, an impulse never before known, and thereby, to the revolutionary element in the tottering feudal society, a rapid development.

24. Engels, *Ludwig Feuerbach and the End of Classical German Philosophy,* in Karl Marx and Friedrich Engels, *Selected Works,* Vol. II (Moscow: Foreign Languages Publishing House, 1962), 386 (fn).

The feudal system of industry, under which industrial production was monopolised by closed guilds, now no longer sufficed for the growing wants of the new markets. The manufacturing system took its place. The guild-masters were pushed on one side by the manufacturing middle class; division of labour between the different corporate guilds vanished in the face of division of labour in each single workshop.

Meantime the markets kept ever growing, the demand ever rising. Even manufacture no longer sufficed. Thereupon, steam and machinery revolutionised industrial production. The place of manufacture was taken by the giant, Modern Industry, the place of the industrial middle class, by industrial millionaires, the leaders of whole industrial armies, the modern bourgeois.

Modern industry has established the world-market, for which the discovery of America paved the way. This market has given an immense development to commerce, to navigation, to communication by land. This development has, in its time, reacted on the extension of industry; and in proportion as industry, commerce, navigation, railways extended, in the same proportion the bourgeoisie developed, increased its capital, and pushed into the background every class handed down from the Middle Ages.

We see, therefore, how the modern bourgeoisie is itself the product of a long course of development, of a series of revolutions in the modes of production and of exchange.

Each step in the development of the bourgeoisie was accompanied by a corresponding political advance of that class. An oppressed class under the sway of the feudal nobility, an armed and self-governing association in the mediaeval commune; here independent urban republic (as in Italy and Germany), there taxable "third estate" of the monarchy (as in France), afterwards, in the period of manufacture proper, serving either the semi-feudal or the absolute monarchy as a counterpoise against the nobility, and, in fact, corner-stone of the great monarchies in general, the bourgeoisie has at last, since the establishment of Modern Industry and of the world-market, conquered for itself, in the modern representative State, exclusive political sway. The executive of the modern State is but a committee for managing the common affairs of the whole bourgeoisie.

The bourgeoisie, historically, has played a most revolutionary part.

The bourgeoisie, wherever it has got the upper hand, has put an end to all feudal, patriarchal, idyllic relations. It has pitilessly torn asunder the motley feudal ties that bound man to his "natural superiors," and has left remaining no other nexus between man and man than naked self-interest, than callous "cash payment." It has drowned the most heavenly ecstasies of religious fervour, of chivalrous enthusiasm, of philistine sentimentalism, in the icy water of egotistical calculation. It has resolved personal worth into exchange value. And in place of the numberless and feasible chartered freedoms, has set up that single, unconscionable freedom—Free Trade. In one word, for exploitation, veiled by religious and political illusions, naked, shameless, direct, brutal exploitation.

The bourgeoisie has stripped of its halo every occupation hitherto honoured and looked up to with reverent awe. It has converted the physician, the lawyer, the priest, the poet, the man of science, into its paid wage labourers.

The bourgeoisie has torn away from the family its sentimental veil, and has reduced the family relation to a mere money relation.

The bourgeoisie has disclosed how it came to pass that the brutal display of vigour in the Middle Ages, which Reactionists so much admire, found its fitting complement in the most slothful indolence. It has been the first to show what man's activity can bring about. It has accomplished wonders far surpassing Egyptian pyramids, Roman aqueducts, and Gothic cathedrals; it has conducted expeditions that put in the shade all former Exoduses of nations and crusades.

The bourgeoisie cannot exist without constantly revolutionising the instruments of production, and thereby the relations of production, and with them the whole relations of society. Conservation of the old modes of production in unaltered form, was, on the contrary, the first condition of existence for all earlier industrial classes. Constant revolutionising of production, uninterrupted disturbance of all social conditions, everlasting uncertainty and agitation distinguish the bourgeois epoch from all earlier ones. All fixed, fast-frozen relations, with their train of ancient and venerable prejudices and opinions, are swept away, all new-formed ones become antiquated before they can ossify. All that is solid melts into air, all that is holy is profaned, and man is at last compelled to face with sober senses, his real conditions of life, and his relations with his kind.

The need of a constantly expanding market for its products chases the bourgeoisie over the whole surface of the globe. It must nestle everywhere, settle everywhere, establish connexions everywhere.

The bourgeoisie has through its exploitation of the world-market given a cosmopolitan character to production and consumption in every country. To the great chagrin of Reactionists, it has drawn from under the feet of industry the national ground on which it stood. All old-established national industries have been destroyed or are daily being destroyed. They are dislodged by new industries, whose introduction becomes a life and death question for all civilised nations, by industries that no longer work up indigenous raw material, but raw material drawn from the remotest zones; industries whose products are consumed, not only at home, but in every quarter of the globe. In place of the old wants, satisfied by the productions of the country, we find new wants, requiring for their satisfaction the products of distant lands and climes. In place of the old local and national seclusion and self-sufficiency, we have intercourse in every direction, universal inter-dependence of nations. And as in material, so also in intellectual production. The intellectual creations of individual nations become common property. National one-sidedness and narrow-mindedness become more and more impossible, and from the numerous national and local literatures, there arises a world literature.

The bourgeoisie, by the rapid improvement of all instruments of production, by the immensely facilitated means of communication, draws all, even the most barbarian, nations into civilisation. The cheap prices of its commodities are the heavy artillery with which it batters down all Chinese walls, with which it forces the barbarians' intensely obstinate hatred of foreigners to capitulate. It compels all nations, on pain of extinction, to adopt the bourgeois mode of production; it compels them to introduce what it calls civilisation into their midst, *i.e.*, to become bourgeois themselves. In one word, it creates a world after its own image.

The bourgeoisie has subjected the country to the rule of the towns. It has created enormous cities, has greatly increased the urban population as compared with the rural, and has thus rescued a considerable part of the population from the idiocy of rural life. Just as it has made the country dependent on the towns, so it has made barbarian and semi-barbarian countries dependent on the civilised ones, nations of peasants on nations of bourgeois, the East on the West.

The bourgeoisie keeps more and more doing away with the scattered state of the population, of the means of production, and of property. It has agglomerated production, and has concentrated property in a few hands. The necessary consequence of this was political centralisation. Independent, or but loosely connected provinces, with separate interests, laws, governments and systems of taxation, became lumped together into one nation, with one government, one code of laws, one national class-interest, one frontier and one customs-tariff.

The bourgeoisie, during its rule of scarce one hundred years, has created more massive and more colossal productive forces than have all preceding generations together. Subjection of Nature's forces to man, machinery, application of chemistry to industry and agriculture, steam-navigation, railways, electric telegraphs, clearing of whole continents for cultivation, canalisation of rivers, whole populations conjured out of the ground—what earlier century had even a presentiment that such productive forces slumbered in the lap of social labour?

We see then: the means of production and of exchange, on whose foundation the bourgeoisie built itself up, were generated in feudal society. At a certain stage in the development of these means of production and of exchange, the conditions under which feudal society produced and exchanged, the feudal organisation of agriculture and manufacturing industry, in one word, the feudal relations of property became no longer compatible with the already developed productive forces; they became so many fetters. They had to be burst asunder; they were burst asunder.

Into their place stepped free competition, accompanied by a social and political constitution adapted to it, and by the economical and political sway of the bourgeois class.

A similar movement is going on before our own eyes. Modern bourgeois society with its relations of production, of exchange and of property, a society that has conjured up such gigantic means of production and of exchange, is like the sorcerer, who is no longer able to control the powers of the nether world whom he has called up by his spells. For many a decade past the history of industry and commerce is but the history of the revolt of modern productive forces against modern conditions of production, against the property relations that are the conditions for the existence of the bourgeoisie and of its rule. It is enough to mention the commercial crises that by their periodical return put on its trial, each time more threateningly, the existence of the entire bourgeois society. In these crises a great part not only of the existing products, but also of the previously created productive forces, are periodically destroyed. In these crises there breaks out an epidemic that, in all earlier epochs, would have seemed an absurdity—the epidemic of over-production. Society suddenly finds itself put back into a state of momentary barbarism; it appears as if a famine, a universal war of devastation had cut off the supply of every means of subsistence; industry and commerce seem to be destroyed; and why? Because there is too much civilisation, too much means of subsistence, too much industry, too much commerce. The productive forces at the disposal of society no longer tend to further the development of the conditions of bourgeois property; on the contrary, they have become too powerful for these conditions, by which they are fettered, and so soon as they overcome these fetters, they bring disorder into the whole of bourgeois society, endanger the existence of bourgeois property. The conditions of bourgeois society are too narrow to comprise the wealth created by them. And how does the bourgeoisie get over these crises? On the one hand inforced destruction of a mass of productive forces; on the other, by the conquest of new markets, and by the more thorough exploitation of the old ones. That is to say, by paving the way for more extensive and more destructive crises, and by diminishing the means whereby crises are prevented.

The weapons with which the bourgeoisie felled feudalism to the ground are now turned against the bourgeoisie itself.

But not only has the bourgeoisie forged the weapons that bring death to itself; it has also called into existence the men who are to wield those weapons—the modern working class—the proletarians.

In proportion as the bourgeoisie, *i.e.*, capital, is developed, in the same proportion is the proletariat, the modern working class, developed—a class of labourers, who live only so long as they find work, and who find work only so long as their labour increases capital. These labourers, who must sell themselves piecemeal, are a commodity, like every other article of commerce, and are consequently exposed to all the vicissitudes of competition, to all the fluctuations of the market.

Owing to the extensive use of machinery and to division of labour, the work of the proletarians has lost all individual character, and consequently, all charm for the workman. He becomes an appendage of the machine, and it is only the most simple, most monotonous, and most easily acquired knack, that is required of him. Hence, the cost of production of a workman is restricted, almost entirely, to the means of subsistence that he requires for his maintenance, and for the propagation of his race. But the price of a commodity, and therefore also of labour, is equal to its cost of production. In proportion therefore, as the repulsiveness of the work increases, the wage decreases. Nay more, in proportion as the use of machinery and division of labour increases, in the same proportion the burden of toil also increases, whether by prolongation of the working hours, by increase of the work exacted in a given time or by increased speed of the machinery, etc.

Modern industry has converted the little workshop of the patriarchal master into the great factory of the industrial capitalist. Masses of labourers, crowded into the factory, are organised like soldiers. As privates of the industrial army they are placed under the command of a perfect hierarchy of officers and sergeants. Not only are they slaves of the bourgeois class, and of the bourgeois State; they are daily and hourly enslaved by the machine, by the over-looker, and, above all, by the individual bourgeois manufacturer himself. The more openly this despotism proclaims gain to be its end and aim, the more petty, the more hateful and the more embittering it is.

The less the skill and exertion of strength implied in manual labour, in other words, the more modern industry becomes developed, the more is the labour of men superseded by that of women. Differences of age and sex have no longer any distinctive social validity for the working class. All are instruments of labour, more or less expensive to use, according to their age and sex.

No sooner is the exploitation of the labourer by the manufacturer, so far, at an end, that he receives his wages in cash, than he is set upon by the other portions of the bourgeoisie, the landlord, the shopkeeper, the pawnbroker, etc.

The lower strata of the middle class—the small tradespeople, shopkeepers, retired tradesmen generally, the handicraftsmen and peasants—all these sink gradually into the proletariat, partly because their diminutive capital does not suffice for the scale on which Modern Industry is carried on, and is swamped in the competition with the large capitalists, partly because their specialized skill is rendered worthless by the new methods of production. Thus the proletariat is recruited from all classes of the population.

The proletariat goes through various stages of development. With its birth begins its struggle with the bourgeoisie. At first the contest is carried on by individual labourers, then by the workpeople of a factory, then by the operatives of one trade, in one locality, against the individual bourgeois who directly exploits them. They direct their attacks not against the bourgeois conditions of production, but against the instruments of production themselves; they destroy imported wares that compete with their labour, they smash to pieces machinery, they set factories ablaze, they seek to restore by force the vanished status of the workman of the Middle Ages.

At this stage the labourers still form an incoherent mass scattered over the whole country, and broken up by their mutual competition. If anywhere they unite to form more compact bodies, this is not yet the consequence of their own active union, but of the union of the bourgeoisie, which class, in order to attain its own political ends, is compelled to set the whole proletariat in motion, and is moreover yet, for a time, able to do so. At this stage, therefore, the proletarians do not fight their enemies, but the enemies of their enemies, the remnants of absolute monarchy, the landowners, the non-industrial bourgeois, the petty bourgeoisie. Thus the whole historical movement is concentrated in the hands of the bourgeoisie; every victory so obtained is a victory for the bourgeoisie.

But with the development of industry the proletariat not only increases in number; it becomes concentrated in greater masses, its strength grows, and it feels that strength more. The various interests and conditions of life within the ranks of the proletariat are more and more equalised, in proportion as machinery obliterates all distinctions of labour, and nearly everywhere reduces wages to the same low level. The growing competition among the bourgeois, and the resulting commercial crises, make the wages of the workers ever more fluctuating. The unceasing improvement of machinery, ever more rapidly developing, makes their livelihood more and more precarious; the collisions between individual workmen and individual bourgeois take more and more the character of collisions between two classes. Thereupon the workers begin to form combinations (Trades Unions) against the bourgeois; they club together in order to keep up the rate of wages; they found permanent associations in order to make provision beforehand for these occasional revolts. Here and there the contest breaks out into riots.

Now and then the workers are victorious, but only for a time. The real fruit of their battles lies, not in the immediate result, but in the ever-expanding union of the workers. This union is helped on by the improved means of communication that are created by modern industry and that place the workers of different localities in contact with one another. It was just this contact that was needed to centralise the numerous local struggles, all of the same character, into one national struggle between classes. But every class struggle is a political struggle. And that union, to attain which the burghers of the Middle Ages, with their miserable highways, required centuries, the modern proletarians, thanks to railways, achieve in a few years.

This organisation of the proletarians into a class, and consequently into a political party, is continually being upset again by the competition between the workers themselves. But it ever rises up again, stronger, firmer, mightier. It compels legislative recognition of particular interests of the workers, by taking advantage of the divisions among the bourgeoisie itself. Thus the ten-hours' bill in England was carried.

Altogether collisions between the classes of the old society further, in many ways, the course of development of the proletariat. The bourgeoisie finds itself involved in a constant battle. At first with the aristocracy; later on, with those portions of the bourgeoisie itself, whose interests have become antagonistic to the progress of industry; at all times, with the bourgeoisie of foreign countries. In all these battles it sees itself compelled to appeal to the proletariat, to ask for its help, and thus, to drag it into the political arena. The bourgeoisie itself, therefore, supplies the proletariat with its own instruments of political and general education, in other words, it furnishes the proletariat with weapons for fighting the bourgeoisie.

Further, as we have already seen, entire sections of the ruling classes are, by the advance of industry, precipitated into the proletariat, or are at least threatened in their conditions of existence. These also supply the proletariat with fresh elements of enlightenment and progress.

Finally, in times when the class struggle nears the decisive hour, the process of dissolution going on within the ruling class, in fact within the whole range of society, assumes such a violent, glaring character, that a small section of the ruling class cuts itself adrift, and joins the revolutionary class, the class that holds the future in its hands. Just as, therefore, at an earlier period, a section of the nobility went over to the bourgeoisie, so now a portion of the bourgeoisie goes over to the proletariat, and in particular, a portion of the bourgeois ideologists, who have raised themselves to the level of comprehending theoretically the historical movement as a whole.

Of all the classes that stand face to face with the bourgeoisie today, the proletariat alone is a really revolutionary class. The other classes decay and finally disappear in the face of Modern Industry; the proletariat is its special and essential product. The lower middle class, the small manufacturer, the shopkeeper, the artisan, the peasant, all these fight against the bourgeoisie, to save from extinction their existence as fractions of the middle class. They are therefore not revolutionary, but conservative. Nay more, they are reactionary, for they try to roll back the wheel of history. If by chance they are revolutionary, they are so only in view of their impending transfer into the proletariat, they thus defend not their present, but their future interests, they desert their own standpoint to place themselves at that of the proletariat.

The "dangerous class," the social scum, that passively rotting mass thrown off by the lowest layers of old society, may, here and there, be swept into the movement by a proletarian revolution; its conditions of life, however, prepare it far more for the part of a bribed tool of reactionary intrigue.

In the conditions of the proletariat, those of old society at large are already virtually swamped. The proletarian is without property; his relation to his wife and children has no longer anything in common with the bourgeois family-relations; modern industrial labour, modern subjection to capital, the same in England as in France, in America as in Germany, has stripped him of every trace of national character. Law, morality, religion, are to him so many bourgeois prejudices, behind which lurk in ambush just as many bourgeois interests.

All the preceding classes that got the upper hand, sought to fortify their already acquired status by subjecting society at large to their conditions of appropriation. The proletarians cannot become masters of the productive forces of society, except by abolishing their own previous mode of appropriation, and thereby also every other previous mode of appropriation. They have nothing of their own to secure and to fortify; their mission is to destroy all previous securities for, and insurances of, individual property.

All previous historical movements were movements of minorities, or in the interests of minorities. The proletarian movement is the self-conscious, independent movement of the immense majority, in the interests of the immense majority. The proletariat, the lowest stratum of our present society, cannot stir, cannot raise itself up, without the whole superincumbent strata of official society being sprung into the air.

Though not in substance, yet in form, the struggle of the proletariat with the bourgeoisie is at first a national struggle. The proletariat of each country must, of course, first of all settle matters with its own bourgeoisie.

In depicting the most general phases of the development of the proletariat, we traced the more or less veiled civil war, raging within existing society, up to the point where that war breaks out into open revolution, and where the violent overthrow of the bourgeoisie lays the foundation for the sway of the proletariat.

Hitherto, every form of society has been based, as we have already seen, on the antagonism of oppressing and oppressed classes. But in order to oppress a class, certain conditions must be assured to it under which it can, at least, continue its slavish existence. The serf, in the period of serfdom, raised himself to membership in the commune, just as the petty bourgeois, under the yoke of feudal absolutism, managed to develop into a bourgeois. The modern laborer, on the contrary, instead of rising with the progress of industry, sinks deeper and deeper below the conditions of existence of his own class. He becomes a pauper, and pauperism develops more rapidly than population and wealth. And here it becomes evident, that the bourgeoisie is unfit any longer to be the ruling class in society, and to impose its conditions of existence upon society as an over-riding law. It is unfit to rule because it is incompetent to assure an existence to its slave within his slavery, because it cannot help letting him sink into such a state, that it has to feed him, instead of being fed by him. Society can no longer live under this bourgeoisie, in other words, its existence is no longer compatible with society.

The essential condition for the existence, and for the sway of the bourgeois class, is the formation and augmentation of capital; the condition for capital is wage-labour. Wage-labour rests exclusively on competition between the laborers. The advance of industry, whose involuntary promoter is the bourgeoisie, replaces the isolation of the labourers, due to competition, by their revolutionary combination, due to association. The development of Modern Industry, therefore, cuts from under its feet the very foundation on which the bourgeoisie produces and appropriates products. What the bourgeoisie, therefore, produces, above all, is its own grave-diggers. Its fall and the victory of the proletariat are equally inevitable.

QUESTIONS ON MARX AND ENGELS

1. How does history manifest an ongoing struggle between and among classes? What is a social *class*? In what sense are the groups mentioned by Marx and Engels classes? How is the domination of a class connected with political power?

2. How has the bourgeoisie played a "revolutionary part" in altering the "motley feudal ties" of an earlier age? How do you understand these "bonds"? (Why might Marx describe these as "motley"?) In what ways do you think markets alter our manner of relating to one another?

3. In what sense do you think that the account of Marx and Engels shows how changes in the (material) forces of production bring about or effect changes in culture and morals? Is it possible that cultural or moral ideas might cause or effect some change in economic production?

4. Marx claims that capitalism not only brings about change but does so in such a way that "All that is solid melts into air." What does Marx mean by this statement? In what way(s) do markets disturb the *status quo*? Do markets challenge the very idea of nationhood?

The Cultural Contradictions of Capitalism

Daniel Bell

Daniel Bell is Henry Ford II Professor of Social Sciences, Emeritus, at Harvard University. The author and editor of some fifteen books and numerous essays, his major works focus on social change. He has written The End of Ideology *(1960),* The Coming of Post-Industrial Society *(1973), and* The Cultural Contradictions of Capitalism *(1976).*

THE MEANING OF CULTURE

Culture, for a society, a group, or a person, is a continual process of sustaining an identity through the coherence gained by a consistent aesthetic point of view, a moral conception of self, and a style of life which exhibits those conceptions in the objects that adorn one's home and oneself and in the taste which expresses those points of view. Culture is thus the realm of sensibility, of emotion and moral temper, and of the intelligence, which seeks to order these feelings.

Historically, most cultures and social structures have exhibited unity, although there have always been small groups expressing esoteric, deviant, usually libertine values. Classical culture expressed its unity through the fusion of reason and will in the pursuit of virtue. Christian culture exhibited consistency in the replication of the ordered ranks of society and the ordered ranks of the church with the hierarchies of heaven and hell, in the quest for salvation both in its social and aesthetic representations. In early modern times, bourgeois culture and bourgeois social structure fused a distinct unity with a specific character structure around the theme of order and work.

Classical social theory (I use the word "classical" here to denote the nineteenth- and early twentieth-century masters) also saw culture as unified with the social structure. Marx, as I have said, argued that the mode of production shaped all the other dimensions of a society. Culture as ideology reflected a substructure and could not have an autonomy of its own. Moreover, in bourgeois society, culture was tied to the economy because culture, too, had become a commodity, to be evaluated by the market and bought and sold through the exchange process. Max Weber argued that thought, conduct, and societal structure were highly integrated, in that all its branches—science, economy, law, and culture—were predominantly rationalistic. Even the modes of art were predominantly rationalistic. For Weber, this was true in a double sense: the cosmological aspects of Western thought and culture were characterized by the elimination of magic (in Schiller's phrase, the "disenchantment of the world"); and the structure and formal organization, the stylistics of the arts, were rational. Weber's particular example was Western harmonic chordal music, which rested on a scale that permitted a maximum of ordered relations, unlike primitive and non-Western music.[1] Finally, Pitirim Sorokin, in his *Social and Cultural Dynamics,* argued that cultures were integrated by mentalities ("the central principle, 'the reason'"), which unite thought and meaning and permeate all aspects of a society. Contemporary society is sensate, in that it is empirical, materialistic, extraverted, oriented to technique, and hedonistic.

Against these views, what I find striking today is the radical disjunction between the social structure (the techno-economic order) and the culture. The former is ruled by an economic principle defined in terms of efficiency and functional rationality, the organization of production through the ordering of things, including men as things. The latter is prodigal, promiscuous, dominated by an anti-rational, anti-intellectual temper in which the self is taken as the touchstone of cultural judgments, and the effect on the self is the measure of the aesthetic worth of experience. The character structure inherited from the nineteenth century, with its emphasis on self-discipline, delayed gratification, and restraint, is still relevant to the demands of the techno-economic structure; but it clashes sharply with the culture, where such bourgeois values have been completely rejected—in part, paradoxically, because of the workings of the capitalist economic system itself. . . .

FROM THE PROTESTANT ETHIC TO THE PSYCHEDELIC BAZAAR

Changes in cultural ideas have an immanence and autonomy because they develop from an internal logic at work within a cultural tradition. In this sense, new ideas and forms derive from a kind of dialogue with, or rebellion against, previous ideas and forms. But changes in cultural practices and life-styles necessarily interact with social structure, since works of art, decoration, records, films, and plays are bought and sold in the market. The market is where social structure and culture cross. Changes in culture as a whole, particularly the emergence of new life-styles, are made possible not only by changes in sensibility, but also by shifts in the social structure itself. One can see this most readily, in American society, in the development of new buying habits in a high consumption economy and the resultant erosion of the Protestant ethic and the Puritan temper, the two codes which sustained the traditional value system of American bourgeois society. It is the breakup of this ethic and temper, owing as much to changes in social structure as to changes in the culture, that has undercut the beliefs and legitimations that sanctioned work and reward in American society. It is this transformation and the lack of any rooted new ethic that are responsible, in good part, for the sense of disorientation and dismay that marks the public mood today. What I propose to do here is to take my general argument about modernism and bourgeois society and trace out the effects more specifically in American society, which has been the exemplar of the bourgeois mode.

The Small-Town Life

The Protestant ethic and the Puritan temper were codes that emphasized work, sobriety, frugality, sexual restraint, and a forbidding attitude toward life. They defined the nature of moral conduct and social respectability. The post-modernist culture of the 1960s has been interpreted, because it calls itself a "counter-culture," as defying the Protestant ethic, heralding the end of Puritanism, and mounting a final attack on bourgeois values. This is too facile. The Protestant ethic and the Puritan temper, as social facts, were eroded long ago, and they linger on as pale ideologies, used more by moralists to admonish and by sociologists to mythologize than as behavioral realities. The breakup of the traditional bourgeois value system, in fact, was brought about by the bourgeois economic system—by the free market, to be precise. This is the source of the contradiction of capitalism in American life.

The Protestant ethic and the Puritan temper in the United States were the world-view of an agrarian, small-town, mercantile and artisan way of life. In the United States, as Page Smith reminds us, "if we except the family and the church, the basic form of social organization up to the early decades of the twentieth century was the small town."[2] The life and character of American society were shaped by the small town, and its religions. They were necessary to enforce strong codes of community sanctions in a hostile environment; they provided meaning and justification for work and restraint in subsistence economics.

If the core values of American society are summed up by the terms "Puritan temper" and "Protestant ethic," they are represented by the two men who stand as exemplars of the early American spirit, Jonathan Edwards as the Puritan and Benjamin Franklin as the Protestant. The thought and homiletics of these two men laid down the specific virtues and maxims of the American character. . . .

The Puritans had signed a covenant which committed each man to an exemplary life. But no person—or doctrine—can live at a fever pitch of intensity for prolonged periods, especially when it means maintaining a life of stern discipline over the springs of impulse. Calvinism, even in the early American colonies, was constantly being nibbled away as new doctrines, such as Arminianism (the basis of Wesley's Methodism), tried to replace absolute predestination with conditional election. What Jonathan Edwards did was to provide a renewal of the Absolute and a psychological mechanism whereby the individual could scrutinize himself and hold himself to account. In *The Great Christian Doctrine of Original Sin Defended* (1758), Edwards attacked those who would relax Calvinism. He argued that depravity is inevitable because the identity of consciousness makes all men one with Adam. He believed in a privileged elect, not of those bearing the outward sign of work but of those who experienced saving grace by some inner illumination, by a transforming experience.

If Jonathan Edwards was the aesthetic and intuitive Puritan, Benjamin Franklin was the pragmatic and utilitarian Protestant. He was a practical man who looked at the world with an unblinking eye, intent mainly on "getting ahead" by frugality, industry, and native shrewdness. Franklin's life exemplified that fundamental American characteristic, self-improvement. Trying to imitate the manner of Addison's *Spectator,* Franklin wrote his own paragraphs, compared them with his mentor, and rewrote them, thus acquiring a vocabulary and fashioning a style of his own. Doggedly, he taught himself French, Italian, Spanish, and Latin. To relieve the "itch" of youthful passions, he entered into a common-law union with his landlady's daughter and had two children by her.

The key word in Franklin's vocabulary was "useful." His one book, the *Autobiography,* was begun as something that might be useful to his son; that purpose served, the book was never finished. He invented a stove, founded a hospital, paved the streets, established a city police force, for all these were useful projects. He believed it was useful to believe in God, for God rewards virtue and punishes vice. In *Poor Richard's Almanack* (1732–1757), Franklin pilfered the world's store of aphorisms and adapted them as homilies for the poor. "As Poor Richard says" became a phrase that gave weight to all the right virtues. There were, Franklin said, 13 useful virtues: temperance, silence, order, resolution, frugality, industry, sincerity, justice, moderation, cleanliness, tranquillity, chastity, and humility. There is perhaps no better inventory of the American creed. Franklin wrote that he gave to each a week's strict attention, setting down in a notebook the measure of daily success achieved in its practice. And thus he went through "a course complete in thirteen weeks and four courses a year."[3]

Yet all this was partly cunning, and perhaps even deceit. While Franklin was thrifty and industrious, his success, like that of many a good Yankee, came from his capacity to make influential friends, an uncanny ability to advertise himself, and the charm and wit reflected in his person and his writing. (Even the "itch" proved renewable, for he sired two more illegitimate children.) He amassed a modest fortune, retired to pursue his interest in natural philosophy and electricity, and for six years Franklin used his leisure for disinterested study before being drawn into public life.

Two images have come down to us as the essence of the American character: the piety and torment of Jonathan Edwards, obsessed with human depravity, and the practicality and expedience of Benjamin Franklin, oriented to a world of possibility and gain. Again, it is Van Wyck Brooks who best portrayed this dualism, writing almost 60 years ago:

> So it is that from the beginning we find two main currents in the American mind running side by side but rarely mingling—a current of overtones and a current of undertones— and both equally unsocial: on the one hand, the transcendental current, originating in the piety of the Puritans, becoming a philosophy in Jonathan Edwards, passing through Emerson, producing the fastidious refinement and aloofness of the chief American writers, and resulting in the final unreality of most contemporary American culture; and on the other hand, the current of catchpenny opportunism, originating in the practical shifts of Puritan life, becoming a philosophy in Franklin, passing through the American

humorists and resulting in the atmosphere of our contemporary business life. . . .[4]

Whatever the irrational mystery at the foundation of Puritan theology, the community itself was ruled by a rational morality in which the moral law was a cold and righteous necessity. The core of Puritanism, once the theological husks are stripped away, was an intense moral zeal for the regulation of everyday conduct, not because the Puritans were harsh or prurient, but because they had founded their community as a covenant in which all individuals were in compact with each other. Given the external dangers and psychological strains of living in a closed world, the individual had to be concerned not only with his own behavior but with the community. One's own sins imperiled not just oneself but the group; by failing to observe the demands of the covenant, one could bring down God's wrath on the community.

The terms of the covenant committed each person to an exemplary life. But the very explicitness of the covenant—and the intimacy of village life—made everyone aware of the sins of temptation and the temptations of the flesh.[5] This made the members more self-scourging, and after being sinners—for there was a considerable amount of illicit sexual activity and a bucolic realism about sex—they were also great repenters. The ritual of confession was at the heart of Puritanism both in New England and, later, in the Midwestern revivalist communities which carried the moral scourging, if not the theology of Puritanism, across the country.

The towns that were established, first in the wilderness and then in the prairies, faced the problem of maintaining some social order among a population that often had a high proportion of social misfits and ne'er-do-wells. A town of a few hundred families could not jail those who deviated from its code, or drive them all out. A system of social control by gossip or shaming, by public confession and repentance, became the means of preventing large-scale break-down in many communities. The idea of respectability—the distrust of light-heartedness, pleasure, drink—became so deeply ingrained that it persisted long after the initial material necessity was gone. If, in the beginning, work and riches were the signs of election, in the next century they became the badges of respectability.

Puritanism as an Ideology

A value system is often diffuse and inchoate. When it is organized into a specific code and formulated as a set of religious dogmas, an explicit covenant, or an ideology, it becomes a means of mobilizing a community, of enforcing discipline or a set of social controls. Why an ideology lingers on and grows even stronger, long after its initial congruence with a social movement has disappeared, is a complicated instance of the sociology of domination: witness the hold of Mormon theology, which grew out of the antinomian doctrine of progressive revelation yet today functions as a source of conservatism; or the ideology of egalitarian Communism in the Soviet Union, half a century after the revolution, to justify the rise of a new class. In such situations, the ideology carries with it the authority and sanctity of the past; it has been instilled into the child and becomes the only conceptual map of the world as well as of the moral norms of conduct. Often, though the original rhetoric and symbols remain, the content has been subtly redefined, over time, to justify the established social codes and social controls that buttress the social power of the predominant class.

This is the *functional* component of an ideology. But there is a cognitive or intellectual component as well. It is in the character of ideologies not only to reflect or justify an underlying reality but, once launched, to take on a life of their own. A truly powerful ideology opens up a new vision of life to the imagination; once formulated, it remains part of the moral repertoire to be drawn upon by intellectuals, theologians, or moralists as part of the range of possibilities open to mankind. Unlike economies or outmoded technologies, they do not disappear. These "moments of consciousness," as Hegel termed them, are renewable; they can be called upon and reformulated throughout the history of a civilization. Thus an ideology gnawed at, worried to the bone, argued about, dissected, and restated by an army of essayists, moralists, and intellectuals becomes a force in its own right.

This was the fate of Puritanism. Long after the harsh environment that fostered the initial ideology had been mitigated, the force of the belief remained. As Van Wyck Brooks once noted so pungently: "When the wine of the Puritans spilled, the aroma became transcendentalism, and the wine itself commercialism." . . .

The New Liberation

The major intellectual attack on Puritanism came in the first decade and a half of the twentieth century from the realm of culture and from the Young Intellectuals, a Harvard College group that included Walter Lippmann, Van Wyck Brooks, John Reed, and Harold Stearns.[6] . . .

There were several facets to the attack on Puritanism. First, there was the desire, expressed principally by Brooks, for a more inclusive culture reflecting the America of the immigrant, the Negro, and the urban scene. If America was to come of age, its culture had to be more cosmopolitan and reflect the vitality of the society. And second was the demand for sexual freedom. "A Puritan," Harold Stearns wrote, "was a sexually inadequate person who, unable to enjoy himself, derived his only satisfaction from interfering with the enjoyment of others." The children of the upper middle class flocked into Greenwich Village to create a new Bohemia. "They had read Nietzsche and Marx and Freud and Krafft-Ebing," Brooks wrote in retrospect. "Many of them wished to try out new ideas of sex, which had hitherto been kept in the cellars of young people's minds. . . ."[7]

The exuberance of life was summed up in a series of catchwords. One of them was "New." There was the New Democracy, the New Nationalism, the New Freedom, the New Poetry, and even the *New Republic* (which was started in 1914). A second was *sex*. Even to use the word openly sent a *frisson* through the readers of the press. Margaret Sanger, in 1913, coined the term "birth control." Ellen Key, the Swedish feminist, argued that marriage should not be a matter of legal or economic compulsion. Emma Goldman, the anarchist, lectured on homosexuality, the "intermediate sex." Floyd Dell celebrated free love, and many of the Young Intellectuals lived in ostentatious unmarried monogamy. And a third catchword was *liberation*. Liberation, as the movement self-consciously called itself, was the wind blowing from Europe, a wind of modernism come to the American shore. In art it was the Fauves and cubism, shown principally in the Armory Show of 1913. In the theater it meant symbolism, suggestion and atmosphere, the acceptance of the nonrealist influence of Maeterlinck, Dunsany, and Synge. In literature there was a vogue for Shaw, Conrad, and Lawrence. But the greatest influence was in "philosophy," where the currents of irrationalism, vitalism, and instinct, refracted through Bergson and Freud, spread rapidly in vulgarized form. . . .

The Young Intellectuals, in their very attack on Puritanism and a crabbed way of life, preached an ethic of hedonism, of pleasure and play—in short, a consumption ethic; yet, ironically—or is it not the trajectory of such "rebellion"—the consumption ethic was to be realized less than a decade later by a capitalism that, without self-consciousness, called itself (was it in faint echo of the "rebellion") the "new capitalism."

If the intellectual justifications of Puritanism had evaporated, its social practices gained new strength in the small towns precisely because of the fear of change. Change in this instance meant the rise of a new way of life—the life of the big cities, turbulent, cosmopolitan, and sinful. A definition of respectability was at stake, and this found its symbol in the idea of Temperance.

A style of life is justified by a set of values, regulated by institutions (church, school, family), and embodied in character structure. Where this style is expressed by a homogeneous set of persons, there exists what sociologists call a "status group." The style of life symbolized by the Temperance movement, though it developed later than Puritanism, had its source in the Protestant doctrines of industry, thrift, discipline, and sobriety; its institutional foundation in the Fundamentalist churches; and its character emphasis in the idea of restraint.

The norm of abstinence had become part of the public morality of American society. It was a device for assimilating the immigrant, the poor, and the deviant into middle-class status, if not into middle-class economic fact. But by the end of the nineteenth century it was no longer voluntary; instead, it was the coercive weapon of a social group whose own style of life was no longer ascendant. For if the new urban groups would not willingly accept temperance as a way of life, then it would have to be imposed by law and made a matter of ceremonial deference to the values of the traditional middle class. . . .

But something else was going on, and this was the transformation of the American social structure, and the end of small-town dominance of American life as a social fact. There was, first, the continuing demographic change, which resulted in the growth of urban centers and the shift in political weight. But more broadly, a consumption society was emerging, with its emphasis on spending and material possessions, and it was undermining the traditional value system, with its emphasis on thrift, frugality, self-control, and impulse renunciation. Integral to both social changes was a technological revolution which, through the automobile, the motion picture, and the radio, broke down rural isolation and for the first time fused the country into a common culture and a national society. This social transformation was responsible for the end of Puritanism as a set of practices that could support the traditional value system. . . .

The Transparent Life

The cultural transformation of modern society is due, singularly, to the rise of mass consumption, or the diffusion of what were once considered luxuries to the middle and lower classes in society. In this process, past luxuries are constantly redefined as necessities, so that it eventually seems incredible that an ordinary object could ever have been considered out of the reach of an ordinary man. For example, because of problems of temperature, homogeneity, and transparency, large windowpanes were once expensive luxuries and rare; yet after 1902, when the Frenchman Fourcault introduced a workable industrial means for manufacturing window glass by extrusion, they became commonplace items in city storefronts or country homes, creating a new range of display and vista.[8]

Mass consumption, which began in the 1920s, was made possible by revolutions in technology, principally the application of electrical energy to household tasks (washing machines, refrigerators, vacuum cleaners, and the like), and by three social inventions: mass production on an assembly line, which made a cheap automobile possible; the development of marketing, which rationalized the art of identifying different kinds of buying groups and whetting consumer appetites; and the spread of installment buying, which, more than any other social device, broke down the old Protestant fear of debt. The concomitant revolutions in transportation and communications laid the basis for a national society and the beginnings of a common culture. Taken all together, mass consumption meant the acceptance, in the crucial area of life-style, of the idea of social change and personal transformation, and it gave legitimacy to those who would innovate and lead the way, in culture as well as in production.

The symbol of mass consumption—and the prime example of the way technology has revolutionized social habits—is, of course, the automobile. Frederick Lewis Allen has observed how hard it is for us today to realize how separate and distant communities were when they depended wholly on the railroad and horse-and-wagon for transportation. A town not near a railroad was really remote. For a farmer who lived five miles out of the county seat it was an event to take the family to town for a Saturday afternoon; a trip to a friend ten miles away was likely to be an all-day expedition, since the horse had to be rested and fed. Each small town, each farm, was dependent mainly on its own resources for amusement and company. Horizons were close, and individuals lived among familiar people and familiar things.

The automobile swept away many sanctions of the closed small-town society. The repressive threats of nineteenth-century morality, as Andrew Sinclair has observed, relied in large measure on the impossibility of escaping from the place, and consequences, of misbehavior. By the middle of the 1920s, as the Lynds observed in Middletown, boys and girls thought nothing of driving 20 miles to dance at a roadhouse, safe from the prying eyes of neighbors. The closed car became the *cabinet particulier* of the middle class, the place where adventurous young people shed their sexual inhibitions and broke the old taboos.[9]

The second major instrument of change in the closed small-town society was the motion picture. Movies are many things—a window on the world, a set of ready-made daydreams, fantasy and projection, escapism and omnipotence—and their emotional power is enormous. It is as a window on the world that the movies have served, in the first instance, to transform the culture. "Sex is one of the things Middletown has long been taught to fear," the Lynds observed when they revisited Middletown ten years later, and "its institutions . . . operate to keep the subject out of sight and out of mind as much as possible." Except in the movies, to which the youngsters flocked.

Adolescents not only enjoyed the movies but went to school there. They modeled themselves after movie stars, repeated movie jokes and gestures, learned the subtleties of behavior between the sexes, and thus developed a veneer of sophistication. And in their efforts to act out this sophistication, to resolve their baffled uncertainties and perplexities by outwardly confident action, the pattern was "not so much . . . the lives of their own cautious parents as . . . the alternative other worlds about them." Films glorified the cult of youth (girls wore bobbed hair and short skirts), and middle-aged men and women were advised "to make hay while the sun shines." The idea of "freedom" was exemplified by the legitimacy of the speakeasy and one's readiness to cut loose at wild parties. "The mockery of ethics, of the old 'inner goodness' of the film heroes and heroines," writes Lewis Jacobs, "was paralleled by the new regard for material things."

The automobile, the motion picture, and radio are technological in origin: advertising, planned obsolescence, and credit are all sociological innovations. David M. Potter has commented that it is as hopeless to understand a modern popular writer without understanding advertising as it would be to understand a medieval troubadour without understanding the cult of chivalry, or a nineteenth-century revivalist without understanding evangelical religion.

The extraordinary thing about advertising is its pervasiveness. What marks a great city if not its lighted signs? Passing over in an airplane one sees, through the refractions of the night sky, the clusters of red, orange, blue, and white signs shimmering like highly polished stones. In the centers of the great cities—Time Square, Piccadilly, the Champs-Elysées, the Ginza—people gather in the streets under the blinking neon signs to share in the vibrancy of the milling crowd. If one thinks about the social impact of advertising, its most immediate, yet usually unnoticed, consequence has been to transform the physical center of the city. In redoing the physical topography, replacing the old *duomos* or municipal halls or palace towers, advertising has placed a "burning brand" on the crest of our civilization. It is the mark of material goods, the exemplar of new styles of life, the herald of new values. As in fashion, advertising has emphasized glamour. A car becomes the sign of the "good life" well lived, and the appeal of glamour becomes pervasive. A consumption economy, one might say, finds its reality in appearances. What one displays, what one shows, is a sign of achievement. Getting ahead is no longer a matter of rising up a social ladder, as it was in the late nineteenth century, but of adopting a specific style of life—country club, artiness, travel, hobbies—which marks one as a member of a consumption community.

In a complex, multi-group, socially mobile society, advertising also takes on a number of new "mediating" functions. The United States was probably the first large-scale society in history to build cultural change into the society, and many status problems arose simply because of the bewildering rapidity of such change. Few societies, in fact, can absorb quick change. The major social institutions—family, church, educational system—were set up to transmit established habits of the society. A society in rapid change inevitably produces confusions about appropriate modes of behavior, taste, and dress. A socially mobile person has no ready guide for acquiring new knowledge on how to live "better" than before, and his guides become the movies, television, and advertising. In this respect, advertising begins to play a more subtle role in changing habits than merely stimulating wants. The advertising in the women's magazines, the house-and-home periodicals, and sophisticated journals like the *New Yorker* was to teach people how to dress, furnish a home, buy the right wines—in short, the styles of life appropriate to the new statuses. Though at first the changes were primarily in manners, dress, taste, and food habits, sooner or later they began to affect more basic patterns: the structure of authority in the family, the role of children and young adults as independent consumers in the society, the pattern of morals, and the different meanings of achievement in the society.

All of this came about by gearing the society to change and the acceptance of cultural change, once mass consumption and a high standard of living were seen as the legitimate purpose of economic organization. Selling became the most striking activity of contemporary America. Against frugality, selling emphasized prodigality; against asceticism, the lavish display.

None of this would have been possible without that revolution in moral habit, the idea of installment selling. Although it had been practiced fitfully in the United States before World War I, installment selling had two stigmas. First, most installment sales were to the poor, who could not afford major expenditures; they paid weekly sums to a peddler who both sold the goods and made the weekly collection. Installment selling was thus a sign of financial instability. Second, installment selling meant debt to the middle class, and going into debt was wrong and dangerous. As Micawber would say, it was a sign of living beyond one's means, and the result would be misery. Being moral meant being industrious and thrifty. If one wanted to buy something, one should save for it. The trick of installment selling was to avoid the word "debt" and emphasize the word "credit." Monthly charges were billed by mail, and the transactions were thus handled on a businesslike basis.

Saving—or abstinence—is the heart of the Protestant ethic. With Adam Smith's idea of parsimony or frugality, and Nassau Senior's idea of abstinence, it was firmly established that saving multiplied future products and earned its own reward by interest. The denouement was the change in banking habits. For years, such was the grim specter of middle-class morality that people were afraid to be overdrawn at the bank, lest a check bounce. By the end of the 1960s, the banks were strenuously advertising the services of cash reserves that would allow a depositor to overdraw up to several thousand dollars (to be paid back in monthly installments). No one need be deterred from gratifying his impulse at an auction or a sale. The seduction of the consumer had become total.

Van Wyck Brooks once remarked about morality in Catholic countries that as long as heavenly virtues are upheld, mundane behavior may change as it will. In America, the old Protestant heavenly virtues are largely gone, and the mundane rewards have begun to run riot. The basic American value pattern emphasized the virtue of achievement, defined as doing and making, and a man displayed his character in the quality of his work. By the 1950s, the pattern of achievement remained, but it had been redefined to emphasize status and taste. The culture was no longer concerned with how to work and achieve, but with how to spend and enjoy. Despite some continuing use of the language of the Protestant ethic, the fact was that by the 1950s American culture had become primarily hedonistic, concerned with play, fun, display, and pleasure—and, typical of things in America, in a compulsive way.

The world of hedonism is the world of fashion, photography, advertising, television, travel. It is a world of make-believe in which one lives for expectations, for what will come rather than what is. And it must come without effort. It is no accident that the successful new magazine of the previous decade was called *Playboy* and that its success—a circulation of 6 million by 1970—is due largely to the fact that it encourages fantasies of male sexual prowess. If, as Max Lerner once wrote, sex is the last frontier in American life, then the achievement motive in a go-go society finds its acme in sex. In the 1950s and the 1960s, the cult of the Orgasm succeeded the cult of Mammon as the basic passion of American life.

Nothing epitomized the hedonism of the United States better than the State of California. A cover story in *Time,* called "California: A State of Excitement," opened:

> California is virtually a nation unto itself, but it holds a strange hope, a sense of excitement—and some terror—for Americans. As most of them see it, the good, godless, gregarious pursuit of pleasure is what California is all about. The citizens of lotusland seem forever to be lolling around swimming pools, sautéing in the sun, packing across the Sierra, frolicking nude on the beaches, getting taller each year, plucking money off the trees, romping around topless, tramping through the redwoods and—when they stop to catch their breath—preening themselves on-camera before the rest of an envious world. "I have seen the future," says the newly returned visitor from California, "and it plays."[10]

Fun morality, in consequence, displaces "goodness morality," which stressed interference with impulses. Not having fun is an occasion for self-examination: "What is wrong with me?" As Dr. Wolfenstein observes: "Whereas gratification of forbidden impulses traditionally aroused guilt, failure to have fun now lowers one's self-esteem."[11]

Fun morality centers, in most instances, on sex. And here the seduction of the consumer has become almost total. The most tell-tale illustration, I believe, was a double-page advertisement by Eastern Airlines in the *New York Times,* in 1973, saying: "Take the Bob and Carol, Ted and Alice, Phil and Anne Vacation." The blatant theme was a takeoff on *Bob and Carol and Ted and*

Alice, a sniggering film about the fumbling attempts of two friendly couples to engage in wife-swapping. Here was Eastern Airlines saying, in effect: "We will fly you down to the Caribbean. We will rent you a cabana. Fly now, pay later." Eastern does not tell you *what* you pay, but you can postpone the money (and forget the guilt) and take the Bob and Carol, Ted and Alice, and (for further titillation another couple is added) Phil and Anne vacation. Compare this with Franklin's 13 useful virtues, which included temperance, frugality, tranquility, and chastity. At the turn of the century, a church in the Midwest might have property on which a brothel was located. And one could then at least say: "Well, we are losing bodies, but we are earning money to save souls." Today, when one sells bodies, one is no longer also saving souls.

What this abandonment of Puritanism and the Protestant ethic does, of course, is to leave capitalism with no moral or transcendental ethic. It also emphasizes not only the disjunction between the norms of the culture and the norms of the social structure, but also an extraordinary contradiction within the social structure itself. On the one hand, the business corporation wants an individual to work hard, pursue a career, accept delayed gratification—to be, in the crude sense, an organization man. And yet, in its products and its advertisements, the corporation promotes pleasure, instant joy, relaxing and letting go. One is to be "straight" by day and a "swinger" by night. This is self-fulfillment and self-realization! . . .

We are now in a position to sum up the process. The erosion of traditional American values took place on two levels. In the realm of culture and ideas, the withering attack on small-town life as constricting and banal was first organized in the 1910s by the Young Intellectuals as a self-consciously defined group, and this attack was sustained in the next decade in the journalistic criticism of H. L. Mencken and in the sketches and novels of Sherwood Anderson and Sinclair Lewis.

But a more fundamental transformation was occurring in the social structure itself: the change in the motivations and rewards of the economic system. The rising wealth of the plutocracy, becoming evident in the Gilded Age, meant that work and accumulation were no longer ends in themselves (though they were still crucial to a John D. Rockefeller or an Andrew Carnegie), but means to consumption and display. Status and its badges, not work and the election of God, became the mark of success.

This is a familiar process of social history with the rise of new classes, though in the past it was military predators whose scions went from spartan to sybaritic living. Yet such parvenu classes could distance themselves from the rest of society, and such social transformations often developed independently of changes in the lives of the classes below. But the real social revolution in modern society came in the 1920s, when the rise of mass production and high consumption began to transform the life of the middle class itself. In effect the Protestant ethic as a social reality and a life-style for the middle class was replaced by a materialistic hedonism, and the Puritan temper by a psychological eudaemonism. But bourgeois society, justified and propelled as it had been in its earliest energies by these older ethics, could not easily admit to the change. It promoted a hedonistic way of life furiously—one has only to look at the transformation of advertising in the 1920s—but could not justify it. It lacked a new religion or value system to replace the old, and the result was disjunction.

In one respect what we see here is an extraordinary historic change in human society. For thousands of years, the function of economics was to provide the daily necessities—the subsistence—of life. For various upper-class groups, economics has been the basis of status and a sumptuary style. But now, on a mass scale, economics had become geared to the demands of culture. Here, too, culture, not as expressive symbolism or moral meanings but as life-style, came to reign supreme.

The "new capitalism" (the phrase was first used in the 1920s) continued to demand a Protestant ethic in the area of production—that is, in the realm of work—but to stimulate a demand for pleasure and play in the area of consumption. The disjunction was bound to widen. The spread of urban life, with its variety of distractions and multiple stimuli; the new roles of women, created by the expansion of office jobs and the freer social and sexual contacts; the rise of a national culture through motion pictures and radio—all contributed to a loss of social authority on the part of the older value system.

The Puritan temper might be described most simply by the term "delayed gratification," and by restraint in gratification. It is, of course, the Malthusian injunction for prudence in a world of scarcity. But the claim of the American economic system was that it had introduced abundance, and the nature of abundance is to encourage prodigality rather than prudence. A higher standard of living, not work as an end in itself, then becomes the engine of change. The glorification of plenty, rather than the bending to niggardly nature, becomes the justification of the system. But all of this was highly incongruent with the theological and sociological foundations of nineteenth-century Protestantism, which was in turn the foundation of the American value system. . . .

THE HINGE OF HISTORY

. . . What is striking about the rise and fall of civilizations—and it was the basis of the philosophy of history of the talented Arabic thinker Ibn Khaldun—is that societies pass through specific phases whose transformations signal decline. These are the transformations from simplicity to luxury (what Plato, who wrote about this in Book 2 of *The Republic,* called the change from the healthy city to the fevered city), from asceticism to hedonism.

It is striking that every new, rising social force—be it a new religion, new military force, or new revolutionary movement—begins as an ascetic movement. Asceticism emphasizes non-material values, renunciation of physical pleasures, simplicity and self-denial, and arduous, purposeful discipline. That discipline is necessary for the mobilization of psychic and physical energies for tasks outside the self, for the conquest and subordination of the self in order to conquer others. As Max Weber remarked: "Discipline acquired during wars of religion was the source of the unconquerableness of both the Islamic and Cromwellian cavalries. Similarly, inner-worldly asceticism and the disciplined quest for salvation in a vocation pleasing to God were the sources of the virtuosity in acquisitiveness characteristic of the Puritans."[12]

The discipline of the old religious "warriors of God" was channeled into military organization and battle. What was historically unique about the Puritan temper was the devotion of this-worldly asceticism to an occupational calling and to work and accumulation. Yet the end of the Puritan's being was not primarily wealth. As Weber remarked, the Puritan got nothing out of his wealth for himself but the proof of his own salvation.[13] And it was this furious energy that built an industrial civilization.

For the Puritan, "the most urgent task" was to destroy spontaneous, impulsive behavior and bring order into the conduct of life. Today one finds asceticism primarily in revolutionary movements and revolutionary regimes. Puritanism, in the psychological and sociological sense, is to be found in Communist China and in the regimes which fuse revolutionary sentiment with Koranic purposes, as in Algeria and Libya.

In the scheme of Khaldun, reflecting in the fourteenth century the vicissitudes of Berber and Arabic civilizations, the sequences of transformation went from the Bedouin to the sedentary to the hedonistic life, and from there, in three generations, to the decline of the society. In the hedonistic life, there is a loss of will and fortitude. More importantly, men become competitive with one another for luxuries, and lose the ability to share and

sacrifice. There then follows, says Khaldun, the loss of *asabîyah,* that sense of solidarity which makes men feel as brothers to one another, that "group feeling which means (mutual) affection and willingness to fight and die for each other."[14]

The basis for *asabîyah* is not only the sense of shared sacrifice and shared danger—the elements which hold platoons of fighting men or underground revolutionary cadres together—but also some moral purpose, a *telos* which provides the moral justifications for the society. At the start, the United States was held together by an implicit convenant, the sense that this was the continent where God's design would be unfolded, a belief which underlay the deism of Jefferson. As this belief receded, what held the society together was a unique polity, an open, adaptive, egalitarian, and democratic system which was responsive to the many claimants that sought inclusion in the society and which respected the principles of law as embodied in the Constitution and abided by the decisions of the Supreme Court. Yet this responsiveness itself was possible largely because of the expansiveness of the economy, and the promise of material wealth as a solvent for social strains. . . . But the deeper and more difficult questions are the legitimations of the society as expressed in the motivations of individuals and the moral purposes of the nation. And it is here that the cultural contradictions—the discordances of character structure and the disjunction of realms—become central.

Changes in culture and moral temper—the fusion of imagination and life-styles—are not amenable to "social engineering" or political control. They derive from the value and moral traditions of the society, and these cannot be "designed" by precept. The ultimate sources are the religious conceptions which undergird a society; the proximate sources are the reward systems and motivations (and their legitimations) which derive from the arena of work.

American capitalism, as I have tried to show, has lost its traditional legitimacy, which was based on a moral system of reward rooted in the Protestant sanctification of work. It has substituted a hedonism which promises material ease and luxury, yet shies away from all the historic implications of a "voluptuary system," with all its social permissiveness and libertinism. The culture has been dominated (in the serious realm) by a principle of modernism that has been subversive of bourgeois life, and the middle-class life-styles by a hedonism that has undercut the Protestant ethic which provided the moral foundation for the society. The interplay of modernism as a mode developed by serious artists, the institutionalization of those played-out forms by the "cultural mass," and the hedonism as a way of life promoted by the marketing system of business, constitutes the cultural contradiction of capitalism. The modernism is exhausted, and no longer threatening. The hedonism apes its sterile japes. But the social order lacks either a culture that is a symbolic expression of any vitality or a moral impulse that is a motivational or binding force. What, then, can hold the society together?

This is joined to a more pervasive problem derived from the nature of modern society. The characteristic style of industrialism is based on the principles of economics and economizing: on efficiency, least cost, maximization, optimization, and functional rationality. Yet it is this very style that is in conflict with the advanced cultural trends of the Western world, for modernist culture emphasizes anti-cognitive and anti-intellectual modes which look longingly toward a return to instinctual sources of expression. The one emphasizes functional rationality, technocratic decision making, and meritocratic rewards; the other, apocalyptic moods and anti-rational modes of behavior. It is this disjunction which is the historic cultural crisis of all Western bourgeois society. This cultural contradiction is, in the longer run, the most fateful division in the society.

ENDNOTES

1. See Max Weber, *The Rational and Social Foundations of Music,* ed. Don Martindale et al. (Carbondale, Ill.: Southern Illinois University Press, 1958).

2. Page Smith, *As a City upon a Hill* (New York: Alfred A. Knopf, 1960), p. vii.

3. In his magisterial work, *The Protestant Ethic and the Spirit of Capitalism,* Max Weber sees Franklin as the embodiment of both. He cites his "sermons," as he calls them (". . . Time is money . . . Remember that credit is money. If a man lets his money lie in my hands after it is done, he gives me the interest . . ."), as marking the characteristic ethos of the "new man." Interestingly, Weber cites Franklin more often than he cites Luther, Calvin, Baxter, Bailey, or any of the other Puritan divines to describe the lineaments of the new ethic. See Max Weber, *The Protestant Ethic and the Spirit of Capitalism,* trans. Talcott Parsons (London: G. Allen & Unwin, 1930).

4. Van Wyck Brooks, *America's Coming of Age* (Garden City, N.Y.: Doubleday Anchor, 1958; orig. ed., 1915), p. 10.

5. Perhaps the most powerful literary illustration of these illicit impulses is Hawthorne's short story "Young Goodman Brown," an oneiromantic vision of a black mass in the woods of Salem. In the story, Young Goodman Brown leaves his wife to go into the woods with the devil (who bears a serpent rod = phallus) to be baptized into the mysteries of sin. To his surprise and horror, he recognizes all the "good" people of the town joyfully moving toward the initiation ceremony, and recognizes, as well, his own young wife Faith. The ceremony and the music have the form of a religious liturgy, but the content is the flowers of evil. In the end it is never clear whether this was, for Goodman Brown, an actual event or a dream in which he was struggling with his own sinful impulses. But his life from then on was miserable. ("On the Sabbath day, when the congregation were singing a holy psalm he could not listen because an anthem of sin rushed loudly upon his ear . . .") He led a cankered and shriveled existence, and his dying hour was gloom. See "Young Goodman Brown," in *The Novels and Tales of Nathaniel Hawthorne* (New York: Modern Library, 1937), pp. 1033–1042.

6. For a discussion of the Young Intellectuals, see Henry F. May, *The End of American Innocence,* pt. 3 (New York: Alfred A. Knopf, 1959). For a characteristic voice, see Harold Stearns, *America and the Young Intellectual* (New York: Doran, 1921).

7. Van Wyck Brooks, *The Confident Years: 1885–1915* (New York: Dutton, 1952), p. 487. The phrase "cellars of young people's minds" came from Ernest Poole's novel *The Harbor,* describing Princeton life in the early 1900s.

8. The illustration is taken from Jean Fourastie, *The Causes of Wealth* (Glencoe, Ill.: Free Press, 1959), p. 127. Professor Fourastie's book, like Siegfried Giedeon's *Mechanization Takes Command* (New York: Oxford University Press, 1948), is a fascinating miscellany of examples of this process.

9. The Lynds quoted one Middle Western observer: "Why on earth do you need to study what's changing this country? . . . I can tell you what's happening in just four letters: A-U-T-O!" Robert S. Lynd and Helen Merrell Lynd, *Middletown* (New York: Harcourt, Brace, 1929), p. 251. In 1890 a pony was the wildest dream of a Middletown boy. By 1923, "the 'horse culture' of Middletown had almost disappeared." The first automobile appeared there in 1900. By 1906 there were "probably 200 in the city and county." At the end of 1923 there were more than 6,200 cars, one for every six persons, or roughly two for every three families. As the Lynds observed: "Group-sanctioned values are disturbed by the inroads of the automobile upon the family budget. A case in point is the not uncommon practice of mortgaging a home to buy an automobile" (p. 254).

10. *Time,* November 7, 1969, p. 60.

11. Martha Wolfenstein, "The Emergence of Fun Morality," in *Mass Leisure,* ed. Eric Larrabee and Rolf Meyersohn (Glencoe, Ill.: Free Press, 1958), p. 86.

12. Max Weber, *The Sociology of Religion,* trans. Ephraim Fischoffs (Boston: Beacon Press, 1963), p. 203.

13. Weber, *Protestant Ethic,* p. 71.

14. Ibn Khaldun, *The Muqaddimah: An Introduction to History,* trans. Franz Rosenthal (New York: Pantheon Books, 1958). The crucial section is in vol. 1, chap. 3; the quotation above is from p. 313.

QUESTIONS ON BELL

1. What is the "cultural contradiction" of capitalism? In what sense is there a *contradiction*? How is this contradiction manifested in daily life?

2. Bell contends that although the Protestant ethic came under attack from intellectuals, the main cause of its demise lies with the market itself. Has some essential aspect or feature of the market generated this effect? Was this effect inevitable, or could it have been prevented?

3. Is there any way in which a "cultural contradiction" can be resolved? Does Bell offer any suggestions on this matter?

4. How do you understand the difference between a hedonistic and an ascetic society? Does capitalism *require* an ascetic morality? Which do you prefer, the hedonist or the ascetic? Why?

The Prevalence of War and *The Loose Individual*

Robert Nisbet

Robert Nisbet (1913–1996) was a Professor of Sociology at Columbia University and the author of The Quest for Community *(1969),* Social Change and History *(1969),* The Social Bond *(1970),* The Twilight of Authority *(1975), and* History of the Idea of Progress *(1980). The excerpts below are from* The Present Age: Progress and Anarchy in Modern America *(1988).*

THE PREVALENCE OF WAR

Of all faces of the present age in America, the military face would almost certainly prove the most astounding to any Framers of the Constitution, any Founders of the Republic who came back to inspect their creation on the occasion of the bicentennial. It is indeed an imposing face, the military. Well over three hundred billion dollars a year go into its maintenance; it is deployed in several dozen countries around the world. The returned Framers would not be surprised to learn that so vast a military has inexorable effects upon the economy, the structure of government, and even the culture of Americans; they had witnessed such effects in Europe from afar, and had not liked what they saw. What would doubtless astonish the Framers most, though, is that their precious republic has become an imperial power in the world, much like the Great Britain they had hated in the eighteenth century. Finally, the Framers would almost certainly swoon when they learned that America has been participant in the Seventy-Five Years War that has gone on, rarely punctuated, since 1914. And all of this, the Framers would sorrowfully find, done under the selfsame structure of government they had themselves built.

Clearly, the American Constitution was designed for a people more interested in governing itself than in helping to govern the rest of the world. The new nation had the priceless advantage of two great oceans dividing it from the turbulences of Europe and Asia. Permanent or even frequent war was the last thing any thoughtful American of the time would think of as a serious threat. Power to declare war could be safely left to the Congress, and leadership of the military to a civilian commander in chief, the president. Let the president have nominal stewardship of foreign policy but let the Senate have the power to advise and consent, and the entire Congress the power of purse over foreign policy and war.

It was ingenious, absolutely ideal for a nation clearly destined to peace and to the cultivation of the arts and sciences. Agriculture, commerce, and manufacture were the proper and highly probable direction of the American future. The states, to which an abundance of powers and rights were left by the Constitution, would be the true motors of American prosperity.

We did a very good job, on the whole, of avoiding the traps and entanglements of the world for the first hundred and twenty-five years, and even made bold to warn the Old World that its presence in the Western Hemisphere, however brief, would be regarded with suspicion. Then things changed.

The present age in American history begins with the Great War. When the guns of August opened fire in 1914, no one in America could have reasonably foreseen that within three years that foreign war not only would have drawn America into it but also would have, by the sheer magnitude of the changes it brought about on the American scene, set the nation on another course from which it has not deviated significantly since. The Great War was the setting of America's entry into modernity—economic, political, social, and cultural. By 1920 the country had passed, within a mere three years, from the premodern to the distinctly and ineffaceably modern. Gone forever now the age of American innocence.

When the war broke out in Europe in 1914 America was still, remarkably, strikingly, pretty much the same country in moral, social, and cultural respects that it had been for a century. We were still, in 1914, a people rooted largely in the mentality of the village and small town, still suspicious of large cities and the styles of living that went with these cities. The states were immensely important, just as the Founding Fathers and the Framers had intended them to be. It was hard to find a truly national culture, a national consciousness, in 1914. The Civil War had, of course, removed forever philosophical, as well as actively political, doubts of the reality of the Union as a sovereign state. But in terms of habits of mind, customs, traditions, folk literature, indeed written literature, speech accent, dress, and so forth, America could still be looked at as a miscellany of cultures held together, but not otherwise much influenced, by the federal government in Washington. For the vast majority of Americans, from east to west, north to south, the principal, if not sole, link with the national government was the postal system—and perhaps also the federal income tax, which was approved at long last by constitutional amendment in 1913.

The Great War changed all of this. By November 1918 after four years of war in Europe and nearly two years of it for America, the whole world was changed, Europe itself ceased in substantial degree to be a contained civilization, and the United States, after close to two years of what can only be called wrenching military nationalism under the charismatic Woodrow Wilson, was brought at last into the modern world of nations. State loyalties and appeals to states' rights would not vanish overnight; they aren't gone yet in constitutional law, and aren't likely to be. But whereas prior to 1914 one still saw the gravamen of American development in the four dozen states, "provinces" in European terms, by 1920, it had shifted to the national culture, with the states becoming increasingly archaic.

The Great War, unwanted by any nation, even Germany, unexpected, really, until it burst devastatingly and irreversibly upon Europe, was at its height by far the largest, bloodiest, cruelest, indeed most savage in history. Churchill wrote:

> All the horrors of all the ages were brought together, and not only armies but whole populations were thrust into the midst of them. . . . Neither peoples nor rulers drew the line at any deed which they thought would help them to win. Germany, having let Hell loose, kept well in the van of terror; but she was followed step by step by the desperate and ultimately avenging nations she had assailed. Every outrage against humanity or international law was repaid by reprisals—often of

a greater scale and of longer duration. No truce or parley mitigated the strife of the armies. The wounded died between the lines: the dead mouldered in the soil. Merchant ships and neutral ships and hospital ships were sunk on the seas and all on board left to their fate or killed as they swam. Every effort was made to starve whole nations into submission without regard to age or sex. Cities and monuments were smashed by artillery. Bombs from the air were cast down indiscriminately. Poison gas in many forms stifled or seared their bodies. Liquid fire was projected upon their bodies. Men fell from the air in flames, or were smothered, often slowly, in the dark recesses of the sea. The fighting strength of armies was limited only by the manhood of their countries. Europe and large parts of Asia and Africa became one vast battlefield on which after years of struggle not armies but nations broke and ran. When all was over, Torture and Cannibalism were the only two expedients that the civilized, scientific, Christian States had been able to deny themselves: and they were of doubtful utility.[1]

The greatest single yield of the First World War was, however, none of the above; it was the Second World War, which came a bare quarter of a century after the First, germinated and let loose by the appalling consequences of 1918, chief among them the spawning of the totalitarian state, first in Russia, then in Italy and, crucially in the end, in Germany under Hitler. World War II was fought, of course, on a much wider front, or set of fronts, than its predecessor. There was no part of the globe that was not touched in one way or other. From the Second World War, officially ended in late 1945, has come a rash of wars during the last forty years, chief among them the Cold War between the Soviet Union and the United States. But we should not overlook the dozens of other wars fought during this period, in Asia, Africa, the Middle East, the Far East, Oceania, and so on. Between the last shot fired in 1945 and the present moment, war, somewhere at some time, has been the rule, peace the exception.

There is every reason for referring to the "Seventy-Five Years War" of the twentieth century, for that is about the length of the period of wars that began in 1914 and, with only brief punctuations of peace, continues through this year, certainly the next, and to what final ending? In so referring to twentieth-century war, we are only following the precedent of what we read routinely in our textbooks of European history about the Hundred Years War at the end of the Middle Ages. That war also had its punctuations of peace, or at least absence of overt hostilities.

War is indeed hell in just about every one of its manifestations through history. But for human beings during the past several thousand years it has plainly had its attractions, and also its boons for humanity. The general who said it is "good that war is so hideous; otherwise we should become too fond of it" spoke knowingly of the mental "wealth" that inheres in most wars along with the mental and physical "illth." So practical and pragmatic a mind as William James believed that we needed a "moral equivalent of war" as the means of attaining the good qualities of war without entailing the evil ones.

Without wars through the ages, and the contacts and intermixtures of peoples they—and for countless aeons they alone—instigated, humanity would quite possibly be mired in the torpor and sloth, the fruits of cultural and mental isolation, with which its history begins. Before trade and commerce broke down cultural barriers and yielded crossbreeding of ideas as well as genetic systems, wars were the sole agencies of such crossbreeding. Individualism, so vital to creativity, was born of mingling of peoples, with their contrasting cultural codes—the very diversity aiding in the release of individuals from prior localism and parochialism, always the price of cultural insularity.

War and change—political and economic foremost, but social and cultural not far behind—have been linked in America from the beginning. War was the necessary factor in the birth of the new American republic, as it has been in the birth of every political state known to us in history. War, chiefly the Civil War, in U.S. history has been a vital force in the rise of industrial capitalism, in the change of America from a dominantly agrarian and pastoral country to one chiefly manufacturing in nature. War, in focusing the mind of a country, stimulates inventions, discoveries, and fresh adaptations. Despite its manifest illth, war, by the simple fact of the intellectual and social changes it instigates, yields results which are tonic to advancement.

By all odds, the most important war in U.S. history, the war that released the greatest number and diversity of changes in American life, was the Great War, the war that began in Europe in August 1914 and engulfed the United States in April 1917. Great changes in America were immediate.

In large measure these changes reflected a release from the sense of isolation, insularity, and exceptionalism that had suffused so much of the American mind during the nineteenth century. The early Puritans had seen their new land as a "city upon a hill" with the eyes of the world on it. It was not proper for the New World to go to the Old for its edification; what was proper was for the Old World, grown feeble and hidebound, to come to America for inspiration. A great deal of that state of mind entered into what Tocqueville called the "American Religion," a religion compounded of Puritanism and ecstatic nationalism.

What we think of today as modernity—in manners and morals as well as ideas and mechanical things—came into full-blown existence in Europe in the final part of the nineteenth century, its centers such cities as London, Paris, and Vienna. In contrast America was a "closed" society, one steeped in conventionality and also in a struggle for identity. This was how many Europeans saw America and it was emphatically how certain somewhat more sophisticated and cosmopolitan Americans saw themselves. The grand tour was a veritable obligation of better-off, ambitious, and educated Americans—the tour being, of course, of Europe.

Possibly the passage of American values, ideas, and styles from "closed" to "open," from the isolated to the cosmopolitan society, would have taken place, albeit more slowly, had there been no transatlantic war of 1914–1918. We can't be sure. What we do know is that the war, and America's entrance into it, gave dynamic impact to the processes of secularization, individualization, and other kinds of social-psychological change which so drastically changed this country from the America of the turn of the century to the America of the 1920s.

War, sufficiently large, encompassing, and persisting, is one of the most powerful media of social and cultural—and also material, physical, and mechanical—change known to man. It was in circumstances of war in primordial times that the political state arose, and at the expense of the kinship order that had from the beginning been the individual's sole community. Ever since, war has had a nourishing effect upon the state; it is "the health of the state," Randolph Bourne observed darkly but accurately, when America went to war in 1917. Werner Sombart, historian of capitalism, devoted a volume to the tonic effects of war on the rise and development of capitalism. But no less true is Max Weber's pronouncement of war and the barracks life of warriors as the true cause of communism. War communism precedes, indeed gives birth to, civil communism, Weber argued. The Communism of Soviet Russia has been based from the very beginning upon war preparation, upon the Red Army and its absolute power in the Soviet state.

War tends to stimulate intellectual and cultural ferment if only because of the mixture of ideas and values that is a by-product of combat, of victory and defeat, in any war. In both world wars, millions of Americans, men and women alike, knew the broadening and enriching effects of travel abroad, of stations in exotic places for the first time, as the result of enlistment or conscription. Granted that some were killed. Far more were not.

War tends to break up the cake of custom, the net of tradition. By so doing, especially in times of crisis, it allows the individual a better chance of being seen and heard in the interstices, in the crevasses opened by the cracking up of old customs, statuses, and conventionalities. This was remarkably true once the European war touched the millions of lives which had been for so long familiar with only the authorities and rhythms of an existence largely rural and pretty much limited to towns of the hinterland.

Lord Bryce, who loved America, was nevertheless forced to devote a chapter in his *The American Commonwealth,* published in the late nineteenth century, to what he called "the uniformity of American life." He was struck by the sameness of the buildings, houses, streets, food, drink, and dress in town after town, village after village, as he crossed and recrossed the country by rail. Not even one great capital, one flourishing city, Bryce felt obliged to report in his classic. That, however, was before the Great War and its transformation of the United States. It brought the literature of "release" in the novels of Sinclair Lewis, Sherwood Anderson, Willa Cather, Ruth Suckow, and others, a literature constructed around the drama and sometimes agony of a protagonist's escape from Main Street or Winesburg or Elmville or wherever, to the freedoms, chilling as these could be, of a Chicago or New York. In postwar New York, America at last got a true world capital. Much of the dreadful sameness began to crack under the force of the Great War. No wonder this war remains popular in American memory; even more popular than the War of Independence with Britain, which, truth to tell, was observed at the time by a majority hostile or at best lukewarm to it. Woodrow Wilson made the war his personal mission, his road to salvation for not only America but the world; and in the process, he made the war the single most vivid experience a large number of Americans had ever known. Even the casualties among American forces (not many compared to those of France, Britain, Russia, and Germany) didn't dampen enthusiasm at home; nor did the passage of legislation which put in the president's hands the most complete thought control ever exercised on Americans.

What the Great War did is what all major wars do for large numbers of people: relieve, if only briefly, the tedium, monotony, and sheer boredom which have accompanied so many millions of lives in all ages. In this respect war can compete with liquor, sex, drugs, and domestic violence as an anodyne. War, its tragedies and devastations understood here, breaks down social walls and by so doing stimulates a new individualism. Old traditions, conventions, dogmas, and taboos are opened under war conditions to a challenge, especially from the young, that is less likely in long periods of peace. The very uncertainty of life brought by war can seem a welcome liberation from the tyranny of the ever-predictable, from what a poet has called the "long littleness of life." It is not the certainties but the uncertainties in life which excite and stimulate—if they do not catastrophically obliterate—the energies of men.

There is a very high correlation between wars in Western history and periods of invention and discovery. If necessity is the mother of invention, then military necessity is the Great Mother. Roger Burlingame was correct when he said that if war were ever to be permanently abolished on earth, then something would have to be found to replace it as the stimulus and the context of inventions—mechanical but also social and cultural inventions. . . . America between 1914 and 1918 was no exception. Inventions of preceding years like the telephone and electric light were brought to a higher degree of perfection; so were the automobile, the radio, and the prototypes of what would become cherished household appliances. The federal government, justified and encouraged by war pressure, was able to do what would have been impossible in time of peace: directly encourage and even help finance new, entrepreneurial ventures such as the airplane and radio, each to revolutionize American life after the war.

Advances in medicine rank high among the benefactions of war. The sheer number of the wounded and sick, the possibility—the necessity—of new and radical techniques of surgery, and the focus of effort that war inevitably brings all combine to make times of war periods of major medical advancement, with incalculable boons for posterity. The whole field of prosthetics, for example, opened up in World War I—to be enormously advanced in the Second War—and with it came widespread relief from the obvious disfigurements of war, so abundant and ubiquitous after the Civil War.

Revolution and reform are common accompaniments of modern national wars. America underwent no political revolution as the consequence of either world war, but in each the acceleration of social and economic reforms and the germination of still other reforms to be accomplished later were striking. Not many wartime reforms long survived the wars, but their pattern was indelibly impressed on the reform mind. Without doubt the long overdue enfranchisement of women, which took place immediately after the First War, as did Prohibition, each the subject of a constitutional amendment, was the fruit in large part of women's conspicuous service during the war in a variety of roles, military and civil, in offices and in factories. The cause of the illiterate was stimulated by the appalling results of the mass literacy tests given recruits in the war; the cause of the unorganized worker was advanced by the special allowance for union labor during the war; the real stimulus to the work toward racial and ethnic equality that has been a prominent part of the social history of the last sixty or so years came from federal agencies in the First World War. It is a matter of frequent note by historians that almost everywhere war needs inspire, in the interest of equity and of social stability, more "socialist" reforms than does the ideology of socialism. . . .

War is a tried and true specific when a people's moral values become stale and flat. It can be a productive crucible for the remaking of key moral meanings and the strengthening of the sinews of society. This is not always the case, as the American scene during the Vietnam War made painfully clear. But that war is more nearly the exception than the rule. Even our divisive, sanguinary, radical Civil War produced a reseating of values, with the nation for the first time exceeding the regions and states in political importance.

Rarely has the sense of national community been stronger than it was in America during the Great War. True, that sense had to be artificially stimulated by a relentless flow of war propaganda from Washington and a few other pricks of conscience, but by the end of the war a stronger national consciousness and sense of cohesion were apparent. But, as we know in today's retrospect, with these gains came distinct losses in constitutional birthright.

All wars of any appreciable length have a secularizing effect upon engaged societies, a diminution of the authority of old religious and moral values and a parallel elevation of new utilitarian, hedonistic, or pragmatic values. Wars, to be successfully fought, demand a reduction in the taboos regarding life, dignity, property, family, and religion; there must be nothing of merely moral nature left standing between the fighting forces and victory, not even, or especially, taboos on sexual encounters. Wars have an individualizing effect upon their involved societies, a loosening of the accustomed social bond in favor of a tightening of the military ethic. Military, or at least war-born, relationships among individuals tend to supersede relationships of family, parish, and ordinary walks of life. Ideas of chastity, modesty, decorum, respectability change quickly in wartime.

They did in Puritan-rooted America during World War I—changed radically in many cases, and irreversibly. Mars and Venus cavorted, as they always had in time of war, and not least in America. When the brave young doughboy in the AEF was about to go overseas, perhaps to his death, couldn't his sweetheart, even the girl next door, both honor and thrill her swain? Of course she could—in life and voluminously in fiction. The relaxation not only of ancient rules and dogmas in the spheres of marriage and family, religion and morals, but also of styles of music, art, literature, and education, although concentrated in the cities, nevertheless permeated the entire nation.

So, above all, did the new spirit of materialistic hedonism, the spirit of "eat, drink, and be merry" with or without the "for tomorrow we die," capture the American mind during the war. The combination of government-mandated scarcities in some areas, as in meat, sugar, and butter, and the vast amount of expendable money from wages and profits in the hands of Americans led to a new consumer syndrome, one that has only widened ever since World War I and has had inestimable impact upon the American economy. Manufacture of consumer goods directed at the individual rather than the family greatly increased, further emphasizing the new individualism and the new hedonism of American life.

The American Way of Life proved both during and after the Great War to be exportable, to peoples all over the world. These peoples may have had an inadequate grasp at the end of the 1920s of just where America was geographically and just what it was made of mentally and morally, but they had acquired during the decade a lively sense of Coca-Cola, the Hamburger, Hollywood Movies, Jazz, Flappers, Bootleg Gin, and Gangsters. The flapper came close to being America's First Lady in the movie houses of India, China, Latin America, and other abodes of what today we call the Third World. On the evidence of tickets bought, they adored what they saw almost as much as did the American people. Despite Prohibition, drinking was in to a degree it had never achieved when legal—that is, among young people of both sexes but generally middle-class by the end of the twenties. The gangster and the cowboy both achieved a fame in that decade earlier denied their prototypes.

The 1920s was par excellence the Age of Heroes. The age had begun in April 1917 when soldiers, from Black Jack Pershing at the top down to Sergeant York, were given novel worship by Americans at home. The spell lasted through the twenties to include heroes of the industrial world like Ford and Rockefeller; of the aviation world like Lindbergh and Earhart; of the sports world like Babe Ruth, Red Grange, Knute Rockne; and of the movies like Chaplin, Fairbanks, Swanson, and Pickford. To this day names such as these are more likely to come off the American tongue than are those of any living heroes.

Almost everyone and everything became larger than life for Americans during the First World War. This began with the armed forces we sent over to Europe, a million and a half strong by the end of the war. Promotions were numerous and so were medals of one degree or other for valor, each with full publicity on the scene and back home. No military breast looked dressed unless rows of ribbons and galaxies of medals adorned it. Rife as decorations were, though, in World War I, these were almost as nothing compared with World War II. And the tendency has heightened immeasurably since that war. One illustration will suffice: In the recent, embarrassingly awkward invasion of tiny Grenada, when three American services, army, navy, and marines, were brought to combat six hundred expatriate Cuban construction workers, less than half of them armed, victory, if that be the word, was celebrated by the issuance of eight thousand decorations—there and back in Washington.

As is so often the case in history, what began in the military spread quickly to nonmilitary society during the First World War. Under George Creel, President Wilson's czar of war propaganda, about whose activities I shall say something in the next chapter, the custom arose of Home Front awards, honors, and decorations. Farmer of the Week, Worker of the Month, Lawyer of the Year, Surgeon of the Decade—these and many, many other honors festooned once quiet, modest, and shy America. The custom lasted, growing spectacularly during the 1920s, slackening somewhat in the 1930s, but regaining speed during World War II and thereafter. Today American professions spend uncountable hours giving awards to themselves. The academic profession probably leads, with journalism a close second, but lawyers, bankers, and dry cleaners are not far behind either.

A possibly more important, more creative change that came with the Great War in America was in language, written as well as spoken. It became obviously bolder than it had ever been in American history—yet another boon, or casualty, of the Great War and its smashing of old icons of respectability and conventionality. In journalism the tabloid flourished, and a newspaper vernacular came close to driving out the statelier papers such as the Boston *Transcript* and the New York *Sun*. Just as newspaper reporters had at last found a prose that brought the realities of war a little closer to readers, so, in the 1920s, they found a prose for the retailing of sex, murder, scandal, and other of the seamier aspects of life that was far more vivid than anything before. One of the great accomplishments of

the respected novelists, dramatists, and critics—Hemingway, Dos Passos, Fitzgerald, Anderson, O'Neill, Mencken, and others—in the twenties was a sharper, terser, more evocative language than had prospered in the Gilded Age.

All in all, the America that came out from a mere year and a half of the Great War was as transformed from its former self as any nation in history. The transformation extended to fashions and styles, to methods of teaching in the schools, to a gradual letting down of the barriers between men and women and between the races, to informalities of language as well as simple habits at home and in the workplace. . . .

THE LOOSE INDIVIDUAL

Repeatedly in history the combination of war and political centralization leads to a fraying effect upon the social fabric. Threads are loosened by the tightening of power at the center. Dr. Johnson once told Boswell of a man in London he knew who "hung loose upon society." Loose in the sense of the loose cannon, the ship that slips its hawser, the dog its leash, the individual his accustomed moral restraints.

Without doubt there are a great many loose individuals in American society at the present time: loose from marriage and the family, from the school, the church, the nation, job, and moral responsibility. What sociologists are prone to call social disintegration is really nothing more than the spectacle of a rising number of individuals playing fast and loose with other individuals in relationships of trust and responsibility. From the right level, it could all look like what physicists call a Brownian movement, one in which molecules fly about in no discernible patterns. It is not entropy, as Henry and Brooks Adams thought, but Brownian. The cause may not lie within the group but in some distant magnet, such as the centralized state or capitalism become seductive, which loosens the individual's relationships with family and other ascribed institutions.

Tocqueville put his finger on political centralization, upon "despotism," in his word, as the principal cause of the waves of egoism, selfishness, and self-seeking which from time to time roll over societies—as has been the case in the West at least since post-Peloponnesian Athens, the age that dismayed Plato and led to *The Republic*. Tocqueville's own France of the early nineteenth century—the France, too, of Balzac and his brilliant landscapes and portraits of the French social and economic scene in *The Human Comedy*—was in many respects like our own at the present time in America.

The chief aspect of the society around him was, for Tocqueville, the eroding away of traditional associations like family, social class, and "craft fraternities" of economic life. With the disappearance of such associations the individual is left freer and freer of the restraints which normally establish checks upon behavior. The government, Tocqueville argues, far from trying to impede this erosion of limits, encourages it in the interest of its own power.

Money becomes the common denominator of human life. It acquires an "extreme mobility" and "everybody is feverishly intent on making money. . . . Love of gain, a fondness for business careers, the desire to get rich at all costs . . . quickly become ruling passions under a despotic government."[2] Government is the primary force in it all; such government weakens where it strengthens: weakens normal social authority as it strengthens itself through laws, prohibitions, and taxes. As the blood rushes to the head of society, it leaves anemic the local and regional extremities.

Others, however, including Burke, Carlyle, and Marx, have made the economic factor central in the process of loosening ties and multiplying loose individuals. It was the vast debt of France, Burke insisted, that formed the background against which "a great monied interest had insensibly grown up, and with it, a great power. . . . The monied power was long looked on with rather an evil eye by the people. They saw it connected with their distresses, and aggravating them. . . . The monied interest is in its nature more ready for any adventure, and its possessors more disposed to new enterprises. Being of recent acquisition, it falls in more naturally with any novelties. It is therefore the kind of wealth which will be resorted to by all who wish for change."[3]

Burke gives the label "new dealers" to the members of this monied class. Later Carlyle, responding to what seemed to him a "spiritual emptiness" of his age, called in the "cash nexus" as the main force. Cash payment, he wrote, is "the sole nexus between man and man." Relationships of kin and neighborhood which had been fundamental in human society for countless ages were of a sudden, as it seemed, transposing themselves into relationships of money alone. Not long after, Marx and Engels in the *Manifesto* wrote of the bourgeoisie that "wherever it has got the upper hand, [it] has put an end to all feudal, patriarchal, idyllic relations. It has pitilessly torn asunder the motley feudal ties that bound man to his 'natural superiors,' and has left remaining no other nexus between man and man than naked self-interest, than callous 'cash payment.'"

Two ideal types come to mind which give emphasis as well as perspective to the kind of society that Carlyle and Marx sought to limn. In the first, possibly the kind that Marx called primitive communism, all relationships in a community are formed solely of the trust, allegiance, fealty, and responsibility which emanate from the kinship roles of the members of the community. No monetary or other denominator exists to dilute the directness of the social bond.

In the second ideal type, there are no such personal, role-determined relationships at all in society. Every act of service, responsibility, protection, and aid to others is an act presupposing or calling for monetary exchange, for cash payment. What individuals do for their spouses, for their children and kinsmen, for neighbors and all other common partners in the business of maintaining family, job, citizenship, and even personal identity itself, rests upon the cash nexus and nothing else.

Most Americans, if asked which of the two ideal types just described most resembles American society at the present time, would doubtless choose the second, and who is to say they are wrong? It is evident that while ancient personal values of trust, loyalty, and selfless service to others have by no means disappeared, they do not count as much in the marketplace as they once did. And "marketplace" as a setting has come to include more and more relationships once declared utterly alien to it. When Balzac said that "the power of a five-franc note has become sovereign," he was referring to the France of the post–Napoleonic age. The power of the five-dollar bill, sufficiently exerted, is enough to open all doors in America today.

The loose individual is a familiar figure in our age. Whether in the role of the deviant, delinquent, alienated, anomic, bored, narcissistic, as the case may be, he displaces a good deal of social atmosphere. Beginning with the economy, I want to suggest in this chapter some of the haunts of our ubiquitous nonhero.

The economy is rich in such figures. I take "economy" in its proper, large sense to include in our day evangelists of the television ministries, who alone form an economic system of profit and loss running into the billions; the baseball, football, and basketball stars; the university, once as noneconomic in function as a monastery, but no longer; and the now thick crowd of ex-generals, ex-admirals, ex-ambassadors, and ex-presidents who, whether in lecture fee, corporate directorship, book authorship, or consulting business, demonstrate how often and quickly the revolving door turns.

I shall come back to these individuals; but let us first look at the economy proper, site of property and profit in the old sense. Almost half a century ago, the distinguished Harvard economist Joseph Schumpeter, in his *Capitalism, Socialism and Democracy,* laid out clearly the essential processes leading to the business and financial scene of the present. Schumpeter referred to an "evaporation" of property; more particularly, an "Evaporation of Industrial Property" and an "Evaporation of Consumer Property," both reflecting a historical trend of tidal proportions that had been going on in the West and especially in America over the past century. The effect of Schumpeter's evaporation of industrial property—looking at the matter solely from the property-holder's viewpoint—was the substitution of the "soft" property of shares of stock and bonds for the "hard" property of land, buildings, and machines that the property-holder had once managed as well as owned in the passive sense and had been very much a part of in its operation. Independently of volition such a property-holder had a distinct stake in society, a role of social responsibility based upon day-to-day mingling with managers, workers, and consumers.

Very different is the "evaporated" property owner, typically possessing shares of stock existing in their own seemingly detached, stock market world, independent of their owner's will beyond the buying and selling of the shares. There is far less stake in society in this kind of property. After all, a single safe-deposit box can hold many millions of dollars of property, the whole requiring little of the attention and responsibility that are mandatory when property exists in the forms of land, buildings, and machinery. An atmosphere of not only impersonality but irresponsibility is created by evaporated property. The fabled miser hoarding his gold must be changed as metaphor to something like the man-about-town enjoying his debentures, if we are to do justice to the present age. Less and less seems to depend upon the traditional virtues of prudence and social responsibility in the husbanding of one's wealth, and more and more depends upon Fortuna. Thus the atmosphere of the gambling casino begins to permeate not only one's economic but also one's familial and community life.

The evaporation of hard property makes for a liquefied atmosphere that alternates in individual lives from trickle to cloudburst. We learn to travel lightly on the principle that he who does so can eat up vaster distances in a lifetime. Above all, travel alone so far as possible; friends, relatives, wards are all hostages to fortune. A house as compared with a condominium or rental is a drag on one's existence. *Ecrasez l'infamie!*

It is evident that as the result of the two evaporations, we have the foundation prepared for a very different kind of capitalism from that of a century ago. More and more capitalism tends to "exalt the monetary unit" over the type of property that theoretically alone gives the monetary unit its value.

Central to this process of evaporation of the two kinds of property, producer and consumer, is the profoundly changed character of the family. Despite the myth of economic man, of the "individual enterpriser," the chief dynamism of capitalism was for a long time provided by the middle-class family—a family that until recently considered itself as inseparable from the future as from present and past. The typical capitalist did not work for himself; he was not a creature of atomistic self-interest. He worked for his family, meaning chiefly his children and their children, and thereby for the future—so vital to long-run investment. Schumpeter writes:

> In order to realize what all this means for the efficiency of the capitalist engine of production we need only recall that the family and the family home used to be the typically bourgeois kind of profit motive. Economists have not always given due weight to this fact. When we look more closely at their idea of the self-interest of entrepreneurs and capitalists, we cannot fail to discover that the results it was supposed to produce are really not at all what one would expect from the rational self-interest of the detached individual or the childless couple who no longer look at the world through the windows of a family home. Consciously or unconsciously they analyzed the behavior of a man whose views and motives are shaped by such a home and who means to work and to save primarily for wife *and children.*[4]

From devotion to family, not from ineluctable, imperishable "instinct to truck and barter," to advance oneself solely in the interest of power and status—thus came the dynamic of capitalism as the West knew it prior to the present day. Thus comes the dynamic of the capitalism of the Western Pacific Rim nations today. From consecration to, and willingness to sacrifice for, the family, then—rather than from religion—came the entrepreneur's motivation and discipline, his willingness to sacrifice for the future. No abstract, amorphous future was involved; it was literally the future as embodied in children, grandchildren, and great-grandchildren that seems to have mattered most to the entrepreneur of old. To work for family—the family-in-time—necessitated forbearance and sacrifice. You chose between spending annual income on self and its desires or on future generations who would carry your name proudly for all posterity. If you chose the first, you were Dr. Johnson's individual "hanging loose upon society"; if the second, you were Thomas Mann's Buddenbrooks of first and founding generation. But forbearance and prudence and an eye to future generations of family did not at all crowd out a certain type of spending: the type manifest in stately town house, perhaps in a house on the seashore for summer use, in a staff, however small, of servants, preferably those living in. As Schumpeter observes, all these and like attributes attested to the stake one had in society, the success with which a possible family dynasty in commerce was being met at an early stage. Even so, ultimate grace was the product of saving and investing, sacrificing in the present for the future. Schumpeter writes:

> The capitalist process, by substituting a mere parcel of shares for the walls of and machines in a factory, takes the life out of property. . . . And this evaporation of what we may term the material substance of property—its visible and touchable reality—affects not only the attitudes of holders but also of the workmen and of the public generally. Dematerialized, defunctionalized and absentee ownership does not impress and call forth moral allegiance as the vital form of property did. Eventually there will be *nobody* left who really cares to stand for it—nobody within and nobody without the precincts of the big concerns.[5]

Morals inevitably suffer, meaning particularly the morals of honesty and loyalty to others. Morals are no emanations from heaven; everywhere, from the beginning of conscience in the human race, from the time when the human mind first made the astounding leap from "is" to "ought," what we call morals are firmly set in what the Romans called the mores, customs and habits of age and sanctity. As a result of the disappearance or sharp reduction of the disciplines upon the self which went inescapably with older kinds of property, and of the rise of the present widely spread monetary unit of property—that is, of liquidity, of cash nexus—morality becomes expendable. Who needs it?

ENDNOTES

1. Cited in Martin Gilbert, *Winston S. Churchill.* Vol. 4, pp. 913–14. Boston: Houghton Mifflin Co., 1966.
2. Alexis de Tocqueville, *The Old Regime and the French Revolution* (1856). Doubleday Anchor Books, 1955. Foreword, xiii.
3. *Reflections on the Revolution in France* (1790). New York: Holt, Rinehart and Winston, 1959. p. 133f.
4. Joseph Schumpeter, *Capitalism, Socialism and Democracy.* New York: Harper and Brothers, 1942, p. 160.
5. Schumpeter, p. 142.

QUESTIONS ON NISBET

1. How did World War I change the societies of Europe and America? How does Nisbet's account of pre–World War I America compare to that offered by Daniel Bell?

2. In what ways did participation in WWI provide the impetus for a new role for the central government? Why does Nisbet believe that the growth of state power "leads to a fraying effect upon the social fabric?" What is meant by this metaphor of a "fabric?" What is a "loose individual?"

3. Nisbet describes how the economic system provides one explanation of the "loose individual." What type of property holding plays a crucial role in altering the norms of capitalism? How do altered conceptions of the family relate to changes in capitalism? Do you think that this analysis is correct?

FOR FURTHER READING

Acton, H. B. *The Morals of Markets and Other Essays.* Edited by David Gordon and Jeremy Shearmur. Indianapolis, Ind.: Liberty Fund, 1993.

Buchanan, James. "Moral Community, Moral Order, or Moral Anarchy." In *Liberty, Market and State.* Brighton, Sussex: Wheatsheaf Books, 1986.

Collier, James. *The Rise of Selfishness in America.* New York: Oxford University Press, 1991.

Dawson, Christopher. *Religion and the Modern State.* London: Sheed & Ward, 1935.

Durkheim, Emile. *The Division of Labor in Society,* translated by George Simpson. New York: The Free Press, 1933.

Ferguson, Adam. *An Essay on the History of Civil Society* [1767], edited by Fania Oz-Salzberger. Cambridge: Cambridge University Press, 1995.

Fukuyama, Francis. *The Great Disruption: Human Nature and the Reconstitution of Social Order.* New York: Simon & Schuster, 1999.

Himmelfarb, Gertrude. *The De-Moralization of Society: From Victorian Virtues to Modern Values.* New York: Vintage, 1996.

Hirsch, Fred. *Social Limits to Growth.* Cambridge: Harvard University Press, 1976.

Hirshman, Albert O. *The Passions and the Interests: Political Arguments for Capitalism Before Its Triumph.* Princeton, N.J.: Princeton University Press, 1977.

————. "Rival Views of Market Society." In *Rival Views of Market Society and Other Essays.* Cambridge: Harvard University Press, 1992.

Horkheimer, Max. *Eclipse of Reason.* New York: Oxford University Press, 1947.

Jacobs, Jane. *Systems of Survival: A Dialogue on the Moral Foundations of Commerce and Politics.* New York: Vintage, 1992.

Klein, Daniel, ed. *Reputation: Studies in the Voluntary Elicitation of Good Conduct.* Ann Arbor: University of Michigan, 1996.

Lippmann, Walter. *The Good Society.* Boston: Little, Brown and Company, 1943.

McClay, Wilfred M. *The Masterless: Self and Society in Modern America.* Chapel Hill: University of North Carolina Press, 1994.

Robertson, William. *View of the Progress of Society in Europe* (1769), edited by Felix Gilbert. Chicago: University of Chicago Press, 1972.

Rousseau, Jean-Jacques. *Discourse on the Sciences and the Arts* and *Discourse on the Origin of Inequality.* In *Jean-Jacques Rousseau: The Basic Political Writings,* translated by Donald Cress. Indianapolis, Ind.: Hackett Publishing, 1983.

Selznick, Philip. *The Moral Commonwealth: Social Theory and the Promise of Community.* Berkeley: University of California, 1992.

Tönnies, Ferdinand. *Community and Society* [1887], translated by Charles P. Loomis. East Lansing: Michigan State University Press, 1957.

Wuthnow, Robert, ed. *Between States and Markets: The Voluntary Sector in Comparative Perspective.* Princeton, N. J.: Princeton University Press, 1991.

Economic Growth, Progress, and Culture

The history of the human race as a whole can be regarded as the realization of a hidden plan of nature to bring about an internally—and for this purpose also externally—perfect political constitution as the only possible state within which all natural capacities of mankind can be developed completely.

Immanuel Kant[1]

The humanistic way of thinking, which has proclaimed itself our guide, did not admit the existence of intrinsic evil in man, nor did it see any task higher than the attainment of happiness on earth. It started modern Western civilization on the dangerous trend of worshipping man and his material needs. Everything beyond physical well-being and the accumulation of material goods, all other human requirements and characteristics of a subtler and higher nature, were left outside the area of attention of state and social systems, as if human life did not have any higher meaning.

Aleksandr I. Solzhenitsyn[2]

Culture may even be described as that which makes life worth living. And it is what justifies other peoples and other generations in saying, when they contemplate the remains and the influence of an extinct civilization, that it was worth while *for that civilization to have existed.*

T. S. Eliot[3]

No nation can last, which has made a mob of itself, however generous at heart. It must discipline its passions, and direct them, or they will discipline it, one day, with scorpion whips. Above all, a nation cannot last as a money-making mob: it cannot with impunity,—it cannot with existence,—go on despising literature, despising science, despising art, despising nature, despising compassion, and concentrating its soul on Pence.

John Ruskin[4]

1. "Idea for a Universal History with a Cosmopolitan Purpose [1784]," in *Kant's Political Writings,* edited by Hans Reiss (Cambridge: Cambridge University Press, 1970), 50.

2. "A World Split Apart," in *Solzhenitsyn at Harvard,* edited by Ronald Berman (Washington, D.C.: Ethics and Public Policy Center, 1980), 16–17.

3. *Notes Towards the Definition of Culture,* in Eliot, *Christianity and Culture* (New York: Harcourt Brace, 1948), 100.

4. "Of Kings' Treasuries," Lecture One of *Sesame and Lilies* [1865], in *Unto This Last and Other Writings,* edited by Clive Wilmer (Harmondsworth: Penguin, 1985), 274.

The idea of progress has never been completely absent from the thought of Western civilization. The ancient Greeks utilized the idea of natural growth, appealing (as did Aristotle) to the notion of the actualization of latent potential. In the first century B.C., the Epicurean thinker, Lucretius, articulated a theory of the progressive development of the universe, including therein an evolutionary account of moral and social order.[5] Ancient Judaism looked forward to a future of perfection, an idea that the early Christians fused with the Greek conception of growth. Drawing from the thought of St. Augustine, who lived in the fourth century, Christianity emphasized the idea that there could be a renewal of earthly life once individuals and societies were free of corruption. However, not until the eighteenth century did the idea of the inevitable improvement or progression of society take hold and animate so many thinkers, growing increasingly popular in the nineteenth century. In 1851, the first international exhibition designed to celebrate human achievement was held at the Crystal Palace in London, and other such exhibitions would continue throughout the remainder of the century. Even today it is the implicit, but no less solid, belief of many of us that, on the whole, the world is developing and improving over time.

The idea of progress did not emerge in isolation from other ideas or events, and therefore it is not surprising that this idea would take hold in the eighteenth century, the century of Enlightenment and of prodigious economic advances. There is no doubt, then, that the modern idea of progress is inextricably linked with the idea of economic growth, technological improvement, intellectual advance, and, in some cases, moral and cultural improvement. Thus, the very idea of progress generates questions concerning culture and whether the culture of progress and economic growth is the culture that we should want. To examine these questions, let us turn first to the idea of progress and its relation to economic growth. We will subsequently examine some questions concerning culture and consumer consumption.

PROGRESS AND ECONOMIC GROWTH

The Very Idea of Progress

The idea of progress entails a specific response to the question of whether history moves in cycles, is merely a series of contingent and unrelated events, or manifests an evolutionary improvement. Thus, implicit in the idea of *progressive* change is the assessment that such change is an improvement; in other words, any judgment that history is moving progressively presupposes the desirability of such change. One of the first scholars of progress, J. G. Bury, states, therefore, that the idea of progress "means that civilization has moved, is moving, and will move in a desirable direction."[6] To examine this concept more fully, let us summarize several aspects of the idea of progress.

There is first the issue of whether progressive change is *inevitable*. Is progress the manifestation of certain laws of history operating in some necessary fashion, or is it a *contingent* series of events which might easily have been otherwise? Second, there may be *types* of progress: technological, intellectual, moral, or cultural. Although many advocates of progress assume that these types move in tandem, it is possible that one aspect of society may progress while another regresses. (Such indeed was the view of Jean-Jacques Rousseau [1712–1778], who argued that despite the progress in the arts and sciences, humanity had undergone a moral degeneration. See the introduction to section CI, pp. 516–517, and below.) A third matter concerns the *rate* of change, whether progress advances slowly and incrementally or whether it occurs in leaps. There remains, finally, the *mechanism* or *agents* of progress. Is the progressive change brought about by human agency (as many of the eighteenth-century thinkers maintained)? Is it the ineluctable outcome of some laws of history (as some nineteenth-century thinkers believed)? Or is it the result of divine agency or providence? These are but a few of the questions to be considered when examining the idea of progress.

The Idea of Economic Growth

The idea of growth, as well as that of progressive improvement, was not unknown prior to the eighteenth century, but it was during this century of Enlightenment and commercial advance that the idea of progress grew so prominent. It is not surprising, therefore, that there is at least a contingent and historical link between the emergence of industry and commerce and the increasing attractiveness of an idea of progress. To examine this connection, let us summarize the nature of economic growth. What is it and how is it manifested? Today we often think of economic growth in relation to a nation's Gross Domestic Product (GDP), a standard measure of growth.

---

5. *On the Nature of Things*, Book V.

6. J. B. Bury, *The Idea of Progress: An Inquiry into Its Origin and Growth* (New York: Macmillan, 1932), 2.

However, what underlies any increase in GDP is an increase in the measurable net output per person. Evidence of economic growth can be found not only in larger incomes per capita but in greater economic security, increased leisure, new and greater opportunities, and improvements in health, housing, safety, and the quality of goods and services. These are some of the typical manifestations of economic growth, but so are these goods which we desire; in that sense, these goods are indicators not just of growth but of progress. That progress is linked to commercial development is a key to understanding the genesis of the modern idea of progress.

Progress and Commerce: The Eighteenth Century

For many eighteenth-century thinkers, especially those of France and Scotland (the twin centers of the Enlightenment) a proper understanding of history revealed that societies progressively developed from a primitive era to a more refined or polished age, usually typified by commercial development. The "stage theory" of social development, which emphasized the importance of a society's economic organization for overall development, was first adumbrated by Turgot, who noted four stages of society: hunting, pastoral, agricultural, and commercial. Later in that century, Condorcet (1743–1794) elucidated a more elaborate theory of progress emphasizing the role of science in abolishing the dead hand of ignorance. And in Prussia, Immanuel Kant (1724–1804) maintained that implicit in history is the continual realization of autonomous reason, whose ultimate attainment requires a peaceful confederation of nations.[7] A group of Scottish thinkers also articulated theories of the progress of nations, including Adam Smith (1723–1790) and others, most of whom adopt the four-stage theory of society, noting that a nation's economic organization had significant consequences on its overall social, cultural and political structures.[8] The eighteenth-century view of history held that progress was an unin-

tended and incremental product of human responses to discrete problems and circumstances. History was progressive, rather than regressive or cyclical, and the agents of the progression were human beings rather than divine forces.

Rousseau's Dissent

Not all of those who developed theories of social development believed that this development was culminating in a beneficial state. In his *Discourse on the Origin of Inequality* (1755), Jean-Jacques Rousseau traces the development of inequality as it emerges from the division of labor and property, exploring how the evolution of modern society moves us ever further from a happier but less developed state. As individuals become dependent on one another, their varying property relations introduce an increasing inequality that alters the manner in which they relate to one another and ultimately leads to despotism. Rousseau is one of the first to challenge the link between economic development and moral progress; this challenge would be renewed in the nineteenth century, kept aloft not only by Karl Marx but also by figures associated with more conservative views.

The Nineteenth Century

In the nineteenth century, those who advocated progress appealed less to human agency than to the laws of history. The German philosopher Georg Hegel (1770–1831) argued that Spirit or *geist* unfolded itself in human society until it reached its zenith in the Prussian state. The Hegelian idea was appropriated and reversed by Karl Marx (1818–1883), who contends that the foundation of progress is not Spirit but matter, specifically, the material forces of economic production. History develops through the ever-changing modes of production and the concomitant conflict of classes, with oppression ending only in the final stage of communism. Although some utopian thinkers, such as Saint Simon (1760–1825) and August Comte (1798–1857)[9] articulated distinct versions

7. Marquis de Condorcet, *Sketch for a Historical Picture of the Progress of the Human Mind* (1795); Immanuel Kant, "Idea for a Universal History with a Cosmopolitan Purpose" and "Perpetual Peace," both in *Kant's Political Writings,* edited by Hans Reiss.

8. See, for example, Adam Smith, *Lectures on Jurisprudence* [1762–3, 1766], edited by R. L. Meek, D. D. Raphael, and P. Stein (Indianapolis, Ind.: Liberty Classics, 1982). Adam Ferguson, in his *An Essay on the History of Civil Society* [1767], edited by Fania Oz-Salzberger (Cambridge: Cambridge University Press, 1995) offers a three-stage version of progress. For an account of eighteenth-century stage theories of progress, see Ronald L. Meek, *Social Science and the Ignoble Savage* (Cambridge: Cambridge University Press, 1976).

9. For the relevant works of Hegel, see *Hegel's Phenomenology of Spirit* [1807], translated by A. V. Miller (Oxford: Oxford University Press, 1977), and *Hegel's Philosophy of Right* [1821], translated by T. M. Knox (Oxford: Oxford University Press, 1967). For a selection of the writings of Saint Simon, see *Selected Writings,* translated by F. M. H. Markham (Oxford: Oxford University Press, 1952). For Comte, see *Introduction to Positive Philosophy,* edited by Frederick Ferré (Indianapolis, Ind.: Hackett Publishing, 1988) or *Auguste Comte and Positivism: The Essential Writings,* edited by Gertrud Lenzer (New Brunswick, N.J.: Transaction, 1998).

of a theory of progress, other thinkers, including some in the twentieth century, began to raise questions as to whether or not economic, social, and political development are equivalent to any sort of genuine progress.

DOUBTS ABOUT PROGRESS

Knowledge and Progress

For a variety of reasons, thinkers began to raise doubts about whether there were negative consequences to the continued development of society. Some of these doubts had to do with the progress of science. Here it is worth recalling that, even prior to the eighteenth century, new discoveries in science sparked new considerations of nature, inspiring thinkers to believe that knowledge would insure progress and motivating them to search for new foundations for science. Thinkers as diverse as Francis Bacon (1561–1626), Thomas Hobbes (1588–1679), and René Descartes (1596–1650) all believed that the application of the proper methodology would permit intellectual advancement and increase our power over nature. For example, Bacon sought to draw a sharp distinction between the new science and that of the past:

> It is idle to expect any great advancement in science from the superinducing and engrafting of new things upon old. We must begin anew from the very foundations, unless we would revolve forever in a circle with mean and contemptible progress.[10]

The French philosopher Descartes, having articulated certain methodological rules by which to inquire into nature, regarded his philosophy as a practical antidote to speculation and asserted that we would now be able to know

> . . . the action of fire, air, and stars, the heavens, and all other bodies in our environment, as distinctly as we know the various crafts of our artisans, and could apply them in the same way to all appropriate uses and thus make ourselves masters and owners of nature.[11]

For some, however, the new scientific account of nature and the ensuing progress in knowledge serve to disenchant the world, leaving human beings in a uni-verse in which nature appears as an alien being. Other thinkers come to doubt that we should be "masters . . . of nature." Apart from these apprehensions associated with the study of nature, others expressed disquiet about the increasing "rationalization" and "bureaucratization" of society. Ferdinand Tönnies (see Section CI, p. 517) suggested, late in the nineteenth century, that the communal organization of *Gemeinschaft* had given way to a more rational organization of society, *Gesellschaft,* whose features included increased trade, urbanization, and the ennobling of reason. At the turn of the century, Max Weber (1864–1920) argued that modern society had become rationalized and bureaucratized, both in the commercial and governmental sphere.

These concerns reveal three types of critical queries concerning progress: (a) Are there side-effects or costs associated with progress? (b) Even if there is little doubt that progress has taken place in some area(s), is it also the case that progress has occurred in all spheres? Or is progress in one sphere a catalyst for *regress* in some other areas? And (c) Even if there is progress in the technological, intellectual, moral, and cultural spheres, is such widespread progress sufficient for happiness? Let us consider this last point more carefully.

Progress and Happiness

It might be assumed that economic growth not only ensures progress but happiness as well. One argument for this conclusion connects economic growth with human welfare. If human well-being, or happiness, is determined by the satisfaction of human preferences, and if economic growth insures ever-increasing satisfaction of preferences, then economic growth insures that human happiness should increase along with economic growth. The problem with this equation is that even if economic growth insures an increasing satisfaction of preferences, it is not obvious that human welfare is reducible to the satisfaction of preferences or, if it is, that economic growth can satisfy enough of the relevant preferences. After all, it seems that happiness involves more than just the acquisition of goods and services available on the market. Certain forms of human relationships, including family or friends, not to mention the experience of love, knowledge, art, and play, may not be describable as the mere satisfaction of preferences; on the other hand, if they are so describable, these preferences are not necessarily included within the goods and services produced on the market. It

---

10. Francis Bacon, *The New Organon* [1620] *and Related Writings,* edited by Fulton H. Anderson (New York: Liberal Arts Press, 1960), aphorism 31.

11. Descartes, *Discourse on the Method of Rightly Directing One's Reason and of Seeking Truth in the Sciences* [1637], in *Descartes: Philosophical Writings,* translated and edited by Elizabeth Anscombe and Peter Thomas Geach (New York: Bobbs-Merrill, 1971), Part VI.

seems plausible, then, that economic growth is one part of welfare but, although relevant to happiness, it is not sufficient for it. None of this is to deny that economic growth (and progress), especially the progress of technology and science, may serve not only to satisfy preferences but to remove significant harms or inconveniences. However, the removal of harm is not the same as the production of something inherently good or valuable and it is there that happiness may reside.[12]

Agrarian Versus Industrial

Some of those to cast doubt on the value of progress, especially in the guise of science and industrialism, were the group of American intellectuals and writers known as the "Southern Agrarians." Writers such as John Crowe Ransom (1888–1974), Robert Penn Warren (1905–1989), Allen Tate (1899–1979), and Donald Davidson (1893–1968) sought to defend an agrarian culture, then situated in the South of the United States, against what they viewed as the overweening pretensions of science, technology, and industrialism. Their collection of essays, published in 1930,[13] sought—without romanticizing the "Old South"—to reaffirm the value of community life, the importance of religious belief, a proper humility toward the natural environment, the importance of the situated place, and the vocation of the farmer. Arrayed against them they perceived a changing world in which individuals were animated by acquisitive impulses, enamored of science and technology, inclined less to religiosity than to rationalism, and encouraged to identify with a centralized state rather than region and place. What many would celebrate as a culture of progress, the agrarians saw as a culture that neglected the very heart of human life.

Indeed, the agrarians' concerns were primarily *cultural* in that their doubts about progress included an unease about the effects of industry on a way of life which, in their view, was congenial to the human spirit. Their concerns point out that the effects of economic growth and progress extend into the culture itself, eliciting a variety of worries, not all of them moral. After all, there are certain matters that we may "care about," matters that have a singular importance but which are not matters of moral concern.[14] Some of these may be matters concerning a way of life, or culture. Historically, these have arisen—as in the early nineteenth century, or in the agrarian South of the early twentieth century—just as economic growth, among other changes (including political), introduces significant transformations into a society. As commerce, technology, and industrialization grew, individuals began to consider more fully the very idea of culture and to evaluate their own culture in light of dramatic social and economic changes. Let us turn to consider the question of culture, especially the extent to which the contemporary society exemplifies a *consumer* culture.

CULTURE AND CONSUMERISM

Culture and Civilization

The concept of *culture* has a variety of meanings, one of the more notable of which is its use as a counterpart to the notion of "civilization." In fact, in the nineteenth century German scholars introduced a distinction between *Kultur* and *Zivilisation,* using the former to refer to the creative activities and products of art, music and literature, the latter to refer to the legal and social structure of a society, as well as more general beliefs and values. In other instances the term "civilization" has been employed to refer, more narrowly, to the underlying norms and legal structure of a society, whereas "culture" has served, more broadly, to indicate creative activities *as well as* the more general knowledge, beliefs, ideals, and values of a society. It is in this sense (admittedly broad) that we employ the term, taking the idea of "culture" to refer to the ideational and symbolic aspects of a society, whether these concern the kinds of knowledge typical of the society, the beliefs and values of the people, or their customs and attitudes. If it is true that, as Richard Weaver writes, a person possesses three levels of reflection, "specific ideas about things, his general beliefs or convictions, and his metaphysical dream of the world,"[15] then these ideas, beliefs,

---

12. The distinction between negative benefits (the removal of some bad) and positive benefits (the introduction of something good) is discussed by Nicholas Rescher, *Unpopular Essays on Technological Progress* (Pittsburgh: University of Pittsburgh Press, 1980), 5.

13. Twelve Southerners, *I'll Take My Stand: The South and the Agrarian Tradition* (New York: Harper & Brothers, 1930).

14. "It can hardly be disputed that, for most of us, the requirements of ethics are not the only things we care about. Even people who care a great deal about morality generally care still more about other things. They may care more, for instance, about their own personal projects, about certain individuals and groups, and perhaps about various ideals to which they accord commanding authority in their lives but which need not be particularly of an ethical nature." Harry G. Frankfurt, "The Importance of What We Care About," in *The Importance of What We Care About* (Cambridge: Cambridge University Press, 1988), 81.

[15]Richard Weaver, *Ideas Have Consequences* (Chicago: University of Chicago Press, 1948), 18.

and dreams are all part of one's culture. It is in this sense that we might agree with T. S. Eliot's description of culture as "not merely the sum of several activities, but a *way of life.*" [16]

The Marxist View

In considering the relation of culture and commerce, one cannot ignore the Marxist view that seeks to relate ideas, cultural norms and beliefs—consciousness—to an underlying material substratum of economic production. Thus, for Marx a cultural outlook is causally determined by an economic system of production.

> We set out from real, active men, and on the basis of their real life-process we demonstrate the development of the ideological reflexes and echoes of this life-process. . . . Morality, religion, metaphysics, all the rest of ideology and their corresponding forms of consciousness, thus no longer retain the semblance of independence. They have no history, no development; but men, developing their material production and their material intercourse, alter, along with this their real existence, their thinking and the products of their thinking. Life is not determined by consciousness, but consciousness by life. [17]

The sense in which consciousness is determined by economic production is, however, rather complicated. Consciousness is determined by economic systems in that, within an economic system, a dominant or ruling class exerts its power through the prevailing beliefs, concepts, and norms. Thus, a culture reflects the material interests of the ruling class.

> The ideas of the ruling class are in every epoch the ruling ideas: i.e., the class which is the ruling *material* force of society, is at the same time its ruling *intellectual* force. The class which has the means of material production at its disposal, has control at the same time over the means of mental production, so that thereby, generally speaking, the ideas of those who lack the means of mental production are subject to it. The ruling ideas are nothing more than the ideal expression of the dominant material relationships, the dominant material relationships grasped as ideas; hence of the relationships which make the one class the ruling one, therefore, the ideas of its dominance. [18]

16. T. S. Eliot, *Notes Towards the Definition of Culture,* 114.

17. *The German Ideology,* in *The Marx-Engels Reader,* 2d ed., edited by Robert C. Tucker (New York: W. W. Norton, 1978), 154–55.

18. *The German Ideology,* 172–73. For a collection of contemporary essays on Marxism and culture, see *Marxism and the Interpretation of Culture,* edited by Cary Nelson and Lawrence Grossberg (Urbana: University of Illinois Press, 1995).

The Marxist view of the relation of economy and culture is, without doubt, a striking and important one. It seems clear that Marx is not claiming that culture is some sort of direct effect of modes of production; rather, the prevailing culture, or consciousness, reflects the interests of the dominant class which seeks, through various beliefs, values, categories, and norms, to legitimate its rule. However, even if the dominant class seeks to employ cultural categories and beliefs to its advantage, that alone does not show that cultural consciousness is *nothing more* than the interests of the dominant class. And it certainly does not tell us whether a way of life is justifiable or not, for the origins of a mode of consciousness do not, by themselves, reveal whether that way of life is worth pursuing or not.

Culture and Commerce

However, isn't there an important point in the Marxist view? For isn't there, after all, a culture characteristic of market societies? Doesn't the economic system of the market tend to produce a certain way of life? What sort of attitudes, beliefs, or ideals tend to dominate in such a society? In the early nineteenth century some thought that the rise of commerce was creating an industrial society that would destroy traditional lifestyles and rural crafts, encourage acquisitive conduct, and create a mass society interested more in material goods than in higher things. [19] The Southern Agrarians, of the twentieth century, held a similar though not identical view. And for George Simmel, the sociologist, the urban metropolis is symbolic of modern capitalist societies, for the psychological characteristics, attitudes, and habits of the urban individual correlate well with the mentality of commerce.

The question of the relation of an economic system to its culture is a difficult causal question. Despite the concerns of Marx and other social critics, it is not obvious to what extent a culture has a specific (or singular) character and whether that character is a result of the market alone. This important question requires careful analysis if only because a cultural outlook or way of life might be a consequence of a variety of causes or influences. Where some might see a certain phenomenon to be generated by the rules and tendencies of markets, others might locate the cause in, say, the egalitarian tendencies of democracies, or the rhetoric of "rights." Some might consider the features of a culture to be the effect of the size or structure of government or its relation to busi-

19. See, for example, Thomas Carlyle, *Signs of the Times* [1829], Samuel Taylor Coleridge, *The Constitution of Church and State* [1837], and Matthew Arnold, *Culture and Anarchy* [1869].

ness or to the subsidiary groups and institutions of society, including the voluntary social organizations that might exist between government and business. Still others might consider the culture to reflect the influence of Enlightenment rationalism or secularism. Just as the market is often taken to be the unique cause of certain moral effects (see Section CI), so must we be cautious in suggesting that there is a single determinative cause of certain cultural effects.

Contemporary Culture How might contemporary culture be described? To do so is to enter upon slippery, controversial, and ever-shifting terrain, but there is some value in articulating one possible account of certain general aspects of contemporary American public culture (public beliefs, values, and ideals) even if we focus, below, on only one aspect: consumerism. There is first an increasing pluralism on matters of morals and values, even as there is a growing valorization of self-expression, feeling and sentiment, and a strong endorsement of democratic equality and participation. The enterprise of science exerts a general influence as the authority of religion—especially revealed religion—has diminished. There is a celebration of the urban, the glamorous, and the stylish, and a denigration of the rural, the functional, the commonplace, and the traditional. Family structures have changed significantly, as have the strength of bonds between husbands and wives, parents and children. No longer is the familial paradigm taken to be that of mother and father, with well-defined roles; familial hierarchies as well as social hierarchies are discouraged. Mobility is encouraged and the idea of a settled place, or homestead, is forgotten. Along with progress in and fascination with technology, there is a plethora of consumer goods and an almost habitual consumption; a widespread fascination with popular entertainment (television, movies, or sports) is matched by a continual concern with health and fitness.

Such is one description of contemporary American culture, a contestable description whose generalities may bear truth even as they are subject to refutation and debate. Some may find this account apt, others may find that it neglects certain aspects or overgeneralizes. Apart from the question of whether the description is true, there is the question of whether we should *want* the description, or some aspect of it, to be or remain true. Some may wish that certain aspects of the culture were different; others may care about values or projects that are not mentioned in this description. In fact, however, one of the features just noted is a pronounced characteristic of contemporary society (one which many believe to be essential to market societies): the consumption of consumer goods. Let us consider the idea of consumerism and explore how it might pose ethical challenges.

Commodification and Consumerism

It is commonly contended that the culture of the market involves the reduction of everything to an economic good, a commodity, to be bought or sold. This idea of "commodification" finds its source in Marx.[20] Marx distinguishes between an economy in which individuals produce for use, laboring with an eye to the use of the product, and an economy of exchange in which one produces in order to exchange. In an exchange economy, a producer does not know by whom, or for what use, a product will be employed; under capitalism, production for exchange is the rule. If the market tends to commodify everything, then any object, relation, or activity is to be bought or sold or is to be comprehended in terms of the concepts and rhetoric of buying and selling. In a market of commodities, the user is the consumer whose relation to these commodities is often described in terms of an "ethic of consumption" or "consumerism." In the selection below from Jean Baudrillard, we find a portrait of the consumer society with its network of objects displayed in environments constructed so as to encourage shopping, as if shopping itself were a form of living. Should a culture be so easily reducible to a culture of consumption?

Consumerism: Four Formulations

The idea of consumerism is less of a description than an indictment, but it is not at all clear in what the charge consists. A consumer is a buyer of goods and, presumably, a user of the goods bought. Given that this is the case, the charge of consumerism focuses on the (buying) habits of the public, but in what way? There are several distinct formulations of the problem of consumerism:

- that we are too devoted to spending money on the purchase of goods; or
- that we buy goods without sufficient regard to what is truly valuable or good; or
- that the goods we buy are not our autonomous choices but are the result of manipulation by an economic elite; or
- that we regard the *activities* of shopping and buying as a good and valuable feature of our society.

---

20. See chapter 1 ("The Commodity") in *Capital*, vol 1 [1867] edited by Friedrich Engels, translated by Samuel Moore and Edward Aveling (London: Lawrence and Wishart, 1974).

Consumption and Self-Control   Each of these claims is distinct from the others, and there are, no doubt, additional or alternative ways of delineating the problem. The first of these claims seems to imply a thesis of excess. Consumerism is a problem of self-control. The consumption of goods in moderation is fine, but we are too devoted to buying, shopping, selling, and having. Although Aristotle considered the virtue of temperance or self-control to be concerned with pleasures of the body, it is not too much of a stretch to view the over-consumption of material goods as an indulgence or excess in which our material desires are no longer under the control of reason. No doubt there are problems of excess, but how do we determine that one's consumption of goods is excessive? Here we need to consider the second formulation.

Consumerism and Value   The second formulation seems to imply that our buying is not grounded in a conception of the good, or perhaps not in a conception that is distinct from that of momentary pleasure. On this view, the problem with a consumer society is not so much that the consumption occurs as that it takes place in a moral vacuum. Consumers do not really buy with a view to acquiring goods that are necessary for a life lived well; rather, consumers buy merely because the product is there, the money is available, and the neighbors already have *two* of these! Of course, an economist might argue that individual preferences are subjective and that these preferences are revealed in consumer expenditures; for this reason, any choices about goods and services are the best possible ones. However, one must recognize that the subjective preferences referred to by the economists are only the consumer's valuations of goods and services. Even if the economic value of goods and services is the result of individual preferences, the question at issue is what these preferences *ought* to be. That economic value is determined by consumer preferences does not entail that consumers should not consider their consumption in light of a standard of goodness or value. After all, commerce and industry may produce items of questionable taste and value, but they also produce items that serve needs and desires essential to a robust conception of a good life.

Shopping as an End   The third claim suggests that our choices are not autonomous choices but are influenced by clever advertisers and corporate manipulation. Since this is a claim taken up in Section BII, we ignore this interpretation of consumerism, moving instead to the final claim, which focuses on consumerism as a problem of the *activities* of purchasing, buying, and shopping. Of course, it is doubtful that many people self-consciously regard buying and spending as a worthwhile end in itself, for surely these activities are merely the means to secure certain goods. However, if the items that people seek and purchase are of limited value, then one might conclude that it is not the items of consumption that we evaluate so positively but the very activity of shopping, seeking, and spending. Given the commodification of "everything," our lives become structured within cycles of shopping and spending so that we delude ourselves into thinking we must respond to new items placed on the market (shopping) and that the failure to do so is, somehow, a bad thing. What is left unclear is the genesis of these attitudes, if they truly exist.

A Positive Case for the Consumer Society   Despite the negative connotation of consumerism, in the above formulations, it might be argued that the astounding variety and types of goods and services is a positive testament to market competition and freedom. The plethora of goods and services is, perhaps, analogous to the wide variety of journals, magazines, books, and newspapers that are available in a free society. Journals and magazines cater to a wide variety of tastes, interests, and concerns: Some deal in truth, others deal in something less than the truth; some are academic, some nonacademic; some are tasteful, others are decidedly lowbrow. But in the welter of magazines of low or questionable taste and value, there are numerous journals and magazines of high quality, significant interest, and real value. Similarly, in the midst of consumer items of low taste, questionable quality, and dubious necessity, there are items of value, ingenuity, and convenience. One cannot ensure that only quality journals exist unless one allows for the publication of magazines of low quality; similarly, one cannot have consumer products of convenience, value, and ingenuity unless one allows for products of low quality that cater to silly desires, dubious necessity, or irrational whim.

Thus, amidst the criticism of consumerism, it is worth recalling that many of the goods we consume do, in fact, provide convenience and relief from drudgery. Those who wish to dispense with consumer goods and opt for the "simple life" should be prepared for the consequences. (Indeed, some of the persons who are most adept at criticizing contemporary habits of consumption all too often exempt from criticism or evaluation their own consumption of such goods as wines, food, coffees, furniture, clothing, or travel.) It is worth remarking that persons who immigrate to, or visit, commercial societies from lands of poverty or from noncommercial societies are often astounded and gratified at the range and quality of items in market societies. Nonetheless, this does not mean that one should consume to excess or consume without any thought to some conception of a good life. Even in a society characterized by widespread commerce, one need not adopt an attitude of blind consumerism, nor need one assume that buying and selling is the end of life. For if one lives in a market society, then one may elect to buy and sell or to refrain from buying and selling; indeed, even the simple life is not precluded.

Choosing a Way of Life If the debate over consumerism reflects a larger debate about ends and purposes and the content of culture, then we should consider the extent to which a society should permit persons to live in and shape the culture they prefer. In one of the readings which follow, Robert Nozick offers an account of utopia that would permit the flourishing of a wide variety of cultures, thereby allowing room for a society of orgiastic consumption, an agrarian social order, or a form of association redolent of the simple and unadorned life. To consider these matters more fully, let us turn to the reading selections, beginning with Turgot's theory of progress.

THE READINGS

Anne-Robert-Jacques Turgot The first person to articulate the eighteenth-century idea of progress, Turgot analogizes the development of society to that of a human being growing from infancy to adulthood. Even though each age of society offers a multitude of divergent events, these are nonetheless linked together by cause and effect. Various and manifold events are caused by human agents motivated by "self-interest, ambition, and vainglory," but over the course of time morals are improved, knowledge grows, and the nations are "brought closer to one another" until all parts of the globe are united commercially and politically. Focusing in particular on the arts and sciences, Turgot maintains that human nature is uniform even though we are not equal in talents, nor born into the same circumstances. Thus, there will be inequality in the progress of the nations even though all have the same potential to progress. Though Turgot does not elucidate the four stages of society he notes how societies progress from barbarism to agriculture to commercial trade. The knowledge essential for such progress is derived from sensation, but our sensory knowledge requires time to develop as well as freedom from the constraints of (false) religion or political authorities. Even during the conflicts that occurred for several centuries during the Medieval period, there is still an imperceptible im-

provement as commercial towns continue, the universities persevere, Arab learning is transferred to the West, and mechanical knowledge and invention proceed. Turgot concludes by noting how new towns are founded, governments grow more stable, new explorations occur, and new languages develop from Latin.

E. J. Mishan Mishan opens his essay with a summation of the outlook of the "Established Enlightenment," an allegedly enlightened outlook whose main emphasis is that progress in knowledge and wealth has provided for greater social welfare. The growth in knowledge and wealth has made possible gains in education, tolerance, free trade, and immigration and mobility. Having summarized the manifestations of progress made possible by technological and economic advance, Mishan maintains that "the products . . . of 200 years of sustained economic growth in the West" include ever growing dissatisfaction and greed, a worsening natural and urban environment, increasingly shallow forms of entertainment and travel, and increased levels of crime and delinquency. Knowledge does not always benefit well-being or generate tolerance and humanity, and specialization may diminish wisdom. Specific technological innovations such as the automobile and the airplane have had particularly harmful effects. And even as innovation produces labor-saving devices there is diminished communication and interaction. Nor can it be said that young persons might alter things for the better, for they, like the old, manifest insatiability and this, more than any claim of materialism, is the essence of the ethos of growth. The attitudes of the young are symptomatic of a "spiritual malaise" that pervades the consumer society. At the close of the essay Mishan doubts whether the radical changes required—including that of controls on scientific inquiry—are politically feasible.

George Simmel For Simmel, modernity is characterized by the plight of the individual forced to adapt to the larger forces and structures of urban society. The person who lives in the metropolis is subjected to an "intensification of emotional life" due to the ever changing external stimuli. The psychological conditions of the city are thus distinct from those of the small town or rural area. The individual protects himself against the metropolis by reacting with reason, not emotion. The quality of reason is manifested in a variety of areas, including commercial life, which has become increasingly impersonal, rational, quantitative, and anonymous. Money is the common demominator of things, and objects are distinguished in terms of a monetary value. To preserve themselves in these conditions, individuals cultivate a reserve toward one another that allows a freedom that could not have been experienced in a small group. The city holds the most advanced division of labor, including an "intellectual individuation of mental qualities" which itself may result from the overwhelming objectivity of modern culture. This objectivity often reduces the individual "to a negligible quantity."

Jean Baudrillard   The longer essay from which this excerpt is drawn offers an elaboration of Marx's account of commodification and includes both a phenomenological description of the abundance of the consumer society as well as a theoretical account of how commodities manifest a structure of communication that incites and constrains our desires. This excerpt includes Baudrillard's description of the phenomenon of consumption, the primary and ubiquitous presence of consumer goods, and the constructed networks of objects which move and constrain us to shop and buy. One of the most prominent characteristics of the consumer society is the profusion of goods, especially in the large department stores, markets, and avenues. The accumulated goods are displayed in stacks, displays, or collections, all within a context that brings to mind other objects and choices, inducing thereby a vision of reality within which the consumer might choose. However, consumer goods "are always arranged to mark out distinctive paths, to orientate the purchasing impulse towards *networks* of objects" so as to "captivate" larger purchases from the consumer. In the case of the shopping mall (or drugstore), an atmosphere is provided in which shopping is turned into of a way of living; anything can be purchased, and all types of goods are organized, homogenous, and constantly available.

Robert Nozick   Nozick offers an account of utopia in which individuals with divergent goals and ends could choose to live in distinct societies with differing ways of life. He begins by constructing a possible world in which individuals would choose the associations in which they would most prefer to live. Applied to the actual world, such a model would permit individuals to enter or to leave any communities they might wish and to construct such communities according to their own goals and ends. Nozick notes three arguments for his account of utopia, the first of which is that people are different in manifold ways (having listed an enormously diverse group of individuals, Nozick asks: "Is there really *one* kind of life which is best for each of these people?"). A second argument for utopia suggests that not all goods can be realized simultaneously in a single so-

ciety; a third argument is that individuals are complex and, even if there is one sort of society best for everyone, the best way to discover what society is best is through a utopian system that permits experimentation. As people design different communities, these will either flourish, disappear, or be altered from within. Some may be communal, others individualistic, some religious, but as individuals choose their communities some associations will be filtered out. Although the decision to join an association is fully voluntary, each community may exercise restrictions over individuals.

A Philosophical Review of the Successive Advances of the Human Mind

Anne-Robert-Jacques Turgot

Anne-Robert-Jacques Turgot (1727–1781), the baron de l'Aulne, was born in Paris and, although he was expected to become a member of the clergy, he elected instead to enter the government. A man of great intellect and wide interests, he is remembered for his work in economics as well as for his reforms that deregulated French industry. The author of On Universal History *(1750) and* Reflections on the Formation and the Distribution of Wealth *(1766), this excerpt is from* A Philosophical Review of the Successive Advances of the Human Mind *(1750).*

The phenomena of nature, governed as they are by constant laws, are confined within a circle of revolutions which are always the same. All things perish, and all things spring up again; and in these successive acts of generation through which plants and animals reproduce themselves time does no more than restore continually the counterpart of what it has caused to disappear.

The succession of mankind, on the other hand, affords from age to age an ever-changing spectacle. Reason, the passions, and liberty ceaselessly give rise to new events: all the ages are bound up with one another by a succession of causes and effects which link the present state of the world with all those that have preceded it. The arbitrary signs of speech and writing, by providing men with the means of securing the possession of their ideas and communicating them to others, have made of all the individual stores of knowledge a common treasure-house which one generation transmits to another, an inheritance which is always being enlarged by the discoveries of each age. Thus the human race, considered over the period since its origin, appears to the eye of a philosopher as one vast whole, which itself, like each individual, has its infancy and its advancement.

We see the establishment of societies, and the formation of nations which in turn dominate other nations or become subject to them. Empires rise and fall; laws and forms of government succeed one another; the arts and the sciences are in turn discovered and perfected, in turn retarded and accelerated in their progress; and they are passed on from country to country. Self-interest, ambition, and vainglory continually change the world scene and inundate the earth with blood; yet in the midst of their ravages manners are softened, the human mind becomes more enlightened, and separate nations are brought closer to one another. Finally commercial and political ties unite all parts of the globe, and the whole human race, through alternate periods of rest and unrest, of weal and woe, goes on advancing, although at a slow pace, towards greater perfection.

In the time placed at my disposal I could not hope to portray for you the whole of so vast a panorama. I shall try merely to indicate the main lines of the progress of the human mind; and this discourse will be wholly taken up with some reflections on the origin and growth of the arts and sciences and the revolutions which have taken place in them, considered in their relation to the succession of historical events.

Holy Writ, after having enlightened us about the creation of the universe, the origin of man, and the birth of the first arts, before long puts before us a picture of the human race concentrated again in a single family as the result of a universal flood. Scarcely had it begun to make good its losses when the miraculous confusion of tongues forced men to separate from one another. The urgent need to procure subsistence for themselves in barren deserts, which provided nothing but wild beasts, obliged them to move apart from one another in all directions and hastened their diffusion through the whole world. Soon the original traditions were forgotten; and the nations, separated as they were by vast distances and still more by the diversity of languages, strangers to one another, were almost all plunged into the same barbarism in which we still see the Americans.

But natural resources and the fertile seeds of the sciences are to be found wherever there are men. The most exalted mental attainments are only and can only be a development or combination of the original ideas, based on sensation, just as the building at whose great height we gaze in wonder necessarily has its foundation in the earth upon which we tread. The same senses, the same organs, and the spectacle of the same universe, have everywhere given men the same ideas, just as the same needs and inclinations have everywhere taught them the same arts.

Now a faint light begins occasionally to penetrate the darkness which has covered all the nations, and step by step it spreads. The inhabitants of Chaldea, closest to the source of the original traditions, the Egyptians, and the Chinese apparently lead the rest of the peoples. Others follow them at a distance, and progress leads to further progress. The inequality of nations increases; in one place the arts begin to emerge, while in another they advance at a rapid rate towards perfection. In some nations they are brought to a standstill in the midst of their mediocrity, while in others the original darkness is not yet dissipated at all. Thus the present state of the world, marked as it is by these infinite variations in inequality, spreads out before us at one and the same time all the gradations from barbarism to refinement, thereby revealing to us at a single glance, as it were, the records and remains of all the steps taken by the human mind, a reflection of all the stages through which it has passed, and the history of all the ages.

But is not nature everywhere the same?—and if she leads all men to the same truths, if even their errors are alike, how is it that they do not all move forward at the same rate along the road which is marked out for them? It is true that the human mind everywhere contains the potential for the same progress, but nature, distributing her gifts unequally, has given to certain minds an abundance of talents which she has refused to others. Circumstances either develop these talents or allow them to become buried in obscurity; and it is from the infinite variety of these circumstances that there springs the inequality in the progress of nations.

Barbarism makes all men equal; and in early times all those who are born with genius are faced with virtually the same obstacles and the same resources. Societies are established and expanded, however; national hatreds and ambition—or rather greed, the only ambition of barbarous peoples—cause war and devastation to increase; and conquests and revolutions mix up peoples, languages, and customs in a thousand different ways. Chains of mountains, great rivers and seas confine the dealings of peoples with one another, and consequently their intermingling, within fixed boundaries. This results in the formation of common languages which become a tie binding several nations together, so that all the nations of the world become divided as it were into a number of different classes. Tillage increases the permanence of settlements. It is able to feed more men than are employed in it, and thus imposes upon those whom it leaves idle the necessity of making themselves either useful or formidable to the cultivators. Hence towns, trade, the useful arts and accomplishments, the division of occupations, the differences in education, and the increased inequality in the conditions of life. Hence that leisure, by means of which genius, relieved of the burden of providing for primary necessities, emerges from the narrow sphere within which these necessities confine it and bends all its strength to the cultivation of the arts. Hence that more rapid and vigorous rate of advance of the human mind which carries along with it all parts of society and which in turn derives additional momentum from their perfection. The passions develop alongside genius; ambition gathers strength; politics lends it ever-widening perspectives; victories have more lasting results and create empires whose laws, customs, and government, influencing men's genius in different ways, become a kind of common education for the nations, producing between one nation and another the same sort of difference which education produces between one man and another.

United, divided, the one raised up on the other's ruins, empires rapidly succeed one another. The revolutions which they undergo cause them to run the whole gamut of possible states, and unite and disunite all the elements of the body politic. Like the ebb and flow of the tide, power passes from one nation to another, and, within the same nation, from the princes to the multitude and from the multitude to the princes. As the balance shifts, everything gradually gets nearer and nearer to an equilibrium, and in the course of time takes on a more settled and peaceful aspect. Ambition, when it forms great states from the remains of a host of small ones, itself sets limits to its own ravages. Wars no longer devastate anything but the frontiers of empires; the towns and the countryside begin to breathe the air of peace; the bonds of society unite a greater number of men; ideas come to be transmitted more promptly and more widely; and the advancement of arts, sciences, and manners progresses more rapidly. Like a storm which has agitated the waves of the sea, the evil which is inseparable from revolutions disappears: the good remains, and humanity perfects itself. Amidst this complex of different events, sometimes favourable, sometimes adverse, which because they act in opposite ways must in the long run nullify one another, genius ceaselessly asserts its influence. Nature, while distributing genius to only a few individuals, has nevertheless spread it out almost equally over the whole mass, and with time its effects become appreciable.

Genius, whose course is at first slow, unmarked, and buried in the general oblivion into which time precipitates human affairs, emerges from obscurity with them by means of the invention of *writing*. Priceless invention!—which seemed to give wings to those peoples who first possessed it, enabling them to outdistance other nations. Incomparable invention!—which rescues from the power of death the memory of great men and models of virtue, unites places and times, arrests fugitive thoughts and guarantees them a lasting existence, by means of which the creations, opinions, experiences, and discoveries of all ages are accumulated, to serve as a foundation and foothold for posterity in raising itself ever higher!

But what a spectacle the succession of men's opinions presents! I seek there for the progress of the human mind, and I find virtually nothing but the history of its errors. Why is its course, which is so sure from the very first steps in the field of mathematical studies, so unsteady in everything else, and so apt to go astray? Let us try to discover the reasons. In mathematics, the mind deduces one from another a chain of propositions, the truth of which consists only in their mutual dependence. It is not the same with the other sciences, where it is no longer from the intercomparison of ideas that truth is born, but from their conformity with a sequence of real facts. To discover and verify truth, it is no longer a question of establishing a small number of simple principles and then merely allowing the mind to be borne along by the current of their consequences. One must start from nature as it is, and from that infinite variety of effects which so many causes, counterbalanced one by the other, have combined to produce. Notions are no longer assemblages of ideas which the mind forms of its own accord and of whose range it has exact knowledge. Ideas emerge and are assembled in our minds almost without our knowing it; we are beset by the images of objects right from the cradle. Little by little we learn to distinguish between them, less by reference to what they are in themselves than by reference to their relation to our habits and needs. The signs of language impress themselves on the mind while it is still undeveloped. At first, through habit and imitation, they become attached to particular objects, but later they succeed in calling up more general notions. This chaotic blend of ideas and expressions grows and becomes more complex all the time; and when man starts to seek for truth he finds himself in the midst of a labyrinth which he has entered blindfold. Should we be surprised at his errors?

Spectator of the universe, his senses show him the effects but leave him ignorant of the causes. And to examine effects in an endeavour to find their unknown cause is like trying to guess an enigma: we think of one or more possible key words and try them in turn until one is found which fulfils all the conditions.

The natural philosopher erects hypotheses, follows them through to their consequences, and brings them to bear upon the enigma of nature. He tries them out, so to speak, on the facts, just as one verifies a seal by applying it to its impression. Suppositions which are arrived at on the basis of a small number of poorly understood facts yield to suppositions which are less absurd, although no more true. Time, research, and chance result in the accumulation of observations, and unveil the hidden connections which link a number of phenomena together.

Ever restless, incapable of finding tranquillity elsewhere than in the truth, ever stimulated by the image of that truth which it believes to be within its grasp but which flies before it, the curiosity of man leads to a multiplication of the number of questions and debates, and obliges him to analyse ideas and facts in a manner which grows ever more exact and more profound. Mathematical truths, becoming from day to day more numerous and hence more fruitful, point the way to the development of hypotheses which are more far-reaching and more precise, and indicate new experiments which, in their turn, present new problems for mathematics to resolve. Thus the need perfects the tool; thus mathematics is sustained by natural philosophy, upon which it sheds its light; thus everything is bound together; thus, in spite of the diversity in their development, all the sciences render mutual aid to one another; thus, by feeling his way, by multiplying systems and draining them, as it were, of their errors, man at last attains to the understanding of a great number of truths.

What ridiculous opinions marked our first steps! How absurd were the causes which our fathers thought up to make sense of what they saw! What sad monuments they are to the weakness of the human mind! The senses constitute the unique source of our ideas: the whole power of our mental faculties is restricted to combining the ideas which they have received from the senses: hardly even can they form combinations of ideas of which the senses do not provide them with a model. Hence that almost irresistible tendency to judge of what one does not know by what one knows; hence those delusive analogies to which the first men in their immaturity abandoned themselves with so little thought; hence the monstrous aberrations of idolatry. Men, oblivious of the original traditions, when affected by sensible phenom-ena, imagined that all effects which were independent of their own action were produced by beings similar to them, but invisible and more powerful, whom they substituted for the Divinity. When they were contemplating nature, it was as if they fixed their gaze on the surface of a deep sea instead of on the sea-bed hidden by the waters, and saw there only their own reflection. All objects of nature had their gods, which, being created after the model of man, shared his attributes and vices. Throughout the world, superstition sanctified the caprices of the imagination; and the only true God, the only God worthy of adoration, was known only in one corner of the earth, by the people whom he had expressly chosen.

In this slow progression of opinions and errors, pursuing one another, I fancy that I see those first leaves, those sheaths which nature has given to the newly-growing stems of plants, issuing before them from the earth, and withering one by one as other sheaths come into existence, until at last the stem itself makes its appearance and is crowned with flowers and fruit—a symbol of late-emerging truth! . . .

[In the paragraphs deleted here, Turgot offers an account of the arts and sciences from ancient Greece to the rise and fall of Rome. Our reading resumes after Turgot has chronicled the first few centuries subsequent to the fall of Rome.]

But nevertheless, from the midst of this barbarism, perfected arts and sciences will one day rise again. Amid all the ignorance, progress is imperceptibly taking place and preparing for the brilliant achievements of later centuries; beneath this soil the feeble roots of a far-off harvest are already developing. The towns among all civilised peoples constitute by their very nature the centres of trade and the backbone of society. They continued to exist; and if the spirit of feudal government, born of the ancient customs of Germany, combined with a number of accidental circumstances, had abased them, this was a contradiction in the constitution of states which was bound to disappear in the long run. Soon we see the towns revive again under the protection of the princes; and the latter, in holding out their hands to the oppressed peoples, reduce the power of their vassals and little by little re-establish their own.

Latin and theology were already being studied in the universities, together with the Aristotelian dialectic. For a long time the Mussulman Arabs had been teaching themselves Greek philosophy, and their learning was spreading to the west. Mathematics had been extended as a result of their work. More independent than the other sciences of the perfection of taste and perhaps even of precision of intellect, one cannot study mathematics without being led to the truth. Always certain, always pure, its truths were emerging, encompassed about by the errors of judicial astrology. The chimerical search for the philosopher's stone, by encouraging the Arab philosophers to separate and to recombine all the elements of bodies, had led to the blossoming under their hands of the vast science of chemistry, and had spread it to all places where men were capable of being imposed upon by their greedy desires. Finally, on all sides, the mechanical arts were coming to be perfected by virtue of the simple fact that time was passing, because even in the decline of the sciences and taste the needs of life preserve them, and because, consequently, among that host of artisans who successively cultivate them it is impossible not to meet every now and then with one of those men of genius who are blended with the rest of mankind as gold is blended with the clay in a mine.

As a result, what a host of inventions unknown to the ancients and standing to the credit of these barbarous ages! Our art of musical notation, our bills of exchange, our paper, window glass, plate glass, windmills, clocks, spectacles, gunpowder, the magnetic needle, and the perfection of navigation and commerce. The arts are nothing but the utilisation of nature, and the practice of the arts is a succession of physical experiments which progressively unveil nature. Facts were accumulating in the darkness of the times of ignorance, and the sciences, whose progress although hidden was no less real, were bound to reappear one day augmented by this new wealth, like those rivers which after disappearing from our view for some time in a subterranean passage, reappear further on swollen by all the waters which have seeped through the earth.

Different series of events take place in different countries of the world, and all of them, as if by so many separate paths, at length come together to contribute to the same end, to raise up once again the ruins of the human spirit. Thus, in the night, we see the stars rise one after the other; they move forward, each in its own orbit; they seem in their common revolution to bear along with them the whole celestial sphere, and to bring in for us the day which follows them. Germany, Denmark, Sweden, and Poland through the efforts of Charlemagne and the Othos, and Russia through trade with the Greek empire, cease to be uncultivated forests. Christianity, in bringing together these scattered savages, in settling them in towns, is going to dry up forever the source of those inundations which have so often been fatal to the sciences. Europe is still barbarous; but the knowledge brought by her to even more barbarous peoples represents for them immense progress. Little by little the customs introduced by Germany into the south of Europe disappear. The na-

tions, amid the quarrels of the nobles and the princes, begin to fashion for themselves the principles of a more stable government, and to acquire, in accordance with the different circumstances in which they find themselves, the particular character which distinguishes them. The wars against the Mussulmans in Palestine, by giving a common interest to all Christian states, teach them to know one another and to unite with one another, and sow the seeds of that modern political state of affairs in which so many nations seem to comprise nothing but one vast republic. Already we see the royal authority reviving again in France; the power of the people establishing itself in England; the Italian towns constituting themselves into republics and presenting the likeness of ancient Greece; the little monarchies of Spain driving the Moors before them and little by little joining up again into one whole. Soon the seas, which have hitherto separated the nations, come to be the link between them through the invention of the compass. The Portuguese in the east and the Spaniards in the west discover new worlds: at last the world as a whole is known.

Already the intermingling of the barbarous languages with Latin has during the course of the centuries produced new languages, of which the Italian, less removed from their common source and less mixed with foreign languages, takes precedence in the elegance of its style and the beauties of its poetry. The Ottomans, spreading through Asia and Europe with the swiftness of a violent wind, end by overthrowing the empire of Constantinople, and disseminate in the west the feeble sparks of those sciences which Greece still preserved.

What new art is suddenly born, as if to wing to every corner of the earth the writings and glory of the great men who are to come? How slow in every sphere is even the least progress! For two thousand years medals have presented to all eyes characters impressed upon bronze—and then, after so many centuries, some obscure individual realises that they can be impressed upon paper. At once the treasures of antiquity, rescued from the dust, pass into all hands, penetrate to every part of the world, bear light to the talents which were being wasted in ignorance, and summon genius from the depths of its retreats.

The time has come. Issue forth, Europe, from the darkness which covered thee! Immortal names of the Medici, of Leo X, of Francis I, be consecrated for ever! May the patrons of the arts share the glory of those who cultivate them! I salute thee, O Italy!—happy land, for the second time the homeland of letters and of taste, the spring from which their waters have spread to fertilise our territories. Our own France still only beholds thy progress from afar. Her language, still tainted by remnants of barbarism, cannot follow it. Soon fatal discords will rend the whole of Europe; audacious men have shaken the foundations of the faith and those of the empires; do the flowered stems of the fine arts grow when they are watered with blood? A day will come, and it is not far off, when they will beautify all the countries of Europe.

Time, spread your swift wings! Century of Louis, century of great men, century of reason, hasten! Already, even amidst the turmoil of heresy, the long-disturbed fortunes of states have ended by settling down, as if as the result of a final shock. Already the unremitting study of antiquity has brought men's minds back again to the point where its progress was arrested; already that host of facts, experiments, instruments, and ingenious exercises which the practice of the arts has accumulated over so many centuries, has been rescued from obscurity through printing; already the productions of the two worlds, brought together before our eyes as the result of a far-flung commerce, have become the foundation of a natural philosophy hitherto unknown, and freed at last from alien speculations; already on every hand attentive eyes are fixed upon nature: the remotest chances, turned to profit, give birth to discoveries. The son of an artisan in Zealand brings together for amusement two convex glasses in a tube; the boundaries of our senses are made to recede, and in Italy the eyes of Galileo have discovered a new firmament. Already Kepler, seeking in the stars for the numbers of Pythagoras, has discovered those two famous laws of the movements of the planets which one day in the hands of Newton will become the key to the universe. Already Bacon has traced out for posterity the road which it must follow.

Who is the mortal who dares to reject the learning of all the ages, and even those notions which he has believed to be the most certain? He seems to wish to extinguish the torch of the sciences in order to relight it all on his own at the pure fire of reason. Does he wish to imitate those peoples of antiquity among whom it was a crime to light at other fires that which was made to burn on the altars of the Gods? Great Descartes, if it was not always given to you to find the truth, at least you have destroyed the tyranny of error.

France, whom Spain and England have already outstripped in the glory of poetry; France, whose genius finishes forming itself only when the philosophical spirit begins to spread, will owe perhaps to this very backwardness the exactitude, the method, and the austere taste of her writers. Rarefied and affected thoughts, and the ponderous display of an ostentatious erudition, still corrupt our literature: a strange difference between our progress in taste and that of the ancients! The real advancement of the human mind reveals itself even in its aberrations; the caprices of Gothic architecture are never found among those who possess nothing but wooden huts. The acquisition of knowledge among the first men and the formation of taste kept pace, as it were, with one another. Hence a crude severity and an exaggerated simplicity were their prerogative. Guided by instinct and imagination, they seized little by little upon those relations between men and the objects of nature which are the sole foundations of the beautiful. In later times, when, in spite of the imperfection of taste, the number of ideas and perceptions was increased, when the study of models and rules had caused nature and feeling to become lost from men's view, it was necessary for them through reflection to take themselves back to where the first men had been led by blind instinct. And who is not aware that it is here that the supreme effort of reason lies?

At last all the shadows are dispelled: and what a light shines out on all sides! What a host of great men in every sphere! What a perfection of human reason! One man, Newton, has subjected the infinite to the calculus, has revealed the properties of light which in illuminating everything seemed to conceal itself, and has put into his balance the stars, the earth, and all the forces of nature. And this man has found a rival. Leibnitz encompasses within his vast intellect all the objects of the human mind. The different sciences, confined at first to a small number of simple notions common to all, can no longer, when as a result of their progress they have become more extensive and more difficult, be envisaged otherwise than separately; but greater progress once again unites them, because there is discovered that mutual dependence of all truths which in linking them together illuminates each through the other; because, if each day adds to the vast extent of the sciences, each day also makes them easier, because methods are multiplied with discoveries, because the scaffolding rises with the building.

O Louis, what majesty surrounds thee! What splendour thy beneficent hand has spread over all the arts! Thine happy people has become the centre of refinement! Rivals of Sophocles, of Menander, and of Horace, gather around his throne! Arise, learned academies, and unite your efforts for the glory of his reign! What a multitude of public monuments, of works of genius, of arts newly invented, and of old arts perfected! Who could possibly picture them? Open your eyes and see! Century of Louis the Great, may your light beautify the precious reign of his successor! May it last for ever, may it extend over the whole world! May men continually make new steps along the road of truth! Rather still, may they continually become better and happier!

In the midst of these vicissitudes of opinions, of sciences, of arts, and of everything which is human, rejoice, gentlemen, in the pleasure of seeing that religion to which you have consecrated your hearts and your talents, always true to herself, always pure, always complete, standing perpetuated in the Church, and preserving all the features of the seal which the Divinity has stamped upon it. You will be her ministers, and you will be worthy of her. The Faculty expects from you her glory, the Church of France her illumination, Religion her defenders. Genius, learning, and piety are united to give ground for their hopes.

QUESTIONS ON TURGOT

1. Turgot writes that "All the ages are bound up with one another by a succession of causes and effects," and he attempts to describe some of the main events in this line of progress. Do you think that Turgot explains successfully the "main lines of the progress of the human mind"?

2. Does Turgot's account of progress depend on the idea of sensation as the source of ideas? What are the motives that move humans to act? What are the circumstances that increase or decrease the rate of progress?

3. In what sense is progress dependent on economic growth? Consider the way in which an agricultural surplus makes possible the development of towns and trade and the way in which towns might serve as the "backbone" of society.

4. For Turgot, progress seems to be a natural process comparable to the growth of a human being. Why should the long-run tendency be toward greater progress rather than the reverse?

Whatever Happened to Progress?

E. J. Mishan

Ezra J. Mishan was a Reader in Economics at The London School of Economics from 1956 to 1977, thereafter lecturing at universities throughout North America. He is the author of The Costs of Economic Growth *(1967),* Cost-Benefit Analysis *(1971), and* Economic Myths and the Mythology of Economics *(1986).*

INTRODUCTION

The idea of Enlightenment can be traced back through the centuries, but for the West the idea is rather more specific and has its origins in what used to be known as the 'European Renaissance,' which, beginning in Italy in the fifteenth century, soon spread to the rest of Europe. The quickening interest in the secular world, the world of art and nature, later took in the 'scientism' of Francis Bacon and Galileo and moved on into the eighteenth century, by which time it appeared to have reached its high point. Influenced by the French philosophers and the encyclopaedists, by Comte and Condorcet, the movement began to associate itself with agnosticism and empiricism, on the one hand, and, on the other, with a boundless optimism about the future and a growing concern for social justice. Not surprisingly, it was during this period, and particularly during the second half of the eighteenth century, that this broadly humanistic and humanitarian movement allied itself with the notion of progress as we understand it today: at first, intellectual and moral progress, which fused into a belief in the perfectibility of man; but later, under the impact of the writings of economists—Cantillon in France and, in the first half of the nineteenth century, the philosophical radicals in Britain, and others too numerous to mention—material progress also. The faith in progress, and especially material progress, reached its apogee in mid-Victorian England, and that faith, although less powerful today, has never lost its hold over the minds of the intellectual guardians of Western civilisation.

The result of these developments has been a continuing climate of 'respectable' intellectual opinion, reaching back at least 200 years—a climate of opinion that (for lack of a better word) we may refer to as the *Established Enlightenment*. Although it has never been so strong as to determine the course of events in opposition to strong vested interests or political repression, the Established Enlightenment could never be wholly ignored by the state. I do not argue that this intellectual climate of opinion could always produce a single view on any contemporary issue, but only that it was the source of inspiration from which flowed an enlightened dialogue—one that continues today between members of the middle class 'intelligentsia.' the professional classes, the scientific and academic community, and the 'higher journalism.' And it is one of the sadder facts of political life that—far from there being a liberal tolerance extended to any arguable point of view at variance with those currently held by the Established Enlightenment—anyone so bold as publicly to challenge any of its cherished preconceptions (as I know to my cost) cannot hope to escape ridicule, abuse and unconscionable misrepresentation.

The thesis I wish to propound here is that, if we are concerned chiefly with social welfare, or with what is loosely spoken of as 'the quality of life,' the benefits espoused by the Established Enlightenment—beliefs that have lighted our way for the past two centuries—are inadequate and inexpedient. They are just beginning to be challenged, perhaps to be challenged too late.

The idea of progress—which, broadly interpreted, encompasses the growing and interacting forces of knowledge and wealth—today holds the key position among the ideas of the Established Enlightenment. The growth of knowledge is pursued almost as an end in itself. (I say *almost,* because the pursuit of knowledge is occasionally justified, albeit briefly, by reference to seemingly accepted but vaguely defined ends, such as 'emancipation' or 'the realisation of human potential,' or as a heroic destiny, a challenge man must not shirk, and so on.) As for the growth of material wealth, its desirability is hardly questioned; it receives occasional benediction in the economic literature from such phrases that depict economic growth as 'widening the area of choices open to men.'

The growth of wealth and knowledge together has made possible the continued advance in universal education—again regarded in the main as a self-evident good, although strengthening its appeal by phrases about 'freeing men from ignorance and superstition,' or about 'promoting increased understanding and tolerance between men,' and justifying its finance by the state as promoting equality of opportunity and encouraging the growth of skills required by modern societies that depend increasingly on sophisticated techniques.

According to the faithful, moreover, with the increased tolerance anticipated from the spread of wealth and knowledge, women will be emancipated from disabilities long and (until recently) patiently endured, social bigotry will disappear, and men and women of diverse races and creeds will live together in harmony.

Closely connected with the presumption by economists in favour of free international trade is that in favour of free migration of peoples—a presumption that, by reference to social justice, extends itself easily enough to the notion of increased mobility, geographical and, of course, also social and occupational. A yet further extension, allied with the presumption that favours the spread of knowledge, or at least of information, reinforces the case for increased media of communication.

A final example is the belief—still widely held, although at one time amounting to an article of faith among the Established Enlightenment—that continued progress will eventually overcome all the chronic social evils; poverty, corruption, crime, war. For sustained material progress not only implies the elimination of poverty, an end that is good in itself, but also the removal of conditions under which delinquency and criminal activity flourish.

These and other 'enlightened' beliefs have been, and to a large extent still are, held by men of otherwise different political ideologies. They are held by socialists, by liberals and by communists. For what separates the liberal (at least the old type liberal) from the socialist or communist lies simply in the deep-seated differences of opinion, amounting to ideological conviction, about the efficiency of the means whereby such believed goods are realised. The old liberal firmly believed in the efficacy of private enterprise and decentralised markets, and in limiting the compass of state activity, as the surest means of promoting economic growth and meeting the wants of citizens and consumers. In contrast, the socialist or communist holds that these ends are more surely realised by centralised planning and state custody. In particular, the communist holds that social justice and the good life require strengthening the state against the 'enemies of the people,' in appropriating the means of communication in order to spread 'the truth' among the masses, and in monopolising education so as to provide equal opportunity and so as to undertake massive scientific research.

Although my own commitment in this imperfect world of disintegrating societies is to a liberal democracy, to a decentralised and institutionally pluralistic order—an order that is increasingly difficult to maintain in the face of rapid technological advance and manifest economies of scale—it is so only on broad political grounds, chiefly as a safeguard against mounting encroachment by the state. Other than that I do not care to choose between the rival ideologies. In particular, it is becoming harder to decide the respective merits of centralised and decentralised planning in terms of economic efficiency, narrowly conceived. Not that it matters much to me anyway, as I am far from enamoured of the economist's idea of economic efficiency or of economic progress as commonly understood.

PHOTO ALBUM OF PROGRESS

Rather than couch my arguments in abstract and general terms, I shall present the reader with a succession of tableaux. First, I shall depict, sparingly, the social scene today compared with the prewar period, and then invoke examples to illustrate how these 'enlightened' beliefs—some of the chief ones and some of the auxiliary ones—are coming to conflict with the basic wants of common aspirations of ordinary men and women. It will be both convenient and instructive, although not necessary, to take our bearings by reference to a Western-type society—one boasting liberal-democratic institutions of a sort, and one in which, although a mixed economic system prevails, there are still the remnants of a presumption in favour of private enterprise and in favour of economic growth. (As a footnote comment I ought to add, however, that the general thrust of my conclusions would not be deflected if I developed my thesis by reference instead to some hypothetical, ideally decentralised, perfectly functioning, market system, as envisaged perhaps by Milton Friedman—one that has the economic textbook virtue of providing the consumer with whatever goods the world market produces at the lowest prices.)

Only if measured by technological achievement and commercial aggrandisement does our civilisation, the civilisation of the West in the 1970s, rate high. Apart from these undeniable technical and commercial achievements, the sort of progress impelled by economic growth, and to some extent influenced by the Established Enlightenment, looks impressive enough only if one does not look at it too closely.

Thus, a quick glance down the credit side of the ledger would reveal the following items: maintenance, until recently, of something close to full employment since the war; a continued rise in 'real' income *per capita;* a phenomenal expansion of higher education, accompanied by a rise in the school-leaving age; a vast proliferation of social welfare services provided by the state; an extension of the suffrage (to younger people in Britain and the United States and, effectively, to many blacks in the southern states of the United States); a reduction of class distinctions and a reduction in regional and racial discrimination; an increased recognition of the rights of self-determination of once subject peoples; a growing awareness by women, and also by some men, that the fair sex was being unfairly treated and, in response, some incipient remedial legislation; the appearance in almost every household of the affluent West of new labour-saving gadgets and television sets; an unprecedented increase of mobility and, over the last two decades especially, increased foreign travel for the multitude. In addition, some possibly controversial, but nonetheless authentic, 'enlightened' measures have been introduced into a number of countries: for in-

stance, the abolition of corporal punishment and of the death penalty, the abolition of theatre censorship, plus a number of smaller legal adjustments making for a more lenient attitude toward sexual deviance, toward juvenile violence, and toward overtly aphrodisiac literature and entertainment.

The traditional liberal, and indeed the nonrevolutionary socialist also, may well be excused for feeling satisfied with the bounty of progress as he surveys these features of national life and compares them with the social scene some fifty or even twenty-five years ago. The fashionable intellectual, he is pleased to observe, is today quite properly a little touchy on the treatment of non-whites in the community. This same trendy spirit, he will also observe, is by and large 'anti-Victorian,' 'anti-imperialist' and condescending of patriotic sentiment and has a marked predilection for debunking past heroes, national myths and anything that savours of 'the glorious days of old.' Withal, it exhibits an impatience of reverence, privilege and ceremony.

Nonetheless, if the advance of a civilisation is associated in our minds with order, with propriety, with a refinement of sensibilities, with the acceptance of norms and procedures, with a sense of things being in place, with ideals of harmony and proportion, then the kind of progress we have experienced over the last few decades can hardly fail to arouse also a great deal of cynicism, if not alarm.

A society has come into being whose members are daily encouraged to make invidious comparisons, and habitually to feel disgruntled at not having more—tendencies that are sometimes euphemistically referred to as 'motivated.' For the momentum of economic growth in the wealthier countries, it is believed, can be sustained only by the unremitting efforts of industry to create dissatisfaction with existing possessions and to promote unbridled covetousness. The resulting restlessness and discontent are accompanied and aggravated by a degenerating environment, and by the movement from the villages and smaller towns to the increasingly congested and polluted metropolises and their suburbs.

Each year sees more massive office blocks erected in our large cities, cheap, nasty and, for the most part, depressing. With the passage of time, once distinguished streets and squares have become tawdry with amusement arcades and sleazy bazaars. The litter of the 'throw-away' society is everywhere in evidence, with the means of sex titillation displayed at every corner news-stand and offered in various doses by the greater number of modern films. With each new summer millions more surge like lemmings toward places that rapidly become like the places they want to get away from. The determination of so many of the young today to look different has come to defy space and time; it has reached proportions where virtually 'anything goes,' and where campuses and sometimes railway stations appear to have been taken over for a marathon tramps' carnival. As trends go, the number of cars on the roads, noise levels in the cities and the number of air passengers are expected to continue to grow year by year. The figures for crime and juvenile violence over the past two decades continue their inexorable climb upward. 'White collar' crime—business theft, embezzlement, bribery, tax frauds—appears to be rampant in the United States. As the young today see it, 'everyone is on the make.'

Some of these unprepossessing features of modern societies—greed, corruption, degenerative activity, public spectacles of sadistic violence—it may be remarked, can be found in one form or another during certain periods of other civilisations, although admittedly on an incomparably smaller scale, since the means of communication were limited, cities fewer and smaller, and populations and their resources then but a fraction of a fraction of those available today. What is today deeply disquieting, however, is not only their unprecedented scale, but also the growing suspicion that all these unhappier features of Western civilisation that have come into prominence since the Second World War are the products, perhaps the inevitable products, of 200 years of sustained economic growth in the West.

Such an outcome was never suspected by the brave reformers and humanists of the eighteenth-century Enlightenment. Nor did such disturbing possibilities ever cloud the splendid visions of those nineteenth-century apostles of progress, who—observing everywhere the spread of industry and knowledge, the establishment of institutions of learning and the introduction of labour-saving contrivances—foretold of a future of universal plenitude, harmony, leisure and culture. To expect that some great good will yet emerge from these unpromising developments—if only we press on with economic growth, with technical innovation, and with more liberal measures of aid and assistance—is to cling more tenaciously to doctrine as the facts become grimmer.

ARE WE APPROACHING HUMAN FULFILMENT?

Concerning human needs, I think there is a fair consensus about them among thoughtful men. Like any other mammal, man has a need for physical activity and exertion. He also needs a sense of security, which depends upon the continuity and stability of institutions, upon a framework of law and custom, and upon his familiarity with places, people and things. Obviously, he also has a strong need of love and trust—a need to love and to be loved, to trust and to be trusted. In all of us too, there is a need for self-respect, allied to the need for love and trust but also deriving from the need for communal esteem; a man wants to feel that he matters to other people. And he craves too a distinct origin—an identity, a destiny, from which arises the desire to belong to a group, a folk, having a common history and a common pride. Irrational though it sounds in these wonderfully scientific times, he also wants to believe in a benevolent deity—in a source of infinite wisdom and compassion.

Finally, although stemming not directly from the same instinctual roots, but from a slow refinement of character and taste brought about by the civilising process, he aspires toward the good life—one offering him more leisure, more space, more margin to his life; one placing him closer to the pulse of nature, yet offering him access to magnificent cities, where each building adds beauty and proportion to the whole and in which concourse and gaiety thrive.

Now, as a result of chance events or in the inherent nature of things, progress in its various manifestations, far from meeting these basic needs or realising our aspirations, has begun to run counter to them. For instance, the pursuit of knowledge for its own sake cannot always be vindicated by reference to human well-being. Unless the search for knowledge is itself motivated by humane ends, it can be destructive of people's contentment. The Copernican theory started a revolution in astronomy that was to displace man from his unique position at the centre of the universe, the chosen and beloved creature of the Lord, and to relegate him to some inconsequential speck of matter whirling about the rim of but one of an uncountable number of star systems in an infinite and inhospitable universe. Three centuries later another dedicated scientist, Charles Darwin, revealed his findings to the world, and in doing so drove another deadly shaft into the heart of men's cherished beliefs. Far from having descended from the angels, our ancestors could be traced through an evolving species back to primeval slime. And all the wonder and variety of nature that once affirmed the infinite wisdom of God was from thence to be understood as the outcome of the mindless forces of natural selection.

Thus, the disinterested pursuit of knowledge saps the spiritual sustenance of men. It destroys also the myths that shore up their morale, the bonds that hold them together, their ideas of kith and kin, their pride in their history and in their folk heroes—beliefs that one by one are doomed to be shattered by troops of eager young historians in search of professional recognition. There is, in short, much knowledge that we should be happier to live without.

As for increase in understanding, tolerance and humanity—the products, supposedly, of universal education—the allegation is blatantly at odds with the facts. Few periods of history reveal such rooted antagonisms based on differences in race and nationality. This is not altogether surprising. Higher education is today overwhelmingly vocational and highly specialised. Its overriding purpose is to produce the manifold skills required by a complex technical society. It teaches men more and more about less and less. It narrows their horizons, weakens their imaginations, perverts their judgments and cramps their spirits.

Finally, the process by which, necessarily, knowledge advances bodes no good for men. The extent and depth of modern knowledge, scholarly and scientific, is beyond the imagination to grasp. Its further progress, on a myriad of fronts, depends above all on a continued splintering of already highly specialised fragments of knowledge. There are signs already of incipient breakdown in communication at various points along the extending frontiers of modern knowledge, although this is not to my purpose just now. What is to the purpose here, however, is that, as specialism grows, wisdom recedes. Not only does the specialist see no more than some of the technical aspects of what is basically a social problem; he also acquires an interest in bringing to bear on it as much of his own technique as possible, so making the world more complex and thus more vulnerable. And his success in doing so brings him his reward, since the greater the number of accidents and breakdowns in any complex technological system, whether foreseeable or unforeseeable, the more scope there is for his expertise and the stronger the case for devoting yet more funds to scientific research.

But to what avail? As one urban expert, Harland Cleveland, said: 'There isn't anything we do not know about the modern city; its demography, its water table, its engineering design, its slums, its economics, its politics. We just don't seem to know how to make it beautiful, accessible, safe, and clean.'

EMERGENT CONSEQUENCES OF THE TRANSPORT AND OTHER REVOLUTIONS

Let us turn now to those technological innovations which have provided us, among other things, with the

means of swift travel both within our own countries and to the furthest part of the earth. We are a generation privileged to enjoy the variety and treasure of the whole world, or at least we thought so in the immediate postwar period. We did not reckon then with the sheer pressure of numbers making itself felt through the automobile and the airliner. As I asserted on a previous occasion, the invention of the automobile is the greatest disaster to have befallen mankind. For sheer irresistible destructive power nothing, save perhaps the airliner, can compete with it. In our towns and cities every principle of architectural harmony has been perverted in the vain struggle to keep the mounting volume of motorised traffic from coming to a standstill. Clamour, dust, fume, congestion and visual distraction are the predominant features in all built-up areas.

Even where styles of architecture differ between cities—and they differ less from one year to the next—these traffic features impinge so blatantly and persistently on the senses as to submerge all other impressions. Whether we are in Paris, Chicago, Tokyo, Milan or Stockholm, or any of 10,000 other towns and cities, it is the choking din, the dust and endless swirl of motorised traffic, that dominate the scene. Yet, such is the hypnotic power of this satanic contrivance that we continue frenziedly to create a physical environment that makes us increasingly dependent upon private motorised transport. Worse, we continue to follow with bated breath the fortunes of the automobile industry, regarded as the prime indicator of economic health and progress.

The social costs of this hapless choice of means of travel include not only the rapid erosion of traditional amenities. They also include such mundane facts that robbery, crime and violence today all depend heavily on the fast getaway car. Motorists kill off other people at the rate of about 140,000 each year (55,000 in the United States alone), and they maim for life well over a million people annually. Through the emission each year of millions of tonnes of foul gases, the automobile's contribution to sickness and death from cancer and from bronchial and other disorders is just beginning to be understood. We are just beginning to understand that perhaps the most impressive example of postwar growth is the increase in the number of places that everyone wants to get away from. What, in contrast, is already fully understood—but about which, for commercial reasons, nothing at all is being done—is the connection between air and motor travel and the greatest holocaust of natural beauty since the dawn of creation. . . .

What may yet be more subversive of social welfare are the kinds of goods that come to be produced by a commercial or consumer-oriented economy and the kinds of innovation favoured by a growth-oriented economy. These are aspects of economic life about which economists do not wish to pass judgment, but such aspects are, of course, critical to my thesis. A word, therefore, about each.

The kinds of goods produced by industry, in order to keep growing at all costs, are no more neutral in their effects on the character and taste of the citizen than are art, literature and entertainment. A society that creates institutions devoted to frenziedly gutting the earth's resources in order to meet that evergreen figment of the business world, 'the needs of industry,' an industry that disposes annually of masses of trivia, can escape a sense of its own abasement only by surreptitiously perverting human instincts and civilised values. And I cannot see the existing economic momentum in the West being maintained over the future except by increasing the outputs of just such trivia—by the production of yet more of those 'luxuries' that are a form of 'neogarbage,' or of goods that are positively inimical to health and sanity.

As for the trend in innovation, both process innovation and product innovation, it is perhaps inevitably of a labour-saving kind. This may seem no more than an economic platitude, yet it is fraught with fearsome consequences for human relationships. For this type of technological innovation, favoured by the growth-oriented economy, is undoubtedly such as to reduce over time the need for direct communication and direct dependence between men. Human contact has declined since the war with the growth of supermarkets, automatic lifts, turnstiles and vending machines, with increased ownership of motor cars, transistors and television sets, and it will continue to decline with the growth of computerisation in offices and patient-monitoring systems in hospitals, with closed circuit television instruction and teaching machines. We are in effect about to enter an era of incredible artifice in the purveying of services and entertainment—a veritable push-button world in which our whims are instantly to be gratified, although at the expense of our deeper human needs. The thought of such a world may elate the businessman and inspire the technocrat. But the inescapable consequence is that the direct flow of communication and sympathy between people becomes even thinner, and to that extent the quality of their lives becomes the poorer.

As a final instance, consider the broad social consequences of economic progress, irrespective of the goods it brings into being. Based as it is on rapid technological change, it is profoundly unsettling to ordinary men. The call by technologists is not merely for yet more change, but for the adoption of a state of continuous rapid change as a way of life in its own right. . . . For the truth is that the psyche of man seeks a settled pattern of life, craves the reassurance of familiar landmarks, the solace of familiar sounds, scenes, faces and accents, a community of shared experiences and shared affection.

Alas for man! In response to the pressures for economic growth, all things about him are in a perpetual state of dissolution. Even if he does not move house or job every few years, the environment around him is continuously and visibly changing. Where there were once open fields or a small copse, there are now rows of new houses. Where once there was a woodland path, there is now a concrete highway. And amid the din of endless drilling, old or historic buildings are being reduced to rubble and their places taken by towering plate-glass office blocks. The sorts of goods a man buys also change year by year—the models, the designs, the packaging, even the flavour of the more common foods. There is no time to form tastes, to learn to discriminate, to come to anticipate the satisfaction of things that are tried and trusted.

In a society that cultivates obsolescence as a prime virtue, nothing lasts long enough to gather affection or evoke memories. And men themselves too live on the brink of obsolescence, apprehensive that the skills and the specialised knowledge they have acquired through diligence and effort over the years will, with some new innovation, become superfluous. Legions of academics and professionals struggle to keep abreast of the relentless advance of knowledge in their specialised fields. There is no respite for fear of being left behind to sink under the waves of anonymity. Thus is the new leisure transmuted into preoccupation and eternal study.

With all their shortcomings, then, as they would appear to a chrome-plated affluent consumer society, we may well envy the small-scale preindustrial communities of the past, steeped in nostalgia and tradition. In those unhurried days familiarity was unfeigned. There was time for the idiosyncracies of life to unfold, time for lasting attachments to form, time to idle and sit around and gossip and take no heed of the morrow.

CAN THE YOUNG SAVE US?

Let me pause to anticipate the reader's remonstrances: that I take too sentimental a view of the past and too gloomy a view of the present. Space does not suffice to defend myself against both charges. I have indicated elsewhere how—by counting centennial disasters, evoking 'black' plagues, quoting 'real' income figures, citing mortality statistics, describing primitive toilet facilities, and so on—a modern historian can easily misjudge the robust sense of well-being common among ordinary people in earlier civilisations. I shall therefore restrict myself briefly to answering the latter charge: that I pay no heed to the more hopeful signs about us.

Thus, notwithstanding the postwar growth in the wealthier countries of the incidence of violence and corruption, the decay of city centres, and the manifest collapse of standards of taste and propriety, optimistic voices can be heard on both sides of the Atlantic. They talk of a new awakening among the young, especially among the middle class young in America, who have become increasingly cynical of the Protestant ethic of their fathers, and who largely reject their materialism and their striving for respectability and status.

As the young themselves see it, they are breaking the fetters of traditional values and seeking a freedom from the pressure of society—a freedom to experiment in life styles, a freedom to 'do their own thing.' 'Hippy' colonies, less popular today than they were in 1970, account only for a small proportion of the growing army of seemingly easygoing footloose youngsters, ready to talk to anyone and to try anything.

If anyone is pinning his hopes for a brighter future on this development, let me urge him to think again. For if the colour of the garment that the young choose to wear differs from that of their parents, the shape is much the same. This becomes clearer once it is understood that the motto I once associated with the spirit of economic growth, 'enough does not suffice,' has relevance not only to the acquisition of material goods, but also to any object or objective that compels the attention of the citizens of the new affluence, old or young. For the essence of the growth ethos is not materialism; it is insatiability. Although there has been a perceptible shift of emphasis from absorption in material accumulation to absorption in 'lifestyles,' there has been no diminution of appetite. The young may preen themselves on being in a different league from their fathers, playing for different prizes. But whatever the prizes, the more of them the better. From head to foot, from crown to toe, they too are maximisers.

Their apparently unlimited tolerance is chiefly a product of the moral vacuum in which they are reared; in the main it reflects their growing insensibility and promiscuity. Their inordinate fondness for 'mixing' with the world takes them by land, sea and air, in every kind of vehicle and in every kind of company, to every city and resort over the globe—there, like disoriented termite colonies, to swarm into parks and squares; to

pour through castles, palaces and galleries; to squat and sprawl, smoke and munch, over the once-hallowed steps of spired cathedrals. Travelling in groups, large or small, they extend their experience from the best hotels to the worst, seeking consciously to be equally at home everywhere; to 'slum' with the rich and 'slum' with the poor; to ape the clothes both of other countries and of other periods of history; to eat the food, borrow the accents, play the instruments and adopt the customs of other cultures; to enter the tabernacles and revel in the rituals, alike of primitive tribes and of ancient civilisations—in short, to be excluded from nothing that may pass for experience, bright or dull, good or evil, sublime or seamy.

Thus, the young of the affluent countries are today among the most ruthless and persistent plunderers of the earth's vanishing variety. Their unchecked gluttony, intensified by commercial interests, is today one of the most active forces at work combining to produce an ad-mass civilisation and to promote a cultural entropy—one that is in the process of dissolving all hierarchies, flattening all barriers, blurring all distinctions, erasing the mosaic pattern of centuries, transforming the once rich diversity of our universe into an inextricably blended monotony.

The effect on the character of the young may seem to be of less consequence, but it is no less pernicious. For this craving for endless experimentation, for savouring new 'lifestyles,' for tasting new experiences, is of the nature of a compulsion among them—a determination to wriggle like mad in every newly detected current of experience in the avid pursuit of hedonic satiation; a determination perhaps partially hindered by the few years' cramming necessary to acquire professional credentials, and later diluted only by economic constraint.

On reflection, I find these new postures, and the attitude that informs them, both less promising and less laudable than the stodgy 'bourgeois' values that are allegedly being rejected. Not only do they entail activities that are, conservatively speaking, no less profligate of natural resources; they also are a good deal further out on the scale of human folly. For after sitting through some bubble-gum courses on 'personality development,' 'self-assertion,' 'relationship enhancement,' 'stereotype avoidance,' 'creative awakening,' 'cognitive amplification' and the like, being offered today by the extracurricular departments of American campuses, the fashion among these newly emancipated spirits is in effect to select their maxims and arrange their thoughts and feelings so as, above all, to be able to 'travel light,' unhampered by affective ties. Indeed, as observed by

H. Hendin in his *Age of Sensation* (1975), all too many of the young at American colleges are unabashedly resolved to avoid falling in love and, generally, to resist surrender to feelings of love and trust, since these feelings are perceived to retard pace and 'turnover,' so encumbering the search for pleasure.

However, these fashionable excesses of the young are, on my interpretation of events, only the tip of the iceberg. Their prodigality is symptomatic of a spiritual malaise that pervades our civilisation. One has only to reflect on the growing range of expendable products, of 'luxuries,' of exhibitionist attire, of extravagant inanities, currently absorbed (despite pockets of destitution) by the consumer society to recognise that today it is less than a half-truth to assert that industry serves the needs of people. For the continuing expansion of modern industry depends directly on its continuing success in enlarging the appetite of the consuming public, so as to enable it to engorge a burgeoning variety and volume of goods. Traditional restraints on self-indulgence must perforce give way. The unrooted society, the permissive society in fact, is one of the preconditions of sustained economic growth.

As I observed in my *Costs of Economic Growth* (1967), the secularisation of society, consequent upon the rising prestige of science and the collapse of ecumenical faith, has also contributed to this transformation. The emerging generation (in spite of its commendable concern with environmental and other causes) lives in a society without religion, without patriotism, without civic pride and apparently without transcendental purpose. Not surprisingly, it is impatient of authority and of any institution believed to impede its claims to immediate gratification. Increasingly, it espouses an 'own ethic' designed to rationalise its conduct, no matter how wayward or deviant, resting its case merely on the depth of its convictions.

Economic determinism is a frightening doctrine. But is it too far-fetched to trace both the animus and the success of women's liberation to those familiar labour-saving innovations that, over the century, have rendered their domestic services increasingly expendable? And what of the permissive society, which, beginning with the joyous rejection of 'Victorian' guilt, progresses to an abandonment of the vestigial sense of shame, moves on to a clamorous rejection of any restraint on appetite and culminates in adopting the experience of pleasure as an infallible guide to the good life? It is surely a providential development by means of which the modern innovative economy, continuously under institutional compulsion to expand, can be kept going.

Yet this seemingly inevitable outcome produces a 'contradiction.' As Fred Hirsch perceived in his *Social Limits to Growth* (1976), the ethos of the permissive society, in so far as it erodes the traditional sense of personal responsibility and obligation, acts also to undermine the efficient working of the economic system itself, whether privately owned, state directed or mixed.

To where does this tend? I have argued elsewhere that economic growth in the West is producing innovations that create unprecedented social conflicts and ecological hazards, both of which demand increasing government control. This consequent trend toward more government is aggravated by the perils of the permissive society. For as the moral restraints on which any civilisation is founded are scrapped in the name of individual emancipation, so, in the name of public safety, must the state expand its powers. Internal repressive mechanisms are replaced by external ones.

The permissive society, it transpires, is the precursor of the totalitarian society.

CAN SOCIETY MOVE OFF THE GROWTH PATH?

If the reader accepts my interpretation of recent developments (although not perhaps without some reservations), and concurs in the broad conclusion that nothing very promising can be detected along the horizon toward which we are moving, he will surely be wondering whether the radical changes required to move us from the growth path are in fact politically feasible. Assuming always that popular opinion becomes increasingly sceptical of the ultimate beneficence of economic growth, will Western civilisation, which has for centuries been guided by the idea of progress—expressed in material plenty, in the advance of knowledge and in free institutions—be able to wrest itself gradually from the responses ingrained in its way of life? Will it be able to place science and technology under permanent constraint and otherwise reshape its institutions, in order to realise a saner society and a more viable economic system?

Attention to three features of the modern world tempt me to doubt it: (1) the conventional rationalisation, (2) entrenched interests, and (3) international distrust. We take them up in that order.

(1) *Conventional rationalisation* can be described as dogged persistence in the belief that, irrespective of the past record of science and technology, it is to science and technology that we must continue to turn for salvation. Certainly, if the application of some new

technology results in distress or disaster, the remedy is invariably sought in more technology, never in less. . . .

. . . From today's massive research, it is hoped, ways and means will eventually be discovered for removing all the pain and frustration from people's lives and for making them whole and beautiful again. There is, then, rationalisation enough in this discontented world of ours for public support of scientific and technological research.

(2) *Entrenched interests* is a term that brings to mind the organised power of wealthy stockholders, business magnates, landlords, bankers, industrial executives and state bureaucrats—supporters of the 'Establishment' all, and fearless growthmen at that. Their vocational purpose, as they see it, is to foster the growth of something, whether private profit, or sales, or revenues, or exports, or numbers of employees, or branches, or customers. . . .

In sum, the seemingly most powerful economic group in the modern nation-state is unwaveringly committed to continued economic growth. It may be 'purified' growth, 'humanised' growth, 'harmonious' growth or any other variety; it may be given a new title, a new set of credentials and 'a new direction.' But growth it has to be.

. . . What is more, with price and wage indices sprouting from every research centre, the members of every pay group have come to take the liveliest interest in their material prospects from one week to another. After three decades of gorging themselves from a cornucopia bulging with 'the good things of life' (enabling them, incidentally, to wreak havoc upon the environment in which they are immersed) and of quaffing periodically at the fount of unlimited expectations, workers in the affluent West are all but convinced that they are entitled by natural law, if not by common law, to a yearly rise in their real incomes. . . .

Now, strong though these economic interests are, they are not the most powerful. They would not, I think, prevail against sustained resistance by today's 'third estate,' the scientific community in the West, whose influence in society is undoubtedly on the ascendant. Despite the emergence of dissident voices over the last ten years, it is within the scientific establishment that the support for economic growth is most deeply entrenched. This support is not expressed directly, of course, not as a crude support for faster rates of gross national product. More fundamentally, it is expressed as a demand for 'freedom of inquiry,' which can be translated today into a demand for continued support and expansion of the immense facilities needed for research and development—facilities that are provided currently by industry,

by governments and by the universities. Add to this sacred principle of 'freedom of inquiry' the spur of 'social need,' the problems galore that in many instances arise from the applications of science itself, and the case for sustaining the expansion of research and development—which, of course, support the scientific community and provide its members with social privilege and influence—becomes irresistible.

But, of course, one of my conclusions is that the continued expansion of research and innovation is ultimately incompatible with the good life. I would not go so far as to argue that, only if *all* scientific and technological progress were to be halted, could there be any hope of creating a good life. To do so would be to claim both too little and too much: too little, because there is already in existence enough of the products of technology to make the good life impossible; too much, because one cannot exclude the possibility of stumbling upon innovations that are wholly beneficial on any reasonable criterion, even though we cannot foresee them. What, instead, I would argue, on the basis of observation and reflection, is that the sum of enduring happiness cannot be much augmented by further scientific discoveries, even under the most favourable circumstances.

If this much were conceded, an essential part of a social policy for the good life would be the enforcement of a general ban on all scientific research, on all new technology and on all new products—exception being made, on appeal, only for research closely directed toward discoveries serving clear humanitarian purposes. If, for example, there were the strongest grounds for believing that specific kinds of research would eventually discover remedies for a particular malignant affliction, permission to undertake or continue it might be granted, provided always that safeguards against possible accidents and side effects were regarded as paramount considerations.

The implied controls on scientific freedom of such a policy would, however, be so drastic as to amount to a virtual ban on empirical research and technological innovation. For all practical purposes economic growth would come to an end.

But imagine the plight of scientists in a steady state economy. Scores of thousands of them would have to move from their prestigious niches in industry or in a university to far humbler tasks. Hundreds of thousands of academics would have to abandon their wistful hopes of status and recognition. The ambitions of an army of technocrats would be permanently thwarted. Design departments in every industry, in every country, would close down. Research laboratories of every size and description would go to rust. Complex and ponderous computers would cease to hum. Sackfuls of learned journals would no longer appear. It would seem to many as if the vital core of society's machinery were being dismantled and that collapse must surely follow. One has but to contemplate the prospect, and the consternation it would produce, to dismiss it almost out of hand—to conclude, then, that scientific research and its translation into technological progress will indeed continue to impel us forward into the future of increasing hazard and anxiety that I have elsewhere described.

(3) *International distrust.* Finally, even if wisdom were somehow to prevail—as a providential result, we could suppose, of a succession of well-publicised near-catastrophes arising from new synthetics or technologies, none of which, mercifully, was fatal to mankind—a policy evolved to establish a steady state economy would run into another formidable obstacle: namely, the universal apprehension that any steady state control of technology would cause the country adopting it to slip behind in 'the arms race.'

I myself doubt whether these apprehensions are warranted. Technological innovation is no longer what it was in earlier times—a product of the spread of enterprise and the growth of markets. Today, it is increasingly the outcome of highly organised research and development, controlled and directed toward specific objectives. Western governments, disposing annually of scores of billions of dollars on military defence, could in principle maintain an up-to-date war technology in virtual independence of the rest of the economy. They could organise research on any required scale and build large scale plants for all specific weapons. . . .

It is not possible, then, to end on a note of even qualified optimism. Nor would it be responsible of me to contrive to do so. But if the outlook is grim indeed, it does not follow that we should feel depressed and impotent. The growth in our understanding of what has happened, and what is happening, to our civilisation, does of itself afford some satisfaction. At least, we are not as sheep lost in the wilderness. Each of us can cling to his individual sanity even amid the collective insanity.

What is more, our forebodings need not encourage an attitude of quietism. And although one possible reaction would be to 'eat, drink and be merry,' for tomorrow comes the holocaust, it is not a reaction that I should expect. For one cannot bring oneself entirely to rule out hope, if only because human beings are incurably obstinate and because they still believe in miracles. Although slender in all conscience, what filament of hope there is depends upon the creation of a growing public awareness of the forces at work in society—awareness of the traditional rationalisations of science and technology, and awareness too of the power of the entrenched material and intellectual interests that support them. Without a growing public awareness, without a growing disbelief in the still prevailing attitude that, by and large, economic growth serves us well—or, with some institutional rearrangements, can be made to serve us well—the little hope that there is for mankind would dwindle to nothing. The best that we could then hope for would be rescue by 'the man on the white horse' and thereafter a social order controlled by a benevolent but repressive bureaucracy.

REFERENCES

Hendin, H. (1975), *Age of Sensation* (Boston, Mass.).

Hirsch, F. (1976), *The Social Limits to Growth* (Cambridge, Mass.).

Mishan, E. J. (1967), *The Costs of Economic Growth* (London: Staples Press).

QUESTIONS ON MISHAN

1. How does Mishan characterize the beliefs of the "Established Enlightenment"? Do you think his characterization is complete (has he left out certain beliefs?) or does he *mis*characterize this core of beliefs?

2. What are some of the positive effects of progress? How does a closer examination of these effects reveal them to be problematic? Do you agree that these are some of the negative consequences of progress?

3. Mishan seems to hover between asserting that the negative effects are necessary or inevitable results of economic progress and saying that they are the result of chance or contingency. Which do you think he intends to say? Can these effects be avoided?

4. What does Mishan mean when he claims that "the essence of the growth ethos is not materialism; it is insatiability"? How does this "insatiability" characterize young people? Do you agree?

The Metropolis and Mental Life

Georg Simmel

Georg Simmel (1858–1918) was one of the most original and influential of the early sociologists, even though much of his work was greeted with disdain and he did not gain an academic appointment until a few years before his death. His works include The Philosophy of Money *(1900),* Conflict *(1908),* The Web of Group-Affiliations *(1922), and other essays. This essay first appeared in 1903.*

The deepest problems of modern life derive from the claim of the individual to preserve the autonomy and individuality of his existence in the face of overwhelming social forces, of historical heritage, of external culture, and of the technique of life. The fight with nature which primitive man has to wage for his *bodily* existence attains in this modern form its latest transformation. The eighteenth century called upon man to free himself of all the historical bonds in the state and in religion, in morals and in economics. Man's nature, originally good and common to all, should develop unhampered. In addition to more liberty, the nineteenth century demanded the functional specialization of man and his work; this specialization makes one individual incomparable to another, and each of them indispensable to the highest possible extent. However, this specialization makes each man the more directly dependent upon the supplementary activities of all others. Nietzsche sees the full development of the individual conditioned by the most ruthless struggle of individuals; socialism believes in the suppression of all competition for the same reason. Be that as it may, in all these positions the same basic motive is at work: the person resists to being leveled down and worn out by a social-technological mechanism. An inquiry into the inner meaning of specifically modern life and its products, into the soul of the cultural body, so to speak, must seek to solve the equation which structures like the metropolis set up between the individual and the super-individual contents of life. Such an inquiry must answer the question of how the personality accommodates itself in the adjustments to external forces. This will be my task today.

The psychological basis of the metropolitan type of individuality consists in the *intensification of nervous stimulation* which results from the swift and uninterrupted change of outer and inner stimuli. Man is a differentiating creature. His mind is stimulated by the difference between a momentary impression and the one which preceded it. Lasting impressions, impressions which differ only slightly from one another, impressions which take a regular and habitual course and show regular and habitual contrasts—all these use up, so to speak, less consciousness than does the rapid crowding of changing images, the sharp discontinuity in the grasp of a single glance, and the unexpectedness of onrushing impressions. These are the psychological conditions which the metropolis creates. With each crossing of the street, with the tempo and multiplicity of economic, occupational and social life, the city sets up a deep contrast with small town and rural life with reference to the sensory foundations of psychic life. The metropolis exacts from man as a discriminating creature a different amount of consciousness than does rural life. Here the rhythm of life and sensory mental imagery flows more slowly, more habitually, and more evenly. Precisely in this connection the sophisticated character of metropolitan psychic life becomes understandable—as over against small town life which rests more upon deeply felt and emotional relationships. These latter are rooted in the more unconscious layers of the psyche and grow most readily in the steady rhythm of uninterrupted habituations. The intellect, however, has its locus in the transparent, conscious, higher layers of the psyche; it is the most adaptable of our inner forces. In order to accommodate to change and to the contrast of phenomena, the intellect does not require any shocks and inner upheavals; it is only through such upheavals that the more conservative mind could accommodate to the metropolitan rhythm of events. Thus the metropolitan type of man—which, of course, exists in a thousand individual variants—develops an organ protecting him against the threatening currents and discrepancies of his external environment which would uproot him. He reacts with his head instead of his heart. In this an increased awareness assumes the psychic prerogative. Metropolitan life, thus, underlies a heightened awareness and a predominance of intelligence in metropolitan man. The reaction to metropolitan phenomena is shifted to that organ which is least sensitive and quite remote from the depth of the personality. Intellectuality is thus seen to preserve subjective life against the overwhelming power of metropolitan life, and intellectuality branches out in many directions and is integrated with numerous discrete phenomena.

The metropolis has always been the seat of the money economy. Here the multiplicity and concentration of economic exchange gives an importance to the means of exchange which the scantiness of rural commerce would not have allowed. Money economy and the dominance of the intellect are intrinsically connected.

They share a matter-of-fact attitude in dealing with men and with things; and, in this attitude, a formal justice is often coupled with an inconsiderate hardness. The intellectually sophisticated person is indifferent to all genuine individuality, because relationships and reactions result from it which cannot be exhausted with logical operations. In the same manner, the individuality of phenomena is not commensurate with the pecuniary principle. Money is concerned only with what is common to all: it asks for the exchange value, it reduces all quality and individuality to the question: How much? All intimate emotional relations between persons are founded in their individuality, whereas in rational relations man is reckoned with like a number, like an element which is in itself indifferent. Only the objective measurable achievement is of interest. Thus metropolitan man reckons with his merchants and customers, his domestic servants and often even with persons with whom he is obliged to have social intercourse. These features of intellectuality contrast with the nature of the small circle in which the inevitable knowledge of individuality as inevitably produces a warmer tone of behavior, a behavior which is beyond a mere objective balancing of service and return. In the sphere of the economic psychology of the small group it is of importance that under primitive conditions production serves the customer who orders the good, so that the producer and the consumer are acquainted. The modern metropolis, however, is supplied almost entirely by production for the market, that is, for entirely unknown purchasers who never personally enter the producer's actual field of vision. Through this anonymity the interests of each party acquire an unmerciful matter-of-factness; and the intellectually calculating economic egoisms of both parties need not fear any deflection because of the imponderables of personal relationships. The money economy dominates the metropolis; it has displaced the last survivals of domestic production and the direct barter of goods; it minimizes, from day to day, the amount of work ordered by customers. The matter-of-fact attitude is obviously so intimately interrelated with the money economy, which is dominant in the metropolis, that nobody can say whether the intellectualistic mentality first promoted the money economy or whether the latter determined the former. The metropolitan way of life is certainly the most fertile soil for this reciprocity, a point which I shall document merely by citing the dictum of the most eminent English constitutional historian: throughout the whole course of English history, London has never acted as England's heart but often as England's intellect and always as her moneybag!

In certain seemingly insignificant traits, which lie upon the surface of life, the same psychic currents characteristically unite. Modern mind has become more and more calculating. The calculative exactness of practical life which the money economy has brought about corresponds to the ideal of natural science: to transform the world into an arithmetic problem, to fix every part of the world by mathematical formulas. Only money economy has filled the days of so many people with weighing, calculating, with numerical determinations, with a reduction of qualitative values to quantitative ones. Through the calculative nature of money a new precision, a certainty in the definition of identities and differences, an unambiguousness in agreements and arrangements has been brought about in the relations of life-elements— just as externally this precision has been effected by the universal diffusion of pocket watches. However, the conditions of metropolitan life are at once cause and effect of this trait. The relationships and affairs of the typical metropolitan usually are so varied and complex that without the strictest punctuality in promises and services the whole structure would break down into an inextricable chaos. Above all, this necessity is brought about by the aggregation of so many people with such differentiated interests, who must integrate their relations and activities into a highly complex organism. If all clocks and watches in Berlin would suddenly go wrong in different ways, even if only by one hour, all economic life and communication of the city would be disrupted for a long time. In addition an apparently mere external factor: long distances, would make all waiting and broken appointments result in an ill-afforded waste of time. Thus, the technique of metropolitan life is unimaginable without the most punctual integration of all activities and mutual relations into a stable and impersonal time schedule. Here again the general conclusions of this entire task of reflection become obvious, namely, that from each point on the surface of existence—however closely attached to the surface alone—one may drop a sounding into the depth of the psyche so that all the most banal externalities of life finally are connected with the ultimate decisions concerning the meaning and style of life. Punctuality, calculability, exactness are forced upon life by the complexity and extension of metropolitan existence and are not only most intimately connected with its money economy and intellectualistic character. These traits must also color the contents of life and favor the exclusion of those irrational, instinctive, sovereign traits and impulses which aim at determining the mode of life from within, instead of receiving the general and precisely schematized form of life from without. Even though sovereign types of personality, characterized by irrational impulses, are by no means impossible in the city, they are, nevertheless, opposed to typical city life. The passionate hatred of men like Ruskin and Nietzsche for the metropolis is understandable in these terms. Their natures discovered the value of life alone in the unschematized existence which cannot be defined with precision for all alike. From the same source of this hatred of the metropolis surged their hatred of money economy and of the intellectualism of modern existence.

The same factors which have thus coalesced into the exactness and minute precision of the form of life have coalesced into a structure of the highest impersonality; on the other hand, they have promoted a highly personal subjectivity. There is perhaps no psychic phenomenon which has been so unconditionally reserved to the metropolis as has the blasé attitude. The blasé attitude results first from the rapidly changing and closely compressed contrasting stimulations of the nerves. From this, the enhancement of metropolitan intellectuality, also, seems originally to stem. Therefore, stupid people who are not intellectually alive in the first place usually are not exactly blasé. A life in boundless pursuit of pleasure makes one blasé because it agitates the nerves to their strongest reactivity for such a long time that they finally cease to react at all. In the same way, through the rapidity and contradictoriness of their changes, more harmless impressions force such violent responses, tearing the nerves so brutally hither and thither that their last reserves of strength are spent; and if one remains in the same milieu they have no time to gather new strength. An incapacity thus emerges to react to new sensations with the appropriate energy. This constitutes that blasé attitude which, in fact, every metropolitan child shows when compared with children of quieter and less changeable milieus.

This physiological source of the metropolitan blasé attitude is joined by another source which flows from the money economy. The essence of the blasé attitude consists in the blunting of discrimination. This does not mean that the objects are not perceived, as is the case with the half-wit, but rather that the meaning and differing values of things, and thereby the things themselves, are experienced as insubstantial. They appear to the blasé person in an evenly flat and gray tone; no one object deserves preference over any other. This mood is the faithful subjective reflection of the completely internalized money economy. By being the equivalent to all the manifold things in one and the same way, money becomes the most frightful leveler. For money expresses all qualitative differences of things in terms of "how

much?" Money, with all its colorlessness and indifference, becomes the common denominator of all values; irreparably it hollows out the core of things, their individuality, their specific value, and their incomparability. All things float with equal specific gravity in the constantly moving stream of money. All things lie on the same level and differ from one another only in the size of the area which they cover. In the individual case this coloration, or rather discoloration, of things through their money equivalence may be unnoticeably minute. However, through the relations of the rich to the objects to be had for money, perhaps even through the total character which the mentality of the contemporary public everywhere imparts to these objects, the exclusively pecuniary evaluation of objects has become quite considerable. The large cities, the main seats of the money exchange, bring the purchasability of things to the fore much more impressively than do smaller localities. That is why cities are also the genuine locale of the blasé attitude. In the blasé attitude the concentration of men and things stimulate the nervous system of the individual to its highest achievement so that it attains its peak. Through the mere quantitative intensification of the same conditioning factors this achievement is transformed into its opposite and appears in the peculiar adjustment of the blasé attitude. In this phenomenon the nerves find in the refusal to react to their stimulation the last possibility of accommodating to the contents and forms of metropolitan life. The self-preservation of certain personalities is brought at the price of devaluating the whole objective world, a devaluation which in the end unavoidably drags one's own personality down into a feeling of the same worthlessness.

Whereas the subject of this form of existence has to come to terms with it entirely for himself, his self-preservation in the face of the large city demands from him a no less negative behavior of a social nature. This mental attitude of metropolitans toward one another we may designate, from a formal point of view, as reserve. If so many inner reactions were responses to the continuous external contacts with innumerable people as are those in the small town, where one knows almost everybody one meets and where one has a positive relation to almost everyone, one would be completely atomized internally and come to an unimaginable psychic state. Partly this psychological fact, partly the right to distrust which men have in the face of the touch-and-go elements of metropolitan life, necessitates our reserve. As a result of this 'reserve' we frequently do not even know by sight those who have been our neighbors for years. And it is this reserve which in the eyes of the small-town people makes us appear to be cold and heartless. Indeed, if I do not deceive myself, the inner aspect of this outer reserve is not only indifference but, more often than we are aware, it is a slight aversion, a mutual strangeness and repulsion, which will break into hatred and fight at the moment of a closer contact, however caused. The whole inner organization of such an extensive communicative life rests upon an extremely varied hierarchy of sympathies, indifferences, and aversions of the briefest as well as of the most permanent nature. The sphere of indifference in this hierarchy is not as large as might appear on the surface. Our psychic activity still responds to almost every impression of somebody else with a somewhat distinct feeling. The unconscious, fluid and changing character of this impression seems to result in a state of indifference. Actually this indifference would be just as unnatural as the diffusion of indiscriminate mutual suggestion would be unbearable. From both these typical dangers of the metropolis, indifference and indiscriminate suggestibility, antipathy protects us. A latent antipathy and the preparatory stage of practical antagonism effect the distances and aversions without which this mode of life could not at all be led. The extent and the mixture of this style of life, the rhythm of its emergence and disappearance, the forms in which it is satisfied—all these, with the unifying motives in the narrower sense, form the inseparable whole of the metropolitan style of life. What appears in the metropolitan style of life directly as dissociation is in reality only one of its elemental forms of socialization.

This reserve with its overtone of hidden aversion appears in turn as the form or the cloak of a more general mental phenomenon of the metropolis: it grants to the individual a kind and an amount of personal freedom which has no analogy whatsoever under other conditions. The metropolis goes back to one of the large developmental tendencies of social life as such, to one of the few tendencies for which an approximately universal formula can be discovered. The earliest phase of social formations found in historical as well as in contemporary social structures is this: a relatively small circle firmly closed against neighboring, strange, or in some way antagonistic circles. However, this circle is closely coherent and allows its individual members only a narrow field for the development of unique qualities and free, self-responsible movements. Political and kinship groups, parties and religious associations begin in this way. The self-preservation of very young associations requires the establishment of strict boundaries and a centripetal unity. Therefore they cannot allow the individual freedom and unique inner and outer develop-

ment. From this stage social development proceeds at once in two different, yet corresponding, directions. To the extent to which the group grows—numerically, spatially, in significance and in content of life—to the same degree the group's direct, inner unity loosens, and the rigidity of the original demarcation against others is softened through mutual relations and connections. At the same time, the individual gains freedom of movement, far beyond the first jealous delimitation. The individual also gains a specific individuality to which the division of labor in the enlarged group gives both occasion and necessity. The state and Christianity, guilds and political parties, and innumerable other groups have developed according to this formula, however much, of course, the special conditions and forces of the respective groups have modified the general scheme. This scheme seems to me distinctly recognizable also in the evolution of individuality within urban life. The small-town life in Antiquity and in the Middle Ages set barriers against movement and relations of the individual toward the outside, and it set up barriers against individual independence and differentiation within the individual self. These barriers were such that under them modern man could not have breathed. Even today a metropolitan man who is placed in a small town feels a restriction similar, at least, in kind. The smaller the circle which forms our milieu is, and the more restricted those relations to others are which dissolve the boundaries of the individual, the more anxiously the circle guards the achievements, the conduct of life, and the outlook of the individual, and the more readily a quantitative and qualitative specialization would break up the framework of the whole little circle.

The ancient *polis* in this respect seems to have had the very character of a small town. The constant threat to its existence at the hands of enemies from near and afar effected strict coherence in political and military respects, a supervision of the citizen by the citizen, a jealousy of the whole against the individual whose particular life was suppressed to such a degree that he could compensate only by acting as a despot in his own household. The tremendous agitation and excitement, the unique colorfulness of Athenian life, can perhaps be understood in terms of the fact that a people of incomparably individualized personalities struggled against the constant inner and outer pressure of a de-individualizing small town. This produced a tense atmosphere in which the weaker individuals were suppressed and those of stronger natures were incited to prove themselves in the most passionate manner. This is precisely why it was that there blossomed in Athens what must be called, without defining it exactly, "the general human character" in the intellectual development of our species. For we maintain factual as well as historical validity for the following connection: the most extensive and the most general contents and forms of life are most intimately connected with the most individual ones. They have a preparatory stage in common, that is, they find their enemy in narrow formations and groupings the maintenance of which places both of them into a state of defense against expanse and generality lying without and the freely moving individuality within. Just as in the feudal age, the "free" man was the one who stood under the law of the land, that is, under the law of the largest social orbit, and the unfree man was the one who derived his right merely from the narrow circle of a feudal association and was excluded from the larger social orbit—so today metropolitan man is "free" in a spiritualized and refined sense, in contrast to the pettiness and prejudices which hem in the small-town man. For the reciprocal reserve and indifference and the intellectual life conditions of large circles are never felt more strongly by the individual in their impact upon his independence than in the thickest crowd of the big city. This is because the bodily proximity and narrowness of space makes the mental distance only the more visible. It is obviously only the obverse of this freedom if, under certain circumstances, one nowhere feels as lonely and lost as in the metropolitan crowd. For here as elsewhere it is by no means necessary that the freedom of man be reflected in his emotional life as comfort.

It is not only the immediate size of the area and the number of persons which, because of the universal historical correlation between the enlargement of the circle and the personal inner and outer freedom, has made the metropolis the locale of freedom. It is rather in transcending this visible expanse that any given city becomes the seat of cosmopolitanism. The horizon of the city expands in a manner comparable to the way in which wealth develops; a certain amount of property increases in a quasi-automatical way in ever more rapid progression. As soon as a certain limit has been passed, the economic, personal, and intellectual relations of the citizenry, the sphere of intellectual predominance of the city over its hinterland, grow as in geometrical progression. Every gain in dynamic extension becomes a step, not for an equal, but for a new and larger extension. From every thread spinning out of the city, ever new threads grow as if by themselves, just as within the city the unearned increment of ground rent, through the mere increase in communication, brings the owner automatically increasing profits. At this point, the quantitative aspect of life is transformed directly into qualitative traits of character. The sphere of life of the small town is, in the main, self-contained and autarchic. For it is the decisive nature of the metropolis that its inner life overflows by waves into a far-flung national or international area. Weimar is not an example to the contrary, since its significance was hinged upon individual personalities and died with them; whereas the metropolis is indeed characterized by its essential independence even from the most eminent individual personalities. This is the counterpart to the independence, and it is the price the individual pays for the independence, which he enjoys in the metropolis. The most significant characteristic of the metropolis is this functional extension beyond its physical boundaries. And this efficacy reacts in turn and gives weight, importance, and responsibility to metropolitan life. Man does not end with the limits of his body or the area comprising his immediate activity. Rather is the range of the person constituted by the sum of effects emanating from him temporally and spatially. In the same way, a city consists of its total effects which extend beyond its immediate confines. Only this range is the city's actual extent in which its existence is expressed. This fact makes it obvious that individual freedom, the logical and historical complement of such extension, is not to be understood only in the negative sense of mere freedom of mobility and elimination of prejudices and petty philistinism. The essential point is that the particularity and incomparability, which ultimately every human being possesses, be somehow expressed in the working-out of a way of life. That we follow the laws of our own nature—and this after all is freedom—becomes obvious and convincing to ourselves and to others only if the expressions of this nature differ from the expressions of others. Only our unmistakability proves that our way of life has not been superimposed by others.

Cities are, first of all, seats of the highest economic division of labor. They produce thereby such extreme phenomena as in Paris the renumerative occupation of the *quatorzième*. They are persons who identify themselves by signs on their residences and who are ready at the dinner hour in correct attire, so that they can be quickly called upon if a dinner party should consist of thirteen persons. In the measure of its expansion, the city offers more and more the decisive conditions of the division of labor. It offers a circle which through its size can absorb a highly diverse variety of services. At the same time, the concentration of individuals and their struggle for customers compel the individual to specialize in a function from which he cannot be readily displaced by another. It is decisive that city life has transformed the struggle with nature for livelihood into an inter-human struggle for gain, which here is not granted by nature but by other men. For specialization does not flow only from the competition for gain but also from the underlying fact that the seller must always seek to call forth new and differentiated needs of the lured customer. In order to find a source of income which is not yet exhausted, and to find a function which cannot readily be displaced, it is necessary to specialize in one's services. This process promotes differentiation, refinement, and the enrichment of the public's needs, which obviously must lead to growing personal differences within this public.

All this forms the transition to the individualization of mental and psychic traits which the city occasions in proportion to its size. There is a whole series of obvious causes underlying this process. First, one must meet the difficulty of asserting his own personality within the dimensions of metropolitan life. Where the quantitative increase in importance and the expense of energy reach their limits, one seizes upon qualitative differentiation in order somehow to attract the attention of the social circle by playing upon its sensitivity for differences. Finally, man is tempted to adopt the most tendentious peculiarities, that is, the specifically metropolitan extravagances of mannerism, caprice, and preciousness. Now, the meaning of these extravagances does not at all lie in the contents of such behavior, but rather in its form of "being different," of standing out in a striking manner and thereby attracting attention. For many character types, ultimately the only means of saving for themselves some modicum of self-esteem and the sense of filling a position is indirect, through the awareness of others. In the same sense a seemingly insignificant factor is operating, the cumulative effects of which are, however, still noticeable. I refer to the brevity and scarcity of the inter-human contacts granted to the metropolitan man, as compared with social intercourse in the small town. The temptation to appear "to the point," to appear concentrated and strikingly characteristic, lies much closer to the individual in brief metropolitan contacts than in an atmosphere in which frequent and prolonged association assures the personality of an unambiguous image of himself in the eyes of the other.

The most profound reason, however, why the metropolis conduces to the urge for the most individual personal existence—no matter whether justified and successful—appears to me to be the following: the development of modern culture is characterized by the preponderance of what one may call the "objective spirit" over the "subjective spirit." This is to say, in language as well as in law, in the technique of production as well as in art, in science as well as in the objects of the domestic environment, there is embodied a sum of spirit. The individual in his intellectual development follows the growth of this spirit very imperfectly and at an ever increasing distance. If, for instance, we view the immense culture which for the last hundred years has been embodied in things and in knowledge, in institutions and in comforts, and if we compare all this with the cultural progress of the individual during the same period—at least in high status groups—a frightful disproportion in growth between the two becomes evident. Indeed, at some points we notice a retrogression in the culture of the individual with reference to spirituality, delicacy, and idealism. This discrepancy results essentially from the growing division of labor. For the division of labor demands from the individual an ever more one-sided accomplishment, and the greatest advance in a one-sided pursuit only too frequently means dearth to the personality of the individual. In any case, he can cope less and less with the overgrowth of objective culture. The individual is reduced to a negligible quantity, perhaps less in his consciousness than in his practice and in the totality of his obscure emotional states that are derived from this practice. The individual has become a mere cog in an enormous organization of things and powers which tear from his hands all progress, spirituality, and value in order to transform them from their subjective form into the form of a purely objective life. It needs merely to be pointed out that the metropolis is the genuine arena of this culture which outgrows all personal life. Here in buildings and educational institutions, in the wonders and comforts of space-conquering technology, in the formations of community life, and in the visible institutions of the state, is offered such an overwhelming fullness of crystallized and impersonalized spirit that the personality, so to speak, cannot maintain itself under its impact. On the one hand, life is made infinitely easy for the personality in that stimulations, interests, uses of time and consciousness are offered to it from all sides. They carry the person as if in a stream, and one needs hardly to swim for oneself. On the other hand, however, life is composed more and more of these impersonal contents and offerings which tend to displace the genuine personal colorations and incomparabilities. This results in the individual's summoning the utmost in uniqueness and particularization, in order to preserve his most personal core. He has to exaggerate this personal element in order to remain audible even to himself. The atrophy of individual culture through the hypertrophy of objective culture is one reason for the bitter hatred which the preachers of the most extreme individualism, above all Nietzsche, harbor against the metropolis. But it is, indeed, also a reason why these preachers are so passionately loved in the metropolis and why they appear to the metropolitan man as the prophets and saviors of his most unsatisfied yearnings.

If one asks for the historical position of these two forms of individualism which are nourished by the quantitative relation of the metropolis, namely, individual independence and the elaboration of individuality itself, then the metropolis assumes an entirely new rank order in the world history of the spirit. The eighteenth century found the individual in oppressive bonds which had become meaningless—bonds of a political, agrarian, guild, and religious character. They were restraints which, so to speak, forced upon man an unnatural form and outmoded, unjust inequalities. In this situation the cry for liberty and equality arose, the belief in the individual's full freedom of movement in all social and intellectual relationships. Freedom would at once permit the noble substance common to all to come to the fore, a substance which nature had deposited in every man and which society and history had only deformed. Besides this eighteenth-century ideal of liberalism, in the nineteenth century, through Goethe and Romanticism, on the one hand, and through the economic division of labor, on the other hand, another ideal arose: individuals liberated from historical bonds now wished to distinguish themselves from one another. The carrier of man's values is no longer the "general human being" in every individual, but rather man's qualitative uniqueness and irreplaceability. The external and internal history of our time takes its course within the struggle and in the changing entanglements of these two ways of defining the individual's role in the whole of society. It is the function of the metropolis to provide the arena for this struggle and its reconciliation. For the metropolis presents the peculiar conditions which are revealed to us as the opportunities and the stimuli for the development of both these ways of allocating roles to men. Therewith these conditions gain a unique place, pregnant with inestimable meanings for the development of psychic existence. The metropolis reveals itself as one of those great historical formations in which opposing streams which enclose life unfold, as well as join one another with equal right. However, in this process the currents of life, whether their individual phenomena touch us sympathetically or antipathetically, entirely transcend

the sphere for which the judge's attitude is appropriate. Since such forces of life have grown into the roots and into the crown of the whole of the historical life in which we, in our fleeting existence, as a cell, belong only as a part, it is not our task either to accuse or to pardon, but only to understand.*

ENDNOTE

* The content of this lecture by its very nature does not derive from a citable literature. Argument and elaboration of its major cultural-historical ideas are contained in my *Philosophie des Geldes* [*The Philosophy of Money;* München and Leipzig: Duncker und Humblot, 1900].

QUESTIONS ON SIMMEL

1. According to Simmel, how does the character of the metropolitan way of life differ from that of a rural mode of life? How does Simmel account for the causes of these differences?

2. In what ways does commerce emphasize the rational? How does commerce relate to metropolitan life? What is the basis for Simmel's assertion that the "money economy and the domination of the intellect" stand in close relation? What is this relation and how does Simmel support his conclusion?

3. What does Simmel mean when he states that the "indifference toward the distinctions between things" is the "correct subjective reflection of a complete money economy"? Do you think that this is correct?

4. Which of Simmel's claims can be confirmed by empirical observation? How does he justify his assertions?

The Consumer Society

Jean Baudrillard

Jean Baudrillard was born in Reims in 1929 and is the author of numerous books and essays. Since the 1980s he has been a well-known representative of postmodernism. Influenced by both Freud and Marx, he is the author of Consumer Society *(1970),* For a Critique of the Political Economy of the Sign *(1972),* Symbolic Exchange and Death *(1976), as well as a diary of travels in the United States,* America *(1988).*

PROFUSION

There is all around us today a kind of fantastic conspicuousness of consumption and abundance, constituted by the multiplication of objects, services and material goods, and this represents something of a fundamental mutation in the ecology of the human species. Strictly speaking, the humans of the age of affluence are surrounded not so much by other human beings, as they were in all previous ages, but by **objects.** Their daily dealings are now not so much with their fellow men, but rather—on a rising statistical curve—with the reception and manipulation of goods and messages. This runs from the very complex organization of the household, with its dozens of technical slaves, to street furniture and the whole material machinery of communication; from professional activities to the permanent spectacle of the celebration of the object in advertising and the hundreds of daily messages from the mass media; from the minor proliferation of vaguely obsessional gadgetry to the symbolic psychodramas fuelled by the nocturnal objects which come to haunt us even in our dreams. The two concepts 'environment' and 'ambience' have doubtless only enjoyed such a vogue since we have come to live not so much alongside other human beings—in their physical presence and the presence of their speech—as beneath the mute gaze of mesmerizing, obedient objects which endlessly repeat the same refrain: that of our dumbfounded power, our virtual affluence, our absence one from another. Just as the wolf-child became a wolf by living among wolves, so we too are slowly becoming functional. We live by object time: by this I mean that we live at the pace of objects, live to the rhythm of their ceaseless succession. Today, it is we who watch them as they are born, grow to maturity and die, whereas in all previous civilizations it was timeless objects, instruments or monuments which outlived the generations of human beings.

Objects are neither a flora nor a fauna. And yet they do indeed give the impression of a proliferating vegetation, a jungle in which the new wild man of modern times has difficulty recovering the reflexes of civilization. We have to attempt rapidly to describe this fauna and flora, which man has produced and which comes back to encircle and invade him as it might in a bad science fiction novel. We have to describe these things as we see and experience them, never forgetting, in their splendour and profusion, that they are *the product of a human activity* and are dominated not by natural ecological laws, but by the law of exchange-value.

> The busiest streets of London are crowded with shops whose show cases display all the riches of the world, Indian shawls, American revolvers, Chinese porcelain, Parisian corsets, furs from Russia and spices from the tropics, but all of these worldly things bear odious, white paper labels with Arabic numerals and the laconic symbols £.s.d. This is how commodities are presented in circulation. (Marx)[1]

Profusion and the Package

Profusion, piling high are clearly the most striking descriptive features. The big department stores, with their abundance of canned foods and clothing, of foodstuffs and ready-made garments, are like the primal landscape, the geometrical locus of abundance. But every street, with its cluttered, glittering shop-windows (the least scarce commodity here being light, without which the merchandise would be merely what it is), their displays of cooked meats, and indeed the entire alimentary and vestimentary feast, all stimulate magical salivation. There is something more in this piling high than the quantity of products: the manifest presence of surplus, the magical, definitive negation of scarcity, the maternal, luxurious sense of being already in the Land of Cockaigne. Our markets, major shopping thoroughfares and superstores also mimic a new-found nature of prodigious fecundity. These are our Valleys of Canaan where, in place of milk and honey, streams of neon flow down over ketchup and plastic. But no matter! We find here the fervid hope that there should be not enough, but too much—and too much for everyone: by buying a piece of this land, you acquire the crumbling pyramid of oysters, meats, pears or tinned asparagus. You buy the part for the whole. And this metonymic, repetitive discourse of consumable matter, of the *commodity,* becomes once again, through a great collective metaphor—by virtue of its very excess—the image of the *gift,* and of that inexhaustible and spectacular prodigality which characterizes the *feast.*

Beyond stacking, which is the most rudimentary yet cogent form of abundance, objects are organized in *packages* or *collections.* Almost all the shops selling clothing or household appliances offer a *range* of differentiated objects, evoking, echoing and offsetting one another. The antique dealer's window provides the aristocratic, luxury version of these sets of objects, which evoke not so much a superabundance of substance as a *gamut* of select and complementary objects presented for the consumer to choose among, but presented also to create in him a psychological chain reaction, as he peruses them, inventories them and grasps them as a total category. Few objects today are offered *alone,* without a context of objects which 'speaks' them. And this changes the consumer's relation to the object: he no longer relates to a particular object in its specific utility, but to a set of objects in its total signification. Washing machine, refrigerator and dishwasher taken together have a different meaning from the one each has individually as an appliance. The shop-window, the advertisement, the manufacturer and the *brand name,* which here plays a crucial role, impose a coherent, collective vision, as though they were an almost indissociable totality, a series. This is, then, no longer a sequence of mere objects, but a chain of *signifiers,* in so far as all of these signify one another reciprocally as part of a more complex super-object, drawing the consumer into a series of more complex motivations. It is evident that objects are never offered for consumption in absolute disorder. They may, in certain cases, imitate disorder the better to seduce, but they are always arranged to mark out directive paths, to orientate the purchasing impulse towards *networks* of objects in order to captivate that impulse and bring it, in keeping with its own logic, to the highest degree of commitment, to the limits of its economic potential. Clothing, machines and toiletries thus constitute object *pathways,* which establish inertial constraints in the consumer: he will move *logically* from one object to another. He will be caught up in a *calculus* of objects, and this is something quite different from the frenzy of buying and acquisitiveness to which the simple profusion of commodities gives rise.

The Drugstore

The synthesis of profusion and calculation is the drugstore. The drugstore (or the new shopping centre) achieves a synthesis of consumer activities, not the least of which are shopping, flirting with objects, playful wandering and all the permutational possibilities of these: In this respect, the drugstore is more representative of modern consumption than the department stores. There, the quantitative centralization of the products leaves less margin for ludic exploration, the arrangement of departments and products imposing a more utilitarian path on the consumer. And, generally, the large stores retain something of the period in which they emerged, when broad classes of the population were first gaining access to *everyday* consumer goods. There is a quite different meaning to the drugstore: it does not juxtapose categories of merchandise, but *lumps signs together indiscriminately,* lumps together all categories of commodities, which are regarded as partial fields of a sign-consuming totality. In the drugstore, the cultural center

becomes part of the shopping centre. It would be simplistic to say that culture is 'prostituted' there. It is *culturalized.* Simultaneously, commodities (clothing, groceries, catering etc.) are also culturalized in their turn, since they are transformed into the substance of play and distinction, into luxury accessories, into one element among others in the general *package* of consumables.

> A new art of living, a new way of living, say the adverts—a 'switched-on' daily experience. You can shop pleasantly in a single air-conditioned location, buy your food there, purchase things for your flat or country cottage—clothing, flowers, the latest novel or the latest gadget. And you can do all this in a single trip, while husband and children watch a film, and then all dine together right there.

There's a café, a cinema, a bookshop, places to buy trinkets, clothing and lots more in the shopping centres: the drugstore takes in everything in kaleidoscopic mode. If the department store offers the fairground spectacle of commodities, the drugstore presents the subtle recital of consumption, the whole 'art' of which consists in playing on the ambiguity of the sign in objects, and sublimating their status as things of use and as commodities in a play upon 'ambience.' This is generalized neo-culture, where there is no longer any difference between a delicatessen and an art gallery, between *Playboy* and a treatise on palaeontology. And the drugstore is to modernize itself to the point of introducing 'grey matter':

> Just selling products doesn't interest us. We want to put a bit of grey matter in there too . . . Three levels. A bar, a dance-floor and sales outlets. Knick-knacks, records, paperback books, intellectual books, a bit of everything. But we aren't trying to flatter the clientele. We are really offering them 'something.' A language laboratory operates on the second level. Among the records and books, you can find the major movements which are stirring our society. Experimental music, tomes which explain our times. This is the 'grey matter' that goes with the products we sell. It's a drugstore, then, but a new-style drugstore with something extra—a little intelligence, perhaps, and a bit of human warmth.

The drugstore can become a whole town: this is the case with Parly 2 with its giant shopping centre in which 'art and leisure mingle with everyday life' and each group of residences radiates out from its swimming-pool, where the local clubhouse becomes its focus. A church built 'in the round,' tennis courts ('the least we could do'), elegant boutiques and a library. The tiniest ski resort borrows this 'universalist' model of the drugstore: all activities there are encapsulated in, systematically combined around and centred on the basic concept of 'ambience.' Thus Flaine-la-Prodigue offers you a complete, all-purpose, combinatorial existence:

> Our Mont Blanc, our spruce forests; our Olympic runs, our children's 'plateau'; our architecture carved, chiselled and polished like a work of art; the purity of the air we breathe; the refined ambience of our Forum (modelled on the forums of Mediterranean towns. A lively time is to be had there after a day on the slopes. Cafés, restaurants, shops, skating-rinks, a night club, a cinema and a cultural and amusement centre are all located in the Forum to make the life you live off-piste particularly rich and varied); our internal TV system; our world-scale future (we shall soon be listed as a cultural monument by the Arts Ministry).[2]

We are at the point where consumption is laying hold of the whole of life, where all activities are sequenced in the same combinatorial mode, where the course of satisfaction is outlined in advance, hour by hour, where the 'environment' is total—fully air-conditioned, organized, culturalized. In the phenomenology of consumption, this general 'air-conditioning' of life, goods, objects, services, behaviour and social relations represents the perfected, 'consummated' [*consommé*] stage of an evolution which runs from affluence pure and simple, through interconnected networks of objects, to the total conditioning of action and time, and finally to the systematic atmospherics built into those cities of the future that are our drugstores, Parly 2s and modern airports.

Parly 2
'The biggest shopping centre in Europe.'

'Printemps, BHV, Dior, Prisunic, Lanvin, Franck et Fils, Hédiard, two cinemas, a drugstore, a Suma supermarket, a hundred other shops—all in a single location!'

In the choice of shops, from grocery to high fashion, two imperatives: commercial dynamism and aesthetic sense. The famous slogan, 'Ugliness doesn't sell,' is now *passé*. It might be replaced by: 'The beauty of the setting is the prime requirement for happy living.'

A two-storey structure organized around a central mall, which is the split-level main thoroughfare—the triumphal avenue. Small- and large-scale traders reconciled. The modern pace of life reconciled with age-old idle wandering.

The unprecedented comfort of strolling among shops whose tempting wares are openly displayed on the mall, without even a shop-window for a screen, the mall itself being a combination of the rue de la Paix and the Champs-Elysées. Adorned with fountains, artificial trees, pavilions and benches, it is wholly exempt from changes of season or bad weather: an exceptional system of climate control, requiring 13 kilometres of air-conditioning ducts, makes for perpetual springtime.

Not only can you buy anything here, from shoelaces to an airline ticket; not only can you find insurance companies and cinemas, banks or medical services, bridge clubs and art exhibitions, but you are not a slave to the clock. The mall, like any street, is accessible night and day, seven days a week.

Naturally, for those who want it, the centre has introduced the most modern style of payment: the 'credit card.' This frees shoppers from cheques or cash—and even from financial difficulties. To pay, you just show your card and sign the bill. There's nothing more to it. And every month you get a statement which you can pay off in full or in monthly instalments.

In this marriage of comfort, beauty and efficiency, the Parlysians are discovering the material conditions of happiness which our anarchic cities denied them.

We are here at the heart of consumption as total organization of everyday life, total homogenization, where everything is taken over and superseded in the ease and translucidity of an abstract 'happiness,' defined solely by the resolution of tensions. The drugstore writ large in the form of the shopping centre, the city of the future, is the *sublimate* of all real life, of all objective social life, in which not only work and money disappear, but also the seasons, those distant vestiges of a cycle which has at last also been homogenized! Work, leisure, nature and culture: all these things which were once dispersed, which once generated anxiety and complexity in real life, in our 'anarchic and archaic towns and cities,' all these sundered activities, these activities which were more or less irreducible one to another, are now at last mixed and blended, climatized and homogenized in the same sweeping vista of perpetual shopping. All are now rendered sexless in the same hermaphroditic ambience of fashion! All at last *digested* and turned into the same homogeneous faecal matter (naturally enough, this occurs precisely under the sign of the disappearance of *liquid cash*—too visible a symbol still of the *real* faecality of real life, and of the economic and social contradictions which once inhabited it). That is all over now. *Controlled,* lubricated, *consumed* faecality has passed into things; it seeps everywhere into the indistinctness of things and social relations. Just as the gods of all countries coexisted syncretically in the Roman Pantheon in an immense 'digest,' so all the gods—or demons—of consumption have come together in our Super Shopping Centre, which is our Pantheon—or Pandaemonium. In other words, all activities, labour, conflicts and seasons have been united and abolished in the same abstraction. The substance of life unified in this way, in this universal digest, can no longer have in it any *meaning:* what constituted the dreamwork, the labour of poetry and of meaning—in other words, the grand schemata of displacement and condensation, the great figures of metaphor and contradiction, which are based on the living interconnection of distinct elements—is no longer possible. The eternal substitution of homogeneous elements now reigns unchallenged. There is no longer any symbolic function, but merely an eternal combinatory of 'ambience' in a perpetual springtime.

ENDNOTES

1. K. Marx, *A Contribution to the Critique of Political Economy,* Lawrence and Wishart, London, 1971, p. 87.
2. Contrary to a rather odd assertion in Mark Poster's book *Jean Baudrillard: Selected Writings* (Polity, 1988, p. 55, note 4), Flaine is not 'Baudrillard's parody of suburban communities around Paris' but a genuine ski resort in Haute-Savoie (Tr.).

QUESTIONS ON BAUDRILLARD

1. Baudrillard claims that "the humans of the age of affluence are surrounded not so much by other human beings . . . but by **objects.**" What does he mean by this claim? In what sense, if any, is this true?

2. In what ways are consumer objects displayed so as to function as "networks" of objects? Do networks of objects constrain decision making? Are they merely helpful in forming a choice? Or are they seductive?

3. How does Baudrillard explain that consumption has now "grasped the whole of life"? Is there a sense in which this is true? What are some of the problems of consumption?

A Framework for Utopia

Robert Nozick

Robert Nozick, Pellegrino University Professor of Philosophy at Harvard University, is the author of Philosophical Explanations *(1981),* The Examined Life *(1990),* The Nature of Rationality *(1993),* Socratic Puzzles *(1997), and* Invariances *(2001). This excerpt is from Part III of* Anarchy, State, and Utopia *(1974).*

No state more extensive than the minimal state can be justified. But doesn't the idea, or ideal, of the minimal state lack luster? Can it thrill the heart or inspire people to struggle or sacrifice? Would anyone man barricades under its banner?[1] It seems pale and feeble in comparison with, to pick the polar extreme, the hopes and dreams of utopian theorists. Whatever its virtues, it appears clear that the minimal state is no utopia. We would expect then that an investigation into utopian theory should more than serve to highlight the defects and shortcomings of the minimal state as the end of political philosophy. Such an investigation also promises to be intrinsically interesting. Let us then pursue the theory of utopia to where it leads.

THE MODEL

The totality of conditions we would wish to impose on societies which are (preeminently) to qualify as utopias, taken jointly, are inconsistent. That it is impossible simultaneously and continually to realize all social and political goods is a regrettable fact about the human condition, worth investigating and bemoaning. Our subject here, however, is the best of all possible worlds. For whom? The best of all possible worlds for me will not be that for you. The world, of all those I can imagine, which I would most prefer to live in, will not be precisely the one you would choose. Utopia, though, must be, in some restricted sense, the best for all of us; the best world imaginable, for each of us. In what sense can this be?

Imagine a possible world in which to live; this world need not contain everyone else now alive, and it may contain beings who have never actually lived. Every rational* creature in this world you have imagined will have the same rights of imagining a possible world for himself to live in (in which all other rational inhabitants have the same imagining rights, and so on) as you have. The other inhabitants of the world you have imagined may choose to stay in the world which has been created for them (they have been created for) or they may choose to leave it and inhabit a world of their own imagining. If they choose to leave your world and live in another, your world is without them. You may choose to abandon your imagined world, now without its emigrants. This process goes on; worlds are created, people leave them, create new worlds, and so on.

Will the process go on indefinitely? Are all such worlds ephemeral or are there some stable worlds in which all of the original population will choose to remain? If this process does result in some stable worlds, what interesting general conditions does each of them satisfy?

---

*I use "rational" or "rational creature" as short for beings having those properties in virtue of which a being has those full rights that human beings have; I do not mean here to say anything about what those properties are.

If there are stable worlds, each of them satisfies one very desirable description by virtue of the way the worlds have been set up; namely, *none* of the inhabitants of the world can *imagine* an alternative world they would rather live in, which (they believe) would continue to exist if all of its rational inhabitants had the same rights of imagining and emigrating. This description is so very attractive that it is of great interest to see what other features are common to all such stable worlds. So that we continually do not have to repeat long descriptions, let us call a world which all rational inhabitants may leave for any other world they can imagine (in which all the rational inhabitants may leave for any other world they can imagine in which . . .) an *association;* and let us call a world in which some rational inhabitants are not permitted to emigrate to some of the associations they can imagine, an *east-berlin.* Thus our original attractive description says that no member of a stable association can imagine another association, which (he believes) would be stable, that he would rather be a member of.

What are such stable associations like? Here I can offer only some intuitive and overly simple arguments. You will not be able to set up an association in which you are the absolute monarch, exploiting all the other rational inhabitants. For then they would be better off in an association without you, and, at the very least, they all would choose to inhabit that one containing all of them minus you, rather than remain in your creation. No stable association is such that everyone (but one) in it jointly would leave for their own association; for this would contradict the assumption that the original association was stable. This reasoning applies as well to two or three or *n* persons whom everyone else in an association would be better off without. Thus we have as a condition of stable associations: if A is a set of persons in a stable association then there is no proper subset S of A such that each member of S is better off in an association consisting only of members of S, than he is in A. For if there were such a subset S, its members would secede from A, establishing their own association. . . .

THE MODEL PROJECTED ONTO OUR WORLD

In *our* actual world, what corresponds to the model of possible worlds is a wide and diverse range of communities which people can enter if they are admitted, leave if they wish to, shape according to their wishes; a society in which utopian experimentation can be tried, different styles of life can be lived, and alternative visions of the

good can be individually or jointly pursued. The details and some of the virtues of such an arrangement, which we shall call the *framework,* will emerge as we proceed. There are important differences between the model and the model's projection onto the actual world. The problems with the operation of the framework in the actual world stem from the divergencies between our earthbound actual life and the possible-worlds model we have been discussing, raising the question of whether even if the realization of the model itself would be ideal, the realization of its pale projection *is* the best we can do here.

1. Unlike the model, we cannot create all the people whose existence we desire. So that even if there were a possible maximally mutually valuing association containing you, its other members actually may not exist; and the other persons among whom you actually live will not constitute your best fan club. Also there may be a particular kind of community you wish to live in, yet not enough other actual people (can be persuaded to) wish to live in such a community so as to give it a viable population. In the model, for a diverse range of nonexploitative communities, there are always enough other persons who wish to live in one.

2. Unlike the model, in the actual world communities *impinge* upon one another, creating problems of foreign relations and self-defense and necessitating modes of adjudicating and resolving disputes between the communities. (In the model, one association impinges upon another only by drawing away some of its members.)

3. In the actual world, there are information costs in finding out what other communities there are, and what they are like, and moving and travel costs in going from one community to another.

4. Furthermore, in the actual world, some communities may try to keep some of their members ignorant of the nature of other alternative communities they might join, to try to prevent them from freely leaving their own community to join another. This raises the problem of how freedom of movement is to be institutionalized and enforced when there are some who will wish to restrict it. . . .

THE FRAMEWORK

It would be disconcerting if there were only one argument or connected set of reasons for the adequacy of a particular description of utopia. Utopia is the focus of so many different strands of aspiration that there must be many theoretical paths leading to it. Let us sketch some of these alternate, mutually supporting, theoretical routes.*

The first route begins with the fact that people are different. They differ in temperament, interests, intellectual ability, aspirations, natural bent, spiritual quests, and the kind of life they wish to lead. They diverge in the values they have and have different weightings for the values they share. (They wish to live in different climates—some in mountains, plains, deserts, seashores, cities, towns.) There is no reason to think that there is *one* community which will serve as ideal for all people and much reason to think that there is not.

We may distinguish among the following theses:

I. For each person there is a kind of life that objectively is the best for him.
   a. People are similar enough, so that there is one kind of life which objectively is the best for each of them.
   b. People are different, so that there is *not* one kind of life which objectively is the best for everyone, and,
      1. The different kinds of life are similar enough so that there *is* one kind of community (meeting certain constraints) which objectively is the best for everyone.
      2. The different kinds of life are so different that there is *not* one kind of community (meeting certain constraints) which objectively is the best for everyone (no matter which of these different lives is best for them).

II. For each person, so far as objective criteria of goodness can tell (insofar as these exist), there is a wide range of very different kinds of life that tie as best; no other is objectively better for him than any one in this range, and no one within the range is objectively better than any other.[2] And there is not one community which objectively is the best for the living of each selection set from the family of sets of not objectively inferior lives.

For our purposes at this point either of Ib2 or II will serve.

Wittgenstein, Elizabeth Taylor, Bertrand Russell, Thomas Merton, Yogi Berra, Allen Ginsburg, Harry Wolfson, Thoreau, Casey Stengel, The Lubavitcher Rebbe, Picasso, Moses, Einstein, Hugh Heffner, Socrates, Henry Ford, Lenny Bruce, Baba Ram Dass, Gandhi, Sir Edmund Hillary, Raymond Lubitz, Buddha, Frank Sinatra, Columbus, Freud, Norman Mailer, Ayn Rand, Baron Rothschild, Ted Williams, Thomas Edison, H. L. Mencken, Thomas Jefferson, Ralph Ellison, Bobby Fischer, Emma Goldman, Peter Kropotkin, you, and your parents. Is there really *one* kind of life which is best for each of these people? Imagine all of them living in any utopia you've ever seen described in detail. Try to describe the society which would be best for all of these persons to live in. Would it be agricultural or urban? Of great material luxury or of austerity with basic needs satisfied? What would relations between the sexes be like? Would there be any institution similar to marriage? Would it be monogamous? Would children be raised by their parents? Would there be private property? Would there be a serene secure life or one with adventures, challenges, dangers, and opportunities for heroism? Would there be one, many, any religion? How important would it be in people's lives? Would people view their life as importantly centered about private concerns or about public action and issues of public policy? Would they be single-mindedly devoted to particular kinds of accomplishments and work or jacks-of-all-trades and pleasures or would they concentrate on full and satisfying leisure activities? Would children be raised permissively, strictly? What would their education concentrate upon? Will sports be important in people's lives (as spectators, participants)? Will art? Will sensual pleasures or intellectual activities predominate? Or what? Will there be fashions in clothing? Will great pains be taken to beautify appearance? What will the attitude toward death be? Would technology and gadgets play an important role in the society? And so on.

The idea that there is one best composite answer to all of these questions, one best society for *everyone* to live in, seems to me to be an incredible one. (And the idea that, if there is one, we now know enough to describe it is even more incredible.) No one should attempt to describe a utopia unless he's recently reread, for example, the works of Shakespeare, Tolstoy, Jane Austen, Rabelais and Dostoevski to remind himself of how different people are. (It will also serve to remind him of how complex they are; see the third route below.)

Utopian authors, each very confident of the virtues of his own vision and of its singular correctness, have differed among themselves (no less than the people listed above differ) in the institutions and kinds of life they present for emulation. Though the picture of an ideal so-

---

*In order to keep the line of argument here independent of the first two parts of this book, I do not discuss here the moral arguments for individual liberty.

ciety that each presents is much too simple (even for the component communities to be discussed below), we should take the fact of the differences seriously. No utopian author has everyone in his society leading exactly the same life, allocating exactly the same amount of time to exactly the same activities. *Why not?* Don't the reasons also count against just one kind of community?

The conclusion to draw is that there will not be *one* kind of community existing and one kind of life led in utopia. Utopia will consist of utopias, of many different and divergent communities in which people lead different kinds of lives under different institutions. Some kinds of communities will be more attractive to most than others; communities will wax and wane. People will leave some for others or spend their whole lives in one. Utopia is a framework for utopias, a place where people are at liberty to join together voluntarily to pursue and attempt to realize their own vision of the good life in the ideal community but where no one can *impose* his own utopian vision upon others.[3] The utopian society is the society of utopianism. (Some of course may be content where they are. Not *everyone* will be joining special experimental communities, and many who abstain at first will join the communities later, after it is clear how they actually are working out.) Half of the truth I wish to put forth is that utopia is meta-utopia: the environment in which utopian experiments may be tried out; the environment in which people are free to do their own thing; the environment which must, to a great extent, be realized first if more particular utopian visions are to be realized stably.

If, as we noted at the beginning of this chapter, not all goods can be realized simultaneously, then trade-offs will have to be made. The second theoretical route notes that there is little reason to believe that one unique system of trade-offs will command universal assent. Different communities, each with a slightly different mix, will provide a range from which each individual can choose that community which best approximates *his* balance among competing values. (Its opponents will call this the smorgasbord conception of utopia, preferring restaurants with only one dinner available, or, rather, preferring a one-restaurant town with one item on the menu.)

DESIGN DEVICES AND FILTER DEVICES

The third theoretical route to the framework for utopia is based on the fact that people are complex. As are the webs of possible relationships among them. Suppose (falsely) that the earlier arguments are mistaken and that *one* kind

of society *is* best for all. How are we to find out what this society is like? Two methods suggest themselves, which we shall call design devices and filter devices.

Design devices construct something (or its description) by some procedure which does not essentially involve constructing descriptions of others of its type. The result of the process is one object. In the case of societies, the result of the design process is a description of one society, obtained by people (or a person) sitting down and thinking about what the best society is. After deciding, they set about to pattern everything on this one model.

Given the enormous complexity of man, his many desires, aspirations, impulses, talents, mistakes, loves, sillinesses, given the *thickness* of his intertwined and interrelated levels, facets, relationships (compare the thinness of the social scientists' description of man to that of the novelists), and given the complexity of interpersonal institutions and relationships, and the complexity of coordination of the actions of many people, it is enormously unlikely that, even if there were one ideal pattern for society, it could be arrived at in this *a priori* (relative to current knowledge) fashion. And even supposing that some great genius *did* come along with the blueprint, who could have confidence that it would work out well?*

Sitting down at this late stage in history to dream up a description of the perfect society is not of course the same as starting from scratch. We have available to us partial knowledge of the results of application of devices other than design devices, including partial application of the filter device to be described below. It is helpful to imagine cavemen sitting together to think up what, for all time, will be the best possible society and then setting out to institute it. Do none of the reasons that make you smile at this apply to us?

Filter devices involve a process which eliminates (filters out) many from a large set of alternatives. The two key determinants of the end result(s) are the particular

---

*No person or group I (or you) know of could come up with an adequate "blueprint" (much less be trusted to do so) for a society of beings as complex personally and interpersonally as they themselves are. ["In fact, no utopia has ever been described in which any sane man would on any conditions consent to live, if he could possibly escape." Alexander Gray, *The Socialist Tradition* (New York: Harper & Row, 1968), p. 63.] In view of this, it is strategically shrewd of groups who wish totally to remake all of society according to one pattern to eschew stating that pattern in detail and to keep us in the dark about how things will work after their change. ("No blueprints.") The behavior of the followers is less easy to understand, but perhaps the more vague the picture, the more each person can assume that it is really *exactly* what he wants that is planned and will be brought about.

nature of the filtering out process (and what qualities it selects against) and the particular nature of the set of alternatives it operates upon (and how this set is generated). Filtering processes are especially appropriate for designers having limited knowledge who do not know precisely the nature of a desired end product. For it enables them to utilize their knowledge of specific conditions they don't want violated in judiciously building a filter to reject the violators. It might turn out to be impossible to design an appropriate filter, and one might try another filter process for this task of design. But generally, it seems, less knowledge (including knowledge of what is desirable) will be required to produce an appropriate filter, even one that converges uniquely upon a particular kind of product, than would be necessary to construct only the product(s) from scratch. . . .

A filtering process for specifying a society which might come to mind is one in which the people planning out the ideal society consider many different kinds of societies and criticize some, eliminate some, modify the descriptions of others, until they come to the one they consider best. This no doubt is how any design team would work, and so it should not be assumed that design devices exclude filtering features. (Nor need filter devices exclude design aspects, especially in the generating process.) But one cannot determine in advance which people will come up with the best ideas, and all ideas must be tried out (and not merely simulated on a computer) to see how they will work.* And some ideas will come only as we are (*post facto*) trying to describe what patterns have evolved from the spontaneous coordination of the actions of many people.

If the ideas must actually be tried out, there must be many communities trying out different patterns. The filtering process, the process of eliminating communities, that our framework involves is very simple: people try out living in various communities, and they leave or slightly modify the ones they don't like (find defective). Some communities will be abandoned, others will struggle along, others will split, others will flourish, gain members, and be duplicated elsewhere. Each community must win and hold the voluntary adherence of its members. No pattern is *imposed* on everyone, and the

result will be one pattern if and only if everyone voluntarily chooses to live in accordance with that pattern of community.[4]

The design device comes in at the stage of generating specific communities to be lived in and tried out. Any group of people may devise a pattern and attempt to persuade others to participate in the adventure of a community in that pattern. Visionaries and crackpots, maniacs and saints, monks and libertines, capitalists and communists and participatory democrats, proponents of phalanxes (Fourier), palaces of labor (Flora Tristan), villages of unity and cooperation (Owen), mutualist communities (Proudhon), time stores (Josiah Warren), Bruderhof,[5] kibbutzim,[6] kundalini yoga ashrams, and so forth, may all have their try at building their vision and setting an alluring example. It should not be thought that every pattern tried will be explicitly designed *de novo*. Some will be planned modifications, however slight, of others already existing (when it is seen where they rub), and the details of many will be built up spontaneously in communities that leave some leeway. As communities become more attractive for their inhabitants, patterns previously adopted as the best available will be rejected. And as the communities which people live in improve (according to their lights), ideas for new communities often will improve as well.

The operation of the framework for utopia we present here thus realizes the advantages of a filtering process incorporating mutually improving interaction between the filter and the surviving products of the generating process, so that the quality of generated and non-rejected products improves.* Furthermore, given people's historical memories and records, it has the feature that an already rejected alternative (or its slight modification) can be *retried*, perhaps because new or changed conditions make it now seem more promising or appropriate. This is unlike biological evolution where previously rejected mutations cannot easily be recalled when conditions change. Also, evolutionists point out the advantages of genetic heterogeneity (polytypic and polymorphic) when conditions change greatly. Similar advantages adhere to a system of diverse communities, organized along different lines and perhaps encouraging different types of character, and different patterns of abilities and skills. . . .

---

*For some writers, the most interesting points come after they think they've thought everything through and have begun to set it down. Sometimes, at this stage, there is a change in point of view, or a realization that it is something different one must write (on what, before writing, one assumed was a subsidiary and clear subject). How much greater will be the differences between a plan (even one written down) and the working out in detail of the life of a society.

*This framework is not the only possible filter process for the task of arriving at a desirable or the best society (though I cannot think of another which would have the special interaction virtues to so great an extent), so the general virtues of filter processes over design devices do not argue *uniquely* for it.

COMMUNITY AND NATION

The operation of the framework has many of the virtues, and few of the defects, people find in the libertarian vision. For though there is great liberty to choose among communities, many particular communities internally may have many restrictions unjustifiable on libertarian grounds: that is, restrictions which libertarians would condemn if they were enforced by a central state apparatus. For example, paternalistic intervention into people's lives, restrictions on the range of books which may circulate in the community, limitations on the kinds of sexual behavior, and so on. But this is merely another way of pointing out that in a free society people may contract into various restrictions which the government may not legitimately impose upon them. Though the framework is libertarian and laissez-faire, *individual communities within it need not be,* and perhaps no community within it will choose to be so. Thus, the characteristics of the framework need not pervade the individual communities. In *this* laissez-faire system it could turn out that though they are permitted, there are no actually functioning "capitalist" institutions; or that some communities have them and others don't or some communities have some of them, or what you will.* . . .

HOW UTOPIA WORKS OUT

"Well, what exactly will it all turn out to be like? In what directions will people flower? How large will the communities be? Will there be some large cities? How will economies of scale operate to fix the size of the communities? Will all of the communities be geographical, or will there be many important secondary associations, and so on? Will most communities follow particular (though diverse) utopian visions, or will many communities themselves be open, animated by no such particular vision?"

I do not know, and you should not be interested in my guesses about what would occur under the framework in the near future. As for the long run, I would not attempt to guess.

"So is this all it comes to: Utopia is a free society?" Utopia is *not* just a society in which the framework is realized. For who could believe that ten minutes after the framework was established, we would have utopia?

Things would be no different than now. It is what grows spontaneously from the individual choices of many people over a long period of time that will be worth speaking eloquently about. (Not that any particular stage of the process is an end state which all our desires are aimed at. The utopian process is substituted for the utopian end state of other static theories of utopias.) Many communities will achieve many different characters. Only a fool, or a prophet, would try to prophesy the range and limits and characters of the communities after, for example, 150 years of the operation of this framework.

Aspiring to neither role, let me close by emphasizing the dual nature of the conception of utopia being presented here. There is the framework of utopia, and there are the particular communities within the framework. Almost all of the literature on utopia is, according to our conception, concerned with the character of the particular communities within the framework. The fact that I have not propounded some particular description of a constituent community does *not* mean that (I think) doing so is unimportant, or less important, or uninteresting. How could that be? We *live* in particular communities. It is here that one's nonimperialistic vision of the ideal or good society is to be propounded and realized. Allowing us to do that is what the framework is *for.* Without such visions impelling and animating the creation of particular communities with particular desired characteristics, the framework will lack life. Conjoined with many persons' particular visions, the framework enables us to get the best of all possible worlds.

The position expounded here totally rejects planning in detail, in advance, one community in which everyone is to live yet sympathizes with voluntary utopian experimentation and provides it with the background in which it can flower; does this position fall within the utopian or the antiutopian camp? My difficulty in answering this question encourages me to think the framework captures the virtues and advantages of each position. (If instead it blunders into combining the errors, defects, and mistakes of both of them, the filtering process of free and open discussion will make this clear.)

UTOPIA AND THE MINIMAL STATE

The framework for utopia that we have described is equivalent to the minimal state. . . .

The minimal state treats us as inviolate individuals, who may not be used in certain ways by others as means or tools or instruments or resources; it treats us as persons having individual rights with the dignity this constitutes.

*It is strange that many young people "in tune with" nature and hoping to "go with the flow" and not force things against their natural bent should be attracted to statist views and socialism, and are antagonistic to equilibrium and invisible-hand processes.

Treating us with respect by respecting our rights, it allows us, individually or with whom we choose, to choose our life and to realize our ends and our conception of ourselves, insofar as we can, aided by the voluntary cooperation of other individuals possessing the same dignity. How *dare* any state or group of individuals do more. Or less.

ENDNOTES

1. "A state which was really morally neutral, which was indifferent to all values, other than that of maintaining law and order, would not command enough allegiance to survive at all. A soldier may sacrifice his life for Queen and Country, but hardly for the Minimum State. A policeman, believing in Natural Law and immutable right and wrong, may tackle an armed desperado but not if he regards himself as an employee of a Mutual Protection and Assurance Society, constructed from the cautious contracts of prudent individuals. Some ideals are necessary to inspire those without whose free cooperation that State would not survive." J. R. Lucas, *The Principles of Politics* (Oxford at the Clarendon Press, 1966), p. 292. Why does Lucas assume that the employees of the minimal state cannot be devoted to the rights it protects?

2. Compare John Rawls, *Theory of Justice* (Cambridge, Mass.: Harvard University Press, 1971), sect. 63, n. 11. It is not clear how extensively Rawls' later text would have to be revised to take this point explicitly into account.

3. Some theories underlying such imposition are discussed by J. L. Talmon in *The Origins of Totalitarian Democracy* (New York: Norton, 1970) and *Political Messianism* (New York: Praeger, 1961).

4. An illuminating discussion of the operation and virtues of a similar filter system is found in F. A. Hayek, *The Constitution of Liberty* (Chicago: University of Chicago Press, 1960), chaps. 2, 3. Some utopian endeavors have fit this, to some extent. "[The nondoctrinaire character of the origins of the Jewish communal settlements in Palestine] also determined their development in all essentials. New forms and new intermediate forms were constantly branching off—in complete freedom. Each one grew out of the particular social and spiritual needs as these came to light—in complete freedom, and each one acquired, even in the initial stages, its own ideology—in complete freedom, each struggling to propagate itself and spread and establish its proper sphere—all in complete freedom. The champions of the various forms each had his say, the pros and cons of each individual form were frankly and fiercely debated. . . . The various forms and intermediate forms that arose in this way at different times and in different situations represented different kinds of social structure . . . different forms corresponded to different human types and . . . just as new forms branched off from the original Kvuza, so new types branched off from the orig-

inal Chaluz type, each with its special mode of being and each demanding its particular sort of realization. . . ." Martin Buber, *Paths in Utopia* (New York: Macmillan, 1950), pp. 145–146.

The people involved need not be trying to discover the best possible community; they may merely be attempting to improve their own situation. Some persons, however, may consciously set out to use and streamline the filtering process of people's choices to arrive at what they (tentatively) judge to be the best community. Compare Karl Popper's account of the filtering process of scientific method, self-consciously used and participated in to get closer to the truth [*Objective Knowledge* (New York: Oxford University Press, 1972)]. Since some persons who participate in filtering processes (or equilibrium processes) will have as an objective reaching the final end, while others won't, we might refine the notion of an invisible-hand process to admit of degrees.

5. See Benjamin Zablocki, *The Joyful Community* (Baltimore: Penguin Books, 1971).

6. For a recent account see Haim Barkai, "The Kibbutz: an Experiment in Micro-socialism," in *Israel, the Arabs, and the Middle East,* ed. Irving Howe and Carl Gershman (New York: Bantam Books, 1972).

QUESTIONS ON NOZICK

1. What is a "framework for utopia"? How does Nozick's account of utopia differ from other utopias?

2. How does the argument of individual difference support the idea of Nozick's "framework for utopia"? Why should the claim that individuals are different support such a utopia rather than, say, a democratic welfare state?

3. In what sense does Nozick's framework allow for the realization of different values and outlooks? Do you think that this framework would allow for both capitalist communities and socialistic communities? Industrial and agrarian societies?

———————

FOR FURTHER READING

Progress

Bury, J. B. *The Idea of Progress: An Inquiry into Its Origin and Growth.* New York: Macmillan, 1932.

Hirsch, Fred. *Social Limits to Growth.* Cambridge: Harvard University Press, 1976.

Kant, Immanuel. "Idea for a Universal History with a Cosmopolitan Purpose." In *Kant's Political Writ-*

ings, edited by Hans Reiss. Cambridge: Cambridge University Press, 1970.

Lane, Robert E. *The Loss of Happiness in Market Democracies.* New Haven, Conn.: Yale University Press, 2000.

Lanier, Lyle. "A Critique of the Philosophy of Progress." In *I'll Take My Stand.* New York: Harper and Brothers, 1930.

Lasch, Christopher. *The True and Only Heaven: Progress and Its Critics.* New York: W.W. Norton, 1991.

Laslett, Peter. *The World We Have Lost.* London: Methuen, 1965.

Manuel, Frank. *Shapes of Philosophical History.* Stanford, Conn.: Stanford University Press, 1965.

Marx, Leo, and Bruce Mazlish, eds. *Progress: Fact or Illusion?* Ann Arbor: University of Michigan Press, 1996.

Moore, Stephen, and Julian Simon. *It's Getting Better All the Time: The 100 Greatest Trends of the 20th Century.* Washington, D.C.: Cato Institute, 2000.

Nisbet, Robert A. *History of the Idea of Progress.* New Brunswick, N.J.: Transaction, 1994.

Passmore, John. *The Perfectibility of Man.* London: Duckworth, 1970.

Postrel, Virginia. *The Future and Its Enemies: The Growing Conflict Over Creativity, Enterprise, and Progress.* New York: The Free Press, 1998.

Simon, Julian, ed. *The State of Humanity.,* Cambridge, Mass.: Basil Blackwell, 1995.

Culture

Agar, Herbert, and Allen Tate, eds. *Who Owns America? A New Declaration of Independence.* Wilmington, Del.: ISI Books, 1999.

Arnold, Matthew. *Culture and Anarchy* [1869], edited by Stefan Collini. Cambridge: Cambridge University Press, 1993.

Bell, Bernard Iddings. *Crowd Culture: An Examination of the American Way of Life* [1952]. Wilmington, Del.: ISI Books.

Berry, Wendell. *The Unsettling of America: Culture and Agriculture.* San Francisco: Sierra Club Books, 1977.

Collier, James Lincoln. *The Rise of Selfishness in America.* New York: Oxford University Press, 1991.

Eliot, T. S. *Notes Towards the Definition of Culture* in *Christianity and Culture.* New York: Harcourt Brace, 1948.

Gray, John. *Enlightenment's Wake: Politics and Culture at the Close of the Modern Age.* London: Routledge, 1995.

Habermas, Jürgen. *The Structural Transformation of the Public Sphere: An Inquiry into a Category of Bourgeois Society,* translated by Thomas Burger, with Frederick Lawrence. Cambridge: MIT Press, 1991.

Hayek, F. A. "Individualism: True and False." In *Individualism and Economic Order.* Chicago: University of Chicago Press, 1948.

Kracauer, Siegfried. *The Mass Ornament,* translated and edited by Thomas Y. Levin. Cambridge: Harvard University Press, 1995.

Leach, William. *Country of Exiles: The Destruction of Place in American Life.* New York: Vintage Books, 1999.

Lukacs, John. "To Hell with Culture." *Chronicles* (September 1994).

Nelson, Cary, and Lawrence Grossberg, eds. *Marxism and the Interpretation of Culture.* Urbana: University of Illinois Press, 1988.

Nisbet, Robert. *Twilight of Authority.* New York: Oxford University Press, 1975.

Pieper, Josef. *Leisure: The Basis of Culture,* translated by Alexander Dru. London: Faber and Faber, 1952.

Rieff, Philip. "Toward a Theory of Culture." In *The Feeling Intellect: Selected Writings,* edited by Jonathan B. Imber. Chicago: University of Chicago Press, 1990.

Riesman, David. *The Lonely Crowd.* New Haven, Conn.: Yale University Press, 1950.

Scitovsky, Tibor. *The Joyless Economy.* New York: Oxford University Press, 1976.

Taylor, Charles. *Sources of the Self: The Making of the Modern Identity.* Cambridge: Harvard University Press, 1989.

Teichgraeber, Richard F., and Thomas L. Haskell, eds. *The Culture of the Market: Historical Essays.* Cambridge: Cambridge University Press, 1993.

Weaver, Richard. "Two Types of American Individualism." In *The Southern Essays of Richard Weaver,* edited by George M. Curtis III and James J. Thompson, Jr. Indianapolis, Ind.: Liberty Press, 1987, 77–103.

Williams, Raymond. *Culture and Society, 1780–1950.* New York: Columbia University, 1960.

Consumerism

Cross, Gary. *An All Consuming Century: Why Commercialism Won in Modern America.* New York: Columbia University Press, 2000.

Fine, Ben, and Ellen Leopold. *The World of Consumption.* New York: Routledge, 1993.

Frank, Robert H. *Luxury Fever: Money and Happiness in an Era of Excess.* Princeton, N.J.: Princeton University Press, 2000.

Galbraith, John Kenneth. *The Affluent Society.* Boston: Houghton Mifflin, 1976.

McKendrick, Neil, John Brewer, and J. H. Plumb. *The Birth of a Consumer Society: The Commercialization of Eighteenth-Century England.* Bloomington: Indiana University Press, 1982.

Packard, Vance. *The Hidden Persuaders.* New York: D. McKay, 1957.

Radin, Margaret Jane. *Contested Commodities.* Cambridge: Harvard University Press, 1996.

Twitchell, James. *Lead Us Into Temptation: The Triumph of American Materialism.* New York: Columbia University Press, 1999.

Veblen, Thorstein. *The Theory of the Leisure Class* [1899]. New York: New American Library, 1953.

CIII

Commerce and the Arts

As in economics, so in art: laissez-faire within a capitalist economy (or within any economy) merely abandons art to the chances of unrestricted competition, and the devil take the hindmost. It means that art becomes one more commodity on the free-market, and that to succeed it must practice all the wiles of salesmanship—mass appeal, sex appeal, adulteration, and the sacrifice of quality to cheapness.

Herbert Read[1]

Kitsch is a product of the industrial revolution which urbanized the masses of Western Europe and America and established universal literacy. . . . Kitsch has not been confined to the cities in which it was born, but has flowed out over the countryside, wiping out folk culture. Nor has it shown any regard for geographical and national-cultural boundaries. Another mass product of Western industrialism, it has gone on a triumphal tour of the world, crowding out and defacing native cultures in one colonial country after another, so that it is now by way of becoming a universal culture, the first universal culture ever beheld.

Clement Greenberg[2]

Business art is the step that comes after Art. I started as a commercial artist, and I want to finish as a business artist. After I did the thing called 'art' or whatever it's called, I went into business art. I wanted to be an Art Businessman or a Business Artist. Being good in business is the most fascinating kind of art. During the hippie era people put down the idea of business—they'd say, 'Money is bad,' and 'Working is bad,' but making money is art and working is art and good business is the best art.

Andy Warhol[3]

[A]lmost all the artists who have done . . . first-rate work have been thoroughly bourgeois people.

Roger Fry[4]

1. "Culture and Liberty," *Nation* 152 (2 April 1941), 438.

2. "Avant-Garde and Kitsch," in *Art and Culture: Critical Essays* (Boston, Mass.: Beacon Press, 1961), 9, 12.

3. *The Philosophy of Andy Warhol* (San Diego: Harcourt Brace Jovanovich, 1975), 92.

4. "The Artist and Psycho-Analysis," in *Hogarth Essays,* compiled by Leonard S. Woolf and Virginia S. Woolf (Freeport, NY: Books for Libraries Press, 1928), 290–91.

Economic systems are often evaluated only in terms of their justice or in terms of their productivity in goods and services. However, as we have seen in the preceding sections (CI and CII), economic systems, including that of the market, can be evaluated in terms of the nature of their noneconomic *effects,* whether these be moral or, broadly speaking, cultural. But apart from the consideration of these kinds of effects, one might also consider whether commerce has positive or negative effects on the arts (or "culture" in a more specific sense than that used in the preceding chapter).

Although the market is often recognized for its amazing productivity and efficiency, that same market has just as often been criticized for having negative effects on the arts. The quotation from Herbert Read serves as a reminder of the judgment, not at all rare, that markets (or capitalism) lead(s) to a decline in the production and appreciation of fine arts. If the claim is correct, then one might wish to reevaluate one's estimation of market institutions, or one might wish to consider exactly which aspects of markets contribute to the decline of art. On the other hand, the claim might not be correct at all. It might be the case that the historical periods of greatest artistic achievement are precisely those periods in which commercial relations have intruded into the artistic sphere, or in which commerce has provided sufficient wealth to enable individuals to create works of art and to permit others to enjoy them. If there is to be any plausible claim about the connection between markets and the arts, then we must first have some sense of what these "arts" are. Only with some account of "art" can one make any sense of an assertion as to a relation between the economic system of a market and the quality, kind, or accessibility of the art produced within that system.

WHAT IS ART?

The Need for an Account

If one is to investigate the relation between commerce and the arts, one must be able to differentiate works of art from (other) economic goods and services; in plain words, this means one must be able to distinguish between, say, the manufacture of shoes and the creation of art, between the construction of advertising jingles and the composition of serious music. That there are clear and convincing cases of art—the statues of the classical Greek sculptor, Praxiteles; the paintings of Giotto, Caravaggio, or Rembrandt; the novels of Jane Austen, George Eliot, or Dostoevski; the music of Purcell,

Mozart, or Bach; or the poetry of Wordsworth, Whitman, or Rabindranath Tagore—does not tell us how to distinguish art from that which is not art. Clearly the arts must include fine sculpture, painting, literature, drama, and music, not to mention certain forms of dance as well as opera. Even if we agree that certain works or even certain specific artistic genres are examples of art, that does not give us a criterion by which to distinguish art from nonart, nor does it provide guidance as to whether avant-garde works, which challenge commonplace assumptions, should be classified as works of art. Marcel Duchamp's *Fountain* (1917), a urinal (originally produced by industrial manufacture and perhaps the most famous of what he called his "ready-mades") is one of the earliest challenges to a traditional conception of art. In music, John Cage offers his *4′33″* (1952), a piece for piano, in which the pianist sits quietly at a piano for four minutes and thirty-three seconds. More recently the work of the British artist Tracey Emin, whose 1999 exhibit, "My Bed" (in London's Tate Gallery), featured a disheveled double bed with stained sheets and assorted paraphernalia of hygiene, sex, and alcohol, reaffirms, by example, the continuing challenge to the conventional assumptions about art. Do such challenges expand our conception of art? Or are these examples, and the many others like them, not objects of art but objects which, under the rubric of art, aim at little more than provocation or protest? Even aside from the avant-garde, a form of creativity that hardly appeals to the widest public, what about the creative products which have mass appeal? Does the entertainment offered on television or the popular music of the radio and dance hall provide examples of art? If we are to consider the relation of art to commerce, we should have some sense of the sort of things that we mean when we speak of "art."

Attempts at Definition

Some critics and philosophers have attempted to provide definitions of art such that if some object fulfilled the conditions limned by the definition, then that object would be an art object. For example, some have suggested that art is defined in terms of some property of the art object. The art critic Clive Bell argued a version of *formalism* in which a work of art was distinguished by its evocation of an aesthetic emotion which, he believed, was brought about by a quality or property of the work, namely, its "Significant Form."[5] Leo Tolstoy argued for a species of *expressivism* which suggested that an art ob-

---

5. Clive Bell, *Art* (London: Chatto and Windus, 1947), 8.

ject expressed an emotion of the creator.[6] On this view, articulable in a variety of ways, the artist produces a work which is intentionally constructed to express an emotion and which communicates this emotion to a spectator or audience. As opposed to those who define art in terms of the properties of an object or in terms of the expression of emotion, there are those who believe that art can be distinguished from nonart in terms of the type of *response* that individuals have to the object, a response that is not reducible to some property of the object. On this view, the properties that suffice to render something a work of art are not properties inherent to the object but are determined by the response to the object of certain persons and institutions. One version of this view is the "institutional" theory of art, forwarded by George Dickie, which states that a work of art is whatever artifact the art critics, historians, institutions, and museums have deemed to be a worthy candidate for appreciation.[7]

Can Art Be Defined?

These attempts to define art, as well as numerous others, have been subject to discussion, counterexample, and criticism. However, one might argue that the very concept of art is not set or limited, that there are no necessary and sufficient conditions that qualify one thing as a work of art, another not. The point of this argument is not that it is *difficult* to define the idea of art, but that there are no common properties of those works which we understand as art.[8] This conclusion, if correct, does not imply that we have no clear sense of what is to count as a work of art, only that we may not be able to *define* the art object in terms of certain universal properties.

It is at this point that some will want to suggest we be content with stipulating that art is whatever an individual declares as art. However, this stipulation seems unwise. Just as no one truly believes that some object is an X simply because an individual announces the object to be an X, so does it seem that no one truly believes an object is a work of art merely because an individual stipulates that it is. If an individual says something is art, he or she must be saying so on *some* grounds; that is, the

individual must have some reasons for asserting that the object in question is art rather than something else. To claim that some object is art merely because one vows it to be art is a linguistic stomp of the foot. If we reject this peremptory stipulation, then we must return to the consideration of the idea of "art," but this time we will seek not a definition but coherent understanding of the idea that will allow us to proceed in our inquiry.

Minimal Criteria of Art

What, then, shall we consider as art objects? Instead of providing a definition or a set of necessary and sufficient conditions, let us stipulate that in speaking about the arts we wish our remarks to include all of those works that may be considered standard or paradigm cases of art (for example, the paintings of Caravaggio, the plays of Shakespeare, the symphonies of Beethoven). We want our use of the term "art" to include these paradigm cases as well as other less obvious cases. How can we specify, then, what the term shall include? To begin we shall stipulate three general characteristics of the relevant sense of art: that the object is an *artifact* of human creation, exhibiting *imagination* and manifesting *form.* Morris Weitz contends, similarly, that certain conditions are typically required for describing something as a work of art:

> Thus, mostly, when we describe something as a work of art, we do so under the conditions of there being present some sort of artifact, made by human skill, ingenuity, and imagination, which embodies in its sensuous, public medium—stone, wood, sounds, words, etc.—certain distinguishable elements and relations.[9]

These generalities provide some means of distinguishing art from that which is not art, but these criteria do not yet allow us to distinguish a television comedy from a work of fine drama, or a silly advertising jingle from a piano concerto. Something is clearly missing from our criteria.

To further refine our account, let us reconsider why we are even posing the question, "What is art?" We want to examine the relation between commerce and the arts in order to determine whether the market serves to encourage or discourage the arts. And we are interested in this question because we attach a significant *value* to the arts. What is still missing from our account is some explicit mention of that aspect of art that reveals it to be not only an artifact of form and imagination, but an object worthy of our concern and deliberation.

6. Leo Tolstoy, *What Is Art?* [1897–1898] *and Essays on Art,* translated by Aylmer Maude (London: Oxford University Press, 1975), esp. 231–250.

7. George Dickie, "Defining Art," *American Philosophical Quarterly* 2 (1965): 219–28.

8. On this account of the concept of "art" see Morris Weitz, "The Role of Theory in Aesthetics," *The Journal of Aesthetics and Art Criticism* 15 (September 1956): 27–35.

9. Morris Weitz, "The Role of Theory in Aesthetics," 33.

Serious Art

What is it that concerns the person who wonders about the relation between art and commerce? Of the myriad artifacts manifesting imagination and form, which works are the concern of this person? Surely the person is not considering whether commerce can produce objects of entertainment, provocative or eye-catching stories, jingles, pictures, or popular musical productions. The market is quite adept at providing these, and so it seems relatively noncontroversial to maintain that the market is a marvelous system for producing entertainment art. Second, the person interested in the relation between commerce and art is not concerned, solely, with whether market societies encourage or discourage art whose only value is reducible to some political, social, or religious message. The person concerned with art and commerce has something else in mind, namely that sort of art whose value lies in something other than mere entertainment or mere politics. The sort of art in question is what one philosopher refers to as "serious art."

The distinctions just noted are developed by the philosopher, John Passmore, who distinguishes between entertainment art, telic art, and serious art. Entertainment art may include television, plays, and music, but its primary feature is to serve as "an enjoyable interlude from care."[10] Telic art (from the Greek term *telos,* meaning purpose or end) serves to increase our care about some political, religious, or social issue. However, a serious work of art is "a candidate for a special kind of critical examination, in terms which would be inappropriate to what is purely a work of entertainment."[11] Of course, serious art may entertain, just as it may also serve—as most art has—a religious or political purpose; these categories are not mutually exclusive. Nonetheless, the artistic (or aesthetic) value of serious art lies beyond its entertainment value or its political or moral message. Since it is this type of art that is the focus of those concerned with the relation between markets and art, our discussion will, henceforth, focus on the type of art that might be deemed *serious*.

DIVERGENT CLAIMS

It is important to distinguish some of the various ways in which the (serious) arts might be affected by commerce and markets. For example, as an economic sys-

tem the market might have differential effects on either the production, distribution, or enjoyment of arts. Some of the most interesting claims concern the *quality* of art that is produced. Is the art of commercial societies of greater or lesser quality than the art of some other economic system? For example, one might argue that the market provides conditions in which freedom, diversity, and competition ensure that the most talented individuals will seek to produce art of the highest quality. Others have argued that the very conditions of the market tend to ensure that serious and fine art is neglected in favor of entertainment art or the popular art of the masses. According to this view, the market is very good at providing products that entertain, but it is less adept at supplying serious art; thus, the art of commercial societies is dominated less by aesthetic and more by entertainment values. Let us consider more fully some of the types of claims that have been made about art and commerce, considering, first, some arguments concerning the production and distribution of art.

The Distribution of Art

One of the first, and perhaps most obvious claim, relies on a distinction between the *production* of art and its *distribution* or *reproduction*: the market tends to ensure that whatever art is produced is widely available. This sort of claim points less to the art than to its reproduction, availability, and distribution. Defenders of the market might here point out how easily and widely one can find inexpensive reproductions of literary masterpieces, performances of fine music (including obscure works), or reprints of paintings. The market proves to be a powerful vehicle for the production and distribution of created works of art and is able to cater to a wide variety of artistic tastes. Market competition, as noted by Cowen in one of the following readings, has also diminished the costs of painting supplies, photography equipment, and musical instruments, and has reduced the costs of staging theatrical productions.

New Materials and Techniques

A related claim, reflective of the power of innovation and market competition, focuses on how the market has insured the development of new materials and techniques. Some of these new techniques include the relatively recent innovations of photography and film, but there were important innovations during other periods as well. For example, the new commercial wealth of the Italian Renaissance not only allowed for the purchase and trans-

---

10. *Serious Art* (La Salle, Illinois: Open Court, 1991), 7.

11. *Serious Art,* 11.

portation of marble but generated an increase in paper production (which gave rise to sketching), and inaugurated painting in oil (an improvement that allowed artists to move beyond tempera and fresco paintings).[12]

Enjoyment and Appreciation: The Question of Class

Even if commerce generates new materials for art, increases its production, and distributes it more widely, it may nonetheless be argued that the art of commercial societies is not of the highest quality. One version of this argument suggests that commerce and industrialization (often in conjunction with democratization) serve to break apart hierarchical social structures that maintain an upper class or elite capable of appreciating, creating, and preserving art. In the nineteenth century, Alexis de Tocqueville (1805–1859) argued that the American nation had made comparatively little progress in the fine arts or the sciences. This was due, he said, to its Puritan temper, to the commercial impulse of the nation, and, most important, to its democratic equality, which diminishes the number of persons with the knowledge or leisure to cultivate the finest of the arts even as there are an increasing number who may pursue them.[13] This is but one instance of the more general view that market economies are destructive of those social structures that establish or maintain a class of cultured and educated persons who will patronize and appreciate certain forms of serious art. That high culture, or serious art, requires a class that has the leisure to develop and appreciate it was also the view of Matthew Arnold (1822–1888), who argued that high culture was the harmonious perfection of the human being, a view seconded by John Ruskin (1819–1900), who complained of his own country "that good Art has only been produced by nations who rejoiced in it . . . they made it to keep, and we to sell."[14] In this century this view has been maintained by the literary critic F. R. Leavis (1895–1978) and the poet and critic T. S. Eliot (1888–1965), for whom the breakdown of a common literary tradition was one of the crucial problems of the modern era.[15]

Mass Art

A different thesis, which need not be attached to any claim about class, suggests that commerce tends to reduce all art to the entertainment art of the masses: television, movies, bestselling novels, and kitsch. Not only does commerce tend to reduce art to mass art, but mass art is of a decidedly poorer type. When it is not formulaic, it requires very little thought or attention from the spectator, and perhaps even less from the artist.[16] Mass art tends to dominate the entire culture even as other serious art is produced and neglected. Some of the most vigorous defenders of this view have been individuals associated with the Frankfurt School, who credit the low taste of modern culture not to the demise of class but to the erosion of traditional folk cultures and the dominance of market-based entertainment and advertising. A "culture industry" has not only commodified art but has produced a popular culture that is debased and hollow.[17]

Bourgeois Art

That the modern form of capitalism has created a mass art of low quality is an instance of the broader claim that all art, in its production, and in its appreciation, reflects the social and economic conditions in which it arose. One non-Marxist version of this claim asserts that the art of a period reflects the social, cultural, and religious outlook of that age. Of course, art may reflect the spirit, interests, or conditions of a society or period simply because *some* art is a response to patrons or clients and *all* art is the creative product of a person who, undoubtedly, will reflect the society in which he or she lives. (For example, prior to the nineteenth century, the major themes of European painting were stories from history, mythology, religion.) On a certain level it seems trivial to assert that art reflects its own particular epoch. Yet one often needs to be

---

12. For an account of these developments, see Cowen, "The Wealthy City as a Center for Western Art," in *In Praise of Commercial Culture* (Cambridge: Harvard University Press, 1998), 83–128.

13. Alexis de Tocqueville, *Democracy in America,* edited by Richard D. Heffer (New York: New American Library, 1956), esp. Part Two: Book I, chapters 19–23.

14. "Cambridge Inaugural Address [1858]," in *The Complete Works of John Ruskin,* edited by E. T. Cook and Alexander Wedderburn, vol. 16 (London: George Allen, 1905), §8 (p. 184). For Arnold, see *Culture and Anarchy* [1869], edited by Stefan Collini (Cambridge: Cambridge University Press, 1993).

15. Leavis, *Mass Civilization and Minority Culture* (Cambridge: Cambridge University Press, 1930); see Eliot, *The Idea of a Christian Society* and *Notes Towards the Definition of Culture,* esp. chapter II, "The Class and the Elite," in *Christianity and Culture* (New York: Harcourt Brace & Company, 1948).

16. For a critique of these criticisms of popular art, see Noël Carroll, *A Philosophy of Mass Art* (Oxford: Clarendon Press, 1998).

17. Theodor Adorno and Max Horkheimer, "The Culture Industry: Enlightenment as Mass Deception," in *Dialectic of Enlightenment* [1947], translated by John Cumming (New York: Herder and Herder, 1972).

reminded of this seemingly trivial point, and on not a few occasions the reminder provides insight, as when Matthew Arnold asserts that the poetry of Alexander Pope "is the poetry of the builders of an age of prose and reason."[18]

However, there is a stronger, Marxist interpretation of this view: Art reflects material or economic conditions in that it reflects (or reacts against) the dominant forces in society, thus ensuring that certain themes, styles, or genres predominate. Marx writes:

> In the social production of their life, men enter into definite relations that are indispensable and independent of their will, relations of production which correspond to a definite stage of development of their material productive forces. The sum total of these relations of production constitutes the economic structure of society, the real foundation, on which rises a legal and political superstructure and to which correspond definite forms of social consciousness. The mode of production of material life conditions the social, political and intellectual life process in general. It is not the consciousness of men that determines their being, but, on the contrary, their social being that determines their consciousness.[19]

Within the capitalist mode of production the ownership of the means of production lies with the capitalist class, a class whose outlook is necessarily shaped by the economy, which requires a self-denying calculation. Thus, Marx condemns capitalist political economy, exclaiming that,

> Self-denial, the denial of life and of all human needs, is its cardinal doctrine. The less you eat, drink and read books; the less you go to the theatre, the dance hall, the public-house; the less you think, love, theorize, sing, paint, fence, etc., the more you *save*—the *greater* becomes your treasure which neither moths nor dust will devour—your *capital*.[20]

In the reading to follow, Ernst Fischer expresses the Marxist point of view, asserting at one point that "capitalism was basically foreign to the arts," a point that seems to imply that there would be little art in a market society. And yet what Fischer finds is that there is art of the Romantic variety, but it is an art born of the artist's rebellion against the constraints of a capitalist system of production.

Even if art is socially conditioned it may nonetheless express universal qualities. That art is socially conditioned is not the same, moreover, as the claim that the market produces more art, or less art, or art of a particular quality. In sum, that art is socially conditioned does not tell us whether the art that is produced manifests qualities of excellence. However, it could be argued that the bourgeois art of market societies is of a lesser or greater quality. For example, Herbert Read (1893–1968) contends that the type of Puritan capitalism typical of England produced little art of any value. Moreover, in Read's view "art is only healthy in a communal type of society, where within one organic consciousness all modes of life, all senses and faculties, function freely and harmoniously."[21]

Art for Art's Sake?

Counter to the idea of socially conditioned art is the idea of art as autonomous enterprise with its own rationale. One version of this view is that the true artist is concerned with *form* alone, and this constitutes a distinct aesthetic motive. This idea, which was not consistently articulated until the nineteenth century, might have surprised many artists, critics, and patrons for whom art was almost always interwoven with religious, political, or ethical conceptions. However, perhaps the idea of autonomous art is itself conditioned by a certain period and context:

> [T]he *autonomy of art* is a category of bourgeois society. It permits the description of art's detachment from the context of practical life as a historical development—that among the members of those classes which, at least at times, are free from the pressures of the need for survival, a sensuousness could evolve that was not part of any means-ends relationships. Here we find the moment of truth in the talk about the autonomous work of art. What this category cannot lay hold of is that this detachment of art from practical contexts is a *historical process,* i.e., that it is socially conditioned. And here lies the untruth of the category, the element of distortion that characterizes every ideology, provided one uses this term in the sense the early Marx does when he speaks of the critique of ideology. The category 'autonomy' does not permit the understanding of its referent as one that developed historically. The relative dissociation of the work of art from the praxis of life in bourgeois society thus becomes transformed into the (erroneous) idea that the work of art is totally independent of society. In the strict meaning of the

18. Arnold, "The Study of Poetry [1880]," in *The Works of Matthew Arnold,* vol. 4, *Essays in Criticism* (London: MacMillan, 1903), 31.

19. "Marx on the History of His Opinions" (Preface to *A Contribution to the Critique of Political Economy*), in *The Marx-Engels Reader,* edited by Robert C. Tucker (New York: W. W. Norton, 1972), 4.

20. *Economic and Philosophic Manuscripts of 1844,* in Tucker, *The Marx-Engels Reader,* 96–97.

21. Herbert Read, "Why We English Have No Taste," in *Anarchy and Order: Essays in Politics* (Boston, Mass.: Beacon Press, 1971), 73.

term, 'autonomy' is thus an ideological category that joins an element of truth (the apartness of art from the praxis of life) and an element of untruth (the hypostatization of this fact, which is a result of historical development as the 'essence' of art).[22]

ART, BUSINESS, AND THE STATE

Art and Commerce in History

Some of the periods of greatest artistic achievement have been periods of commerce. During the sixteenth and seventeenth centuries the great growth in wealth funded new buildings and lavish furnishings; it was commercial prosperity that commissioned portraits and supplemented the continuing demand for religious art. In addition there was an increased demand for music ("music that had to be bought and learned, became part of the texture of festival and ceremony"[23]) and a growing demand for more drama productions, as for-profit theaters opened in major cities such as London, Madrid, and Paris (with Shakespeare's Globe theatre opening in 1599). That there was some connection between commercial prosperity and the production of the arts is not doubtable, though what that connection was is unclear. John Hale concludes:

> Capital investment in printing presses, theatres and workshop and studio space responded to demand and quickened productivity. Prosperity stimulated demand. Demand offered opportunity which attracted talent. But we must remember that there was no *necessary* connection between the economy and creativity, between money and genius. In the Florentine generations of Botticelli, Leonardo, Raphael, Michelangelo, Ficino, Pico della Mirandola and Machiavelli, nearby Genoa was as commercially active but produced no artist or thinker of note. The prosperity that built country houses and filled the theatres left Elizabethan England a net importer of fine and decorative arts. . . . But overall, taking into account the greater purchasing power of Europeans in a period of lively commercial activity, social and educational change, and an in-

tense concern with status and fashionableness, the power of money helps to explain the increased consumption that gave works of genius a better chance of being produced and appreciated than ever before.[24]

From the sixteenth century on, art flourished in great commercial centers, including Amsterdam, Paris, and New York.[25] By the latter part of the nineteenth century, the sale of visual art grew into a specific business practice, and private art dealers emerged in number. In France the impressionist painters arrayed themselves against government-sanctioned exhibitions and awards, appealing to a freedom that "paralleled the freedom from prior restraints that entrepreneurs were pleading for."[26] Many of their paintings portrayed the new commercial middle class enjoying leisure, as in Pierre Auguste Renoir's *Le Moulin de la Galette* (1876), Édouard Manet's *A Bar at the Folies-Bergère* (1882), or Georges Seurat's *Sunday Afternoon on the Island of La Grande Jatte* (1884–1886). Yet despite the interconnections between commerce and serious art, the modern period has been witness to a widespread antipathy between artists and businesspersons.

The Antipathy of the Artists

Despite the value we place on art, the artist has not always looked with favor on commerce or on commercial societies. For example, the businessperson is rarely treated sympathetically in a literary work; indeed, the very decision to enter business is regarded, somehow, as less worthy than the decision to be an artist. The economist Deirdre McCloskey notes (Section BI, esp. pp. 264–66) how artists and intellectuals have often identified themselves with freedom and creativity, disdaining business as an activity demanding nothing more than utilitarian reason and hardly worthy of any sustained literary or artistic exploration at all. That the achievements of commerce are often disparaged by the literary and the artistic is exemplified in the sardonic lines that open Sinclair Lewis' novel *Main Street* (1920):

> Main Street is the climax of civilization. That this Ford car might stand in front of the Bon Ton Store, Hannibal invaded Rome and Erasmus wrote in Oxford cloisters.[27]

22. Peter Bürger, "On the Problem of the Autonomy of Art," in *Art in Modern Culture: An Anthology of Critical Texts,* edited by Francis Frascina and Jonathan Harris (New York: Icon Editions, HarperCollins, 1992), 56–57.

23. John Hale, *The Civilization of Europe in the Renaissance* (New York: Atheneum, 1994), 273. Information on the Renaissance is drawn from Hale's chapter "Cash and Culture," 259–81. On the commercial customs of fifteenth-century Italian painting, see Michael Baxandall, *Painting and Experience in Fifteenth-Century Italy* (Oxford: Oxford University Press, 1972), esp. chapter 1, "The Conditions of Trade."

24. Hale, *The Civilization of Europe in the Renaissance,* 280.

25. See Cowen's account, "The Wealthy City as a Center for Western Art," in *In Praise of Commercial Culture.*

26. Robert L. Herbert, "Impressionism, Originality and Laissez-Faire," *Radical History Review* 38 (1987): 11.

27. Sinclair Lewis, *Main Street* (New York: Library of America, 1992), 3.

It is not every artist that looks so disparagingly on business; after all, a few of them worked in business: The poet T. S. Eliot worked in the Lloyds Bank for several years and both Wallace Stevens (1879–1955), the poet, and Charles Ives (1874–1954), the composer, worked in the insurance industry. And yet these isolated instances shed no light on the more general antipathy of the artist toward the vocation of commerce. (This is especially true of the hostility that exsists between serious art and business, for popular art is much more connected to the aims and methods of business than is high art. In the sixties, Andy Warhol (1928–1987) viewed himself not only as challenging the distinction between high and low art, serious and popular, but doing so as a businessman!) Why might business life be viewed so negatively by the artist? Could there be differences between the commercial and artistic life which might explain this disdain?

Business *versus* Art: Creativity

Part of the hostility that exists between the artist and the businessperson may lie in the different goals, methods, and conditions in which the artist and the businessperson work.[28] The artist may work alone, whereas the person in commerce may work within an organization in which there is a structured division of labor, allotting to each person a specific function or set of tasks. In the case of work within large business organizations, there may be a relatively diminished need for individual insight, creativity, and independent imagination. However, that does not mean that the individual business-owner or entrepreneur merely plods along exercising little or no creativity as he or she engages in a pedestrian and mechanical optimization of the ends decreed by the autonomous market. This view of business not only ignores the way in which imagination and creativity play a role in successful commerce but simultaneously equates the ideal artist with the typical artist, ignoring the extent to which art may be unimaginative, formulaic, and plodding.

It is, nonetheless, true that economic theory as well as popular portrayals of business suggest that the manager or owner has but *one* task: to optimize the means to produce some given service or end. Although such optimization may require ingenuity and creativity—whether these be manifested in advertising, new methods of production, or innovative structures of organization—there is another realm of business enterprise that is often over-

looked—that of the creative entrepreneur.[29] As discussed in Section BIII (pp. 443–44), it is the entrepreneur who *discovers* new kinds of services or new types of goods, for it is the entrepreneur who is alert to and recognizes opportunities or situations in which profits can be made.

Motives in Business and Art

Of course, the criteria of success may be different in business than in art. After all, the economic measure of success in business is profit. The criterion of artistic success may not be profit, but what is it? This raises the question of motivation. The businessperson, it might be said, is motivated by a material interest, but the artist is motivated by some ideal of beauty or goodness. Such a description, so flattering to the romantic artist, seems to ignore just how various the motives of artists and businesspersons can be. It is unrealistic to suppose that the motives of the artist are, in some sense, always of a more pure type than those of the businessperson. The prospect of fame may motivate the artist just as it may motivate the aspiring businessperson. Similarly, an artist may paint in order to make money just as the businessperson works in order to acquire funds. On the other hand, the businessperson may also work in order to produce a product of importance and value, just as an artist may compose or create in order to create a work of beauty and imagination.

And yet, even if the difference between the businessperson and the artist may not lie in their motives, there is one motivation that, if it exists, may distinguish the (true) artist from the businessperson—the aesthetic motive, the desire to produce a work that bears the qualities and marks of beauty and perfection. As Iris Murdoch states, "The true artist is obedient to a conception of perfection to which his work is constantly related and re-related in what seems an external manner."[30] Such is the obedience of the *true* artist, but it is worth asking whether the *true* businessperson might also regard his or her work in relation to a conception of perfection—or is this idea of perfection to be relegated to certain products and creations only, excluding thereby the products and services of the commercial realm?

---

28. An excellent account of these differences can be found in Robert N. Wilson, "Business and the Creative Arts," in *The Business of America,* edited by Ivar Berg (New York: Harcourt Brace, 1968), 388–405.

29. Israel Kirzner has emphasized effectively the importance of entrepreneurship. See *Competition and Entrepreneurship* (Chicago: University of Chicago Press, 1973), esp. chapters 1 and 2; see also Kirzner, "The Primacy of Entrepreneurial Discovery," in *Prime Mover of Progress: The Entrepreneur in Capitalism and Socialism.* (London: Institute of Economic Affairs, 1980), 3–28.

30. *The Sovereignty of Good* (New York: Schocken Books, 1971), 62.

Arts and the State: The Case of France

The relation between art and business has often been an unhappy one, but the relation between artists and the state has often been equally fraught (even though artists have often received the patronage or subsidy of governments). The case of France provides some illustration of early and energetic intervention into the arts. The Royal Academy of Painting and Sculpture, founded in 1648, ensured not only an enforcement of standards but a certain cultural uniformity in that artists would be granted work, receive commissions, enter art school, or exhibit in the official salons (including the Paris Salon) only with official sanction. It was thus that in the seventeenth century the Academy (in addition to other academies established for Architecture, Music, Language, and Literature) served as a branch of the government, issuing and enforcing principles of content and otherwise ensuring the dominance of French classical style and taste. However, during the nineteenth century the French government's support of the visual arts was challenged.

The French government had supported a number of artists of renown, including Eugène Delacroix, but it had also sponsored a large class of artists who, remaining within the government-supported institutions, received sufficient funds and awards to make a living, even if their art was increasingly unoriginal. However, exhibition at the Paris Salon was crucial for carrying on a life in painting, and in 1863 a host of rejected painters, including Édouard Manet, organized the *Salon des Refusés,* which though widely attended was not a striking artistic success. However, the very existence of this *Salon* lent credence to the view that artists had a right to exhibit their work regardless of what the official schools might decree. Thus, in 1874, when the French government refused to support the work of the Impressionists, this group of artists held the First Impressionist Exhibition, the first large exhibition held independent of the French government. This exhibition, which included works of Monet, Degas, Pissarro, Renoir, and Sisley, proved to be a significant challenge to the state's authority over the content and style of art; by the end of the century, the exhibitions of the state-sanctioned French Academy had become relatively minor events.

Two Types of Government Policy

This historical aside does not answer a significant question concerning the relation between the state and the arts: Should the state promote or subsidize the arts? There seem to be at least two modes of government support. The first type, utilized by the French government, is direct support or subsidy given to organizations, in-

stitutions, museums, or individuals. This type of support, to which we return below, is more controversial, but there is an alternative policy that does not involve a direct subsidy. This second and indirect means of assistance occurs via the tax code, permitting individuals (or corporations) to take tax deductions for charitable contributions to nonprofit organizations, including those concerned with the arts. Unlike direct subsidies, which ultimately require that the government, or some officially sanctioned body, make decisions about which organizations or individuals receive subsidies, tax deductions allow individuals to make decisions as to which kinds of art they wish to support. This policy permits aesthetic decisions to occur in a decentralized manner, thereby lessening the probability of the sort of uniformity and stagnation that may occur if funding is centralized into a governmental body. Moreover, it helps to prevent the possibility that artists will create art that is compatible only with the views and outlooks of those in government ("Whoever takes the king's shilling sings the king's song").

Even though tax deductions provide notable support for a variety of institutions, it is often argued that this is insufficient and that direct subsidies are required. Indeed, some contend that the creative products of serious art are akin to public goods—goods that are *nonrivalrous* (one person's consumption does not diminish the availability of the goods for others) and *non-exclusive* (nonpayers cannot be excluded from enjoying the good). It is not clear, however, that works of art are public goods. Even so, if works of art are private goods, capable of being produced on the market, it might be argued that if the goods of art are left to the market, then individuals will get less of these than if they were subsidized. Advocates of government subsidies may point out, further, that the percentage of public funds given to the arts has been and will be relatively minuscule. On the other hand, those who are opposed to such funding may argue that any such subsidies may allow the state to support only those arts that cohere with the dominant political and cultural elite, thus converting a program for the arts into something akin to a special interest program.

State Neutrality and the Arts

And yet, for many the issue remains whether the state has a *moral* justification for providing direct subsidies to the arts. If one adopts a position that the state should be neutral and not seek to advance any particular version of the good life (any substantive view about what is good) then insofar as art itself is a substantive good, or insofar as art works may advance (or denigrate) specific ends, then any direct subsidy could be a violation of state neutrality. The power of art to represent, encourage, or celebrate ideals and visions should be obvious; that is one reason the content of art has so often focused on religious themes. However, it should also be clear that art has perhaps an equal power to denigrate and discourage ideals and visions. Andrés Serrano's photograph of a crucifix immersed in urine, *Piss Christ (1989),* which received a government-funded award of $15,000, may have aesthetic qualities worthy of note, but many would consider it to denigrate their view of the good, specifically the beliefs of Christians or the very practice of religion more generally. Because art may form part of one's conception of the good life, or because art may forward particular views about good or evil, many liberals argue that the state should not provide direct support to the arts. According to this argument, just as the state should *not* seek to support particular ideals of goodness or character (even if the state does provide the economic and social means to insure human flourishing) *neither* should it support works of art that contribute to these ideals. Thus the egalitarian liberal John Rawls (see Section AII), who adumbrates a theory of justice grounded in a conception of fairness, argues one case for neutrality:

> While justice as fairness allows that in a well-ordered society the values of excellence are recognized, the human perfections are to be pursued within the limits of the principle of free association. Persons join together to further their cultural and artistic interests in the same way that they form religious communities. They do not use the coercive apparatus of the state to win for themselves a greater liberty or larger distributive shares on the grounds that their activities are of more intrinsic value. Perfectionism is denied as a political principle. Thus the social resources necessary to support associations dedicated to advancing the arts and sciences and culture generally are to be won as a fair return for services rendered, or from such voluntary contributions as citizens wish to make, all within a regime regulated by the two principles of justice.[31]

Is there, in contrast to the argument of Rawls, a neutralist argument *in favor* of government support of the arts? One important thinker who has argued this point is Ronald Dworkin. He contends that state support of the arts (whether by subsidy or by tax exemptions) should not be understood as funding particular *content* but as supporting the "structural aspects" of culture, including diversity and innovation in art as well as forms or institutions of art that might prove too expensive for private support. Dworkin summarizes this outlook:

> We should try to define a rich cultural structure, one that multiplies distinct possibilities or opportunities of value, and count ourselves trustees for protecting the richness of our culture for those who will live their lives in it after us. We cannot say that in so doing we will give them more pleasure, or provide a world they will prefer as against alternative worlds we could otherwise create. That is the language of the economic approach, and it is unavailable here. We can, however, insist—how can we deny this?—that it is better for people to have complexity and depth in the forms of life open to them, and then pause to see whether, if we act on that principle, we are open to any objection of elitism or paternalism.[32]

The difficult question of whether the state should or should not subsidize the arts is, in effect, a question that should follow upon a consideration of the relation between commerce and the arts. To that end, let us turn to consider Ernst Fischer's Marxist account of "capitalist art," Donald Davidson's defense of an agrarian view of the role of art in industrial society, Tyler Cowen's defense of the capacity of markets to generate worthy works of art, and Dwight MacDonald's notable consideration of mass art.

THE READINGS

Ernst Fischer   Fischer states that in a capitalist economy, constituted by a division of labor and moved by anonymous forces, art too becomes a commodity: The capitalist pushes for accumulation of capital but regards art as "an embellishment of his private life or else as a good investment." And yet capitalism has favored the arts in certain respects, generating new ideas and styles, as well as new means and techniques. In the nineteenth century the arts enter a more developed period of capitalist commodity production in which there is alienation, the division of labor, and increased impersonalization. In this environment, the estrangement of the artist is revealed in the rise of Romanticism, a movement Fischer holds to be "the most complete reflection in philosophy, literature, and art of the contradictions of developing capitalist society." Romanticism manifests the plight of the individual who seeks, in the midst of rationalized

---

31. John Rawls, *A Theory of Justice* (Cambridge: Harvard University Press, 1971), 328–29.

32. "Can a Liberal State Support Art?" in *A Matter of Principle* (Cambridge: Harvard University Press, 1985), 229.

capitalism, a coherent and reconciled order. Fischer also notes how the modern view encourages further this sense of estrangement. For the progression of capitalism produces nihilism, a mode of thought that denies the possibility of any moral or artistic foundations and serves to divert the masses from revolution. The enormous and incomprehensible social processes of late capitalism, with its mechanization and specialization, produce an art that is dehumanized and fragmented. Indeed, desocialization and dehumanization lead millions to seek escape from the drudgery of their daily lives, an escape fueled further by the mass production of items of entertainment and "barbaric trash."

Donald Davidson   Davidson holds that the advance of industrialism not only diminishes the arts but eliminates the very conditions and values—religious and agrarian—that would enable artistic activity. Industrialism celebrates "material values" too removed from nature to allow art to flourish. According to theories of industrial progress, the arts should flourish as commerce and industrialization proceed apace. There will be more leisure, works of art will be easily and cheaply available, and the artist will be more free and productive than ever before. However, as Davidson remarks, industrial leisure is not true leisure, and although industry allows for the distribution of art, it will be an art that appeals to the masses ("Henry Ford's hired hands do not hum themes from Beethoven as they go to work"). Indeed, mass art will extend itself throughout the culture, ensuring a corruption of art and taste. Davidson rejects the view that a genuine appreciation for art can be acquired by market means or by education, especially if education is only vocational or technological. Nor will art museums provide a means of inculcating art precisely because museums manifest how far the civilization has removed itself from art and how far art has lost its connection with daily life. Romantic art arises in an industrial society in which the artist is out of place. To restore harmony between artist and society, the society itself must be harmonized. The artist should ally himself with agrarianism and to those parts of the nation, such as the South, that are "provincial, conservative, agrarian." Davidson admits that the South has not produced "great art," but he doubts that the criterion of any civilization should be whether or not it produces "great art."

Tyler Cowen   Espousing "cultural optimism," Cowen begins with the discussion of the interaction between artists, consumers, and distributors of art. Capitalism generates wealth that allows artists to produce and allows for "niche" markets in which artists can find means to fund their projects. He notes that artists of the Italian Renaissance were businessmen and that other notable geniuses were interested in the money they might reap from their art. The falling costs of materials help explain, says Cowen, why art has moved away from the popular and accessible. Cowen believes that technological progress benefits the arts. The development of markets supports a diversity of art forms, styles, and tastes, and this has occurred as artists have become less dependent on patronage and better able to appeal to a wide variety of funding. This has liberated the artist from common tastes, for one need not produce a bestselling item in order to profit handsomely. The competition of the market and the desire of artists for larger incomes or greater renown serve to increase artistic innovation. Cowen rejects the view that the arts and modern culture are dominated by the tastes of the masses, for the market for art is diverse enough to support niches. Cowen allows for a distinction between high and low culture and argues that the division is supported by economic factors. Those fields that are capital intensive must hew to standardized tastes, but as these popular forms of entertainment grow, they may exhibit greater instances of high culture.

Dwight MacDonald   MacDonald contends that there is a division between "High Culture" and "Mass Culture." Though mass culture is not necessarily the culture of the market (there was, says MacDonald, a mass culture in the Soviet Union), American mass culture is a culture of mass commerce. Within high culture there is good art and bad, but mass culture (or masscult) is distinguished not by being bad art but by being "nonart." Masscult should not be confused with art that is popular; rather, masscult, unlike genuine art, demands no effort on the part of its audiences, for it provides a uniform product that offers no communication between artist and audience but is aimed at an impersonal and abstract mass. The diversity of a culture, a diversity made real by individual qualities and not by uniformity, is essential to creativity and the stimulation of talent. Masscult functions as a dynamic force that destroys and dissolves traditional standards and distinctions and degrades high culture. Masscult, unlike the folk culture existing prior to the Industrial Revolution, is a product of business technicians and is a force for domination. For those who lack knowledge and taste, masscult is easy to consume. At its best, masscult is a vulgarized version of high culture, but it is also a competitor, a matter that is especially crucial in a society that does not have clear divisions of class. Today, the great danger is less from masscult than from "midcult," which "pretends to respect the standards of High Culture while in fact it waters them down and vulgarizes them." In this sense, midcult is a corruption of High Culture. MacDonald concludes that the masses can have masscult, but it should be kept distinct from High Culture; there must be a self-conscious and coherent establishment enforcing the standards of High Culture and doing so in distinction from masscult and midcult.

Art and Capitalism

Ernst Fischer

Ernst Fischer (1899–1972) was born in Austria, joining the Communist Party in 1934. A philosopher and literary critic, Fischer was the founder and, until 1959, the chief editor of Neues Osterreich. *He is the author of* Art Against Ideology *(1969), among other works. This excerpt is taken from* The Necessity of Art *(1963).*

The artist in the capitalist age found himself in a highly peculiar situation. King Midas had turned everything he touched into gold: capitalism turned everything into a commodity. With a hitherto unimaginable increase in production and productivity, extending the new order dynamically to all parts of the globe and all areas of human experience, capitalism dissolved the old world into a cloud of whirling molecules, destroyed all direct relationships between producer and consumer, and flung all products on to an anonymous market to be bought or sold. Previously the artisan had worked to order for a particular client. The commodity producer in the capitalist world now worked for an unknown buyer. His products were swallowed up in the competitive flood and carried away into uncertainty. Commodity production extending everywhere, the increasing division of labour, the splitting up of the job itself, the anonymity of the economic forces—all this destroyed the directness of human relationships and led to man's increasing alienation from social reality and from himself. In such a world art, too, became a commodity and the artist a commodity producer. Personal patronage was superseded by a free market whose workings were difficult or impossible to comprehend, a conglomerate of nameless consumers, the so-called 'public.' The work of art was subjected more and more to the laws of competition.

For the first time in the history of mankind the artist became a 'free' artist, a 'free' personality, free to the point of absurdity, of icy loneliness. Art became an occupation that was half-romantic, half-commercial.

For a long time capitalism regarded art as something suspect, frivolous, and shady. Art 'did not pay.' Pre-capitalist society had tended towards extravagance, carefree spending on a vast scale, lavish entertainments and the promotion of the arts. Capitalism meant sober calculation and the puritanical slide-rule. Wealth in its pre-capitalist form had been volatile and expansive; capitalist wealth demanded constant accumulation and concentration, incessant self-increase. Karl Marx gives this description of the capitalist:

> Fanatically bent upon the expansion of value, he relentlessly drives human beings to production for production's sake, thus bringing about a development of social productivity and the creation of those material conditions of production which can alone form the real basis of a higher type of society, whose fundamental principle is the full and free development of every individual. Only as the personification of capital is the capitalist respectable. As such, he shares with the miser the passion for wealth as wealth. But that which in the miser assumes the aspect of mania, is in the capitalist the effect of the social mechanism in which he is only a driving-wheel. Furthermore, the development of capitalist production necessitates a continuous increase of the capital invested in an industrial undertaking; and capitalism subjects every individual capitalist to the immanent laws of capitalist production as external coercive laws. Competition forces him continually to extend his capital for the sake of maintain it, and he can only extend it by means of progressive accumulation.[1]

And further on:

> Accumulate! Accumulate! That is Moses and all the prophets, 'Industry furnishes the material which saving accumulates' (Adam Smith, *Wealth of Nations*). Therefore you must save, you must save, you must reconvert the largest possible proportion of surplus value or surplus product into capital. Accumulation for accumulation's sake, production for production's sake, this was the formula by which the classical political economists gave expression to the historical mission of the bourgeois period.

Of course the capitalist's increasing wealth also brought new luxuries with it, but, as Marx pointed out, '. . . the capitalist's extravagance never has the genuine character of unbridled prodigality which was typical of certain feudal magnates . . . behind it there lurk sordid avarice and anxious calculation.' For the capitalist, luxury may mean the purely private satisfaction of his desires, but it also means the chance of displaying his wealth for prestige reasons. Capitalism is not essentially a social force that is well-disposed to art or that promotes art; in so far as the average capitalist needs art at all, he needs it as an embellishment of his private life or else as a good investment. On the other hand, it is true that capitalism released tremendous forces of artistic as well as economic production. It brought into being new feelings and ideas and gave the artist new means with which to express them. It was no longer possible to cling rigidly to any fixed, slowly evolving style; the local limitations within which such styles are formed had been overcome, and art developed in expanded space and accelerated time. And so, while capitalism was basically foreign to the arts, it nevertheless favoured their growth and the production of an enormous range of many-sided, expressive, and original works.

Furthermore, the acutely problematic condition of the arts in the capitalist world did not become fully manifest so long as the bourgeoisie was a rising class and the artist who affirmed bourgeois ideas was still part of an active progressive force.

During the Renaissance, on the first wave of the bourgeois advance, social relationships were still relatively transparent, the division of labour had not yet taken the rigid and narrow forms it was to assume later, and the wealth of new productive forces was still stored up as a potential within the bourgeois personality. The newly successful bourgeois and the princes who collaborated with him were generous patrons. Whole new worlds were then open to a man of creative gifts. Naturalist, discoverer, engineer, architect, sculptor, painter, and writer were often combined in one person, who passionately affirmed the age in which he lived and whose fundamental attitude was summed up in: 'What joy it is to be alive!' The second wave came with the bourgeois-democratic revolt which reached its climax in the French Revolution. Here again, the artist in his proud subjectivity expressed the ideas of the age, for it was precisely this subjectivity of the free man championing the cause of humanity and of the unification of his own country and mankind as a whole in a spirit of liberty, equality, and fraternity that was the banner of the age, the ideological programme of the rising bourgeoisie.

True, the inner contradictions of capitalism were already at work. It proclaimed liberty while practising its own peculiar idea of freedom in the form of wage slavery. It subjected the promised free play of all human capabilities to the jungle law of capitalist competition. It forced the many-sided human personality into narrow specialization. And these contradictions were beginning to pose problems even then. The sincere humanist artist was bound to feel profound disillusionment when faced with the thoroughly prosaic, thoroughly sobering, yet disquieting results of the bourgeois-democratic revolution. And after 1848, the year of that revolution's collapse in Europe, we may speak of something like a disenchantment in the arts. The brilliant artistic period of the bourgeoisie was at an end. The artist and the arts entered the fully developed world of capitalist commodity production with its total alienation of the human being, the externalization and materialization of all human relationships, the division of labour, the fragmentation, the rigid specialization, the obscuring of social connexions, the increasing isolation and denial of the individual.

The sincere humanist artist could no longer affirm such a world. He could no longer believe with a clear conscience that the victory of the bourgeoisie meant the triumph of humanity.

ROMANTICISM

Romanticism was a movement of protest—of passionate and contradictory protest against the bourgeois capitalist world, the world of 'lost illusions,' against the harsh prose of business and profit. The harsh criticism by Novalis, the German Romantic, of Goethe's *Wilhelm Meister* was characteristic of this attitude (although Friedrich Schlegel, another Romantic, was full of praise for the great novel). In *Wilhelm Meister*, Goethe presents bourgeois values in a positive spirit and traces the path from aestheticism to an active life within the prosaic bourgeois world. Novalis would have none of this.

> Adventurers, comedians, courtesans, shopkeepers and philistines are the ingredients of this novel. Whoever takes it properly to heart will never read another.

From Rousseau's *Discourses* until *The Communist Manifesto* of Marx and Engels, Romanticism was the dominant attitude of European art and literature. Romanticism, in terms of the petty-bourgeois consciousness, is the most complete reflection in philosophy, literature, and art of the contradictions of developing capitalist society. Only with Marx and Engels did it become possible to recognize the nature and origin of those contradictions, to understand the dialectic of social development, and to realize that the working class was the only force which could surmount them. The Romantic attitude could not be other than confused, for the petty bourgeoisie was the very embodiment of social contradiction, hopeful of sharing in the general enrichment yet fearful of being crushed to death in the process, dreaming of new possibilities yet clinging to the old security of rank, and order, its eyes turned towards the new times yet often also, nostalgically, towards the 'good old' ones.

To begin with, Romanticism was a petty-bourgeois revolt against the Classicism of the nobility, against rules and standards, against aristocratic form, and against a content from which all 'common' issues were excluded. For these Romantic rebels there were no privileged themes: everything was a fit subject for art.

> The extremes and excrescences [Goethe, the admirer of Stendhal and Mérimée, said as an old man on 14 March 1830] will gradually disappear; but at last this great advantage will remain—besides a freer form, richer and more diversified subjects will have been attained, and no object of the broadest world and the most manifold life will be any longer excluded as unpoetical.[2]

Opposed though he was to everything that Goethe stood for, Novalis, too, saw that Romanticism encouraged the poetic treatment of hitherto forbidden themes. 'Romanticizing,' he wrote, 'means giving a lofty significance to that which is common, a mysterious appearance to the ordinary, and the dignity of the unknown to the familiar.' Shelley wrote in *The Defence of Poetry:* 'Poetry . . . makes familiar objects appear as if they were not familiar.' Romanticism led out of the well-tended park of Classicism into the wilderness of the wide world.

Yet Romanticism opposed not only Classicism but also the Enlightenment. In many cases it was not a total opposition but one directed only against mechanistic ideas and optimistic simplifications. It is true that Chateaubriand, Burke, Coleridge, Schlegel, and many others—especially among the German Romantic school—solemnly dismissed the Enlightenment; but Shelley, Byron, Stendhal, and Heine, whose insight into the contradictions of social development was more profound, carried on the Enlightenment's work.

One of the basic experiences of Romanticism was that of the individual emerging alone and incomplete from the ever-increasing division of labour and specialization and the consequent fragmentation of life. Under the old order, a man's rank had been a kind of intermediary in his relations with other men and with society at large. In the capitalist world the individual faced society alone, without an intermediary, as a stranger among strangers, as a single 'I' opposed to the immense 'not-I.' This situation stimulated powerful self-awareness

and proud subjectivism, but also a sense of bewilderment and abandon. It encouraged the Napoleonic 'I' and at the same time an 'I' whimpering at the feet of holy effigies, an 'I' ready to conquer the world yet overcome by the terror of loneliness. The writer's and artist's 'I,' isolated and turned back upon itself, struggling for existence by selling itself in the market-place, yet challenging the bourgeois world as a 'genius,' dreamed of a lost unity and yearned for a collective imaginatively projected either into the past or into the future. The dialectic triad—*thesis* (unity of origin), *antithesis* (alienation, isolation, fragmentation), and *synthesis* (removal of contradictions, reconciliation with reality, identity of subject and object, paradise regained)—was the very core of Romanticism.

All the contradictions inherent in Romanticism were carried to their extreme by the revolutionary upheaval of which the American War of Independence was the prologue and Waterloo the final act. The revolution and the attitudes adopted to it as a whole and to its separate phases are a key-subject of the Romantic movement. Again and again, at each turning-point of events, the movement split up into progressive and reactionary trends. Each time the petty bourgeoisie proved itself to be, as Marx wrote to Schweitzer, 'contradiction incarnate.'

What all the Romantics had in common was an antipathy to capitalism (some viewing it from an aristocratic angle, others from a plebeian), a Faustian or Byronic belief in the insatiability of the individual, and the acceptance of 'passion in its own right' (Stendhal). In proportion as material production was officially regarded more and more as the quintessence of all that was praiseworthy, and as a crust of respectability formed round the dirty core of business, artists and writers attempted more and more intensively to reveal the heart of man and to hurl the dynamite of passion in the face of the apparently well-ordered bourgeois world. And as the relativity of all values was made increasingly clear by capitalist production methods, so passion—intensity of experience—became increasingly an absolute value. Keats said that he believed in nothing so much as in the 'heart's affection.' In the preface to *The Cenci,* Shelley wrote: 'Imagination is as the immortal God made flesh for the redemption of mortal passion.' Géricault, 'extreme in all things' as Delacroix said of him, wrote in an essay of the 'fever of exultation which overthrows and overwhelms everything,' and of the 'fire of a volcano which must irrepressibly break through to the light of day.'

Romanticism was indeed a gigantic breakthrough. It led to the wild and the exotic, to limitless horizons:

but it also led back to one's own people, one's own past, one's own specific nature. The greatest of the Romantics all admired Napoleon, the 'cosmic self,' the unbounded personality; yet at the same time the Romantic revolt merged with the national liberation struggles. Foscolo greeted Napoleon with an ode entitled *A Bonaparte Liberatore*. In 1802 he pleaded with Napoleon to proclaim the independence of the Cisalpine Republic, i.e. of Italy. In the end he turned, full of loathing, against Napoleon the conqueror. Leopardi, similarly embittered and disillusioned by the French liberator's failure to set his country free, exclaimed in the *Canzoni*:

> . . . *l'armi, qua l'armi! io solo*
> *Combatteró, procomberó sol io.*
> *Dammi, o ciel, che sia faco*
> *Agli italici petti il sangue mio.*

Arms, bring arms! I alone shall fight, I alone shall fall. Heaven provide that my blood be an inspiration to Italian hearts.

And in Eastern Europe, where capitalism had not yet triumphed and where the people were still labouring under the yoke of a decaying medievalism, Romanticism meant rebellion pure and simple, a trumpet call to the people to rise against foreign and home-bred oppressors, an appeal to national consciousness, a struggle against feudalism, absolutism, and foreign rule. Byron carried these countries by storm. The Romantic idealization of folk lore and folk art became a weapon for stirring up the people against degrading conditions, Romantic individualism a means of freeing the human personality from medieval bondage. The bourgeois-democratic revolution, as yet unaccomplished in the East, flashed like distant lightning through the works of the Romantic artists of Russia, Hungary, and Poland.

But for all these differences in its manifestation in various countries, Romanticism everywhere had certain features in common: a sense of spiritual discomfort in a world with which the artist could not identify himself, a sense of instability and isolation out of which grew the longing for a new social unity, a preoccupation with the people and their songs and legends ('the people' being endowed with an almost mystical unity in the artists' minds), and the celebration of the individual's absolute uniqueness, the unbounded Byronic subjectivism. The 'free' writer rejecting all ties, setting himself up as an opponent of the bourgeois world, and at the same time, though himself unaware of this, recognizing the bourgeois principle of production for the market, made his first appearance at the time of Romanticism. In their

Romantic protest against bourgeois values and in their emancipation which ultimately forced them into the role of Bohemians, such writers made of their works precisely what they wanted to denounce: a market commodity. Despite its invocation of the Middle Ages, Romanticism was an eminently bourgeois movement, and all the problems regarded as modern today were already implicit in it. . . .

ALIENATION

. . . Hegel and the young Marx developed the concept of alienation philosophically. Man's alienation begins when he parts company with nature through work and production. Through his work 'man makes himself twofold, not only intellectually, as in the conscience, but in reality, through his work, and hence contemplates himself within a world made by himself . . .' (Karl Marx). As man becomes more and more capable of mastering and transforming nature and the entire world around him, so does he confront himself more and more as a stranger in his own work, and find himself surrounded by objects which are the product of his activity yet which have a tendency to grow beyond his control and to become more and more powerful in their own right.

This alienation, necessary for Man's development, needs to be continually overcome, so that men can become conscious of themselves in the process of work, find themselves again in the product of their work, and create new social conditions so as not to be the slaves of their own production but its masters. The artisan, who is creative, can feel at home in his work and can have a personal feeling for his product. But with the division of labour in industrial production this becomes impossible. The wage-earner can have no sense of unity with his work or with himself to set against his 'alienation.' His attitude towards the product of his work is that 'towards an alien object having power over him.' He is alienated from the thing he makes and from his own self, lost in the act of production. Then, as Marx puts it,

> activity appears as suffering, strength as powerlessness, production as emasculation, and the worker's *own* physical and spiritual energy, his personal life—for what is life if not activity?—as an activity turned against himself, independent from himself, and not belonging to himself.

. . . Those engaged in commercial exchange are totally alienated from one another, and the product is likewise totally alienated from the man who puts it on the market. Bertolt Brecht makes this point very strikingly in the 'Trader's Song' from *Die Massnahme*:

> How should I know what rice is?
> How should I know who knows what it is?
> I've no idea what rice is.
> I only know its price.

We speak of price trends, stock-exchange prices, and by so doing we acknowledge the inhuman, autonomous movement of objects, a movement that carries human beings along as a stream carries twigs of wood. In a world governed by commodity production, the product controls the producer, and objects are more powerful than men. Objects become the strange thing that casts long shadows, they become 'density' and the *daemon ex machina*.

Industrial society is distinguished not only by this *objectification* of social relationships, but also by an increasing division of labour and specialization. Man as he works becomes fragmented. His connexion with the whole is lost; he becomes a tool, a small accessory to a huge apparatus. And as this division of labour makes a man's role more partial, so his field of vision becomes more limited; the more ingenious the work process, the less intelligent is the work required and the more acute the individual's alienation from the whole. The tag from Terence—'*Nihil humanum mihi alienum est*'—is reversed, and the tremendous expansion of production is accompanied by a shrinkage of the personality. . . .

Not only is the human being more and more obliterated by his own special knowledge and training—by his existence as a *detail*—but also the social relationships and conditions around him become more and more difficult to comprehend.

> Men's living together has become so broad and thick [wrote Robert Musil in *The Man Without Qualities*] and their relationships are so endlessly intertwined, that no eye and no will can any longer penetrate an area of any size, and every man outside the narrowest circle of his activities must remain dependent on others like a child; never before was the underling's mind so limited as it is today, when it rules all.

In a note on Rousseau, Musil wrote:

> The great undivided life-force must be preserved. . . . The culture of social and psychological division of labour which smashes this unity into innumerable fragments is the greatest peril for the soul.

Ulrich, the 'man without qualities,' remarks that in the past 'one had an easier conscience about being a person than one has today.' Responsibility today, he finds, 'has its centre of gravity not in the human being but in relationships between objects . . . .' And elsewhere he says: 'The inner drought, the uncanny mixture of keenness about details and indifference to the whole, the human being's immense abandonment in a desert of detail. . . .'

. . . The contradiction between the findings of modern science and the backwardness of social understanding also encourages a sense of alienation. Modern knowledge about the structure of the atom, the Quantum and Relativity theories, the new science of cybernetics, have made the world an uneasy place for the man in the street—far uneasier than the discoveries of Galileo, Copernicus, and Kepler made the world for medieval man. The palpable becomes impalpable, the visible becomes invisible, behind the reality perceived by the senses there is a vast reality that escapes the imagination and can only be expressed by mathematical formulae. Vigorous, forceful reality with all its shapes and colours—the 'nature' Goethe saw as a scientist as well as a poet—has become an immense abstraction. Ordinary men no longer feel at home in such a world. The icy breath of the incomprehensible chills them. A world that can only be understood by scientists is a world from which they are alienated.

There are moments when technical achievements—the flight into the cosmos, which is the realization of an ancient, magic dream—can enchant men. But it is precisely this same power over the forces of nature that also intensifies a sense of powerlessness and arouses apocalyptic fears. And indeed the discrepancy between social consciousness and technical achievement is alarming. A single misreading of a radar report, a mistake by a simple technician may mean world disaster. Humanity may be destroyed and no one will have wanted it to happen.

Alienation has had a decisive influence on the arts and literature of the twentieth century. It has influenced the great writings of Kafka, the music of Schoenberg, the Surrealists, many abstract artists, the 'anti-novelists' and 'anti-dramatists,' Samuel Beckett's sinister farces; and also the poetry of the American beatniks, one of which reads:

> Now listen to this
> a do-it-yourself laparectomy set
> the hydrogen strophe
> the best fallout possible.
> Think of the funny embryonic mutations
> generous, genial, genocide.

It's democratic too
it'll take fragmented man
everyone will move upward
in the free world
equally
in that final illumination. . . .

(Carl Forsberg: *Lines on a Tijuana John*)

The sense of total alienation veers into total despair, veers into nihilism.

NIHILISM

Nietzsche, who understood decadence if anyone did, recognized nihilism as one of its essential features. He announced the 'rise of nihilism': 'The whole of our European culture has been moving, for a long time past, with a tortured tension that increases from decade to decade, towards something like a catastrophe: restlessly, violently, precipitously. . . .' And this is how he described the times into which we have been 'thrown' (this idea of being 'thrown' into one's time was to become one of the themes of existentialism):

. . . a time of great inner decay and disintegration. . . . Radical Nihilism [he declared] means being convinced that existence is absolutely untenable. . . . Nihilism is an intermediary pathological state (the colossal generalization, the conclusion that there is *no sense at all* is purely pathological): whether it be that the productive forces are not yet strong enough—whether it be that decadence is still hesitating and has not yet found its auxiliary means. . . . Nihilism is not a cause but only the logic of decadence.

Here nihilism is clearly diagnosed as a result, an expression of decadence. But, blind to social dialectics, Nietzsche failed to recognize the connexion with outworn capitalism. Nihilism, already foreshadowed by Flaubert, is a genuine attitude for many artists and writers in the late bourgeois world. But we must not overlook the fact that it helps many uneasy intellectuals to reconcile themselves to iniquitous conditions—that its radical nature is often only a form of dramatized opportunism. The nihilist writer says to us: 'The capitalist bourgeois world is wretched. I say so without mercy and I carry my opinion to its most extreme consequences. There is no limit to this barbarity. And whoever believes that there is something in this world worth living for or worthy of mankind is a fool or a swindler. All human beings are stupid and wicked, the oppressed as much as the oppressors, those who fight for freedom as much as the tyrants. To say this needs

courage.' Let me continue now with words actually written by Gottfried Benn:

The thought occurs to me that it is perhaps far more radical, far more revolutionary, far more of a challenge to a man who is strong, hard and fit, to tell mankind: You are like that and you will never be any different; this is how you live, have lived, and always shall live. If you have money, you keep your health; if you have power, you need not perjure yourself; if you are strong, you are doing right. That is history! *Ecce historia!* . . . Whoever cannot bear this thought lies among the worms that nest in the sand and in the dampness which the earth lays upon them. Whoever boasts, as he looks into his children's eyes, that he still has a hope, is covering the lightning with his hand, yet cannot save himself from the night that snatches the nations away from their cities. . . . All these catastrophes born from destiny and freedom: useless blossoms, powerless flames, and behind them the impenetrable with its boundless No.

All this sounds much more radical than any Communist Manifesto—and yet the ruling class only occasionally has any objection to such 'radicalism.' More than that: in times of revolutionary upheaval, nihilism such as this becomes virtually indispensable to the ruling class, more useful, indeed, than direct eulogies of the bourgeois world. Direct eulogies provoke suspicion. But the radical tone of the nihilist's accusation strikes 'revolutionary' echoes and so can channel revolt into purposelessness and create a passive despair. Only when the ruling class thinks itself unusually secure, and particularly when it is preparing a war, does its satisfaction with anti-capitalist nihilism evaporate: at such times it requires direct apologetics and references to 'eternal values.' Nihilistic radicalism then runs the risk of being branded as 'degenerate art.'

The nihilist artist is generally not aware that he is, in effect, surrendering into the hands of the capitalist bourgeois world, that in condemning and denying *everything* he condones that world as a fit setting for universal wretchedness. For many of these artists, who are subjectively sincere, it is by no means easy to grasp things that have not yet come fully into being and to translate these things into art. There are two good reasons why it is not easy: first, the working class itself has not remained entirely uncorrupted by imperialistic influences in the capitalist world; secondly, the overcoming of capitalism, not only as an economic and social system but also as a spiritual attitude, is a long and painful process, and the new world does not come forth gloriously perfect but scarred and disfigured by the past. A high degree of social consciousness is needed in order to distinguish between the death-throes of the old world and the birth-pangs of the new, between the ruin and the as yet unfinished edifice. Equally a high degree of social consciousness is needed in order to portray the new in its totality without ignoring, or worse still idealizing, its ugly features. It is far easier to notice only the horrible and inhuman, only the ravaged foreground of the age, and to condemn it, than to penetrate into the very essence of what is about to be—the more so as decay is more colourful, more striking, more immediately fascinating than the laborious construction of a new world. And one last word: nihilism carries no obligation. . . .

THE FLIGHT FROM SOCIETY

The de-socialization of art and literature produces the recurring motif of flight: the motif of deserting a society which is felt to be catastrophic in order to attain a supposed state of 'pure' or 'naked' being. . . .

. . . Millions of people, particularly young people, seek to escape from unsatisfying jobs, from daily lives they feel to be empty, from a boredom prophetically analysed by Baudelaire, from all social obligations and ideologies, away, away on roaring motor-cycles, intoxicated by a speed that consumes every feeling and thought, away from their own selves, into a Sunday or holiday in which the whole meaning of life is somehow concentrated. As though driven by approaching disaster, as though sensing an imminent storm, whole generations in the capitalist world flee from themselves, to put up, somewhere in the midst of the unknown, a flimsy tent where it will be brighter inside than it is in the outer darkness.

What makes the problems of the de-socialization and dehumanization of the arts all the more acute is the fact that the improving techniques of mechanical reproduction, which began with photographs and records, have created a colossal entertainment industry serving vast masses of art consumers. The barbaric character, anti-humanist content, and brutal sensationalism of many artistic items manufactured for mass consumption under capitalism are well known; to analyse such products and their effects would require a book in itself. I should like to make only two points. First, writers and artists of some stature often supply the models that are later imitated, in cruder form and cheaper execution, by the art-manufacturing industries—so that, as it were, the *haute couture* of anti-humanism influences the mass-producing trade. Secondly, an art which arrogantly ignores the needs of the masses and glories in being understood only by a select few opens the floodgates for the rubbish produced by the entertainment industry. In pro-

portion as artists and writers withdraw more and more from society, more and more barbaric trash is unloaded on to the public. The 'new brutalism' extolled as an admirable quality of modern art by certain aesthetes has in fact a free commercial run in the late bourgeois world.

REALISM

The feature common to all significant artists and writers in the capitalist world is their inability to come to terms with the social reality that surrounds them. All social systems have had their great apologists in art (side by side with their rebels and accusers): only under capitalism has *all* art above a certain level of mediocrity always been an art of protest, criticism, and revolt. Man's alienation from his environment and from himself has become so overwhelming under capitalism, the human personality released from the bonds of the medieval system of guilds and classes is so violently aware of having been cheated of the freedom and fullness of life it might have enjoyed, the transformation of all earthly goods into market commodities, the all-embracing utilitarianism, the total commercialization of the world, have provoked such intense repugnance in anyone possessed of an imagination that the imaginative have inevitably found themselves emphatically rejecting the victorious capitalist system. . . .

ENDNOTES

1. *Capital,* Allen & Unwin, 1928.
2. Goethe: *Conversations with Eckermann.* Everyman Edition, J. M. Dent & Sons, London and Toronto, 1930.

QUESTIONS ON FISCHER

1. Fischer states that romanticism is the reflection of capitalist society. Why does the romantic artist seek to rebel against capitalism? Under what form does romanticism exist in Eastern Europe, where "capitalism had not yet triumphed"?

2. How does Fischer portray dehumanization and alienation? If his description of these phenomena is correct, are these the effects of markets alone? Are there any other cultural, social, political, or religious forces that might account for these?

3. What is nihilism, and why does Fischer believe that it is a product of capitalism? Are there other reasons why nihilism might emerge?

A Mirror for Artists

Donald Davidson

Born in Tennessee, Donald Davidson (1893–1968) was Professor of English at Vanderbilt University. A poet and a founder of The Fugitive, *an important literary journal, Davidson's books of poetry include* The Outland Piper *(1924),* The Tall Men *(1927) and* Lee in the Mountains and Other Poems *(1938). Other works include* The Attack on Leviathan: Regionalism and Nationalism in the United States *(1938) and* "Still Rebels, Still Yankees" and Other Essays *(1972). The essay reprinted here is from* I'll Take My Stand *(1930), the manifesto of Agrarianism, authored by "Twelve Southerners."*

What is the industrial theory of the arts? It is something to which industry has not turned its corporate brains in any large measure. Yet however unformulated, there seems to be the phantom of a theory in the air; perhaps it may materialize into some formidable managerial body which will take care of the matter for us—a United States Chamber of Art or a National Arts Council, with a distinguished board of directors and local committees in every state. In the absence of the reassuring information which it would undoubtedly be the function of such a body to collect and disseminate, I must beg leave to define the industrial theory of the arts as best I can.

Whenever it is attacked for dirtying up the landscape and rendering human life generally dull, mechanical, standardized, and mean, industrialism replies by pointing out compensatory benefits. In the field of the arts, these are the benefits that a plodding Mæcenas might think about without greatly agitating his intellect: When material prosperity has finally become permanent, when we are all rich, when life has been reduced to some last pattern of efficiency, then we shall all sit down and enjoy ourselves. Since nice, civilized people are supposed to have art, we shall have art. We shall buy it, hire it, can it, or—most conclusively—manufacture it. That is a sufficient answer to the whole question, so far as the industrial Mæcenas is concerned—and he does not, of course, realize what a strange part he plays in the rôle of Mæcenas. The *nouveau riche* is never sensible of his own errors. If the industrial Mæcenas were alone to be considered, I should not be writing this essay. Other people, some of them persons of learning and thoughtfulness, hold essentially the same theory. They talk of "mastering the machine" or "riding the wild horses" of industrial power, with the idea that industri-

alism may furnish the basis for a society which will foster art. It is a convenient doctrine, and a popular one.

The contention of this essay is that such theories are wrong in their foundation. Industrialism cannot play the rôle of Mæcenas, because its complete ascendancy will mean that there will be no arts left to foster; or, if they exist at all, they will flourish only in a diseased and disordered condition, and the industrial Mæcenas will find himself in the embarrassing position of having to patronize an art that secretly hates him and calls him bad names. More completely, the making of an industrialized society will extinguish the meaning of the arts, as humanity has known them in the past, by changing the conditions of life that have given art a meaning. For they have been produced in societies which were for the most part stable, religious, and agrarian; where the goodness of life was measured by a scale of values having little to do with the material values of industrialism; where men were never too far removed from nature to forget that the chief subject of art, in the final sense, is nature.

It is my further contention that the cause of the arts, thus viewed, offers an additional reason among many reasons for submitting the industrial program to a stern criticism and for upholding a contrary program, that of an agrarian restoration; and that, in America, the South, past and present, furnishes a living example of an agrarian society, the preservation of which is worth the most heroic effort that men can give in a time of crisis.

Let us recall the song of the sirens, which Sir Thomas Browne ventured to say was not beyond conjecture. . . . Whatever the words and melody, the song of the sirens must have had this meaning: "You shall enjoy beauty without the toil of winning it, if you will forsake your ship and dwell with us." It was an alluring promise, and few of those who yielded thought of the condition on which it was made. They were attracted by the first clause and forgot the second, which implied, yet revealed not that alien shore where the bones of victims littered the rocks. For the sirens were cannibals; their embrace was death.

Industrialism makes the promise of the sirens, though of course with no real malignancy—rather with a mild innocence which we could forgive if it were not so stupid. Industrialism wants to take a short-cut to art. Seeing the world altogether in terms of commodities, it simply proposes to add one more commodity to the list, as a concession to humanity's perfectly unaccountable craving, or as just one more market—why not? It will buy art, if any fool wants art. And industrialism is quite unconscious that the bargain (which the Middle Ages would have described as a devil's bargain, ending in the delivery of the soul to torment) involves the destruction of the thing bargained for. The takers of the bargain, if there are any, are likely to be equally unconscious of what is happening to them, except as they are vaguely aware of being somehow betrayed. Hence results a situation that might be put into a dialogue:

"Incompetent wretch," says the industrialist, "is this sorry product what I bargained for? Have I not endowed you with leisure and comfort in which to produce your masterpieces? Do I not reward you with great wealth and provide you with all the proper facilities in all manner of institutions? Yet you perform no great works, but oddly prefer to indulge in maudlin ravings that no sensible person can understand or in obscene scoldings that no right-minded citizen can approve."

"You do not understand the nature of genius," the artist answers, haughtily. "I am what I am. I do not expect to be appreciated in my lifetime, anyway, and certainly not by vulgar persons unlearned in the modern theories of art. Art makes its own rules, which are not the rules of commerce. If you want to play my game, you must play it by my rules."

The industrialist, reorganizing society according to theories of material progress, avows his good intentions. He naturally expects the arts to flourish as a matter of course, perhaps even more joyously and quickly than in the past. For he thinks his dispensation sets men free to use the blessings of art, however minor and incidental these may be in his cosmic scheme. The artist, who is in spirit dissociated from the industrialist's scheme of society but forced to live under it, magnifies his dissociation into a special privilege and becomes a noble exile.

Do the arts require leisure for their creation and enjoyment? The industrialist claims that he increases the sum-total of human leisure through machines that save labor; furthermore, that this leisure is more widely distributed than ever before in history, and that the proportion of leisure to labor and the extent of its distribution are bound to increase as industrialism waxes mightier and ever more efficient. With leisure goes physical security—greater length of life, freedom from disease and poverty, increase of material comforts. If, under this benevolent dispensation, men do not spontaneously devote themselves to art, then the further presumption is that industrial philanthropy will be equal to the emergency, for its accumulations of surplus capital can be used for promoting the "finer things of life."

Through his command over nature the modern man can move his art about at will. Literary masterpieces, chosen by the best critics that can be hired, can be distributed once a month to hundreds of thousands of disciples of culture. Symphony concerts, heavily endowed and directed by world-famous experts, can be broadcast to millions. Much as the Red Cross mobilizes against disease, the guardians of public taste can mobilize against bad art or lack of art; one visualizes caravans of art, manned by regiments of lecturers, rushed hastily to future epidemic centers of barbarism when some new Mencken discovers a Sahara of the Bozart. Or, *vice versa,* modern man can move himself to the place where art is—to the Louvre, to the cathedrals, to the pagodas, to meetings of the Poetry Society of America. Through power of accumulated wealth, in public or private hands, he can bring precious canvasses and sculptures together for multitudes to stare at. He can build immense libraries or put little libraries on wheels—the flying library may be looked for eventually. The millionaire can retain an expert to buy his gallery of Corots—or of the newest, surest masters declared by modern dealers. Or, as wealth trickles down to humbler hands, the shop girl can get a ten-cent print of Corot to hang above her dressing-table, or buy her dollar edition of Shakespeare, with an introduction by Carl Van Doren. Between the shop girl and the millionaire will of course be a universal art-audience of all the people, introduced to the classics through schemes of mass-education and trained from babyhood (in nursery schools) in all varieties of art-appreciation.

In short, the artist is to have a freer and fuller opportunity than he has ever known before. With leisure to enjoy art, with command over the materials of art, with remarkable schemes for communicating, distributing, manufacturing, and inculcating art—how can the creative spirit fail to respond to the challenge? Why not a golden age of the arts, wherein ideal cities, grandiosely designed, shelter a race of super-beings who spend all their unemployed moments (destined to be numerous, when production is finally regulated) in visiting art museums, reading immortal works, and dwelling in beautiful homes adorned with designs approved by the best interior decorators?

What a shame if, with all this tremendous array of compulsions, the stubborn pig still refuses to get over the stile! Yet that is what happens. The arts behave with piggish contrariness. They will not budge, or they run crazily off into briar patches and mud puddles, squealing hideously.

It is common knowledge that, wherever it can be said to exist at all, the kind of leisure provided by industrialism is a dubious benefit. It helps nobody but merchants and manufacturers, who have taught us to use it in industriously consuming the products they make in great excess over the demand. Moreover, it is spoiled, as leisure, by the kind of work that industrialism compels. The furious pace of our working hours is carried over into our leisure hours, which are feverish and energetic. We live by the clock. Our days are a muddle of "activities," strenuously pursued. We do not have the free mind and easy temper that should characterize true leisure. Nor does the separation of our lives into two distinct parts, of which one is all labor—too often mechanical and deadening—and the other all play, undertaken as a nervous relief, seem to be conducive to a harmonious life. The arts will not easily survive a condition under which we work and play at cross-purposes. We cannot separate our being into contradictory halves without a certain amount of spiritual damage. The leisure thus offered is really no leisure at all; either it is pure sloth, under which the arts take on the character of mere entertainment, purchased in boredom and enjoyed in utter passivity, or it is another kind of labor, taken up out of a sense of duty, pursued as a kind of fashionable enterprise for which one's courage must be continually whipped up by reminders of one's obligation to culture.

The promise of distribution is equally deceptive. One thing has obviously happened that nobody counted on when industrialism first appeared as Messiah. It has been generally assumed that the art to be distributed will naturally be good art. But it is just as easy to distribute bad art—in fact, it is much easier, because bad art is more profitable. The shop-girl does not recite Shakespeare before breakfast. Henry Ford's hired hands do not hum themes from Beethoven as they go to work. Instead, the shop-girl reads the comic strip with her bowl of patent cereal and puts on a jazz record while she rouges her lips. She reads the confession magazines and goes to the movies. The factory hand simply does not hum; the *Daily Mirror* will do for him, with pictures and titles that can be torpidly eyed. The industrialists in art—that is, the Hollywood producers, the McFadden publications, the Tin Pan Alley crowd, the Haldeman-Julius Blue Books—will naturally make their appeal to the lowest common denominator. They know the technique of mass-production, which, if applied to the arts, must invariably sacrifice quality to quantity. Small margins of profit, large sales, the technique of forcing the market through salesmanship and high-pressure advertising, will all work havoc; nor have we much reason to hope that the ravages will eventually be limited to the vulgar enterprises I have named, of which the movies offer perhaps the most convincing example. What have we to hope for when eminent critics sell their prestige and ability to book clubs whose entire scheme of operations is based on the technique of mass-production; when publishers begin to imitate the methods of William Wrigley and Lydia E. Pinkham? What but a gradual corruption of integrity and good taste, a preference for the mediocre and "safe," if not for the positively bad. The magnificent possibilities for distributing art become appalling opportunities for distributing bad art. One has only to glance at magazines of large circulation, at the advertising columns of reviews (if not at the articles themselves), at the general critical confusion of New York, to see what inroads have already been made.

At this point somebody might argue that the lower classes never produced or enjoyed good art, anyway; and the number of persons of good taste is steadily increasing.

This objection would ask us to view good art as an aristocratic affair. It cannot be granted without ignoring history, which shows that art in its great periods has rarely been purely aristocratic. It has generally been also "popular" art in a good sense and has been widely diffused. The "popular" art that has survived for inspection is good art, certainly as compared with the McFadden publications. Furthermore, this objection would at once subtract from consideration one of the major claims of industrialism, which proposes to enlarge and not to diminish the audience of the artist—even to make his audience universal. And even if there should be proved to be, by actual census, a larger number of people who enjoy good art through the agency of industrialism than in past times, I should still suspect the validity of the process by which they achieved good taste. For good taste cannot be had by simply going into the market for it. It will be but a superficial property, the less valued because it was easily got; and it will be dangerous to society if society is merely gilded with culture and not permeated. Such an aristocracy, if it could be achieved, would reign very insecurely; and it would always be more likely that its manners would be perverted by the "lower" class than that the manners of the "lower" class would be raised. . . .

As to art museums and other philanthropic schemes for promoting art, I do not speak against them in any denunciatory sense. Yet one cannot help but fear that they too only serve to emphasize the discrepancy between our life and our art. Alone, they can hardly supply the impulses which a thousand other influences are negating and destroying. It is futile to imagine that the arts will penetrate our life in exact proportion to the number of art galleries, orchestras, and libraries that philanthropy may endow. Rather it is probable that a multiplication of art galleries (to take a separate example) is a mark of a diseased, not a healthy civilization. If paintings and sculptures are made for the purpose of being viewed in the carefully studied surroundings of art galleries, they have certainly lost their intimate connection with life. What is a picture for, if not to put on one's own wall? But the principle of the art gallery requires me to think that a picture has some occult quality in itself and for itself that can only be appreciated on a quiet anonymous wall, utterly removed from the tumult of my private affairs.

The art gallery or art museum theory of art to which philanthropists and promoters would persuade us views art as a luxury quite beyond the reach of ordinary people. Its attempt to glorify the arts by setting them aside in specially consecrated shrines can hardly supply more than a superficial gilding to a national culture, if the private direction of that culture is ugly and materialistic—Keyserling would say, animalistic. The proposition is as absurd as this: Should we eat our meals regularly from crude, thick dishes like those used in Greek restaurants, but go on solemn occasions to a restaurant museum where somebody's munificence would permit us to enjoy a meal on china of the most delicate design? The truly artistic life is surely that in which the æsthetic experience is not curtained off but is mixed up with all sorts of instruments and occupations pertaining to the round of daily life. It ranges all the way from pots and pans, chairs and rugs, clothing and houses, up to dramas publicly performed and government buildings. Likewise public libraries, which tend ever to become more immense and numerous, pervert public taste as much as they encourage it. For the patrons are by implication discouraged from getting their own books and keeping them at home. Their notion is that the state—or some local Mæcenas—will take care of their taste for them, just as the police take care of public safety. Art galleries and libraries are fine enough in their way, but we should not be deceived into putting our larger hope in them.

The final evidence of the false promise of industrialism is in the condition of the arts themselves. That they have in our time a real excellence as arts I should be the last to deny. I am, however, not so much concerned with defining that excellence as with discovering their general status in relation to the profound changes which industrialism has brought into human society. Those who study the modern arts seriously and disinterestedly are obliged to note that their excellence is maintained somewhat desperately and defiantly. It has a back-against-the-wall heroism. It has the fierce courage that flares up when one is cornered by an overwhelming adversary, or it has the malaise of defeat. . . .

. . . Romantic writers, from William Blake to T. S. Eliot, are not so much an advance guard leading the way to new conquests as a rear guard—a survival of happier days when the artist's profession was not so much a separate and special one as it is now. Romantic writers—and modern writers, who are also romantic—behave like persons whose position is threatened and needs fresh justification. The rebellion against tradition, so marked in some kinds of Romanticism, is thus an abandonment of one untenable fortress in order to take a new position that the artist hopes will be unassailable. In turn it too is besieged, and a new manœuvre must be attempted. Yet every time it is not merely Neoclassic art or Victorian art that is invaded. It is art itself, as art, that is being attacked by an enemy so blind and careless that he does not know what citadel he is approaching.

Mr. Babbitt, Mr. More, and other critics of the Humanist school have dragged the weaknesses of Romantic art into the light, but seemingly fail to realize that if there is to be any art at all under the conditions of modern life, it must probably be Romantic art, and must have the weaknesses of Romantic art, with such excellences as may be allowed to the unvictorious. . . .

Unpredictable though the great artist may be, no study of the past can fail to reveal that social conditions to a large extent direct the temper and form of art. . . .

Eighteenth Century society, which pretended to classicism artistically and maintained a kind of feudalism politically, was with all its defects a fairly harmonious society in which the artist was not yet out of place, although he was already beginning to be. But in the middle of the eighteenth century, democracy and the industrial revolution got under way almost simultaneously. The rise of the middle classes to power, through commercial prosperity, prepared the way for the one; scientific discovery, backed by eighteenth century rationalism, prepared for the other, and society speedily fell into a disharmony, where it has remained. Political democracy . . . left social democracy unrealized. The way was clear for the materialistic reorganization of society that in effect brought a spiritual disorganization.

Thus arise the works of the Romantic school, in which the artist sets forth "the fundamental contradiction of principle" between himself and society. The artist is no longer *with* society, as perhaps even Milton, last of classicists, was. He is *against* or *away from* society, and the disturbed relation becomes his essential theme, always underlying his work, no matter whether he evades or accepts the treatment of the theme itself. . . .

Wordsworth's hope that the objects of science—such as, presumably, dynamos, atoms, skyscrapers, knitting-machines, and chemical reactions—might one day become materials of art, when they are as familiar as trees and rocks, seems as far from realization as ever. The attempt to sublimate them, which has something of the attitude of the realist without his method, does not yet show much promise of success. The objects appear in art, of course, but that art is already conditioned by the social trends that machines and scientific theories have caused. They become a part of the background of artistic interpretation or they furnish motives, but their rôle is mainly Satanic. Since their influence on humanity is to dehumanize, to emphasize utilitarian ends, to exalt abstraction over particularity and uniformity over variety, the artist tends to view them as evil. He cannot accept them as offering an approach to some "new" art unless he adopts the resolution of Satan, "Evil, be thou my good!" A world committed to some hypothetical and as yet unheard-of-form of art-science can today be visioned only as a monstrous and misshapen nightmare which we pray we may not survive to witness. Whether or not science and art are actually hostile to each other, as I have argued, it is certainly true that they have no common ground; they are as far apart as science and religion.

In short, the condition of the arts themselves, in whatever field, gives little ground for thinking that they are actually cherished in an industrial civilization. The sporadic vitality that they show is probably not a mark of abundant health, but of a lingering and lusty capacity to survive every disaster and disease short of complete extinction. The ultimate disaster of extinction must honestly be faced—unless the arts accept a rôle inferior to anything they have previously enjoyed, so greatly in contrast to their old state as to make them appear slavish and parasitical.

In his *Portrait of the Artist as American* Matthew Josephson has shown to what an astonishing extent the careers of American artists have been distorted and erratic. Rarely if ever in America do we find a great artist slowly maturing his powers in full communion with a society of which he is an integral part. Instead we have seclusionists like Emily Dickinson, retiring within a narrow subjective cell; or at the other extreme exiles like Henry James and Lafcadio Hearn who sought salvation in flight. Van Wyck Brooks has tended, in such cases, to blame the insufficiency of the artists themselves—that is, Mark Twain should not have let himself be gentled; Henry James should have drawn strength from his native earth. Rightly, I think, Mr. Josephson finds that American society was to blame, and not the artists, for their defeatism was but a corollary of their dislocated re-lation to society. The rule of mechanism, though it began early in America, promised for a while to be checked by the New England group who might have established a society hospitable to the arts. But New England idealism failed in the débâcle of the Civil War that it egged on. Thenceforth industrialism, which had been long resisted by the agrarian South and its old ally, the West of the transition period, held strong sway. The schism between the artist and society, already foreshadowed in the inherent weaknesses of New England, became more and more exaggerated until today France and England harbor veritable colonies of expatriates, while at home new tribes of artists repeat the subjective tragedy of Emily Dickinson or Poe, or with a vain assurance attempt like Whitman to adumbrate the glory of a democratic, muscular future that forever recedes in mists of retreating hope.

Mr. Josephson makes a strong case, but states it too narrowly. His America is New England or New York; he is blissfully oblivious to the agrarian South, past and present. He does not realize that the malady he pictures appears in the United States only in its most exaggerated and obvious form. Geographically, it covers Western civilization wherever industrialism has fully entered. Historically, its ravages may be studied throughout the nineteenth century. The long list from Byron to Tennyson to Eliot, from Hugo to the Symbolists, from Goethe to the Expressionists, will reveal the lamentable story of dissociation and illustrate profusely, with examples of exile, distortion, sensibility, Mr. Josephson's dictum, "Under mechanism, the eternal drama of the artist becomes *resistance to the milieu.*"

It is significant, as I have previously indicated, that the Romanticism which could be defined under this principle begins almost simultaneously with the industrial revolution. Democracy began its great rule at the same time; but we should do wrong to blame democracy too much, as Mr. Josephson does, for the bad estate of the artist. Democracy did not, after all, disturb society unduly. It was a slow growth, it had some continuity with the past, and in an agrarian country like pre-Civil War America it permitted and favored a balanced life. Industrialism came suddenly and marched swiftly. It left a tremendous gap. Only as democracy becomes allied with industrialism can it be considered really dangerous, as when, in the United States, it becomes politically and socially impotent; or, as in the extreme democracy of the Soviets, where, converted into equalitarianism within class limits, it threatens the existence of man's humanity. Democracy, if not made too acquisitive by industrialism, does not appear as an enemy to the arts. Industrialism does so appear, and has played its hostile rôle for upwards of a hundred and fifty years. As socialism in its various forms may be considered the natural political antitoxin that industrialism produces, Romanticism is the artistic antitoxin and will appear inevitably if the artist retains enough courage and sincerity to function at all. To yield to industrialism means to surrender the artistic function, to play the clown at Dives' feast, to become a kind of engineer—which is, for example, just what the architects of skyscrapers have become. Not to yield means to invite and even to exploit the unbalance that is a unique characteristic of modern Romanticism, all the more marked because of the modern tendency to exalt the separate rôle of the artist as artist and to make art itself sacrosanct and professional.

There is but one other possibility. The supremacy of industrialism itself can be repudiated. Industrialism can be deposed as the regulating god of modern society.

This is no doubt a desperate counsel. But the artist may well find in it more promise for his cause than in all the talk of progressivists about "mastering the machine." Mastery of the machine, he will reflect, can only begin with a despisal of the machine and the supposed benefits it offers. He has no reason to hope that those who hold the machine in awe will ever subdue it. Lonely exile though he be, he must be practical enough to distrust the social philosophers who promise him a humble corner in the Great Reconstruction that they are undertaking to produce for our age.

Harmony between the artist and society must be regained; the dissociation must be broken down. That can only be done, however, by first putting society itself in order. In this connection we must realize that discussions of what is good or bad art, no matter how devoted or learned, cannot avail to reëstablish the arts in their old places. Criticism, for which Arnold and others have hoped so much, is futile for the emergency if it remains wholly aloof from the central problem, which is the remaking of life itself. . . . But we cannot hope . . . that we can win men to beauty by simply loving the beautiful and preaching its merits as they are revealed to us in an admirable body of tradition. . . . [F]or our whole powerful economic system rests on mass motives—the motives of society's lowest common denominator. This counsel leads us toward fastidiousness, dilettantism, at best a kind of survival on sufferance.

As in the crisis of war, when men drop their private occupations for one supreme task, the artist must step into the ranks and bear the brunt of the battle against the common foe. He must share in the general concern as to the conditions of life. He must learn to understand and must try to restore and preserve a social economy that is in danger of being replaced altogether by an industrial economy hostile to his interests.

For strategic purposes, at least, I feel he will ally himself with programs of agrarian restoration. Out of conviction he should do so, since only in an agrarian society does there remain much hope of a balanced life, where the arts are not luxuries to be purchased but belong as a matter of course in the routine of his living. Again, both strategy and conviction will almost inevitably lead him to the sections of America that are provincial, conservative, agrarian, for there only will he find a lingering preference for values not industrial. The very wilderness is his friend, not as a refuge, but as an ally. But he does not need to go into the wilderness. There are American communities throughout the country from the West, even to the fringes of the industrialized East, that are in the industrial sense backward, and are naturally on his side. Negatively to his advantage are the discontent and confusion in the heart of industrialism itself.

The largest and most consistent exhibit of such communities is in the South. For a century and a half the South has preserved its agrarian economy. On one occasion it fought to the death for principles now clearly defined, in the light of history, as representing fundamentally the cause of agrarianism against industrialism. The South lost its battle. What was worse for the nation, it lost the peace—first in the Reconstruction, second by temporarily conforming, under the leadership of men like Walter H. Page and Henry W. Grady, to "new South" doctrines subversive of its native genius. Yet the agrarian South did not vanish. Only at this late day has it given any general promise of following the industrial program with much real consent. The danger of such consent is real. So far as industrialism triumphs and is able to construct a really "new" South, the South will have nothing to contribute to modern issues. It will merely imitate and repeat the mistakes of other sections. The larger promise of the South is in another direction. Its historic and social contribution should be utilized.

It offers the possibility of an integrated life, American in the older rather than the newer sense. Its population is homogeneous. Its people share a common past, which they are not likely to forget; for aside from having Civil War battlefields at their doorsteps, the Southern people have long cultivated a historical consciousness that permeates manners, localities, institutions, the very words and cadence of social intercourse. This consciousness, too often misdescribed as merely romantic and gallant, really signifies a close connection with the eighteenth-century European America that is elsewhere forgotten. In the South the eighteenth-century social inheritance flowered into a gracious civilization that, despite its defects, was actually a civilization, true and indigenous, well diffused, well established. Its culture was sound and realistic in that it was not at war with its own economic foundations. It did not need to be paraded loudly; it was not thought about particularly. The manners of planters and countrymen did not require them to change their beliefs and temper in going from cornfield to drawing-room, from cotton rows to church or frolic. They were the same persons everywhere. There was also a fair balance of aristocratic and democratic elements. Plantation affected frontier; frontier affected plantation. The balance might be illustrated by pairings; it was no purely aristocratic or purely democratic South that produced Thomas Jefferson and Andrew Jackson, Robert E. Lee and Stonewall Jackson, John C. Calhoun and Andrew Johnson, Poe and Simms. There was diversity within unity. There were also leisureliness, devotion to family and neighborhood, local self-sufficiency and self-government, and a capacity, up through the 'sixties, for developing leaders.

Above all, the South was agrarian, and agrarian it still remains very largely. Whether it still retains its native, inborn ways is a question open to argument in the minds of those who know the South mainly from hearsay. In the South itself, especially in its scattering and deluded industrial centres, there is much lip-service to progress—the more because industrialism makes a very loud noise, with all its extravagant proclamations of better times; and the South has known hard times only too well. Yet probably the secret ambition of most Southern city-dwellers, especially those in apartment houses, is to retire to the farm and live like gentlemen. There are still plenty of people who find the brassy methods of tradesmen a little uncouth. The Southern tradition is probably more vital than its recent epitaphists have announced. If it were not alive, even in the younger generations, this book would never be written. But these are considerations which are touched upon elsewhere. My business is to consider to what extent it offers the kind of society we are looking for.

One must allow that the South of the past, for all its ways of life, did not produce much "great" art. An obvious retort to such a criticism would be, "Neither did the rest of America." Also I might say, as it is frequently said, that the long quarrel between Southern agrarianism and Northern industrialism drove the genius of the South largely into the political rather than the artistic field. A good case might be made out, indeed, for polit-ical writing itself as a kind of art in which the South excelled, as in forensic art.

Yet this is not the whole story. So far as the arts have flourished in the South, they have been, up to a very recent period, in excellent harmony with their milieu. The South has always had a native architecture, adapted from classic models into something distinctly Southern; and nothing more clearly and satisfactorily belongs where it is, or better expresses the beauty and stability of an ordered life, than its old country homes, with their pillared porches, their simplicity of design, their sheltering groves, their walks bordered with boxwood shrubs. The South has been rich in the folk-arts, and is still rich in them—in ballads, country songs and dances, in hymns and spirituals, in folk tales, in the folk crafts of weaving, quilting, furniture-making. Though these are best preserved in mountain fastnesses and remote rural localities, they were not originally so limited. They were widespread; and though now they merely survive, they are certainly indicative of a society that could not be termed inartistic. As for the more sophisticated arts, the South has always practised them as a matter of course. I shall not attempt to estimate the Southern contribution to literature with some special array of names; the impassioned scholars who are busily resurrecting Chivers, Kennedy, Byrd, Longstreet, Sut Lovengood, and such minor persons, in their rediscovery of American literature, will presently also get around again to Cooke, Page, Cable, Allen, and the like. What I should particularly like to note is that the specious theory that an "independent" country ought to originate an independent art, worthy of its national greatness, did not originate in the South. Emerson fostered such a theory, Whitman tried to practice it, and the call for the "great American novel" has only lately died of its own futility. Since the day when Southerners read Mr. Addison or got Mr. Stuart to paint grandfather's portrait, they have not, on the whole, been greatly excited over the idea that America is obliged to demonstrate its originality by some sharp divorce from the European tradition.

What might have happened, had not the Civil War disrupted the natural course of affairs, I cannot venture to say. Certainly an indigenous art would have had a good chance to spring up in the South, as the inevitable expression of modes of life rather favorable to the arts. What kind of art it might have been, or whether it would have been "great," I do not know. We should, however, recognize that the appearance or non-appearance of a "great" art or a "great" artist can hardly be accepted as a final criterion for judging a society. That is a typically modern view, implying that society merely exists to produce the artist, and it is wrong. Certainly the "great" art cannot be made by fiat; it probably hates compulsion. But an artistic life, in the social sense, is achievable under right conditions; and then, probably when we least expect it, the unpredictable great art arrives. If art has any real importance in life, it is as a significant and beautiful way of shaping whatever there is to be shaped in life, secular and religious, private and public. Let me go back to my thesis. I do not suggest that the South itself is about to become the seat of some grand revival of the arts—though such might happen. I do suggest that the South, as a distinct, provincial region, offers terms of life favorable to the arts, which in the last analysis are a by-product anyway and will not bear too much self-conscious solicitude.

Our megalopolitan agglomerations, which make great ado about art, are actually sterile on the creative side; they patronize art, they merchandise it, but do not produce it. The despised hinterland, which is rather carefree about the matter, somehow manages to beget the great majority of American artists. True, they often migrate to New York, at considerable risk to their growth; they as often move away again, to Europe or some treasured local retreat. Our large cities affect a cosmopolitan air but have little of the artistic cosmopolitanism that once made Paris a Mecca. They do not breed literary groups; the groups appear in the hinterland. We have only to examine the biographies of our artists to learn how provincial are the sources of our arts. The Mid-Western excitement of some years ago was a provincial movement, as is today the Southern outburst. Zona Gale, Robert Frost, James Branch Cabell, Julia Peterkin, Sherwood Anderson, Willa Cather, and many others are provincialists. The Little Theater movement is provincial; it has decentralized dramatic art and broken the grip of Broadway.

And certainly the provincial artist ought to enjoy special blessings. More nearly than his big-city colleague, he should be able to approximate a harmonious relation between artist and environment. Especially to his advantage is his nearness to nature in the physical sense—which ought to mean, not that he becomes in the narrow sense an artist "of the soil," dealing in the picturesque, but that nature is an eternal balancing factor in his art, a presence neither wholly benign nor wholly hostile, continually reminding him that art is not a substitute for nature. Likewise he is far from the commercial fury and the extreme knowingness of the merchandising centers. He works unaware of critical politics; he is ignorant of how this or that career was "put over," he does not have to truckle and wear himself out at drink-ing bouts and literary teas, he is not obliged to predict cleverly the swings of the artistic pendulum before they fairly begin to swing.

Even so, he cannot escape the infection of the cities by mere geographical remoteness. The skepticism and malaise of the industrial mind reach him anyway, though somewhat subdued, and attack his art in the very process of creation. Unself-conscious expression cannot fully be attained. It is conditioned by the general state of society, which he cannot escape. It is inhibited by the ideals of the market place, which are, after all, very powerful. . . .

. . . For many reasons the Southern tradition deserves rehabilitation, but not among them is the reason that it would thus enable Southern artists to be strictly Southern artists. If the Southern tradition were an industrial tradition, it would deserve to be cast out rather than cherished. It happens, however, to be an agrarian tradition. And so it needs to be defined for the present age, as a mode of life congenial to the arts which are among the things we esteem as more than material blessings. In the emergency it needs, in fact, to be consciously studied and maintained by artists, Southern or not, as affording a last stand in America against the industrial devourer—a stand that might prove to be a turning-point.

The artist should not forget that in these times he is called on to play the part both of a person and of an artist. Of the two, that of person is more immediately important. As an artist he will do best to flee the infection of our times, to stand for decentralization in the arts, to resist with every atom of his strength the false gospels of art as a luxury which can be sold in commercial quantities or which can be hallowed by segregation in discreet shrines. But he cannot wage this fight by remaining on his perch as artist. He must be a person first of all, even though for the time being he may become less of an artist. He must enter the common arena and become a citizen. Whether he chooses, as citizen-person, to be a farmer or to run for Congress is a matter of individual choice; but in that general direction his duty lies.

QUESTIONS ON DAVIDSON

1. Davidson states that if art becomes a commodity then it ceases to be art. What reasons does he give for this claim? In what sense is this true?

2. In what sense is leisure necessary for the production and enjoyment of art? How does Davidson characterize the leisure of industrial society? Do you agree with this description?

3. Davidson maintains that the economic system depends on "mass motives—the motives of society's lowest common denominator." What are these motives? Why should one assume that they are present in the economic system and not present elsewhere?

4. What are the conditions which make an agrarian society more conducive to art? What evidence does Davidson provide for his conclusion? What *is* the value of art for Davidson?

Masscult and Midcult

Dwight MacDonald

Dwight MacDonald (1906–1982), a graduate of Yale University, was for eight years an associate editor of Fortune. *In 1937 he became editor of the radical political and literary journal* Partisan Review, *which he left in 1943 in a protest of its support of the second World War. One of the "New York Intellectuals," his works include numerous essays, as well as* Memoirs of a Revolutionist *(1957),* Politics Past *(1970),* Discriminations *(1974), and a collection of his essays entitled* Against the American Grain *(1962).*

For about two centuries Western culture has in fact been two cultures: the traditional kind—let us call it High Culture—that is chronicled in the textbooks, and a novel kind that is manufactured for the market. This latter may be called Mass Culture, or better Masscult, since it really isn't culture at all. Masscult is a parody of High Culture. In the older forms, its artisans have long been at work. In the novel, the line stretches from the eighteenth-century "servant-girl romances" to Edna Ferber, Fannie Hurst and such current ephemera as Burdick, Drury, Mechener, Ruark and Uris; in music, from Hearts and Flowers to Rock 'n Roll; in art, from the chromo to Norman Rockwell; in architecture, from Victorian Gothic to ranch-house moderne; in thought, from Martin Tupper's *Proverbial Philosophy* ("Marry not without means, for so shouldst thou tempt Providence;/But wait not for more than enough, for marriage is the DUTY of most men.") to Norman Vincent Peale. (Thinkers like H. G. Wells, Stuart Chase, and Max Lerner come under the head of Midcult rather than Masscult.) And the enormous output of such new media as the radio, television and the movies is almost entirely Masscult.

I

This is something new in history. It is not that so much bad art is being produced. Most High Culture has been undistinguished, since talent is always rare—one has only to walk through any great art museum or try to read some of the forgotten books from past centuries. Since only the best works still have currency, one thinks of the past in their terms, but they were really just a few plums in a pudding of mediocrity.

Masscult is bad in a new way: it doesn't even have the theoretical possibility of being good. Up to the eighteenth century, bad art was of the same nature as good art, produced for the same audience, accepting the same standards. The difference was simply one of individual talent. But Masscult is something else. It is not just unsuccessful art. It is non-art. It is even anti-art.

> There is a novel of the masses but no Stendhal of the masses; a music for the masses but no Bach or Beethoven, whatever people say . . . [André Malraux observes in "Art, Popular Art and the Illusion of the Folk"—(*Partisan Review,* September–October, 1951).] It is odd that no word . . . designates the common character of what we call, separately, bad painting, bad architecture, bad music, etc. The word "painting" only designates a domain in which art is possible. . . . Perhaps we have only one word because bad painting has not existed for very long. There is no bad Gothic painting. Not that all Gothic painting is good. But the difference that separates Giotto from the most mediocre of his imitators is not of the same kind as that which separates Renoir from the caricaturists of *La Vie Parisienne.* . . . Giotto and the Gaddi are separated by talent, Degas and Bonnat by a schism, Renoir and "suggestive" painting by what? By the fact that this last, totally subjected to the spectator, is a form of advertising which aims at selling itself. If there exists only one word . . . it is because there was a time when the distinction between them had no point. Instruments played real music then, for there was no other.

But now we have pianos playing Rock 'n Roll and *les sanglots longs des violons* accompanying torch singers.

Masscult offers its customers neither an emotional catharsis nor an aesthetic experience, for these demand effort. The production line grinds out a uniform product whose humble aim is not even entertainment, for this too implies life and hence effort, but merely distraction. It may be stimulating or narcotic, but it must be easy to assimilate. It asks nothing of its audience, for it is "totally subjected to the spectator." And it gives nothing.[1]

Some of its producers are able enough. Norman Rockwell is technically skilled, as was Meissonier—though Degas was right when he summed up the cavalry charge in *Friedland, 1806:* "Everything is steel except the breastplates." O. Henry could tell a story better than many contributors to our Little Magazines. But a work of High Culture, however inept, is an expression of feelings, ideas, tastes, visions that are idiosyncratic and the audience similarly responds to them as individuals. Furthermore, both creator and audience accept certain standards. These may be more or less traditional; sometimes they are so much less so as to be revolutionary, though Picasso, Joyce and Stravinsky knew and respected past achievements more than did their academic contemporaries; their works may be seen as a heroic breakthrough to earlier, sounder foundations that had been obscured by the fashionable gimcrackery of the academies. But Masscult is indifferent to standards. Nor is there any communication between individuals. Those who consume Masscult might as well be eating ice-cream sodas, while those who fabricate it are no more expressing themselves than are the "stylists" who design the latest atrocity from Detroit.

The difference appears if we compare two famous writers of detective stories, Mr. Erle Stanley Gardner and Mr. Edgar Allan Poe. It is impossible to find any personal note in Mr. Gardner's enormous output—he has just celebrated his centenary, the hundredth novel under his own name (he also has knocked off several dozen under pseudonyms). His prose style varies between the incompetent and the nonexistent; for the most part, there is just no style, either good or bad. His books seem to have been manufactured rather than composed. . . . He is marketing a standard product, like Kleenex, that precisely because it is not related to any individual needs on the part of either the producer or the consumer appeals to the widest possible audience. . . .

Like Mr. Gardner, Mr. Poe was a money-writer. (That he didn't make any is irrelevant.) The difference, aside from the fact that he was a good writer, is that, even when he was turning out hack work, he had an extraordinary ability to use the journalistic forms of his day to express his own peculiar personality, and indeed, as Marie Bonaparte has shown in her fascinating study, to relieve his neurotic anxieties. . . .

It is important to understand that the difference between Mr. Poe and Mr. Gardner, or between High Culture and Masscult, is not mere popularity. From *Tom Jones* to the films of Chaplin, some very good things have been popular; *The Education of Henry Adams* was the top nonfiction best seller of 1919. Nor is it that Poe's detective stories are harder to read than Gardner's, though I suppose they are for most people. The difference lies in the qualities of Masscult already noted: its impersonality and its lack of standards, and

"total subjection to the spectator." The same writer, indeed the same book or even the same chapter, may contain elements of both Masscult and High Culture. In Balzac, for instance, the most acute psychological analysis and social observation is bewilderingly interlarded with the cheapest, flimsiest kind of melodrama. In Dickens, superb comedy alternates with bathetic sentimentality, great descriptive prose with the most vulgar kind of theatricality. All these elements were bound between the same covers, sold to the same mass audience, and, it may well be, considered equally good by their authors—at least I know of no evidence that either Dickens or Balzac was aware of when he was writing down and when he was writing up. Masscult is a subtler problem than is sometimes recognized.

"What is a poet?" asked Wordsworth. "He is a man speaking to men . . . a man pleased with his own passions and volitions, and one who rejoices more than other men in the spirit of life that is in him." It is this human dialogue that Masscult interrupts, this spirit of life that it exterminates. Evelyn Waugh commented on Hollywood, after a brief experience there: "Each book purchased for motion pictures has some individual quality, good or bad, that has made it remarkable. It is the work of a great array of highly paid and incompatible writers to distinguish this quality, separate it and obliterate it." This process is called "licking the book"—i.e., licking it into shape, as mother bears were once thought to lick their amorphous cubs into real bears; though here the process is reversed and the book is licked not into but out of shape. The other meaning of "licked" also applies; before a proper Hollywood film can be made, the work of art has to be defeated.

II

The question of Masscult is part of the larger question of the masses. The tendency of modern industrial society, whether in the USA or the USSR, is to transform the individual into the mass man. For the masses are in historical time what a crowd is in space: a large quantity of people unable to express their human qualities because they are related to each other neither as individuals nor as members of a community. In fact, they are not related *to each other* at all but only to some impersonal, abstract, crystallizing factor. In the case of crowds, this can be a football game, a bargain sale, a lynching; in the case of the masses, it can be a political party, a television program, a system of industrial production. The mass man is a solitary atom, uniform with the millions of other atoms that go to make up "the lonely crowd," as David Riesman well calls our society. A community, on the contrary, is a group of individuals linked to each other by concrete interests. Something like a family, each of whose members has his or her special place and function while at the same time sharing the group's economic aims (family budget), traditions (family history), sentiments (family quarrels, family jokes), and values ("That's the way we do it in *this* family!"). The scale must be small enough so that it "makes a difference" what each person does—this is the first condition for human, as against mass, existence. Paradoxically, the individual in a community is both more closely integrated into the group than is the mass man and at the same time is freer to develop his own special personality. Indeed, an individual can only be defined in relation to a community. A single person in nature is not an individual but an animal; Robinson Crusoe was saved by Friday. The totalitarian regimes, which have consciously tried to create the mass man, have systematically broken every communal link—family, church, trade union, local and regional loyalties, even down to ski and chess clubs—and have reforged them so as to bind each atomized individual directly to the center of power.

The past cultures I admire—Periclean Greece, the city-states of the Italian Renaissance, Elizabethan England, are examples—have mostly been produced by communities, and remarkably small ones at that. Also remarkably heterogeneous ones, riven by faction, stormy with passionate antagonisms. But this diversity, fatal to that achievement of power over other countries that is the great aim of modern statecraft, seems to have been stimulating to talent. . . . A mass society, like a crowd, is inchoate and uncreative. Its atoms cohere not according to individual liking or traditions or even interests but in a purely mechanical way, as iron filings of different shapes and sizes are pulled toward a magnet working on the one quality they have in common. Its morality sinks to the level of the most primitive members—a crowd will commit atrocities that very few of its members would commit as individuals—and its taste to that of the least sensitive and the most ignorant.

Yet this collective monstrosity, "the masses," "the public," is taken as a human norm by the technicians of Masscult. They at once degrade the public by treating it as an object, to be handled with the lack of ceremony of medical students dissecting a corpse, and at the same time flatter it and pander to its taste and ideas by taking them as the criterion of reality (in the case of the questionnaire-sociologists) or of art (in the case of the Lords of Masscult). . . .

Whenever a Lord of Masscult is reproached for the low quality of his products, he automatically ripostes, "But that's what the public wants, what can I do?" A simple and conclusive defense, at first glance. But a second look reveals that (1) to the extent the public "wants" it, the public has been conditioned to some extent by his products, and (2) his efforts have taken this direction because (a) he himself also "wants" it—never underestimate the ignorance and vulgarity of publishers, movie producers, network executives and other architects of Masscult—and (b) the technology of producing mass "entertainment" (again, the quotes are advised) imposes a simplistic, repetitive pattern so that it is easier to say the public wants this than to say the truth which is that the public gets this and so wants it. The March Hare explained to Alice that "I like what I get" is not the same thing as "I get what I like," but March Hares have never been welcome on Madison Avenue.

For some reason, objections to the giving-to-the-public-what-it-wants line are often attacked as undemocratic and snobbish. Yet it is precisely because I do believe in the potentialities of ordinary people that I criticize Masscult. For the masses are not people, they are not The Man in the Street or The Average Man, they are not even that figment of liberal condescension, The Common Man. The masses are, rather, man as nonman, that is man in a special relationship to other men that makes it impossible for him to function as man (one of the human functions being the creation and enjoyment of works of art). "Mass man," as I use the term, is a theoretical construction, an extreme toward which we are being pushed but which we shall never reach. For to become wholly a mass man would mean to have no private life, no personal desires, hobbies, aspirations, or aversions that are not shared by everybody else. One's behavior would be entirely predictable, like a piece of coal, and the sociologists could at last make up their tables confidently. It is still some time to 1984 but it looks unlikely that Orwell's anti-Utopia will have materialized by then, or that it will ever materialize. Nazism and Soviet Communism, however, show us how far things can go in politics, as Masscult does in art. And let us not be too smug in this American temperate zone, unravaged by war and ideology. "It seems to me that nearly the whole Anglo-Saxon race, especially of course in America, have lost the power to be individuals. They have become social insects like bees and ants." So Roger Fry wrote years ago, and who will say that we have become less again?

III . . .

IV

The historical reasons for the rise of Masscult are well known. There could obviously be no mass culture until there were masses, in our modern sense. The industrial revolution produced the masses. It uprooted people from their agrarian communities and packed them into factory cities. It produced goods in such unprecedented abundance that the population of the Western world has increased more in the last two centuries than in the preceding two millennia—poor Malthus, never has a brilliantly original theorist been so speedily refuted by history! And it subjected them to a uniform discipline whose only precedent was the "slave socialism" of Egypt. But the Egypt of the Pharaohs produced no Masscult any more than did the great Oriental empires or the late Rome of the proletarian rabble, because the masses were passive, inert, submerged far below the level of political or cultural power. It was not until the end of the eighteenth century in Europe that the majority of people began to play an active part in either history or culture.

Up to then, there was only High Culture and Folk Art. To some extent, Masscult is a continuation of Folk Art, but the differences are more striking than the similarities. Folk Art grew mainly from below, an autochthonous product shaped by the people to fit their own needs, even though it often took its cue from High Culture. Masscult comes from above. It is fabricated by technicians hired by businessmen. They try this and try that and if something clicks at the box office, they try to cash in with similar products, like consumer-researchers with a new cereal, or like a Pavlovian biologist who has hit on a reflex he thinks can be conditioned. It is one thing to satisfy popular tastes, as Robert Burns's poetry did, and quite another to exploit them, as Hollywood does. Folk Art was the people's own institution, their private little kitchen-garden walled off from the great formal park of their masters.[2] But Masscult breaks down the wall, integrating the masses into a debased form of High Culture and thus becoming an instrument of domination. If one had no other data to go on, Masscult would expose capitalism as a class society rather than the harmonious commonwealth that, in election years, both parties tell us it is.

The same goes even more strongly for the Soviet Union. Its Masscult is both worse and more pervasive than ours, a fact which is often not recognized because in form Soviet Masscult is just the opposite, aiming at propaganda and pedagogy rather than distraction. But like ours, it is imposed from above and it exploits rather than satisfies the needs of the masses—though, of course, for political rather than commercial reasons. Its quality is even lower.

Our Supreme Court building is tasteless and pompous but not to the lunatic degree of most Soviet architecture; post-1930 Soviet films, with a few exceptions, are far duller and cruder than our own; the primitive level of *serious* Soviet periodicals devoted to matters of art or philosophy has to be read to be believed, and as for the popular press, it is as if Hearst or Colonel McCormick ran every periodical in America. Furthermore, while here individuals can simply turn their back on Masscult and do their own work, there no such escape is possible; the official cultural bodies control all outlets and a *Doctor Zhivago* must be smuggled out for foreign publication.

V. . . VI. . . VII. . .

VIII

Let us, finally, consider Masscult first from the standpoint of consumption and then from that of production.

As a marketable commodity, Masscult has two great advantages over High Culture. One has already been considered: the post-1750 public, lacking the taste and knowledge of the old patron class, is not only satisfied with shoddy mass-produced goods but in general feels more at home with them (though on unpredictable occasions, they will respond to the real thing, as with Dickens' novels and the movies of Chaplin and Griffith). This is because such goods are standardized and so are easier to consume since one knows what's coming next—imagine a Western in which the hero loses the climactic gun fight or an office romance in which the mousy stenographer loses out to the predatory blonde. But standardization has a subtler aspect, which might be called The Built-In Reaction. As Clement Greenberg noted in "Avant-garde and *Kitsch*" many years ago in *Partisan Review,* the special aesthetic quality of *Kitsch*—a term which includes both Masscult and Midcult—is that it "predigests art for the spectator and spares him effort, provides him with a shortcut to the pleasures of art that detours what is necessarily difficult in the genuine art" because it includes the spectator's reactions in the work itself instead of forcing him to make his own responses. That standby of provincial weddings, "I Love You Truly," is far more "romantic" than the most beautiful of Schubert's songs because its wallowing, yearning tremolos and glissandos make it clear to the most unmusical listener that something very tender indeed is going on. It does his feeling for him; or, as T. W. Adorno has observed of popular music, "The composition hears for the listener." Thus Liberace is a much more "musical" pianist than Serkin, whose piano is not adorned with antique candelabra and whose stance at it is as business-like as Liberace's is "artistic." So, too, our Collegiate Gothic, which may be seen in its most resolutely picturesque (and expensive) phase at Yale, is more relentlessly Gothic than Chartres, whose builders didn't even know they *were* Gothic and so missed many chances for quaint effects.[3] And so, too, Boca Raton, the millionaires' suburb that Addison Mizener designed in Palm Beach during the Great Bull Market of the 'twenties, is so aggressively Spanish Mission that a former American ambassador to Spain is said to have murmured in awe, "It's more Spanish than anything I ever saw in Madrid." The same Law of the Built-In Reaction also insures that a smoothly air-brushed pin-up girl by Petty is more "sexy" than a real naked woman, the emphasis of breasts and thighs corresponding to the pornographically exaggerated Gothic details of Harkness. More *sexy* but not more *sexual,* the relation between the terms being similar to that of *sentimentality* to *sentiment* or *modernistic* to *modern,* or *arty* to *art.*

The production of Masscult is a subtler business than one might think. We have already seen in the case of Poe that a serious writer will produce art even when he is trying to function as a hack, simply because he cannot help putting himself into his work. The unhappy hero of James's story, "The Next Time," tried again and again to prostitute his talents and write a best seller to support his family, but each time he created another unprofitable masterpiece; with the best will in the world, he was simply unable to achieve a low enough standard. The reverse is also true: a hack will turn out hack stuff even when he tries to be serious. Most of these examples will come later under Midcult, but Masscult also has its little tragedies. When I was in Hollywood recently, I was told by one of the most intelligent younger directors, Stanley Kubrick: "The reason movies are often so bad out here isn't because the people who make them are cynical money hacks. Most of them are doing the very best they can; they really want to make good movies. The trouble is with their heads, not their hearts." This was borne out by the film I was there to write about, a mawkish travesty of Nathanael West's *Miss Lonelyhearts* that was written and produced by Dore Schary with the noblest intentions.

There seem to be two main conditions for the successful production of *Kitsch.* One is that the producer must believe in what he is doing. A good example is Norman Rockwell, who since 1916 has painted over three hundred covers for the *Saturday Evening Post.* When a fellow illustrator remarked that their craft was just a way to make a living—"You do your job, you get your check, and nobody thinks it's art"—Rockwell was horrified. "Oh no no no. How can you say that? No man

with a conscience can just bat out illustrations. He's got to put all of his talent, all of his feelings into them." Having just seen a most interesting exhibition of Rockwell's techniques at a local bank, I think he was telling the truth. He makes dozens of careful, highly competent pencil sketches, plus oil renderings of details, for just one *Post* cover; if genius were really "an infinite capacity for taking pains," Norman Rockwell would be a genius. The trouble is that the final result of all this painstaking craftsmanship is just—a *Post* cover, as slick and cliché in execution as in content. "There's this magazine cover," says the comedian Mort Sahl, "and it shows this kid getting his first haircut you know and a dog is licking his hand and his mother is crying and it's Saturday night in the old home town and people are dancing outside in the streets and the Liberty Bell is ringing and, uh, did I miss anything?" . . .

The other condition for success in Masscult is that the writer, artist, editor, director or entertainer must have a good deal of the mass man in himself, as was the case with Zane Grey, Howard Chandler Christy, Mr. Lorimer of the *Post,* Cecil B. DeMille, and Elvis Presley. This is closely related to sincerity—how can he take his work seriously if he doesn't have this instinctive, this built-in vulgar touch? Like Rockwell, he may know that art is good and honorable and worthy of respect, and he may pay tribute to it. But knowing it is one thing and feeling it is another. A journalistic entrepreneur like Henry Luce—by no means the worst—has the same kind of idle curiosity about the Facts and the same kind of gee-whiz excitement about rather elementary ideas (see *Life* editorials passim) as his millions of readers have. When I worked for him on *Fortune* in the early 'thirties, I was struck by three qualities he had as an editor: his shrewdness as to what was and what was not "a story," his high dedication to his task, and his limited cultural background despite, or perhaps because of, his having attended Yale College. All three are closely interrelated in his success: a more sophisticated editor would have gotten out of step with his millions of readers, a less idealistic one would have lacked the moral oomph to attract them, and he knew a "story" when he saw one because what interested them interested him.

IX. . .

X

We are now in a more sophisticated period. The West has been won, the immigrants melted down, the factories and railroads built to such effect that since 1929 the problem has been consumption rather than production. The work week has shrunk, real wages have risen, and never in history have so many people attained such a high standard of living as in this country since 1945. College enrollment is now well over four million, three times what it was in 1929. Money, leisure and knowledge, the prerequisites for culture, are more plentiful and more evenly distributed than ever before.

In these more advanced times, the danger to High Culture is not so much from Masscult as from a peculiar hybrid bred from the latter's unnatural intercourse with the former. A whole middle culture has come into existence and it threatens to absorb both its parents. This intermediate form—let us call it Midcult—has the essential qualities of Masscult—the formula, the built-in reaction, the lack of any standard except popularity— but it decently covers them with a cultural figleaf. In Masscult the trick is plain—to please the crowd by any means. But Midcult has it both ways: it pretends to respect the standards of High Culture while in fact it waters them down and vulgarizes them.[4]

The enemy outside the walls is easy to distinguish. It is its ambiguity that makes Midcult alarming. For it presents itself as part of High Culture. Not that coterie stuff, not those snobbish inbred so-called intellectuals who are only talking to themselves. Rather the great vital mainstream, wide and clear though perhaps not so deep. You, too, can wade in it for a mere $16.70 pay nothing now just fill in the coupon and receive a full year six hard-cover lavishly illustrated issues of *Horizon: A Magazine of the Arts,* "probably the most beautiful magazine in the world . . . seeks to serve as guide to the long cultural advance of modern man, to explore the many mansions of the philosopher, the painter, the historian, the architect, the sculptor, the satirist, the poet . . . to build bridges between the world of scholars and the world of intelligent readers. It's a good buy. Use the coupon *now.*" *Horizon* has some 160,000 subscribers, which is more than the combined circulations, after many years of effort, of *Kenyon, Hudson, Sewanee, Partisan, Art News, Arts, American Scholar, Dissent, Commentary,* and half a dozen of our other leading cultural-critical magazines.

Midcult is not, as might appear at first, a raising of the level of Masscult. It is rather a corruption of High Culture which has the enormous advantage over Masscult that while also in fact "totally subjected to the spectator," in Malraux's phrase, it is able to pass itself off as the real thing. Midcult is the Revised Standard Version of the Bible, put out several years ago under the aegis of the Yale Divinity School, that destroys our greatest monument of English prose, the King James Version, in order to make

the text "clear and meaningful to people today," which is like taking apart Westminster Abbey to make Disneyland out of the fragments. Midcult is the Museum of Modern Art's film department paying tribute to Samuel Goldwyn because his movies are alleged to be (slightly) better than those of other Hollywood producers—though why they are called "producers" when their function is to prevent the production of art (cf., the fate in Hollywood of Griffith, Chaplin, von Stroheim, Eisenstein and Orson Welles) is a semantic puzzle. Midcult is the venerable and once venerated *Atlantic*—which in the last century printed Emerson, Lowell, Howells, James, and Mark Twain—putting on the cover of a recent issue a huge photograph of Dore Schary, who has lately transferred his high-minded sentimentality from Hollywood to Broadway and who is represented in the issue by a homily, "To A Young Actor," which synthesizes Jefferson, Polonius and Dr. Norman Vincent Peale, concluding: "Behave as citizens not only of your profession but of the full world in which you live. Be indignant with injustice, be gracious with success, be courageous with failure, be patient with opportunity, and be resolute with faith and honor." Midcult is the Book-of-the-Month Club, which since 1926 has been supplying its members with reading matter of which the best that can be said is that it could be worse, i.e., they get John Hersey instead of Gene Stratton Porter. Midcult is the transition from Rodgers and Hart to Rodgers and Hammerstein, from the gay tough lyrics of *Pal Joey,* a spontaneous expression of a real place called Broadway, to the folk-fakery of *Oklahoma!* and the orotund sentimentalities of *South Pacific.*[5] Midcult is or was, "Omnibus," subsidized by a great foundation to raise the level of television, which began its labors by announcing it would "be aimed straight at the average American audience, neither highbrow nor lowbrow, the audience that made the *Reader's Digest, Life,* the *Ladies' Home Journal,* the audience which is the solid backbone of any business as it is of America itself" and which then proved its good faith by programming Gertrude Stein and Jack Benny, Chekhov and football strategy, Beethoven and champion ice skaters. "Omnibus" failed. The level of television, however, was not raised, for some reason.

XI. . . XVIII. . .

XIX

What is to be done? Conservatives like Ortega y Gasset and T. S. Eliot argue that since "the revolt of the masses" has led to the horrors of totalitarianism and of California roadside architecture, the only hope is to rebuild the old class walls and bring the masses once more under aristocratic control. They think of the popular as synonymous with the cheap and vulgar. Marxian radicals and liberal sociologists, on the other hand, see the masses as intrinsically healthy but as the dupes and victims of cultural exploitation—something like Rousseau's "noble savage." If only the masses were offered good stuff instead of *Kitsch*, how they would eat it up! How the level of Masscult would rise! Both these diagnoses seem to me fallacious because they assume that Masscult is (in the conservative view) or could be (in the liberal view) an expression of *people*, like Folk Art, whereas actually it is, as I tried to show earlier in this essay, an expression of *masses*, a very different thing.

The conservative proposal to save culture by restoring the old class lines has a more solid historical basis than the liberal-cum-Marxian hope for a new democratic, classless culture. Politically, however, it is without meaning in a world dominated by the two great mass nations, the USA and the USSR, and a world that is becoming more industrialized and mass-ified all the time. The only practical thing along those lines would be to revive the spirit of the old avant-garde, that is to re-create a cultural—as against a social, political or economic—elite as a countermovement to both Masscult and Midcult. It may be possible, in a more modest and limited sense than in the past—I shall return to this point later—but it will be especially difficult in this country where the blurring of class lines, the lack of a continuous tradition and the greater facilities for the manufacturing and distribution of *Kitsch,* whether Masscult or Midcult, all work in the other direction. Unless this country goes either fascist or communist, there will continue to be islands above the flood for those determined enough to reach them and live on them; as Faulkner has shown, a writer can use Hollywood instead of being used by it, if his purpose be firm enough. But islands are not continents.

The alternative proposal is to raise the level of our culture in general. Those who advocate this start off from the assumption that there has already been a great advance in the diffusion of culture in the last two centuries—Edward Shils is sure of this, Daniel Bell thinks it is probably the case—and that the main problem is how to carry this even further; they tend to regard such critics of Masscult as Ernest van den Haag, Leo Lowenthal or myself as either disgruntled. Left romantics or reactionary dreamers or both. Perhaps the most impressive—and certainly the longest—exposition of this point of view appears in Gilbert Seldes' *The Great Audience.* Mr. Seldes blames the present sad state of our Masscult on (1) the stupidity of the Lords of *Kitsch* (who underestimate the mental age of the public), (2) the arrogance of the intellectuals (who make the same mistake and so snobbishly refuse to try to raise the level of the mass media), and (3) the passivity of the public itself (which doesn't insist on better Masscult). This diagnosis seems to me superficial because it blames everything on subjective, moral factors: stupidity (the Lords of *Kitsch*), perversity (the intellectuals), or failure of will (the public). My own notion is that—as in the case of the "responsibility" of the German (or Russian) people for the horrors of Nazism (or of Soviet Communism)—it is unjust and unrealistic to blame large social groups for such catastrophes. Burke was right when he said you cannot indict a people. Individuals are caught up in the workings of a mechanism that forces them into its own pattern; only heroes can resist, and while one can hope that everybody will be a hero, one cannot demand it.

I see Masscult—and its recent offspring, Midcult—as a reciprocating engine, and who is to say, once it has been set in motion, whether the stroke or the counterstroke is responsible for its continued action? The Lords of *Kitsch* sell culture to the masses. It is a debased, trivial culture that avoids both the deep realities (sex, death, failure, tragedy) and also the simple, spontaneous pleasures, since the realities would be too real and the pleasures too lively to induce what Mr. Seldes calls "the mood of consent": a narcotized acceptance of Masscult-Midcult and of the commodities it sells as a substitute for the unsettling and unpredictable (hence unsalable) joy, tragedy, wit, change, originality and beauty of real life. The masses—and don't let's forget that this term includes the well-educated fans of *The Old Man and the Sea, Our Town, J.B.,* and *John Brown's Body*—who have been debauched by several generations of this sort of thing, in turn have come to demand such trivial and comfortable cultural products. Which came first, the chicken or the egg, the mass demand or its satisfaction (and further stimulation), is a question as academic as it is unanswerable. The engine is reciprocating and shows no signs of running down.

XX

"Our fundamental want today in the United States," Walt Whitman wrote in 1871, "is of a class and the clear idea of a class, of native authors, literatures, far different, far higher in grade than any yet known, sacerdotal, modern, fit to cope with our occasions, lands, permeating the whole mass of American mentality, taste, belief, breathing into it a new life, giving it decision, affecting politics far more than the popular superficial suffrage. . . . For know you not, dear, earnest reader, that the people of our land may all read and write, and may all possess the right to vote—and yet the main things may be entirely lacking? . . . The priest departs, the divine literatus comes."

The divine literatus is behind schedule. Masscult and Midcult have so pervaded the land that Whitman's hope for a democratic culture shaped by a sacerdotal class at once so sublime and so popular that they can swing elections—that this noble vision now seems absurd. But a more modest aspiration is still open, one adumbrated by Whitman's idea of a new cultural class and his warning that "the main things may be entirely lacking" even though everybody knows how to read, write and vote. This is to recognize that two cultures have developed in this country and that it is to the national interest to keep them separate. The conservatives are right when they say there has never been a broadly democratic culture on a high level. This is not because the ruling class forcibly excluded the masses—this is Marxist melodrama—but quite simply because the great majority of people at any given time (including most of the ruling class for the matter) have never cared enough about such things to make them an important part of their lives. So let the masses have their Masscult, let the few who care about good writing, painting, music, architecture, philosophy, etc., have their High Culture, and don't fuzz up the distinction with Midcult.

Whitman would have rejected this proposal as undemocratic, which it is. But his own career is a case in point: he tried to be a popular bard but the masses were not interested, and his first recognition, excepting Emerson's lonely voice, came from the English pre-Raphaelites, a decadent and precious group if ever there was one. If we would create a literature "fit to cope with our occasions," the only public the writer or artist or composer or philosopher or critic or architect should consider must be that of his peers. The informed, interested minority—what Stendhal called "We Happy Few." Let the majority eavesdrop if they like, but their tastes should be firmly ignored.

There is a compromise between the conservative and liberal proposals which I think is worth considering—neither an attempt to re-create the old avant-garde nor one to raise the general level of Masscult and Midcult. It is based on the recent discovery—since 1945—that there is not One Big Audience but rather a number of smaller, more specialized audiences that may still be commer-

cially profitable. (I take it for granted that the less differentiated the audience, the less chance there is of something original and lively creeping in, since the principle of the lowest common denominator applies.) This discovery has in fact resulted in the sale of "quality" paperbacks and recordings and the growth of "art" cinema houses, off-Broadway theatres, concert orchestras and art museums and galleries. The mass audience is divisible, we have discovered—and the more it is divided, the better. Even television, the most senseless and routinized expression of Masscult (except for the movie newsreels), might be improved by this approach. One possibility is pay-TV, whose modest concept is that only those who subscribe could get the program, like a magazine; but, also like a magazine, the editors would decide what goes in, not the advertisers; a small gain but a real one. The networks oppose this on philanthropic grounds—they don't see why the customer should pay for what he now gets free. But perhaps one would rather pay for bread than get stones for nothing.

As long as our society is "open" in Karl Popper's sense—that is unless or until it is closed by a mass revolution stimulated by the illusion of some "total solution" such as Russian-type Communism or Hitler-type Fascism, the name doesn't really matter—there will always be happy accidents because of the stubbornness of some isolated creator. But if we are to have more than this, it will be because our new public for High Culture becomes conscious of itself and begins to show some *esprit de corps,* insisting on higher standards and setting itself off—joyously, implacably—from most of its fellow citizens, not only from the Masscult depths but also from the agreeable ooze of the Midcult swamp.

In "The Present Age," Kierkegaard writes as follows:

> In order that everything should be reduced to the same level it is first of all necessary to procure a phantom, a monstrous abstraction, an all-embracing something which is nothing, a mirage—and that phantom is the public. . . .
> The public is a concept which could not have occurred in antiquity because the people *en masse in corpore* took part in any situation which arose . . . and moreover the individual was personally present and had to submit at once to applause or disapproval for his decision. Only when the sense of association in society is no longer strong enough to give life to concrete realities is the Press able to create that abstraction, "the public," consisting of unreal individuals who never are and never can be united in an actual situation or organization—and yet are held together as a whole.
> The public is a host, more numerous than all the peoples together, but it is a body which can never be reviewed; it cannot even be represented because it is an abstraction. Nevertheless, when the age is reflective [i.e., the individual

sees himself only as he is reflected in a collective body] and passionless and destroys everything concrete, the public becomes everything and is supposed to include everything. And . . . the individual is thrown back upon himself. . . .

A public is neither a nation nor a generation nor a community nor a society nor these particular men, for all these are only what they are through the concrete. No single person who belongs to the public makes a real commitment; for some hours of the day, perhaps, he belongs to a real public—at moments when he is nothing else, since when he really is what he is, he does not form part of the public. Made up of such individuals, of individuals at the moment when they are nothing, a public is a kind of gigantic something, an abstract and deserted void which is everything and nothing. But on this basis, any one can arrogate to himself a public, and just as the Roman Church chimerically extended its frontiers by appointing bishops *in partibus infidelium,* so a public is something which every one can claim, and even a drunken sailor exhibiting a peep-show has dialectically the same right to a public as the greatest man. He has just as logical a right to put all those noughts *in front of* his single number.

This is the essence of what I have tried to say.

ENDNOTES

1. "Distraction is bound to the present mode of production, to the rationalized and mechanized process of labor to which . . . the masses are subject. . . . People want to have fun. A fully concentrated and conscious experience of art is possible only to those whose lives do not put such a strain on them that in their spare time they want relief from both boredom and effort simultaneously. The whole sphere of cheap commercial entertainment reflects this dual desire."—T. W. Adorno: *On Popular Music.*

2. And if it was often influenced by High Culture, it did change the forms and themes into its own style. The only major form of Folk Art that still persists in this country is jazz, and the difference between Folk Art and Masscult may be most readily perceived by comparing the kind of thing heard at the annual Newport Jazz Festivals to Rock 'n Roll. The former is musically interesting and emotionally real; the latter is—not. The amazing survival of jazz despite the exploitative onslaughts of half a century of commercial entrepreneurs, is in my opinion, due to its folk quality. And as the noble and the peasant understood each other better than either understood the bourgeois, so it seems significant that jazz is the only art form that appeals to both the intelligentsia and the common people. As for the others, let them listen to *South Pacific.*

3. When I lived in Harkness Memorial Quadrangle some thirty years ago, I noticed a number of cracks in the tiny-paned windows of my room that had been patched with picturesquely wavy strips of lead. Since the place had just been built, I thought this peculiar. Later I found that after the windows had been installed, a special gang of artisans had visited them; one craftsman had delicately cracked every tenth or twentieth pane with a little hammer and another had then repaired the cracks. In a few days, the windows of Harkness had gone through an evolution that in backward places like Oxford had taken centuries. I wonder what they do in Harkness when a window is broken by accident.

4. It's not done, of course, as consciously as this suggests. The editors of the *Saturday Review* or *Harper's* or the *Atlantic* would be honestly indignant at this description of their activities, as would John Steinbeck, J. P. Marquand, Pearl Buck, Irwin Shaw, Herman Wouk, John Hersey and others of that remarkably large group of Midcult novelists we have developed. One of the nice things about Zane Grey was that it seems never to have occurred to him that his books had anything to do with literature.

5. An interesting Midcult document is the editorial the *New York Times* ran August 24, 1960, the day after the death of Oscar Hammerstein 2nd:

. . . The theatre has lost a man who stood for all that is decent in life. . . . The concern for racial respect in *South Pacific,* the sympathy and respect for a difficult though aspiring monarch in *The King and I,* the indomitable faith that runs through *Carousel* were not clever bits of showmanship. They represented Mr. Hammerstein's faith in human beings and their destiny. . . .

Since he was at heart a serious man, his lyrics were rarely clever. Instead of turning facetious phrases he made a studious attempt to write idiomatically in the popular tradition of the musical theatre, for he was a dedicated craftsman. But the style that was apparently so artless has brought glimpses of glory into our lives. "There's a bright, golden haze on the meadow," sings Curly in *Oklahoma!* and the gritty streets of a slatternly city look fresher. "June is bustin' out all over," sing Carrie and Nettie in *Carousel* and the harshness of our winter vanishes. . . . To us it is gratifying that he had the character to use his genius with faith and scruple.

The contrast of faith (good) with cleverness (bad) is typical of Midcult, as is the acceptance of liberalistic moralizing as a satisfactory substitute for talent. Indeed, talent makes the midbrow uneasy: "Since he was a serious man, his lyrics were rarely clever." The death of Mr. Hart did not stimulate the *Times* to editorial elegy.

QUESTIONS ON MACDONALD

1. How does MacDonald differentiate mass culture, midculture, and high culture? Do you find these distinctions persuasive?

2. In what sense is mass culture dependent on the market? Do you think that markets help or hinder high culture?

3. How does MacDonald characterize the "conservative" and the "liberal" solution to the problems of Masscult? With which of these does MacDonald express greatest sympathy? Do you agree with his analysis?

————————

The Arts in a Market Economy

Tyler Cowen

Tyler Cowen holds the Holbert Harris Chair in Economics at George Mason University. The editor of The Theory of Market Failure: A Critical Examination *(1988), he is the author of* What Price Fame? *(2000). The selection below is taken from the first chapter of* In Praise of Commercial Culture *(2000).*

Art markets consist of artists, consumers, and middlemen, or distributors. Artists work to achieve self-fulfillment, fame, and riches. The complex motivations behind artistic creation include love of the beautiful, love of money, love of fame, personal arrogance, and inner compulsions. Creators hold strong desires to be heard and witnessed. Joshua Reynolds, in his *Discourses on Art,* pronounced that "The highest ambition of every Artist is to be thought a man of Genius." More generally, I treat artists as pursuing a complex mix of pecuniary and nonpecuniary returns.

Consumers and patrons stand as the artist's silent partners. We support creators with our money, our time, our emotions, and our approbation. We discover subtle nuances in their work that the artists had not noticed or consciously intended. Inspired consumption is a creative act that further enriches the viewer and the work itself. Art works provoke us to reexamine or reaffirm what we think and feel, and consumer and patron demands for artworks finance the market.

Distributors bring together producer and consumer, whether the product be beauty soap, bread, or Beethoven. The resultant meeting of supply and demand fuels the creative drive and disseminates its results. Neither producers nor consumers of art can flourish without the other side of the market. No distributor can profit without attracting both artists and consumers. The interactions between producers, consumers, and distributors provide the basic setting for the analysis of this book.

Creators respond to both internal and external forces. Internal forces include the artist's love of creating, demands for money and fame, and the desire to work out styles, aesthetics, and problems posed by previous works. External forces include the artistic materials and media available, the conditions of patronage, the distribution network, and opportunities for earning income. When translated into the terminology of economics or rational choice theory, the internal forces correspond to preferences and external forces represent opportunities and constraints. These internal and external forces interact to shape artistic production.

Psychological motivations, though a driving force behind many great artworks, do not operate in a vacuum, independent of external constraints. Economic circumstances influence the ability of artists to express their aesthetic aspirations. Specifically, artistic independence requires financial independence and a strong commercial market. Beethoven wrote: "I am not out to be a musical usurer as you think, who writes only to become rich, by no means! Yet, I love an independent life, and this I cannot have without a small income."[1]

Capitalism generates the wealth that enables individuals to support themselves through art. The artistic professions, a relatively recent development in human history, flourish with economic growth. Increasing levels of wealth and comfort have freed creative individuals from tiresome physical labor and have supplied them with the means to pursue their flights of fancy. Wealthy societies usually consume the greatest quantities of nonpecuniary enjoyments. The ability of wealth to fulfill our basic physical needs elevates our goals and our interest in the aesthetic. In accord with this mechanism, the number of individuals who can support themselves as full-time creators has risen steadily for centuries.

Perhaps ironically, the market economy increases the independence of the artist from the immediate demands of the culture-consuming public. Capitalism funds alternative sources of financial support, allowing artists to invest in skills, undertake long-term projects, pursue the internal logic of their chosen genre or niche, and develop their marketing abilities. A commercial society is a prosperous and comfortable society, and offers a rich variety of niches in which artists can find the means to satisfy their creative desires.

Many artists cannot make a living from their craft, and require external sources of financial support. Contrary to many other commentators, I do not interpret this as a sign of market failure. Art markets sometimes fail to recognize the merits of great creators, but a wealthy economy, taken as a whole, is more robust to that kind of failure in judgment than is a poor economy. A wealthy economy gives artists a greater number of other sources of potential financial support.

Private foundations, universities, bequests from wealthy relatives, and ordinary jobs, that bane of the artistic impulse, all have supported budding creators. Jane Austen lived from the wealth of her family, T. S. Eliot worked in Lloyd's bank, James Joyce taught languages, Paul Gauguin accumulated a financial cushion through his work as a stockbroker, Charles Ives was an insurance executive, Vincent van Gogh received support from his brother, William Faulkner worked in a power plant and later as a Hollywood screenwriter, and Philip Glass drove a taxi in New York City. William Carlos Williams worked as a physician in Rutherford, New Jersey, and wrote poetry between the visits of his patients.[2]

Wallace Stevens, the American poet, pursued a full-time career in the insurance industry. "He was a very imaginative claims man," noted one former colleague. When offered an endowed chair to teach and write poetry at Harvard University, Stevens declined. He preferred insurance work to lecturing and did not wish to sacrifice his position in the firm. At one point a co-worker accused Stevens of working on his poetry during company time. He replied: "I'm thinking about surety problems Saturdays and Sundays when I'm strolling through Elizabeth Park, so it all evens out."[3]

Parents and elderly relations have financed many an anti-establishment cultural revolution. Most of the leading French artists of the nineteenth century lived off family funds—usually generated by mercantile activity—for at least part of their careers. The list includes Delacroix, Corot, Courbet, Seurat, Degas, Manet, Monet, Cézanne, Toulouse-Lautrec, and Moreau. French writers Charles Baudelaire, Paul Verlaine, and Gustave Flaubert went even further in their anti-establishment attitudes, again at their parents' expense.[4]

Even the most seclusive artists sometimes rely furtively on capitalist wealth. Marcel Proust sequestered himself in a cork-lined room to write, covering himself in blankets and venturing outside no more than fifteen minutes a day. Yet he relied on his family's wealth, obtained through the Parisian stock exchange. Paul Gauguin left the French art world for the tropical island of Tahiti, knowing that his pictures would appreciate in value in his absence, allowing for a triumphal return. Gauguin never ceased his tireless self-promotion, and during his Pacific stays he constantly monitored the value of his pictures in France.[5]

Wealth and financial security give artists the scope to reject societal values. The bohemian, the avant-garde, and the nihilist are all products of capitalism. They have pursued forms of liberty and inventiveness that are unique to the modern world.

PECUNIARY INCENTIVES

Many artists reject the bohemian lifestyle and pursue profits. The artists of the Italian Renaissance were businessmen first and foremost. They produced for profit, wrote commercial contracts, and did not hesitate to walk away from a job if the remuneration was not sufficient. Renaissance sculptor Benvenuto Cellini, in his autobiography, remarked, "You poor idiots, I'm a poor goldsmith, and I work for anyone who pays me."[6]

Bach, Mozart, Haydn, and Beethoven were all obsessed with earning money through their art, as a reading of their letters reveals. Mozart even wrote: "Believe me, my sole purpose is to make as much money as possible; for after good health it is the best thing to have." When accepting an Academy Award in 1972, Charlie Chaplin remarked: "I went into the business for money and the art grew out of it. If people are disillusioned by that remark, I can't help it. It's the truth." The massive pecuniary rewards available to the most successful creators encourage many individuals to try their hand at entering the market.[7]

Profits signal where the artist finds the largest and most enthusiastic audience. British "punk violinist" Nigel Kennedy has written: "I think if you're playing music or doing art you can in some way measure the amount of communication you are achieving by how much money it is bringing in for you and for those around you." Creators desiring to communicate a message to others thus pay heed to market earnings, even if they have little intrinsic interest in material riches. The millions earned by Prince and Bruce Springsteen indicate how successfully they have spread their influence.[8]

Beethoven cared about money as a means of helping others. When approached by a friend in need, he sometimes composed for money: "I have only to sit down at my desk and in a short time help for him is forthcoming." Money, as a general medium of exchange, serves many different ends, not just greedy or materialistic ones.[9]

FUNDING ARTISTIC MATERIALS

Artists who chase profits are not always accumulating wealth for its own sake. An artist's income allows him or her to purchase the necessary materials for artistic creation. Budding sculptors must pay for bronze, aluminum, and stone. Writers wish to travel for ideas and background, and musicians need studio time. J. S. Bach used his outside income, obtained from playing at weddings and funerals, to buy himself out of his commitment to teach Latin, so that he would have more time to compose. Robert Townsend produced the hit film *Hollywood Shuffle* by selling the use of his credit cards to his friends. Money is a means to the ends of creative expression and artistic communication.[10]

Capitalist wealth supports the accouterments of artistic production. Elizabethan theaters, the venues for Shakespeare's plays, were run for profit and funded from ticket receipts. For the first time in English history, the theater employed full-time professional actors, production companies, and playwrights. Buildings were designed specifically for dramatic productions. Shakespeare, who wrote for money, earned a good living as an actor and playwright.[11]

Pianos, violins, synthesizers, and mixers have all been falling in price, relative to general inflation, since their invention. With the advent of the home camcorder, even rudimentary movie-making equipment is now widely available. Photography blossomed in the late nineteenth century with technological innovations. Equipment fell drastically in price and developing pictures became much easier. Photographers suddenly were able to work with hand cameras, and no longer needed to process pictures immediately after they were taken. Photographic equipment no longer weighed fifty to seventy pounds, and the expense of maintaining a traveling darkroom was removed.[12]

Falling prices for materials have made the arts affordable to millions of enthusiasts and would-be professionals. In previous eras, even paper was costly, limiting the development of both writing and drawing skills to relatively well-off families. Vincent van Gogh, an ascetic loner who ignored public taste, could not have managed his very poor lifestyle at an earlier time in history. His nonconformism was possible because technological progress had lowered the costs of paints and canvas and enabled him to persist as an artist.

Female artists, like Berthe Morisot and Mary Cassatt, also took advantage of falling materials costs to move into the market. In the late nineteenth century women suddenly could paint in their spare time without having to spend exorbitant sums on materials. Artistic willpower became more important than external financial support. This shift gave victims of discrimination greater access to the art world. The presence of women in the visual arts, literature, and music has risen steadily as capitalism has advanced.

Falling materials costs help explain why art has been able to move away from popular taste in the twentieth century. In the early history of art, paint and materials were very expensive; artists were constrained by the need to generate immediate commissions and sales. When these costs fell, artists could aim more at innovation and personal expression, and less at pleasing buyers and critics. Modern art became possible. The impressionists did not require immediate acceptance from the French Salon, and the abstract expressionists could continue even when Peggy Guggenheim was their only buyer.

The artist's own health and well-being, a form of "human capital," provides an especially important asset. Modernity has improved the health and lengthened the lives of artists. John Keats would not have died at age twenty-six of tuberculosis with access to modern medicine. Paula Modersohn-Becker, one of the most talented painters Germany has produced, died from complications following childbirth, at the age of thirty-one. Mozart, Schubert, Emily Brontë, and many others who never even made their start also count as medical tragedies who would have survived in the modern era. The ability of a wealthy society to support life for greater numbers of people, compared to pre-modern societies, has provided significant stimulus to both the supply and demand sides of art markets.

Most advances in health and life expectancy have come quite recently. In the United States of 1855, one of the wealthiest and healthiest countries in the world at that time, a newly born male child could expect no more than 39 years of life. Yet many of the greatest composers, writers, and painters peak well after their fortieth year.[13]

Birth control technologies, generally available only for the last few decades, have given female creators greater control over their lives and domestic conditions. Most of the renowned female painters of the past, for various intentional or accidental reasons, had either few children or no children at all. Childbearing responsibilities kept most women out of the art world. Today, budding female artists can exercise far greater control over whether and when they wish to have children. The increasing prominence of women in music, literature, and the visual arts provides one of the most compelling arguments for cultural optimism. For much of human history, at least half of the human race has been shut out from many prominent artistic forms, and women are only beginning to redress the balance. . . .[14]

MECHANISMS IN SUPPORT OF ARTISTIC DIVERSITY

Well-developed markets support cultural diversity. A quick walk through any compact disc or book superstore belies the view that today's musical and literary tastes are becoming increasingly homogeneous. Retail outlets use product selection and diversity as primary strategies for bringing consumers through the door. Even items that do not turn a direct profit will help attract business and store visits, thereby supporting the ability of the business to offer a wide variety of products.

The successive relaxation of external constraints on internal creativity tends to give rise to a wide gamut of emotions and styles. Contemporary culture has proved itself optimistic, celebratory, and life-affirming. The songs of Buddy Holly, Howard Hodgkin's paintings, and Steven Spielberg's *Close Encounters of the Third Kind* show positive cultural forces with great vigor. The songs of Hank Williams, Isaac Bashevis Singer's stories, and Ingmar Bergman's *Persona* depict a sadder, more shattering aesthetic, although not without the possibility of redemption. And for a dark and ecstatic experience we are drawn to the works of Mark Rothko. Depravity and excess, exquisitely executed, can be found in the photography of Robert Mapplethorpe, the Sex Pistols's music, and Bernardo Bertolucci's *Last Tango in Paris.*

The available variety of artistic products should come as no surprise. Adam Smith emphasized that the division of labor, and thus the degree of specialization, is limited by the extent of the market. In the case of art, a large market lowers the costs of creative pursuits and makes market niches easier to find. In the contrary case of a single patron, the artist must meet the tastes of that patron or earn no income.

Growing markets in music, literature, and the fine arts have moved creators away from dependence on patronage. A patron, as opposed to a customer, supports an artist with his or her own money, without necessarily purchasing the artistic output. Samuel Johnson, writing in the eighteenth century, referred to a patron as "a wretch who supports with insolence, and is paid with flattery." Even Johnson, however, did not believe that patrons were intrinsically bad; the problem arises only when artists are completely dependent upon a single patron. Patronage relationships, which today stand at an all-time high, have become more beneficial to artistic creativity over time. The size and diversity of modern funding sources gives artists bargaining power to create space for their creative freedom.[15]

Growth of the market has liberated artists, not only from the patron, but also from the potential tyranny of mainstream market taste. Unlike in the eighteenth century, today's books need not top the bestseller list to remunerate their authors handsomely. Artists who believe that they know better than the crowd can indulge their own tastes and lead fashion. Today it is easier than ever before to make a living by marketing to an artistic niche and rejecting mainstream taste.

The wealth and diversity of capitalism have increased the latitude of artists to educate their critics and audiences. Starting in the late nineteenth century, many painters deliberately refused to produce works that were easily accessible to viewers. At first Manet, Monet, and Cézanne shocked the art world with their paintings but eventually they converted it. The financial support they received from their families and customers was crucial to this struggle. The twentieth-century American Pop artists, such as Andy Warhol, Roy Lichtenstein, Robert Rauschenberg, and Jasper Johns, also made initial sacrifices to elevate our tastes. Today we enjoy their brilliant pictures while taking the once-shocking approach for granted.

In the realm of culture, market mechanisms do more than simply give consumers what they want. Markets give producers the greatest latitude to educate their audiences. Art consists of a continual dialogue between producer and consumer; this dialogue helps both parties decide what they want. The market incentive to conclude a profitable sale simultaneously provides an incentive to engage consumers and producers in a process of want refinement. Economic growth increases our ability to develop sophisticated and specialized tastes. . . .

Competition and Complementarity as Forces for Innovation

Artists offer new products to increase their income, their fame, and their audience exposure. They seek to avoid duplicating older media and styles, which become played out and filled with previous achievements. Picasso had the talent to master many styles, but won greater accolades with his innovations than he would have achieved by copying the French impressionists. Rather than safely performing Haydn and Beethoven, four young talented performers decided to become the Kronos Quartet, and to perform music by Glass and Riley and African music. As a leader in a new line of production, the quartet has earned especially high profits. The Arditti Quartet has not earned the profits of Kronos, but nonetheless has staked out its position as a preeminent string quartet for contemporary chamber music.

Innovation enables artists to overcome their fear of being compared to previous giants. A century of German and Austrian musicians—Schumann, Schubert, Brahms, and Bruckner—dreaded comparison with Beethoven and pursued new directions. Brahms avoided composing symphonies for many years, instead writing songs and vocal ensembles. These works surpassed Beethoven's vocal music. Brahms turned to symphonies much later in life: He had once written, "You don't know what it is like always to hear that giant marching along behind me." Beethoven refused to hear the operas of Mozart for this reason, but even Beethoven could not escape being intimidated by his own achievements. Rather than finishing a tenth symphony, which might have paled in comparison to his ninth, he wrote his innovative late string quartets. . . .[16]

Critics often write premature obituaries for changing styles and genres. The writing of epic poetry has not ceased but lives on in the works of Derek Walcott, who emulates Homer. Lawrence Kasdan's *Body Heat* and Paul Verhoeven's *Basic Instinct* follow the film *noir* tradition of the 1940s or 1950s. Many of the most popular bands of the last several years—like Nirvana, Pearl Jam, and Smashing Pumpkins—have created a deliberately retrograde sound, hearkening back to the 1970s. In classical music, Arvo Pärt resurrects the medieval tradition and in jazz George Gruntz has revitalized the big band.[17]

The pastiche of today's so-called "postmodern" style responds to two market incentives. First, an increasing number of past styles accumulate over time. It becomes harder to create works that do not refer to past styles in some fashion. Second, both creators and audiences come to know more past styles over time, due to the success of markets in preserving and disseminating cultural creations. Performers find themselves increasingly able to establish rapport with their audiences by referring to past works. Warhol could reproduce Chairman Mao, Marilyn Monroe, or the Mona Lisa in silkscreen form, but Leonardo da Vinci had a smaller number of established icons—primarily religious—to draw upon.

Some new artistic developments turn their back on the futuristic and high-tech and embrace earlier, more naturalistic forms of art. Witness the recent trend of rock stars to go "unplugged" and produce acoustic albums and concerts. Andy Goldsworthy and Robert Smithson, two contemporary sculptors, have worked with objects taken from nature, such as stones, tree branches, and ice. The artist Cy Twombly uses crayon to great effect. Artists increase their income and fame by reaching audiences, and they will not hesitate to cast off electronic gadgetry and draw upon earlier styles to achieve that end.

Standing still is one tactic that artists cannot prosper by in a dynamic market economy. Artists stake out niche positions but they are not protected against competition for long. Picasso and Braque introduced cubism but eventually had to contend with competitors who built on their work. Declining eminence and profits, combined with threatening competition, often induce the original artist to innovate again. Stravinsky, Picasso, and the Beatles outpaced their competitors, at least for a while, by undergoing several metamorphoses of style.

Eventually most artists lose the drive or depth to meet challenges and consequently give up their place as industry leaders. Andy Warhol set up The Factory and sold studio-made prints and silkscreens under his own name, Maria Callas did not take sufficient care with her voice, and Rossini ceased composing operas altogether. E. M. Forster published his last novels in the 1920s, even though he did not die until 1970. "I have nothing more to say," was his explanation. These artists ceded their places on the cutting edge of their respective fields.[18]

New innovations do not always eclipse older, more established artistic forms, but they do inevitably change them. Outside competition shakes up older forms and spurs ingenuity. Renaissance sculpture communicated the idea of depth perspective to painters, jazz crept into the rhythms of classical music, and movies have sped up the pacing of the best-selling novel. Sometimes a new medium pushes other works in the opposite direction. The need to compete with television prompted film directors to develop the big-screen movie with spectacular special effects. Photography created a cheap substitute for portraiture, which induced painters to direct their talents to more abstract and less realistic themes.[19]

Artistic fertilizations and innovations also occur backwards in time, as later works improve the quality of earlier ones by changing their meaning. Verdi's opera *Otello* and Orson Welles's film *Othello* tell us more about Shakespeare's *Othello* than does any piece of literary criticism. These variations on the work, through different media and presentation, enable us to see Shakespeare's work anew. Verdi's music brings out the aspect of terror in the text and influences how we read the play. Subsequent contributions and adaptations thus make Shakespeare's work richer, just as Shakespeare's original *Othello* now contributes to the depth of the later versions. Art Tatum's piano improvisations, Lichtenstein's takeoffs on French and abstract expressionist paintings, and Beethoven's *Diabelli Variations* all shed light on previous artworks to an especially high degree. T. S. Eliot, who focused on this mechanism in his essay "Tradition and the Individual Talent," has been prominent on both sides of such exchanges. . . .

Outsiders as Innovators

Outsiders and marginalized minorities often drive artistic innovation. Much of the dynamic element in American culture, for instance, has been due to blacks, Jews, and gays, as Camille Paglia has noted.

Outsiders have less stake in the status quo and are more willing to take chances. They face disadvantages when competing on mainstream turf, but a differentiated product gives them some chance of obtaining a market foothold. Individuals who will not otherwise break into the market are more inclined to take risks, since they have less to lose. Were an all-black orchestra or black conductor to record the umpteenth version of Mozart's *Jupiter* symphony, the racially prejudiced would have no reason to promote or purchase the product. (Few individuals know the name or the works of the most critically renowned black conductor of our century, Dean Dixon.) The cost of indulging discriminatory taste is low when the market offers the virtuosic Herbert von Karajan and Karl Boehm, both former Nazi supporters. But when black performers played "Take the A Train" or "Maybellene," even many racists were impelled to support the outsider with their dollars.

The most influential African-American contributions have not come in the most established cultural forms, such as letters and landscape paintings. Instead, America's black minority has dominated new cultural areas—jazz, rhythm and blues, breakdancing, and rap.

Minority innovators bring novel insights to cultural productions. Their atypical background provides ideas and aesthetics that the mainstream does not have and, initially, cannot comprehend. Minorities also must rationalize their outsider status. They deconstruct their detractors, reexamine fundamentals, and explore how things might otherwise be. They tend to bring the upstart, parvenu mentality necessary for innovation. Jazz musician Max Roach pointed out: "Innovation is in our blood. We [blacks] are not people who can sit back and say what happened a hundred years ago was great, because what was happening a hundred years ago was shit: slavery. Black people have to keep moving."[20]

Capitalism has allowed minority groups to achieve market access, despite systematic discrimination and persecution. Black rhythm and blues musicians, when they were turned down by the major record companies, marketed their product through the independents, such as Chess, Sun, Stax, and Motown. The radio stations that favored Tin Pan Alley over rhythm and blues found themselves circumvented by the jukebox and the phonograph. These decentralized means of product delivery allowed the consumer to choose what kind of music would be played.

The French impressionist painters, rejected by the government-sponsored academy, financed and ran their own exhibitions. In the process modern art markets were born. Jews were kept out of many American businesses early in this century, but they developed the movie industry with their own capital, usually earned through commercial retail activity. Women cracked the fiction market in eighteenth century England once a wide public readership replaced the system of patronage. Innovators with a potentially appealing message usually can find profit-seeking distributors who are willing to place money above prejudice or grudges.

Innovations in Preserving Past Culture

The diversity of the contemporary world includes our unparalleled ability to preserve and market the cultural contributions of the past. Markets provide profits to those who successfully preserve and market the cultural contributions of previous artists.

Today's consumers have much better access to the creations of Mozart than listeners of that time did, even if we restrict the comparison to Europe. More people saw Wagner's Ring cycle on public television in 1990 than had seen it live in all Ring productions since the premiere in 1876. Recorded boxed sets and complete editions of little-known composers are now common. Once-obscure operas and symphonies are available in profusion. Compact disc reissues of classic performances have exceeded all expectations; record companies eagerly reissue obscure recordings that sell only a few thousand copies.[21]

Old movies, including many silents, can be rented on videocassette for a pittance. The video laser disc, likely to fall drastically in price, will provide new and better access to movies and musical performances. Many classic symphonic and instrumental performances have been reissued on compact disc. New and definitive editions of many literary works, or better translations, are being published for the first time. The classics are available in cheap paperback editions. Television, video stores, and bookstores give modern fans much better access to Shakespeare than the Elizabethans had.

Even lesser painters now have their own one-man shows with published catalogs full of beautiful color plates. Wealthy American art collectors have enabled New York's Museum of Modern Art and Metropolitan Museum of Art to become world leaders in preserving the art of our century and of centuries past. The Getty and Norton Simon museums in California have been assembled in recent times from two large private donations. Even the government-run National Gallery of Art assembled most of its holdings from private collections like those of the Mellon, Kress, Dale, and Widener families—paintings that were headed for museums in any case.

Live performance, as a means of preserving the past, also has flourished. Today's concertgoers can sample a range of musical periods, instruments, and styles with an ease that previous ages would have envied. While conductors are mastering twentieth century idioms, they are also refining "original performance" presentations of Renaissance, baroque, and classical styles. American symphony orchestras in Cleveland, Boston, New York, Philadelphia, and other cities have outpaced many of their European competitors. From 1965 to 1990 America grew from having 58 symphony orchestras to having nearly 300, from 27 opera companies to more than 150, and from 22 non-profit regional theaters to 500. . . .[22]

Is Modernity an Age of Mass Culture?

Many commentators see the modern age as the age of mass culture, where large numbers of individuals unthinkingly consume the same products. But the mass culture model applies, at most, to the fields of television and sports. These areas are highly visible and therefore easy to focus on. I see television and sports as special cases where competitive pressures have been partially stifled; they do not, therefore, represent the vanguard or the high points of modern culture.

Post-war American television, by and large, has not provided cultural riches. Television programs entertain us and present appealing characters, but a canonic list of the best television programs would not, in this author's opinion, stand up to a comparable list from music, painting, or literature. My personal and purely idiosyncratic nominations for the best television products ever—Britain's Monty Python troupe and Ingmar Bergman's *The Magic Flute*—both were produced for government-owned stations, rather than for the market-based American system. I concur with Robert Hughes, who notes that several hours of American television provide the best argument against market-supplied culture.

The influence of the television market also has had some consequences for other cultural media, such as motion pictures. Today a considerable percentage of the profits from a movie come from the sale of television rights. Moviemakers, to some degree, have shifted their attention away from more specialized moviegoers to the more general television audience. Television helps fund movies that would otherwise not be made, but it also exerts a negative influence on movie quality.[23]

I do not intend the above remarks as an anti-television polemic. Television—even its lower brow forms—provides a useful medium for presenting social issues and showing audiences by example how people can deal with their personal problems. The rapid and healthy increase in social and sexual openness, which blossomed in the 1960s and 1970s, is due partly to television. Television also provides a variety of other non-artistic services, ranging from news to Sesame Street in Spanish to nature documentaries.

Legal restrictions on cable television are partly to blame for the cultural shortcomings of television. For many years the American government gave monopoly power to the three major networks and certain privileged local stations. The Federal Communications Commission also holds the power to revoke the licenses of stations that do not broadcast in the so-called "public interest." Television has not been able to develop the diversity necessary to support innovative and visionary cultural products. The quality of television is especially vulnerable to restrictions on competition because TV programs have no other outlet. Music, in contrast, has been less affected by the limitations of radio. Live performance, phonographs, and jukeboxes have provided alternate marketing outlets. There are also more radio stations than television channels.

If mass taste had controlled other genres as it has controlled television, they too would fare little or no better. A society with three major outlets for books, distributing common products for all who wish to read, would not have produced Vladimir Nabokov's *Lolita* or Franz Kafka's *Metamorphosis*. The virtues of cultural markets lie not in the quality of mass taste but rather in the ability of artists to find minority support for their own conceptions. Even Michael Jackson, an unparalleled cultural phenomenon whose *Thriller* album has sold fifty million copies worldwide, has never commanded the allegiance of most Americans.

With the widespread advent of cable and satellite television, the reign of mass taste in television programming has begun to decline. The competitive rivalry of market forces tends to "de-massify" the media, to borrow a phrase from Alvin Toffler. The television audience is fragmenting as special interest stations proliferate on cable. In the last fifteen years, the three major networks have lost thirty million viewers—a third of their audience. Diverse products appealing to market niches can exploit the vulnerability of bland products aimed at mass audiences. Cable subscriptions frequently give individuals access to 150 stations or more, and the number is growing steadily.[24]

It nonetheless remains an open question how much cultural inspiration television will produce in the future. The American experience with cable television has disappointed many expectations. Many cable channels focus on repackaging traditional network programs; we now can view reruns of situation comedies at all times of the day. Much of cable's diversity has supported evangelists, Home Shopping Network, personal advertisements in search of romance, ongoing weather reports, airline schedules, and soap operas in various languages. These products are useful to consumers but they are unlikely to provide culture that will stand the test of time. Cable channels have produced fewer new programs than many observers had expected. Even when the number of available channels is large, creators still must cover their production and marketing costs by bringing in a sizable audience. . . .[25]

GOVERNMENT AS CUSTOMER

Music and the arts have been moving away from government funding since the Middle Ages. The Renaissance, the Enlightenment, the nineteenth century romantic movement, and twentieth century modernism all brought art further into the market sphere. Today, most of the important work in film, music, literature, painting, and sculpture is sold as a commodity. Contemporary art is capitalist art, and the history of art has been a history of the struggle to establish markets. These trends will not be reversed in any foreseeable course for the current world, regardless of our opinion of government funding for the arts. Most countries in the world are not contemplating reversions to socialism.

The arguments of this book, taken alone, cannot determine which side is correct in the American political debates over government funding of the arts. Rather, I wish to challenge the common premise of cultural pessimism behind both sides. Funding critics argue that the National Endowment for the Arts (NEA) is corrupting American culture, while funding advocates claim that eliminating the NEA would critically damage American culture. I see American culture, and the culture of the free world, as fundamentally healthy in any case.

The real choice today is between two alternate optimistic visions of our cultural future. In one vision, government funding plays a minor but supportive role by creating niches for artists who might otherwise fall between the cracks. Government serves as one of many entrepreneurs in the cultural marketplace. In the second vision, even small amounts of government funding will more likely corrupt the arts than improve them. The costs of politicizing art might outweigh the benefits from additional government funding of art. Governments, even democratic ones, tend to favor the cultural status quo that put them in power, or to shape a new status quo that will cement their power.

Contrary to the claim of Alexis de Tocqueville, democracy need not prove an inferior system for the arts, compared to aristocracy. At most democratic *government* might be inferior for the arts, compared to aristocratic government. Democratic systems as a whole do extraordinarily well when they allow an accompanying capitalistic market to fund their artistic activities. The cultural rise of the American nation, which occurred largely after Tocqueville wrote, provides the strongest argument against his thesis. After the second World War, America has been a clear world leader in film, painting, and popular music, and has had a strong presence, arguably second to none, in literature, poetry, and music composition. Among other factors, Tocqueville overlooked the rise of the steamship, which brought America in closer touch with Europe in the late nineteenth century, and facilitated beneficial cultural exchange.[26]

The state does best in promoting the arts when it acts as simply another customer, patron, or employer, rather than as a bureaucracy with a public mandate. Direct government funding works best when it serves as private funding in disguise, such as when Philip IV hired Velázquez to serve as his court painter. In similar fashion, the royal court of Louis XIV supported Moliére and the German municipalities of Weimar, Cöthen, and Leipzig hired Johann Sebastian Bach to serve as town musician. We can find many cases where monarchs. Popes, municipalities, guilds, and other governmental or quasi-governmental institutions commissioned or otherwise supported notable works.

We should not, however, overestimate the successes of government funding. For every Velázquez, governments have supported hundreds of unknown court painters. Autocracy will sometimes place substantial resources in the hands of an artistic superstar, but, more often than not, will promote mediocre hacks. The purse strings are in the hands of politicians who seek personal power for themselves, and flattery and obedience from others. For this reason aristocratic government does not guarantee artistic success, even though we can point to some inspired aristocratic buyers.

Whether government funding for the arts should be discontinued, maintained, or extended brings two sets of incommensurable values into conflict. On one hand, the case against funding makes two valid points. First, tax-supported funding forces consumers to forgo goods and services that they would prefer more than art. Second, many individuals believe it is unjust to force conservative Christians to support an exhibit of Robert Mapplethorpe, to draw an example from the U.S. context. On the other hand, funding supporters point out that more money will support more artists, more art, and, if done with reasonable care, will improve our artistic heritage. Neither side has succeeded in showing that its favored values are more important than the values favored by the other side.[27]

Government arts funding cannot be restructured to avoid this clash of artistic versus non-artistic values. Artistic buyers must be liberated from accountability to the masses, if they are to have a good chance of influencing the market in a positive direction. Art and democratic politics, although both beneficial activities, operate on conflicting principles. In the field of art new masterpieces usually bring aesthetic revolutions, which tend to offend majority opinion or go over its head. In the field of politics we seek stability, compromise, and consensus. This same conservatism, so valuable in politics, stifles beauty and innovation in art.

The current American political debate has confronted the NEA with an impossible task. The NEA is supposed to deliver the benefits of privileged spending while receiving its funding from a democratic system based on political accountability. The result is an agency whose best and most innovative actions—such as funding exhibits of Robert Mapplethorpe and Andrés Serrano—are precisely those that offend its taxpaying supporters.

Ironically, the massive publicity generated by NEA critics may have done more for the arts than the NEA itself. Jesse Helms, with his virulent, prejudiced attacks on Robert Mapplethorpe, did far more for that artist than the Washington arts establishment has. Mapplethorpe's name is now a household word. In his lifetime, Mapplethorpe did not need government assistance; he became a millionaire by selling his photographs in the marketplace. Jesse Helms, however, did bring Mapplethorpe his current fame.

The American government has done a good deal to support the arts, but most of the successes have come from outside of the NEA. The entire NEA budget, at its peak, fell well short of the amount of money required to produce Kevin Costner's *Waterworld* epic. NEA expenditures have never exceeded seventy cents per capita, and the NEA has never been vital to American artistic success. Before 1965, when the NEA was created, American culture—even the preservation of high culture—flourished. The best American symphony orchestras and museums were created well before 1965 and without NEA involvement.[28]

The bulk of American governmental support for the arts has come in two other forms. First, the tax deduction for contributions to artistic non-profits has greatly benefited museums, opera companies, and other artistic activities that rely on private donations. Government also exempts not-for-profit institutions from income taxation. Tax deductibility allows government to support the arts without making judgments about the relative artistic merits of different projects. Just as tax deductibility has succeeded in supporting American religion or the American housing market, so has it improved the quantity and quality of American culture.

Second, federal and state governments provide massive indirect support to the arts through subsidies to higher education. Many of today's cutting-edge composers and writers rely on university positions for part- or full-time support while they pursue their craft. While the number of writers and composers in university jobs may have overly academized American culture, professorships have been the only available source of support for many of these creators. Whether American higher educational policies have been effective, all things considered, falls outside the scope of this book. But seen as cultural policy, government subsidies for higher education are far more significant than the small sums spent by the NEA.

Governments often support creativity most effectively by providing a large number of jobs where individuals are not expected to work very hard. Many leading eighteenth century writers, for instance, worked for the government bureaucracy. These individuals pursued their creative interests either in their spare time or while "on the job." John Gay, Daniel Defoe, and Jonathan Swift, to name but a few examples, all received substantial income from government employment. Goethe spent much of his life working as a government administrator while writing in his spare time. The university has now stepped into the role once provided by the bureaucracy—in many cases teaching posts give talented individuals financial security with a relative minimum of daily responsibilities.[29]

The funding model of Western Europe differs from that of the United States. Germany and France, for instance, deliberately sacrifice contemporary popular culture to both older, high culture and to the contemporary avant-garde. These governments restore old cathedrals and subsidize classic opera and theater, while simultaneously supporting the extreme avant-garde, such as Boulez, Stockhausen, and Beuys. Yet European popular culture, especially in cinema and music, is largely moribund and lacking in creativity. Germany and France have not escaped the bureaucratization of culture. The French Ministry of Culture, for instance, spends $3 billion a year and employs 12,000 bureaucrats. Yet France has lost her position as a world cultural leader, and few other countries embrace American popular culture with such fervor.

Government involvement in cultural preservation involves costs beyond the immediate tax burden—state support makes the arts more bureaucratic and less dynamic. Government, when it acts as customer on a very large scale, often pushes out beneficial market influences. The American market has less government funding but receives much more funding from consumers and private donors. As in the American debate, European arts funding brings a clash of potentially incommensurable values and does not admit of resolution through positive analysis alone.[30]

One alternative (minority) vision suggests that government funding can create a useful target for radical artists. American painter John Sloan said "Sure, it would be fine to have a Ministry of the Fine Arts in this country. Then we'd know where the enemy is."[31]

ENDNOTES

1. Cited in Alexander Thayer, *Life of Beethoven* (Princeton: Princeton University Press, 1967), p. 500. See also H. L. Mencken, *Prejudices: Third Series* (New York: Alfred Knopf, 1922), pp. 17–18, and the writings of Ayn Rand, such as *Atlas Shrugged* (New York: Random House, 1957). On psychological approaches to creativity, see the survey by Jock Abra, *Assaulting Parnassus: Theoretical Views of Creativity* (Lanham, Md.: University Press of America, 1988).

2. On Williams, see David Perkins, *A History of Modern Poetry* (Cambridge, Mass.: Belknap Press of Harvard University Press, 1976), vol. 1, pp. 544–554. On Ives, see Frank R. Rossiter, *Charles Ives and His America* (New York: Liveright, 1975).

3. On Wallace Stevens, see Peter Brazeau, *Parts of a World: Wallace Stevens Remembered* (San Francisco: North Point Press, 1985), pp. 57, 67. On Stevens's refusal of the Harvard position, see Perkins, *A History of Modern Poetry,* p. 535.

4. Monet also received initial financial support from his family, although his father cut off the stipend when he learned that Claude refused to break with his pregnant mistress. On Delacroix and Courbet, see Alan Bowness, *The Conditions of Success: How the Modern Artist Rises to Fame* (London: Thames and Hudson, 1989), p. 60; on Corot, see Madeleine Hours, *Jean-Baptiste-Camille Corot* (New York: Harry N. Abrams, 1972), pp. 11–30. On Degas's sustenance, see Roy McMullen, *Degas: His Life, Times, and Work* (Boston: Houghton Mifflin Company, 1984), pp. 242, 249, 260, 373. On Seurat's family wealth, see Ralph E. Shikes and Paula Harper, *Pissarro: His Life and Work* (New York: Horizon Press, 1980), p. 209. On Cezanne, see John Rewald, *Studies in Impressionism* (New York: Harry N. Abrams, 1985), p. 99, and Harrison C. White and Cynthia A. White, *Canvases and Careers: Institutional Change in the French Painting World* (Chicago: University of Chicago Press, 1993), p. 129. On Manet, see F. W. J. Hemmings, *Culture and Society in France, 1848–1898, Dissidents and Philistines* (London: B.T. Batsford, 1971), p. 162. On Toulouse-Lautrec, see Riva Castleman and Wolfgang Wittrock, eds., *Henri de Toulouse-Lautrec: Images of the 1890's* (New York: Museum of Modern Art, 1985), pp. 21, 45. On Moreau, see John Rewald, *Studies in Post-Impressionism* (New York: Harry N. Abrams, 1986), p. 256. On Monet's father and his funds, see Jacques Letheve, *Daily Life of French Artists in the Nineteenth Century* (New York: Praeger Publishers, 1972), p. 154. On Verlaine, see Jerrold Seigel, *Bohemian Paris: Culture, Politics, and the Boundaries of Bourgeois Life, 1830–1930* (New York: Penguin, 1986), p. 249. On Baudelaire, see A. E. Carter, *Charles Baudelaire* (Boston: Twayne, 1977), pp. 30, 36, 52. On Flaubert, see Benjamin F. Bart, *Flaubert* (Syracuse, N.Y.: Syracuse University Press, 1967), p. 7. On the rise of "hobby science" following the wealth of the Industrial Revolution, see Terence Kealey, *The Economic Laws of Scientific Research* (New York: St. Martin's Press, 1996), pp. 75–77.

5. On Proust, see Ronald Hayman, *Proust: A Biography* (New York: Carroll & Graf, 1990), pp. 335, 337, 347, 411. On the role of pecuniary incentives in the life of Gauguin, see Paul Gauguin, *The Writings of a Savage,* ed. by Daniel Guérin (New York: Viking, 1978), and Belinda Thomson, *Gauguin* (London: Thames and Hudson, 1987).

6. Benvenuto Cellini, *The Treatises of Benvenuto Cellini on Goldsmithing and Sculpture* (New York: Dover Publications, 1967 [1568]), p. 165.

7. On Mozart's letter, written in 1781 to his father, see Alan Steptoe, *The Mozart-DaPonte Operas* (Oxford: Clarendon Press, 1988), p. 63. On Chaplin, see James Twitchell, *Carnival Culture* (New York: Columbia University Press, 1992), p. 132.

8. See Nigel Kennedy, *Always Playing* (London: Mandarin Paperbacks, 1992), pp. 52–53.

9. On Beethoven's writing for his friends, see H. C. Robbins Landon, *Beethoven: His Life, Work and World* (London: Thames and Hudson, 1992), p. 87.

10. On Bach's Latin class, see Otto L. Bettmann, *Johann Sebastian Bach as His World Knew Him* (New York: Birch Lane Press, 1995), p. 56.

11. On the rise of commercialized Elizabethan theater, see Gerald Eades Bentley, *The Profession of Dramatist in Shakespeare's Time, 1590–1642* (Princeton: Princeton University Press, 1971), and Douglas Bruster, *Drama and the Market in the Age of Shakespeare* (Cambridge: Cambridge University Press, 1992).

12. On the late nineteenth-century revolution in photography, see C. J. Gover, *The Positive Image: Women Photographers in Turn of the Century America* (Albany: State University of New York Press, 1988).

13. See William J. Baumol, Sue Anne Batey Blackman, and Edward N. Wolff, *Productivity and American Leadership: The Long View* (Cambridge, Mass.: MIT Press, 1989), p. 52.

14. See Tyler Cowen, "Why Women Succeed, and Fail, in the Arts," *Journal of Cultural Economics,* 20 (1996): 93–113.

15. For more detail on Johnson and patronage, see chapter 2 of this work.

16. On Brahms, see Malcolm MacDonald, *Brahms* (New York: Schirmer Books, 1990), p. 245. On the idea that artists are held back by their own contributions, see Alexander Gerard, *An Essay on Taste* (New York: Garland Publishing, 1970 [1754]), pp. 115–116. On Beethoven's refusal to hear Mozart, see Landon, *Beethoven,* p. 81. For other examples of this phenomenon, see David Lowenthal, *The Past Is a Foreign Country* (Cambridge: Cambridge University Press, 1985), chapter 2.

17. On the importance of emulation to the arts, see the discussion in Howard D. Weinbrot, *Britannia's Issue: The Rise of British Literature from Dryden to Ossian* (Cambridge: Cambridge University Press, 1993), chapter 3.

18. On Forster, see Francis King, *E. M. Forster and His World* (New York: Charles Scribner's Sons, 1978), p. 76.

19. On painting and portraiture, see Remi Clignet, *The Structure of Artistic Revolutions* (Philadelphia: University of Pennsylvania Press, 1985), p. 57, and Jean Gimpel, *The Cult of Art: Against Art and Artists* (New York: Stein and Day, 1969), chapter 11.

20. Cited in Havelock Nelson and Michael A. Gonzales, *Bring the Noise: A Guide to Rap Music and Hip-Hop Culture* (New York: Harmony Books, 1991), p. 261. On the tendency of those at the bottom of the socioeconomic ladder to innovate, see Reuven Brenner, *Rivalry, in Business Science, among Nations* (Cambridge: Cambridge University Press, 1987), pp. 30–33.

21. "Public Television: The Taxpayer's Wagner," *Economist,* May 30, 1992, p. 41. Contrary to some people's impressions, public television is funded primarily by the private sector; government grants account for only 17 percent of the public television budget.

22. See Richard Bolton, ed., *Culture Wars: Documents from the Recent Controversies in the Arts* (New York: New Press, 1992), p. 266. On the success of the private art museum in America, see Perry T. Rathbone, "Influences of Private Patrons: The Art Museum as an Example," in W. McNeil Lowry, ed., *The Arts and Public Policy in the United States* (Englewood Cliffs, N.J.: Prentice-Hall, 1984), pp. 38–56. On the American tradition of privately-funded symphony orchestras, see Philip Hart, *Orpheus in the New World: The Symphony Orchestra as an American Cultural Institution* (New York: W. W. Norton, 1973).

23. On this latter point, see the perceptive analysis of Pauline Kael, "Why are Movies So Bad? Or, the Numbers," in *For Keeps* (New York: Dutton, 1994), pp. 817–829.

24. For the statistic on the decline of the networks' audiences, see Michael Medved, *Hollywood vs. America: Popular Culture and the War on Traditional Values* (New York: Harper and Row, 1992), p. 5.

25. This point is emphasized by Gene F. Jankowski and David C. Fuchs, two cable skeptics, in their *Television Today and Tomorrow: It Won't Be What You Think* (New York: Oxford University Press, 1995).

26. On the role of the steamship, see Norman F. Cantor, *Twentieth-Century Culture: Modernism to Deconstruction* (New York: Peter Lang, 1988), p. 30.

27. For a look at these debates, see Bolton, *Culture Wars.*

28. More generally, subsidies from all levels of government in America provide only 15 percent of the yearly budgets of American arts institutions. Private and corporate donors give $6.4 billion annually, and many millions pay the admissions fees. If we look at privately-run museums only, direct federal support accounts for less than 2 percent of the budget. American opera productions are growing like never before, due largely to increasing demand, not increasing subsidies. See Bill Kauffman, "Subsidies to the Arts: Cultivating Mediocrity," Cato Institute Policy Analysis no. 137, August 8, 1990, p. 9, and Martin Feldstein, "Introduction," in *The Economics of Art Museums,* Martin Feldstein, ed. (Chicago: University of Chicago Press, 1991), p. 6.

29. On this theme, see Robert Wuthnow, *Communities of Discourse: Ideology and Social Structure in the Reformation, the Enlightenment, and European Socialism* (Cambridge, Mass.: Harvard University Press, 1989), especially pp. 215, 243, 259.

30. For data on French expenditures, see William Drozdiak, "The City of Light, Sans Bright Ideas," *The Washington Post,* October 28, 1993, pp. D1, D6. On cultural policies in other European countries, see Milton C. Cummings Jr. and Richard Katz, *The Patron State: The Government and the Arts in North America, Europe, and Japan* (New York: Oxford University Press, 1987). On the ability of government

funding to push out private donations, see Heilbrun and Gray, *The Economics of Art and Culture,* pp. 241–242.

31. Cited in Kauffman, "Subsidies to the Arts: Cultivating Mediocrity," p. 3.

QUESTIONS ON COWEN

1. In what sense can it be said that the markets support the arts? Exactly what features of markets has Cowen isolated?

2. What does Cowen believe that the market will produce? A variety of art, and in great quantity? Or superb art, regardless of variety or quantity?

3. How do you understand the distinction between high and low culture? How does Cowen contend that the market supports high culture as well as low culture? Do you agree with this account?

FOR FURTHER READING

Adorno, Theodor, and Max Horkheimer. "The Culture Industry: Enlightenment as Mass Deception." In *Dialectic of Enlightenment,* translated by John Cumming. New York: Herder and Herder, 1972.

Arnold, Matthew. *Culture and Anarchy* [1869] *and Other Writings.* Cambridge: Cambridge University Press, 1993.

Banfield, Edward C. *The Democratic Muse: Visual Arts and the Public Interest.* New York: Basic Books, 1984.

Benjamin, Walter. "The Work of Art in the Age of Mechanical Reproduction." In *Illuminations,* translated by Harry Zohn. London: Jonathan Cape, 1970.

Blaug, Mark, ed. *The Economics of the Arts.* Boulder, Colo.: Westview Press, 1976.

Carroll, Noël. *A Philosophy of Mass Art.* Oxford: Clarendon Press, 1998.

Cantor, Paul. *Gilligan Unbound: Pop Culture in the Age of Globalization.* Lanham, Md.: Rowman and Littlefield, 2001.

Collingwood, R. G. *The Principles of Art.* Oxford: Oxford University Press, 1938.

Frascina, Francis, and Jonathan Harris, eds. *Art in Modern Culture: An Anthology of Critical Texts.* New York: HarperCollins, 1992.

Gans, Herbert. *Popular Culture and High Culture: An Analysis and Evaluation of Taste.* New York: Basic Books, 1974.

Grampp, William. *Pricing the Priceless: Art, Artists, and Economics.* New York: Basic Books, 1989.

Graña, César. *Bohemian versus Bourgeois.* New York: Basic Books, 1964.

Greenberg, Clement. "The Plight of Culture." In *Art and Culture: Critical Essays.* Boston, Mass.: Beacon Press, 1961.

Heilburn, James, and Charles Gray, *The Economics of Arts and Culture: An American Perspective.* Cambridge: Cambridge University Press, 1993.

Henry, William A. *In Defense of Elitism.* New York: Doubleday, 1994.

Kaufmann, David. *The Business of Common Life: Novels and Classical Economics Between Revolution and Reform.* Johns Hopkins, 1995.

Levine, Lawrence W. *Highbrow/Lowbrow: The Emergence of Cultural Hierarchy in America.* Cambridge: Harvard University Press, 1988.

Lifshitz, Mikhail. *The Philosophy of Art of Karl Marx.* New York: Critics Group, 1938.

Lowenthal, Leo. *Literature, Popular Culture and Society.* Englewood Cliffs, N.J.: Prentice Hall, 1961.

Luhmann, Niklas. *Art as a Social System.* Translated by Eva M. Knodt. Stanford, Conn.: Stanford University Press, 2000.

von Mises, Ludwig. *The Anti-Capitalist Mentality.* South Holland, Ill.: Libertarian Press, 1972.

Munson, Lynne. *Exhibitionism: Art in an Era of Intolerance.* Chicago: Ivan R. Dee, 2000.

Paglia, Camille. *Sexual Personae: Art and Decadence from Nefertiti to Emily Dickinson.* New Haven, Conn.: Yale University Press, 1990.

Robbins, Lionel. "Art and the State." In *Politics and Economics: Papers in Political Economy.* London: Macmillan and Company, 1963.

Rosenberg, Bernard, and David Manning White, eds. *Mass Culture: The Popular Arts in America.* New York: The Free Press, 1957.

Warren, Robert Penn. *Democracy and Poetry.* Cambridge: Harvard University Press, 1975.

Williams, Raymond. *Marxism and Literature.* Oxford: Oxford University Press, 1977.

Wilson, Robert N. "Business and the Creative Arts." In *The Business of America,* edited by Ivar Berg. New York: Harcourt Brace, 1968.

Business, Technology, and Environmental Ethics

And God said, Let us make man in our image, after our likeness: and let them have dominion over the fish of the sea, and over the fowl of the air, and over the cattle, and over all the earth, and over every creeping thing that creepeth upon the earth.

Genesis, 1: 26

Here I am tempted to construct a little fairy tale: Once upon a time, there was a bumbling and kind-hearted old father named Science, and he had a smart, brawny son who found the father's way of life dull, and so set forth to make his fortune. Not far on his journey he met a beautiful golden-haired lady with a bewitching smile. Her name was Money. Now Money had a bad reputation in certain quarters, especially among old, stuffy folk, and it was even rumored that she had borne several bastards. But bastards or no, she had never lost her girlishly lissome figure, delicious complexion, promising smile, and eye for brawny young fellows. Of course this young fellow, having been raised in so retired a way, knew nothing of the gossip about the lady.

So they got married and lived happily ever after—at least, until right now—for he was blind to her little private diversions and was wrapped up in a beautiful, thriving little son who grew as fast as a beanstalk and whose name was Business Culture. I forgot to tell you that the brawny young fellow who married the durable lady was named Technology.

Robert Penn Warren[1]

Like economic reasoning, ecological reasoning is reasoning about equilibria and perturbations that keep systems from converging on equilibria. Like economic reasoning, ecological reasoning is reasoning about competition and unintended consequences, and the internal logic of systems, a logic that dictates how a system responds to attempts to manipulate it. Environmental activism and regulation do not automatically improve the environment. It is a truism in ecology, as in economics, that well-intentioned interventions do not necessarily translate into good results. Ecology (human and nonhuman) is complicated, our knowledge is limited, and environmentalists are themselves only human.

David Schmidtz[2]

1. *Democracy and Poetry* (Cambridge: Harvard University Press, 1975), 52.

2. "Natural Enemies: An Anatomy of Environmental Conflict," *Environmental Ethics* 22 (2000): 406.

Over the past two hundred fifty years, the pace of knowledge and technological change has shown a dramatic change from previous centuries. Innovations in science, technology, and industry have brought about manifold improvements (and opportunities) that have granted us freedom from ignorance, disease, burdensome labor, and unpredictable nature. The enormous growth in industry could not have occurred without numerous technological innovations that owe much to a market framework that allowed individuals to explore, produce, and exchange new applications of knowledge. For many persons, industrial and technological innovation is synonymous with progress itself, but the very growth of industry and technology has raised questions not only about the environmental consequences of commercial activity but also about whether or not the technology associated with much of that activity comes without significant costs.

Industry and technology have altered not only our perception of nature but nature itself. In fact, the enormous growth in industry has been often accompanied by numerous negative effects on the natural environment, including water and air pollution, toxic wastes, the loss of wilderness areas and natural species, and the depletion of natural resources. From this list, or some similar and expanded list, it might be concluded that human beings live in an antagonistic relation to nature. One might assume, further, that environmental problems are a result of Western attitudes (philosophical or religious), technology, capitalism, or some combination of these ("modernity"). However, things are rarely as simple as they sometimes seem. It is not obvious that human beings, even in advanced industrial societies, live in some peculiarly antagonistic relation to nature, nor is it incontestable that the harm and damage that has occurred to the environment are the results of some deep religious or philosophical outlook or that environmental degradation is the inevitable outcome of technological or capitalistic societies. If we are to explore these questions carefully, it is wise to consider both (a) the beneficial and negative consequences of technology and (b) the environmental consequences of commerce and industry. Since both of these topics concern our use of and attitudes toward the natural world, let us begin first with a brief consideration of Western attitudes toward nature, followed by a summary of the emergence of the modern scientific and technological outlook.

WESTERN ATTITUDES TO NATURE

Some have argued that our dependence on technology as well as most environmental problems result from certain deep-seated attitudes about nature; as a result, any moderation of technological dependence or any amelioration of environmental problems will require an alteration of these attitudes and views. Whether or not our dependence on technology is problematical or whether environmental problems emerge out of such attitudes, it is nonetheless true that these attitudes—which have both a religious and philosophical background—may inform the conceptual framework of our deliberations.

Biblical Views: Despotism or Stewardship?

What is the status of nature in relation to human beings? The Bible states that God created, *ex nihilo,* the heaven and the earth, subsequently forming the human being in God's image. At various points in the Genesis narrative of creation—beginning with the separation of the earth and the waters and continuing with God's command that the earth bring forth grass, trees and fruit—it is written, "and God saw that it was good," a phrase which seems to refer to a goodness in creation *prior* to the creation of the human being. Once man and woman are created, then it is written that the human being is to have "dominion" over creation. As in Genesis, so in Psalms 8:6 it is written that "Thou madest him to have dominion over the works of thy hands; thou hast put all *things* under his feet." Some have argued that this sort of view not only separates humankind from nature but grants us a despotic right to use nature as we see fit.[3] However, it is not clear that this "despotic" view is the only, or best, way to interpret certain Biblical passages. Although we may have dominion, it is not at all obvious that we may simply do as we wish with God's creation. For God has created a world in which He has provided for the animals as well as for people: "He sendeth the springs into the valleys, which run among the hills. They give drink to every beast of the field: the wild asses quench their thirst." (Psalms 104:11–12). (The story of Noah and the Flood shows, for example, that God seeks to preserve animals.) It is not obvious that human dominion establishes either that humanity may act toward nature without constraint or that nature is without value. Indeed, some argue that the second book of Genesis provides a basis for the view that human beings are to be *stewards* of nature. For example, in the second chapter, sometimes referred to as the second creation story, God places man into the Garden of Eden "to dress it and to keep it" (Genesis 2:15), thus implying that the human being has a duty of stewardship toward the natural realm.

3. See, for example, Lynn White, Jr., "The Historical Roots of Our Ecological Crisis," *Science* 155 (10 March 1967): 1203–7. White suggests that St. Francis articulates an alternative Christian view.

The Medieval View

In the medieval period, between the fall of Rome and the Renaissance, Greek philosophy would intermingle with and influence Biblical interpretation, affecting the medieval cast of mind in important ways. Whereas the Biblical view was that the human being was made in the image of God (under God's commands but higher than the animals and the plants), the easily assimilable Greek view was that the human being was the rational animal—another way of understanding the preeminence of the human being. Influenced by the thought of Aristotle (384–322 B.C.), the medieval mind understood nature to exemplify an ordered hierarchy of beings or kinds, each kind exhibiting certain natural tendencies or characteristics and having a particular place or station in the world. The four simple elements of earth, air, fire and water each had their particular natures that directed their movements, and animal and plant organisms each had their own inner principles of motion and growth. It was not only assumed that the earth was in the center of the universe, but it was also accepted that human beings had a divinely ordained place in the natural world, just as each particular natural kind had, as Aristotle had pointed out, a particular (natural) tendency or purpose (*telos*).

MODERN SCIENCE AND TECHNOLOGY

Despite some mathematical advances and technological progress, the medieval age was not a period of scientific experimentation or widespread commercial growth. The era of modern science begins with the work of Copernicus (1473–1543), who challenged the reigning beliefs by embracing a heliocentric account of the universe in which the earth revolves on its axis and moves around the sun. Galileo (1564–1642), like Johannes Kepler (1571–1630), not only defends the Copernican system but suggests that nature is to be understood not in terms of some inner natural principle (Aristotle's idea of a *telos*), but through the language of mathematics. However, a mathematical description of nature requires that we conceive and understand nature in terms of properties that are quantifiable, such as size, number, velocity, shape, and temporal and spatial location. Thus does Galileo help to inaugurate a new manner of regarding nature: No longer is the natural world understood as a purposive system, apprehensible largely via the senses; rather, nature is to be understood as matter in motion—quantifiable, mechanical, and impersonal—whose mathematical qual-

ities provide the foundation for a strict science and for progress.

Science and Human Control

Clearly, the rise of modern science proved to shift our thinking. Although most scientists of the early modern era see themselves as exploring the order of God's creation, they also adopt a view of nature in which knowledge is linked to control and predictability. The forces of nature are understood to be distinct from the human subject; nature is purely material and mechanical. For René Descartes (1596–1650), this would be as true of animals as it was of ocean, wind, and fire. And like Francis Bacon (1560–1626) and others, Descartes not only believed that a correct methodology of learning would allow us to increase our knowledge but that such knowledge could be used to control and predict natural events.

> For these general notions show me that it is possible to arrive at knowledge that is very useful in life and that in place of the speculative philosophy taught in the Schools, one can find a practical one, by which, knowing the force and the actions of fire, water, air, stars, the heavens, and all the other bodies that surround us, just as we understand the various skills of our craftsmen, we could, in the same way, use these objects for all the purposes for which they are appropriate, and thus make ourselves, as it were, masters and possessors of nature.[4]

In many ways, the philosophical assumptions of Bacon and Descartes provide the background for modern science, technological innovation, and the Industrial Revolution.

Science and Technology

What is technology? And is its growth the result of scientific progress? In the modern era there is an important relation between science and technology, though it is important to recognize that scientific knowledge is not *essential* for technology. The enterprise of science seeks to discover and articulate the general principles for explaining and predicting the phenomena of the natural world. Any application of these principles to specific tasks, goals, and problems involves devising tools, devices, machines, and instruments of all kinds. Such implements are technological. However, we should not assume that the creation of technological artifacts *requires* scientific the-

---

4. *Discourse on the Method for Rightly Conducting One's Reason and for Seeking Truth in the Sciences* [1637], translated by Donald Cress (Indianapolis, Ind.: Hackett Publishing, 1993), Part Six (p. 35).

ory or expertise, even if such expertise may serve to increase the rate of technological discovery. Many technological achievements were brought about by trial and error and were dependent not on scientific principles or knowledge but on the nontheoretical knowledge and skill of ordinary workmen concerned with particular problems and tasks. Thus does Frederick Ferré conclude that technology should be defined in terms of "practical implementations of intelligence," thereby emphasizing the way in which technology "involves (i) implements used as (ii) means to practical ends that are somehow (iii) manifested in the material world as (iv) expressions of intelligence."[5]

Technology and the Market

A definition such as this may also help us to understand how institutional conditions may affect the rate of technological growth. Scientific knowledge spurs technological innovation, but the generation of such knowledge may require laws and institutions that permit scientific discussion, exploration, and experimentation. Moreover, if the laws and institutions also allow for individuals to create businesses and enterprises, then the persons in these firms can apply their intellects—whether informed by science or by personal experience—to the production of technologies that are tailored for practical purposes. Indeed, the economist F. A. Hayek (1899–1993) makes the argument that economic competition is an institutional means by which we can discover facts, techniques, needs, and opportunities which would otherwise be left unknown or produced at a higher cost and a slower pace.[6] Hayek suggests that we are ignorant of the wide variety of matters that must be known if a diversity of goods and services is to be produced as cheaply as possible. It is because of this ignorance—shared by *all* persons—that a system of experimentation is necessary by which we can draw upon the dispersed knowledge and skills of individuals working with differing goals, in diverse circumstances. Through experimentation at the level of the firm or by the individual, the research, manufacture, and sale of goods and services is encouraged most effectively. Establishing appropriate rules and laws that allow for competition is, therefore, to institutionalize a procedure for discovery and innovation.

Technology and the Technological Outlook

The growth of technology has brought new products to many, including items of necessity and of convenience. However, the emergence of technology has often raised worries. Some have associated the rise of technology and mass production with the demise of traditional crafts. Others have questioned whether or not the point of technological innovations was anything other than change itself. Commenting on the fabulous array of new machines on display at the International Exhibition of 1876, in Philadelphia, the biologist Thomas Henry Huxley exclaimed, "The great issue about which hangs a true sublimity, and the terror of overhanging fate, is what are you going to do with all these things?"[7] Such is one of the questions posed by Jacques Ellul, who asks of that particular kind of technology called gadgetry: Of what use is this?

Other thinkers have expressed concerns about the manner in which technology and, more important, technological thinking has affected our very outlook. Writing in the 1920s, Romano Guardini (1885–1968) distinguished between that form of human ingenuity which cooperates with nature and that which overcomes nature, the latter offering a drastic alteration in the very way in which we are situated within the world. Thus does Guardini differentiate between, for example, the sailing vessel and that vessel powered by an engine:

> It grieves me when I see built into one of these vessels, these noble creations, a gasoline engine, so that with upright mast but no sails the vessel clatters through the waves like a ghost of itself. Go even further and the sailing vessel becomes a steamer, a great ocean liner—culture indeed, a brilliant technological achievement! And yet a colossus of this type presses on through the sea regardless of wind and waves. It is so large that nature no longer has power over it; we can no longer see nature on it.[8]

The German philosopher Martin Heidegger (1889–1976) contends that the attitude typical of the modern individual is an *a priori* technological attitude according to which we approach nature as that which can be understood, controlled, and utilized for our purposes.[9] Similarly, Jacques Ellul maintains that technology, which he believes has its

5. Frederick Ferré, *Philosophy of Technology* (Englewood Cliffs, N.J.: Prentice Hall, 1988), 26 and 25, respectively.

6. See Hayek, "Competition as a Discovery Procedure," in *New Studies in Philosophy, Politics, Economics, and the History of Ideas* (Chicago: University of Chicago Press, 1978), 179–90.

7. As quoted in Daniel Boorstin, *The Republic of Technology: Reflections on Our Future Community* (New York: Harper & Row, 1978), 5.

8. *Letters from Lake Como: Explorations in Technology and the Human Race* [1926], translated by Geoffrey W. Bromiley (Grand Rapids, Mich.: William B. Eerdmans, 1994), 13. See also, Lewis Mumford, *Technics and Civilization* (New York: Harcourt, Brace, 1934).

9. See *The Question Concerning Technology,* translated by William Lovitt (New York: Harper & Row, 1977), 13–15.

own internal momentum and comes to encompass all spheres of society and all societies, carries with it the idea of organizational efficiency, the idea of *technique:*

> The term *technique,* as I use it, does not mean machines, technology, or this or that procedure for attaining an end. In our technological society, *technique* is the totality of methods rationally arrived at and having absolute efficiency (for a given stage of development) in every field of human activity. Its characteristics are new; the technique of the present has no common measure with that of the past.[10]

Modern Success

Despite these concerns, and cognizant of how the infatuation with technology may be symptomatic of *hubris,* it is, nonetheless, worth recalling that we have the benefit of considering the question of technology, and corollary questions concerning the natural environment, precisely *because* we have succeeded in controlling and predicting natural events. And this, it might be suggested, has been accomplished not through some wistful communion *with* nature but through analytical science, markets, experimentation, and technological innovation. Not only can we predict the weather, protect against a large number of diseases, grow food more efficiently than ever before, and live without fear of wild animals, but we also enjoy an extraordinary level of comfort and ease—from the use of refrigerators, heating systems, air conditioners, mechanized tools, automobiles, and household appliances—that is a direct result of the technology spawned from scientific advance and commercial exchange and production.[11]

KINDS OF ENVIRONMENTALISM

It is worth asking, nonetheless, whether these advances, if they are such, have come at a cost, one of which is the degradation of the natural environment. It is important to recognize that the claims of environmental destruction must be analyzed carefully. For the problems of the environment raise a host of questions, including these:

10. Jacques Ellul, *The Technological Society* (New York: Random House, 1967), xxv.

11. It is important to keep in mind that it is not at all obvious that all nonindustrial or pre-technological societies held some uniform view of nature that ensured that humans coexisted in harmony with the natural world. Although this may be true of some pre-technological societies, it is incorrect to think it true of all and it ignores the extent to which many of these societies were in fact destructive of nature. See Martin W. Lewis, *Green Delusions: An Environmental Critique of Radical Environmentalism* (Durham: Duke University Press, 1992), 59–81.

Scientific questions: Has some specific event or sequence occurred? (Or how probable is its occurrence?) To what extent is there damage? And what are the long-term consequences for human beings and for natural systems?

Ethical questions: What is the value of nature? Does nature have value only insofar as it is an instrument for human well-being?

Political questions: What institutional rules offer the best means of preserving natural resources, wildlife, or wilderness areas? Are regulations helpful? Should there be greater public control of lands? Or should we maintain or increase private control of land, resources, and animals?

Common Assumptions

It is often assumed that the institutions of property and exchange, which undergird markets and commerce, must be altered if we are to preserve and improve our prospects for living with nature, for if we allow private owners to engage in manufacture and commerce, then they will do so without regard to the condition of the natural environment or to the depletion of resources. However, some have argued that matters are, in fact, quite the reverse. Environmental degradation is much more likely to occur when ownership is not individual but collective (witness the degradation that occurred in the socialist nations of Eastern Europe and the Soviet Union); hence, the best way to protect the natural environment is to employ market incentives to encourage individuals to care about the air, land, and water around them.

It should be clear, then, that environmental problems are not merely scientific or technical but have a moral and political dimension. Moreover, it should be taken into account that there are no perfect solutions, that all policies have benefits as well as costs, and that just as there exists the possibility of "market failure," so does there exist the possibility of "government failure." To understand some of the distinct approaches to ameliorating environmental problems, let us distinguish three alternative perspectives on the proper relation between human beings and nature.

Three Perspectives

We can consider each of these distinct perspectives as responding to this question: Does nature have value only because of its relation to human beings, or is there an intrinsic value in natural organisms and natural systems that is *independent* of any human valuation or use? The human-centered or anthropocentric outlook understands the value of nature to be a function of, or dependent on, its value for human beings. On this view nature may have a very high value, but that value is not *intrinsic* to it but derives from some human end or purpose. The biocentric perspective (the "deep ecological" view) maintains that nature has an intrinsic value that is independent of any human value, purpose, or utility. Between these two kinds of environmentalism, one can discern an extension of the first, a position according to which some characteristic or property that gives human beings special standing is shared by (some) other creatures; because of this, the moral standing that human beings have should be extended to these creatures as well.[12] For example, the capacity to feel pain is shared by humans *and* animals. Thus, the architect of the theory of utilitarianism, Jeremy Bentham (1748–1832) argued that the most important moral quality is neither reason or free will—two characteristics that would pertain to human beings but not to most other creatures—but the capacity to feel pleasure or pain. Clearly, the extensionist point of view would encompass the sort of utilitarian moral criterion raised by Bentham and proffered more recently by Peter Singer.[13] However, the extensionist point of view does not, typically, take into account or allot moral standing to trees, rocks, and clouds.

Biocentrism

Of these three perspectives the most radical approach is offered by biocentrism. Articulated by a number of thinkers, including Aldo Leopold (1887–1948) and Arne Naess,[14] this point of view seeks to ground environmental issues in the axiom that the nonhuman has intrinsic value that is independent of human purposes; that part of this value includes the complex diversity of whole ecosystems; and that nonhuman creatures, objects, and ecosystems have moral standing. In addition, biocentrists "favour diversity of human ways of life, of cultures, of occupations, of economies. They support the fight against economic and cultural, as much as military, invasion and domination, and they are opposed to the annihilation of seals and whales as much as to that of human tribes or cultures."[15]

What should be obvious is that the biocentric view poses particular challenges to any religious outlook in which the human being is created in "the image of God," or to any secular philosophy that accords primacy to reason or to freedom of the will. And, indeed, what one typically encounters in the biocentric outlook is a more general rejection of the traditional Western outlook, if not modernity as a whole. Thus does Luc Ferry critically remark:

> Thus the humanist era is being brought to a close; and this is the main objective for these new zealots of nature. Its oddities aside . . . the debate on the rights of trees, islands, or rocks is based on no other grounds: it is a matter of determining whether the only legal subject is man, or whether, on the contrary, legal status should extend to what is today called the 'biosphere' or the 'ecosphere,' formerly known as the 'cosmos.' From every point of view—ethical, legal, or ontological—man would be but one element among others, and the least *sympathetic* one at that, being the least *symbiotic* with the harmonious and orderly universe into which he is constantly, by his excess, by his '*hubris*,' introducing the worst disorder.[16]

The biocentric point of view is often taken to be a point of view of the political left, but it has also proved attractive to some thinkers on the authoritarian right as well. Nonetheless, Hans Jonas (1903–1993), a philosopher whose thought has influenced many biocentrists, remarks that "only a maximum of politically imposed social discipline can ensure the subordination of present advantages to the long-term exigencies of the future," an imposition he believes is more likely under a Marxist than under a capitalist regime.[17] On the other hand, an anthropocentric point of view may include the perspective of contemporary environmentalists, including those who seek to improve the environment through legislative and regulatory efforts, but it may also include free-market environmentalists, who believe that many, if not all environmental problems are better dealt with via market mechanisms or property rights than through so-called "command and control" regulations.

12. The term "extensionism" is employed in J. Baird Callicott, "The Search for an Environmental Ethic," in *Matters of Life and Death: New Introductory Essays in Moral Philosophy*, 2d ed., edited by Tom Regan (New York: Random House, 1980), 392.

13. *Animal Liberation*, 2d ed. (New York: New York Review Book, 1990).

14. "[T]he equal right to live and blossom is an intuitively clear and obvious value axiom. Its restriction to humans is an anthropocentrism with detrimental effects upon the life quality of humans themselves. This quality depends in part upon the deep pleasure and satisfaction we receive from close partnership with other forms of life." Arne Naess, "The Shallow and the Deep, Long-Range Ecology Movement. A Summary," *Inquiry* 16 (1973): 96. Leopold, *A Sand County Almanac* (Oxford: Oxford University Press, 1949).

15. Naess, "The Shallow and the Deep. . . ," 96.

16. *The New Ecological Order*, translated by Carol Volk (Chicago: University of Chicago Press, 1995), xix–xx.

17. *The Imperative of Responsibility: In Search of an Ethics for the Technological Age* (Chicago: University of Chicago Press, 1984), 142.

MARKETS AND THE ENVIRONMENT

It is often assumed that the economic system of the market is to blame for most environmental problems. Thus, the first sentence in the introduction to one important collection of essays states that it is "widely known that western industrial nations are polluting their rivers, contaminating the soil, exterminating wildlife, and using up the world's natural resources." The author then proceeds to assert that this is a testament to "the failures of a social order in which technological policy has been determined more by private profit than by human welfare."[18] What is striking in such claims as these is not only that they seem to ignore the astonishing environmental degradation that has occurred in noncapitalist nations (whose economic systems have not been oriented toward profit), but that they also assume, without argument, that market institutions are to blame for environmental problems. However, it might be argued that the institutions of markets are precisely the best institutions for preserving the environment and avoiding harm to nature. To what extent are environmental problems understandable as economic problems or as related to economic institutions? To explore this question let us first summarize why someone might blame market institutions for environmental degradation and then summarize why someone might argue that market institutions are the best means for preserving and restoring the natural environment.

The Argument Against the Market

The basic argument against the market rests upon the idea that markets tend to allow owners to *use* their property as they wish, a fact that may allow one to destroy that part of nature under one's ownership (or to inflict harm against natural goods that one does not own). The market allows individuals to own land and resources and to use these as they see fit, perhaps thereby destroying a habitat, utilizing scarce resources, or altering the landscape in some detrimental fashion. More generally, individuals may pursue profits at the expense of the environment and at the expense of other persons, as when a manufacturing plant discharges sewage into a river or pollutes the air with smoke. On this view, it is not simply that one may alter or destroy the land or resources within one's control; it is also argued that market transactions allow businesses to affect, negatively, those who are not parties to their market transactions (negative externalities).

The Argument for the Market

In many ways the environmental argument for the market stresses the same points as the argument against, except that market environmentalism, as it is often called, emphasizes how commercial incentives may work to thwart or counteract actions destructive of air, land, water, and natural resources more generally. For example, in the case of negative externalities it is argued that there is no necessary connection between negative externalities and markets, for if property rights are in fact observed, then no two transacting parties should be permitted to affect negatively the person or property of a third party. The market defense may often appeal to property rights. For example, in the case of scarce resources the defender of the market contends that if persons have property rights in valuable resources, then they are eager to husband these resources for the future, much more willing to do so than would persons in a political office or in government administrative positions. In those instances or circumstances in which it is not possible to enact, enforce, or otherwise articulate property rights, it is contended that the correct resolution is one that takes advantage of the rules and incentives of human interaction within the marketplace.

To understand more fully the relation between markets and the environment, let us consider more carefully the central idea of market failure. For even if markets are very good at producing certain goods and services, are there circumstances in which markets might generate effects destructive of the natural environment? To answer this question economists typically refer to the idea of "market failure."

Market Failure

There are generally considered to be at least three major candidates for market failure: monopoly, public goods, and externalities, of which the latter two have particular relevance to questions concerning the environment. A public good is typically understood in terms of two attributes: nonexcludability and nonrivalrous consumption. (Rivalrous consumption occurs when one person's consumption of the good diminishes the availability of the good for others.) For example, even if the market is able to produce and sell "private goods" (those for which a nonpayer can be excluded and for which consumption is "rivalrous"), it is not clear that markets can produce (or

---

18. Ian Barbour, "Introduction," in *Western Man and Environmental Ethics,* edited by Ian Barbour (Reading, Mass.: Addison-Wesley, 1973), 1.

maintain) public goods—such as clean air—for which it is inefficient to exclude nonpayers and for which any number of consumers can enjoy the good. The features of nonexcludability and nonrivalrous consumption are relevant to understanding how it might be claimed that markets allow for the destruction of the environment, but we shall not assume that both features must be present to generate an environmental problem. For as we will see, even if a good is not, strictly speaking, a public good which exhibits *both* attributes, any good which merely exhibits the property of nonexcludability may generate significant environmental problems. To see how this might be so, we must consider the classic case of a "commons."

The Tragedy of the Commons

We can think of a "commons" as a good that exhibits nonexcludability but is rivalrous, for, it is not possible for all who wish to do so to enjoy the goods of the commons. In a famous article, Garrett Hardin describes "the tragedy of the commons."

> Picture a pasture open to all. It is to be expected that each herdsman will try to keep as many cattle as possible on the commons. Such an arrangement may work reasonably satisfactorily for centuries because tribal wars, poaching, and disease keep the numbers of both man and beast well below the carrying capacity of the land. Finally, however, comes the day of reckoning, that is, the day when the long-desired goal of social stability becomes a reality. At this point, the inherent logic of the commons remorselessly generates tragedy.
>
> . . . [T]he rational herdsman concludes that the only sensible course for him to pursue is to add another animal to his herd. And another; and another. . . . But this is the conclusion reached by each and every rational herdsman sharing a commons. Therein is the tragedy. Each man is locked into a system that compels him to increase his herd without limit—in a world that is limited.[19]

What does Hardin's story imply? Each shepherd is acting independent of all other shepherds, and so there are no relations among the shepherds that might regulate their conduct. As a result, each shepherd finds it to be in his interest to add another sheep to the land, but each shepherd concludes the same. Thus each adds sheep and, as a result, overfeeding occurs, thereby ruining the commons for all. To solve the problem of the commons there must be some system of excludability; in other words, some system of rationing is needed, either via property rights or some other norms or institutions.

19. Garrett Hardin, "The Tragedy of the Commons," *Science* (13 December 1968): 1244.

The Commons and the Environment

How does the commons mirror certain problems of the environment? Consider that in the case of the shepherds, nonexcludability produces an overusage of the commons. The phenomena of the commons might appear in the case of the open seas in which there arise problems of overfishing and resource depletion. However, the problem of the commons might also appear in the case of water and air pollution, because the problem of nonexcludability may arise here as well. Because there are no rules, norms, or institutions of excludability, individuals find it in their interests to dump or discharge their pollutants into the commons of a river or that of the atmosphere.

PROTECTING THE ENVIRONMENT

Norms and Agreements

One proposal for counteracting the tragedy of the commons recommends that individuals behave according to moral norms that would limit the use of the commons so as to benefit, for example, either the greatest number or the most deserving. Some have argued that where there are small groups with iterated contacts, such norms could emerge spontaneously, thereby averting the conditions for a tragedy of the commons. That such norms might evolve is not impossible, though it is not clear whether they would persist, at least without government enforcement, in any large group with anonymous interactions. For example, individuals might seek to limit their use of the commons through some sort of reciprocal agreement; however, when businesses and industries have attempted to do this they have often run afoul of antitrust provisions of the law. A notable instance of this was brought to court, *Gulf Coast Shrimpers and Oystermans Association v. United States* (1956), after a group of fishermen had sought to conserve the harvest of fish by limiting the numbers of fishermen. The fishermen claimed conservation but the government charged, via the Sherman Antitrust act, that theirs was an effort to monopolize markets.[20]

Prohibitions, Regulations, Taxes

Are there other policies for dealing with the problems of the commons? One option is simply to ban all activity in the commons or to ban any activity beyond a certain threshold. However, these prohibitions come at a high

20. For an interesting account of this case, sympathetic to the fishermen's plea of conservation, see Bruce Yandle, "Antitrust and the Commons: Cooperation or Collusion?" *The Independent Review* 3 (Summer 1998): 37–52.

cost, not only because any such bans will be difficult to enforce but because any *successful* enforcement might ban industrial activities that are productive of necessary goods. A second, and not always successful, option is some form of regulation that seeks to limit externalities either by directly limiting their output or by indirectly prescribing a certain process of production, the effect of which is to limit the externalities. This alternative, which often sets stiffer standards for new entrants to the market than for current producers, may serve as a barrier to entry or, more generally, as a means by which a current industry may seek to thwart potential competition. A third and interesting alternative is one that seeks to use the incentives of the market, as well as the pricing mechanism, to ameliorate environmental problems. This alternative may involve levying a tax on the producer of the externality sufficient to cover the cost imposed on others. This option would not mean the end of the externality, but, if successful, it would reduce pollution to the point at which it costs the polluter more in pollution taxes than is gained by selling the products that generate the side-effect of pollution. Thus, if we consider the air to be a commons, then we could levy taxes or set a price on air pollution. In the readings that follow, Larry Ruff offers one possible means of doing so.

Property Rights and Negative Externalities

Another solution to the problem of the commons is to convert the commons from collective to private ownership. Property rights limit the commons, as John Locke (1632–1704) points out in his *Second Treatise of Government*,[21] but it is precisely the limits on use that allow for a greater good for all. It can be argued that the very absence of clearly defined ownership rights generates both the problem of the commons and allows for the occurrence of negative externalities. The externality occurs insofar as the effects of the exchange are not contained or internalized to the transacting parties. If there are effects that are external to the transaction, then the transacting parties do not bear all of the costs or benefits of the exchange, and thus neither party is taking into account all of the costs which actually occur.

Thus, pollution can also be understood as a negative externality, for an industry whose pollutants affect third parties is an industry whose goods are priced to cover only the internal but not the external cost. Some have suggested that externalities result because property rights are not clearly defined or consistently enforced. Note that there are two alternative approaches to the matter of property rights. R. H. Coase has argued[22] that in the case of externalities it simply does not matter to whom the property rights are assigned. This may sound surprising, but Coase argues that whoever receives the right—whether it is a right to impose costs or whether it is the right to be free of some externality—is irrelevant so long as the individuals could then bargain over the cost (or price) of allowing an externality, thereby achieving an efficient outcome. An alternative property rights approach would also allow bargaining, but this approach holds that the original assignation of property rights is not irrelevant but should be decided on the basis of justice.[23]

Preserving and Privatizing

The property rights approach to overcoming the conditions of the commons (or that of externalities) is problematical in those areas for which we do not have clear intuitions or indications about how to define or articulate property rights. Such cases would include rights to air and water, for example. Nonetheless, that does not mean that the property rights approach is unworkable, for it might be possible for such rights to evolve if there are no legal or institutional barriers to establishing such.[24] However, one might argue that we do not want to establish property rights over nature; that doing so is a precise expression of valuing nature only in terms of human desires and values. For example, even if there is evidence that private ownership of wildlife offers a means of protecting and preserving creatures which might otherwise be destroyed,[25] one might argue that the very act of *owning* wild animals alters our relationship to the animals in such a way that we destroy the very value which we seek to preserve. For if nature, in particular wild animals, can be owned, then an

---

21. "God gave the world to men in common; but since he gave it to them for their benefit and for the greatest conveniences of life they were capable to draw from it, it cannot be supposed he meant it should always remain common and uncultivated." *Second Treatise of Government* [1689–1690], edited by C. B. MacPherson (Indianapolis, Ind.: Hackett Publishing, 1980) chapter V, § 34.

22. "The Problem of Social Cost," *Journal of Law and Economics* 3 (October 1960): 1–45.

23. See, for example, Murray Rothbard, "Law, Property Rights, and Air Pollution," *The Cato Journal* 2 (Spring 1982): 55–99.

24. A discussion of the property rights approach can be found in Terry L. Anderson and Donald R. Leal, *Free Market Environmentalism* (San Francisco: Pacific Research Institute for Public Policy, 1991), esp. 24–36.

25. Terry L. Anderson and Peter J. Hill, editors, *Wildlife in the Marketplace* (Lanham, Md.: Roman and Littlefield, 1995).

essential aspect of their status has been destroyed, namely, that they are *wild* animals which are *unowned*.

It should be clear that whether one adopts the view of regulation, pricing, or property rights, one cannot expect a perfect solution to the problems we encounter as human beings acting within the natural system. To consider these matters more fully, we turn, in the readings which follow, to two opposing views about the promise of technology. Subsequent to these readings we examine problems of environmental ethics. The first of the readings on the environment forwards the view that nature should not be valued only insofar as it contributes to human wishes; in the second of the readings on the environment, we turn to an economist's account of how we might ameliorate the problems of pollution by using the incentives of the market. The last reading offers a provocative challenge to the widespread view that our resources are finite and diminishing.

THE READINGS

Emmanuel G. Mesthene   Mesthene contends that our age is distinguished by the amount of physical power available to us and the fact that we are consciously aware of that power. For millennia nature had exerted its power over human thought and action, but now invention and technology create new possibilities, giving us more freedom and the opportunity to "be more human." However, even if technology is liberating, many are fearful of it. Technology may not only destroy some values but it may also reveal the hidden brutality of much of human experience and complicate the world by extending to us greater opportunities for choice. These negative concerns should not give way to despair or irrational fear. In fact we should not want to discontinue scientific and technological inquiry because we are human beings who have an innate desire to learn. The moral question that confronts us is this: How are we to use our knowledge to render our lives good?

Jacques Ellul   Ellul asks about the use of the new gadgets on which we seem to be so reliant. Drawing a distinction between basic and natural needs and those which are secondary and artificial, Ellul contends that "technique" (the idea of rational and efficient procedure) has brought about the multiplication of our needs and has rendered happiness more difficult to achieve. What are some of the objects to which we assert a need? These gadgets range from quartz watches, to flat screen televisions, to computers. Although Ellul recognizes that the computer has some useful operations, it may also serve to reinforce

centralized power (without serving as a catalyst for freedom or nonconformity). The computer cannot substitute for human judgment and decision making, and serves to render society more rather than less vulnerable.

W. Michael Hoffman   Asserting that there are "ominous" signs of environmental degradation, Hoffman suggests that any environmental policy debate must focus on three questions: the obligations of business, the proper relationship between business and government, and the rationale for protecting the environment. In Hoffman's view, corporations have expertise on environmental problems and an ethical responsibility to to do more than to merely follow the current environmental laws. What standard or criterion would justify the responsibility of business? Although Hoffman doesn't oppose the movement to ensure that environmental policy is compatible with profit-making enterprise, he nonetheless holds that this view may be dangerous for environmental ethics. Ethics may require "that we place the interests of others ahead of or at least on par with our own interests." Moral action should not be identified with or reduced to acting in our private interests. What is the underlying rationale for responsible behavior to the environment? Hoffman maintains that instead of maintaining an anthropocentric (or homocentric) outlook, we should adopt a biocentric ethic which holds that things other than human beings have intrinsic value. Environmental arguments which favor only human interests may diminish the sense of obligation which originally animated the concern for the environment.

Larry E. Ruff   In Ruff's view the problem of pollution must be treated as an economic problem. There are two key ideas in economics, *marginalism* and the self-regulating market. The concept of *marginalism* involves comparing additional costs to additional benefits, with the aim of discovering that point at which the net gain from some activity is maximized, namely, that point at which the marginal cost for expanding the activity equals the marginal benefit. To apply the ideas of marginalism to pollution is to ask at what point the costs of abating pollution exceed the benefits. A self-regulating market is one in which prices convey sufficient information for everyone to act in such a way that marginal costs equal marginal benefits. In the case of pollution, however, certain prices do not reflect the total costs of the polluting activity, and this inefficiency "*is the fundamental cause of pollution of all types.*" If we could make an estimate of the social cost of pollution, then we would need to make another estimate of the costs of pollution abatement. These could be estimated by a Pollution Control Board that determines the costs of abatement for each source of pollution, finally determining that point at which the marginal costs of abatement equal the benefit of less pollution. Once the optimal level of pollution is determined then the Pollution Control Board would need to impose a price on any pollution that approximated the marginal social cost. Polluters will then make adjustments in their pollution until any further reduction costs more than the price of the pollution.

Julian L. Simon   It is a common assumption that natural resources are finite and should, therefore, be conserved, but Simon argues the counterintuitive claim that there is no meaningful economic sense in which resources could be asserted to be finite. For example, if Alpha Crusoe, who has a single copper mine on an island, continues to use and make items of copper, then the copper in the mine will become more difficult to get because it will be deeper in the ground. If we assume that Crusoe does not recycle and if we introduce a second person on the island, then copper becomes more scarce unless they can mine more efficiently, look for new lodes, discover new methods of obtaining copper from the original mine, or find a copper substitute. However, these inventions or discoveries result from the very shortage of copper; its increased cost motivates a more efficient use of the mineral. "So increased scarcity causes the development of its own remedy," and thus a more efficient use of a resource effectively increases the stock of the unused resource, just as the discovery of a substitute resource is a positive benefit (or externality) for future generations. In sum, a short term scarcity of resources causes their prices to rise, which offers an incentive to inventors and discoverers to search for solutions, after which the price of the previously scarce resource is reduced. Simon also suggests that we should conceptualize natural resources in terms of their services, and since we cannot make any appropriate count of the services that we might obtain from a resource, these services should not be considered finite.

Technology and Wisdom

Emmanuel G. Mesthene

Emmanuel G. Mesthene (1920–1990) served as the Director of the Harvard Program on Technology and Society from 1964 to 1974, subsequently serving as Dean of Livingston College of Rutgers University, and as a professor of philosophy and of management. He is the author of Technological Change: Its Impact on Man and Society *(1970) as well as other books and articles.*

My objective is to suggest some of the broader implications of what is new about our age. It might be well to start, therefore, by noting what is new about our age.

The fact itself that there is something new is not new. There has been something new about every age, otherwise we would not be able to distinguish them in history. What we need to examine is what in particular is new about our age, for the new is not less new just because the old was also at one time new.

The mere prominence in our age of science and technology is not strikingly new, either. A veritable explosion of industrial technology gave its name to a whole age two centuries ago, and it is doubtful that any scientific idea will ever again leave an imprint on the world so penetrating and pervasive as did Isaac Newton's a century before that.

It is not clear, finally, that what is new about our age is the rate at which it changes. What partial evidence we have, in the restricted domain of economics, for example, indicates the contrary. The curve of growth, for the hundred years or so that it can be traced, is smooth, and will not support claims of explosive change or discontinuous rise. For the rest, we lack the stability of concept, the precision of intellectual method, and the necessary data to make any reliable statements about the rate of social change in general.

I would, therefore, hold suspect all argument that purports to show that novelty is new with us, or that major scientific and technological influences are new with us, or that rapidity of social change is new with us. Such assertions, I think, derive more from revolutionary fervor and the wish to persuade than from tested knowledge and the desire to instruct.

Yet there is clearly something new, and its implications are important. I think our age is different from all previous ages in two major respects: first, we dispose, in absolute terms, of a staggering amount of physical power; second, and most important, we are beginning to think and act in conscious realization of that fact. We are therefore the first age who can aspire to be free of the tyranny of physical nature that has plagued man since his beginnings.

I

The consciousness of physical impossibility has had a long and depressing history. One might speculate that it began with early man's awe of the bruteness and recalcitrance of nature. Earth, air, fire, and water—the eternal, immutable elements of ancient physics—imposed their requirements on men, dwarfed them, outlived them, remained indifferent when not downright hostile to them. The physical world loomed large in the affairs of men, and men were impotent against it. Homer celebrated this fact by investing nature with gods, and the earliest philosophers recognized it by erecting each of the natural elements in turn—water, air, earth, and fire—into fundamental principles of all existence.

From that day to this, only the language has changed as successive ages encountered and tried to come to terms with physical necessity, with the sheer "rock-bottomness" of nature. It was submitted to as fate in the Athenian drama. It was conceptualized as ignorance by Socrates and as metaphysical matter by his pupils. It was labeled evil by the pre-Christians. It has been exorcised as the Devil, damned as flesh, or condemned as illicit by the Church. It has been the principle of nonreason in modern philosophy, in the form of John Locke's Substance, as Immanuel Kant's formless manifold, or as Henri Bergson's pure duration. It has conquered the mystic as nirvana, the psyche as the Id, and recent Frenchmen as the blind object of existential commitment.

What men have been saying in all these different ways is that physical nature has seemed to have a structure, almost a will of its own, that has not yielded easily to the designs and purposes of man. It has been a brute thereness, a residual, a sort of ultimate existential stage that allowed, but also limited, the play of thought and action.

It would be difficult to overestimate the consequences of this recalcitrance of the physical on the thinking and outlook of men. They have learned, for most of history, to plan and act *around* a permanent realm of impossibility. Man could travel on the sea, by sail or oar or breast stroke. But he could not travel *in* the sea. He could cross the land on foot, on horseback, or by wheel, but he could not fly over it. Legends such as those of Daedalus and Poseidon celebrated in art what men could not aspire to in fact.

Thinking was similarly circumscribed. There were myriad possibilities in existence, but they were not unlimited, because they did not include altering the physical structure of existence itself. Man could in principle know all that was possible, once and for all time. What else but this possibility of complete knowledge does Plato name in his Idea of the Good ? The task of thought was to discern and compare and select from among this fixed and eternal realm of possibilities. Its options did not extend beyond it, anymore than the chess player's options extend beyond those allowed by the board and

the pieces of his game. There was a natural law, men said, to which all human law was forever subservient, and which fixed the patterns and habits of what was thinkable.

There was, occasionally, an invention during all this time that did induce a physical change. It thus made something new possible, like adding a pawn to the chess game. New physical possibilities are the result of invention; of technology, as we call it today. That is what *invention* and *technology* mean. Every invention, from the wheel to the rocket, has created new possibilities that did not exist before. But inventions in the past were few, rare, exceptional, and marvelous. They were unexpected departures from the norm. They were surprises that societies adjusted to after the fact. They were generally infrequent enough, moreover, so that the adjustments could be made slowly and unconsciously, without radical alteration of world views, or of traditional patterns of thought and action. The Industrial Revolution, as we call it, was revolutionary precisely because it ran into attitudes, values, and habits of thought and action that were completely unprepared to understand, accept, absorb, and change with it.

Today, if I may put it paradoxically, technology is becoming less revolutionary, as we recognize and seek after the power that it gives us. Inventions are now many, frequent, planned, and increasingly taken for granted. We were not a bit surprised when we got to the moon. On the contrary, we would have been very surprised if we had not. We are beginning to use invention as a deliberate way to deal with the future, rather than seeing it only as an uncontrolled disrupting of the present. We no longer wait upon invention to occur accidentally. We foster and force it, because we see it as a way out of the heretofore inviolable constraints that physical nature has imposed upon us in the past.

Francis Bacon, in the sixteenth century, was the first to foresee the physical power potential in scientific knowledge. We are the first, I am suggesting, to have enough of that power actually at hand to create new possibilities almost at will. By massive physical changes deliberately induced, we can literally pry new alternatives out of nature. The ancient tyranny of matter has been broken, and we know it. We found, in the seventeenth century, that the physical world was not at all like what Aristotle had thought and Aquinas had taught. We are today coming to the further realization that the physical world need not be as it is. We can change it and shape it to suit our purposes.

Technology, in short, has come of age, not merely as technical capability, but as a social phenomenon. We have the power to create new possibilities, and the will to do so. By creating new possibilities, we give ourselves more choices. With more choices, we have more opportunities. With more opportunities, we can have more freedom, and with more freedom we can be more human. That, I think, is what is new about our age. We are recognizing that our technical prowess literally bursts with the promise of new freedom, enhanced human dignity, and unfettered aspiration. Belatedly, we are also realizing the new opportunities that technological development offers us to make new and potentially big mistakes.

II

At its best, then, technology is nothing if not liberating. Yet many fear it increasingly as enslaving, degrading, and destructive of man's most cherished values. It is important to note that this is so, and to try to understand why. I can think of four reasons.

First, we must not blink at the fact that technology does indeed destroy some values. It creates a million possibilities heretofore undreamed of, but it also makes impossible some others heretofore enjoyed. The automobile makes real the legendary foreign land, but it also makes legendary the once real values of the ancient market place. Mass production puts Bach and Brueghel in every home, but it also deprives the careful craftsman of a market for the skill and pride he puts into his useful artifact. Modern plumbing destroys the village pump, and modern cities are hostile to the desire to sink roots into and grow upon a piece of land. Some values are unquestionably bygone. To try to restore them is futile, and simply to deplore their loss is sterile. But it is perfectly human to regret them.

Second, technology often reveals what technology has not created: the cost in brutalized human labor, for example, of the few cases of past civilization whose values only a small elite could enjoy. Communications now reveal the hidden and make the secret public. Transportation displays the better to those whose lot has been the worse. Increasing productivity buys more education, so that more people read and learn and compare and hope and are unsatisfied. Thus technology often seems the final straw, when it is only illuminating rather than adding to the human burden.

Third, technology might be deemed an evil, because evil is unquestionably potential in it. We can explore the heavens with it, or destroy the world. We can cure disease, or poison entire populations. We can free enslaved millions, or enslave millions more. Technology spells only possibility, and is in that respect neutral.

Its massive power can lead to massive error so efficiently perpetrated as to be well-nigh irreversible. Technology is clearly not synonymous with the good. It *can* lead to evil.

Finally, and in a sense most revealing, technology is upsetting, because it complicates the world. This is a vague concern, hard to pin down, but I think it is a real one. The new alternatives that technology creates require effort to examine, understand, and evaluate them. We are offered more choices, which makes choosing more difficult. We are faced with the need to change, which upsets routines, inhibits reliance on habit, and calls for personal readjustments to more flexible postures. We face dangers that call for constant re-examination of values and a readiness to abandon old commitments for new ones more adequate to changing experience. The whole business of living seems to become harder.

This negative face of technology is sometimes confused with the whole of it. It can then cloud the understanding in two respects that are worth noting. It can lead to a generalized distrust of the power and works of the human mind by erecting a false dichotomy between the modern scientific and technological enterprises, on the one hand, and some idealized and static prescientific conception of human values, on the other. It can also color discussion of some important contemporary issues, that develop from the impact of technology on society, in a way that obscures rather than enhances understanding, and that therefore inhibits rather than facilitates the social action necessary to resolve them.

Because the confusions and discomfort attendant on technology are more immediate and therefore sometimes loom larger than its power and its promise, technology appears to some an alien and hostile trespasser upon the human scene. It thus seems indistinguishable from that other, older alien and hostile trespasser; the ultimate and unbreachable physical necessity of which I have spoken. Then, since habit dies hard, there occurs one of those curious inversions of the imagination that are not unknown to history. Our new-found control over nature is seen as but the latest form of the tyranny of nature. The knowledge and therefore the mastery of the physical world that we have gained, the tools that we have hewed from nature and the human wonders we are building into her, are themselves feared as rampant, uncontrollable, impersonal technique that must surely, we are told, end by robbing us of our livelihood, our freedom, and our humanity.

It is not an unfamiliar syndrome. It is reminiscent of the long-term prisoner who may shrink from the responsibility of freedom in preference for the false security of his accustomed cell. It is reminiscent even more of Socrates, who asked about that other prisoner, in the cave of ignorance, whether his eyes would not ache if he were forced to look upon the light of knowledge, "so that he would try to escape and turn back to the things which he could see distinctly, convinced that they really were clearer than these other objects now being shown to him." Is it so different a form of escapism from that, to ascribe impersonality and hostility to the knowledge and the tools that can free us finally from the age-long impersonality and hostility of a recalcitrant physical nature?

Technology has *two* faces: one that is full of promise, and one that can discourage and defeat us. The freedom that our power implies from the traditional tyranny of matter—from the evil we have known—carries with it the added responsibility and burden of learning to deal with matter and to blunt the evil, along with all the other problems we have always had to deal with. That is another way of saying that more power and more choice and more freedom require more wisdom if they are to add up to more humanity. But that, surely, is a challenge to be wise, not an invitation to despair.

An attitude of despair can also, as I have suggested, color particular understandings of particular problems, and thus obstruct intelligent action. I think, for example, that it has distorted the public debate about the effects of technology on work and employment.

The problem has persistently taken the form of fear that machines will put people permanently out of work. That fear has prevented recognition of a distinction between two fundamentally different questions. The first is a question of economic analysis and economic and manpower policy about which a great deal is known, which is susceptible to analysis by well-developed and rigorous methods, and on the dimensions and implications of which there is a very high degree of consensus among the professionally competent.

That consensus is that there is not much that is significantly new in the probable consequences of automation on employment. Automation is but the latest form of mechanization, which has been recognized as an important factor in economic change at least since the Industrial Revolution. What *is* new is a heightened social awareness of the implications of machines for men, which derives from the unprecedented scale, prevalence, and visibility of modern technological innovation. That is the second question. It, too, is a question of work, to be sure, but it is not one of employment in the economic connotation of the term. It is a distinct question, that has been too often confused with the economic

one because it has been formulated, incorrectly, as a question of automation and employment.

This question is much less a question of whether people will be employed than of what they can most usefully do, given the broader range of choices that technology can make available to them. It is less a technical economic question than a question of the values and quality of work. It is not a question of what to do with increasing leisure, but of how to define new occupations that combine social utility and personal satisfaction.

I see no evidence, in other words, that society will need less work done on some day in the future when machines may be largely satisfying its material needs, or that it will not value and reward that work. But we are, first, a long way still from that day, so long as there remain societies less affluent than the most affluent. Second, there is a work of education, integration, creation, and eradication of disease and discontent to do that is barely tapped so long as most people must labor to produce the goods that we consume. The more machines can take over what we do, the more we can do what machines cannot do. That, too, is liberation: the liberation of history's slaves, finally to be people. . . .

III

Such basically irrational fears of technology have a counterpart in popular fears of science itself. Here, too, anticipatory despair in the face of some genuine problems posed by science and technology can cloud the understanding.

It is admittedly horrible, for example, to contemplate the unintentional evil implicit in the ignorance and fallibility of man as he strives to control his environment and improve his lot. What untoward effects might our grandchildren suffer from the drugs that cure our ills today? What monsters might we breed unwittingly while we are learning to manipulate the genetic code? What are the tensions on the human psyche of a cold and rapid automated world? What political disaster do we court by providing 1984's Big Brother with all the tools he will ever need? Better, perhaps, in Hamlet's words, to

> . . . bear those ills we have
> Than fly to others that we know not of.

Why not stop it all? Stop automation! Stop tampering with life and heredity! Stop the senseless race into space! The cry is an old one. It was first heard, no doubt, when the wheel was invented. The technologies of the bomb, the automobile, the spinning jenny, gunpowder, printing, all provoked social dislocation accompanied by similar cries of "Stop!" Well, but why not stop now, while there may still be a minute left before the clock strikes twelve?

We do not stop, I think, for three reasons: we do not want to; we cannot, and still be men; and we therefore should not.

It is not at all clear that atom bombs will kill more people than wars have ever done, but energy from the atom might one day erase the frightening gap between the more and less favored peoples of the world. Was it more tragic to infect a hundred children with a faulty polio vaccine than to have allowed the scourge free reign forever? It is not clear that the monster that the laboratory may create, in searching the secret of life, will be more monstrous than those that nature will produce unaided if its secrets remain forever hidden. Is it really clear that rampant multiplication is a better ultimate fate for man than to suffer, but eventually survive, the mistakes that go with learning? The first reason we do not stop is that I do not think we would decide, on close examination, that we really want to.

The second reason is that we cannot so long as we are men. Aristotle saw a long time ago that "man by nature desires to know." He will probe and learn all that his curiosity prompts him to and his brain allows, so long as there is life within him. The stoppers of the past have always lost in the end, whether it was Socrates, or Christ, or Galileo, or Einstein, or Bonhoeffer, or Boris Pasternak they tried to stop. Their intended victims are the heroes.

We do not stop, finally, because we would not stop being men. I do not believe that even those who decry science the loudest would willingly concede that the race has now been proved incapable of coping with its own creations. That admission would be the ultimate in dehumanization, for it would be to surrender the very qualities of intelligence, courage, vision, and aspiration that make us human. "Stop," in the end, is the last desperate cry of the man who abandons man because he is defeated by the responsibility of being human. It is the final failure of nerve.

I am recalling that celebrated phrase, "the failure of nerve," in order to introduce a third and final example of how fear and pessimism can color understanding and confuse our values. It is the example of those who see the sin of pride in man's confident mastery of nature. I have dealt with this theme before, but I permit myself to review it briefly once more, because it points up the real meaning of technology for our age.

The phrase, "the failure of nerve," was first used by the eminent classical scholar, Gilbert Murray, to characterize the change of temper that occurred in Hellenistic civilization at the turn of our era. The Greeks of the fifth and fourth centuries B.C. believed in the ultimate intelligibility of the universe. There was nothing in the nature of existence or of man that was inherently unknowable. They accordingly believed also in the power of the human intelligence to know all there was to know about the world, and to guide man's career in it.

The wars and mixing of cultures that marked the subsequent period brought with them vicissitude and uncertainty that shook this classic faith in the intelligibility of the world and in the capacity of men to know and to do. There was henceforth to be a realm of knowledge and action available only to God, not subjected to reason or to human effort. Men, in other words, more and more turned to God to do for them what they no longer felt confident to do for themselves. That was the failure of nerve.

The burden of what I have been saying is that times are changing. We have the power and will to probe and change physical nature. No longer are God, the human soul, or the mysteries of life improper objects of inquiry. We are ready to examine whatever our imagination prompts us to. We are convinced again, for the first time since the Greeks, of the essential intelligibility of the universe: there is nothing in it that is in principle not knowable. As the sociologist Daniel Bell has put it, "Today we feel that there are no inherent secrets in the universe, and this is one of the significant changes in the modern moral temper." That is another way of stating what is new about our age. We are witnessing a widespread recovery of nerve.

Is this confidence a sin? According to Gilbert Murray, most people "are inclined to believe that without some failure and sense of failure, without a contrite heart and conviction of sin, man can hardly attain the religious life." I would suspect that this statement is still true of most people, although it is clear that a number of contemporary theologians are coming to a different view. To see a sense of failure as a condition of religious experience is a historical relic, dating from a time when an indifferent nature and hostile world so overwhelmed men that they gave up thought for consolation. To persist in such a view today, when nature is coming increasingly under control as a result of restored human confidence and power, is both to distort reality and to sell religion short. It surely does no glory to God to rest his power on the impotence of man.

The challenge of our restored faith in knowledge and the power of knowledge is rather a challenge to wisdom—not to God.

Some who have seen farthest and most clearly in recent decades have warned of a growing imbalance between man's capabilities in the physical and in the social realms. John Dewey, for example, said: "We have displayed enough intelligence in the physical field to create the new and powerful instrument of science and technology. We have not as yet had enough intelligence to use this instrument deliberately and systematically to control its social operations and consequences." Dewey said this more than thirty years ago, before television, before atomic power, before electronic computers, before space satellites. He had been saying it, moreover, for at least thirty years before that. He saw early the problems that would arise when man learned to do anything he wanted before he learned what he wanted.

I think the time Dewey warned about is here. My more thoughtful scientific friends tell me that we now have, or know how to acquire, the technical capability to do very nearly anything we want. Can we . . . control our biology and our personality, order the weather that suits us, travel to Mars or to Venus? Of course we can, if not now or in five or ten years, then certainly in twenty-five, or in fifty or a hundred.

But if the answer to the question What can we do? is "Anything," then the emphasis shifts far more heavily than before onto the question What should we do? The commitment to universal intelligibility entails moral responsibility. Abandonment of the belief in intelligibility two thousand years ago was justly described as a failure of nerve because it was the prelude to moral surrender. Men gave up the effort to be wise because they found it too hard. Renewed belief in intelligibility two thousand years later means that men must take up again the hard work of becoming wise. And it is much harder work now, because we have so much more power than the Greeks. On the other hand, the benefits of wisdom are potentially greater, too, because we have the means at hand to *make* the good life, right here and now, rather than just to go on contemplating it in Plato's heaven.

The question What should we do? is thus no idle one but challenges each one of us. That, I think, is the principal moral implication of our new world. It is what all the shouting is about in the mounting concern about the relations of science and public policy, and about the impact of technology on society. Our almost total mastery of the physical world entails a challenge to the public intelligence of a degree heretofore unknown in history.

QUESTIONS ON MESTHENE

1. How would you characterize Mesthene's understanding of the very idea of "technology"? In what ways is our age different from previous ages and how is this a result of technology?

2. What are some of the reasons that people fear technology? What are the "two faces" of technology? How does Mesthene attempt to connect technology and wisdom? What sort of institutions might be needed if this wisdom is to be realized or employed?

3. Why does Mesthene claim that we cannot stop the progress of science and technology? Do you agree that "there is nothing in it [the universe] that is in principle not knowable"?

What Use? The World of Gadgets

Jacques Ellul

Jacques Ellul (1912–1994) was a Professor of the History of Law at the University of Bordeaux. The author of some forty books and hundreds of articles, Ellul was a Marxist who became a Christian. His main concern is the threat to freedom and to religion via the forces of technology. His most important work is The Technological Society *(1964). This excerpt is from* The Technological Bluff *(1988).*

When I was twenty years old, the question that I am asking in this chapter—"What use?"—was for me the horror of horrors. In the period from 1925 to 1935 only the abominable middle class, which was materialistic in fact though idealistic in word, incessantly asked and repeated this question. Everywhere I came up against their triumphant logic: poetry, art—what good are they? They could admire Picasso because his work was beginning to sell at high prices. But history and Latin—what use are they? We must certainly learn to count; that makes sense. But change society? To what end? This was the question of the philistine. The important thing then was to find a place in society. Being red or leftist not only served no useful purpose; it was definitely bad. "What use?" was the absurdly triumphant question of a middle class which no longer believed either in values or in God, which had a positive but no less limited spirit, and which regarded the making of money as the only useful activity. Anything that might contribute to this was useful; the rest was of no account.

By way of reaction I was one of the generation that was greatly influenced by the surrealists and by Gide, who proclaimed the value of gratuitous acts, which were of value simply because they served no useful purpose and had neither origin nor goal but *were* simply because they *were*. All this prepared the ground for existentialism and the philosophy of the absurd. But at that time we had to crush the dreadful mentality of vulgar utilitarianism. A little later, however, I myself had to put the same question but from a different angle. The first time the issue was faster trains and automobiles. When meeting a man who had driven 100 kilometers per hour (in 1928) and cut fifteen minutes off some journey, I asked him what he had done with the fifteen minutes that he had saved. He looked at me with astonishment. Then when I heard that the Concorde had cut four hours off the flight across the Atlantic, or that the high-speed train had saved two hours on the run from Paris to Lyons, I asked again what people were doing with the time that they saved. Were they beginning a symphony or a sonnet, or thinking up a new experiment in chemistry? Were they simply enjoying the freedom of a stroll with no particular goal but in all the joy of liberty? But no one was ever able to give me any answer. They had perhaps taken a drink but in effect they had done nothing and had no vital experience. They had simply filled up the time in an empty and insignificant way. Or else they had profited by the time saved, as when a busy executive might squeeze three interviews into a heavy schedule, thus hastening the day of his or her heart attack. And always with the anxious proviso to the very end of the journey that the airplane or train had to arrive on time!

The time saved is empty time. I am not denying that on rare occasions speed might be of use, for example, to save an injured person, or to rejoin a loved one, or to go back to one's family, or for the sake of peace in a decisive meeting. But how few are the times when it is really necessary to save time. The truth is that going fast has become a value on its own, as is now acknowledged. What we have here is *L'homme pressé,* as P. Morand so well describes him, but not really "pressed" by anything. The media extol every gain in speed as a success, and the public accepts it as such. But experience shows that the more time we save, the less we have. The faster we go, the more harassed we are. What use is it? Fundamentally, none. I know that I will be told that we need to have all these means at our disposal and to go as fast as we can because modern life is harried. But there is a

mistake here, for modern life is harried just because we have the telephone, the telex, the plane, etc. Without these devices it would be no more harried than it was a century ago when we could all walk at the same pace. "You are denying progress then?" Not at all; what I am denying is that *this* is progress!

Another incident that made me raise the question "What use?" was that of the first great massacres of the peasants, the kulaks, in the USSR. I asked many friends who were close to communism what purpose was served by killing these peasants, who had no real idea what was happening in their country. The embarrassed reply was always the same: They were capitalists. But all the evidence we had showed that this was not so. They were counterrevolutionaries, then, who did not want their land to be collectivized. This was half true, but did it justify mass killings? Did the reign of social justice, equity, peace, and freedom have to be inaugurated by massacres of which we knew both the horror and the extent in spite of censorship? At that time I was still an innocent in politics, but even though I was taking up the despised bourgeois question I could not stop myself from putting it. It is along the same lines that face-to-face with the fabulous technical progress of our day I put the same banal and vulgar question: What is the use of this immense mobilization of intelligence, money, means, and energies? Of what use *in truth?* The immediate utility is plain enough—dishwashers and robots save us time. It always comes back to that. But it is quickly seen that we are invaded not merely by objects, as Perec showed, but by innumerable working gadgets. There are individual gadgets and collective gadgets and gadgets of society as a whole, so that when I criticize them I stir up great, scandalized protests. But before taking a look at gadgets we must first give a summary sketch of our needs. For if objects are useful and correspond to true and original needs, they are not mere gadgets.

NEEDS

The search for happiness is not new. It is written into the U.S. Constitution, which is significant because the modern world opened with that declaration. But long ago I showed that there is a great difference between the ideology of happiness (or the utopia) found among past millenarians and our own ideology of happiness. It is a matter of means. Previously, the means did not exist to make people happy. The quest for happiness was thus an individual matter, a matter of culture, spirituality, asceticism, and choice of life-style. But for the last two centuries we have had the (technical) means to put happiness within the reach of all. Yet this is not, of course, the same thing. Happiness now consists of meeting needs, assuring well-being, gaining wealth and also culture and knowledge. It is not an inner state but an act of consumption. Above all, it is a response to needs. Though it may be a commonplace, it is worth recalling that we must make a distinction (contested) between basic, primary, natural needs and new, secondary, artificial needs. The lively argument against this distinction is that so-called natural needs are in fact modeled on a given culture. All needs, it is said, are cultural, so that a supposedly artificial need, when absolutely anchored in a culture (like the need for a car), is just as pressing as a "natural" need. As a rule, technical growth, in countries in which it has occurred, has enabled us to respond to the natural needs of food, drink, clothing, protection against heat and cold, shelter from bad weather. I know that there will be reaction to this simple statement, for it is not true that in our world everybody finds these natural needs met. My reply is also simple. The difference from past centuries is that then, if there was famine, people had to accept it as fate and do the best they could to survive, but today famine, or the existence of the Fourth World, is a scandal that we must immediately halt.

The difference in attitude brings to light the extraordinary change brought about by technique as regards access to happiness through the satisfying of primary needs. But the same technical explosion incessantly produces new needs.[1] That is the difficulty. Happiness is harder to achieve because of the acceleration of the production of new and different needs which become the more intense as primary needs are met. A young person wants a Walkman or a Honda because he or she does not lack food. The new needs are also multiplying. There are needs to compensate for the destruction of the traditional order: expenditures on nature, communication, cars, social life, leisure, sport. There are the needs of desire which are triggered by technical progress and which are in rhythm with the proposed objects: the desire for pleasure, for leisure, for longevity, for health. Though these needs are abstract and exist only because there are technical instruments, they are the constituents of happiness. There is need of music for the Walkman, need of the computer, need of the telephone, etc. E. Morin rightly says that the progress of technical and industrial development is the constant creation of new needs.[2] In other words, it transforms and extends our notion of well-being. The transformation is more by quantitative increase than by qualitative modification. Yet there are also qualitative modifications: an expansion of the conception of the consumption of the make-believe (cinema, television), and

expansion of leisure in which eros plays a big part, so that life is eroticized.

Finally, there is also the creation of a need to compensate in the form of techniques of well-being (jogging, dieting, yoga, camping, etc.). In this case needs lead to well-being. This is not done only for consumption; one is searching for a "better life" (according to the banal slogan), or for being "in shape" (pushed by advertising). But there is a close connection between the better life or being in shape and technique, for we have to be in shape to be able to work. An ethic of production finds inner expression in the concern for a better life. . . .

THE WORLD OF GADGETS

What do I mean by gadgets? In this context I am referring to mechanical or electrical objects which are amusing or entertaining and which we can take up or leave as we please. The electric knife to carve up the roast is a gadget; the gas-powered corkscrew that opens a bottle all by itself is a gadget. Always there is something of a game about them. They correspond to an older reality. I would say that the mechanical products of the 18th century were the first true gadgets.[3] These were marvels of invention, finesse, material skill, and mechanical knowledge. They might claim to be a scientific approach to the human mechanism. But they could serve only to astonish, to provoke admiration, to surprise court ladies, and to divert philosophers. They did not respond to any need, even a need for knowledge. Whether we like it or not, they were games, learned and noble games, but still games.

In its private dimension the gadget still has very largely the character of a game. But I will not study this aspect here because I will deal at length with the question of play in our society in part IV below. I will talk here only about useful gadgets. What then, are the features of a gadget? It is a technically very complex instrument which represents much intelligence, a combination of learned techniques, and considerable investment. It is now the main industrial product and an unlimited source of profit. It is an object which always involves "very advanced composition," and always (according to an absurd usage which is hallowed by tradition) very sophisticated. But a second feature is that the result of these efforts and skills does not correspond to any real need. By the very nature of a gadget, its utility is totally out of proportion to the considerable investment that it involves. Its services are completely out of step with the prodigious technical refinement of its conception. In other words, it entails an application of high tech for almost zero utility. This disproportion is what constitutes a gadget in the present sense. This being so, it will be apparent that for me the gadget is more than an odd little personal object. Yet I will begin with some examples from this area.

We have quartz watches, which will not break down, which tell us the exact time without varying more than a second in a year. What good are they? Will they get us to meetings exactly on time? Will they help us to get up in the morning more easily? Will meetings we attend end precisely at the time announced? Not at all! These watches are no use whatever except perhaps for navigators (to plot their position). What is more, they also come with remarkable extra features which might waken us up to a charming melody or enable us to do astonishing calculations. An admiring friend told me one day that thanks to his watch, if I told him the day and year of my birth, he could tell me on what day of the week I was born and how many days I had lived thus far. I thanked him for his kindness but had no interest in such data. What is the point of so ingenious and learned an instrument when it obtains such absurd results?

Many engineers, each more skilled than the other, are working on a flat-screen television so as to prevent the slight distortion caused by the curve. Are we such lovers of art, such concerned aesthetes, that we cannot tolerate that slight distortion of the picture? Let us go ahead then! But if others are like myself, ordinary watchers, they are quite satisfied with what they see. What use, then, is a flat screen? None at all to anybody.[4] The same applies to the famous compact disc. It will give you an hour of music without stop, and its use of the laser produces no background noise, no static. What a marvel! And we had it presented to us on French television (March 21, 1986) by some idiot who raved about the beauty, the grandeur, the technical progress which has made possible the reduction of size and noise, and who finished his stupid address by telling us to throw away our old music and our outdated recordings. Advertising, of course; people had to be induced to buy the discs. But are we such informed musicologists or such lovers of music that the slightest speck of dust causes us to start? What good, then, is all this buffoonery, this creation of pure music, this deifying of the laser?

In reality, technique produces more technique whether it makes sense or not, whether it is needed or not. We are pressed to buy it. Thus there is the remarkable invention which enables us to see in a small corner of our television sets what is happening on other channels, so that we can better choose. Another fine invention for nothing! Then there is the remarkable oven

which has a computer to tell us when the roast is cooked, or the microwave which cooks without heating up, as if there were the slightest need to invent a gadget of this kind except perhaps out of curiosity to see if it would sell! Are our meals better? Are our roasts better cooked? Is our gratin better? Obviously not! The end result, then, is nothing. There are also the household appliances furnished with "programs": electric ovens, washing machines, electric irons, etc. Those who work them have to find the right button in increasingly complex operations, the usefulness coming to light only as they grow accustomed to them, that is, when the need has been created. These things make life easier? Not at all! They go wrong, or we press the wrong buttons. And what about the freezer, which one out of three households in France now has? It enables us to do our shopping (by car, of course) once a week. What a simplifying of life! How it lightens our burdens! But how can we say that it really makes life better, shutting people up at home and breaking off many social contacts? I concede that in the case of big-game hunters the freezer makes it possible to keep large pieces of meat for many months, or in the case of those with many fruit trees, it enables them to keep the fruit (also vegetables) "fresh" for a time. But is this worth the cost? (I could quote from memory the millions of dollars worth of food that was lost with the famous blackout in New York, not to speak of the lesser one in Lyons, but these, of course, were accidents!) . . .

Let us continue our slaughter of the innocents. What use is the telephone which will enable us to see who is talking? Is this so important (except in the case of two lovers)? It does, no doubt, enable us to catch fleeting expressions which might change the meaning of words. But all this gadgetry for a mere image! There is, however, a better use for the videophone. One simple call on it and we can be electronically guided through a town by the Tourist Office, arrange for a video, reserve a film for the desired hour, and make a doctor's appointment. All that! As Mitterrand has assured us, we have here the most advanced electronics and the true vehicle of economic recovery. No more than that!

Again, what use is the video recorder? It enables us to see films as we want and to record television programs that interest us. But do we not spend enough time in front of the television without adding to it, without doubling the brutalizing and dispossessing of the self which four hours of daily viewing produce? As regards television, what good is the ability to capture by satellite programs from all round the world?[5] Do we really need to see television from China, Pakistan, or Finland? Do we understand these languages? I have been in many countries where I did not know the language and the television sets in the hotels were totally useless. Yet attempts are made to justify channels that receive foreign programs even though they could be suppressed without loss. Is the price of a satellite worth the ability to listen to Dutch radio? Absurd! Pure gadgetry! Another worthless gadget is the all-terrain vehicle with four-wheel drive and big tires. I concede that it is useful for ethnologists, but the rest of the time all that it does is crush the undergrowth, destroy silence and nature, rush about beaches, bring down sand dunes, and poison the pure forest air—and all this to save walking a mile or two on foot. What use, except to wreck what is not already wrecked?

It is on vehicles that the imagination of (very serious) inventors of gadgets has had free play. One such gadget is the power window, which is useful only to spare us the exertion of turning the handle. A computer at least ought to be on hand for such a noble task! But that is nothing. Seats can be adjusted electronically with four different "memories" so that different drivers can find at once the right position. On-board computers can tell us how long we have been traveling, what our average speed is, what our gasoline consumption is, whether we are ahead of our schedule or behind it, and whether we are going faster than we planned. Then there are remote controls which enable us to lock and unlock the car doors or to control the heating and cooling, so that the car will be just the right temperature in the morning even though we leave it out overnight. . . .

In the past pages readers might have smiled and shrugged, thinking I was making much ado about very little. But what we are now going to discuss should make us angry. I refer to social or collective gadgets, that is, objects of great collective importance which are still no more than gadgets. The two main ones in our society are those connected with space and the computer. Now, I am not saying that these are no use at all. My point is that their value is small compared to the investment of intelligence, skill, money, and labor that goes into their creation. Remember that it is this disproportion that makes a gadget. Naturally, I recognize the great space achievements: walking on the moon, etc.[6] But what do they really amount to? What real value is the enormous, gigantic, ruinous growth of booster rockets and satellites put into orbit? . . .

The second great collective gadget in our advanced world is the computer, which has the peculiarity of being able to link individual gadgets to the great universal gadget. Naturally, I know as I write this that it will be found scandalous. For all our hopes rest on this gigantic worldwide instrument. We must begin by taking note of all the propaganda and publicity which incessantly promotes the merits of the computer and especially the microcomputer (Lussato's "Little Kettle"), as though the macrocomputer no longer existed. Yet in reality it is the latter on which laboratories, banks, insurance companies, multinational corporations, and governments depend. We forget it because it is embarrassing, a centralizing organism which we cannot dress up, which we cannot come to grips with. That said, what is the usual line on the computer? First, the possibility of "decolonizing" it,[7] of bringing in a new world order of information, so that nondeveloped peoples will not be totally dependent for information on Western centers. Communication has been changed into a system of signals and commands which can increase the power of the large machines. Freedom of information was always accepted in theory, but was never possible for lack of means. Today the computer makes it possible. The modern technology of signs allows of pure and simple transfer. Nonaligned countries do not want a new order of closed information. What is needed is a pluralism of sources. This demands a truly universal expansion of means. Thanks to the free flow of data,[8] underdeveloped countries can finally get moving, there can be new activity and employment on a planetary scale, and the prices of raw materials can be prorated.

The computer smashes any monopoly in information or techniques. The computer can transform information and knowledge into useful operations. It is the tool of a twofold revolution, in both communication and economics. We are witnessing an astonishing growth in its applications: letters, accounts, forecasts, microprocessing. The computer figures in office automation, telematics, robotics, and factory automation. The computer can be used in scores of ways: for household accounts, for orders, for information, as office equipment for the execution and even the conception of work. Informational tasks can be automated so as to increase productivity, to speed up the rate of economic growth, to raise the level of education, to improve medical services, and to reduce the rate of pollution. Thanks to fantastic progress in perfecting the computer, everything seems to be possible. The creation of smart cards, computerized banking, electronic mail, data banks: all are available to help in the search for information.

It is estimated that by 1995 the equipment available for each inhabitant in France will have the power of dealing with 100 million instructions per second (100 mips) and of storing 20 million characters. In 1984 the total power was only 9 mips. But 200 mips are now expected, with a central memory capacity of 50 million characters.

The sending of one page of 2,000 characters takes 20 seconds. The communication (by satellite) between two computers will be 1 billion characters in 20 minutes. A coaxial cable can carry 50 images or 1 million characters per second, and an optical fiber ten times as many. At the same time the price of these marvels is rapidly decreasing. Computers in charge of specific functions can cooperate with one another. Texts can be changed into vocal messages and vice versa. Simplified languages make it possible to get in touch directly with data banks. Telematics systems are also increasingly rapidly. In France in 1984 there were 800,000 videotex terminals in operation and more than 1,000 operational services with some 8 million calls a month.

Progress is incessant and seems to be unlimited. One might say that it involves an economic transformation, an intellectual transformation, and a communications transformation. All the services and institutions that are the framework of a nation are undergoing transformation. Everything has to be adapted. The computer will supposedly end all mindless and boring work. "Teletel [an electronic telephone directory] will open up our minds and spirits. It is said to be bringing a power to earth that will illumine everything with its light. We see a new omnipotence on earth. The ideal of socialized omnipotence is incarnate in modern technique and will bring great benefits to life."[9] Things are moving too fast to leave time for decisions. A debate on Teletel was suggested but technical progress moved so much faster than discussion that videotex was being integrated before there was time to consider the related details or problems. The experiment was thus initiated without debate. Confronted by this evidence of progress and utility, how do I have the audacity to talk of gadgets? I am not arguing that computers are not efficient or that they have not become indispensable for accounting or budgeting or juggling with fantastic figures or keeping track of sales or stocks. They play a useful part in economic and financial management.

Computers are also indispensable for calculations in modern astronomy and mathematics. We simply note once again that technique makes possible a certain development in science without our really knowing whether the new knowledge makes sense. I will undoubtedly be told that the uses I have cited are minor and relate only to calculations when in fact the handling of information has far greater economic impact. The future of the computer is supposedly more oriented to the manipulating of information, of which only a small part has to do with figures. But it is pre-

cisely in this regard that I ask whether the computer has any *real* use and not merely a fictional, phantasmagoric, supererogatory use.

No one denies that data banks contain a vast amount of information. But who consults them? Do we really believe that 50 million French people are using these services? Only intellectuals, engineers, and journalists do so. In this way the gap between the upper level and the rest widens. We have only to consider the difficulty for houses equipped with videotex. A whole propaganda campaign was needed to get people to buy this equipment. Vitalis pinpointed the problem. We were invited to live as free, autonomous, rational subjects who could find the answer to our problems by asking the system, but also to live as submissive subjects conforming to the bureaucracy. In response to the latter demand we practiced diversion; in response to the former we resisted merely as objects with hyperconformism, dependence, and passivity.[10] . . .

Gadgets to detect pollen so as to guard against allergies are useful, as are also those for surveys, or for assembling data in the case of oil slicks, but they simply do much faster what can be done already. Gadgets for constructing computer graphics, which are very costly, are mostly ridiculous. Some graphics, for example, those for engineers or architects which can represent in three dimensions what they have in mind, are also useful, but the same can hardly be said of advertising graphics, or especially of artistic graphics, like the dreadful portrait of Montaigne by M. Combes (of the Center for Contemporary Plastic Arts) at the opening of the Bordeaux Museum of Contemporary Art. This computer portrait of Montaigne is not in the least bit like him, makes him out to be ignoble and stupid, and forms a kind of antithesis to his *Essais*. It is an interesting illustration of the aesthetic capacity of the computer, and all its creations seem to be of the same order. Of its musical creations I have spoken elsewhere.[11] Here again we need to distinguish between an acceptable use by engineers and a totally superfluous, absurd, snobbish use in which the computer is merely a gadget.

In another area I will simply recall briefly a much debated issue that cannot be decided. In its political impact, is the computer an instrument of unequalled centralization or a means of remarkable decentralization? There are as many arguments for the one side as the other. But the reference is to mainframes in the one case, to microcomputers in the other. Furthermore, the only two orientations that seem to be serious are as follows. Thus far the only applications have been for the reinforcing of central power, and I do not know of a single example of decentralization by computer. But second, different conditions are needed for the two different results. As regards centralization, whether in Africa, Asia, or the USA, centralization already exists, and the computer has simply to go with the tide. As regards decentralization, it would have to swim against the tide, opposing usages, institutions, habits, and the demands of the social body, and doing a creative work of freedom. But to make this possible we would need thousands of people and associations that are autonomous, that are nonconformist (whether left or right), that think for themselves, that stand for something specific, and that do not share the current commonplaces. This would demand an enormous effort. We have mentioned already the lamentable failure of independent local radio stations in this regard. A hundred times more quality and will would be needed for decentralization by computer. Thus far we have been shown what individuals might create thanks to it, but when reference is made to the transmitting of information, we are not told *what* information. All that we really have is the invention of games.

The case is self-evident. The idea that the computer is a creator of freedom is a myth pure and simple.[12] The information that it handles is that which *this* society uses and can use. The computer can only confirm it. To be amortized, the heavy investment in computers demands that the system already installed be preserved. The methods of analysis and programming do not permit an evolution of services already in place. There is no computer revolution. There is simply a computer shock that impels the socio-technical system to move faster in its own direction.

In general, we may say that we have had some experience of the choices that are available when a technique is at work. Always and in all circumstances technique has historically gone along with centralization and the concentration of power. "Without automobiles, planes, and loudspeakers," said Hitler in October 1935, "we could not have taken over Germany." "By the magic of the telephone and telex, centralization is even easier today. Orders come down smoothly from superiors to the lower echelons. Information circulates rapidly and discreetly, making possible both increased surveillance of citizens and total concentration of decision. Totalitarianism goes hand in hand with modern gadgetry."[13] "Totalitarian societies seem to be simple, logical exaggerations of the technological state of modern society."[14] "What would the new order be without the transmitting capacity of modern instruments . . . which is constantly

growing. The Nazi government launched a big advertising campaign to get all Germans to buy radio sets. In May 1935 they could legitimately triumph, for in two years more than 800,000 sets had been sold."[15] These experiences seem to me to be conclusive, confirming a reasonable evaluation. Yet I cannot think that all the talk of the possibility of decentralization by such technical means as the microcomputer is a lie. There is no intention to deceive. It is a major example of technological bluff. It is a bluff that ensnares democrats and liberals, and that is all it is.

"The computer is not a means that can be used in the service of new social ends."[16] Once again, I am not doubting the marvels performed by computers and especially microcomputers. I am simply trying to show that these marvels do not really change existing society (except to speed it up and, as we shall see, to make it more fragile). Nor do they truly better the individual lot. The use of a touch screen instead of the traditional keyboard did not really change anything. The visual information terminal is a masterpiece, but it does not really change anything. In the politico-social realm it is simply an aid to decision and office automation.

As regards the aid to decision, we must differentiate between this and ideas which receive help from computers. The latter kind of help is incontestable. An engineer has the idea of circuits and the computer designs them on the screen. If the engineer agrees he gives the green light and the computer, linked up with precision instruments, makes sure that the circuit is made properly. We have here the particular case of a graphic representation of an idea. The same process can be helpful in the routing of planes or cars. Technique aids technique. But the aiding of decisions is very different. We enter here the domain of economics and politics. According to an old idea, computers can register all the information concerning an issue. They can encompass all the parameters. The dream twenty years ago, then, was that computers would make useful, right, and wise decisions. Knowing all the data and all the rules, why should they not be able to decide definitively? They could also foresee various scenarios and combine factors in different ways. They could be told what the goal was. They would then point out the most appropriate scenario. Since they could not make a mistake, we ought to follow them.

That is a dream. First, our human models are always incomplete. Second, qualitative imponderables that the computer cannot know enter into all political and economic issues: How much bombardment can a population stand? What will be the level of courage of the last German troops? How apt are Japanese workers to mobilize? The next theory, then, is that of the aided decision. Politicians will make the decision but only after having received all the data that the computer can provide. In my view, we have here a great mistake, for people who are deluged by information become incapable of making decisions. An excess of information and parameters results in total paralysis of the process of decision. . . .

We will conclude with some more general reflections. The first is that this whole field of computers is making society more vulnerable. The risks extend to the public and daily life. We are vulnerable financially. We are vulnerable to strikes by a very small number of people. We run the risk of greater social control and a levelling of behavior.[17] To be acceptable to electronic machines and to calculators, models of human behavior have to be reductionist. In relation to both things and people analyses and data have to be in simple classes for easy expression and comparison. A specialist tells us that; Chamoux is a specialist on network security and has founded a private research center. We have here the counterpart of the supposed "conviviality" of the computer, but no one, of course, talks about this.

In reality, we have to pay for the gain in efficiency with the risk of enslavement on the one side and actual vulnerability on the other. But let us pass on to what seem to be more sophisticated reflections of a different kind. Neirynck has noted that the world of computers fulfils all the conditions of a cult of initiates. It has every quality as well. It is clean. It uses little energy. It deals with immaterial things. We increasingly need its information in our society. To the public it is very mysterious. It corresponds to an ancient dream of humanity, that of constructing an automaton that will perfectly imitate humanity. Having shown why there is this passion for the computer, Neirynck then asks what use it really is. Does it better the lives of individuals? Does the spread of personal or domestic computers meet a real need? Or is the manufacturing of well-marketed microcomputers a solution in search of a problem? Do robots really make life easier for workers? In principle they do, but in practice they do not. (We shall look at the problem of productivity later.) Having noted the ineluctable march toward centralization, Neirynck concludes that the greatest danger of the computer is ideological. The less comprehensible it is, the more extravagant the statements to which it gives rise. In particular, it supposedly liberates us from the constraints of energy, reversing entropy! This idea rests on a confusion which Neirynck analyzes in detail. By giving

pure computer information to a closed system, we do not diminish entropy. The real truth is simply that we can get spectacularly better energy performance by the computer. A computer linked to a network of electrical distribution can avoid the loss of power by better transit planning. This is valuable, and the computer is a remarkable tool in constructing a technical system at a low rate of entropy growth.[18]

To return to the human level, the computer can hardly fail to pose anew the question of time. It is a machine which greatly compresses the time needed for planning, production, and management. As programming advances, a society is set up that is fully synchronous with a generalized synchronization of which the computer is the founding myth and omnipresent organizer. Real time is now looped in advance and works in an instant. The search for ever more synchronization weighs heavily on workers, as we shall see at length in relation to productivity. Chesneaux has given a detailed description of the impact upon human life at all levels of this instantaneity to which the computer accustoms us and which it progressively forces upon us. "The computer is the instrument of the absolute primacy of the present over the future and the past. It is the central benchmark of social duty, which must adjust its rhythm to generations of computers."[19] . . .

ENDNOTES

1. Several authors are aware of this fact even though they are not critical of technique. Thus M. Mirabail, *Les Cinquante mots clés de la télématique* (Privat, 1981), writes: "The offer of services anticipates a demand for them. Technology thus induces new needs." I would find this hard to contest!

2. There is even a supposed "need for communication between computers." We must weigh the terms here. The fact that computers can communicate with one another directly has become a "need"!

3. Cf. the learned work of J.-C. Beaune, *L'Automate et ses Mobiles* (Flammarion, 1980), though he tends to make over-profound philosophical inferences.

4. I know that some say a flat screen is necessary to receive satellite transmissions. We will return to that.

5. See C. Akrich, "Les satellites de télévision directe," *La Recherche* 140 (Jan. 1983).

6. Behind them, of course, is national prestige and competition. Cf. P. Langereux, "L'Europe spatiale à la croisée des chemins," *La Recherche* 138 (Nov. 1982).

7. Cf. the three articles of J. Deornoey, "Empire des signes et signes de l'empire," *Le Monde,* Aug. 1983.

8. See *Les Flux trans-frontières de données* (Paris: La Documentation française, 1983).

9. Quotations in Marchand and Ancelin, eds., *Télématique* (Paris: La Documentation française, 1984).

10. A. Vitalis, *Les Enjeux sociopolitiques et culturels du système télématique* (Telem, 1983); idem, *Informatique, Pouvoir et Libertés* (Economica, 1981).

11. See J. Ellul, *L'Empire du non-sens* (Paris: Press Universitaires, 1980).

12. See J. L. Leonhardt, "Informatique et société," in *Une société informatisée—Pourquoi? Pour qui? Comment?* (Presses universitaires de Namur, 1982) (forty-five essential studies).

13. See D. Pelassy, *Le Règne nazi* (Paris: Fayard, 1982).

14. See C. Friedrich and Z. Brzezinski, *Totalitarian Dictatorship and Autocracy* (Cambridge: Harvard University Press, 1956).

15. D. Pelassy, *Le Règne nazi*.

16. Ohrenbuch in *Travaux de l'Institut d'Informatique*.

17. See J.-P. Chamoux, *Menaces sur l'ordinateur*, p. 211.

18. J. Neirynck, *Le Huitième Jour de la Création. Introduction à l'entropologie* (Presses polytechniques romanes, 1986), pp. 208–12.

19. Chesneaux, *De la modernité* (Maspero, 1983), pp. 35–49.

QUESTIONS ON ELLUL

1. How does Ellul characterize "gadgetry"? Why does he claim that gadgets do not, in fact, respond to a primary *need?* In what sense, if any, does his argument rest on a distinction between needs and the "needs of desires"?

2. Ellul implies that we cannot live without our gadgets but that our gadgets nonetheless transform our lives for the worse. In what ways are we dependent on the technology of gadgetry? Does this technology alter, for the worse, our relationships to one another or to nature itself?

3. Ellul claims that the computer is a gadget. Do you agree? Does the computer work to enforce conformity, authority, and bureaucratization? Or is the computer a technological force for freedom?

Business and Environmental Ethics

W. Michael Hoffman

W. Michael Hoffman is Professor of Philosophy and Executive Director of the Center for Business Ethics at Bentley College, Massachusetts. He has written or ed- *ited numerous books and articles in business ethics including* Ethics Matters: How to Implement Values-Driven Management *(with Dawn-Marie Driscoll, 2000), and has consulted with corporations and institutions of higher learning on business ethics.*

The business ethics movement, from my perspective, is still on the march. And the environmental movement, after being somewhat silent for the past twenty years, has once again captured our attention—promising to be a major social force in the 1990s. Much will be written in the next few years trying to tie together these two movements. This is one such effort.

Concern over the environment is not new. Warnings came out of the 1960s in the form of burning rivers, dying lakes, and oil-fouled oceans. Radioactivity was found in our food, DDT in mother's milk, lead and mercury in our water. Every breath of air in the North American hemisphere was reported as contaminated. Some said these were truly warnings from Planet Earth of eco-catastrophe, unless we could find limits to our growth and changes in our lifestyle.

Over the past few years Planet Earth began to speak to us even more loudly than before, and we began to listen more than before. The message was ominous, somewhat akin to God warning Noah. It spoke through droughts, heat waves, and forest fires, raising fears of global warming due to the buildup of carbon dioxide and other gases in the atmosphere. It warned us by raw sewage and medical wastes washing up on our beaches, and by devastating oil spills—one despoiling Prince William Sound and its wildlife to such an extent that it made us weep. It spoke to us through increased skin cancers and discoveries of holes in the ozone layer caused by our use of chlorofluorocarbons. It drove its message home through the rapid and dangerous cutting and burning of our primitive forests at the rate of one football field a second, leaving us even more vulnerable to greenhouse gases like carbon dioxide and eliminating scores of irreplaceable species daily. It rained down on us in the form of acid, defoliating our forests and poisoning our lakes and streams. Its warnings were found on barges roaming the seas for places to dump tons of toxic incinerator ash. And its message exploded in our faces at Chernobyl and Bhopal, reminding us of past warnings at Three Mill Island and Love Canal.

Senator Albert Gore said in 1988: "The fact that we face an ecological crisis without any precedent in historic times is no longer a matter of any dispute worthy of recognition."[1] The question, he continued, is not whether there is a problem, but how we will address it.

This will be the focal point for a public policy debate which requires the full participation of two of its major players—business and government. The debate must clarify such fundamental questions as: (1) What obligation does business have to help with our environmental crisis? (2) What is the proper relationship between business and government, especially when faced with a social problem of the magnitude of the environment crisis? And (3) what rationale should be used for making and justifying decisions to protect the environment? Corporations, and society in general for that matter, have yet to answer these questions satisfactorily. In the first section of this paper I will briefly address the first two questions. In the final two sections I will say a few things about the third question.

I

. . . At the Center's First National Conference on Business Ethics, Harvard Business School Professor George Cabot Lodge told of a friend who owned a paper company on the banks of a New England stream. On the first Earth Day in 1970, his friend was converted to the cause of environmental protection. He became determined to stop his company's pollution of the stream, and marched off to put his new-found religion into action. Later, Lodge learned his friend went broke, so he went to investigate. Radiating a kind of ethical purity, the friend told Lodge that he spent millions to stop the pollution and thus could no longer compete with other firms that did not follow his example. So the company went under, 500 people lost their jobs, and the stream remained polluted.

When Lodge asked why his friend hadn't sought help from the state or federal government for stricter standards for everyone, the man replied that was not the American way, that government should not interfere with business activity, and that private enterprise could do the job alone. In fact, he felt it was the social responsibility of business to solve environmental problems, so he was proud that he had set an example for others to follow.

The second story portrays another extreme. A few years ago "Sixty Minutes" interviewed a manager of a chemical company that was discharging effluent into a river in upstate New York. At the time, the dumping was legal, though a bill to prevent it was pending in Congress. The manager remarked that he hoped the bill would pass, and that he certainly would support it as a responsible citizen. However, he also said he approved of his company's efforts to defeat the bill and

of the firm's policy of dumping wastes in the meantime. After all, isn't the proper role of business to make as much profit as possible within the bounds of law? Making the laws—setting the rules of the game—is the role of government, not business. While wearing his business hat the manager had a job to do, even if it meant doing something that he strongly opposed as a private citizen.

Both stories reveal incorrect answers to the questions posed earlier, the proof of which is found in the fact that neither the New England stream nor the New York river was made any cleaner. . . . Although the paper company owner and the chemical company manager had radically different views of the ethical responsibilities of business, both saw business and government performing separate roles, and neither felt that business ought to cooperate with government to solve environmental problems.[2]

If the business ethics movement has led us anywhere in the past fifteen years, it is to the position that business has an ethical responsibility to become a more active partner in dealing with social concerns. Business must creatively find ways to become a part of solutions, rather than being a part of problems. Corporations can and must develop a conscience, as Ken Goodpaster and others have argued—and this includes an environmental conscience.[3] Corporations should not isolate themselves from participation in solving our environmental problems, leaving it up to others to find the answers and to tell them what not to do.

Corporations have special knowledge, expertise, and resources which are invaluable in dealing with the environmental crisis. Society needs the ethical vision and cooperation of all its players to solve its most urgent problems, especially one that involves the very survival of the planet itself. Business must work with government to find appropriate solutions. It should lobby for good environmental legislation and lobby against bad legislation, rather than isolating itself from the legislative process. . . . It should not be ethically quixotic and try to go it alone, as our paper company owner tried to do, nor should it be ethically inauthentic and fight against what it believes to be environmentally sound policy, as our chemical company manager tried to do. Instead business must develop and demonstrate moral leadership.

There are examples of corporations demonstrating such leadership, even when this has been a risk to their self-interest. In the area of environmental moral leadership one might cite DuPont's discontinuing its Freon products, a $750-million-a-year-business, because of their possible negative effects on the ozone layer, and Proctor and Gamble's manufacture of concentrated fabric softener and detergents which require less packaging. But some might argue . . . that the real burden for environmental change lies with consumers, not with corporations. If we as consumers are willing to accept the harm done to the environment by favoring environmentally unfriendly products, corporations have no moral obligation to change so long as they obey environmental law. This is even more the case, so the argument goes, if corporations must take risks or sacrifice profits to do so.

This argument fails to recognize that we quite often act differently when we think of ourselves as *consumers* than when we think of ourselves as *citizens*. Mark Sagoff, concerned about our over-reliance on economic solutions, clearly characterizes this dual nature of our decision making.[4] As consumers, we act more often than not for ourselves; as citizens, we take on a broader vision and do what is in the best interests of the community. I often shop for things I don't vote for. I might support recycling referendums, but buy products in nonreturnable bottles. I am not proud of this, but I suspect this is more true of most of us than not. To stake our environmental future on our consumer willingness to pay is surely shortsighted, perhaps even disastrous.

I am not saying that we should not work to be ethically committed citizen consumers, and investors for that matter. I agree . . . that "consumers bear a far greater responsibility for preserving and protecting the environment than they have actually exercised,"[5] but activities which affect the environment should not be left up to what we, acting as consumers, are willing to tolerate or accept. To do this would be to use a market-based method of reasoning to decide on an issue which should be determined instead on the basis of our ethical responsibilities as a member of a social community.

Furthermore, consumers don't make the products, provide the services, or enact the legislation which can be either environmentally friendly or unfriendly. Grass roots boycotts and lobbying efforts are important, but we also need leadership and mutual cooperation from business and government in setting forth ethical environmental policy. . . . I am suggesting that corporate moral leadership goes far beyond public educational campaigns. It requires moral vision, commitment, and courage, and involves risk and sacrifice. I think business is capable of such a challenge. Some are even engaging in such a challenge. Certainly the business ethics movement should do nothing short of encouraging such leadership. I feel morality demands such leadership.

II

If business has an ethical responsibility to the environment which goes beyond obeying environmental law, what criterion should be used to guide and justify such action? Many corporations are making environmentally friendly decisions where they see there are profits to be made by doing so. They are wrapping themselves in green where they see a green bottom line as a consequence. This rationale is also being used as a strategy by environmentalists to encourage more businesses to become environmentally conscientious. In December 1989 the highly respected Worldwatch Institute published an article by one of its senior researchers entitled "Doing Well by Doing Good" which gives numerous examples of corporations improving their pocketbooks by improving the environment. It concludes by saying that "fortunately, businesses that work to preserve the environment can also make a buck."[6]

In a recent Public Broadcast Corporation documentary entitled "Profit the Earth," several efforts are depicted of what is called the "new environmentalism" which induces corporations to do things for the environment by appealing to their self-interest. The Environmental Defense Fund is shown encouraging agribusiness in Southern California to irrigate more efficiently and profit by selling the water saved to the city of Los Angeles. This in turn will help save Mono Lake. EDF is also shown lobbying for emissions trading that would allow utility companies which are under their emission allotments to sell their "pollution rights" to those companies which are over their allotments. This is for the purpose of reducing acid rain. Thus the frequent strategy of the new environmentalists is to get business to help solve environmental problems by finding profitable or virtually costless ways for them to participate. They feel that compromise, not confrontation, is the only way to save the earth. By using the tools of the free enterprise system, they are in search of win-win solutions, believing that such solutions are necessary to take us beyond what we have so far been able to achieve.

I am not opposed to these efforts; in most cases I think they should be encouraged. There is certainly nothing wrong with making money while protecting the environment, just as there is nothing wrong with feeling good about doing one's duty. But if business is adopting or being encouraged to adopt the view that good environmentalism is good business, then I think this poses a danger for the environmental ethics movement—a danger which has an analogy in the business ethics movement. . . .

Is the rationale that good ethics is good business a proper one for business ethics? I think not. One thing that the study of ethics has taught us over the past 2500 years is that being ethical may on occasion require that we place the interests of others ahead of or at least on par with our own interests. And this implies that the ethical thing to do, the morally right thing to do, may not be in our own self-interest. What happens when the right thing is not the best thing for the business?

Although in most cases good ethics may be good business, it should not be advanced as the only or even the main reason for doing business ethically. When the crunch comes, when ethics conflicts with the firm's interests, any ethics program that has not already faced up to this possibility is doomed to fail because it will undercut the rationale of the program itself. We should promote business ethics, not because good ethics is good business, but because we are morally required to adopt the moral point of view in all our dealings—and business is no exception. In business, as in all other human endeavors, we must be prepared to pay the costs of ethical behavior.

There is a similar danger in the environmental movement with corporations choosing or being wooed to be environmentally friendly on the grounds that it will be in their self-interest. There is the risk of participating in the movement for the wrong reasons. But what does it matter if business cooperates for reasons other than the right reasons, as long as it cooperates? It matters if business believes or is led to believe that it only has a duty to be environmentally conscientious in those cases where such actions either require no sacrifice or actually make a profit. And I am afraid this is exactly what is happening. I suppose it wouldn't matter if the environmental cooperation of business was only needed in those cases where it was also in business' self-interest. But this is surely not the case, unless one begins to really reach and talk about that amorphous concept "long-term" self-interest. Moreover, long-term interests, I suspect, are not what corporations or the new environmentalists have in mind in using self-interest as a reason for environmental action.

I am not saying we should abandon attempts to entice corporations into being ethical, both environmentally and in other ways, by pointing out and providing opportunities where good ethics is good business. And there are many places where such attempts fit well in both the business and environmental ethics movements. But we must be careful not to cast this as the proper guideline for business' ethical responsibility. Because when it is discovered that many ethical actions are not necessarily good for business, at least in the short-run, then the rationale based on self-interest will come up morally short, and both ethical movements will be seen as deceptive and shallow.

III

What is the proper rationale for responsible business action toward the environment? A minimalist principle is to refrain from causing or prevent the causing of unwarranted harm, because failure to do so would violate certain moral rights not to be harmed. There is, of course, much debate over what harms are indeed unwarranted due to conflict of rights and questions about whether some harms are offset by certain benefits. Norm Bowie, for example, uses the harm principle, but contends that business does not violate it as long as it obeys environmental law. Robert Frederick, on the other hand, convincingly argues that the harm principle morally requires business to find ways to prevent certain harm it causes even if such harm violates no environmental law.[7]

However, Frederick's analysis of the harm principle is largely cast in terms of harm caused to human beings and the violation of rights of human beings. Even when he hints at the possible moral obligation to protect the environment when no one is caused unwarranted harm, he does so by suggesting that we look to what we, as human beings, value.[8] This is very much in keeping with a humanistic position of environmental ethics which claims that only human beings have rights or moral standing because only human beings have intrinsic value. We may have duties with regard to nonhuman things (penguins, trees, islands, etc.) but only if such duties are derivative from duties we have toward human beings. Nonhuman things are valuable only if valued by human beings.

Such a position is in contrast to a naturalistic view of environmental ethics which holds that natural things other than human beings are intrinsically valuable and have, therefore, moral standing. Some naturalistic environmentalists only include other sentient animals in the framework of being deserving of moral consideration; others include all things which are alive or which are an integral part of an ecosystem. This latter view is sometimes called a biocentric environmental ethic as opposed to the homocentric view which sees all moral claims in terms of human beings and their interests.

Some characterize these two views as deep *versus* shallow ecology.

The literature on these two positions is vast and the debate is ongoing. The conflict between them goes to the heart of environmental ethics and is crucial to our making of environmental policy and to our perception of moral duties to the environment, including [those of] business. I strongly favor the biocentric view. And although this is not the place to try to adequately argue for it, let me unfurl its banner for just a moment.

A version of R. Routley's "last man" example[9] might go something like this: Suppose you were the last surviving human being and were soon to die from nuclear poisoning, as all other human and sentient animals have died before you. Suppose also that it is within your power to destroy all remaining life, or to make it simpler, the last tree which could continue to flourish and propagate if left alone. Furthermore you will not suffer if you do not destroy it. Would you do anything wrong by cutting it down? The deeper ecological view would say yes because you would be destroying something that has value in and of itself, thus making the world a poorer place.

It might be argued that the only reason we may find the tree valuable is because human beings generally find trees of value either practically or aesthetically, rather than the atoms or molecules they might turn into if changed from their present form. The issue is whether the tree has value only in its relation to human beings or whether it has a value deserving of moral consideration inherent in itself in its present form. The biocentric position holds that when we find something wrong with destroying the tree, as we should, we do so because we are responding to an intrinsic value in the natural object, not to a value we give to it. This is a view which argues against a humanistic environmental ethic and which urges us to channel our moral obligations accordingly.

Why should one believe that nonhuman living things or natural objects forming integral parts of ecosystems have intrinsic value? One can respond to this question by pointing out the serious weaknesses and problems of human chauvinism.[10] More complete responses lay out a framework of concepts and beliefs which provides a coherent picture of the biocentric view with human beings as a part of a more holistic value system. But the final answer to the question hinges on what criterion one decides to use for determining moral worth—rationality, sentience, or a deeper biocentric one. Why should we adopt the principle of attributing intrinsic value to all living beings, or even to all natural objects, rather than just to human beings? I suspect Arne Naess gives as good an answer as can be given.

Faced with the ever returning question of 'Why?,' we have to stop somewhere. Here is a place where we well might stop. We shall admit that the value in itself is something shown in intuition. We attribute intrinsic value to ourselves and our nearest, and the validity of further identification can be contested, and *is* contested by many. The negation may, however, also be attacked through a series of 'whys?' Ultimately, we are in the same human predicament of having to start somewhere, at least for the moment. We must stop somewhere and treat where we then stand as a foundation.[11]

In the final analysis, environmental biocentrism is adopted or not depending on whether it is seen to provide a deeper, richer, and more ethically compelling view of the nature of things.

If this deeper ecological position is correct, then it ought to be reflected in the environmental movement. Unfortunately, for the most part, I do not think this is being done, and there is a price to be paid for not doing so. Moreover, I fear that even those who are of the biocentric persuasion are using homocentric language and strategies to bring business and other major players into the movement because they do not think they will be successful otherwise. They are afraid, and undoubtedly for good reason, that the large part of society, including business, will not be moved by arguments regarding the intrinsic value and rights of natural things. It is difficult enough to get business to recognize and act on their responsibilities to human beings and things of human interest. Hence many environmentalists follow the counsel of Spinoza:

> . . . [I]t is necessary that while we are endeavoring to attain our purpose . . . we are compelled . . . to speak in a manner intelligible to the multitude . . . For we can gain from the multitude no small advantages. . . .[12]

I understand the temptation of environmentalists employing a homocentric strategy, just as I understand business ethicists using the rationale that good ethics is good business. Both want their important work to succeed. But just as with the good ethics is good business tack, there are dangers in being a closet ecocentrist. The ethicists in both cases fail to reveal the deeper moral base of their positions because it's a harder sell. Business ethics gets marketed in terms of self-interest, environmental ethics in terms of human interest.

A major concern in using the homocentric view to formulate policy and law is that nonhuman nature will not receive the moral consideration it deserves. It might be argued, however, that by appealing to the interests and rights of human beings, in most cases nature as a whole will be protected. That is, if we are concerned about a wilderness area, we can argue that its survival is important to future generations who will otherwise be deprived of contact with its unique wildlife. We can also argue that it is important to the aesthetic pleasure of certain individuals or that, if it is destroyed, other recreational areas will become overcrowded. In this way we stand a chance to save the wilderness area without having to refer to our moral obligations to respect the intrinsic value of the spotted owl or of the old-growth forest. This is simply being strategically savvy. To trot out our deeper ecological moral convictions runs the risk of our efforts being ignored, even ridiculed, by business leaders and policy makers. It also runs head-on against a barrage of counter arguments that human interests take precedence over nonhuman interests. In any event it will not be in the best interest of the wilderness area we are trying to protect. Furthermore, all of the above homocentric arguments happen to be true—people will suffer if the wilderness area is destroyed.

In most cases, what is in the best interests of human beings may also be in the best interests of the rest of nature. After all, we are in our present environmental crisis in large part because we have not been ecologically intelligent about what is in our own interest—just as business has encountered much trouble because it has failed to see its interest in being ethically sensitive. But if the environmental movement relies only on arguments based on human interests, then it perpetuates the danger of making environmental policy and law on the basis of our strong inclination to fulfill our immediate self-interests, on the basis of our consumer viewpoints, on the basis of our willingness to pay. There will always be a tendency to allow our short-term interests to eclipse our long-term interests and the long-term interest of humanity itself. Without some grounding in a deeper environmental ethic with obligations to nonhuman natural things, then the temptation to view our own interests in disastrously short-term ways is that much more encouraged. The biocentric view helps to block this temptation.

Furthermore, there are many cases where what is in human interest is not in the interest of other natural things. Examples range from killing leopards for stylish coats to destroying a forest to build a golf course. I am not convinced that homocentric arguments, even those based on long-term human interests, have much force in protecting the interests of such natural things. Attempts to make these interests coincide might be made, but the point is that from a homocentric point of view the leopard and the forest have no morally relevant interests to consider. It is simply fortuitous if nonhuman natural interests coincide with human interests, and are thereby

valued and protected. Let us take an example from the work of Christopher Stone. Suppose a stream has been polluted by a business. From a homocentric point of view, which serves as the basis for our legal system, we can only correct the problem through finding some harm done to human beings who use the stream. Reparation for such harm might involve cessation of the pollution and restoration of the stream, but it is also possible that the business might settle with the people by paying them for their damages and continue to pollute the stream. Homocentrism provides no way for the stream to be made whole again unless it is in the interests of human beings to do so. In short it is possible for human beings to sell out the stream.[13]

I am not saying that human interests cannot take precedence over nonhuman interests when there are conflicts. For this we need to come up with criteria for deciding on interspecific conflicts of interests, just as we do for intraspecific conflicts of interest among human beings.[14] But this is a different problem from holding that nonhuman natural things have no interests or value deserving of moral consideration. There are times when causing harm to natural things is morally unjustifiable when there are no significant human interests involved and even when there are human interests involved. But only a deeper ecological ethic than homocentrism will allow us to defend this.

Finally, perhaps the greatest danger that biocentric environmentalists run in using homocentric strategies to further the movement is the loss of the very insight that grounded their ethical concern in the first place. This is nicely put by Laurence Tribe:

> What the environmentalist may not perceive is that, by couching his claim in terms of human self-interest—by articulating environmental goals wholly in terms of human needs and preferences—he may be helping to legitimate a system of discourse which so structures human thought and feeling as to erode, over the long run, the very sense of obligation which provided the initial impetus for his own protective efforts.[15]

Business ethicists run a similar risk in couching their claims in terms of business self-interest.

The environmental movement must find ways to incorporate and protect the intrinsic value of animal and plant life and even other natural objects that are integral parts of ecosystems. This must be done without constantly reducing such values to human interests. This will, of course, be difficult, because our conceptual ideology and ethical persuasion is so dominantly homocentric; however, if we are committed to a deeper biocentric ethic, then it is vital that we try to find appropriate ways to promote it. Environmental impact statements should make explicit reference to nonhuman natural values. Legal rights for nonhuman natural things, along the lines of Christopher Stone's proposal, should be sought.[16] And naturalistic ethical guidelines, such as those suggested by Holmes Rolston, should be set forth for business to follow when its activities impact upon ecosystems.[17]

At the heart of the business ethics movement is its reaction to the mistaken belief that business only has responsibilities to a narrow set of its stakeholders, namely its stockholders. Crucial to the environmental ethics movement is its reaction to the mistaken belief that only human beings and human interests are deserving of our moral consideration. I suspect that the beginnings of both movements can be traced to these respective moral insights. Certainly the significance of both movements lies in their search for a broader and deeper moral perspective., If business and environmental ethicists begin to rely solely on promotional strategies of self-interest, such as good ethics is good business, and of human interest, such as homocentrism, then they face the danger of cutting off the very roots of their ethical efforts.

ENDNOTES

1. Albert Gore, "What Is Wrong With Us?" *Time* (January 2, 1989), 66.
2. Robert Frederick, Assistant Director of the Center for Business Ethics, and I have developed and written these points together. Frederick has also provided me with invaluable assistance on other points in this paper.
3. Kenneth E. Goodpaster, "Can a Corporation have an Environmental Conscience," *The Corporation, Ethics, and the Environment,* edited by W. Michael Hoffman, Robert Frederick, and Edward S. Petry, Jr. (New York: Quorom Books, 1990).
4. Mark Sagoff, "At the Shrine of Our Lady of Fatima, or Why Political Questions Are Not All Economic," found in *Business Ethics: Readings and Cases in Corporate Morality,* 2nd edition, edited by W. Michael Hoffman and Jennifer Mills Moore (New York: McGraw-Hill, 1990), pp. 494–503.
5. Norman Bowie, "Morality, Money, and Motor Cars," *Business, Ethics, and the Environment: The Public Policy Debate,* edited by W. Michael Hoffman, Robert Frederick, and Edward S. Petry, Jr. (New York: Quorum Books, 1990), p. 94.
6. Cynthia Pollock Shea, "Doing Well By Doing Good," *World-Watch* (November/December, 1989), p. 30.
7. Robert Frederick, "Individual Rights and Environmental Protection," presented at the Annual Society for Business Ethics Conference in San Francisco, August 10 and 11, 1990.
8. Frederick.
9. Richard Routley, and Val Routley, "Human Chauvinism and Environmental Ethics," *Environmental Philosophy,* Monograph Series, No. 2, edited by Don Mannison, Michael McRobbie, and Richard Routley (Australian National University, 1980), pp. 121 ff.
10. See Paul W. Taylor, "The Ethics of Respect for Nature," found in *People, Penguins, and Plastic Trees,* edited by Donald VanDeVeer and Christine Pierce (Belmont, California: Wadsworth, 1986), pp. 178–183. Also see R. and V. Routley, "Against the Inevitability of Human Chauvinism," found in *Ethics and the Problems of the 21st Century,* edited by K. E. Goodpaster and K. M. Sayre (Notre Dame: University of Notre Dame Press, 1979), pp. 36–59.
11. Arne Naess, "Identification as a Source of Deep Ecological Attitudes," *Deep Ecology,* edited by Michael Tobias (San Marcos, California: Avant Books, 1988), p. 266.
12. Benedict de Spinoza, "On the Improvement of the Understanding," found in *Philosophy of Benedict de Spinoza,* translated by R. H. M. Elwes (New York: Tudor Publishing Co., 1936), p. 5.
13. Christopher D. Stone, "Should Trees Have Standing?—Toward Legal Rights for Natural Objects," found in *People, Penguins, and Plastic Trees,* pp. 86–87.
14. See Donald VanDeVeer, "Interspecific Justice," *People, Penguins, and Plastic Trees,* pp. 51–66.
15. Lawrence H. Tribe, "Ways Not to Think about Plastic Trees: New Foundations for Environmental Law," found in *People, Penguins, and Plastic Trees,* p. 257.
16. Stone, pp. 83–96.
17. Holmes Rolston, III, *Environmental Ethics* (Philadelphia: Temple University Press, 1988), pp. 301–313.

QUESTIONS ON HOFFMAN

1. Hoffman contends that "mutual cooperation" between business and government is needed if the environment is to be protected. What might such cooperation involve? Are there any risks in having business and government cooperate? Which businesses would be most likely to want to work with the government?

2. What is the distinction between homocentric justification and a biocentric one? What is Hoffman's justification for aiding the environment? Do you think that his justification is sound?

3. In what sense could it be true that the natural environment has an "intrinsic value"? Is this intrinsic value independent of the human valuer? Would nature have any value if there were no human beings?

The Economic Common Sense of Pollution

Larry E. Ruff

Larry E. Ruff was a Professor of Economics at the University of California, San Diego and now is a managing director of an economic and management consulting firm. This essay was originally published in 1970 in The Public Interest.

We are going to make very little real progress in solving the problem of pollution until we recognize it for what, primarily, it is: an economic problem, which must be understood in economic terms. Of course, there are *noneconomic* aspects of pollution, as there are with all economic problems, but all too often, such secondary matters dominate discussion. Engineers, for example, are certain that pollution will vanish once they find the magic gadget or power source. Politicians keep trying to find the right kind of bureaucracy; and bureaucrats maintain an unending search for the correct set of rules and regulations. Those who are above such vulgar pursuits pin their hopes on a moral regeneration or social revolution, apparently in the belief that saints and socialists have no garbage to dispose of. But as important as technology, politics, law, and ethics are to the pollution question, all such approaches are bound to have disappointing results, for they ignore the primary fact that pollution is an economic problem.

Before developing an economic analysis of pollution, however, it is necessary to dispose of some popular myths.

First, pollution is not new. Spanish explorers landing in the sixteenth century noted that smoke from Indian campfires hung in the air of the Los Angeles basin, trapped by what is now called the inversion layer. Before the first century B.C., the drinking waters of Rome were becoming polluted.

Second, most pollution is not due to affluence, despite the current popularity of this notion. In India, the pollution runs in the streets, and advice against drinking the water in exotic lands is often well taken. Nor can pollution be blamed on the self-seeking activities of greedy capitalists. Once-beautiful rivers and lakes which are now open sewers and cesspools can be found in the Soviet Union as well as in the United States, and some of the world's dirtiest air hangs over cities in Eastern Europe, which are neither capitalist nor affluent. In many ways, indeed, it is much more difficult to do anything about pollution in noncapitalist societies. In the Soviet Union, there is no way for the public to become outraged or to exert any pressure, and the polluters and the courts there work for the same people, who often decide that clean air and water, like good clothing, are low on their list of social priorities. . . .

Most discussions of the pollution problem begin with some startling facts: Did you know that 15,000 tons of filth are dumped into the air of Los Angeles County every day? But by themselves, such facts are meaningless, if only because there is no way to know whether 15,000 tons is a lot or a little. It is much more important for clear thinking about the pollution problem to understand a few economic concepts than to learn a lot of sensational-sounding numbers.

MARGINALISM

One of the most fundamental economic ideas is that of *marginalism,* which entered economic theory when economists became aware of the differential calculus in the nineteenth century and used it to formulate economic problems as problems of "maximization." The standard economic problem came to be viewed as that of finding a level of operation of some activity which would maximize the net gain from that activity, where the net gain is the difference between the benefits and the costs of the activity. As the level of activity increases, both benefits and costs will increase; but because of diminishing returns, costs will increase faster than benefits. When a certain level of the activity is reached, any further expansion increases costs more than benefits. At this "optimal" level, "marginal cost"— or the cost of expanding the activity—equals "marginal benefit," or the benefit from expanding the activity. Further expansion would cost more than it is worth, and reduction in the activity would reduce benefits more than it would save costs. The net gain from the activity is said to be maximized at this point.

This principle is so simple that it is almost embarrassing to admit it is the cornerstone of economics. Yet intelligent men often ignore it in discussion of public issues. Educators, for example, often suggest that, if it is better to be literate than illiterate, there is no logical stopping point in supporting education. Or scientists have pointed out that the benefits derived from "science" obviously exceed the costs and then have proceeded to infer that their particular project should be supported. The correct comparison, of course, is between *additional* benefits created by the proposed activity and the *additional* costs incurred.

The application of marginalism to questions of pollution is simple enough conceptually. The difficult part lies in estimating the cost and benefits functions, a question to which I shall return. But several important qualitative points can be made immediately. The first is that the choice facing a rational society is *not* between clean air and dirty air, or between clear water and polluted water, but rather between various *levels* of dirt and pollution. The aim must be to find that level of pollution abatement where the costs of further abatement begin to exceed the benefits.

The second point is that the optimal combination pollution control methods is going to be a very complex affair. Such steps as demanding a 10 percent reduction in pollution from all sources, without considering the relative difficulties and costs of the reduction, will certainly be an inefficient approach. Where it is less costly to reduce pollution, we want a greater reduction, to a point where an additional dollar spent on control anywhere yields the same reduction in pollution levels.

MARKETS, EFFICIENCY, AND EQUITY

A second basic economic concept is the idea—or the ideal—of the self-regulating economic system. Adam Smith illustrated this ideal with the example of bread in London: the uncoordinated, selfish actions of many people—farmer, miller, shipper, baker, grocer—provide bread for the city dweller, without any central control and at the lowest possible cost. Pure self-interest, guided only by the famous "invisible hand" of competition, organizes the economy efficiently.

The logical basis of this rather startling result is that, under certain conditions, competitive prices convey all the information necessary for making the optimal decision. A builder trying to decide whether to use brick or concrete will weigh his requirements and tastes against the prices of the materials. Other users will do the same, with the result that those whose needs and preferences for brick are relatively the strongest will get brick. Further, profit-maximizing producers will weigh relative production costs, reflecting society's productive capabilities, against relative prices, reflecting society's tastes and desires, when deciding how much of each good to produce. The end result is that users get brick and cement in quantities and proportions that reflect their individual tastes and society's production opportunities. No other solution would be better from the standpoint of all the individuals concerned.

This suggests what it is that makes pollution different. The efficiency of competitive markets depends on the identity of *private* costs and *social* costs. As long as the brick-cement producer must compensate somebody for every cost imposed by his production, his profit-maximizing decisions about how much to produce, and how, will also be socially efficient decisions. Thus, if a producer dumps wastes into the air, river, or ocean; if he pays nothing for such dumping; and if the disposed wastes have no noticeable effect on anyone else, living or still unborn; then the private and social costs of disposal are identical and nil, and the producer's private decisions are socially efficient. *But if these wastes do affect others, then the social costs of waste disposal are not zero. Private and social costs diverge, and private profit-maximizing decisions are not socially efficient.* Suppose, for example, that cement production dumps large quantities of dust into the air, which damages neighbors, and that the brick-cement producer pays these neighbors nothing. In the social sense, cement will be over-produced relative to brick and other products because users of the products will make decisions based on market prices which do not reflect true social costs. They will use cement when they should use brick, or when they should not build at all.

This divergence between private and social costs is the fundamental cause of pollution of all types, and it arises in any society where decisions are at all decentralized—which is to say, in any economy of any size which hopes to function at all. Even the socialist manager of the brick-cement plant, told to maximize output given the resources at his disposal, will use the People's Air to dispose of the People's Wastes; to do otherwise would be to violate his instructions. And if instructed to avoid pollution "when possible," he does not know what to do: how can he decide whether more brick or cleaner air is more important for building socialism? The capitalist manager is in exactly the same situation. Without prices to convey the needed information, he does not know what action is in the public interest, and certainly would have no incentive to act correctly even if he did know.

Although markets fail to perform efficiently when private and social costs diverge, this does not imply that there is some inherent flaw in the idea of acting on self-interest in response to market prices. Decisions based on private cost calculations are typically correct from a social point of view; and even when they are not quite correct, it often is better to accept this inefficiency than to turn to some alternative decision mechanism, which may be worse. Even the modern economic theory of socialism is based on the high correlation between managerial self-interest and public good. There is no point in trying to find something—some omniscient and omnipotent *deus ex machina*—to replace markets and self-interest. Usually it is preferable to modify existing institutions, where necessary, to make private and social interest coincide. . . .

ESTIMATING THE COSTS OF POLLUTION

Both in theory and practice, the most difficult part of an economic approach to pollution is the measurement of the cost and benefits of its abatement. Only a small fraction of the costs of pollution can be estimated straight-forwardly. If, for example, smog reduces the life of automobile tires by 10 percent, one component of the cost of smog is 10 percent of tire expenditures. It has been estimated that, in a moderately polluted area of New York City, filthy air imposes extra costs for painting, washing, laundry, etc., of $200 per person per year. Such costs must be included in any calculation of the benefits of pollution abatement, and yet they are only a part of the relevant costs—and often a small part. Accordingly it rarely is possible to justify a measure like river pollution control solely on the basis of costs to individuals or firms of treating water because it usually is cheaper to process only the water that is actually used for industrial or municipal purposes, and to ignore the river itself.

The costs of pollution that cannot be measured so easily are often called "intangible" or "noneconomic," although neither term is particularly appropriate. Many of these costs are as tangible as burning eyes or a dead fish, and all such costs are relevant to a valid economic analysis. Let us therefore call these costs "nonpecuniary."

The only real difference between nonpecuniary costs and the other kind lies in the difficulty of estimating them. If pollution in Los Angeles harbor is reducing marine life, this imposes costs on society. The cost of reducing commercial fishing could be estimated directly: it would be the fixed cost of converting men and equipment from fishing to an alternative occupation, plus the difference between what they earned in fishing and what they earn in the new occupation, plus the loss to consumers who must eat chicken instead of fish. But there are other, less straightforward costs: the loss of recreation opportunities for children and sportsfishermen and of research facilities for marine biologists, etc. Such costs are obviously difficult to measure and may be very large indeed; but just as surely as they are not zero, so too are they not infinite. Those who call for immediate action and damn the cost, merely because the spiney starfish and furry crab populations are shrinking, are putting an infinite marginal value on these creatures. This strikes a disinterested observer as an overestimate.

The above comments may seem crass and insensitive to those who, like one angry letter-writer to the Los Angeles *Times,* want to ask: "If conservation is not for its own sake, then what in the world *is* it for?" Well, what *is* the purpose of pollution control? Is it for its own sake? Of course not. If we answer that it is to make the air and water clean and quiet, then the question arises: what is the purpose of clean air and water? If the answer is, to please the nature gods, then it must be conceded that all pollution must cease immediately because the cost of angering the gods is presumably infinite. But if the answer is that the purpose of clean air and water is to further human enjoyment of life on this planet, then we are faced with the economists' basic question: given the limited alternatives that a niggardly nature allows, how can we best further human enjoyment of life? And the answer is, by making intelligent marginal decisions on the basis of costs and benefits. Pollution control is for lots of things: breathing comfortably, enjoying mountains, swimming in water, for health, beauty, and the general delectation. But so are many other things, like good food and wine, comfortable housing and fast transportation. The question is not which of these desirable things we should have, but rather what combination is most desirable. To determine such a combination, we must know the rate at which individuals are willing to substitute more of one desirable thing for less of another desirable thing. Prices are one way of determining those rates.

But if we cannot directly observe market prices for many of the costs of pollution, we must find another way to proceed. One possibility is to infer the costs from other prices, just as we infer the value of an ocean view from real estate prices. In principle, one could estimate the value people put on clean air and beaches by observing how much more they are willing to pay for property in nonpolluted areas. Such information could be obtained; but there is little of it available at present.

Another possible way of estimating the costs of pollution is to ask people how much they would be willing to pay to have pollution reduced. A resident of Pasadena might be willing to pay $100 a year to have smog reduced 10 or 20 percent. In Barstow, where the marginal cost of smog is much less, a resident might not pay $10 a year to have smog reduced 10 percent. If we knew how much it was worth to everybody, we could add up these amounts and obtain an estimate of the cost of a marginal amount of pollution. The difficulty, of course, is that there is no way of guaranteeing truthful responses. Your response to the question, how much is pollution costing *you,* obviously will depend on what you think will be done with this information. If you think you will be compensated for these costs, you will make a generous estimate; if you think that you will be charged for the control in proportion to these costs, you will make a small estimate.

In such cases it becomes very important how the questions are asked. For example, the voters could be asked a question of the form: Would you like to see pollution reduced x percent if the result is a y percent increase in the cost of living? Presumably a set of questions of this form could be used to estimate the costs of pollution, including the so-called "measurable" costs. But great care must be taken in formulating the questions. For one thing, if the voters will benefit differentially from the activity, the questions should be asked in a way which reflects this fact. If, for example, the issue is cleaning up a river, residents near the river will be willing to pay more for the cleanup and should have a means of expressing this. Ultimately, some such political procedure probably will be necessary, at least until our more direct measurement techniques are greatly improved.

Let us assume that, somehow, we have made an estimate of the social cost function for pollution, including the marginal cost associated with various pollution levels. We now need an estimate of the benefits of pollution—or, if you prefer, of the costs of pollution abatement. So we set the Pollution Control Board (PCB) to work on this task.

The PCB has a staff of engineers and technicians, and they begin working on the obvious question: for each pollution source, how much would it cost to reduce pollution by 10 percent, 20 percent, and so on. If the PCB has some economists, they will know that the cost of reducing total pollution by 10 percent is *not* the total cost of reducing each pollution source by 10 percent. Rather, they will use the equimarginal principle and find the pattern of control such that an additional dollar spent on control of any pollution source yields the same reduction. This will minimize the cost of achieving any given level of abatement. In this way the PCB can generate a "cost of abatement" function, and the corresponding marginal cost function.

While this procedure seems straightforward enough, the practical difficulties are tremendous. The amount of information needed by the PCB is staggering; to do this job right, the PCB would have to know as much about each plant as the operators of the plant themselves. The cost of gathering these data is obviously prohibitive, and, since marginal principles apply to data collection too, the PCB would have to stop short of complete information, trading off the resulting loss in efficient control against the cost of better information. Of course, just as fast as the PCB obtained the data, a technological change would make it obsolete.

The PCB would have to face a further complication. It would not be correct simply to determine how to control existing pollution sources given their existing locations and production methods. Although this is almost certainly what the PCB would do, the resulting cost functions will overstate the true social cost of control. Muzzling existing plants is only one method of control. Plants can move, or switch to a new process, or even to a new product. Consumers can switch to a less-polluting substitute. There are any number of alternatives, and the poor PCB engineers can never know them all. This could lead to some costly mistakes. For example, the PCB may correctly conclude that the cost of installing effective dust control at the cement plant is very high and hence may allow the pollution to continue, when the best solution is for the cement plant to switch to brick production while a plant in the desert switches from brick to cement. The PCB can never have all this information and therefore is doomed to inefficiency, sometimes an inefficiency of large proportions.

Once cost and benefit functions are known, the PCB should choose a level of abatement that maximizes net gain. This occurs where the marginal cost of further abatement just equals the marginal benefit. If, for example, we could reduce pollution damages by $2 million at a cost of $1 million, we should obviously impose that $1 million cost. But if the damage reduction is only $1/2 million, we should not and in fact should reduce control efforts.

This principle is obvious enough but is often overlooked. One author, for example, has written that the national cost of air pollution is $11 billion a year but that we are spending less than $50 million a year on control; he infers from this that "we could justify a tremendous strengthening of control efforts on purely economic grounds." That *sounds* reasonable, if all you care about are sounds. But what is the logical content of the statement? Does it imply we should spend $11 billion on control just to make things even? Suppose we were spending $11 billion on control and thereby succeeded in reducing pollution costs to $50 million. Would this imply we were spending too *much* on control? Of course not. We must compare the *marginal* decrease in pollution costs to the *marginal* increase in abatement costs.

DIFFICULT DECISIONS

Once the optimal pollution level is determined, all that is necessary is for the PCB to enforce the pattern of controls which it has determined to be optimal. (Of course, this pattern will not really be the best one, because the PCB will not have all the information it should have.)

But now a new problem arises: how should the controls be enforced?

The most direct and widely used method is in many ways the least efficient: direct regulation. The PCB can decide what each polluter must do to reduce pollution and then simply require that action under penalty of law. But this approach has many shortcomings. The polluters have little incentive to install the required devices or to keep them operating properly. Constant inspection is therefore necessary. Once the polluter has complied with the letter of the law, he has no incentive to find better methods of pollution reduction. Direct control of this sort has a long history of inadequacy; the necessary bureaucracies rarely manifest much vigor, imagination, or devotion to the public interest. Still, in some situations there may be no alternative. . . .

Clearly, the PCB has a big job which it will never be able to handle with any degree of efficiency. Some sort of self-regulating system, like a market, is needed, which will automatically adapt to changes in conditions, provide incentives for development and adoption of improved control methods, reduce the amount of information the PCB must gather and the amount of detailed control it must exercise, and so on. This, by any standard, is a tall order.

PUTTING A PRICE ON POLLUTION

And yet there is a very simple way to accomplish all this. *Put a price on pollution.* A price-based control mechanism would differ from an ordinary market transaction system only in that the PCB would set the prices, instead of their being set by demand-supply forces, and that the state would force payment. Under such a system, anyone could emit any amount of pollution so long as he pays the price which the PCB sets to approximate the marginal social cost of pollution. Under this circumstance, private decisions based on self-interest are efficient. If pollution consists of many components, each with its own social cost, there should be different prices for each component. Thus, extremely dangerous materials must have an extremely high price, perhaps stated in terms of "years in jail" rather than "dollars," although a sufficiently high dollar price is essentially the same thing. In principle, the prices should vary with geographical location, season of the year, direction of the wind, and even day of the week, although the cost of too many variations may preclude such fine distinctions.

Once the prices are set, polluters can adjust to them any way they choose. Because they act on self-interest they will reduce their pollution by every means possible up to the point where further reduction would cost more than the price. Because all face the same price for the same type of pollution, the marginal cost of abatement is the same everywhere. If there are economies of scale in pollution control, as in some types of liquid waste treatment, plants can cooperate in establishing joint treatment facilities. In fact, some enterprising individual could buy these wastes from various plants (at negative prices— i.e., they would get paid for carting them off), treat them, and then sell them at a higher price, making a profit in the process. (After all, this is what rubbish removal firms do now.) If economies of scale are so substantial that the provider of such a service becomes a monopolist, then the PCB can operate the facilities itself.

Obviously, such a scheme does not eliminate the need for the PCB. The board must measure the output of pollution from all sources, collect the fees, and so on. But it does not need to know anything about any plant except its total emission of pollution. It does not control, negotiate, threaten, or grant favors. It does not destroy incentive because development of new control methods will reduce pollution payments.

As a test of this price system of control, let us consider how well it would work when applied to automobile pollution, a problem for which direct control is usually considered the only feasible approach. If the price system can work here, it can work anywhere.

Suppose, then, that a price is put on the emissions of automobiles. Obviously, continuous metering of such emissions is impossible. But it should be easy to determine the average output of pollution for cars of different makes, models, and years, having different types of control devices and using different types of fuel. Through graduated registration fees and fuel taxes, each car owner would be assessed roughly the social cost of his car's pollution, adjusted for whatever control devices he has chosen to install and for his driving habits. If the cost of installing a device, driving a different car, or finding alternative means of transportation is less than the price he must pay to continue his pollution, he will presumably take the necessary steps. But each individual remains free to find the best adjustment to his particular situation. It would be remarkable if everyone decided to install the same devices which some states currently require; and yet that is the effective assumption of such requirements.

Even in the difficult case of auto pollution, the price system has a number of advantages. Why should a person living in the Mojave desert, where pollution has little social cost, take the same pains to reduce air pollution as a person living in Pasadena? Present California law, for example, makes no distinction between such areas; the price system would. And what incentive is there for auto manufacturers to design a less polluting engine? The law says only that they must install a certain device in every car. If GM develops a more efficient engine, the law will eventually be changed to require this engine on all cars, raising costs and reducing sales. But will such development take place? No collusion is needed for manufacturers to decide unanimously that it would be foolish to devote funds to such development. But with a pollution fee paid by the consumer, there is a real advantage for any firm to be first with a better engine, and even a collusive agreement wouldn't last long in the face of such an incentive. The same is true of fuel manufacturers, who now have no real incentive to look for better fuels. Perhaps most important of all, the present situation provides no real way of determining whether it is cheaper to reduce pollution by muzzling cars or industrial plants. The experts say that most smog comes from cars; but *even if true, this does not imply that it is more efficient to control autos rather than other pollution sources.* How can we decide which is more efficient without mountains of information? The answer is, by making drivers and plants pay the same price for the same pollution, and letting self-interest do the job.

In situations where pollution outputs can be measured more or less directly (unlike the automobile pollution case), the price system is clearly superior to direct control. A study of possible control methods at the Delaware estuary, for example, estimated that, compared to a direct control scheme requiring each polluter to reduce his pollution by a fixed percentage, an effluent charge which would achieve the same level of pollution abatement would be only half as costly—a saving of about $150 million. Such a price system would also provide incentive for further improvements, a simple method of handling new plants, and revenue for the control authority.

In general, the price system allocates costs in a manner which is at least superficially fair: those who produce and consume goods which cause pollution, pay the costs. But the superior efficiency in control and apparent fairness are not the only advantages of the price mechanism. Equally important is the ease with which it can be put into operation. It is not necessary to have detailed information about all the techniques of pollution reduction, or estimates of all costs and benefits. Nor is it necessary to determine whom to blame or who should pay. All that is needed is a mechanism for estimating, if only roughly at first, the pollution output of all polluters, together with a means of collecting fees. Then we can simply pick a price—any price—for each category of pollution, and we are in business. The initial price should be chosen on the basis of some estimate of its effects but need not be the optimal one. If the resulting reduction in pollution is not "enough," the price can be raised until there is sufficient reduction. A change in technology, number of plants, or whatever, can be accommodated by a change in the price, even without detailed knowledge of all the technological and economic data. Further, once the idea is explained, the price system is much more likely to be politically acceptable than some method of direct control. Paying for a service, such as garbage disposal, is a well-established tradition, and is much less objectionable than having a bureaucrat nosing around and giving arbitrary orders. When businessmen, consumers, and politicians understand the alternatives, the price system will seem very attractive indeed.

WHO SETS THE PRICES?

An important part of this method of control obviously is the mechanism that sets and changes the pollution price. Ideally, the PCB could choose this price on the basis of an estimate of the benefits and costs involved, in effect imitating the impersonal workings of ordinary market forces. But because many of the costs and benefits cannot be measured, a less "objective," more political procedure is needed. This political procedure could take the form of a referendum, in which the PCB would present to the voters alternative schedules of pollution prices, together with the estimated effects of each. There would be a massive propaganda campaign waged by the interested parties, of course. Slogans such as "Vote NO on 12 and Save Your Job," or "Proposition 12 Means Higher Prices," might be overstatements but would contain some truth, as the individual voter would realize when he considered the suggested increase in gasoline taxes and auto registration fees. But the other side, in true American fashion, would respond by overstating *their* case: "Smog Kills, Yes on 12," or "Stop *Them* From Ruining *Your* Water." It would be up to the PCB to inform the public about the true effects of the alternatives; but ultimately, the voters would make the decision. . . .

If the democratic principle upon which the above political suggestions are based is rejected, the economist cannot object. He will still suggest the price system as a tool for controlling pollution. With any method of decision—whether popular vote, representative democracy, consultation with the nature gods, or a dictate of the intellectual elite—the price system can simplify control and reduce the amount of information needed for decisions. It provides an efficient, comprehensive, easily understood, adaptable, and reasonably fair way of handling the problem. It is ultimately the only way the problem will be solved. Arbitrary, piecemeal, stop-and-go programs of direct control have not and will not accomplish the job. . . .

. . . But the strongest argument for the price system is not found in idle speculation but in the real world, and in particular, in Germany. The Rhine River in Germany is a dirty stream, recently made notorious when an insecticide spilled into the river and killed millions of fish. One tributary of the Rhine, a river called the Ruhr, is the sewer for one of the world's most concentrated industrial areas. The Ruhr River valley contains 40 percent of German industry, including 80 percent of coal, iron, steel and heavy chemical capacity. The Ruhr is a small river, with a low flow of less than half the flow on the Potomac near Washington. The volume of wastes is extremely large—actually exceeding the flow of the river itself in the dry season! *Yet people and fish swim in the Ruhr River.*

This amazing situation is the result of over forty years of control of the Ruhr and its tributaries by a hierarchy of regional authorities. These authorities have as their goal the maintenance of the quality of the water in the area at minimum cost, and they have explicitly applied the equimarginal principle to accomplish this. Water quality is formally defined in a technological rather than an economic way; the objective is to "not kill the fish." Laboratory tests are conducted to determine what levels of various types of pollution are lethal to fish, and from these figures an index is constructed which measures the "amount of pollution" from each source in terms of its fish-killing capacity. This index is different for each source, because of differences in amount and composition of the waste, and geographical locale. Although this physical index is not really a very precise measure of the real economic *cost* of the waste, it has the advantage of being easily measured and widely understood. Attempts are made on an *ad hoc* basis to correct the index if necessary—if, for example, a nonlethal pollutant gives fish an unpleasant taste.

Once the index of pollution is constructed, a price is put on the pollution, and each source is free to adjust its operation any way it chooses. Geographical variation in prices, together with some direct advice from the authorities, encourage new plants to locate where pollution is less damaging. For example, one tributary of the Ruhr has been converted to an open sewer; it has been lined with concrete and landscaped, but otherwise no attempt is made to reduce pollution in the river itself. A treatment plant at the mouth of the river processes all these wastes at low cost. Therefore, the price of pollution on this river is set low. This arrangement, by the way, is a rational, if perhaps unconscious, recognition of marginal principles. The loss caused by destruction of *one* tributary is rather small, if the nearby rivers are maintained, while the benefit from having this inexpensive means of waste disposal is very large. However, if *another* river were lost, the cost would be higher and the benefits lower; one open sewer may be the optimal number.

The revenues from the pollution charges are used by the authorities to measure pollution, conduct tests and research, operate dams to regulate stream flow, and operate waste treatment facilities where economies of scale make this desirable. These facilities are located at the mouths of some tributaries, and at several dams in the Ruhr. If the authorities find pollution levels are getting too high, they simply raise the price, which causes polluters to try to reduce their wastes, and provides increased revenues to use on further treatment. Local governments influence the authorities, which helps to maintain recreation values, at least in certain stretches of the river.

This classic example of water management is obviously not exactly the price system method discussed earlier. There is considerable direct control, and the pollution authorities take a very active role. Price regulation is not used as much as it could be; for example, no attempt is made to vary the price over the season, even though high flow on the Ruhr is more than ten times larger than low flow. If the price of pollution were reduced during high flow periods, plants would have an incentive to regulate their production and/or store their wastes for release during periods when the river can more easily handle them. The difficulty of continuously monitoring wastes means this is not done; as automatic, continuous measurement techniques improve and are made less expensive, the use of variable prices will increase. Though this system is not entirely regulated by the price mechanism, prices are used more here than anywhere else, and the system is much more successful than any other.[1] So, both in theory and in practice, the price system is attractive, and ultimately must be the solution to pollution problems. . . .

ENDNOTES

1. For a more complete discussion of the Ruhr Valley system, see Allen V. Kneese, *The Economics of Regional Water Quality Management* (Baltimore, Md.: Johns Hopkins Press, 1964).

QUESTIONS ON RUFF

1. Explain what is meant by "marginalism." How do market prices solve the problems of economics?

2. How does Ruff seek to justify his conclusion that we should put a price on pollution? Is Ruff's account an anthropocentric account? Is this the best way to think about environmental questions?

3. Why is it difficult to measure pollution costs? Do you think that Ruff has provided an adequate set of institutions by which to price pollution?

Can the Supply of Natural Resources Be Finite?

Julian L. Simon

Julian L. Simon (1932–1998) was a Professor of Business Administration at the University of Maryland. Among numerous other works, he wrote The Ultimate Resource *(1981),* Theory of Population and Economic Growth *(1986),* Population and Development in Poor Countries *(1992), and edited* The State of Humanity *(1995). This excerpt is from* The Ultimate Resource 2 *(1996).*

. . . Natural resources are not finite. Yes, you read correctly. This chapter shows that the supply of natural resources is not finite in any economic sense, which is one reason why their cost can continue to fall indefinitely.

On the face of it, even to inquire whether natural resources are finite seems like nonsense. Everyone "knows" that resources are finite. And this belief has led many persons to draw unfounded, far-reaching conclusions about the future of our world economy and civilization. A prominent example is the *Limits to Growth* group, who open the preface to their 1974 book as follows.

> Most people acknowledge that the earth is finite. . . . Policy makers generally assume that growth will provide them tomorrow with the resources required to deal with today's problems. Recently, however, concern about the consequences of population growth, increased environmental pollution, and the depletion of fossil fuels has cast doubt upon the belief that continuous growth is either possible or a panacea.[1]

(Note the rhetorical device embedded in the term "acknowledge" in the first sentence of the quotation. It suggests that the statement is a fact, and that anyone who does not "acknowledge" it is simply refusing to accept or admit it.) For many writers on the subject, the inevitable depletion of natural resources is simply not open to question. A political scientist discussing the relationship of resources to national security refers to "the incontrovertible fact that many crucial resources are nonrenewable."[2] A high government energy official says that views that "the world's oil reserves . . . are sufficient to meet the worlds' needs" are "fatuities."[3]

The idea that resources are finite in supply is so pervasive and influential that the President's 1972 Commission on Population Growth and the American Future (the most recent such report) based its policy recommendations squarely upon this assumption. Right at its beginning the report asked,

> What does this nation stand for and where is it going? At some point in the future, the finite earth will not satisfactorily accommodate more human beings—nor will the United States. . . . It is both proper and in our best interest to participate fully in the worldwide search for the good life, which must include the eventual stabilization of our numbers.[4]

The assumption of finiteness indubitably misleads many scientific forecasters because their conclusions follow inexorably from that assumption. From the *Limits to Growth* team again, this time on food: "The world model is based on the fundamental assumption that there is an upper limit to the total amount of food that can be produced annually by the world's agricultural system."[5] . . .

Nor is it only noneconomists who fall into this error (although economists are in less danger here because they are accustomed to expect economic adjustment to shortages). John Maynard Keynes's contemporaries thought that he was the cleverest person of the century. But on the subject of natural resources—and about population growth, as we shall see later—he was both ignorant of the facts and stupid (an adjective I never use except for the famously clever) in his dogmatic logic. In his world-renowned *The Economic Consequences of the Peace*, published just after World War I, Keynes wrote that Europe could not supply itself and soon would have nowhere to turn:

> [B]y 1914 the domestic requirements of the United States for wheat were approaching their production, and the date was evidently near when there would be an exportable surplus only in years of exceptionally favorable harvest. . . .
>
> Europe's claim on the resources of the New World was becoming precarious; the law of diminishing returns was at last reasserting itself, and was making it necessary year by year for Europe to offer a greater quantity of other

commodities to obtain the same amount of bread . . . If France and Italy are to make good their own deficiencies in coal from the output of Germany, then Northern Europe, Switzerland, and Austria . . . must be starved of their supplies.[6]

All these assertions of impending scarcity turned out to be wildly in error. So much for Keynes's wisdom as an economist and a seer into the future. Millions of plain American farmers had a far better grasp of the agricultural reality in the 1920s than did Keynes. This demonstrates that one needs to know history as well as technical facts, and not just be a clever reasoner. . . .

But because the ideas in this chapter are counterintuitive does not mean that there is not a firm theoretical basis for holding them.

THE THEORY OF DECREASING NATURAL-RESOURCE SCARCITY

People's response to the long trend of falling raw-material prices often resembles this parody: We look at a tub of water and mark the water level. We assert that the quantity of water in the tub is "finite." Then we observe people dipping water out of the tub into buckets and taking them away. Yet when we re-examine the tub, lo and behold the water level is higher (analogous to the price being lower) than before. We believe that no one has reason to put water into the tub (as no one will put oil into an oil well), so we figure that some peculiar accident has occurred, one that is not likely to be repeated. But each time we return, the water level in the tub is higher than before—and water is selling at an ever cheaper price (as oil is). Yet we simply repeat over and over that the quantity of water must be finite and cannot continue to increase, and that's all there is to it.

Would not a prudent person, after a long series of rises in the water level, conclude that perhaps the process may continue—and that it therefore makes sense to seek a reasonable explanation? Would not a sensible person check whether there are inlet pipes to the tub? Or whether someone has developed a process for producing water? Whether people are using less water than before? Whether people are restocking the tub with recycled water? It makes sense to look for the cause of this apparent miracle, rather than clinging to a simple-minded, fixed-resources theory and asserting that it cannot continue.

Let's begin with a simple example to see what contrasting possibilities there are. (Such simplifying abstraction is a favorite trick of economists and mathematicians.) If there is only Alpha Crusoe and a single

copper mine on an island, it will be harder to get raw copper next year if Alpha makes a lot of copper pots and bronze tools this year, because copper will be harder to find and dig. And if he continues to use his mine, his son Beta Crusoe will have a tougher time getting copper than did his daddy, because he will have to dig deeper.

Recycling could change the outcome. If Alpha decides in the second year to replace the old tools he made in the first year, he can easily reuse the old copper and do little new mining. And if Alpha adds fewer new pots and tools from year to year, the promotion of cheap, recycled copper can rise year by year. This alone could mean a progressive decrease in the cost of copper, even while the total stock of copper in pots and tools increases.

But let us for the moment leave the possibility of recycling aside. Consider another scenario: If suddenly there are not one but two people on the island, Alpha Crusoe and Gamma Defoe, copper will be more scarce for each of them this year than if Alpha lived there alone, unless by cooperative efforts they can devise a more complex but more efficient mining operation—say, one man getting the surface work and one getting the shaft. (Yes, a joke.) Or, if there are two fellows this year instead of one, and if copper is therefore harder to get and more scarce, both Alpha and Gamma may spend considerable time looking for new lodes of copper.

Alpha and Gamma may follow still other courses of action. Perhaps they will invent better ways of obtaining copper from a given lode, say a better digging tool, or they may develop new materials to substitute for copper, perhaps iron.

The cause of these new discoveries, or the cause of applying ideas that were discovered earlier, is the "shortage" of copper—that is, the increased cost of getting copper. So increased scarcity causes the development of its own remedy. This has been the key process in the supply of natural resources throughout history. (This process is explored for energy in chapter 11. Even in that special case there is no reason to believe that the supply of energy, even of oil, is finite or limited.)

Interestingly, the pressure of *low* prices can also cause innovation, as in this story:

> [In the] period 1984 to 1986 . . . the producer price of copper hovered around 65 cents per pound. In terms of constant dollars, this was the lowest price since the great depression of the 1930s. . . . [S]ome companies . . . analyzed what needed to be done to be profitable even if the price of copper remained low. . . .

Major copper companies have found ways of reducing their costs. Phelps Dodge . . . will improve the efficiency of its transportation of rock by use of computer monitoring and by installing an in-pit crusher. . . . [It] has improved the efficiency of its copper concentration process by employing analytic instrumentation, including x-ray fluorescence. The most effective move . . . has been to install equipment that permits inexpensive . . . production of pure copper from leachates of wastes and tailings.[7]

Improved efficiency of copper use not only reduces resource use in the present, but effectively increases the entire stock of unused resources as well. For example, an advance in knowledge that leads to a 1 percent decrease in the amount of copper that we need to make electrical outlets is much the same as an increase in the total stock of copper that has not yet been mined. And if we were to make such a 1 percent increase in efficiency for all uses every year, a 1 percent increase in demand for copper in every future year could be accommodated without any increase in the price of copper, even without any other helpful developments.

Discovery of an improved mining method or of a substitute such as iron differs, in a manner that affects future generations, from the discovery of a new lode. Even after the discovery of a new lode, on the average it will still be more costly to obtain copper, that is, more costly than if copper had never been used enough to lead to a "shortage." But discoveries of improved mining methods and of substitute products can lead to lower costs of the services people seek from copper.

Please notice how a discovery of a substitute process or product by Alpha or Gamma benefits innumerable future generations. Alpha and Gamma cannot themselves extract nearly the full benefit from their discovery of iron. (You and I still benefit from the discoveries of the uses of iron and methods of processing made by our ancestors thousands of years ago.) This benefit to later generations is an example of what economists call an "externality" due to Alpha and Gamma's activities, that is, a result of their discovery that does not affect them directly.

If the cost of copper to Alpha and Gamma does not increase, they may not be impelled to develop improved methods and substitutes. If the cost of getting copper does rise for them, however, they may then bestir themselves to make a new discovery. The discovery may not immediately lower the cost of copper dramatically, and Alpha and Gamma may still not be as well off as if the cost had never risen. But subsequent generations may be better off because their ancestors Alpha and Gamma suffered from increasing cost and "scarcity."

This sequence of events explains how it can be that people have been cooking in copper pots for thousands of years, as well as using the metal for many other purposes, yet the cost of a pot today is vastly cheaper by any measure than it was one hundred or one thousand or ten thousand years ago.

Now I'll restate this line of thought into a theory that will appear again and again: More people, and increased income, cause resources to become more scarce in the short run. Heightened scarcity causes prices to rise. The higher prices present opportunity and prompt inventors and entrepreneurs to search for solutions. Many fail in the search, at cost to themselves. But in a free society, solutions are eventually found. And in the longrun *the new developments leave us better off than if the problems had not arisen.* That is, prices eventually become lower than before the increased scarcity occurred.

It is all-important to recognize that discoveries of improved methods and of substitute products are not just luck. They happen in response to an increase in scarcity—a rise in cost. Even after a discovery is made, there is a good chance that it will not be put into operation until there is need for it due to rising cost. This is important: Scarcity and technological advance are not two unrelated competitors in a Malthusian race; rather, each influences the other.

Because we now have decades of data to check its predictions, we can learn much from the 1952 U.S. governmental inquiry into raw materials—the President's Materials Policy Commission (the Paley Commission), organized in response to fears of raw-material shortages during and just after World War II. Its report is distinguished by having some of the right logic, but exactly the wrong forecasts.

There is no completely satisfactory way to measure the real costs of materials over the long sweep of our history. But clearly the man hours required per unit of output declined heavily from 1900 to 1940, thanks especially to improvements in production technology and the heavier use of energy and capital equipment per worker. This long-term decline in real costs is reflected in the downward drift of prices of various groups of materials in relation to the general level of prices in the economy.

[But since 1940 the trend has been] soaring demands, shrinking resources, the consequences [being] pressure toward rising real costs, the risk of wartime shortages, the strong possibility of an arrest or decline in the standard of living we cherish and hope to share.[8]

The commission went on to predict that prices would continue to rise for the next quarter-century. However, prices declined rather than rose.

There are two reasons why the Paley Commission's predictions were topsy-turvy. First, the commission reasoned from the notion of finiteness and used a static technical analysis of the sort discussed in chapter 2.

> A hundred years ago resources seemed limitless and the struggle upward from meager conditions of life was the struggle to create the means and methods of getting these materials into use. In this struggle we have by now succeeded all too well. The nature of the problem can perhaps be successfully over-simplified by saying that the consumption of almost all materials is expanding at compound rates and is thus pressing harder and harder against resources which whatever else they may be doing are not similarly expanding.[9]

The second reason the Paley Commission went wrong is that it looked at the wrong facts. Its report placed too much emphasis on the trends of costs over the short period from 1940 to 1950, which included World War II and therefore was almost inevitably a period of rising costs, instead of examining the longer period from 1900 to 1940, during which the commission knew that "the man-hours required per unit of output declined heavily."[10]

Let us not repeat the Paley Commission's mistakes. We should look at trends for the longest possible period, rather than focusing on a historical blip; the OPEC-led price rise in all resources after 1973 and then the oil price increase in 1979 are for us as the temporary 1940–1950 wartime reversal was for the Paley Commission. We should ignore them, and attend instead to the long-run trends which make it very clear that the costs of materials, and their scarcity, continuously decline with the growth of income and technology.

RESOURCES AS SERVICES

As economists or as consumers we are interested, not in the resources themselves, but in the particular services that resources yield. Examples of such services are a capacity to conduct electricity, an ability to support weight, energy to fuel autos or electrical generators, and food calories.

The supply of a service will depend upon (a) which raw materials can supply that service with the existing technology, (b) the availabilities of these materials at

various qualities, (c) the costs of extracting and processing them, (d) the amounts needed at the present level of technology to supply the services that we want, (e) the extent to which the previously extracted materials can be recycled, (f) the cost of recycling, (g) the cost of transporting the raw materials and services, and (h) the social and institutional arrangements in force. What is relevant to us is not whether we can find any lead in existing lead mines but whether we can have the services of lead batteries at a reasonable price; it does not matter to us whether this is accomplished by recycling lead, by making batteries last forever, or by replacing lead batteries with another contraption. Similarly, we want intercontinental telephone and television communication, and, as long as we get it, we do not care whether this requires 100,000 tons of copper for cables, or a pile of sand for optical fibers, or just a single quarter-ton communications satellite in space that uses almost no material at all.[11] And we want the plumbing in our homes to carry water, if PVC plastic has replaced the copper that formerly was used to do the job—well, that's just fine.

This concept of services improves our understanding of natural resources and the economy. To return to Crusoe's cooking pot, we are interested in a utensil that one can put over the fire and cook with. After iron and aluminum were discovered, quite satisfactory cooking pots—and perhaps more durable than pots of copper—could be made of these materials. The cost that interests us is the cost of providing the cooking service rather than the cost of copper. If we suppose that copper is used only for pots and that (say) stainless steel is quite satisfactory for most purposes, as long as we have cheap iron it does not matter if the cost of copper rises sky high. (But as we have seen, even the prices of the minerals themselves, as well as the prices of the services they perform, have fallen over the years.)*

Here is an example of how we develop new sources of the sources we seek Ivory used for billiard balls threatened to run out late in the nineteenth century. As a result of a prize offered for a replacement material, celluloid was developed, and that discovery led directly to

---

*Here is an example of how new developments increase the amount of services we get from a given amount of ore: Scientists have recently rediscovered the "superplastic" steel used in ancient Damascus blades. This causes a large reduction in the amount of scrap that is left over in machining parts, and hence a large decrease in the amount of material needed, as well as the amount of energy used, in metal fabrication processes (*Chemecology*, March 1992, p. 6).

the astonishing variety of plastics that now gives us a cornucopia of products (including billiard balls) at prices so low as to boggle the nineteenth-century mind. We shall discuss this process at greater length in the context of energy in chapter 11.

ARE NATURAL RESOURCES FINITE?

Incredible as it may seem at first, the term "finite" is not only inappropriate but is downright misleading when applied to natural resources, from both the practical and philosophical points of view. As with many important arguments, the finiteness issue is "just semantic." Yet the semantics of resource scarcity muddle public discussion and bring about wrongheaded policy decisions.

The ordinary synonyms of "finite," the dictionary tells us, are "countable" or "limited" or "bounded." This is the appropriate place to start our thinking on the subject, keeping in mind that the appropriateness of the term "finite" in a particular context depends on what interests us. Also please keep in mind that we are interested in material benefits and not abstract mathematical entities per se. (Mathematics has its own definition of "finite," which can be quite different from the common sort of definition we need here.)*

The quantity of the services we obtain from copper that will ever be available to us should not be considered finite because there is no method (even in principle) of making an appropriate count of it, given the problem of the economic definition of "copper," the possibility of using copper more efficiently, the possibility of creating copper or its economic equivalent from other materials, the possibility of recycling copper, or even obtaining

copper from sources beyond planet Earth, and thus the lack of boundaries to the sources from which "copper" might be drawn. That is, one cannot construct a working definition of the total services that we now obtain from copper and that can eventually be obtained by human beings.[12]

This is easier to see now than ever before. After centuries of slow progress and the use of mostly the familiar materials such as stone, wood, and iron, science is attaining undreamed-of abilities to create new materials. This includes syntheses of known compounds and also "materials that do not exist in nature. . . . Instead of trying to modify existing materials, scientists now are learning to assemble atoms and molecules systematically into new materials with precisely the properties they need for designs too demanding for off-the-shelf resources."[13] The first auto engine parts made of silicon and carbon—water-pump seal rings—are now being installed in Volkswagens, and engines could soon be made of silicon carbide, cutting weight and emissions in addition to replacing metals.[14] Palladium instead of platinum can now be used in auto exhaust emission systems.[15] Organic plastics can now be blended with glass to yield a material as strong as concrete but flexible and much lighter.[16] And a feasible way has been found to make heat-resistant plastics using gallium chloride.[17] Ceramics engineering is exploding with new knowledge, finally putting an end to past generations' worries about running out of metals.

Plastics are now made only from fossil fuels or oils from plants grown in fields, but researchers have recently found ways to convert such agricultural products as potatoes and corn into direct sources of plastics by inserting special plastic-producing genes into them.[18]

---

*The word "finite" is frequently used in mathematics, in which context we all learn it as schoolchildren. The definition of "finite" used in this book, however, applies not to mathematical entities but rather to physical entities. Therefore, arguments about the mathematical entities and the mathematical definition of "finite" are not germane here, even though the notion of infinity may be originally of mathematical origin.

In the first edition, I wrote that even in mathematics the word "finite" can be confusing. (I appreciate a discussion of this point with Alvin Roth.) For example, consider whether a one-inch line segment should be considered finite. The *length* of a one-inch line is finite in the sense that it is bounded at both ends. But the line within the endpoints contains an infinite number of points which have no defined size and hence cannot be counted. Therefore, *the number of points* in that one-inch segment is not finite. My point, as I wrote, was that the appropriateness of the term "finite" depends upon what interests us. This paragraph elicited much criticism, and because it is not necessary to the argument, I leave it out this time.

When I wrote about a line's finiteness in the first edition, I did not intend to suggest that the supply of copper should be considered to be not finite because it could be subdivided ever more finely; however, what I wrote caused some confusion. I meant to say that if we cannot state *how to count* the total amount of a resource that could be available in the future, it should not be considered finite. But in one important sense the notion of subdivision *is* relevant. With the passage of time and the accumulation of technical knowledge, we learn how to obtain a given amount of service from an ever-smaller amount of a resource. It takes much less copper now to pass a given message than a hundred years ago. And much less energy is required to do a given amount of work than in the past; the earliest steam engines had an efficiency of about 2 percent, but efficiencies are many times that high now.

This sort of gain in efficiency fits with Baumol's line of thought, discussed above, that an improvement in productivity not only reduces resource use in the present, but increases the future services from the entire stock of resources.

In light of these extraordinary developments—which continue the line of discoveries since humankind thousands of years ago found a way to convert iron into a resource by learning how to work with it—concern about running out of materials such as copper seems ever less sensible.

Consider this remark about potential oil and gas from an energy forecaster. "It's like trying to guess the number of beans in jar without knowing how big the jar is." So far so good. But then he adds, "God is the only one who knows—and even He may not be sure."[19] Of course he is speaking lightly, but the notion that some mind *could* know the "actual" size of the jar is misleading, because it implies that there is a fixed quantity of standard-sized beans. The quantity of a natural resource that might be available to us—and even more important the quantity of the services that can eventually be rendered to us by that natural resource—can never be known even in principle, just as the number of points in a one-inch line can never be counted even in principle. Even if the "jar" were fixed in size, it might yield ever more "beans." Hence, resources are not finite in any meaningful sense.

The entire notion of the nonfiniteness of resources such as copper, energy, and living space may so boggle the mind of some readers as to turn them away from the rest of the book. If this is so for you, please notice that one can reach the same practical conclusions from current data and economic theory, without making the stronger argument about infinite resources, as long as one accepts that it is silly to worry now about any implications of the proposition that energy will run out in (say) seven billion years. If the notion of finitude is quite irrelevant for you, as it is for me, please skip the rest of the discussion on the subject. But for some other, I cannot leave out discussion of the issue, because it is the basis of their thinking.

Well-wishers have advised me to "admit" that resources are limited to the capacities of the planet, thinking that this will keep me from "losing credibility." And I seem pigheaded to them when I do not follow their advice. But this is why I continue to argue that these quantities are not finite: The rhetorical difficulty is that as soon as one would "admit" that there are only (say) seven billion years of energy, some doomsters begin to work backward to argue that the sun's measurable size and rate of energy output means that the supply of energy is finite for next year. But that's physical estimate—it's not an economic definition of "energy," any more than copper atoms in the Earth's crust is a useful *economic* definition of "copper."

Objections to the notion of nonfiniteness often come from a mathematical background. Yet there is ample justification even within mathematics itself for taking the point of view that I do, and mathematical statisticians such as Barrow and Tipler affirm this. As Tipler puts it, "The laws of physics do not forbid perpetual economic growth."[20]

I continue to stand on the ground of nonfiniteness because I have found that leaving that ground leads to more bad arguments than standing on it, even though it seems so strange to many, and I doubt that many people's judgment will be affected by what I write on this particular issue. Hence there is little temptation to trim my sails to this wind, and do that which is offensive to me—to "admit" something that I do not believe is so.

But what if I am wrong? Certainly it is possible that the cosmos has a countable amount of mass/energy. How should we continue with that line of thought?

We have seen that even if energy is the relevant constraint for fabricating new kinds of "raw" materials, one would need to take into account, at the very least, all the mass/energy in the solar system. This amount is so huge relative to our use of energy, even by many multiples of the present population and many multiples of our present rates of individual use, that the end of the solar system in seven billion years or whenever would hardly be affected by our energy use now. This should be reason enough to ignore the issue of finitude.

Even if human population and the rate of using energy and materials should increase vastly so as to controvert the previous paragraph, there is the possibility that humans will come to exploit the resources of other parts of the cosmos, which is so huge relative to the solar system as to render calculations irrelevant under any conceivable rates of growth. If so, further discussion would seem frivolous.

Physicist Freeman Dyson, in his book, *Infinite in All Directions,* takes this mode of thought much further and theorizes that even if the world were to get progressively colder forever, it would be possible for human beings to adapt in such fashion as to stay ahead of the cooling; consequently, he writes, "Boiled down to one sentence, my message is the unboundedness of life and the consequent unboundedness of human destiny."[21] And physicist Frank Tipler argues, on the basis of the established body of contemporary knowledge of physics, that the ultimate constraint is not energy but rather information. Because we can increase the stock of information without limit, there is no need to consider our existence finite.* Of course these arguments are exceedingly abstract, and far from contemporary concerns. I cite these ideas not as proof that the future of humanity is not finite, but rather as showing that the doomsayers' arguments from physics that human existence is *not* finite are not consistent with a solid body of reasoning by physicists.

To restate: A satisfactory operational definition—which is an estimate—of the quantity of a natural resource, or of the services we now get from it, is the only sort of estimate that is of any use in policy decision. The estimate must tell us about the quantities of a resource (or of a particular service) that we can expect to receive in any particular year to come, at each particular price, conditional on other events that we might reasonably expect to know (such as use of the resource in prior years). And there is no reason to believe that at any given moment in the future the available quantity of any natural resource or service at present prices will be much smaller than it is now, let alone nonexistent. Only one-of-a-kind resources such as an Arthur Rubinstein concert or a Michael Jordan basketball game, for which there are no close replacements, will disappear in the future and hence are finite in quantity.

The term "finite" is not meaningful when applied to resources because we cannot say with any practical surety where the bounds of a relevant resource system lie, or even if there are any bounds. The bounds for Crusoes are the shores of their island, and so it was for early humans. But then Crusoes find other islands. Humankind traveled farther and farther in search of resources—finally to the bounds of continents, and then to other continents. When America was opened up, the world, which for Europeans had been bounded by Europe and perhaps by Asia too, was suddenly expanded. Each epoch has seen a shift in the bounds of the relevant resource system. Each time, the old ideas about "limits," and the calculations of "finite resources" within those bounds, were thereby falsified. Now we have begun to explore the sea, which contains amounts of metallic and perhaps energy resources that dwarf any deposits we know about on land. And we have begun to explore the moon. Why shouldn't the boundaries of the system from which we derive resources continue to expand in such directions, just as they have expanded in the past? This is one more reason not to regard resources as "finite" in principle.

Why do we become hypnotized by the word "finite"? That is an interesting question in psychology, education, and philosophy. One likely reason is that the word "finite" seems to have a precise and unambiguous meaning in any context, even though it does not. Second, we learn the word in the context of simple mathematics, where all propositions are tautologous definitions and hence can be shown logically to be true or false. But scientific subjects are empirical rather than definitional, as twentieth-century philosophers have been at great pains to emphasize. Mathematics is not a science in the ordinary sense because it does not deal with facts other than the stuff of mathematics itself, and hence such terms as "finite" do not have the same meaning elsewhere that they do in mathematics.

Third, much of our daily life about which we need to make decisions is countable and finite—our salaries, the amount of gas in a full tank, the width of the backyard, the number of greeting cards you sent out last year, or those you will send out next year. Since these quantities are finite, why shouldn't the world's total possible salary in the future, or the gasoline in the possible tanks in the future, or the number of cards you ought to send out, also be finite? Though the analogy is appealing, it is not sound. And it is in making this incorrect extension that we go astray in using the term "finite."

I think we can stop here. I'm sorry to have taken up your time with this unless you were seriously worried beforehand about what will happen seven billion years from now. . . .

---

*The amount of knowledge would not be finite in any meaningful sense, because the stock of knowledge can grow at a faster rate than the stock of energy can decline, which would eventuate in a cushion much greater than necessary to accommodate the possible growth in human population. (I do not give the specifics of such a calculation because doing so would be a waste of time.)

In order to show that we ought to take account of finitude, one would first have to show that the previous issue—the eventual domination of knowledge rather than energy—is wrong. Then one would have to show that the probabilities of a nonfinite universe and the future exploitation of the cosmos outside the solar system are very low, then show some reasonable basis for saying that events beyond (say) a thousand or million or more years, all the way to seven billion years, would matter for our economic choices now, then show that the likelihood is low that our present understanding of the mass/energy relationship is wrong, then show that there is little likelihood that it is possible to get our needs serviced with ever-smaller amounts of energy. Without some reasonable argument about *every* link in that chain, discussion of the finitude of energy that will be available to humans seems misplaced.

AFTERNOTE 1

A Dialogue on "Finite"

The notion of nonfinite natural resources is sufficiently important, and sufficiently difficult to think through, that it is worth taking the time for an imaginary dialogue between Peers Strawman (PS) and Happy Writer (HW).

PS: Every natural resource is finite in quantity, and therefore any resource must get more scarce as we use more of it.

HW: What does "finite" mean?

PS: "Finite" means "countable" or "limited."

HW: What is the limit for, say, copper? What is the amount that may be available in the future?

PS: I don't know.

HW: Then how can you be sure it is limited in quantity?

PS: I know that at least it must be less than the total weight of the Earth.

HW: If it were only slightly less than the total weight of the Earth, or, say a hundredth of that total weight would there be reason for us to be concerned?

PS: You're getting off the track. We're only discussing whether it is theoretically limited in quantity, not whether the limit is of practical importance.

HW: Okay. Would you say that copper is limited in quantity if we could recycle it 100 percent?

PS: I see what you're saying. Even if it is limited in quantity, finiteness wouldn't matter to us if the material could be recycled 100 percent or close to it. That's true. But we're still talking about whether it is limited in quantity. Don't digress.

HW: Okay again. Would copper be limited in quantity if everything that copper does could be done by other materials that are available in limitless quantities?

PS: The quantity of copper wouldn't matter then. But you're digressing again.

HW: We're talking about scarcity for the future, aren't we? So what matters is not how much copper there is now (whatever the word "is" means) but the amounts in future years. Will you agree to that?

PS: That I'll buy.

HW: Then, is copper limited for the future if we can create copper from other materials, or substitute other materials for copper?

PS: The size of the Earth would still constitute a limit.

HW: How about if we can use energy from outside the Earth—from the sun, say—to create additional copper the way we grow plants with solar energy?

PS: But is that realistic?

HW: Now it's you who are asking about realism. But as a matter of fact, yes, it is physically possible, and also likely to be feasible in the future. So will you now agree that at least *in principle* the quantities of copper are not limited even by the weight of the Earth?

PS: Don't make me answer that. Instead, let's talk realism. Isn't it realistic to expect resources such as copper to get more scarce?

HW: Can we agree to define scarcity as the cost of getting copper?

[Here an extended dialogue works out the arguments about scarcity and price given in chapter 1. Finally PS says "okay" to defining scarcity as cost.]

HW: Future scarcity will depend, then, on the recycling rate, on the substitutes we develop, on the new methods we discover for extracting copper, and so on. In the past, copper became progressively less scarce, and there is no reason to expect that trend to change, no matter what you say about "finiteness" and "limits," as we just agreed. But there is more. Do you really care about copper, or only about what copper does for you?

PS: Obviously what matters is what copper can do for us, not copper itself. [Now you know why the name is Strawman].

HW: Good. Then can we agree that the outlook for the services that copper provides is even better than for copper itself?

PS: Sure, but all this *can't* be true. It's not natural. How can we use more of something and have it get less scarce?

HW: Well, this is one of those matters that defies common sense. That's because the common-sense view applies only when the resource is arbitrarily limited—for example, limited to the copper wire in your cellar. But that quantity is only fixed as long as you don't make another trip to the hardware store. Right?

PS: I may be Strawman but my patience is limited.

And so we close.

ENDNOTES

1. Dennis L. Meadows, William W. Behrens III, Donella H. Meadows, Roger F. Naill, Jorgen Randers, and Erich K. O. Zahn, *Dynamics of Growth in a Finite World* (Cambridge, Mass.: Wright-Allen, 1974), p. vii.
2. Ted Robert Gurr, "On the Political Consequences of Scarcity and Economic Decline," *International Studies Quarterly* 29 (1985), p. 52.

3. James E. Akins, "The Oil Crisis: This Time the Wolf is Here," in *Economics of Energy,* edited by Leslie E. Grayson (Princeton: The Darwin Press, 1975), p. 289.

4. U.S. The White House, Population and the American Future, *The Report of the Commission on Population Growth and the American Future* (New York: Signet, 1972), pp. 2–3.

5. Meadows, et al., 1974, p. 265.

6. John Maynard Keynes, *The Economic Consequences of the Peace* (New York: Harcourt, Brace, 1920), pp. 24, 25, 94.

7. Philip Abelson, *Science,* November 11, 1988, p. 837, editorial.

8. U.S. The White House, summary of vol. 1, *Resources for Freedom,* 4 vols. The President's Materials Policy Commission (The Paley Commission) (Washington, D.C.: GPO, June 1952), pp. 12–13; idem, p. 1.

9. Ibid., p. 2.

10. Ibid., p. 1.

11. Buckminster Fuller, *Utopia or Oblivion: The Prospect for Humanity* (New York: Bantam, 1969), p. 4, quoted by James A. Weber, *Grow or Die!* (New Rochelle, N.Y.: Arlington House, 1977), p. 45.

12. For discussion of operational or working definitions, see a text on research methods, such as Julian L. Simon and Paul Burstein, *Basic Research Methods in Social Science,* 3rd ed. (New York: Random House, 1985).

13. Ivan Amato, "New Alchemy: Fooling Mother Nature," *Washington Post,* August 20, 1989, p. B3.

14. *Wall Street Journal,* November 11, 1988, p. B4.

15. *Washington Post,* May 31, 1991, p. D1.

16. *Wall Street Journal,* August 30, 1991, p. B1.

17. *Wall Street Journal,* August 30, 1991, p. B1.

18. *Business Week,* August 19, 1991, p. 110.

19. Sheldon Lambert, quoted in *Newsweek,* June 27, 1977, p. 71.

20. Telephone conversation about June 8, 1994. Tipler goes even further and says that the laws of physics *mandate* perpetual growth, but that goes far beyond anything discussed here—as indeed do *any* laws of physics have little or nothing to do with change within the economic horizon of this book.

21. Freeman Dyson, *Infinite in All Directions* (New York: Harper and Row, 1988), p. vii.

QUESTIONS ON SIMON

1. What does Simon mean when he says that natural resources are not finite in an economic sense? Is there another sense in which these resources are finite?

2. Why does a more efficient use of some resource entail that the entire stock of unused resources has grown?

3. How does short-term scarcity provide incentives for discovery? Why might Simon assume solutions to scarcity are easily found in a free society? Is Simon overly optimistic?

_____

FOR FURTHER READING

Science, Technology and the Economy

Bell, Daniel. *The Coming of the Post-Industrial Society.* New York: Basic Books, 1983.

Ferré, Frederick. *Philosophy of Technology.* Englewood Cliffs, N.J.: Prentice Hall, 1988.

Fuller, Buckminster. *No More Secondhand God and Other Writings.* Garden City, N.Y.: Doubleday, 1963.

Giedion, Siegfried. *Mechanization Takes Command.* Oxford: Oxford University Press, 1948.

Guardini, Romano. *Letters from Lake Como: Explorations in Technology and the Human Race.* Translated by Geoffrey W. Bromiley. Grand Rapids, Mich.: William B. Eerdmans, 1994.

Heidegger, Martin. *The Question Concerning Technology and Other Essays.* Translated by William Lovitt. New York: Harper and Row, 1977.

Kealey, Terence. *The Economic Laws of Scientific Research.* New York: St. Martin's Press, 1996.

Marcuse, Herbert. *One-Dimensional Man: Studies in the Ideology of Advanced Industrial Society.* Boston: Beacon Press, 1964.

Mumford, Lewis. *The Myth of the Machine.* New York: Harcourt, Brace, and World, 1967–1970.

———. *Technics and Civilization.* New York: Harcourt, Brace, 1934.

Noble, D. F. *The Religion of Technology: The Divinity of Man and the Spirit of Invention.* New York: Knopf, 1997.

Petroski, Henry. *The Evolution of Useful Things.* New York: Vintage Books, 1992.

Postrel, Virginia. *The Future and Its Enemies: The Growing Conflict over Creativity, Enterprise, and Progress.* New York: The Free Press, 1998.

Rosenberg, Nathan. *Inside the Black Box: Technology and Economics.* Cambridge: Cambridge University Press, 1982.

Tenner, E. *Why Things Bite Back: Technology and the Revenge of Unintended Consequences.* Cambridge: Harvard University Press, 1997.

Winner, Langdon. *The Whale and the Reactor: A Search for Limits in an Age of High Technology.* Chicago: University of Chicago Press, 1986.

The Environment

Anderson, Terry L., and Peter J. Hill, eds. *Wildlife in the Marketplace.* Lanham, Md: Rowman and Littlefield, 1995.

Baxter, William F. *People or Penguins: The Case for Optimal Pollution.* New York: Columbia University Press, 1974.

Beckerman, Wilfred. *Green-Colored Glasses: Environmentalism Reconsidered.* Washington, D.C.: Cato Institute, 1996.

Berry, Wendell. *The Gift of Good Land: Further Essays, Cultural and Agricultural.* San Francisco, Calif.: North Point Press, 1981.

Botkin, Daniel B. *Discordant Harmonies: A New Ecology for the Twenty-first Century.* New York: Oxford University Press, 1990.

Bramwell, Anna. *Ecology in the 20th Century: A History.* New Haven, Conn.: Yale University Press, 1989.

Chase, Alston. *In a Dark Wood: The Fight Over Forests and the Myths of Nature.* New Brunswick, N.J.: Transaction, 2000.

Cronin, William, ed. *Uncommon Ground: Rethinking the Human Place in Nature.* New York: Norton, 1995.

Douglas, Mary, and Aaron Wildavsky. *Risk and Culture: The Selection of Technical and Environmental Dangers.* Berkeley: University of California Press, 1982.

Dorfman, Robert and Nancy, eds. *Economics of the Environment: Selected Readings.* 3d ed. New York: W. W. Norton, 1993.

Ferry, Luc. *The New Ecological Order.* Translated by Carol Volk. Chicago: University of Chicago Press, 1995.

Fumento, Michael. *Science Under Siege: Balancing Technology and the Environment.* New York: Morrow, 1993.

Greve, Michael S., and Fred L. Smith, Jr., eds. *Environmental Politics: Public Costs, Private Rewards.* New York: Praeger, 1992.

Hess, Karl. *Visions Upon the Land: Man and Nature on the Western Range.* Covelo, Calif.: Island Press, 1992.

Huber, Peter W. *Hard Green: Saving the Environment from the Environmentalists.* New York: Basic Books, 1999.

Johnson, Lawrence E. *A Morally Deep World: An Essay on Moral Significance and Environmental Ethics.* Cambridge: Cambridge University Press, 1991.

Jonas, Hans. *The Imperative of Responsibility: In Search of an Ethics for the Technological Age.* Chicago: University of Chicago Press, 1984.

Kaufman, Wallace. *No Turning Back: Dismantling the Fantasies of Environmental Thinking.* New York: Basic Books, 1994.

Lehr, Jay. *Rational Readings on Environmental Concerns:* New York: Van Nostrand, 1992.

Leopold, Aldo. *A Sand County Almanac.* Oxford: Oxford University Press, 1949.

Lomborg, Bjorn. *The Skeptical Environmentalist: Measuring the Real State of the World.* Cambridge: Cambridge University Press, 2001.

Luke, Timothy W. *Capitalism, Democracy, and Ecology: Departing from Marx.* Urbana: University of Illinois Press, 1999.

Nash, Roderick. *The Rights of Nature: A History of Environmental Ethics.* Madison: University of Wisconsin Press, 1989.

Nash, Roderick. *Wilderness and the American Mind.* New Haven, Conn.: Yale University Press, 1973.

Ostrom, Elinor. *Governing the Commons.* New York: Cambridge University Press, 1990.

Passmore, John. *Man's Responsibility for Nature: Ecological Problems and Western Traditions.* London: Duckworth, 1974.

Rolston, Holmes, III. *Environmental Ethics.* Philadelphia, Pa.: Temple University Press, 1988.

Sagoff, Mark. "At the Shrine of Our Lady of Fatima, or Why Political Questions Are Not All Economic." *Arizona Law Review* 23 (1981): 1283–98.

Schmidtz, David, and Elizabeth Willott, eds. *Environmental Ethics: What Really Matters, What Really Works.* New York: Oxford University Press, 2001.

Simmons, Randy T., Fred L. Smith, Jr., and Paul Georgia. *The Tragedy of the Commons Revisited: Politics vs. Private Property.* Washington, D.C.: Competitive Enterprise Institute, 1996.

Stone, Christopher. *Should Trees Have Standing?* Los Altos, Calif.: William Kaupmann, 1974.

Yandle, Bruce. *The Political Limits of Environmental Quality Regulation.* Westport, Conn.: Quorum, 1987.

Credits

Section B

BI

Page 248: From Samuel Smiles, "Men of Business," in *Self-Help: With Illustrations of Character and Conduct,* pp. 208-232 (Harper and Brothers, 1860). **Page 254:** From Robert C. Solomon in *Business as a Humanity,* edited by Thomas Donaldson and R. Edward Freeman, copyright © 1994 by Oxford University Press. Used by permission of Oxford University Press, Inc. **Page 259:** From Deirdre Mc-Closekey, "Bourgeois Virtue" in *The American Scholar,* Volume 63, No. 2, Spring 1994, pp. 177-191. Reprinted by permission of The American Scholar. **Page 270:** Excerpts from Ayn Rand in *Atlas Shrugged,* 1957, pp. 387-452. **Page 275:** From Philip Wicksteed, "Business and the Economic Nexus" in *The Common Sense of Political Economy,* 1933, pp. 162-181. Reprinted by permission of Routledge and Kegan Paul, a division of Taylor & Francis Books Ltd. **Page 284:** From Adam Smith, "Of Prudence," in *The Theory of Moral Sentiments,* VI:1. **Page 286:** From H.J.N. Horsburgh, "Prudence" in *Proceedings of the Aristotelian Society* 36, Supplement, 1962, 65-76. Reprinted by courtesy of the Editor of the Aristotelian Society: © 1962. **Page 293:** From Aristotle, "Liberality" in *Nicomachean Ethics,* Book VI:1. **Page 295:** From Tibor Machan, "Dimensions of Generosity" in *Generosity: Virtue in Civil Society,* 1998, pp. 1-52. Reprinted by permission of the Cato Institute, Washington D.C. **Page 305:** From Sarah Buss, "Appearing Respectful: The Moral Significance of Manners" in *Ethics* 109 (July 1999); excerpt 795-805 (from the whole article 795-826). Reprinted by permission of The University of Chicago Press and Sarah Buss. **Page 311:** From H. Tristam Engelhardt, Jr., "Why Do It? Because That's What *We* Do: Manners in the Ruins of Community" in *Gentility Recalled: 'Mere' Manners and the Making of Social Order,* Digby Anderson, ed., 1996,

pp. 181-194. Reprinted by permission of The Social Affairs Unit.

BII

Page 323: From Daniel Defoe, *The Complete English Tradesman,* volume 1, chapters xix-xx, pp. 177-198. **Page 326:** From LYING by Sissela Bok, copyright © 1978 by Sissela Bok, pp. 19-30. Used by permission of Pantheon Books, a division of Random House, Inc. **Page 331:** Reprinted by permission of *Harvard Business Review,* excerpts from "Is Business Bluffing Ethical?", pp. 143-153 by Carr, Jan/Feb 1968. Copyright © 1968 by the Harvard Business School Publishing Corporation; all rights reserved. **Page 339:** From John G. Jones, "Character and Caliber in Salesmanship" in *Salesmanship and Management,* pp. 146-171 (New York: Alexander Hamilton Institute, 1918). **Page 336:** From David Holley, "A Moral Evaluation of Sales Practices" in *Business & Professional Ethics Journal* 5, number 1 (1987): 3-21. Reprinted by permission of the author. **Page 352:** From Israel Kirzner in *The Freeman* (September 1972). Reprinted with permission. **Page 358:** From "Advertising and Behavior Control" by Robert Arrington in *Journal of Business Ethics* 1 (1982), pp. 3-12. Reprinted by permission of Kluwer Academic/Plenum Publishers. **Page 368:** From Gabriele Taylor, "Integrity" in *Proceedings of the Aristotelian Society,* Supplement volume LV (1981): 143-159. Reprinted by courtesy of the Editor of the Aristotelian Society: © 1981. **Page 374:** Josiah Royce, "Loyalty" in *The Philosophy of Loyalty,* pp. 38-48 (New York: MacMillan, 1915). **Page 377:** From Ronald Duska, "Whistleblowing and Employee Loyalty" from Desjardins and McCall, *Contemporary Issues in Business Ethics,* 4/e, 2000, pp. 167-172. Reprinted by permission of the author. **Page 379:** From Mike Martin, "Whistle Blowing: Professionalism, Personal Life, and Shared Responsibility," in *Business & Professional Ethics Journal* 11, number 2 (summer 1992): 21-40. Reprinted by permission of the author.

BIII

Page 391: " 'I Only Work Here': Mediation and Irresponsibility" by John Lachs, from *Ethics, Free Enterprise, and Public Policy,* edited by Richard T. DeGeorge & Joseph A. Pichler, pp. 201-213, copyright © 1978 by Oxford University Press. Used by permission of Oxford University Press, Inc. **Page 396:** From Michael O. Hardimon, "Role Obligations" in *The Journal of Philosophy* 91, number 7 (July 1994): 333-363. Reprinted by permission of *The Journal of Philosophy* and the author. **Page 405:** From Milton Friedman, "The Social Responsibility of Business Is to Increase Its Profits" in *New York Times Magazine* (September 13, 1970). Copyright © 1970 by the New York Times Co. Reprinted by permission. **Page 409:** From R. Edward Freeman, "A Stakeholder Theory of the Modern Corporation" from *Ethical Theory and Business,* 6/e, edited by T.L. Beauchamp and N.E. Bowie, pp. 56-66. Reprinted by permission of R. Edward Freeman. **Page 416:** From Michael E. DeBow, "The Ethics of Rent-Seeking?: A New Perspective on Corporate Social Responsibility" in *The Journal of Law and Commerce* 12 (Fall 1992): 1-21. Reprinted by permission of The Journal of Law and Commerce. **Page 428:** From *Benjamin Franklin Reader,* edited by Nathan G. Goodman, pp. 301-310 (New York: Thomas Y. Crowell, 1945). **Page 431:** Dorothy Sayers, "Why Work?" in *Creed or Chaos?*", 1949, pp. 46-62. Reprinted by permission of David Higham Associates Limited. **Page 435:** From Adam Smith, *The Theory of Moral Sentiments,* I.iii.2-3. **Page 445:** From Aristotle in *Nicomachean Ethics,* Book III: 6-9. **Page 448:** Reprinted by permission of the publisher from *The Theory of Economic Development* by Joseph A. Schumpeter, translated by Redvers Opie, pp. 75-94, Cambridge, Mass.: Harvard University Press, Copyright © 1934 by the President and Fellows of Harvard College. **Page 453:** From N. Scott Arnold, "Why Profits are Deserved" in *Ethics* 97 (1987): 387-402. Reprinted by permis-

Section C

CI

CII

CIII

CIV

Index